WORD
BIBLICAL
COMMENTARY

General Editors
Bruce M. Metzger
David A. Hubbard †
Glenn W. Barker †

Old Testament Editor
John D. W. Watts

New Testament Editor
Ralph P. Martin

Associate Editors
James W. Watts, *Old Testament*
Lynn Allan Losie, *New Testament*

WORD
BIBLICAL
COMMENTARY

Volume 52C

Revelation 17–22

DAVID E. AUNE

THOMAS NELSON PUBLISHERS

Nashville

Word Biblical Commentary
Revelation 17–22
Copyright © 1998 by Thomas Nelson, Inc.

Library of Congress Cataloging-in-Publication Data
Main entry under title:

Word biblical commentary.

Includes bibliographies.
  1. Bible—Commentaries—Collected works.
BS491.2.W67   22.2 '7   81–71768
ISBN 0–8499–1545–7 (v. 52C) AACR2

Printed in the United States of America

The author's own translation of the Scripture text appears in italic type under the heading *Translation*.

3 4 5 6 QPV 02 01 00 99

To
Peder and Inger Borgen
and
Martin and Marianne Hengel

Contents

Editorial Preface   x
Author's Preface   xi
Abbreviations   xiii
Commentary Bibliography   xxviii
General Bibliography   xxx

INTRODUCTION
    Section 1: Authorship   xlvii
    Section 2: Date   lvi
    Section 3: Genre   lxx
    Section 4: Literary Structure   xc
    Section 5: Source Criticism   cv
    Section 6: Text   cxxxiv
    Section 7: Syntax   clx
    Section 8: Vocabulary   ccvii

TEXT AND COMMENTARY
The Inscription   3
  I. Prologue (1:1–8)   5
    A. Title: The Revelation of Jesus Christ (1:1–2)   5
    B. Beatitude (1:3)   5
    C. Epistolary Prescript (1:4–5c)   23
      Excursus 1A: The Tripartite Divine Name in the Targumim   32
      Excursus 1B: The Spirit in Revelation   36
    D. Doxology (1:5d–6)   41
    E. Two Prophetic Oracles (1:7–8)   50
  II. John's Vision and Commission (1:9–3:22)   60
    A. Vision of "One like a Son of Man" (1:9–20)   60
      Excursus 1C: The "Angels" of the Seven Churches   108
      Excursus 1D: The Tripartite Prophecy Formula   112
      Excursus 1E: The Number Seven   114
    B. Proclamations to the Seven Churches (2:1–3:22)   117
      1. The Proclamation to Ephesus (2:1–7)   132
        Excursus 2A: The Nicolaitans   148
      2. The Proclamation to Smyrna (2:8–11)   156
      Excursus 2B: Anatolian Jewish Communities and Synagogues   168
      Excursus 2C: Ancient Wreath and Crown Imagery   172
      3. The Proclamation to Pergamon (2:12–17)   176
      Excursus 2D: Eating Food Sacrificed to Idols   191
      4. The Proclamation to Thyatira (2:18–29)   195
      5. The Proclamation to Sardis (3:1–6)   214
      6. The Proclamation to Philadelphia (3:7–13)   228
      7. The Proclamation to Laodicea (3:14–22)   245

Excursus 3A: The Sayings of Jesus in Revelation   264
III. The Disclosure of God's Eschatological Plan (4:1–22:9)   266
  A. John's Heavenly Ascent (4:1–2a)   266
  B. The Sovereignty of God, the Investiture of the Lamb, and the First Six
     Seals (4:2b–7:17)   266
    1. Vision of the Heavenly Throne Room (4:2b–5:14)   266
     a. The Heavenly Worship of God (4:2b–11)   266
       Excursus 4A: The Twenty-Four Elders   287
       Excursus 4B: Hymns in Revelation   314
       Excursus 4C: The Cosmology of Ancient Ascent Narratives   317
     b. The Investiture of the Lamb (5:1–14)   319
       Excursus 5A: Christ as the Lamb   367
    2. The Lamb Breaks the First Six Seals (6:1–17)   377
     Excursus 6A: Ancient Prodigies and the Plagues of Revelation   416
    3. The Protective Sealing of the 144,000 (7:1–17)   424
    Excursus 7A: Marking, Branding, and Tattooing in the Ancient World   456
     Excursus 7B: The Order of the Tribes in Rev 7:4–8   464
  C. The Seventh Seal and the First Six Trumpets (8:1–11:14)   480
    1. The Seventh Seal (8:1)   480
    2. Vision of the First Six Trumpets (8:2–9:21)   480
    3. The Angel and the Little Scroll (10:1–11)   547
    4. The Temple and the Two Witnesses (11:1–14)   575
  D. The Seventh Trumpet and the Seven Bowls (11:15–16:21)   632
    1. The Seventh Trumpet (11:15–18)   632
    2. The Woman, the Child, and the Dragon (11:19–12:17)   647
     Excursus 12A: Michael the Archangel   693
     Excursus 12B: The Commandments of God and the Torah   710
    3. The Two Beasts (12:18–13:18)   713
     Excursus 13A: The Nero Redux or Redivivus Legend   737
     Excursus 13B: The Eschatological Antagonist   751
     Excursus 13C: 666 and Gematria   771
     Excursus 13D: The Provincial League (Koinon) of Asia   773
     Excursus 13E: The Roman Imperial Cult in Asia Minor   775
    4. Visions of Eschatological Salvation and Judgment (14:1–20)   781
     Excursus 14A: Celibacy in Antiquity   818
    5. The Seven Bowls (15:1–16:21)   849
     Excursus 16A: Rome and Parthia   **891**
  E. Revelations of the Judgment of Babylon (17:1–19:10)   **905**
    1. Introduction to the Revelations (17:1–2)   **905**
    2. The Allegorical Vision of Babylon as the Great Whore (17:3–18)   **905**
     Excursus 17A: The Biography of the Beast   **941**
    Excursus 17B: Alternate Ways of Counting the Roman Emperors   **947**
    3. The Destruction of Babylon (18:1–24)   **961**
    4. Heavenly Throne-Room Audition (19:1–8)   **1012**
    5. Concluding Angelic Revelation (19:9–10)   **1012**

F. The Final Defeat of God's Remaining Foes (19:11–21:8)   **1040**
   1. The Divine Warrior and His Conquests (19:11–21)   **1040**
   2. The Final Defeat of Satan (20:1–10)   **1069**
   3. Vision of the Judgment of the Dead (20:11–15)   **1069**
      Excursus 20A: The Temporary and the Eternal Kingdom   **1104**
   4. The Transition to the New Order (21:1–8)   **1108**
G. The Vision of the New Jerusalem (21:9–22:9)   **1133**
   1. Introduction to the Vision (21:9–10a)   **1133**
   2. The Seer Visits the New Jerusalem (21:10b–22:5)   **1133**
   3. Transitional Conclusion (22:6–9)   **1133**
      Excursus 21A: Jerusalem and the Temple in Early Judaism
      and Early Christianity   **1188**
      Excursus 21B: Ancient Utopias and the Paradise Myth   **1191**
IV. Epilogue (22:10–21)   **1195**
A. Concluding Parenesis (22:10–20)   **1195**
B. Epistolary Postscript (22:21)   **1238**
The Subscription   **1242**

INDEXES   **1243**

Editorial Preface

The launching of the *Word Biblical Commentary* brings to fulfillment an enterprise of several years' planning. The publishers and the members of the editorial board met in 1977 to explore the possibility of a new commentary on the books of the Bible that would incorporate several distinctive features. Prospective readers of these volumes are entitled to know what such features were intended to be; whether the aims of the commentary have been fully achieved time alone will tell.

First, we have tried to cast a wide net to include as contributors a number of scholars from around the world who not only share our aims but are in the main engaged in the ministry of teaching in university, college, and seminary. They represent a rich diversity of denominational allegiance. The broad stance of our contributors can rightly be called evangelical, and this term is to be understood in its positive, historic sense of a commitment to Scripture as divine revelation and the truth and power of the Christian gospel.

Then, the commentaries in our series are all commissioned and written for the purpose of inclusion in the *Word Biblical Commentary*. Unlike several of our distinguished counterparts in the field of commentary writing, there are no translated works, originally written in a non-English language. Also, our commentators were asked to prepare their own rendering of the original biblical text and to use those languages as the basis of their own comments and exegesis. What may be claimed as distinctive with this series is that it is based on the biblical languages, yet it seeks to make the technical and scholarly approach to the theological understanding of Scripture understandable by—and useful to—the fledgling student, the working minister, and colleagues in the guild of professional scholars and teachers as well.

Finally, a word must be said about the format of the series. The layout, in clearly defined sections, has been consciously devised to assist readers at different levels. Those wishing to learn about the textual witnesses on which the translation is offered are invited to consult the section headed *Notes*. If the readers' concern is with the state of modern scholarship on any given portion of Scripture, they should turn to the sections on *Bbiliography* and *Form/Structure/Setting*. For a clear exposition of the passage's meaning and its relevance to the ongoing biblical revelation, the *Comment* and concluding *Explanation* are designed expressly to meet that need. There is therefore something for everyone who may pick up and use these volumes.

If these aims come anywhere near realization, the intention of the editors will have been met, and the labor of our team of contributors rewarded.

General Editors: *Bruce Metzger*
David A. Hubbard†
Glenn W. Barker†
Old Testament: *John D. W. Watts*
New Testament: *Ralph P. Martin*

Author's Preface

Serious research on this commentary began in 1982–83, when I spent the academic year at the University of Trondheim, as a Fulbright guest professor in the Department of Religious Studies. Professor Peder Borgen was my host, and I am grateful to him and his wife, Inger, for the kindness, hospitality, and friendship shown to my family and me during that exciting year. Work on the commentary was all but completed some twelve years later in 1994–95 at the University of Tübingen, where I continued my research as the recipient of an Alexander von Humboldt Forschungspreis. Professor Martin Hengel (whom I first met when he gave a lecture at the University of Trondheim in the spring of 1983) was my host, and my wife and I experienced the gracious hospitality of the Hengels and Professor and Mrs. Peter Stuhlmacher on many occasions. I must also express my appreciation to Dr. Jörg Frey, Professor Hengel's research assistant, for his ready help in dealing with many practical details at the Theologicum in Tübingen. Since the years at Trondheim and Tübingen were critical for the commencement and completion of this commentary, I have dedicated it in gratitude to the Borgens and the Hengels. I am, of course, profoundly grateful both to the Council for International Exchange of Scholars for the Fulbright award and to the Alexander von Humboldt Stiftung for the award of a Forschungspreis, as well as to Loyola University Chicago for providing me with a subsidized leave of absence during the 1994–95 academic year.

A number of colleagues and students have made important contributions to this commentary. Colleagues who have read and offered critiques of portions of the commentary include Professors Lee Levine of Hebrew University, Jan Willem van Henten of the University of Amsterdam, and Bruce Metzger of Princeton Theological Seminary. Some of the material that found its way into the commentary was originally formulated and delivered as lectures at the University of Aberdeen (February 1983), the University of Oslo and the Baptist Theological Seminary in Oslo (March 1983), Washington University (February 1990), and the University of Utrecht (March 1995). I also profited greatly by participating in various seminars on Revelation, including the Seminar on Early Christian Apocalypticism (1983–87), chaired by Professor Adela Yarbro Collins, the Seminar on Reading the Apocalypse (1991–97), chaired by Professor David Barr, both under the auspices of the Society of Biblical Literature, and the Seminar on Apocalyptic in the New Testament, chaired by a succession of scholars including Professors Traugott Holtz, Elizabeth Schüssler Fiorenza, Charles H. Giblin, and Jens Taeger, under the auspices of the Studiorum Novi Testamenti Societas. Three graduate research assistants, Peter Sibilio (spring 1994), Paul Hartog (fall 1995), and Kevin McCruden (Spring 1997), have waded through countless pages of text and saved me from hundreds of errors.

My own interest in Revelation began in connection with earlier work on issues relating to early Christiain prophecy that came to fruition in a book entitled *Prophecy in Early Christianity and the Ancient Mediterranean World* (Grand Rapids, MI:

Eerdmans, 1983). It seemed a natural continuation of that interest to focus on a detailed study of the Revelation of John. I am grateful for the confidence that Professor Ralph Martin had in my work, which led to the issuing of the contract that made this commentary part of the Word Biblical Commentary series.

The writing of a commentary on any book of the Bible is a daunting task, particularly so in the case of the Revelation of John. Though the bibliography of books and articles on Revelation is enormous (extensive as the bibliographies in this commentary are, they are far from exhaustive), I am particularly indebted to the rich and creative commentaries of Wilhelm Bousset and R. H. Charles, and to the very detailed and painstaking textual work of H. C. Hoskier and Josef Schmid. In the words of J. W. v. Goethe:

> Seh ich die Werke der Meister an,
> So seh ich das, was sie getan;
> Betracht ich meine Siebensachen,
> Seh ich, was ich hätt sollen machen.

The *Notes* sections in this commentary contain discussions of the grammar and text of Revelation. Readers who have a special interest in the text of Revelation are urged to read Section 6 of the *Introduction,* where a full explanation of the many abbreviations of manuscripts and families of manuscripts can be found.

Jeff Hubing, my graduate research assistant for the 1997–98 academic year helped with the task of reading and correcting the page proofs of volume 52B, while the enormous task of compiling the indexes included in volume 52C was completed with the help of Hans Svebakken, my graduate assistant for the fall semester of 1998, and my wife, Mary Lou. I am also grateful for the competent editorial help provided by Thomas Nelson in the persons of Melanie McQuere and Lynn Losie; both have gone over the manuscript meticulously and introduced improvements and corrections too numerous to mention.

DAVID E. AUNE

September 1998
Loyola University Chicago

Abbreviations

A. General Abbreviations

abs.	absolute	neut.	neuter
acc.	accusative	no.	number
adj.	adjective, adjectival	nom.	nominative
adv.	adverb, adverbial	n.s.	new series
aor.	aorist	NT	New Testament
Aram.	Aramaic	obj.	object, objective
ca.	*circa*, about	OL	Old Latin
cent.	century	OT	Old Testament
cf.	*confer*, compare	par.	parallel
chap(s).	chapter(s)	pass.	passive
d.	deceased	PEnteux	*Enteuxeis* Papyri (Cairo)
dat.	dative	pf.	perfect
DSS	Dead Sea Scrolls	PGiss	Giessen Papyri
ed.	editor, edited by	PKöln	Kölner Papyri
e.g.	*exempli gratia*, for example	pl.	plural
ET	English translation	plupf.	pluperfect
et. al.	*et alii*, and others	PLond	London Papyri
fem.	feminine	poss.	possessive
fig.	figure	POxy	Oxyrhynchus Papyri
fl.	*floruit*, flourished	prep.	preposition
fol.	folio	PRoss	Papyri russischer und
FS	*Festschrift*, volume written		georgischer
	in honor of		Sammlungen
fut.	future	ptcp.	participle
gen.	genitive	PWash	Washington University
Gk.	Greek		Papyri
hap. leg.	*hapax legomenon*, sole	repr.	reprint
	occurrence	rev.	revised, reviser, revision
Heb.	Hebrew	sc.	*scilicet*, namely
id.	*idem*, the same	ser.	series
i.e.	*id est*, that is	sing.	singular
imper.	imperative	s.v.	*sub verbo*, under the word
impf.	imperfect	Sync	Syncellus
ind.	indicative	Theod	Theodotion
inf.	infinitive	tr.	translator, translated by,
lit.	literally		translation
LXX	Septuagint	UP	University Press
masc.	masculine	v, vv	verse, verses
MS(S)	manuscript(s)	*var. lect.*	*varia(e) lectio(nes)*,
MT	Masoretic Text		"variant reading(s)"
n.	note	vol.	volume
n.d.	no date	x	times (2x = two times)

B. Abbreviations for Translations and Paraphrases

ASV	American Standard Version, American Revised Version (1901)	NAV	New Authorized Version
		NEB	New English Bible
		NIV	New International Version
AV	Authorized Version = KJV	NRSV	New Revised Standard Version
KJV	King James Version (1611) = AV		
		REB	Revised English Bible
NASB	New American Standard Bible	RSV	Revised Standard Version

C. Abbreviations of Commonly Used Periodicals, Reference Works, and Serials

AAA	R. A. Lipsius and M. Bonnet (eds.), *Acta Apostolorum Apocrypha*	*AOT*	H. F. D. Sparks (ed.), *The Apocryphal Old Testament*
AB	Anchor Bible	AramBib	Aramaic Bible (Wilmington, DE: Glazier)
ABD	D. N. Freedman (ed.), *Anchor Bible Dictionary*, 6 vols.	*ARW*	*Archiv für Religionswissenschaft*
AC	*Antike und Christentum*	*AsSeign*	*Assemblées du Seigneur*
AcCl	*Acta Classica*	*ASTI*	*Annual of the Swedish Theological Institute*
AD	I. J. Gelb et al. (eds), *The Assyrian Dictionary of the Oriental Institute of the University of Chicago*, 21 vols.	ATANT	Abhandlung zur Theologie des Alten und Neuen Testaments
		ATR	*Anglican Theological Review*
		Aug	*Augustinianum*
AHI	G. I. Davies (ed.), *Ancient Hebrew Inscriptions: Corpus and Concordance*	AUSDDS	Andrews University Seminary Doctoral Dissertation Series
AJA	*American Journal of Archaeology*	*AUSS*	*Andrews University Seminary Studies*
AJAH	*American Journal of Ancient History*		
AJBI	Annual of the Japanese Biblical Institute	*BA*	*Biblical Archaeologist*
		BAGD	W. Bauer, W. F. Arndt, F. W. Gingrich, and F. W. Danker, *A Greek-English Lexicon of the NT*, 2nd ed.
AJP	*American Journal of Philology*		
ALUOS	Annual of Leeds University Oriental Society		
AnBib	Analecta biblica	*BAR*	*Biblical Archaeologist Reader*
AnBoll	Analecta Bollandiana	*BARev*	*Biblical Archaeology Review*
ANEP	J. B. Pritchard (ed.), *The Ancient Near East in Pictures*	BARevSup	*BARev* Supplementary Series
		BASOR	*Bulletin of the American Schools of Oriental Research*
ANET	J. B. Pritchard (ed.), *Ancient Near Eastern Texts*	BASORSup	*BASOR* Supplementary Studies
ANRW	*Aufsteig und Niedergang der römischen Welt*	Bauer-Aland	W. Bauer, *Griechisch-deutsches Wörterbuch zum den Schriften des Neuen Testaments und der frühchristlichen Literatur*, 6th ed., rev. K. and B. Aland
ANTF	Arbeiten zur neutestamentlichen Textforschung		
AOB	Acta Orientalia Beligica		

BCH	Bulletin de Correspondance Hellénique	ByzNeugrJb	Byzantinisch-neugriechische Jahrbücher
BDB	F. Brown, S. R. Driver, and C. A. Briggs, *Hebrew and English Lexicon of the OT*	BZ	*Biblische Zeitschrift*
		BZAW	Beihefte zur *ZAW*
		BZNW	Beihefte zur *ZNW*
BDF	F. Blass, A. Debrunner, and R. W. Funk, *A Greek Grammar of the NT*	CA	*Classical Antiquity*
		CAH	*Cambridge Ancient History*
BDR	F. Blass, A. Debrunner, and F. Rehkopf, *Grammatik des neutestamentlichen Griechisch* (1984)	CBQ	*Catholic Biblical Quarterly*
		CBQMS	Catholic Biblical Quarterly— Monograph Series
BETL	Bibliotheca ephemeridum theologicarum lovaniensium	CCL	Corpus Christianorum, Series Latina
		CH	*Church History*
BEvT	Beiträge zur Evangelischen Theologie	Checklist	J. F. Oates, R. S. Bagnall, W. H. Willis, and K. A. Worp, *Checklist of Editions of Greek Papyri and Ostraca,* 3rd ed.
BG	W. C. Till (ed.), *Die gnostischen Schriften des koptischen Papyrus Berolinensis 8502*		
		CIG	*Corpus Inscriptionum Graecarum,* 4 vols.
BGBE	Beiträge zur Geschichte der biblischen Exegese	CIJ	*Corpus Inscriptionum Judaicarum*
BHS	*Biblia hebraica stuttgartensia*	CIL	*Corpus Inscriptionum Latinarum*
BHT	Beiträge zur historischen Theologie	CIMRM	M. J. Vermaseren (ed.), *Corpus Inscriptionum et Monumentorum Religionis Mithraicae,* 2 vols.
Bib	*Biblica*		
BibLeb	*Bibel und Leben*		
BibReal	K. Galling (ed.), *Biblisches Reallexikon,* 2nd ed.	CJ	*Classical Journal*
BJRL	*Bulletin of the John Rylands University Library of Manchester*	CMIR	J. R. Cayón, *Compendio de las Monedas del Imperio Romano,* 2 vols.
BJS	Brown Judaic Studies	ConBNT	Coniectanea biblica, NT series
BK	*Bibel und Kirche*		
BMC	H. Mattingly, *Coins of the Roman Empire in the British Museum*	ConBOT	Coniectanea biblica, Old Testament
		ConNT	Coniectanea neotestamentica
BMI	*British Museum Inscriptions*		
BN	*Biblische Notizen*	CP	*Classical Philology*
BR	*Biblical Research*	CPJ	V. A. Tcherikover, A. Fuks, and M. Stern (eds.), *Corpus Papyrorum Judaicorum,* 3 vols.
BSac	*Bibliotheca Sacra*		
BT	*The Bible Translator*		
BTB	*Biblical Theology Bulletin*		
BurH	*Buried History*	CQ	*Classical Quarterly*
BVC	*Bible et vie chrétienne*	CQR	*Church Quarterly Review*
BWANT	Beiträge zur Wissenschaft vom Alten und Neuen Testament	CREBM	H. Mattingly and R. A. G. Carson, *Coins of the Roman Empire in the*

British Museum, 6 vols.

CRINT	Compendia Rerum Iudaicarum ad Novum Testamentum
CSCA	California Studies in Classical Antiquity
CSCO	Corpus scriptorum christianorum orientalium
CSEL	Corpus scriptorum ecclesiasticorum latinorum
CTA	A. Herdner, Corpus des tablettes en cunéiformes alphabétiques
CTM	Concordia Theological Monthly
CTQ	Concordia Theological Quarterly
CTR	Criswell Theological Review
DACL	F. Cabrol (ed.), Dictionnaire d'archéologie chrétienne et la liturgie, 15 vols.
DBSup	Dictionnaire de la Bible, Supplément
DCH	D. J. A. Clines (ed.), The Dictionary of Classical Hebrew
DDD	K. van der Toorn, B. Becking, and P. W. van der Horst (eds.), Dictionary of Deities and Demons in the Bible
DJD	Discoveries in the Judaean Desert
DJPA	M. Sokoloff, A Dictionary of Jewish Palestinian Aramaic of the Byzantine Period
DSD	Dead Sea Discoveries
DTT	Dansk teologisk tidsskrift
EDNT	H. Balz and G. Schneider (eds.), Exegetical Dictionary of the New Testament, 3 vols.
EEC	Angelo Di Berardino (ed.), Encyclopedia of the Early Church, 2 vols.
EncJud	Encyclopedia Judaica, 16 vols.
EncRel	M. Eliade (ed.), The Encyclopedia of Religion

EPRO	Études préliminaires aux religions orientales dans l'empire romain
ERE	J. Hastings (ed.), Encyclopedia of Religion and Ethics
ErFor	Erträge der Forschung
ESAR	T. Frank (ed.), An Economic Survey of Ancient Rome, 5 vols.
EstBib	Estudios bíblicos
ETL	Ephemerides theologicae lovanienses
ETR	Études théologiques et religieuses
EvQ	Evangelical Quarterly
EvT	Evangelische Theologie
EWNT	H. Balz and G. Schneider (eds.), Exegetisches Wörterbuch zum Neuen Testament, 3 vols.
ExpTim	Expository Times
FHJA	C. R. Holladay (ed.), Fragments from Hellenistic Jewish Authors, 4 vols.
FNT	Filologia Neotestamentaria
FOTL	The Forms of the Old Testament Literature
FrGrHist	F. Jacoby (ed.), Die Fragmente der griechischen Historiker
FRLANT	Forschungen zur Religion und Literatur des Alten und Neuen Testaments
FuF	Forschungen und Fortschritte
FVS	H. Diels and W. Kranz, Die Fragmente der Vorsokratiker, 3 vols.
GCS	Griechischen christlichen Schriftsteller
GELS	J. Lust, E. Eynikel, and K. Hauspie, A Greek-English Lexicon of the Septuagint
GGR	M. P. Nilsson, Geschichte der griechischen Religion, vol. 1, 3rd ed. (1967); vol. 2, 2nd ed. (1961)
GHÅ	Göteborgs Högskolas Årsskrift
GKC	Gesenius' Hebrew Grammar, ed. E. Kautzsch, tr. A. E. Cowley
GL	Geist und Leben

GNS	Good News Studies		*Inscriptiones Latinae Selectae*
GR	*Greece and Rome*	*IM*	*Istanbuler Mitteilungen*
GRBS	*Greek, Roman, and Byzantine Studies*	*Int*	*Interpretation*
		ISBE	G. W. Bromiley (ed.),
GTJ	*Grace Theological Journal*		*International Standard Bible Encyclopedia*, rev., 4 vols.
HAT	Handbuch zum Alten Testament	*ITQ*	*Irish Theological Quarterly*
HCNT	M. E. Boring, K. Berger, and C. Colpe, *Hellenistic Commentary to the NT*	*JAAR*	*Journal of the American Academy of Religion*
		JAC	Jahrbuch für Antike und Christentum
HDA	H. Bächtold-Stäubli with E. Hoffmann-Krayer (eds.), *Handwörterbuch des deutschen Aberglaubens*	*JAF*	*Journal of American Folklore*
		JAOS	*Journal of the American Oriental Society*
HDR	Harvard Dissertations in Religion	*JBL*	*Journal of Biblical Literature*
		JBR	*Journal of Bible and Religion*
HeyJ	*Heythrop Journal*	*JE*	*Jewish Encyclopedia*
HibJ	*Hibbert Journal*	*JEA*	*Journal of Egyptian Archaeology*
HNT	Handbuch zum Neuen Testament	*JES*	*Journal of Ecumenical Studies*
		JETS	*Journal of the Evangelical Theological Society*
HSCP	*Harvard Studies in Classical Philology*	*JHS*	*Journal of Hellenic Studies*
HSM	Harvard Semitic Monographs	*JIGRE*	W. Horbury and D. Noy (eds.), *Jewish Inscriptions of Graeco-Roman Egypt*
HSS	Harvard Semitic Studies		
HTR	*Harvard Theological Review*	*JJS*	*Journal of Jewish Studies*
HTS	Harvard Theological Studies	*JMS*	*Journal of Mithraic Studies*
HUCA	*Hebrew Union College Annual*	*JNES*	*Journal of Near Eastern Studies*
HUT	Hermeneutische Untersuchungen zur Theologie	*JP*	*Journal of Philology*
		JPOS	*Journal of Palestine Oriental Society*
		JQR	*Jewish Quarterly Review*
IBM	*Ancient Greek Inscriptions in the British Museum*, 4 vols.	*JR*	*Journal of Religion*
		JRS	*Journal of Roman Studies*
IDB	G. A. Buttrick (ed.), *Interpreter's Dictionary of the Bible*, 4 vols.	*JSJ*	*Journal for the Study of Judaism in the Persian, Hellenistic and Roman Period*
IDBSup	Supplementary Volume to *IDB*	*JSNT*	*Journal for the Study of the New Testament*
IEJ	*Israel Exploration Journal*	JSNTSup	Journal for the Study of the New Testament— Supplement Series
I. Eph.	H. Wankel (ed.), *Die Inschriften von Ephesos*, IGSK, 8 vols.		
		JSOT	*Journal for the Study of the Old Testament*
IGRom	R. Cagnat et al., *Inscriptiones Graecae ad res Romanas pertinentes*, 4 vols.	JSOTSup	Journal for the Study of the Old Testament— Supplement Series
IGSK	Inschriften griechischer Städte aus Kleinasien	*JSP*	*Journal for the Study of the Pseudepigrapha*
ILS	H. Dessau (ed.),		

JSPSup	Supplement to *JSP*	*MGWJ*	*Monatsschrift für Geschichte und Wissenschaft des Judentums*
JSS	*Journal of Semitic Studies*		
JTC	*Journal for Theology and the Church*	*MIR*	I. G. Mazzini, *Monete Imperiale Romane*, 4 vols.
JTS	*Journal of Theological Studies*	MM	J. H. Moulton and G. Milligan, *The Vocabulary of the Greek Testament*
KAT	Kommentar zum Alten Testament		
KAV	Kommentar zu den Apostolischen Vätern	*MQ*	*McCormick Quarterly*
		Mus	*Le Muséon*
KB³	L. Koehler and W. Baumgartner, *Hebräisches und Aramäisches Lexikon zum Alten Testament*, 3rd ed., 4 vols.	NCB	New Century Bible
		NEAEHL	E. Stern (ed.), *The New Encyclopedia of Archaeological Excavations in the Holy Land*, 4 vols.
KD	*Kerygma und Dogma*		
Kleine Pauly	K. Ziegler and W. Sontheimer, *Der Kleine Pauly: Lexikon der Antike*, 5 vols.	*NedTTs*	*Nederlands theologisch tijdschrift*
		Neot	*Neotestamentica*
		Nestle-Aland²⁶	E. Nestle, K. Aland, et al. (eds.), *Novum Testamentum Graece*, 26th ed.
LB	*Linguistica Biblica*		
LCL	Loeb Classical Library	Nestle-Aland²⁷	E. Nestle, K. Aland, et al. (eds.), *Novum Testamentum Graece*, 27th ed.
LexÄgypt	W. Helck and E. Otto (eds.), *Lexikon der Ägyptologie*		
LIMC	*Lexicon Iconographicum Mythologiae Classicae*	Neuer Wettstein	G. Strecker and U. Schnelle (eds.), *Neuer Wettstein: Texte zum Neuen Testament aus Griechentum und Hellenismus:* vol. 2/2. *Texte zur Briefliteratur und zur Johannes-apokalypse*
Louw-Nida	J. P. Louw and E. A. Nida, *Greek-English Lexicon of the New Testament Based on Semantic Domains*, 2 vols.		
LQHR	*London Quarterly and Holburn Review*	New Docs	G. H. R. Horsley and S. R. Llewelyn (eds.), *New Documents Illustrating Early Christianity*
LR	*Lutherische Rundschau*		
LSJ	H. G. Liddell, R. Scott, H. S. Jones, and R. McKenzie, *A Greek-English Lexicon*, 9th ed.		
		NGM	*National Geographic Magazine*
		NHS	Nag Hammadi Studies
		NICNT	New International Commentary on the New Testament
MAMA	W. M. Calder and J. M. R. Cormack (eds.), *Monumenta Asiae Minoris Antiqua*	*NIDNTT*	C. Brown (ed.), *The New International Dictionary of New Testament Theology*
		NKZ	*Neue kirchliche Zeitschrift*
MDAIRA	*Mitteilungen des deutschen archaeologischen Instituts, Römische Abteilung*	*NorTT*	*Norsk Teologisk Tidsskrift*
		NovT	*Novum Testamentum*
MeyerK	H. A. W. Meyer, *Kritischexegetischer Kommentar über das Neue Testament*	NovTSup	Novum Testamentum, Supplements
		NRT	*La nouvelle revue théologique*

NTA	E. Hennecke and W. Schneemelcher (eds.), *New Testament Apocrypha,* rev. ed.	*RAC*	*Reallexikon für Antike und Christentum*
		RArch	*Revue archéologique*
NTAbh	Neutestamentliche Abhandlungen	*RÄRG*	H. Bonnet (ed.), *Reallexikon der ägyptischen Religionsgeschichte,* 2nd ed.
NTOA	Novum Testamentum et Orbis Antiquus	*RB*	*Revue biblique*
		RBén	*Revue bénédictine*
NTS	*New Testament Studies*	*RCT*	*Revista Catalana de Teologia*
NumenSup	Supplements to *Numen*	*RE*	*Realencyklopädie für protestantische Theologie und Kirche*
NumZ	*Numismatische Zeitschrift*		
OBO	Orbis biblicus et orientalis	*REA*	*Revue des études anciennes*
OCD [2]	*Oxford Classical Dictionary,* 2nd ed. (1975)	*REG*	*Revue des études grecques*
		REJ	*Revue des études juives*
OGIS	W. Dittenberger, *Orientis Graeci Inscriptiones Selectae,* 2 vols.	*ResQ*	*Restoration Quarterly*
		RevExp	*Review and Expositor*
		RevistB	*Revista bíblica*
OLD	P. G. W. Glare (ed.), *Oxford Latin Dictionary*	*RevQ*	*Revue de Qumran*
		RevThom	*Revue thomiste*
OrChr	*Oriens christianus*	*RF*	*Rivista di Filologia*
ORPB	*Oberrheinisches Pastoralblat*	*RGG*	*Religion in Geschichte und Gegenwart*
OTL	Old Testament Library		
OTP	J. H. Charlesworth (ed.), *The Old Testament Pseudepigrapha*	RGRW	Religions in the Graeco-Roman World (formerly EPRO)
OTS	*Oudtestamentische Studiën*	*RHPR*	*Revue d'histoire et de philosophie religieuses*
OTS	Old Testament Studies		
		RHR	*Revue de l'histoire des religions*
PAAJR	*Proceedings of the American Academy of Jewish Research*	*RIC*	H. Mattingly, E. A. Sydenham, et al., *Roman Imperial Coinage,* 8 vols.
PBA	*Proceedings of the British Academy*		
		RivB	*Rivista biblica*
PDM	H. D. Betz (ed.), *The Greek Magical Papyri in Translation, including the Demotic Spells*	*RMP*	*Rheinisches Museum für Philologie*
		RQ	*Römische Quartalschrift für christliche Altertumskunde und Kirchengeschichte*
PEQ	*Palestine Exploration Quarterly*		
PG	J.-P. Migne, *Patrologia graeca*	RQSup	Supplement to *RQ*
PGL	G. H. W. Lampe (ed.), *A Patristic Greek Lexicon*	*RSR*	*Recherches de science religieuse*
		RVV	*Religionsgeschichtliche Versuche und Vorarbeiten*
PGM	K. Preisendanz (ed.), *Papyri graecae magicae,* 2nd ed., 2 vols.		
		SB	F. Preisigke et al. (eds.), *Sammelbuch griechischer Urkunden aus Ägypten*
PL	J.-P. Migne, *Patrologia latina*		
PW	Pauly-Wissowa, *Real-Encyclopädie der classischen Altertumswissenschaft*	*SBFLA*	*Studii Biblici Franciscani Liber Annuus*
PWSup	Supplement to PW	SBL	Society of Biblical Literature

SBLDS	SBL Dissertation Series	SUNT	Studien zur Umwelt des Neuen Testaments
SBLMS	SBL Monograph Series		
SBM	Stuttgarter biblische Monographien	SVF	J. von Arnim, *Stoicorum Veterum Fragmenta*, 4 vols.
SBS	Stuttgarter Bibelstudien	SVTG	Septuaginta: Vetus Testamentum Graecum
SBT	Studies in Biblical Theology		
SC	Sources chrétiennes		
SCHNT	Studia ad corpus hellenisticum Novi Testamenti	*TAPA*	*Transactions of the American Philological Association*
ScrT	*Scripta Theologica*	*TBA*	*Tübinger Beiträge zur Altertumswissenschaft*
SEÅ	*Svensk exegetisk årsbok*	*TBei*	*Theologische Beiträge*
SE	*Studia Evangelica* 1, 2, 3 (= TU 73 [1959], 87 [1964], 88 [1964], 102 [1968], 103 [1968], 112 [1973])	*TBl*	*Theologische Blätter*
		TCGNT[1]	B. M. Metzger, *A Textual Commentary on the Greek New Testament*
SD	Studies and Documents	*TCGNT*[2]	B. M. Metzger, *A Textual Commentary on the Greek New Testament*, 2nd ed.
SEG	*Supplementum Epigraphicum Graecum*		
SGU	Studia Graeca Upsaliensia	*TDNT*	G. Kittel and G. Friedrich (eds.), *Theological Dictionary of the New Testament*, 10 vols.
SIG	W. Dittenberger (ed.), *Sylloge Inscriptionum Graecarum*, 3rd ed., 4 vols.		
SJLA	Studies in Judaism in Late Antiquity	*TDOT*	G. J. Botterweck and H. Ringgren (eds.), *Theological Dictionary of the Old Testament*
SJT	*Scottish Journal of Theology*		
SKI	Studien zu Kirche und Israel		
SNT	Studien zum Neuen Testament	TextsS	Texts and Studies
		TGl	*Theologie und Glaube*
SNTSMS	Society for New Testament Studies Monograph Series	*TGL*	H. Stephanus, *Thesaurus Graecae Linguae*
SNTU	*Studien zum Neuen Testament und seiner Umwelt*	*THAT*	E. Jenni and C. Westermann (eds.), *Theologisches Handwörterbuch zum Alten Testament*
SO	*Symbolae osloenses*		
SPA	*Studia Philonica Annual*	THKNT	Theologischer Handkommentar zum Neuen Testament
SPap	*Studia papyrologica*		
SPB	Studia postbiblica		
SR	*Studies in Religion/Sciences religieuses*	*TLNT*	C. Spicq, *Theological Lexicon of the New Testament*, tr. J. D. Ernst, 3 vols.
ST	*Studia theologica*		
STDJ	Studies on the Texts of the Desert of Judah	*TLZ*	*Theologische Literaturzeitung*
		TPQ	*Theologisch-praktische Quartalschrift*
Str-B	[H. Strack and] P. Billerbeck, *Kommentar zum Neuen Testament aus Talmud und Midrash*	*TQ*	*Theologische Quartalschrift*
		TRE	*Theologische Realenzyklopädie*
		TRu	*Theologische Rundschau*
StudP	*Studia Patristica*	*TS*	*Theological Studies*

TSK	*Theologische Studien und Kritiken*	WBC	Word Biblical Commentary
TT	*Theologisk Tijdskrift*	WHort	B. F. Westcott and F. J. A. Hort, *The New Testament in the Original Greek*
TThQ	*Tübinger theologische Quartalschrift*		
TTZ	*Trierer theologische Zeitschrift*	WMANT	Wissenschaftliche Monographien zum Alten und Neuen Testament
TU	Texte und Untersuchungen		
TWAT	G. J. Botterweck, H. Ringgren, and H.-J. Fabry (eds.), *Theologisches Wörterbuch zum Alten Testament*	*WO*	*Die Welt des Orients*
		WTJ	*Westminster Theological Journal*
		WUNT	Wissenschaftliche Untersuchungen zum Neuen Testament
TWNT	G. Kittel and G. Friedrich (eds.), *Theologisches Wörterbuch zum Neuen Testament*	*ZASA*	*Zeitschrift für Ägyptische Sprache und Altertumskunde*
		ZAW	*Zeitschrift für die alttestamentliche Wissenschaft*
TynBul	*Tyndale Bulletin*		
TZ	*Theologische Zeitschrift*		
		ZKT	*Zeitschrift für katholische Theologie*
UBSGNT³	K. Aland et al. (eds.), United Bible Societies *Greek New Testament*, 3rd ed.	*ZNW*	*Zeitschrift für die neutestamentliche Wissenschaft*
UBSGNT⁴	K. Aland et al. (eds.), United Bible Societies *Greek New Testament*, 4th ed.	*ZPE*	*Zeitschrift für Papyrologie und Epigraphie*
		ZRGG	*Zeitschrift für Religions- und Geistesgeschichte*
VC	*Vigiliae Christianae*	*ZST*	*Zeitschrift für systematische Theologie*
VCaro	*Verbum caro*		
VD	*Verbum domini*	*ZTK*	*Zeitschrift für Theologie und Kirche*
VoxEv	*Vox Evangelica*		
VT	*Vetus Testamentum*	*ZVS*	*Zeitschrift für vergleichende Sprachforschung*
VTG	Vetus Testamentum Graecum		
VTSup	Supplements to *Vetus Testamentum*	*ZWT*	*Zeitschrift für wissenschaftliche Theologie*
		ZZ	*Zeichen der Zeit*

D. Abbreviations for Books of the Bible with Aprocrypha

OLD TESTAMENT

Gen	1–2 Kgs	Cant	Obad
Exod	1–2 Chr	Isa	Jonah
Lev	Ezra	Jer	Mic
Num	Neh	Lam	Nah
Deut	Esth	Ezek	Hab
Josh	Job	Dan	Zeph
Judg	Ps(s)	Hos	Hag
Ruth	Prov	Joel	Zech
1–2 Sam	Eccl	Amos	Mal

NEW TESTAMENT

Mark	1–2 Cor	1–2 Thess	Jas
Luke	Gal	1–2 Tim	1–2 Pet
John	Eph	Titus	1–2–3 John
Acts	Phil	Philem	Jude
Rom	Col	Heb	Rev

APOCRYPHA

1 Kgdms	1 Kingdoms		(Wisdom of Jesus the
2 Kgdms	2 Kingdoms		son of Sirach)
3 Kgdms	3 Kingdoms	Bar	Baruch
4 Kgdms	4 Kingdoms	Ep Jer	Epistle of Jeremiah
1–2 Esdr	1–2 Esdras	S Th Ch	Song of the Three
Tob	Tobit		Children (or Young Men)
Jdt	Judith	Sus	Susanna
Add Esth	Additions to	Bel	Bel and the Dragon
	Esther	Pr Azar	Prayer of Azariah
4 Ezra	4 Ezra	1 Macc	1 Maccabees
Wis	Wisdom of	2 Macc	2 Maccabees
	Solomon	3 Macc	3 Maccabees
Sir	Ecclesiasticus	4 Macc	4 Maccabees

E. Abbreviations of Pseudepigrapha and Early Jewish Literature

Adam and Eve	*Books of Adam and Eve* or *Vita Adae et Evae*	*Jos. As.*	*Joseph and Aseneth*
		Jub.	*Jubilees*
Apoc. Abr.	*Apocalypse of Abraham*	*Mart. Isa.*	*Martyrdom of Isaiah*
2–3 Apoc. Bar.	*Syriac, Greek Apocalypse of Baruch*	*Par. Jer.*	*Paraleipomena Jeremiou* or *4 Baruch*
Apoc. Sedr.	*Apocalypse of Sedrach*	*Pr. Man.*	*Prayer of Manassis*
Apoc. Zeph.	*Apocalypse of Zephaniah*	*Pss. Sol.*	*Psalms of Solomon*
Bib. Ant.	Ps.-Philo, *Biblical Antiquities*	*Sib. Or.*	*Sibylline Oracles*
		T. Job	*Testament of Job*
1–2–3 Enoch	Ethiopic, Slavonic, Hebrew *Enoch*	*T. Mos.*	*Testament of Moses (Assumption of Moses)*
Ep. Arist.	*Epistle of Aristeas*	*T. 12 Patr.*	*Testaments of the Twelve Patriarchs*
Jos. Ag. Ap.	Josephus *Against Apion*		
Ant.	*The Jewish Antiquities*	*T. Levi*	*Testament of Levi*
J. W.	*The Jewish War*	*T. Benj.*	*Testament of Benjamin*
Life	*The Life*	*T. Reub.*	*Testament of Reuben*, etc.

F. Abbreviations of Dead Sea Scrolls

CD	Cairo (Genizah text of the) *Damascus* (*Document*)	Mas	Masada texts
		MasShirShabb	*Songs of Sabbath*
Ḥev	Naḥal Ḥever texts	*Sacrifice,* or	*Angelic*
8 Ḥev XIIgr	Greek Scroll of the Minor Prophets from Naḥal Ḥever	*Liturgy* from	Masada
		Mird	Khirbet Mird texts
		Mur	Wadi Murabbaʿat texts

p	pesher (commentary)	4QMMT	*Miqsat Ma'aseh Torah* from Qumran Cave 4
Q	Qumran	4QPhyl	Phylacteries from Qumran Cave 4
1Q, 2Q, 3Q, etc.	Numbered caves of Qumran	4QPrNab	*Prayer of Nabonidus* from Qumran Cave 4
QL	Qumran literature	4QPssJosh	*Psalms of Joshua* from Qumran Cave 4
1QapGen	*Genesis Apocryphon* of Qumran Cave 1		
1QH	*Hôdāyôt (Thanksgiving Hymns)* from Qumran Cave 1	4QShirShabb	*Songs of Sabbath Sacrifice,* or *Angelic Liturgy* from Qumran Cave 4
1QpHab	*Pesher on Habakkuk* from Qumran Cave 1	4QTestim	*Testimonia* text from Qumran Cave 4
1QM	*Milḥāmāh (War Scroll)*	4QTLevi	*Testament of Levi* from Qumran Cave 4
1QS	*Serek hayyaḥad (Rule of the Community, Manual of Discipline)*	11QMelch	*Melchizedek* text from Qumran Cave 11
1QSa	Appendix A (*Rule of the Congregation*) to 1QS	11QShirShabb	*Songs of Sabbath Sacrifice,* or *Angelic Liturgy* from Qumran Cave 11
1QSb	Appendix B (*Blessings*) to 1QS	11QTemple	*Temple Scroll* from Qumran Cave 11
3Q15	*Copper Scroll* from Qumran Cave 3	11QpaleoLev	Copy of Leviticus in paleo-Hebrew script from Qumran Cave 11
4QFlor	*Florilegium* (or *Eschatological Midrashim*) from Qumran Cave 4	11QtgJob	*Targum of Job* from Qumran Cave 11
4QMess ar	Aramaic "Messianic" text from Qumran Cave 4		

G. Philo

Abr.	*De Abrahamo*	*Mut.*	*De mutatione nominum*
Aet.	*De aeternitate mundi*	*Op.*	*De opificio mundi*
Agr.	*De agricultura*	*Plant.*	*De plantatione*
Cher.	*De cherubim*	*Post.*	*De posteritate Caini*
Conf.	*De confusione linguarum*	*Praem.*	*De praemiis et poenis*
Congr.	*De congressu eruditionis gratia*	*Prov.*	*De providentia*
Decal.	*De decalogo*	*Quaest. in Gn.*	*Questiones et solutiones in Genesin*
Det.	*Quod deterius potiori insidiari solet*	*Quaest. in Ex.*	*Questiones et solutiones in Exodum*
Ebr.	*De ebrietate*	*Quis Her.*	*Quis rerum divinarum heres sit*
Flacc.	*In Flaccum*	*Quod Deus*	*Quod Deus sit immutabilis*
Fug.	*De fuga et inventione*	*Quod Omn.*	*Quod omnis Probus Prob. Liber sit*
Gig.	*De gigantibus*		
Hyp.	*Hypothetica/Apologia pro Iudaeis*	*Sac.*	*De Sacrificiis Abelis et Caini*
Jos.	*De Josepho*	*Sob.*	*De sobrietate*
Leg.	*De legatione ad Gaium*	*Som.*	*De somniis*
Leg. All.	*Legum allegoriarum*	*Spec. Leg.*	*De specialibus legibus*
Mig.	*De migratione Abrahami*	*Virt.*	*De virtute*
Mos.	*De vita Mosis*	*Vit. Cont.*	*De vita contemplativa*

H. Abbreviations of Early Christian Literature

Acts Pil.	Acts of Pilate	Justin Apol.	Justin 1 Apology
Acts Scill.	Acts of the Scillitan Martyrs	2 Apol.	2 Apology
Apoc. Pet.	Apocalypse of Peter	Dial.	Dialogue with Trypho
Apost. Const.	Apostolic Constitutions	Mart. Agape	The Martyrdom of Agape,
Asc. Isa.	Ascension of Isaiah		Irene, Chione, Companions
Barn.	Barnabas	Mart. Apollo-	The Martyrdom
1–2 Clem.	1–2 Clement	nius	of Apollonius
Corp. Herm.	Corpus Hermeticum	Mart. Carpus	Martyrdom of Saints
Did.	Didache		Carpus, Papylus, and
Diogn.	Diognetus		Agathonice
Ep. Lugd.	Epistula ecclesiarum apud	Mart. Dasius	The Martyrdom of Dasius
	Lugdunum et Viennam =	Mart. Fruct.	The Martyrdom of Bishop
	Letter of the Churches of Lyons		Fructuosus and his
Eusebius	Eusebius Historia		Deacons, Augurius and
Hist. ecc.	Ecclesiastica		Eulogius
Praep.	Praeparatio evangelica	Mart. Julius	The Martyrdom of Julius the
Gos. Eb.	Gospel of the Ebionites		Veteran
Gos. Heb.	Gospel of the Hebrews	Mart. Justin	The Martyrdom of Saints
Gos. Naass.	Gospel of the Naassenes		Justin, Chariton, Charito,
Gos. Pet.	Gospel of Peter		Evelpistus, Hierax,
Herm. Mand.	Hermas Mandate(s)		Paeon, Liberian, and
Sim.	Similitude(s)		Their Community
Vis.	Vision(s)	Mart. Mont.	Martyrdom of Saints
Ign. Eph.	Ignatius Letter to the		Montanus and Lucius
	Ephesians	Mart.	The Martyrdom of Perpetua
Magn.	Letter to the Magnesians	Perpetua	and Felicitas
Phld.	Letter to the Philadelphians	Mart. Pionius	The Martyrdom of Pionius
Pol.	Letter to Polycarp	Mart. Pol.	The Martyrdom of Polycarp
Rom.	Letter to the Romans	Odes Sol.	Odes of Solomon
Smyrn.	Letter to the Smyrnaeans	Pol. Phil.	Polycarp, Letter to the
Trall.	Letter to the Trallians		Philippians
Iren. Adv.	Irenaeus Against	Prot. Jas.	Protevangelium of James
Haer.	All Heresies	Tert. De	Tertullian, On the
Jos. Ag. Ap.	Josephus Against Apion	Praesc, Haer.	Proscribing of Heretics
Ant.	The Jewish Antiquities	Test. Forty	The Testament of the Forty
J.W.	The Jewish War	Martyrs	Martyrs of Sebaste
Life	The Life		

I. Abbreviations of Targumic Material

Tg. Onq.	Targum Onqelos	Tg. Neof.	Targum Neofiti I
Tg. Neb.	Targum of the Prophets	Tg. Ps.-J.	Targum Pseudo-Jonathan
Tg. Ket.	Targum of the Writings	Tg. Esth. I, II	First or Second Targum of
Tg. Isa.	Targum of Isaiah		Esther
		Tg. Ezek.	Targum of Ezekiel

J. Abbreviations of Nag Hammadi Tractates

Acts Pet. 12 Apost.	*Acts of Peter and the Twelve Apostles*	*Marsanes*	*Marsanes*
Allogenes	*Allogenes*	*Melch.*	*Melchizedek*
Ap. Jas.	*Apocryphon of James*	*Norea*	*Thought of Norea*
Ap. John	*Apocryphon of John*	*On Bap. A–B–C*	*On Baptism A–B–C*
Apoc. Adam	*Apocalypse of Adam*	*On Euch A–B*	*On Eucharist A–B*
1–2 Apoc. Jas.	*1–2 Apocalypse of James*		
Apoc. Paul	*Apocalypse of Paul*	*Orig. World*	*On the Origin of the World*
Apoc. Pet.	*Apocalypse of Peter*	*Paraph. Shem*	*Paraphrase of Shem*
Asclepius	*Asclepius 21–29*	*Pr. Paul*	*Prayer of the Apostle Paul*
Auth. Teach.	*Authoritative Teaching*	*Pr. Thanks.*	*Prayer of Thanksgiving*
Dial. Sav.	*Dialogues of the Savior*	*Sent. Sextus*	*Sentences of Sextus*
Disc. 8–9	*Discourse on the Eighth and Ninth*	*Soph. Jes. Chr.*	*Sophia of Jesus Christ*
		Steles Seth	*Three Steles of Seth*
Ep. Pet. Phil.	*Letter of Peter to Philip*	*Teach. Silv.*	*Teachings of Silvanus*
Eugnostos	*Eugnostos the Blessed*	*Testim. Truth*	*Testimony of Truth*
Exeg. Soul	*Exegesis on the Soul*	*Thom. Cont.*	*Book of Thomas the Contender*
Gos. Eg.	*Gospel of the Egyptians*		
Gos. Phil.	*Gospel of Philip*	*Thund.*	*Thunder, Perfect Mind*
Gos. Thom.	*Gospel of Thomas*	*Treat. Res.*	*Treatise on Resurrection*
Gos. Truth	*Gospel of Truth*	*Treat. Seth*	*Second Treatise of the Great Seth*
Great Pow.	*Concept of Our Great Power*		
Hyp. Arch.	*Hypostasis of the Archons*	*Tri. Trac.*	*Tripartite Tractate*
Hypsiph.	*Hypsiphrone*	*Trim. Prot.*	*Trimorphic Protennoia*
Interp. Know.	*Interpretation of Knowledge*	*Val. Exp.*	*A Valentinian Exposition*
		Zost.	*Zostrianos*

K. Manuscripts of Revelation

Andr or Andreas   Andreas, or Andrew, a bishop of Caesarea in Cappadocia, wrote a commentary on Revelation, ca. A.D. 600 (J. Schmid, ed., *Studien*, part 1: *Der Apokalypse-Kommentar des Andreas von Kaisareia*). "Andreas" means that the reading is in the text of Schmid. "Andr," when followed by a letter, e.g., "a," refers to a group of Andreas MSS (listed in the *Introduction*, Section 6: Text); when a letter is followed by a superscript number, e.g., Andreas f[051], only that MS in the group has the reading; when a letter is followed by a super script prefixed with a minus sign, e.g., f[2023], only that MS in the group lacks the reading.

Apringius   Apringius of Beja, a Spanish biblical interpreter (mid-sixth century A.D.) who wrote a commentary on Revelation; portions on Rev 1:5–7; 18:7–22:20 survive.

Arethas   Arethas (ca. 850–944), a native of the Peloponnesus who became the bishop of Caesarea in 902, wrote a commentary on Revelation that was a revision of the commentary of Andreas of Caesarea.

arm Armenian version of the NT; F. C. Conybeare, *Armenian Version.* arm[1] = Bodleian Codex (Conybeare, 115–134, appendix 1–189); arm[2] = British Museum Codex (Conybeare, 135–37); arm[3] = Bibliotheque Nationale (Conybeare, 135–37)); arm[4] = Armenian Convent Codex (Conybeare, 95–114).

Beatus Beatus of Liebana, d. 798, was a Spanish abbot who compiled a commentary on Revelation, chiefly from the now lost commentary of Tyconius. The Tyconian text of Beatus is printed in Vogels, *Untersuchungen,* 194–208. For the modern critical edition of Beatus, *Commentarius in Apocalypsin,* see Romero-Pose, *Sancti Beati.*

bo Bohairic version of Coptic NT.

Byz Byzantine family of MSS. When followed by an arabic numeral and superscript arabic numbers, e.g., Byz 1[920 1859], this refers to family 1 of the Byzantine recension (as described by Schmid, *Studien*), and specifically to MSS 920 and 1859 within that family.

Byzantine When most MSS in the Byzantine, or Koine, recension support a reading, the designation is spelled out in full.

Compl. Complutensian group of MSS.

cop Coptic version of the NT; used when the Sahidic (sa) and Bohairic (bo) agree.

eth Variants discussed by J. Hofmann, *Die äthiopische Johannes-Apokalypse.*

eth[comm] Commentaries on the Ethiopic version of Revelation published by R. W. Cowley, *Ethiopian Orthodox.*

Fulgentius Bishop of Ruspe in North Africa (A.D. 468–533); Latin text of Revelation in Vogels, *Untersuchungen,* 217–19.

Irenaeus[Lat] Irenaeus, bishop of Lyons, died ca. A.D. 200; evidence for his use of the Old Latin version is collected in Sanday-Turner, *Nouum Testamentum.*

Oecumenius Greek bishop of Tricca (early seventh century) and author of a commentary on Revelation; see in H. C. Hoskier, ed., *Oecumenius.* As used in the *Notes,* Oecumenius refers to the reading in Hoskier's text, while the citation of a particular MS with a superlinear number, e.g., Oecumenius[2053], refers to a specific MS.

Prom *De promissionibus et praedictionibus dei,* anonymous composition with Latin quotations from Revelation (in Vogels, *Untersuchungen,* 215–17).

sa Sahidic version of the NT.

syr   Syriac version of the NT.

TR   The so-called *Textus Receptus*, "Received Text," of the NT, consisting of
               Erasmus' edition of the Greek NT of 1516 based largely on minuscule
               codex 1 (twelfth–thirteenth century) of the NT.

Tyc   Tyconius, died ca. A.D. 400, was a Donatist who wrote a commentary
               on Revelation, which exists only in fragments and excerpts. Tyc[1] = Turin
               fragments of Tyconius (first edited by the Benedictines of Monte Cassino in
               the third volume of the *Spicilegium Casinense* [reproduced in Vogels,
               Untersuchungen, 179–82] but more recently edited by F. Lo Bue, *Tyconius*),
               containing only Rev 2:18–4:1; 7:16–12:6; Tyc[2] = Tyconius text of the Ps.-
               Augustine Homily (Vogels, *Untersuchungen,* 182–90); Tyc[3] = Tyconius text of
               the *Summa Dicendorum* of Beatus (Vogels, *Untersuchungen,* 190–93).

Victorinus   Victorinus of Petovium (died ca. 304 B.C.) wrote the first commentary on
               Revelation; see in J. Haussleiter, ed., *Victorinus.*

vg   Vulgate: *Biblia sacra iuxta Vulgatam versionem,* ed. R. Weber.

Note: Some textual notes and numbers are drawn from the apparatus criticus of *Novum Testamentum Graece,* ed. E. Nestle, K. Aland, et al., 26th ed. (Stuttgart: Deutsche Bibelgesellschaft, 1979); from *Novum Testamentum Graece,* ed. E. Nestle, K. Aland, et al., 27th ed. (Stuttgart: Deutsche Bibelgesellschaft, 1994), designated Nestle-Aland[26] and Nestle-Aland[27]; and from *The Greek New Testament,* ed. K. Aland, M. Black, C. Martini, B. M. Metzger, and A. Wikgren. 4th ed. (New York: United Bible Societies, 1994), designated UBSGNT[4]. These three identical editions of the Greek New Testament are the bases for the *Translation* sections.

Commentary Bibliography

References to commentaries are by author's last name and page number.

Alford, H. "Apocalypse of John." In *The Greek Testament.* Chicago: Moody, 1958. 4:544–750.
Allo, E. B. *L'Apocalypse du Saint Jean.* Paris: Gabalda, 1933. **Beasley-Murray, G. R.** *Revelation.* Rev. ed. NCB. London: Marshall, Morgan & Scott, 1978. **Beckwith, I. T.** *The Apocalypse of John.* New York: Macmillan, 1919. **Behm, J.** *Die Offenbarung des Johannes.* Göttingen: Vandenhoeck & Ruprecht, 1935. **Böcher, O.** *Die Johannesapokalypse.* 2nd ed. ErFor 41. Darmstadt: Wissenschaftliche Buchgesellschaft, 1980. **Boring, M. E.** *Revelation.* Interpretation. Louisville: John Knox, 1989. **Bousset, W.** *Die Offenbarung Johannis.* 6th ed. Kritisch-exegetischer Kommentar zum Neuen Testament 16. Göttingen: Vandenhoeck & Ruprecht, 1906. ———. *Die Offenbarung Johannis.* 5th ed. Kritisch-exegetischer Kommentar zum Neuen Testament 16. Göttingen: Vandenhoeck & Ruprecht, 1896. **Brütsch, C.** *Die Offenbarung Jesu Christi: Johannes-Apokalypse.* 2nd ed. 3 vols. Zürcher Bibelkommentare. Zürich: Zwingli, 1970. **Buchanan, G. W.** *The Book of Revelation: Its Introduction and Prophecy.* Mellen Biblical Commentary, NT Series 22. Lewiston, NY: Mellen Biblical, 1993. **Caird, G. B.** *A Commentary on the Revelation of St. John the Divine.* Harper's/Black's New Testament Commentaries. New York: Harper & Row, 1966. **Charles, R. H.** *A Critical and Exegetical Commentary on the Revelation of St. John.* 2 vols. Edinburgh: T. & T. Clark, 1920. **Delebecque, É.** *L'Apocalypse de Jean.* Paris: Mame, 1992. **Eichhorn, J. G.** *Commentarius in Apocalypsin Joannis.* 2 vols. Göttingen: Dieterich, 1791. **Ford, J. M.** *Revelation: Introduction, Translation and Commentary.* AB 38. Garden City, NY: Doubleday, 1965. **Giblin, C. H.** *The Book of Revelation: The Open Book of Prophecy.* GNS 34. Collegeville, MN: Liturgical, 1991. **Giesen, H.** *Johannes-Apokalypse.* 2nd ed. Stuttgarter kleiner Kommentar NT 18. Stuttgart: Katholisches Bibelwerk, 1989. ———. *Die Offenbarung des Johannes.* Regensburger Neues Testament. Regensburg: Pustet, 1997. **Glasson, T. F.** *The Revelation of John.* CBC. Cambridge: Cambridge UP, 1965. **Hadorn, D. W.** *Die Offenbarung des Johannes.* THKNT 18. Leipzig: Deichert, 1928. **Harrington, W. J.** *Revelation.* Sacra Pagina 16. Collegeville: Liturgical, 1993. **Hendricksen, W.** *More Than Conquerors.* Grand Rapids, MI: Baker, 1944. **Hengstenberg, E. W.** *The Revelation of St. John.* Edinburgh: T. & T. Clark, 1851. **Hort, F. J. A.** *The Apocalypse of St John I–III.* London: Macmillan, 1908. **Kiddle, M.,** and **Ross, M. K.** *The Revelation of St. John.* London: Hodder & Stoughton, 1946. **Kraft, H.** *Die Offenbarung des Johannes.* HNT 16a. Tübingen: Mohr-Siebeck, 1974. **Krodel, G. A.** *Revelation.* Augsburg Commentary on the New Testament. Minneapolis: Augsburg, 1989. **Ladd, G. E.** *A Commentary on the Revelation of John.* Grand Rapids, MI: Eerdmans, 1972. **Lange, J. P.** *Die Offenbarung des Johannes.* 2nd ed. Bielefield/Leipzig:Velhagen und Klasing, 1878. **Lohmeyer, E.** *Die Offenbarung des Johannes.* 3rd ed. HNT 16. Tübingen: Mohr-Siebeck, 1970. **Lohse, E.** *Die Offenbarung des Johannes.* Göttingen: Vandenhoeck & Ruprecht, 1976. **Loisy, A.** *L'Apocalypse de Jean.* Paris: Nourry, 1923. **Moffatt, J.** "The Revelation of St. John the Divine." In *The Expositor's Greek Testament,* ed. W. R. Nicoll. London: Hodder & Stoughton, 1910. 5:297–494. **Mounce, R. H.** *The Book of Revelation.* NICNT. Grand Rapids, MI: Eerdmans, 1977. **Müller, U. B.** *Die Offenbarung des Johannes.* Gütersloh: Mohn, 1984. **Prigent, P.** *L'Apocalypse de Saint Jean.* 2nd ed. Geneva: Labor et Fides, 1988. **Rissi, M.** "The Revelation of St. John the Divine: Introduction and Exegesis." In *The Interpreter's Bible,* ed. G. A. Buttrick et al. New York; Nashville: Abingdon, 1957. 12:345–613. **Roloff, J.** *Die Offenbarung des Johannes.* Zürcher Bibelkommentare NT 18. Zürich: Theologischer, 1984. ———. *The Revelation of John.* Tr. J. E. Alsup. Continental Commentaries. Minneapolis: Fortress, 1993 (hereafter Roloff, ET). **Romero-Pose, E.** *Sancti Beati a Liebana Commentarius in Apocalypsin.* 2 vols. Rome: Typis

Officinae Polygraphicae, 1985. **Rowland, C.** *Revelation.* Epworth Commentaries. London: Epworth, 1993. **Spitta, F.** *Die Offenbarung des Johannes.* Halle: Waisenhaus, 1889. **Stuart, M.** *Commentary on the Apocalypse.* 2 vols. Andover: Allen, Morrill and Wardwell, 1845. **Sweet, J. P. M.** *Revelation.* Philadelphia: Westminster, 1979. **Swete, H. B.** *The Apocalypse of John.* 3rd ed. London: Macmillan, 1908. **Talbert, C. H.** *The Apocalypse: A Reading of the Revelation of John.* Louisville: Westminster John Knox, 1994. **Völter, D.** *Die Offenbarung Johannis neu untersucht und erläutert.* 2nd ed. Strassburg: Heitz & Mundel, 1911. **Weiss, J.**, and **Heitmüller, W.** "Die Offenbarung des Johannes." In *Die Schriften des Neuen Testaments.* 3rd ed. Göttingen: Vandenhoeck & Ruprecht, 1920. 4:229–319. **Wikenhauser, A.** *Die Offenbarung Johannes.* 3rd. ed. Das Neue Testament 9. Regensburg: Pustet, 1959. **Zahn, T.** *Die Offenbarung des Johannes.* 1st to 3rd ed. 2 vols. Kommentar zum Neuen Testament 18. Leipzig; Erlangen: Deichert, 1924.

General Bibliography

Abbott, E. A. *Johannine Grammar.* London: Adam & Charles Black, 1906. **Aberbach, M.,** and **Grossfeld, B.** *Targum Onkelos to Genesis.* New York: Ktav, 1982. **Abrahams, I.** *Studies in Pharisaism and the Gospels.* 1924. Repr. New York: Ktav, 1967. **Achelis, H.** *Hippolyt's kleinere exegetische und homiletische Shriften.* GCS 1.2. Leipzig: Hinrichs, 1897. **Adler, A.,** ed., *Suidae Lexicon.* Leipzig: Teubner, 1928–38. **Aejmelaeus, A.** *Parataxis in the Septuagint: A Study of the Renderings of the Hebrew Coordinate Clauses in the Greek Pentateuch.* Helsinki: Suomalainen Tiedeakatemia, 1982. **Albright, W. F.** *Archaeology and the Religion of Israel.* Baltimore: Johns Hopkins UP, 1956. ———. *Yahweh and the Gods of Canaan.* Garden City, NY: Doubleday, 1969. **Alföldi, A.** "Die Ausgestaltung des monarchischen Zeremoniells am römischen Kaiserhofe." *MDAIRA* 49 (1934) 1–118. ———. *Die monarchische Repräsentation im römischen Kaiserreiche.* Darmstadt: Wissenschaftliche Buchgesellschaft, 1970. **Allen, J. H.,** and **Greenough, J. B.** *A Latin Grammar: Founded on Comparative Grammar.* Rev. ed. Boston: Ginn and Heath, 1884. **Andersen, F. I.** *The Sentence in Biblical Hebrew.* The Hague: Mouton, 1974. ——— and **Freedman, D. N.** *Amos.* New York: Doubleday, 1989. **Attridge, H. W.** *The Epistle to the Hebrews.* Philadelphia: Fortress, 1989. ———. *First-Century Cynicism in the Epistles of Heraclitus.* HTS 29. Missoula, MT: Scholars, 1976. ———, ed. *Nag Hammadi Codex I (The Jung Codex).* NHS 22. Leiden: Brill, 1985. ———, ed. *Nag Hammadi Codex I (The Jung Codex) Notes.* NHS 23. Leiden: Brill, 1985. ——— and **Oden, R. A.** *Philo of Byblos: The Phoenician History.* CBQMS 9. Washington, DC: The Catholic Biblical Association, 1981. ——— and **Oden, R. A.** *The Syrian Goddess (De Dea Syria).* Missoula, MT: Scholars, 1976. **Audet, J.-P.** *La Didachè: Instructions des Apôtres.* Paris: Gabalda, 1958. **Aune, D. E.** "The Apocalypse of John and Graeco-Roman Revelatory Magic." *NTS* 33 (1987) 481–501. ———. "Charismatic Exegesis in Early Judaism and Early Christianity." In *The Pseudepigrapha and Early Biblical Interpretation,* ed. J. H. Charlesworth and C. A. Evans. Sheffield: JSOT, 1993. 126–50. ———. "De esu carnium orationes I and II (Moralia 933A–999B)." In *Plutarch's Theological Writings and Early Christian Literature,* ed. H. D. Betz. SCHNT 3. Leiden: Brill, 1975. ———. *The New Testament in Its Literary Environment.* Philadelphia: Westminster, 1987. ———. "The Odes of Solomon and Early Christian Prophecy." *NTS* 28 (1982) 435–60. ———. "Prolegomena to the Study of Oral Tradition in the Hellenistic World." In *Jesus and the Oral Gospel Tradition,* ed. H. Wansbrough. JSNTSup 64. Sheffield: Sheffield Academic, 1991. 59–106. ———. *Prophecy in Early Christianity and the Ancient Mediterranean World.* Grand Rapids, MI: Eerdmans, 1983. **Avigad, N.** *Beth She'arim: Report on the Excavations during 1953–1958.* Vol. 3. New Brunswick, NJ: Rutgers UP, 1976. **Bailey, C.** *Titi Lucreti Cari De Rerum Natura Libri Sex.* 3 vols. Oxford: Clarendon, 1947. **Baillet, M.** *Qumran Grotte 4.* Vol. 3. DJD 7. Oxford: Clarendon, 1982. **Bakker, W. F.** *The Greek Imperative: An Investigation into the Aspectual Differences between the Present and Aorist Imperatives in Greek Prayer from Homer up to the Present Day.* Amsterdam: Hakkert, 1966. ———. *Pronomen Abundans and Pronomen Coniunctum: A Contribution to the History of the Resumptive Pronoun with the Relative Clause in Greek.* Amsterdam: North-Holland, 1974. **Balsdon, J. P. V. D.** *Romans and Aliens.* Chapel Hill: University of North Carolina, 1979. **Barr, J.** *The Semantics of Biblical Language.* Oxford: Oxford UP, 1961. **Barrett, C. K.** *The Gospel According to St. John.* 2nd ed. London: SPCK, 1978. **Barton, J.** *Oracles of God: Perceptions of Ancient Prophecy in Israel after the Exile.* New York: Oxford UP, 1988. **Bauckham, R. J.** *The Climax of Prophecy: Studies on the Book of Revelation.* Edinburgh: T. & T. Clark, 1993. ———. *Jude, 2 Peter.* WBC 50. Waco, TX: Word, 1983. ———. *The Theology of the Book of Revelation.* Cambridge: Cambridge UP, 1993. **Bauer, W.,** and **Paulsen, H.** *Die Briefe des Ignatius von Antiochia und des Polykarp von Smyrna.* 2nd ed. HNT 18. Tübingen: Mohr-Siebeck, 1985. **Baumgarten, A. I.** *The Phoenician History of Philo* *of Byblos: A Commentary.* Leiden: Brill, 1981. **Beagley, A. J.** *The 'Sitz im Leben' of the Apocalypse with Particular Reference to the Role of the Church's Enemies.* BZNW 50. Berlin; New York: de Gruyter, 1987. **Beale, G. K.** *The Use of Daniel in Jewish Apocalyptic Literature and in the Revelation of John.* Lanham: University Press of America, 1984. **Beck, R.** *Planetary Gods and Planetary Orders in the Mysteries of Mithras.* EPRO 109. Leiden: Brill, 1988. **Bell, A. A.** "The Date of John's Apocalypse." *NTS* 25 (1978) 98–99. **Benoit, P., Milik, J. T.,** and **Vaux, R. de.** *Les Grottes de Murabaʿat.* DJD 2. Oxford: Clarendon, 1961. **Berger, A.** *Encyclopedic Dictionary of Roman Law.* Philadelphia: American Philosophical Society, 1953. **Berger, K.** *Die Amen-Worte Jesu: Eine Untersuchung zum Problem der Legitimation in apokalyptischer Rede.* BZNW 39. Berlin: de Gruyter, 1970. ⸻. *Formgeschichte des Neuen Testaments.* Heidelberg: Quelle & Meyer, 1984. ⸻. *Die griechische Daniel-Diegese: Eine altkirchliche Apokalypse: Text, Übersetzung und Kommentar.* SPB 27. Leiden: Brill, 1976. ⸻, **Boring, M. E.,** and **Colpe, C.** *Hellenistic Commentary to the New Testament.* Minneapolis: Fortress, 1995. **Bergman, J.** *Ich bin Isis: Studien zum memphitischen Hintergrund der griechischen Isisaretalogien.* Lund: Berlingska Boktryckeriet, 1968. **Bergmeier, R.** "Jerusalem, du hochgebaute Stadt." *ZNW* 75 (1984) 86–106. **Berlin, A.** *Zephaniah.* AB 25A. New York: Doubleday, 1994. **Beskow, P.** *Rex Gloriae: The Kingship of Christ in the Early Church.* Stockholm: Almqvist & Wiksell, 1962. **Betz, H. D.** *Galatians: A Commentary on Paul's Letter to the Churches in Galatia.* Philadelphia: Fortress, 1979. ⸻. *Lukian von Samosata und das Neue Testament: Relgionsgeschichtliche und Paränetische Parallelen.* Berlin: Akademie, 1961. ⸻, ed. *The Greek Magical Papyri in Translation Including the Demotic Spells.* 2nd ed. Chicago: University of Chicago, 1992. ⸻, ed. *Plutarch's Ethical Writings and Early Christian Literature.* Leiden: Brill, 1978. ⸻, ed. *Plutarch's Theological Writings and Early Christian Literature.* Leiden: Brill, 1975. **Beyer, K.** *Die aramäischen Texte vom Toten Meer.* Göttingen: Vandenhoeck & Ruprecht, 1984. ⸻. *Die aramäischen Texte vom Toten Meer: Ergänzungsband.* Göttingen: Vandenhoeck & Ruprecht, 1994. ⸻. *Semitische Syntax im Neuen Testament.* Göttingen: Vandenhoeck & Ruprecht, 1962. **Beyerlin, J.** *Near Eastern Religious Texts Relating to the Old Testament.* Philadelphia: Westminster, 1978. **Bidez, J.,** and **Cumont, F.** *Les mages hellénisés: Zoroastre, Ostanes et Hystaspe d'après la tradition grecque.* 1938. Repr. New York: Arno, 1975. **Bietenhard, H.** *Die himmlische Welt im Urchristentum und Spätjudentum.* Tübingen: Mohr-Siebeck, 1951. ⸻. *Der Tosefta-Traktat Soṭa: Hebräischer Text mit kritischem Apparat, Übersetzung, Kommentar.* Bern; Frankfurt am Main; New York: Lang, 1986. **Bihlmeyer, K.** *Die apostolischen Väter.* 2nd ed. Part 1. Tübingen: Mohr-Siebeck, 1956. ⸻. *Die apostolischen Väter: Neubearbeitung der funkschen Ausgabe.* 2nd ed. Ed. W. Schneemelcher. Tübingen: Mohr-Siebeck, 1956. **Birt, T.** *Das antike Buchwesen in seinem Verhältnis zur Literatur.* Berlin: W. Hertz, 1882. **Black, M.** *An Aramaic Approach to the Gospels and Acts.* 3rd ed. Oxford: Clarendon, 1967. ⸻. *The Book of Enoch or 1 Enoch: A New English Edition with Commentary and Textual Notes.* Leiden: Brill, 1985. ⸻. *The Scrolls and Christian Origins.* London: Thomas Nelson, 1961. ⸻, ed. *Apocalypsis Henochi Graeci.* Leiden: Brill, 1970. **Blakeney, E. H.,** ed. and tr. Laetantius, *Epitome institutionem divinarum.* London: S.P.C.K., 1950. **Blomqvist, J.** *Das sogennante KAI adversitivum: Zur Semantik einer griechischen Partikel.* SGU 13. Stockholm, 1979. **Blümner, H.** *The Home Life of the Ancient Greeks.* Tr. A. Zimmern. New York: Cooper Square, 1966. **Böcher, O.** "Johanneisches in der Apokalypse des Johannes." *NTS* 27 (1981) 310–21. ⸻. *Kirche in Zeit und Endzeit: Aufsätze zur Offenbarung des Johannes.* Neukirchen: Neukirchener, 1983. **Bodenmann, R.** *Naissance d'une Exégèse: Daniel dans l'Église ancienne de trois premiers siècles.* BGBE 28. Tübingen: Mohr-Siebeck, 1986. **Böhlig, A., Wisse, F.,** and **Labib, P.** *Nag Hammadi Codices II,2 and IV,2: The Gospel of the Egyptians.* NHS 4. Leiden: Brill, 1975. **Boll, F.** *Aus der Offenbarung Johannis: Hellenistische Studien zum Weltbild der Apokalypse.* Leipzig; Berlin: Teubner, 1914. **Bömer, F.** *Untersuchungen über die Religion der Sklaven in Griechenland und Rom.* 4 vols. Wiesbaden: Steiner, 1958–63. ⸻. *Untersuchungen über die Religion der Sklaven in Griechenland und Rom. Dritter Teil: Die wichtigsten Kulte der Griechischen Welt.* 2nd ed. with P. Herz. Stuttgart: Steiner, 1990. **Bonner, C.** *Studies in Magical Amulets Chiefly Graeco-Egyptian.* Ann Arbor: University of Michigan, 1950. **Boring, M. E.** *Sayings of the Risen Jesus:*

Christian Prophecy in the Synoptic Tradition. SNTSMS 46. Cambridge: Cambridge UP, 1982. **Bornkamm, G.** "Die Komposition der apocalyptischen Visionen in der Offenbarung Johannis." *ZNW* 36 (1937) 132–49. **Borsch, F. H.** *The Christian and Gnostic Son of Man.* SBT 2nd ser. 14. London: SCM, 1970. **Bouché-Leclerq, A.** *Histoire de la divination dans l'antiquité.* 4 vols. 1879–82. Repr. Aalen: Scientia, 1978. **Boulluec, A. Le,** and **Sandevoir, P.** *L'Exode.* Vol. 2 of *La Bible d'Alexandrie.* Paris: Cerf, 1980. **Bousset, W.** *Textkritische Studien zum Neuen Testament.* TU 11/4. Leipzig: Hinrichs, 1894. ——— and **Gressmann, H.** *Die Religion des Judentums im späthellenistischen Zeitalter.* 4th ed. Tübingen: Mohr-Siebeck, 1966. **Bowersock, G.** *Augustus and the Greek World.* Oxford: Clarendon, 1965. **Bowker, J.** *The Targums and Rabbinic Literature.* Cambridge: Cambridge UP, 1969. **Bratcher, R. G.,** and **Hatton, H. A.** *A Handbook on the Revelation to John.* New York: United Bible Societies, 1993. **Braude, W. G.** *The Midrash on Psalms.* 2 vols. New Haven, CT: Yale UP, 1959. **Brenk, F. E.** *In Mist Apparelled: Religious Themes in Plutarch's Moralia and Lives.* Leiden: Brill, 1977. **Brettler, M. Z.** *God Is King: Understanding an Israelite Metaphor.* JSOTSup 76. Sheffield: JSOT, 1989. **Briscoe, J.** *A Commentary on Livy, Books XXXIV–XXXVI.* Oxford: Clarendon, 1981. **Brown, R. E.** *The Epistles of John: A New Translation with Introduction and Commentary.* AB 30. Garden City, NY: Doubleday, 1982. ———. *The Gospel according to John.* 2 vols. Garden City, NY: Doubleday, 1966–70. **Brownlee, W. H.** *Ezekiel.* WBC 28. Waco, TX: Word, 1986. **Bruce, F. F.** "The Spirit in the Apocalypse." In *Christ and Spirit in the New Testament.* FS C. F. D. Moule, ed. B. Lindars and S. Smalley. Cambridge: Cambridge UP, 1973. 333–44. **Bultmann, R.** *Die Geschichte der synoptischen Tradition.* 8th ed. Göttingen: Vandenhoeck & Ruprecht, 1970. ———. *Die Geschichte der synoptischen Tradition: Ergänzungsheft.* Rev. G. Theissen and P. Vielhauer. 4th ed. Göttingen: Vandenhoeck & Ruprecht, 1971. ———. *The History of the Synoptic Tradition.* Tr. J. Marsh. New York: Harper & Row, 1963. **Burkert, W.** *Ancient Mystery Cults.* Cambridge: Harvard UP, 1987. ———. *Greek Religion.* Tr. J. Raffan. Cambridge: Harvard UP, 1985. ———. *Homo Necans: The Anthropology of Ancient Greek Sacrificial Ritual and Myth.* Tr. P. Bing. Berkeley; Los Angeles: University of California Press, 1983. ———. *Structure and History in Greek Mythology and Ritual.* Berkeley: University of California, 1979. **Burney, C. F.** *The Aramaic Origin of the Fourth Gospel.* Oxford: Clarendon, 1922. **Burton, E. DeW.** *Syntax of the Moods and Tenses in New Testament Greek.* 3rd ed. Edinburgh: T. & T. Clark, 1898. **Buttmann, A.** *A Grammar of the New Testament Greek.* Andover: Warren F. Draper, 1878. **Cadbury, H. J.** *The Making of Luke-Acts.* London: SPCK, 1958. **Caley, E. R.** *Orichalcum and Related Ancient Alloys: Origin, Composition and Manufacture, with Special Reference to the Coinage of the Roman Empire.* New York: American Numismatic Society, 1964. **Carr, W.** *Angels and Principalities.* SNTSMS 42. Cambridge: Cambridge UP, 1981. **Casson, L.** *The Periplus Maris Erythraei Text: with Introduction, Translation and Commentary.* Princeton: Princeton UP, 1989. **Cathcart, K. J.,** and **Gordon, R. P.** *The Targum of the Minor Prophets: Translated, with a Critical Introduction, Apparatus, and Notes.* AramBib 14. Wilmington, DE: Glazier, 1989. **Cayón, J. R.** *Compendio de las monedas del Imperio Romano.* 4 vols. Madrid: J. R. Cayón, 1985–90. **Charles, R. H.** *The Book of Enoch.* 2nd ed. Oxford: Clarendon, 1912. ———. *The Greek Versions of the Testaments of the Twelve Patriarchs.* Oxford: Clarendon, 1908. ———. *Studies in the Apocalypse: Being Lectures Delivered before the University of London.* Edinburgh: T. & T. Clark, 1913. **Chilton, B. D.** *The Isaiah Targum: Introduction, Translation, Apparatus, Notes.* AramBib. Wilmington, DE: Glazier, 1987. **Chilver, G. E. F.** *A Historical Commentary on Tacitus' Histories I and II.* Oxford: Clarendon, 1979. **Clemen, C. C.** *Religionsgeschichtliche Erklärung des Neuen Testaments.* Giessen: Töpelmann, 1924. **Collins, J. J.** *The Apocalyptic Vision of the Book of Daniel.* Missoula, MT: Scholars, 1977. ———. *Daniel: A Commentary on the Book of Daniel.* Minneapolis: Fortress, 1993. ———. *The Sibylline Oracles of Egyptian Judaism.* Missoula, MT: Scholars, 1972. **Comblin, J.** *Le Christ dans l'Apocalypse.* Paris; Tournai: Desclée, 1965. **Conybeare, F. C.** *The Armenian Version of Revelation.* London: The Text and Translation Society, 1907. ——— and **Stock, St. G.** *Grammar of Septuagint Greek.* 1905. Repr. Peabody, MA: Hendrickson, 1988. **Conzelmann, H.** *1 Corinthians: A Commentary on the First Epistle to the Corinthians.* Tr. J.

W. Leitch; ed. G. W. MacRae. Philadelphia: Fortress, 1975. ———. *An Outline of the Theology of the New Testament.* Tr. J. Bowden. New York; Evanston, IL: Harper & Row, 1969. **Copley, F. O.** *Vergil, The Aeneid.* 2nd ed. Indianapolis: Bobbs-Merrill, 1975. **Copenhaver, B. P.** *Hermetica: The Greek Corpus Hermeticum and the Latin Asclepius in a New English Translation with Notes and Introduction.* Cambridge: Cambridge UP, 1992. **Court, J.** *Myth and History in the Book of Revelation.* Atlanta: John Knox, 1979. **Cousar, C. B.** *A Theology of the Cross: The Death of Jesus in the Pauline Letters.* Minneapolis: Fortress, 1990. **Cowley, A.** *Aramaic Papyri of the Fifth Century B.C.* Oxford: Clarendon, 1923. **Cowley, R. W.** *The Traditional Interpretation of the Apocalypse of St John in the Ethiopian Orthodox Church.* Cambridge: Cambridge UP, 1983. **Cranfield, C. E. B.** *Romans.* 2 vols. Edinburgh: T. & T. Clark, 1975–79. **Cross, F. M.** *Canaanite Myth and Hebrew Epic.* Cambridge, MA: Harvard UP, 1973. **Crossan, J. D.** *In Fragments: The Aphorisms of Jesus.* San Francisco: Harper & Row, 1983. **Cullmann, O.** *Early Christian Worship.* Tr. A. S. Todd and J. B. Torrance. London: SCM, 1953. **Cumont, F.** *The Mysteries of Mithra.* New York: Dover, 1956. ———. *Oriental Religions in Roman Paganism.* New York: Dover, 1956. ———. *Recherches sur le Symbolisme Funéraire des Romains.* Paris: Geuthner, 1942. **Cuss, D.** *Imperial Cult and Honorary Terms in the New Testament.* Fribourg: The University Press, 1974. **Dalman, G.** *Aramäisch-Neuhebräisches Handwörterbuch zu Targum, Talmud und Midrasch.* 2nd ed. Göttingen: Vandenhoeck & Ruprecht, 1938. ———. *Grammatik des jüdisch-palästinischen Aramäisch.* Leipzig: Hinrichs, 1905. ———. *Die Worte Jesu mit Berücksichtigung des nachkanonischen jüdischen Schrifttums und der Aramäischen Sprache.* 2nd ed. 1930. Repr. Darmstadt: Wissenschaftliche Buchgesellschaft, 1965. **Danby, H.** *The Mishnah.* London: Oxford UP, 1933. **Daniel, R. W.,** and **Maltomini, F.** *Supplementum Magicum.* Vol. 1. Papyrologica Coloniensia 16.1. Oppladen: Westdeutscher, 1990. Vol. 2. Papyrologica Coloniensia 16.2. Oppladen: Westdeutscher, 1992. **Daniélou, J.** *The Theology of Jewish Christianity.* Tr. J. A. Baker. London: Darton, Longman & Todd, 1964. **Danker, F. W.** *Benefactor: Epigraphic Study of a Graeco-Roman and New Testament Semantic Field.* St. Louis: Clayton, 1982. **Davies, P. R.** *1QM, the War Scroll from Qumran: Its Structure and History.* Rome: Biblical Institute, 1977. ———. *The Damascus Covenant.* JSOTSup 25. Sheffield: JSOT, 1983. **Davies, W. D.** *Paul and Rabbinic Judaism: Some Rabbinic Elements in Pauline Theology.* Rev. ed. New York; Evanston: Harper & Row, 1955. ——— and **Allison, D. C., Jr.** *A Critical and Exegetical Commentary on the Gospel according to Saint Matthew.* 2 vols. ICC. Edinburgh: T. & T. Clark, 1988, 1991. **Day, J.** *God's Conflict with the Dragon and the Sea.* Cambridge: Cambridge UP, 1985. **Debord, P.** *Aspects Sociaux et économiques de la vie religieuse dans l'Anatolie greco-romaine.* Leiden: Brill, 1982. **Deichgräber, R.** *Gotteshymnus und Christushymnus in der frühen Christenheit: Untersuchungen zu Form, Sprache und Stil der frühchristlichen Hymnen.* Göttingen: Vandenhoeck & Ruprecht, 1967. **Deissmann, A.** *Bible Studies.* Edinburgh: T. & T. Clark, 1901. ———. *Light from the Ancient East.* New York; London: Hodder & Stoughton, 1910. **Delatte, A.** *Anecdota Atheniensia.* Paris, Champion, 1927. ——— and **Derchain, Ph.** *Les intailles magiques gréco-égyptiennes.* Paris: Bibliothèque Nationale, 1964. **Delling, G.** *Jüdische Lehre und Frömmigkeit in den Paralipomena Jeremiae.* BZAW 100. Berlin: Töpelmann, 1967. ———. *Worship in the New Testament.* Tr. P. Scott. Philadelphia: Westminster, 1962. **Delobel, J.** "Le texte de l'Apocalypse: Problemes de méthode." In *L'Apocalypse,* ed. J. Lambrecht. 151–66. **Denis, A.-M.** *Concordance Grecque des Pseudépigraphes d'ancien Testament: Concordance, Corpus des textes, Indices.* Louvain-la-Neuve: Université Catholique de Louvain, 1987. ———. *Fragmenta Pseudepigraphorum quae supersunt Graeca.* Leiden: Brill, 1970. **Denniston, J. D.** *The Greek Particles.* 2nd ed. Oxford: Clarendon, 1954. ———. *Greek Prose Style.* Oxford: Clarendon, 1952. **Dexinger, F.** *Henochs Zehnwochenapokalypse und offene Probleme der Apokalyptikforschung.* SPB 29. Leiden: Brill, 1977. **Dibelius, M.,** and **Greeven, H.** *James: A Commentary on the Epistle of James.* Tr. M. A. Williams. Philadelphia: Fortress, 1976. **Dick, K.** *Der schriftstellerische Plural bei Paulus.* Halle: Niemeyer, 1900. **Dieterich, A.** *Abraxas: Studien zur Religionsgeschichte.* Leipzig: Teubner, 1891. ———. *Eine Mithrasliturgie.* 2nd ed. Leipzig; Berlin: Teubner, 1910. **Diobouniotis, C.,** and **Harnack, A.** *Der Scholien-Kommentar des Origenes zur Apokalypse-Johannis.*

TU 38/3. Leipzig: Hinrichs, 1911. **Dodd, C. H.** *According to the Scriptures.* Digswell Place: James Nisbet, 1952. ———. *The Interpretation of the Fourth Gospel.* Cambridge: Cambridge UP, 1965. **Dogniez, C.,** and **Harl, M.** *Le Deutéronome.* La Bible d'Alexandrie 5. Paris: Cerf, 1992. **Doran, R.** *Temple Propaganda: The Purpose and Character of 2 Maccabees.* CBQMS 12. Washington DC: Catholic Biblical Association, 1981. **Dornseiff, F.** *Das Alphabet in Mystik und Magie.* 2nd ed. Leipzig; Berlin: Teubner, 1925. **Dothan, M.** *Hammath Tiberias: Early Synagogues and the Hellenistic and Roman Remains.* Jerusalem: Israel Exploration Society, 1983. **Doudna, J. C.** *The Greek of the Gospel of Mark.* Philadelphia: Society of Biblical Literature, 1961. **Dover, K. J.** *Greek Popular Morality.* Berkeley; Los Angeles: University of California, 1974. **Dunn, J. D. G.** *Romans.* 2 vols. WBC 38A–B. Waco, TX: Word, 1988. **Durham, J. I.** *Exodus.* WBC 3. Waco, TX: Word, 1987. **Durling, R. J.** *A Dictionary of Medical Terms in Galen.* SAM 5. Leiden: Brill, 1993. **Eckhardt, K. A.** *Der Tod des Johannes.* Berlin: de Gruyter, 1961. **Ehrenberg, V.,** and **Jones, A. H. M.** *Documents Illustrating the Reigns of Augustus and Tiberius.* 2nd ed. Oxford: Clarendon, 1976. **Eisenman, R. H.,** and **Wise, M.** *The Dead Sea Scrolls Uncovered.* Rockport: Element, 1992. **Eissfeldt, O.** *The Old Testament: An Introduction.* Tr. P. R. Ackroyd. New York; Evanston, IL: Harper & Row, 1965. **Eitrem, S.** *Papyri Osloenses.* Fasc. 1: *Magical Papyri.* Oslo: Dybwad, 1925. ———. *Some Notes on the Demonology in the New Testament.* 2nd ed. Oslo: Universitetsforlaget, 1966. **Eliade, M.** *The Sacred and the Profane: The Nature of Religion.* Tr. W. R. Trask. New York: Harper & Row, 1959. **Elliott, J. H.** *A Home for the Homeless: A Sociological Exegesis of I Peter.* Philadelphia: Fortress, 1981. **Engelmann, H.** *The Delian Aretalogy of Sarapis.* Leiden: Brill, 1975. **Enslin, M. S.,** and **Zeitlin, S.** *The Book of Judith.* Leiden: Brill, 1972. **Epstein, I.,** ed. *Babylonian Talmud.* 35 vols. London: Soncino, 1935–52. **Ernst, J.** *Die eschatologischen Gegenspieler in den Schriften des Neuen Testaments.* Regensburg: Pustet, 1967. **Evans, C. A, Webb, R. L.,** and **Wiebe, R. A.** *Nag Hammadi Texts and the Bible: A Synopsis and Index.* Leiden: Brill, 1993. **Fanning, B. M.** *Verbal Aspect in New Testament Greek.* Oxford: Clarendon, 1990. **Farrer, A.** *A Rebirth of Images: The Making of St John's Apocalypse.* Albany: State University of New York, 1986. **Fee, G.** *The First Epistle to the Corinthians.* Grand Rapids, MI: Eerdmans, 1987. **Fekkes, J.** *Isaiah and Prophetic Traditions in the Book of Revelation.* JSNTSup 93. Sheffield: JSOT, 1994. **Ferrar, W. J.,** ed. and tr. *Eusebius, The Proof of the Gospel.* 2 vols. New York: Macmillan, 1920. **Festugière, A.-J.** *La révélation d'Hermès Trismégiste.* 4 vols. Paris: J. Gabalda, 1950–54. **Fiedler, P.** *Die Formel "Und Siehe" im Neuen Testament.* Munich: Kosel, 1969. **Field, F.** *Origenis Hexaplorum quae supersunt; sive Veterum Interpretum Graecorum in totus Veius Testamentum Fragmenta.* 2 vols. Oxford: Clarendon, 1875. **Finegan, J.** *The Archaeology of the New Testament.* Princeton: Princeton UP, 1969. **Finley, M. I.** *The Ancient Economy.* Berkeley; Los Angeles: University of California, 1985. ———. *The World of Odysseus.* Rev. ed. New York: Penguin, 1979. **Fitzmyer, J. A.** *The Gospel according to Luke.* 2 vols. Garden City, NY: Doubleday, 1979–83. **Fontenrose, J.** *The Delphic Oracle: Its Responses and Operations with a Catalogue of Responses.* Berkeley; Los Angeles: University of California, 1978. ———. *Didyma: Apollo's Oracle, Cult, and Companions.* Berkeley: University of California, 1988. **Forestell, J. T.** *Targumic Traditions and the New Testament.* Chico, CA: Scholars, 1979. **Fraenkel, E.** *Aeschylus, Agamemnon.* Oxford: Clarendon, 1950. ———. *Horace.* Oxford: Clarendon, 1957. **Frank, T.,** ed. *An Economic Survey of Ancient Rome.* 6 vols. Baltimore: Johns Hopkins, 1933–40. **Fraser, P. M.,** and **Matthews, E.** *A Lexicon of Greek Personal Names.* Vol. 1: *The Aegean Islands, Cyprus, Cyrenaica.* Oxford: Clarendon, 1987. **Freedman, H.,** and **Simon, M.,** eds. *Midrash Rabbah.* 3rd ed. 10 vols. London; New York: Soncino, 1983. **Friesen, S. J.** *Twice Neokoros: Ephesus, Asia and the Cult of the Flavian Imperial Family.* Leiden: Brill, 1993. **Frisk, H.** *Griechisches Etymologisches Wörterbuch.* 3 vols. Heidelberg: Winter, 1960. ———. *Le Périple de la Mer Érythrée suivi d'une étude sur la tradition et la langue.* Göteborg: Elander, 1927. **Frost, S. B.** *Old Testament Apocalyptic.* London: Epworth, 1952. **Fustel de Coulanges, N. D.** *The Ancient City.* Baltimore: Johns Hopkins UP, 1980. **Gallop, D.** *Plato, Phaedo: Translated with Notes.* Oxford: Clarendon, 1975. **García Martínez, F.** *The Dead Sea Scrolls Translated.* Leiden: Brill, 1994. ———. *Qumran and*

Apocalyptic: Studies on the Aramaic Texts from Qumran. Leiden: Brill, 1994. **Geissen, A.** *Der Septuaginta-Text des Buches Daniel nach dem Kölner Teil des Papyrus 967: Kap. V-XII.* Bonn: Habelt, 1968. **Georgi, D.** *Die Gegner des Paulus im 2. Korintherbrief.* WMANT 11. Neukirchen: Neukirchener, 1964. **Gibson, J. C. L.** *Canaanite Myths and Legends.* 2nd ed. Edinburgh: T. & T. Clark, 1978. ———. *Hebrew and Moabite Inscriptions.* Vol. 1 of *Textbook of Syrian Semitic Inscriptions.* Oxford: Clarendon, 1973. **Giet, S.** *L'Apocalypse et l'histoire: Étude historique sur l' Apocalypse johannique.* Paris: Presses universitaires de France, 1957. **Gignac, F. T.** *A Grammar of the Greek Papyri of the Roman and Byzantine Periods.* 2 vols. Milan: Cisalpino-Goliardica, 1976–81. **Ginzberg, L.** *The Legends of the Jews.* Philadelphia: Jewish Publication Society of America, 1909. **Goldin, J.** *The Fathers according to Rabbi Nathan.* 1955. Repr. New York: Schocken, 1974. **Goldingay, J. E.** *Daniel.* WBC 30. Dallas: Word, 1989. **Gollinger, H.** *Die Kirche in der Bewährung: Eine Einführung in die Offenbarung des Johannes.* Aschaffenburg: Pattloch, 1973. **Goodenough, E. R.** *Jewish Symbols in the Greco-Roman Period.* 12 vols. New York: Bollingen Foundation, 1953–65. ———. "The Menorah among Jews of the Roman World." *HUCA* 23 (1950–51) 449–92. **Goodspeed, E. J.** *Problems of New Testament Translation.* Chicago: University of Chicago, 1945. **Gow, A. S. F.,** and **Page, D. L.** *The Greek Anthology: Hellenistic Epigrams.* 2 vols. Cambridge: Cambridge UP, 1965. **Grant F. C.,** ed. *Hellenistic Religions: The Age of Syncretism.* New York: Liberal Arts, 1953. **Grant, R. M.** *Early Christianity and Society.* New York: Harper & Row, 1977. **Grese, W. C.** *Corpus Hermeticum XII and Early Christian Literature.* SCHNT 5. Leiden: Brill, 1979. **Gressmann, H.** *Altorientalische Texte zum Alten Testament.* 2nd ed. Berlin; Leipzig: de Gruyter, 1926. **Griffiths, J. G.** *Apuleius of Madauros, The Isis-Book (Metamorphoses, Book XI).* Leiden: Brill, 1975. **Gross, W.** *Die Pendenskonstruktion im biblischen Hebräisch.* St. Ottilien: EOS, 1987. **Grossfeld, B.** *The First Targum to Esther.* New York: Sepher-Hermon, 1983. ———. *The Targum Sheni to the Book of Esther.* New York: Sepher-Hermon, 1994. ———. *The Two Targums of Esther.* AramBib 18. Wilmington, DE: Glazier, 1991. ———. *Targum Onqelos to Exodus.* AramBib 7. Wilmington, DE: Glazier, 1988. ———, tr. *The Targum Onqelos to Leviticus and The Targum Onqelos to Numbers.* AramBib 8. Wilmington, DE: Glazier, 1988. **Grotius, H.** *Annotationes in Novum Testamentum.* 8 vols. Groningen: Zuidema, 1830. **Gruen, E. S.** *The Hellenistic World and the Coming of Rome.* 2 vols. Berkeley: University of California, 1984. **Gruenwald, I.** *Apocalyptic and Merkavah Mysticism.* Leiden: Brill, 1980. **Guelich, R. A.** *Mark 1–8:26.* WBC 34A. Dallas: Word, 1989. **Gunkel, H.** *Schöpfung und Chaos in Urzeit und Endzeit: Eine religionsgeschichtliche Untersuchung über Gen 1 und Ap Joh 12.* Göttingen: Vandenhoeck & Ruprecht, 1921. ———. *Zum religionsgeschichtlichen Verständnis des Neuen Testaments.* Göttingen: Vandenhoeck & Ruprecht, 1903. **Guthrie, D.** *New Testament Introduction.* Downers Grove, IL: Inter-Varsity Press, 1970. **Gwynn, J.** *The Apocalypse of St. John, in a Syriac Version Hitherto Unknown.* 1897. Repr. Amsterdam: APA-Philo, 1981. **Hachlili, R.** *Ancient Jewish Art and Archaeology in the Land of Israel.* Leiden: Brill, 1988. **Hadas, M.** *The Third and Fourth Books of Maccabees.* New York: Harper & Brothers, 1953. **Hadas-Lebel, M.** *Jérusalem contre Rome.* Paris: Cerf, 1990. **Haelst, J. van.** *Catalogue des papyrus littéraires Juifs et Chrétiens.* Paris: Publications de la Sorbonne, 1976. **Haenchen, E.** *A Commentary on the Gospel of John.* 2 vols. Hermeneia. Philadelphia: Fortress, 1984. **Hafemann, S. J.** *Paul, Moses, and the History of Israel.* WUNT 81. Tübingen: Mohr-Siebeck, 1995. ———. *Suffering and the Spirit: An Exegetical Study of II Cor. 2:14–3:3 within the Context of the Corinthian Correspondence.* WUNT 2/19. Tübingen: Mohr-Siebeck, 1986. **Hahn, F.** "Die Rede von der Parusie des Men-schensohnes Markus 13." In *Jesus und der Menschensohn,* ed. R. Pesch and R. Schnackenburg. Freiburg: Herder & Herder, 1975. ———. *Mission in the New Testament.* London: SCM, 1965. **Hals, R. M.** *Ezekiel.* FOTL 19. Grand Rapids, MI: Eerdmans, 1989. **Hands, A. R.** *Charities and Social Aid in Greece and Rome.* Ithaca, NY: Cornell UP, 1968. **Hannestad, N.** *Roman Art and Imperial Policy.* Aarhus: Aarhus UP, 1988. **Hanson, A. T.** *The Wrath of the Lamb.* London: S.P.C.K., 1957. **Hanson, P. D.** *The Dawn of Apocalyptic.* Philadelphia: Fortress, 1975. **Haran, M.** *Temples and Temple-Service in Ancient Israel.* Oxford: Clarendon, 1978. **Hare, D. R. A.** *The Son of Man Tradition.*

Minneapolis: Fortress, 1990. **Harnisch, W.** *Verhängnis und Verheißung der Geschichte: Untersuchungen zum Zeit- und Geschichtsverständnis im 4. Buch Esra und in der syr. Baruchapokalypse.* FRLANT 97. Göttingen: Vandenhoeck & Ruprecht, 1969. **Harrington, D. J.**, and **Saldarini, A. J.** *Targum Jonathan of the Former Prophets: Introduction, Translation and Notes.* AramBib 10. Wilmington, DE: Glazier, 1987. **Harrington, W. J.** *Understanding the Apocalypse.* Washington, DC; Cleveland: Corpus Books, 1969. **Hartman, L.** *Prophecy Interpreted: The Formation of Some Jewish Apocalyptic Texts and of the Eschatological Discourse Mark 13 par.* ConBNT 1. Lund: Gleerup, 1966. **Harvey, W. W.** *Sancti Irenaei Episcopi Lugdunensis Libros quinque adversus Haereses.* 2 vols. Cambridge: Typis Academicis, 1857. **Hatch, E.** *Essays in Biblical Greek.* Oxford: Oxford UP, 1889. **Haussleiter, J.** *Victorinus Episcopi Petavionensis Opera.* Leipzig: Freytag, 1916. **Hay, D. M.** *Glory at the Right Hand: Psalm 110 in Early Christianity.* Nashville: Abingdon, 1973. **Hayward, R.** *The Targum of Jeremiah: Translated, with a Critical Introduction, Apparatus, and Notes.* AramBib 12. Wilmington, DE: Glazier, 1987. **Heidel, A.** *The Gilgamesh Epic and Old Testament Parallels.* 2nd ed. Chicago: University of Chicago, 1949. **Heiler, F.** *Prayer: A Study in the History and Psychology of Religion.* Tr. S. McComb. London; New York: Oxford UP, 1932. **Heinemann, J.** *Prayer in the Talmud.* Berlin; New York: de Gruyter, 1977. **Helbing, R.** *Die Kasussyntax der Verba bei den Septuaginta: Ein Beitrag zur Hebraismenfrage und zur Syntax der Κοινή.* Göttingen: Vandenhoeck & Ruprecht, 1928. **Hellholm, D.** "The Problem of Apocalyptic Genre and the Apocalypse of John." In *Early Christian Apocalypticism: Genre and Social Setting,* ed. A. Yarbro Collins. *Semeia* 36 (1986) 13–64. ———, ed. *Apocalypticism in the Mediterranean World and the Near East.* Tübingen: Mohr-Siebeck, 1983. **Hemer, C. J.** *The Letters to the Seven Churches of Asia in Their Local Setting.* JSNTSup 11. Sheffield: JSOT, 1986. **Hengel, M.** *The Charismatic Leader and His Followers.* New York: Crossroad, 1981. ———. *Eigentum und Reichtum in der frühen Kirche: Aspekte einer frühchristlichen Sozialgeschichte.* Stuttgart: Calwer, 1973 (ET: *Property and Riches in the Early Church: Aspects of a Social History of Early Christianity.* Philadelphia: Fortress, 1974). ———. *Judaism and Hellenism.* Philadelphia: Fortress, 1974. ———. *The Zealots: Investigations into the Jewish Freedom Movement in the Period from Herod I until 70 A.D.* Tr. D. Smith. Edinburgh: T. & T. Clark, 1989. **Hercher, R.** *Epistolographi graeci.* 1873. Repr. Amsterdam: Hocker, 1965. **Heubeck, A., West, S.,** and **Hainsworth, J. B.** *A Commentary on Homer's Odyssey.* Vol. 1. Oxford: Clarendon, 1988. **Hilhorst, A.** *Sémitismes et Latinismes dans le Pasteur d'Hermas.* Nijmegen: Dekker and Van de Vegt, 1976. **Hill, D.** *New Testament Prophecy.* Atlanta: John Knox, 1979. ———. "Prophecy and Prophets in the Revelation of St. John." *NTS* 18 (1971–72) 401–18. **Hillers, D.** *Treaty-Curses and the Old Testament Prophets.* Rome: Pontifical Biblical Institute, 1964. **Himmelfarb, M.** *Ascent to Heaven in Jewish and Christian Apocalypses.* New York; Oxford: Oxford UP, 1993. ———. *Tours of Hell: An Apocalyptic Form in Jewish and Christian Literature.* Philadelphia: University of Pennsylvania, 1983. **Hobbs, T. R.** *2 Kings.* WBC 13. Waco, TX: Word, 1985. **Hofmann, J.** *Die äthiopische Johannes-Apokalypse kritisch Untersucht.* CSCO 297. Louvain: Secrétariat du CorpusSCO, 1969. **Holladay, W. L.** *Jeremiah 1.* Philadelphia: Fortress, 1986. **Hollander, H. W.,** and **Jonge, M. de.** *The Testaments of the Twelve Patriarchs: A Commentary.* Leiden: Brill, 1985. **Holmberg, B.** *Sociology and the New Testament.* Minneapolis: Fortress, 1990. **Holtz, T.** *Die Christologie der Apokalypse des Johannes.* 2nd ed. Berlin: Akademie, 1971. **Hopfner, T.** *Griechisch-Ägyptischer Offenbarungszauber.* 2 vols. Leipzig: Haessel, 1921–24. **Horgan, M. P.** *Pesharim: Qumran Interpretations of Biblical Books.* CBQMS 8. Washington, DC: Catholic Biblical Association of America, 1979. **Horst, J.** *Proskynein: Zur Anbetung im Urchristentum nach ihrer religionsgeschichtlichen Eigenart.* Gütersloh: Bertelsmann, 1932. **Horst, P. W. van der.** *Ancient Jewish Epitaphs.* Kampen: Kok Pharos, 1991. ———. *Aelius Aristides and the New Testament.* SCHNT 6. Leiden: Brill, 1980. **Hoskier, H. C.** *The Complete Commentary of Oecumenius on the Apocalypse.* Ann Arbor: University of Michigan, 1928. ———. *Concerning the Date of the Bohairic Version Covering a Detailed Examination of the Text of the Apocalypse.* London: Quaritch, 1911. ———. *Concerning the Text of the Apocalypse.* 2 vols. London: Quaritch, 1929. **Houtman,**

C. *Der Himmel im Alten Testament: Israels Weltbild und Weltanschauung.* Oudtestamentische Studiën 30. Leiden: Brill, 1993. **Hurtado, L.** *One God, One Lord: Early Christian Devotion and Ancient Jewish Monotheism.* London: SCM, 1988. **Hvalvik, R.** *The Struggle for Scripture and Covenant: The Purpose of the Epistle of Barnabas and Jewish-Christian Competition in the Second Century.* WUNT 2/82. Tübingen: Mohr-Siebeck, 1996. **Isbell, C. D.** *Corpus of the Aramaic Incantation Bowls.* SBLDS 17. Missoula, MT: Scholars, 1975. **Jacobson, H.** *The Exagoge of Ezekiel.* Cambridge: Cambridge UP, 1983. **James, M. R.** *The Psalms of Solomon.* Cambridge: Cambridge UP, 1891. **Jastrow, M.** *A Dictionary of the Targumim, the Talmud Babli and Yerushalmi and the Midrashic Literature.* 2 vols. New York: Ktav, 1950. **Jellicoe, S.** *The Septuagint and Modern Study.* 1968. Repr. Winona Lake, IN: Eisenbrauns, 1989. **Jellinek, A.,** ed. *Bet Ha-Midrasch.* 3rd ed. 6 vols. Jerusalem: Sifre Vahrman, 1967. **Jeremias, A.** *Babylonisches im Neuen Testament.* Leipzig: Hinrichs, 1905. **Jeremias, C.** *Die Nachtgeschichte des Sacharja.* FRLANT 117. Göttingen: Vandenhoeck & Ruprecht, 1977. **Jeremias, Joachim.** *The Eucharistic Words of Jesus.* New York: Scribner's Sons, 1966. ———. *Jerusalem in the Time of Jesus.* Tr. F. H. and C. H. Cave. Philadelphia: Fortress, 1969. ———. *The Parables of Jesus.* Rev. ed. New York: Scribner, 1964. ———. *The Prayers of Jesus.* Philadelphia: Fortress, 1978. ———. *New Testament Theology.* New York: Scribner's Sons, 1971. ——— and **Strobel, A.** *Die Briefe an Timotheus und Titus, Der Brief an die Hebräer.* 12th ed. Göttingen: Vandenhoeck & Ruprecht, 1981. **Jeremias, Jörg.** *Theophanie: Die Geschichte einer alttestamentlichen Gattung.* WMANT 10. 2nd ed. Neukirchen: Neukirchener, 1977. **Johannessohn, J.** *Der Gebrauch der Kasus und der Präpositionen in der Septuaginta.* Berlin: Friedrich-Wilhelms-Universität, 1910. **Jones, A. H. M.** *The Cities of the Eastern Roman Provinces.* Oxford: Clarendon, 1937. ———. *The Greek City from Alexander to Justinian.* Oxford: Clarendon, 1940. **Jones, C. P.** *The Roman World of Dio Chrysostom.* Cambridge: Harvard UP, 1978. **Jonge, M. de.** *The Testaments of the Twelve Patriarchs: A Critical Edition of the Greek Text.* Leiden: Brill, 1978. **Jörns, K.-P.** *Das hymnische Evangelium: Untersuchungen zu Aufbau, Funktion und Herkunft der hymnischen Stücke in der Johannesoffenbarung.* Gütersloh: Mohn, 1971. **Joüon, P.** *A Grammar of Biblical Hebrew.* 3 vols. Rome: Pontifical Biblical Institute, 1991. **Kahn, C. H.** *The Art and Thought of Heraclitus: An Edition of the Fragments with Translation and Commentary.* Cambridge: Cambridge UP, 1979. **Karrer, M.** *Die Johannesoffenbarung als Brief: Studien zu ihrem literarischen, historischen und theologischen Ort.* Göttingen: Vandenhoeck & Ruprecht, 1986. **Kaufmann, Y.** *The Religion of Israel: From Its Beginnings to the Babylonian Exile.* Tr. M. Greenberg. Chicago: University of Chicago, 1960. **Kavanagh, M. A.** *Apocalypse 22:6–21 as Concluding Liturgical Dialogue.* Rome: Pontifical Gregorian University, 1984. **Keel, O.** *Die Welt der altorientalischen Bildsymbolik und das Alte Testament.* Zürich: Benziger; Neukirchen: Neukirchener, 1972. **Kees, H.** *Der Götterglaube im alten Aegypten.* Leipzig: Hinrichs, 1941. **Kilmer, A. D., Crocker, R. L.,** and **Brown, R. R.** *Sounds from Silence: Recent Discoveries in Ancient Near Eastern Music.* Berkeley: Bit Enki, 1976. **Klein, M. L.** *The Fragment-Targums of the Pentateuch according to their Extant Sources.* AnBib 76. 2 vols. Rome: Biblical Institute, 1980. **Klein, R.** *1 Samuel.* WBC 10. Waco, TX: Word, 1983. **Kloppenborg, J. S.** *The Formation of Q: Trajectories in Ancient Wisdom Collections.* Philadelphia: Fortress, 1987. **Knibb, M. A.** *The Ethiopic Book of Enoch: A New Edition in the Light of the Aramaic Dead Sea Fragments.* 2 vols. Oxford: Clarendon Press, 1978. ———. *The Qumran Community.* Cambridge: Cambridge UP, 1987. **Koch, G.,** and **Sichtermann, H.** *Römische Sarkophage.* Munich: Beck, 1982. **Koch, K.** *The Growth of the Biblical Tradition.* New York: Scribner's Sons, 1969. **Koep, L.** *Das himmlische Buch in Antike und Christentum: Eine religionsgeschichtliche Untersuchung zur altchristlichen Bildersprache.* Bonn: Hanstein, 1952. **Koester, H.** *Introduction to the New Testament.* 2 vols. Philadelphia: Fortress, 1982. **Korpel, M. C. A.** *A Rift in the Clouds: Ugaritic and Hebrew Descriptions of the Divine.* Münster: UGARIT-Verlag, 1990. **Kraabel, A. T.** "Judaism in Western Asia Minor under the Roman Empire, with a Preliminary Study of the Jewish Community at Sardis, Lydia." Diss., Harvard, 1968. **Kraeling, C. H.** *The Synagogue. The Excavations at Dura Europas 8/1.* New Haven, CT: Yale UP, 1956. **Kraft, R. A.** *The Testa-*

ment of Job according to the SV Text. Missoula, MT: Scholars, 1974. **Kraus, H.-J.** *Theology of the Psalms.* Tr. K. Crim. Minneapolis: Augsburg, 1986. ———. *Worship in Israel: A Cultic History of the Old Testament.* Richmond: John Knox, 1966. **Krause, M.,** and **Labib, P.** *Die drei Versionen des Apokryphon des Johannes.* Wiesbaden: Harrassowitz, 1962. **Krauss, F. B.** *An Interpretation of the Omens, Portents, and Prodigies Recorded by Livy, Tacitus, Suetonius.* Philadelphia: University of Pennsylvania, 1930. **Krauss, S.** *Talmudische Archäologie.* Leipzig: Fock, 1910–12. **Kreitzer, L. J.** *Jesus and God in Paul's Eschatology.* Sheffield: JSOT, 1987. **Kroll, J.** *Die Lehren des Hermes Trismegistos.* 2nd ed. Münster: Aschendorff, 1928. **Kropp, A. M.** *Ausgewählte Koptische Zaubertexte.* 3 vols. Bruxelles: Égyptologique Reine Élisabeth, 1930–31. **Krüger, G.,** and **Ruhbach, G.** *Ausgewählte Märtyrerakten.* 4th ed. Tübingen: Mohr-Siebeck, 1965. **Kuhn, P.** *Offenbarungsstimmen im Antiken Judentum: Untersuchungen zur Bat Qol und verwandten Phänomenen.* Texte und Studien zum Antiken Judentum 20. Tübingen: Mohr-Siebeck, 1989. **Kuhnen, H.-P.** *Nordwest-Palästina in hellenistisch-römischer Zeit: Bauten und Gräber im Karmelgebiet.* Weinheim: VCH Verlagsgesellschaft, 1987. **Kühner, R.** and **Gerth, B.** *Ausführliche Grammatik der griechischen Sprache: Satzlehre.* 2 vols. 3rd ed. Hannover: Hahsche, 1898–1904. **Kümmel, W. G.** *Introduction to the New Testament.* Rev. ed. Tr. H. C. Kee. Nashville: Abingdon, 1975. **Lambrecht, J.,** ed. *L'Apocalypse johannique et l'Apocalyptique dans le Nouveau Testament.* Leuven: Leuven UP, 1980. **Lancellotti, A.** *Uso delle forme verbali nell'Apocalisse alla luce ella sintassi ebraica.* Assisi: Studio Teologico "Porziuncola," 1964. **Lange, N. M. R. de.** *Origen and the Jews.* Cambridge: Cambridge UP, 1976. **Lattimore, R.** *Themes in Greek and Latin Epitaphs.* Urbana: University of Illinois, 1962. **Laughlin, T. C.** *Solecisms of the Apocalypse.* Princeton: C. S. Robinson, 1902. **Lauterbach, J. Z.** *Mekilta De-Rabbi Ishmael.* 3 vols. Philadelphia: Jewish Publication Society of America, 1935. **Leaney, A. R. C.** *The Rule of Qumran and Its Meaning.* Philadelphia: Westminster, 1966. **Lee, D.** "The Narrative Asides in the Book of Revelation." Diss., Chicago Theological Seminary, 1990. **Levey, S. H.** *The Targum of Ezekiel: Translated, with a Critical Introduction, Apparatus, and Notes.* AramBib 13. Wilmington, DE: Glazier, 1987. **Levy, J.** *Wörterbuch über die Talmudim und Midraschim.* 4 vols. Darmstadt: Wissenschaftliche Buchgesellschaft, 1963. **Lieberman, S.** *Hellenism in Jewish Palestine.* New York: The Jewish Theological Seminary of America, 1962. **Liebeschuetz, J. H. W. G.** *Antioch: City and Imperial Administration in the Later Roman Empire.* Oxford: Clarendon, 1972. ———. *Continuity and Change in Roman Religion.* Oxford: Clarendon, 1979. **Lifshitz, B.** *Donateurs et fondateurs dans les synagogues juives.* Paris: Gabalda, 1967. **Lightfoot, J.** *Horae Hebraicae et Talmudicae.* 4 vols. Oxford UP, 1959. **Lightfoot, J. B.** *The Apostolic Fathers: Clement, Ignatius, and Polycarp.* Two parts in 5 vols. London: Macmillan, 1889–90. **Lindars, B.** *Jesus Son of Man: A Fresh Examination of the Son of Man Sayings in the Gospels in the Light of Recent Research.* Grand Rapids, MI: Eerdmans, 1983. ———. *New Testament Apologetic: The Doctrinal Significance of the Old Testament Quotations.* London: SCM, 1961. **Lindblom, J.** *Gesichte und Offenbarungen: Vorstellungen von göttlichen Weisungen und übernatürlichen Erscheinungen im ältesten Christentum.* Lund: Gleerup, 1968. **Lindemann, A.** *Die Clemensbriefe.* HNT 17. Tübingen: Mohr-Siebeck, 1992. ———. *Paulus im ältesten Christentum.* BHT 58. Tübingen: Mohr-Siebeck, 1979. **Ljungvik, H.** *Beiträge zur Syntax der spätgriechischen Volkssprache.* Uppsala: Almqvist & Wiksell; Leipzig: Harrassowitz, 1932. **Lo Bue, F.** *The Turin Fragments of Tyconius' Commentary on Revelation,* ed. G. G. Willis. Cambridge: Cambridge UP, 1963. **Lohse, E.** *Colossians and Philemon.* Philadelphia: Fortress, 1971. **Louw, J. P.** "On Greek Prohibitions." *AcCl* 2 (1959) 43–57. **Lücke, F.** *Versuch einer vollständigen Einleitung in die Offenbarung des Johannes oder Allgemeine Untersuchungen über die apokalyptischen Literatur überhaupt und die Apokalypse des Johannes insbesondere.* 2nd ed. Bonn, 1852. **Luterbacher, F.** *Der Prodigienglaube und Prodigienstil der Römer.* Burgdorf: Langlois, 1880. **MacDonald, D. R.,** ed. *The Acts of Andrew and The Acts of Andrew and Matthias in the City of the Cannibals.* Atlanta: Scholars, 1990. **Mach, M.** *Entwicklungsstadien des jüdischen Engelglaubens in vorrabbinischer Zeit.* Tübingen: Mohr-Siebeck, 1992. **Macho, A. D.** *Neophyti: Targum Palestinense Ms de la Biblioteca Vaticana.* Vol. 1. Madrid; Barcelona: Consejo Superior de Investigaciones Científicas, 1968. **MacMullen, R.** *Paganism in the Roman Empire.* New Haven, CT: Yale UP, 1981. **Magie, D.** *Roman Rule in Asia Minor to the End of the Third Century after Christ.* 2 vols. Princeton: Princeton UP, 1950. **Maher, M.** *Targum Pseudo-Jonathan: Genesis.* AramBib 1b. Wilmington, DE: Glazier, 1992. **Maier, J.** *The Temple Scroll.* JSOTSup 34. Sheffield: JSOT, 1985. **Malherbe, A. J.** *Moral Exhortation: A Greco-Roman Sourcebook.* Library of Early Christianity. Philadelphia: Westminster, 1986. ———. *Social Aspects of Early Christianity.* 2nd ed. Philadelphia: Fortress, 1983. **Malina, B. J.** *On the Genre and Message of Revelation: Star Visions and Sky Journeys.* Peabody, MA: Hendrickson, 1995. **Maloney, E. C.** *Semitic Interference in Marcan Syntax.* Chico, CA: Scholars, 1981. **Marcovich, M.,** ed. *Hippolytus Refutatio Omnium Haeresium.* Patristische Texte und Studien 25. Berlin; New York: de Gruyter, 1986. **Martin, J.** *Commodiani Carmina.* CCL 128. Turnholti: Typographi Brepols Editores Pontificii, 1960. **Martin, R. H.** *Tacitus.* Berkeley: University of California, 1981. **Mason, H. J.** *Greek Terms for Roman Institutions: A Lexicon and Analysis.* Toronto: Hakkert, 1974. **Mateos, J.** *El Aspecta Verbal en el Neuevo Testamento.* Madrid: Ediciones Cristiandad, 1977. **Matthiae, K.,** and **Schönert-Geiss, E.** *Münzen aus der urchristlichen Umwelt.* Berlin: Evangelische, 1981. **Maurer, C.** *Ignatius von Antiochien und das Johannesevangelium.* Zürich: Zwingli, 1949. **Mayser, E.** *Satzlehre.* Vol. 2/3 of *Grammatick der griechischen Papyri aus der Ptolemäerzeit.* Berlin; Leipzig: de Gruyter, 1934. **Mazzaferri, F. D.** *The Genre of the Book of Revelation from a Source-critical Perspective.* BZNW 54. Berlin; New York: de Gruyter, 1989. **McDonald, M. F.,** tr. *Lactantius: The Divine Institutes.* Washington, DC: The Catholic University of America, 1964. **McKay, K. L.** *Greek Grammar for Students: A Concise Grammar of Classical Attic with Special Reference to Aspect in the Verb.* Canberra: Australian National University, 1974. **McNamara, M.** *The New Testament and the Palestinian Targum to the Pentateuch.* Rome: Pontifical Biblical Institute, 1966. ———. *Targum and Testament.* Grand Rapids, MI: Eerdmans, 1972. ———. *Targum Neofiti 1: Leviticus.* Collegeville: Liturgical, 1994. ——— and **Clarke, E. G.** *Targum Neofiti 1: Numbers.* AramBib 4. Wilmington, DE: Glazier, 1995. ———, **Hayward, R.,** and **Maher, M.** *Targum Neofiti 1: Exodus and Targum Pseudo-Jonathan: Exodus.* AramBib 2. Wilmington, DE: Glazier, 1984. ———, **Hayward, R.,** and **Maher, M.** *Targum Neofiti 1: Leviticus and Targum Pseudo-Jonathan: Leviticus.* AramBib 3. Wilmington, DE: Glazier, 1994. **Meiggs, R.,** and **Lewis, D.** *A Selection of Greek Historical Inscriptions to the End of the Fifth Century B.C.* Oxford: Clarendon, 1969. **Mellor, R.** ΘΕΑ 'ΡΩΜΗ: *The Worship of the Goddess Roma in the Greek World.* Göttingen: Vandenhoeck & Ruprecht, 1975. **Ménard, J. E.** *L'Évangile de Vérité: Rétroversion Grecque et Commentaire.* Paris: Letouzey & Ané, 1962. ———. *L'Évangile selon Thomas.* Montélimar: Marsanne, 1974. **Merk, A.,** ed. *Novum Testament: Graece et Latine.* 10th ed. Rome: Pontifical Biblical Institute, 1984. **Meshorer, Y.** *Jewish Coins of the Second Temple Period.* Tr. I. H. Levine. Tel-Aviv: Am Hassefer, 1967. **Metzger, B. M.** *Breaking the Code: Understanding the Book of Revelation.* Nashville: Abingdon, 1993. ———. *Manuscripts of the Greek Bible.* New York; Oxford: Oxford UP, 1981. ———. *The Text of the New Testament: Its Transmission, Corruption and Restoration.* 2nd. ed. New York: Oxford UP, 1968. ———. *A Textual Commentary on the Greek New Testament:* Stuttgart: United Bible Societies, 1975. **Meyer, E.** *Ursprung und Anfänge des Christentums.* 3 vols. 1923. Repr. Darmstadt: Wissenschaftliche Buchgesellschaft, 1962. **Michaels, J. R.** *1 Peter.* WBC 49. Waco, TX: Word, 1988. ———. *Interpreting the Book of Revelation.* Grand Rapids, MI: Baker, 1992. **Michl, J.** *Die Engelvorstellung in der Apokalypse.* Munich: Hueber, 1937. **Milik, J. T.** *The Books of Enoch: Aramaic Fragments of Qumran Cave 4.* Oxford: Clarendon, 1976. **Millar, F.** *The Emperor in the Roman World (31 B.C.–A.D. 337).* Ithaca, NY: Cornell UP, 1977. ———. *The Roman Near East 31 B.C.–A.D. 337.* Cambridge: Harvard UP, 1993. **Miller, A. M.** *From Delos to Delphi: A Literary Study of the Homeric Hymn to Apollo.* Leiden: Brill, 1986. **Minear, P. S.** *I Saw a New Earth: An Introduction to the Visions of the Apocalypse.* Washington DC; Cleveland: Corpus, 1968. **Mitchell, S.** *Anatolia: Land, Men, and Gods in Asia Minor.* 2 vols. Oxford: Clarendon, 1993. **Mommsen, T.** *Römisches Staatsrecht.* 3rd ed. Graz: Akademische Druck- und Verlagsanstalt, 1952. ——— and **Krueger, P.** *The Digest of Justinian.* Tr. and ed. Alan Watson. 4 vols. Philadelphia: University of Pennsylvania, 1985. **Montgomery, J. A.** *Aramaic Incantation Texts from Nippur.* Philadelphia: The University Museum, 1909. ———. *A Critical and Exegetical Commentary on the Book of Daniel.* Edinburgh: T. & T. Clark, 1927. **Moore, C. A.** *Judith: A New Translation with Introduction and Commentary.* AB 40. Garden City, NY: Doubleday, 1985. **Moore, G. F.** *Judaism in the First Centuries of the Christian Era: The Age of the Tannaim.* 3 vols. Cambridge: Harvard UP, 1927. **Moran, H. E.** *The Consolations of Death in Ancient Greek Literature.* Washington, DC: The Catholic University of America, 1917. **Morenz, S.** *Egyptian Religion.* Tr. A. E. Keep. Ithaca, NY: Cornell UP, 1973. **Morgan, M. A.,** tr. *Sepher ha-Razim: The Book of the Mysteries.* Chico, CA: Scholars, 1983. **Moule, C. F. D.** *An Idiom-Book of New Testament Greek.* 2nd ed. Cambridge: Cambridge UP, 1959. **Moulton, J. H.** *A Grammar of New Testament Greek.* 3 vols. Edinburgh: T. & T. Clark, 1908–76. ———. *Prolegomena.* Vol. 1 of *A Grammar of New Testament Greek.* 3rd ed. Edinburgh: T. & T. Clark, 1908. ——— and **Howard, W. F.** *Accidence and Word-Formation.* Vol. 2 of *A Grammar of New Testament Greek.* Edinburgh: T. & T. Clark, 1928. **Mowinckel, S.** *Offersang og Sangoffer.* Oslo: Universitetsforlaget, 1951. ———. *The Psalms in Israel's Worship.* 2 vols. New York; Nashville: Abingdon, 1967. **Müller, U. B.** "Literarische und formgeschichtliche Bestimmung der Apokalypse des Johannes als einem Zeugnis frühchristlicher Apokalyptic." In *Apocalypticism,* ed. D. Hellholm. 599–620. ———. *Messias und Menschensohn in jüdischen Apokalypsen und in der Offenbarung des Johannes.* SNT 6. Gütersloh: Mohn, 1972. ———. *Prophetie und Predigt im Neuen Testament: Formgeschichtliche Untersuchungen zur urchristlichen Prophetie.* Gütersloh: Mohn, 1975. ———. *Zur frühchristlichen Theologiegeschichte: Judenchristentum und Paulinismus in Kleinasien an der Wende vom ersten zum zweiten Jahrhundert n. Chr.* Gütersloh: Mohn, 1976. **Muraoka, T.** *A Greek-English Lexicon of the Septuagint (Twelve Prophets).* Louvain: Peeters, 1993. **Mussies, G.** *Dio Chrysostom and the New Testament.* Leiden: Brill, 1972. ———. "Identification and Self-Identification of Gods in Classical and Hellenistic Times." In *Knowledge of God in the Graeco-Roman World,* ed. R. van den Broek, T. Baarda, and J. Mansfeld. EPRO 112. Leiden: Brill, 1988. 1–18. ———. *The Morphology of Koine Greek as Used in the Apocalypse of John: A Study in Bilingualism.* Leiden: Brill, 1971. **Musurillo, H.** *The Acts of the Christian Martyrs.* Oxford: Clarendon, 1972. **Myers, J. M.** *I and II Esdras.* AB 42. Garden City, NY: Doubleday, 1974. **Nachmanson, E.** *Partitives Subjekt im Griechischen.* Göteborg: Elanders Boktryckeri, 1942. **Nauck, A.** *Tragicorum graecorum fragmenta.* Leipzig: Teubner, 1856. **Naveh, J.,** and **Shaked, S.** *Amulets and Magic Bowls: Aramaic Incantations of Late Antiquity.* Jerusalem: Magnes; Leiden: Brill, 1985. **Neusner, J.,** ed. *Pesiqta de Rab Kahana.* 2 vols. BJS 122–23. Atlanta: Scholars, 1987. **Newsom, C.** *Songs of the Sabbath Sacrifice: A Critical Edition.* Atlanta: Scholars, 1985. **Nickelsburg, G. W. E.** *Jewish Literature between the Bible and the Mishnah.* Philadephia: Fortress, 1981. **Niederwimmer, K.** *Die Didache.* KAV 1. Göttingen: Vandenhoeck & Ruprecht, 1989. **Niggemeyer, J.-H.** *Beschwörungsformeln aus dem 'Buch der Geheimnisse' (Sefär ha-razîm).* Hildesheim; New York: Olms, 1975. **Nock, A. D.** *Essays on Religion and the Ancient World,* ed. Z. Stewart. 2 vols. Oxford: Clarendon, 1972. ——— and **Festugière, A.-J.,** eds. *Corpus Hermeticum.* 6th ed. Paris: Société d'édition "Les belles lettres," 1983. ——— and **Festugière, A.-J.** *Hermès Trismégiste.* 4 vols. Paris: Société d'édition 'Les belles lettres,' 1954–60. **Norden, E.** *Agnostos Theos: Untersuchungen zur Formengeschichte religiöser Rede.* Darmstadt: Wissenschaftliche Buchgesellschaft, 1956. **Nussbaum, M.** *The Therapy of Desire: Theory and Practice in Hellenistic Ethics.* Princeton: Princeton UP, 1994. **Odelain, O.,** and **Séguineau, R.** *Lexikon der Biblischen Eigennamen.* Düsseldorf: Patmos; Neukirchen: Neukirchener, 1981. **Olyan, S. M.** *A Thousand Thousands Served Him: Exegesis and the Naming of Angels in Ancient Judaism.* Tübingen: Mohr-Siebeck, 1993. **Otto, E.** *Die biographischen Inschriften der ägyptischen Spätzeit: Ihre geisteschichtiche und literarische Bedeutung.* Leiden: Brill, 1954. **Palmer, L. R.** *The Greek Language.* Atlantic Highlands, NJ: Humanities, 1980. **Parker, R.** *Miasma: Pollution and Purification in Early Greek Religion.* Oxford: Clarendon, 1983. **Pax, E.** *Epiphaneia: Ein religionsgeschichtlier Beitrag zur biblischen Theologie.* Munich: Münchener Theologische Studien, 1955. **Peerbolte, L. J. L.** *The Antecedents of Antichrist: A*

Traditio-Historical Study of the Earliest Christian Views on Eschatological Opponents. Leiden: Peerbolte, 1995. **Perrin, M.,** ed. *Épitomé des institutions divines, [par] Lactance.* SC 335. Paris: Cerf, 1987. **Perrin, N.** *Rediscovering the Teaching of Jesus.* New York; Evanston, IL: Harper & Row, 1967. **Pesch, R.** *Das Markus-evangelium.* 2 vols. Freiburg: Herder, 1977. ———. *Naherwartungen: Tradition und Redaktion in Mk 13.* Düsseldorf: Patmos, 1968. **Peterson, E.** *Εἷς Θεός: Epigraphische, formgeschichtliche und religionsgeschichtliche Untersuchungen.* Göttingen: Vandenhoeck & Ruprecht, 1926. **Pétrement, S.** *A Separate God: The Christian Origins of Gnosticism.* San Francisco: Harper & Row, 1990. **Petzl, G.** *Die Inschriften von Smyrna.* Part 1: *Grabinschriften, postume Ehrungen, Grabepigramme. Inschriften griechischer Städte aus Kleinasien,* vol. 23. Bonn: Habelt, 1982. ———. *Die Inschriften von Smyrna.* Part 2, vol. 2. Bonn: Habelt, 1990. **Philipp, H.** *Mira et Magica: Gemmen im ägyptischen Museum der staatlichen Museen, preussischer Kulturbesitz Berlin-Charlottenburg.* Mainz am Rhein: von Zabern, 1986. **Philonenko, M.** *Joseph et Aséneth.* Leiden: Brill, 1968. **Pietersma, A.** *The Apocryphon of James and James the Magician.* RGRW 119. Leiden: Brill, 1994. ——— et al., eds. and trs. *The Apocalypse of Elijah: Based on P. Chester Beatty 2018.* Atlanta: Scholars, 1981. **Ploeg, J. P. M. van der,** and **Woude, A. S. van der,** eds. *Le Targum de Job de la grotte XI de Qumran.* Leiden: Brill, 1971. **Pohlenz, M.** *Vom Zorne Gottes: Eine Studie über den Einfluss der griechischen Philosophie auf das alte Christentum.* FRLANT 12. Göttingen: Vandenhoeck & Ruprecht, 1909. **Pollitt, J. J.** *Art in the Hellenistic Age.* Cambridge: Cambridge UP, 1986. **Porten, B.** *Archives from Elephantine: The Life of an Ancient Jewish Military Colony.* Berkeley; Los Angeles: University of California, 1968. ——— and **Yardeni, A.** *Textbook of Aramaic Documents from Ancient Egypt.* 3 vols. Jerusalem: Hebrew University, 1986–93. **Porter, S. E.** *Verbal Aspect in the Greek of the New Testament with Reference to Tense and Mood.* Frankfurt/M.; Berne; New York: Lang, 1978. **Qimron, E.,** and **Strugnell, J.** *Qumran Cave 4.* Vol. V: *Miqsat Maʿase ha-Torah.* DJD 10. Oxford: Clarendon, 1994. **Rad, G. von.** *Old Testament Theology.* 2 vols. New York; Evanston, IL: Harper & Row, 1962–65. ———. *Wisdom in Israel.* Nashville; New York: Abingdon, 1972. **Radermacher, L.** *Neutestamentliche Grammatik.* 2nd ed. Tübingen: Mohr-Siebeck, 1925. **Rahlfs, A.** *Septuaginta: Id est Vetus Testamentum graece iuxta LXX interpretes.* 8th ed. 2 vols. Stuttgart: Würtembergische Bibelanstalt, 1935. **Ramsay, W. M.** *The Cities of St. Paul: Their Influence on His Life and Thought.* London: Hodder and Stoughton, 1907. ———. *The Letters to the Seven Churches.* London: Hodder & Stoughton, 1904. **Reader, W. W.** "Die Stadt Gottes in der Johannesapokalypse." Diss., Göttingen, 1971. **Reardon, B. P.,** ed. *Collected Ancient Greek Novels.* Berkeley: University of California, 1989. **Rehm, B.** *Die Pseudoklementinen.* Vol. 1: *Homilien.* GCS. Berlin: Akademie, 1953. **Reichelt, G.** *Das Buch mit den sieben Siegeln in der Apokalypse des Johannes.* Göttingen: Georg-August-Universität zu Göttingen, 1975. **Reichelt, H.** *Angelus Interpres-Texte in der Johannes-Apokalypse.* Frankfurt am Main: Lang, 1994. **Reicke, B.** *The New Testament Era: The World of the Bible from 500 B.C. to A.D. 100.* Philadelphia: Fortress, 1968. ———. *Die zehn Worte in Geschichte und Gegenwart.* BGBE 13. Tübingen: Mohr-Siebeck, 1973. **Rendtorff, R.** *Studien zur Geschichte des Opfers im alten Israel.* Neukirchen: Neukirchener, 1967. **Reynolds, J.** *Aphrodisias and Rome.* London: Society for the Promotion of Roman Studies, 1982. ——— and **Tannenbaum, R.** *Jews and Godfearers at Aphrodisias.* Cambridge: Cambridge Philological Society, 1987. **Rijksbaron, A.** *The Syntax and Semantics of the Verb in Classical Greek: An Introduction.* Amsterdam: Gieben, 1984. **Rissi, M.** *The Future of the World: An Exegetical Study of Revelation 19.11–22.15.* SBT 23. Naperville, IL: Allenson, n.d. ———. *Die Hure Babylon und die Verführung der Heiligen: Eine Studie zur Apokalypse des Johannes.* BWANT 136. Stuttgart: Kohlhammer, 1995. ———. "The Kerygma of the Revelation to John." *Int* 22 (1968) 3–17. ———. *Zeit und Geschichte.* Zürich: Zwingli, 1952. ———. *Time and History: A Study on the Revelation.* Tr. G. C. Winsor. Richmond, VA: Knox, 1966. **Robert, L.** *Hellenica: Recueil d'epigraphie de numismatique et d'antiquities grecques.* 13 vols. Limoges: Bontemps, 1940–65. ———. *Nouvelles inscriptions de Sardes.* Paris: Librairie d'Amérique et d'Orient, 1964. **Robertson, A. T.** *A Grammar of the Greek New Testament in the Light of Historical Research.*

Nashville: Broadman, 1934. **Robinson, J. A. T.** *Redating the New Testament.* Philadelphia: Westminster, 1976. **Robinson, J. M.,** ed. *The Nag Hammadi Library.* Rev. ed. San Francisco: Harper & Row, 1988. **Roloff, J.** *Das Kerygma und der irdische Jesus: Historische Motive in den Jesus-Erzählungen der Evangelien.* Göttingen: Vandenhoeck & Ruprecht, 1970. **Romero-Pose, E.,** ed. *Sancti Beati a Liebana Commentarius in Apocalipsin.* Rome: Typis officinae polygraphicae, 1985. **Rordorf, W.,** and **Tuilier, A.** *La Doctrine des douze Apôtres (Didachè).* SC 248. Paris: Cerf, 1978. **Roscher, W. H.** *Ausführliches Lexikon der griechischen und römischen Mythologie.* 6 vols. Leipzig: Teubner, 1884–1937. **Rosenstiehl, J.-M.** *L'Apocalypse d'Elie.* Paris: Geuthner, 1972. **Rosenthal, F.** *A Grammar of Biblical Aramaic.* Wiesbaden: Harrassowitz, 1963. **Rostovtzeff, M.** *The Social and Economic History of the Roman Empire.* 2nd ed. by P. M. Fraser. 2 vols. Oxford: Clarendon, 1957. **Roueché, C.** *Aphrodisias in Antiquity.* London: Society for the Promotion of Roman Studies, 1989. **Ruckstuhl, E.,** and **Dschulnigg, P.** *Stilkritik und Verfasserfrage im Johannesevangelium.* Göttingen: Vandenhoeck & Ruprecht; Freiburg: Universitätsverlag, 1991. **Rudolf, K.** *Gnosis: The Nature and History of Gnosticism.* Tr. R. McL. Wilson. San Francisco: Harper & Row, 1983. **Rusam, F.** "Hymnische Formeln in Apokalypse 1." Diss., Christian-Albrechts-Universität zu Kiel, 1970. **Russell, D. S.** *The Method and Message of Jewish Apocalyptic.* Philadelphia: Westminster, 1964. **Rydbeck, L.** *Fachprosa, Vermeintliche Volkssprache und Neues Testament.* Uppsala: Berlingska Boktryckeriet, 1967. **Sanday, W.,** and **Headlam, A. C.** *Romans.* 5th ed. Edinburgh: T. & T. Clark, 1902. ——— and **Turner, C. H.** *Nouum Testamentum Sancti Irenaei Episcopi Lugdunensis.* Old-Latin Biblical Texts 7. Oxford: Clarendon, 1923. **Sanders, E. P.** *Jesus and Judaism.* Philadelphia: Fortress, 1985. **Sanders, J. T.** *The New Testament Christological Hymns: Their Historical Religious Background.* SNTSMS 15. Cambridge: Cambridge UP, 1971. **Sandnes, K. O.** *Paul—One of the Prophets? A Contribution to the Apostle's Self-Understanding.* WUNT 2/43. Tübingen: Mohr-Siebeck, 1991. **Satake, A.** *Die Gemeindeordnung in der Johannesapokalypse.* WMANT 21. Neukirchen: Neukirchener, 1966. **Sattler, W.** "Das Buch mit sieben Siegeln: Studien zum literarischen Aufbau der Offenbarung Johannis." *ZNW* 20 (1921) 231–40. **Sauter, F.** *Der römische Kaiserkult bei Martial und Statius.* Stuttgart; Berlin: Kohlhammer, 1934. **Schäfer, P.** *Rivalität zwischen Engeln und Menschen: Untersuchungen zur rabbinischen Engelvorstellung.* SJ 8. Berlin; New York: de Gruyter, 1975. ———. *Synopse zur Hekhalot-Literatur.* Tübingen: Mohr-Siebeck, 1981. **Schiffman, L. H.,** and **Swartz, M. D.** *Hebrew and Aramaic Incantation Texts from the Cairo Genizah: Selected Texts from Taylor-Schechter Box K1.* Sheffield: Sheffield Academic, 1992. **Schlatter, A.** *Das Alte Testament in der johanneischen Apokalypse.* Gütersloh: Bertelsmann, 1912. **Schlier, H.** *Der Brief an die Galater.* 12th ed. Göttingen: Vandenhoeck & Ruprecht, 1962. **Schmid, J.** *Studien zur Geschichte des griechischen Apokalypse-Textes.* 2 vols. Munich: Zink, 1955. **Schmidt, C.,** and **MacDermot, V.** *The Books of Jeu and the Untitled Text in the Bruce Codex.* NHS 13. Leiden: Brill, 1978. ——— and **MacDermot, V.** *Pistis Sophia.* NHS 9. Leiden: Brill, 1978. ——— and **Till, W.** *Koptisch-gnostische Schriften.* Vol. 1: *Die Pistis Sophia, Die beiden Bücher des Jeu, Unbekanntes altgnostisches Werk.* GCS 13. 3rd ed. Berlin: Akademie, 1962. **Schmidt, F.** *Le Testament grec d'Abraham.* Tübingen: Mohr-Siebeck, 1986. **Schnackenburg, R.** *The Gospel according to St. John.* 3 vols. Vol. 1: New York: Herder & Herder, 1968; Vol. 2: New York: Seabury, 1980; Vol. 3: New York: Crossroad, 1982. **Schoedel, W. R.** *Ignatius of Antioch: A Commentary on the Letters of Ignatius of Antioch.* Philadelphia: Fortress, 1985. **Schowalter, D. N.** *The Emperor and the Gods: Images from the Time of Trajan.* HDR 28. Minneapolis: Fortress, 1993. **Schrenk, G.** *Die Weissagung über Israel im Neuen Testament.* Zürich: Gotthelf, 1951. **Schröder, S.** *Plutarchs Schrift De Pythiae oraculis. Text, Einleitung und Kommentar.* Stuttgart: Teubner, 1990. **Schürer, E.** *The History of the Jewish People in the Age of Jesus Christ.* 4 vols. Ed. G. Vermes, F. Millar, and M. Goodman. Edinburgh: T. & T. Clark, 1973–87. **Schüssler Fiorenza, E.** "Apokalypsis and Propheteia: The Book of Revelation in the Context of Early Christian Prophecy." In *L'Apocalypse johannique et l'Apocalyptique dans le Nouveau Testament,* ed. J. Lambrecht. Leuven: Leuven UP, 1980. 105–28. ———. *The Book of Revelation: Justice and Judgment.* Philadelphia: Fortress, 1985. ———. "Composition and Structure of the Book of Revelation." *CBQ* 39 (1977) 344–66. ———. "The Eschatology and Composition of the Apocalypse." *CBQ* 30 (1968) 564. ———. *Priester für Gott: Studien zum Herrschafts- und Priestermotiv in der Apokalypse*. NTAbh 7. Münster: Aschendorf, 1972. ———. "The Quest for the Johannine School: The Apocalypse and the Fourth Gospel." *NTS* 23 (1976–77) 402–27. **Schwemer, A. M.** "Studien zu den frühjüdischen Prophetenlegenden: Vitae Prophetarum." 2 vols. Diss., Tübingen, 1993. **Scott, W.** *Hermetica: The Ancient Greek and Latin Writings Which Contain Religious or Philosophic Teachings Ascribed to Hermes Trismegistus*. 4 vols. 1924–36. Repr. Boston: Shambhala, 1985. **Scullard, H. H.** *Festivals and Ceremonies of the Roman Republic*. Ithaca, NY: Cornell UP, 1981. **Sellin, E.,** and **Fohrer, G.** *Introduction to the Old Testament*. Tr. D. E. Green. Nashville: Abingdon, 1968. **Shepherd, M. H.** *The Paschal Liturgy and the Apocalypse*. Richmond: John Knox, 1960. **Sherk, R. K.** *Roman Documents from the Greek East: Senatus Consulta and Epistulae to the Age of Augustus*. Baltimore: Johns Hopkins UP, 1969. **Sherwin-White, A. N.** *The Letters of Pliny: A Historical and Social Commentary*. Oxford: Clarendon, 1966. **Sickenberger, J. B.** *Erklärung der Johannesapokalypse*. Bonn: Hanstein, 1940. **Simon, M.** *Verus Israel: A Study of the Relations between Christians and Jews in the Roman Empire (A.D. 135–425)*. Oxford: Oxford UP, 1986. **Simpson, M.,** tr. *Gods and Heroes of the Greeks: The Library of Apollodorus*. Amherst: University of Massachusetts, 1976. **Skarsaune, O.** *The Proof from Prophecy: A Study in Justin Martyr's Proof-Text Tradition: Text-Type, Provenance, Theological Profile*. NovTSup 56. Leiden: Brill, 1987. **Skehan, W., Ulrich, E.,** and **Sanderson, J. E.** *Qumran Cave 4*. Vol. 4: *Palaeo-Hebrew and Greek Biblical Manuscripts*. DJD 9. Oxford: Clarendon, 1992. **Skutsch, O.** *The Annals of Quintus Ennius*. Oxford: Clarendon, 1985. **Smalley, S. S.** *Thunder and Love: John's Revelation and John's Community*. Milton Keynes: Nelson Word, 1994. **Smith, J. Z.** "The Prayer of Joseph." In *Religions in Antiquity*, ed. J. Neusner. NumenSup 14. Leiden: Brill, 1968. 253–94. **Smith, K. F.** *The Elegies of Albius Tibullus*. New York: American Book Company, 1913. **Smith, M.** *Tannaitic Parallels to the Gospels*. SBLMS 6. 2nd ed. Philadelphia: Society of Biblical Literature, 1968. **Smyth, H. W.** *Greek Grammar*. Rev. G. M. Messing. Cambridge: Harvard UP, 1956. **Soden, H. F. von.** *Das lateinische Neue Testament in Afrika zur Zeit Cyprians*. TU 33. Leipzig: Hinrichs, 1909. ———. *Text mit Apparat*. Part 2 of *Die Schriften des Neuen Testaments in ihrer ältesten erreichbaren Textgestalt*. Göttingen: Vandenhoeck & Ruprecht, 1913. **Söder, R.** *Die apokryphen Apostelgeschichten und die romanhafte Literatur der Antike*. Stuttgart: Kohlhammer, 1932. **Soisalon-Soininen, I.** *Die Infinitive in der Septuagints*. Helsinki: Suomalainen Tiedeakatemia, 1965. **Sokolowski, F.** *Lois sacrées de l'Asie Mineure*. Paris: de Boccard, 1955. **Sollamo, R.** *Renderings of Hebrew Semiprepositions in the Septuagint*. Helsinki: Suomalainen Tiedeakatemia, 1979. **Souza Nogueira, P. A. de.** "Der Widerstand gegen Rom in der Apokalypse des Johannes: Eine Untersuchung zur Tradition des Falls von Babylon in Apokalypse 18." Diss., Heidelberg, 1991. **Spengel, L.** *Rhetores Graeci*. 3 vols. Leipzig: Teubner, 1853–56. **Sperber, A.** *The Bible in Aramaic*. 4 vols. Leiden: Brill, 1959–73. **Spicq, C.** *Notes de lexicographie Néo-testamentaire*. 3 vols. Göttingen: Vandenhoeck & Ruprecht, 1978–82. **Stegemann, W.** *Zwischen Synagoge und Obrigkeit: Zur historischen Situation der lukanischen Christen*. Göttingen: Vandenhoeck & Ruprecht, 1991. **Stengel, P.** *Die griechischen Kultusaltertümer*. 3rd ed. Munich: Beck, 1920. **Stone, M. E.** *Fourth Ezra: A Commentary on the Book of Fourth Ezra*. Minneapolis: Fortress, 1990. **Stoneman, R.** *Palmyra and Its Empire: Zenobia's Revolt against Rome*. Ann Arbor: University of Michigan, 1992. **Strobel, A.** "Apokalypse des Johannes." In *Theologische Realenzyklopädie*. Vol. 3. New York; Berlin: de Gruyter, 1978. **Stroker, W. D.** *Extracanonical Sayings of Jesus*. Atlanta: Scholars, 1989. **Stuckenbruck, L. T.** *Angel Veneration and Christology: A Study in Early Judaism and the Apocalypse of John*. Tübingen: Mohr-Siebeck, 1995. **Stuhlmann, R.** *Das eschatologische Maß im Neuen Testament*. Göttingen: Vandenhoeck & Ruprecht, 1983. **Swartz, M. D.** *Mystical Prayer in Ancient Judaism: An Analysis of Ma'aseh Merkavah*. Tübingen: Mohr-Siebeck, 1992. **Swete, H. B.** *Introduction to the Old Testament in Greek*. Cambridge: Cambridge UP, 1914. **Syme, R.** *Tacitus*. 2 vols. Oxford: Clarendon, 1958. **Tagawa, K.** *Miracles et Évangile: la pensée personelle de* *l'évangeliste Marc*. Paris: Presses universitaires de France, 1966. **Tajra, H. W.** *The Martyrdom of St. Paul: Historical and Judicial Context, Traditions and Legends*. WUNT 2/67. Tübingen: Mohr-Siebeck, 1994. **Taylor, L. R.** *The Divinity of the Roman Emperor*. Middletown: American Philological Association, 1931. **Tcherikover, V.** *Hellenistic Civilisation and the Jews*. Philadelphia: Jewish Publication Society of America, 1961. **Thackeray, H. St. J.** *A Grammar of the Old Testament in Greek*. Cambridge: Cambridge UP, 1909. ———. *Josephus the Man and the Historian*. New York: Ktav, 1967. **Thayer, J. H.** *A Greek-English Lexicon of the New Testament*. Grand Rapids, MI: Zondervan, n.d. **Theisohn, J.** *Der auserwählte Richter: Untersuchungen zur traditionsgeschichtlicher Ort der Menschensohngestalt der Bilderreden des Äthiopisch Henoch*. Göttingen: Vandenhoeck & Ruprecht, 1976. **Theissen, G.** *The Gospels in Context: Social and Political History in the Synoptic Tradition*. Minneapolis: Fortress, 1991. ———. *The Miracle Stories of the Early Christian Tradition*. Philadelphia: Fortress, 1983. **Theodor, J.,** and **Albeck, Ch.** *Midrash Bereshit Rabba: Critical Edition with Notes and Commentary*. 3 vols. Jerusalem: Vahrman, 1965. **Thompson, L. L.** *The Book of Revelation: Apocalypse and Empire*. New York: Oxford UP, 1990. **Thompson, S.** *The Apocalypse and Semitic Syntax*. SNTSMS 52. Cambridge: Cambridge UP, 1985. ———. *Motif-Index of Folk-Literature*. 6 vols. 1932–34. Repr. Bloomington: Indiana UP, 1983. **Tischendorf, C.** *Novum Testamentum Graece*. 8th ed. 2 vols. Leipzig: Giesecke & Devrient, 1872. **Tödt, H. E.** *The Son of Man in the Synoptic Tradition*. Tr. D. M. Barton. Philadelphia: Westminster, 1965. **Toit, A. du.** "Vilification as a Pragmatic Device in Early Christian Epistolography." *Bib* 75 (1994) 403–12. **Torrey, C. C.** *The Apocalypse of John*. New Haven: Yale UP, 1958. **Touilleux, P.** *L'Apocalypse et les cultes de Domitien et de Cybèle*. Paris: Librairie Orientaliste Paul Geuthner, 1935. **Tov, E.** *The Greek Minor Prophets Scroll from Nahal Ḥever (8ḤevXIIgr, The Seiyal Collection I)*. DJD 8. Oxford: Clarendon, 1990. **Trebilco, P.** *Jewish Communities in Asia Minor*. SNTSMS 69. Cambridge: Cambridge UP, 1991. **Trites, A. A.** *The New Testament Concept of Witness*. Cambridge: Cambridge UP, 1977. **Tromp, J.** *The Assumption of Moses: A Critical Edition with Commentary*. Leiden: Brill, 1992. **Turner, N.** *Grammatical Insights into the New Testament*. Edinburgh: T. & T. Clark, 1965. ———. *Style*. Vol. 4 of *A Grammar of New Testament Greek*, ed. J. H. Moulton. Edinburgh: T. & T. Clark, 1976. ———. *Syntax*. Vol. 3 of *A Grammar of New Testament Greek*, ed. J. H. Moulton. Edinburgh: T. & T. Clark, 1963. **Ulrichsen, J. H.** *Die Grundschrift der Testamente der zwölf Patriarchen: Eine Untersuchung zu Umfang, Inhalt und Eigenart der ursprünglichen Schrift*. Uppsala: Almqvist & Wiksel, 1991. **Urbach, E. E.** *The Sages: Their Concepts and Beliefs*. Cambridge: Harvard UP, 1987. **VanderKam, J. C.** *The Book of Jubilees: A Critical Text*. CSCO 510; Scriptores Aethiopici 87. Louvain: Peeters, 1989. ———. *Enoch and the Growth of an Apocalyptic Tradition*. CBQMS 16. Washington, DC: Catholic Biblical Society of America, 1984. **Vanhoye, A.** "L'utilisation du livre d'Ézéchiel dans l'Apocalypse. *Bib* 43 (1962) 436–76. **Vanni, U.** *L'Apocalisse: Ermeneutica, Esegesi, Teologia*. Bologna: Editzioni Dehoniane, 1988. ———. *La struttura letteraria dell'Apocalisse*. 2nd ed. Napoli: Morcelliana, 1980. **Vaux, R. de.** *Ancient Israel: Its Life and Institutions*. Tr. J. McHugh. New York: McGraw-Hill, 1961. **Vermaseren, M. J.** *Mithraica III: The Mithraeum at Marino*. EPRO 16. Leiden: Brill, 1982. ———. *Mithras the Secret God*. London: Chatto & Windus, 1963. **Vermes, G.** *The Dead Sea Scrolls in English*. 3rd rev. and aug. ed. London: Penguin, 1987. ———. *Jesus the Jew*. New York: Macmillan, 1973. **Vermeule, C. C.** *Roman Imperial Art in Greece and Asia Minor*. Cambridge: Harvard UP, 1968. **Vermeule, E.** *Aspects of Death in Early Greek Art and Poetry*. Berkeley: University of California, 1979. **Versnel, H. S.** "Religious Mentality in Ancient Prayer." In *Faith, Hope and Worship: Aspects of Religious Mentality in the Ancient World*. Leiden: Brill, 1981. 1–64. ———. *Triumphus: An Inquiry into the Origin, Development and Meaning of the Roman Triumph*. Leiden: Brill, 1970. **Vielhauer, P.** *Geschichte der urchristlichen Literatur*. Berlin; New York: de Gruyter, 1975. **Vischer, E.** *Die Offenbarung Johannis: eine jüdische Apokalypse in christlicher Bearbeitung*. TU 2/3. Leipzig: Hinrichs, 1886. **Vlastos, G.** *Socrates: Ironist and Moral Reformer*. Cambridge: Cambridge UP, 1991. **Vogels, H. J.** *Untersuchungen zur Geschichte der lateinischen Apokalypse-Übersetzung*. Düsseldorf: Schwann, 1920. **Vögtle, A.** *Das Neue Testament und die Zukunft des Kosmos*. Düsseldorf: Patmos, 1970. ———. *Die Tugend-*

und Lasterkataloge im Neuen Testament. NTAbh 16. Münster: Aschendorff, 1936. **Völter, D.** *Die Entstehung der Apokalypse.* 2nd ed. Freiburg: Mohr-Siebeck, 1882. **Volz, P.** *Die Eschatologie der jüdischen Gemeinde.* Tübingen: Mohr-Siebeck, 1934. **Vos, L. A.** *The Synoptic Traditions in the Apocalypse.* Kampen: Kok, 1965. **Votaw, C. W.** *The Use of the Infinitive in Biblical Greek.* Chicago: Votaw, 1896. **Vuyst, J. de.** *De structuur van de apokalyps.* Kampen: Kok, 1968. **Walbank, F. W.** *A Historical Commentary on Polybius.* 3 vols. Oxford: Clarendon, 1957–79. **Watson, A.,** ed. *The Digest of Justinian.* Philadelphia: University of Pennsylvania, 1985. **Weber, R.** ed., *Biblia sacra iuxta Vulgatam versionem.* 2 vols. Stuttgart: Deutsche Bibelgesellschaft, 1969. **Wehr, L.** *Arznei der Unsterblichkeit: Die Eucharistie bei Ignatius von Antiochien und im Johannesevangelium.* NTAbh 18. Münster: Aschendorff, 1987. **Weiser, A.** *The Psalms: A Commentary.* Philadelphia: Westminster, 1962. **Weiss, B.** *Die Johannes-Apokalypse: Textkritische Untersuchungen und Textherstellung.* TU 7.1. Leipzig: Hinrichs, 1892. **Weiss, H.-F.** *Untersuchungen zur Kosmologie des hellenistischen und palästinischen Judentums.* TU 97. Berlin: Akademie, 1966. **Weiss, J.** *Der erste Korintherbrief.* 8th ed. Göttingen: Vandenhoeck & Ruprecht, 1910. ———. *Die Offenbarung des Johannes: Ein Beitrag zur Literatur- und Religionsgeschichte.* Göttingen: Vandenhoeck & Ruprecht, 1904. **Wellhausen, J.** *Analyse der Offenbarung Johannis.* Berlin: Weidmann, 1907. ———. *Skizzen und Vorarbeiten.* 6 vols. 1884–99. Repr. Berlin; New York: de Gruyter, 1985. **Wellmann, M.,** ed. *Pedanii Dioscurides Anazarbei, De material medica libri quinque.* 3 vols. Berlin: Weidmann, 1958. **Wengst, K.** *Schriften des Urchristentums: Didache (Apostellehre), Barnabasbrief, Zweiter Klemensbrief, Schrift an Diognet.* Munich: Kösel, 1984. **Werner, E.** *The Sacred Bridge: Liturgical Parallels in Synagogue and Early Church.* New York: Columbia UP, 1959. **West, M. L.** *Hesiod, Theogony: Edited with Prolegomena and Commentary.* Oxford: Clarendon, 1966. **Westcott, B. F.** *A General Survey of the History of the Canon of the New Testament.* 6th ed. Grand Rapids, MI: Baker, 1980. ——— and **Hort, F. J. A.** *Introduction to the New Testament in the Original Greek.* New York: Harper, 1882 (*indicates pages in the Appendix). **Westermann, C.** *Genesis: A Commentary.* Tr. J. J. Scullion. 3 vols. Minneapolis: Augsburg, 1984–86. ———. *The Praise of God in the Psalms.* Tr. K. R. Crim. Richmond: John Knox, 1965. **Wettstein, J. J.** *Novum Testamentum Graecum.* 2 vols. 1752. Repr. Graz: Akademische Druck- und Verlaganstalt, 1962. **Weyland, W. G. J.** *Omwerkings en Compilatie-Hypothesen toegepast op de Apokalypse van Johannes.* Groningen: Wolters, 1888. **White, R. J.** *The Interpretation of Dreams: Oneirocritica by Artemidorus.* Park Ridge, NJ: Noyes, 1975. **Wilken, R. L.** *The Christians as the Romans Saw Them.* New Haven; London: Yale UP, 1984. **Williams, F.** *Callimachus, Hymn to Apollo: A Commentary.* Oxford: Clarendon, 1978. **Wilson, W. T.** *The Mysteries of Righteousness: The Literary Composition and Genre of the Sentences of Pseudo-Phocylides.* Tübingen: Mohr-Siebeck, 1994. **Winer, G. B.** *A Treatise on the Grammar of New Testament Greek.* Tr. W. F. Moulton. 3rd ed. rev. Edinburgh: T. & T. Clark, 1882. **Winston, D.** *The Wisdom of Solomon.* Garden City, NY: Doubleday, 1979. **Wissowa, G.** *Religion und Kultus der Römer.* 2nd ed. Munich: Beck, 1912. **Witt, R. E.** *Isis in the Graeco-Roman World.* Ithaca, NY: Cornell UP, 1971. **Wolff, C.** *Jeremia im frühjudentum und Urchristentum.* TU 118. Berlin: Akademie, 1976. **Wolff, H. W.** *Joel and Amos.* Hermeneia. Philadelphia: Fortress, 1977. **Wülker, L.** *Die geschichtliche Entwicklung des Prodigienwesens bei den Römern: Studien zur Geschichte und Überlieferung der Staatsprodigien.* Leipzig: Glausch, 1903. **Yarbro Collins, A.** *The Combat Myth in the Book of Revelation.* Missoula, MT: Scholars, 1975. ———. *Crisis and Catharsis: The Power of the Apocalypse.* Philadelphia: Westminster, 1984. ———. "The Political Perspective of the Revelation to John." *JBL* 96 (1977) 241–56. ———. "The 'Son of Man' Tradition and the Book of Revelation." In *The Messiah: Developments in Earliest Judaism and Christianity,* ed. J. H. Charlesworth. Minneapolis: Fortress, 1992. 536–68. **Ysebaert, J.** *Die Amtsterminologie im Neuen Testament und in der Alten Kirche: Eine lexicographische Untersuchung.* Breda: Eureia, 1994. **Zahn, T.** *Ignatii et Polycarpi Epistolae Marytia Fragmenta.* Vol. 2 of *Patrum Apostolicorum Opera.* Leipzig: Hinrichs, 1876. ———. *Introduction to the New Testament.* 3 vols. Grand Rapids, MI: Kregel, 1953. ———, ed. *Forschungen zur Geschichte des neutestamentlichen Kanons und der altkirchlichen Literatur.* Erlangen: Deichert, 1891. **Zazoff, P.** *Die antike Gemmen.* Munich: Beck, 1983.

Zerwick, M. *Biblical Greek.* Tr. J. Smith, S.J. Rome: Pontifical Biblical Institute, 1963. ——— and **Grosvenor, M.** *A Grammatical Analysis of the Greek New Testament.* 2 vols. Rome: Biblical Institute, 1974. **Ziegler, J.,** ed. *Duodecim prophetae.* VTG 13. Göttingen: Vandenhoeck & Ruprecht, 1943. ———, ed. *Ezechiel.* Septuaginta: VTG 16/1. Göttingen: Vandenhoeck & Ruprecht, 1952. ———, ed. *Susanna, Daniel, Bel et Draco.* VTG 16/2. Göttingen: Vandenhoeck & Ruprecht, 1954. **Ziegler, K.-H.** *Die Beziehungen zwischen Rom und dem Partherreich.* Wiesbaden: Steiner, 1964. **Zimmerli, W.** *Ezekiel.* Tr. R. E. Clements. 2 vols. Philadelphia: Fortress, 1979–83.

Revelation
17:1–22:21

E. Revelations of the Judgment of Babylon (17:1–19:10)
1. Introduction to the Revelations (17:1–2)
2. The Allegorical Vision of Babylon as the Great Whore (17:3–18)

Bibliography

Bachmann, M. "Offb 17,5: Hurenmutter?" In *Religionspädagogische Grenzgänge.* FS E. Bochinger and M. Widmann, ed. G. Büttner and J. Thierfelder. Stuttgart: Calwer, 1988. 95–98. **Bartsch, S.** *Decoding the Ancient Novel: The Reader and the Role of Description in Heliodorus and Achilles Tatius.* Princeton: Princeton UP, 1989. **Bauckham, R.** "Nero and the Beast." In R. Bauckham, *Climax.* 384–452. **Beagley, A. J.** *The "Sitz im Leben" of the Apocalypse, with Particular Reference to the Role of the Church's Enemies.* Berlin/New York: de Gruyter, 1987. **Beale, G. K.** "The Danielic Background for Revelation 13:18 and 17:9." *TynBul* 31 (1980) 163–70. ———. "The Origin of the Title 'King of Kings and Lord of Lords' in Revelation 17:14." *NTS* 31 (1985) 618–20. **Beauvery, R.** "L'Apocalypse au risque de la numismatique: Babylone, la grande Prostituée et le sixième roi Vespasien et la déesse Rome." *RB* 90 (1983) 243–60. **Becker, A. S.** "Reading Poetry through a Distant Lens: Ecphrasis, Ancient Greek Rhetoricians, and the Pseudo-Hesiodic 'Shield of Herakles.'" *AJP* 113 (1992) 5–24. **Bergmeier, R.** "Die Erzhure und das Tier: Apk 12.18–13.18 und 17f.: Eine quellen- und redaktionskritische Analyse." *ANRW* II, 25/5:3899–3916. **Bird, P.** "'To Play the Harlot': An Inquiry into an Old Testament Metaphor." In *Gender and Difference in Ancient Israel,* ed. P. L. Day. Minneapolis: Fortress, 1989. 75–94. **Bishop, J.** *Nero: The Man and the Legend.* London: R. Hale, 1964. **Brelich, A.** *Die geheime Schutzgottheit von Rom.* Zürich: Rhein, 1949. **Brown, D. F.** *Temples of Rome as Coin Types.* New York: The American Numismatic Society, 1940. **Brun, L.** "Die römische Kaiser in der Apokalypse." *ZNW* 26 (1927) 128–51. **Bruns, J. E.** "The Contrasted Women of Apocalypse 12 and 17." *CBQ* 26 (1964) 459–63. **Calza, G.** "La figurazione di Roma nell' arte antica." *Dedalo* 7 (1926–27) 663–88. **Castagnoli, F.** "Note Numistiche." *Archeologia Classica* 5 (1953) 104–11. **Chilver, G. E. F.** "The Army in Politics, A.D. 68–70." *JRS* 47 (1957) 29–35. **Cohen, H.** *Description historique des monnaies frappées sous l'Empire Romain.* 2nd ed. 8 vols. Paris; London: Rollin & Feuardent, 1880–92. **Coppens, J.** "L'Élu et les élus dans les Écritures Saintes et les Écrits de Qumrân." *ETL* 57 (1981) 120–24. **Davidson, M.** "The Thematic Use of Ekphrasis in the Ancient Novel." In *Erotica Antiqua: Acta of the International Conference on the Ancient Novel.* Bangor: University of Wales, 1977. **Downey, G.** "Ekphrasis." *RAC* 4 (1959) 921–44. **Dürbeck, H.** *Zur Charakteristik der griechischen Farbenbezeichnungen.* Bonn: Habelt, 1977. **Fayer, J. C.** *Il culto della dea Rome: Origine e diffusione nell' Impero.* Pescara: Trimestre, 1976. ———. "La 'dea Roma' sulle monete greche." *Studi Romani* 23 (1975) 273–88. **Fitzgerald, J. T.,** and **White, L. M.** *The Tabula of Cebes.* Chico: Scholars, 1983. **Franke, P. R.** *Kleinasien zur Römerzeit: Griechisches Leben im Spiegel der Münzen.* Munich: Beck, 1968. **Fridh, Å.** "Mons and Collis." *Eranos* 91 (1993) 1–12. **Galling, K.,** and **Altaner, B.** "Babylon." *RAC* 1 (1950) 1118–34. **Gardner, P.** *The Types of Greek Coins: An Archaeological Essay.* Cambridge: Cambridge UP, 1883. **Garofalo, S.** "'Sette monti su cui siede la donna' (Apoc. 17,9)." In *Kirche und Bibel.* FS E. Schick. Paderborn: Schoningh, 1979. 97–104. **Gelsomino, R.** *Varrone e i sette colli di Roma.* Rome: Universita' degli Studi di Siena, 1975. **Giblin, C. H.** "Structural and Thematic Correlations in the Theology of Revelation 16–22." *Bib* 55 (1974) 487–504. **Griffiths, J. G.** "Βασιλεὺς βασιλέων: Remarks on the History of a Title." *CP* 48 (1953) 145–54. **Holwerda, D.**

"Ein neuer Schlüssel zum 17. Kapitel der johanneischen Offenbarung." *EstBib* 53 (1995) 387–96. **Hommel, H.** "Domina Roma." In *Symbola*. Vol. 1: *Kleine Schriften zur Literatur- und Kulturgeschichte der Antike*, ed. B. Gladigow. Hildesheim: Olms, 1976. 331–64. **Huntzinger, C.-H.** "Babylon als Deckname für Rom und die Datierung des 1. Petrusbriefes." In *Gottes Wort und Gottes Land*. FS H.-W. Hertzberg, ed. H. G. Reventlow. Göttingen: Vandenhoeck & Ruprecht, 1965. 66–77. **Inan J.,** and **Alföldi-Rosenbaum, E.** *Römische und frühbyzantinische Porträtplastik aus der Türkei: Neue Funde*. Mainz am Rhein: von Zabern, 1979. **Joly, R.** *Le Tableau de Cébe et la philosophie religieuse*. Bruxelles-Berchem: Latomus, 1963. **Mattingly, H.,** and **Carson, R. A. G.** *Coins of the Roman Empire in the British Museum*. 6 vols. London: The British Museum, 1923–62. **May, H. G.** "Some Cosmic Connotations of *MAYIM RABBIM*, 'Many Waters.'" *JBL* 74 (1955) 9–21. **Mellor, R.** "The Goddess Roma," *ANRW* II, 17/2:950–1030. ———. ΘΕΑ ΡΩΜΗ: *The Worship of the Goddess Roma in the Greek World*. Göttingen: Vandenhoeck & Ruprecht, 1975. **Momigliano, A.** *Claudius: The Emperor and His Achievement*. Westport: Greenwood, 1981. **Moore, R. D.** "Personification of the Seduction of Evil: 'The Wiles of the Wicked Woman.'" *RQ* 10 (1979–81) 505–19. **Muehsam, A.** *Coin and Temple: A Study of the Architectural Representation on Ancient Jewish Coins*. Leiden: Brill, 1966. **Otto, E.** *Die biographischen Inscriften der ägyptischen Spätzeit: Ihre geistesgeschichtliche und literarische Bedeutung*. Leiden: Brill, 1954. **Palm, J.** "Bemerkungen zur Ekphrase in der griechischen Literatur." *Kungliga Humanistika Vetenskaps-Samfundet i Uppsala, Årsbok, 1965–66*. 1:108–211. **Platner, S. B.** "Mons and Collis." *CP* 2 (1907) 433–34. **Reicke, B.** "Die jüdische Apokalyptik und die johanneische Tiervision." *RSR* 60 (1972) 173–92. **Reinhold, M.** *The History of Purple as a Status Symbol in Antiquity*. Brussels: Latomus, 1970. **Robinson, H. S.** "A Monument of Roma in Corinth." *Hesperia* 43 (1974) 470–84. **Skehan, P. W.** "King of Kings, Lord of Lords (Apoc 19, 16)." *CBQ* 10 (1948) 398. **Slater, T. B.** "'King of Kings and Lord of Lords' Revisited." *NTS* 39 (1993) 159–60. **Strobel, A.** "Abfassung und Geschichtstheologie der Apokalypse nach Kap. XVII.9–12." *NTS* 10 (1963–64) 433–45. **Taylor, C.** "Hermas and Cebes." *JP* 27 (1901) 276–319; 28 (1903) 24–38, 94–98. **Towner, W. S.** *The Rabbinic "Enumeration of Scriptural Examples": A Study of a Rabbinic Pattern of Discourse with Special Reference to Mekhilta d'R. Ishmael*. Leiden: Brill, 1973. **Trell, B. L.** *The Temple of Artemis of Ephesus*. New York: American Numismatic Society, 1945. **Uhlig, S.** "Die typologische Bedeutung des Begriffs Babylon." *AUSS* 12 (1974) 112–25. **Ulrichsen, J. H.** "Dyret i Åpenbaringen: En skisse til tidshistorisk forståelse av kapitlene 13 og 17." *NorTT* 87 (1986) 167–77. ———. "Die sieben Häupter und die zehn Hörner: Zur Datierung der Offenbarung des Johannes." *ST* 39 (1985) 1–20. **Unnik, W. C. van.** "ΜΙΑ ΓΝΩΜΗ, Apocalypse of John XVII,13.17." In *Studies in John*. FS J. N. Sevenster. Leiden: Brill, 1970. 209–20. **Vermeule, C. C.** *The Goddess Roma in the Art of the Roman Empire*. 2nd ed. London: Spink and Son, 1974.

Translation

[1]*Now one of*[a] *the seven angels with the seven bowls came and spoke with me,*[b] *saying,*[c] *"Come, I will show you the judgment of* [d]*the great whore* [d] *seated by* [e] [f]*many waters,*[f] [2] [a]*with whom the kings of the earth have fornicated,*[a] [b]*and with whom* [b] *the inhabitants of the earth have become drunk from the wine* [c]*which is* [c] *her immorality."*

[3]*He then carried me to the desert in* [a] *a prophetic trance. I* [b] *saw* [c]*a woman* [c] *sitting on* [d]*a scarlet beast* [d] [e]*covered with blasphemous* [f] *names,*[e] *with* [g] *seven heads and ten horns.* [4]*Now the woman was* [a] *dressed in purple* [b] *and scarlet and* [c] *adorned with gold ornaments,*[d] [e]*precious stones,*[e] *and pearls. She was holding a golden cup in her hand,* [f]*filled* [g] *with abominations and the impurities* [f] *of her* [h] *fornication.* [5] [a]*Upon her forehead a mysterious name was written, "Babylon the great, the mother of whores* [b] *and of earthly abominations."* [6]*And I saw the woman drunk* [a]*on the blood of* [b] *God's people* [b] *and the blood of the witnesses to* [c]*Jesus.*[d]

I was ^every perplexed ^e when I saw her. ⁷*Thereupon the angel said to me, "Why are you perplexed?* ^a*I will explain to you^a the ^bsecret meaning^b of the woman and the beast with seven heads and ten horns which bears her.* ⁸*The beast that you saw was and is not and is about to ascend from the abyss and^ais headed^a for destruction. The inhabitants ^bof the earth,^b whose names^c have not been inscribed in the book of life since the creation^d of the world, will be amazed^e when they see^f the beast because it was and is and is not^gand will be present again.^g* ⁹*This requires deep insight.*

"The seven heads are seven mountains upon which the woman is seated.^a They are also ^bseven kings,^c ¹⁰*of whom five have fallen,^a one is living, the other has not yet come. When he comes, he can remain for only a short while.* ¹¹*The beast which was and is not, ^ahe^b is the eighth^c and is ^done of the seven^d and is headed for destruction.* ¹²*And ^athe ten horns^a that you saw are ten kings, who^b have ^cnot yet^c ^dbecome kings,^d but they will receive royal authority, together with the beast, for one hour.* ¹³*They^a are of one accord and relinquish^b their power and ^cauthority to the beast.* ¹⁴*They will fight against the Lamb, and the Lamb will conquer them, because he is Lord of lords and King of kings,^a and those with him are ^bcalled and^c elect and faithful."^b*

¹⁵*Continuing, he said^a to me, ^b"The waters^b that you saw, ^cwhere the whore resides,^c ^d are ^epeoples and crowds and nations and languages.* ¹⁶*The ten horns that you saw and the beast will hate the whore and make her desolate^aand naked^{ab} and will devour her flesh and will burn her^cwith fire.* ¹⁷*For^aGod prompted^b ^cthem^a to do his^d will^eand to be in one accord^e and to surrender their royal power to the beast until the words of God^fwill have been fulfilled.^f*

¹⁸*"And the woman that you saw is the great city that has dominion over the^akings^bof the earth."*

Notes

1.a. Variant: (1) ἐκ before τῶν ἑπτὰ ἀγγέλων] Hippolytus (*de Ant.* 36; MSS E R). (2) omit ἐκ] ℵ fam 1006^{106 1841} Hippolytus (*de Ant.* 36).

1.b. On the Septuagintism λαλεῖν μετ᾽ ἐμοῦ, see *Note* 1:12.b-b.

1.c. Variant: (1) omit μοι] ℵ A 025 046 fam 1611¹⁶¹¹ Andr f l 94 2019 Hippolyus Victorinus Cyprian Primasius Tyc³ Beatus. (2) insert μοι] fam 1611^{1854 2344} Andreas.

1.d-d. Since the phrase τῆς πόρνης τῆς μεγάλης, "the great whore," is articular, though the author refers to this figure here for the first time, he evidently expects his readers to be familiar with her. The next four references to her all have the anaphoric article (17:5, 15, 16; 19:2).

1.e. The prep. ἐπί + gen. can be used with a literal spatial significance to mean "on, upon" (Bauer-Aland, 579; Louw-Nida, § 83.23; e.g., Matt 9:9; 14:25; Luke 22:30; Rev 3:20), but here it makes more sense if it is construed as "by, beside" (e.g., Matt 21:19; John 21:1), for how is one to visualize the whore *on* many waters (NRSV)? Still less justified is the NEB: "enthroned above the ocean."

1.f-f. Variants: (1) ὑδάτων πολλῶν] ℵ A 025 fam 1006 fam 1611 Oecumenius^{2053 2063}. (2) τῶν ὑδάτων τῶν πολλῶν] 2030 Andr f²⁰²³ 94 Byzantine. (3) ὑδάτων τῶν πολλῶν] 𝔓⁴⁷. (4) τῶν ὑδάτων πολλῶν] Andr n²⁴²⁹.

2.a-a. Variant: ἐποίησαν πορνείαν] ℵ Andr l. The phrase πορνεύειν μετά is problematic because the verb is normally intransitive; however, the phrase also occurs in Rev 18:3, 9, thereby binding the two chaps. together stylistically. There is, however, a single occurrence of the phrase μετὰ σοῦ πεπορνεύκασιν, translating the phrase וְאַחֲרַיִךְ לֹא זֻנָּה *wĕ᾽aḥărayik lō᾽ zûnnâ*, in LXX Ezek 16:34. K. G. C. Newport suggests that since the meaning is figurative rather than literal, it might be appropriate to translate the phrase something like "chased after," particularly in 18:3. Since sexual immorality is a frequent metaphor for idolatry, the phrase πορνεύειν μετά is perhaps one way of rendering זָנָה אַחֲרֵי *zānâ ᾽aḥărê*, rendered ἐκπορνεύσει ὀπίσω θεῶν ἀλλοτρίων, "they lusted after other gods" or "they chased after other gods," in LXX Deut 31:16 and ἐξεπόρνευσαν ὀπίσω θεῶν ἑτέρων, "they lusted after other gods" or "they ran after other gods," in LXX Judg 2:17 ("Semitic Influence on Revelation," *BT* 37 [1986] 331–32).

2.b-b. Here the relative clause is continued with καὶ … αὐτῆς, which therefore functions as a relative clause (Zerwick, *Greek*, § 455ε).

2.c-c. The noun phrase τῆς πορνείας αὐτῆς, lit. "of her fornication," is construed here as epexegetical or explanatory and is therefore translated "which is."

3.a. Variants: (1) omit ἐν] 2030 Byzantine. (2) τῷ instead of ἐν] Andr c.

3.b. The καί that introduces this sentence is left untranslated because it lacks semantic value and functions as a discourse marker indicating the beginning of a new sentence clause.

3.c-c. γυναῖκα, "woman," is anarthrous, which means that she is unknown to the readers; the second and following occurrences of γυνή are all articular as one would expect (17:4, 6, 7, 9, 18).

3.d-d. Since the phrase θηρίον κόκκινον, "red animal," is anarthrous, the author is not (apparently) referring to the beast from the sea first mentioned in 13:1. The articular use of θηρίον in 17:7, 8(2x), 11, 12, 13, 16, 17, is anaphoric, referring back to the first mention of this beast in 17:3.

3.e-e. Variants: (1) γέμον ὀνόματα] Byzantine; Merk, *NT;* Schmid, *Studien* 2:235–36. (2) γέμον ὀνομάτων] Andreas Hippolytus (*de Ant.* 36; MSS E R); TR. (3) γέμων ὀνόματα] fam 1006¹⁰⁰⁶ Andr e⁻²⁰⁵⁷ f²⁰³¹ h i²⁰⁸² 598 Andr/Byz 2a Andr/Byz 3²⁰⁶¹ Andr/Byz 4a⁶¹⁶ Byz 3⁴²⁹ Byz 5⁸⁰⁸ Byz 17⁴⁶⁹ ¹⁸⁵² ²⁰¹⁷ Byz 19¹⁰⁹⁴. (4) γέμωντα ὀνόματα] fam 1611²³²⁹. (5) γέμοντα ὀνόματα] A (lacunae in C and 𝔓⁴⁷) ℵ* 025 Oecumenius²⁰⁵³; Tischendorf, *NT Graece;* WHort; Swete, 214; Bousset (1906) 403; Charles, 2:338; Hadorn, 168. Nestle-Aland²⁷ and UBSGNT⁴ read γέμον[τα]. (6) γέμον τὰ ὀνόματα] Hippolytus (*de Ant.* 36; MS H). ὀνόματα in readings (1), (3), (4), (5), and (6) is a neut. pl. acc. dependent on a ptcp. form of γέμειν, where a gen. of material or content is expected (cf. BDF § 159.1; 172; BDR § 172.2). γέμειν is used seven times in Revelation, six times with the gen. of material or content (4:6, 8; 5:8; 15:7; 17:4; 21:9), once with the acc. (17:3), and once with a gen. and an acc. (17:4). Since there are no other known instances of γέμειν with the acc., this usage may reflect a lit. translation of the Heb. verb מָלֵא *mālēʾ*, "to fill," used with the acc. of material (BDB, 570), construed with אֶת *ʾet-* (GKC § 117z; cf. Exod 8:17). Variant (2) is clearly a correction. However, note that 17:4 reads γέμον βδελυγμάτων καὶ τὰ ἀκάθαρτα, "filled with abominations and the impurities," a clause that includes *both* a gen. and an acc. dependent on γέμον (see *Note* 17:4.f-f.). For examples of verbs meaning "to fill" with the acc. in both the LXX and Gk. literature, cf. Helbing, *Kasussyntax*, 147–49 (though he gives no examples of γέμειν with the acc. of that which is filled). Exod 1:7 reads ἐπλήθυνεν δὲ ἡ γῆ αὐτούς, "the earth was filled with them" (αὐτῶν is expected). Another example is found in Ezek 39:20, καὶ ἐμπλησθήσεσθε ἐπὶ τῆς τραπέζης μου ἵππον καὶ ἀναβάτην, "And you will be filled at my table with horse and rider."

B. Weiss (*Johannes-Apokalypse,* 206) is alone in construing γέμοντα ὀνόματα of variant (5) like variant (6) by separating -τα from γέμοντα and reading it as a definite article, arguing that the definite article is anaphoric, referring back to the anarthrous use of ὄνομα in 13:1. The variant *could* be read this way; however, spaces between words were not used in papyri and uncial MSS, and thus γεμονταονοματα could be divided γεμοντα/ονοματα as in (5) or γεμον/τα/ονοματα as in (6). In variant (5), the ptcp. γέμοντα, "covered, filled" (which can be construed as a present masc. sing. acc. or a present neut. pl. nom. or acc.), must be a *masc.* sing. acc. modifying the *neut.* sing. acc. noun θηρίον. This is an example of the *constructio ad sensum* in which the fact that the θηρίον symbolizes a male often influences the gender of the ptcps. and pronouns modifying θηρίον in Revelation (n.b. the masc. pronouns used to refer to θηρίον in 17:11, 16). It is possible, however, that an original γέμον was erroneously copied as γέμοντα under the influence of the following word ὀνόματα. The reading γέμον found in variants (1) and (2) has strong internal corroboration in that 13:1 reads θηρίον … ἔχον, 13:2 reads τὸ θηρίον ὅ, and 17:11 has τὸ θηρίον ὅ (i.e., the neut. ptcp. and neut. pronouns are used to modify θηρίον in readings that are certainly original), and in 11:7 and 13:11 in which neut. ptcps. modifying θηρίον are very probably original (Schmid, *Studien* 2:233–34). On the other hand, in alternate readings (1) and (2), γέμον (present neut. *sing.* acc. ptcp.) could be a correction to modify θηρίον, "beast."

3.f. Variants: (1) βλασφημίας] Hippolytus (*de Ant.* 36; MSS e R). (2) omit βλασφημίας] Hippolytus (*de Ant.* 36). In the phrase ὀνόματα βλασφημίας, lit. "names of blasphemy," βλασφημίας is a qualitative gen. used in place of an adj. (BDR § 165.2; Mussies, *Morphology*, 96).

3.g. The pres. masc. sing. nom. ptcp. ἔχων, "with, having," is a solecism since it modifies θηρίον, "beast" (neut. sing. acc.), and should therefore have the form ἔχον (neut. sing. nom. or acc. ptcp.), which is the corrected reading of 051 Byzantine Andreas Hippolytus (*de Ant.* 36), though it is possible that because of the o = ω interchange (see Gignac, *Grammar* 1:275–77), ἔχον was pronounced ἔχων (cf. BDF § 28; BDR § 28; B. Weiss, *Johannes-Apocalypse*, 54 n. 1). If the masc. ptcp. is original, this is also an example of John's tendency to use the nom. of apposition when modifying an oblique case, particularly with a ptcp. (cf. ζῷον ἔχων in 4:7–8). A further reason for the use of ἔχων is that in apocalyptic language, beasts symbolize human beings and nations. The variant reading ἔχοντα (pres. masc. sing. acc. ptcp. or present neut. pl. nom. or acc. ptcp.) is found in ℵ P and in the important minuscules 2053 and 2062 (both equivalent to A and C in value), though only in the commentary, not the text itself. The reading ἔχων is supported by A (C and 𝔓⁴⁷ have lacunae here) and more than forty minuscules, including 1006 2319 2344. Schmid regards the minuscule evidence for ἔχων to be the result of scribal error in copying ἔχων, leaving A as the only independent witness for ἔχων (*Studien* 2:235–36).

4.a. Variants: (1) ἦν] ℵ A (lacuna in C) 025 046 051 Hippolytus syr^ph. (2) ἦν] fam 1611²³²⁹.

4.b. Variants: (1) πορφυροῦν] ℵ A 025 046 Oecumenius²⁰⁵³comm 2062comm fam 1006 fam 1611¹⁶¹¹ ¹⁸⁵⁴ ²³²⁹. (2) πορφύραν] 051 Andreas. (3) πορφύρον] Oecumenius²⁰⁵³txt 2062txt. (4) πορφύρας] syr^ph.

4.c. Variants: (1) insert καί] ℵ A fam 1611¹⁶¹¹ ¹⁸⁵⁴²³²⁹ Oecumenius²⁰⁵³ ²⁰⁶² 2030 Andr a c l 94 1773 2019 latt syr^h. (2) omit καί] 025 046 051 Andreas Byzantine Hippolytus (*de Ant.* 36); 051 syr^ph. See Rev 18:16.

4.d. χρυσίον means "object or objects made of gold," i.e., "gold jewelry, gold ornaments" (Louw-Nida, § 6.189). Variants: (1) χρυσίῳ] A (lacuna in C) 046 Oecumenius²⁰⁵³txt 2062txt. (2) χρυσῷ] ℵ 051 fam 1006 fam 1611¹⁶¹¹ ²³²⁹ ²³⁴⁴ Andreas Hippolytus (*de Ant.* 36).

4.e-e. The phrase λίθῳ τιμίῳ, lit. "precious stone," is a collective sing.; cf. 18:16.

4.f-f. The phrase γέμον βδελυγμάτων καὶ τὰ ἀκάθαρτα is peculiar since the verb γέμειν, "to fill," is normally followed by a gen. of material or content indicating that with which something is filled. Here, however, γέμειν is first followed by a gen. (which is idiomatic Gk.) and then followed by an acc., which would be idiomatic in Heb. (but cf. 17:3 where γέμειν is followed by the acc. ὀνόματα βλασφημίας). The use of the acc. of material after a verb of filling is the usual construction in Heb. (e.g., BDB, 570). A close parallel to Rev 17:4 (suggested by Laughlin, *Solecisms*, 12–13) is found in 2 Sam 23:7, ואיש יגע בהם ימלא ברזל ועץ חנית *wĕ'îš yiggaʿ bāhem yimmālē' barzel wĕʿēṣ ḥănût*, "A person will [not] touch them; he will be filled [i.e., his hand?] with [a weapon of] iron and the shaft of a spear." This is a problematic passage in which ימלא *yimmālē'*, "he will be filled," has been emended (following the Lucianic recension of the LXX, which reads ἐὰν μή) to read לא אם *'im lō'*, "except," by K. McCarter, *II Samuel*, AB 9 [Garden City: Doubleday, 1984] ad loc., an emendation presupposed by the REB: "none touch them but with a tool of iron or of wood." Despite the problems with the MT, the LXX translates the Heb. phrase quoted above in this way: καὶ ἀνὴρ οὐ κοπιάσει ἐν αὐτοῖς, καὶ πλῆρες σιδήρου καὶ ξύλον δόρατος, "And a man will not toil among them, except armed with iron and the shaft of a spear." Here the adj. πλῆρες, lit. "filled," is appropriately followed by the gen. noun σιδήρου, "with iron" (reflecting idiomatic Gk. usage). But πλῆρες also governs ξύλον δόρατος, "shaft of a spear," which is placed in the acc. in accordance with the lit. Heb. idiom. 2 Kgdms 23:7 is therefore a very close syntactical parallel to Rev 17:4 since a verb of filling is followed first by a gen. then by an acc., both connected with καί.

4.g. Variants: (1) γέμον] Hippolytus (*de Ant.* 36; MS R). (2) γέμων] ℵ* fam 1006¹⁰⁰⁶ ¹⁸⁵⁴ Hippolytus (*de Ant.* 36). (3) γέμοντα] Oecumenius²⁰⁵³ ²⁰⁶² fam 1611²³⁴⁴.

4.h. Variants: (1) αὐτῆς] A fam 1006¹⁰⁰⁶ fam 1611²³⁴⁴ vg syr^ph. (2) τῆς γῆς] fam 1611¹⁶¹¹ ¹⁸⁵⁴²³²⁹ 2030 Oecumenius²⁰⁵³ ²⁰⁶² Byzantine it^gig arm³ Hippolytus (*de Ant.* 36). (3) αὐτῆς καὶ τῆς γῆς] ℵ (cop^sa bo). Reading (2) is apparently the result of a error in copying, while reading (3) is a conflation of readings (1) and (2) (*TCGNT*¹, 756; *TCGNT*², 681–82).

5.a. Variant: omit καί] Hippolytus (*de Ant.* 36; MSS E R).

5.b. The reading πορνῶν, from the fem. noun ἡ πόρνη, meaning "(female) prostitute," is the (probably) correct reading chosen by all modern texts of the Gk. NT. There is, however, surprisingly strong support for the reading πόρνων, from the masc. noun ὁ πόρνος, meaning "(male) prostitute" (fifty MS witnesses to this reading are listed in Hoskier, *Text* 2:449). The evidence is reviewed and assessed in R. Borger, "NA²⁶ und die neutestamentliche Textkritik," *TRu* 52 (1987) 48–50. Since for the most part accents were not part of the uncial texts of NT MSS for the first few centuries A.D., the reading ΠΟΡΝΩΝ would have been generically ambiguous. It is entirely possible that the variant reading πορνειῶν, from the abstract fem. noun ἡ πορνεία, "fornication, prostitution," arose in an attempt to resolve the ambiguity by translating πορνῶν/πόρνων with *fornicationum* in the Latin versions found in some commentaries (Tyconius, Primasius, Beatus).

6.a. Variants: (1) ἐκ τοῦ αἵματος] majority of witnesses, including Andreas Byzantine Hippolytus (*de Ant.* 37; MSS E R); TR. (2) τῷ αἵματι] ℵ* And l¹⁶⁷⁸ ¹⁷⁷⁸ ²⁰²⁰. (3) τοῦ αἵματος] ℵ² 046 P 94 Oecumenius²⁰⁵³ fam 1611¹⁸⁵⁴ ²³²⁹ 2030 2062 Byzantine; Hippolytus (*de Ant.* 37). Here μεθύειν + ἐκ + gen. expresses an instrumental notion, as the identical expression does in v 2 (cf. 14:8). Reading (3), the simple gen., is clearly a correction of (1) in the direction of classical usage (Plato *Symp.* 203b; cf. Helbing, *Kasussyntax*, 150; BDR § 195). Reading (2) is a more radical correction in which the dat. of instrument, more characteristic of Hellenistic Gk. (cf. Eph 5:18; Lucian *De dea Syr.* 22), is substituted for the Hebraic ἐκ + gen. (though ἀπό is preferred in the LXX; cf. Deut 32:42; Isa 34:7; Jer 26:10[MT 46:10]; Ps 35:9[MT 36:9]; Sir 1:16).

6.b-b. On translating οἱ ἅγιοι, lit. "saints, holy ones," as "God's people," see *Comment* on 5:8.

6.c. Variant: τοῦ before Ἰησοῦ] Hippolytus (*de Ant.* 37; MSS E R).

6.d. In the phrase τῶν μαρτύρων Ἰησοῦ, lit. "the witnesses of Jesus," Ἰησοῦ is an obj. gen., i.e., "witnesses *to* Jesus."

6.e-e. The phrase ἐθαύμασα . . . θαῦμα μέγα, lit. "I was astonished with great astonishment," is an example of a cognate acc. (Winer, *Grammar,* 280–83; Robertson, *Grammar,* 478; Turner, *Syntax,* 245–46; BDR § 153.2); cf. Mark 4:41, ἐφοβήθησαν φόβον μέγαν, "they were filled with awe" (rsv); "they were awestruck" (reb). Since this is a very common Gk. construction, it is not quite correct to claim that this construction is more common in Semitic than in Gk. (as does Maloney, *Marcan Syntax,* 189–90). The cognate acc. occurs frequently in the LXX (Conybeare-Stock, *Septuagint,* § 56); cf. Gen 12:17; Judg 16:23; 1 Kgs 17:25; Zech 1:2, 14, 15; 8:2; Dan 11:2 (cf. S. Thompson, *Apocalypse,* 80), though the dat. is more frequently found. Another cognate acc. occurs in Rev 16:9 and perhaps also in 18:6. Mussies observes (*Morphology,* 99, 323–24) that in the LXX, Gk. verbs are often linked with accs. of content, instrumental dats., or ptcps. that are based on cognate forms. These often represent literal translations of a Heb. finite verb and absolute inf., used to intensify the meaning of the verb. Since the abs. inf. had disappeared from Heb. and was rare in Aram., John's uses of this idiom in 17:6, 16:9, and 18:6 may be imitations of Septuagint Gk. or Masoretic Heb. In Rev 17:6 and 16:9, the value of intensification is conveyed through the adj. μέγα.

The meaning of θαυμάζειν here is problematic. It normally means "to wonder, to be amazed, to marvel" (Louw-Nida, § 25.213), and since the context determines whether this reaction is positive or negative, the suggestion that θαυμάζειν here means "appalled, dumbfounded" (S. Thompson, *Apocalypse,* 12) is derived from the context and should not be considered a definition of the word. I have translated θαυμάζειν with the verb "perplexed" because it is clear that the narrator is not simply "amazed" or "astonished," in the usual sense of the term, but rather "wonders" about the meaning and significance of the female figure he has seen.

7.a-a. Variants: (1) ἐρῶ σοι] A 046 fam 1006 fam 1611[1611] Oecumenius[2053txt 2062] Hippolytus vg it[gig]. (2) σοὶ ἐρῶ] ℵ 051 fam 1611[1854 2329 2344] Andreas. (3) σοὶ φήσιν ἐρῶ τι ἐστί] Oecumenius[2053comm].

7.b-b. τὸ μυστήριον, lit. "the mystery," actually means "secret meaning" or "symbolic significance" (Hatch, *Essays,* 59–62); cf. the more extended discussion under *Comment* on 1:20.

8.a-a. Variants: (1) ὑπάγει] A (lacuna in C) fam 1611[1611] Oecumenius[2053 2062] Irenaeus[Lat] (*vadit*); Hippolytus (*de Ant.* 37); Primasius (*vadit*); Tyc[2] (*ibit*); *De promissionibus* (*itura*); it[gig] (*ibit*); vg; B. Weiss, *Johannes-Apokalypse,* 106; Charles, 2:340; Merk, *NT;* WHort; Nestle-Aland[27]; UBSGNT[4]. (2) ὑπάγειν] ℵ (lacuna in 𝔓[47]) 025 046 051 fam 1006 fam 1611[1854 2050 2329] Andreas Byzantine Hippolytus (*de Ant.* 37; MSS E R S); Beatus (*ire*); syr[h] TR; Bousset (1906) 405 (ν bracketed); Charles, 2:340 (margin). ὑπάγει, a present ind., is the *lectio difficilior* and could easily have been changed to ὑπάγειν, since final ν is often represented simply by a horizontal stroke over the preceding letter (*TCGNT*[1], 756; *TCGNT*[2], 682). Assimilation to the inf. in the preceding periphrasis (μέλλει ἀναβαίνειν) is more probable than a change from the inf. to a present ind. (Schmid, *Studien* 2:92–93).

8.b-b. Variant: τὴν γῆν] 2030 Andr c n[2429] Byzantine.

8.c. Variants: (1) τὸ ὄνομα] A 94 Byzantine. (2) τὰ ὀνόματα] ℵ 051 fam 1611[2329 2344] Andreas lat syr[ph] cop[sa].

8.d. For καταβολή as "creation," see *Note* 13:8.d.

8.e. Variants: (1) θαυμασθήσονται] A 025 1611. (2) θαυμάσονται] ℵ 051 Andreas Byzantine. (3) θαυμάζουσιν] Hippolytus (*de Ant.* 37). (4) θαυμάσουσιν] Hippolytus (*de Ant.* 37; MSS E R). θαυμασθήσονται should be understood as a true fut. ind. rather than a lit. rendering of Semitic impf. (contra S. Thompson, *Apocalypse,* 46) because (unlike the aor. pass. ἐθαυμάσθη in 13:3) here the action described is fut. since the vision is based on the interpretation of a *static* scene rather than a narrative description of actions.

8.f. The gen. pl. ptcp. βλεπόντων is problematic. Though it can be understood as a syntactical error for βλέποντες, perhaps influenced by the gen. pl. relative pronoun ὧν (Buttmann, *Grammar,* 306; Bousset [1906] 406; Beckwith, 698; Charles, 2:68; Robertson, *Grammar,* 718–19; Schmid, *Studien* 2:247), it can more naturally be construed as a gen. abs. with αὐτῶν understood (B. Weiss, *Johannes-Apokalypse,* 207; Winer, *Grammar,* 260; BDR §§ 423.3, 9). Variant: βλέποντες] fam 1611[1854] 94 792 1773 2019 Andr a c f n[2429] Hippolytus (*de Ant.* 37); TR. This is certainly a scribal correction.

8.g-g. Variants: (1) καὶ παρέσται] A 025 Andr b d f g 1 94 1773 2019 Byzantine Hippolytus (*de Ant.* 37). (2) καὶ πάλιν παρέσται] ℵ*. (3) καὶ πάρεστιν] ℵ[2] Andreas. (4) καὶ ὅτι πάρεστιν] fam 1611[1854].

9.a. In the adv. phrase ὅπου ἡ γυνὴ κάθηται ἐπ᾽ αὐτῶν, lit. "where the woman sits upon them," ἐπ᾽ αὐτῶν is a resumptive pronoun used in place of a resumptive adv. such as ἐκεῖ. The antecedent of ὅπου is ἑπτὰ ὄρη, which the relative clause defines as the place where the woman is seated; the clause is therefore essential or dependent. This use of a resumptive pronoun, more properly called a *pronomen abundans*, is often considered a Semitism (cf. Bakker, *Pronomen Abundans*, 42), though there are parallels in pagan Gk. This construction occurs nine times in Revelation (3:8; 7:2, 9; 12:6, 14; 13:8, 12; 17:9; 20:8). For a detailed discussion, see *Note* 3:8.c. and *Introduction*, III. Syntax, Pronouns, pp. clxvi–clxvii. On the use of resumptive advs. in Revelation (which occur only in 12:6, 14), see *Note* 12:6.a-a.

9.b. Variant: insert αἱ before ἑπτά] Hippolytus (*de Ant.* 38).

9.c. The term βασιλεῖς, usually translated "kings," can also be translated "emperors" (see *Comment* on 17:9).

10.a. Variants: (1) ἔπεσαν] Oecumenius²⁰⁵³. (2) ἔπεσον] fam 1006⁹⁵ ¹⁰⁰⁶ ¹⁸⁴¹ fam 1611¹⁶¹¹ ¹⁸⁵⁴ Hippolytus (*de Ant.* 38; MS H; *Comm. in Dan.* 4.23).

11.a. Variant: omit καί] ℵ itᵃ vgᵐˢˢ Hippolytus (*de Ant.* 38; MS S).

11.b. Variants: (1) αὐτός] Hippolytus (*de Ant.* 38). (2) οὗτος] ℵ fam 1006¹⁰⁰⁶ ¹⁸⁴¹ 2030 Byzantine syrʰ. In both readings the masc. nom. sing. forms modify the neut. noun τὸ θηρίον and so are solecisms. Here αὐτός is an emphatic use of the nom. (Mussies, *Morphology*, 169–70).

11.c. The masc. predicate adj. ὄγδοος agrees in gender, number, and case with its antecedent αὐτός, but not with τὸ θηρίον, the antecedent of αὐτός (see *Note* 11.b.).

11.d-d. The phrase ἐκ τῶν ἑπτά ἐστιν is a partitive gen. in which the predicate nom. εἷς (in apposition to ὄγδοος) is understood, "*one* of the seven" (cf. BAGD, 230; Bauer-Aland, 464–65).

12.a-a. Variants: (1) τὰ δέκα κέρατα] *lectio originalis*. (2) τὰ κέρατα τὰ δέκα] Hippolytus (*de Ant.* 38).

12.b. οἵτινες, the nom. pl. form of ὅστις, is here simply an interchangeable equivalent of the relative pronoun οἵ.

12.c-c. Variants: (1) οὔπω] Oecumenius²⁰⁶² Hippolytus (*de Ant.* 38). (2) οὕτω] ℵ*. (3) οὐκ] A 296 (copy of printed TR); vgᵐˢˢ Hippolytus (*de Ant.* 38; MS S).

12.d-d. The phrase λαμβάνειν βασιλείαν, lit. "to take a rule," is an idiom meaning "to become a king" (Louw-Nida, § 37.65); cf. Luke 19:12, 15; Jos. *Ant.* 13.220; *Mart. Isa.* 3:1 (Denis, *Fragmenta*, 108, Μανασσῆς ὁ υἱὸς παραλαμβάνειν βασιλείαν, "Manasseh his son became king"); cf. *Ep. Arist.* 36. Similar idioms are κτᾶσθαι βασιλείαν, "to acquire kingship," i.e., "to become king" (Jos. *Ant.* 17.220), and λαμβάνειν τὴν ἀρχήν, "to take ruling power" (Jos. *J.W.* 1.284).

13.a. Variants: (1) omit οὗτοι] Hippolytus (*de Ant.* 38). (2) καί instead of οὗτοι] Hippolytus (*de Ant.* 38; MS S).

13.b. Variants: (1) διδόασιν] Hippolytus (*de Ant.* 38). (2) δίδωσιν] Hippolytus (*de Ant.* 38; MSS E R). (3) δώσουσιν] 2036 vg cop Primasius.

13.c. Variant: τήν before ἐξουσίαν] ℵ 051 fam 1611¹⁶¹¹ ¹⁸⁵⁴ Oecumenius²⁰⁵³ ²⁰⁶² Andreas Hippolytus (*de Ant.* 38).

14.a. The phrase "king of kings" has been understood as a periphrasis for the superlative, i.e., "most powerful king," because it conforms to the Heb. idiom of expressing the superlative by placing a noun in the construct state before pl. forms of the same noun, e.g., שׁיר הַשִּׁירִים *šîr haššîrîm*, "song of songs" or "most excellent song" (GKC § 133i, where the NT passages containing the phrase "king of kings," 1 Tim 6:15, Rev 17:14, and 19:16, are specifically mentioned; cf. Turner, *Style*, 153). Winer (*Grammar*, 308–9) argues that βασιλεὺς βασιλέων is not a pure Hebraism but is simply more emphatic than ὁ μέγιστος βασιλεύς.

14.b-b. Variants: (1) κλητοὶ καὶ πιστοὶ καὶ ἐκλεκτοί] Andr i Andr/Byz 4b⁻¹⁸⁸⁸ ²⁰³². (2) κλητοὶ ὅτι πιστοὶ καὶ ἐκλεκτοί] Andr m. (3) κλητοὶ ὅτι ἐκλεκτοὶ καὶ πιστοί] Andr a b. (4) *electi et fideles et vocati*] Primasius. (5) ἐκλεκτοὶ καὶ πιστοί] Byz 12¹¹⁰ itᵍⁱᵍ (*electi et fideles*).

14.c. Variants: (1) ὅτι] Andr a b m. (2) omit καί] vg.

15.a. The verb λέγει is a historical present, translated as "said" in conformity with Eng. usage; on the historical present in Revelation, see *Introduction*, VII. The Verb, B. The Tenses of the Verb, pp. clxxxiv–clxxxv.

15.b-b. Variants: (1) ταῦτα] ℵ* fam 1611¹⁸⁵⁴ ²³²⁹ Beatus. (2) ταῦτα τὰ ὕδατα] ℵ¹.

15.c-c. Variants: (1) omit ἡ] ℵ*. (2) κάθηται ἡ πόρνη] Hippolytus (*de Ant.* 39) Primasius arm⁴.

15.d. The verb καθῆσθαι, "to sit," is used four times in Rev 17, three times followed by the prep. ἐπί, with the resultant meaning "to sit upon" (vv 1, 3, 9; cf. Louw-Nida, § 17.12), while here καθῆσθαι is used without ἐπί and probably means "reside" (Louw-Nida, § 85.63).

15.e. Variant: insert καί] ℵ.

16.a-a. Variants: (1) καὶ γυμνήν] ℵ A 025 Andr c²⁰⁶⁹ g i l; 94 Byzantine. (2) omit καὶ γυμνήν] 046 Andreas.

16.b. Variant: insert ποιήσουσιν αὐτήν] 046 051 Andr c²⁰⁶⁹ f⁰⁵¹ ²⁰²³ ²⁰⁷³ Byzantine (ποιήσωσιν); 2030 Byzantine. This poetic addition to the text repeats the phrase ποιήσουσιν αὐτήν governing ἠρημωμένην.

16.c. Variant: omit ἐν] ℵ 025 046.

17.a-a. The phrase ὁ θεὸς ἔδωκεν εἰς τὰς καρδίας αὐτῶν, lit. "God put it into their hearts," is a Septuagintism in which εἰς indicates the indirect obj., reflecting the Heb. phrase אֶל־לִבּוֹ נָתַן *nātan 'el-libbô* or נָתַן בְּלִבּוֹ *nātan bĕlibbô*, with God as subject, found several times in the OT: Neh 2:12 and 7:5 (where it is used of the divine guidance that Nehemiah received in planning to rebuild the walls of Jerusalem); Exod 36:2 ("every wise man in whose mind the Lord had put wisdom [נָתַן יהוה חָכְמָה בְּלִבּוֹ] *nātan YHWH ḥokmâ bĕlibbô*]"); 1 Kgs 10:24 and 2 Chr 9:23 (Solomon's wisdom "which God had put in his mind [אֲשֶׁר־נָתַן (ה)אלהים בְּלִבּוֹ] *'ăšer-nātan (hā)ʾĕlōhîm bĕlibbô*]"); 1QpHab 2:8 (where the author claims that God has put understanding in the heart [נָתַן אֵל בְּ(לִבּוּ בִּינָ)ה] *nātan 'ēl bĕ (libbô bînā)h;* following W. H. Brownlee, *The Midrash Pesher of Habakkuk*, SBLMS 24 (Missoula, MT: Scholars, 1979), 53] of the Teacher of Righteousness, i.e., revealed to him the true meaning of the biblical prophets); and 1QH 14:8 ("[I give Thee thanks,] O Adonai, who hast put understanding into the heart of Thy servant [הֲנוֹתֵן בְּלֵב עֶבֶ(דְּכָה) בִּינָה] *hannôtēn bēlēb 'ab(dĕkâ) bînâ*]"). Variant: τὴν καρδίαν] Hippolytus (*de Ant.* 39).

17.b. ἔδωκεν is an aor., which is used to describe the certain occurrence of future events and functions like a plupf. (Mussies, *Morphology*, 329).

17.c. Variant: insert βουλήν after ἔδωκεν] 2329. Unique scribal correction.

17.d. Variant: αὐτῶν for αὐτοῦ] ℵ² 2329. Scribal error based on the other two occurrences of αὐτῶν in this verse.

17.e-e. Variant: omit καὶ ποιῆσαι μίαν γνώμην] A 94 254 792 2329 Andr c²⁰²⁸ ²⁰²⁹ ²⁰³³ ²⁰⁴⁴ i m²⁰³⁷ ²⁰⁴⁶ Andr/Byz 2b⁵⁸² Andr/Byz 3¹²⁴⁸ ¹³⁸⁴ it^sig vg Tyc² Beatus. The collation of 2329 by N. Beis, "Die Kollation der Apokalypse Johannis mit dem Kodex 573 des Meteorklosters," *ZNW* 13 (1912) 260–65 (which Hoskier did not see; cf. *Text* 1:637), does not mention the absence of this phrase from the MS.

17.f-f. Variant: (1) τελεσθήσονται] ℵ A C 025 051 Oecumenius²⁰⁵³ ²⁰⁶² fam 1611¹⁸⁵⁴ ²³²⁹ ²³⁴⁴ Hippolytus (*de Ant.* 39). (2) τελεσθῶσιν] fam 1006 fam 1611¹⁶¹¹ 2030 Byzantine. (3) τελεσθῇ τὰ ῥήματα] 296 TR. The conjunction ἄχρι or ἄχρι οὖ in Revelation is ordinarily used with an aor. subjunctive (e.g., 2:25; 7:3; 15:8; 20:3, 5; cf. Schmid, *Studien* 2:223), with the exception here in 17:17, where the external attestation is overwhelming. τελεσθήσονται is a fut. that functions like a subjunctive; for other examples in Revelation, see 4:9; 8:3; 14:13; 18:14; 22:14 (Mussies, *Morphology*, 341).

18.a. Variant: βασιλείων] ℵ syr^ph.

18.b. Variant: insert ἐπί] 046 2030 Byzantine.

Form/Structure/Setting

I. OUTLINE

D. Revelations of the judgment of Babylon (17:1–19:10)
  1. Introduction to the visions (17:1–2)
    a. Appearance of one of the seven bowl angels (v 1a)
    b. Invitation to witness the judgment of the great whore (v 1b)
    c. Description of the great whore (vv 1c–2)
      (1) Location: seated by many waters
      (2) The metaphorical characterization of her transgressions (v 2)
        (a) The metaphor of sexual immorality: kings have fornicated with her (v 2a)
        (b) The metaphor of intoxication: the people of the earth have become drunk from the wine of her fornication (v 2b)
  2. The allegorical vision of Babylon as the great whore (17:3–18)
    a. The vision of the whore (vv 3–6a)
      (1) Angel transports John (v 3a)
        (a) Means: in a prophetic trance
        (b) Destination: a wilderness
      (2) The vision of the woman (vv 3b–6a)

        (a) Description of beast on which the woman is seated (v 3bc)
           [1] Scarlet in color
           [2] Covered with blasphemous names
           [3] Seven heads
           [4] Ten horns
        (b) Description of the woman (vv 4–6a)
           [1] Luxuriously clothed (v 4a)
               [a] Purple garments
               [b] Scarlet garments
           [2] Adorned with jewelry (v 4a)
               [a] Gold ornaments
               [b] Precious stones
               [c] Pearls
           [3] Holding a full golden cup (v 4b)
               [a] Containing abominations
               [b] Containing the impurities of her fornication
           [4] A mysterious name on her forehead: "Babylon the
               great" (v 5)
               [a] Mother of whores
               [b] Mother of earthly abominations
           [5] The woman appears drunk (v 6a)
               [a] With the blood of saints
               [b] With the blood of the witnesses to Jesus
  b. The interpretation of the vision (vv 6b–18)
    (1) Introduction to the interpretation (vv 6b–7)
        (a) John reacts with amazement (v 6b)
        (b) The angelic guide offers to interpret the details of the vision
           (v 7)
           [1] The mystery of the woman
           [2] The mystery of the beast who bears her
               [a] With seven heads
               [b] With ten horns
    (2) The angel's interpretation (vv 8–18)
        (a) The mystery of the beast (vv 8–17)
           [1] The story of the beast and the inhabitants of the earth
               (vv 8–9a)
               [a] The biographical riddle of the beast (vv 8a)
                   {1} He was
                   {2} He is not
                   {3} He will ascend from the abyss
                   {4} He goes to destruction
               [b] The role of the inhabitants of the earth (v 8bc)
                   {1} Identity: their names are not in the book of life
                      (v 8b)
                   {2} Response to the beast: amazement (worship)
                      (v 8b)
                   {3} The second biographical riddle of the beast
                      (v 8c)

{a} He was

{b} He is not

{c} He is to come

[c] Wisdom needed to understand this riddle (v 9a)

[2] The meaning of the seven heads (vv 9b–10)

[a] Seven mountains on which woman is seated (v 9b)

[b] Seven kings (vv 9c–10)

{1} Five have fallen

{2} One is living

{3} The other (the seventh) has not yet come

{4} The seventh can remain a short time

[3] Interjection about the beast who was and is not: the riddle of v 8 amplified (v 11)

[a] He is the eighth (king)

[b] He is one of the seven (kings)

[c] He is headed for destruction

[4] The ten horns are ten kings (vv 12–17)

[a] The brief reign of the ten kings (v 12)

{1} They do not yet reign (v 12a)

{2} They will become kings (v 12b)

{a} For one hour

{b} With the beast

[b] The ten kings and the beast (v 13)

{1} They are of one accord

{2} They willingly subject themselves to the beast

{a} Their power

{b} Their authority

[c] Their opposition to the Lamb (v 14)

{1} They will fight the Lamb (v 14a)

{2} The Lamb will conquer them (v 14bc)

{a} Identity of Lamb as the reason for his victory (v 14b)

<1> King of kings

<2> Lord of lords

{b} Identity of those with him (v 14c)

<1> Called

<2> Elect

<3> Faithful

[(b) Interjection: The meaning of the waters: the people of the world v 15)]

[d] Their hostility toward the whore (v 16)

{1} They hate the whore

{2} They will make her desolate and naked

{3} They will devour her flesh

{4} They will burn her with fire

[e] God's sovereign control (v 17)

{1} God caused them

{a} To do his will (v 17a)

{b} To act in harmony (v 17b)
{c} To surrender their royal power to the beast (v 17b)
{2} Purpose: until His words are fulfilled (v 17b)
(c) The mystery of the woman (v 18)
[1] She represents the great city
[2] The great city rules "over the kings of the earth"

II. LITERARY ANALYSIS

Rev 17:1–18, though a relatively independent textual unit, has been integrated into a larger section dealing with the fall of Babylon/Rome (17:1–19:10). The larger unit, consisting of 17:1–19:10, has a structure strikingly parallel to the structure of Rev 21:9–22:9 (Giblin, *Bib* 55 [1974] 488–91), which similarly consists of several originally distinct textual units. Therefore, Rev 17:1–3a should be understood as an introduction not to the vision of Rev 17 only (as Charles, 2:55, assumes, but cf. 62) but rather to the entire unit of text from 17:3b to 19:10. When the angel promises in 17:1 to show John the judgment of the great whore, that judgment is summarily predicted in 17:1 but is in fact delayed until Rev 18, where it becomes the focus of attention. In Rev 19:2 there is a retrospective mention of this motif when it is said that "he has judged the great whore who corrupted the earth with her fornication," referring to Rev 18 while reflecting the vocabulary of Rev 17:1. While the beast is only a subsidiary figure in 17:3–6a, the focus in vv 8–14 is on the beast itself.

In the setting of the entire book, Rev 17 is unusual in that it is the only vision paired with a detailed interpretation, a feature common in Jewish apocalyptic literature (n.b. that the vision with which it is paired through parallel literary structures in 21:9–22:9 contains no corresponding angelic interpretation of the vision of the New Jerusalem). Rev 17 also contains the first narrative appearance in Revelation of an *angelus interpres,* "interpreting angel," a stock figure in early Jewish apocalyptic literature first mentioned in Rev 1:1 (see *Comment* there). Elsewhere in Revelation John's interlocutors include the exalted Christ (1:9–20; 4:1) and one of the twenty-four elders (7:13–14). Either the same or a different *angelus interpres* is introduced in Rev 21:9 (the author does not make their identity clear); this angel provides John with a guided tour of the New Jerusalem in 21:9–22:5 but has no comments to make apart from introductory remarks in 21:9.

Rev 17:1–18 contains three main sections: (1) the introduction to the visions of 17:3–19:10 (vv 1–2), (2) the vision of the woman seated on a scarlet beast (vv 3–6), and (3) the interpretation of the vision (vv 7–18). A more detailed literary analysis of these sections follows.

1. Rev 17:1–2: Summary Introduction. This introductory unit consists of two structural parts that are closely connected: (a) an invitation by the bowl angel to see the judgment of the great whore seated by many waters (a summary of visions in 17:3–18 and 18:1–24) and (b) a twofold indictment of the whore: (i) the kings of the earth have fornicated with her, and (ii) the inhabitants of the earth have become intoxicated from the wine that is her fornication. While it is possible to regard vv 1–2 as the introduction to vv 3–18 alone, the structural parallels between 17:1–19:10 and 21:9–22:9 make it more likely that 17:1–2 should be understood as introducing the whole of 17:3–19:10. This is likely in view of the obvious parallelism between 17:1–2 and 21:9–10a, which introduces a parallel text unit that concludes with 22:9. This introductory section summarizes the themes of 17:3–18, 18:1–24, and 19:1–8. The secondary character of this summary (by "secondary" I mean simply that the author has prefixed this introductory summary to 17:3–18 with the intention of linking it more closely with 18:1–24, both of which were existing compositions) is suggested by several factors: (a) the beast with seven heads and ten horns (the focus of vv 7–17) is not mentioned; (b) the *judgment* of the great whore refers not primarily to Rev 17 (though her judgment is briefly narrated in 17:16) but to Rev 18, and this judgment is referred to as completed in 19:2; and (c) v 2 appears to be modeled on 18:3, though the order of the four constituent elements has been reversed:

Rev 17:2	*Rev 18:3*
a μεθ' ἧς ἐπόρνευσαν with whom fornicated	d ὅτι ἐκ τοῦ οἴνου τοῦ θυμοῦ because of the wine which is the wrath
	c τῆς πορνείας αὐτῆς of her fornication
b οἱ βασιλεῖς τῆς γῆς the kings of the earth	πέπτωκαν πάντα τὰ ἔθνη all nations have collapsed
c καὶ ἐμεθύσθησαν and they have become drunk	
οἱ κατοικοῦντες τὴν γῆν the inhabitants of the earth	b καὶ οἱ βασιλεῖς τῆς γῆς for the kings of the earth
d ἐκ τοῦ οἴνου τῆς πορνείας αὐτῆς from the wine which is her fornication	a μετ' αὐτῆς ἐπόρνευσαν fornicated with her

It is striking that the term πόρνη, "whore," is not applied directly to the woman within the vision narrated in 17:3b–6a, though it can be inferred since her golden cup is filled with "fornication" and the "crime" tatooed on the forehead of the woman is "mother of whores" (v 5). However, the verb πορνεύειν, "to fornicate" (17:2; 18:3, 9), and the noun πορνεία, "fornication" (17:2, 4; 18:3; 19:2), both occur several times in the larger textual unit in 17:1–19:10. In many respects the πορν-cognates provide the catchwords about which this entire section has been formed.

2. *Rev 17:3–6: The Vision of the Woman Seated on a Scarlet Beast.* This section consists of three distinct units: (a) introduction: the transport of John "in the spirit," i.e., in an ecstatic state, to a wilderness (17:3a); (b) the vision (17:3b–6a), which focuses on a woman sitting on a scarlet beast, covered with blasphemous names and having seven heads and ten horns; and (c) conclusion: the reaction of the seer (17:6b). The vision described in vv 3b–6a is designed to be allegorically interpreted in vv 7–18.

3. *Rev 17:7–18: The Interpretation of the Vision.* This interpretation begins in v 7 with a summary description of the vision, intended to underline the four salient

features of the vision: "I will explain to you the secret meaning of the *woman* and the *beast* with *seven heads* and *ten horns* which bears her." In introducing the allegorical meaning of each major feature of the vision, John uses a stereotypical formula consisting of the appropriate relative pronoun and the aorist verb εἶδες, "you saw," which occurs in connection with three of the four explanations that begin with a lemma summarizing the content of the vision followed by an allegorical interpretation:

v 8:	"The beast that you saw [ὃ εἶδες] was . . ."
[v 9b:	"The seven heads are . . ."]
v 12:	"And the ten horns that you saw [ἃ εἶδες] are . . ."]
v 15:	"the waters that you saw [ἃ εἶδες] . . . are . . ."
v 16:	"the ten horns that you saw [ἃ εἶδες]. . ."
v 18:	"and the woman that you saw [ἣν εἶδες] is . . ."

The aorist form of the verbs indicates that the vision of vv 3b–6 is no longer being seen but is being interpreted as a vision seen in the past. This suggests the literary character of the vision since it would have been more appropriate for the author-editor to describe aspects of the vision in the present tense. This pattern indicates that the author has chosen to deal with the salient features of the vision summarized in v 7 in two complexes in reverse order. First, he explains the significance of the *beast—seven heads—ten horns*, and then he turns briefly to the *woman*, the interpretation of whom leads into Rev 18. The extraneous element in this scheme is v 15, with its reference to the waters that John saw, which symbolize the peoples of the world. This verse is clearly a gloss since the waters are not part of the vision in vv 3b–6a (they are, however, part of the summary of the anticipated vision given by the angelic guide in v 1b, suggesting that the gloss in v 15 was added when vv 1–2 were prefixed to the vision report), and "the waters" are not mentioned in the summary of the four central features of the vision listed by an *angelus interpres* in v 7.

III. SOURCE-CRITICAL ANALYSIS

The literary analysis of Rev 17 reveals a number of inconsistencies and compositional problems, particularly in vv 7–18, which suggests either that materials from several sources have been combined in a new way or that this section has undergone a series of revisions. The latter proposal appears to be the most likely. It was noted above that the interpretation of "the waters" in 17:15 appears to be out of place (in the detailed outline of Rev 17 provided above, v 15 was labeled an "interjection" because it appears to interrupt the interpretive narrative of the activities of the ten kings). Though it is not possible to retrace every step of the author-editor in the various stages of the composition and revision reflected in this chapter, several major revisions are still visible in the final product. Malina argues that since the author was not at all concerned with allegory, vv 8–18 are probably a later interpolation (*Revelation*, 75). This is unlikely.

There are several other uneven features of the composition of vv 7–18 that suggest the amplification or revision of an earlier composition. (1) One of the most obvious is v 14, which provides a succinct narrative of the war waged by the ten kings against the Lamb and their defeat. There are several reasons for thinking that this verse does not fit the context, making it likely that it is a later interjection or interpolation: (a) Though the coalition of ten kings (apparently with the beast) are defeated, they appear again in v 16, where they destroy the whore. (b) The mention of the Lamb is abrupt at this point, and the Lamb is mentioned elsewhere in 17:1–19:10 only in 19:7, 9 in a very different connection. It is likely that the author-editor inserted 17:14 in connection with the final arrangement of 17:1–19:10, when he also referred to the Lamb in 19:7, 9. (c) The titles of the Lamb, "Lord of lords" and "King of kings," which are the titles of the rider on the white horse in 19:16, appear to be derived (in reverse order) from the latter passage (see *Comments* on 17:14 and 19:16). (d) Along with v 15, v 14 interrupts the interpretation of the ten horns in vv 12–17. In v 16a, the phrase καὶ τὰ δέκα κέρατα ἃ εἶδες, "and the ten horns that you saw," is a verbatim repetition of v 12a, which suggests that v 16a is a framing repetition, i.e., a literary device for picking up the threads of a narrative interrupted by an excursus or an interpolation. (2) An interpretation of the eschatological events of 17:12–16 is found in v 17, where for the first time these events are interpreted as divinely arranged in accordance with the sovereign will of God. Two events are interpreted in this way, the miraculous harmony exhibited by the ten kings (referring to v 13a) and transference of their independent royal authority to the beast (referring to v 13b). (3) Further, v 8 appears to be a later interpretive gloss that can be eliminated without any disruption of the sense of the passage. One indication is that the beast is suddenly understood as an individual rather than as a nation. The description of this beast as one who "was and is not and is about to ascend from the abyss and is headed for destruction" (v 8a) and as one "who was and is not and will be present again" (v 8c) is clearly presented as the antithesis of the Lord God Almighty "who is and who was [and who is to come]" (1:4, 8; 4:8; 11:17; 16:5).

Bousset distinguished in Rev 17 a source from the time of Vespasian, perhaps of Jewish origin, which consisted of 17:1–7, 9–11, 15–18 and in which the beast was identified with Nero *redux*, who would return with the Parthian kings and destroy Rome ([1906] 415). According to Bousset, this source was reworked by the final redactor of Revelation, who contributed vv 8, 12–14 and several words and phrases in vv 6, 9, and 11, who thought in terms of Nero *redivivus*, and who conceived of him as the satanic counterpart to the Lamb ([1906] 414–15). Charles (2:54–62) argued that Rev 17 is constructed from two sources, one underlying 17:1–10 (which originally identified the beast with the Roman empire) and another underlying 17:11–18 (which identified the beast with the emperor).

M. Rissi, in a monograph devoted to Rev 17, argues that the original text of the vision and its interpretation concern the figure of the woman, not the beast (*Babylon*, 50). The danger threatening the Christian community is not the political and social pressure exerted on it by the Roman empire but the more pressing internal Christian problem of capitulating to the seductive syncretistic religious practices of the cities in Asia Minor, which threaten faith (*Babylon*, 51). Therefore, the traditional interpretation of the woman or the beast as Rome with its emperor cult, which threatened the Christian communities in Roman Asia, is not correct (*Babylon*, 55). The godless political power in Revelation is not Rome, which destroyed Jerusalem and the temple, but rather "the kings of the earth" and "the kings of the whole world." Revelation was not written in a situation of persecution, although persecution has been experienced in the past and will again occur in the future (*Babylon*, 57–58). Rather, Revelation was written in a situation of general uncertainty and anxiety (*Babylon*, 67–68). Rissi bases his reading on the conviction that Rev 17:9–17 consists of secondary interpretations that have been added to the text in two independent stages and that serve to shift the focus from the whore to the beast (*Babylon*, 61–73). The first addition is found in vv 9–14, while the second consists of vv 15–17. The first addition, vv 9–14, like that in 13:18, focuses on concrete historical places and persons, something the author of Revelation never does (*Babylon*, 62). The second addition, vv 15–17, does not appear to have originated with a Christian author; rather, it was probably a piece of Jewish tradition, like parts of the *Sibylline Oracles*, focusing on the destruction of the enemies of Israel.

IV. REV 17:1–18 AS AN *EKPHRASIS*

A. *Distinctive Features of Rev 17*

Vision reports in apocalyptic literature characteristically contain lengthy detailed descriptions of the highly symbolic dreams or visions that the apocalyptist has purportedly experienced, together with their decoded meaning. Frequently the apocalyptist is accompanied by an angelic guide with whom he carries on a dialogue, with the apocalyptist asking simple-minded questions and the *angelus interpres* providing profound answers. Revelation departs from this literary pattern, for the apocalyptist *never* asks the meaning of anything he sees, though occasionally meanings are volunteered by supernatural revealers (1:20; 7:13–14), or the author-editor glosses the text with meanings and definitions of his own (4:5; 5:6, 8; 11:4; 14:4; 17:4; 20:5, 14). There are several features of Rev 17 that are either unique or very distinctive within the context of the whole book. One such unique feature is that only here does the *angelus interpres* provide John with a running allegorical interpretation of the details of the vision he sees (note that the angelic guide in Rev 21:9–22:9 shows John the New Jerusalem but does not explain anything to him). This may reveal the importance of Rev 17 in the estimation of the author-editor, who emphasizes the revelatory role of the *angelus interpres* at the beginning and end of the book (1:1; 22:6, 8–9), although this angel in fact appears only in Rev 17:1–18; 19:9–10 and (if it is the same angel) in 21:9–22:9. A second unique feature is that the vision report in 17:3b–6 is *static;* i.e., it does not consist of any movement or action but rather has the character of a *tableau*. Only the vision of the New Jerusalem in 21:10–22:5 is somewhat comparable, but even there the vision has some movement: the seer sees the holy city καταβαίνουσαν, "descending," from heaven (21:10; cf. 3:12; 21:2); he sees the water of life ἐκπορευόμενον, "flowing," from the throne of God and the Lamb (22:1); and the trees of life ποιοῦν, "produce," twelve kinds of fruit and ἀποδιδοῦν, "yield," their fruit monthly (22:2; other movements in this vision belong to the future, as the tenses in 21:24–27 and 22:3–5 indicate). Rev 17 is also peculiar in that the real focus of the interpretive section (vv 7–18) is the beast rather than the woman, for even though the woman dominates the visual imagery in vv 1b–6, she is interpreted only briefly in v 18 (a passage leading to the portrayal of Babylon personified as a woman in 18:4–24) and mentioned only tangentially in v 7. Finally, the visionary imagery of vv 1b–6 is thoroughly symbolic or allegorical, though such allegorical imagery is conspicuous by its rarity in Revelation (the only two examples of allegorical imagery are 1:9–20 and 10:8–10).

B. The Dea Roma Coin

An important key for understanding the static character of the vision of the whore and the beast in Rev 17 may lie in a coin minted in A.D. 71 in the Roman province of Asia during the reign of Vespasian (A.D. 69–79); see plate 1.

Plate 1. IMP CAESAR VESPASIANVS . . . (Cohen, *Description* 1:398 [no. 404]).

A number of scholars have independently recognized a connection between the description in Rev 17:9 of the whore seated on seven mountains and a particular sestertius (Castagnoli, *Archeologia Classica* 5 [1953] 110–11; Beauvery, *RB* 90 [1983] 243–60; Bergmeier [with D. Mannsperger], *ANRW* II, 25/5, Tafel I, following p. 3910). The obverse depicts a realistic portrait of the emperor with the inscription IMP CAESAR VESPASIANVS AVG PM TP PP COS III, standard abbreviations for "Emperor Caesar Vespasian Augustus, Pontifex Maximus ['Greatest Priest,' i.e., head of the college of pontifices], Tribunicia Potestas ['Tribunal Power'], Pater Patriae ['Father of the Fatherland'], Consul for the Third Time." The reverse depicts the goddess Roma in military dress (some think in the guise of Athena, others as an Amazon, while still others as a combination of the two), sitting on Rome's Seven Hills with a parazonium (small sword) in her left hand resting on her left knee, a symbol of the military might of Rome (C. C. Vermeule, *Goddess Roma,* 41, describes this object incorrectly as an eagle-topped scepter). She is flanked on the left and right fields by the abbreviations "S" and "C," standing for *senatus consultum,* i.e., "a resolution of the senate." There are two other figures on the reverse. The anthropomorphic figure of the river god Tiber reclines against the Seven Hills at the right (the right foot of the goddess extends toward him, apparently touching him). A group consisting of a miniature she-wolf with the twins Romulus and Remus suckling is located on the lower left. This coin is described and depicted in the following catalogues: Cohen, *Description* 1:398 (no. 404); Mattingly et al., *RIC* 2:69, no. 442 (plate II, 301); Roscher, *Lex.* 4:154 (fig. 12); Mattingly-Carson, *Coins,* 2:187 (no. 774; plate 34.5); Cayón, *Compendio* 1:215 (no. 100); Mazzini, *MIR* 1:204 (no. 404), plate LXXII, no. 404; C. C. Vermeule, *Goddess Roma,* plate III, 24; Beauvery, *RB* 90 (1983) 260, plate 1. Small variations in detail indicate that a number of different coins of this basic type were minted (Beauvery, *RB* 90 [1983] 246 n. 9).

The scene described in Rev 17 is very probably *static* because the framework for the vision in Rev 17 is an *ekphrasis* or description of an ancient work of propagandistic Roman art very similar, if not identical, to that depicted on the sestertius (see below). Though the original (or originals, since it probably existed in many generic variants) is no longer extant, representations of it apparently survive only on the reverse of the sestertius minted in A.D. 71 during the reign of Vespasian. The work of art itself, which may have been a marble or bronze relief, was dominated by the seated figure of Dea Roma, the goddess who personified Rome for the Greek world. C. C. Vermeule (*Goddess Roma*, 41) proposed with the following arguments that the reverse of this coin is a copy of an actual marble or bronze frieze:

> The treatment of the rocks, the plasticity of the drapery, and the closeness of the background suggest that a marble relief might have inspired this creation, an effectively balanced composition, even to the point of introducing a vertical stabilizer and cross balance in the form of Tiber at the right.

One could also argue that the depiction of the figure of the god Tiber, also reclining against the Seven Hills, would be redundant in a painting, and therefore appears to represent another sculpture. A base for a statue of Roma that may have resembled that depicted on the sestertius minted under Vespasian has been discovered in Corinth, and each of the canonical Seven Hills was part of the base, as indicated by the inscriptions on it (Robinson, *Hesperia* 43 [1974] 470–84). Since imperial artists who worked for the mints regularly reproduced actual monuments, temples, and statues in their engravings, it is reasonable to suppose that the goddess Roma seated on the Seven Hills of Rome is also a copy of an otherwise unknown work of art (C. C. Vermeule, *Goddess Roma*, 41; Robinson, *Hesperia* 43 [1974] 482–83; Beauvery, *RB* 90 [1983] 246). However, the extreme view that buildings and statues depicted on Roman coins *always* imitate reality cannot be substantiated. This view is argued by B. Trell, who claims that "the architectural order is always represented with absolute reliability" (Trell, *Temple*, 3, 44–45; cf. Muehsam, *Coin and Temple*, 2–3), but the argument is not convincing (cf. T. Drew-Bear, "Representations of Temples on the Greek Imperial Coinage," *The American Numismatic Society, Museum Notes* 19 [1974] 27–63; G. Fuchs, *Architecturdarstellungen auf römischen Münzen* [Berlin: de Gruyter, 1969] 92–129; Brown, *Temple*, 14, observes, "the essential features of the buildings are faithfully reproduced"). Yet with regard to statues, Gardner (*Types*, 177) has observed, "It is a rule, I think without exceptions, that when a figure thus appears in a building on coins, it is a copy of the cultus-statue which was the central point of the building." The same conventions (seated goddess, hill[s], and river god) were used by other cities, particularly in Asia Minor. On a coin from Side/Pamphylia (A.D. 225–26), the goddess Tyche of Antiochia holds grain and is seated on a rock or rocks with the river god Melas below her (Franke, *Kleinasien*, 23, fig. 214).

Though depictions on coins of a seated goddess Roma before or after the time of Vespasian are known, Roma *seated on the Seven Hills of Rome* is an innovation in the coinage of Vespasian with no parallels in the coins of other Flavian emperors or of later emperors. The seated Roma, however, is found on coins issued by eight cities in Pontus and Bithynia, ca. 60 B.C. (cf. the temple of Roma and Augustus in Bithynia depicted on a coin of Hadrian: Mazzini, *MIR* 2:75 [nos. 246, 247], plate XXVI, nos. 246, 247), following Pompey's departure to Rome (Mellor, *ANRW* II, 17/2:962–63); Roma is depicted in a helmet, seated on a pile of shields with a Nike (Victory) in her right hand. The seated Roma is also found on some republican issues (Roscher, *Lex.*, 4:146). From Nero (A.D. 54–68) through Constantius Chlorus

(d. A.D. 306), the goddess Roma was depicted on the reverse of coins seated on a pile of shields or other types of armor and holding a parazonium, i.e., a dagger worn at the waist (Roscher, *Lex.* 4:152–54). The oval shapes of the shields are replaced by the oval shapes of the Seven Hills.

C. Dea Roma in Asia Minor

There was a particularly close connection between Dea Roma and Asia Minor, for the Smyrneans claimed to be the first to worship Roma (Mellor, ΘΕΑ ΡΩΜΗ, 20). In fact most of the cities to which John addressed his circular epistolary apocalypse had active cults of Dea Roma (Mellor, ΘΕΑ ΡΩΜΗ, 127). While the author-editor used this widespread cultic image as a basis for attacking Rome, the general populace of Roman Asia held a very positive view of Rome and the goddess who personified it (cf. Dio Chrysostom *Or.* 41.9).

Hadrian introduced the cult of Roma into Rome by erecting a cult statue of Roma Aeterna into a temple shared by Roma and Venus Felix (the temple, though not the cult statue, is depicted on the reverse of a coin of Hadrian shown in Brown, *Temples,* plate IV, 5; cf. Mazzini, *MIR* 2:150, plate LII, nos. 1421–22). This statue of a seated (enthroned) Roma became the model for cult statues of Dea Roma, all of which have perished (C. C. Vermeule, *Goddess Roma,* 29; Mazzini, *MIR* 2:82–83, plate XXVIII, nos. 337–51; for a survey of known types of Dea Roma figures in ancient Roman art, see Calza, *Dedalo* 7 [1926–27] 663–68). The temple of Venus and Roma, with the cult statue of the seated Dea Roma, is depicted frequently on coins and medallions after Septimus Severus (A.D. 193–211) and is the only representation of a temple and cult statue on fourth-century Roman coins (Brown, *Temples,* 8, plates VIII, 4, 5; IX, 1, 3, 5–8).

Roma, as a personification of Rome, was essentially a Greek goddess serving Greek purposes (Nilsson, *GGR* 2:177 n. 2). The goddess Roma was not known in Rome itself before the beginning of the second century A.D. Hadrian (A.D. 117–38) was the first emperor actually to introduce the cult of Roma to the city of Rome (Mellor, *ANRW* II, 17/2:1027–28; cf. Walbank, *Polybius* 3:421–42). The earliest attestation of Roma in the Greek world is on a late third-century coin from Locri Epizephyrii in Magna Graecia in central Italy (Mellor, *ANRW* II, 17/2:961). The earliest attested *temple* of Roma was founded in Smyrna in 195 B.C. (Tacitus *Annals* 4.56). Ambassadors from the city of Alabanda in Caria in 170 B.C. claimed that their city had founded a temple in honor of Roma and instituted a festival called the Romaia, i.e., Ῥωμαῖα (Livy 43.6.5). There is also evidence for a temple of Roma in Miletus (Mellor, *ANRW* II 17/2:960). In 164 B.C. the city of Rhodes erected a colossal statue (forty-five feet high) of the *Demos,* "People," of the Romans (Polybius 31.4.4; cf. Walbank, *Polybius* 3:470). Plutarch quotes a hymn sung to Roma, Zeus, and the Roman general Titus Flamininus in 191 B.C. (*Flam.* 16). One statue of Roma from the Greek east survives, on Delos, and Roma has been conjecturally identified in friezes found in Ephesus, Stratonicea, and Aphrodisias (Mellor, *ANRW* II, 17/2:960–61, 1012). In 30–29 B.C., the Greek cities of Asia and Bithynia asked permission to establish cults to Octavian; Augustus allowed four temples to be dedicated to Roma and himself, two in Asia (Pergamon and Ephesus) and two in Bithynia (Nicea and Nicomedia); cf. Dio Cassius 51.20; Tacitus *Annals* 4.37. For a list of cults of Roma alone and Roma together with Augustus, see Magie, *Roman*

Rule 2:1613–14. The origin of the conception of Roma as a goddess is connected with the cult of rulers and benefactors that was widespread in the eastern Mediterranean during the Hellenistic period (Mellor, *ANRW* II 17/2:957–58).

D. Ekphrasis *as a Literary Form*

Rev 17 constitutes an *ekphrasis*, or "detailed description [of a work of art]," a literary form that often occurs as a digression within a literary narrative. *Ekphraseis* were not discussed by rhetorical theorists until the first or second century A.D., when the *ekphrasis* was included in the basic rhetorical exercises called *progymnasmata* (Theon *Progym.* 11 [Spengel, *Rhetores* 2:118–20]; Hermogenes *Progym.* 10 [Spengel, *Rhetores* 2:16–17]; Aphthonius *Progym.* 12 [Spengel, *Rhetores* 2:46–49]; Nicolaus *Progym.* 12 [Spengel, *Rhetores* 3:491–93]; on *ekphraseis* in the rhetoricians, cf. Palm, "Bemerkungen," 108–15). The term ἔκφρασις, "description," itself is not regularly used of this rhetorical and literary form until the Second Sophistic; the only two uses of the term previously are found in Dionysius of Halicarnasus *De imitatione* fr. 6.3.2 and *Ars rhetorica* 10.17 (Bartsch, *Decoding*, 8). Theon defines *ekphrasis* as "a descriptive account bringing what is illustrated vividly before one's sight" (*Progym.* 11; Spengel, *Rhetores* 2:118; tr. Bartsch, *Decoding*, 9). Theon later observes, "the virtues of ecphrasis are in particular clarity and vividness, such that one can almost see the things narrated" (Spengel, *Rhetores* 2:119; tr. Bartsch, *Decoding*, 111). Nicolaus suggests that "ecphrasis undertakes to fashion spectators out of auditors" (Spengel, *Rhetores* 3:491; tr. Bartsch, *Decoding*, 111). Though *ekphrasis* is commonly defined as "the rhetorical description of a work of art" (*OCD*, 377), which is certainly appropriate for our hypothesis about Rev 17, such a definition is unduly restrictive, for the rhetorical handbooks listing the topics appropriate for *ekphraseis* include persons, circumstances, places, periods of time, customs, festivals, assemblies, statues, and paintings (Bartsch, *Decoding*, 10–14, esp. 12–13 n. 12, where a classified list of *ekphraseis* found in the Greek novels is given). *Ekphraseis* were used very elaborately in Greek literature long before they became the subject for rhetorical discussion. The first literary *ekphraseis* occur in Homer (the shield of Achilles in *Iliad* 18.478–608; the cup of Nestor in *Iliad* 11.632–35), and these became models for later authors. Many *ekphraseis* are detailed descriptions of works of art, such as magnificent garments or decorated shields (e.g., the mantle of Jason in Apollonius Rhodius *Argonautica* 1.721–67, the shield of Dionysus in Nonnus *Dionysiaca* 25.380–567, and the shield of Eurypylus in Quintus Smyrn. *Posthomerica* 6.196–293), or places such as palaces, gardens, harbors, and caves (e.g., the palace and garden of Alkinoos in *Odyssey* 7.84–132, the palace of Aeëtes in Apollonius Rhodius *Argonautica* 3.213–48, and the cave of the nymphs in Quintus Smyrn. *Posthomerica* 6.471–92).

The *ekphrasis* was eventually transformed from a constituent literary form used as a digression in narrative passages into an independent literary form, evident in such literary works as the *Imagines*, "Paintings," of Philostratus Major, the *Imagines* of Philostratus Minor, Cebes *Tabula*, and Callistratus *Statuarum descriptiones* (late third century A.D.). In the Roman period *ekphrasis* became a relatively popular literary form. By the second century A.D., descriptions of paintings were frequently used to introduce entire compositions or large sections of compositions (M. C. Mittelstadt, "Longus: Daphnis and Chloe and Roman Narrative

Painting," *Latomus* 26 [1967] 757 n. 1). A painting depicting the story of Europa and the bull (closely corresponding to similar scenes on coins from Phoenician Sidon) is described at the beginning of Achilles Tatius *Leucippe and Clitophon* 1.1–2, and later the author describes paintings of Perseus and Andromeda (3.6–7) and Prometheus (3.8); for a comprehensive approach to *ekphrasis* in the novels, see Bartsch, *Decoding*. One influential work, the *Tabula* of Cebes (first century A.D.), consists of a lengthy discussion of the contents and significance of a picture on a votive tablet in a temple; the work is essentially a discussion of popular morality. The *Tabula* is a dialogical *ekphrasis* in which a group of visitors to a temple see a votive tablet with a picture on it they cannot understand; i.e., they are confused about its meaning. An old man offers to explain the meaning of the picture and provides a moralizing allegorical explanation for the various figures, making frequent use of the demonstrative pronouns οὗτος, "this," and ἐκεῖνος, "that," and the interrogative pronouns τίς, "who," and τί, "what," in the explanations, a stylistic feature characteristic of many Jewish apocalypses. There is a close relationship between the literary form exhibited in the *Tabula* and that found in Rev 17. Both are descriptions of works of art, and both find allegorical significance in the details of the picture.

By the time of the Second Sophistic (second century A.D.), there were two major approaches to the use of *ekphrasis* in ancient literature. One approach centers on the necessity of understanding and interpreting the work itself. The other (found in Cebes and Lucian) focuses on the hidden meanings conveyed by the picture or work of art, which are usually uncovered through an allegorical mode of interpretation (Bartsch, *Decoding*, 22–31). There are two types of such allegorical descriptions: those whose meaning is obvious (as in Lucian *De mercede cond.* 42 [in which the *Tabula* of Cebes is specifically mentioned] and *Calumniae* 4–5) and those whose meaning must be carefully explained (Lucian *Hercules;* Cebes *Tabula*). In the last two compositions, the narrator is puzzled over the meaning of the representation, not unlike the surprise and wonder expressed by John in Rev 17:6b over what he has just seen in 17:3–6a.

Though *ekphraseis* occur much less frequently in the OT than in Greek literature (literary descriptions of impressive buildings and works of art are, of course, found throughout the ancient world and are not originally related to similar phenomena in Greek tradition), the OT does contain detailed descriptions of the temple (1 Kgs 6:14–36; 7:15–50) and of Solomon's palace (1 Kgs 7:2–12); Josephus expanded and embellished both in *Ant.* 8.63–98; 8.133–40. *Ekphraseis* become relatively common only in Jewish apocalyptic literature, where the detailed description of metaphorical visions plays a very significant role (Downey, *RAC* 4 [1959] 932).

Several scholars have proposed that the Shepherd of Hermas contains *ekphraseis* dependent on Cebes, particularly in Hermas *Vis.* 3, and *Sim.* 6, 9 (Taylor, *JP* 27 [1901] 276–319; 28 [1903] 24–38; 94–98; Joly, *Tableau*). The real issue, however, is whether Hermas (like John in Rev 17) adapted the *ekphrasis* genre by basing literary vision reports on allegorical interpretations of pictures. The static character of at least one of Hermas's visions (e.g., *Vis.* 4) suggests that this too is probably an *ekphrasis* based on an unknown picture. Another lengthy *ekphrasis* is found in *Apoc. Abr.* 21:7–29:21, probably written ca. A.D. 80–100 and surviving only in old Slavonic. In this passage God explains the meaning of a picture of creation that remains static in *Apoc. Abr.* 21.7–26.7. After God shows the picture to Abraham in 21.1–7,

Abraham asks (22.1), "Eternal, Mighty One! What is this picture of creation?" An explanation follows from 22.2 to 26.7. Thereafter, it begins to move, and various actions are described (27.1–29.21).

E. *Components of the* Ekphrasis *Form in Rev 17*

The basic visual imagery presented by the apocalyptist in Rev 17:1b–6 occurs in two parts. (1) In the first part, vv 1–2, which serve as the introduction to the larger textual unit consisting of 17:3–19:10, the bowl angel describes the subject of the vision as "the judgment of the great whore seated by many waters." (2) This is followed by a short commentary providing two reasons for the judgment of the great whore: (a) the kings of the earth have committed fornication with the whore (v 2a), and (b) the inhabitants of the earth have become drunk from the wine of that fornication (v 2b). In the vision proper (vv 3b–6), the apocalyptist sees a woman dressed in purple and scarlet, wearing a lot of expensive jewelry and seated on a scarlet beast who is covered with blasphemous names and has seven heads and ten horns. The woman holds a golden cup and has a mysterious name written on her forehead: "Babylon the great, mother of whores and of earthly abominations." The interpretation volunteered by the *angelus interpres* follows in vv 6b–18.

The artificial composite literary character of this vision (which one would expect of an *ekphrasis*) is suggested by several factors. First, in v 15 "the waters" by which the apocalyptist saw the whore sitting are interpreted by the *angelus interpres* as "peoples and crowds and nations and languages," an interpretation that has nothing to do with what precedes or follows. Further, the apocalyptist did not "see" the waters in his vision (reported in vv 3b–6); they were simply mentioned to him by the *angelus interpres* as what he was invited to see (vv 1b–2). Second, the stereotypical aorist verb εἶδον, "I saw," used five times to introduce portions of the interpretation (vv 8, 12, 15, 16, 18), suggests that the apocalyptist has seen the vision in the past, not that he is presently viewing it, as vv 3b–6 seem to imply.

The imagery of the vision segments in vv 1b–2 and 3b–6 has several elements that are related to the Vespasian sestertius and several elements that are drawn from elsewhere (e.g., Jer 51); the descriptions are therefore composite:

1. The central important figure of the woman can easily be identified with the figure of Dea Roma on the coin, though there appears to be nothing immediately evident from the image on the coin that would associate Dea Roma with a prostitute. However, on the lower left-hand field of the reverse, there is a representation of the well-known Roman legend of the infants Romulus and Remus being nursed by a she-wolf. The Latin term *lupa*, "she-wolf," had the connotation "prostitute" and might have contributed to a subversive joke that was transferred to Roma as the female personification of Rome. The clothing and jewelry of the great whore in v 4a are also not evident on the portrait of Roma on the sestertius but are drawn from the stereotypical description of prostitutes in ancient literature, which was sometimes applied to cities. Pericles is reported to have condemned the extensive building program in Athens by comparing the city to a gaudy prostitute (*Pericles* 12.2; LCL tr. with modifications): "We are gilding and beautifying our city which, like a shameless woman [ὥσπερ ἀλαζόνα γυναῖκα], adds to her wardrobe precious stones and costly statues and temples worth millions."

2. The woman is described as "seated by many waters" (vv 1b, 15). The Vespasian sestertius depicts Dea Roma as touching the Tiber river with her right foot, personified as a reclining bearded male figure, a gesture that reflects the historical location of Rome on the river Tiber. This descriptive feature, however, is also characteristic of historical Babylon, for LXX Jer 28:13 (MT 51:13) describes Babylon as "you who dwell near many waters [Hebrew מִים רַבִּים *rabbîm mayim;* Greek ἐφ' ὕδασι πολλοῖς] in the multitude of her treasures."

3. In the interpretive section (vv 8–18), the seven heads of the beast are interpreted in v 9 as "seven mountains on which the woman is seated." While this suggests, somewhat awkwardly, that the woman is seated on seven heads that represent seven hills, in the vision itself she is depicted as seated on the beast, not on his seven heads. However, if the seven hills on the coin were considered representations of "heads" of the beast, then it makes perfect sense to speak of the woman as "seated" on the seven heads = seven hills. The image of the woman seated on seven hills is certainly the most striking link between the Vespasian sesterius and Rev 17, though it must be emphasized that it is not part of the primary imagery of the vision in vv 3b–6 but rather part of the interpretation in v 9.

4. The golden cup "filled with the abominations and the impurities of her fornication" (v 4b) has no obvious corresponding representation on the Vespasian sestertius. This metaphor is in part an allusion to LXX Jer 28:7 (MT 51:7), though there the golden cup is a metaphor for Babylon itself: "Babylon was a golden cup in the Lord's hand, making all the earth drunken; the nations drank of her wine; therefore the nations went mad." In *Tg. Jer.* 51:7 (tr. Hayward), however, the cup is turned into a metaphor for the *sin* of Babylon, which is precisely the symbolism of the cup in Rev 17:4, "Behold like the cup of gold which was precious among all the vessels, so is the sin of Babylon exalted!" However, there is a relatively close parallel in Cebes *Tabula* 5.1–3, where a woman named Ἀπάτη, "Deceit," seated on a throne, holds a cup and leads astray people who drink of it (i.e., those who are about to enter the world through the gateway of life). This parallel is quite significant because it too is part of an elaborate *ekphrasis.*

5. The mysterious name inscribed on the forehead of the whore in v 5 may be connected to the label "ROMA" on the Vespasian sestertius. The city of Rome was itself regarded as a deity with a carefully concealed name. By the end of the first century A.D., there is evidence to suggest that many were aware that Rome had a secret name (Plutarch *Quaest. Rom.* 61; Pliny *Hist. nat.* 28.4.18; Macrobius *Saturn.* 3.9.3). The reason for concealing the true name of Rome is suggested by Servius (*Comm. in Verg. Aen.* 2.351):

> The Romans wished to keep secret the identity of the god who cared for Rome, and therefore their priestly regulations decreed that the gods of Rome should not be invoked by their proper names that they might not be enticed away.

Johannes Lydus (sixth century A.D.) maintained that Rome had three names, a political name known to all (Roma), a hieratic name also widely known (Flora), and a ritual name used only by the Roman priests (*De mensibus* 4.73). Lydus thought that Rome's ritual name was *Amor,* "Love," i.e., Roma spelled backwards. This view was also held by Aelius Aristides *Roman Oration* 8 (mid-second century A.D.) and is also found in a graffito made on the wall of a house in Pompey (destroyed A.D. 79):

```
R   O   M   A
O           M
M           O
A   M   O   R
```

Since Romans regarded themselves as descendants of Aeneas, who was the son of Venus/Aphrodite, the goddess of love and sexuality, the name *Amor* is not inappropriate. While the actual secret name of Rome (if there ever was such a name) will never be known, *Amor* was widely thought to be that name. Since John depicts Dea Roma as a prostitute, he may be consciously dragging the popular view in the dirt.

6. The vision presents the woman as drunk with the blood of the saints and the witnesses to Jesus (v 6). Even though this may be a later interpolation into the text, the fact that Dea Roma is depicted on the Vespasian sesterius holding a parazonium (representing the power of Rome) might have called to mind the many Christians and Jews who had been killed by representatives of Rome.

7. The puzzled narrator is often a literary motif in *ekphraseis*, "descriptions," of pictures with hidden allegorical significance. In v 6b, the apocalyptist says that "when I saw her, I was greatly amazed." The expression of confusion and perplexity is juxtaposed with the introduction of the learned interpreter, a stock figure usually found conveniently at the narrator's elbow (Bartsch, *Decoding*, 25–27). After describing a strange picture of Heracles, the narrator of Lucian's *Hercules* says (*Herc.* 4; LCL tr.), "I had stood for a long time, looking, wondering [θαυμάζων] and fuming," when a Celt offers to explain the riddle of the picture (λύσω τῆς γραφῆς τὸ αἴνιγμα). A similar confusion is expressed by the narrator of Cebes *Tabula* 2.1, who sees a painting he cannot understand; fortunately, an old man is standing by who can explain what the painting means. Again in Callistratus *Imagines* 6, the narrator describes a statue of Lysippus and then states, "Such was the marvel [θαῦμα], as it seemed to us; but a man who was skilled in the arts" explained the meaning of the statue (LCL tr.). In Achilles Tatius *Leucippe and Clitophon* 5.3–5, a picture of the rape of Philomela is described by the narrator. A puzzled Leukippe asks, "What does this picture mean?" The narrator then explains the meaning of the picture. Menelaos, one of the characters in the story, has earlier observed (5.4; tr. Reardon, *Novels*), "Interpreters of signs tell us to consider the story of any painting we chance to see as we set out on business." That is, the allegorical meaning of pictures may serve as a means of divine revelation. Other examples of this pattern (*ekphrasis*—puzzled viewer—informed interpreter) are found in Philostratus *Vita Apoll.* 4.28 and Lucian *Amores* 8.

F. Conclusions and Implications

The evidence reviewed above suggests that the author did in fact adapt the literary convention of the *ekphrasis* in order to provide a framework for the visionary imagery and interpretations included in Rev 17. The recognition of the presence of this literary form provides some insight into the peculiar static quality of the vision in vv 3b–6a, as well as into the process of composition the author-editor used to incorporate earlier material (which focused almost exclusively on the vision of the beast and its meaning) into the *ekphrasis* that centered on Dea Roma seated on seven hills. The literary framework provided by the *ekphrasis* is restricted to vv 1b–2 (the angel's introductory description of the vision, with its mention of the great whore seated by many waters), vv 3b–6a (the vision itself, with its primary emphasis on the description of the woman), vv 6b–7 (with the motif of surprise and puzzlement coupled with the angel's offer to interpret the vision), v 9b (the interpretation of the seven heads of the beast as seven hills), and v 18 (the interpretation of the woman as the great city that has authority over the kings of the earth). The fact that the elements of *ekphrasis* provide the literary framework for Rev 17 makes it possible to formulate a source-critical analysis of the passage.

There are also some geographical and chronological implications of the apocalyptist's use of the sculpture group depicted on the Vespasian sestertius. The minting of the coin in Roman Asia suggests that the sculpture was particularly prominent in that region, and it would have been there that the apocalyptist became acquainted with it. While the date of A.D. 71 does not mean that the author-editor *must* have become acquainted with the sculpture only after that date, it does suggest the relative chronological conclusion that the author *probably* became acquainted with it after that date.

Comment

1a Καὶ ἦλθεν εἷς ἐκ τῶν ἑπτὰ ἀγγέλων τῶν ἐχόντων τὰς ἑπτὰ φιάλας, "Now one of the seven angels with the seven bowls came." This phrase is replicated verbatim in 21:9 (along with v 1b) with the additional descriptive phrase τῶν γεμόντων τῶν ἑπτὰ πληγῶν τῶν ἐσχάτων, "filled with the seven last plagues." The attributive participial clause τῶν ἐχόντων τὰς ἑπτὰ φιάλας, "with the seven bowls," formally ties this section to the narrative of the pouring out of the seven bowls of God's wrath in Rev 16. Since Rev 17 was originally unconnected with the series of seven bowl plagues narrated in Rev 16, this verbal link is strictly formal and does not guarantee the thematic continuity of Rev 17 with Rev 16 (contra Souza Nogueira, *Widerstand*, 114). This phrase is, therefore, an analeptic gloss designed to unify Rev 17 with Rev 15–16.

1b καὶ ἐλάλησεν μετ᾽ ἐμοῦ λέγων· δεῦρο, δείξω σοι τὸ κρίμα τῆς πόρνης τῆς μεγάλης, "and spoke with me, saying, 'Come, I will show you the judgment of the great whore.'" The phrase καὶ ἐλάλησεν μετ᾽ ἐμοῦ λέγων· δεῦρο, δείξω σοι, "and he spoke with me, saying, 'Come I will show you,'" also occurs (along with v 17:1a) verbatim in 21:9. A close parallel is found in *3 Apoc. Bar.* 2:6 in a statement made by Baruch's angelic tour guide, δεῦρο καὶ ὑποδείξω σοι μείζονα μυστήρια, "come and I will show you greater mysteries" (this apocalypse was probably composed in the second century A.D.). One of the indications that 17:1–3 belongs to the final stages in the redaction of Revelation is the use of the term δεικνύναι, "to show," which occurs just eight times in Revelation, always in sections of the text that appear to belong to the last editorial level of the book (1:1; 4:1; 17:1; 21:9, 10; 22:1, 6, 8). In each instance the subject of δεικνύναι is an *angelus interpres*, "interpreting angel," according to Rev 1:1 and 22:6, 8, the primary mediator of revelation to John. The role of the *angelus interpres* according to the literary frame of Revelation (1:1–8 and 22:6–21) appears to be based at least in part on the role of the angelic guide(s) in 17:1–22:6, suggesting that the author put the finishing literary touches on 17:1–22:6 before bracketing Revelation with 1:1–8 and 22:6–21. The term τῆς πόρνης, "the whore," is an objective genitive, while τῆς μεγάλης, "the great," is a descriptive genitive. The phrase ἡ πόρνη ἡ μεγάλη, "the great whore," is found here and in 19:2; the author also uses the unmodified noun ἡ πόρνη, "whore," three times in vv 5, 15, and 16. Rome as πόρνη, then, is restricted to Rev 17 with the exception of 19:2 (see *Comment* there for the possible significance of this fact). The image of the prostitute is frequently found in the OT, where it is applied to godless cities (Isa 1:21 [Jerusalem]; Isa 23:16–17 [Tyre]; Nah 3:4 [Nineveh]). Idolatrous and disobedient Israel is also compared to a prostitute (Jer 3:6–10; Ezek 16:15–22; 23:1–49; Hos 4:12–13; 5:3). Bruns (*CBQ* 26 [1964] 459–63) has suggested that while the great whore represents Rome, it might secondarily refer to the Roman empress Messalina, wife of Claudius, who indulged in a variety of sexual escapades, including an infamous drunken sexual orgy (Tacitus *Annals* 11.31; Juvenal *Satires* 6.116–24). The problem with this proposal, however, is that it is based on rumor preserved in a few literary sources and, despite its possible currency in Rome, would in all probability not have been widely known or reported in the provinces.

On prostitution in the Greco-Roman world, see J. M. Ford, "Prostitution in the Ancient World," *BTB* 23 (1993) 128–34; L. Basserman, *The Oldest Profession: A History of Prostitution*, tr. J. Cleugh (New York: Stein & Day, 1967); H. Herter, "Die Sociologie der antiken Prostitution im Lichte des heidnischen und christlichen Schrifttums," *JAC* 3 (1960) 70–111; A. Rousselle, *Porneia: On Desire and the Body in Antiquity*, tr. F. Pheasant (Oxford: Blackwell, 1988).

Nothing on the sestertius of Vespasian with the goddess Roma on the reverse (described above under *Form/Structure/Setting*) explicitly links that figure with prostitution or sexuality. However, Beauvery (*RB* 90 [1983] 257) has pointed out that the Latin term for the "she-wolf" depicted on the coin is *lupa*, a term that also meant "prostitute" (*OLD*, 1051). This *lupa*, with the nursing twins Romulus and Remus, was depicted in a variety of ways in plastic arts throughout the Roman empire and perhaps was the basis for a subversive joke based on the double meaning of the term.

1c τῆς καθημένης ἐπὶ ὑδάτων πολλῶν, "seated by many waters." The "many waters" is interpreted in v 15 as "peoples and crowds and nations and languages," based in part on an OT metaphor in which peoples or armies are symbolized by "(many) waters" (Ps 144:7; Isa 8:6–7; 17:12–14; 28:17; Jer 47:2). This is particularly clear in Isa 17:12–14, where the comparison of the roaring of many peoples or nations is like the roaring of "many waters." Ps 29 is striking because it depicts Yahweh as enthroned on many waters. The phrase "many waters" occurs in the OT (see May, *JBL* 74 [1955] 9–21), with the suggestion of chaos and disorder that are sometimes in conflict with Yahweh and therefore are occasionally used as an equivalent to the dragon or Rahab (Pss 18:16; 29:3; 32:6; 77:19 ["many waters" = Red Sea]; 93:4; 144:7; Ezek 32:13 [the Nile]; Hab 3:15). The sestertius of Vespasian on which the goddess Roma is shown seated on the Seven Hills (described above under *Form/Structure/Setting*) also shows her with her right foot touching the Tiber river, personified as a reclining bearded male figure. This descriptive feature, however, is also characteristic of historical Babylon, which was surrounded by a moat filled with water (Herodotus 1.178). In addition, the Euphrates river flowed through the middle of the city (Herodotus 1.185; Strabo 16.1.5), and the surrounding region was criss-crossed with canals and irrigation ditches (Strabo 16.1.9). LXX Jer 28:13(MT 51:13) describes Babylon as "you who dwell near many waters [Hebrew מים רבים *mayim rabbîm;* misunderstood by the Greek translator as ἐφ᾽ ὕδασι πολλοῖς] in the multitude of her treasures." The wealth of Babylon briefly mentioned here in Jeremiah may be expanded on in Rev 17:4 (C. Wolff, *Jeremia,* 167).

The fact that the woman is *sitting* is obviously an important feature of the description since the verb καθῆσθαι, "to sit," is used of the woman's posture also in vv 3, 9, and 15, i.e., four times in all. Sitting in these contexts is primarily an indication of enthronement. According to v 9, "the seven heads are seven mountains, on which the woman is seated." Several denominations of coins minted during the reign of Nero show the goddess Roma, dressed in military garments, with a miniature winged victory in her right hand and a parazonium in her left, and seated (Cayón, 1:141 [no. 29], 149 [nos. 58–60], 152 [no. 69], 158 [no. 94]).

2a μεθ' ἧς ἐπόρνευσαν οἱ βασιλεῖς τῆς γῆς, "with whom the kings of the earth have fornicated." Though the previous phrase in v 3a is an allusion to Jer 51:7 (LXX 28:7), this particular phrase has no counterpart in Jeremiah, except for the interpretive expansion found in *Tg. Jer.* 51:7 (tr. Hayward), "All the kings of the nations are about to be inebriated from her with langour, and the nations shall drink from the cup of her punishment." The phrase also has two close parallels in Rev 18:3 and 9; 19:2 (all allusions to Isa 23:17):

Rev 17:2: μεθ' ἧς ἐπόρνευσαν οἱ βασιλεῖς τῆς γῆς
with whom the kings of the earth have fornicated

Rev 18:3 καὶ οἱ βασιλεῖς τῆς γῆς μετ' αὐτῆς ἐπόρνευσαν
for the kings of the earth fornicated with her

Rev 18:9 οἱ βασιλεῖς τῆς γῆς οἱ μετ' αὐτῆς πορνεύσαντες
the kings of the earth, who fornicated with her

Rev 19:2 ἥτις ἔφθειρεν τὴν γῆν ἐν τῇ πορνείᾳ αὐτῆς
who corrupted the earth with her fornication

It is clear that the author is dependent on the Hebrew text of Isa 23:17, וזנתה את־כל־ממלכות הארץ *wĕzānâ 'et-kol-mamlĕkôt hā'āreṣ,* "and she [Tyre] fornicated with all the kingdoms of the earth," for the LXX contains quite a different reading, καὶ ἔσται ἐμπόριον πάσαις ταῖς βασιλείαις τῆς οἰκουμένης, "and will be a market for all the kingdoms of the earth." In the OT the term זנה *zānâ,* "fornicate, be a prostitute," is frequently used in a figurative sense of Israel's faithless behavior toward Yahweh as manifested in her frequent lapses into idolatry. This is based on the analogy of the covenant between Yahweh and Israel and marriage contracts (Lev 17:7; 20:5–6; Num 14:33; 15:39; Deut 31:16; Judg 2:17; 8:27; 1 Chr 5:25; 2 Chr 21:11; Ps 73:27), a metaphor found with particular frequency in the prophets Hosea (1:2; 2:4[MT: 6]; 4:15; 9:1), Jeremiah (2:20; 3:2, 9, 13; 5:7, 11; 13:27), and Ezekiel (6:9; 16; 23; 43:7, 9); see Erlandsson, *TDOT* 4:101–4.

Considered against this OT background, the metaphor of sexual immorality appears at first sight to have little to do with the author's condemnation of Babylon-Rome. In a very few places in the OT, however, there are instances in which the commercial trade of a city is described with the metaphor of prostitution (Kuhn, *TDNT* 1:515 n. 11), doubtless because economic relationships frequently led to the exchange of religious practices (Mic 1:7; Nah 3:4; 2 Kgs 9:22). In Isa 23:17, Tyre's commercial contacts are called "prostitution," and the profits of such trade are called "the price of a prostitute" (similar language is used of Nineveh in Nah 3:4). However, the historical context of both Isa 23:17 and Nah 3:4 suggests that neither prophet is interested in Tyre or Nineveh in themselves; rather the prophets condemn the negative influences the cities have exerted on the Near East, particularly on Israel.

If we ask why John used the metaphor of sexual immorality to characterize the relationship between Babylon and the kings of the earth, it seems reasonable to suppose that he is denouncing the *political* alliances between Babylon and her client kingdoms. The fact that Babylon-Rome, under the metaphor of a prostitute, is blamed for the immoral behavior of the kings of the earth is a striking reminder of the ancient and modern double standard that places the blame for an illicit sexual union more on the woman than on her male partner. Such alliances inevitably had significant economic, social, and religious implications and usually worked to the detriment of the kingdoms involved. If we press the matter further and ask why the author is so outraged by such political alliances, it is reasonable to suppose that he shares the hostility that many Jews from Palestine had toward the Romans and the various rulers of Judea that the Romans manipulated from 63 B.C. on to the first Jewish revolt of A.D. 66–73 and that he has universalized his outrage on the basis of his experiences and historical legacy as a Palestinian Jew who may have known Roman violence firsthand.

Diplomatic contacts between the Romans and the Jews (with either the Hasmoneans or Hellenizing Jewish leaders) may go back as far as 164 B.C., during the reign of Judas Maccabaeus (2 Macc 11:34–38), and a treaty may have been concluded shortly thereafter in 161 B.C. (1 Macc 8:1–32; 12:1–4, 16; Jos. *Ant.* 13.163–65, 169; Gruen, *Hellenistic World* 2:745–51). Pompey conquered Syria and then Palestine in 63 B.C., conquering Jerusalem, desecrating the temple by slaughtering priests and people in the temple and by entering the holy of holies, and earned Jewish hatred in the process (Jos. *Ant.* 14.37–79). He then installed Hyrcanus as a puppet monarch. Hyrcanus was taken prisoner by the Parthians in 40 B.C., providing the Roman senate with an excuse to declare Herod king of Judea (on the condition that he subdue it, which he did by 37 B.C.). The nobility in Judea, however, regarded Antigonus as the legitimate king and Herod as a usurper. Gaius Caligula's plans to erect a statue of himself in the temple in A.D. 40, vehemently opposed by Jews (Jos. *Ant.* 18.263, 270), was prevented only by Caligula's death. Events leading up to the first revolt in A.D. 66–73 resulted in a complete meltdown of Roman-Judean relations. The revolt itself was a political and religious disaster of enormous proportions for Palestinian Judaism. On the complexities of Roman-Judean relations from 164 B.C. on, see M. Smallwood, *The Jews under Roman Rule* (Leiden: Brill, 1976); U. Baumann, *Rom und die Juden: Die römisch-jüdaischen Beziehungen von Pompeius bis zum Tode des Herodes (63 v. Chr– 4 v. Chr.)* (Frankfurt am Main: Lang, 1983); A. N. Sherwin-White, *Roman Foreign Policy in the East* (London, 1984); M. Goodman, *The Ruling Class of Judaea: The Origins of the Jewish Revolt against Rome A.D. 66–70* (Cambridge: Cambridge UP, 1987); R. D. Sullivan, *Near Eastern Royalty and Rome, 100–30 B.C.* (Toronto: University of Toronto, 1990); L. L. Grabbe, *Judaism from Cyrus to Hadrian,* 2 vols. (Minneapolis: Fortress, 1992). For a broader approach to the problem see W. Dahlheim, *Gewalt und Herrschaft: Das provinziale Herrschaftssystem der römischen Republik* (Berlin; New York: de Gruyter, 1977); M. Stahl, *Imperial Herrschaft und provinziale Stadt* (Göttingen: Vandenhoeck & Ruprecht, 1978).

2b καὶ ἐμεθύσθησαν οἱ κατοικοῦντες τὴν γῆν ἐκ τοῦ οἴνου τῆς πορνείας αὐτῆς, "and with whom the inhabitants of the earth have become drunk from the wine which is her immorality." The phrase "the inhabitants of the earth" occurs frequently in Revelation (3:10; 6:10; 8:13; 13:8, 14; 17:8), but only here is the phrase τὴν γῆν in the accusative, and only here is the preposition ἐπί missing. In this clause the author combines the metaphor of sexual immorality (= disastrous political alliances; cf. v 2a) with the metaphor of intoxication, which suggests the victimization of the people of the world by Rome, as mediated by their kings. In the OT passages that speak of the "cup of wrath," Yahweh is presented as compelling his enemies to drink a cup resulting in their drunkenness, which itself is considered a judgment (Isa 51:17–23; Jer 13:13–14; 25:15–29 [in vv 28–29 becoming drunk from God's cup of wrath is explicitly called punishment]; 48:26; 51:39, 57; Lam 4:21; see Holladay, *Jeremiah 1*, 673). This is the second major transgression of Babylon-Rome that will result in her judgment by God (for the first, see v 2a). This transgression of Babylon-Rome is expressed in several related ways; all of the instances but the first are restricted to 17:1–19:10:

Rev 14:8:	ἣ ἐκ τοῦ οἴνου τοῦ θυμοῦ τῆς πορνείας αὐτῆς who of the wine which is her immoral passion
	πεπότικεν πάντα τὰ ἔθνη gave all nations to drink
Rev 17:2b:	καὶ ἐμεθύσθησαν οἱ κατοικοῦντες τὴν γῆν and the inhabitants of the earth have become drunk
	ἐκ τοῦ οἴνου τῆς πορνείας αὐτῆς from the wine which is her immorality
Rev 18:3a:	ἐκ τοῦ οἴνου τοῦ θυμοῦ τῆς πορνείας αὐτῆς From the wine which is her immoral passion
	πέπτωκαν πάντα τὰ ἔθνη all nations have collapsed.
Rev 19:2	ἥτις ἔφθειρεν τὴν γῆν ἐν τῇ πορνείᾳ αὐτῆς who corrupted the earth with her immorality

Rev 17:2b is an allusion to LXX Jer 28:7 (MT 51:7), ἀπὸ τοῦ οἴνου αὐτῆς ἐπίοσαν ἔθνη, "from her wine the nations drank" (also alluded to in Rev 14:8; cf. Isa 51:7–23), while the consequences of this intoxication are stated in LXX Jer 28:7b (but not mentioned in Rev 17:2), διὰ τοῦτο ἐσαλεύθησαν, "because of this they are unstable." For the targumic version of Jer 51:7, see above (*Comment* on v 2a). *Pss. Sol.* 8:14, after narrating the sins of the people of Israel, alludes to Isa 51:7–23 (Charlesworth, *OTP* 2:659), "Because of this God mixed them (a drink) of a wavering spirit, and gave them a cup of undiluted wine to make them drunk." A thematic parallel is found in *Odes Sol.* 38:9–14 (tr. Sparks, *AOT*, 726):

[9]And the corruptor of corruption
I saw while the bride who is corrupted was adorning herself,
Even the bridegroom who corrupts and is corrupted;
[10]And I asked Truth, Who are these? And he said to me,

This is the Deceiver, and that is Error;
[11]And they imitate the Beloved One and his bride,
And cause the world to err, and corrupt it;
[12]And they invite many to a banquet,
And give them to drink of the wine of their intoxication,
[13]And they cause them to vomit their wisdom and understanding,
And they render them irrational;
[14]And then they abandon them,
But they go about raving and corrupting,
Because they are without understanding,
For neither do they seek it.

Here a bride and bridegroom are metaphors for Error and Deceit, and they imitate the Beloved One and his bride. The wine served at the wedding feast makes the guests drunk, and they vomit out the understanding they previously had. The allegorical figures of the corrupt bride and bridegroom have many similarities to the female figures used to personify Virtue and Vice (cf. the myth of Prodicus in Xenophon *Memorabilia* 2.1.21–34), Kingship and Tyranny (Dio Chrysostom *Or.* 1.69–84, an adaptation of the Prodicus myth), or Philosophy and Error (Lucian *Piscator* 11ff.). Ovid (*Art. amat.* 3.23; LCL tr.) observes, "Virtue too herself is by dress and name a woman." In *Amores* 3.1, Ovid uses two female figures, Elegy and Tragedy (the former described using features drawn from the courtesan motif), to depict a struggle within the artist between these two genres (cf. L. P. Wilkinson, *Ovid Recalled* [Cambridge: Cambridge UP, 1955], 115–16). Female figures can personify entire nations; in Aeschylus *Persians* 176–99, Atossa queen of Persia describes a dream in which two beautiful women represent Persia and the Dorian Greeks, respectively.

3a καὶ ἀπήνεγκέν με εἰς ἔρημον ἐν πνεύματι, "He then carried me to the desert in a prophetic trance." The phrase (ἐγενόμην) ἐν πνεύματι, "(I fell) into a prophetic trance," is a stereotypical formula used to introduce vision reports and occurs four times in Revelation (1:10; 4:2; 17:3; 21:10). The closest parallel to 17:3 is 21:10, καὶ ἀπήνεγκέν με ἐν πνεύματι ἐπὶ ὄρος μέγα καὶ ὑψηλόν, "He then carried me in prophetic ecstasy to a great and high mountain." The term ἔρημος, "uninhabited place, the desert," is used pejoratively here (in 12:6, 14 it has positive associations as a place of refuge and protection), in contrast to the positive associations with "a great and high mountain" in 21:10. The Shepherd of Hermas contains two extensive vision reports that are introduced by similar supernatural journeys to remote locations. According to Hermas *Vis.* 1.1.3, καὶ πνεῦμά με ἔλαβεν καὶ ἀπήνεγκέ με δι' ἀνοδίας τινός, δι' ἧς ἄνθρωπος οὐκ ἐδύνατο ὁδεῦσαι, "Then a spirit took me and carried me through a trackless region through which a person could not travel" (here the spirit referred to functions like the angel in Rev 17:3; 21:10). The second vision is introduced similarly (2.1.1): καὶ πάλιν με αἴρει πνεῦμα καὶ ἀποφέρει εἰς τὸν αὐτὸν τόπον, "And again a spirit takes me and carries me to the same place." Yet here the spirit is conceived of as an external force, very similar to the conception behind a stereotypical formula found five times in Ezekiel: ותשאני רוח *wattiśśāʾēnî rûaḥ* (LXX καὶ ἀνέλαβέν με πνεῦμα), "Then a spirit took me up" (3:12; 8:3; 11:1, 24; 43:5). He also uses the phrase ורוח נשאתני ותקחני *wěrûaḥ něśāʾatnî wattiqqāḥēnî* (LXX καὶ τὸ πνεῦμα ἐξῆρέν με καὶ ἀνέλαβέν με), "Then the spirit took me up and carried me" (Ezek 3:14; cf. 2:2). This language of being carried off by the spirit (*rûaḥ*), probably originally meaning "disappear," is also found in 1 Kgs 18:12 and 2 Kgs 2:16, where Elijah was reportedly transported by the יהוה רוח *rûaḥ YHWH*, the "wind of the Lord" (n.b. that יהוה רוח *rûaḥ YHWH* is construed with masculine verbs, though רוח *rûaḥ* is a feminine noun), and Ezekiel was reportedly transported by the רוח *rûaḥ*, "spirit" or "wind" (Ezek 3:12, 14; 8:3; 11:1, 24; 37:1; 43:5; construed with feminine verbs); cf. M. Greenberg, *Ezekiel 1–20*, AB 22 (Garden City: Doubleday, 1983) 70. For the notion of physical transport "in the spirit," John is dependent on Ezekiel, as Ezekiel was dependent on the Elijah tradition.

3b καὶ εἶδον γυναῖκα καθημένην ἐπὶ θηρίον κόκκινον, "I saw a woman sitting on a scarlet beast." (On καὶ εἶδον, "I saw," see *Comment* on 5:1.) The woman's seated position indicates that she is enthroned, though the author substitutes the beast for the expected throne. The term θηρίον, "beast," occurs nine times in this chapter. In the Greco-Roman moralist writers, the vice against which one struggles is sometimes described metaphorically as the conquest of a θηρίον, "beast," as in Cebes *Tabula* 22–23. The interpretation of the woman is not made explicit until v 18 (see *Comment* there), where it is simply said that she represents the great city that rules over the kings of the earth. While most commentators understand the woman to represent Rome (Bousset [1906] 464; Müller, 288), some maintain the unlikely view that she represents Jerusalem (Beagley, *Church's Enemies*, 92–108; Ford, 285–86; Holwerda, *EstBib* 53 [1995] 387–89), or more abstractly the godlessness of the syncretistic religions of the world (Rissi, *Babylon*, 55–60). On the scarlet color of the beast (which coordinates with the wardrobe of the whore; cf. v 4), see *Comments* on 12:3 and 18:16. In *Sib. Or.* 8.88, Nero *redivivus* is referred to as a "purple dragon" (πορφύρεός τε δράκων), an appropriate parallel since the beast represents the Roman principate.

3c γέμον ὀνόματα βλασφημίας ἔχον κεφαλὰς ἑπτὰ καὶ κέρατα δέκα, "covered with blasphemous names, with seven heads and ten horns." This phrase is derived from 13:1, "and on its heads were blasphemous names" (see *Comment* on 13:1). The phrase "with ten horns and seven heads" was derived from 13:1, though the order is reversed. See *Comment* on 13:1. In *Sib. Or.* 3.175–76, Rome is referred to as λευκὴ καὶ πολύκρανος, "white and many-headed."

4a καὶ ἡ γυνὴ ἦν περιβεβλημένη πορφυροῦν καὶ κόκκινον καὶ κεχρυσωμένη χρυσίῳ καὶ λίθῳ τιμίῳ καὶ μαργαρίταις, "Now the woman was dressed in purple and scarlet and adorned with gold ornaments, precious stones, and pearls." This description has an extremely close verbal correspondence to Rev 18:16:

> ἡ πόλις ἡ μεγάλη, ἡ περιβεβλημένη βύσσινον καὶ πορφυροῦν
> The great city, clothed with linen and purple

> καὶ κόκκινον
> and scarlet

> καὶ κεχρυσωμένη ἐν χρυσίῳ καὶ λίθῳ τιμίῳ καὶ μαργαρίτῃ.
> and adorned with gold and precious stones and pearls.

While here the *woman* is described as dressed elegantly and bejewelled, in 18:16 the same language explicitly describes the elegance of the *city*, symbolized by the woman.

The term πορφυροῦς, usually translated "purple," actually describes a spectrum of colors in antiquity from red to purple to black (Dürbeck, *Charakteristik*, 129–39). Purple garments were worn in antiquity to symbolize status and particularly royalty (Judg 8:26; Esth 8:15; Lam 4:5; Dan 5:7, 16, 29; 1 Macc 10:20, 62, 64; 11:58; 14:43; Sir 40:4; Mark 15:17; John 19:2; *Gos. Pet.* 3.5; see Reinhold, *Purple*). Porphyry, on the other hand (whose own name was derived from the word πορφυροῦς), associated the color purple with carnality (*De antro* 14). Scarlet, however, does not represent royalty (the χλαμὺς κοκκίνη, "scarlet cloak," in Matt 27:28, where Mark 15:17 has πορφύρα, "purple," may also represent royalty) so much as the status associated with wealth (2 Sam 1:24; Prov 31:21; Jer 4:30; Epictetus 3.22.10; 4.11.34).

The description of the woman is drawn at least in part from the ancient courtesan *topos*, as the author suggests by using the phrase ἡ πόρνη ἡ μεγάλη, "the great whore," in v 1b. Courtesans were used, particularly by moralist writers, as personifications of the vices, including incontinence, profligacy, covetousness, and flattery (Cebes *Tabula* 9.1–4; Fitzgerald-White, *Tabula*, 142 n. 33). They had a recognizable way of dressing (Cebes *Tabula* 9.1) and are often depicted as conspicuously well dressed (Lucian *Dial meretr.* 286, 294; Alciphron *Ep. court.* 9.1). Successful courtesans could be very rich (Lucian *Dial. meretr.* 295) and sported gaudy jewelry (Lucian *Piscator* 12; *Dial. meretr.* 296–97, 321; Alciphron *Ep. court.* 12.2), exacted from their lovers (Alciphron *Ep. court.* 17.5). Plutarch records a speech condemning Pericles's building program in mid-fifth century B.C. Athens (*Pericles* 12.2; LCL tr. with modifications): "We are gilding and beautifying our city which, like a shameless woman [ὥσπερ ἀλαζόνα γυναῖκα], adds to her wardrobe precious stones and costly statues and temples worth millions." Here these anonymous critics compare the city of Athens with a prostitute's expensive and gaudy wardrobe.

The figure of the harlot is also used in the OT and early Jewish literature. A poetic text (4Q*184*) in J. Allegro, ed., *Qumran Cave 4*, DJD 5 (Oxford: Clarendon, 1968) 82–85, on "The Wiles of the Wicked Woman," is a pastiche of harlotry passages from Proverbs (2:16–19; 5:3–6; 6:24–35; 7:5–27; 22:14; 23:27–28; cf. R. D. Moore, *RQ* 10 [1979–81] 505–6). The harlot described in the poem may symbolize the enemy of the community, or she may be used not for polemical purposes but for an exposition of theological truth (as Moore argues, *RQ* 10 [1979–81] 506–7).

4b ἔχουσα ποτήριον χρυσοῦν ἐν τῇ χειρὶ αὐτῆς γέμον βδελυγμάτων καὶ τὰ ἀκάθαρτα τῆς πορνείας αὐτῆς, "She was holding a golden cup in her hand, filled with abominations and the impurities of her fornication." This is in part an allusion to LXX Jer 28:7 (MT 51:7), though there the golden cup is a metaphor for Babylon itself: "Babylon was a golden cup in the Lord's hand, making all the earth drunken; the nations drank of her wine; therefore the nations went mad." In *Tg. Jer.* 51:7 (tr. Hayward), however, the cup is turned into a metaphor for the *sin* of Babylon, which is precisely the symbolism of the cup in Rev 17:4, "Behold like the cup of gold which was precious among all the vessels, so is the sin of Babylon exalted!" The golden cup held by the woman is described as filled with two ingredients: "what is detestable" and "the impurities of her fornication" (repeated in v 5), i.e., an allegorical explanation that is presented as if it is inherent in the vision itself, though it is obviously the kind of interpretive addition appropriate for an *ekphrasis*. Both terms occur in LXX Job 15:16, ἐβδελυγμένος καὶ ἀκάθαρτος, "one who is detestable and impure," arguably a hendiadys. A shift in meaning appears to have occurred between v 2 and vv 4–5, for since the βδελύγματα, "abominations," of vv 4–5 refer primarily to pagan religious practices (i.e., idolatry) and have no deeper allegorical significance, the phrase "impurities of her fornication" probably refers not to political alliances (as in v 2a) but rather to pagan sexual immorality. The term βδέλυγμα (see *TDNT* 1:598–600), "that which is disgusting, abhorrent, detestable" (cf. Frisk, *Wörterbuch* 1:229–30), occurs three times in Revelation (17:4, 5; 21:27). Elsewhere in the NT (in addition to Luke 16:15), the term occurs twice in the eschatological discourse in Mark 13:14 = Matt 24:15 (where the phrase τὸ βδέλυγμα [τῆς] ἐρημώσεως, "the abomination of desolation," is an allusion to LXX Dan 12:11; cf. 9:27; 11:31), where it means a sacrilegious object or rite causing the desecration of a sacred place (*GELS* 1:79). In Dan 9:27 and 1 Macc 1:54, βδέλυγμα clearly refers to an idol, while in LXX Zech 9:7 it refers to sacrificial meat offered to idols (Muraoka, *Septuagint,* 36). In the LXX βδέλυγμα and βδελύγματα are designations for idols (e.g., Jer 13:27; 39:35[MT 32:35]; 51:22[MT 44:22]; Ezek 5:9, 11; 6:9; 20; 11:18). In v 6 Babylon is described as drunk with the blood of the martyrs of Jesus, which apparently has no connection with the "wine" in the gold cup that she holds, which has been given quite a different meaning in v 4 (on the widespread ancient association between wine and blood, see *Comment* on v 6a). A close parallel occurs in Cebes *Tabula* 5.1–3, where a woman, named Ἀπάτη, "Deceit," seated on a throne, holds a cup and leads people astray who drink of it (i.e., those who are about to enter the world through the gateway of life). This parallel is quite significant because it too is part of an elaborate *ekphrasis,* or description of a work of art.

5a καὶ ἐπὶ τὸ μέτωπον αὐτῆς ὄνομα γεγραμμένον, μυστήριον, Βαβυλὼν ἡ μεγάλη, "Upon her forehead a mysterious name was written, 'Babylon the great.'" It is grammatically possible to construe μυστήριον, "mystery, secret meaning," as part of the inscription with Βαβυλὼν ἡ μεγάλη ἡ μήτηρ τῶν πορνῶν, "Babylon the great, the mother of whores," in apposition to μυστήριον, i.e., "and upon her forehead was written a name, 'Mystery, Babylon the Great the Mother of Whores'" (Zahn, 2:554; Mounce, 306–7; AV; NIV), and in support of this the Greek text can be punctuated ὄνομα γεγραμμένον· μυστήριον, "name written: mystery" (Tischendorf, *NT Graece*). Or it is possible to construe μυστήριον as part of the preceding clause in apposition to ὄνομα, "name," i.e., "and upon her forehead was written a name, a mystery, 'Babylon the great, the mother of whores'" (Charles, 2:428, RSV; NRSV; REB), with the punctuation ὄνομα γεγραμμένον, μυστήριον· Βαβυλών, "name written, a mystery: Babylon" (von Soden, *Text*). The text can also be punctuated ambiguously, as in Nestle-Aland[27] and UBSGNT[4]: ὄνομα γεγραμμένον, μυστήριον, Βαβυλών, "a name written, (a) mystery, Babylon." Since the angel offers to explain "the mystery of the woman" in v 7, it is probable that the term μυστήριον, "mystery," is not part of what is written on the woman's forehead in v 5 but a way of indicating that the phrase "Babylon the great, the mother of whores" itself is a mystery in need of interpretation. μυστήριον, "mystery" (used also in 1:20; 16:7; 17:7), indicates that "Babylon" is a name that must be understood symbolically, as are the names "Balaam" (2:14), "Jezebel" (2:20), and the city that is understood figuratively as "Sodom and Egypt" (11:8). The inscription on the forehead of this female figure suggests that, in addition to being a whore, she is "a whore of the most degraded kind, a tattooed slave" (C. P. Jones, "*Stigma:* Tattooing and Branding in Graeco-Roman Antiquity," *JRS* 77 [1987] 151); for a discussion of ancient branding and tattooing on the face and forehead, cf. *Excursus 7A*. This recumbent female figure represents Rome, often personified in the female divinity Dea Roma, "the goddess

Rome." Though Jupiter Optimus Maximus was the patron god of Rome, the city itself was regarded as a deity with a carefully concealed name (see the discussion above in *Form/Structure/Setting*, IV. E. Components of the *Ekphrasis* Form in Rev 17).

On the title "Babylon the Great," which occurs in LXX and Theod Dan 4:30, see *Comment* on 14:8. Greeks conceived of the various kings of Babylon as effeminate people who lived like women, wore dresses, makeup, and jewels, and were therefore regarded negatively as examples of unmanly living.

5b ἡ μήτηρ τῶν πορνῶν καὶ τῶν βδελυγμάτων τῆς γῆς, "'the mother of whores and of earthly abominations.'" These two categories of sinfulness refer to sexual promiscuity and idolatry and repeat the two ingredients that fill the golden cup in v 4. In the phrase "the mother of whores," the term μήτηρ, "mother," is a figurative extension that means something like "archetype," i.e., something "anticipating a later reality and suggesting a derivative relationship" (Louw-Nida § 58.64), or that indicates the source or origin of some activity or quality. In Hos 2:2–5 (cf. Isa 50:1), Israel is personified as a "mother" who has played the whore and has bastard children. The word is used with this meaning in Greek, Jewish, and Christian literature: Tob 4:13 ("shiftlessness is the mother of famine"); *T. Sim.* 5:3 ("fornication is the mother of all wicked deeds"); Gal 4:26; Hermas *Vis.* 3.8.5; Ps.-Phocylides 42; Hierocles 11; Clement Alex. *Strom.* 2.5; Gregory Thaum. *Pan. or.* 12; Cyril *Hom. pasch.* 4; Pindar *Ol.* 8.1; Aeschylus *Septem contra Thebas* 225. It is also possible that the phrase "mother of whores" is used in a superlative sense meaning "the most depraved whore." In Jer 27:12 (MT: 50:12), Babylon is called "mother" in the context of a prophetic judgment oracle (the *Tg. Jer.* 50:12 substitutes a word meaning "assembly" for "mother"). If Rome is the great whore, it is likely that the whores referred to here are cities under the domination of Rome. Perhaps the specific cities in Asia Minor that had temples and cults in honor of Dea Roma are intended.

6a καὶ εἶδον τὴν γυναῖκα μεθύουσαν ἐκ τοῦ αἵματος τῶν ἁγίων καὶ ἐκ τοῦ αἵματος τῶν μαρτύρων Ἰησοῦ, "And I saw the woman drunk on the blood of God's people and the blood of the witnesses to Jesus." (On καὶ εἶδον, "I saw," see *Comment* on 5:1.) The motif of "becoming drunk on blood" is found in Ezek 39:18–19; Jdt 6:4 (cf. Isa 49:26). LXX Jer 26:10 (MT 46:10) has the metaphor of the sword of the Lord "being drunk from their blood [μεθυσθήσεται ἀπὸ τοῦ αἵματος αὐτῶν]," i.e., the blood of God's enemies. In Pliny *Hist. nat.* 14.148, Mark Antony is described before the battle of Actium as *ebrius iam sanguine civium*, "drunk with the blood of his compatriots" (*Neuer Wettstein*, ad Rev 16:6). A different but related motif of "drinking the cup of God's wrath" (cf. Isa 51:17, 22) is also found in Revelation (see *Comment* on 14:10). The *topos* of the courtesan usually depicts her as a moderate drinker for business reasons (Lucian *Dial. meretr.* 294), though drinking bouts with lovers are also a standard part of the *topos* (Alciphron *Ep. court.* 13.11, 18; 13.3, 7).

Since it is difficult to distinguish between "God's people" (literally "the holy ones"; see *Comment* on 5:8) and "those killed for their loyalty to Jesus," it is possible that the καί, "and," connecting the two noun phrases is epexegetical and should therefore be understood as "with the blood of the saints, *that is,* with the blood of those killed for their loyalty to Jesus," thereby understanding the second phrase as a further explanation of the first (E. Schweizer, *Church Order in the New Testament* [London: SPCK, 1961] 134–35). However, the parallel in 16:6, "they poured out the blood of the saints and prophets," suggests rather that the terms "prophets" and "witnesses" (i.e., "those killed for their loyalty") should be equated (Hill, *NTS* 18 [1971–72] 409).

There is a shift in meaning of the cup metaphor when it is said that the harlot is "drunk on the blood" of the saints, which suggests that the cup is filled with blood symbolizing the murder of her opponents. There was a widespread ancient association between blood and wine reflected in such expressions as αἷμα σταφυλῆς, "the blood of the grape" (see Gen 49:11; Deut 32:14; Sir 39:26; 50:15; 1 Macc 6:34; *ANET,* 133; Achilles Tatius 2.2; Clement Alex. *Paed.* 2.19.3; 2.29.1; *Strom.* 5.8.48.8; Pliny *Hist. nat.* 14.58; Burkert, *Homo Necans,* 224 n. 38), undoubtedly because the juice of red grapes resembled blood (Stephanus, *TGL* 1:972). The phrase "with the blood of the saints and the blood of those killed for their loyalty to Jesus" appears to be a gloss added during the final revision of Revelation (cf. J. Weiss, *Offenbarung,* 31) since it is not a description of what could be seen in a vision but rather an allegorical interpretation of the drunkenness of the woman based on a shift in metaphors. In v 4 the contents of the cup are described as "full of abominations and the impurities of her fornication." The reference to the blood of saints and prophets in 16:6 is also redactional (see *Comment* on 16:6).

In Seneca *Hercules Oetaeus* 657–58, a similar theme occurs:

> It is in the cup of gold alone
> That blood is mingled with the wine.

Here, however, *both* blood and wine are said to be mixed in one cup. This couplet means that the rich, rarely the poor, are guilty of crimes of violence and murder.

The term μάρτυς, used here in the plural, clearly connotes those who have been killed because of loyalty to their beliefs, i.e., the classic definition of a martyr (Louw-Nida, § 20.67, where it belongs to the semantic subdomain of "kill"). Yet the same can also be said of the term ἅγιοι, "saints."

6b καὶ ἐθαύμασα ἰδὼν αὐτὴν θαῦμα μέγα, "I was very perplexed when I saw her." The narrator's description of his own wonder at seeing the vision in 17:1–6a is also intended to convey his puzzlement over the meaning of the vision. This is clear from the explanation provided by the angel in vv 7–18. The puzzled narrator is often a literary motif in *ekphraseis,* "descriptions," of pictures with hidden allegorical significance; the expression of confusion and perplexity is juxtaposed with the introduction of the learned interpreter, a stock figure usually found conveniently at the narrator's elbow (Bartsch, *Decoding,* 25–27). See further discussion in *Form/ Structure/Setting,* IV. E. Components of the *Ekphrasis* Form in Rev 17.

Dreams, particularly those of an oracular or revelatory nature, are usually descriptive and just as often require interpretation (cf. Artemidorus *Oneirocritica;* Aelius Aristides *Or.* 47–52 [*Sacred Tales*]; cf. Bartsch, *Decoding,* 32–35). According to Artemidorus (*Oneir.* 1.2), dreams can be either literal (θεωρηματικός, "to be interpreted as seen," LSJ, 796) or allegorical (ἀλληγορικός). The dreams interpreted in the stories of Joseph and Daniel in the OT are all described before they are interpreted. S. Thompson (*Apocalypse,* 12) has suggested that LXX Dan 4:19 is parallel to Rev 17:6; in Dan 4:19, after Nebuchadrezzar has narrated his dream to Daniel, the narrator says that "Daniel ... was dismayed for a moment [μεγάλως δὲ ἐθαύμασεν ὁ Δανιήλ]" (cf. LXX Dan 8:27). Neither of these passages, however, conveys a lack of understanding or perplexity in Daniel, for it is Daniel himself who provides the interpretation of these dreams. A closer parallel to Rev 17:6 is found in Dan 7:15, where Daniel's perplexity causes him to seek an interpretation of the vision narrated in 7:1–14 (cf. Dan 8:15).

7a καὶ εἶπέν μοι ὁ ἄγγελος· διὰ τί ἐθαύμασας; "Thereupon the angel said to me, 'Why are you perplexed?'" See *Form/Structure/Setting*, IV. E. Components of the *Ekphrasis* Form in Rev 17, in which the stock figure of the interpreter of an enigmatical picture is discussed.

7b ἐγὼ ἐρῶ σοι τὸ μυστήριον τῆς γυναικὸς καὶ τοῦ θηρίου τοῦ βαστάζοντος αὐτὴν τοῦ ἔχοντος τὰς ἑπτὰ κεφαλὰς καὶ τὰ δέκα κέρατα, "I will explain to you the secret meaning of the woman and the beast with seven heads and ten horns which bears her." The vision is divided into two main subjects, the woman and the beast, while two subordinate features of the beast are emphasized, the seven heads and ten horns. The term μυστήριον, "mystery, secret meaning," occurs four times in Revelation (1:20; 10:7; 17:5, 7); see *Comment* on 1:20a.

8a τὸ θηρίον ὃ εἶδες ἦν καὶ οὐκ ἔστιν καὶ μέλλει ἀναβαίνειν ἐκ τῆς ἀβύσσου καὶ εἰς ἀπώλειαν ὑπάγει, "The beast that you saw was and is not and is about to ascend from the abyss and is headed for destruction." The phrase ὃ εἶδες, "that you saw," is the first of five occurrences of this stereotypical expression (relative pronoun + aorist verb εἶδες) in the interpretive section of Rev 17 (vv 8–18). The phrase is repeated in vv 12, 15, 16, 18. The aorist tense of εἶδες suggests that he is no longer seeing the vision presented in vv 3b–6 (in contrast to the present tenses used in describing the New Jerusalem in 21:9–22:5). This suggests the literary character of the passage. The beast itself is the only important symbol not explicitly interpreted in Rev 17, though in v 11 it is paradoxically stated that the beast is the eighth (head = king), but actually one of the seven (heads = kings). This formulation is repeated twice more in vv 8b and 11a; see the following synoptic comparison:

Rev 17:8a	*Rev 17:8b*	*Rev 17:11a*
τὸ θηρίον . . . The beast . . .	τὸ θηρίον . . . The beast . . .	τὸ θηρίον . . . The beast . . .
ἦν καὶ οὐκ ἔστιν was and is not	ἦν καὶ οὐκ ἔστιν was and is not	ἦν καὶ οὐκ ἔστιν . . . was and is not . . .
καὶ μέλλει ἀναβαίνειν and will ascend	καὶ παρέσται and will be present	
ἐκ τῆς ἀβύσσου καὶ from the abyss and		
εἰς ἀπώλειαν ὑπάγει goes to destruction		καὶ εἰς ἀπώλειαν ὑπάγει and goes to destruction

The threefold varied repetition of this formula within the immediate context is striking, not least because it is not used of the beast elsewhere in Revelation. This formulation is designed by the author as a parody of his predication of God as ὁ ὢν καὶ ὁ ἦν καὶ ὁ ἐρχόμενον, "the One who is and who was and who is coming" (1:4, 8), or ὁ ἦν καὶ ὁ ὢν καὶ ὁ ἐρχόμενον, "The One who was and who is and who is the coming One" (4:8), where ὁ ἦν, "who was," and ὁ ὢν, "who is," are reversed, as in 17:8 (in 11:17 and 16:5 a bipartite formula occurs in the same order as the longer formula in 1:4, 8: ὁ ὢν καὶ ὁ ἦν); see *Comment* on 1:4. The emphasis on God as "the One who comes" (1:4, 8; 4:8) refers to the eschatological "visitation" of God, and so the beast who "is about to ascend from the abyss and go to destruction" also refers to the "coming" and "going" of the one playing this eschatological role. Here in 17:8, "was" and "is not" really mean "who lived" and "who no longer lives [i.e., 'is dead']," reflecting an epitaph used widely in the ancient world: "I was not, I became, I am not" (ὅστις οὐκ ἤμην καὶ ἐγενόμην, οὐκ εἰμί; Lattimore, *Epitaphs*, 76, 84–85). For the formula and its variants, cf. F. Cumont, "Non fui, fui, non sum," *Musée Belge* 32 (1928) 73–85. The formula occurs frequently in Latin epitaphs, e.g., *non fui, fui, non sum, non desidero*, "I was not, I was, I am not, I do not care" (Lattimore, *Epitaphs*, 84), and occurs also on Greek epitaphs: οὐκ ἤμην, ἐγενόμην, ἤμην, οὐκ εἰμί· τοσαῦτα, "I was not, I was born, I was, I am not; so much for that." If this parody is to have any force, it must refer to a person who both died and returned from the dead (or was expected to do so), and it is therefore probably a reference to the Nero *redivivus* myth (Yarbro Collins, *Combat Myth*, 174).

The phrase καὶ μέλλει ἀναβαίνειν ἐκ τῆς ἀβύσσου, "and is about to ascend from the abyss," is closely parallel to 11:7, τὸ θηρίον τὸ ἀναβαῖνον ἐκ τῆς ἀβύσσου, "the beast who ascends from the abyss," and to 13:1, ἐκ τῆς θαλάσσης θηρίον ἀναβαῖνον, "a beast ascending from the sea [sea = abyss]" (both 11:7 and 13:1 appear to have been derived from 17:8). On the meaning of "abyss," see *Comment* on 9:1b. The phrase καὶ εἰς ἀπώλειαν ὑπάγει, "and goes to destruction," is repeated verbatim in 17:11 (thus framing vv 8–11) and refers specifically to the casting of the beast into the lake of fire (19:20). The term ἀπώλειαν, "destruction," appears to be a play on words, since in 9:11 the angel of the abyss (τῆς ἀβύσσου) is called Ἀπολλύων, "Destroyer" (a formation from the Greek verb ἀπολλύναι, "to destroy"), a Greek translation of the Hebrew name אֲבַדּוֹן *'ăbaddôn* (also mentioned in 9:11), which is translated ἀπώλεια in the LXX (Job 26:6; 28:22; Ps 88:11; Prov 15:11); cf. BAGD, 1. This reflects the principle of *lex talionis*, i.e., the "law of retributive justice," in that the Destroyer is himself destroyed.

8b καὶ θαυμασθήσονται οἱ κατοικοῦντες ἐπὶ τῆς γῆς ὧν οὐ γέγραπται τὸ ὄνομα ἐπὶ τὸ βιβλίον τῆς ζωῆς ἀπὸ καταβολῆς κόσμου, "The inhabitants of the earth, whose names have not been inscribed in the book of life since the creation of the world, will be amazed." The people of the earth are amazed that the beast "was and is not and will be present again"; i.e., it has returned from the dead. In the closely parallel passage in 13:3b, people's reaction of amazement to the beast is elicited by the healing of the fatal wound suffered by one of the heads of the beast. (It is implied that amazement is tantamount to worship, a notion made explicit in 13:3–4.) This phrase is a doublet of the one in 13:8, though there the gloss τοῦ ἀρνίου τοῦ ἐσφαγμένου, "the Lamb slain," has been inserted between ζωῆς, "life," and ἀπό, "since," with the result that the meaning of the phrase has been transformed, suggesting that the author derived the phrase in 13:8 from 17:8b. Here the peculiar negative formulation of the phrase ("whose names have not been recorded in the book of life since the creation of the world") suggests that the author has simply negated a positive formulation, i.e., "whose names have been recorded in the book of life since the creation of the world." This predestinarian view is similar to that expressed in Eph 1:4, "He chose us in him before the creation of the world." On the phrase "the inhabitants of the earth," see *Comment* on 3:10. On the various uses of the stereotypical phrase "since/before the creation of the earth," see *Comment* under 13:8.

8c βλεπόντων τὸ θηρίον ὅτι ἦν καὶ οὐκ ἔστιν καὶ παρέσται, "when they see the beast because it was and is not and will be present again." The enigmatic statement that "it was not and is not and will be present again" is said to cause the amazement of those who see the beast. This statement is made three times within this context in vv 8a, 8c, and 11a (see *Comment* on 17:8a). This means "[the beast] lived, died, and will live again." The verb παρεῖναι, "to be present," here may suggest a parody of the resurrection of Jesus.

9a ὧδε ὁ νοῦς ὁ ἔχων σοφίαν, "This requires deep insight." This statement does not introduce what follows (as in the NRSV where it introduces a new paragraph) but refers to the narrative riddle of the beast proposed in v 8. That it refers to what has already been said is confirmed by literary parallels. One such parallel expression is found in 13:18, ὧδε ἡ σοφία ἐστίν, "Here is wisdom." The parallel sayings in both 13:18 and 17:9 *conclude* a riddle and function to emphasize that a mysterious set of apocalyptic symbols requires interpretation. An important parallel outside Revelation is found in the apocalyptic discourse in Mark 13:14, where the author breaks in and directly addresses the reader with a parenthetical comment, "Let the reader understand," a saying that *follows* the apocalyptic symbol of the "desolating sacrilege." With this editorial statement the author calls attention to the immediately preceding prophecy of Jesus and implicitly underlines the difficulty of the saying. Similarly, in *Barn.* 4:6a, the author concludes a section in which he cites Dan 7:24 and 7:7–8 as prophecies referring to the present time with the saying συνιέναι οὖν ὀφείλετε, "you ought to understand," again emphasizing the difficulty of interpreting the apocalyptic symbols in Daniel. Beale (*TynBul* 31 [1980] 163–70) argues that the Hebrew counterparts of νοῦς, "mind, understanding," and σοφία, "wisdom," שׂכל *śēkel* and בִּין *bîn*, occur together five times in Daniel (1:4, 17; 9:22; 11:33; 12:10) and that since this combination is rare in the Hebrew Bible and early Jewish apocalyptic literature, the idea of eschatological insight in Daniel is the background against which v 9 must be understood. Yet these Hebrew terms do not have any consistent translation in the LXX or Theod, and it is simply not true that terms meaning "wisdom" and "understanding" are absent from early Jewish apocalyptic literature. The phrase ὁ νοῦς καὶ ἡ διάνοια, "mind and understanding," occurs in *T. Reub.* 46, and the phrase νοὸς σοφός, "wise mind," occurs in an oracular context in *Sib. Or.* 5.286. The combined qualities of σύνεσις καὶ σοφία, "understanding and wisdom," are prayed for in *T. Zeb.* 6:1 (cf. *1 Clem.* 32:4). In the *Pistis Sophia* 1.40 (ed. Schmidt-Till, p. 41, lines 3f. = ed. Schmidt-MacDermot, p. 65), the mystery of the fourth repentance of Sophia is emphasized by this statement attributed to Jesus, "now at this time let him who understands [νοεῖν] understand [νοεῖν]," and is followed by an interpretation of the mystery.

Excursus 17A: The Biography of the Beast

The figure of the beast is mentioned in four narrative passages in Revelation (longest to shortest: 13:1–18; 17:3–17; 20:7–10; 19:17–21; 11:7), elsewhere in discrete sayings on the brand of the beast and the worship of his image (14:9; 15:2; 16:2), and two more times in a variety of brief miscellaneous notices (16:10, 13). A synoptic comparison of the main narratives about the beast indicate that the author had experimented with a basic "biographical" conception.

Rev 11:7	Rev 13:1–18			Rev 16:10–16	Rev 17:3–17			Rev 19:17–21	Rev 20:7–10
					Beast was (8a)	Beast was (8c)	Beast was (11a)		
					Beast is not (8a)	Beast is not (8c)	Beast is not (11a)		
Ascends from the abyss (7a)	Beast ascends from sea (1a)				Beast ascends from abyss (8a)	Beast is to come (8c)	Beast is the eighth (11b)		
					Color scarlet: (3b)				
	Has 10 horns (1b)				Has 10 horns (3d, 7c, 12, 16)	Has 10 horns (7c)			
						10 horns = 10 kings (12a)			
	Has 7 heads (1c)				Has 7 heads (3c)	Has 7 heads (7c)			
						7 heads = 7 hills (9c)			
						7 heads = 7 kings (9d)			
	Has blasphemous name on its heads (1b)				Beast full of blasphemous names (3b)				
	Looks like leopard, feet like bear, mouth like lion (2a)								
	Dragon gives beast his power, his throne, great authority (2b)			[Fifth bowl plague poured on throne of beast (10a)]					
	One of his heads appeared fatally wounded (3a)	The first beast, whose mortal wound (12b)	The beast who was wounded by the sword (14b)						
	Fatal wound healed (3b)	Was healed (12b)	But lived (14b)						
	Whole earth amazed and followed beast (3c)				Inhabitants of earth amazed (8b)				
	People worshiped dragon (4a)								
	People also worshiped beast (4b)								
	Beast permitted to say proud and blasphemous things (5a)	Blasphemed God and those who dwell in heaven (6a)							

Rev 11:7	Rev 13:1–18		Rev 16:10–16	Rev 17:3–17			Rev 19:17–21	Rev 20:7–10
	Given authority to be active 42 months (5b)			Beast in power for one day, with 10 kings (12b)				
The beast will fight, conquer and kill 2 witnesses (7b)	Fights against saints; conquers them (7a)							
	Given authority over every tribe, people, language, and nation (7b)			Waters where whore seated are peoples, crowds, nations, and languages (15)				
	All inhabitants of earth will worship him (8a)	Second beast makes people worship first beast (12b)		All inhabitants of earth will be amazed at beast (8b)				
	Those whose names not written in book of life (8b)			Those whose names not written in book of life (8b)				
			Kings of world assembled for battle (14), at Armageddon (16)	10 kings give their power and authority to the beast (13)	10 kings give royal power to the beast (17a)		Beast and kings of earth gather to fight the rider and his army (19)	[Satan deceives nations and gathers them for battle (8)]
				10 kings and beast fight against the Lamb (14a)				Army surrounds the camp of the saints and the beloved city (9a)
				Lamb will conquer them (14b)			Beast and false prophet captured (20)	Fire from heaven consumes them (9b)
				10 horns and beast will hate and destroy the whore (16)				
				Beast headed for destruction (8a)		Beast headed for destruction (11b)	Beast thrown into lake of fire (20b)	[Devil thrown into lake of fire with beast and false prophet (10)]

Though it is difficult to untangle the literary process followed by the author-editor in inserting this material into his composition, several facets of this process seem clear: (1) The longest narrative, 13:1–18, appears to be the latest, not only because it is the most complex but also because it includes the supplementary figure of the beast from the land, later referred to as the false prophet. (2) Further, while the beast in 13:1–18 is described as having ten horns and seven heads (v 1a), the meaning of these symbols remains uninterpreted, suggesting that 17:3–17 represents an earlier stage of tradition or composition in which those symbols were mentioned because the author-editor thought it important to interpret them explicitly. The interpretation of the heads as kings is presupposed in 13:3, however, where it is said that one of the beast's heads had suffered a fatal wound. (3) It is striking that while 17:14 refers to the alliance of ten kings and the beast waging war against the *Lamb,* the parallel in 19:17–21 does not mention the Lamb; rather it refers to the leader of the righteous army as simply the rider on the white horse (19:19, 21; cf. vv 11–16), though in both contexts he is identified as Lord of lords and King of kings (17:14) or King of kings and Lord of lords (19:16).

9b αἱ ἑπτὰ κεφαλαὶ ἑπτὰ ὄρη εἰσὶν ὅπου ἡ γυνὴ κάθηται ἐπ᾽ αὐτῶν, "The seven heads are seven mountains upon which the woman is seated." This is one of *two* interpretations of the seven horns of the scarlet beast (the second immediately follows in v 9c and interprets the seven horns as seven kings). This strongly suggests that the author has revised an earlier source (compiled by himself or another), for such double interpretations are not found in other apocalypses. Charles (2:68–69), for example, regards the phrase ὄρη εἰσὶν ὅπου ἡ γυνὴ κάθηται ἐπ᾽ αὐτῶν καί, "they are mountains where the woman is seated and," as a later interpolation. The phrase "seven hills" or "seven mountains" was widely used during the late first century B.C. (after Varro) and the first century A.D. and would be instantly recognizable as a metaphor for Rome. This phrase may be a gloss on the text (Charles, 2:69; Loisy, 308).

The phrase "seven hills" as a symbol for Rome occurs frequently in writers following the mid-first century B.C. (Juvenal *Satires* 9.130; Propertius 3.11.57; Horace *Carmen saeculare* 5; Ovid *Tristia* 1.5.69; Pliny *Hist. nat.* 3.66–67; Claudian *Bell. Gild.* 104; *VI cons. Hon.* 617). The location of Rome, according to Varro, was called the *Septimontium;* his list of the Seven Hills includes (*De lingua Latina* 5.41–54): (1) Capitol (previously called Tarpeian and earlier Saturnian), (2) Aventine, (3) Caelian, (4) Esquiline, (5) Quirinal, (6) Viminal, and (7) Palatine. In the seventh century B.C., settlers on seven hills near the Tiber in central Italy united (Palatium, Velia, Fagutal, Germalus, Caelius, Oppius, and Cispius); the Germalus and the Palatium were sections of the Palatine, and the Oppius, Cispius, and Fagutal were sections of the Esquiline (*CAH* 7/2:83; the list is preserved by Paulus *Fest.* 341M). These seven areas were therefore not the same as the canon of the traditional Seven Hills later identified by M. Terentius Varro (*CAH* 7/2:84). There is evidence to suggest that the canon of the Seven Hills of Rome was in fact *invented* by Varro, 116–27 B.C. (Gelsomino, *Varrone,* 37–54, 81–83). Varro wrote a book, now lost, entitled *Hebdomades,* in which he indulged in elaborate speculations on the significance of the number seven (Aulus Gelius *Noctes Atticae* 3.10). Varro also refers to the *dies Septimontium,* "Septimontium day," a festival only for people who live on the *septem montes* (*De lingua Latina* 6.24). However, these are not identical with the traditional Seven Hills (Servius *Comm. in Verg. Aen.* 6.783; Scullard, *Festivals,* 203–4; *CAH* 7/2:83–84; Gelsomino, *Varrone,* 27–31). Domitian was responsible for reviving the *Septimontia* (Suetonius *Dom.* 4.5). According to Dionysius of Halicarnassus, the Seven Hills of Rome were included within the *pomerium,* "boundaries," of Rome by stages during the monarchy (1.31.3–4: Palatine; 1.34.1: Capitoline [earlier called Saturnian]; 2.62.5: Quirinal;

3.1.5: Caelian; 3.43.1: Aventine; 3.69.4: Capitoline [formerly called Tarpeian]; 4.13.2: Viminal and Esquiline). The traditional list of Seven Hills is also found in Strabo (63–21 B.C.): Capitoline, Palatine, Quirinal, Caelian, Aventine, Esquiline, and Viminal (5.3.7). Cicero, writing ca. 52–51 B.C., refers simply to the Esquiline and Quirinal hills among others, but does not mention seven hills or use the term *Septimontium* (Gelsomino, *Varrone*, 31–35). After Varro, however, the tradition of the Seven Hills became an enormously popular image for Rome (Gelsomino, *Varrone*, 55–66). Vergil (70–19 B.C.) twice refers to the Seven Hills enclosed by a single wall (*Aeneid* 6.783; *Georgics* 2.535). The traditional Seven Hills are listed on an inscription from Corinth on the base of a statue erected during the first half of the second century A.D., probably depicting Dea Roma seated or standing on the Seven Hills of Rome (H. S. Robinson, "A Monument of Roma at Corinth," *Hesperia* 43 [1974] 470–84, plates 101–6): "PALATINUS / MONS, ESQUILINUS / MONS, AVENTINUS / MONS, CAELIUS / MONS, COLLIS VIMINALIS, [COLLIS / QUIRINALIS], CAPITOLINUS / MONS."

Roman writers often used the terms *mons*, "mountain," and *collis*, "hill," interchangeably when referring to the Seven Hills of Rome (cf. Horace *Carm. saec.* 7, who refers to the seven *colles;* Tibullus 2.5.55–56 refers to the seven *montes;* Livy 1.44.3; see Platner, *CP* 2 [1907] 433–34, and Fridh, *Eranos* 91 [1993] 1–12), while the canonical nomenclature used the term *collis* of the Quirinal and the Viminal and *mons* of each of the other hills.

The depiction of the woman seated on seven mountains has an antithetical parallel in the two versions of Enoch's vision of the seven mountains in *1 Enoch* 18:6–8 and 24:1–25:3 (Black, *1 Enoch*, 158, 169). In *1 Enoch* 18:8, the middle mountain is said to reach to heaven, like the throne of the Lord. In *1 Enoch* 24:3, the seven mountains appear to form a throne where the Lord of Glory will sit when he comes to visit the earth (25:3).

An unconvincing alternative solution to the identity of the seven hills has been proposed by Holwerda, who interprets vv 10–11 in light of the Galilean phase of the first Jewish revolt (A.D. 66–73). Holwerda understands the seven hills as seven important strongholds in northern Palestine, six in Galilee (Jotapata, Tarichea, Tiberias, Sepphoris, Fischala, and Tabor) and one in Gaulanitis (Gamala) (*EstBib* 53 [1995] 392–93).

9c καὶ βασιλεῖς ἑπτά εἰσιν, "They are also seven kings." Though the seven horns have already been interpreted as seven hills (i.e., the city of Rome), an unprecedented second interpretation explains the seven horns as seven kings (i.e., emperors of Rome); this suggests that the author has revised an earlier source, whether by himself or another. In apocalyptic tradition there is a tendency to associate the heads of many-headed creatures seen in dreams or visions with rulers. In Dan 7:6, the four-headed leopard represents Persia, while the four heads apparently represent four kings (Dan 11:2), though it is not clear precisely *which* four kings are in view. In CD^a 8:11 and CD^b 19:23–24, the "head of the cruel, harsh asps" in Deut 32:33 (note the differences with the MT) is interpreted as follows: "the asps' head is the head of the kings of Greece" (tr. García Martínez, *Dead Sea Scrolls*, 38). In 4 Ezra 12:22–26, the three heads of the eagle are said to represent three kings. Similarly, when the existence of a three-headed male creature was reported to Apollonius of Tyana, he reportedly interpreted this phenomenon to represent three emperors, Galba, Otho, and Vitellius (Philostratus *Vita Apoll.* 5.13). Some of the golden crowns worn by priests of the imperial cult (see *Comment* on 4:4) are depicted with the busts of *seven* figures (see J. Inan and E. Alföldi-Rosenbaum, *Römische und frühbyzantinische Porträtplastik aus der Türkei: Neue Funde* ([Mainz am Rhein: von Zabern, 1979] vol. 1, no. 230 [pp. 252–53], plate in vol. 2, no. 164).

The term βασιλεῖς, usually translated "kings," and the most elevated title of Hellenistic monarchs, can equally well be translated "emperors." However, βασιλεύς is not widely used as a Greek translation of the Latin term *imperator,* "emperor," until the second century A.D. (Mason, *Greek Terms,* 120–21). For references, see 1 Pet 2:13; 1 Tim 2:2; *Acta Alex.* IV.iii.5, 15; XI.ii.6; XII.10 (Musurillo, *Acts,* 19, 66, 71); BAGD, 136; Bauer-Aland, 272. The term αὐτοκράτωρ was normally used as an exact translation equivalent of *imperator.* Antipater of Thessaly used βασιλεύς to refer to Augustus in an epigram (*Anth. Pal.* 10.26). When Plutarch refers to the Ῥωμαίων βασιλεῖς, he probably means "kings of Rome" (i.e., the seven kings before the beginning of the Republic in 586 B.C.) rather than "emperors of Rome" (*De tranqilitate* 6.467E).

The identity of these seven kings has been the subject of speculation, though no single solution has found wide support among scholars (see *Excursus 17B: Alternate Ways of Counting the Roman Emperors*). There are at least three approaches to interpreting vv 9c–11: (1) the *historical* approach, (2) the *symbolic* approach, and (3) a combination of the *historical and symbolic* approaches.

1. The historical approach. Many commentators have attempted to identify the kings mentioned in Rev 17:9–11 with specific Roman emperors and on that basis to suggest a specific date for the composition of Revelation (see *Excursus 17B* below, where the main options are summarized). One matter of importance is the way in which the ancient Greeks and Romans themselves enumerated the Roman emperors. Some considered Julius Caesar the first of the Roman emperors, while others regarded Augustus as the first. In the enumeration of nineteen emperors through the numerical value of their names in *Sib. Or.* 5.12–51, the list begins with Julius Caesar and concludes with Marcus Aurelius. Since the generic term Caesar was derived from the name of Julius Caesar, it was natural for ancients to consider him the first Roman emperor. Suetonius (born ca. A.D. 70; died after 122) began his *Lives of the Caesars* with the biography of Julius Caesar. Dio Chrysostom (ca. A.D. 40– after 112) refers in *Or.* 34.7 to Augustus as ὁ δεύτερος Καῖσαρ, "the second Caesar" (Mussies, *Dio,* 253), just as Josephus referred to Augustus as the δεύτερος Ῥωμαίων αὐτοκράτωρ, "the second emperor of the Romans" (*Ant.* 18.32), both clearly implying that Julius Caesar was the first emperor. On the other hand, Suetonius reports that Claudius wrote a history of Rome that began with the death of Julius Caesar (*Claud.* 41; see Momigliano, *Claudius,* 6–7), suggesting that he regarded Augustus as the first emperor. Similarly, Tacitus began his *Annals* with Augustus, whom he considered the first emperor. While Rev 17:9c seems relatively clear, scholars have interpreted this text in a bewildering number of ways (for surveys, see Beckwith, 704–8; Yarbro Collins, *Crisis and Catharsis,* 58–64). Following the assumption that Rev 17:9b–11 refers to Roman history, it is logical to assume that if one begins to calculate the seven kings or emperors beginning with Julius Caesar (see *Excursus 17B: Alternate Ways of Counting the Roman Emperors*), and *includes* the three short-term emperors who reigned briefly in A.D. 68–69, then Galba (October 68 to 15 January 69) would be the "other," i.e., the seventh emperor who would appropriately be said to reign "for only a short time." However, if one begins counting with Julius Caesar but *excludes* the three emperors who reigned briefly in A.D. 68–69 (as many scholars do), then Claudius would be the fifth emperor, and Nero (13 October 54 to 9 June 68) the sixth emperor, the "one [who] is living" (Wilson, *NTS* 39 [1993] 599), and Vespasian (1 July 69 to 23 June 79) would be the "other," the seventh emperor who will reign "for only a short while" (though in fact

Vespasian ruled for eleven years). On the other hand, if one begins with Augustus as the first of the kings who have fallen, and if one includes the three emperors who reigned briefly during the tumultuous years A.D. 68–69, then the fifth emperor would be Nero, the "one [who] is living" would be Galba, and the "other" who will reign "for only a short while" would be Otho (5 January 69 to 16 April 69). However, if the three emperors of A.D. 68–69 are excluded, Nero would be the fifth emperor, the "one [who] is living" would be Vespasian, and the "other" who will reign "for only a short while" would be Titus (23 June 79 to 13 September 81), who was apparently known to be in ill health (Plutarch *De tuenda san. praec.* 123d). Since the phrase "one is living" seems to refer to the emperor whose reign was contemporaneous with the composition of Rev 17:9–11, the main options are Nero or Galba (Weiss-Heitmüller, 302; Beckwith, 704; Bishop, *Nero*, 173; Wilson, *NTS* 39 [1993] 605), while the questionable procedure of omitting the three so-called interregum emperors would point to either Vespasian (A.D. 69–79) or Titus (A.D. 79–81).

Excursus 17B: Alternate Ways of Counting the Roman Emperors

	a	b	c	d	e	f	g	h	i
Julius Caesar (101–44 B.C.)	1[a]	1[b]						1[h]	
Augustus (27 B.C.–A.D. 14)	2	2	1[c]	1[d]				2	
Tiberius (A.D. 14–37)	3	3	2	2					
Gaius (A.D. 37–41)	4	4	3	3	1[e]				1[i]
Claudius (A.D. 41–54)	5	5	4	4	2			3	2
Nero (A.D. 54–68)	6	6	5	5	3	1[f]			3
Galba (June A.D. 68–Jan. 69)	7	–	6	–	4	2	1[g]		–
Otho (A.D. 69)	8	–	7	–	5	3	2		–
Vitellius (A.D. 69)	–	–	8	–	6	4	3		–
Vespasian (A.D. 69–79)	–	7	–	6	7	5	4	4	4
Titus (A.D. 79–81)	–	–	–	7	8	6	5	5	5
Domitian (A.D. 81–96)	–	–	–	8	–	7	6	6	6
The "other" (17:10b)									7
[Neronic Antichrist]								7	8
Nerva (A.D. 96–98)							7		

Notes

[a]Sequentially with Julius Caesar first (Dio Chrysostom *Or.* 34.7; Jos. *Ant.* 18.32 [in the parallel passage in Jos. *J.W.* 2.168, Augustus and his successor Tiberius are mentioned but not enumerated]; Suetonius *De vita Caesarum; Sib. Or.* 5.12; 4 Ezra 12:15; Theophilus *Ad Autolycum* 3.27; Meyer, *Christentum* 3:525–26 n. 4). *Barn.* 4:3–6a probably begins with Julius Caesar also; see Hvalvik, *Struggle*, 27–32. The three short-lived emperors of 68–69, Galba, Otho, and Vitellius, are included in Suetonius *De vita Caesarum; Sib. Or.* 5.35; Jos. *J.W.* 4.491–99, but are often dismissed because Suetonius refers to their brief reigns as *rebellio trium principum*, "rebellion of the three emperors" (Suetonius *Vesp.* 1), as if their short reigns were *interregna*.

[b]Julius Caesar first; three short-lived emperors of A.D. 68–69 omitted; Nero is the "one who is" (17:10a), Vespasian is "the other one who has not yet come" (17:10b); Giet, *L'Apocalypse*, 77, 224–25; Ford, 290.

[c]Sequentially with Augustus first (Vergil *Aeneid* 6.789–97; Tacitus *Annals* 1.1); Torrey, *Apocalypse*, 58–66; Eckhardt, *Johannes*, 64; J. A. T. Robinson, *Redating*, 248–53.

[d]Augustus first; three short-lived emperors of A.D. 68–69 omitted (Swete, 220–21; Wellhausen, *Analyse*, 28; Bousset [1906] 415; Hadorn, 175; Giblin, 165; Smalley, *Thunder*, 47–48).

^eBegins with Gaius, infamous for his treatment of Jews (Brun, *ZNW* 26 [1927] 128–51; Prigent, 261; Ulrichsen, *ST* 39 [1985] 1–20). Perhaps because he is the first emperor to reign following the death and resurrection of Jesus, Gaius's reign has been regarded as the point at which the old age is concluded and the new age begun.

^fBegins with Nero, infamous for his treatment of Christians (Allo, 248–49, 270, 281–82; Reicke, *RSR* 60 [1972] 175–81; Court, *Myth and History*, 126–28). This position is often based on Rev 13:3, where μίαν ἐκ τῶν κεφαλῶν αὐτοῦ is translated "the first of his heads" rather than "one of his heads."

^gScheme of Victorinus, *Comm. in Apoc.* 17.9–11 (Haussleiter, *Victorinus*, 118–19). Tacitus began his *Histories* with 1 January 69, the reign of Galba (*Hist.* 1.1; see Chilver, *Tacitus*, 33–34).

^hFirst five emperors deified by the senate, followed by Domitian, who claimed divinity while living.

ⁱEmperors who died violently (17:10: ἔπεσαν), either actually or in rumor (Gaius was the first emperor to "fall" in the sense of dying a violent death, if one discounts Julius Caesar). Gaius is the first emperor to reign after the death of Christ ca. A.D. 30, signaling the decisive turning point in history (Strobel, *NTS* 10 [1963–64] 437–45).

2. *The symbolic approach.* Some have maintained, I think correctly, that John is not referring to seven specific kings; rather he is using the number seven as an apocalyptic symbol, a view that has become increasingly popular among scholars (Beckwith, 704–8; Kiddle-Ross, 350–51; Lohmeyer, 143; Beasley-Murray, 256–57; Caird, 218–19; Lohse, 95; Guthrie, *Introduction*, 959; Mounce, 315; Sweet, 257; Harrington, 172; Giblin, 164–65; Talbert, 81). For several reasons, the *symbolic* rather than the *historical* approach to interpreting the seven kings is convincing. (a) Seven, a symbolic number widely used in the ancient world, occurs fifty-three times in Revelation to reflect the divine arrangement and design of history and the cosmos. The enumeration of just *seven* kings, therefore, suggests the propriety of a symbolic rather than a historical interpretation. (b) The *seven* heads of the beast, first interpreted as seven hills and then as seven kings, is based on the archaic mythic tradition of the seven-headed dragon widely known in the ancient world (see *Comment* on 12:3). Since the author is working with traditional material, this again suggests that precisely *seven* kings should be interpreted symbolically. (c) Rome, founded in 753 B.C. according to Varro (several alternate dates are suggested by other ancient authors), was an Etruscan monarchy until the expulsion of the last Etruscan king, Tarquinius Superbus, in 508 B.C. From the perspective of canonical Roman tradition, there were exactly *seven* kings in all: Romulus, Numa Pompilius, Tullus Hostilius, Ancus Marcus, Tarquinus Priscus, Servius Tullius (the only king of Latin origin), and Tarquinius Superbus (though it is true that Lars Porsenna, the Etruscan king of Clusium, controlled Rome briefly after the expulsion of Tarquinius Superbus [Tacitus *Hist.* 3.72; Pliny *Hist. nat.* 34.139]). While there were probably more than seven historical kings (Momigliano, *CAH* 7/2:96), Roman and Etruscan historians identified minor figures with major ones to maintain the canonical number. The number seven was referred to frequently in that connection (Appian *Bell. civ. praef.* 14; bk. 1, frag. 2; a magical prayer in Demotic found in *PDM* XIV.299 is addressed to the seven kings, though what this means is impossible to say). There is also occasional reference to the seven archons who rule the seven planetary spheres (the sun, the moon, and five planets) as *kings* (*Ap. John* II/1 11.4–6).

3. *The combined symbolic and historical approach.* Some combine the two ways of construing vv 9c–11 because, although the enumeration of *seven* kings has a good claim to be understood symbolically, the reference in v 10a to the sixth emperor who is now living would be readily identifiable by the audience to whom John

addressed his apocalypse. Since the focus of vv 9c–10 is on the king who is now living and on the one who will come shortly but remain for only a little while, the identity of the first five kings is irrelevant and probably does not refer to five specific kings (Bauckham, *Climax*, 406–7). Further, the statement that the king who will come shortly will reign for *only a short time* is a stereotypical apocalyptic motif that emphasizes the nearness of the end.

10a οἱ πέντε ἔπεσαν, ὁ εἷς ἔστιν, ὁ ἄλλος οὔπω ἦλθεν, "of whom five have fallen, one is living, the other has not yet come." ἔπεσαν, "have fallen" (from πίπτειν, "to fall"), does not simply mean "died" but carries the connotation of being overthrown or being killed violently (Lohmeyer, 143; Strobel, *NTS* 10 [1963–64] 439). "To fall" is commonly used in the euphemistic metaphorical sense of a person's violent death, usually in war, in both Israelite-Jewish and Greek literature (Exod 32:28; 1 Sam 4:10; 2 Sam 1:19, 25, 27; 3:38; 21:22; Job 14:10 [LXX only]; 1 Chr 5:10; 20:8; 1 Macc 3:24; 4:15, 34; 2 Macc 12:34; Jdt 7:11; *Gk. 1 Enoch* 14:6; 1 Cor 10:18; *Barn.* 12:5; *Iliad* 8.67; 10.200; 11.157, 500; Xenophon *Cyr.* 1.4.24; Herodotus 9.67; see Louw-Nida, § 23.105), though the use of the metaphor "fallen" for death has nothing to do with the rank of the person (contra Beckwith, 699). Many of the Roman emperors died violent deaths: Julius Caesar was assassinated by being stabbed twenty-three times (Plutarch *Caesar* 66.4–14; Suetonius *Julius* 82; Dio Cassius 44.19.1–5); Caligula was stabbed repeatedly with swords (Suetonius *Caligula* 58; Tacitus *Annals* 11.29; Jos. *Ant.* 19.104–113; Dio Cassius 59.29.4–7; Seneca *Dial.* 2.18.3; *Ep.* 4.7); Claudius was poisoned (Suetonius *Claudius* 44–45; Tacitus *Annals* 12.66–67; 14.63; Pliny *Hist. nat.* 2.92; 11.189; 22.92); Nero committed suicide (Suetonius *Nero* 49; Jos. *J.W.* 4.493); Galba was stabbed to death by many using swords, decapitated, and his corpse mutilated (Tacitus *Hist.* 1.41.2; Plutarch *Galba* 27); Otho committed suicide with a dagger (Plutarch *Otho* 17; Suetonius *Otho* 11); Vitellius was beaten to death (Suetonius *Vit.* 17–18; Tacitus *Hist.* 3.84–85; Jos. *J.W.* 4.645; Cassius Dio 64.20.1–21.2); and Domitian was assassinated with a dagger (Suetonius *Dom.* 18).

The phrase "one is living" appears to suggest that the person who formulated this statement was contemporaneous with the sixth king and wrote during his reign; the statement that the seventh king "has not yet come" constitutes a prophecy. Weiss-Heitmüller (302) thought that 17:10 meant that Revelation was written during the reign of the sixth emperor, whom they believed to be Galba. Unfortunately, "the one who is living" is ultimately ambiguous since he can variously be identified as Nero, Galba, Vitellius, Vespasian, Titus, or Domitian (see *Excursus 17B* and *Comment* on v 9c). A further complication is the possibility that the final author of Rev 17 did not write during the reign of the sixth emperor, "who is living," but revised and updated a document that was written at an earlier time (see *Introduction*, Section 2: Date, pp. lxi–lxii). It has also been proposed that the seven "kings" are the seven commanders of seven cities in northern Palestine during the beginning of the first Jewish revolt (A.D. 66–73), and the "eighth" is John of Gischala (Holwerda, *EB* 53 [1995] 394–95). The "five who have fallen" are the five fortresses in northern Palestine with their commanders: Sepphoris, Jotapata, Tiberias, Tarichea, and Mount Tabor.

10b καὶ ὅταν ἔλθῃ ὀλίγον αὐτὸν δεῖ μεῖναι, "When he comes, he must remain for only a short while." Galba, who reigned briefly from October 68 to 15 January 69, was the seventh emperor if all the emperors beginning with Julius Caesar are counted. However, according to Victorinus, the seventh king is Nerva, who reigned for "a short while," i.e., less than two years (16 September 96 to 25 January 98). Kraft (222) also argues that Nerva is the emperor referred to here, noting that Nerva adopted Trajan in September 97, giving him authority nearly equal to his own. Another emperor who reigned a very short time was Titus, 23 June 79 to 13 September 81, important as the general who supervised the destruction of Jerusalem in A.D. 70 (Wellhausen, *Analyse*, 28).

11a καὶ τὸ θηρίον ὃ ἦν καὶ οὐκ ἔστιν, "The beast which was and is not." This descriptive statement, with close parallels in vv 8a and 8c (see *Comment* on v 8a), is clearly a parody of the divine title "who is and who was and who is to come" (1:4, 8; 4:8; 11:17; 16:5).

11b καὶ αὐτὸς ὄγδοός ἐστιν καὶ ἐκ τῶν ἑπτά ἐστιν καὶ εἰς ἀπώλειαν ὑπάγει, "he is the eighth and is one of the seven and is headed for destruction." The masculine singular pronoun αὐτός, "he," is used with the neuter noun θηρίον, "beast," since it symbolizes a male person (Mussies, *Morphology*, 138; cf. the same grammatical phenomenon in 5:6, 12; 9:5; 11:4; 13:8, 14; 17:3, 16). Victorinus, who considered this eighth king to be Nero, was apparently the first commentator on Revelation to identify Nero with the Antichrist (*Comm. in Apoc.* XVII.16; Haussleiter, *Victorinus*, 120–21). There is widespread agreement that this king does indeed represent Nero and reflects the Nero *redivivus* legend (Rev 13:3, 12, 14; 17:8; see *Excursus 13A: The Nero* Redux *or* Redivivus *Legend*). A number of authors regarded Domitian as a second Nero (Juvenal 4.37–38; Martial 11.33; Pliny *Pan.* 53; see Tertullian *Apol.* 5; *De pall.* 4). The symbolic significance of the number *eight* is relevant since the beast is called the "eighth." In early Judaism and early Christianity, eight has eschatological significance since it represents the eighth day of the new creation after the seven days of the old creation have concluded (*2 Enoch* 33:1–2; *Barn.* 15:9), and Sunday in early Christian tradition is occasionally called the eighth day (*Barn.* 15:9; Justin *Dial.* 24.1; 41.4; 138.1; see Bauckham, "Nero," 396–97). Bauckham also calls attention to a Hebrew idiom called the "graded numerical saying," which uses two consecutive numbers as parallels ("Nero," 405; Towner, *Rabbinic*, 6–8), with two examples of seven and eight used in this manner: Eccl 11:2, "Give a portion to seven or even to eight," and Mic 5:4, "And this shall be peace, when the Assyrian comes into our land and treads upon our soil, that we will raise against him seven shepherds and eight princes of men." Smalley (*Thunder*, 100, 135–36), even though he thinks Revelation was written before A.D. 70 under the reign of Vespasian, suggests that the "eighth king" is probably Domitian as Nero *redivivus*, indicating that the text of Revelation was slightly revised, ca. A.D. 85.

12a καὶ τὰ δέκα κέρατα ἃ εἶδες δέκα βασιλεῖς εἰσιν, οἵτινες βασιλείαν οὔπω ἔλαβον, "And the ten horns that you saw are ten kings, who have not yet become kings." The imagery of ten horns = ten kings is derived from Dan 7:7–8, 20, 24 (also alluded to in *Sib. Or.* 3.387–400 and *Barn.* 4:3–5), where they probably refer to ten successive (rather than ten contemporaneous) kings (J. J. Collins, *Comm. Daniel*, 320–21). Here they are presented as contemporaneous rather than successive (according to v 14 they make war on the Lamb and are conquered by the Lamb), and since they "have not yet received a kingdom" (on λαμβάνειν βασιλείαν as "become king," see *Note* 17:12.d-d.), the author is emphasizing that they belong to the *future*. This same imagery from Daniel is used in *Barn.* 4:4–5, apparently for ten successive Roman emperors (but see Reeves, "Citation," 267–69, who argues that *Barn.* 4:3–5 is based on the *Oracles of Hystaspes,* preserved in part in Lactantius *Div. Inst.* 7.16.1–3, "There will be no rest from deadly wars until ten kings arise at the same time who will divide the world, not to govern, but to consume it"). Ulrichsen (*ST* 39 [1985] 1–20) has argued that the ten horns signify the Roman emperors following Caligula, including the three emperors of A.D. 68–69 (Galba, Otho, and Vitellius), and that Revelation was written during the reign of the *sixth* king of Rev 17:10 and the *ninth* horn of Rev 13:1 and 17:12–14, i.e., Domitian. There is also a late tradition of ten successive kings who ruled the entire world, a tradition found in slightly different versions in *2 Tg. Esth.* 1.1 (Grossfeld, *Two Targums,* 96–97; cf. Grossfeld, *Sheni,* 23) and *Pirqe R. El.* 11 (10).

Here the ten kings represent Roman client kings. Roman generals in the Greek east, particularly Pompey and Antony, developed an elaborate system of client kingship. Various kings and dynasts were sanctioned or elevated in order to serve as an inexpensive and effective means for controlling their regions, some of which were reorganized as provinces. Mark Antony appointed Herod and Phasael tetrarchs of Judea in 42 B.C. (Jos. *J.W.* 1.243–44), and upon his recommendation the senate was convened and passed a *senatus consultum* giving Herod the title "king" (Jos. *J.W.* 1.282–85). Herod's son Archelaus traveled to Rome to obtain the title of king as his father's successor (Jos. *Ant.* 17.208–22; *J.W.* 2.18), and Antipas, his rival for the throne, went to Rome for the same purpose (Jos. *J.W.* 2.20–22). Augustus, however, gave Archelaus only the title "ethnarch" and gave Antipas and Philip (the other sons of Herod) the title of "tetrarch" (Jos. *J.W.* 2.93–94). Augustus thus continued the institution of client kingship begun late in the republican period. Some of the major client kingdoms at various periods included Bosporus, Pontus, Paphlagonia, Galatia, Cappadocia, Judea, Nabatea, Commagene, Emesa, Armenia, Osrhoene, Adiabene, Thrace, and Mauretania; see G. W. Bowersock, *Augustus and the Greek East* (Oxford: Clarendon, 1965) 42–61; Millar, *Near East,* index. There were also many client kingdoms subject to Parthia east of the Euphrates. While there were numerous dynastic kingdoms in the Near East during the reign of Augustus, by the early second century all those west of the Euphrates had disappeared. With the death of some of these client kings, or as a result of dynastic squabbling, their kingdoms were reorganized as Roman provinces (e.g., Galatia in 25 B.C., Paphlagonia in 6 B.C., Judea in A.D. 6; Emesa in the 70s A.D.; Commagene in A.D. 17 and again in A.D. 72 or 73 [i.e., it was made part of the province of Syria in A.D. 17; then king Antiochus IV was reinstated in A.D. 38, and Commagene was conquered in A.D. 72 or 73 and again made part of the Roman province of Syria], Nabatea in A.D. 106 [Dio Cassius 68.14.5], Osrhoene with its capital in Edessa in A.D. 212–13, and Adiabene, which perhaps became the province of Assyria for a short time, beginning in A.D. 116). The conception of ten kings subordinate to the beast thus coheres with an informal political institution fostered by Rome during the late republican and early imperial periods. The Roman board of *decemviri,* "ten men," appointed in 451 B.C. to codify Roman law, is described in a famous inscription containing parts of a speech by Claudius as a "tenfold kingship" (Dessau, *ILS,* 212).

12b ἀλλὰ ἐξουσίαν ὡς βασιλεῖς μίαν ὥραν λαμβάνουσιν μετὰ τοῦ θηρίου, "but they will receive royal authority, together with the beast, for one hour." The limited tenure of the ten kings suggests that they receive authority to become kings ultimately from God, a view confirmed by v 17. Augustus had bestowed kingdoms on subordinate rulers (*Res Gestae* 33): "The nations of the Parthians and Medes received their kings from my hand." Later the emperor Gaius (A.D. 37–41) established six kings in the east, including Agrippa I (Jos. *Ant.* 18.237), Antiochus IV of Commagene and Cilicia (Dio Cassius 59.8.2; see Jos. *J.W.* 7.219ff., 234ff.), and Soemus of Iturea (Dio Cassius 59.12.2). Three sons of Antonia Tryphaena were established as kings of Armenia Minor, Thrace and Pontus, and the Bosporus (Dio Cassius 59.12.2). On Roman kingmaking before the principate, see R. D. Sullivan, *Near Eastern Royalty and Rome, 100–30 B.C.* (Toronto: University of Toronto, 1990). The term ὥρα, literally "hour" (and the Hebrew עֵת *ʿēt*, literally "time, season," translated with ὥρα twenty-four times in the LXX), is frequently used for a short period of time and only rarely for the twelfth part of the day or night (cf. 3 Macc 5:13, 14; Matt 20:3, 5, 6, 9; 27:45; John 1:39; 4:6; Acts 2:15). The phrase μία ὥρα also occurs in 18:10, 17, 19, in the fixed phrase μιᾷ ὥρᾳ, literally "in one hour"; cf. Epictetus 1.15.8, where μιᾷ ὥρᾳ is parallel to ἄφνω, "suddenly." The term "hour" is also used for "the time appointed by God" (Matt 24:36, 44, 50; 25:13).

13 οὗτοι μίαν γνώμην ἔχουσιν καὶ τὴν δύναμιν καὶ ἐξουσίαν αὐτῶν τῷ θηρίῳ διδόασιν, "They are of one accord and relinquish their power and authority to the beast." As van Unnik ("ΜΙΑ ΓΝΩΜΗ") has shown, this idiom is very nearly a technical term drawn from the sphere of politics and is part of the larger *topos* of ὁμόνοια, "concord," that happy state in which citizens are united in an agreement of thought and opinion, a condition for which people pray and which is thought to occur only through the intervention of the gods. μία γνώμη, "one accord," is used of concord *within* a city or state (Dio Chrysostom *Or.* 36. 22;39.8; Isocrates *Or.* 4.138; Thucydides 1.122.2; 6.17.4; Demosthenes *Or.* 10.59), as well as of concord or unanimity *between* nations (Dionysius Hal. *Ant. Rom.* 6.77.1); for a collection of parallels, see van Unnik, "ΜΙΑ ΓΝΩΜΗ," 211–18, and van der Horst, *Aelius Aristides*, 83–84. For an instance of five kings whose concord and mutual friendship were interpreted by the *legatus* of Syria, Domitius Marsus, as contrary to the interests of Rome, see Josephus *Ant.* 19.338–41. Ten different autonomous kings surrendered their power to the beast, not because they were forced but because they found themselves in full agreement with the beast. Yet Rev 17:17 indicates that it was through divine intervention that the miracle of a single opinion was achieved.

There are a number of other idioms that express the unanimity of the will of a group of people: (1) αὐτὸς νοῦς, "the same mind" (1 Cor 1:10); (2) αὐτὴ γνώμη, "the same judgment" (1 Cor 1:10); (3), καρδία μία, "one heart" (Acts 4:23); (4) ψυχὴ μία, "one mind" (Acts 4:32; Phil 1:27); (5) αὐτὸ πνεῦμα, "one spirit" (2 Cor 12:18); (6) ἰσόψυχος, "having the same attitude" (Phil 2:20); and (7) σύμψυχος, "harmonious, one in mind" (Phil 2:2; see M. Silva, "Semantic Change and Semitic Influence in the Greek Bible," Ph.D. Thesis, University of Manchester, 1972, 147).

14a οὗτοι μετὰ τοῦ ἀρνίου πολεμήσουσιν καὶ τὸ ἀρνίον νικήσει αὐτούς, "They will fight against the Lamb, and the Lamb will conquer them." Though the geographical location of the Lamb is left unspecified, it appears that he is accompanied by the faithful, possibly the messianic army of 144,000 (see *Form/Structure/Setting* under Rev 7 [WBC 52B, 440–45]). This attack of ten kings against the Lamb has several parallels in Revelation (16:14–16; 19:19; 20:8–9) and numerous parallels in the OT and Jewish apocalyptic literature (Ezek 38:7–16; 39:2; Ps 2; *1 Enoch 56:5–6; 4* Ezra 13:33–34; *Sib. Or.* 3.663–68). There is a striking problem in composition here in that the Lamb destroys the armies of the ten allied kings before they are depicted as destroying Rome in v 16. Even though this is a future event, the chronological order of the vision is disturbed. It is therefore apparent that this entire verse is a secondary redactional addition coincident with the final revision of Revelation (cf. J. Weiss, *Offenbarung*, 27, 31; Charles, 2:74). The first mention of the gathering of this eschatological army occurs in connection with the pouring out of the sixth bowl in 16:12–16. This pericope is somewhat awkward because, apart from the interpolated 17:14, the eschatological battle itself is not mentioned until 19:11–21, with a doublet in 20:7–10, though preparations for the battle are briefly narrated in 16:12–16, and 17:12–14 can be read as a continuation of this passage. This brief interpolation appears to be a succinct summary of 19:11–21, where the essential features of 17:14 are described with greater detail, though the Lamb is not mentioned there (another indication of the relative lateness of the interpolation in 17:14).The opponents here are the ten kings and their armies, while in 16:12 they are called "the kings of the east" and in 16:14 "the kings of the whole world." In the eschatological scenario in 20:7–10, the enemy is alternatively decribed as "the nations in the four quarters of the earth" (v 8) and "the hosts of Gog and Magog" (v 9) led by the devil, the beast, and the false prophet (v 10).

14b ὅτι κύριος κυρίων ἐστὶν καὶ βασιλεὺς βασιλέων, "because he is Lord of lords and King of kings." These two titles are attributed to the Lamb here, while the same two titles occur in reverse order in 19:16 (whence they were derived, for this appears to be another literary device to link 17:1–19:10 to an earlier version of Revelation), where they are used of the heavenly rider on the white horse. At this literary level these two figures are meant to be equated. Together with v 14a, the inclusion of this title is probably redactional (Müller, *Messias*, 166). This suggests the identity of the rider on the white horse of 19:11–16 and the Lamb here in 17:14, at least for the final revision of Revelation. In 1 Tim 6:15, a similar double title, "King of kings and Lord of lords [ὁ βασιλεὺς τῶν βασιλευόντων καὶ κύριος τῶν κυριευόντων]," is applied to God (n.b. the close parallel with the Greek version of *1 Enoch* 9:4, ὁ βασιλεὺς τῶν βασιλευόντων, "King of kings"). The title occurs in a polemical context in *Acts Scill.* 6, where the martyr Speratus, asked by proconsul P. Vigellius Saturninus to swear by the genius of the emperor, replies (tr. Musurillo, *Acts*), "I acknowledge my lord who is the emperor of kings [*imperatorem regum*] and of all nations" (three MSS have the reading *regem regum et imperatorem*, "king of kings and emperor"). In *Pr. Paul* I A.14, Jesus Christ is called (tr. J. M. Robinson, *Nag Hammadi*, 27) "[the Lord] of Lords, the King of the ages." This double title first appears in early Jewish literature in *1 Enoch* 9:4, where it is applied to God: (ὁ) κύριος τῶν κυρίων καὶ ὁ βασιλεὺς τῶν βασιλευόντων, "Lord of lords and King of kings." The Ethiopic text may be translated (Knibb, *Enoch*, 85–86) "Lord of Lords, God of Gods, King of Kings!" Black emends the text, in light of the Aramaic fragments, to read "Lord of the ages, Lord of lords and God of gods and King of the ages" (*1 Enoch*, 29), suggesting that the phrases "Lord of lords" and "God of gods" were added in the Greek and Ethiopic texts through dependence on such OT titles as those found in LXX (Deut 10:17; Ezek 26:7; Dan 2:37; Ezra 7:12; see Black, *1 Enoch*, 130).

A close verbal parallel is LXX Dan 4:37, "he is the God of gods and Lord of lords and King of kings" (cf. LXX Dan 2:37, 47). Beale (*NTS* 31 [1985] 618–20; supported by Slater, *NTS* 39 [1993] 159–60) argues that LXX Dan 4:37 (which is a Greek addition to the Aramaic text) was the source of the title in v 14a on the basis of both

verbal and contextual arguments (few commentators have mentioned this relatively close parallel): (1) The wording of the title in LXX Dan 4:37 "is *almost
identical*" to the one in Rev 17:14. (2) The context of the title in Dan 4:37 and Rev
17:14 is similar, for it is used "as the causal basis of the divine power to take away
the rule of evil kings." (3) "*Almost* the same title" occurs in LXX Dan 2:37, 47; 3:2,
suggesting that these texts would have made a collective impression on John, with
4:37 uppermost in his mind. (4) The fourfold expression of universality following
Rev 17:14 ("people and multitudes and nations and languages") is found in almost
the same terms following LXX Dan 4:37 in LXX Dan 4:37a, 37b, 37c. (5) Dan 4 is
the probable background for the title since allusions to Dan 4 and 7 occur in the
context of Rev 17:14. Perhaps the argument from word order should also be added,
for the phrase "Lord of lords and King of kings" occurs in that order in LXX Dan
4:37. Even though Beale is correct that the title in Rev 17:14 has its closest verbal
parallel in LXX Dan 4:37, his arguments are nevertheless problematic: (1) There
is no clear evidence elsewhere in Revelation for allusions to LXX Daniel (as
opposed to Theod Daniel; see Swete, *Old Testament in Greek*, 48; Jellicoe, *Septuagint*,
87). (2) The title occurs as an address to God at the beginning of a prayer in *1 Enoch*
9:4 and in a context of praise to God in LXX Dan 4:37, i.e., in very similar contexts.
(3) It is not possible to determine whether LXX Dan 4:37 influenced *1 Enoch* 9:4
or whether *1 Enoch* 9:4 influenced LXX Dan 4:37 (the date of both translations is
problematic; the existence of a translation of all or part of *1 Enoch* in the first
century A.D. is rendered probable by the quotation of *1 Enoch* 1:9 in Jude 14–15).

The title "King of kings" is also applied to Yahweh in early Jewish literature (2
Macc 13:4; 3 Macc 5:35; *1 Enoch* 9:4; 63:4; 84:2; 1QM 14:16; 4Q*491* = 4QM^a frags. 8–
10, line 13; 4Q*381* = 4QNon-Canonical Psalms B frags. 76–77, line 7; Philo *Spec. Leg.*
1.18; *Decal.* 41; *T. Mos.* 8:1). It is also a title for God found in the Mishnah (*m. Sanh.*
4:5), as is the even more comprehensive title "King of kings of kings" (*m. 'Abot* 3:1;
4:22; *Ma'aseh Merkavah* §§ 551, 552, 555, 558; see Swartz, *Prayer*, 119 n. 40). Other
relevant parallels in the OT and early Jewish literature include Deut 10:17, "For the
Lord our God, he is God of gods and Lord of lords"; Ps 136:3, "Lord of lords"; LXX
Dan 11:36, "God of gods"; Bel 7, "God of gods"; *1 Enoch* 63:2, "Lord of kings"; 63:4,
"Now we realize that we ought to praise and bless the Lord of kings and the one who
is king over all kings"; 63:7, "Lord of kings"; 84:2, "King of kings" (cf. Bousset-
Gressmann, *Religion des Judentums*, 313 n. 2).

The title "King of kings" has strong Near Eastern associations, and its origin is
often traced to Achaemenid Persia and the phrase χšayaθiya χšayaθiyanam, "king of
kings," found in the Behistan inscription (*CAH* 4:185; v. Schoeffer, PW vol. 5 [1897]
80–81). The later Parthian kings also described themselves using this title (E. H.
Minns, "Parchments of the Parthian Period from Arroman in Kurdistan," *JHS* 35
[1915] 38–39). The Parthian king Phraates III was accustomed to being addressed
as "king of kings," though Pompey refused to use this title; i.e., he dropped "of
kings" in letters to Phraates, thereby insulting him (Plutarch *Pompey* 38.2; Dio
Cassius 37.6.1–3). It was against this background that Antony proclaimed his two
sons by Cleopatra to be "kings of kings" (Plutarch *Antony* 54.4) when he made them
rulers over Armenia, Media, and Parthia. The title *šar šarrani*, "king of kings," is also
attested in Assyrian sources, where it is a title of both Assyrian gods and kings
(Griffiths, *CP* 48 [1953] 148). The title "king of kings" is also used of Egyptian
pharoahs (Griffiths, *CP* 48 [1953] 150–51), and Deissmann cites evidence showing

that the title was used of royalty in Armenia, the Bosporus, and Palmyra (Deissmann, *Light*, 368). The title "lord of kings" (מרא מלכן *mārēʾ malkin*) was applied to the Egyptian Pharaoh in a seventh-century B.C. Aramaic letter (A1.1, lines 1, 6 in Porten-Yardeni, *Textbook* 1:6). It is often claimed that the titles "great king" and "king of kings" had precise political significance in terms of territorial sovereignty. Griffiths argues that the titles were originally used of deities and that they were only later and secondarily applied to earthly kings (*CP* 48 [1953] 152). The Greek inscription of the decree of Darius Hystaspes (521–486 B.C.), addressed to the satrap Gadatas, begins with the title βασιλεῦ [βα]σιλέων, "king of kings" (Meiggs-Lewis, *Inscriptions*, no. 12). The ancient Persian title for king, *χšayaθiya χšayaθiyanam*, "king of kings," is reflected in those parts of the OT that were composed during the Persian period (539–332 B.C.); cf. S. A. Cook, *A Glossary of the Aramaic Inscriptions* (Hildesheim/New York: Olms, 1974) 77. In the OT and the Jewish apocrypha, the title "king of kings" is used in two ways (Griffiths, *CP* 48 [1953] 151): (1) as a designation assumed by Neo-Babylonian kings (e.g., of Nebuchadrezzar in Ezek 26:7 and Dan 2:37) and (2) as a designation of Persian kings (Artaxerxes in Ezra 7:12). Titles of this type are not strictly limited to Jewish and ancient Near Eastern sources, however. Zeus is called βασιλεὺς βασιλέων, "king of kings," in Dio Chrysostom (*Or.* 2.75), and ἄναξ ἀνάκτων, "king of kings," in Aeschylus *Suppl.* 524, which, however, has a superlative meaning since it is parallel to the phrase μακάρων μακάρτατε, "most blessed of the blessed ones [i.e., 'the gods']" (Aeschylus *Suppl.* 524–25). Yet it is true that the Greeks were most familiar with the title as one used by the Persians (Griffiths, *CP* 48 [1953] 146). Several parallels also occur in the Greek magical papyri, primarily in invocations; cf. *PGM* II.53, "god of gods, king of kings"; *PGM* XIII.605, "king of kings, tyrant of tyrants"; and *PGM* XIII.606, βασιλεῦ βασιλέων, τύραννε τυράννων, "king of kings, tyrant of tyrants" (two objective genitives indicating that this divine king reigns over all other kings and this tyrant reigns over all other tyrants). The magical name "Marmaroth," found in Greek transliteration as ΜΑΡΜΑΡΑΙΩΘ or ΜΑΡΜΑΡΑΩΘ (and other spelling variations), occurs with some frequency in magical texts and particularly on magical gems and is based on an Aramaic phrase מר מרותא *mār mārûtāʾ*, meaning "lord of lords," or מר מאורות *mār mĕʾôrôt*, "lord of lights" (Hopfner, *Offenbarungszauber*, vol. 1, § 746; Kroll, *Koptische Zaubertexte* 3:124–25; Peterson, *Εἷς Θεός*, 307–8; Bonner, *Magical Amulets*, 154, 182–83; Philipp, *Mira et Magica*, 47, no. 41; cf. Delatte-Derchain, *Les intailles magiques*, no. 320; Naveh-Shaked, *Amulets*, Amulet 4, lines 24–25). The same Aramaic phrase is found in the magical papyri, e.g., Θεὲ θεῶν, Μὰρ μαριὼ Ἰάω, "God of gods, Lord of lords, Iaô" (*PGM* IV.1201; cf. IV.366; XII.72, 187, 289; XLIII.7). The even more comprehensive phrase "king of kings of kings [מלך מלכי המלכים *melek malkê hammēlākîm*]" frequently occurs in rabbinic literature (Jastrow, *Dictionary*, 791a) and also as a divine title on Jewish magical amulets (Naveh-Shaked, *Amulets*, Amulet 1, line 24; Amulet 12, line 20).

14c καὶ οἱ μετ᾽ αὐτοῦ κλητοὶ καὶ ἐκλεκτοὶ καὶ πιστοί, "and those with him are called and elect and faithful." This clause may have been added to the text, as suggested by the fact that the adjectives κλητός, "called," and ἐκλεκτός, "elect," occur only here in Revelation. The terms "called" and "elect" also occur together in Matt 22:14. While in the OT the term "elect" was used of Israel in general, in the literature from Qumran it was used to refer to members of the community (1QpHab 5:4; 9:12; 4QpPs 37 1:5; 2:5; 4QpIsaᵃ 3); see Coppens, *ETL* 57 [1981] 120–24.

Bauckham has suggested that eschatological holy-war traditions took two forms (Bauckham, "The Apocalypse as a Christian War Scroll," in *Climax*, 210–11). In one form the victory is won by God alone or by God accompanied by his heavenly armies (the tradition that predominates in apocalyptic), which I will call the *passive* model, while in the other the people of God play an active role in physical warfare against their enemies (a striking example of which is found in 1QM), which I will call the *active* model. The few apocalyptic texts in which the righteous act as agents of divine retribution include *1 Enoch* 90:19; 91:12; 95:3, 7; 96:1; 98:12; *Jub.* 23:30; *Apoc. Abr.* 29.17–20; cf. 1 Cor 6:2–3. While it is not explicitly said that "those with him" participate in the battle, this seems to be implied, making this brief narrative an example of the *active* model of the final eschatological battle. With the possible exception of this verse, most apocalytic texts that depict the final eschatological war tend to emphasize the *passive* model, i.e., the role of God and his angels in the eschatological battle, ignoring the role, if any, of the people of God in the conflict. (For an argument that the saints are enjoined to seek vengeance on their enemies in Rev 18:6–7, see S. M. Elliott, "Who Is Addressed in Revelation 18:6–7?" *BR* 40 [1995] 98–113.) 1QM is the most striking example in Jewish eschatological literature of the *active* model of the eschatological war, while Revelation reflects a much more complex combination of sometimes contradictory eschatological perspectives. The *active* model is reflected (or presupposed) in Rev 7:1–9; 14:1–5; 17:14, while the *passive* model appears in Rev 16:12–16; 19:11–21; 20:8–9.

15 καὶ λέγει μοι· τὰ ὕδατα ἃ εἶδες οὗ ἡ πόρνη κάθηται λαοὶ καὶ ὄχλοι εἰσὶν καὶ ἔθνη καὶ γλῶσσαι, "Continuing, he said to me, 'The waters that you saw, where the whore resides, are peoples and crowds and nations and languages.'" Though the author-editor uses the stereotypical interpretation formula ἃ εἶδες, "that you saw," which is part of the structure of Rev 17 (8, 12, 15, 18), v 15 is an interjection into the text that has no organic relationship to the preceding or following context (this is made clear by the outline on p. 914). The vision narrated in vv 3b–6 does not mention that the whore is either seated upon the waters or dwelling by the water since that bit of information is contained only in the angelic guide's invitation to John in 17:1. It is likely, therefore, that v 15, like v 14, is a secondary insertion into the text made when the author was linking 17:3b–18 to form a textual unit consisting of 17:1–19:10 (J. Weiss, *Offenbarung*, 27; Charles, 2:72).

In Isa 8:6–8 and Jer 47:2, "waters" is a metaphor for an invading foreign army; in Isa 8:7, the phrase מֵי הַנָּהָר *mê hannāhār*, "waters of *the* river," undoubtedly refers to the Euphrates and symbolizes the nations east and north of that great river. A similar metaphor is used of the Persian army in Aeschylus *Persians* 87–92. In 4Q169 = 4QNahum Pesher frags. 1–2, lines 3–4, the "sea" of Nah 1:4 is interpreted to mean the Kittim (= Romans). On the four ethnic groups used to emphasize universality, see *Comment* on 5:9.

16a καὶ τὰ δέκα κέρατα ἃ εἶδες καὶ τὸ θηρίον, "The ten horns that you saw and the beast." This phrase, which repeats the phrase introducing v 12, with the addition of "and the beast," is redactional since it links vv 16–17 with vv 8–13, which have been interrupted by the two interpolations, v 14 and v 15.

16b οὗτοι μισήσουσιν τὴν πόρνην καὶ ἠρημωμένην ποιήσουσιν αὐτὴν καὶ γυμνὴν καὶ τὰς σάρκας αὐτῆς φάγονται καὶ αὐτὴν κατακαύσουσιν ἐν πυρί, "they will hate the whore and make her desolate and naked and will devour her flesh and will burn her with fire." This is an allusion to Ezek 23:26–29, where Jerusalem is compared to a woman stripped naked, and to Ezek 23:25, where the survivors of Jerusalem will be burned with fire. Several OT prophets (mentioned by Hillers, *Treaty-Curses*) also threaten the harlot Judah with being stripped naked (Jer 13:26–27; Ezek 16:37–38; 23:10, 29; Hos 2:5, 12). The prophet Nahum threatens Nineveh, a graceful courtesan, with being stripped naked (Nah 3:5; cf. Isa 3:17; 47:3; Jer 13:22; Lam 1:8).

The ten horns (the nations allied with Rome) and the beast (a Roman emperor, presumably Nero) will turn on the city of Rome and destroy it. This prediction may reflect the rumor that Nero would return from the east with Parthian allies to conquer Rome (on Rome and Parthia, see *Excursus 16A*). This is the only reference in Revelation that implies the conquest of Babylon-Rome by armies of allied nations. The same theme occurs in *Tg. Jer.* 51:55 (tr. Hayward; additions to MT indicated by italics), "For the Lord has plundered Babylon, and has destroyed out of her *many troops; and the troops of many nations shall be gathered against her, and* they shall *lift up* their voice *with roaring.*" The theme of the destruction of Babylon by her enemies recurs throughout Jer 51 and is amplified in the *Targum of Jeremiah*. There is an obvious tension between this prophecy and the description of the destruction of Babylon-Rome in 18:8–9, where she is destroyed through plagues, pestilence, famine, and fire (18:8), for there the kings of the earth are not the agents of her destruction, for they mourn her passing (18:9–10), nor is there any mention of the role of the beast in her destruction.

Since the whore is a city, the phrase ἠρημωμένην ποιήσουσιν αὐτήν, "they will make her desolate," i.e., depopulate her, is appropriate. However, in the full phrase ἠρημωμένην ποιήσουσιν αὐτὴν καὶ γυμνήν, "they will make her desolate and naked," the last part is particularly appropriate, for it reflects Assyrian treaty curses that use the curse of being stripped like a prostitute (Hillers, *Treaty-Curses*, 58–60).

The phrase "they shall devour her flesh" is clearly a metaphor. In the ancient world one would expect *dogs* to devour unburied corpses in cities and birds in the country (1 Kgs 14:11; 16:4). This phrase is probably an allusion to the fate of Jezebel, who was reportedly thrown from a window and eaten by wild dogs in the street (1 Kgs 21:23–24; 2 Kgs 9:10, 36–37). The author of Revelation has a particular interest in Jezebel (cf. 2:19–29), which suggests that this phrase might have been added when the final edition of Revelation was completed. One might expect κύνες, "dogs," to be the subject of φάγονται, "devour," implying the figurative use of κύων, "dog," in a manner similar to 22:15; cf. the figurative use of "dog" to describe people opposed to the gospel (Matt 7:6), Paul's Judaizing opponents (Phil 3:2), and heretics (2 Pet 2:22; Ign. *Eph.* 7:1).

The burning of the whore (Rome) is mentioned in the context of a late version of the Nero *redivivus* myth in *Sib. Or.* 8.36–42, and the OT prescribes burning as the punishment for a priest's daughter who is a prostitute (Lev 21:9; this law was subject to a great deal of discussion among the rabbis: *m. Ter.* 7:2; *m. Sanh.* 7:2; 9:1; *b. Pesaḥ.* 75a; *b. Sanh.* 50a; 51a; 51b; 52b; 66b; 76a).

17a ὁ γὰρ θεὸς ἔδωκεν εἰς τὰς καρδίας αὐτῶν ποιῆσαι τὴν γνώμην αὐτοῦ, "For God prompted them to do his will." V 17 provides a commentary on some, but not all, of the events predicted in vv 12–16. This commentary is expressed through three infinitive clauses, all objects of the verb ἔδωκεν, "prompted": (1) ποιῆσαι τὴν γνώμην αὐτοῦ, "to do his will" (v 17a), (2) ποιῆσαι μίαν γνώμην, "to be in one accord" (v 17b), and (3) δοῦναι τὴν βασιλείαν αὐτῶν τῷ θηρίῳ, "to surrender their royal power to the beast" (v 17b). The first infinitive clause ποιῆσαι τὴν γνώμην αὐτοῦ, "to do his will," is very general in nature and reveals that the events predicted in vv 12–16 are all controlled by the sovereign will and purpose of God, while the next two clauses are more specific (see below).

The phrase διδόναι εἰς τὰς καρδίας αὐτῶν, literally "to put into their hearts," is a Semitic idiom not found elsewhere in Revelation, but it occurs a few times in the OT and more frequently in ancient Near Eastern texts. In Neh 2:12; 7:5 the phrase נתן אל־לבב *nātan 'el lēbāb*, "to put in the heart," refers to the divine guidance given to Nehemiah in his plans for Jerusalem (the same idiom occurs in Exod 35:30–35, esp. v 34; Ezra 7:27; 1 Esdr 8:25). For additional parallels, see G. von Rad, "Die Nehemia-Denkschrift," *ZAW* 76 (1964) 176–87. The eight parallels he cites are from late Egyptian inscriptions (twenty-second to twenty-sixth dynasties) collected and discussed in Otto, *Die biographischen Inschriften*, 22, 141, 148–49, 158, 162–63, 177–78, 184; e.g., 22, "I have daily done what your Ka loves, because you have put it into my heart," and 148–49, "God put it in my heart to make my life on earth glorious." These inscriptions frequently reflect the idea that good or evil action depends on a god who puts good or evil thoughts into the heart of a person (Otto, *Inscriften*, 21–22). The idiom also occurs in 1QpHab 2:8, where the Teacher of Righteousness is described as "the priest into whose heart God placed understanding [הכוהן אשר נתן אל ב(לבו בינ)ה *hakkôhēn 'ăšer nātan 'ēl bĕ(libbô bînā)h*] to interpret all the words of his servants the prophets."

17b καὶ ποιῆσαι μίαν γνώμην καὶ δοῦναι τὴν βασιλείαν αὐτῶν τῷ θηρίῳ ἄχρι τελεσθήσονται οἱ λόγοι τοῦ θεοῦ, "and to be in one accord and to surrender their royal power to the beast until the words of God will have been fulfilled." The two infinitive clauses in this partial verse (ποιῆσαι μίαν γνώμην, "to be in one accord," and δοῦναι τὴν βασιλείαν αὐτῶν τῷ θηρίῳ, "to surrender their royal power to the beast") are the objects (along with the infinitive clause ποιῆσαι τὴν γνώμην αὐτοῦ, "to do his will," in v 17a) of ἔδωκεν, "prompted," in v 17a. These two infinitive clauses detail the two ways in which God has caused the ten kings to do his will. The clause ποιῆσαι μίαν γνώμην, "to be in one accord," is a reference to v 13a, where it is simply stated οὗτοι μίαν γνώμην ἔχουσιν, "they [the ten kings] are of one accord." Since, according to the ancient view, the political achievement of "one accord" is a desirable state but one unattainable without the intervention of the gods, this clause indicates that it is none other than God himself who has brought about this state of political harmony.

The third infinitive clause, δοῦναι τὴν βασιλείαν αὐτῶν τῷ θηρίῳ, "to surrender their royal power to the beast," refers back to v 13b, τὴν δύναμιν καὶ ἐξουσίαν αὐτῶν τῷ θηρίῳ διδόασιν, "they are of one accord and relinquish their power and authority to the beast." Here βασιλείαν, "royal authority," is an alternate way of expressing ἡ δύναμις καὶ ἐξουσία, "power and authority," two terms governed by a single article, connected by καί, and therefore clearly referring to a single reality.

Finally, the phrase ἄχρι τελεσθήσονται οἱ λόγοι τοῦ θεοῦ, "until the words of God will have been fulfilled," is an oblique reference to the destruction of the whore in v 16, which is presented there as an anticipated historical event, while here it is disclosed that this event not only fulfills God's sovereign will in controlling history (the primary emphasis in the three infinitive clauses dependent on ἔδωκεν in vv 17ab) but also fulfills prophecy. Here the phrase τελεσθήσονται οἱ λόγοι τοῦ θεοῦ is essentially parallel to the phrase ἐτελέσθη τὸ μυστήριον τοῦ θεοῦ, "the secret plan of God will have been fulfilled" (10:7b), where it goes on to state explicitly that this "secret plan" was announced to God's servants the prophets.

18 καὶ ἡ γυνὴ ἣν εἶδες ἔστιν ἡ πόλις ἡ μεγάλη ἡ ἔχουσα βασιλείαν ἐπὶ τῶν βασιλέων τῆς γῆς, "And the woman that you saw is the great city that has dominion over the kings of the earth." It is striking that the very *first* thing the seer saw (though in the description of the woman in vv 3b–6, she is interpreted as "Babylon," i.e., a city) is the very *last* thing to be explained by the interpreting angel. On the relationship between Babylon-Rome and the kings of the earth, see *Comments* on 16:14; 17:12–14; 18:9. While "the great city" is applied to Jerusalem in 11:8 (see *Comment*), in Rev 17–18 the phrase "the great city" refers clearly to Rome, implicitly or explicitly designated "Babylon" (17:18; 18:10, 16, 18, 19, 21; cf. 16:19). While various other ancient cities were variously designated "the great city" (see *Comment* on 11:8), it was inevitable that the title, either implicitly or explicitly, would be applied to Rome. Rome was called *princeps urbium*, "the greatest of cities" (Horace *Carm.* 4.3.13), and Aelius Aristides referred to her as ἡ μεγάλη πόλις, "the great city" (*Or.* 26.3; cf. 26.9). See also the extensive collection of texts in *Neuer Wettstein*, ad Rev 17:18 (Dio Cassius 76.4.4–5; *Anth. Pal.* 9.236; Dion Periegetes 352–56; Athenaeus 1.208b; 3.98c; Porphyry *De abst.* 2.56.9 [ἡ μεγάλη πόλις]; Procopius *Goth.* 3.22; Vergil *Aeneid* 1.601–6; 7.272–82; *Eclogues* 1.19–25; Livy 1.16.6–7; Ovid *Fasti* 5.91–100; *Metam.* 15.439–49; Manilius 4.686–95, 773–77; Pliny *Hist. nat.* 3.38; Silius 3.505–10, 582–87; Martial 1.3.1–6; 10.103.7–12; Ammianus Marc. 14.6.5–6).

Explanation

Rev 17:1–18 is a self-contained textual unit that introduces a larger section centering on the fall of Babylon/Rome (17:1–19:10), with vv 1–3a serving as an introduction to the entire unit. The author links this unit to the previous section (15:1–16:21) by specifying that this vision was mediated and explained by one of the bowl angels. Rev 17 has a strikingly different character than the other visions in the book since it is one of the few in which the constituent elements have allegorical or symbolic meaning and it is the only one in which an *angelus interpres*, "interpreting angel," interprets the significance of aspects of the vision. This visionary episode is distinctive in another way also, for unlike the other vision sequences in Revelation, it describes a *static* scene, or tableau. The reason is simply that John's vision of "Babylon" belongs to the Hellenistic literary genre of *ekphrasis*, i.e., a detailed description of a work of art. Though the works of art on which the description is based have perished (probably a marble or bronze relief existing in many copies), a visual representation has survived on several ancient coins. These coins, minted during the reign of Vespasian, depict Dea Roma (the goddess Rome) seated on Rome's Seven Hills with a dagger resting on her right knee, the river god Tiber reclining at her feet at the right, and the she-wolf with Romulus and Remus at the lower left. The goddess Dea Roma was particularly popular in Anatolia from the mid-second century B.C. on. In fact, most of the seven cities addressed by John had active cults dedicated to this female personification of the city of Rome. John used this widespread artistic representation of the glory of Rome as a means for attacking Rome and contrasting her with the New Jerusalem.

Rev 17:1–18 contains three main sections: (1) the introduction to 17:3–19:10 (vv 1–2), (2) the vision of the woman seated on a scarlet beast (vv 3–6), and (3) the interpretation of the vision (vv 7–18). In the introductory summary (vv 1–2), one of the bowl angels invites the author to visit the scene of the judgment of the great whore seated (i.e., enthroned) by many waters (later interpreted in v 15 as symbolizing the people of the world). This judgment is based on two patently allegorical charges: (1) the kings of the earth have "fornicated" with her, and (2) the inhabitants of the earth have become "intoxicated" from her "wine" (i.e., her "fornication"). "Fornication" or "sexuality immorality" is emphasized as the primary crime of Babylon-Rome in 17:3–19:10. While various forms of sexual immorality are used in the OT as a metaphor for Israel's lapses into idolatry, and some non-Israelite trade and commerce centers such as Tyre and Nineveh were denounced under the metaphor of prostitution (probably because economic ties resulted in Israel's importation of new religious practices), here sexual immorality is a metaphor for the political alliances between Babylon-Rome and her client kingdoms and allies, and "intoxication" suggests the victimization of the people of the world by Rome.

The second part of Rev 17 focuses on a description of the vision of the scarlet beast covered with blasphemous names and having seven heads and ten horns (vv 3–6). This symbolic vision is clearly set up by the author-editor to be allegorically interpreted. It begins with the transport of the seer in a prophetic trance to the wilderness, where he sees a woman sitting on a scarlet beast full of blasphemous names with seven heads and ten horns (v 3), the beast from the sea (13:1). The woman is decked out like a successful prostitute and holds in her hand a golden cup filled with the filth of her fornication (v 4). She is drunk on the blood of Christian martyrs. On her forehead is written "a name of mystery" (RSV), "Babylon the great, the mother of whores and of earthly abominations" (v 5). The name "Babylon" first appeared in 14:8 and 16:19, anticipating the more lengthy sections on the punishment of Babylon in Rev 17–18. Babylon was a great ancient Mesopotamian city important for Judaism chiefly because the short-lived Neo-Babylonian empire (605–539 B.C.) captured Judea and Jerusalem and destroyed the temple in 586 B.C. In the OT it became a symbol for the current "superpower," while in some post-A.D. 70 Jewish and early Christian writings, "Babylon" became a cryptic name for Rome since Rome, like Babylon before, had successfully captured Jerusalem and destroyed the second temple during the first Jewish revolt (A.D. 66–70). The author's reaction of perplexity (v 6b) is a literary device enabling his angelic guide to explain what this sight means.

The largest section of the chapter centers on the interpretation of the vision (vv 7–18). This interpretation begins in v 7 with a short description of the vision, which emphasizes the four important features of the vision on which the interpretation will concentrate: "I will explain to you the secret meaning of the *woman* [v 18] and the *beast* [v 8] with *seven heads* [v 9b] and *ten horns* [vv 12, 16] which bears her." The only feature missing in this list is the *waters* (interpreted in v 15), mentioned only in the introductory summary in v 2 and not in the account of the vision itself in vv 3b–6a. Enigmatically, the angel explains that the beast "was and is not and is to come" (v 8a; a riddle repeated in vv 8c, 11). This way of describing the beast both suggests the legend of Nero's return already encountered in 13:3 and parodies the attributes of the God who "is and was and is to come." While the woman herself is "the great city" who has worldwide dominion, i.e., Rome (v 18), in v 9 the angel interprets the seven heads as the seven mountains on which the woman sits (by the fourth century B.C. Rome was situated on the traditional Seven Hills, three isolated heights, the Capitoline, Palatine, and Aventine, with four connected elevations, the Quirinal, Viminal, Esquiline, and Caelian). The Seven Hills, we learn, are really seven kings; five have fallen, one is, and the other has not yet come (v 10). The beast is an eighth king but belongs to the seven (v 11). There has been endless speculation about the identity of these kings = emperors (see *Excursus 17B*), for many have assumed that it is possible to date Revelation precisely if only the correct list of emperors can be constructed. Yet if the seventh king is Nero (who when he returns will be the eighth), who are the previous six? No matter how the list of Roman emperors from Julius Caesar to Domitian is juggled, they do not neatly fit John's scheme of seven. This suggests that the number seven may simply be a schematic representation for the complete number of Roman emperors (who were generally called "kings" in the eastern provinces). Actually, according to tradition, Rome did have seven kings, no more and no less. These belonged to the Roman monarchy beginning with Romulus (traditionally in 753 B.C.) and ending with the expulsion of the seventh king, Tarquinius Superbus, in 508 B.C. The number seven, laced with Etruscan and Roman fatalism, led to the widespread Roman belief that the period of kings had been destined to conclude with the reign of the seventh king in the seventh *saeculum,* "generation," "reign." The ten horns are ten client kings of Rome who are of "one mind" (RSV), or "one accord," an ancient technical term for the kind of concord within a city and unanimity among nations brought about by the benevolence of the gods (in this case ordained by God; 17:17). These client kings, therefore, are not coerced into an alliance with Rome but join her because they are in full agreement with her. Their united forces will unsuccessfully war against the Lamb, who will conquer them (v 14). The angel then interprets the *waters* (i.e., the Tiber) under the harlot as representative of all humanity over which Rome has temporary control (v 15). In vv 16–17 the *ten horns* are interpreted as a coalition of ten kings allied with the beast, who will mount a concerted attack on the harlot and destroy her. The Nero legends anticipated the return of Nero from the east with a great army that would destroy his enemies in Rome. During the period of the late republic (133–41 B.C.), Rome experienced almost continual internal disorder, aided and abetted by a relatively independent army of professional soldiers under the control of strong leaders (e.g., Marius, Sulla, Pompey, and Caesar). Rome was captured by Sulla (88 B.C.), then by Cinna and Marius (87 B.C.), then again by Sulla (82 B.C.), followed by the mass murder of thousands of Sulla's opponents. Add to this the instability revealed by the year of the three emperors (A.D. 68–69), and the scenario imagined for the returned Nero had ample precedent in Roman history.

3. The Destruction of Babylon (18:1–24)

Bibliography

Alexiou, M. *The Ritual Lament in Greek Tradition.* Cambridge: Cambridge UP, 1974. **Bauckham, R.** "The Economic Critique of Rome in Revelation 18." In R. Bauckham, *Climax.* 338–83.

Beagon, M. *Roman Nature: The Thought of Pliny the Elder.* Oxford: Clarendon, 1992. **Begley, V.,** and **De Puma, R. D.,** eds. *Rome and India: The Ancient Sea Trade.* Madison: University of Wisconsin, 1991. **Black, M.** "Some Greek Words with Hebrew Meanings in the Epistles and Apocalypse." In *Biblical Studies in Honour of William Barclay,* ed. J. R. McKay and J. F. Miller. London: Collins, 1976. 135–46. **Blundell, M. W.** *Helping Friends and Harming Enemies: A Study of Sophocles and Greek Ethics.* Cambridge: Cambridge UP, 1989. **Borger, R.** "NA²⁶ und die neutestamentliche Textkritik." *TRu* 52 (1987) 1–58. **Casson, L.** *Ancient Trade and Society.* Detroit: Wayne State UP, 1984. ———. *Ships and Seamanship in the Ancient World.* Princeton: Princeton UP, 1971. **Charlesworth, M. P.** *Trade-Routes and Commerce of the Roman Empire.* Cambridge: Cambridge UP, 1924. **Conzelmann, H.** *Acts of the Apostles.* Hermeneia. Philadelphia: Fortress, 1987. ———. "Miszelle zu Apk 18:17." *ZNW* 66 (1975) 288–90. **D'Arms, J. H.** *Commerce and Social Standing in Ancient Rome.* Cambridge, MA: Harvard UP, 1981. **Elliott, J. K.** "The Citation of Manuscripts in Recent Printed Editions of the Greek New Testament." *NovT* 25 (1983) 97–132. **Elliott, S. M.** "Who Is Addressed in Revelation 18:6–7?" *BR* 40 (1995) 98–113. **Fohrer, G.** "Die Gattung der Berichte über symbolische Handlungen der Propheten." *ZAW* 64 (1952) 101–20. ———. *Die symbolischen Handlungen der Propheten.* Zürich: Zwingli, 1953. **Friedrichsen, A.** "Sprachliches und Stilistisches zum Neuen Testament." In A. Friedrichsen. *Exegetical Writings: A Selection,* ed. C. C. Caragounis and T. Fornberg. WUNT 76. Tübingen: Mohr-Siebeck, 1994. 282–91. **Garnsey, P.** *Famine and Food Supply in the Graeco-Roman World: Responses to Risk and Crisis.* Cambridge: Cambridge UP, 1988. ———, **Hopkins, K.,** and **Whittaker, C. R.** *Trade in the Ancient Economy.* Berkeley; Los Angeles: University of California, 1983. **Goldsmith, R. W.** "An Estimate of the Size and Structure of the National Product of the Early Roman Empire." *Review of Income and Wealth* 30 (1984) 263. **Grobel, K.** "Σῶμα as 'Self, Person' in the LXX." In *Neutestamentliche Studien.* FS R. Bultmann. Berlin: Töpelmann, 1954. 52–59. **Harris, W. V.** "Towards a Study of the Roman Slave Trade." In *The Seaborne Commerce of Ancient Rome: Studies in Archaeology and History.* Rome: American Academy in Rome, 1980. 117–40. **Hillers, D.** "*Hoy* and *Hoy*-Oracles: A Neglected Syntactic Aspect." In *The Word of the Lord Shall Go Forth,* ed. C. Meyers and M. O'Connor. Winona Lake, IN: Eisenbrauns, 1983. 185–88. **Hirzel, R.** *Die Person: Begriff und Name derselben im Altertum.* Munich: Königlich Bayerischen Akademie der Wissenschaften, 1914. **Hopkins, K.** "Taxes and Trade in the Roman Empire." *JRS* 70 (1980) 101–25. **Isager, J.** *Pliny on Art and Society.* Odense: Odense UP, 1991. **Jahnow, H.** *Das hebräische Leichenlied im Rahmen der Völkerdichtung.* BZAW 36. Giessen: Töpelmann, 1923. **Jones, A. H. M.** "Asian Trade in Antiquity." In *The Roman Economy,* ed. P. A. Brunt. Oxford: Blackwell, 1974. 140–50. ———. "The Cloth Industry under the Roman Empire." In *The Roman Economy,* ed. P. A. Brunt. Oxford: Blackwell, 1974. 350–64. **Martino, F. de.** *Wirtschaftsgeschichte des alten Rom.* Munich: Beck, 1985. **Meiggs, R.** *Trees and Timber in the Ancient Mediterranean World.* Oxford: Clarendon, 1982. **Miller, J. I.** *The Spice Trade of the Roman Empire.* Oxford: Clarendon, 1969. **Mussies, G.** "Pagans, Jews, and Christians at Ephesus." In *Studies on the Hellenistic Background of the New Testament,* by P. W. van der Horst and G. Mussies. Utrecht: Rijksuniversiteit te Utrecht, 1990. 177–94. **Nestle, E.** *Einführung in das griechische Neue Testament.* 3rd ed. Göttingen: Vandenhoeck & Ruprecht, 1909. **Oliver, J. H.** *The Ruling Power: A Study of the Roman Empire in the Second Century after Christ through the Roman Oration of Aelius Aristides.* Philadelphia: American Philosophical Society, 1953. **Pleket, H. W.** "Urban Elites and Business in the Greek Part of the Roman Empire." In *Trade in the Ancient Economy,* ed. P. Garnsey, K. Hopkins, and C. R. Whittaker. Berkeley: University of California, 1983. 131–44. **Provan, I.** "Foul Spirits, Fornication and Finance: Revelation 18 from an Old Testament Perspective." *JSNT* 64 (1996) 81–100. **Raschke, M. G.** "New Studies in Roman Commerce with the East." *ANRW* II, 9/2:604–1378. **Reinhold, M.** *History of Purple as a Status Symbol in Antiquity.* Brussels: Latomus, 1970. **Rickman, G.** "The Grain Trade under the Roman Empire." In *The Seaborne Commerce of Ancient Rome: Studies in Archaeology and History.* Rome: American Academy in Rome, 1980. 261–76. **J. Rougé.** *Ships and Fleets of the Ancient Mediterranean.* Trans. S. Frazer. Middletown:

Wesleyan UP, 1975. ———. *Recherches sur l'organisation du commerce maritime en Méditerranée sous l'Empire romain.* Paris: S.E.V.P.E.N., 1966. **Ruiz, J.-P.** *Ezekiel in the Apocalypse: The Transformation of Prophetic Language in Revelation 16,17–19,10.* Frankfurt am Main; New York: Lang, 1989. **Schmidt, T. E.** *Hostility to Wealth in the Synoptic Gospels.* JSNTSup 15. Sheffield: JSOT, 1987. **Scholl, R.** *Corpus der ptolemäischen Sklaventexte.* 3 vols. Stuttgart: Steiner, 1990. **Shea, W. H.** "Chiasm in Theme and by Form in Revelation 18." *AUSS* 20 (1982) 249–56. **Souza Nogueira, P. A. de.** "Der Widerstand gegen Rom in der Apokalypse des Johannes: Eine Untersuchung zur Tradition des Falls von Babylon in Apokalypse 18." Diss., Heidelberg, 1991. **Steigerwald, G.** "Die antike Purpurfärberei nach dem Bericht Plinius des Alteren in seiner 'Naturalis Historia.'" *Traditio* 42 (1986) 1–57. **Strand, K. A.** "Some Modalities of Symbolic Usage in Revelation 18." *AUSS* 24 (1986) 37–46. ———. "Two Aspects of Babylon's Judgment Portrayed in Revelation 18." *AUSS* 20 (1982) 53–60. **Ward-Perkins, J.** "The Marble Trade and Its Organization: Evidence from Nicomedia." In *The Seaborne Commerce of Ancient Rome: Studies in Archaeology and History.* Rome: American Academy in Rome, 1980. 325–38. ———. "Tripolitania and the Marble Trade." *JRS* 41 (1951) 96–102. **Warmington, E. H.** *The Commerce between the Roman Empire and India.* Cambridge: Cambridge UP, 1928. **Yarbro Collins, A.** "Revelation 18: Taunt-Song or Dirge?" In *L'Apocalypse*, ed. J. Lambrecht. 185–202.

Translation

[1] [a]*After this I saw another angel with extraordinary authority descending from heaven, and the earth was illuminated by his splendor.* [2]*Then he cried out* [a] *with* [b] *a mighty voice, saying,*

> *"Fallen, fallen* [c] *is Babylon the great.*
> *It* [d] *has become the habitation of demons,* [e]
> [f]*a* [d] *preserve* [g] *for every type of unclean spirit,* [h][f]
> [i]*a* [d] *preserve* [g] *for every type of unclean and hateful bird.* [i][j]
> [3] *For all nations have collapsed* [a] *because* [b]*of the wine*
>   *that is her immoral* [c]*passion.* [b]
> *For* [d] *the kings of the earth fornicated* [e] *with her,*
> *and* [f] *the merchants of the earth became rich* [g] [h]*from her*
>   *excessive luxury."* [h]
> [4]*Then I heard another voice from heaven,* [a] *saying,*
> [b]*"My people,* [c] *come* [d] *out of her,* [b]
> *lest you participate in her sins,*
> *and lest you share* [e]*her* [f]*suffering.* [e]
> [5] *For* [a]*her sins* [a] *have reached to heaven,* [b]
> *and God remembered her crimes.*
> [6] *Render to her as she* [a] *has rendered,* [b]
> *and repay her* [c]*twice* [d] *as much as she has done.* [c]
> *In the cup* [e]*in which* [e] *she mixed,*
> *mix for her* [f] *a double portion.*
> [7] *As she glorified herself* [a] *and lived sensually,*
> *so give to her torment* [b]*and grief.* [b]
> *For in her heart she says,*
>   *'I sit* [c] [d]*as queen.* [d]
>   *I am not a widow;*
>   *sorrow will I never see.'"*
> [8]*Because of this her plagues will come in one day, pestilence* [a] *and sorrow and*

famine, and she will be burned with fire, because mighty is the [b]*Lord God* [b] *who has judged* [c] *her.*

[9]*The kings of the earth,* [a]*who committed immorality with her* [b]*and lived luxuriously* [b] *with her,* [c]*will weep* [ac] [de]*and wail over her,* [f] *when* [g] [h]*they see* [h] *the smoke of her* [i]*burning,* [10]*standing far off because of fear of her torment, saying,*

    [a]*"Alas, alas,* [a] [b]*you great city,*
    Babylon, you mighty city, [b]
    because your reckoning came [c] [d]*in a moment."* [d]

[11]*And the merchants of the earth* [a]*weep and mourn* [a] [b]*over her,* [b] *because no one buys their merchandise any longer,* [12]*merchandise consisting of gold,* [a] *and silver, and precious stones, and pearls,* [b] *and* [c]*fine linen cloth,* [c] *and purple material, and silk, and scarlet material,* [d]*all kinds of* [d] *citron-wood products, and all kinds of products* [e] *made of ivory, and all kinds of products* [f]*made of* [f] *expensive* [g]*wood, and of brass, and of iron,* [h]*and of marble,* [h] [13]*and cinnamon,* [a] [b]*and amomum,* [b] *and incense,* [c] *such as* [d] *myrrh and frankincense,* [e]*and wine,* [e] *and oil, and fine flour, and grain, and cattle, and sheep, and horses, and carriages,* [f] *and slaves,* [g] *namely,* [h] *human beings.*

[14]*And the ripe fruit* [a] [b]*which you* [c] *desired* [b] *has gone from you, and all the* [d]*expensive and* [e]*beautiful trinkets* [d] [f]*are lost* [f] *to you so that* [g] *people* [h] [i]*will never find them* [i] *again.* [15]*The merchants* [a] [b]*in these commodities,* [b] [c]*who have become wealthy* [c] [d]*by means of her,* [d] *stand far off because of the fear of her torment, weeping and mourning,* [16a]*saying,*

    [b]*"Alas, alas,* [b] *you great city,* [c]
    who were dressed in [d]*fine linen* [d] *and purple* [e] *and scarlet*
    and [f] [g]*were adorned with* [h] *gold* [gi] *and* [j]*precious stones* [j] *and pearls,* [k]
 [17] *for* [a]*in a moment* [a] *such fabulous wealth was destroyed."*

And every shipmaster [b]*and every* [c]*seafarer,* [db] *and sailors and all those who make their living on the sea, they stood at a great a distance* [18]*and exclaimed* [a] *when they saw the smoke from her incineration,*

    "What city [b] *is like the great city?"*

[19]*And they threw* [a] *dust on their heads and cried, weeping and mourning,*

    [b]*"Alas, alas,* [b] *you great city,* [c]
    through whom all those who have [d]*ships on the sea became rich from her wealth,*
    for [e]*in a moment* [e] *she has been destroyed."*

[20] *Rejoice over* [a] *her,* [b] *heaven,*
    and you [c]*people of God* [c] *and apostles* [d] *and prophets,* [e]
    for [f]*God has condemned her for condemning you.* [f]

[21]*A certain* [a] *mighty angel picked up a stone resembling a huge* [b]*millstone and threw it into the sea, saying,*

"In the same way will that great city Babylon be overthrown with sudden violence and will no longer exist. [c]

[22] *And the sound of the kitharists and the singers* [a] *and the flutists and the trumpeters*
    [b]*will never be heard* [b] *in you again;*
    and no [c] *craftsman* [d]*of any occupation* [d]
    [e]*will ever be found* [e] *in you* [f]*again;*
    the sound of the mill
    [g]*will never be heard* [g] *in you again;* [f]
[23] *the light of a lamp*
    [a]*will never be seen* [a] *in you again;*

the voices ᵇ *of the bridegroom and* ᶜ*the bride*
ᵈ*will never be heard* ᵈ *in you again;*
for your merchants were the prominent people of the world;
for all the nations were deluded by your magic spells.
²⁴*And in her was found the blood* ª *of the prophets and of the* ᵇ*people of God* ᵇ *and of all those slaughtered upon the earth.* "

Notes

1.a. Variants: (1) omit καί] *lectio originalis*. (2) insert καί] 051 Andreas latt syrᵖʰ copᵇᵒ. (3) insert καὶ εἶδον] Andr/Byz 3¹⁵⁰³ ¹⁷³². Reading (2) is an insertion based on the frequency of sentences beginning with καί in Revelation.

2.a. Variant: ἐκέκραξεν] A cop.

2.b. Variants: (1) ἐν ἰσχυρᾷ φωνῇ] A (lacuna in C) 025 051 fam 1006¹⁰⁰⁶ ¹⁸⁴¹ fam 1611¹⁶¹¹ ¹⁸⁵⁴ ²³²⁹ Oecumenius²⁰⁵³ ²⁰⁶² Andr i. (2) ἰσχυρᾷ φωνῇ] א 046 fam 1611⁹¹¹ 2030 Andr e²⁰²⁶ f 94 itª. (3) ἰσχυρᾷ φωνῇ μεγάλῃ] Hippolytus (*de Ant.* 40; MSS E R); Andr a b c d g l. (4) ἐν ἰσχυρᾷ φωνῇ μεγάλῃ] Andreas (ἐν bracketed); Byzantine. (5) ἐν ἰσχύι φωνῇ μεγάλῃ] Hippolytus (*de Ant.* 40). The omission of ἐν from (2) could have arisen as an error of haplography since the previous word ends with -εν, while (1) could have arisen as an error of dittography. The fact that φωνῇ μεγάλῃ occurs eighteen times in Revelation accounts for its insertion in (3) and (4). However, the simple dat. form φωνῇ μεγάλῃ occurs seven times (5:12; 6:10; 7:2, 10; 8:13; 10:3; 14:18), while ἐν φωνῇ μεγάλῃ occurs five times (5:2; 14:7, 9, 15; [19:17]). Reading (1) can be judged original only on the basis of the superiority of the MS attestation.

2.c. Variants: (1) omit ἔπεσεν] א fam 1611¹⁸⁵⁴ 2030 Byzantine cop. (2) insert a third ἔπεσεν] 025.

2.d. The καί that begins this line has been left untranslated since it has no independent semantic value but functions as a discourse marker indicating the beginning of a new clause or sentence.

2.e. Variant: δαιμόνων] Andreas Byzantine.

2.f-f. Variant: omit καὶ φυλακὴ παντὸς πνεύματος ἀκαθάρτου] fam 1611¹⁶¹¹ Andr c²⁰⁶⁹* g 2019.

2.g. The term φυλακή (which occurs three times in v 2), here translated "preserve," is translated "haunt" in BAGD, 868 (though no passages other than Rev 18:12 are cited); RSV, "dwelling place" (v 2a), "haunt" (v 2bc); NIV, "home" (v 2a), "haunt" (v 2bc); and NEB, "dwelling" (v 2a), "haunt" (v 2b). Cf. Michaels, *1 Peter*, 207–9, who suggests for both 1 Peter 3:18 and Rev 18:2 that φυλακή can mean confinement for the purpose of incarceration or protection and can therefore mean "prison," on the one hand, and "refuge, haven," on the other.

2.h. Variants: (1) insert καὶ μεμισημένου after ἀκαθάρτου] A 2080 itᵍⁱᵍ syrᵖʰ Hippolytus (*de Ant.* 40); Andr l²⁰⁸⁰; [Bousset (1906) 418]. (2) insert καὶ μισημένου after ἀκαθάρτου] Hippolytus (*de Ant.* 40; MS H).

2.i-i. Variant: omit καὶ φυλακὴ παντὸς ὀρνέου ἀκαθάρτου] A 025 Andreas syrᵖʰ Hippolytus.

2.j. Variants: (1) omit καὶ φυλακὴ παντὸς θηρίου ἀκαθάρτου] א 051 Oecumenius²⁰⁵³ᵗˣᵗ Andreas Byzantine vg copᵇᵒ Beatus; AV; RSV; NRSV; REV; Tischendorf, *NT Graece;* B. Weiss, *Johannes-Apokalypse*, 209; von Soden, *Text;* Charles, 2:343; [Nestle-Aland²⁷]; [UBSGNT⁴]; NRSVᵐᵍ. (2) insert καὶ φυλακὴ παντὸς θηρίου ἀκαθάρτου] A fam 1611¹⁶¹¹ ²³²⁹ Oecumenius²⁰⁵³ᶜᵒᵐᵐ Hippolytus (*de Ant.* 40); itᵍⁱᵍ vgˢᵗ copᵇᵒ; NRSV. Important MS witnesses have lacunae at this point: C 𝔓⁴⁷ fam 1611²³⁴⁴. This text problem is discussed in some detail in Schmid, *Studien* 2:142–46; *TCGNT* ¹, 756–57; *TCGNT* ², 682–83. Though it is easier to account for the omission of reading (2), due to an error of the eye (ἀκαθάρτου also concludes the previous phrase), than for its subsequent insertion, and though the MS evidence is evenly divided, reading (2) should probably be considered a later addition to the text. There is doubtless an error in Bousset (1906) 418, where he reverses the two clauses without comment: καὶ φυλακὴ παντὸς θηρίου ἀκαθάρτου καὶ μεμισημένου καὶ φυλακὴ παντὸς ὀρνέου ἀκαθάρτου καὶ μεμισημένου.

3.a. Variants: (1) πέπτωκαν (3rd pl. pf. from πίπτειν)] A C Andr f²⁰³¹ WHort. (2) πεπτώκασι(ν) (3rd pl. pf. from πίπτειν)] א 046 fam 1006¹⁰⁰⁶ ¹⁸⁴¹ fam 1611¹⁶¹¹ 2030 Andr d f²⁰⁵⁶ g l⁻¹⁶⁷⁸ Byzantine; Hippolytus (*de Ant.* 40); cop. (3) πέπτωκε(ν)] fam 1611¹⁸⁵⁴ Oecumenius²⁰⁵³ ²⁰⁶² Andr h⁻²³⁰² n⁻²⁴²⁹. (4) πέπωκε(ν)] 051 Andreas. (5) πεπώκασιν] Bousset (1906) 419. (6) πέπωκαν (3rd pl. pf. from πίνειν)] fam 1611²³²⁹ Andr/Byz 2b¹⁸²⁸ syrʰ; Tischendorf, *NT Graece;* B. Weiss, *Johannes-Apokalypse*, 137; von Soden, *Text;* Nestle-Aland²⁷; UBSGNT⁴; *TCGNT* ¹, 757–58; *TCGNT* ², 683. (7) πέποκε(ν)] 025 Andr a f²⁰²³ 598. (8) πεπότικεν] 94 2042 2065 2432 syrᵖʰ; Charles, 1:96, 344; UBSGNT¹; UBSGNT². The variants divide among those derived from πίπτειν, variants (1) through (3), those derived from πίνειν, variants (4) through (7), and those derived from ποτίζειν, variant (8). Variant (1), the unusual pf. form πέπτωκαν, has been corrected in readings (2) and (3) (Schmid, *Studien* 2:141). Variant (7), πέποκεν, is an orthographical variant of πέπωκεν, variant (4). Reading (1), πέπτωκαν, the reading with the strongest external attestation, is also the *lectio difficilior*.

In spite of the strong MS attestation of πέπτωκαν or πεπτώκασιν (both 3rd pl. pfs. that differ morphologically [see below] but are semantically identical), they are rejected as semantically impossible or inappropriate by most modern critical texts and commentators, with the exception of WHort. Several versions support either reading with the translation "have fallen" (syr^ph cop^sa bo arm eth). Of the two morphological variants, πέπτωκαν is probably the more original, since by the first century A.D. the 3rd pl. aor. ind. ending -αν increasingly replaced the 3rd pl. pf. ind. ending -ασιν (i.e., the pf. was in process of assimilation to the aor.; Gignac, *Grammar* 2:354–55), e.g., εἴρηκαν in Rev 19:3 and γέγοναν in 21:6. Since the older ending -ασιν is found in Revelation only in 8:2 (ἐστήκασιν), πέπτωκαν is probably the original reading. The reading πέπωκαν, "drank," a 3rd pl. pf. ind. from πίνειν, "to drink," is preferred by most modern critical texts and most commentators who comment on the text (e.g., Charles, vol. 2). See the brief discussion in *TCGNT*[1], 757–58 (n.b. that MS 2321, containing only the Gospels, is erroneously cited for 2329; the error was noticed by J. K. Elliott, *NovT* 25 [1983] 128, and corrected by Borger, *TRu* 52 [1987] 50–51, but nonetheless carried over into *TCGNT*[2], 683); more extensive discussions are found in Schmid, *Studien* 2:141–43, and Borger, *TRu* 52 (1987) 50–51. Yet the MS attestation for this reading is extremely weak (versions that read "have drunk" include it^gig vg Tyconius Beatus syr^ph). Nevertheless, it has been preferred since a verb meaning "to drink" makes much more sense than one meaning "to fall."

Rev 14:8 (see 17:2) provides an extremely close parallel: ἐκ τοῦ οἴνου τοῦ θυμοῦ τῆς πορνείας αὐτῆς πεπότικεν πάντα τὰ ἔθνη, "all nations have drunk from the wine, namely the wrath of her fornication." Here the pf. ind. active πεπότικεν (3rd sing. in agreement with the neut. pl. subject; see BDR § 133.1) from ποτίζειν clearly indicates the propriety of reading πέπωκαν, πεπώκασι(ν), or even πεπότικεν in 18:3. Yet it can also be argued that an original πέπτωκαν in 18:3 (clearly the *lectio difficilior*) could have been corrected from 14:8 (that this in fact occurred is clear in my opinion from the weakly supported variant πεπότικεν in 18:3, supported only by 94 2042 2065 2432 and syr^ph, even though it appeared in the text of UBSGNT[1] and UBSGNT[2] and was earlier supported by Charles, 1:96, 344).

How could the more difficult reading πέπτωκαν or πεπτώκασι have replaced an original πέπωκαν or πεπώκασι? Possibly through assimilation to the verbs ἔπεσεν, ἔπεσεν in 18:2; i.e., as Babylon fell, so did the nations (Charles, 1:96; *TCGNT*[1], 757–58). Schmid rejects as not fully convincing the possibility of an error of the eye or hand in copying πέπτωκαν instead of the very similar but original πέπωκαν; he rather suggests that the original reading πέπωκαν completely disappeared through misreading, i.e., an error of the ear, and that it was corrected probably through the influence of 14:8 (*Studien* 2:143). Yet since πέπτωκαν or πεπτώκασι is the reading in so many MSS and versions, it is clearly not as "impossible" as many suppose (Charles, 1:96). There is, in fact, a progression from πεπότικεν, "had drunk," of 14:8, to ἐμεθύσθησαν, "were intoxicated," of 17:2, to πέπτωκαν, "had collapsed," of 18:3.

3.b-b. Variants: (1) τοῦ οἴνου τοῦ θυμοῦ τῆς πορνείας] ℵ 046 fam 1006^1006 Andreas 94 1773 Byzantine it^dem cop^sa bomss. (2) τοῦ θυμοῦ τοῦ οἴνου τῆς πορνείας] 051 Andreas it^gig cop^bopart Hippolytus (*de Ant.* 40). (3) τοῦ θυμοῦ τῆς πορνείας] A fam 1611^1611 Oecumenius^2053 2062 it^a vg^st cop^bomss. (4) τοῦ οἴνου τῆς πορνείας] fam 1611^1854 syr^ph Primasius Beatus. (5) τῆς πορνείας τοῦ θυμοῦ] C. A, C, and Oecumenius reflect the omission of τοῦ οἴνου through scribal carelessness (*TCGNT*[1], 757; *TCGNT*[2], 683), an omission presupposed in reading (2), where it has been restored but at an incorrect location (Schmid, *Studien* 2:93).

3.c. τοῦ θυμοῦ is a gen. of apposition or an epexegetical gen. providing, in effect, an allegorical interpretation of τοῦ οἴνου. In the noun clause τοῦ θυμοῦ τῆς πορνείας αὐτῆς, the second articular noun is a gen. of quality functioning like an adj.: "her immoral passion" (Zerwick, *Greek*, 40; BDF § 165). θυμός has two distinct meanings; here (and in 14:8, a close parallel) it means "intense desire" (Louw-Nida, § 25.19), while in 14:10 it means "fury, intense anger" (Louw-Nida, § 88.178).

3.d. Since καί here and in the following clause introduces a clause that provides the reason for the action in the preceding clause, it functions syntactically as a causal particle and can therefore be translated "for, because." Charles (2:431 n. 1) considers this an example of a Hebraic circumstantial clause (see GKC § 156) literally reproduced in Gk.; for similar uses of καί in Revelation, see 12:11 (with a detailed discussion in *Note* 12:11.c.) and 19:3.

3.e. ἐπόρνευσαν is an aor. with the value of a pf. (Mussies, *Morphology*, 338).

3.f. See *Note* 3.d.

3.g. ἐπλούτησαν is an aor. with the value of a pf. (Mussies, *Morphology*, 338).

3.h-h. In the phrase ἐκ τῆς δυνάμεως τοῦ στρήνους αὐτῆς, δύναμις means "wealth," but combined with στρῆνος, "sensuality, luxury," it emphasizes degree, hence "excessive luxury" (BAGD, 208). στρῆνος here means "luxury" rather than "sensuality" since it is connected with the verb ἐπλούτησαν.

4.a. Variant: τῶν οὐρανῶν] Hippolytus (*de Ant.* 40).

4.b-b. Variants: (1) ὁ λαός μου ἐξ αὐτῆς] C ℵ 025 Andr d l; Nestle-Aland²⁷; UBSGNT⁴. (2) ἐξ αὐτῆς ὁ λαός μου] A [Andreas] Byzantine WHort^mg; Charles, 2:345^mg. (3) ὁ λαός μου] Andr a b e f h 598 1773. (4) λαός μου] Andr b e h 598 1773.

4.c. The articular noun ὁ λαός, "people," functions as a vocative; there are eighteen other occurrences of this construction in Revelation (see *Note* 4:11a.).

4.d. Variants: (1) ἐξέλθατε] A ℵ Andreas (ἐξέλθετε); Hippolytus (*de Ant.* 40); all modern editions. (2) ἐξελθε] C 046 fam 1611¹⁶¹¹ 2030 Oecumenius²⁰⁵³ ²⁰⁶² (2062 reads καὶ ἔξελθε); Andr l 94 Byzantine; Cyprian Primasius. In spite of the strong attestation of variant (2), it is very probably a correction of the *constructio ad sensum* found in variant (1), which is the *lectio difficilior* (Schmid, *Studien* 2:106). The 2nd plur. aor. imper. ἐξέλθατε has ὁ λαός as its subject. The author considers λαός, a collective noun that is grammatically sing., to be pl., requiring a pl. verb form. This is an example of one type of *constructio ad sensum;* for similar examples see *Notes* 7:9.g.; 8:9.b.; 9:18.a.; 13:4.a.; 19:1.d. and *Introduction*, Section 7: Syntax.

4.e-e. Variants: (1) καὶ ἐκ τῶν πληγῶν αὐτῆς] A C fam 1006 fam 1611^-1854 Oecumenius²⁰⁵³ Andr a^1corr c d e²⁰²⁶ f²⁰²³ g h i¹⁶⁸⁵ ²⁰³⁶ 194 1773 2019 Byzantine. (2) omit καὶ ἐκ τῶν πληγῶν αὐτῆς] 025 051 fam 1611¹⁸⁵⁴ Andreas.

4.f. πληγή here means "distress, suffering" and is a figurative extension of the lit. meaning of πληγή, "plague, disease, pestilence" (Louw-Nida, § 22.13).

5.a-a. Variants: αἱ ἁμαρτίαι αὐτῆς] Hippolytus (*de Ant.* 40). This scribal correction restores the author's normal word order, in which a poss. pronoun follows the noun it qualifies. In the majority of witnesses the pronoun αὐτῆς precedes rather than follows the substantive αἱ ἁμαρτίαι. In 302 instances in Revelation, a poss. pronoun in the gen. *follows* an articular noun, as opposed to just eleven occurrences of a personal pronoun in the gen. *preceding* an articular noun. Seven of these eleven instances are concentrated in Rev 2–3 (2:9, 19; 3:1, 2, 8[2x], 18), while the other four instances occur in 10:9; 14:18; 18:5, 14.

5.b. τοῦ οὐρανοῦ here means "heaven" (the dwelling place of God), not "the sky," since the imagery here is that the enormous number of transgressions came to the attention of God himself.

6.a. Though the LXX and NT often use the nom. forms of αὐτός in an unemphatic way, that usage does not occur in Revelation. For the emphatic use of the nom. forms of αὐτός, see 3:20; 6:11; 12:11; 14:17; 17:11; 18:6; 19:12, 15(2x); 21:3.

6.b. Variants: (1) omit ὑμῖν] ℵ A C 025 046. (2) insert ὑμῖν] 051 Andreas it^gig vg^clem.

6.c-c. For this translation, see Louw-Nida, § 59.70.

6.d. διπλώσατε τὰ διπλᾶ, "to pay back double," is an instance of an idiom frequently found in the LXX, in which a verb is followed by a cognate acc. of content (used to translate a Heb. finite verb followed by an abs. inf.) to *intensify* the meaning of the verb. The same idiom occurs in pagan Gk., but less frequently than in the LXX (see BDR § 153; Robertson, *Grammar*, 477–79). Two other instances of this idiom occur in Revelation (16:9; 17:6). This may be an imitation of the style of Septuagint Gk. or Masoretic Heb. since the idiom had disappeared from late Heb. and is rare in Jewish Aram. (Mussies, *Morphology*, 99). Here διπλώσατε τὰ διπλᾶ may not refer to exactly *double;* it may simply mean "much more" (Louw-Nida, § 60.75).

6.e-e. The relative pronoun ᾧ has been attracted to the dat. case of ποτηρίῳ, which immediately precedes, though it could have been put in the acc. case (Buttmann, *Grammar*, 285–86; Schmid, *Studien* 2:206). The prep. can also be omitted before a relative pronoun if the prep. has already been used before the antecedent noun (BAGD, 584), so that this clause is elliptical for ἐν τῷ ποτηρίῳ ἐν ᾧ, "in the cup in which."

6.f. αὐτῇ is a dat. of disadvantage.

7.a. Variants: (1) αὐτήν] ℵ* A C 025 046 051. (2) ἑαυτήν] ℵ¹ fam 1006 fam 1611¹⁸⁵⁴ ²³²⁹ ⁽ᵉᵃᵘᵗῇ⁾ Andreas. (3) omit αὐτήν] 046. The unaspirated form of reading (1) is preferred by *TCGNT* ¹, 758.

7.b-b. Variant: omit καὶ πένθος] 051 [Andreas].

7.c. Variants: (1) κάθημαι] *lectio originalis.* (2) καθώς] Byzantine. (3) καθίω] 046. (4) κάθημαι ὡς] Andr n. Reading (4) is a conflation of (1) and (2).

7.d-d. βασίλισσα is an independent nom. in which the nom. does not refer specifically to the speaker but indicates some kind of connection with the speaker referred to in the 1st sing. verb (Mussies, *Morphology*, BDR § 143; Robertson, *Grammar*, 456–61).

8.a. On θάνατος as "pestilence, plague," see *Note* 6:8.m.

8.b-b. Variants: (1) κύριος ὁ θεός] ℵ² C 025 051 fam 1611¹⁶¹¹ ¹⁸⁵⁴ Andreas Byzantine itᵍⁱᵍ ᵐ syrʰ arm Hippolytus Cyprian Tyconius Beatus. (2) ὁ θεός] A fam 1006¹⁰⁰⁶ ¹⁸⁴¹ Oecumenius²⁰⁵³ᶜᵒᵐᵐ Andr l itᵃ vg. (3) ὁ κύριος] Oecumenius²⁰⁵³ᵗᵉˣᵗ ²⁰⁶² Primasius. (4) ὁ θεὸς ὁ κύριος] ℵ*. (5) insert παντοκράτωρ after θεός] Andr i. The order in reading (4) occurs nowhere else in Revelation, and reading (1) has the strongest external support (*TCGNT*¹, 758). κύριος ὁ θεός occurs five times in Revelation (1:8; 4:8; 19:6; 21:22; 22:5). The phrase κύριε ὁ θεός is found in 11:17; 15:3; 16:7, while ὁ κύριος ὁ θεός occurs once in 22:6.

8.c. ὁ κρίνας is an aor. substantival ptcp. that functions as a pf. (Mussies, *Morphology*, 338).

9.a-a. In the phrase οἱ μετ᾽ αὐτῆς πορνεύσαντες καὶ στρηνιάσαντες, n.b. that the author places a prep. phrase between the article and its substantive (in this case a substantival ptcp.) and that a single article with two substantival ptcps. linked by καί indicates that the same group is in view.

9.b-b. Variant: omit καὶ στρηνιάσαντες] ℵ* Beatus. The verb στρηνιᾶν here means "to live in luxury" because it is parallel to the phrase "became rich from her excessive luxury" in v 3.

9.c-c. Variants: (1) κλαύσουσιν] C 025 046 fam 1006¹⁰⁰⁶ fam 1611¹⁸⁵⁴ Andreas Byzantine; B. Weiss, *Johannes-Apokalypse*, 210; Bousset (1906) 421; Nestle-Aland²⁷; UBSGNT⁴. (2) κλαύσονται] A ℵ fam 1006 ⁻¹⁰⁰⁶ Oecumenius²⁰⁵³ ²⁰⁶² Andr a b c d g 598 2019 Hippolytus; Tischendorf, *NT Graece;* WHortᵐᵍ; von Soden, *Text;* Charles, 2:346. (3) κλαύσωσιν] Andr f²⁰²³ h 94. Reading (2) is not a conformation to the following κόψονται (as argued by B. Weiss, *Johannes-Apokalypse*, 100–101) but a correction of the unusual fut. active (Schmid, *Studien* 2:107).

9.d. Variants: (1) omit αὐτήν] A C ℵ 046 latt cop syrʰ Hippolytus. (2) insert αὐτήν] 025 046 051 fam 1611¹⁸⁵⁴ Andreas Byzantine syrᵖʰ.

9.e. Variant: insert καὶ πενθήσουσι] fam 1611¹⁶¹¹ syrʰ.

9.f. Variant: αὐτῇ] A fam 1006 fam 1611¹⁶¹¹ ²³²⁹ Oecumenius²⁰⁵³ ²⁰⁶² Andreas.

9.g. ὅταν refers here to a specific rather than repeated action (see Mussies, *Morphology*, 345).

9.h-h. Variants: (1) ἴδωσιν] ℵ Andr l. (2) βλέπουσι] 051 Andr e 598.

9.i. Variant: πτώσεως] ℵ*.

10.a-a. The phrase οὐαὶ οὐαί with the nom. phrase ἡ πόλις ἡ μεγάλη, which functions as a vocative identifying the one to whom the lament is addressed, is repeated in vv 16 and 19 (for examples of this usage, see LXX Isa 1:24; 5:11, 18, 20, 21, 22; 31:1; Amos 5:18; Hab 2:6, 12, 19; Zeph 2:5; *Barn.* 4:11; for οὐαί with the vocative, see LXX 3 Kgdms 12:24; 13:30; Jer 22:18; 41:5[MT 34:5]). Elsewhere the author uses οὐαί with the acc. (8:13; 12:12; see *Notes* 8:13.e-e. and 12:12.e.). There is a tendency in prophetic writers to arrange "woe" oracles in series (*TDOT* 3:359–64; Andersen-Freeman, *Amos*, 520; Hillers, "Hoy," 185–88).

10.b-b. In the phrase ἡ πόλις ἡ μεγάλη, Βαβυλὼν ἡ πόλις ἡ ἰσχυρά, the anarthrous Βαβυλών is a vocative, while the first ἡ πόλις is an articular nom. functioning as a vocative (although the vocative πόλι was in use), while the second ἡ πόλις is a nom. in apposition to the vocative βαβυλών and therefore functions as a vocative. In the LXX, the interjection οὐαί is used with articular noms. used as vocatives (Zech 2:5; Isa 1:24; 5:8, 11, 18, 20, 21, 22; 31:1). There are eighteen other articular noms. that function as vocatives in Revelation (see 18:4, 10, 16, 19, 20 [3x]); for a complete list see *Note* 4:11.a.

10.c. Variant: omit ἦλθεν] A.

10.d-d. Variants: (1) μιᾷ ὥρᾳ] ℵ C Byzantine Andreas. (2) μίαν ὥραν] A fam 1006 fam 1611 Oecumenius²⁰⁵³ ²⁰⁶² Andr f²⁰⁷³ n; WHortᵐᵍ. (3) ἐν μιᾷ ὥρᾳ] fam 1611²³²⁹ 1773 Andr a b c d l TR. The fact that A has only μίαν ὥραν in Rev 18:17, 19 strongly suggests that A has changed μιᾷ ὥρᾳ (a dat. of time) to an acc. of extent of time (Schmid, *Studien* 2:107). Reading (3) is a simple amplification of the dat. The Gk. expression ὥραν μίαν in LXX Dan 4:19 (MT 4:16; for the Aram. חדה כשעה kěšaʿâ ḥǎdâ) is an idiom in Aram. meaning "in a moment," i.e., "Daniel . . . was dismayed *for a moment*" (Torrey, *Apocalypse*, 113). Similarly, the idiom μιᾷ ὥρᾳ (Rev 18:10, 17, 19) means "instantly," "*in* a short time" (G. Delling, *TDNT* 9:680; see *T. Job* 7.12). The phrase ἐν μιᾷ ὥρᾳ also occurs in the document Denis calls *Vita Adae et Evae* 25.2 (Denis, *Concordance*, 816), though this is often labeled the *Apocalypse of Adam* (Charlesworth, 2:283, where the phrase is incorrectly translated "on that occasion"). The phrase μίαν ὥραν, on the other hand, means "*for* a short time" (Rev 17:10). The phrase μιᾷ ὥρᾳ in Rev 18:10, 17, then, means "in a moment" or "in a flash" (M. Black, "Some Greek Words," 141–42).

11.a-a. Variants: (1) κλαύσουσιν καὶ πενθήσουσιν] fam 1611²³²⁹ 2030 Byzantine itᵃ vg cop. (2) κλαύσουσι καὶ πενθοῦσιν] Andr i²⁰³⁶ l¹⁷⁷⁸. (3) κλαύσονται καὶ πενθοῦσιν] Andr i²⁰³⁶. (4) omit καὶ πενθοῦσιν] Andr e²⁰²⁶ i⁻¹⁶⁸⁵.

11.b-b. Variants: (1) ἐπ᾽ αὐτήν] ℵ C 025 fam 1611¹⁶¹¹ Andr b²⁰⁸¹ 94. (2) ἐν αὐτῇ] A fam 1611²³²⁹. (3) ἐπ᾽ αὐτῇ] fam 1006 Oecumenius²⁰⁵³ Andr f²⁰²³, ²⁰⁷³ g i¹⁶⁸⁵ l n 1773 Byzantine. (4) ἐφ᾽ ἑαυτούς] Andreas. (5) ἐφ᾽ αὐτούς] 051 Andr f²⁰⁷³ᵗˣᵗ 598. (6) ἐφ᾽ ἑαυτοῖς] Andr a²¹⁸⁶ c d e²⁰²⁶ h²³⁰² 2019. (7) ἐν ἑαυτοῖς] Andr a¹ i⁻¹⁶⁸⁵. (8) σε] Oecumenius²⁰⁶². Readings (3) and (4) represent independent corrections of an earlier form of the text (Schmid, *Studien* 2:71). The attestation of reading (1) is strongest, and the other variants are a combination of accidental and deliberate modifications of the text (*TCGNT*[1], 758).

12.a. The noun χρυσοῦ (from χρυσός, "gold") is a gen. of material or content (as are the next seven nouns or noun groups in the list), not a gen. of apposition as Turner claimed (*Syntax*, 214–15).

12.b. The case and number of the word translated "pearls" is problematic (Schmid, *Studien* 2:80). There are four possibilities: (1) μαργαριτῶν] ℵ 792 fam 1006[1006 1841] fam 1611[1611] Andr l[1678] it[gig] syr Primasius; Tischendorf, *NT Graece;* WHort; Charles, 2:348; Nestle-Aland[27]; UBSGNT[4]; it conforms to its immediate context because it is surrounded by seven other gens. dependent on γόμον. (2) μαργαρίταις] A alone has the dat. form, certainly the *lectio difficilior* (see Mussies, *Morphology,* 99) but probably not original since the dat. makes no obvious sense in this context and appears to be a scribal error based on the reading preserved in C and 025, μαργαρίτας (see Schmid, *Studien* 2:93). (3) μαργαρίτας] C 025 Hippolytus (*de Ant.* 41) have the acc. pl. (grammatically possible, yet both MSS also have three other accs. in the context (χρυσοῦν, ἀργυροῦν, λίθους τιμίους), which severely weakens the probability that they preserve the originally correct form μαργαρίτας. (4) μαργαρίτου] Andreas Byzantine; probably a correction designed to fit the case and number of the nouns in the context.

12.c-c. Variants: (1) βυσσίνου] 025 Andr l[2080]. (2) βύσσους] Hippolytus (*de Ant.* 41). (3) βυσσίνων] ℵ Andr l[1678 1778]. (4) βύσσου] 051 fam 1611[1854] Andreas it[a] vg syr[h].

12.d-d. Here πᾶς without the article means "every (kind of)"; see Zerwick, *Greek,* § 188.

12.e. The term σκεῦος refers to "any kind of instrument, tool, weapon, equipment, container, or property," i.e., "thing," "object" (Louw-Nida, § 6.1), and since the things referred to with the prep. ἐκ (see *Note* 12.f-f.) refer to the material from which various objects were made or manufactured, the translation "products" is appropriate.

12.f-f. The phrase καὶ πᾶν σκεῦος ἐκ, "all kinds of products made of," is followed by four nouns or noun groups in the gen., which with the prep. ἐκ can refer to the material of which something is made (BAGD, 235); here the prep. is essentially redundant since the gen. can function in such a way without the prep. (see *Note* 18:12.a.). The relationship, ἐκ + gen. for indicating the material of which things are made is found occasionally both in Gk. literature (LSJ, 499) and in the OT. The Heb. prefix מִן *min-* ("from" = Gk. ἐκ) is used to designate the material out of which something is made or derived. The LXX often translated such expressions using ἐκ + the gen.: "And God made from the soil [מִן־הָאֲדָמָה *min-hā'ădāmâ;* LXX ἐκ τῆς γῆς] all the beasts of the field" (LXX Gen 2:19; see Gen 2:23; Exod 25:31, 35, 36; Isa 41:24; Hos 13:2).

12.g. Variant: λίθου] A fam 1006[1006 1841] it[a] vg. Scribal correction (*TCGNT*[2], 684).

12.h-h. Variants: (1) omit καὶ μαρμάρου] ℵ Andr a. (2) καὶ μαργάρου] Andr e[2057] l[1778 2080].

13.a. Variant: κινναμώμου] ℵ fam 1611[1854] Oecumenius[2053 2062] Byzantine Hippolytus (*de Ant.* 41).

13.b-b. Variant: omit καὶ ἄμωμον] ℵ[2] 1006 1841 2030 Oecumenius[2053 2062] Byzantine vg[cl] syr[ph] Hippolytus (*de Ant.* 41); Primasius.

13.c. Variant: θυμίαμα] Hippolytus (*de Ant.* 41).

13.d. The καί here appears to be epexegetical since θυμιάματα is a generic term for incense or spices, while μύρον and λίβανον are two specific types of spice.

13.e-e. Variant: omit καὶ οἶνον] Byzantine.

13.f. Variants: (1) ῥεδῶν] *lectio originalis;* vg[ww] (*redarum*). (2) ῥαιδῶν] 051[txt] fam 1006 fam 1611[2329] vg[FG]. The gen. form of the Latin loanword ἡ ῥαίδη is usually written ῥεδῶν (Moulton-Howard, *Accidence,* 155; BDF § 5[1] n. 3). Reading (2), ῥαιδῶν, is the form that one would have expected (Westcott-Hort, *Introduction,* *150–51). A ῥέδη, originally a Celtic word (Quintilian *Inst.* 1.5.57; cf. Caesar *Gall.* 1.51; 6.30) transliterated into Latin (= Latin *raeda* or *reda*) and then to Gk., was a four-wheeled, horse-drawn carriage used by the wealthy for personal travel (Pliny *Hist. nat.* 33.140; Martial 3.62).

13.g. The term σώματα, lit. "bodies," meant "slaves" (see Dittenberger, *OGIS,* 345, 9, 10, 13, 16; MM, 621; P.Cair.Zen. I, 59015 [verso], line 17; V, 59804, lines 2, 8; J. Reynolds, *Aphrodisias and Rome,* no. 12 = SEG XXXII 1128.12 [Ephesus, 39–38 B.C.]); see Y. Garlan, *Slavery in Ancient Greece* (Ithaca, NY: Cornell UP, 1988) 21.

13.h. καί, translated "namely," is epexegetical, indicating that the phrase ψυχὰς ἀνθρώπων, "human beings," is in apposition to σώματα (lit. "bodies" but idiomatically "slaves") and therefore defines σώματα more specifically.

14.a. ὀπώρα, the ripe fruit of plants, is used here figuratively for "good things of life" (Louw-Nida, § 3.34).

14.b-b. The phrase σου τῆς ἐπιθυμίας τῆς ψυχῆς, lit. "the desire of your soul," occurs several times in the LXX (Deut 12:20, 21; Jer 2:24; sometimes found in the verbal form ἐπιθυμεῖ ἡ ψυχή, Deut 12:20; 14:26; 1 Kgs 2:16; Job 33:20). While σου is a poss. gen., τῆς ἐπιθυμίας is a subjective gen., the obj. of which is ὀπώρα. σοῦ τῆς ψυχῆς is a Hebraic idiom meaning "you," and τῆς ψυχῆς can also be construed as a subjective gen. whose obj. is τῆς ἐπιθυμίας.

14.c. The sing. gen. poss. pronoun σοῦ occurs three times in this verse, indicating that Babylon is addressed directly in an apostrophe. Rev 18 is primarily couched in the third person, though the second person sing. occurs here and in the apostrophes that constitute v 10 and vv 22–23. Here the poss. pronoun σοῦ precedes an articular noun, whereas the author's usual pattern is to place it after the substantive; see *Note* 18:5.a-a. For this reason the placing of σοῦ in the post-position in Andreas and Byzantine must be regarded as a correction in conformity with the author's usual style: τῆς ἐπιθυμίας τῆς ψυχῆς σου (Schmid, *Studien* 2:81).

14.d-d. πάντα τὰ λιπαρὰ καὶ τὰ λαμπρά, lit. "all the expensive things and the beautiful things," is a hendiadys, i.e., two words connected with καί that refer to the same thing. The phrase can therefore be translated "expensive and beautiful trinkets."

14.e. τά before λαμπρά is omitted by ℵ C fam 1611[1611 2329] Oecumenius[2053 2062], an omission that can be regarded as the result of stylistic improvement (leaving a single article with two nouns connected with καί); see Schmid, *Studien* 2:107, 194.

14.f-f. The sing. verb ἀπώλετο has two neut. pl. verbs as subjects in accordance with the rule, strictly adhered to in Attic Gk., that sing. verbs are used with neut. pl. subjects (BDF § 133). This syntactical phenomenon occurs several times in Revelation (e.g., 1:19; 14:13; 20:5, 7; 21:12), but neut. pl. subjects are more frequently used with pl. verbs (e.g., 4:8, 9, 11; 5:14; 11:13, 18).

14.g. The καί introducing this clause functions as an introduction to a coordinate result clause.

14.h. εὑρήσουσιν, lit. "they will find," is a 3rd pl. fut. active ind., which functions as an indefinite pl.: "people will find" (this phenomenon occurs elsewhere in Revelation; see 2:24; 12:6; 13:16; 16:15; 20:4; see *Note* 2:24.a-a.).

14.i-i. Variants: (1) οὐ μὴ αὐτὰ εὑρήσουσιν (3rd pl. fut. ind.)] ℵ A Andr l Andr/Byz 4b Hippolytus. (2) αὐτὰ οὐ μὴ εὑρήσουσιν] C 025 fam 1611[1611] Byz 2; Hippolytus (*de Ant.* 41). (3) αὐτὴν οὐ μὴ εὑρήσουσιν] Oecumenius[2053]. (4) οὐ μὴ εὑρήσεις αὐτά (2nd sing. fut. ind.)] 051 Andreas it[gig] Primasius Beatus. (5) οὐ μὴ εὑρήσῃς αὐτά (2nd sing. 1st aor. subjunctive)] Andr b f[051? -2073?] TR. (6) αὐτὰ οὐ μὴ εὕρῃς (2nd sing. 2nd aor. subjunctive)] fam 1006[1006 1841] fam 1611[1854 2329] 2030 Andr d f[2031] h i 94 2019 Byzantine. The 2nd pl. verbs in readings (4), (5), and (6) must be considered attempts to correct the impersonal 3rd pl. Reading (5) is an itacism based on reading (4); see Mussies, *Morphology*, 294 n. 3. οὐ μή occurs with both the aor. subjunctive and the fut. ind., though the latter occurs only rarely (Moulton, *Prolegomena*, 187–92; BDR § 365) and just twice in Revelation (3:5 and 18:14; see *Note* 3:5.b-b.). The variant readings often waver between aor. subjunctive and fut. ind. (see Rev 9:6; 13:5; BDR § 365.3). Here εὑρήσουσιν must be original since a simple phonetic change could not turn it into an acceptable subjunctive (the aor. subjunctive form is εὕρωσιν); see Mussies, *Morphology*, 341.

15.a. Variant: σοῦ instead of τούτων] Hippolytus (*de Ant.* 41; MSS E and R have τούτων).

15.b-b. τούτων is an obj. gen., i.e., "the traders *in these commodities.*"

15.c-c. The aor. substantival ptcp. οἱ πλουτήσαντες functions as a pf. (Mussies, *Morphology*, 338).

15.d-d. ἀπ᾽ αὐτῆς can be construed as a gen. of *means,* though ἀπό/ἐκ + gen. can also be understood as a marker of cause or reason with an emphasis on source, "because of her" (Louw-Nida, § 89.25).

16.a. Variant: insert καί before λέγοντες] Hippolytus (*de Ant.* 41).

16.b-b. See *Note* 18:10.a-a.

16.c. The articular noun ἡ πόλις functions as a vocative; see *Note* 18:10.b-b. For a list of the other eighteen occurrences of this construction in Revelation, see *Note* 4:11.a.

16.d-d. Variant: βύσσον] 2030 Byzantine it[a] vg syr.

16.e. Variant: πορφύραν] 025 Andr b[2059] d g 2019. See *Note* 17:4.b. and *Comment* on v 4a.

16.f. Variant: omit καί] Andreas].

16.g-g. The phrase κεχρυσωμένη ἐν χρυσίῳ is pleonastic since χρυσοῦν itself means "to overlay with gold." There are, however, parallels in both pagan Gk. (cf. Herodotus 2.132, κεχρυσωμένα . . . χρυσῷ, "covered with gold") and biblical Gk. (Exod 25:11, 13; 26:32; 2 Chr 3:10) that indicate that χρυσοῦν χρυσίῳ τι means "to cover something with gold" (see BAGD, 889; Charles, 2:64).

16.h. Variants: (1) omit ἐν] A 025 fam 1006[1006 1841] fam 1611[1854 2329] 2030 Oecumenius[2053 2062] Byzantine latt; Charles, 2:349. (2) ἐν before χρυσίῳ] ℵ C 051 0229 fam 1611[1611] Andreas Hippolytus (*de Ant.* 41); [WHort]; von Soden, *Text;* B. Weiss, *Johannes-Apokalypse,* 131; [Bousset (1906) 423]; [Nestle-Aland[27]]; [UBSGNT[4]]. The insertion of ἐν as a correction makes more sense than its deletion, though its deletion can be considered an attempt to conform to the absence of ἐν before χρυσίῳ in 17:4 (B. Weiss, *Johannes-Apokalypse*).

16.i. Variant: χρυσῷ] ℵ 051 0229 fam 1611[1611 2329] Oecumenius[2053 2062] Andreas.

16.j-j. The phrase λίθῳ τιμίῳ, lit. "precious stone," is a collective sing., as is μαργαρίτῃ; see *Comment* on 17:4.

16.k. Variants: (1) μαργαρίτῃ] ℵ A C 025 0229 fam 1006 fam 1611¹⁶¹¹ ²³²⁹ Oecumenius²⁰⁵³ ²⁰⁶² 1773 Primasius; WHort. (2) μαργαρίταις] 051 Andreas Byzantine lat syr cop^bo; B. Weiss, *Johannes-Apokalypse*, 137–38. (3) μαργαρίτας] Andr h. This text is closely parallel to 17:4, where all MSS read μαργαρίταις; therefore reading (2) arose through conforming reading (1) to that text. See Schmid, *Studien* 2:80.

17.a-a. See *Note* 10.d-d.

17.b-b. Variants: (1) καὶ πᾶς ὁ ἐπὶ τόπον πλέων] A C fam 1006 (Nestle-Aland²⁶ incorrectly lists 1611, a mistake not repeated in *TCGNT*¹, 759) fam 1611¹⁸⁵⁴ ²³²⁹ 2030 Andr l²⁰²⁰ Ø⁹⁴ Byz 1⁹²⁰ ¹⁸⁵⁹ ²⁰²⁷ Byz 2⁻⁹¹⁹ Byz 3 Byz 4⁻¹⁴²⁴ Byz 5⁸⁰⁸ Byz 6¹³⁵² Byz 7²⁰⁷⁹ Byz 8⁻¹⁸⁰ Byz 9⁻⁴⁶⁷ ⁻²⁰²¹ Byz 10⁻¹⁸⁷⁰ Byz 11 Byz 12 Byz 13 Byz 14⁻¹⁸⁵⁷ Byz 15 Byz 16 Byz 17⁸² ⁹³ ²⁴¹ ⁶³² ⁶⁹⁹ ¹⁸⁵² Byz 18²⁵⁶ Andr/Byz 1⁹²² Andr/Byz 2a¹⁰⁴ ⁶⁸⁰ Andr/Byz 2b³³⁶ ⁶²⁸ Andr/Byz 4à⁻¹⁸⁸⁸ ⁻²⁰³² Andr/Byz 4c²⁰²² ²⁰⁷⁰. (2) καὶ πᾶς ὁ ἐπὶ τὸν τόπον πλέων] ℵ 046 0229 fam 1611¹⁶¹¹ (-ὁ); (Nestle-Aland²⁶ mistakenly lists 2329, a mistake not repeated in *TCGNT*¹, 759); Andr l. (3) καὶ πᾶς ὁ ἐπὶ τῶν πλοίων πλέων] 024 051 Andr d f²⁰²³ᶜᵒʳʳ ²⁰⁷³ᶜᵒʳʳ 94 2019 (omit ὁ before ἐπί) Andreas. (4) καὶ πᾶς ὁ ἐπὶ τὸν ποταμὸν πλέων ("everyone who sails on a river")] Oecumenius²⁰⁵³ ²⁰⁶² cop^sa. (5) καὶ πᾶς ἐπὶ τῶν πλοίων ὁ ὅμιλος ("the whole crowd of people who travel on ships")] Andr a¹ ²¹⁸⁶ 296 and 2049 (copies of printed TR); TR. (6) καὶ πᾶς ὁ ἐπὶ πόντον πλέων ("and everyone who travels by sea")] 469 582 2073^mg Primasius cop^bo; conjecture Nestle, *Einführung*, 181. (7) καὶ πᾶς ἐπὶ τῶν πλοίων] Hippolytus (*de Ant.* 41). Though (1) is probably original, it is a notoriously difficult phrase (though with a close parallel in Acts 27:2), which has produced many variant readings (*TCGNT*¹, 684; *TCGNT*², 759). The phrase was slightly corrected by the addition of the definite article before τόπον in variant (2). The next most frequent (and simpler) reading is (3), "and everyone who sails in boats," in which the unusual term (τὸν) τόπον was replaced with τῶν πλοίων (*TCGNT*¹, 759). Finally, with (6) E. Nestle conjectured that the original reading was ἐπὶ πόντον, "on the sea," a proposal supported only by a very few MSS. However, though τόπος usually means "place" or "region," it can be used more specifically in the sense of "port." In the anonymous *Periplus Maris Rubri*, the term τόπος occurs more than forty times to indicate localities. Conzelmann (*Acts*, 215), discussing the occurrence of τόπος in Acts 27:2, claims that several times it is used in the sense of "port" (citing *Periplus Maris Rubri*, ed. Frisk, *Périple*, 8 [p. 3, line 26], 10 [p. 4, line 9], 17 [p. 6, line 16]; these citations are more specific than the "8, 10, 17, etc." mentioned by Conzelmann). However, while the term τόπος is often used of a "place" also designated as a "port" (λιμήν) or a "harbor" (ὅρμος) or a "port of trade" (ἐμπόριον), it cannot properly be said that τόπος means "port" or "harbor" or "port of trade" (for a discussion this terminology, see Casson, *Periplus*, 271–77: "Appendix 1. Harbors and Ports").

17.c. Variants: (1) ὁ before ἐπί] Andreas d f²⁰²³ᶜᵒʳʳ ²⁰⁷³ᶜᵒʳʳ l 94 2019. (2) omit ὁ before ἐπί] 051 1611 Andreas Hippolytus (*de Ant.* 41).

17.d. Variants: (1) τόπον πλέων] A C fam 1006 fam 1611¹⁶¹¹ ¹⁸⁵⁴ 94 2030 Byzantine. (2) τὸν τόπον πλέων] ℵ 046 0229 fam 1611²³²⁹ Andr l it^gig. (3) τὸν ποταμὸν πλέων] Primasius (*omnis super mare navigans*). (4) τῶν πλοίων πλέων] Andreas. (5) τόπον ὁ ὅμιλος] Andr a Hippolytus. (6) τόπον ὅμιλος] Andr c.

18.a. Variants: (1) ἔκραξαν] A C 025 051 598 fam 1006 fam 1611¹⁶¹¹ ²³²⁹ Andr l¹⁶⁷⁸ ²⁰⁸⁰ Hippolytus (*de Ant.* 41); WHort; Bousset (1906) 423; Charles, 2:350. (2) ἔκραζον] Andreas. (3) omit καὶ ἔκραξαν] Andr l¹⁷⁷⁸ ²⁰²⁰. According to Bousset ([1906] 169), the author does not seem to have used κράζειν in the impf., though the MS evidence varies considerably. For certain uses of aor. forms of κράζειν, see 6:10; 7:2; 10:3; 18:2; 19:17. The aor. is probably the correct reading at 18:18 and 18:19.

18.b. The interrogative particle τίς is a fem. sing. nom. since the predicate ὁμοία is also a fem. sing. nom. (ὅμοια is masc. and neut. nom. and acc.) and therefore refers to a city (πόλις, a fem. nom. sing.) with which Babylon can be compared.

19.a. Variants: (1) ἔβαλον] TR. (2) ἔβαλαν] C 1828 Hippolytus (*de Ant.* 41). (3) ἔβαλλον] 025 051. (4) ἐπέβαλον] A fam 1006¹⁰⁰⁶ ¹⁸⁴¹ Byz 17⁴⁶⁹.

19.b-b. See *Note* 18:10.a-a.

19.c. The articular noun phrase ἡ πόλις ἡ μεγάλη functions as a vocative; see 18:4, 10, 16, 20[3x] and especially *Note* 18:10.b-b. For a complete list of the occurrences of this construction in Revelation, see *Note* 4:11.a.

19.d. Variant: omit τά before πλοῖα] 051 fam 1611¹⁸⁵⁴ Oecumenius²⁰⁵³ Andreas Hippolytus (*de Ant.* 41).

19.e-e. See *Note* 18:10.d-d.

20.a. εὐφραίνεσθαι with ἐπί + dat. of cause indicates the cause or reason for rejoicing (Helbing, *Kasussyntax*, 257; BDR § 196.3; Louw-Nida, § 89.27). The *dativus causae* with verbs of strong emotion can also be used with ἐν (see Acts 7:41). For LXX examples of εὐφραίνεσθαι ἐπί + *dativus causae*, see Deut 28:63; 30:9; Isa 62:5.

20.b. Variant: αὐτήν] Hippolytus (*de Ant.* 42).

20.c-c. οἱ ἅγιοι functions as a vocative (see *Note* 18:10.b-b.); the article is always added to nom. forms used in apposition to a vocative (here in apposition to οὐρανέ).

20.d. οἱ ἀπόστολοι functions as a vocative (see *Note* 18:10.b-b.); the article is always added to nom. forms used in apposition to a vocative (here in apposition to οὐρανέ).

20.e. οἱ προφῆται functions as a vocative (see *Note* 18:10.b-b.); the article is always added to nom. forms used in apposition to a vocative (here in apposition to οὐρανέ).

20.f-f. A more literal translation of the phrase ἔκρινεν ὁ θεὸς τὸ κρίμα ὑμῶν ἐξ αὐτῆς is "God has judged the condemnation of you by her [i.e., 'Babylon']." This translation construes ὑμῶν as an obj. gen., i.e., "the condemnation of you," while ἐξ αὐτῆς indicates the *agency* (with little if any emphasis on the source) from which the condemnation came, i.e., "by her." The claim that the expression κρίνειν τὸ κρίμα is an idiom found in the LXX, apparently meaning "to pronounce judgment" (LXX Zech 7:9; 8:16; Ezek 44:24), is misleading (BAGD, 450–51.5.a; Bauer-Aland, 915.5.a) since in none of those LXX passages is κρίμα used as a cognate acc. with the meaning "to pronounce judgment." Charles understands ἔκρινεν τὸ κρίμα ὑμῶν ἐξ αὐτῆς to mean "hath judged your case against her" (2:112) and points to Lam 3:59 (שָׁפְטָה מִשְׁפָּטִי *šopṭâ mišpaṭî*, translated ἔκρινας τὴν κρίσιν μου in the LXX), "judge my case." However, understanding ἐξ αὐτῆς as "against her" is problematic. Further, it is less satisfying to construe ἐκ + gen. as indicating the source of an activity or state with the implication of something coming from the source (so Louw-Nida, § 90.16: "because God condemned her for what she did to you"). While the translation of Louw-Nida is correct, their understanding of ἐξ αὐτῆς is less helpful.

21.a. The cardinal number εἷς could be used as a substitute for the adj. use of τίς, so that it functions as a definite article. The phrase εἷς ἄγγελος ἰσχυρός should therefore be translated "a [certain] mighty angel." For a more extensive discussion, see *Note* 8:13.a.

21.b. Variants: (1) μύλινον] A Oecumenius[2053 2062]; WHort; Charles, 2:351. (2) μυλικόν] C; B. Weiss, *Johannes-Apokalypse*, 211 (he prints this in his text, though he regards it as the result of clear scribal error, p. 61). (3) μύλον] Andreas Byzantine Hippolytus (*de Ant.* 42); Tischendorf, *NT Graece;* Bousset (1906) 424; von Soden, *Text;* Merk, *NT.* (4) λίθον] ℵ (λίθον ἰσχυρὸς ὡς λίθον μέγα). Bousset ([1906] 424 n. 2) regards reading (1) as an error, which was corrected by (4). Mussies (*Morphology,* 137) considers μύλινον, meaning "mill*stone*," as an implicit transposition of an adj. to a substantive; see MM, 419.

21.c. This is the aor. subjunctive pass. verb εὑρεθῇ, from εὑρίσκεσθαι, "to be found to be, exist" (Louw-Nida, § 13.7, a deponent present, which they distinguish lexically from εὑρίσκειν). When the pass. form is used with a negation, it can mean "disappear" (i.e., can no longer be found); see BAGD, 325.1.a; Bauer-Aland, 657.1.a. The verb εὑρεθῇ, used with οὐ μή, is the subjunctive of emphatic negation.

22.a. μουσικός here probably means "singer" (Louw-Nida, § 14.84).

22.b-b. The subjunctive mood of the verb used with the emphatic negative particles οὐ μή is the subjunctive of emphatic negation (see v 21 and the four more occurrences in vv 22–23).

22.c. The phrase πᾶς . . . οὐ μή is used in place of the negative pronoun οὐδείς and is therefore a Hebraism, or perhaps a Septuagintalism, i.e., an imitation of LXX style (D. Tabachovitz, *Die Septuaginta und das Neue Testament: Stilstudien* [Lund: Gleerup, 1956] 90–91). In Heb. there are no equivalents to the Gk. terms οὐδείς, μηδείς, οὔποτε, μήποτε, οὐδέτερος, and μηδέτερος, which must be used in Gk. to negate generalities. A normal Gk. expression is οὐδεὶς θέλει, "no one wishes," while πᾶς οὐ θέλει, lit. "each does not wish," i.e., "no one wishes," reflects a lit. translation of a normal Heb. or Aram. phrase (A. Hilhorst, *Sémitismes,* 132–33). πᾶς . . . οὐ corresponds to the Heb. combination of כֹּל *kōl,* "each," with לֹא *lōʾ,* "not"; see Mussies, *Morphology,* 183. A parallel construction in Revelation is found only in 22:3, though the related כֹּל/לֹא *kōl/lōʾ* or πᾶς/οὐ pattern is found in 7:16; 9:4; 21:27. The πᾶς . . . οὐ idiom occurs with some frequency in the NT (Matt 12:25; Mark 7:18; Luke 14:33; John 3:16; 6:39; 11:26; 12:46; Acts 5:42; Rom 10:11; Eph 4:29; 5:5; 2 Pet 1:20; 1 John 2:16, 21; 3:6[2x], 9, 10, 15; 4:3; 5:18; 2 John 9). It occurs three times in Hermas (*Vis.* 3.6.1; *Mand.* 10.3.2; 11.5).

22.d-d. Variants: (1) πάσης τέχνης] C 025 046 051 fam 1006[1006] fam 1611[1611 1854 2344] it[dem gig] vg syr[h] cop[sa] Primasius Beatus. (2) omit πάσης τέχνης] ℵ A fam 1611[2329] cop[bo]. (3) καὶ πάσης τέχνης] Oecumenius[2053] it[c div haf]. The omission reflected in reading (2) is probably accidental, while (3) lends support to (1), which is the *lectio originalis* (*TCGNT*[1], 759; *TCGNT*[2], 684).

22.e-e. See *Note* 22.b-b.

22.f-f. Variant: omit ἔτι καὶ φωνὴ μύλου οὐ μὴ ἀκουσθῇ ἐν σοὶ ἔτι] Hippolytus (*de Ant.* 42; MS S).

22.g-g. See *Note* 22.b-b.

23.a-a. See *Note* 22.b-b.

23.b. φωνή is used in a distributive sense, i.e., something possessed by each member of a particular group, and is therefore translated as a pl.

23.c. Variant: φωνή before νύμφης] C fam 1611²³²⁹ Byz 1⁹²⁰ ¹⁸⁵⁹ ²²⁵⁶ Byz 17⁹¹³ Hippolytus (*de Ant.* 42). Correction by assimilation to the stereotyped phrase in the OT to which this passage alludes: "the voice of mirth and the voice of gladness, the voice of the bridegroom and the voice of the bride" (Jer 7:34; 16:9; 25:10; 40:11[MT 33:11]; Bar 2:23); this phrase is consistently used in a negative context; i.e., it refers to things that will cease. *Tg. Jer.* 7:34 differs from the MT primarily in the use of the pl.: "the sound of bride-grooms and the sound of brides" (tr. Hayward).

23.d-d. See *Note* 22.b-b.

24.a. Variants: (1) αἷμα προφητῶν] ℵ A C Oecumenius²⁰⁵³ ²⁰⁶² Andr a i l 94 2019; WHort; Bousset (1906) 424; Charles, 2:113, 353; Merk, *NT;* Nestle-Aland²⁷; UBSGNT⁴. (2) αἵματα προφητῶν] 046 051 fam 1006⁹¹¹ ¹⁰⁰⁶ ¹⁸⁴¹ fam 1611¹⁶¹¹ ¹⁸⁵⁴ Andreas Byzantine; Tischendorf, *NT Graece.* Aside from the strong witness for reading (1), the pl. form in reading (2) is contrary to the style of the author, since αἷμα occurs nineteen times in Revelation and always in the sing. (see *Note* 16:6.b., where αἵματα is a variant found in ℵ Andr/Byz 2b). The sing. αἷμα can refer to blood as a liquid, as well as "drop of blood" or "case of bloodshed," both of which can have the figurative meaning of "death." The latter two meanings can be expressed in the pl. form αἵματα; see John 1:13 (see Euripides *Ion* 693), where an original pl. has sing. variants (Mussies, *Morphology,* 82). Thus αἵματα can mean the deaths of several people (see LXX Hab 2:8); see BDR § 141.10.

24.b-b. On translating οἱ ἅγιοι, lit. "saints," as "people of God," see *Comment* on 5:8.

Form/Structure/Setting

I. OUTLINE

3. The destruction of Babylon (18:1–24)
   a. An angelic taunt song (vv 1–3)
      (1) Vision of an angel descending from heaven (v 1ab)
         (a) Possessing extraordinary authority (v 1b)
         (b) His splendor illuminates the earth (v 1b)
      (2) The angel's taunt song (vv 2–3)
         (a) Announcement of Babylon's fall (v 2a)
         (b) Description of fallen Babylon (v 2bc)
            [1] A habitation of demons
            [2] A preserve for unclean spirits
            [3] A preserve for unclean birds
         (c) Reasons for Babylon's fall (v 3)
            [1] Nations have become drunk from the wine of her fornication
            [2] Kings fornicated with her
            [3] Merchants have enriched themselves through her
   b. Speech by the unidentified heavenly voice (vv 4–20)
      (1) Speaker: "another voice" from heaven (v 4a)
      (2) Summons to flight (vv 4b–8)
         (a) Appeal to flee (v 4b)
         (b) Reasons for flight (vv 4c–5)
             [1] To avoid participating in her sins (v 4c)
            [2] To avoid sharing her suffering (v 4c)
            [3] Babylon's imminent punishment (v 5)
               [a] Her sins have reached to heaven
               [b] God remembered her crimes
         (c) The threat of judgment (vv 6–8)

[1] Reiterated summons for revenge against Babylon (v 6)
  [a] Render to her as she has rendered (v 6a)
  [b] Repay her double for what she has done (v 6a)
  [c] Mix her a double portion in the cup she used
     (v 6b)
[2] Reason for judgment: excessive pride and
    complacency (v 7)
  [a] As she glorified herself and lived sensually, so give
     her torment and grief (v 7a)
  [b] Babylon's soliloquy of self-condemnation (v 7b)
     {1} I rule as queen
     {2} I am not a widow
     {3} I will never see sorrow
[3] The sudden destruction of Babylon (v 8)
  [a] Her plagues will come in one day (v 8a)
     {1} Pestilence
     {2} Sorrow
     {3} Famine
  [b] She will be burned with fire (v 8a)
  [c] How is such a sudden judgment possible? The
     might of God (v 8b)
(3) Three songs of lament (vv 9–20)
  (a) The kings of the earth and their lament (vv 9–10)
    [1] Their relationship to Babylon (v 9a)
     [a] They fornicated with her
     [b] They lived luxuriously with her
    [2] Their reaction to her destruction (vv 9a–10a)
     [a] They weep and wail (v 9a)
     [b] They stand at a distance for fear of her torment
      (v 10a)
    [3] Their lament (v 10bc)
     [a] Babylon was a great and mighty city
     [b] Yet her destruction was quick and sudden
  (b) The merchants and their lament (vv 11–17a)
    [1] They weep and mourn in reaction to her destruction
     (vv 11–14)
     [a] Reason: no one buys their goods (v 11b)
     [b] Excursus: list of luxury goods (vv 12–13)
     [c] Commodities no longer available (v 14)
      {1} Ripe fruit
      {2} Expensive, beautiful trinkets
    [2] Relationship to Babylon: they owe their wealth to her
     (v 15a)
    [3] Their reaction to her destruction (v 15b)
     [a] They stand at a distance, fearing her torment
     [b] They weep and mourn
    [4] Their lament (vv 16–17a)

[a] Past: The great city described as a wealthy woman
(v 16)
[b] Present: Her fabulous wealth was destroyed in a
moment (v 17a)
(c) The sea captains and sailors and their lament (vv 17b–20)
[1] Their reaction to her destruction (vv 17c–19a)
[a] They stand at a distance (v 17c)
[b] They exclaim "What city is like the great city?"
(v 18)
[c] They throw dust on their heads (v 19a)
[d] They weep and mourn (v 19a)
[2] Their lament (v 19bc)
[a] Past: The great city enriched the ship owners
[b] Present: She has been destroyed in a moment
[3] Interjection (v 20)
[a] Call for rejoicing (v 20ab)
{1} Heaven
{2} People of God
{3} Apostles
{4} Prophets
[b] Reason: God has punished her for condemning
you (v 20c)
c. Vision of the symbolic destruction of Babylon (vv 21–24)
(1) Symbolic action: a mighty angel threw a huge stone into the
sea (v 21a)
(2) Primary interpretation (v 21b)
(a) So will Babylon the great be overthrown with sudden
violence
(b) Babylon will exist no longer
(3) The interpretation elaborated: negative vignettes of
Babylon's fate (vv 22–23b)
(a) No kitharists, singers, flutists, trumpeters (v 22a)
(b) No craftsmen (v 22b)
(c) No sound of the mill (v 22c)
(d) No lamp light (v 23a)
(e) No voices of bridegrooms and brides (v 23b)
(4) Babylon's past economic power: her merchants were world
power brokers (v 23c)
(5) Babylon's universal evil influence (v 23d)
(6) Babylon's murderous past (v 24)
(a) Responsible for the murder of prophets and saints (v 24a)
(b) Responsible for everyone killed on the earth (v 24b)

II. Literary Analysis

In this chapter the author presents the events surrounding the fall of Babylon,
not in chronological order or in logical sequence but rather in such a way as to
create an emotional effect on the hearers. Rev 18 consists of three closely related

textual units that are formally presented as three speeches, the first by "another angel" (vv 1–3), the second by "another voice" (vv 4–20), and the third by "a mighty angel" (vv 21–24). The chapter begins with the announcement that Babylon has fallen (vv 1–3). The entire section that follows in vv 4–20 is a speech uttered by the unidentified heavenly voice in v 4 (Yarbro Collins, "Revelation 18," 193; Bauckham, "Revelation 18," 340). This speech consists of two parts: the first deals with events *preceding* the fall of Babylon (vv 4–8), including the future consequences of the wickedness of Babylon (note the future tenses following διὰ τοῦτο, "because of this," in v 8: ἥξουσιν, "will come"; κατακαυθήσεται, "will be burned"). Thereafter the focus is on events *following* her fall (vv 9–20), first in future tenses (v 8, ἥξουσιν, κατακαυθήσεται; v 9, κλαύσουσιν, "will weep," κόψονται, "will wail"; v 11, κλαίουσιν, "weep," πενθοῦσιν, "mourn," ἀγοράζει, "buys" [all futuristic presents in v 11]) and then (after v 18) in past tenses. Finally, in v 21, the prophecy that Babylon will be destroyed is reiterated. The angels who announce the events (18:1, 4, 21) are not explicitly described as coming after one another (as are the angelic figures in 8:7, 8, 10, 12; 9:1, 13; 11:15). Babylon's fall is not the only theme linking these various segments together. A reiterated motif is that her fall takes place "in a single day" (18:8) or "in a single hour" (18:10, 17, 19); i.e., God's vengeance upon her will take place quickly and unexpectedly.

In Rev 18 three different types of poetic compositions are linked together by the common theme of the fall of Babylon: (1) the ritual lament (vv 1–3, 9–20), which has striking similarities to the ritual laments over Tyre in Ezek 26:15–18 and 27:1–8, 26–36 (Jahnow, *Leichenlied*, 210–18), interrupted by (2) the command to flee (vv 4–8), and followed by (3) a symbolic action and interpretation (vv 21–24). As so often in Revelation, the formal structure imposed on the material does not cohere well with an analysis of the content. Perhaps the most striking feature is the dependence on the imagery more typical of the OT writing prophets than that found in apocalyptic literature. Three stanzas within vv 9–20 are examples of ἠθοποιία, i.e., a "speech in character": first the lament of the kings of the earth (18:10), second the lament of the merchants of the earth (18:14, 16), and third those involved in shipping (18:18b–20).

The first section, vv 1–3, though often referred to as a funeral dirge or lament, is in fact a *prophetic taunt song*, though the latter is very probably a development of the former with the addition of a mocking tone (Eissfeldt, *Introduction*, 91); the victory song is also similar in that it incorporates themes from the taunt song. The angel serves as the leader of the ritual lament by making a public announcement of the "death," a formal feature of ancient Israelite ritual laments (Jahnow, *Leichenlied*, 101, 138, 167). Taunt songs have no fixed form but are characterized by derision and joy over the (past, present, or future) misfortunes and shortcomings of others (see 1 Sam 17:43, 44; Jer 22:14–15; Isa 23:15–16). In Isa 37:22–29, for example, Hezekiah taunts Sennacherib. Taunt songs were taken up by OT prophets for deriding the enemies of Israel and announcing their downfall (Isa 23–24, 47; Jer 50–51; Ezek 26–27). This taunt consists first of an angelic announcement anticipating the fall of Babylon (vv 1–3). The opening words, "Fallen, fallen is Babylon the great," are derived from Isa 21:9, yet the *form* of 18:1–3 is closer to Amos 5:1–3 (Jahnow, *Leichenlied*, 219), which is also cast in the form of the funerary lament, where the initial announcement of the fall of Israel is followed by a clause providing the *reason* for that fall:

> Hear this word which I take up over you in lamentation, O house of Israel:
> "Fallen [נפלה *nāpĕlâ*/ἔπεσεν], no more to rise,
>   is the virgin Israel;
> forsaken on her land,
>   with none to raise her up."
> For [כי *kî*/διότι] thus says the Lord God:
> "The city that went forth a thousand
>   shall have a hundred left,
> and that which went forth a hundred
>   shall have ten left
>   to the house of Israel." (RSV)

Here in Amos 5:1–3 (as in Rev 18:1–3) the statement that Israel has fallen is a prophetic anticipation of a future event that will surely come to pass. In this taunt song and in the three laments found in vv 9–19, the rhetorical strategy of the author focuses on the stark contrast between past glory and present devastation. This emphasis on contrast characterizes ritual laments over cities and nations throughout the ancient Mediterranean world.

Formally considered, Rev 18:1–3 is an *angelic speech,* a form that occurs nine times in Revelation (7:2–3; 10:1–7; 14:6–7; 14:8; 14:9–11; 14:14–16; 14:18–20; 18:1–3; 19:17–18; see *Form/Structure/Setting* on Rev 7) and is often inserted immediately after an *angelic epiphany* (see also *Form/Structure/Setting* on Rev 7). The *angelic speech* in Revelation exhibits the following structural features: (1) introductory phrase: καὶ εἶδον, "I saw" (18:1; see 7:2; 10:1; 14:6; 14:14; 19:17); (2) object of vision: ἄλλον ἄγγελον, "another angel" (18:1; see 7:2; 10:1; 14:6; 14:8; 14:9; 14:15; 14:18; 19:17); (3) the angel moves (ascends, descends, flies, emerges) to the center of the action (18:1; see 7:2; 10:1; 14:6; 14:8; 14:9; 14:15; 14:18; 19:17); (4) the angel "cries with a loud voice" (18:2a; see 7:2; 10:3; 14:7; 14:9; 14:15; 14:18; 19:17); and (5) the angel utters a brief statement (18:2b–3; see 7:3; 10:3; 14:7; 14:8; 14:9b–11; 14:15b; 14:18b; 19:17b–18). The frequent occurrence of this literary form in Revelation and its general absence elsewhere strongly suggest that 18:1–3 comes from the hand of the author-editor of Revelation.

Rev 18:4–8, which interrupts the continuity of the ritual lament in vv 1–3 and 9–20, is attributed to an unidentified "heavenly voice," which mentions the future fall of Babylon. It conforms to a particular prophetic form found in the OT, the *summons to flight* (*Aufforderung zur Flucht*), consisting of an initial summons to flee (vv 4–5) followed by a threat of judgment (vv 6–8). Though found in earlier historical narratives (1 Sam 15:6; 22:5), the form is most often found in the writing prophets, particularly Jeremiah (e.g., Jer 4:4–5; 6:1; 48:6–8). Flight from Babylon is specifically enjoined in Jer 50:8–10; 51:6–10; 51:45–48 (a later addition to the Hebrew text); Isa 48:20–22 (using imagery from the flight from Egypt); and Isa 52:11–12. The form is also found in Christian prophecies (Mark 13:14–20; Eusebius *Hist. eccl.* 3.5.3; Epiphanius *Haer.* 29.7; 30.2; *De mens. et pond.* 15 [Migne, *PG,* 43.261B]; see Matt 2:13, 19–20; Aune, *Prophecy,* 311–12). The command "Come out of her!" (v 4b) is followed by the reason for the command (v 5), an encouragement to pay back Rome double for what she has done (v 6). The reason for leaving the city is because of the imminent arrival of plagues: disease, famine, and conflagration (vv 4cd, 8). In the present context these plagues must be those associated with the seven trumpets and seven bowls. Sandwiched in between the threats of v 6 and v 8 is a brief monologue attributed to Babylon-Rome in v 7b, intended to dramatize the claim made in v 7a that she has "glorified herself and lived sensually" and should therefore be repaid by torment and grief. In v 7b Babylon-Rome personified says in her heart, "I sit as queen. / I am not a widow; / sorrow will I never see." The hybris of Babylon-Rome is brought home to the reader clearly and forcefully through this brief speech. A similar rhetorical device is the more lengthy monologue attributed to Jerusalem personified as a widow and as a mother bereft of her children in Bar 4:9b–16. The humility and degradation of this speech contrast vividly with the pride of the speech of Babylon-Rome in 18:7b.

The ritual lament begun in vv 1–3 is resumed in vv 9–20. However, vv 9–20 have a different literary character than vv 1–3, since the latter exhibit the features of a lament that has been transformed into a *taunt song*, while the element of mockery is completely absent from the three ritual laments in vv 9–20 (their ritual character, however, is revealed by the stereotypical features they contain). The motif of different mourners speaking in the first person probably belongs to the ancient form of the ritual lament in which different parts were assigned to solo voices or choral groups, a motif that is later transposed into third-person descriptions (Jahnow, *Leichenlied*, 102, 219). The historical lament for the fall or destruction of cities is a poetic form (later adapted to prose) with a long history in both the Greek world (Alexiou, *Ritual Lament*, 83–101) and in Israel and the ancient Near East (Eissfeldt, *Introduction*, 91–98). The funeral dirge, originally used to lament the death of an individual (e.g., David's lament for Jonathan in 2 Sam 1:17–27 and David's lament for Abner in 2 Sam 3:1–3), was extended to apply to the defeat and destruction of communities or societies in which their downfall was spoken of as their "death" (see the three laments over the fall of Jerusalem in Lam 1, 2, and 4). A prophetic adaptation of the lament over a fallen nation is found in Amos 5:1–3, and an example of the prophetic adaptation of the taunt song is found in Isa 14:4–23.

In vv 9–20 John has incorporated three laments spoken in the *personae* of those sympathetic to Babylon, i.e., those enriched by their dealings with the city, and the content of each threnody is determined by the role assumed by the speaker: (1) The kings of the earth (vv 9–10; cf. Ezek 26:15–18) express the most impersonal of the laments and stand the farthest away from the destruction of Babylon. (2) The merchants of the earth (vv 15–17a), who weep and mourn because they have lost their single best customer, sing of the luxurious commodities that inhabitants of the city once enjoyed. Their lament is prefaced in vv 12–13 by a list of luxury goods (cf. Ezek 27:12–24) that are no longer marketable in Babylon-Rome. (3) The sea captains and sailors (vv 17b–19; cf. Ezek 27:29b–36) lament that the flourishing lucrative maritime trade with Babylon-Rome is over. Particularly in the last two laments, vv 15–17a and 17b–19, the emphasis is on the contrast between past and present conditions.

Each of these three brief threnodies (vv 9–10, 15–17a, 17b–19) consists of four stereotyped elements: (1) Each group is said to "stand afar off" (v 10, ἀπὸ μακρόθεν ἑστηκότες, "standing far off"; v 15, ἀπὸ μακρόθεν στήσονται, "will stand far off"; and v 17, ἀπὸ μακρόθεν ἔστησαν, "stand far off"). Note how the author achieves variety of expression only by varying the form of the verb. (2) Each group is described as weeping and wailing or mourning; kings: κλαύσουσιν καὶ κόψονται, "will weep and wail" (v 9a); merchants: κλαίουσιν καὶ πενθοῦσιν, "weep and mourn" (v 11a);

κλαίοντες καὶ πενθοῦντες, "weeping and mourning" (v 15b); sea captains and sailors: κλαίοντες καὶ πενθοῦντες, "weeping and mourning" (v 19a). (3) Each lament begins with the formula οὐαὶ οὐαί, "Alas! alas!" (vv 10, 16, 19). (4) Each lament concludes with the formula ὅτι μιᾷ ὥρᾳ, "for in one hour," characterizing the suddenness of Babylon's fall (vv 10b, 17a, 19b). While these three laments are in part modeled after Ezek 26–28, there are also a number of other features in Rev 18:9–20 that have been adapted from other ritual laments in the OT and perhaps even from the laments used in the Greek world. Two formulas characterize the lament in the OT: (1) They often begin with the term אֵיךְ *'êk* or אֵיכָה *'êkâ*, "alas! how!" (e.g., 2 Sam 1:19, 25, 27; Ezek 26:17; Lam 1:1; 2:1; 4:1; all translated by πῶς in the LXX). (2) They often contain imperative forms of verbs meaning "to weep, mourn." The Hebrew terms for this mocking adaptation of the lament are מָשָׁל *māšāl*, "taunt song" (Isa 14:4), and קִינָה *qînâ*, "lament" (Ezek 27:2; 28:12; 32:2, 16). The Greek tradition of poetic laments for cities or nations follows slightly different conventions. They characteristically begin with a rhetorical question introduced by the interrogative adverb ποῦ, "where?" in the first line of a stanza, with the answer provided in the last line of the stanza, e.g., the epigram of Antipater of Sidon (*Pal. Anth.* 9.151; LCL tr.):

Where [ποῦ] is thy celebrated beauty, Doric Corinth?
Where [ποῦ] are the battlements of thy towers and thy ancient possessions?
Where [ποῦ] are the temples of the immortals, the houses and the matrons of the town of Sisyphus, and her myriads of people?
Not even a trace is left of thee, most unhappy of towns, but war has seized on and devoured everything.

For other examples, see Agathias Scholasticus in *Pal. Anth.* 9.153; Aelius Aristides *Or.* 18, a μονῳδία, or prose "lament," over Smyrna when destroyed by an earthquake early in 178 A.D., with a θρηνῳδία, "dirge, lament," in 18.7–10; and an anonymous fragment of a tragedy quoted in Alexiou, *Ritual Lament*, 84–85. Very similar to the laments in Rev 18:9–19, however, is the lament over the fall of Persia in Aeschylus *Persians* 249–52 (LCL tr.):

O [ὦ] ye cities of all the land of Asia,
O [ὦ] realm of Persia, and bounteous haven of wealth,
How at a single stroke [ὡς ἐν μιᾷ πληγῇ] has all your plenteous weal been shattered, and the flower of the Persians fallen and perished!

The group of three dirges concludes with a cry of joy in v 20, a taunt motif thematically linked to the taunt of vv 2–3 with which the chapter begins, thus providing a literary frame for vv 4–19. This cry of joy is appended to earlier material by the author and calls for the rejoicing of heaven, saints, apostles, and prophets over the fate of Babylon.

Rome is presented in vv 11–14 using the *topos* of the central world market, first found in Isocrates (*Panegyricus* 42), who describes the Piraeus as the center of Hellas, just as Strabo refers to Alexandria as the greatest emporium of the world (17.1.13); see Oliver, *Ruling Power*, 910. The extensive Roman trade in silver, gold, ivory, amber, crystal, ebony, jewelry, and rare dyes was proverbial (Dio Chrysostom *Or.* 13.34–36; Aelius Aristides *Or.* 17.11–13). The cities of Roman Asia, primarily located on waterways, were important trade routes from the Anatolian interior to the sea. The major products of Asia Minor, many of which were exported through Ephesus, included many of those listed in 18:12–13, such as wine, oil, marble, pottery, parchment, timber, horses, emeralds, gold, silver, iron, wool, linen, dyed fabrics, and tapestry. Aelius Aristides, writing in praise of Rome (*Or.* 26.11–13; tr. C. A. Behr, LCL), emphasizes her wealth and role in world trade:

> Here [Rome] is brought from every land and sea all the crops of the seasons and the produce of each land, river, lake, as well as of the arts of the Greeks and barbarians, so that if someone should wish to view all these things, he must either see them by traveling over the whole world or be in this city. It cannot be otherwise than that there always be here an abundance of all that grows and is manufactured among each people. So many merchant ships arrive here, conveying every kind of goods from every people every hour and every day, so that the city is like a factory common to the whole earth. It is possible to see so many cargoes from India and even from Arabia Felix, if you wish, that one imagines that for the future the trees are left bare for the people there and that they must come here to beg for their own produce if they need anything. Again there can be seen clothing from Babylon and ornaments from the barbarian world beyond, which arrive in much larger quantity and more easily than if merchantmen bringing goods from Naxus or Cythnus had only put into Athens. Your farmlands are Egypt, Sicily, and all of Africa which is cultivated. The arrivals and departures of the ships never stop, so that one would express admiration for the harbor, but even the sea. . . . So everything comes together here, trade, seafaring, farming, the scourings of the mines, all the crafts that exist or have existed, all that is produced and grown. Whatever one does not see here, is not a thing which has existed or exists, so that it is not easy to decide which has the greater superiority, the city in regard to the present day cities, or the empire in regard to the empires which have gone before.

In Seneca's tragedy *Hercules Oetaeus* 659–69 (tr. F. J. Miller, LCL), the author characterizes the life of the poor man's wife as innocent of luxuries, implicitly condemning luxury for the simple older ways:

> The poor man's wife no necklace wrought
> Of costly pearls, the red sea's gift,
> May wear; no gems from eastern shores
> Weigh down her ears; nor does she wear
> Soft scarlet wools in Tyrian dye
> Twice dipped; not hers with Lydian art
> To 'broider costly silks whose threads
> The Serians under sunlit skies
> From orient treetops gather; she
> With common herbs must dye the web
> Which she with unskilled hands has wov'n.

The list of twenty-eight types of trade goods brokered by the merchants of the earth in vv 12–13 has some similarities with the list in Ezek 16:9–13 (an allegory about Jerusalem, described as a young girl who has become queen and wears a luxurious costume, features completely obscured in *Tg. Jer.* 16:9–13), and particularly with Ezek 27:5–24 (describing in luxurious detail the wealth of the king of Tyre, all of which will sink into the depths of the sea like the ship that brought them from afar [Ezek 27:25–36]). In Rev 18:12–13, however, the extensive list of luxurious trade goods consumed by Rome takes the form of a litany consisting of twenty-nine items, each connected to the previous item with the conjunctive particle καί, "and," making the whole list an example of polysyndeton (see Aune, "De esu carnium," 309, with examples of *polysyndeton* from Hellenistic literature; BDF § 460; see also Rev 5:12). Polysyndeton produces the effect of "extensiveness and abundance by means of an exhaustive summary" (BDF § 460); i.e., it rhetorically emphasizes the conspicuous consumption of Rome. For other examples of polysyndeton in Revelation, see 4:11; 5:12, 13; 7:12. Using this rhetorical device, the author deftly conveys the profound materialism of Rome/Babylon.

The list begins with the phrase γόμον χρυσοῦ, "merchandise consisting of gold" (χρυσοῦ, "of gold," here is a genitive of apposition, as are the seven nouns or noun groups that follow it). Of the twenty-eight types of goods, the first eight are genitives, concordant with χρυσοῦ, and fourteen are nouns or noun groups in the accusative, the objects (like γόμον, "merchandise") of the verb ἀγοράζειν, "buy" (the third of these fourteen nouns or noun groups governs four nouns in the genitive governed by the single preposition ἐκ, "of, from," following the phrase πᾶν σκεῦος ἐκ, "every kind of vessel of": ξύλου τιμιωτάτου, "fine wood," χαλκοῦ, "brass," σιδήρου, "iron," and μαρμάρου, "marble." Then the author concludes the list with three plural genitives of apposition (picking up again the concordance with χρυσοῦ). Finally, he ends with the phrase καὶ ψυχὰς ἀνθρώπων, and here καί is epexegetical so that the phrase should be translated "namely, human souls." This oscillation from genitive to accusative to genitive to accusative is an example of *oratio variata*, i.e., heterogeneous structure (see Robertson, *Grammar*, 440–44).

In one passage Pliny makes a list of the most valuable products from various parts of the natural world outside Italy (*Hist. nat.* 37.204; LCL tr. with modifications); thirteen of the twenty-eight items found in Rev 18:12–13 are mentioned (those found in Rev 18:12–13 are italicized):

The most costly product of the sea is the *pearl;* of the earth's surface, rock-crystal; of the earth's interior, *diamonds, emeralds, gemstones* [Revelation uses the generic expression "precious stones"] and vessels of fluor-spar of the earth's increase, the scarlet kermes-insect and silphium, with spikenard and *silks* from leaves, *citrus wood,* balsam, *myrrh* and *frankincense,* which exude from trees or shrubs, and costus from roots. As for animals... the most costly product found on land is the *elephant's tusk* [ivory], and on sea the turtle's shell. Of the hides and coats of animals, the most costly are the pelts dyed in China and the Arabian she-goat's tufted beard which we call "ladanum." Of creatures that belong to both land and sea, the most costly products are *scarlet* and *purple* dyes made from shell-fish. . . . We must not forget to mention that *gold* for which all mankind has so mad a passion, comes scarcely tenth in the list of valuables, while *silver,* with which we purchase gold, is almost as low as twentieth.

For similar lists of luxury imports see Statius *Silvae* 5.1.60–61, 210–16. As many as five of the luxury products mentioned in Rev 18:12–13 are found in the brief account in *T. Abr.* (Rec. A) 4:2–3 (tr. E. P. Sanders, *OTP* 1:883 with modifications), where Abraham requests that his best possessions be used in entertaining his angelic guest:

Prepare for us there a dining couch and a lampstand and a *table* [τράπεζαν] with an abundance of everything good. Beautify the chamber, my child, and spread linen and *purple cloth* [πορφύραν] and *fine linen* [βύσσον] underfoot. Burn every valuable and prized *incense*, and bring fragrant plants from the garden to fill our house. Light seven lamps filled with *oil* so that we may make merry . . . .

In this context all these items are clearly associated with extravagance.

Martial (9.59) satirizes a shopping spree of a wealthy Roman named Mamurra, in which he examines and rejects as inferior many of the goods catalogued by John. Similarly, Dio Chrysostom (*Or.* 13.34; LCL tr.) tells the Athenians that material resources without moral resources are worthless (one of his favorite themes; see his advice to Tarsus in *Or.* 33.23; C. P. Jones, *Chrysostom*, 73) in a polysyndetic catalogue of ten luxury items:

> For only then, I continued, will your city be great [ἡ πόλις μεγάλη; cf. Rev 18:10, 21] and strong and truly imperial, since at present its greatness arouses distrust and is not very secure. For in proportion as courage, justice, and temperance increase among you, in that degree there will be less silver and gold and furniture of ivory and of amber, less of crystal and citron-wood and ebony and women's adornments and embroideries and dyes of many hues; in short, all the things which are now considered in your city precious and worth fighting for, you will need in smaller quantities, and when you have reached the summit of virtue, not at all.

The stanza of four poetic lines in Rev 18:16–17a is very carefully arranged. The first list consists of two expressions of lamentation linked to a noun and an adjective: οὐαὶ οὐαί, ἡ πόλις ἡ μεγάλη, "Alas, alas, you great city" (the same line occurs verbatim in vv 10b and 19b). Each of the next two lines begins with a feminine perfect passive participle followed by three polysyndetic dependent nouns or adjectives functioning as nouns (the author frequently lists items in groups of three), the first line focusing on luxurious garments, the second on expensive jewelry:

16b	ἡ περιβεβλημένη	βύσσινον	πορφυροῦν	κόκκινον
	Dressed in	fine linen	purple	scarlet
16c	κεχρυσωμένη	χρυσίῳ	λίθῳ τιμίῳ	μαργαρίτῃ
	Adorned with	gold	precious stones	pearls

The καί linking περιβεβλημένη with κεχρυσωμένη indicates that the definite article goes with both substantival participles, which then describe a single reality. The economy of these lines suggests the secondary character of ἐν before χρυσίῳ attested in some MSS (see *Note* 18:16.h.). The adjectives πορφυροῦν and κόκκινος link this verse with the description of the clothing of the whore in 17:4 (where the adjectives occur in the same order), suggesting a connection before the final redaction of Rev 17 and that of Rev 18 (17:4 was probably adapted to 18:16). Finally, the fourth line announces the juridical fulfillment of the announcement of judgment implied in the first line: "for in a moment such fabulous wealth was destroyed."

An angel then throws a millstone into the sea, an action symbolizing the downfall of "Babylon" (vv 21–24). Fohrer (*Handlungen*, 17) enumerates thirty-two examples of symbolic prophetic actions in the OT (e.g., 1 Kgs 22:11; 2 Kgs 13:14–19; Isa 7:10–17; 8:1–4; 20:2–6; Jer 19:1–5; 28:10–11; 32:6–44; Ezek 4:1–3, 4–8, 9–17; 5:1–17). The angel's action here contains two of the three elements typical of the "reports of prophetic symbolic actions" found in OT prophets (see Fohrer, *ZAW* 64 [1952]

101–20; id., *Handlungen,* 17–19, 20–71): (1) a report of a symbolic act performed by a prophet (v 21a) and (2) an interpretation of the prophetic action (vv 21b–23). The element that normally occurs first in the OT examples of such symbolic prophetic acts, the command of Yahweh, is missing. The first element in v 21a is unlike OT symbolic prophetic acts in that here in the setting of apocalyptic prophecy an *angel,* rather than a prophet, performs the action, which John has modeled after a similar action reported in Jer 51:63–64, where Jeremiah is told to throw a stone into the Euphrates, symbolizing Babylon who will sink to rise no more. The second element in vv 21b–23 is unlike typical OT symbolic acts in that the author has used the interpretation as a basis for a series of plaintive vignettes of city life that are gone forever. This text unit is composed with extreme care. The statement that Babylon exists no longer (καὶ οὐ μὴ εὑρεθῇ ἔτι) in v 21c is used as the basis for vv 22–23b, which contain five couplets in which the first line refers to a typical feature of urban life and the second has the stereotypical phrase οὐ μὴ . . . ἐν σοὶ ἔτι, "will never be [heard, found, seen] in you again." Babylon is referred to in the third person by the angel in v 21. After addressing Babylon directly in the second person singular in vv 22–23 (cf. v 14), the author resumes the third person again, referring to Babylon with the pronoun αὐτῇ, "her," in v 24. This inclusio is further marked by the use of the verb εὑρεθῆναι, "be found," in both v 21 and v 24, though with two different meanings.

III. The Influence of Jeremiah

The depiction of the judgment of Babylon-Rome in Rev 18:2–8, 21–24 includes a number of allusions to Jer 50–51 (LXX 27–28), where the focus is on the judgment of Babylon (C. Wolff, *Jeremia,* 167–69). While each of of these allusions is discussed in more detail below under *Comment,* they are listed here in tabular form to convey the pervasive influence that Jer 50–51 has had on Rev 18:

18:2a	Jer 51:8(LXX 28:8); Isa 21:9
18:2b	Jer 51:37(LXX 28:37)
18:3	Jer 51:7(LXX 28:7)
18:4	Jer 51:6(LXX 28:6)
18:5	Jer 51:9(LXX 28:9)
18:6	Jer 50:29(LXX 27:29); cf. Jer 16:18
18:8	cf. Jer 50:32, 34; 51:30, 32, 58
18:20	Jer 51:48 (not in LXX)
18:21	Jer 51:64(LXX 28:64)
18:22c–23b	Jer 25:10
18:23b	Jer 7:34; 16:9; 25:10; 33:11; cf. Bar 2:23
18:24	Jer 51:49(LXX 28:49)

IV. Source-Critical Analysis

R. H. Charles (2:87–95) proposed that Rev 18:2–23 was based on a Jewish source originally written in Hebrew but available to the author in a Greek translation during the reign of Vespasian. Charles based his view on the following arguments: (1) The diction of this section differs from the rest of the book. (2) This section contains none of the author's characteristic abnormal Greek constructions found in the rest of the book. (3) This section contains constructions that are wholly against the author's normal usage: (a) The construction οὐαί + nominative (18:10[2x], 16[2x], 19[2x]) is used rather than οὐαί + accusative (8:13; 12:12); and (b) ἐν ἰσχυρᾷ φωνῇ (18:2) has the order adjective + noun. With the exception of 16:1, elsewhere the author uses the order noun + adjective in the analogous phrase φωνὴ μεγάλη (1:10; 5:2, 12; 6:10; 7:2, 10; 8:13; 10:3; 11:12, 15; 12:10; 14:7, 9, 15, 18; 16:17; 19:1, 17; 21:3), and he never uses the adjective ἰσχυρός elsewhere with φωνή (though note that φωνὴ μεγάλη occurs in *Par. Jer.* 2:2, alongside μεγάλη φωνή in *Par. Jer.* 5:32; 7:15). (4) The order of this section is much less Semitic than passages in the rest of the book. While these arguments suggest that Rev 18 was not composed at the same time as the rest of the book, they are not adequate to demonstrate that the author has incorporated a document he has not written into the larger composition.

There are numerous aporias and other compositional features in Rev 18 that suggest the author has incorporated an existing text into the larger context of Rev 17:1–19:10. (1) Rev 18:1–3 is an *angelic speech,* a form that occurs nine times in Revelation (see the discussion above under II. Literary Analysis and *Form/Structure/ Setting* on Rev 7) but rarely elsewhere in apocalyptic literature. That this literary form occurs so frequently in Revelation and rarely elsewhere indicates that 18:1–3 was certainly composed by the author-editor of Revelation as an introduction to 18:4–24 as well as a link to 17:1–18. (2) Rev 18:12–13, the list of luxury trade goods that the merchants of the earth can no longer ship to Babylon-Rome, appears to be a later excursus inserted into an earlier text at this point. (3) Rev 18:14 is a fragment of a speech directed to Babylon-Rome in the style of 18:21–23 but lacks any identification of the speaker or speakers (unless one is to assume that it is spoken by the merchants), and it is not introduced with a verb of saying or speaking as are the other speeches in Rev 18 (vv 10, 16, 19, 21). This fragment deals with luxury goods (ripe fruit, expensive and beautiful trinkets) that are no longer available to the populace of Babylon-Rome. Both vv 12–13 and v 14 are framed by the phrases κλαίουσιν καὶ πενθοῦσιν, "they weep and wail" (v 11a), and κλαίοντες καὶ πενθοῦντες, "weeping and wailing" (v 15b). (4) The description of the luxurious garments and jewels of Babylon-Rome given in the lament of the merchants in v 16 is closely parallel to 17:4 and appears to have been borrowed from that context and inserted in 18:16 in order to link the two chapters. (5) Rev 18:20 and 18:24 are the only explicitly Christian features in Rev 18 and therefore appear to be later additions by the author-editor as an attempt to connect this chapter with other themes in Revelation. (6) The plaintive poetic description in vv 22–23b ends abruptly with the mention in v 23c that the merchants of Babylon were the power brokers of the world. There is no obvious relationship between this line and its context, nor is it obvious why the statement that all nations were deceived by Babylon's magic is included in v 23d.

On the basis of this brief analysis, it appears that the earliest textual unit underlying Rev 18 in its present form consisted of (1) the summons to flight (vv 4–8), (2) the three songs of lament (vv 9–11, 15, 17–19), and (3) the symbolic destruction of Babylon (vv 21–23).

Comment

1a μετὰ ταῦτα εἶδον ἄλλον ἄγγελον καταβαίνοντα ἐκ τοῦ οὐρανοῦ ἔχοντα ἐξουσίαν μεγάλην, "After this I saw another angel with extraordinary authority descending from heaven." The phrase "after this I saw" is used in Revelation to introduce new textual units (4:1; 7:1, 9; 15:5; 19:1), and the phrase "another angel" is an editorial link referring back to the interpreting angel in 17:1, 3, 7, 15. The verb εἶδον, "I saw," also marks the following textual unit (vv 1–3) as a *vision* (while vv 4–20 are introduced as an *audition*). The perception that the angel wielded great authority is obviously a commentary by the author rather than a visible part of the angelophany.

1b καὶ ἡ γῆ ἐφωτίσθη ἐκ τῆς δόξης αὐτοῦ, "and the earth was illuminated by his splendor." This phrase is a relatively close rendering of the Hebrew text of Ezek 43:2, "the earth shone with his glory" (referring, however, to Yahweh), which exhibits several differences from the LXX version (Vanhoye, *Bib* 43 [1962] 437). This is the only instance in Revelation in which an angelic being is described as having δόξα, "glory, splendor," a term usually reserved as a designation for the presence of God (Rev 15:8; 21:11, 23; see *Comment* on 15:8). The attribution of δόξα or כבוד *kābôd* to angelic beings occurs in Ezek 9:3; 10:4, 18, 22; Heb 9:5; cf. Sir 49:8.

2a καὶ ἔκραξεν ἐν ἰσχυρᾷ φωνῇ λέγων, ἔπεσεν ἔπεσεν Βαβυλὼν ἡ μεγάλη, "Then he cried with a mighty voice, saying, 'Fallen, fallen is Babylon the great.'" This phrase, which also occurs in 14:8 (see the more extensive *Comment* there), is probably an allusion to Isa 21:9 (Fekkes, *Isaiah*, 204–5, 213–14); cf. Jer 51:8(LXX 28:8), καὶ ἄφνω ἔπεσεν Βαβυλών, "And immediately Babylon fell." In LXX Isa 21:9 the double verb occurs in MS B (and two lesser MSS): πέπτωκεν πέπτωκεν Βαβυλών, "Babylon has fallen, fallen," though this is a literal rendering of the Hebrew נָפְלָה נָפְלָה בָּבֶל *nāpĕlâ nāpĕlâ bābel*, "fallen, fallen, is Babylon." The aorist verbs ἔπεσεν ἔπεσεν, "fallen, fallen," emphasize the certainty of the fall of Babylon-Rome, which, from the standpoint of the speaker, is an event that has not yet occurred (this same phrase also occurs in Rev 14:8). This is an example of the *perfectum propheticum*, "prophetic perfect," used to describe a future event with a verb in the past tense as if it had already happened (GKC § 106n; Mussies, *Morphology*, 338). The phrase "fallen, fallen is so-and-so" originated as a lament uttered upon the death of an individual and is transferred to the actual or anticipated demise of a political unit such as a tribe, city, or nation (Eissfeldt, *Introduction*, 91–92; Yarbro Collins, "Revelation 18," 192–93). The term πίπτειν, "fall," was frequently used in the ancient world in the metaphorical sense of a person's violent death, usually in war (Exod 32:28; 1 Sam 4:10; 2 Sam 1:19, 25, 27; 3:38; 21:22; Job 14:10 [LXX only]; 1 Chr 5:10; 20:8; 1 Macc 3:24; 4:15, 34; 2 Macc 12:34; Jdt 7:11; Gk. *1 Enoch* 14:6; 1 Cor 10:18; *Barn.* 12:5; *Iliad* 8.67; 10.200; 11.157, 500; Xenophon *Cyr.* 1.4.24; Herodotus 9.67). The name "Babylon" occurs several times in Revelation (14:8; 16:19; 17:5; 18:2, 10, 21). (On the title "Babylon the great," see *Comment* on 14:8.) While most commentators assume that "Babylon" is a code name for Rome (Bousset [1906] 384; Charles, 2:62–63; Müller, 267, 288–89), Lohmeyer rejects the view that Rome is specifically in view, since "Babylon" is a term used in the OT and Judaism for the earthly power opposed to God; no more specification is necessary (138–39, 147). Kraft identifies Rome with the "Babylon" of Rev 17 but not that of Rev 18 (229, 234), and other scholars understand "Babylon" of Rev 18 to represent Jerusalem (Ford, 285–86, 296–307; Beagley, *Apocalypse*, 92–102; Provan, *JSNT* 64 [1996] 91–97). The historical fall of Rome occurred in August of A.D. 410 when the city was pillaged by Alaric and his army of Goths.

2b καὶ ἐγένετο κατοικητήριον δαιμονίων καὶ φυλακὴ παντὸς πνεύματος ἀκαθάρτου, "It has become the habitation of demons, / a preserve for unclean spirits." This and what follows is an allusion to Isa 13:21–22a, where the devastation following the destruction of Babylon is graphically depicted using the *topos* of the deserted city as a dwelling place for wild animals:

> [21]But wild animals will lie down there,
>   and its houses will be full of howling creatures;
> there ostriches will live,
>   and there goat-demons will dance.
> [22a]Hyenas will cry in its towers,
>   and jackals in the pleasant palaces. (NRSV)

It is also possible that there is an allusion here to Jer 51:37 (LXX 28:37), a possibility made more likely by the presence of seven other allusions to Jer 51 in Rev 18 (see *Form/Structure/Setting* on Rev 18, III. The Influence of Jeremiah). The MT text of Jer 51:37, which is longer than the LXX text (which probably represents an earlier Hebrew text), is represented here by the RSV:

> And Babylon shall become a heap of ruins,
>   the haunt of jackals,
> a horror and a hissing,
>   without inhabitant.

The aftermath of the destruction of Nineveh is described similarly in Zeph 2:14 (NRSV):

> Herds shall lie down in it [Nineveh],
>   every wild animal;
> the desert owl and the screech owl
>   shall lodge on its capitals;
> the owl shall hoot at the window,
>   the raven croak on the threshold;
> for its cedar work will be laid bare.

The same *topos* is used to gloat over the destruction of Tyre in Isa 23:1 and Edom in Isa 34:11–15 (n.b. that Edom eventually became a code name for Rome in Jewish tradition; see 4 Ezra 6:7–10; *Gen. Rab.* 65.21). The emptiness and aridity of the location of a city punished by Yahweh is mentioned in Jer 50:12; 51:43. In Bar 4:35 it is predicted that the enemy of Israel will be destroyed by fire and inhabited by demons. Demons were associated with unsettled and desolate places (Isa 13:21; 34:14; Tob 8:3; Matt 12:43 = Luke 11:24; Mark 5:10). The threat of desolation is a frequently occurring theme in prophetic denunciations of nations and cities, including Judah and Jerusalem (Jer 4:26–27; 9:10–12; 22:5–6; Ezek 6:14; Hos 2:3; Joel 3:19; Zeph 2:13; Mal 1:3–4).

2c καὶ φυλακὴ παντὸς ὀρνέου ἀκαθάρτου καὶ μεμισημένου, "a preserve for every type of unclean and hateful bird." This may continue the allusion to Jer 51:37 (LXX 28:37), "And Babylon shall become a heap of ruins, the haunt of jackals, a horror and a hissing, without inhabitant." Yet similar phrases are used of Jerusalem in Jer 9:11, "I will make Jerusalem a heap of ruins, a lair of jackals; and I will make the cities of Judah a desolation, without inhabitant." It is of interest that when Trajan visited the famous Mesopotamian Babylon, ca. 115 A.D., he found it largely deserted, consisting mainly of mounds, stones, and ruins (Dio Cassius 68.30).

3a ὅτι ἐκ τοῦ οἴνου τοῦ θυμοῦ τῆς πορνείας αὐτῆς πέπτωκαν πάντα τὰ ἔθνη, "For all nations have collapsed because of the wine that is her immoral passion." The initial ὅτι, "for," introduces the first reason given for the devastation of Babylon, which centers on her negative influence on the nations. This negative influence is expressed differently in v 23: "For all the nations were deluded by your magic spells" (see *Comment* on v 23). The two additional clauses that are part of the ὅτι clause are given in v 3bc and constitute two additional reasons for the judgment of Rome (see *Comment* on v 3bc). This lament over the fall of Babylon is structured much like the lament over the impending fall of Israel in Amos 5:1–3, where the reason (introduced by יכּ *kî,* "for" in v 3) is provided by an oracle from Yahweh (see the analysis of H. W. Wolff, *Joel and Amos,* 231–32). Just as Israel had not yet fallen when Amos uttered that prophetic lament, so Rome had not yet fallen when John wrote Rev 18:1–3. The term θυμός, which means "intense desire" here (Louw-Nida, § 25.19), can also mean "fury," "intense anger" (Louw-Nida, § 88.178).

This verse replicates part of Rev 14:8: "Fallen, fallen is Babylon the great who gave all nations to drink of the wine of her passionate lust [ἐκ τοῦ οἴνου τοῦ θυμοῦ τῆς πορνείας αὐτῆς]." In the LXX the phrase πίνειν ἀπό, "drink from," + genitive occurs frequently, while πίνειν ἐκ, "drink from," + genitive occurs just once, in the expression πίνειν ἐκ τοῦ οἴνου, "drink from the wine" (LXX Gen 9:21; see Helbing, *Kasussyntax,* 134). Close parallels are found in several LXX texts: Jer 28:7[MT 51:7], ποτήριον χρυσοῦν Βαβυλὼν ἐν χειρὶ κυρίου μεθύσκον πᾶσαν τὴν γῆν· ἀπὸ τοῦ οἴνου αὐτῆς ἐπίοσαν ἔθνη, "Babylon is a golden cup in the hand of the Lord causing the entire earth to become drunken; from her wine the nations drank." In *Tg. Jer.* 51:7 the cup is not Babylon herself but rather the *sin* of Babylon, and mention is made (as in Rev 18:3) of the kings of the earth (tr. Hayward with italicized portions indicating additions to the Hebrew text):

> *Behold, like* the cup of gold *which was precious among all the vessels, so is the sin of* Babylon *exalted! Therefore mighty punishment is about to come to her from before the* Lord. All *the kings of the nations are about to be* inebriated from *her with langour, and* the nations shall drink *from the cup of her punishment:* therefore the nations shall be confused.

LXX Jer 32:15(MT 25:15) (cf. 32:17[MT 25:17]) says, Λαβὲ τὸ ποτήριον τοῦ οἴνου τοῦ ἀκράτου τούτου ἐκ χειρός μου καὶ ποτιεῖς πάντα τὰ ἔθνη, "Take the cup of this unmixed wine from my hand and cause all the nations to drink." Isa 51:17 uses the metaphor τὸ ποτήριον τοῦ θυμοῦ, "the cup of wrath." Greeks typically mixed wine with water in a vessel called a κρατήρ, "mixer"; they considered unmixed wine extremely potent (Diodorus Siculus 4.3.4; Athenaeus *Deipn.* 2.38c).

The term πέπτωκαν, "they collapsed," is used here with a double meaning since literal drunkenness can cause a person "to fall down," while metaphorically nations can "fall" or "suffer ruin" through their association with Babylon. On the fixed phrase πάντα τὰ ἔθνη, "all nations," see *Comment* on 12:5.

3b καὶ οἱ βασιλεῖς τῆς γῆς μετ᾽ αὐτῆς ἐπόρνευσαν, "For the kings of the earth fornicated with her." This is the second of three "reasons" for Babylon's fall introduced by the ὅτι clause in v 3a, though this appears to be an extremely flimsy reason for her fall. Who is to blame for committing fornication, the kings of the earth or Babylon? This can only be construed as a reason for Babylon's fall given the ancient and modern double standard that holds the woman rather than the man responsible for violating sexual mores. Given the occurrence of a parallel phrase in v 9, it is probable that that phrase was not originally part of the text but has been incorporated into the introduction to this pericope by the author. This is an allusion to Isa 23:17, also alluded to in v 9 and 17:2 (see *Comment* on 17:2), a formal feature that links Rev 17 and 18. V 3bc constitutes a synonymous couplet that is repeated with some variation in v 9:

Rev 18:3	*Rev 18:9*
καὶ οἱ βασιλεῖς τῆς γῆς for the kings of the earth	οἱ βασιλεῖς τῆς γῆς the kings of the earth
μετ᾽ αὐτῆς ἐπόρνευσαν fornicated with her,	οἱ μετ᾽ αὐτῆς πορνεύσαντες who fornicated with her
καὶ οἱ ἔμποροι τῆς γῆς and the merchants of the earth	καὶ and
ἐκ τῆς δυνάμεως τοῦ στρήνους αὐτῆς from her excessive luxury	στρηνιάσαντες lived in luxury [with her]
ἐπλούτησαν became rich.	

In this instance the author is clearly dependent on the Hebrew text of Isa 23:17 (see *Comment* on 17:2). In the OT, the term זנה *zānâ*, "fornicate, be a prostitute," is frequently used in a figurative sense of Israel's faithless behavior through frequent lapses into idolatry, a judgment based on the larger metaphor of the "marriage" between Yahweh and Israel presupposed in many OT texts (Lev 17:7; 20:5–6; Num 14:33; 15:39; Deut 31:16; Judg 2:17; 8:27; 1 Chr 5:25; 2 Chr 21:11; Ps 73:27; Hos 1:2; 2:4[MT 6]; 4:15; 9:1; Jer 2:20; 3:2, 9, 13; 5:7, 11; 13:27; Ezek 6:9; 16; 23; 43:7, 9; see Erlandsson, *TDOT* 4:101–4). However, since Yahweh and Babylon have no such "marriage" relationship, this language has nothing to do with the author's condemnation of Babylon-Rome. There are instances in the OT where the metaphor of prostitution is applied instead to the commercial trade of a city (Kuhn, *TDNT* 1:515 n. 11), perhaps because economic ties frequently led to the exchange of religious practices (Mic 1:7; Nah 3:4; 2 Kgs 9:22). In Isa 23:17, Tyre's commercial contacts are called "prostitution," and the profits of such trade are called "the price of a prostitute," while in Nah 3:4–7 Nineveh is denounced for her sexual debauchery and sorcery.

3c καὶ οἱ ἔμποροι τῆς γῆς ἐκ τῆς δυνάμεως τοῦ στρήνους αὐτῆς ἐπλούτησαν, "and the merchants of the earth became rich from her excessive luxury." This is the third of three reasons for the fall of Babylon introduced by the ὅτι, "for," clause in v 3a, and like v 3b, it too does not appear at first sight to be a valid reason. The "merchants of the earth," however, must include those involved with seafaring (see *Comments* on vv 17b–19) since that was the primary means for transporting merchandise from east to west. The Romans (paradigmatic landlubbers) had a fear of the sea that was reflected in Latin literature in a constellation of related *topoi* (K. F. Smith, *Tibullus*, 246–47; Beagon, *Roman Nature*, 159–61, 177–201). The unpredictable and destructive character of the sea meant that seafarers were fools attempting to do what was contrary to nature and against the will of the gods, and therefore impious (Horace *Odes* 1.3.23; Propertius 1.17.13; Seneca *Medea* 328; Pliny *Hist. nat.* 12.87; 19.3–6). Every ship was an insult to the sea and a deliberate challenge to the gods (Seneca *Medea* 340, 605, 668; Lucan 3, 193). The primary motive for seafaring was thought to be *greed:* "Nature has spread out the sea as a trap for the covetous" (Propertius 3.7.37 [tr. G. Lee, *Tibullus: Elegies*, 2nd ed. (Liverpool: Cairns, 1982) ad loc.]; Tibullus 1.3.39–40; cf. 1.9.9; 2.3.39; Euripides *Iphigeneia Taur.* 410; Seneca *Medea* 361; Pliny *Hist. nat.* 2.118). Conceptions of the golden age pointedly did not include seafaring: *improba navigii ratio tum caeca iacebat,* "Then the wanton art of sailing lay as yet unknown" (Lucretius *De rerum natura* 5.1006; cf. 2.552–68; 5.1000–13; Tibullus 1.3.35–40; Seneca *Hipp.* 530; Hesiod *Works* 236). The Roman view that seafarers were moral reprobates (Cicero *De officiis* 1.150) is also reflected in Hellenistic authors such as Philostratus *Vita Apoll.* 4.32 (LCL tr.; cf. Wettstein, *Novum Testamentum* 2:831):

> Well, and can you mention any rabble of people more wretched and ill-starred than merchants and skippers? In the first place they roam from sea to sea, looking for some market that is badly stocked; and then they sell and are sold, associating with factors and brokers, and they subject their own heads to the most unholy rate of interest in their hurry to get back the principal; and if they do well, their ship has a lucky voyage, and they tell you a long story of how they never wrecked it either willingly or unwillingly; but if their gains do not balance their debts, they jump into their long boats and dash their ships onto the rocks, and make no bones as sailors of robbing others of their substance, pretending in the most blasphemous manner that it is an act of God.

The clause in Rev 18:3c was probably drawn from v 15 (οἱ ἔμποροι τούτων οἱ πλουτήσαντες ἀπ' αὐτῆς, "the merchants in these commodities who have become wealthy by means of her") when vv 1–3 were prefixed to vv 4–23 by the author-editor. The theme of the wealth of Babylon-Rome occurs four times in this chapter: vv 3, 9, 16–17, and 19. This wealth was based on tax revenue, approximately 10 percent of the gross national product of the empire, from a low estimate of ca. 112 million silver *denarii* under Augustus (Frank, *Economic Survey* 5:7) to as much as 200 million silver *denarii* (Hopkins, *JRS* 70 [1980] 119). The inflow of tribute cash from the provinces was approximately balanced by the outflow of cash in private trade; that is, it caused the volume of trade in the Roman empire to increase greatly (Hopkins, *JRS* 70 [1980] 126; cf. Goldsmith, *Review of Income and Wealth* 30 [1984] 263; Millar, *Near East*, 49–50). The city of Rome, the center of imperial government, and the outer ring of provinces required an expensive military presence. They were not self-supporting but depended on imported tax revenues from the richer provinces such as Spain, northern Africa, southern Gaul, Asia Minor, Syria, and Egypt (Hopkins, *JRS* 70 [1980] 101). It is certainly interesting that no allusion to Roman taxation, including the sometimes excessive zeal and extortionate practices of the tax farmers, occurs in Rev 18. Of course, taxes could be sent to Rome in cash or in kind (e.g., olive oil from Spain; wheat from Egypt and North Africa), though the transportation of such goods was expensive. Taxes in kind, as opposed to taxes in currency, did not stimulate trade since they flowed from the taxpayer to the tax-consumer.

The *wealth* and *luxury* of Babylon-Rome is referred to four times in this chapter (18:3, 9, 16–17, 19), reflecting the fourfold mention of wealth found in Ezek 27 (vv 12, 18, 27, 33), which served as a literary model for much of Rev 18. The OT and subsequent Jewish literature contain occasional denunciations of the wealthy for a variety of reasons (cf. Hengel, *Eigentum,* 20–27 [ET 12–22])—their dishonest and violent practices (Amos 5:11; LXX Ps 75.5; Sir 13:13), their complacency (Amos 6:4–6), and their arrogance (Isa 2:7–9; 3:16–26; 5:8–10; Sir 13:20; *1 Enoch* 46:7; 94:8; 97:8–9; *Sib. Or.* 3.179–82, 350–488)—though wealth in and of itself does not have a negative connotation (Schmidt, *Wealth,* 49–60 [OT], 61–102 [Jewish non-canonical sources]). Schmidt argues convincingly that positive and negative evaluations of wealth exist side by side in Jewish as well as Greco-Roman prophetic, wisdom, and philosophical texts because hostility to wealth is a fundamental religious-ethical tenet that exists independently of actual socio-economic circumstances (*Wealth,* 164 and passim). Similarly, the OT and early Jewish literature contain occasional denunciations of merchants, not for their wealth but for the dishonest practices they used to gouge the poor (Jer 5:26–28; Hos 12:7; Amos 8:4–6; Mic 6:10–12; Sir 26:29–27:3; 37:11; 42:5). The term "poor" (עָנִי *ʿānî*), meaning one wrongfully impoverished, is the antonym of "violent," not "rich" (Bammel, *TDNT* 6:888). However, the wealth of political units (primarily cities) is occasionally criticized for the pride and self-satisfaction that accompany such wealth, as in Hos 12:8, "Ephraim has said, 'Ah, I am rich, I have gained wealth for myelf; in all of my gain no offense has been found in me that would be sin'" (cf. *1 Enoch* 98:2–3). The teaching of Jesus, however, does contain a radical critique of wealth (Luke 12:13 = Matt 6:24; Luke 7:22 = Matt 11:5; Luke 6:20; Luke 6:24–25; 12:16–21; Mark 10:23–25 = Matt 19:23–24 = Luke 18:24–25; 2 Cor 8:9; see Hengel, *Eigentum,* 31–38 [ET 23–30]; Schmidt, *Wealth,* 102–62). Nowhere in Rev 18, however, is there a hint of an economic reversal of the type occasionally found in Jewish apocalyptic texts (*Sib. Or.* 3.531–32, 657, 750, 783; *2 Apoc. Bar.* 70:4). In fact, Rev 18 does not deal with the issue of economic exploitation at all (Provan, *JSNT* 64 [1996] 87). Latin literature itself contains occasional denunciations of the Roman desire for luxury, often seen as a betrayal of the spartan values of the earlier Roman republic (Petronius *Satyricon* 119.1–36).

4a καὶ ἤκουσα ἄλλην φωνὴν ἐκ τοῦ οὐρανοῦ λέγουσαν, "Then I heard another voice from heaven, saying." For a discussion of the motif of the unidentified voice in Revelation, see *Comment* on 10:4. The introduction of this new voice indicates the beginning of a new textual subunit. While vv 1–3 are presented as a *vision* (similarly, a vision is implied in vv 21–24), vv 4–20 are introduced as an *audition.* The identification of the speaker is problematic, though the reference in v 4b to "my people" suggests that the speaker is God or Christ (Bousset [1906] 419; Swete, 228; Beckwith, 714; Charles, 2:97; Loisy, 317). The reference to God in the third person in v 5b, however, suggests that it is perhaps more logical to identify the speaker as Christ (Charles, 2:97; Allo, 290; Harrington, 215).

4b ἐξέλθατε ὁ λαός μου ἐξ αὐτῆς, "My people, come out of her." V 4 introduces a prophetic speech form in vv 4–8, the "summons to flight" (*Aufforderung zur Fluch*), found with some frequency in the OT prophetic books (see *Form/Structure/Setting,* II. Literary Analysis). The call for the people of God to leave Babylon in order not to partake of her sins and plagues alludes to several prophetic passages in the OT prophets, particularly Jer 51:45 (which is not found in the LXX): "Go out of the midst of her, my people" (see also Jer 50:8[LXX 27:8]; 51:6[LXX 28:6]; Isa 48:20; 52:11). The second-person plural aorist imperative ἐξέλθατε, "come out," is a *constructio ad sensum* (BDF § 134) that regards the singular noun group ὁ λαός μου, "my people," as a collective singular requiring a plural verb. The subjects of the four second-person plural imperatives in vv 6–7 are problematic (see *Comments* below on vv 6–7). It is generally agreed among commentators that the αὐτῆς, "her," from which the people of God are to flee, is Babylon, personified as a woman, used as a code name for Rome. If "Rome" is understood as the city of Rome (cf. 17:9, 18; 18:10, 16, 18, 21), the possibility is raised that this "summons to flight" is addressed specifically to the Christian community (or communities) of the *city* of Rome or the Roman *empire*. Since it is impossible to flee from the latter, Rissi argues that "Babylon" cannot symbolize Rome (*Babylon*, 55–56). It appears more likely, however, that the summons to flee from the city is used symbolically, with the city referring to the demonic social and political power structure that constituted the Roman empire, while the summons to flight refers to the necessity of Christians disentangling themselves and distancing themselves morally, and perhaps even socially, from the corrupt and seductive influences of Roman rule in Asia (Souza Nogueira, "Widerstand," 208–9). A parallel instance of a symbolic use of the prophetic "summons to flight" is found in 2 Cor 6:17, where Paul exhorts the Corinthians "to come out from them and be separate" (an allusion to Isa 52:11–12, which contains a literal prophetic "summons to flight"), i.e., to abstain from the idolatrous practices of pagan society (though no impending catastrophe is in view).

Though this "other voice" mentioned in v 4a is not identified, it must be the voice of either God or Christ (probably the former) since Christians are addressed as ὁ λαός μου, "my people" (a vocative in nominative form; see *Note* 4:11.a. for a more detailed discussion of this phenomenon in Revelation; see also 18:4, 10, 16, 19, 20[3x]).

4c ἵνα μὴ συγκοινωνήσητε ταῖς ἁμαρτίαις αὐτῆς, καὶ ἐκ τῶν πληγῶν αὐτῆς ἵνα μὴ λάβητε, "lest you participate in her sins, / and lest you share her suffering." The clause καὶ ἐκ τῶν πληγῶν αὐτῆς ἵνα μὴ λάβητε, "and lest you share her suffering," is very unusual in that the partitive genitive phrase that functions as the object of the verb λάβητε, "share," is placed before the ἵνα, "in order that," whereas in all other ἵνα clauses in Revelation (as in Greek usage generally) the subjects, objects, and indirect objects of the verbs governed by the ἵνα clause follow the ἵνα. The only obvious reason for this violation of normal Greek word order is to construct a poetic chiasm consisting of the abb'a' pattern:

a   ἵνα μὴ συγκοινωνήσητε
    Lest you participate

b   ταῖς ἁμαρτίαις αὐτῆς
       in her sins

b'   καὶ ἐκ τῶν πληγῶν αὐτῆς
       and in her sufferings

a' ἵνα μὴ λάβητε
    lest you share

V 4c may allude to the sense, if not the phraseology, of Jer 51:6b, where the people are warned to escape Babylon to avoid the imminent judgment of God: "Be not cut off in her punishment, / for this is the time of the Lord's vengeance, / the requital he is rendering her" (RSV). The unusual verb συγκοινωνεῖν, "participate in," occurs in the NT only here and in Eph 5:11, in both places in a similar context: καὶ μὴ συγκοινωνεῖτε τοῖς ἔργοις τοῖς ἀκάρποις τοῦ σκότους, "do not participate in the unfruitful deeds of darkness."

5a ὅτι ἐκολλήθησαν αὐτῆς αἱ ἁμαρτίαι ἄχρι τοῦ οὐρανοῦ, "For her sins have reached to heaven." This clause is an allusion to Jer 51:9, "for her [Babylon's] judgment has reached up to heaven [שְׁחָקִים šĕḥāqîm, literally 'clouds']." *Tg. Jer.* 51:9 reads (tr. Hayward), "for her destruction comes near to heaven, and is carried up to the heaven of heavens." According to Ezra 9:6, in the context of a penitential prayer, Ezra confesses that the peoples' "iniquities have risen higher than our heads, and our guilt has mounted up to the heavens" (see Jonah 1:2; 4 Ezra 11:43). The metaphor "to the heavens" is a hyperbolic way of emphasizing the magnitude of something (Gen 11:4; Deut 1:28; 9:1; 2 Chr 28:9). The conception of sins reaching heaven is a metaphor for the magnitude of sin with the implication that it threatens the sovereignty of God (Houtman, *Himmel,* 358). This metaphor is not restricted to the world of the OT and early Judaism, for in *Odyssey* 15.329, the swineherd Eumaios, commenting on the behavior of the suitors in the house of Odysseus, says that "their excessive pride and violence reaches to the iron heavens" (*Neuer Wettstein,* ad Rev 18:5), the term "iron" emphasizing that the gods have not acted to punish the suitors.

5b καὶ ἐμνημόνευσεν ὁ θεὸς τὰ ἀδικήματα αὐτῆς, "and God remembered her crimes." Only here in the NT is God the subject of a verb meaning "remember." The imperative form זְכֹר zĕkôr, or μνήσθητι, "remember," is often used in prayers in the OT in which the petitioner asks God to remember him or her (Judg 16:28; 2 Kgs 20:3; 2 Chr 6:42; Job 7:7; 10:9; Pss 74:2[LXX 73:2]; 89:50[LXX 88:50]; Isa 38:3). Similarly, the response of God to prayer is often presented in terms of his "remembering" his servants (Gen 8:1; 19:29; 30:22; 1 Sam 1:19; *Pss. Sol.* 5:16). God is said to come to the rescue of his people who are in dire circumstances by "remembering" his covenant with them (CDᵃ 1:4; 6:2). Sometimes (as in Rev 18:5 and 16:19) God "remembers" the wicked acts of the enemies of Israel and takes vengeance on them (Pss 25:7; 137:7; 1 Macc 7:38; see *TDNT* 4:675). The theme of remembering (μνήμη in inscriptions) appears in prayers that are inscribed on votive offerings (Versnel, "Ancient Prayer," 59ff.). Here that motif is used in an ironic sense, for it is the sins that have reached heaven, analogous to the smoke of sacrifices or incense or the prayers of the worshipers, and have provoked a response.

6a ἀπόδοτε αὐτῇ ὡς καὶ αὐτὴ ἀπέδωκεν καὶ διπλώσατε τὰ διπλᾶ κατὰ τὰ ἔργα αὐτῆς, "Render to her as she has rendered, / and repay her twice as much as she has done." This is an allusion to Jer 50:29b (LXX 27:29b), "Requite to her according to her deeds; do to her according to all that she has done [ἀνταπόδοτε αὐτῇ κατὰ τὰ ἔργα αὐτῆς, κατὰ πάντα ὅσα ἐποίησεν, ποιήσατε αὐτῇ]." The notion of a *double* recompense, which cannot be regarded as just retaliation (Exod 21:24–25; Lev 24:19–20; Deut 19:21), is probably based on Jer 16:18, καὶ ἀνταποδώσω διπλᾶς τὰς ἀδικίας αὐτῶν, "I will recompense their iniquities twofold" (cf. Isa 40:2). The idea of paying people back *double* for the evil they have done occurs with some frequency in Greek literature, though it is never claimed that this is just (Hesiod *Works* 709–11; *Iliad* 13.445–47; Theognis 1189–90; Sophocles *Oedipus Rex* 1320; Aeschylus

Agamemnon 537; Plato *Laws* 642e; Xenophon *Anabasis* 1.9.11; *Memorabilia* 2.6.35; cf. Blundell, *Enemies*, 30; Dover, *Morality*, 184, calls this "a head for an eye"). This is perhaps the reversal of the principle of generosity whereby someone is paid back double for what has been borrowed or taken from them (*T. Job* 4.7–8; cf. Luke 19:8, where Zacchaeus promises to pay back anyone he has defrauded *fourfold* the original amount). The notion of a sevenfold return of evil is found in Ps 79:12. In Greek literature the harming of one's enemy to the fullest extent allowed by the law is a commonplace (Solon *Frag.* 1 [ed. E. Diehl, *Anthologia Lyrica Graeca*, 3rd ed. (Leipzig: Teubner, 1954)]; Euripides *Medea* 807–10; *Ion* 1046–47; Plato *Meno* 71E; Isocrates *Ad Dem.* 26; Pindar *Pyth.* 2.83–85; Blundell, *Enemies*, 26–31), and the notion of τὸ ἀντιπεπονθός, "to suffer in return," i.e., *lex talionis*, is found among the Pythagoreans (Aristotle *Nic. Ethics* 1132b) and among other Greeks (Aeschylus *Choephoroi* 309–14; Thucydides 3.40.7; Aristotle *Top.* 113a; *Rhet.* 1367a). On the phrase κατὰ τὰ ἔργα, "according to [her] deeds," "as [she] has done," in a context of judgment, which occurs four times in Revelation (2:23; 18:6; 20:12, 13), see *Comment* on 2:23.

Variations on the retributive justice proverb "each will be repaid [frequently using the verbs ἀποδιδόναι or διδόναι] in accordance with his or her works [regularly κατὰ τὰ ἔργα]" occur frequently in the OT, early Jewish literature, and early Christian literature (LXX Pss 27:4[2x]; 61:13; Prov 24:12; Sir 16:12, 14; *Pss. Sol.* 2:34; 17:8; Isa 3:11; Jer 27:29; Lam 3:64; Rom 2:6; 2 Cor 11:15; 2 Tim 4:14; Ign. [longer rec.] *Ad Magnesios* 11:3; *2 Clem.* 17:4). The principle of *lex talionis* (i.e., "proportional retribution") from the Latin legal term *talio*, "payment in kind" (cf. A. Dihle, *Die goldene Regel: Eine Einführung in die Geschichte der antiken und frühchristlichen Vulgarethik* [Göttingen: Vandenhoeck & Ruprecht, 1962] 13–40), and exemplified by the OT phrase "an eye for an eye and a tooth for a tooth" (Exod 21:23–25; cf. Demosthenes 24.140–41; Diodorus 12.17.4), is a frequent motif in the prophetic judgment speeches of OT prophets (Isa 34:8; 59:18; 65:6–7; Ezek 9:10; 11:21; 16:43; 17:19; 22:31; 23:49; Hos 4:9; 12:2; Joel 3:4, 7[MT 4:4, 7]; Obad 15–16; see Prov 24:12) and early Jewish literature (Sib. Or. 3.312–14; *Apoc. Abr.* 29.19). It is also a motif in eschatological contexts in the NT (Matt 7:1–2 = Luke 6:37; 16:27; 2 Tim 4:14). A similar motif occurs in the farewell testament of Mattathias in 1 Macc 2:68, "Pay back the Gentiles in full [ἀνταπόδοτε ἀνταπόδομα τοῖς ἔθνεσιν]." In Ps 137:8 (LXX 136:8), the principle of *lex talionis* is applied to Babylon: "O daughter of Babylon, you devastator! Happy shall he be who requites you what you have done to us [ὃς ἀνταποδώσει σοι τὸ ἀνταπόδομά σου, ὃ ἀνταπέδωκας ἡμῖν]."

The important moral distinction between punishment and revenge is not reflected in this passage, though it is found in Greek sources as early as Protagoras (Plato *Protagoras* 324A–B). The Socrates in the dialogues of Plato (*Crito* 49B–C) argues that "we should never return an injustice [οὐδαμῶς δεῖ ἀδικεῖν]" and that "we should never return evil for evil [ἀντικακουργεῖν]" (cf. Vlastos, *Socrates*, 179–99). This view is presented much later in the teachings of Jesus (Matt 5:38–42 = Luke 6:27–31) and a few times elsewhere in the NT (Rom 12:17; 1 Cor 6:7; 1 Pet 2:19–20; 3:9).

The subject of the two second-person plural aorist imperatives ἀπόδοτε, "render," and διπλώσατε, "repay twice as much," is not immediately clear (nor is the subject of the other two imperatives, κεράσατε, "mix," in v 6b and δότε, "give," in v 7a). There are three main possibilities (see Elliott, *BR* 40 [1995] 98–113): (1) The most obvious possibility is that *Christians* are enjoined to take vengeance on Babylon (though this view is often rejected by commentators because it is thought to violate the NT teaching on love of enemies and non-retaliation); that is, the subjects of these imperatives are Christians who are encouraged to take revenge against Rome (Souza Nogueira, "Widerstand," 213). There are two main arguments for this view: (a) The first is a grammatical argument. The phrase ὁ λαός μου, "my people," in v 4, is certainly the subject of the second-person plural aorist imperative ἐξέλθατε, "come out," in v 4 (a *constructio ad sensum* in which the collective singular λαός is given a plural verb) and the second-person plural aorist subjunctives συγκοινωνήσητε, "participate," and λάβητε, "share," in v 4 (Minear, *New Earth*, 145; Court, *Myth and History*, 143). Likewise, it is logical to understand ὁ λαός μου as the subject of ἀπόδοτε and διπλώσατε here in v 6. (b) The righteous do occasionally act as agents of divine retribution in Jewish apocalyptic literature, perhaps in part as a legacy of the holy-war tradition (*1 Enoch* 90:19; 91:12; 95:3, 7; 96:1; 98:12; *Jub.* 23:30; *Apoc. Abr.* 29.17–20). According to the expectation expressed in *1 Enoch* 38:5 (tr. Knibb), "the mighty kings will at that time be destroyed and given into the hand of the righteous and the holy." In 1 Cor 6:2–3, Paul expects Christians to play an active role in judgment, though the motif of revenge is lacking. (2) The most popular proposal is that the subject of the imperatives is the "angels of punishment" (*Strafengeln*), variously specified as "spirits of vengeance" (Beckwith, 714), "ministers of Divine Justice" (Swete, 229), or "angelic agents of retribution" (Caird, 224). Angels of punishment who act as agents of divine judgment are familiar figures in early Jewish literature (*1 Enoch* 53:3; 56:1; 62:11; 63:1; 66:1; *3 Enoch* 31:2; 32:1; 33:1; *b. Šabb.* 55a; 88a; cf. P. S. Alexander, *OTP* 1:285 n. 31f; K. E. Grözinger, "Engel III," *TRE* 9:591; Michl, "Engel II," *RAC* 5:75–76). The weakness of this view lies in the abrupt shift from the "people" as collective subjects of the plural verbs in v 4 to another group that is never explicitly mentioned in the text. (3) Another proposal is that the subject of the imperatives is a group of people who are destined to act as divine agents in the destruction of Babylon, such as the ten kings of 17:16 (Bousset [1906] 420; Zahn, 573; Goppelt, *TDNT* 6:152). This view shares the same weakness as (2). (4) It has also been suggested that no particular group is addressed (Ruiz, *Ezekiel*, 403). Of these four possibilities, the arguments for the first are clearly the strongest. The main argument against Christians as agents of divine retribution, i.e., that this would violate the NT teaching on love for enemies and nonretaliation, is based not on the exegesis of the text but rather on a theological norm that was in all probability not uniformly espoused in early Christianity.

6b ἐν τῷ ποτηρίῳ ᾧ ἐκέρασεν κεράσατε αὐτῇ διπλοῦν, "In the cup in which she mixed, / mix for her a double portion." In the phrase ᾧ ἐκέρασεν, "which she mixed," the relative pronoun ᾧ, "which," is the only example in Revelation of a pronoun attracted to its antecedent (τῷ ποτηρίῳ, "the cup"). See Charles, 1:xxix, where he claims this phenomenon *never* occurs, though see 1:cxxii n. 2, where he admits that it occurs in Rev 18:6, though he regards this as a source.

7a ὅσα ἐδόξασεν αὐτὴν καὶ ἐστρηνίασεν, τοσοῦτον δότε αὐτῇ βασανισμὸν καὶ πένθος, "As she glorified herself and lived sensually, / so give to her torment and grief." In the biblical tradition, δόξα, "glory, honor, praise," is something that one properly ascribes to God (Deut 32:3; Josh 7:19; Isa 42:8; Jer 13:16; *T. Abr.* 15:5; *T. Jud.* 25:5; *T. Jos.* 8:5; *T. Job* 16.7; Matt 9:8; 15:31; Mark 2:12; John 9:24; Rom 4:20;

11:36; 1 Cor 6:20; 1 Pet 2:12; cf. Rom 1:21). Though one should not seek δόξα for oneself (Matt 6:2; John 12:43; 1 Thess 2:6), one can accept it from others if it is spontaneous and unsolicited (1 Thess 2:20; but cf. Acts 12:23) or if it is bestowed by God (Dan 5:18; *T. Iss.* 5:7; *T. Jos.* 10:3), which is the only kind of honor that can legitimately be sought after (John 5:44; 12:43). This tradition is encapsulated in Luke 14:11, "The one who exalts himself will be humbled, and the one who humbles himself will be exalted" (cf. Prov 29:23; Dan 5:20; Matt 18:4; 23:12; Luke 18:14; 2 Cor 11:7; Jas 4:10).

In the phrase ἐδόξασεν αὐτήν, "she glorified herself," the reflexive pronoun αὐτήν, "herself," is used as the object of an active verb (cf. John 7:18), while the same notion can be conveyed through the use of the middle voice, as in *T. Iss.* 1:9, where Leah says to Rachel, μὴ καυχῶ καὶ μὴ δοξάζου, "do not boast and do not glorify yourself" (see also *T. Benj.* 4:4). Of course, δόξα, "glory," and δοξάζειν, "to glorify," constitute just one set of cognates that can be used to express ὕβρις, the excessive pride condemned in Judeo-Christian as well as Greco-Roman moral thought (*NIDNTT* 3:27–28; *2 Apoc. Bar.* 12:3). Excessive pride is one of the hallmarks of the eschatological antagonist (see *Comment* on 13:5).

7b ὅτι ἐν τῇ καρδίᾳ αὐτῆς λέγει ὅτι κάθημαι βασίλισσα καὶ χήρα οὐκ εἰμὶ καὶ πένθος οὐ μὴ ἴδω, "For in her heart she says, 'I sit as queen. / I am not a widow; / sorrow will I never see.'" Babylon, personified as a woman, is represented in this soliloquy as claiming (in her heart) that she is a queen who will never be a widow and experience mourning. This soliloquy is based on Isa 47:8, "Now therefore hear this, you lover of pleasures, who sit securely, who say in your heart, 'I am, and there is no one besides me; I shall not sit as a widow or know the loss of children.'" This may be designated a *hybris soliloquy*, a short literary form that occurs several times in the OT and early Jewish and early Christian literature, as well as in Greco-Roman literature. I cite six examples: (1) Ezek 28:2, "Because your heart is proud, / and you have said, 'I am a god; I sit in the seat of the gods, / in the heart of the seas'"; (2) Jer 5:12, "They have spoken falsely of the Lord, / and have said, 'He will do nothing; / no evil will come upon us, / nor shall we see sword or famine'"; (3) *Sib. Or.* 5.173 (tr. J. Collins, *OTP* 1:397), "But you [i.e., Rome personified as a woman] said, 'I alone am, and no one will ravage me'"; (4) Rev 3:17, "Because you say, 'I am wealthy and I have become rich and need nothing'"; (5) *2 Tg. Esth.* 1.1, "Nebuchadnezzar became self-conceited and said, 'There is no king or rule but I'" (Grossfeld, *Two Targums*, 98). (6) A lengthier hybris soliloquy with some striking similarities to Rev 18:7 is attributed to Niobe in Ovid *Metam.* 6.170–202 (Wettstein, *Novum Testamentum* 2:826), as these excerpts reveal (LCL tr.):

> I am queen of Cadmus' royal house. . . . Surely I am happy. Who can deny it? And happy I shall remain. This also who can doubt? My very abundance has made me safe. I am too great for Fortune to harm; though she should take many from me, still many more will she leave to me.

Much of this speech demeans the goddess Leto, who reacts angrily to Niobe's hybris by killing her and her children.

In the the first two laments over the fall of Jerusalem in Lam 1 and 2, Jerusalem is personified as a suffering woman. She speaks in Lam 1:9c, 11c–16, 18–22; 2:20–22 (W. F. Lanahan, "The Speaking Voice in the Book of Lamentations," *JBL* 93

[1974] 41–49). This has the effect of personalizing the suffering of a great number of people. In Rev 18:7, on the other hand, the excessive pride of Babylon is personalized in the brief soliloquy in which Babylon is presented as boasting in the *persona* of a proud queen. This proud boast may be an intentional allusion to the theme of the eternal permanence of Rome in imperial propaganda (Vergil *Aeneid* 6.781–82; Rutilius Namatianus *De red.* 1.115–40). For Vergil the Romans are *rerum domini*, "lords of the world," and have an *imperium sine fine*, "an empire without end." Frontinus (*De aquis* 2.88.1) refers to Rome as *regina et domina orbis*, "queen and mistress of the world."

The emphasis on widowhood is appropriate since one of the frequent results of war in ancient times (and all times) was the slaughter of adult males, many of whom were husbands and fathers. Widows (and orphans) were extremely vulnerable and disadvantaged in ancient Israel because they were deprived of the protection and financial support afforded them by husbands and their families, and consequently often experienced extreme hardship and oppression (Job 22:8–9; 24:2–3, 21; Ps 94:6; Isa 10:1–2; Ezek 22:7; Mark 12:40; Luke 18:1–5; Jas 1:27). In the OT, the notion of "widow" (אַלְמָנָה *'almānâ*) has exclusively negative connotations. "Widow" was an appropriate metaphor for cities and nations who were defeated in war and consequently desolated (Babylon: Isa 47:9; Jerusalem: Isa 54:4; Lam 1:1; 5:3–4; see Hoffner, *TDOT* 1:291).

8a διὰ τοῦτο ἐν μιᾷ ἡμέρᾳ ἥξουσιν αἱ πληγαὶ αὐτῆς θάνατος καὶ πένθος καὶ λιμός, καὶ ἐν πυρὶ κατακαυθήσεται, "Because of this her plagues will come in one day, pestilence and sorrow and famine, and she will be burned with fire." The allusion to Isa 47 continues, this time from Isa 47:9, referring to Babylon (NRSV): "both of these things [widowhood, loss of children] shall come upon you in a moment, in one day [LXX 47:8: ἐν μιᾷ ἡμέρᾳ]." The specific plagues mentioned, pestilence, mourning, famine, and burning with fire, though not found in Isa 47, are all part of the ancient *topos* used in describing the capture of a city (Dio Chrysostom *Or.* 11.29–30). Pestilence and famine were the common results of a prolonged siege (e.g., the siege of Agrigentum by Rome [Polybius 1.19.7]), mourning is linked with the death of the inhabitants, and burning with fire is the final act of destruction by the conquerors. λιμός, "hunger, famine," can mean anything from hunger to death by starvation, either for a few or for many (Garnsey, *Famine*, 19). λιμός is used here of "life-threatening hunger," and it is used by ancient historians to describe various catastrophic food crises in cities (Agrigentum: Polybius 1.19.7; Rome: Cassius Dio 55.27.1–3; 55.31.3–4; Appian *Bell. civ.* 5.67). The destruction of Rome by fire is predicted in *Sib. Or.* 2.15–19; 3.52–62; 5.158–61. The burning of Babylon-Rome was referred to in 17:16, and it is mentioned again in 18:8, 18. The burning of a besieged city following its capture was a typical act of retribution in the ancient world (Jer 34:22).

8b ὅτι ἰσχυρὸς κύριος ὁ θεὸς ὁ κρίνας αὐτήν, "because mighty is the Lord God who has judged her." The term ἰσχυρός, "mighty," is used as an explicit attribute of God only here in the NT (cf. 1 Cor 1:25; 10:22; Eph 1:18). Here the emphasis on the might or power of God is appropriate in light of the anticipated scale and suddenness of the destruction of Babylon-Rome. It seems clear that this clause should be taken with v 8a, rather than as a concluding comment that applies to vv 4–8 as a whole. The statement answers a question implied by v 8a: How is such a sudden and complete overthrow of Babylon-Rome possible? Answer: It is possible by the might and power of God. Eros and Ananke are called ἰσχυροτάτω, "most mighty," in Aelius Aristides *Or.* 43.16 (van der Horst, *Aristides*, 84).

9a καὶ κλαύσουσιν καὶ κόψονται ἐπ' αὐτὴν οἱ βασιλεῖς τῆς γῆς οἱ μετ' αὐτῆς πορνεύσαντες καὶ στρηνιάσαντες, "The kings of the earth, who committed immorality with her and lived luxuriously with her, will weep and wail over her." This allusion to Isa 23:17 (also alluded to in 17:2 and 18:3) again mentions the kings of the earth, and the immorality of Babylon-Rome repeats a theme already mentioned in v 3b (see *Comments* on 17:2 and 18:3).

9b ὅταν βλέπωσιν τὸν καπνὸν τῆς πυρώσεως αὐτῆς, "when they see the smoke of her burning." On the burning of Babylon-Rome, see *Comment* on 17:16 (the punishment for a prostitute) and 18:8a.

10a ἀπὸ μακρόθεν ἑστηκότες διὰ τὸν φόβον τοῦ βασανισμοῦ αὐτῆς λέγοντες, "standing far off because of the fear of her torment, saying." This is a literary device used by the author to present an external view of the destruction of Babylon so that the readers or hearers will imaginatively view Babylon from the perspective of a series of characters that have previously profited from her existence. The reactions of those who pass by such a deserted city is a commonplace in OT prophetic texts (Jer 18:16, "All who pass by it are horrified and shake their heads"; cf. Jer 19:8; 49:17; 50:13; Ezek 5:14–15; 36:34; Lam 2:15; 2 Chr 7:21), though another related commonplace (not used in Revelation) is to claim that no one passes by it any more (Isa 34:10; 60:15; Jer 9:10; Ezek 14:15; 33:28; 35:7; Zeph 3:6).

The phrase ἀπὸ μακρόθεν, "from a distance," is repeated three times in this text unit (vv 10, 15, 17) and characterizes the stance of each of the three groups who witness the destruction of Babylon: kings, merchants, and the maritime professionals. This spatial separation from Babylon not only expresses the horror they feel at its sudden and unexpected destruction; it also reflects their attempt to distance themselves from a judgment they deserve to share (*TDNT* 4:373).

10b οὐαὶ οὐαί, ἡ πόλις ἡ μεγάλη, Βαβυλὼν ἡ πόλις ἡ ἰσχυρά, "Alas, alas, you great city, / Babylon, you mighty city." The phrase οὐαὶ οὐαί, ἡ πόλις ἡ μεγάλη, "alas, alas, you great city," is repeated verbatim twice more in vv 16 and 19 in phrases in which the articular nominative functions as a vocative identifying the one to whom the lamentation is addressed (LXX Isa 1:24; 5:11, 18, 20, 21, 22; 31:1; Amos 5:18; Hab 2:6, 12, 19; Zeph 2:5; *Barn.* 4:11; for οὐαί with the vocative, see LXX 3 Kgdms 12:24; 13:30; Jer 22:18; 41:5 [MT 34:5]). Elsewhere the author uses οὐαί with the accusative of those to whom the woe or lamentation is addressed (8:13; 12:12); the mention of the three woes or plagues in 8:13 is referred to in 9:12; 11:14. Elsewhere the author uses οὐαί with the accusative (8:13; 12:12; see *Notes* 8:13.e–e. and 12:12.e.). There is a tendency for OT prophetic writers to arrange "woe" oracles in series (*TDOT* 3:359–64; Andersen-Freeman, *Amos,* 520; Hillers, "*Hoy,*" 185–88).

The phrase ἡ πόλις ἡ μεγάλη, "the great city," occurs in 11:8, where it clearly refers to Jerusalem. This is part of the larger argument advanced by several scholars that Jerusalem, not Rome, is addressed in Rev 18 (Ford, 285–86; Beagley, *Apocalypse,* 92–102; Provan, *JSNT* 64 [1996] 91–96).

10c ὅτι μιᾷ ὥρᾳ ἦλθεν ἡ κρίσις σου, "because your reckoning came in a moment." The phrase μιᾷ ὥρᾳ, literally "in one hour," occurs four times in Revelation (17:10; 18:10, 17, 19) and means "a short time" (G. Delling, *TDNT* 9:680). The phrase ἐν ὥρᾳ μιᾷ τῆς ἡμέρας occurs in LXX Dan 4:17a, with the literal meaning of one hour in the day. Probably the phrase ἐν γὰρ μιᾷ ὥρᾳ ἀπέρχομαι, "for in one hour I will depart" (in *T. Job* 7.10 [ed. R. A. Kraft]), should be understood similarly, though usually the term is used metaphorically. The phrase is a figure of speech for an unexpectedly quick destruction, as in Josephus *J.W.* 3.227–28, when the Jews burn up the Roman siege machines "in one hour" (ἐπὶ μιᾶς ὥρας), or in *J.W.* 2.457, which reports that the residents of Caesarea slaughtered the Caesarean Jews "in one hour" (ὑπὸ μίαν ὥραν).

11a καὶ οἱ ἔμποροι τῆς γῆς κλαίουσιν καὶ πενθοῦσιν ἐπ' αὐτήν, "And the merchants of the earth weep and mourn over her." The merchants of the earth were mentioned in v 3c. On the relatively low social status of the ἔμπορος, "merchant," in the Greco-Roman world, see Pleket, "Urban Elites," 131–44. In later antiquity, merchants played a very limited role in cities such as Antioch. In Libanius they "appear to be humble landless men who are trying to make a living out of such resources as they have" (Liebeschuetz, *Antioch,* 82). On the other hand, owning a ship or a fleet of ships could be a very profitable enterprise (see Lucian *Nav.* 13).

11b ὅτι τὸν γόμον αὐτῶν οὐδεὶς ἀγοράζει οὐκέτι, "because no one buys their merchandise any longer." The reason for the weeping and wailing of the merchants is not pity for the fate of Babylon but the self-pity of those who have lost their best customer.

12a γόμον χρυσοῦ καὶ ἀργύρου καὶ λίθου τιμίου καὶ μαργαριτῶν, "merchandise consisting of gold, and silver, and precious stones, and pearls." Vv 12–13, which contain an extensive polysyndetic list of luxury trade goods (cf. Rev 5:12; BDF § 460; Aune, "De esu carnium," 309), serve as a preface to the lament of the merchants and therefore read like a later insertion of the author into an earlier text made to underscore the enormous wealth of both Babylon and the merchants who tried to satisfy her expensive and extravagant tastes. This list is limited to luxury trade goods primarily for the consumption of the very wealthy (Müller, 307; Wikenhauser, 136; Hadorn, 181). The first four luxury products are grouped together because of their similarity; they are all precious metals or precious stones. Gold and silver were products of the Roman empire; Spain was the primary source of both metals until the end of the first century A.D. (Strabo 3.2.10; Tacitus *Annals* 3.53; 6.19), but shortly thereafter the Balkans became the chief source of gold. With regard to λίθου τιμίου, "precious stones," a detailed discussion of ancient gems is found in Pliny *Hist. nat.* 37.54–195 (see Isager, *Pliny,* 212–20). Precious stones were not the products of any particular place in the Roman empire itself. Ultimately they came from India, where they were exported to Alexandria to be cut and polished. Pearls (which were found in the Persian Gulf and the Indian Ocean, both part of what was called "the Red Sea" in antiquity [Aelian *De nat. anim.* 10]) were regarded as the most valuable of precious stones in antiquity (Pliny *Hist. nat.* 9.54; Athenaeus *Deipn.* 3.93).

12b καὶ βυσσίνου καὶ πορφύρας καὶ σιρικοῦ καὶ κοκκίνου, "and fine linen cloth, and purple material, and silk, and scarlet material." This second group of four luxury products consists of varieties of expensive fabric. There is no way of determining whether the author has yard goods in mind. He could as easily be speaking of linen yarn and raw silk or finished garments, though yard goods seem more likely, and the translation reflects that understanding. Gold-embroidered rugs and gold-colored cloth were products of Alexandria and Syria (Pliny *Hist. nat.* 19.4).

Linen: The Edict of Diocletian (A.D. 301) provides a great deal of detail on the prices of wool and linen yarn, the varieties of garments and the wages of workers, though admittedly much later than the composition of Revelation. Linen garments of high quality were associated with famous weaving centers such as Scythopolis (*Cod. Theod.* 10.20.8), Tarsus (see Dio Chrysostom *Or.* 34.21), Alexandria (*Hist. Aug. Saturnius* 8), Byblos, and Laodicea (*Ed. Diocl.* 26–28). Linen tunics (στίχαι) from Scythopolis are listed at seven thousand denarii, while the same product from Alexandria commanded just two thousand denarii (A. H. M. Jones, "Cloth Industry," 353).

Purple: The term πορφύρα was used of purple cloth and clothing rather than of the dye itself (BAGD, 694; Bauer-Aland, 1390–91; Louw-Nida, § 6.169; see Appian *Pun.* 66, where πορφύρα clearly refers to a garment). Purple cloth was a very expensive industrial product requiring a heavy investment, which was offset by the high prices demanded for the finished products (Pliny *Hist. nat.* 9.124–41; Pleket, "Urban Elites," 142; Steigerwald, *Traditio* 42 [1986] 1–57). Purple *woolens* in particular were highly prized and enormously expensive (*Ed. Diocl.* 24.16; A. H. M. Jones, "Cloth Industry," 363). The purple dye from Tyre was judged the most desirable in antiquity (Strabo 16.2.23).

Silk: Procopius (*Anecdota* 25.14) observes that silk had been produced since ancient times in Beirut and Tyre in Phoenicia. There was an overland northern silk route connecting the Mediterranean with China that flourished particularly from A.D. 90 to 130 (Charlesworth, *Trade-Routes,* 97–111). In about A.D. 90 the Chinese began to control the Tarim Basin and were able to export silk to Rome via the Kushan kingdom and Parthia. Chinese merchants stopped at Merv in Parthia, and the Parthians bought the silk and sent it to western markets. In the annals of the Han Dynasty (A.D. 25–220), in the ninth year of Yung-Yuan of Hoti (A.D. 97), Kan-Ying was sent as a messenger to Ta-ts'in (Syria) to make arrangements for the silk trade between China and the Roman empire (de Martino, *Wirtschaftsgeschichte,* 357–58; Hermann, PW 11:51). During the first part of the first century A.D., Pliny estimated the total Roman trade with India, China, and Arabia at one hundred million sesterces (Pliny *Hist. nat.* 12.41.84), fifty-five million with India (*Hist. nat.* 6.26.101), leaving forty-five million for trade with China (de Martino, *Wirtschaftsgeschichte,* 356–57). Yet since such land routes were under the control of the Parthians, sea routes were generally preferred. Procopius relates a story of how Emperor Justinian (ca. A.D. 482–565) instituted an imperial monopoly on the silk trade and limited the price on silk to eight gold pieces per pound (*Anecdota* 25.16).

Since it was a time-honored virtue for Roman women to weave cloth at home, during the time of Nero one Roman writer complained that women bought expensive clothes rather than weave the cloth and produce the garments themselves (Columella *De re rustica* 12.*praef.* 9–10). However, in other parts of the empire it is clear that even poor people normally bought clothes ready to wear (A. H. M. Jones, "Cloth Industry," 352). According to Jones ("Cloth Industry," 355), "The famous weaving towns, then, which produced high class garments from high quality material catered only for the rich; their products, since they were highly priced rarities, no doubt travelled far and commanded a widely-spread market."

12c καὶ πᾶν ξύλον θύϊνον καὶ πᾶν σκεῦος ἐλεφάντινον, "all kinds of citron-wood products, and all kinds of products made of ivory." The wood from the citron (Latin *citrus*) or thyine (Greek θύον) tree (*Callitris quadrivalvis* Vent), native to north Africa, was highly prized in antiquity (Pliny *Hist. nat.* 37.204, cf. 16.66), and Pliny considered it the most valuable type of wood. The use of citron wood in antiquity is discussed in detail by Meiggs, *Trees and Timber,* 286–91. Pliny the Elder (*Hist. nat.*

13.91–102) discussed this tree and the valuable tables made from its wood in great detail. It is a hardwood with beautiful grain patterns and is decay resistant and stain resistant (important for serving wine). The roots of this tree were particularly valued for their elaborate grain patterns and color variations. According to Theophrastus, a great variety of valuable articles were made from this wood (*Hist. plant.* 5.3.7). Citron-wood wine tables, particularly prized by wealthy Romans (Cicero *Verr.* 4.37), sometimes had ivory legs (Martial 14.3; Dio 61.10.3). Pliny (*Hist. nat.* 13. 91) speaks of the *mensarum insania*, "table craze," among wealthy Roman men, which gave their wives an offensive weapon against their husbands' complaints that they were pearl crazy. Again, according to Pliny (*Hist. nat.* 13.100; LCL tr.), "Few things supplying the apparatus of a more luxurious life rank with this tree." The luxurious character of citron-wood wine tables is suggested by the prices that particularly fine specimens commanded. Cicero reportedly paid 500,000 sesterces for one table (= $2,500,000); Gallus Asinius paid 1,000,000 sesterces ($5,000,000) for another; King Juba of Mauretania auctioned off two such tables, one for 1,200,000 sesterces ($6,000,000) and another for a little less (Pliny *Nat. hist.* 92; four sesterces = one denarius, and since one denarius was a laborer's daily wage, then one denarius would roughly equal $40).

Ivory was imported into the Roman world from Africa (*Periplus Mari Erythraei* 4; cf. commentary in Casson, *Periplus,* 108) and India. For more information on ivory trade, see H. Scullard, *The Elephant in the Greek and Roman World* (Ithaca: Cornell UP, 1974).

12d καὶ πᾶν σκεῦος ἐκ ξύλου τιμιωτάτου καὶ χαλκοῦ καὶ σιδήρου καὶ μαρμάρου, "and all kinds of products made of expensive wood, and of brass, and of iron, and of marble." This is another grouping of four products, all manufactured from wood, metal, or stone. Each of these four nouns is a genitive of material dependent on the preposition ἐκ, "from." τιμιωτάτου, "expensive," is one of only two superlatives found in Revelation; the other is τιμιωτάτῳ, the same word in the dative case, in 21:11; both have "elative" rather than superlative value, and both mean "costly, precious" (Mussies, *Morphology,* 128, 138). The only comparative adjective, πλείονα, "better than," is found in Rev 2:19.

Wood: The most valuable types of wood in the ancient Mediterranean world were used for furniture, sculpture (primarily during the archaic period), and interior paneling. Various types of wood were prized for their resistance to decay and insects, for their beautiful grains, for their resistance to cracking and splitting, and finally for their aromatic properties (Meiggs, *Trees and Timber,* 300). One of the most valued types of wood, θύον, or "citron wood," has already been mentioned above. Other valued types of wood included boxwood, ebony, cedar, and cypress (Meiggs, *Trees and Timber,* 280–99). Further, expensive wood products were often embellished with legs of ivory or silver, and the technique of veneering was widely practiced during the early empire.

Bronze: On the highly prized Corinthian bronze (Pliny *Hist. nat.* 34.1; 34.3.6–8; Petronius *Sat.* 119; Plutarch *De Pyth. orac.* 395b–d; Suetonius *Tiberius* 34; Pausanias 2.3.3; Orosius *Hist. adv. pag.* 5.3.7; Schröder, *Plutarch,* 118–21), see H. Blümner, *Technologie und Terminologie der Gewerbe und Künste bei Griechen und Römern* (Leipzig: Teubner, 1886) 4:1, 183ff.; J. Murphy-O'Connor, "Corinthian Bronze," *RB* 90 (1983) 80–93; T. L. Shear, "A Hoard of Coins found in Corinth in 1930," *AJA* 25 (1931) 139–51 (subjected to metalurgical analysis).

Iron: Highly valued in antiquity, iron deposits were found in Greece (Athens and the Isthmus cities were centers for the fabrication of iron articles). During the republican period of Rome, iron from Spain was highly prized, and after A.D. 40, Noricum (a Roman alpine province south of the Danube) became the chief source for Roman iron. Because iron was harder than bronze, it was widely used for weapons, particularly knives and swords. Statues were also cast with iron.

Marble: Of the many types of marble available in the ancient world, λύγδος, "white marble" (Pliny *Hist. nat.* 36.62; *Periplus Mari Erythraei* 24), came in pieces just large enough for carving into plates, bowls, unguent jars, and boxes. The marble to which Pliny refers is probably Parian marble (O. Rubensohn, "Paros," *RE* [1949] 1794; see Isager, *Pliny,* 144–205). Phrygia had quarries from which a white marble with purple marks was taken, some of which was used for sarcophagi in Asia but the bulk of which was shipped to Rome (Magie, *Roman Rule* 1:50; 2:815 n. 96). In fact, imports account for most of the marble trade up until the Flavian period, A.D. 69–98 (Ward-Perkins, "Marble Trade," 96–102).

13a καὶ κιννάμωμον καὶ ἄμωμον καὶ θυμιάματα καὶ μύρον καὶ λίβανον, "and cinnamon, and amomum, and incense, such as myrrh and frankincense." These four products (assuming that the καί following "incense" is epexegetical) are the major spices popular throughout the Mediterranean world. They were extremely expensive because they were imported from distant lands to the south and east. Roman merchant fleets based in Egypt made annual voyages to the ports in Somaliland and east Africa in order to procure myrrh and frankincense, which were used in incense, perfumes, and medicines (Miller, *Spice Trade,* 281–84).

Cinnamon: a term for cassia. The wood of the plant, as well as the bark and shoots, or cinnamon proper, was used for perfume, medicine, incense, and a flavoring for wine. Cinnamon was imported from east Africa, Arabia, and India; see Casson, "Cinnamon and Cassia in the Ancient World," in *Ancient Trade,* 225–46.

Amomum: a fragrant smelling spice imported from south India (Warmington, *Commerce,* 184–85).

Myrrh: Greeks and Romans used myrrh, imported from Somalia (*Periplus Mari Erythraei* 7) and south Arabia (*Periplus Mari Erythraei* 24), in perfume, as incense and spice, as a deodorant, and in medicines. The Egyptians used it in the embalming process. Pliny (*Hist. nat.* 12.70) observed that myrrh cost from 11 to 16.5 denarii per Roman pound, which made it very expensive (twice the price of the best frankincense, which was 6 denarii per Roman pound). On myrrh in the ancient world, see A. Steier, "Myrrha," *RE* (1935); on myrrh and frankincense, see G. Van Beek, "Frankincense and Myrrh in Ancient South Arabia," *JAOS* 78 (1958) 141–52.

Frankincense: Like myrrh, frankincense was imported into the Roman world from Somalia (*Periplus Mari Erythraei* 8) and south Arabia (*Periplus Mari Erythraei* 27; Pliny *Hist. nat.* 12.51); see Vergil *Georgics* 1.57. Pliny (*Hist. nat.* 12.65) observed that the best quality of frankincense from Arabia sold for 6 denarii per Roman pound or less, thus making it the cheapest of all the imported spices (see Casson, *Periplus,* 162). Cf. W. Müller, "Weihrauch," *RESup* 15 (1978); N. Hepper, "Arabian and African Incense Frankincense Tree," *JEA* 55 (1969) 66–72. It was often used at funerals (Pliny *Hist. nat.* 12.82–83).

13b καὶ οἶνον καὶ ἔλαιον καὶ σεμίδαλιν καὶ σῖτον καὶ κτήνη καὶ πρόβατα, καὶ ἵππων καὶ ῥεδῶν, καὶ σωμάτων, καὶ ψυχὰς ἀνθρώπων "and wine, and oil, and fine flour, and grain, and cattle, and sheep, and horses, and carriages, and slaves, namely, human beings." The first six items on this list cannot be considered luxury items. Wine, oil, and grain were the staples of the ancient world, though "fine flour" must be considered an expensive import item not available to most consumers. *Wine:* Wine was imported from Spain, Sicily, and Greece in great quantities; cf. Petronius *Sat.* 76; Athenaeus *Deipn.* 1–10; Columella *De re rust.* 12; Pliny *Hist. nat.* 14. The Greeks recognized three types of wine, the Romans four: white wine (λευκός; *albus*), brown wine (κιρρός; *fulvus*), and red wine (ἐρυθρός, μέλας), divided by the Romans into light red (*sanguineus*) and dark red (*niger*). *Oil:* Olive oil was produced in Italy and imported from north Africa and Spain.

Fine flour: Fine flour was produced in Italy and also imported from Egypt (Pliny *Hist. nat.* 18.82). *Grain:* Egypt and Africa provided most of Rome's supply of wheat (Jos. *J.W.* 2.283, 386), and since the late republic, about 200,000 recipients, i.e., adult males, of the citizens of Rome (population ca. 750,000 to 1,000,000) had been provided with a free distribution of grain (*frumentationes*) (August *Res Gestae* 15; Dio Cassius 55.26.3), i.e., 80,000 tons of grain annually (Rickman, "Grain," 263). It took thousands of ships to import the required amount of grain to Rome (Lucian *Navig.* 5; Rougé, *Maritime*, 69–71).

Slaves: The phrase "slaves, namely, human beings" is apparently dependent on Ezek 27:13, which has the Hebrew phrase בְּנֶפֶשׁ אָדָם *běnepeš ʾādām* (LXX ἐν ψυχαῖς ἀνθρώπων). The term σῶμα, meaning "slave," is a Greek idiom that occurs in the classical period with various qualifiers in phrases such as οἰκετικὰ σώματα (Aeschines Or. 1.16, 99), or *persona servilis* (*Digest* 50.17.22), i.e., "domestic slaves," and αἰχμάλωτα σώματα, "captives" (Demosthenes Or. 20.77); see R. Hirzel, *Die Person: Begriff und Name derselben im Altertum* (Munich: Königlich Bayerischen Akademie der Wissenschaften, 1914) 19 n. 3. Hirzel (20–24) is critical of the indiscriminate translation of σῶμα with "slave," where "person" would be more appropriate. σῶμα occasionally means "slave" in the LXX (Gen 34:29; 36:6 [the only place in the LXX where נְפָשׁוֹת *napšôt* means "slaves"]; Tob 10:10 [MSS A B]; 2 Macc 8:11; Bel 32) and in Hellenistic Greek (Polybius 12.16.5; Jos. *Ant.* 14.321). For evidence from the papyri, see Scholl, *Sklaventexte* 3:1122 (*sub* σώματα); some interesting occurrences of σώματα = παῖδες = slaves are in *Sklaventexte* 1:157, 183. The contention that the use of the term σώματα, "bodies," for slaves indicates the contemptuous degradation of a human being to the level of a thing (maintained, for example, by Grobel, "Σῶμα," 56, and more emphatically by R. H. Gundry, *Sōma in Biblical Theology*, SNTSMS 29 [Cambridge: Cambridge UP, 1976] 27) is doubtful. It is, of course, true that in the ancient world slaves were chattel and were treated much like livestock. For the occurrence of the term σώματα, "slaves," *last* on a list of trade goods, see *Periplus Maris Erythraei* 36 (tr. Casson): "Both ports of trade export to Barygaza and Arabia pearls in quantity but inferior to the Indian; purple cloth; native clothing; wine; dates in quantity; gold; slaves [σώματα]." Cf. *Periplus Maris Erythraei* 8, 31. According to Artemidorus, slave traders could make huge profits from their trade (*Oneirocritica* 3.17; see Pleket, "Urban Elites," 139). The phrase ψυχαὶ ἀνθρώπων, "human beings," however, is a Hebrew idiom (see Gen 12:5, where ψυχαί means "people"). The number of slaves in the Roman empire in the first century A.D. has been estimated at ca. ten million, i.e., 16.6 percent to 20 percent of the population, the majority of whom were male (Harris, "Slave," 118). The primary methods of obtaining slaves were the enslavement of prisoners of war and brigandage on land and sea (Dio Chrysostom 15.25), though during the 60s B.C. there was a marked decline in piracy, which naturally reduced the slave supply from that major source. According to Josephus, 97,000 Jewish prisoners were enslaved following the first Jewish revolt of A.D. 66–73 (*J.W.* 6.420). Asia Minor, with the exception of the Roman province of Asia, was one of the regions most heavily exploited for slaves (Harris, "Slave," 122). Large-scale slave trade took place regularly in the major cities of the Roman empire, with Rome as the greatest of all slave markets (Harris, "Slave," 125–28).

14a καὶ ἡ ὀπώρα σου τῆς ἐπιθυμίας τῆς ψυχῆς ἀπῆλθεν ἀπὸ σοῦ, "And the ripe fruit which you desired has gone from you." V 14 is problematic because it is a fragmentary speech directly addressed to the ruined Babylon in the style of the angelic speech of vv 21–24, though the speaker or speakers are not explicitly identified unless one is to assume that they are the merchants. The fragmentary character of this isolated speech is indicated by the lack of a verb of saying or speaking, which introduces each of the other speeches in this chapter (vv 10, 16, 19, 21). Here the phrase translated "the ripe fruit which you desired" can be rendered more literally "the ripe fruit of the desire of your soul." The phrase reflects the Semitic idiom אַוַּת נַפְשֶׁךָ *'awwat napšekā*, "your soul desired" (the piel of אָוָה *'awwâ*, "to desire," regularly occurs with נֶפֶשׁ *nepeš* as its subject; Deut 12:15, 20, 21; 14:26; cf. Charles, 1:108), and is translated τὴν ἐπιθυμίαν τῆς ψυχῆς σου, "the desire of your soul," in the LXX (Deut 12:20, 21; 14:26; cf. LXX Ps 9:24[MT 10:3]; LXX Ps 20:3[MT 21:2]; Jer 2:24; 4 Macc 2:1; *Pss. Sol.* 2:24; *T. Reub.* 4:9). The closely related expression תַּאֲוַת־נֶפֶשׁ *ta'ăwat-nāpeš*, "desire of soul," also occurs (Isa 26:8; Ps 10:3). "Ripe fruit" here is a metaphor for the good things of life; cf. POxy 2.298, "there has not been much fruit [ὑπώρα, i.e., 'results'] in Memphis up to the present" (MM, 454). Terms for "fruit" in the OT and NT (Hebrew פְּרִי *pĕrî;* Greek καρπός) are frequently used in metaphorical senses (D. G. Burke, "Fruit," *ISBE* 2:364–66; F. Hauck, *TDNT* 3:614–16). Charles also thinks this verse out of place, but relocates it after v 21 (1:108).

14b καὶ πάντα τὰ λιπαρὰ καὶ τὰ λαμπρὰ ἀπώλετο ἀπὸ σοῦ, "and all the expensive and beautiful trinkets are lost to you." Here λιπαρά and λαμπρά are juxtaposed in a type of assonance based on alliteration or ὁμοιοπρόφορος, i.e., similarity in the pronunciation of the initial letter of a word (cf. Martianus Capella 5.167); interestingly, lambda is one of the less frequently occurring letters of the Greek alphabet. The REB tries to convey this initial alliteration in English: "all the glitter and glamor." Other uses of alliteration in the NT include Heb 1:1 (six π-words); 11:28 (five π- words); 12:11 (four π- words); cf. 2:2; 7:25; 13:19 (three π-words); see also 2 Pet 1:16–17, 19–21; 2:4–9; 3:13. Alliteration is not as common in Greek rhetoric as many have supposed; see Denniston, *Prose*, 126–29.

14c καὶ οὐκέτι οὐ μὴ αὐτὰ εὑρήσουσιν, "so that people will never find them again." The emphatic negative phrase οὐκέτι οὐ μή, an awkward, overly strong expression in Greek, occurs just three times in the LXX (Tob [B, A] 6:8; Odae 11:11; Jer 38:40), and eight more times as variant readings (Ps 38:13[MT 39:13]; Mic 4:3; Isa 23:12; 30:20; 32:5[2x]; 38:11[2x]; Ezek 7:13), as translations of אֵין *'ên*, לֹא *lō'*, or לֹא עוֹד *lō' 'ôd*. The phrase occurs four times in the NT and early Christian literature (Mark 14:25; Rev 18:14; Justin *Dial.* 81.1 [quoting LXX Isa 65:19, which reads οὐκέτι μή + aorist subjunctive]; Origen *Exp. in Prov.* 17.233) and once as a variant reading (Luke 22:16); see BDR § 437.3; Joachim Jeremias, *Euch.,* 182.

15 οἱ ἔμποροι τούτων οἱ πλουτήσαντες ἀπ' αὐτῆς ἀπὸ μακρόθεν στήσονται διὰ τὸν φόβον τοῦ βασανισμοῦ αὐτῆς κλαίοντες καὶ πενθοῦντες, "The merchants in these commodities, who have become wealthy by means of her, stand far off because of the fear of her torment, weeping and mourning." The metaphor not only involves those who see someone in deep distress and do not know how to offer any solace; it also implies the attempt to distance themselves from a judgment in which they also deserve to share. On the phrase ἀπὸ μακρόθεν, "from a distance," which occurs three times in this text unit, 18:10, 15, 17, see *Comment* on 18:17.

16a λέγοντες· οὐαὶ οὐαί, ἡ πόλις ἡ μεγάλη, "saying, 'Alas, alas, you great city.'" This is a refrain repeated three times in this text unit, in vv 10, 16, 19; see *Comment* on v 10.

16b ἡ περιβεβλημένη βύσσινον καὶ πορφυροῦν καὶ κόκκινον, καὶ κεχρυσωμένη ἐν χρυσίῳ καὶ λίθῳ τιμίῳ καὶ μαργαρίτῃ, "who were dressed in fine linen and purple and scarlet / and were adorned with gold and precious stones and pearls." This is a repetition, with a few changes, of the description of the whore in Rev 17:4, as this synoptic comparison indicates:

Rev 17:4	Rev 18:16b
περιβεβλημένη dressed	ἡ περιβεβλημένη who were dressed
πορφυροῦν καὶ κόκκινον in purple and scarlet	βύσσινον καὶ πορφυροῦν καὶ κόκκινον in fine linen and purple and scarlet
καὶ κεχρυσωμένη and adorned	καὶ κεχρυσωμένη and adorned
χρυσίῳ καὶ λίθῳ τιμίῳ with gold and precious stones	ἐν χρυσίῳ καὶ λίθῳ τιμίῳ with gold and precious stones
καὶ μαργαρίταις and pearls	καὶ μαργαρίτῃ and pearls

On the extraordinary wealth and luxury of Rome, see Tacitus *Annals* 3.52.1–54.5; Seneca *Moral Epistles* 86.1–7; Pliny *Hist. nat.* 9.58.117–18; 13.29.92; Petronius *Satyricon* 31.3–34.4; Pliny *Ep.* 2.17; F. Christ, *Die römische Weltherrschaft in der antiken Dichtung* (Stuttgart: Kohlhammer, 1938) 4–64.

17a ὅτι μιᾷ ὥρᾳ ἠρημώθη ὁ τοσοῦτος πλοῦτος, "for in a moment such fabulous wealth was destroyed." (On the phrase "in a moment," see *Comment* on 18:10.) The noun πλοῦτος, "wealth" (which occurs elsewhere in Revelation only in 5:12), refers to the literal wealth and luxury of Babylon-Rome and belongs to the same semantic domain as τιμιότης, "wealth," in v 19 (the verb πλουτεῖν, "become rich, wealthy," is used in 18:3, 15, 19).

17b καὶ πᾶς κυβερνήτης καὶ πᾶς ὁ ἐπὶ τόπον πλέων καὶ ναῦται καὶ ὅσοι τὴν θάλασσαν ἐργάζονται, "And every shipmaster and every seafarer, and sailors and all those who make their living on the sea." The kings of the earth (vv 9–10) and the merchants (vv 11–17a) were both mentioned earlier in v 3 and are part of an elaborate adaptation of Ezek 27:33–35, where the merchants are mentioned first and then the kings. The reference to those who live and work on the sea in vv 17b–19 is similarly a reworking of Ezek 27:25–32 (particularly vv 29–30) and continues the reversal by placing those who work on the sea last. The phrase that has exercised commentators and challenged ancient scribes (see *Notes* 18:17.b–b. and 18:17.d.) is καὶ πᾶς ὁ ἐπὶ τόπον πλέων, literally "and every one who sails to a place" (NRSV: "seafarers"). The context consists of three types of people whose livelihood is linked to the sea: the κυβερνήτης, "shipmaster, captain," the ναύτης, "sailor," and the miscellaneous category ὅσοι τὴν θάλασσαν ἐργάζονται, "those whose with maritime professions," probably fishermen, a phrase with parallels in classical literature (Dionysius Hal. *Antiq. Rom.* 3.46.3; Appian *Pun.* 1.2). Several commentators have assumed that καὶ πᾶς ὁ ἐπὶ τόπον πλέων is corrupt and have suggested emendations: (1) Nestle (*Einführung*, 181) conjectured that the original reading was ὁ ἐπὶ πόντον πλέων, "one who sails on the sea" (πόντον can be abbreviated as πō̄τον, with a horizontal line over the first omicron), a proposal supported only by a very few MSS. It was, however, the reading preferred by Primasius: *omnis super mare navigans*, "all who sail on the sea." (2) Kraft (236) also assumed that the text is corrupt and suggested several conjectures based on LXX Ezek 27:29, settling on "boatswain" (*Bootsmann*), an intermediate position between the shipmaster and the sailor. The list of marine grades in Plutarch *Praec. ger. reip.* 807b, however, simply lists ναύκληρος, "shipowner," κυβερνήτης, "captain," and ναύτης, "sailor." (3) Friedrichsen ("Sprachliches," 282–91), too, assumed that ὁ ἐπὶ τόπον πλέων was corrupt and suggested the simple expedient of reading the phrase as ὁ ἐπίτοπον πλέων, i.e., "the one who has the opportunity to sail," i.e., the passenger (cf. Acts 27:6, which illustrates that passengers could only sail if they happened to find space on some vessel going their way). In this instance, however, emendation does not seem to be necessary.

πλεῖν ἐπί + accusative of place does occur, though rarely (see Thucydides 1.53.2; 4 Macc 7.3; *SIG*, 409.4ff.), and though τόπος usually means "place" or "region," it can be used more specifically in the sense of "port." In the anonymous *Periplus Maris Rubri*, the term τόπος occurs more than forty times to indicate localities or ports. Conzelmann (*Acts*, 215; cf. id., *ZNW* 66 [1975] 288–90) discusses the occurrence of τόπος in Rev 18:17 and Acts 27:2 and argues that τόπος is used several times in the sense of "port" in the *Periplus Maris Rubri* (ed. Frisk, 8 [p. 3, line 26], 10 [p. 4, line 9], 17 [p. 6, line 16]). However, while the term τόπος is often used of a "place" that can also designated as a "port" (λιμήν) or a "harbor" (ὅρμος) or a "port of trade" (ἐμπόριον), it cannot properly be said that τόπος has the semantic *meaning* "port" or "harbor" or "port of trade" (for a discussion this terminology, see Casson, *Periplus*, 271–77: "Appendix 1. Harbors and Ports"). The term τόποι ἀποδεδειγμένοι, "designated places," really means "designated ports" (P. Ross. Georg. 2.18, 33, 133, 196 [A.D. 140]; P. Hib. 198.110–22 [2nd century B.C.]; cf. Casson, *Periplus*, 273–74).

Long ago Swete (237) was on the right track when he translated ὁ ἐπὶ τόπον πλέων as "he who sails for (any) port," which he understood to refer to the merchant who goes with his goods or the chance passenger (*vector*); i.e., the two major options for understanding ὁ ἐπὶ τόπον πλέων are as (1) seagoing merchants or (2) seafarers or travelers. On the basis of the use of τόπος in the *Periplus Maris Rubri*, Conzelmann suggested the translation *Seekaufleute*, i.e., "seagoing merchants" (*ZNW* 66 [1975] 290). This is probably incorrect, however, for if the author had intended merchants, he would probably have used one of the three common terms for port or harbor (λιμήν, ὅρμος, ἐμπόριον). It is, therefore, more appropriate to translate the phrase as

Küstenfahrer, "coastal traveler," as is done by Weiss-Heitmüller, 305; Bousset (1906) 423; and Bauer-Aland, col. 1343. Similarly, Lohmeyer (151), followed by Koester (*TDNT* 8:203), translates the phrase ὁ ἐπὶ τόπον πλέων, as " *der (von Ort zu Ort fahrende) Küstenfahrer,* " "the coastal traveler (who travels from place to place)."

Attempts to construe τόπος as a physical part of a ship do not make good sense (Kraft, 236); the catalogue of ship components found in Athenaeus *Deipn.* 204a (frequently cited in this regard) does not use the term τόπος. Finally, it is of interest that sea captains and sailors are widely portrayed as charlatans in Philostratus *Vita Apoll.* 4.32.

17c–18a ἀπὸ μακρόθεν ἔστησαν καὶ ἔκραζον βλέποντες τὸν καπνὸν τῆς πυρώσεως αὐτῆς λέγοντες, τίς ὁμοία τῇ πόλει τῇ μεγάλη, "they stood at a great distance and exclaimed when they saw the smoke of her incineration, 'What city is like the great city?'" On the phrase ἀπὸ μακρόθεν, "at a distance," repeated three times in 18:10, 15, 17, see *Comment* on 18:10. The rhetorical question "What city is like the great city?" which focuses on the incomparable character of the fall of Babylon, has a counterpart in Ezek 27:32b, where the mariners and pilots of the sea ask: "Who was ever destroyed like Tyre in the midst of the sea?" (see Jahnow, *Leichenlied,* 221). The form of this rhetorical question (interrogative pronoun + ὅμοιος) occurs again in 13:4; it is intended to elicit the answer "no one" or "nothing" (see Exod 15:11; Deut 33:29; Pss 35:10[LXX 34:10]; 71:19[LXX 70:19]; Sir 48:4). Sometimes the point is made more directly through a declarative sentence: οὐκ ἔστιν ὅμοιος, "there is no one like" or "there is nothing like" (1 Kgs 10:24; 1 Chr 17:20; 2 Chr 6:14; Ps 86:8[LXX 85:8]).

An enormous and tremendously destructive fire broke out in Rome in A.D. 64 and burned for more than six days, destroying much of ten of the fourteen districts of the city (Tacitus *Annals* 15.38–41). Eckhardt speculates that the author was on board a ship on the Tiber or near the mouth of the Tiber when the burning of Rome occurred under Nero in A.D. 64, and this became a model for his anticipation of the eschatological destruction of Rome (*Johannes,* 63, 72–73).

19a καὶ ἔβαλον χοῦν ἐπὶ τὰς κεφαλὰς αὐτῶν καὶ ἔκραζον κλαίοντες καὶ πενθοῦντες λέγοντες, "And they threw dust on their heads and cried, weeping and mourning." This specific action is based on another allusion to Ezek 27, this time in v 30, where the mariners and pilots of the sea stand on the shore and look at the ruined Tyre, wailing bitterly and throwing dust on their heads. The custom of throwing dust on one's head was an act of mourning or sorrow (Josh 7:6; Job 2:12; Lam 2:10; 1 Macc 11:71), repentance (Job 42:6), or contrition when accompanied by prayer (2 Macc 10:25; 14:15; 3 Macc 1:18; Maximus Tyrius 5.7f–h; Ovid *Metam.* 8.530; cf. *Neuer Wettstein,* ad Rev 18:19).

19b οὐαὶ οὐαί, ἡ πόλις ἡ μεγάλη, ἐν ᾗ ἐπλούτησαν πάντες οἱ ἔχοντες τὰ πλοῖα ἐν τῇ θαλάσσῃ ἐκ τῆς τιμιότητος αὐτῆς, "Alas, alas, you great city, / through whom all those who have ships on the sea became rich from her wealth." This is the third repetition of the refrain "Alas, alas, you great city," in this text unit; see *Comment* on v 10.

19c ὅτι μιᾷ ὥρᾳ ἠρημώθη, "for in a moment she has been destroyed." The phrase μιᾷ ὥρᾳ, literally "in a single hour," is used three times in this text unit, vv 10, 17, 19; see *Comment* on v 10.

20a εὐφραίνου ἐπ᾽ αὐτῇ, οὐρανέ, "Rejoice over her, heaven." V 20 is a call to rejoice (Deichgräber, *Gotteshymnus,* 55; Jörns, *Evangelium,* 140–43), an abrupt interjection that should not be regarded as part of the lament of the shipmasters and sailors in v 19. It belongs to the final version of Revelation (both v 20 and v 24 are very probably later interpolations with a clearly Jewish-Christian character). The character of v 20, rejoicing over the downfall of one's enemy, has a close parallel in 19:1–4, the heavenly rejoicing over Babylon's fall, which can be considered the response to the call for rejoicing in 18:20. The imperative εὐφραίνου, "rejoice," is in the second-person singular because it precedes a series of subjects, the first of which (οὐρανέ, "heaven") is singular (BDF § 135; see 1:7; 7:16; 8:7; 9:2, 17; 11:18; 12:10; 3:10; 19:20; 20:11; 21:27). This phrase is parallel to Rev 12:12, though there are significant verbal differences. Here an aspect of the universe is depicted anthropomorphically as rejoicing; see Ps 96:11, "Let the heaven be glad, and let the earth rejoice." V 20 does not fit the dirge of the sailors and shipowners in 18:17b–19; therefore, it (like v 24) appears to be a subsequent addition to the text.

20b καὶ οἱ ἅγιοι καὶ οἱ ἀπόστολοι καὶ οἱ προφῆται, "and you people of God and apostles and prophets." (On translating οἱ ἅγιοι, literally "saints, holy ones," as "people of God," see *Comment* on 5:8.) This polysyndetic list consists of three separate groups, as the definite articles with each substantive indicates. The groups "apostles" and "prophets" are also closely linked in many early Christian texts (Luke 11:49, 1 Cor 12:28–29; Eph 2:20; 3:5; 4:11; 2 Pet 3:2; *Did.* 11:3 and Ign. *Phld.* 9:1). In each of these texts, οἱ ἀπόστολοι is a technical term referring to the twelve apostles. The term ἀπόστολος occurs three times in Revelation, once of charlatans who claim the name "apostle" (2:2) and twice of the twelve apostles (18:20; 21:14; see *Comment* on 21:14). Eph 3:5 contains a very close parallel containing the three terms ἅγιοι, "saints, people of God," ἀπόστολοι, "apostles," and προφῆται, "prophets." The Ephesians passage can be construed several ways: ὡς νῦν ἀπεκαλύφθη τοῖς ἁγίοις ἀποστόλοις αὐτοῦ καὶ προφήταις, "as has now been revealed to his holy apostles and prophets" (taking ἁγίοις, "holy," as an adjective modifying τοῖς ἀποστόλοις καὶ προφήταις, "the apostles and prophets," the most likely solution since the article τοῖς "the," is most naturally construed as belonging to ἀποστόλοις καὶ προφήταις) or "as has now been revealed to the saints, that is, to his apostles and prophets" (taking ἁγίοις as a substantive, "holy [ones], saints," with ἀποστόλοις καὶ προφήταις forming a hendiadys in apposition to τοῖς ἁγίοις). The author of Ephesians has apparently combined the phrase νῦν δὲ ἐφανερώθη τοῖς ἁγίοις αὐτοῦ, "but now has been manifested to his saints" (Col. 1:26), with οἱ ἀπόστολοι καὶ προφῆται from Eph 2:20 to form the more complex phrase in Eph 3:5 (Sandnes, *Paul,* 231). The same phrase occurs in 2 Pet 3:2, τῶν ἁγίων προφητῶν καὶ τῆς τῶν ἀποστόλων, "the holy prophets and apostles," probably referring to OT prophets and NT apostles, though it is not always certain whether OT prophets or early Christian prophets are in view. The fact that saints and apostles and prophets are enjoined to rejoice that God has avenged them suggests that members of all three groups have suffered martyrdom (17:6; 19:2; cf. 6:9–11) and are present in heaven. Probably both Peter and Paul were martyred in Rome during the Neronian persecution that began in A.D. 64 (see *1 Clem.* 5:3–7; Ign. *Rom.* 4:3; Dionysius in Eusebius *Hist. eccl.* 2.25.8; Irenaeus *Adv. haer.* 3.1.1; Origen in Eusebius *Hist. eccl.* 3.1.2–3; *Acts Peter* 9.30–41; *Acts Paul* 11.1–7).

While "apostles" is obviously a designation for a particular Christian group, the meaning of "prophets" is not as clear. Since it is preceded by "apostles," it would be natural to understand it to refer to Christian prophets rather than OT prophets, as it must in 1 Cor 12:28–28, Eph 4:11, and *Did.* 11:3 (the two roles are reversed in Luke 11:49 and 2 Pet 3:2, suggesting that OT prophets are referred to in those

passages), just as the phrase "apostles and prophets" in Eph 2:20 and 3:5 must refer
to Christian prophets (Sandnes, *Paul*, 233).

20c   ὅτι ἔκρινεν ὁ θεὸς τὸ κρίμα ὑμῶν ἐξ αὐτῆς, "for God has condemned her
for condemning you." This clause is somewhat awkwardly phrased. It can be
translated more literally as "because God judged the condemnation of you by her"
(see *Note* 18:20.f-f.). The principle of *lex talionis*, i.e., the law of retribution in kind,
is evident here through the use of paronomasia; i.e., τὸ κρίμα, "the condemnation"
(the verbal idea is clear here since the noun takes an objective genitive), was
exercised by Babylon against Christians, and now God has judged (ἔκρινεν) her.
Other examples of paranomasia in Revelation are found in 2:2(2x), 22; 3:10; 11:18;
14:8; 18:6(3x), 21; 22:18, 19 (see BDF § 488.1; Turner, *Syntax*, 148).

21a   καὶ ἦρεν εἷς ἄγγελος ἰσχυρὸς λίθον ὡς μύλινον μέγαν, "A certain mighty angel
picked up a stone resembling a huge millstone." This is part of an adaptation of Jer
51:63–64(LXX 28:63–64). (On the phrase "mighty angel," see *Comment* on 5:2.) In
the Hellenistic and Roman periods, there were oil mills as well as grain mills. The mill
consisted of a large round stone with a circular track in which a smaller doughnut-
shaped rotary stone revolved, driven by a horizontal beam that extended through the
middle of the rolling stone to an upright beam set in the base stone; the horizontal
beam was driven by human or animal power (drawing in Kuhnen, *Nordwest-Palästina*,
45; see *ADB* 4:831–32). The kind of millstone referred to here would be similar in size,
shape, and weight to the μύλος ὀνικός, "donkey's millstone" (Mark 9:42; Matt 18:6),
so called because it was turned by a donkey or mule.

21b   καὶ ἔβαλεν εἰς τὴν θάλασσαν λέγων· οὕτως ὁρμήματι βληθήσεται Βαβυλὼν
ἡ μεγάλη πόλις καὶ οὐ μὴ εὑρεθῇ ἔτι, "and threw it into the sea, saying, 'In the same
way will that great city Babylon be overthrown with sudden violence and will no
longer exist.'" In this prophetic action of the angel, note the occurrence of
paranomasia: first the literal meaning of βάλλειν, "to throw," then the figurative
meaning in the passive of βάλλεσθαι, "to be overthrown" (for other examples of
paronomasia that alternates between the literal and figurative meanings of the
same word, see *Comment* on 18:20). This verse alludes to Jer 51:63–64(LXX 28:63–
64), "When you finish reading this book, bind a stone to it, and cast it into the midst
of the Euphrates, and say, 'Thus shall Babylon sink, to rise no more, because of the
evil that I am bringing upon her.'"

22a   καὶ φωνὴ κιθαρῳδῶν καὶ μουσικῶν καὶ αὐλητῶν καὶ σαλπιστῶν οὐ μὴ ἀκουσθῇ
ἐν σοὶ ἔτι, "And the sound of the kitharists and the singers and the flutists and the
trumpeters will never be heard in you again." The motif of the cessation of the
sounds of musical instruments as a poetic way of describing desolation also occurs
in Isa 24:8 and 1 Macc 3:45. A more remote parallel is found in *Sib. Or.* 8.113–19
(tr. J. J. Collins, *OTP* 1:420), which may be dated ca. A.D. 175 and in which a strong
antipathy to musical accompaniment at ritual occasions is expressed:

> They do not pour blood on altars in libations or sacrifices.
> No drum sounds, no cymbal,
> no flute of many holes, which has a sound that damages the heart,
> no pipe, which bears an imitation of the crooked serpent,
> no savage-sounding trumpet, herald of wars,
> none who are drunk in lawless revels or dances,
> no sound of the lyre, no evil-working device.

22b καὶ πᾶς τεχνίτης πάσης τέχνης οὐ μὴ εὑρεθῇ ἐν σοὶ ἔτι, "and no craftsman of any occupation / will ever be found in you again." The presence of various crafts was an essential feature of the ancient city. The crafts typically included metalworking, brick-making, glassmaking, carpentry, perfume-making, tent-making, spinning, weaving, tanning, dyeing, pottery-making, carving, sculpture, and stonemasonry.

22c καὶ φωνὴ μύλου οὐ μὴ ἀκουσθῇ ἐν σοὶ ἔτι, "the sound of the mill / will never be heard in you again." This clause is the beginning of an allusion to Jer 25:10, which contains various elements used in a different order (see v 23), including the absence of "the sound of the millstones." The Hebrew phrase קוֹל רֵחַיִם *qôl rēḥayim*, "sound of the handmill," is erroneously translated ὀσμὴν μύρου, "smell of perfume," in LXX Jer 25:10, indicating that the author of Revelation is dependent on the Hebrew text. The dual form רֵחַיִם *rēḥayim* indicates that these handmills consisted of two implements (KB³, 1134), a concave bottom stone (פֶּלַח תַּחְתִּית *pelaḥ taḥtît,* Job 41:24[MT 41:16]) and a small loaf-shaped "rider" stone (פֶּלַח רֶכֶב *pelaḥ rekeb,* Judg 9:53; 2 Sam 11:21), which was moved back and forth by hand to crush the grain in the bottom stone (*ADB* 4:831–32). Because meal and flour were staples, milling was a daily activity performed by slaves (Exod 11:5; Judg 16:21) or the woman (and daughters) of the household (Isa 47:2), and the possession of a handmill was absolutely essential (Deut 24:6; Jos. *Ant.* 4.270). This incessant scraping sound of the handmill, a normal and frequent sound coming from all homes, is referred to here.

23a καὶ φῶς λύχνου οὐ μὴ φάνῃ ἐν σοὶ ἔτι, "the light of a lamp / will never be seen in you again." This clause alludes to Jer 25:10, "Moreover I will banish from them . . . the light of the lamp." This phrase is found only here in Jeremiah, making it certain that the allusions in Rev 18:22–23 are primarily dependent on Jer 25:10. In *Tg. Jer.* 25:10 this becomes "And I will destroy from them . . . the sound of travelling-companies who rejoice with the light of a candle." Lamp light in the early evening, seen through the windows of homes in a city, indicates the presence of people and of life.

23b καὶ φωνὴ νυμφίου καὶ νύμφης οὐ μὴ ἀκουσθῇ ἐν σοὶ ἔτι, "the voices of the bridegroom and the bride / will never be heard in you again." This is part of a longer stereotyped couplet in Jer 25:10, to which this passage alludes. There the couplet is used in a negative context of divine judgment: "the voice of mirth and the voice of gladness, the voice of the bridegroom and the voice of the bride" (also in Jer 7:34; 16:9; 25:10; 40:11[MT 33:11]; cf. Bar 2:23). In *Tg. Jer.* these passages consistently have the plural forms "the sound of the bridegrooms and the sound of brides." The prophecy of Joshua ben Ananias (uttered ca. A.D. 62), which anticipated the destruction of Jerusalem, contains one line that reads "A voice against the bridegroom and the bride" (Jos. *J.W.* 6.301), i.e., a metaphor that represents the vitality of a thriving city as well as a harbinger for its future prosperity used as a threat of destruction in prophetic speech. The metaphor of the bridegroom and the bride is closely associated with joy and rejoicing, and the notion of "rejoicing" has connotations of sexual enjoyment; cf. the fifth and sixth blessings of R. Judah (*b. Ketub.* 8a; tr. Epstein, *Babylonian Talmud*):

> Blessed art Thou, O Lord our King, God of the universe, who has created joy and gladness, bridegroom and bride, rejoicing, song, mirth, and delight, love, and brotherhood, and peace, and friendship. Speedily, O Lord our God, may be heard in the cities

of Judah, and in the streets of of Jerusalem, the voice of joy and the voice of gladness, the voice of the bridegroom and the voice of the bride, the voice of the singing of bridegrooms from their canopies and of youths from their feasts of song. Blessed are Thou, O Lord, who maketh the bridegroom to rejoice with the bride.

23c ὅτι οἱ ἔμποροί σου ἦσαν οἱ μεγιστᾶνες τῆς γῆς, "for your merchants were the prominent people of the world." This clause alludes to Isa 23:8, part of an oracle against Tyre (NRSV): "whose merchants were princes, whose traders were the honored of the earth," with the omission of "were princes, whose traders" (see Fekkes, *Isaiah,* 221–23). It is not at all obvious why this causal clause (a ὅτι clause) has been inserted at this point. Charles (2:112) speculates that it might originally have been read after the first clause in v 11. Though the stereotypical poetic pattern of vv 22–23a is not continued here, this clause (and the one immediately following in v 23d) does continue the apostrophic style of directly addressing Babylon in the phrase "your merchants." Though merchants have been mentioned in vv 11–17a, they are not referred to as "your [i.e., Babylon's] merchants."

Rome is condemned for her economic domination of the Mediterranean world, which is viewed from the perspective of exploitation. While exploitation did occur (e.g., in Egypt following the tradition of the Ptolemies), the economic infrastructure of the Roman world was the primary reason for the prosperity of much of the Mediterranean world, particularly Roman Asia.

23d ὅτι ἐν τῇ φαρμακείᾳ σου ἐπλανήθησαν πάντα τὰ ἔθνη, "for all the nations were deluded by your magic spells." This is the second of two causal clauses (see v 23c), though it is not at all obvious how it follows the preceding text. The apostrophic style of vv 22–23a is continued in the phrase "*your* magic spells," though the rest of the poetic pattern in vv 22–23a is not used. In Rev 18:3, the first reason given for the fall of Babylon is extremely convoluted: all nations have become drunk from the wine that is the wrath of her fornication (see *Comment* on 18:3). V 23d is probably an allusion to Isa 47:9 (see *Comment* above on 18:8, 9; cf. Fekkes, *Isaiah,* 220 n. 74), where the defeat of Babylon is prophesied (NRSV): "in spite of your many sorceries and the great power of your enchantments [LXX ἐν τῇ φαρμακείᾳ σου ἐν τῇ ἰσχύι τῶν ἐπαοιδῶν σου σφόδρα]" (cf. v 12). Nineveh is denounced in Nah 3:4 under the imagery of a harlot who is a mistress of sorcery who practices sorcery. In *Sib. Or.* 5.165 (before A.D. 132), Rome is charged with desiring sorcery (ὅτι φαρμακίην ἐπόθησας). In Cebes *Tabula* 5.2, as part of an allegorical interpretation of a picture found on a tablet, a female figure named Ἀπάτη, "Deceit," holds a cup in her hand, and it is said that she leads all people astray (ἡ πάντας τοὺς ἀνθρώπους πλανῶσα); cf. Rev 17:2; 18:3. The mention of magical spells at this point suggests that the power and success of Rome in conquering and dominating the Mediterranean world, like that of ancient Babylon, was such that it could only be attributed to magic. On the fixed phrase πάντα τὰ ἔθνη, "all nations," see *Comment* on 12:5.

24 καὶ ἐν αὐτῇ αἷμα προφητῶν καὶ ἁγίων εὑρέθη καὶ πάντων τῶν ἐσφαγμένων ἐπὶ τῆς γῆς, "And in her was found the blood of the prophets and God's people and of all those slaughtered upon the earth." This concluding couplet is striking in that the apostrophic style of vv 22–23 has been dropped and Babylon is referred to in the third person, as in v 21. The "prophets and God's people" (on the latter as a translation of οἱ ἅγιοι, see *Comment* on 5:8) include all the Christian martyrs, while the parallel line, "those slaughtered on the earth," may refer to all those put to death by Babylon-Rome (cf. Tacitus *Annals* 1.10.4). There is a likely allusion here to Jer 51:49, in which Babylon is blamed not only for the slaughter of Israelites but also for that of other peoples as well: "Babylon must fall for the slain of Israel, as for Babylon have fallen the slain of all the earth." John's Jewish origins may have made him sensitive to the slaughter of Jews right after the beginning of the first Jewish revolt and the enormous slaughter following it (A.D. 66–73). 1,100,000 people, probably an exaggerated figure, were reportedly killed (Jos. *J.W.* 6.420; John Malalas *Chron.* 10.45). After the revolt began in A.D. 66, fighting erupted in the Greek cities of Palestine (Caesarea, Philadelphia, Esbous, Gerasa, Pella, Gadara, Hippos, Gaulanitis, Tyre, Ptolemais, Gaga, Sebaste, Ascalon, Anthedon, Gaza, Scythopolis, and Damascus [where 10,500 Jews died]), resulting in the slaughter of scores of thousands of Jews (Jos. *J.W.* 2.457–86, 559–61). The victorious Titus took Jewish captives to Caesarea Philippi, Berytus, and Antioch, where they were thrown to wild animals and forced to fight and die as gladiators (Jos. *J.W.* 7.2.23–24; 3.37–40; 5.100–111). There is a change from the second person to the third person here (ἐν αὐτῇ, "in her," instead of the expected ἐν σοί, "in you"), which together with the motif of martyrdom, i.e., "the blood of the prophets and God's people" (which is not even hinted at until this concluding verse), suggests that this verse belongs to the final redaction of this chapter within the book as a whole (Wellhausen, *Analyse*, 29). The same motif is clearly redactional in 16:6 and 17:6, suggesting a dramatic change in the historical situation in which persecution had been intensified to the point of actual executions (i.e., either the Neronian persecution, A.D. 64–68, or a perceived crisis during the reign of Domitian at the end of the first century A.D.). A parallel is found in Matt 23:35, in a woe of Jesus directed to the scribes and Pharisees (NRSV): "so that upon you may come all the righteous blood shed on earth [ἐκχυννόμενον ἐπὶ τῆς γῆς]." See also *1 Enoch* 9:1: Michael, Gabriel, Ouriel, Raphael, and Gabriel look down from heaven and see αἷμα πολὺ ἐκχυννόμεν[ον] ἐπὶ τῆς γῆς, "much blood shed upon the earth" (cf. *1 Enoch* 9:9: ὅλη ἡ γῆ ἐπλήθη αἵματος καὶ ἀδικίας, "the whole earth was filled with blood and iniquity"). 5 Ezra 1:32 (NRSV) reflects the notion that those who shed the blood of the prophets will eventually pay for their crime: "I sent to you my servants the prophets, but you have taken and killed them and torn their bodies in pieces; I will require their blood of you, says the Lord."

Explanation

Rev 18 continues the focus on the destruction of Babylon-Rome, anticipated in 14:8 and then dealt with in a preliminary way in Rev 17. There are three closely related textual units in Rev 18, formally presented as three speeches: (1) The first speech is attributed to "another angel" (i.e., one different from the interpreting angel of Rev 17), who announces that Babylon has fallen. The speech takes the form of a ritual lament or prophetic taunt song (vv 1–3), with the *topos* of the deserted city, which the angel uses to gloat over Babylon's destruction. The threat of desolation is a theme adapted from OT prophetic speeches. Three reasons are given for God's judgment of Babylon (v 3): (a) her corrupting influence on the nations of the world, (b) the kings of the earth fornicated with her (cf. 17:2), and (c) the merchants of the earth shared her excessive wealth (seafarers were thought to be motivated primarily by greed). (2) The next speech is attributed to an unidentified heavenly voice (vv 4–20), though the phrase "my people" (v 4) suggests that the speaker is God. This speech begins with a "summons to flight" (a speech form found in the classical prophets) encouraging the innocent inhabitants of Babylon to leave before it is too late (vv 4–8), referring not to physical flight but rather to the avoidance of the temptations of the corrupt features of Greco-Roman culture. Babylon's punishment is viewed not merely in terms of *lex talionis*, i.e., the principle of limited retaliation. Rather, Babylon will be repaid *double* for what she has inflicted on the nations of the world. The brief soliloquy, in which an attitude of excessive pride or hybris is abundantly evident, is attributed to Babylon personified as a queen. The speech then takes the form of a second ritual lament in vv 9–20, with a series of different mourners (the kings of the earth, the merchants of the earth, and those who sail the seas) expressing their reactions in brief first-person threnodies. The theme of the sudden and unexpected destruction of Babylon-Rome is emphasized, and a list of the luxury trade goods that flow into the city stresses her excessive wealth (vv 12–13). (3) The final speech is attributed to "a mighty angel" acting like a prophet who performs a symbolic prophetic act (vv 21–24). He picks up a great millstone and throws it into the sea to illustrate how Babylon will be suddenly destroyed. All of the normal sights and sounds of an inhabited city will be noticeably absent from Babylon, a theme that picks up the emphasis on the deserted city *topos* from v 2.

4. Heavenly Throne-Room Audition (19:1–8)
5. Concluding Angelic Revelation (19:9–10)

Bibliography

Batey, R. A. *New Testament Nuptial Imagery.* Leiden: Brill, 1971. **Bauckham, R.** "The Worship of Jesus." In R. Bauckham, *Climax.* 118–49. **Bruce, F. F.** "The Spirit in the Apocalypse." In *Christ and the Spirit in the New Testament.* FS C. F. D. Moule, ed. B. Lindars and S. Smalley. Cambridge: Cambridge UP, 1973. 333–44. **Chavasse, C.** *The Bride of Christ: An Enquiry into the Nuptial Element in Early Christianity.* London: Faber & Faber, 1939. **Cothenet, E.** "L'esprit de prophétie dans le corpus Johannique." *DBSup* 8 (1972) col. 1330. **Fekkes, J.** "'His Bride Has Prepared Herself': Revelation 19–21 and Isaian Nuptial Imagery." *JBL* 109 (1990) 269–87. **Ford, J. M.** "'For the Testimony of Jesus Is the Spirit of Prophecy' (Rev. 19:10)." *ITQ* 42 (1975) 284–91. **Francis, F. O.** "Humility and Angel Worship in Col. 2:18." *ST* 16 (1962) 109–34. **Giblin, C. H.** "Structural and Thematic Correlations in the Theology of Revelation 16–22." *Bib* 55 (1974) 487–504. **Gnilka, J.** "Bräutigam—spätjüdisches Messiasprädikat?" *TTZ* 69 (1960) 298–301. **Gunkel, H.** *The Psalms: A Form Critical Introduction.* Philadelphia: Fortress, 1967. **Hayward, R.** *Divine Name and Presence: The Memra.* Totowa, NJ: Allenheld, Osmun, 1981. ———. "The *Memra* of YHWH and the Development of Its Use in Targum Neofiti I." *JJS* 25 (1974) 412–18. **Johnston, S. I.** "Riders in the Sky: Cavalier Gods and Theurgic Salvation in the Second Century A.D." *CP* 87 (1992) 303–21. **Lampe, G. W. H.** "The Testimony of Jesus Is the Spirit of Prophecy (Rev. 19,10)." In *The New Testament Age.* FS B. Reicke, ed. W. Weinrich. 2 vols. Macon, GA: Mercer UP, 1984. 245–58. **Lohse, E.,** ed. *Die Texte aus Qumran: Hebräisch und Deutsch.* 2nd ed. Munich: Kösel, 1971. **Mazzaferri, F.** *"Martyria Iesou* Revisited."

BT 39 (1988) 114–22. **Priest, J.** "A Note on the Messianic Banquet." In *The Messiah: Developments in Earliest Judaism and Christianity,* ed. J. H. Charlesworth. Minneapolis: Fortress, 1992. 222–38. **Prigent, P.** "Une tradition messianique relative à Juda." *La Monde de la Bible* 11 (1979) 46. **Rissi, M.** "Die Erscheinung Christi nach Off. 19,11–16." *TZ* 21 (1965) 81–95. **Sheppard, A. R. R.** "Pagan Cults of Angels in Roman Asia Minor." *Talanta* 12–13 (1980–81) 77–101. **Simon, M.** "Remarques sur l'angélolâtrie juive au début de l'Ére Chrétienne." In *Le Christianism antique et son contexte religieux.* WUNT 23. Tübingen: Mohr-Siebeck, 1981. 2:450–64. **Skehan, P. W.** "King of Kings, Lord of Lords (Apoc 19, 16)." *CBQ* 10 (1948) 398. **Slater, T. B.** "'King of Kings and Lord of Lords' Revisited." *NTS* 39 (1993) 159–60. **Smith, D.** "Messianic Banquet." *ADB* 4:788–91. ———. "The Messianic Banquet Reconsidered." In *The Future of Early Christianity.* FS H. Koester, ed. B. A. Pearson. Minneapolis: Fortress, 1991. 64–73. **Sokolowski, F.** "Sur le Culte d'Angelos dans le paganisme grec et romain." *HTR* 53 (1960) 225ff. **Teixidor, J.** *The Pagan God: Popular Religion in the Greco-Roman Near East.* Princeton: Princeton UP, 1977. **Torrey, C. C.** "Armageddon." *HTR* 31 (1938) 237–48. **Vermez, P.** "Buber's Understanding of the Divine Name Related to Bible, Targum and Midrash." *JJS* 24 (1973) 147–66. **Williams, A. L.** "The Cult of Angels at Colossae." *JTS* 10 (1909) 413–38.

Translation

¹ᵃ*After this I heard* ᵇ*what sounded like* ᵇ *the* ᶜ*loud noise* ᶜ *of a huge crowd in heaven, saying,*ᵈ

"Hallelujah! ᵉ

Victory ᶠ *and* ᵍ*glory and power* ᵍ *belong to* ʰ *our God,*

² *because* ᵃ *true and just are his judgments,*

because ᵇ *he judged the great whore*

who ᶜ*corrupted the earth with her immorality,*

and he avenged the deaths ᵈ *of his servants* ᵉ*caused by* ᶠ*her."* ᵉ

³*Then they said* ᵃ *a second* ᵇ *time,*

"Hallelujah!

For ᶜ *her smoke ascends for ever."*

⁴*Then the twenty-four elders and the four cherubim fell prostrate and worshiped* ᵃ *God* ᵇ *who is seated on the throne, singing,*

"Amen!

Hallelujah!"

⁵*A*ᵃ ᵇ*voice came from the throne, saying,*ᵇ

ᶜ*"Praise* ᵈ*our God* ᵈ ᶜ ᵉ*all you his servants,*

even ᶠ *you who fear him, both small and great."* ᵉ

⁶*Then I heard* ᵃ*what sounded like* ᵃ *the sound of a great multitude or like the sound of many waters or like the sound of loud thunder, saying,*ᵇ

"Hallelujah!

For ᶜ*the Lord our God* ᶜ ᵈ*the Almighty* ᵈ ᵉ*has begun to reign.*ᵉ

⁷ *Let us rejoice* ᵃ *and exult* ᵇ *and give* ᶜ *glory to him,*

for ᵈ*the wedding day of the Lamb has arrived,*ᵉ

and his ᶠ *wife* ᵍ *has prepared herself;*

⁸ *for* ᵃ*she was permitted to wear* ᵃ

fine linen, ᵇ*shining and pure"*

(for the fine linen ᵇ *represents the righteous deeds of the* ᶜ*people of God* ᶜ*).*

⁹*Then he said to me, "Write,*ᵃ ᵇ *'How fortunate* ᵇ *are* ᶜ*those who have been invited* ᶜ *to*

the ᵈ*wedding feast* ᵈ *of the Lamb.'"* ᵉ*He said to me,*ᵉ *"This is the* ᶠ ᵍ*true message from God."* ᵍ ¹⁰ *Then I fell before* ᵃ*his feet to worship* ᵃ ᵇ*him, but* ᶜ *he said to me, "Don't do that!* ᵈ *I am a fellow servant with you and your brothers* ᵉ *and sisters* ᵉ *who maintain the testimony concerning* ᶠ*Jesus.*ᵍ *Worship* ʰ *God. For the testimony concerning Jesus* ⁱ *is the Spirit of prophecy."*

Notes

1.a.   Variant: omit καί] ℵ A C 025 046 fam 1006 fam 1611²⁰⁵⁰ ⁻²³⁴⁴ Oecumenius²⁰⁵³ ²⁰⁶².

1.b-b.   Variants: (1) ὡς] ℵ A C 025 046 fam 1006¹⁸⁴¹ fam 1611²⁰⁵⁰⁻²³⁴⁴ Andr fᵒ⁵¹ᶜᵒʳ²⁰²³²⁰⁷³ i l n Cassiodorus vg. (2) omit ὡς] 051* fam 1006¹⁰⁰⁶ Oecumenius²⁰⁵³ ²⁰⁶² Andreas Primasius Tyc² Tyc³ Beatus itᵍⁱᵍ syr. The phrase ἤκουσα ὡς φωνήν occurs just twice elsewhere, in places disputed by many of the same witnesses: 6:6 (omitted by fam 1006 fam 1611¹⁶¹¹ Oecumenius²⁰⁵³ Andreas syr cop) and 19:6 (omitted by 1006 Andreas itᵍⁱᵍ Primasius). John's more usual idiom is either ἤκουσα φωνήν (6:7; 9:13; 10:4; 12:10; 14:2) or ἤκουσα φωνῆς (11:2; 14:13; 21:3; cf. 16:1). The evidence for reading (1) is very strong. In addition, it is awkward in Gk. and thus the *lectio difficilior,* making it a prime candidate for scribal correction (as also in 6:6 and 19:6). ἤκουσα ὡς is analogous to εἶδον ὡς (Heb. כְּאֵרְאֶה *wā'ēre' kĕ*), "I saw something like," in Ezek 1:27(2x).

1.c-c.   Variants: (1) φωνὴν μεγάλην] ℵ A C 025 046 051 fam 1006¹⁸⁴¹ ²⁰⁴⁰ fam 1611¹⁶¹¹ ¹⁸⁵⁴ ²³²⁹ Oecumenius²⁰⁵³ Andr f²⁰³¹ ⁻²⁰⁵⁶ g l n 2019. (2) φωνήν] fam 1611²³⁴⁴ Andreas vgᶜˡᵉᵐ; Primasius Apringius Beatus. (3) φωνῆς] Andr b²⁰⁸¹ d i l²⁰⁸⁰ 1773.

1.d.   λεγόντων, a present gen. masc. pl. ptcp., should be governed by the fem. acc. sing. noun phrase φωνὴν μεγάλην and thus have the form λέγουσαν. However, this is a *constructio ad sensum,* congruent in gender and case (though not number) with the preceding noun phrase ὄχλου πολλοῦ, which the author considers a collective noun that should receive a pl. ptcp. form. Mussies (*Morphology,* 138) states that there are only two *constructiones ad sensum* in Revelation, 7:9 and 19:1; yet see 8:9; 9:18; 13:3–4; 18:4. The *constructio ad sensum* is relatively common in Koine Gk. For NT examples, cf. pl. verbs with ὄχλος: Matt 21:8; John 6:2; Acts 6:7; pl. ptcp. with ὄχλος: Matt 15:31; pl. ptcps. with πλῆθος: Luke 2:13; Acts 5:16; 21:36 (cf. BDR § 134).

1.e.   The term ἀλληλουϊά, which occurs four times in Revelation (19:1, 3, 4, 6), exhibits some thoughtless spelling inconsistency in modern editions of the Gk. NT. The term ἀλληλουϊά with an initial *spiritus lenis* is found in Tischendorf, *NT Graece,* von Soden, *Text,* and Nestle-Aland²⁵ at 19:1, 3, 4, 6, while ἁλληλουϊά with a *spiritus asper* is found in Nestle-Aland²⁶ ²⁷ as well as in WHort and UBSGNT⁴ at 19:1, 3, 4, 6. The form with the *spiritus asper* is found in BAGD, 39, while in Bauer-Aland, 76, the variations in orthography are mentioned but not explained. In fact, the *spiritus lenis* and *asper* readings are simply modern guesswork since they are rarely represented in the MS traditions. The rule of thumb is that א (') and ע (') are transliterated into Gk. with the *spiritus lenis,* while ה (*h*) and ח (*ḥ*) are transliterated with the *spiritus asper.*

1.f.   On the translation of σωτηρία as "victory," see *Comment* on 7:10.

1.g-g.   Variants: (1) ἡ δόξα καὶ ἡ δύναμις] ℵ A C 025 051 fam 1006¹⁰⁰⁶¹⁸⁴¹ fam 1611¹⁶¹¹ Oecumenius²⁰⁵³ ²⁰⁶² Andreas Tyc² Beatus Apringius copˢᵃ vg. (2) ἡ δόξα καὶ ἡ τιμὴ καὶ ἡ δύναμις] fam 1611²³²⁹ Andr a b c d g 2019 copᵇᵒ. (3) ἡ δύναμις καὶ ἡ δόξα] fam 1611¹⁸⁵⁴ 2030 Andr f²⁰²³ 94 Byzantine itᵍⁱᵍ. (4) ἡ δύναμις] ℵ* itᵃ.

1.h.   Variants: (1) τοῦ θεοῦ] ℵ A C 025 046 051 fam 1006¹⁰⁰⁶ ¹⁸⁴¹ fam 1611¹⁶¹¹ ¹⁸⁵⁴ ²³²⁹ 1862 1678 Oecumenius²⁰⁵³ᵗᵉˣᵗ. (2) κυρίῳ τῷ θεῷ] Andr a c d TR. (3) τῷ θεῷ] Andr b d⁷⁴³ ²⁰⁵⁵. Here the three attributes are in the nom. (ἡ σωτηρία, ἡ δόξα, and ἡ δύναμις) in a nominal sentence, while the predicate is in the gen., τοῦ θεοῦ ἡμῶν, requiring that a verb such as εἰσί be supplied: "[are] our God's," or "[belong to] our God" (cf. 6:6). Here one might have expected (as the scribal corrections indicate) a dat. of poss. (τῷ θεῷ ἡμῶν, "[belong to] our God"), as in 1:6; 5:13; 7:10, 12; cf. Luke 2:15), the more common construction in doxologies in which the verb εἰσί is omitted (*Did.* 9:2, 3; 10:2; *1 Clem.* 20:12; 32:4; 38:4; 43:6; 45:7; 50:7; 58:2; 61:3; 64:1; 65:2). Yet the construction in 19:10, i.e., an attribute in the nom. with a gen. of poss., has a close parallel in Rev 12:10 and is an alternate construction for doxologies; cf. Matt 6:13 (*var. lect.* 1253); *Did.* 8:2; 9:4; 10:5; cf. Rom 9:5.

2.a.   Torrey (*Apocalypse,* 42) regarded ὅτι as a mistranslation of the Aram. particle דִּי *dî,* which can be translated as a relative pronoun ("who, which") or as a causal particle ("because"). In his view, this clause should therefore be translated "*whose* judgments are true and righteous."

2.b. See *Note* 2.a. This clause could then be translated "*who* has judged the great whore."

2.c. Variants: (1) ἔφθειρεν] *lectio originalis.* (2) διέφθειρεν] fam 1611¹⁸⁵⁴ ²³²⁹ 2030 Andr d⁰⁵¹ ²⁰²³ ²⁰⁷³ f 94 Byzantine.

2.d. Here τὸ αἷμα, "the blood," is a metaphorical way of referring to deaths caused by Babylon = Rome; here "death" is the deep structural meaning of τὸ αἷμα (cf. J. P. Louw, *Semantics of New Testament Greek* [Chico, CA: Scholars, 1982] 76–77).

2.e-e. The phrase ἐκ χειρὸς αὐτῆς, lit. "by her hand," is a *phraseological* Hebraism found only here in Revelation (the two other occurrences of ἐκ χειρός, "from the hand," in 8:4 and 10:10 are lit. references to hands). Here ἐκ χειρός functions as a compound prep. governing αὐτῆς, which must be construed as a gen. of *agency* (the alternative is to regard χειρός as a gen. of agency or means and αὐτῆς as a poss. gen.). In the LXX the phrases ἐκ/ἀπὸ [τοῦ] χειρός are frequently used to translate the Heb. semiprep. מיָּד *miyyad,* "from the hand" (see Sollamo, *Semiprepositions,* 194–98, 340–42). The noun χείρ is redundant, so the phrases ἐκ χειρός and ἀπὸ χειρός can be translated "by" or "from." A close parallel is found in 2 Kgs 9:7 (cf. Charles, 2:119): καὶ ἐκδικήσεις τὰ αἵματα τῶν δούλων μου τῶν προφητῶν καὶ τὰ αἵματα πάντων τῶν δούλων κυρίου ἐκ χειρὸς Ἰεζάβελ [מיד איזבל *miyyad 'îzābel*], "And you will avenge the deaths of my servants the prophets and the deaths of all the servants of the Lord caused by Jezebel." K. G. C. Newport ("The Use of ἐκ in Revelation: Evidence of Semitic Influence," *AUSS* 24 [1986] 223–24) thinks that the NIV captures this idiomatic use of ἐκ χειρός: "He has avenged *on her* the blood of his servants [emphasis mine]." This is incorrect, however, since ἐκ χειρός in Rev 19:2 and in 2 Kgs 9:7 is used in a causal or instrumental sense.

2.f. Variant: insert τῆς before χειρός] 051 Oecumenius²⁰⁵³ ²⁰⁶² fam 1611²³⁴⁴ Andreas. Although parts of the body are normally articular, the tendency in Classical and Hellenistic Gk. is to omit the article in prep. phrases (Smyth, *Greek Grammar,* § 1128), a phenomenon encouraged by the fact that the OT Heb. term מיָּד *miyyad,* "from the hand," is always anarthrous.

3.a. Variants: (1) εἴρηκαν] ℵ A fam 1611²³²⁹ Andreas. (2) εἴρηκεν] fam 1611¹⁸⁵⁴ ²³⁴⁴ Andr f²⁰²³ g Andr 0¹⁷⁷³ 2019 Byzantine cop^bo. (3) εἰρήκασιν] Oecumenius²⁰⁵³ Andr d e²⁰⁵⁷ f²⁰⁷³ n. (4) εἶπαν] C. (5) εἶπον] Andr l. Readings (1), (2), and (3) are the *lectiones difficiliores* since they are perfects; reading (3) is a correction of the later 3rd pl. pf. ending -αν to the earlier and more distinctive ending -ασιν (found only in Rev 8:2; cf. Mussies, *Morphology,* 265). A similar correction from εἴρηκα to εἶπον is found in Rev 7:14 (see *Note* 7:14.b.). The 3rd sing. verb in reading (2) represents a correction based on understanding ὄχλου πολλοῦ in v 1 as a collective *sing.,* whereas the 3rd pl. verbs in (1), (3), (4), and (5) understand ὄχλου πολλοῦ as a collective *pl.,* as does the ptcp. λεγόντων. Reading (1) is the best attested, is the *lectio difficilior,* and is congruent with the way the author understands ὄχλου πολλοῦ as reflected by λεγόντων. εἴρηκαν is a 3rd pl. pf. ind. used as an aor. (Mussies, *Morphology,* 265). The subject of εἴρηκαν is not made explicit, though it must logically be the ὄχλος πολύς in v 1a, so this is an instance of a *constructio ad sensum.* There are three other examples of this use of the pf. in Rev: 5:7; 7:13; 8:5.

3.b. δεύτερον here means "a second time" (BAGD, 177.2; Mussies, *Morphology,* 220).

3.c. The clause introduced by καί provides the reason or circumstances for the preceding Hallelujah, so καί functions as a causal or (more broadly considered) circumstantial particle, which should be translated "for, because." For a more extensive discussion, cf. *Notes* 12:11.c. and 18:3.d. (cf. Charles, 1:cxlviii; 2:120).

4.a. The subject of the 3rd pl. verb προσεκύνησαν includes τὰ τέσσαρα ζῷα, a neut. nom. pl. Pl. neut. nouns are used with pl. (instead of sing.) verbs if they refer to living beings; cf. 4:8, 9; 5:8, 14; 19:21 (Mussies, *Morphology,* 231–32; BDR § 133).

4.b. On the use of προσκυνεῖν + dat. or acc. in Revelation, see *Note* 4:10.b.

5.a. The καί with which this sentence begins is left untranslated because it lacks independent semantic value and functions as a discourse marker indicating the beginning of a new sentence.

5.b-b. Variants: (1) φωνὴ ἀπὸ τοῦ θρόνου ἐξῆλθεν λέγουσα] A C Oecumenius²⁰⁵³ vg^WW; von Soden, *Text.* (2) φωνὴ ἐκ τοῦ θρόνου ἐξῆλθεν λέγουσα] 025 051; Tischendorf, *NT Graece.* (3) φωνὴ ἐκ τοῦ θρόνου ἐξῆλθεν] Andreas. (4) φωνὴ ἀπὸ τοῦ οὐρανοῦ ἐξῆλθεν λέγουσα] 046 Primasius. (5) φωναὶ ἐξῆλθον ἐκ τοῦ θρόνου λέγουσαι] ℵ*. (6) φωναὶ ἐξῆλθεν ἀπὸ τοῦ θρόνου λέγουσαι] 0229.

5.c-c. Though the verb αἰνεῖν normally takes a direct obj. in the acc. (LXX 2 Esdr 3:10; Neh 5:13; Jdt 13:14; Job 33:30; Luke 2:13, 20; 19:37; 2:47; 3:8, 9; Rom 15:11; *Sib. Or.* 5.403; *T. Levi* 2.3B9 [de Jonge, *Testaments,* 25]; *Vit. Proph.* 15.7; *Pr. Man.* 15 [2.22.14]; Denis, *Fragmenta*]; see the correction in *Note* 19:5.d-d.), here it takes a dat. of direct obj., reflecting the Heb. הוֹדָה לְ *hôdâ lě* or הִלֵּל לְ *hillēl lě* (BAGD, 23). This is reflected in the LXX and in Greco-Jewish literature about one hundred times; see Jer 4:2; 20:13; 1 Chr 16:36; 23:5; 2 Chr 5:13; 7:3; 20:19; 2 Esdr 3:11; Sir 51:12; Dan 2:23; 4:34; *Pss. Sol.* 5:1; 10:5.

5.d-d. Variants: (1) τῷ θεῷ] ℵ A C 025 046 051 0229 fam 1611²³²⁹ ²³⁴⁴ Andr b²⁰⁵⁹* ²⁰⁸¹* f²⁰²³ i²⁰³⁶ 2019 lat;

all modern editions. (2) τὸν θεόν] Oecumenius²⁰⁵³ Andreas Byzantine. Reading (2) corresponds to the customary style of the LXX (see 1 Chr 16:36; 23:5; 2 Chr 20:19; 2 Esdr 3:10–11; Jer 4:2; 20:13; *Pss. Sol.* 5:1; 10:5) and the Gk. of the NT and must therefore be regarded as a correction (Schmid, *Studien* 2:81).

5.e-e. πάντες οἱ δοῦλοι αὐτοῦ καὶ οἱ φοβούμενοι αὐτόν, οἱ μικροὶ καὶ οἱ μεγάλοι is a string of four articular pl. noms. functioning as vocatives. Twelve other articular noms. are used as vocatives in Revelation; cf. *Note* 4:11.a. for a complete list.

5.f. Variants: (1) insert καί] A 046 051 fam 1006¹⁰⁰⁶ ¹⁸⁴¹ fam 1611¹⁶¹¹ ¹⁸⁵⁴ ²³²⁹ ²³⁴⁴ Oecumenius²⁰⁵³ ²⁰⁶² Andreas Byzantine latt syrᵖʰ copᵇᵒ arm Primasius Beatus; B. Weiss, *Johannes-Apokalypse*, 126; Charles, 2:356; [Bousset (1906) 427]; [von Soden, *Text*]; [Merk, *NT*]; [Nestle-Aland²⁷]; [UBSGNT⁴]; R. Boismard, "L'Apocalypse ou les Apocalypses de s. Jean," *RB* 56 (1949) 519–20. (2) omit καί] ℵ C 025 copˢᵃ ᵇᵒᵐˢˢ eth; Tischendorf, *NT Graece;* WHort. While *TCGNT* ¹, 759–60, and *TCGNT* ², 684, regard the external evidence as balanced, the evidence is actually stronger for reading (1), which is probably original. The καί here is epexegetical, indicating that "his servants" are not different from, but rather are further defined by, "those who fear him, both small and great." Schmid (*Studien* 2:108) notes that it is not at all clear who these Godfearers are.

6.a-a. Variants: (1) ὡς] *lectio originalis.* (2) omit ὡς] fam 1006¹⁰⁰⁶ Andreas itᵍⁱᵍ Primasius. The regular use of ὡς as a comparative particle is verb + obj. + ὡς + substantive.

6.b. Variants: (1) λεγόντων (gen. pl. masc. present ptcp.)] A 025 0229 fam 1006¹⁰⁰⁶ ¹⁸⁴¹ fam 1611¹⁶¹¹ ²³²⁹ Oecumenius²⁰⁵³ ²⁰⁶² latt; WHort; Charles, 2:356; Merk, *NT;* Nestle-Aland²⁷; UBSGNT⁴. (2) λεγουσῶν] ℵ (lends support to reading [1]). (3) λέγοντας (acc. pl. masc. present ptcp.)] 051 Andreas. (4) λέγοντες (nom. pl. masc. present ptcp.)] fam 1611¹⁸⁵⁴ 2030 Byzantine; Tischendorf, *NT Graece;* WHortᵐᵍ; B. Weiss, *Johannes-Apokalypse,* 137 (argues that λεγόντων conforms mechanically to the preceding gen. pl. forms); Bousset (1906) 427. λεγόντων, a present active masc. gen. pl. ptcp., *should* be congruent in gender, number, and case with φωνήν, and so have the form λέγουσαν (present active fem. acc. sing.), though it is noteworthy that this reading is found in no known MS (Hoskier, *Text* 2:519). However, φωνήν occurs *three* times in this verse, the first governing the noun phrase ὄχλου πολλοῦ (masc. gen. sing.; cf. 19:1), the second governing ὑδάτων πολλῶν (neut. gen. pl.), and the third governing βροντῶν ἰσχυρῶν (fem. gen. pl.). This appears to be a *constructio ad sensum* (contra Schmid, *Studien* 2:232; Mussies, *Morphology,* 138); however, since the author obviously considers ὄχλου πολλοῦ to be the most important antecedent and since he considers it a collective noun that is congruent with a pl. verb form (cf. *Note* 1.d. for references), he uses the ptcp. form λεγόντων.

6.c-c. Variants: (1) κύριος ὁ θεός] A fam 1006¹⁰⁰⁶ ¹⁸⁴¹ itᵗ syrᵖʰ copᵇᵒ ˢᵃᵐˢˢ; Charles, 2:126, 356. (2) κύριος ὁ θεὸς ἡμῶν] ℵ² 025 046 fam 1611 Oecumenius²⁰⁵³ ²⁰⁶² Andr c f²⁰²³ ²⁰⁷³ i l¹⁶⁷⁸ n 94 1773 2019 Byzantine itᵃʳ ᶜ ᵈᵉᵐ ᵈⁱᵛ ʰᵃᶠ vg syrʰ copˢᵃᵐˢˢ ; Cyprian (von Soden, *Das lateinische Neue Testament*, 587); Aphraates; Tyconius; Ps-Ambrose; Beatus; Arethas; Tischendorf, *NT Graece;* WHort [ἡμῶν]; B. Weiss, *Johannes-Apokalypse*, 213; von Soden, *Text;* Bousset (1906) 427; Nestle-Aland²⁵; Nestle-Aland²⁷ [ἡμῶν]; UBSGNT⁴ [ἡμῶν]. (3) ὁ θεὸς ἡμῶν] 051 Andreas. (4) ὁ θεὸς ὁ κύριος ἡμῶν] ℵ Andr l¹⁷⁷⁸ ²⁰⁸⁰. (5) ὁ θεός, ὁ θεὸς ἡμῶν] Andr e²⁰⁵⁷ 598. (6) ὁ θεός] 1 Andr a n²⁴²⁹ arm. (7) κύριος] syrᵖʰ* copᵇᵒᵐˢˢ Primasius. The phrase κύριος ὁ θεὸς ὁ παντοκράτωρ occurs several times in Revelation (4:8; 11:17; 15:3; 16:7; 21:22; cf. 1:8), suggesting that the addition of ἡμῶν does not agree with the author's usual style (Charles, 2:126; Schmid, *Studien* 2:81; *TCGNT* ¹, 760; *TCGNT* ², 685). It may have been imported from the phrase ὁ θεὸς ἡμῶν, which occurs in 19:1, 5.

6.d-d. Variant: omit ὁ παντοκράτωρ] itᵍⁱᵍ.

6.e-e. ἐβασίλευσεν, lit. "he became king," "he reigned," is an ingressive aor. emphasizing the beginning of a state and can therefore be understood as "he has begun to reign"; see *Note* 11:17.f-f.

7.a. Variant: χαίρομεν] Oecumenius²⁰⁵³ fam 1611²³²⁹ Andr b²⁰⁵⁹* e²⁰²⁶ i²⁰³⁶ ²⁰⁷⁴* l¹⁷⁷⁸ n⁻²⁴²⁹ 2019 arm.

7.b. Variants: (1) ἀγαλλιῶμεν] *lectio originalis.* (2) ἀγαλλιώμεθα] 2030 Andr c f²⁰²³ Byzantine.

7.c. Variants: (1) δῶμεν (aor. subjunctive)] ℵ* 046 94 fam 1006¹⁰⁰⁶ ¹⁸⁴¹ fam 1611¹⁶¹¹ ¹⁸⁵⁴ 2030 itᵍⁱᵍ vg syr cop eth Arethas Cyprian Primasius Andr a c f⁰⁵¹ ²⁰²³ ²⁰⁷³ g l Byzantine; Tischendorf, *NT Graece;* Bousset (1906) 427; von Soden, *Text;* Merk, *NT.* (2) δώσομεν (fut. ind.)] ℵ² A (lacuna in C) Oecumenius²⁰⁵³ Andr d i²⁰⁴² n; WHort; B. Weiss, *Johannes-Apokalypse*, 116; Charles, 2:356; Nestle-Aland²³. (3) δώσωμεν (irregular form of aor. subjunctive)] 025 fam 1611²³²⁹ ²³⁴⁴ Andreas; Nestle-Aland²⁷; UBSGNT⁴. (4) δοξάζωμεν] 598. Reading (2), though the *lectio difficilior,* follows two hortatory subjunctives and is impossible Gk.; therefore, it is clearly the result of a scribal error (Schmid, *Studien* 2:133; *TCGNT* ¹, 760; *TCGNT* ², 685). However, note the frequent o = ω interchange (Gignac, *Grammar* 1:275–77). *TCGNT* ¹, 760, and *TCGNT* ², 685, regard reading (3) as least objectionable despite relatively poor external MS support, though it is easy to construe reading (2) as an error based on reading (3). Note the identical constellation of variants in Mark 6:37: δώσομεν (𝔓⁴⁵ A B L Δ; Nestle-Aland²⁷); δῶμεν (W Θ f¹ Byzantine); δώσωμεν (ℵ D N f¹³ 28 33 565 892 1424).

7.d. Variant: insert ἡ δόξα καί before ὁ γάμος] fam 1611²³²⁹. Unique reading.

7.e. ἦλθεν is an aor. used here with a perfective value (Mussies, *Morphology*, 339).

7.f. Variant: omit αὐτοῦ] Andr a b g.

7.g. Variant: νύμφη] ℵ² it^gig (*sponsa*); cop^(sa bo) (*sheleet*); Apringius. Variant the result of assimilation to Rev 21:2, 9, 17.

8.a-a. καὶ ἐδόθη αὐτῇ ἵνα περιβάληται, lit. "and it was given to her that she wear." However, διδόναι + inf. or διδόναι + ἵνα + subjunctive means "to allow, permit."

8.b-b. Variant: omit λαμπρὸν καθαρόν· τὸ γὰρ βύσσινον] Oecumenius²⁰⁵³ ²⁰⁶². Scribal omission through homoioteleuton. There is a slight grammatical problem in that τὰ δικαιώματα (neut. pl.) is in apposition to τὸ βύσσινον (neut. sing.), which is solved by this omission. The relevant sentence in Oecumenius²⁰⁵³ implies that a period is placed after the clause ἵνα περιβάληται βύσσινον, "to wear fine linen," so that the next sentence consists of τὰ δικαιώματα τῶν ἁγίων ἐστιν, "righteousness deeds belong to the people of God."

8.c-c. On translating οἱ ἅγιοι, lit. "saints," as "God's people," see *Comment* on 5:8.

9.a. Variants: (1) omit γράψον] Andr a b e f²⁰³¹ ²⁰⁵⁶ g²⁰⁴⁵* h 598. (2) omit γράψον . . . μοι] Cassiodorus Beatus.

9.b-b. On the translation "how fortunate," see *Note* 1:3.b.

9.c-c. An extensive prep. phrase, εἰς τὸ δεῖπνον τοῦ γάμου τοῦ ἀρνίου, is inserted between the article οἱ and the substantival ptcp. κεκλημένοι, contrary to the usual practice of the author; i.e., he normally avoids placing a prep. phrase between an article and its substantive (Bousset [1906] 176; Charles, 1:clvii). However, this is precisely the pattern in each of the *adscriptiones* in the proclamations to the seven churches (2:1, 8, 12, 18; 3:1, 7, 14). See also *Notes* 2:1.a-a. and 14:14.b-b.

9.d-d. Variants: (1) τοῦ γάμου] ℵ¹ A 025 fam 1006¹⁰⁰⁶ fam 1611 Oecumenius²⁰⁵³ ²⁰⁶² Andr c d f⁰⁵¹ ²⁰²³ ²⁰⁷³ l n⁻²⁴²⁹ Byzantine. (2) omit τοῦ γάμου] ℵ fam 1006¹⁸⁴¹ Andreas it^gig t cop^bo.

9.e-e. Variant: omit καὶ λέγει μοι] ℵ*.

9.f. Variants: (1) οἱ before ἀληθινοί] A (lacuna in C) Andr e²⁰⁵⁷ Byz 5⁸⁰⁸ Byz 10¹⁷³⁴ Byz 18⁹¹ ²⁴² ¹⁹³⁴; WHort^mg; B. Weiss, *Johannes-Apokalypse*, 107 (who claims that it was omitted by some copyists on analogy with 21:5; 22:6); [Bousset (1906) 428]; Charles, 2:357. (2) omit οἱ] ℵ Andreas Byzantine; Tischendorf, *NT Graece;* WHort; von Soden, *Text;* Nestle-Aland²⁷; UBSGNT⁴. Reading (1) is probably original since it is syntactically necessary; it was omitted through carelessness (Schmid, *Studien* 2:93, 196). In the apparently similar phrases in 21:5 and 22:6, the adj. ἀληθινοί (along with πιστοί) is a *predicate*, while in 19:9 ἀληθινοί is in the attributive position and should therefore be articular in conformity with the author's style.

9.g-g. Variants: (1) ἀληθινοὶ τοῦ θεοῦ εἰσιν] A (ἀληθεινοί); 025 046 fam 1611¹⁸⁵⁴ Oecumenius²⁰⁵³ ²⁰⁶² Byzantine. (2) ἀληθινοί εἰσιν τοῦ θεοῦ] ℵ* 051 Andreas Primasius. (3) τοῦ θεοῦ ἀληθινοί εἰσιν] ℵ² fam 1006¹⁰⁰⁶ ¹⁸⁴¹ fam 1611²³²⁹ Andr n. Since the phrase τοῦ θεοῦ is found in three different places in the MS tradition and is absent from parallel phrases (21:5; 22:6), Bousset speculates that they have been interpolated ([1906] 428).

10.a-a. Variant: omit ποδῶν αὐτοῦ προσκυνῆσαι] fam 1611²³²⁹.

10.b. On the use of προσκυνεῖν with the dat. and acc., see *Note* 4:10.b.

10.c. καί is translated as "but" since the two clauses it coordinates have an adversative relationship; this is an instance of καί *adversativum*.

10.d. Variant: insert ποιήσῃς] fam 1006 Andr f²⁰⁷³ n. The same variant occurs in a similar context in 22:9.

10.e-e. "And sisters" added to indicate inclusiveness of "your brothers."

10.f. The gen. Ἰησοῦ is translated here as an obj. gen. (see *Comment* on 19:10).

10.g. Variant: add: Χριστοῦ] fam 1611²³²⁹.

10.h. See *Note* 19:10.b.

10.i. See *Note* 19:10.e.

Form/Structure/Setting

I. Outline

4. Heavenly throne-room audition (19:1–8)
   a. Two-part hymn of praise and the response (vv 1–4)

(1) First part of the hymn of praise (vv 1–2)
    (a) The singers: a great multitude in heaven (v 1a)
    (b) The hymn (vv 1b–2)
        [1] Introduction: Hallelujah! (v 1b)
        [2] Attributes ascribed to God (v 1b)
            [a] Salvation
            [b] Glory
            [c] Power
        [3] Reason for the praise: God's judgments are true and
            just (v 2a)
            [a] He has judged the great whore (v 2b)
            [b] He avenged on her the blood of his servants (v 2c)
(2) Second part of the hymn of praise (v 3)
    (a) The singers: great heavenly multitude (v 3a)
    (b) The hymn (v 3b)
        [1] Introduction: Hallelujah!
        [2] Judgment of the great whore: her smoke rises eternally
(3) The response of the heavenly court (v 4)
    (a) The respondents (v 4a)
        [1] The twenty-four elders
        [2] The four cherubim
    (b) Nature of their response (v 4a–c)
        [1] Physical response: they fall prostrate (v 4a)
        [2] Verbal response: They worship God who is seated on
            the throne by saying (v 4bc)
            [a] Amen!
            [b] Hallelujah!
b. Call to praise and hymnic response (vv 5–8)
  (1) The voice from the throne (v 5a)
    (a) Exhortation to praise God (v 5b)
    (b) Those exhorted to praise (v 5b)
        [1] All you his servants
        [2] All those who fear him
            [a] The small
            [b] The great
  (2) The hymn of praise (vv 6–8)
    (a) Description of the sound (v 6a)
        [1] Like a great multitude of people
        [2] Like many waters
        [3] Like loud thunder
    (b) Their hymn of praise (vv 6b–8)
        [1] Introduction: Hallelujah! (v 6b)
        [2] Reason for praise: the Lord God Almighty reigns
            (v 6b)
        [3] Three exhortations (v 7a)
            [a] Let us rejoice
            [b] Let us exult
            [c] Let us give God glory

[4] Reason (vv 7b–8)
    [a] The wedding of the Lamb has come
    [b] The bride is ready (vv 7b–8)
        {1} God has granted her a special linen dress (v 8a)
            {a} Bright
            {b} Pure
        {2} Allegorical meaning of dress: the righteousness
            of the saints (v 8b)
5. Concluding angelic revelation (vv 9–10)
    a. Angel commands John to write a beatitude (v 9)
        (1) A blessing for those invited to the marriage supper of the
            Lamb (v 9a)
        (2) This is the true message from God (v 9b)
    b. John worships the angelic guide (v 10a)
    c. John is rebuked by the angel (v 10b)
        (1) Angel forbids John's worship
        (2) The role claimed by the angel
            (a) A fellow servant of John
            (b) A fellow servant of John's brothers and sisters who hold the
                testimony of Jesus
        (3) Angel directs John to worship God
    d. Concluding saying: the testimony of Jesus is the spirit of
        prophecy (v 10c)

II. Literary Analysis

Rev 19:1–8 and 19:9–10 are textual units, both of which function as transitions from 17:1–18:24 (which focuses on the judgment of Babylon-Rome) to 21:9–22:5 (on the bride, i.e., the holy city). This section is framed by the introductory formula μετὰ ταῦτα ἤκουσα, "after this I heard" (v 1), and the more common introductory formula καὶ εἶδον, "then I saw" (v 11), which introduces the next unit of text in 19:11–21.

The unit in 19:1–8 in turn consists of two complex subunits: (1) 19:1–4, a two-part hymn of praise and the response, which focuses on the judgment of the whore and serves as a conclusion for 17:7–18:24, and (2) 19:5–8, a call to praise and hymnic response, a hymnic continuation of the throne scene in 19:1–4. This second subunit now introduces a new subject, the marriage of the Lamb and his bride.

Finally, 19:9–10 is the fifth and concluding textual unit in 17:1–19:10; it consists of a brief angelic revelation introduced by καὶ λέγει μοι, "and he said to me." The identity of the speaker is not at all evident, though it is apparently the *angelus interpres* of 17:1–18, who is not part of the intervening units of text in 18:1–19:8. This short section (which forms a conclusion to 17:1–19:8) bears several verbal and thematic similarities with 22:6–9. In both, an angel commissions John to write, a beatitude is pronounced, and John tries to, but is discouraged from, worshiping the angelic revealer. The angelic claim that "these are the true words of God" (v 9b) refers to the entire section 17:1–19:8. This angelic revelation also consists of three parts, each introduced by καὶ λέγει μοι. Kraft (244) regards v 9 as the original conclusion of Revelation and speculates that the speaker is the revelatory angel mentioned in 1:1.

The overall structure of 21:9–22:9 must first be considered in relation to the parallel structure in 17:1–19:10, both of which have been carefully and convincingly analyzed as paired angelic revelations by Giblin (*Bib* 55 [1974] 487–504). This can best be understood by looking at a synoptic comparison of the parallel texts that frame these units, i.e., Rev 17:1–3, 19:9–10, and 21:9–10, 22:6–9:

Rev 17:1–19:10	*Rev 21:9–22:9*
¹⁷:¹καὶ ἦλθεν εἷς ἐκ τῶν ἑπτὰ Then came one of the seven	²¹:⁹καὶ ἦλθεν εἷς ἐκ τῶν ἑπτὰ Then came one of the seven
ἀγγέλων τῶν ἐχόντων τὰς ἑπτὰ angels with the seven	ἀγγέλων τῶν ἐχόντων τὰς ἑπτὰ angels with the seven
φιάλας bowls	φιάλας τῶν γεμόντων τῶν ἑπτὰ bowls full of the seven
	πληγῶν τῶν ἐσχάτων last plagues
καὶ ἐλάλησεν μετ' ἐμοῦ λέγων and spoke with me, saying,	καὶ ἐλάλησεν μετ' ἐμοῦ λέγων and spoke with me, saying,
δεῦρο, δείξω σοι "Come, I will show you	δεῦρο, δείξω σοι "Come, I will show you
τὸ κρίμα τῆς πόρνης τῆς μεγάλης. . . . the judgment of the great whore. . . ."	τὴν νύμφην τὴν γυναῖκα τοῦ ἀρνίου the bride, the wife of the Lamb."
¹⁷:³καὶ ἀπήνεγκέν με He then transported me	²¹:¹⁰καὶ ἀπήνεγκέν με He then transported me
εἰς ἔρημον to the desert	
ἐν πνεύματι in a prophetic trance.	ἐν πνεύματι in a prophetic trance
	ἐπὶ ὄρος μέγα καὶ ὑψηλόν to a great and high mountain.
καὶ εἶδον Then I saw	καὶ ἔδειξέν μοι Then he showed me . . . .
[Body of vision]	[Body of vision]
¹⁹:⁹ᵃμακάριοι. . . . [see 22:7] How fortunate. . . .	
¹⁹:⁹ᵇκαὶ λέγει μοι Then he said to me,	²²:⁶καὶ εἶπέν μοι Then he said to me,
οὗτοι οἱ λόγοι ἀληθινοὶ "This is the true message	οὗτοι οἱ λόγοι πιστοὶ καὶ "This message is faithful and

τοῦ θεοῦ εἰσιν. . . .
from God. . . ."

ἀληθινοί. . . .
true . . ."

22:7μακάριος. . . . [see 19:9a]
Fortunate. . . .

22:8bκαὶ ὅτε ἤκουσα καὶ ἔβλεψα
And when I heard and saw them,

19:10καὶ ἔπεσα ἔμπροσθεν
Then I fell before

ἔπεσα προσκυνῆσαι ἔμπροσθεν
I fell to worship before

τῶν ποδῶν αὐτοῦ
his feet

τῶν ποδῶν τοῦ ἀγγέλου
the feet of the angel

τοῦ δεικνύοντός μοι ταῦτα.
who revealed them to me.

προσκυνῆσαι αὐτῷ.
to worship him,

καὶ λέγει μοι·
but he said to me,

καὶ λέγει μοι·
But he said to me,

ὅρα μή·
"Don't do that!

ὅρα μή·
"Don't do that!

σύνδουλός σού εἰμι
I am a fellow servant with you

σύνδουλός σού εἰμι
I am a fellow servant with you

καὶ τῶν ἀδελφῶν σου τῶν ἐχόντων
and your brothers and sisters who maintain

καὶ τῶν ἀδελφῶν σου τῶν προφητῶν
and your brothers and sisters, the prophets

τὴν μαρτυρίαν Ἰησοῦ·
the testimony concerning Jesus.

καὶ τῶν τηρούντων τοὺς λόγους
and those who obey the commands

τοῦ βιβλίου τούτου.
in this book.

τῷ θεῷ προσκύνησον.
Worship God."

τῷ θεῷ προσκύνησον.
Worship God."

III. ANALYSIS OF THE HYMNS

Rev 19:1–8 is the longest, most complex, and final hymnic section in Revelation, containing five hymnic text units. This lyrical section has aptly been described as a great hymnic finale to Revelation (Deichgräber, *Gotteshymnus*, 56; Jörns, *Evangelium*, 144, 159), though in fact the section functions as an *intermezzo,* composed to connect two sections of the composition by concluding 17:1–18:24 and introducing 21:9–22:9

(n.b. that it does not introduce 19:11–21:8, the section that immediately follows!).
Rev 19:1–10 does not reflect liturgical hymns or hymnic pieces used in churches but
was expressly composed to fit its present literary context, even though some elements
may have been drawn from Jewish and Christian liturgical tradition (Deichgräber,
Gotteshymnus, 58). Vv 1–4 focus on anticipatory celebration of the judgment of the
great whore proleptically narrated in 18:1–24, while vv 5–8 anticipate the marriage
of the Lamb and the readiness of his bride, metaphors for the descent of the New
Jerusalem to earth in 21:9–22:9. Among the distinctive features of this hymnic section
is the occurrence of the transliterated Hebrew liturgical formula "hallelujah" four
times (vv 1, 3, 4, 6).

The first strophe occurs in Rev 19:1–4 and consists of three distinct elements.
The *first* element is a "judgment doxology" in vv 1b–2, a genre that was used twice
before in 16:5–6 and 16:7 (see *Comments* on 16:5–6). Following the introductory
"hallelujah!" a *cry of victory* (similar to those already met in 7:10, 11:15, and 12:10)
occurs in v 1b, followed by the general reason for the celebration of God's victory,
namely, the truth and justice of his acts of judgment. This is followed by the specific
reason for emphasizing God's justice, the judgment of Babylon that has been
proleptically narrated in 18:1–24. The *second* element appears in v 3 and is
essentially a narrative continuation of the specific reason for celebrating God's just
judgment in v 2. The same singers, the "huge crowd" in heaven mentioned in v 1a,
chant a second hymn, which, like the first, is introduced with a "hallelujah" and
followed by a reference to the eternal destruction of Babylon. The *third* element
centers on a responsory scene of worship in the heavenly court in which the twenty-
four elders and the four cherubim fall prostrate in worship of God crying "Amen!
Hallelujah!" This entire strophe clearly functions as a victorious conclusion to the
destruction of Babylon narrated in 18:1–24.

The second strophe occurs in Rev 19:5–8 and consists of two subunits. The *first*
subunit, in v 5, is a *summons to praise* directed to the people of God on earth, referred
to as his servants or those who fear him, people of all social stations. The *second*
subunit is the *hymn of praise* in vv 6–8, the only hymn in Revelation that conforms
fully to the OT genre (K. Berger, *Formgeschichte*, 241–42).

Two Hebrew terms for the hymn of praise are תְּהִלָּה *tĕhillâ* (see *TDOT* 3:410; note
that the Hebrew Psalter is entitled תהלים *tĕhillîm*, indicating a broader use of the
term) and תּוֹדָה *tôdâ* (see *TDOT* 5:427–43). The hymn of praise typically consists of
three parts (Gunkel, *Psalms*, 10–13; Mowinckel, *Psalms* 1:81–105; Eissfeldt, *Introduction*, 105–9; Weiser, *Psalms*, 52–66; K. Koch, *Tradition*, 159–70): (1) The *invitation
to song* or *hymnic introduction* can be in the imperative, jussive, or cohorative and
constitutes a summons to begin praising Yahweh ("Hallelujah!" in v 6b). (2) The
thematic sentence is a transitional section beginning with a term meaning "for" or
"because" that introduces the theme of the hymn ("For the Lord our God the
Almighty has begun to reign" in v 6b). (3) The main part of the hymn consists of
the report of the actions of God to indicate the basis or motivation for the praise
(vv 7–8). In this case, the call for joy and rejoicing (v 7a) is grounded in the
imminent marriage of the Lamb and the readiness of his bride (vv 7b–8a), an event
of the future rather than the past. The concluding explanatory line of prose in v
8b does not belong to the body of the hymn itself but is an editorial addition to it.

Vv 7–8 of this hymn are clearly modeled after Isa 61:10, which comprises three
parallel couplets:

I will greatly *rejoice* in the Lord,
  my soul shall *exult* in my God;
for *he has clothed me* with the *garments* of salvation,
  he has covered me with the *robe of righteousness*,
as a bridegroom decks himself with a garland,
  and as a bride adorns herself with her jewels. (RSV)

While the prophet is speaking in Isa 61:10, a change in speakers is clearly indicated in *Tg. Isa.* 61:10, where the targumist begins "Jerusalem said." This means that *Jerusalem* is clothed with the garments of salvation, i.e., with the "robe of righteousness."

In Rev 19:7–8, words for "rejoice" and "exult" are combined in a single stichos, while the author uses the stichos τὸ γὰρ βύσσινον τὰ δικαιώματα τῶν ἁγίων ἐστίν, "for the fine linen is the righteous deeds of the people of God," as an explanatory comment. Since such commentary is rarely introduced with γάρ, "for," this may indicate that this particular comment was part of the original hymn composed by the author and not a secondary interpolation (against Charles, 2:127–28).

IV. SOURCE-CRITICAL ANALYSIS

According to Bousset, Rev 19:1–8 is the product of the final editor of Revelation because it reflects features found throughout the rest of the book ([1906] 428): v 1 (7:9); v 2a (15:6; 16:5); v 2b (chaps. 17–18; cf. 11:18); v 2c (6:10); v 3 (14:11); v 4 (chap. 4); v 5 (11:18); v 6 (14:1–5); and vv 7–8 (chap. 21). In the interest of considering 19:1–8 as a "hymnic finale" to Revelation, Jörns (*Evangelium,* 160) lists terms that occur in 19:1–8 and are also found in earlier hymnic portions: (1) δόξα, "glory" (19:1; cf. 4:11), (2) δύναμις, "power" (19:1; cf. 4:11; 11:17; 12:10), (3) ἔκρινεν, "he judged" (19:2; cf. 16:5; 18:20), (4) ἔφθειρεν, "she corrupted" (19:2; cf. 11:18), and (5) ἐξεδίκησεν, "he avenged" (19:2; cf. 16:6; 6:10). This list is not very impressive, however, and hardly proves that 19:1–8 is a "grand finale" that gathers together elements from earlier hymns. The hymns in this section differ from others in Revelation in that the transliterated Hebrew term "hallelujah" occurs only in this section (in vv 1, 3, 4, 6), though it can be argued that this provides the final hymn with a greater liturgical solemnity than the earlier hymns possessed.

There are several reasons for suspecting that 19:9–10 has been inserted at the end of 19:1–8 (Bousset [1906] 429): (1) The introduction of this section at the conclusion of the hymnic section in 19:1–8 seems abrupt (the identity of the speaker in 19:1 is not immediately obvious). (2) The syntax of the phrase "those who have been invited to the wedding feast of the Lamb" (v 9) is unusual. (3) This section has a doublet in 22:6–9. (4) The three-part literary form in vv 9–10 centers on a beatitude, and many of the other beatitudes in Revelation (14:13; 16:15; 20:6) are probably secondary insertions.

Comment

1a μετὰ ταῦτα ἤκουσα ὡς φωνὴν μεγάλην ὄχλου πολλοῦ ἐν τῷ οὐρανῷ λεγόντων, "After this I heard what sounded like the loud noise of a huge crowd in heaven, saying." The introductory phrase "after this I heard" occurs nowhere else in

Revelation, though the phrase μετὰ ταῦτα/τοῦτο εἶδον, "after this I saw," occurs five times (4:1; 7:1, 9; 15:5; 18:1). The phrase ὄχλος πολύς, "huge crowd," occurs just three times in Revelation, once in 7:9 and twice in a similar formulation in 19:1, 6 (ἤκουσα ὡς φωνὴν [μεγάλην] ὄχλου πολλοῦ, "I heard something like the [loud] noise of a huge crowd"). The great heavenly multitude probably refers to heavenly beings (see 5:11).

1b   ἀλληλουϊά· ἡ σωτηρία καὶ ἡ δόξα καὶ ἡ δύναμις τοῦ θεοῦ ἡμῶν, "Hallelujah! / Victory and glory and power belong to our God." The term ἀλληλουϊά, "hallelujah," is a Greek transliteration of the Hebrew liturgical formula הַלְלוּ־יָהּ *halĕlû-yāh*, meaning "praise Yahweh" (occurring twenty-four times in the MT), which was taken over into Christian hymns and occurs for the first time in Christian literature in Rev 19:1–6 (J. Hempel, "Hallelujah," *IDB* 2:514–15). The "Hallelujah!" exclamation here in v 1b is apparently understood by the author as a call to praise introducing the *judgment doxology* that follows in vv 1b–2 (Deichgräber, *Gotteshymnus,* 56). In the NT, the term ἀλληλουϊά is found just four times in Revelation, all in chap. 19, where it is used three times to introduce hymns (vv 1, 3, 6) and once as an antiphonal response (v 4b).

The introductory function of hallelujah is evident in Tob 13:18. The term "hallelujah" is used in the Psalms both in the *titles* to individual psalms (Pss 106:1; 111:1; 112:1; 113:1; 135:1; 146:1; 147:1; 148:1; 149:1; 150:1; ἀλληλουϊά is added to the titles of several psalms in the LXX: 114:1; 115:1; 116:1; 117:1; 118:1; 145:1) and as *conclusions* to individual psalms (Pss 104:35; 105:45; 106:48 [where it concludes the fourth book of the Psalter]; 113:9; 115:18; 116:19; 117:2; 146:10; 147:20; 148:14; 149:9; 150:6; it is omitted in the LXX from all these passages with the exception of Ps 150:6). Hallelujah is also a concluding cry in 3 Macc 7:13, and in *Apoc. Moses* 43:4 it is used with a doxology to conclude the work: ἀλληλουϊά. ἅγιος ἅγιος ἅγιος κύριος εἰς δόξαν θεοῦ πατρός. ἀμήν, "Halleluia! Holy, holy, holy is the Lord to the glory of God the Father. Amen" (for a brief discussion of the many variants, see M. D. Johnson, *OTP* 2:295 n. 43.c). Hallelujah is transliterated into Syriac in the conclusion of each of the *Odes of Solomon*.

The rabbis puzzled about the absence of the word "hallelujah" in the Psalter before Ps 104 (*Midr. Ps.* 104.27; *t. Ber.* 9b; see Str-B, 2:725; 3:497; on the two ways of spelling "hallelujah," see Str-B, 3:822). In the LXX, the Greek transliterated form occurs twenty times in the Psalms as well as in Tob 13:18 and 3 Macc 7:13. The term occurs only rarely in other Greco-Jewish literature (*Apoc. Moses* 43:4; *Vit. Proph.* 15.7 [*var. lect.*], where it is interpreted to mean αἰνεῖτε τὸν θεόν, "praise God"). The phrase ἀλληλουϊά, ἀμήν, "hallelujah, amen," is used to conclude a spell in a magical papyrus that shows Jewish influence (*PGM* VII.271). The term occurs infrequently in early Christian literature (*Odes Sol.* 11:24; *PGM* 10.33; see *PGL,* 75). In *Apoc. Paul* 29–30, "hallelujah" occurs seven times, and it is also defined as meaning *"tecel. cat. marith. macha,"* which is interpreted to mean "Let us bless him all together."

The song sung in Rev 19:1b–2, like the angelic taunt of 18:1–3, focuses on the judgment of "Babylon" (and the vindication of the martyrs) as an accomplished fact (vv 1b–4). Although vv 1b–2 are similar to a doxology (for a discussion of the form of the doxology, see *Form/Structure/Setting* on 1:5b–6), they in fact constitute a *judgment doxology,* similar to the two judgment doxologies in 16:5–6 and 16:7 (Deichgräber, *Gotteshymnus,* 56). The clause "Victory and glory and power belong to our God" is *a cry of victory* formula similar to those found in 7:10, 11:15, and 12:10, all in the third-person *er-Stil*, "he style." The clause ἡ σωτηρία . . . τοῦ θεοῦ ἡμῶν, "victory . . . belongs to our God," is closely parallel to the relatively rare OT formula ליהוה הישועה *lĕYHWH hayĕšûʿâ*, "victory belongs to Yahweh" (Ps 3:9; Jonah 2:9; cf. *TDOT* 6:458), also found in 7:10 and 12:10 (see *Comment* on 7:10). Strings of similar substantives are used in inscriptions honoring Greco-Roman benefactors, in this case the emperor Constantius II: "For the *health* and *safety* and *(for)tune* and *victory* and *eternal endurance* [ὑπὲρ ὑγιείας καὶ σωτηρίας καὶ (τύ)χης καὶ νίκης καὶ αἰωνίου διαμονῆς] of our master, Flavius Julius Constantius [i.e., Emperor Constantius II] . . ." (Roueché, *Aphrodisias*, 35–39, inscription 19).

2a ὅτι ἀληθιναὶ καὶ δίκαιαι αἱ κρίσεις αὐτοῦ, "because true and just are his judgments." The first of two reasons or motivations for ascribing victory to God is introduced by ὅτι, "for, because," corresponding to the Hebrew causal particle כִּי *kî*, "for, because, indeed, truly" (cf. *TDOT* 5:434), and is extremely general in the sense that it does not refer to a particular act of God. This statement has a general parallel in 15:3 in reverse order ("just and true are your ways") but a verbatim parallel in 16:7b, ἀληθιναὶ καὶ δίκαιαι αἱ κρίσεις σου, "true and just are your judgments." There is a parallel in *Apoc. Moses* 27:5: "Then the angels fell on the ground and worshipped the Lord saying, 'You are just, O Lord, and you judge rightly.'" On the paired divine attributes ἀληθινός, "true," and δίκαιος, "just," see *Comment* on 16:7b.

2b ὅτι ἔκρινεν τὴν πόρνην τὴν μεγάλην, ἥτις ἔφθειρεν τὴν γῆν ἐν τῇ πορνείᾳ αὐτῆς, "because he judged the great whore / who corrupted the earth with her immorality." This is the second of two reasons for ascribing victory to God, and like the first in v 2b, it is also introduced by the causal particle ὅτι, "because." This basis for praise, however, refers very specifically to an event of the narrative past (hence the aorist verb ἔκρινεν, "judged"), the judgment, i.e., destruction of the great whore (referring back to 18:20, ἔκρινεν ὁ θεὸς τὸ κρίμα ὑμῶν ἐξ αὐτῆς, "for God has condemned her for condemning you"). The unmodified word πόρνη as a metaphor for Rome is used only in 17:5, 15, 16, while the phrase ἡ πόρνη ἡ μεγάλη, "the great whore," occurs elsewhere only in 17:1, where it is part of the introduction or title to the text unit that follows. The phrase "who corrupted the earth with her immorality" constitutes the crime for which Babylon was judged by God. Parallels to this phrase are found in 18:3, "because all nations have collapsed because of the wine which is her immoral passion," and 14:8, "who gave all nations to drink of the wine which is her immoral passion." The use of the verb φθείρειν, "to corrupt," recalls 11:18, where the verb διαφθείρειν is used: καὶ διαφθεῖραι τοὺς διαφθείροντας τὴν γῆν, "and to ruin utterly those who ruin the earth."

2c καὶ ἐξεδίκησεν τὸ αἷμα τῶν δούλων αὐτοῦ ἐκ χειρὸς αὐτῆς, "and he avenged the deaths of his servants caused by her." The verb ἐκδικεῖν, "to avenge," occurs only here and in 6:10 (see *Comment* on 6:10). This is a clear, though somewhat contracted, allusion to 4 Kgdms 9:7, καὶ ἐκδικήσεις τὰ αἵματα τῶν δούλων μου τῶν προφητῶν καὶ τὰ αἵματα πάντων τῶν δούλων κυρίου ἐκ χειρὸς Ἰεζάβελ, "And you will avenge the deaths of my servants the prophets and the deaths of all the servants of the Lord at the hand of Jezebel." The LXX phrase ἐκ χειρὸς Ἰεζάβελ clearly means that blood was shed "by [the hand of] Jezebel," not that vengeance would be taken upon her. The underlying Hebrew phrase in 2 Kgs 9:7 is:

ונקמתי דמי עבדי הנביאים . . . מיד איזבל
wĕniqqamtî dĕmê ʿăbāday hannĕbîʾîm . . . miyyad ʾîzābel
and I will avenge the blood of my servants the prophets . . . shed by Jezebel (NIV).

This way of understanding the Hebrew text is supported by BDB, 668, and Hobbs, *2 Kings*, 107: "and avenge the blood of my servants the prophets . . . who suffered at the hand of Jezebel." Josephus (*Ant.* 9.108) rewrites 2 Kgs 9:7, in which he idiomatically translates the phrase ἐκ χειρὸς Ἰεζάβελ: "that he might avenge the blood of the prophets murdered unlawfully by Jezebel [ὑπὸ Ἰεζαβέλας]." Though John eliminates the name "Jezebel" from his allusion, it is nevertheless clear that he saw a parallel between the infamous "Jezebel" of Thyatira and the great whore (Babylon = Rome).

3 καὶ δεύτερον εἴρηκαν· ἀλληλουϊά, καὶ ὁ καπνὸς αὐτῆς ἀναβαίνει εἰς τοὺς αἰῶνας τῶν αἰώνων, "Then they said a second time, 'Hallelujah! / For her smoke ascends for ever.'" While it seems obvious that the "they" of the verb εἴρηκαν, "they said," refers to the same group to which the judgment doxology of vv 1b–2 is ascribed, the "huge crowd" of v 1a, some have improbably argued that a second (unidentified) group is in view (Kraft, 243).

The major interpretive problem in this passage is whether "hallelujah" should be understood as a conclusion to the judgment doxology in vv 1b–2 or as the introduction to a second hymnic text in v 3. The text could be framed by the introductory and concluding hallelujahs (Deichgäber, *Gotteshymnus*, 56–57). Similar framing devices occur in some of the Psalms. LXX Ps 150 begins and ends with hallelujahs, and Pss 113(LXX 112) and 146–50 begin and end with הַלְלוּ יָהּ *halĕlû yāh,* "praise Yah," while Ps 117(LXX 116) begins with אֶת־יְהוָה הַלְלוּ *halĕlû ʾet-YHWH,* "praise Yahweh," and ends with הַלְלוּ יָהּ *halĕlû yāh,* "praise Yah." Alternatively, "hallelujah" may serve to introduce a second hymnic text found in the remainder of v 3 (Charles, 2:120; Kraft, 243; Jörns, *Evangelium*, 150), the more likely view.

This verse is an allusion to Isa 34:10, part of a prophecy against Edom: "its smoke shall go up forever," clearly closer to the Hebrew text (לְעוֹלָם יַעֲלֶה עֲשָׁנָהּ *lĕʿôlām yaʿăleh ʿăšānāh*) than the LXX text. A doublet occurs in 14:11: "The smoke of their [i.e., those who worship the beast] torment ascends for ever." The more immediate reference, however, is to the fiery destruction of Babylon mentioned in 18:9, 18 with the phrase ὁ καπνὸς τῆς πυρώσεως αὐτῆς, "the smoke of her burning." Both Isa 34:10 and Rev 19:3 share the same hyperbole, which portrays the destruction as lasting *forever,* i.e., emphasizing the finality and totality of the destruction. A similar hyperbole describes the fires of judgment as unquenchable (Isa 66:24; Jer 4:4; 17:27; Ezek 20:48), and similar statements are made of the fire of hell or Gehenna (Mark 9:43 = Matt 18:8; Mark 9:48 [an allusion to Isa 66:24]; Matt 25:41; *Sib. Or.* 1.103).

4a καὶ ἔπεσαν οἱ πρεσβύτεροι οἱ εἴκοσι τέσσαρες καὶ τὰ τέσσαρα ζῷα, "Then the twenty-four elders and the four cherubim fell prostrate." In Revelation, scenes of heavenly worship are often used as part of the narrative framework of hymns set in the heavenly court to introduce, punctuate, or conclude them (4:10; 5:8, 14; 7:11; 11:16; 19:4). Here the twenty-four elders and the four cherubim participate in the heavenly adoration of God, just as in 5:14.

4b καὶ προσεκύνησαν τῷ θεῷ τῷ καθημένῳ ἐπὶ τῷ θρόνῳ, "and worshiped God who is seated on the throne." Vv 4a and 4b constitute a couplet that appears to exhibit *synthetic parallelism* in that both cola describe a complete action. The verbs πίπτειν, "to fall down," and προσκυνεῖν, "to worship," are two ways of describing two stages of a single act of adoration and thus are very nearly synonymous (they are also paired in 4:10; 5:14; 7:11; 11:16; 19:10; 22:8; this pairing is widely attested: Ps 72:11; Dan 3:5, 6, 10, 11, 15; Matt 2:11; 4:9; 18:26; Acts 10:25; 1 Cor 14:25; *Apoc. Moses* 27:5; *Jos. As.* 28:9; *T. Job* 40.6; *Jos. Ant.* 7.95; 9.11; 10.213). Nevertheless, v 4a focuses on the worshipers and v 4b on the one who is worshiped, and therefore it is not correct to categorize the parallelism in this couplet as synonymous (Jörns, *Evangelium*, 151).

4c λέγοντες· ἀμὴν ἀλληλουϊά, "singing, 'Amen! / Hallelujah!'" The term "amen" has a concluding function here, just as in 5:14. The combination "Amen! Hallelujah!" concludes the fourth book of the Psalter (Ps 106:48, ואמר כל־העם אמן הללו־יה *wĕʾāmar kol-hāʿām ʾāmēn halĕlû-yāh*, "And all the people said, 'Amen, Hallelujah'!"), though in the LXX (105:48) these formulas are translated γένοιτο γένοιτο, "may it be so, may it be so." Similar concluding expressions are found in 1 Chr 16:36 ("Then all the people said 'Amen!' and praised the Lord") and Neh 5:13 ("And all the assembly said 'Amen' and praised the Lord"). Ἀμὴν ἀλληλουϊά occurs in *Mart. Matt.* 26:39 (Lipsius-Bonnet, *AAA* 2/1:255). "Hallelujah, Amen" concludes a spell in a magical papyrus that exhibits Jewish influence (*PGM* VII.271), and at the conclusion of a sequence of *voces magicae* in a magical amulet we find the sequence Ἀμήν· οὐ Ἀμήν· Ἀληουϊά, "Amen; Amen; Aleouia," the last word of which is a slightly garbled version of "Allelouia" (Delatte-Derchain, *Les intailles magiques*, 332–33). In *PGM* 10.33, a Christian magical papyrus, τὸ ἀμὴν καὶ τὸ ἀλληλουϊά are hypostasized.

5a καὶ φωνὴ ἀπὸ τοῦ θρόνου ἐξῆλθεν λέγουσα, "A voice came from the throne, saying." The phrase ἀπὸ τοῦ θρόνου, "from the throne," occurs only here and in 16:17 in Revelation, while the phrase ἐκ τοῦ θρόνου, "from the throne," is used as the source of an unidentified heavenly voice in 21:3 (there is no discernible difference in meaning between the two locutions). On the motif of the unidentified heavenly voice, see *Comment* on 10:4. Though one might assume that a voice "from the throne" would be the voice of God (but cf. 5:6), the brief speech that follows in vv 3b–4 with the phrase αἰνεῖτε τῷ θεῷ ἡμῶν, "praise our God," seems to exclude that possibility since it refers to God in the third person. In Exod 25:22, God promises to speak to Moses from the mercy seat between the two cherubim on the ark (see Philo *Quaest. in Ex.* 2.68; *Fug.* 101; *Quis Her.* 166). Some commentators attribute this voice to one of the four cherubim or one of the twenty-four elders (Beckwith, 721; Charles, 2:124; Mounce, 338), while others attribute it to Christ, the Lamb (Bousset, 427), even though the phrase "my God" would be more appropriate than "our God" in this case. Kraft suggests that the speaker is "the angel of the throne" (243). Since there can be no satisfactory answer to this question, it is perhaps better to conclude simply that the phrase "from the throne" at the very least indicates the divine authorization of the speaker.

5b αἰνεῖτε τῷ θεῷ ἡμῶν πάντες οἱ δοῦλοι αὐτοῦ καὶ οἱ φοβούμενοι αὐτόν, οἱ μικροὶ καὶ οἱ μεγάλοι, "Praise our God, all you his servants, / even you who fear him, both small and great." This summons to praise is directed to those on earth, in contrast to vv 1b–4, which are directed to those who dwell in heaven. This same pattern is found in Ps 148, in which vv 1–6 center on the praise of God from the heavens and vv 7–14 focus on the praise of God from the earth. In this injunction to praise God, the voice from the throne acts as a choir director in commanding the servants of God to praise him. Similarly, in Callimachus *Hymns* 2.25–31, the speaker turns to the choir and commands them to sing the paean to Apollo (cf. Williams, *Callimachus*, 35).

The phrase αἰνεῖτε τῷ θεῷ ἡμῶν, "praise our God," is very close to the OT formula הַלְלוּ־אֵל *halĕlû-ʾēl*, "praise God" (Ps 150:1), translated αἰνεῖτε τὸν θεόν in the LXX. Very similar is the formula הוֹדוּ לַיהוָה *hôdû laYHWH*, "praise Yahweh" (Pss 33:2; 105:1; 106:1; 107:1; 1 Chr 16:34; Isa 12:4; see Jörns, *Evangelium*, 152). The phrase הַלְלוּ אֶת־יְהוָה *halĕlû ʾet-YHWH*, "praise Yahweh," in Ps 117:1 (LXX 116:1: αἰνεῖτε τὸν κύριον, "praise the Lord") suggests that αἰνεῖτε τῷ θεῷ is a relatively close way of rendering "hallelujah." The phrase הַלְלוּ לֵאלֹהֵינוּ *halĕlû lēʾlōhênû* represents a literal retroversion of αἰνεῖτε τῷ θεῷ ἡμῶν into Hebrew (Charles, 2:124; Lohmeyer, 154), though this expression is nowhere found in the Hebrew Bible. αἰνεῖν, which occurs only here in Revelation, is part of a rich liturgical vocabulary of thanks and praise (on the words in these two semantic domains, see Louw-Nida, §§ 33.349–64) inherited by early Christianity from Judaism and the Greco-Roman world (on αἰνεῖν, see *TDNT* 1:177–78; on הוֹדָה *hôdâ*, see *TDOT* 3:352–56; on translating הוֹדָה *hôdâ* as "to praise," rather than "to thank," see Westermann, *Praise*, 26–27).

The articular substantives οἱ μικροί, literally, "small ones," and οἱ μεγάλοι, literally, "great ones," are idioms meaning "low status" and "high status," respectively (Louw-Nida, § 87.22, 58), which can be translated "those of every station in life." On "small and great" in other contexts in Revelation, see *Comment* on 13:16.

6a καὶ ἤκουσα ὡς φωνὴν ὄχλου πολλοῦ καὶ ὡς φωνὴν ὑδάτων πολλῶν καὶ ὡς φωνὴν βροντῶν ἰσχυρῶν λεγόντων, "Then I heard what sounded like the sound of a great multitude or like the sound of many waters or like the sound of loud thunder, saying." The fact that φωνή is anarthrous suggests that the author does not think that this group is identical with the group mentioned in 19:1. Three metaphors are used here for the singing the author is about to report, the *roaring of a huge crowd* (cf. v 1; *Pss. Sol.* 8:2), the *roaring and crashing of the sea* (cf. 1:15; 14:2; Isa 17:12; Ezek 1:24), and the *crash of thunder* (6:1; 14:2; *3 Apoc. Bar.* 11:3; 14:1–2). While loud speaking or singing is normally described by the phrase φωνὴ μεγάλη, here three metaphors are clustered to emphasized the loudness of the sound heard (two metaphors occur together in 14:2).

6b ἀλληλουϊά, ὅτι ἐβασίλευσεν κύριος ὁ θεὸς [ἡμῶν] ὁ παντοκράτωρ, "Hallelujah! / For the Lord our God the Almighty has begun to reign." The introductory hallelujah is not used simply as a liturgical formula but corresponds in meaning to "praise our God" in v 5b, for it is immediately followed by the general reason introduced by ὅτι, namely, that God has begun to reign (K. Berger, *Formgeschichte*, 241). Vv 6b–8 constitute a *hymn of praise* that conforms to the OT genre of hymn frequently found in the Psalter. The hymn consists of three parts (Gunkel, *Psalms*, 10–13; Mowinckel, *Psalms* 1:81–105; Weiser, *Psalms*, 52–66; K. Koch, *Tradition*, 159–70): (1) the *invitation to song* or hymnic introduction (here represented by "Hallelujah!"), (2) the *thematic sentence*, generally introduced by "for" (here the ὅτι clause, reflecting the Hebrew כִּי *kî*, which can be rendered in a variety of ways; see *TDOT* 5:434), and (3) the main part of the hymn, which describes God's historical acts (vv 7–8).

The verb βασιλεύειν, "to reign," with God as subject occurs just twice elsewhere in Revelation (11:15, 17). The verb is twice used in the future tense in the phrase κύριος ὁ θεὸς βασιλεύσει, "the Lord God will reign," in *Jos. As.* 19:5, 8. On the divine title κύριος ὁ θεὸς ὁ παντοκράτωρ, which occurs five times in Revelation (4:8; 11:17; 15:3; 16:7; 21:22), see *Comment* on 4:8.

7a χαίρωμεν καὶ ἀγαλλιῶμεν καὶ δώσωμεν τὴν δόξαν αὐτῷ, "Let us rejoice and exult and give glory to him." This passage contains a possible allusion to Isa 61:10 (which is again alluded to in Rev 21:2), "I will greatly rejoice [שׂוֹשׂ אָשִׂישׂ *śôś 'āśîś*] in the Lord; my soul shall exult [תָּגֵל *tāgēl*] in my God, for [כִּי *kî*]. . . ." If the author is dependent on Isa 61:10a at this point (which seems likely in view of the imagery that follows), he has rendered it freely and shows no dependence on the LXX (Fekkes, *Isaiah*, 231–38). Tob 13:15–17 (perhaps also influenced by Isa 61:10), which may also have influenced the description of the New Jerusalem in Rev 21:18–21, begins (in MSS A B) χάρηθι καὶ ἀγαλλίασαι ἐπὶ τοῖς υἱοῖς τῶν δικαίων, "give thanks and rejoice in the sons of the righteous," after which follows a description of the eschatological Jerusalem. The verbal parallels that follow suggest that the expression was relatively fixed in Greek-speaking Judaism. The same two verbs also occur together followed by ὅτι in Matt 5:12: χαίρετε καὶ ἀγαλλιᾶσθε ὅτι, "rejoice and be glad, for." Cf. LXX Ps 117:24 (MT 118:24), ἀγαλλιασώμεθα καὶ εὐφρανθῶμεν, "let us rejoice and be glad" (cf. Pss 97:1[LXX 96:1]; 118:24[LXX 117:24]; Joel 2:23). See also *1 Enoch* 104:13 (M. Black, *Apocalypsis*, 43), "All the righteous will be glad and rejoice [χαρήσονται καὶ ἀγαλλιάσονται] in them." The verbs χαίρειν, "rejoice," and ἀγαλλιᾶν, "exult," are used together with some frequency in other early Jewish texts as well (*T. Abr.* [Rec. A] 11:7, 8, 10; *Par. Jer.* 6:17, χαῖρε καὶ ἀγαλλιῶ, ὅτι, "rejoice and be glad, for"; here the first imperative is cleverly used to introduce a letter [thus conveying a double meaning], for which the normal salutation would be χαίρειν).

7b ὅτι ἦλθεν ὁ γάμος τοῦ ἀρνίου καὶ ἡ γυνὴ αὐτοῦ ἡτοίμασεν ἑαυτήν, "for the wedding day of the Lamb has arrived, / and his wife has prepared herself." The reason for rejoicing and giving God the glory is introduced with this ὅτι, "for," clause, which constitutes an announcement of the impending wedding, while v 9 mentions the wedding supper and the invitations to the wedding. The phrase ὁ γάμος τοῦ ἀρνίου, "the wedding of the Lamb," occurs only here in vv 7, 9, while the image of the "wife" occurs in 19:7 and 21:9 and the related metaphor of the "bride" (νύμφη) is used of the New Jerusalem in 21:2, 9 (see 22:17). It is important to observe that the notion of "the wife" of the Lamb is mentioned enigmatically but not further defined or described. The mention of a wedding at this point is entirely unexpected, and the theme is not touched again until 21:2, 9. The verb ἑτοιμάζειν, "to prepare," is also used of the appearance of the bride = New Jerusalem as it descends from heaven as from a bridal chamber.

The metaphor of Christ as the bridegroom and the people of God as the bride was quite widespread in early Christianity. The metaphor of the (Corinthian) church as a chaste virgin betrothed to Christ as husband occurs in 2 Cor 11:2: "I betrothed you to one husband, to present you as a chaste virgin [παρθένος ἁγνή, i.e., *virgo intacta*] to Christ." The "betrothal" presumably occurred with the conversion of the Corinthians, while the "presentation" to Christ will presumably occur at his coming; during the interim the Church, like a betrothed virgin, must maintain her purity and faithfulness to her *one* husband. The use of γυνή, "wife," at this point (see *Note* 19:7.g.) fits Jewish marriage customs in which engagement was a legally binding initiation of marriage consummated by the wedding (see Deut 22:23–24; Matt 1:18–25; *Jos. As.* 21:1; Fekkes, *Isaiah*, 234 n. 26). This metaphor is developed further in Eph 5:25–32, where the archetype for the appropriate relationship between husbands and wives is the self-sacrificing love Christ had for the Church. By his death he could then cleanse her so that eventually he could "present" her as a pure bride to himself at his return. Mark 2:20 (= Matt 9:15b; Luke 5:35; cf. *Gos. Thom.* 104) appears to equate the figure of the bridegroom with Christ (on 2:20 as a secondary expansion of 2:19, see Roloff, *Kerygma,* 229–34). The bridegroom as an allegory for Christ also occurs in the parable of the ten virgins in Matt 25:1–13 (Joachim Jeremias, *Parables,* 51–53; J. R. Donahue, *The Gospel in Parable* [Philadelpha: Fortress, 1988] 101–5). In subsequent early Christian literature, the metaphor of Christ as bridegroom and the Church as bride occurs frequently (*2 Clem.* 14:2; Tertullian *Contra Marc.* 5.18; Clement of Alex. *Strom.* 3.6; Methodius *Symp.* 7.7; Augustine *Serm.* 40.6; see *PGL,* 928).

In dealing with the origins of this imagery, it is important to distinguish between the OT and early Jewish metaphor of the marriage of Yahweh to Israel and the (rarely attested) marriage of the Messiah to Israel (Hos 2:19–20; Jer 3:20; Ezek 16:8–14; Isa 49:18; 50:1; 54:1–6; 62:5; *Tg. Ket.* Ps 48; see Str-B, 3:822). By the first century A.D., Canticles was understood to refer allegorically to Israel as the bride of God (*Tg. Cant.;* Joachim Jeremias, *TDNT* 4:1102; Stauffer, *TDNT* 1:654); this view was taken over and elaborated by Origen (R. Lawson, *Origen, The Song of Songs: Commentary and Homilies* [Philadelphia: Westminster, 1957]). The supposed notion of the Messiah as the bridegroom of Israel occurs only rarely in early Judaism (Gnilka, *TTZ* 69 [1960] 298–301; Joachim Jeremias, *TDNT* 4:1101–2; id., *Parables,* 52 n. 13, can find only a single example; Chavasse, *Bride,* 36–37, overemphasizes this notion).

8a καὶ ἐδόθη αὐτῇ ἵνα περιβάληται βύσσινον λαμπρὸν καθαρόν, "for she was permitted to wear / fine linen, shining and pure." This refers to the trousseau of the bride, though only her garments are mentioned. Clothing is also mentioned in Isa 61:10 (alluded to in v 7), though there is no verbal correspondence: "He has clothed me with the garments of salvation, and covered me with the robe of righteousness." In 21:2 the phrase "prepared as a bride adorned for her husband" also refers to the bridal trousseau but is more general and probably refers to both clothing and jewelry. The implied "jewelry" is explicitly referred to in 21:18–21 as the various precious stones out of which the foundations, walls, and gates (which ring the city as necklaces encircle the neck of a bride) were constructed. For the Church as bride, cf. 2 Cor 11:2, "I betrothed you to one husband, to present a pure virgin to Christ"; Eph 5:22–33. βύσσινον, "fine linen," was a luxury item in the ancient world, a fact made clear by its inclusion in the list of luxury trade goods in 18:12 and by the depiction of Babylon-Rome as clothed in "fine linen and purple and scarlet [garments]" in 18:16. There is an intentional contrast here between the "fine linen" of Babylon-Rome (a symbol of decadence and opulence) and the "fine linen, shining and pure" of the bride of the Lamb.

8b τὸ γὰρ βύσσινον τὰ δικαιώματα τῶν ἁγίων ἐστίν, "(for the fine linen represents the righteous deeds of the people of God)." This is an explanatory interpolation to make the symbolic significance of the "linen, shining and pure" even more obvious. This explanation was apparently thought necessary because βύσσινον was used earlier in 18:16 of the garments of Babylon-Rome. This is one of several passages within Revelation in which the symbolic significance of a person or thing is explained to the hearers and readers (see 1:20; 4:5; 8:3; 13:6; 14:10; 17:9, 12, 15, 18) and may be a later addition or explanatory gloss to the text (Wellhausen, *Analyse,* 29; Bousset [1906] 428; Charles, 2:127–28; Lohmeyer, 155; Lohse, 97; Jörns, *Evangelium,* 155).

The term δικαίωμα (which usually means "ordinance, decree" in the LXX

[*GELS,* 115] and early Jewish and early Christian literature) occurs also in 15:4. Here it means "righteous act" (Bar 2:19; see BAGD, 198; Louw-Nida, § 88.14), while in 15:4 it means "sentence of condemnation" (BAGD, 198); see *Comment* on 15:4. This clause may be a later addition since only here is the term τὰ δικαιώματα used of Christians, whereas elsewhere δικαι- terminology is used only of God.

9a καὶ λέγει μοι· γράψον· μακάριοι οἱ εἰς τὸ δεῖπνον τοῦ γάμου τοῦ ἀρνίου κεκλημένοι, "Then he said to me, 'Write, "How fortunate are those who have been invited to the wedding feast of the Lamb."'" This is the fourth of seven beatitudes or makarisms in Revelation (see 1:3; 14:13; 16:15; 20:6; 22:7, 14; for a discussion of the form, see *Form/Structure/Setting* on 1:1–3). There are striking formal similarities between 14:13 and 19:9. Both exhibit (1) an introductory formula, (2) a command to write, (3) a beatitude, and (4) a second introductory formula followed by (5) a further statement (see Kavanagh, *Liturgical Dialogue,* 54):

Rev 14:13	*Rev 19:9*
καὶ ἤκουσα φωνῆς ἐκ τοῦ οὐρανοῦ Then I heard a voice from heaven,	καὶ Then
λεγούσης saying,	λέγει μοι he said to me,
γράψον "Write,	γράψον "Write,
μακάριοι 'How fortunate	μακάριοι 'How fortunate
οἱ νεκροὶ οἱ ἐν κυρίῳ ἀποθνήσκοντες are the dead who die in the Lord.	οἱ εἰς τὸ δεῖπνον τοῦ γάμου τοῦ ἀρνίου are those who to the wedding feast of the Lamb
	κεκλημένοι. are invited.'"
ἀπαρτὶ λέγει τὸ πνεῦμα, Truly, says the Spirit,	καὶ λέγει μοι Then he said to me,
ἵνα ἀναπαήσονται ἐκ τῶν κόπων αὐτῶν, that they might rest from their labors,	οὗτοι οἱ λόγοι ἀληθινοὶ "This is the true message
τὰ γὰρ ἔργα αὐτῶν ἀκολουθεῖ for their works follow	τοῦ θεοῦ εἰσιν. from God."
μετ' αὐτῶν. after them.'"	

The identity of the speaker is not immediately apparent, though we learn from v 10 that it is probably the bowl angel of 17:1 (Bousset [1906] 428; Lohmeyer, 154; Kraft, 244–45; Müller, 319). However, the abruptness with which vv 9–10 are introduced, as well as the existence of a doublet in 22:6–9, suggests that this passage is a seam in the text (Reichelt, *Angelus*, 98) and very probably an interpolation (Ford, 311; Bousset [1906] 429). Bousset conjectured that both 19:9–10 and 22:6–9 were based on a source used twice by the author in these two places ([1906] 456–57).

The phraseology of this beatitude has close parallels in Luke 14:15, "Blessed is he who shall eat bread in the kingdom of God" (cf. Eichhorn, 2:260), and in the much later *Acts Phil.* 135 (Lipsius-Bonnet, *AAA* 2/1:67), ἰδοὺ τὸ δεῖπνον ἕτοιμον καὶ μακάριος ὁ καλούμενος, "Behold, the dinner is prepared, and blessed is the one who has been invited." There are three additional instances in Revelation in which the initial phrase in v 9a is repeated with variations:

19:9a:　　　καὶ λέγει μοι· γράψον
　　　　　　　And he said to me, "Write."

19:9b:　　　καὶ λέγει μοι· οὗτοι οἱ λόγοι ἀληθινοὶ τοῦ θεοῦ εἰσιν
　　　　　　　And he said to me, "This is the true message from God."

21:5b:　　　καὶ λέγει· γράψον, ὅτι οὗτοι οἱ λόγοι πιστοὶ καὶ ἀληθινοί εἰσιν
　　　　　　　And he said, "Write, 'This is the faithful and true message.'"

22:6a:　　　καὶ εἶπέν μοι· οὗτοι οἱ λόγοι πιστοὶ καὶ ἀληθινοί
　　　　　　　And he said to me, "This is the faithful and true message."

The phrase οἱ εἰς τὸ δεῖπνον τοῦ γάμου τοῦ ἀρνίου κεκλημένοι, "those who have been invited to the wedding feast of the Lamb," is unusual since only rarely in Revelation is a prepositional phrase placed between an article and the substantive it governs (see *Note* 19:9.c-c.). Furthermore, the theme of the eschatological wedding *feast* is found only here in Revelation. The author has balanced this heavenly announcement of the impending wedding banquet with an angelic invitation to the birds to feast on the corpses of the enemies defeated by the rider on the white horse (19:17–21). The "seven years of God" (Ezek 39:9) were interpreted in rabbinic Judaism as a time for the righteous to prepare for the age to come, and in that regard *Lev. Rab.* 11.2 quotes a proverb: "Whoever actively participates in wedding preparations will partake of the banquet." While determining the object of the verb γράψον, "write," is problematic, in this instance it probably refers only to the beatitude.

The term δεῖπνον, "dinner," occurs only here and in v 17 in Revelation, where it refers to very different things; the wedding banquet of the Lamb (v 9) is consciously formulated in antithesis to the destruction of the enemies of God who are devoured by wild animals (v 17). The metaphor of the wedding banquet is based on the social convention of inviting friends and relatives to a wedding feast (Matt 22:1–10 = *Gos. Thom.* 64 [a feast for an unspecified reason rather than specifically a wedding feast is in view here]; Matt 25:10; Luke 12:36; 14:8; *Acts Thom.* 4–5, 7, 13; 4 Ezra 9:47; *Jos. As.* 21:8; *Apoc. Ezek.* [Epiphanius *Haer.* 64.70.7; Denis, *Fragmenta*, 121]; Diodorus Siculus 13.84.1; Diogenes Laertius 3.2; see Blümner, *Greeks*, 138–39), usually referred to by the plural form γάμοι, "wedding celebrations." It is often claimed (with some exaggeration) that the motif of the messianic banquet is a common theme in apocalyptic literature (Russell, *Apocalyptic*, 322). While there are a number of references to eating and drinking in the kingdom of God or the heavenly world in early Jewish and early Christian literature, these passages appear to preserve several traditions that exhibit relative independence from each other. (1) The primeval monsters Behemoth and Leviathan will serve as food for the righteous in the eschaton (*2 Apoc. Bar.* 29:4; 4 Ezra 6:52; *b. B. Bat.* 74). This tradition may be based on Ps 74:14 and Ezek 32:4, where God killed Leviathan and gave him as food for wild animals (see Volz, *Eschatologie*, 389; Frost, *OT Apocalyptic*, 152–53). (2) According to Isa 25:6–8, God will provide a sumptuous feast for all people on the mountain of the Lord in the eschaton. In one passage in Q (Matt 8:11 = Luke 13:29) the Messiah is missing, but the motifs of *gathering, Jews and Gentiles,* and *table fellowship* are present (following the Matthaean order; see Kloppenborg, *Formation of Q,* 226–27):

Matt 8:11–12	*Luke 13:29, 28*
[11]I tell you, many will come from east and west	[29]And men will come from east and west, and from north and south,
and sit at table with Abraham, Isaac, and Jacob in the kingdom of heaven, [12]while the sons of the kingdom will be thrown into the outer darkness; there men will weep and gnash their teeth.	and sit at table in the kingdom of God. [28]There you will weep and gnash your teeth, when you see Abraham and Isaac and Jacob and all the prophets in the kingdom of God and you yourselves thrust out.

In the narrative of the Last Supper, Jesus speaks of drinking new wine with the disciples in the Father's kingdom (Mark 14:25 = Matt 26:29; cf. Luke 22:18), perhaps reflecting the tradition of a messianic banquet. Some scholars argue that the meals Jesus shared with "tax collectors and sinners" were intended by Jesus to serve as anticipations of the final eschatological banquet (J. P. Meier, *Mentor, Message and Miracles,* vol. 2 of *A Marginal Jew* [New York: Doubleday, 1994] 302–9). In an enigmatic passage in Luke 14:15, a blessing is pronounced on those who will eat bread in the kingdom of God. A late Christian interpolation in 4 Ezra (often designated 5 Ezra) 2:38 exhorts, "Rise and stand, and see at the feast of the Lord the number of those who have been sealed." Similarly, the Christian edition of *T. Isaac* 6:22 observes that the righteous "shall be present from the first moment of the millennial banquet." (3) In an apparent development of the last type, the Messiah becomes the one who provides nourishment for the righteous in the eschaton. It is this tradition that finds expression in *1 Enoch* 62:14 (tr. Knibb), where it is said that the righteous will dwell with the Son of man "and eat, and lie down, and rise up for ever and ever." In Luke 22:28–30, Jesus says that those disciples who persevere will eat and drink at his table in his kingdom (though it is questionable whether Jesus functions as the Messiah in this passage). In *3 Enoch* 48A:10, the gathering of Israel to Jerusalem from among the Gentiles is followed by commensality (tr. P. Alexander, *OTP* 1:302): "Moreover, the kingdom of Israel, gathered from the four quarters of the world, shall eat with the Messiah, and the gentiles shall eat with them." (4) Access to the fruit of the tree of life is a metaphor for eschatological salvation (Rev 2:7; 22:14). (5) Eschatological manna is an eschatological symbol of salvation for the righteous (see *Comment* on 2:17).

The metaphor of the "wedding feast" of the Lamb mentioned in Rev 19:9 is a single event (as one might expect for such singular occasions), whereas the meal mentioned in *1 Enoch* 62:14 (perhaps alluding to Zeph 3:13) continues indefinitely. A feature of the so-called divine warrior hymn is the concluding victory banquet (P. D. Hanson, *Dawn*, 300–322). In Greek and Roman sources a festive meal was sometimes similarly used to symbolize the happy afterlife (Plato 2.363c–d; Lattimore, *Epitaphs*, 52).

The term κεκλημένοι, "invited," refers to a formal summons to friends and relatives to join in the festive occasion. In this instance, since the bride mentioned in 19:7 represents faithful Christians, the bride and those invited must be identical, making the metaphor somewhat awkward. According to *b. B. Bat.* 75b (tr. Epstein), "Rabbah said in the name of R. Johanan: Jerusalem of the world to come will not be like Jerusalem of the present world. To Jerusalem of the present world, anyone who wishes goes up, but to that of the world to come only those invited [מְקְרָאֶיהָ *miqrā'eyhā*] will go."

9b καὶ λέγει μοι· οὗτοι οἱ λόγοι ἀληθινοὶ τοῦ θεοῦ εἰσιν, "He said to me, 'This is the true message from God.'" Who is the speaker in the two occurrences of the phrase καὶ λέγει μοι, "and he said to me," in this verse (9a and 9b)? It appears to be the bowl angel introduced in 17:1, who speaks in 17:1–2, 7–14, 15–18 (Allo, 276; Lohmeyer, 155; Caird, 33). Though this view is widespread among commentators, it is not without difficulty, particularly since 18:1–19:8 has introduced a great many other possibilities. Several other speakers are introduced in Rev 18, including "another angel" (18:1–3), "another voice" (18:4–20), and the "mighty angel" (18:21–24).

A second problem in this verse is the meaning of the expression οὗτοι οἱ λόγοι, "these words." How much of what precedes does this statement intend to include? The phrase οὗτοι οἱ λόγοι ἀληθινοὶ τοῦ θεοῦ εἰσιν, "this is the true message from God," has close parallels in 21:5 (οὗτοι οἱ λόγοι πιστοὶ καὶ ἀληθινοί εἰσιν, "this is the faithful and true message") and 22:6 (οὗτοι οἱ λόγοι πιστοὶ καὶ ἀληθινοί, "this is the faithful and true message").

10a καὶ ἔπεσα ἔμπροσθεν τῶν ποδῶν αὐτοῦ προσκυνῆσαι αὐτῷ, "Then I fell before his feet to worship him." On the combination of πίπτειν and προσκυνεῖν, see *Comment* on 4:10. The motif of prostration following a divine revelation (found here and in 22:8 in contexts that are very similar; see the synoptic comparison below) occurs occasionally in early Jewish and early Christian literature (Dan 2:46; *Asc. Isa.* 7.21–22; *Pistis Sophia* 1.27 [ed. Schmidt-Till, p. 24, lines 20–23 = ed. Schmidt-MacDermot, pp. 39–40]; 4.138 [ed. Schmidt-Till, p. 235, lines 19–22 = ed. Schmidt-MacDermot, p. 357]). A parallel episode occurs in *Asc. Isa.* 7.21 (Hennecke-Schneemelcher, *NTA* 2:654):

> And I fell on my face to worship him, and the angel who conducted me did not allow me, but said to me, "Worship neither angel nor throne which belongs to the six heavens—for this reason I was sent to conduct thee—till I tell thee in the seventh heaven."

This parallel is a much broader prohibition that interdicts the worship of both angel and throne (a metaphor for a type of angelic being; see Col 1:16; *T. Levi* 3:8).

Another parallel is even more telling in the same document, *Asc. Isa.* 8:5, where the *angelus interpres,* after being called "Lord" by Isaiah, responds, "I am not your Lord, but your companion" (a response strikingly similar to the response of the angel in Rev 19:10b and 22:9). Bauckham argues that the angel who refuses worship is a traditional apocalyptic motif that functions to safeguard monotheism ("Worship," 120–32). He identifies two stock reactions in apocalyptic literature to angelophanies, *involuntary collapse* (*T. Abr.* [Rec. A] 9; *2 Enoch* [Rec. J and A] 21:2; *3 Enoch* 1:7; Matt 28:4; Tob 12:16–22; see *Comment* on 1:17) and *voluntary prostration in worship* (*Apoc. Zeph.* 6:11–15; *2 Enoch* 1:7). *Apoc. Zeph.* 6:11–15 (second century A.D.) is striking because it contains a description of the angel Eremel, a passage with similarities to both Dan 10:5–14 and Rev 1:13–18, and contains as well the motif of the refusal of an angel to accept worship (tr. Wintermute, *OTP* 1:513):

> Then I arose and stood, and I saw a great angel standing before me with his face shining like the rays of the sun in its glory since his face is like that which is perfected in its glory. And he was girded as if a golden girdle were upon his breast. His feet were like bronze which is melted in a fire. And when I saw him, I rejoiced, for I thought that the Lord Almighty had come to visit me. I fell upon my face, and I worshipped him. He said to me, "Take heed. Don't worship me. I am not the Lord Almighty, but I am the great angel Eremel, who is over the abyss and Hades."

These obscure and late texts hardly constitute evidence for an *apocalyptic* literary tradition. Rather, mistaking a human being for a deity appearing in human form is a motif found frequently in Greek and Hellenistic literature (*Iliad* 6.108–9, 128–29; Nonnos *Dionysiaca* 7.226–54; 10.196–216; 42.158–63). In Greek mythic tradition the gods appear in various guises and sometimes, but not always, are recognizable (*Odyssey* 13.311–13; 17.485; *Hymn to Demeter* 1.111; Mussies, "Identification," 1–18), a tradition repeated in a Judaized form in Heb 13:2 and Philo *Som.* 1.232, "To souls which are still in a body, God gives himself the likeness of angels [ἀγγέλοις εἰκαζόμενον]." Mistaking heroes or otherwise exceptional people for deities is a motif found frequently in both Hellenistic novels (Xenophon *Ephesiaca* 1.12; Chariton 1.14.1) and early Christian apocryphal acts (*Acts Pet.* 10; *Acts Thom.* 109); see Söder, *Apostelgeschichten,* 95–102. A relatively close verbal parallel to Rev 19:10 occurs in Acts 10:25, where Cornelius greets Peter by falling at his feet and worshiping him (πεσὼν ἐπὶ τοὺς πόδας προσεκύνησεν), only to be rebuked by Peter, who says that he is a human being. This passage combines the three motifs of falling down, worship, and rebuke (cf. Acts 14:11–15). A parallel from Hellenistic literature is found in Lucian *Icaromenippus* 13 (LCL tr.), which combines the motifs of worship and rebuke, suggesting that this combination was not restricted to early Jewish or early Christian literature:

> I was downcast and almost in tears when the philosopher Empedocles came and stood behind me, looking like a cinder, as he was covered with ashes and all burned up. On catching sight of him I was a bit startled, to tell the truth, and thought I beheld a lunar spirit; but he said, "Don't be alarmed, Menippus, 'No god am I: why liken me to them?' I am the natural philosopher Empedocles."

This text is a satirical version of the conventional Greek conception that gods could masquerade as human beings; here a human being is thought to be a god.

Many scholars understand Rev 19:10 and its parallel in 22:8–9 as a polemically motivated attempt to counter the practice of angel worship or angel veneration in the Christian congregations of Asia Minor (Bousset [1906] 493; Swete, 248, 304; Kiddle-Ross, 382; Boring, 194; Sweet, 280; Roloff [ET] 213). This view is not unproblematic, and there are several related issues that need consideration. First of all, the motif of the angel who refuses worship from a seer in the context of an angelic revelation (as in Rev 19:10 and 22:9) is a *literary* motif with many parallels in apocalyptic literature, though the motif is not restricted to apocalyptic. As a *literary* motif, it is difficult if not impossible to claim that the constituent motif of the *fear* attributed to the recipient of angelic revelations is anything more than a formal part of this literary motif (against Stuckenbruck, *Angel,* 87–92).

A related issue is the problem of whether a cult of angels existed in Judaism, affirmed by some scholars (Schäfer, *Rivalität,* 67) but denied by others (Carr, *Angels,* 69–71; Hurtado, *One God,* 27–35). Philo thought that those who worshiped angels were in error (*Fug.* 212), yet he also thought that God revealed himself in angelic form (*Som.* 1.232, 238), which creates some tension in his system. The "worship of angels" (θρησκεία τῶν ἀγγέλων) is mentioned in Col 2:18 as an error, which many scholars maintain to reflect a cult of angels purportedly Jewish in origin (Simon, *Verus Israel,* 345; Williams, *JTS* 10 [1909] 413–38), though what may be meant here is participation in angelic worship of God (Francis, "Angel Worship," 109–34); see the review of research in Stuckenbruck, *Angel,* 111–19. The role of angels is particularly prominent in Jewish magical texts such as the *Sepher ha-Razim* (see also Jos. *J.W.* 2.142). There are, however, a number of passages in rabbinic literature that prohibit images, sacrifices, prayer, and veneration directed toward angels (*b. Sanh.* 38b; *y. Ber.* 9.13a–b; *Exod. Rab.* 32.4; see Schäfer, *Rivalität,* 65–72; Stuckenbruck, *Angels,* 52–75).

Angels had a prominent place in early Jewish Christianity (Daniélou, *Jewish Christianity,* 117–46). According to Origen, his Jewish teacher claimed that the two seraphim spoken of in Isa 6 were the Son of God and the Holy Spirit (*De principiis* 1.3.4; 4.3.14). Celsus charged that the Jews "worship angels and are addicted to sorcery" (*Contra Celsum* 1.26) and that they "worship the heaven and the angels in it" (*Contra Celsum* 5.6), though it is likely that he culled these views from Greco-Jewish literature; see Lange, *Origen,* 42. Origen is quick to rebut such charges (*Contra Celsum* 1.26; 5.6), but other early Christian writers seem to echo this view (Aristides *Apol.* 14.4; *Kerygma Petri* in Clement Alex. *Strom.* 6.5.41; cf. Origen *Comm. Joh.* 13.17). It is possible that these Christian writers were slandering Judaism by characterizing their observance of the Torah as the "worship of angels" (see Stuckenbruck, *Angels,* 142).

It is worth noting, however, that a Greco-Roman cult of angels did in fact exist in Anatolia and that worship was accorded them (see Sokolowski, *HTR* 53 [1960] 225ff.; Sheppard, *Talanta* 12–13 [1980–81] 77–101; Mitchell, *Anatolia* 2:46; for a review of this phenomenon, see Stuckenbruck, *Angels,* 181–91). Similarly, Teixidor (*Pagan God,* 14–15) notes that various cults of angels were known in the ancient Near East, such as the "Angel of Bel" (*Malakbel*) and the "Holy Angels of Baal Shamin" at Palmyra, the "Angels of Holiness" at Coptos, and the "Angel" of Milkastart, revered near Tyre.

Rev 22:8b–9 is a doublet of 19:10 as this synoptic comparison indicates:

Rev 19:10	*Rev 22:8b–9*
[καὶ] ἔπεσα ἔμπροσθεν [Then] I fell before	ἔπεσα προσκυνῆσαι ἔμπροσθεν I fell to worship before
τῶν ὁδῶν [αὐτοῦ] [his] feet	τῶν ποδῶν [τοῦ ἀγγέλου] the feet [of the angel]
προσκυνῆσαι [αὐτῷ] to worship [him],	[τοῦ δεικνύοντός μοι ταῦτα]. [who revealed them to me].
καὶ λέγει μοι· ὅρα μή· but he said to me, "Don't do that!	καὶ λέγει μοι· ὅρα μή· But he said to me, "Don't do that!
σύνδουλός σού εἰμι I am a fellow servant with you	σύνδουλός σού εἰμι I am a fellow servant with you
καὶ τῶν ἀδελφῶν σου and your brothers and sisters	καὶ τῶν ἀδελφῶν σου and your brothers and sisters
[τῶν ἐχόντων [who maintain	[τῶν προφητῶν [the prophets
τὴν μαρτυρίαν Ἰησοῦ]. the testimony concerning Jesus].	καὶ τῶν τηρούντων τοὺς and those who obey the
	λόγους τοῦ βιβλίου τούτου]· commands in this book].
τῷ θεῷ προσκύνησον. Worship God."	τῷ θεῷ προσκύνησον. Worship God."

The bracketed portions in 19:10 and 22:8b–9 show how distinctive statements have been intercalated into the same basic formulaic framework. While 19:10 suggests that John's brothers are those who maintain their testimony about Jesus, 22:9 indicates that John's brothers are the prophets and those who obey the commands in this book. Revelation contains a restricted amount of material that can be construed as words or commands that can be obeyed, and that emphasis is found in 22:9, but not 19:10. Strictly speaking, such material (following our hypothesis of two editions of Revelation) is generally restricted to the parenetic sections of Rev 2–3, 22:6–21, and a few scattered commands inserted into the body of the work as part of the author's revision (13:9–10; 14:12; 16:15; 18:4; 21:7–8). It appears that the author-editor has used 19:10 as the source for 22:8b–9 (Kraft, 227) rather than 22:8b–9 as the source for 19:10 (against Vischer, *Offenbarung*, 44–45; Charles, 2:130; Bergmeier, *ZNW* 75 [1984] 87). Some commentators explain the doublet by maintaining that the repetition serves as a structural framework (Karrer, *Brief*, 175), which of course is also true. Since Revelation contains a limited amount of material that can be construed as words or commands that can be obeyed, and that material is almost exclusively restricted to Rev 1–3 and 22:6–21, it is probable that the emphasis on obeying the commands in "this book" (22:9) belongs to the final redactional stage of composition.

10b καὶ λέγει μοι· ὅρα μή· σύνδουλός σού εἰμι καὶ τῶν ἀδελφῶν σου τῶν ἐχόντων τὴν μαρτυρίαν Ἰησοῦ· τῷ θεῷ προσκύνησον, "but he said to me, 'Don't do that! I am a fellow servant with you and your brothers and sisters who maintain the testimony concerning Jesus. Worship God." This passage has a close parallel in 22:9, except that the phrase "who maintain the testimony concerning Jesus" is there replaced with "the prophets and those who obey the commands of this book" (see *Comment* on v 10a). Rev 22:9 (which belongs to the final revision of Revelation) was very probably drawn from 19:10 (the reverse is argued by Vischer, *Offenbarung*, 44–45; Charles 2:130; Bergmeier, *ZNW*75 [1984] 87), and for that reason v 10c was added as an explanatory gloss (Bousset [1906] 429 n. 2; a possibility also suggested by Charles, 2:130).

The words of the angelic guide in claiming to be a fellow servant with John and his brothers and sisters have a close parallel in *Asc. Isa.* 8:4–5, where "Isaiah" addresses his angelic guide and receives a mild rebuke (tr. Knibb, *OTP* 2:168): "'What (is) this which I see, my lord?' And he said to me, 'I am not your lord, but your companion.'" Another apparent parallel is found in the reason for not worshiping the sun, moon, and stars in Philo *Decal.* 64, "Let us . . . refrain from worshipping those [i.e., the heavenly bodies] who by nature are our brothers [τοὺς ἀδελφοὺς φύσει μὴ προσκυνῶμεν], even though they have been given a substance purer and more immortal than ours." The emphasis on worshiping God rather than the angelic messenger has a parallel in the reaction of Joseph when his brothers did obeisance before him in Gen 50:19, "Do not be afraid! Am I in the place of God?" (a rhetorical question rejected by *Tg. Ps.-J., Tg. Onq.,* and *Tg. Neof.* on Gen 50:19). Similarly, when Barnabas and Paul rejected the worship of the people from Lystra who thought that they were gods, they said, "Gentlemen, why are you doing this? We are people just like you" (Acts 14:15).

10c ἡ γὰρ μαρτυρία Ἰησοῦ ἐστιν τὸ πνεῦμα τῆς προφητείας, "For the testimony concerning Jesus is the Spirit of prophecy." The phrase ἡ μαρτυρία Ἰησοῦ occurs several times in Revelation (1:2, 9; 12:17; 19:10b; 20:4). Several other parallel or otherwise related phrases occur: (1) ἡ μαρτυρία αὐτῶν, "their testimony" (11:7 and 12:11), (2) τὴν μαρτυρίαν ἣν εἶχον, "the testimony which they bore" (6:9), (3) τοῦ αἵματος τῶν μαρτύρων Ἰησοῦ, "the blood of the witnesses to Jesus" (17:6), and (4) τὴν πίστιν Ἰησοῦ, "faith in (or, faithfulness to) Jesus" (14:12). The genitive form of Ἰησοῦ, "Jesus," here is ambiguous since it can be either an objective (i.e., "the witness to Jesus") or a subjective genitive (i.e., "the witness borne by Jesus"). Many commentators think that Ἰησοῦ in this context is a subjective genitive (Beckwith, 729; Kiddle-Ross, 383; Caird, 238; Kraft, 215; Trites, *Witness*, 155–59). However, if the testimony borne by Jesus is in view here, that presumably would refer to the testimony he maintained during his trial (Matt 27:11–14; Mark 15:1–5; Luke 23:1–12; John 18:19–24, 33–38), characterized by evasive answers (except for Mark 14:62), by silence, or by the rather profound response in John 18:33–38. Further, construing ἡ μαρτυρία Ἰησοῦ as a subjective genitive would mean that it would be one of the very few references to the historical Jesus in Revelation (along with 1:5; 2:8; 5:6; 11:8). Finally, the references noted above in 6:9, 11:7, 12:11, and 17:6 all unambiguously emphasize that the testimony is borne by Christians, presumably about Jesus and explicitly about Jesus in 17:6. For these reasons, then, Ἰησοῦ should be taken as an objective genitive and the phrase ἡ μαρτυρία Ἰησοῦ should be understood to mean "the testimony about Jesus," which believers should bear (Charles, 2:130–31; Glasson, 107–8; Bruce, "Spirit," 338; Lampe, "Testimony," 253–58).

The connection with prophecy found in this verse has parallels with the inspiration promised to those who will be called before various assemblies to answer for their faith in Christ (Mark 13:11; Matt 10:20; Luke 12:11–12; 21:15; Eusebius *Hist. eccl.* 5.3.3; Tertullian *Ad mart.* 1.3; Cyprian *Ep.* 81.2; see Lampe, "Testimony," 245–58). The subject of prophetic speech in early Christianity is frequently the exalted status of Jesus (1 Cor 12:3; 1 John 4:2–3; John 15:26–27). Here the striking character of the "testimony concerning Jesus" is that it is equated with the "spirit of prophecy"; i.e., since true prophecy witnesses to Jesus, any witness to Jesus can be identified as prophecy, and thus prophecy is not limited to those who are designated "prophets" in a special sense. Since 22:9 was based on 19:10, this phrase in 22:9 is probably a gloss to show the connection between "the testimony concerning Jesus" and prophecy (a possibility suggested by Charles, 2:130).

The phrase τὸ πνεῦμα τῆς προφητείας, "the Spirit of prophecy," occurs only here in Revelation and is therefore certainly not characteristic of the author. The genitive phrase τῆς προφητείας, "of prophecy," suggests that the Spirit is chiefly characterized by prophetic manifestations, a view of the Spirit that is characteristic of late second temple Judaism and taken over by early Christianity. The phrase should probably be understood as "the prophetic Spirit," i.e., the power that allows certain individuals to have visionary experiences and gives them revelatory insights not available to ordinary people (Schweizer, *TDNT* 6:449). It is parallel to the expression τὸ πνεῦμα προφητικόν, "the prophetic Spirit," a phrase that occurs with some frequency in second- and third-century Christian authors as a way of referring to a mode of prophetic inspiration (Justin *1 Apol.* 6:2; 13.3; 31.1; *Dial.* 55.1; Athenagoras *Leg.* 10.4; 18.2; Irenaeus *Adv. haer.* 1.13.4 [used of Marcus]; Clement of Alex. *Protrep.* 9). Another striking parallel occurs in Hermas *Mand.* 11.9 in the phrase "the angel [or messenger] of the prophetic spirit [ὁ ἄγγελος τοῦ προφητικοῦ πνεύματος (*var. lect.* τοῦ προφήτου)]." The phrase "spirit of prophecy" occurs occasionally in early Jewish texts (though it is does not appear to be present in the DSS), particularly in the targums, as in *Tg. Isa* 61:1 (Sperber, *Aramaic* 3:121), "The prophet said, the spirit of prophecy [רוח נבואה *rûaḥ něbûʾâ*] from before the Lord God is upon me." In two parallel texts in *Tg. Onq.* Gen 41:38 and *Tg. Ps.-J.* Gen 41:38, Pharaoh describes Joseph as "a man in whom there is the spirit of prophecy from before the Lord [גבר דרוח נבואה מן יי ביה *gbr drwḥ nbwʾh mn yy byḥ*]" (the MT has אשר רוח אלהים בו *ʾăšer rûaḥ ʾělōhîm bô*, "in whom the spirit of God dwells"); see Aberbach-Grossfeld, *Targum Onkelos*, 240–41. The phrase רוח נבואה *rûaḥ něbûʾâ*, "spirit of prophecy," also occurs in *Tg. Onq.* Num 11:25, 26, 29; 24:2; 27:18; *Tg. Neof.* Exod 2:12 (MS M); 31:3 (spirit of a prophet?).

Explanation

Rev 19:1–10 consists of two textual units, a heavenly throne-room audition consisting of five hymnic units (vv 1–8) and a concluding angelic revelation (vv 9–10), the fifth and final section of the larger unit in 17:1–19:10. The unit in 19:1–8 is the last and most complex hymnic section in Revelation and has been called the hymnic finale of the book. This section consists of two complex subunits: (1) Vv 1–4, a two-part hymn of praise and the response, celebrate the proleptic judgment of the whore (Babylon) narrated in 18:1–24, with a judgment doxology (vv 1b–2; cf. 16:5–6, 7), an appended hymnic text (v 3), and the prostration in worship of the twenty-four elders, who respond with a concluding amen (v 4). (b) Vv 5–8 constitute a call to praise of those who dwell on earth together with a hymnic response, actually a hymnic continuation of the throne scene in 19:1–4 but one that looks forward to the future marriage of the Lamb and the prepared- ness of his bride, references to the descent of the New Jerusalem to earth (21:9– 22:9). Those who respond with song in v 6 are a huge multitude (different from the one in v 1), and their loud singing is compared with the roaring sea and booming thunder. The song they sing is a hymn of praise (vv 6b–8), a type found often in the Psalms, and the reason for their praise is the imminence of the marriage of the Lamb.

The concluding unit in 19:9–10 is abruptly introduced with the phrase "he said to me," by an unidentified speaker, presumably the interpreting angel of 17:1– 18. He pronounces a blessing on those who are invited to the marriage feast of the Lamb and declares that "these are the true words of God" (v 9b), probably referring to the entire section 17:1–19:8. John responds by falling down and worshiping the angelic messenger, but he is rebuked and directed rather to worship God (see 22:9).

F. The Final Defeat of God's Remaining
Foes   (19:11–21:8)
1. The Divine Warrior and His
Conquests   (19:11–21)

Bibliography

Alexander, P. J. "Letters and Speeches of the Emperor Hadrian." *HSCP* 49 (1938) 141–77. **Aune, D. E.** "The Significance of the Delay of the Parousia for Early Christianity." In *Current Issues in Biblical and Patristic Interpretation.* FS M. C. Tenney, ed. G. F. Hawthorne. Grand Rapids, MI: Eerdmans, 1975. 87–109. **Benoit, P.** "Ἅγιοι en Colossiens 1.12: Hommes ou Anges?" In *Paul and Paulinism,* ed. M. D. Hooker and S. G. Wilson. London: SPCK, 1982. 83–99. **Bietenhard, H.** *Das Tausendjährige Reich.* 2nd ed. Zürich: Zwingli, 1955. **Den Boer, W.** "Trajan's Deification." In *Proceedings of the XIV International Congress of Papyrologists.* London: The British Academy, 1975. 85–90. **Dunn, J. D. G.** *Christology in the Making.* Philadelphia: Westminster, 1980. **Fekkes, J.** "'His Bride Has Prepared Herself': Revelation 19–21 and Isaian Nuptial Imagery." *JBL* 109 (1990) 269–87. **Frey, J.** "Erwägungen zum Verhältnis der Johannesapokalypse zu den übrigen Schriften des Corpus Johanneum." In *Die johanneische Frage: Ein Lösungsversuch,* by M. Hengel. Tübingen: Mohr-Siebeck, 1993. 326–449. **Grelot, P.** "L'exégese messianique d'Isaïe LXIII,1–6." *RB* 70 (1963) 371–80. **Griffin, J.** *Homer on Life and Death.* Oxford:

Clarendon, 1980. **Griffiths, J. G.** "Βασιλεὺς Βασιλέων: Remarks on the History of a Title." *CP* 48 (1953) 145–54. **Güntert, H.** *Von der Sprache der Götter und Geister: Bedeutungsgeschichtliche Untersuchungen zur homerischen und eddischen Göttersprache.* Halle (Saale): Niemeyer, 1921. **Hayward, R.** *Divine Name and Presence: The Memra.* Totowa, NJ: Allenheld, Osmun, 1981. ⸺. "The *Memra* of YHWH and the Development of Its Use in Targum Neofiti I." *JJS* 25 (1974) 412–18. **Jeremias, Joachim.** "Zum Logos-Problem." *ZNW* 59 (1968) 82–85. **Lentzen-Deis, F. L.** "Das Motiv der 'Himmelsöffnung' in verschiedenen Gattungen der Umweltliteratur des Neuen Testaments." *Bib* 50 (1969) 301–27. ⸺. *Die Taufe Jesu nach den Synoptikern: Literarkritische und gattungsgeschichtliche Untersuchungen.* Frankfurt am Main: Knecht, 1970. **MacCormack, S.** "Change and Continuity in Late Antiquity: The Ceremony of Adventus." *Historia* 21 (1972) 721–52. **Mealy, J. W.** *After the Thousand Years: Resurrection and Judgment in Revelation 20.* Sheffield: Sheffield Academic, 1992. **Miller, P. D., Jr.** *The Divine Warrior in Early Israel.* Cambridge: Harvard UP, 1973. **Noth, M.** "The Holy Ones of the Most High." In *The Laws in the Pentateuch.* London: Oliver and Boyd, 1966. 215–28. **Priest, J. B.** "A Note on the Messianic Banquet." In *The Messiah: Developments in Earliest Judaism and Christianity,* ed. J. H. Charlesworth. Minneapolis: Fortress, 1992. 222–38. **Rissi, M.** "Die Erscheinung Christi nach Off. 19:11–16." *TZ* 21 (1965) 81–95. **Skehan, P. W.** "King of Kings, Lord of Lords (Apoc. 19:16)." *CBQ* 10 (1948) 398. **Syrén, R.** *The Blessings in the Targums: A Study of the Targumic Interpretations of Genesis 49 and Deuteronomy 33.* Åbo: Åbo Akademi, 1986. **Torrey, C. C.** "Armageddon." *HTR* 31 (1938) 237–48. **Zandee, J.** *Death as an Enemy according to Ancient Egyptian Conceptions.* Leiden: Brill, 1960. 14–16, 133–42.

Translation

[11]*I then saw heaven open, and behold,* [a]*a white steed* [a] *and the person mounted on it* [b]*is faithful* [c]*and true.*[cb] *With justice he judges* [d] *and wages war.* [12]*Now* [a] *his eyes* [b] *were like* [c] *brilliant flame,*[d] *and on his head were many diadems* [e]*with* [f] *a name* [g]*inscribed*[he] *that no one* [g] *knows but he himself.*[i] [13]*He was dressed* [a] *in a garment* [b]*stained with* [c]*blood,*[b] *and* [d]*his name was called* [d] *"the* [e] *Word of God."* [14]*The* [a] *heavenly armies followed* [b] *him on white steeds, wearing* [c] *white, pure linen.* [15]*From his mouth projected a sharp sword that he might smite the nations with it, and he himself will rule* [a] *them with an iron crook, and he himself* [b] *will tread* [c]*the winepress,* [d]*representing the furious wrath* [d] *of God the Almighty.* [c] [16]*And he has* [a]*upon his robe,* [b]*that is,*[a] *upon his thigh,* [c] *a name inscribed,*[d] [e]*"King of kings and Lord of lords."* [e]

[17]*Then I saw an* [a] *angel standing on the sun, and he cried* [b] *with* [c] *a loud voice to all the birds flying in midheaven,*[d] *"Come, gather together at* [e]*the great* [e] [f]*supper of God* [18]*to eat the carrion* [a] *of kings and the carrion of generals and the carrion of the powerful and the carrion of horses and their* [b] *riders and the carrion of all, free* [c] *and slave,* [d]*and the unimportant* [d] [e]*and the* [f]*important."*

[19]*I saw the beast and the kings of the earth and their* [a] *armies assembled to wage* [b]*war with the one mounted on the steed and with his army.* [20]*The beast was captured and*[a]*with him the* [a] *false prophet who performed signs* [b]*on his authority,*[b] *by which he deceived those who received the brand* [c] *of the beast and who worshiped his* [d]*cultic image;* [d] *they were both hurled* [e] *alive into the lake of fire burning*[f] *with sulfur.* [21]*The rest were slain with the sword projecting from the mouth of the one mounted on the steed, and all the birds feasted*[a] *on their carrion.*

Notes

11.a-a. ἵππος λευκός is a nom. because it is the author's practice to introduce a nom. after καὶ ἰδού (see 4:1; 6:2, 5, 8; 7:9; 11:14; 12:3; 14:1, 14; 21:3).

11.b-b. Variants: (1) πιστὸς καὶ ἀληθινός] A (lacuna in C) 025 051 Andreas; von Soden, *Text.* (2) καλούμενος πιστὸς καὶ ἀληθινός] 046 fam 1006[1006 1841] fam 1611[1854 2030] Oecumenius[2053 2062] Andr f[2023 2073] j[1685] l n 94 1773 Byzantine Irenaeus[Lat] Origen Cyprian Primasius Victorinus (Haussleiter, *Victorinus*, 137); it[dem] div haf t vg[Θ K O Πc S U V W] syr[ph h] ; Tischendorf, *NT Graece;* Nestle-Aland[27] [καλούμενος] UBSGNT[4] [καλούμενος]; *TCGNT*[1], 760–61; Bousset (1906) 430 [καλούμενος]; Charles, 2:358 [καλούμενος]. (3) πιστὸς καλούμενος καὶ ἀληθινός] א; B. Weiss, *Johannes-Apokalypse,* 134; WHort [καλούμενος]; *TCGNT*[1], 761; *TCGNT*[2], 686 (dissenting view of B. Metzger). (4) πιστὸς καὶ ἀληθινὸς καλούμενος] Andr c[2028] it[ar]. (5) πιστος καλούμενος] fam 1611[2329]. (6) *Vocabatur fidelis, et verax vocatur*] it[c] vg[A C G I Π* T]. Schmid argues that א inserted καλούμενος under the influence of the Byzantine text (*Studien* 2:130). The UBSGNT Committee argues that καλούμενος was accidentally or deliberately omitted (*TCGNT*[1], 760–61). While a *deliberate* omission is improbable, an *accidental* omission is conceivable if καλούμενος was followed by καί as in reading (3), which is the argument of B. Weiss, *Johannes-Apokalypse,* 134. However, since the insertion of καλούμενος is easier to account for than its omission, and the emphasis on naming the rider here is in apparent tension with v 12c, and the placement of καλούμενος has no parallel in the style of Revelation, reading (1) is probably the *lectio originalis,* and the titular use, implied by the addition of καλούμενος, was derived from Rev 3:14.

11.c-c Variant: omit καὶ ἀληθινός] fam 1611[2329]. Omission through haplography (καὶ πιστὸς καί).

11.d. κρίνειν, "to judge," is used here in the sense of "to rule." The Heb. verb שׁפט *šāpaṭ* can mean "to rule, govern," as well as "to judge." In LXX Judg 3:10; 1 Sam 8:20; LXX Theod Dan 9:12, שׁפט *šāpaṭ* means "rule" and is translated with κρίνειν; see Luke 22:30 (Fitzmyer, *Luke* 2:1419).

12.a. Descriptions of the exalted Christ are twice introduced with δέ in Revelation, here and 1:14.

12.b. οἱ ὀφθαλμοί is in the nom. because it is coordinated with the three other nom. substantives following καὶ εἶδον . . . καὶ ἰδού in v 11; see *Note* 19:13.a.

12.c. Variants: (1) ὡς] A (lacuna in C); fam 1006[-911] latt syr cop[sa bo] Irenaeus[Lat] Andr c f[2073] l n; Andr/ Byz 4a[250] Andr/Byz 4b[172]; Primasius (*ut*); it[gig] (*sicut*); Tyc[2] (*ut*); Beatus (*velut*); Cyprian (*tamquam*); vg (*sicut*); WHort[mg]; Charles, 2:358; [Nestle-Aland[27]]; [UBSGNT[4]]. (2) omit ὡς] א 025 046 051 fam 1611[1611 1854 2329] Oecumenius[2053 2062] Andreas Byzantine arm Hippolytus; Tischendorf, *NT Graece;* WHort; B. Weiss, *Johannes-Apokalypse,* 77 (ὡς inserted to conform to 1:14); Merk, *NT;* Nestle-Aland[23]. If ὡς was original (as the phrase ὡς φλὸξ πυρός in 1:14 and 2:18 suggests), its later omission is difficult to explain, except as an accidental omission; ὡς is probably original in 14:3 (though accidentally omitted in 𝔓[47] א Byzantine) and original in 19:6 (though omitted in Andreas; see Schmid, *Studien* 2:93–94). Evidence for and against the presence of ὡς is nearly equal (*TCGNT*[1], 761; *TCGNT*[2], 686), though its insertion is easier to explain than its omission.

12.d. In the phrase φλὸξ πυρός, lit. "flame of fire," πυρός is either an epexegetical gen. ("a flame, that is, fire") or (less probably) a descriptive gen. ("a fiery flame"). Either can be rendered "a glowing flame" or "a brilliant flame."

12.e-e. Variants: (1) ἔχων ὀνόματα γεγραμμένα καί] fam 1006[1006 1841] fam 1611[1854] 2030 Andr c d e[2026] f[2023] g n Byzantine. (2) ἔχοντα ὄνομα γεγραμμένον· καὶ ὄνομα] 2329. These variants are attempts to resolve the problem caused by the mention of many diadems followed by the inscription of a single secret name (there are many more variants, each attested in only one or two MSS; see Hoskier, *Text* 2:529). Variant (1) assumes that the "inscribed names" are on the rider himself (as the masc. sing. ἔχων suggests), while variant (2) assumes that the names are inscribed on the diadems.

12.f. ἔχων (present ind. masc. nom. ptcp.) is apparently governed by the masc. nom. sing. substantival ptcp. ὁ καθήμενος in v 11. Since v 12b has no main verb (κέκληται in v 13 is actually an independent [coordinate] clause that functions as a separate sentence), the ptcp. ἔχων functions as a finite verb (Mussies, *Morphology,* 325). For similar instances of ἔχων functioning as a finite verb, see 1:16; 4:7, 8; 6:2, 5; 9:17, 19; 10:2; 12:2; 21:12.

12.g-g. Variant: omit γεγραμμένον ὃ οὐδείς] א*. Probably an error of the eye; perhaps the omission of an entire line.

12.h. The pf. ptcp. γεγραμμένον, "inscribed," is in apposition to ὄνομα, which is the obj. of the ptcp. ἔχων; the pattern ἔχειν + obj. + pf. ptcp. occurs several times in Revelation (12:6; 14:1; 19:12, 16; 21:12); see *Note* 12:6.d.

12.i. αὐτός is used here emphatically as it regularly is in Revelation (see 3:20; 6:11; 12:11; 14:17; 17:11; 18:6; 19:12, 15[2x]; 21:3, 7). There are no instances of the unemphatic use of the nom. forms of αὐτός (see Mussies, *Morphology,* 169–70).

13.a. περιβεβλημένος is a pf. pass. masc. nom. ptcp. congruent with the three other substantives following καὶ ἰδού: (1) ἵππος λευκός, (2) ὁ καθήμενος, and (3) οἱ ὀφθαλμοί.

13.b-b. Variants: (1) βεβαμμένον (acc. sing. neut. pf. pass. ptcp. from βάπτειν)] A (lacuna in C); 046 051 fam 1611¹⁸⁵⁴ cop^sa syr Arethas Andreas Byzantine; B. Weiss, *Johannes-Apokalypse*, 123; von Soden, *Text;* Charles, 2:359; Merk, *NT;* Nestle-Aland²⁷; UBSGNT⁴. (2) ῥεραντισμένον (acc. sing. neut. pf. pass. ptcp. from ῥαντίζειν)] 025 2019 fam 1611²³²⁹ Hippolytus Origen; WHort (ῥεραντισμένον). (3) ἐρραντισμένον (acc. sing. neut. pf. pass. ptcp. from ῥαντίζειν)] fam 1006⁹¹¹ ¹⁰⁰⁶ 792 Oecumenius²⁰⁵³. (4) περιρεραμμένον (acc. sing. neut. pf. pass. ptcp. from περι[ρ]ραίνειν)] ℵ* Irenaeus; Tischendorf, *NT Graece.* (5) περιρεραντισμένον (acc. sing. neut. pf. pass. ptcp. from περιραντίζειν)] ℵ¹ Cyprian. (6) ἐρραμμένον (acc. sing. neut. pf. pass. ptcp. from ῥαίνειν)] Oecumenius²⁰⁵³text&comm; Oecumenius²⁰⁶² (text: ἐραμμένον; commentary: ἐρραμένον). (7) ῥεραμμένον (acc. sing. neut. pf. pass ptcp. from ῥαίνειν)] fam 1611¹⁶¹¹. Readings (2), (3), (6), and (7) reflect readings in which the pf. reduplicated either ερ- or ρε- (BDF § 68; BDR § 68; Moulton-Howard, *Accidence*, 192–93). According to B. Weiss (*Johannes-Apokalypse*, 123), reading (1) was changed to reading (2) because of the unusual use of the dat. αἵματι without ἐν. Though WHort print reading (2), elsewhere they suggest that reading (7) would account for all the textual variations (Westcott, *Introduction*, Appendix, 139–40; see Moulton-Howard, *Accidence*, 256). The evidence from the versions is not really helpful, except that the Latin words used to translate the Gk. terms in 19:13 are *sparsam, aspersam,* or *conspersam* (with various endings), which seem to point to ῥαίνειν, ῥαντίζειν, or compounds with περι-, rather than to βάπτειν. According to *TCGNT*¹, 761–62, and *TCGNT*², 686–87, reading (1) has the strongest external support and is also the reading most likely to provoke change. βάπτειν (like ἐμβάπτειν) means "to dip in" (Louw-Nida, § 47.11), followed by the gen. (Luke 16:24) or the dat. (4 Kgdms 8:15; *PGM* XII.200) of that in which something is dipped, or εἰς + acc. (LXX Lev 9:9; 11:32; 14:51; Josh 3:15; 1 Kgdms 14:27; Ezekiel *Exagoge* 186 [Jacobson, *Exagoge*, 62]: εἰς αἷμα βάψαι, "to dip in blood"; cf. *PGM* XII.199–200, βάψον εἰς χάλκανθον), or ἐν + dat. (LXX Deut 33:24; Ruth 2:14; Job 9:31; Ps 67:24[MT 68:23]). βάπτειν can also mean "to dye, stain," and so the phrase βεβαμμένον αἵματι can mean "dyed with blood" or "stained with blood" (BAGD, 133; Bauer-Aland, 266).

13.c. Variant: αἷμα] fam 1611²³²⁹.

13.d-d. The phrase κέκληται τὸ ὄνομα αὐτοῦ, lit. "his name was called," is awkward in Gk. because of the unnecessary use of τὸ ὄνομα αὐτοῦ. This idiom occurs frequently in the LXX, however (see Gen 3:20; 11:9; 1611, 13, 15; 17:5, 15, 19; 19:22, 37, 39; 21:3; 25:26, 30; 29:32, 33, 34, 35), though the pf. form of καλεῖν, "to call," is never used in such contexts.

13.e. The author has transposed the phrase ὁ λόγος τοῦ θεοῦ into a proper name, which yet retains its semantic significance. Normally "names" such as this coined by the author are anarthrous because they are as yet unknown to the readers (see 9:11; titles in Revelation are regularly anarthrous; see Mussies, *Morphology*, 190), yet here the article is retained because it was part of a previously existing phrase (Mussies, *Morphology*, 195–96). Origen read a text in which λόγος was anarthrous and argues that this means that Christ is the Logos absolutely and that there cannot therefore be many λόγοι (*Comm. in Jo.* 2.4).

14.a. Variants: (1) τά before ἐν τῷ οὐρανῷ] 025 051 fam 1006¹⁰⁰⁶ ¹⁸⁴¹ fam 1611¹⁸⁵⁴ 2030 Andr d f²⁰³⁰ ²⁰⁵⁶ l²⁰⁸⁰; Byzantine lat cop^sa Cyprian; WHort; B. Weiss, *Johannes-Apokalypse*, 115; Bousset (1906) 431; Charles, 2:359; [Nestle-Aland²⁷]; [UBSGNT⁴]. (2) omit τά] ℵ A 046 fam 1611¹⁶¹¹ ²³²⁹ ²³⁴⁴ Oecumenius²⁰⁵³ ²⁰⁶² Andreas; Tischendorf, *NT Graece;* von Soden, *Text.* Reading (1) is probably original in view of the author's tendency to nominalize prep. phrases with an attributive article (textually secure instances of article + noun + article + prep. phrase: 1:4; 2:24; 5:5; 8:3; 11:16).

14.b. Variants: (1) ἠκολούθει (3rd sing. impf. active)] *lectio originalis.* (2) ἠκολούθουν (3rd pl. impf. active)] Andreas. Reading (1) follows the rule, generally observed in Revelation (Schmid, *Studien* 2:230–31), that a pl. neut. substantive takes a 3rd sing. verb (BDR § 133).

14.c. ἐνδεδυμένοι, a masc. nom. pl. pf. pass. ptcp., modifies τὰ στρατεύματα (neut. nom. pl.) and should therefore have the form ἐνδεδυμένα. However, the author probably understands the members of these "troops" as male riders and so switches from the neut. to the masc. gender.

15.a. ποιμανεῖ, "to herd, tend, guide, rule," is clearly an allusion to LXX Ps 2:9 but is problematic here; see *Note* 2:27.a-a.

15.b. αὐτός is the nom. form of the intensive pronoun used here in the emphatic sense (see 3:20; 6:11; 12:11; 14:17; 17:11; 18:6; 19:12, 15[2x]; 21:3, 7). The unemphatic use of nom. forms of αὐτός, found in the LXX and NT, is absent from Revelation (Mussies, *Morphology*, 169–70).

15.c-c. τὴν ληνὸν τοῦ οἴνου τοῦ θυμοῦ τῆς ὀργῆς τοῦ θεοῦ τοῦ παντοκράτορος, "the winepress, representing the furious wrath of God the Almighty." This string of five gens. is the longest such string in Revelation (see *Comment* under Rev 15:5). τοῦ οἴνου, "of the wine," is a descriptive gen. or gen. of quality functioning as an adj. modifying ληνός, "press, vat"; τοῦ θυμοῦ, "the wrath," is an appositive or epexegetical gen.; τῆς ὀργῆς, "the anger," is a qualitative gen. functioning as an adj., which intensifies the meaning of θυμός; τοῦ θεοῦ, "God," is a poss. gen., while τοῦ παντοκράτορος, "Almighty," is an appositive or epexegetical gen.

15.d-d. Variants: (1) τοῦ θυμοῦ τῆς ὀργῆς] A 025 046 051 Andr f[2031-2056]; Andr l 94. (2) τῆς ὀργῆς τοῦ θυμοῦ] ‫ א‬2329 cop[sa] Origen. (3) τοῦ θυμοῦ καὶ τῆς ὀργῆς] fam 1611[2344] Andreas TR. (4) τοῦ θεοῦ τῆς ὀργῆς] Oecumenius[2053]. In reading (4), τοῦ θεοῦ is clearly an error for τοῦ θυμοῦ.

16.a-a. Variants: (1) omit ἐπὶ τὸ ἱμάτιον καί] A eth. (2) ἐπὶ τὸ μέτωπον καί] fam 1006[911] Andr n. (3) ἐπὶ τὸν ἵππον] conjecture of Wellhausen, Analyse, 30. The omission of the phrase ἐπὶ τὸ ἱμάτιον καί by A is attractive because of the problem of precisely what ἐπὶ τὸν μηρὸν αὐτοῦ, "on his thigh," means; Charles (2:137) regards ἐπὶ τὸ ἱμάτιον as a marginal gloss. Wellhausen regards the text as garbled and conjectures that it originally read "on his horse, that is, on its haunch." B. Weiss (Johannes-Apokalypse, 215) thinks that μηρός refers to the "hip" of the rider. The term μηρός can be used to refer to the haunch of a horse (Ps.-Callisthenes 1.15.2) or to the thigh of animals (PLond 1132b, line 5).

16.b. καί is probably epexegetical here, so the second phrase functions as an explanation of the first; i.e., it refers to the part of the robe where the name was inscribed, the part that covered the thigh of the rider (Beckwith, 733–34).

16.c. Torrey (Apocalypse, 153–54; id., HTR 31 [1938] 237–48) has proposed that since ‫ ר‬r and ‫ ד‬d are not distinguished in written Aram., the translator has mistaken דגלה dglh, "his banner," for רגלה rglh, "his leg," and then has located the name inscribed as high on the "leg" as possible, on the μηρός, the thigh.

16.d. The pf. ptcp. γεγραμμένον is in apposition to ὄνομα, which is the obj. of ἔχει; the pattern ἔχειν + obj. + pf. ptcp. occurs several times in Revelation (12:6; 14:1; 19:12, 16; 21:12); see Notes 19.12.h. and 12:6.d.

16.e-e. Variants: (1) Rex regum et dominus dominantium] it[gig] vg Ambrose. (2) Rex regum et dominus dominorum] Irenaeus Cyprian Primasius. The Gk. phrase Βασιλεὺς βασιλέων καὶ κύριος κυρίων is in the nom., but since it is in apposition to the acc. sing. ὄνομα γεγραμμένον, "an inscribed name," and so a solecism, it might be considered a quotation of a title.

17.a. The cardinal number εἷς came to be used as a substitute for the indefinite adj. τὶς, so that it functioned as an indefinite article. The phrase ἕνα ἄγγελον should therefore be translated "a [certain] angel." For a more extensive discussion, see Note 8:13.a.

17.b. Variants: (1) ἔκραξεν] ‫ א‬A (lacuna in C) Andreas Byzantine. (2) ἔκραζεν] 046. The aor. of reading (1), like the parallels in 6:10; 10:3; 18:2, represents the original text (Schmid, Studien 2:208). The present tense of κράζειν is original in 12:2 but questionable in 7:2 and 18:18, 19.

17.c. Variants: (1) omit ἐν before φωνῇ] A (lacuna in C) 051 fam 1006[1006 1841] fam 1611[1611 2329 2344] Oecumenius[2053 2062] Andreas latt TR; Charles, 2:360. (2) ἐν before φωνῇ] ‫ א‬046 fam 1611[1854] 2030 Andr h; Byzantine; Tischendorf, NT Graece; [WHort]; B. Weiss, Johannes-Apokalypse, 134; [Bousset (1906) 432]; Merk, NT; [Nestle-Aland²⁷]; [UBSGNT⁴]. There are several places in Revelation in which the phrase ἐν φωνῇ μεγάλῃ occurs (5:2; 14:7, 9, 15; 16:17), and several other places in which φωνῇ μεγάλῃ is used instrumentally without ἐν (5:12; 6:10; 7:2, 10; 8:13; 10:3; 14:8). ἐν is used when the phrase is preceded by λέγων, but it is missing when preceded by κράζειν (6:10; 7:2, 10; 10:3) or φωνεῖν (14:18); Schmid, Studien 2:133. Therefore, ἐν must be rejected as secondary both here and in 18:2.

17.d. Variant: μεσωουρανίματι] fam 1611[2329].

17.e. Variants: (1) τὸ μέγα τοῦ] ‫ א‬A 025 046 Andr d f 94 1773. (2) τοῦ μεγάλου] Andreas. (3) τὸν μέγαν] Andr l; fam 1611[2329].

17.f. Variant: τὸν before δεῖπνον] 025 046 fam 1006[911] fam 1611[2329] Andr b[2059ª] e[2057] f[2031] i l.

18.a The acc. pl. form σάρκας of the fem. noun σάρξ occurs five times in this verse and in the gen. pl. σαρκῶν in v 21. While the noun σάρξ can be used as a distributive sing., here it is used of the sum total of such things and can be appropriately rendered in Eng. by "corpses" or "carcasses," or even as "carrion."

18.b. Variant: (1) αὐτῶν] lectio originalis. (2) αὐτούς] A. (3) αὐτοῖς] ‫ א‬Byz 17[469 2078 2436] Andr/Byz 3[1617] latt.

18.c. Variants: (1) omit πάντων after ἐλευθέρων] Andr a b c d. (2) πάντων after ἐλευθέρων] Andreas.

18.d-d. Variants: (1) καὶ μικρῶν] fam 1611[2329]. (2) μικρῶν (omit καί)] 046 fam 1611[1611] Oecumenius[2053 2062] Andr e g h i[2042] 1 598 2019 vg[mss].

18.e. Variant: τε before καί] 051 fam 1611[1854] 2030 Oecumenius[2053] Andr e[2026] f[2031-2056] g l 94 2019 Byzantine.

18.f. Variant: τῶν before μεγάλων] ‫ א‬fam 1006 fam 1611[1611] Byz 17[469] cop.

19.a. Variants: (1) αὐτῶν] lectio originalis. (2) αὐτοῦ] A (lacuna in C) Byz 19 cop[sa] arm²; B. Weiss,

Johannes-Apokalypse, 106; Charles, 2:138, suggests that this might be correct, intended to make it clear that the assembled armies are those of the beast and not those of the kings that he has summoned. Weiss argues that the change to αὐτῶν was intentional in order to associate the armies with the kings of the earth as well as the beast. (3) omit αὐτῶν] Byz 9⁴⁶⁷ cop^boms.

19.b. Variant: omit τόν] 046 051 fam 1006¹⁰⁰⁶ ¹⁸⁴¹ fam 1611¹⁶¹¹ ²³²⁹ ²³⁴⁴ Oecumenius²⁰⁵³ ²⁰⁶² Andreas.

20.a-a. Variants: (1) μετ' αὐτοῦ ὁ] ℵ 1773 2019 2329 Andr c d e²⁰⁵⁷ i l. (2) ὁ μετ' αὐτοῦ] fam 1006¹⁰⁰⁶ ¹⁸⁴¹ 2030 Andr f²⁰²³* ²⁰⁷³ 94 Byzantine it^gig cop^samss Tertullian. (3) μετὰ τούτου ὁ] Andreas. (4) ὁ μετ' αὐτοῦ ὁ] 025 Andr e²⁰²⁶. (5) οἱ μετ' αὐτοῦ ὁ] A. In reading (5), the insertion of οἱ is a scribal error, so (5) in effect supports (1). Readings (2) and (3) are obvious corrections, while reading (4) is a conflation of readings (1) and (2).

20.b-b. The prep. ἐνώπιον, which lit. means "in the presence of, before," here means "by the authority of, on behalf of" (BAGD, 271) or "at the commissioning of" (H. Krämer, *EDNT* 1:462). See also *Notes* 13:12.c-c. and 13:14.a-a.

20.c. On this translation, see *Note* 13:16.b.

20.d-d. Variants: (1) τῇ εἰκόνι] ℵ¹ fam 1611²³²⁹. (2) τὴν εἰκόνα] ℵ* fam 1611¹⁶¹¹ Oecumenius²⁰⁵³ ²⁰⁶² Andr i¹³⁸⁴ ¹⁷³² l Byz 1⁻¹⁸⁷² latt. (3) τὸ χάραγμα] 046. On the use of προσκυνεῖν + dat. or acc., see *Note* 4:10.b.

20.e. Variants: (1) ἐβλήθησαν] ℵ A Oecumenius²⁰⁵³ Andr f²⁰³¹ ⁻²⁰⁵⁶ g²⁰⁹ ²⁰⁴⁵ i n 94. (2) βληθήσονται] Andreas. (3) βληθέντες] 1773.

20.f. In the phrase τὴν λίμνην τοῦ πυρὸς τῆς καιομένης, the articular τῆς καιομένης appears to be a solecism congruent with the case of τοῦ πυρός (a neut. noun) rather than with τὴν λίμνην (a fem. noun), i.e., with the word the author considered the most important of the two nouns (see Mussies, *Morphology,* 139). Mussies thinks this instance indicates that the author was uncertain in using categories alien to his own language (*Morphology,* 98). However, if the article τῆς = ταύτης or αὐτῆς (BDR § 249.2), then καιομένης can be construed as a gen. abs. (BDR § 423.10) dependent on εἰς τὴν λίμνην. Torrey (*Apocalypse,* 51) proposes another explanation. In the Aram. phrase בגפרתא יקדא ד נרא ד ליממא *lymm' d nr' d yqd' bgprt',* "lake of fire which burns with sulphur," ליממא *lymm',* "lake," is masc., and נרא *nr',* "fire," is fem., while the ptcp. יקד *yqd',* "burning," is fem. but introduces a new clause and modifies the fem. noun גפרתא *gprt',* "sulphur." G. J. Weyland simply observes that the Heb. word behind λίμνη is masc., while that behind πῦρ is fem., though he does not specify which Heb. terms he has in mind (*Omwerkings- en Compilatie-Hypothesen toegepast op de Apokalypse van Johannes* [Groningen: Wolters, 1888] 136–37).

21.a. τὰ ὄρνεα, a neut. nom. pl. noun, is the subject of ἐχορτάσθησαν, a 3rd pl. aor. pass. verb, since there is a tendency in the NT to use pl. verbs with neut. pl. substantives when the latter refer to living beings (see Mussies, *Morphology,* 231; BDR § 133).

Form/Structure/Setting

I. OUTLINE

E. The final defeat of God's remaining foes (19:11–21:8)
   1. The divine warrior and his conquests (19:11–21)
      a. Description of the divine warrior (19:11–16)
         (1) Summary of vision (19:11)
            (a) Rider called faithful and true (v 11b)
            (b) He judges and makes war in righteousness (v 11c)
         (2) Description of the rider (vv 12–16)
            (a) Eyes like a fiery flame (v 12a)
            (b) Many diadems on his head (v 12b)
            (c) He alone knows his name (v 12c)
            (d) Wears robe stained with blood (v 13a)
            (e) His name: Word of God (v 13b)
            (f) Accompanied by the armies of heaven (v 14)
            (g) Sharp sword issues from his mouth with which he smites the nations (v 15a)

        (h) He rules the nations with a rod of iron (v 15b)

        (i) He will treat the winepress of God's judgment (v 15c)

        (j) His name: King of kings and Lord of lords (v 16)

    b. The divine warrior defeats the beast and his armies (vv 17–21)

        (1) Angelic prophetic invitation (vv 17–18)

            (a) Context of announcement (v 17)

                [1] Location of angel: standing in the sun (v 17a)

                [2] Means of announcement: loud voice (v 17b)

                [3] Audience: birds of midheaven (v 17b)

            (b) The message of the angel (vv 17c–18)

                [1] Invitation to gather for the great supper of God (v 17c)

                [2] Invitation to devour the bodies of the defeated enemies of God (v 18)

        (2) Vision of the assembled armies (v 19)

            (a) Leaders: the beast and the kings of the earth (v 19a)

            (b) Purpose: to fight the rider on the white horse and his armies (v 19b)

        (3) The defeat of the hostile armies (vv 20–21)

            (a) The leaders captured (v 20)

                [1] The beast (v 20a)

                [2] The false prophet (v 20a)

                    [a] Who had performed signs (v 20b)

                    [b] These signs had deceived people (v 20b)

                        {1} Those who had received the mark of the beast

                        {2} Those who worshiped its image

            (b) The punishment of the defeated enemies (vv 20c–21)

                [1] The beast and the false prophet were thrown into the lake of fire (v 20c)

                [2] The fate of the rest (v 21)

                    [a] Killed by the sword issuing from the mouth of the rider (v 21a)

                    [b] The birds gorge on their flesh (v 21b)

II. LITERARY ANALYSIS

Rev 19:11–21 consists of two textual units that constitute a literary pair: (1) 19:11–16 depicts the eschatological coming of the divine warrior to destroy the nations, and (2) 19:17–21 (omitting any battle scene) describes the capture of the beast and the false prophet and the destruction of the army they led.

A. Rev 19:11–16: The Rider on the White Horse

There is general agreement among commentators that this pericope is a description of the return or Parousia of Jesus Christ. At the same time this perspective is problematic because the pericope contains no features clearly derived from traditional early Christian conceptions of the Parousia of Jesus. The view that Rev 19:11–16 presents Christ as the royal bridegroom, based on the royal wedding song in Ps 45 (Farrer,

Images, 169–70; Mealy, *Thousand Years,* 64–65), is suggestive. Ps 45:7–8 is quoted in Heb 1:8–9 and given a christological interpretation. The unit of text in vv 11–16 is framed by the phrase καὶ εἶδον, "then I saw," in vv 11 and 17a (where it introduces the next unit of text, vv 17–21). The first καὶ εἶδον has as its object the accusative noun cluster τὸν οὐρανὸν ἠνεῳγμένον, "the heaven opened," which is a motif widespread in apocalyptic literature to introduce a vision or revelation (see *Comment* on v 11).

The literary form of this unit is the *symbolic description,* which focuses on the *description, identity,* and *tasks* of the rider on the white horse (see *Comment* on the symbolic description in 1:12–16). (1) His description: (a) his eyes are like a fiery flame (v 12); (b) he has many diadems on his head (v 12); (c) he wears a robe dipped in blood (v 13); and (d) a sharp sword issues from his mouth (v 15a). (2) His identity (names): (a) he is "faithful and true" (v 11); (b) he has a name inscribed, which he alone knows (v 12b); (c) his name is "the Word of God" (v 13b); and (d) on his robe and on his thigh he has a name inscribed: "King of kings and Lord of lords" (v 16). (3) His tasks: (a) he judges in righteousness (v 11b); (b) he wages war in righteousness (v 11b); (c) he smites the nations with the sharp sword projecting from his mouth (v 15a); (d) he will rule the nations with a rod of iron (v 15b); and (e) he will tread the winepress of the fury of the wrath of God the Almighty. The indicators of the *symbolic* nature of this description include the mention of the sharp sword that proceeds from his mouth (v 15a) and the metaphorical interpretation of the wine that is pressed as "the fury of the wrath of God the Almighty" (v 15c).

B. *Rev 19:17–21*

This unit of text is framed by the formulas καὶ εἶδον ἕνα ἄγγελον, "then I saw an angel" (v 17a), and καὶ εἶδον ἄγγελον, "then I saw an angel" (20:1a, where it introduces the next unit of text), and by the references to birds in vv 17 and 21. This narrative unit consists of an apocalyptic scenario, based on the tradition of the inviolability of Zion, in which the kings of the earth gather in an unsuccessful attempt to conquer Jerusalem. One of the primary models for this scenario is the Gog and Magog oracle of Ezek 38–39 (also referred to in 1QM 11:16–17). There are two major variants of this apocalyptic scenario: (1) the hostile nations are destroyed by divine intervention before they actually conquer Jerusalem (Rev 19:17–21; 20:7–10; cf. Pss 46; 48:1–8; 76:1–9; Isa 17:12–14; 29:1–8; Ezek 38:1–23; 39:1–6; Joel 3:1–17; Zech 12:1–9; *Sib. Or.* 3.657–701; *1 Enoch* 56:5–8; 100:1–6; 4 Ezra 13:5–11, 29–38; Lactantius *Div. Inst.* 7.17), and (2) the hostile nations temporarily conquer Jerusalem but are eventually repulsed by divine intervention (Rev 11:2; Zech 14:1–11; *Pss. Sol.* 17:11–25; Luke 19:41–44; 21:20–24).

The unsuccessful attempt of the nations to conquer Jerusalem occurs in three variants in Revelation (16:12–16; 19:11–17; 20:7–10). The last two passages have been strongly influenced by the Gog and Magog oracle of Ezek 38–39. Notice the parallels between Rev 19:17–18 and Ezek 39:17–18a:

Rev 19:17–18	*Ezek 39:17–18a*
Then I saw an angel standing in the sun,	As for you, son of man, thus says the Lord God:

and with a loud voice he called
    to all the birds that fly in
    midheaven,
"Come, gather for the great supper
    of God

"Speak to the birds of
    every sort and to all
    the beasts of the field,
'Assemble and come, gather
from all sides to the sacrificial feast
    which I am preparing
    for you,
a great sacrificial feast
    upon the mountains of
    Israel,
and you shall eat flesh
    and drink blood.

to eat the flesh of kings,
    the flesh of captains,
    the flesh of horses and
        their riders,
    and the flesh of all men,
        both free and slave,
        both small and great." (RSV)

You shall eat the flesh of
    the mighty,
and drink the blood of the
    princes of the earth.'" (RSV)

III. THE WARRIOR-KING IMAGERY OF 19:11–16

A. *The Eschatological Warrior*

Rev 19:11–16 is a descriptive passage that focuses on the figure of an eschatological warrior king coming to wage war on the nations. The imagery in this passage is very complex and exhibits parallels with a number of texts in the OT and early Judaism in which either God or the Messiah (particularly in the later targumic texts) is depicted as a warrior. The metaphor of God as a bloodstained divine warrior occurs in Isa 63:1–3, a passage that has influenced subsequent descriptions:

> Who is this that comes from Edom,
>   in crimsoned garments from Bozrah,
> he that is glorious in his apparel,
>   marching in the greatness of his strength?
> . . . .
> Why is thy apparel red,
>   and thy garments like his that treads the wine press?
> "I have trodden the wine press alone,
>   and from the peoples no one was with me;
> I trod them in my anger
>   and trampled them in my wrath;
> their lifeblood is sprinkled upon my garments,
>   and I have stained all my raiment." (RSV)

A similar scene, though notably lacking the winepress imagery, is Wis 18:15, in part dependent on Exod 15:3–4:

> Thy all-powerful word [ὁ παντοδύναμός σου λόγος] leaped from
>   heaven, from the royal throne
> into the midst of the land that was doomed,

a stern warrior
carrying the sharp sword [ξίφος ὀξύ] of thy authentic command,
and stood and filled all things with death,
and touched heaven while standing on the earth. (RSV)

This is part of a poetic description of the destruction of the firstborn of Egypt during the Exodus. There are several striking similarities between this passage and Rev 19:11–16: (1) the heavenly figure is called ὁ . . . σοῦ λόγος, "your Word," i.e., the "Word of God," (2) the figure is depicted as a warrior, (3) the warrior dispenses death and destruction, and (4) he wields a sword, which appears to be a metaphor for the powerful word or command of God.

The depiction of God as a warrior, similarly based on Exod 15:3–4, is much more extensive in *Mek. de-Rabbi Ishmael, Shirata* 1, which is a pastiche of martial metaphors from throughout the Hebrew Bible (Lauterbach, 2:30):

> R. Judah says: This is a verse ["The Lord is a Man of War, the Lord is his Name."] replete with meaning, being illustrated by many passages. It tells that He appeared to them with all the implements of war. He appeared to them like a mighty hero girded with a sword [Rev 19:15], as it is said: "Gird thy sword upon thy thigh, O mighty one" (Ps 18:11). He appeared to them like a horseman [Rev 19:11], as it is said: "And He rode upon a cherub, and did fly" (Ps 18:11). He appeared to them in a coat of mail and helmet, as it is said: "and He put on righteousness as a coat of mail, and a helmet of salvation upon His head" (Isa 59:17). He appeared to them with a spear, as it is said: "At the shining of Thy glittering spear" (Hab 3:11). And it also says: "Draw out also the spear and battle-axe," etc. (Ps 35:3). He appeared to them with bow and arrows, as it is said: "Thy bow is made quite bare," etc. (Hab. 3:9). And it also says: "And He sent out arrows, and scattered them," etc. (2 Sam 22:15). He appeared to them with shield and buckler, as it is said: "His truth is a shield and a buckler," etc. (Ps 91:4). And it also says: "Take hold of shield and buckler," etc. (Ps 35:2). I might understand that He has need of any of these measures, it therefore says: "The Lord is His name."—With his name does He fight and has no need of any of these measures.

A closer parallel to Rev 19:11–16, found in almost identical versions in all the Palestinian Targums with the exception of Targum Onqelos (Syrén, *Targums,* 111–12), reveals the influence of the messianic interpretation of Isa 63:1–6 in early Judaism (perhaps influenced also by Joel 3:17–21[MT 4:17–21]; Syrén, *Targums,* 105). Two very similar versions of Gen 49:11 are found in the Fragmentary Targums to the Pentateuch. The first is MS Paris, Bibliothèque nationale Hébr. 110 (M. L. Klein, *Fragment-Targums* 2:31):

> He [i.e., the King Messiah] girds his loins, [and] goes out to battle against those who hate him; and he kills kings and rulers, and reddens the mountains from the blood of their slain; and he whitens his cloak with the fat of their mighty ones; his garments are rolling [מזגובין *mzgzbyn*, "to be clear," is emended by Klein to מעגענין *mᵉgᵉgyn*, "rolling"] in blood.

The second version is found in MS Vatican Ebr. 440, folios 198–227 (M. L. Klein, *Fragment-Targums* 2:119):

> How beautiful is the King Messiah who will arise from the house of Judah! He girds his loins and goes out to battle against those who hate him, and he kills kings and rulers; he reddens the mountains from the blood of their slain; and he whitens his hills from the

fat of their mighty ones; his garments roll in the blood [מעגגין באדמה (מע) לבושוי *lbwšwy* (*m*ᶜ) *m*ᶜ*g*ᶜ*gyn b'dmh*], and he is like one who presses grapes.

While no trace of this tradition occurs in *Tg. Onq.* Gen 49:11, the same interpretation occurs in *Tg. Neof.* Gen 49:11 (Macho, *Neophyti* 1:635):

> How beautiful is the King Messiah who is to arise from among those of the house of Judah. He girds his loins and goes forth to battle against those that hate him; and he kills kings with rulers, and makes the mountains red from the blood of their slain and makes the valleys white from the fat of their warriors. His garments are rolled in blood; he is like a presser of grapes.

M. Black regards the targum on Gen 49:11 as an example of early Aramaic liturgical poetry (*Aramaic*, 308–9).

The original prophecy in Isa 63:1–6 was directed at Edom, a term that was used later as a codeword for Rome (Grelot, *RB* 70 [1963] 373; Volz, *Eschatologie*, 280). Grelot argues in detail for the messianic interpretation of Isa 63:1–6, saying that John did not create this interpretation but rather was dependent on an existing messianic understanding of this OT text, which he incorporated into Rev 19:13–15 (Grelot, *RB* 70 [1963] 371–80).

The description of the coming of the divine warrior to execute judgment on his enemies is also found in *T. Mos.* 10:3–7, which makes elaborate use of theophany imagery (tr. J. Priest, *OTP* 1:932):

> For the Heavenly One will arise from his kingly throne.
> Yea, he will go forth from his holy habitation
>   with indignation and wrath on behalf of his sons.
> And the earth will tremble, even to its ends shall it be shaken.
> And the high mountains will be made low.
> Yea, they will be shaken, as enclosed valleys will they fall.
> The sun will not give light.
> And in darkness the horns of the moon will flee.
> Yea, they will be broken in pieces.
> It will be turned wholly into blood.
> Yea, even the circle of the stars will be thrown into disarray.
> And the sea all the way to the abyss will retire,
>   to the sources of waters which fail.
> Yea, the rivers will vanish away.
> For God Most High will surge forth, the Eternal One alone.
> In full view will he come to work vengeance on the nations.
> Yea, all their idols will he destroy.

Finally, there is the related tradition preserved by Philo (*Praem.* 95 [LCL, 423]):

> "For there shall come forth a man," says the oracle [viz. LXX Num 24:7], "and leading his host to war, he will subdue great and populous nations."

B. Roman Triumph Imagery

Several features of this descriptive passage (which again is a static description of a picture or scene rather than a narrative; see *Form/Structure/Setting* on Rev 17) suggest that the author has incorporated imagery from the Roman triumph into his description: (1) the prominence of the white horse (v 11) and the white horses (v 14), (2) the diadems worn by the rider (v 13), (3) the name or title inscribed on the rider (vv 12–13, 16), (4) the posthumous character of the rider suggested by his robe dipped in blood (v 13), (5) the armies accompanying the rider (v 14), and (6) the predominantly military imagery, which reflects a decisive victory (v 15). The major feature missing is the quadriga or chariot drawn by four horses, yet this is explicable since the setting here is not the celebration of victory but the preparation for a final battle.

PGiss 3, which dates to A.D. 117, appears to be a draft of the official celebration of the ascension of Trajan (i.e., his deification) and the accession of Hadrian to the throne at Heptakomia, the metropolis of the Egyptian nome Apollonopolites (tr. Alexander, *HSCP* 49 [1938] 143):

> Having just mounted aloft with Trajan in my chariot of white horses, I come to you, oh people, I, Phoebus, by no means an unknown god, to proclaim the new ruler Hadrian, whom all things serve on account of virtue and the genius of his divine father [πατρὸς θεοῦ].

This papyrus suggests that Hadrian was proclaimed emperor not by people but by divine revelation. The triumph was a procession in Rome honoring a *triumphator* and his army (on the occasion of a victory in a just war in which at least five thousand of the enemy were killed). The *triumphator* rode in a chariot drawn by four white horses, and a slave held a crown over his head (gold crowns from defeated towns were presented to the *imperator* and displayed in the triumphal procession). He wore the *tunica palmata* (a tunic, originally with a border the width of a hand but later decorated with palmette designs) and the *toga picta* (a toga decorated with designs in gold thread) and was adorned like a god-king, specifically as Jupiter Optimus Maximus. The procession included magistrates, senators, captives, booty, and the *triumphator*.

Triumphal arches (of which about a hundred are known) were erected to memorialize such triumphs. One important example is the posthumous Arch of Titus, which celebrated both his victory over the Jews in A.D. 70 and his apotheosis, or divinization. Each of these events is depicted in a major bas relief (see *Comment* on 5:8). The triumph of Aemilius Paulus in 167 B.C. is described in detail in Plutarch *Aem.* 32–34, and Polybius (30.25) describes a Greco-Syrian adaptation of the Roman triumph by Antiochus IV. Recently it has been demonstrated that the *adventus* ceremony was developed on the basis of the triumph (MacCormack, *Historia* 21 [1972] 725).

Particularly interesting is the phenomenon of the posthumous triumph, which is applicable to Rev 19:11–16. There is both numismatic and literary evidence that Trajan was accorded such a posthumous triumph. Coin legends with *Divus Traianus Parthicus* and *Divo Traiano Parthico* indicate that the deceased emperor received the title Parthicus posthumously, though Den Boer argues that the funeral procession and triumph were separate events ("Trajan's Deification," 85–88). According to *Scriptores Historiae Augustae* (tr. LCL):

> When the senate offered him [Hadrian] the triumph which was to have been Trajan's, he refused it for himself and caused the effigy of the dead emperor to be carried in a

triumphal chariot, in order that the best of emperors might not lose even after death the honour of a triumph.

IV. SOURCE CRITICISM

Though Wellhausen (*Analyse*, 30) thought that 19:1–10 and 19:11–21 came from the hand of the apocalyptist, J. Weiss (*Offenbarung*, 99–100) thought that 19:11–21 could not have stood in the *Grundschrift* of Revelation because (1) it is a doublet of 14:14–20, (2) it is thoroughly Jewish, (3) it is so cruel and vindictive that it could not represent the outlook of the author of the Johannine letters, (4) it constitutes a continuation of the vision of the two beasts in Rev 13, and (5) it identifies the Messiah with the child of Rev 12, which also was not part of the *Grundschrift* of Revelation. These arguments are not persuasive, however, and it appears that both 19:1–10 and 19:11–21 originated with the author.

Comment

11a καὶ εἶδον τὸν οὐρανὸν ἠνεῳγμένον, "I then saw heaven open." καὶ εἶδον, "then I saw," introduces a new vision report here (see *Comment* on 5:1). The motif of the opening of heaven is primarily associated with divine revelation. This motif occurs just once in the OT, in Ezek 1:1 (see Zimmerli, *Ezekiel* 1:116). The motif of "the open heaven," frequently linked to a verb of seeing, is more common in early Jewish apocalyptic literature (*2 Apoc. Bar.* 22:1; 4Q*213–14* Aramaic Testament of Levi 2 ii 19–21 [Eisenman-Wise, *Scrolls*, 136–41]; *T. Levi* 2:6; *Jos. As.* 14:3; *Apoc. Mos.* 35:2 [Eve tells Seth to see "the seven heavens opened"]; *T. Abr.* [Rec. A] 7:3) and early Christianity (Mark 1:10 [= Matt 3:16; Luke 3:21]; John 1:51; Acts 7:56; 10:11; Herm. *Vis.* 1.1.4; *T. Jud.* 24:2 [an allusion to the baptism of Jesus in a chapter that is largely a Christian composition; see Ulrichsen, *Grundschrift*, 174, 315]; Origen *Contra Celsum* 1.41–48; *Ap. John* II/1 1.30–32), where it is frequently used as a way of introducing a divine revelation. On the related motif of the "open door in heaven," see *Comment* on 4:1. This motif is also used to signal the beginning of a scene of divine judgment, the earliest reference to which appears to be Isa 64:1–3 (3 Macc 6:18–19; *T. Levi* 5:1–7 [Levi ascends to heaven after the gates are opened for him by an angel, and he is then commissioned by God to execute vengeance upon Shechem, which he does upon his return to earth; this is judged an interpolation by Ulrichsen, *Grundschrift*, 193]; *T. Levi* 18:6; 4QTestLevi[a] 2:17–18). This motif is found in *PGM* XXXVI.298–300, a magical papyrus with a strong Jewish orientation: "The heaven of heavens opened, and the angels of God descended and overturned the five cities of Sodom and Gomorrah, Admah, Zeboiim, and Segor." The combination of the motifs of the open heavens and the descent of Jesus who radiates light (his first coming) is found in the *Pistis Sophia* 1.4. The motif of "the opening of heaven" is also used in the Greco-Roman world in connection with revelatory signs or omens (Vergil *Aeneid* 9.20, "I see the heavens part asunder [*medium video discedere caelum*]").

11b καὶ ἰδοὺ ἵππος λευκὸς καὶ ὁ καθήμενος ἐπ᾿ αὐτὸν πιστὸς καὶ ἀληθινός, "and behold, a white steed and the person mounted on it is faithful and true." This descriptive style, in which the writer first mentions the object on which a person is seated (a throne or thrones; a horse or horses; a cloud) and then the individual or group of individuals seated on it, occurs frequently in Revelation (4:2, 4; 6:2–8; 14:14; 20:4; see Rissi, *Future,* 18–19). The appearance of the rider on the white horse accompanied by an angelic cavalry is generally, and probably correctly, understood as a dramatization of the Parousia of Jesus. In no other early Christian eschatological scenario that includes the Parousia, however, is Jesus depicted as mounted on a white horse, making it likely that this distinctive conception of the Parousia is adapted from elsewhere. In the Greco-Roman world, the image of the celestial rider was widely understood as a savior who could deliver people from various kinds of trouble (Johnston, *CP* 87 [1992] 307–16). Since this figure rides at the head of a heavenly army (v 14), it would be natural and logical for the reader to construe this rider as Michael, who led an angelic army in battle against the dragon and his angels in 12:7. The color of the mount, however, would seem to point toward identifying the rider of the white horse in Rev 6:2 with the Messiah.

The attributes "faithful and true" are used of Christ elsewhere in Revelation (3:14; πιστός, "faithful," is used with other attributes in 1:5) and are also used of the revelatory message given to John (21:5; 22:6). Both are meanings of the Hebrew term אמן *'mn,* and both πιστός, "faithful," and ἀληθινός, "true," are used in the LXX as translations of אמן *'mn.*

11c καὶ ἐν δικαιοσύνῃ κρίνει καὶ πολεμεῖ, "With justice he judges and wages war." The use of the present tense in the verbs κρίνει, "he judges," and πολεμεῖ, "he wages war" (here the general or gnomic present, used to express customary actions and general truths; see Burton, *Syntax,* § 12), often used in explanatory remarks in Revelation, suggests that this phrase is a narrative aside.

The phrase κρίνειν ἐν δικαιοσύνῃ, "to judge with righteousness," is not used here exclusively in connection with the destruction of the rider's enemies (contra Beckwith, 732; Mounce, 344) but also has the positive connotation of the salvific action of Christ toward his people, i.e., as judge of his Church (Holtz, *Christologie,* 169–70; Rissi, *Future,* 22). When God is described in the OT as "judging with righteousness," it can be applied to the nations as well as to his people (Pss 9:8; 72:2; 96:13; see Prigent, 292). This is an allusion to the Hebrew text of Isa 11:4, a passage in which it is said of the ideal king, the "shoot of Jesse" (mentioned in 11:1), that "he judges with righteousness [וְשָׁפַט בְּצֶדֶק *wĕšāpaṭ bĕṣedeq*]" and then destroys the wicked. Isa: 11:4, which is part of a passage interpreted messianically in Judaism (*Tg. Isa.* 11:1–6; *Pss. Sol.* 17:24–25; 4QpIsaᵃ 8–10; 4 Ezra 3:9–11, 37–38; see Fekkes, *Isaiah,* 117–22), is also alluded to in v 15 and is applied to Christ at his Parousia in 2 Thess 2:8. Variations on the phrase "to judge with righteousness," "to judge with right judgment," i.e., "to judge justly," are extremely important in the OT and early Judaism, for the notion of צדקה *sĕdāqâ* or δικαιοσύνη, "righteousness, justice," is central for defining the relationships between people and between people (both individually and collectively) and God (von Rad, *OT Theology* 1:370–83). It was the moral standard for judges (Deut 1:16; 16:18), for kings (Prov 31:9), and for interpersonal relationships (Zech 7:9), based on the ideal pattern of the completely consistent just and fair judgment that characterizes the actions of God (Ps 7:11; Jer 11:20; Rom 2:5; 2 Tim 4:8; 1 Pet 2:23). In early Christianity it was applied to interpersonal relationships (John 7:24; *Barn.* 19:11). The specific phrase κρίνειν ἐν δικαιοσύνῃ occurs in LXX Pss 9:9; 71:2(MT 72:2); 95:13(MT 96:13); 97:9(MT 98:9); cf. Pss 7:9; 35:24. The same terminology is used of the expected role of the Davidic Messiah in *Pss. Sol.* 17:26 (tr. Sparks, *AOT*), "And he shall gather together a holy people, whom he shall lead in righteousness [ἐν δικαιοσύνῃ], and he shall judge [κρινεῖ] the tribes of the people which has been sanctified by the Lord his God." See also *Pss. Sol.* 17:29, "He [the Davidic Messiah] shall judge [κρινεῖ] peoples and nations in the wisdom of his righteousness [δικαιοσύνης]." This is, therefore, a description of the action of the Messiah.

The verb πολεμεῖ, "wages war," does not simply refer to the chastening or judging of wayward members of the community, as it does in 2:16 (contra Holtz, *Christologie*, 171); rather it refers to the destruction of the wicked, as v 15 makes clear (Prigent, 292; Fekkes, *Isaiah*, 224–25).

12a οἱ δὲ ὀφθαλμοὶ αὐτοῦ [ὡς] φλὸξ πυρός, "Now his eyes were like a brilliant flame." The conjunction δέ, "and, but, now," occurs just seven times in Revelation (1:14; 2:5, 16, 24; 10:2; 9:12; 21:8). δέ is twice used for emphasis when the author begins a description of the appearance of the exalted Christ, here and in 1:14. In 21:8 δέ is used as an adversative particle to introduce the fate of various categories of sinner in contrast to those who are victorious.

The phrase ὡς φλὸξ πυρός, "like a brilliant flame," occurs in 1:14 and 2:18 (ὡς φλόγα πυρός) as well as here in 19:12 and is an allusion to the Aramaic phrase אשׁ די כלפי *kĕlappî dê 'ēš* from LXX Theod Dan 10:6, ὡσεὶ λαμπάδες πυρός, "like flaming torches," where it is part of a more extensive description of a supernatural being, as in Rev 19:12. The phrase ὡς φλὸξ πυρός occurs three times in *Jos. As.*: (1) in *Jos. As.* 14:9 as part of a description of an angel, "the hairs of his head like a flame of fire of a burning torch"; (2) in *Jos. As.* 17:8, "the chariot was like a flame of fire"; and (3) in *Jos. As.* 23:15, "their swords were flashing forth (something) like a flame of fire." φλὸξ πυρός also occurs in *Pr. Man.* frag. (Denis, *Fragmenta*, 117) and in *Apoc. Elijah* frag. c in a description of the Antichrist (Denis, *Fragmenta*, 104): ἡ κεφαλὴ αὐτοῦ φλὸξ πυρός, "his head is a burning flame."

12b καὶ ἐπὶ τὴν κεφαλὴν αὐτοῦ διαδήματα πολλά, "and on his head were many diadems." The dragon has already been depicted as wearing a diadem on each of his seven heads (12:3), doubtless representing a series of seven king-emperors, while the beast from the sea has a diadem on each of his ten horns (13:1). The use of multiple diadems in antiquity often represented sovereignty over as many nations. According to 1 Macc 11:13 and Josephus *J.W.* 13.113, Ptolemy VI Philometer entered Antioch (ca. 169 B.C.) wearing two diadems, one representing Egypt and the other Asia. The many diadems are therefore appropriate for one who is called "King of kings and Lord of lords" (v 16). The allegorical female figure named Τυραννίς, "Tyrant," in Dio Chrysostom *Or.* 1.78–82 (cf. Mussies, *Dio*, 250) is depicted as wearing many diadems in addition to many scepters and tiaras; each of the diadems undoubtedly symbolizes a tyrant. Both Hellenistic kings and Roman generals were often presented crowns by Greek cities as tokens of major victories (Millar, *Emperor*, 140–42). The statue of the mother of Ozymandias (= Ramses II) is said to have worn *three* diadems, indicating that she was daughter, wife, and mother of a king (Diodorus Siculus 1.47.5). The many diadems worn by the rider of the white horse are a literary counterpoint to the diadems worn by the dragon, who is described as having seven heads with a diadem on each head in 12:3, while the beast from the sea is described as having ten horns with a diadem on each horn in 13:1.

12c ἔχων ὄνομα γεγραμμένον ὃ οὐδεὶς οἶδεν εἰ μὴ αὐτός, "with a name inscribed that no one knows but he himself." There is a close verbal parallel in 2:17, where the victorious Christian is promised a white stone ὄνομα καινὸν γεγραμμένον ὃ οὐδεὶς οἶδεν εἰ μὴ ὁ λαμβάνων, "with a new name inscribed that no one but the recipient knows," and 3:12, where the exalted Christ writes the names of God, the name of the heavenly city, and his own "new name" on the conquering Christian. Wellhausen (*Analyse*, 30) and Charles (2:132) correctly regard this phrase as a later addition for several reasons: (1) it interrupts the description, (2) the statement is contradicted in v 13, and (3) omitting it restores the two parallel couplets in vv 12–13:

12a	Now his eyes were like a brilliant flame,
12b	and on his head were many diadems.
13a	He was dressed in a garment stained with blood,
13b	and his name was "the Word of God."

The statement is awkward because the masculine singular participle ἔχων, "having," assumes that the secret name is inscribed on the rider himself, not on the diadems (in 13:1 the blasphemous names are written on the seven heads of the beast from the sea).

Charles's second argument must be qualified, however, for in the magical papyri, after statements emphasizing the secrecy of the name of a divinity, *it is precisely the secret name that is disclosed*, usually in the form of *voces magicae*, "magical words," or *nomina arcana*, "secret names"; for examples, see *PGM* I.216–17, "I invoke your secret name" (followed by a series of *voces magicae* or *nomina arcana* that constitute the secret name); *PGM* XXI.1, "Hear me, Lord, whose secret name cannot be spoken" (also followed by a series of *voces magicae* or *nomina arcana*). In *PGM* IV.277–78, Typhon is requested to perform the desires of the magician for "I tell your true names" (followed by *voces magicae*). *PGM* IV.1266 claims that Aphrodite's name (i.e., her *real* name) cannot be learned quickly, but her name is then given as "Nepheriêri." *PGM* XII.240 (with a close parallel in XIII.763) mentions a "secret, inexpressible name," which again is given in the series of *voces magicae* or *nomina arcana* that immediately follow (see also P. Merton II.58 in Daniel-Maltomini, *Supplementum Magicum* 2:63, lines 11–12, which mentions the deity's τὸ κρυπτόν σου ὄνομα, "your secret name").

The very fact that the rider has a secret name suggests that the rider is either a divine being (see Gen 32:29) or an angelic being (Judg 13:17–18), and that in turn might suggest that if this phrase is a later interpolation by the author (it certainly reflects his style; see 19:16 and 2:17), it is intended to reflect the high Christology of the final edition of Revelation. The secret name of the Son is mentioned in the Coptic-Gnostic tractate *Gos. Phil.* 54.5–7 (tr. J. M. Robinson, *Nag Hammadi*, 142), "One single name is not uttered in the world, the name which the father gave to the son; it is the name above all things." The same tractate refers to "Jesus" as a hidden name, while "Christ" is a revealed name (*Gos. Phil.* 56.3–4). In *Asc. Isa.* 9:5, on the other hand, "Jesus" is the earthly name of the Lord Christ, but his real name cannot be known by his followers until they have ascended out of the body.

The view is expressed in Plato *Cratylus* 400d–e that people do not know the true names of the gods that the gods use of themselves; they can only know those names traditionally used in prayers and invocations. Iamblichus (*De myst.* 7.4; E. des Places, ed., *Les Mysteres d'Egypte [par] Jamblique* [Paris: Les Belles letteres, 1966] 191) observed that some names of the gods are known and others unknown, but those that are known have been revealed by the gods themselves. One feature of Greco-Roman mythological literature is that supernatural beings, as well as other features of the cosmos known to humans, have names by which they are known on earth but also *secret names* that are known only to the gods and to those to whom the gods choose to reveal them: e.g., *Iliad* 1.403–4, "whom the gods call Briareus, but all men Aegaeon" (see also *Iliad* 2.813–14; 14.290–91; 20.74; *Scholia in Hom. Iliad.* 1.403 [ed. W. Dindorf, *Scholia Graeca in Homeri Iliadem* (Oxford: Clarendon, 1875) 1:51]; *Odyssey* 10.305; 12.61; Hesiod, frag. 296 [R. Merkelbach and M. L. West, eds., *Fragmenta Hesiodea* (Oxford: Clarendon, 1967)]; Pindar, *Hymni* frag. 33e [H. Maehler, ed., *Pindari Carmina cum fragmentis,* post B. Suell, 8th ed. (Leipzig: Teubner, 1987–89)]; Athenaeus *Deipn.* 14.643a; Dio Chrysostom *Or.* 10.23; *Prayer of Joseph* [Origen *Comm. in Ioann.* II.31], ὁ κληθεὶς ὑπὸ ἀνθρώπων Ἰακώβ, "called 'Jacob' by people"); *Pistis Sophia* 137 contains a list of the five archons with both their celestial names and the names they are called by humans (see Güntert, *Sprache der Götte,* 102–16, who demonstrates the tendency to regard common terms as human, but uncommon, yet genuine, Greek terms as divine). The fear that the correct name of the god or gods may be unknown is reflected in the ancient liturgical formula ὅστις ποτ' ἐστίν, "whoever he is," used in Greek prayers and invocations (Aeschylus *Agamemnon* 160; Euripides *Troad.* 885–86; Athenaeus 8.334b [used in parody]); see E. Norden, *Agnostos Theos,* 143–47. The *Pistis Sophia* 1.10 (ed. Schmidt-Till, p. 10, lines 20–21; ed. Schmidt-MacDermot, p. 16) refers to a heavenly form of writing as "in the manner of writing of those of the height." The secrecy of divine names also features in some Gnostic documents (e.g., *Gos. Truth* 38.16–32). The same motif occurs in folktales; in the fairy tale about Rumpelstilskin, a famous line runs *Ei wie gut dass niemand weiss, dass ich Rumpelstilzchen heiss,* "Oh, how good that no one knows, that I am named Rumpelstilskin." The secrecy surrounding the name of the heavenly figure in Rev 19:12c has a parallel in *Jos. As.* 15:12 in the speech of the mysterious heavenly revealer (tr. C. Burchard, *OTP* 2:227):

> Why do you seek my name, Aseneth? My name is in the heavens in the book of the Most High, written by the finger of God in the beginning of the book before all (the others), because I am chief of the house of the Most High. And all names written in the book of the Most High are unspeakable, and man is not allowed to pronounce nor hear them in this world.

In a prayer attributed to Baruch in *Par. Jer.* 6:13, the scribe mentions τὸ μέγα ὄνομα, ὃ οὐδεὶς δύναται γνῶναι, "the great name which no one can know." That of course is the Tetragrammaton, the name יהוה or *YHWH,* referred to by Philo (*Mos.* 2.114; LCL tr.): "a name which only those whose ears and tongues are purified may hear or speak in the holy place, and no other person, nor in any other place at all." According to *1 Enoch* 69:14, Michael was asked about the secret name (i.e., the שֵׁם הַמְּפֹרָשׁ *šēm hammĕpōrāš,* "the ineffable name [of God]"; see *Jub.* 36:7) so that it could be used in effective oaths. The mystery of the true name of Jesus is mentioned in a brief dialogue in *Acts Thom.* 163 (tr. Hennecke-Schneemelcher, *NTA* 2:528; see Lipsius-Bonnet, *AAA* 2/2:277):

> "My Lord," says Thomas, "is my master and thine, since he is Lord of heaven and earth." And Misdaeus said: "What is his name?" Judas said: "Thou canst not hear his true name at this time, [. . .] but the name which was bestowed upon him for a season is Jesus, the Christ."

Lactantius (reflecting the widespread view in early Christianity that the gods of the pagans are really demons, so that the names used by benighted worshipers are not the true names of the beings they are worshiping) claims that magicians call upon the true names, the heavenly names, of gods represented by images and statues (*Div. Inst.* 2.17).

13a καὶ περιβεβλημένος ἱμάτιον βεβαμμένον αἵματι, "He was dressed in a garment stained with blood." The blood mentioned here is not primarily a metaphor for the atoning death of Christ (see *Comments* on 1:5; 5:9; 7:14; 12:11) but rather a literal reference to the heavenly warrior whose garment is stained with the blood of those he has slain (Allo, 304–5). The imagery of a bloodstained divine warrior coming to destroy his enemies occurs in a number of texts in the OT and early Judaism (Exod 15; Deut 33; Judg 5; Hab 3; Isa 26:16–27:6; 59:15–20; 63:1–6; Zech 14:1–21; see T. Hiebert, "Warrior, Divine," *ADB* 6:876–80; Miller, *Divine Warrior*), one of the oldest of which is Isa 63:1–3 (quoted above in *Form/Structure/ Setting* on 19:11–21). An even closer parallel to Rev 19:11–16, which reveals the influence of the messianic interpretation of Isa 63:1–6 in early Judaism (perhaps influenced also by Joel 3:17–21 [MT 4:17–21] [Syrén, *Targums*, 105]), is found in almost identical versions in all the Palestinian Targums with the exception of Targum Onqelos (Syrén, *Targums*, 111–12). All three versions of Gen 49:11 in the targums are quoted above in *Form/Structure/Setting* on 19:11–21. The most important of the three, MS Paris, Bibliothèque nationale Hébr. 110 (M. L. Klein, *Fragment-Targums* 2:31) is quoted here:

> He [i.e., the King Messiah] girds his loins, [and] goes out to battle against those who hate him; and he kills kings and rulers, and reddens the mountains from the blood of their slain; and he whitens his cloak with the fat of their mighty ones; his garments are rolling [מזגביין *mzgzbyn*, "to be clear," is emended by Klein to מעגעגין *mᶜgᶜgyn*, "rolling"] in blood.

The striking feature of this targum is the juxtaposition of the declaration that the Messiah "whitens his cloak" with the observation that "his garments are rolling in blood," an antithesis that calls to mind the robes of the followers of Jesus, made white by the blood of the Lamb (Rev 7:14).

It was inevitable that this older image of God as the divine warrior with blood-soaked garments transposed into the Messiah as divine warrior would be understood as a reference to the death of Christ by both the author and his readers when placed in a Christian context. The dress worn in battle by Roman field commanders was traditionally colored red, while in the imperial period the color red or purple was reserved for the emperor (Herodian 2.8.6; Mommsen, *Römisches Staatsrecht* 1:433).

13b καὶ κέκληται τὸ ὄνομα αὐτοῦ ὁ λόγος τοῦ θεοῦ, "and his name was called 'the Word of God.'" This phrase has often been considered a later addition to the text (Wellhausen, *Analyse*, 30; Bousset [1906] 431), under the mistaken assumption that the Logos theology of the Johannine community is reflected. This description of the heavenly warrior has elements that are both explicitly and implicitly allegorical. That a sharp sword issues from his mouth with which to strike the nations (see *Comment* on 19:15) and that with the sword issuing from his mouth he slays enemies (see *Comment* on 19:21) suggest that the sword is a metaphor for the Word of God. According to *Pss. Sol.* 17:24, the Davidic Messiah will "destroy the unlawful nations with the word of his mouth." The phrase ὁ λόγος τοῦ θεοῦ, "the Word of God," occurs five times in Revelation (1:2, 9; 6:9; 19:13; 20:4), the plural form "words of God" twice more (17:17; 19:9); in both singular and plural forms the phrase means "gospel," i.e., the Christian message of salvation. Only here is ὁ λόγος τοῦ θεοῦ, "the word of God," used as a title for Jesus presented as the returning Lord. Since elsewhere in the NT the term ὁ λόγος is used as a christological title only in Johannine literature, the designation of Jesus as the Word is often considered an important link between Revelation and the Corpus Johanneum (see the comprehensive survey and discussion in Frey, "Verhältnis," 403–9). It is important to notice that while the term ὁ λόγος is used of the pre-incarnate Jesus in an absolute form three times in John 1:1, i.e., without being qualified by an adjective or a noun in the genitive (cf. Ign. *Magn.* 8:2), in 1 John 1:1 ὁ λόγος (which appears to be a reinterpretation of ὁ λόγος in John 1:1 to mean the "message [preached by Jesus during his ministry]"; see Brown, *Epistles*, 164–65, 182) is qualified by a noun in the genitive in the phrase ὁ λόγος τῆς ζωῆς, "the word of life." The phrase ὁ λόγος τοῦ θεοῦ, "the word of God," in Rev 19:13 is qualified by the genitive τοῦ θεοῦ, "of God," which has no explicit parallel in either the Fourth Gospel or 1 John, and the title is applied to the returning Lord.

The warrior's name "the Word of God" is one of several names or titles in 19:11–16 ("faithful and true," "a secret name," and "King of kings and Lord of Lords") that are attributed to the victorious warrior Messiah depicted in this passage. The figure of the rider on the white horse has less in common with the Logos of John 1 and 1 John 1 than with the conception found in Wis 18:15–16:

> Thy all-powerful word [ὁ παντοδύναμός σου λόγος] leaped from
>   heaven, from the royal throne
> into the midst of the land that was doomed,
> a stern warrior
> carrying the sharp sword [ξίφος ὀξύ] of thy authentic command,
> and stood and filled all things with death,
> and touched heaven while standing on the earth. (RSV)

Since the context of Wis 18:15–16 is a poetic description of God's slaying of the firstborn in Egypt during the tenth and final plague, it is of some interest that the Hebrew term דבר *dbr* can mean both "word" and "pestilence." This personification of Plague as a messenger of God has a canonical parallel in 1 Chr 21:16:

> David looked up and saw the angel of the Lord standing between earth and heaven, and in his hand a drawn sword stretched out over Jerusalem. (NRSV)

The context is the pestilence that God inflicted on Israel because David had ordered a census taken. The double meaning of דבר *dbr* is also reflected in a striking error in translation in the LXX version of Hab 3:5. While a translation of the Hebrew text reads "Before him [the Lord] went pestilence [דֶּבֶר *dāber*], and plague followed close behind," LXX Hab 3:5 mistakenly has πρὸ προσώπου αὐτοῦ πορεύσεται λόγος, καὶ ἐξελεύσεται, ἐν πεδίλοις οἱ πόδες αὐτοῦ, "Before his presence goes the word, and his feet will follow with plagues." A passage emphasizing divine judgment has been changed into one in which the word arrives in advance of God's punishment.

Despite the common application of ὁ λόγος to Jesus in Rev 19:13, John 1:1, and 1 John 1:1, the title is used in such a different way in Rev 19:13 that it may in fact reflect the earliest stage of the application of the term Logos to Jesus (Joachim Jeremias, *ZNW* 59 [1968] 82–5; Schüssler Fiorenza, *NTS* 23 [1976–77] 415–16). Hayward (*Divine Name*, 132–33) has argued that targumic *Memra* theology (which he thinks may go back to the first century A.D., but which is limited exclusively to the Targums since it never occurs in the Talmud or the midrashim) is probably reflected in this passage. In *Tg. Neof.* Exod 12:42 the *Memra* goes out on the fourth night (the last night of the present evil age) to achieve the redemption of Israel.

14 καὶ τὰ στρατεύματα τὰ ἐν τῷ οὐρανῷ ἠκολούθει αὐτῷ ἐφ᾽ ἵπποις λευκοῖς ἐνδεδυμένοι βύσσινον λευκὸν καθαρόν, "The heavenly armies followed him on white steeds, wearing white, pure linen." This sudden and unanticipated mention of the heavenly army appears intrusive since the description of the rider is resumed in v 15. Within the context of Revelation, it is natural for the reader to identify this heavenly army as the force of angels led by Michael who defeated Satan and his angels in Rev 12:7 (and perhaps even with the army of "holy ones" bivouacked about the beloved city in 20:9). Even though traditional Christian imagery associated with the Parousia is largely absent from 19:11–16, the fact that the rider is accompanied by a heavenly host can be construed as an allusion to the Son of man tradition (Bietenhard, *Reich*, 15 n. 12). It is also possible to construe this heavenly army as equivalent to "the holy ones" or "holy angels" that accompany God as a regular feature of theophanies (Deut 33:3), particularly when he comes in judgment (Zech 14:5; Dan 7:10; Ps 68:17; *1 Enoch* 1:9 [quoted in Jude 14]; see Noth, "Holy Ones"), or those that accompany Christ (Mark 8:38; Matt 16:27; Luke 9:26; *Did.* 16:7). The term ἅγιοι, "holy ones," is ambiguous when used in such contexts, for it could refer to the people of God (see *Comment* on 5:8) or to angels. In the OT and early Judaism, the angels of God are frequently conceptualized as a heavenly army (Gen 32:1–2; Josh 5:14–15 [here the phrase שַׂר צְבָא־יהוה *śar ṣĕbā᾽-YHWH*, "prince of the army of Yahweh," is paralleled in Dan 8:11, where שַׂר־הַצָּבָא *śar-haṣṣābā᾽*, "prince of the army," occurs]; 1 Kgs 22:19; 2 Kgs 6:17; 2 Chr 18:18; Ps 68:18; Dan 7:10; Joel 2:11; *1 Enoch* 1:4; *2 Enoch* 17; *3 Enoch* 35; *T. Levi* 3:3; see Justin *1 Apol.* 6.2, who refers to "an army of good angels"). The divine name יהוה צבאות *YHWH ṣĕbā᾽ōt*, "Yahweh Sebaoth" or "Yahweh of hosts," alludes to Yahweh as a leader of angelic armies (1 Sam 7:45; Isa 21:10; 31:4; 37:16; Amos 3:13; 4:13; 5:27; 6:14). In some early Christian eschatological scenarios, the returning Christ is accompanied by an angelic host (Matt 13:41; 25:31; Mark 8:38 [= Matt 16:27; Luke 9:26]; 13:26–27 [= Matt 24:30–31]; 1 Thess 3:13; 4:16; 2 Thess 1:7; Justin *1 Apoc.* 51.9), while in others these "holy ones" or "saints" have come to be understood as previously deceased Christians (*Did.* 16:7; *Apost. Const.* 7.34.4). *Both* angels and the host of saints accompany Christ in *Asc. Isa.* 4.14–16 and perhaps in *Apoc. Peter* 1; see Benoit, " Ἅγιοι," 83–99. The Parousia is sometimes depicted as a salvific event (e.g., 1

Thess 4:13–18) or as judgment (e.g., 2 Thess 1:7–10); see Aune, "Parousia," 103–9. There is a particularly close parallel with the vision attributed to martyrs just before their death in *Mart. Marian* 12.4 (tr. Musurillo, *Acts*, 211), "there appeared horses in the sky of snow-white brilliance, on which rode young men in white garments" (perhaps a "personal Parousia" on analogy with the vision of Stephen in Acts 7:56). The sight and sound of heavenly armies is a frequent prodigy reported in Roman sources (Pliny *Hist. nat.* 2.58.148; Jos. *J.W.* 6.288; Tacitus *Hist.* 5.13; see *Excursus 6A*).

The phrase "white, *pure* linen" makes it obvious that these white garments symbolize the purity and holiness of this heavenly army. This is the only place in Revelation where heavenly figures are said to wear βύσσινα, "linen garments," though in 15:6 the seven angels with the seven last plagues are described as emerging from the heavenly temple ἐνδεδυμένοι λίνον καθαρὸν λαμπρόν, "wearing pure shining linen." In a magical text the seven virgin Τύχαι, "Fates," are described as ἐν βυσσίνοις, "wearing linen garments" (*PGM* IV.663–64).

15a καὶ ἐκ τοῦ στόματος αὐτοῦ ἐκπορεύεται ῥομφαία ὀξεῖα, ἵνα ἐν αὐτῇ πατάξῃ τὰ ἔθνη, "From his mouth projected a sharp sword that he might smite the nations with it." Variations on the phrase "the sword of his mouth" occur five times in Revelation (1:16; 2:12, 16; 19:15, 21), in two clusters: (1) ῥομφαία, "sword," in 1:16 is anarthrous, while the anaphoric article is used with it in 2:12, 16; (2) in 19:15 ῥομφαία is again anarthrous, while in 19:21 it is articular. In Rev 19:15, 21 (particularly the latter), we have the kind of apocalyptic context appropriate for the transmission of this metaphor; in fact Rev 19:15, 21 is very probably the source of the metaphor used in 1:16; 2:12, 16. The author has drawn on an existing tradition in which Ps 2:9 (alluded to in v 15b; see *Comment* below) and Isa 11:4 (alluded to here in v 15a) are combined and given a messianic interpretation. This is clear from *Pss. Sol.* 17:24, clearly in a messianic context (see Charles, 2:136): "To shatter all their substance with an iron rod [Ps 2:9]; to destroy the unlawful nations with the word of his mouth [Isa 11:4]." A messianic context for understanding Isa 11:4 is also reflected in 4Q*161* = 4QIsaiah Pesher[a] 8–10 iii 15–19 (tr. García Martínez, *Dead Sea Scrolls*, 186):

[He will destroy the land with the rod of his mouth and with the breath of his lips he will execute the evil] . . . [The interpretation of the word concerns the shoot] of David which will sprout [in the final days, since with the breath of his lips he will execute] his enemies.

A very similar early Christian text in which this apocalyptic metaphor occurs is 2 Thess 2:8 (an allusion to Isa 11:4 also alluded to in v 11), "the Lord Jesus will slay him with the breath of his mouth and destroy him by his appearance and coming." Both *Pss. Sol.* 17:24 and 2 Thess 2:8 allude to Isa 11:4, part of a passage interpreted messianically in early Judaism (Dodd, *Scriptures*, 83; Lindars, *Apologetic*, 201–2): "and he shall smite the earth with the rod [MT שֵׁבֶט *šēbet;* LXX τῷ λόγῳ] of his mouth, and with the breath of his lips he shall slay the wicked." Since the precise metaphor of a sword projecting from the mouth of the Messiah occurs nowhere in early Jewish literature, it is likely that it was coined by John himself, perhaps by combining the messianic use of Isa 11:4 with an allusion to Isa 49:2, "He [God] made my mouth like a sharp sword," from the second servant song in Isa 49:1–6. In Heb 4:12 the word of God is compared to a sword: "For the word of God is living and active, sharper than any two-edged sword." In 1QSb 5:24, the "Prince of the Congregation," who is described as a messianic figure, is addressed in the following way, with a clear allusion to Isa 11:4 (tr. Vermes, *Dead Sea Scrolls*): "[May you smite the peoples] with the might of your hand [Lohse, *Die Texte*, reads בעז [פ']כה *běʿōz [pî]kā*, 'with the power of your mouth'] and ravage the earth with your sceptre; may you bring death to the ungodly with the breath of your lips [וברוח שפתיכה *ûbrûaḥ śĕpāteykā*]!" Isa 11:4 is also alluded to in Irenaeus (*Adv. haer.* 4.33.1) in the context of a pastiche of OT messianic passages: "But the second [coming] in which he will come on the clouds [Dan 7:13], bringing on the day which burns as a furnace [Mal 4:1], and smiting the earth with the word of his mouth [Isa 11:4]." The "man from the sea," a messianic figure in 4 Ezra, incinerates his enemies with a stream of fire that proceeds from his mouth (4 Ezra 13:10–11), but this is later softened by interpreting it as a reference to the judgment pronounced by the Messiah based on the Law (4 Ezra 13:37–38); i.e., the fire issuing from the Messiah's mouth becomes a metaphor for the Torah. The same metaphorical motif occurs in *1 Enoch* 62:2 (Knibb, *Enoch*): "the word of his mouth kills all the sinners and all the lawless, and they are destroyed before him." See also *Comment* on 1:16.

In *T. Dan* 5:10 it is said that the Lord's salvation, who will arise from the tribe of Judah, "will make war against Beliar." The "sword of the Lord," which is mentioned so frequently in the OT (Deut 32:41; Isa 34:5–6; Jer 12:12; 47:6; Ezek 21:3–5; 30:24; 32:10; Zech 13:7; Ps 17:13; 1 Chr 21:12), becomes a metaphor for eschatological judgment (Isa 27:1; 66:16; 1QM 6:3; 12:11–12; 15:3; 19:11). This is clear in 4QpIsaᵃ 7–10 iii 26, which speaks of the Davidic Messiah (tr. Horgan, *Pesharim*): "[al]l the peoples will his sword judge." Angelic figures are also depicted as wielding swords; in Josh 5:13, the angelic commander of the army of the Lord is depicted with a sword in hand.

15b καὶ αὐτὸς ποιμανεῖ αὐτοὺς ἐν ῥάβδῳ σιδηρᾷ, "and he himself will rule them with an iron crook." This phrase is an allusion to Ps 2:9, interpreted messianically, together with Isa 11:4 (see v 15a above). Ps 2:9 is alluded to twice elsewhere in Revelation (2:26; 12:5) but nowhere else in the NT (the allusion in 12:5 appears to be a gloss; see *Comment* there). Various passages from Ps 2 are frequently alluded to in Revelation (Ps 2:1 in Rev 11:18; Ps 2:2 in Rev 6:15; 11:15; 17:18; 19:19; Ps 2:5 in Rev 11:18; Ps 2:8 in Rev 2:26; Ps 2:9 in Rev 12:5; 19:15; Ps 2:12 in Rev 11:18). In *Pss. Sol.* 17:23–24, the allusion to Ps 2:9 is clearly interpreted messianically. The allusion to Ps 2:9 assures the messianic understanding of the rider on the white horse. The future tense of ποιμανεῖ, "he will rule," makes it clear that this clause, like the ἵνα, "that," clause in v 15a, is not part of the description of the rider but a messianic interpretation of his role, in which the "sharp sword" is construed as functionally equivalent to the "iron crook."

15c καὶ αὐτὸς πατεῖ τὴν ληνὸν τοῦ οἴνου τοῦ θυμοῦ τῆς ὀργῆς τοῦ θεοῦ τοῦ παντοκράτορος, "and he himself will tread the winepress, representing the furious wrath of God the Almighty." This is an allusion to Isa 63:2–3, where treading the winepress is a metaphor for divine judgment. The enemy who was punished in Isa 63:2–3 was Edom, which became a cipher in Jewish exegesis first for Rome and later for Christians. But who is the enemy punished by the rider on the white horse? Jewish exegetical tradition understood Isa 63:2–3 to refer to the punishment of the nations, i.e., of Gog and Magog and of the four kingdoms (*Midr. Ps.* 8.8.79; tr. Braude, *Midrash* 1:128–29):

This verse [Isa 63:2] refers to the punishment of Gog and Magog and of the four kingdoms upon whom God will tread as in a wine press, as it is written, "Wherefore is Thine apparel red, and Thy garments like his that treadeth in the wine vat?"

In *Tg. Isa.* 63:2–3, the winepress as a metaphor for divine judgment is underscored (tr. Chilton):

Why will mountains be red from the blood of those killed, and plains gush forth like wine in the press? "Behold, as grapes trodden in the press, so shall slaughter increase among the armies of the peoples, and their [*sic*] will be no strength for them before me; I will kill them in my anger and trample them in my wrath.

The awkward string of five genitives found in this verse is the longest such string in Revelation (see *Comment* on 15:5 and *Note* 19:15.c-c.). The sentence is difficult to interpret. Bousset ([1906] 432) and Charles (2:137, apparently following Bousset) observe that the author mixes his metaphors by combining the image of the winepress (cf. 14:19) with that of the cup of wrath (cf. 14:10). The phrase ἡ ὀργὴ τοῦ θεοῦ, "the anger of God," occurs earlier in the forms "your anger" (11:18) and "his anger" (14:10; 16:19); Rev 6:16 extends this concept as "the anger of the Lamb." The phrase "the anger of God" occurs several times in the NT (John 3:36; Rom 1:18; Eph 5:6; Col 3:6), more than two hundred times in the LXX and in Jewish or Christian sepulchral inscriptions (*MAMA* 6, 25), and frequently in early Jewish literature (*Apoc. Zeph.* 12; *T. Isaac* 4:54; *T. Levi* 6:11; *T. Reub.* 4:4; *1 Enoch* 89:33; 99:16; *Sib. Or.* 3.632; 4.159–70; *Jub.* 15:34).

The future tense of πατεῖ, "he will tread," indicates that this is a continuation of the messianic interpretation of the rider, which the author began in vv 15a and 15b. It is, therefore, an embellishment made to an earlier account that was less obviously messianic.

16 καὶ ἔχει ἐπὶ τὸ ἱμάτιον καὶ ἐπὶ τὸν μηρὸν αὐτοῦ ὄνομα γεγραμμένον, Βασιλεὺς βασιλέων καὶ κύριος κυρίων, "And he has upon his robe, that is, upon his thigh, a name inscribed, 'King of kings and Lord of lords.'" This verse is problematic because it appears redundant in view of v 12c, unless that phrase is considered a later interpolation by the same author (see *Comment* above on v 12c).

The place where the name is written is problematic, and a number of proposals have been made in explanation. There are examples in Greco-Roman literature of inscriptions on the thighs of statues. Pausanias (5.27.12) refers to an elegiac couplet written on the thigh of a statue: "but there is a couplet engraved on its thigh [ἐλεγεῖον δὲ ἐπ' αὐτὸ γεγραμμένον ἐστὶν ἐπὶ τοῦ μηροῦ], 'To Zeus, king of the gods, as first-fruits was I placed here, by the Mendeans / who reduced Sipte by might of hand.'" For two other examples of inscriptions on the thighs of statues, see Cicero *Verrine Orations* 4.43 and Justin 15.4.5, 9; cf. *Neuer Wettstein,* ad Rev 19:16. On the magical diagram of a figure in *PGM* XXXVI (Betz, *Greek Magical Papyri,* 269), the legs bear the magical name "Brak" (see Eitrem, *Papyri Osloenses,* 140).

This is the third time in this brief pericope that the *name* of the rider is mentioned, and the mode of expression makes it clear that this is an explanation of the secret name mentioned in v 12. If that is so, then this verse is an explanatory interpolation that has been added to the pericope by the final author-editor. The phrase "King of kings and Lord of lords" appears in reverse order earlier in 17:14 (see the discussion there under *Comment*), though that entire verse is probably an interpolation based in part on the occurrence of this phrase in 19:16. Since the title "King of kings and Lord of lords" is one associated primarily with Yahweh, the transfer of this title to the Messiah appears to cohere well with the enhanced Christology of the final edition of Revelation. Skehan proposed that the name of the rider on the white horse, "King of kings and Lord of lords," has a numerical value of 777, corresponding to 666, the name of the beast according to Rev 13:18. However, since Skehan found it necessary to omit the "and" and to translate the phrase into Aramaic (מלך מלכין מרא מרון *mlk mlkyn mrʾ mrwn*), his suggestion is too speculative.

17a καὶ εἶδον ἕνα ἄγγελον ἑστῶτα ἐν τῷ ἡλίῳ, "Then I saw an angel standing on the sun." καὶ εἶδον, "then I saw," introduces a new vision report here; see *Comment* on 5:1. The angel takes a position in heaven, either "on" the sun or "in" the sun, from which to address an invitation to all the birds flying in midheaven. There are several magical procedures preserved in the *Sepher ha-Razim* 4.31–67 that allow the magician to see the angel of the sun, who is otherwise obscured by the bright rays of the sun. While Boll suggests that the author depicts an angel standing on the sun primarily for literary effect, he does claim that the close connection between the eagle and the sun (as "messenger of the sun") in ancient Syrian tradition indicates that it would be appropriate for the eagle (= angel) to stand on the sun to deliver his message (*Offenbarung*, 38–39). In Jewish tradition, however, angels are closely associated with the sun (in *Sepher ha-Razim* 2.148, an angel whose name is "Sun" is mentioned), and Loisy suggests that it is the angel of the sun who speaks to the birds of the air (343). According to *3 Enoch* 14:4 and 17:4, the angel Gilgalliʾel is in charge of the sun, and in to *3 Apoc. Bar.* 6:2, forty angels draw the chariot of the sun (see *2 Enoch* [Rec. J] 11:4–5). *Sepher ha-Razim* 4.9 (tr. Morgan, 67) says "The angels of fire, girded with strength, surround him (the sun) and lead him during the day."

17b καὶ ἔκραξεν φωνῇ μεγάλῃ λέγων πᾶσιν τοῖς ὀρνέοις τοῖς πετομένοις ἐν μεσουρανήματι, "and he cried with a loud voice to all the birds flying in midheaven." See *Comment* on 8:13.

17c Δεῦτε συνάχθητε εἰς τὸ δεῖπνον τὸ μέγα τοῦ θεοῦ, "Come, gather together at the great supper of God." This invitation is an allusion to Ezek 39:17, where the Lord God tells Ezekiel to say the following: "Assemble and come, gather from all sides to the sacrificial feast which I am preparing for you." This appears to be a parody of ancient dinner invitations to share a sacred meal with various pagan deities such as Sarapis. The phrase "the great supper of God" suggests more specifically that this is a parody of the messianic banquet, a symbol of eschatological joy (Isa 25:6–8; 55:1–2; 65:13–14; *1 Enoch* 62:12–16; *2 Apoc. Bar.* 29:1–8; *m. ʾAbot* 3:20; Matt 8:11; Luke 13:29; 14:15; 22:16, 29–30; see Priest, "Banquet," 222–38, who does not construe Rev 19:17–21 as a parody; D. Smith, "Messianic Banquet," *ADB* 4:788–91). The theme of the messianic banquet has its origins in myths that narrate a great battle between the gods, a battle that concludes with an assembly of the gods to celebrate victory and to share a festive meal (*Enuma Elish* 6.69–94 [Pritchard, *ANET*, 69]; Isa 34:5–7; Zech 9:15). In Zech 9:15 the meal consists of a bloody sacrifice-banquet of defeated enemies (P. D. Hanson, *Dawn*, 322; disputed by R. L. Smith, *Micah-Malachi*, WBC 32 [Waco, TX: Word, 1984] 260, who reads the text positively as a great victory banquet).

18 ἵνα φάγητε σάρκας βασιλέων καὶ σάρκας χιλιάρχων καὶ σάρκας ἰσχυρῶν καὶ σάρκας ἵππων καὶ τῶν καθημένων ἐπ᾽ αὐτῶν καὶ σάρκας πάντων ἐλευθέρων τε καὶ δούλων καὶ μικρῶν καὶ μεγάλων, "to eat the carrion of kings and the carrion of generals and the carrion of the powerful and the carrion of horses and their riders and the carrion of all, free and slave, the unimportant and the important." This is an allusion to Ezek 39:18, "You shall eat the flesh of the mighty, and drink the blood of the princes of the earth." Rev 19:17–18 represents a parody of the Jewish tradition of the eschatological messianic banquet (see Comment on v 17c), because it is an eschatological banquet that consists of feeding on the flesh and blood of dead enemies. Lev. Rab. 11.2 is an exegetical text that links Prov 9:1–6, which focuses on the banquet of wisdom (interpreting the house of wisdom in v 1 as the temple and the seven pillars as the seven years of Gog; cf. Ezek 39:9), to the prophecy of Ezek 39:17–20, which refers to the great sacrifice on the mountains of Israel, where Ezekiel is asked to invite the birds and wild animals to eat the flesh and drink the blood of the men of Gog. In Lev. Rab. 11.2, however, it is the Israelites who are invited to the banquet.

A very similar list of those judged occurs in 6:15 (see the synoptic comparison there under Comment). The list in 13:16 lists "both small and great, both rich and poor, both free and slave." On "small and great," see Comment on 13:16. The use of polysyndeton (i.e., the use of καί, "and," as a connective between lexical units) occurs five times in v 18, four times with the plural accusative σάρκας, "flesh, carrion" (emphasizing the sum total of such things; see Mussies, Morphology, 84).

χιλίαρχος, "chiliarch" (a term already used in Rev 6:15), is a Greek term that means a military commander of one thousand soldiers and is equivalent to the Latin designation tribunus militum, which can be translated "military commander, general." Tribuni militum were the highest officers in the Roman legions, usually of equestrian rank (those of the higher senatorial rank were called tribuni laticlavii). Each legion had six tribuni militum, and during periods of war one of them assumed command of the entire legion. The term is used literally of tribuni militum in Mark 6:21; John 18:21; Acts 21:31–33, 37; 22:24, 26–29; 23:10, 15, 17–19, 22; 25:23; 1 Clem. 37:3.

19a καὶ εἶδον τὸ θηρίον καὶ τοὺς βασιλεῖς τῆς γῆς καὶ τὰ στρατεύματα αὐτῶν συνηγμένα, "I saw the beast and the kings of the earth and their armies assembled." Here the introductory vision formula καὶ εἶδον, "then I saw," functions to focus on a new aspect of a continuing vision report (see Comment on 5:1). According to 16:14, the kings of the whole earth (βασιλεῖς τῆς οἰκουμένης ὅλης) had been previously summoned to gather for battle on the great day of God Almighty, and the threads of that narrative, which abruptly ends in 16:14, are picked up again here. The motif of the gathering and assault of the heathen on the people of God has roots in the OT (Ezek 38:14–16; 39:1–6; Joel 3:2; Zech 12:1–9; 14:2; Ps 2:1–3) and frequently appears in apocalyptic literature (1 Enoch 56:5–6; 90:13–19; 99:4; 2 Apoc. Bar. 48:37; 70:7; 4 Ezra 13:33–38; Jub. 23:23; Syb. Or. 3.663–68; Pss. Sol. 2:1–2; 17:22–23; T. Jos. 19; LXX Esth 11:5–8; 1QM 1:10–11; 15:2–3; Luke 21:20 [the historicization of this motif]; see Hartman, Prophecy Interpreted, 77–101). 4 Ezra 13:5 is a clear example of this motif:

> After this I looked and saw that an innumerable multitude of people were gathered together from the four winds of heaven to make war against the man who came up out of the sea.

The specific presence of the motif of the *assembling* or *gathering together* (συνάγειν) of hostile forces against the people of God in the last days occurs frequently in such eschatological scenes (Rev 16:14, 16; 19:17, 19; 20:8; see Isa 66:18; Ezek 38:7–8; Zech 12:3; 14:2; *1 Enoch* 90:16; 1QM 14:5; 15:3).

19b ποιῆσαι τὸν πόλεμον μετὰ τοῦ καθημένου ἐπὶ τοῦ ἵππου καὶ μετὰ τοῦ στρατεύματος αὐτοῦ, "to wage war with the one mounted on the steed and with his army." In a fragmentary parallel narrative in 17:14, it is said that "these [the ten kings who receive authority for 'one hour' with the beast, 17:12] will make war on the Lamb, and the Lamb will conquer them," though the forces on the side of the Lamb are apparently followers of the Lamb (cf. 14:1–5) who are described as "called and elect and faithful." The conflict between hostile nations and the Messiah is reflected in a Christian interpolation (Ulrichsen, *Grundschrift*, 116, 316) in *T. Jos.* 19:8, "and all the wild animals rushed against him, but the lamb conquered them."

20a καὶ ἐπίασθη τὸ θηρίον καὶ μετ᾽ αὐτοῦ ὁ ψευδοπροφήτης, "The beast was captured and with him the false prophet." Like other battles in the narrative of Revelation, this one omits any reference to the conflict itself and emphasizes only the capture or decimation of the enemy (cf. 17:14; 20:7–10). The army accompanying the rider is again mentioned in v 19b (the earlier reference in v 14 suggests an angelic army), but it apparently plays no part in the conflict. The faithful play no role at all, in sharp contrast with some references to the final eschatological battle in Jewish apocalyptic literature (1QM; Bauckham, "Christian War Scroll," in *Climax*, 210–12; Metzger, *Code*, 92). The passive verb ἐπίασθη, "was captured," refers to the action performed by the rider on the white horse, the Divine Warrior. On the false prophet, see *Comment* on 16:13. Since the false prophet is mentioned in this narrative only at this point, it is likely that he has been added to the scene, though probably on the basis of 16:13.

20b ὁ ποιήσας τὰ σημεῖα ἐνώπιον αὐτοῦ, ἐν οἷς ἐπλάνησεν τοὺς λαβόντας τὸ χάραγμα τοῦ θηρίου καὶ τοὺς προσκυνοῦντας τῇ εἰκόνι αὐτοῦ, "who performed signs on his authority, by which he deceived those who received the mark of the beast and who worshiped his cultic image." On the frequent use of participial phrases to describe various characters in the narrative, see *Comment* on 11:7. This long participial phrase is essentially a digression. On the idiom ποιεῖν σημεῖα, "to perform signs," see *Comment* on 13:13. This explanatory passage is a later gloss that refers back to 13:11–18 since the false prophet mentioned here is clearly identified with the beast from the land, though the designation θηρίον, "beast," is applied to this figure *only* in 13:11.

20c ζῶντες ἐβλήθησαν οἱ δύο εἰς τὴν λίμνην τοῦ πυρὸς τῆς καιομένης ἐν θείῳ, "they were both hurled alive into the lake of fire burning with sulphur." Num 16:33 relates that Korah, Dathan, and Abiram were swallowed by the earth and descended *alive* into Sheol. According to Irenaeus, the Antichrist and his followers will be sent into the lake of fire upon the return of Christ (*Adv. haer.* 5.30.4; see Hippolytus *Comm. in Dan.* 4.56.6). In the context of the final eschatological battle in *1 Enoch* 56:8, it is said that Sheol will open its mouth and swallow the hostile sinners (cf. the fate of Korah and his fellow conspirators in Num 16:30–35; Philo *Mos.* 2.282; *Bib. Ant.* 16:6–7).

The phrase "the lake of fire burning with sulphur" occurs with variations six times in Revelation (here; 20:10, 14–15[3x]; 21:8). The image is problematical for there are no close parallels in the OT, in Jewish literature, or in Greco-Roman literature, particularly when the place of eternal punishment is conceived of as a λίμνη, "lake." Surprisingly, the image of a "lake of fire" occurs in ancient Egyptian texts (*Book of the Dead* 17.40–42; 24.4; 175.15, 20; see Zandee, *Death as an Enemy,* 133–42; "Flammensee," *Lexikon der Aegyptologie* [Wiesbaden: Harrasowitz, 1977] 2:259–60; H. Kees, *Totenglauben und Jenseitsvorstellungen der alten Aegypter* [Leipzig: Hinrichs, 1926] 294–95), where it is located in the underworld. Though the channel of transmission from Egypt to Revelation is unknown, it is instructive to note that another Egyptian underworld myth, "the second death" (see *Comment* on 20:6), not only is associated with the "lake of fire" in Rev 20:14 and 21:8 but is also found closely connected with the "lake of fire" in the *Book of the Dead* (see *Comment* on 20:6). This reinforces the probability that traditional Egyptian underworld mythology has somehow contributed to John's conception of the underworld.

The imagery of fire as a means of eternal punishment was a familiar conception during the second temple period. In ancient Israel, the theophanic imagery of the Sinai tradition (Exod 19) included fire as part of a complex of natural phenomena associated with volcanic activity, wind storms, and earthquakes (see *Comment* on 4:5). Fire continued to be associated with theophanic imagery (Ps 50:3; Ezek 1:4, 13f.), and in particular the metaphor of a "stream of fire" (drawn from volcanic imagery) became associated with mythological depictions of the throne of God (Dan 7:10; *1 Enoch* 14:18). The connection of divine judgment with fire (see *Comment* on 8:7) was common in the OT and early Judaism, and it was but a short step to depict streams of fire pouring down from heaven in judgment (*Sib. Or.* 2.196–205, 286; 3.54, 84–85; 7.120–21; 8:243; *Pss. Sol.* 15:6–7). Fire in the underworld as a means of eternal punishment is first mentioned in Isa 66:24 and frequently thereafter (*1 Enoch* 10:6, 13; Matt 5:22; 13:42, 50; 18:9; 25:41; Mark 9:43, 48). It became natural to think of the underworld as the site for a river of fire (*2 Enoch* 10:2), a tradition that continued to be used in Christian underworld mythology (*Apoc. Paul* 31, 34, 36).

The specific conception of a *lake* of fire, when mentioned in early Christian texts (*Apoc. Peter* [Akhmimic] 23), is clearly dependent on Revelation. The notion of a "lake" or "sea" in the underworld or the heavenly world (Rev 15:2 [see *Comment*] mentions a heavenly sea, a counterpart to the lake of fire) is part of Greco-Roman underworld mythology (Plato *Phaedo* 113D; Plutarch *De gen. Socr.* 590D; *PGM* IV.1461–62, Ἀχερουσίατε λίμνη Ἅιδου, "the Acherusian lake of Hades"; *PGM* VII.517, τῇ ἱερᾷ λίμνῃ τῇ καλουμένῃ ἀβύσσῳ, "the holy lake which is called Abyss"). The Acherusian lake (originally a river in Epirus that formed a lake on the Acherusian plain in ancient times, where an entrance to Hades was believed to be located) was associated with the Elysian fields, and Jewish and Christian texts mention deliverance from fiery torment to the blessings of the Acherusian lake (*Sib. Or.* 2.334–38; *Apoc. Peter* 14; *Apoc. Paul* 22).

Since eternal fire was believed to be located in Hades in both early Judaism and early Christianity, it is possible that John was not dependent on Egyptian underworld traditions but rather himself combined the traditions of fiery punishment in the netherworld with the notion of a "lake of Hades," resulting in a lake of fire. The tradition of a fiery river in Hades is also found in Greek and Roman underworld mythology. According to Plato (*Phaedo* 111D; LCL tr.),

There are everlasting rivers of huge size under the earth, flowing with hot and cold water; and there is much fire, and great rivers of fire, and many streams of mud.

As many as four rivers are connected with Hades (*Odyssey* 10.513; Plato *Phaedo* 112E–113C; Cicero *De natura deorum* 3.43): (1) Styx or Acheron (which separates the realm of the dead from the world of the living), (2) Phlegethon or Pyriphlegethon (meaning "blazing"), (3) Cocytus (in Latin literature), and (4) Lethe ("forgetfulness"). Vergil *Aeneid* 6.550–51 describes one of the sights Aeneas saw during his visit to Hades (tr. Copley, *Vergil*): "A river of swirling flame flowed all around— Phlegethon, rolling a rubble of grinding rocks." Other references to this underworld river are found in Vergil *Aeneid* 6.265; Statius *Theb.* 4.55; Ovid *Met.* 5.544; 15.532. The variant Pyriphlegethon is found in *Odyssey* 10.513; Plato *Phaedo* 113B; Cicero *De nat. deor.* 3.43. According to Plato's myth (*Phaedo* 113E–114B), the curable souls of those in Tartarus who have outraged their parents are carried by the Pyriphlegethon river to the Acherusian lake where they beg forgiveness from those they have wronged. If forgiven, they enter the lake; if not, they are carried back to Tartarus by the fiery river. This punishment is not eternal in Plato, though it is interpreted as such in some Christian apologists (Tertullian *Apol.* 47.12; Minucius Felix *Oct.* 35.1; Arnobius 2.14).

21a καὶ οἱ λοιποὶ ἀπεκτάνθησαν ἐν τῇ ῥομφαίᾳ τοῦ καθημένου ἐπὶ τοῦ ἵππου τῇ ἐξελθούσῃ ἐκ τοῦ στόματος αὐτοῦ, "The rest were slain with the sword projecting from the mouth of the one mounted on the steed." "The rest" refers to the kings of the earth and the armies they led mentioned in v 19a. To be slain by the sword that projected from the mouth of the warrior on the white steed certainly invites metaphorical interpretation; i.e., the "sword" must be the words spoken by the warrior (on the sword as a metaphor for the word of God, see Heb 4:12). In *Pss. Sol.* 17:24, the Davidic Messiah destroys "the unlawful nations with the word of his mouth," and in 1Q*28* = 1QRule of the Blessings 5:24–25 we read (tr. García Martínez, *Dead Sea Scrolls*, 433), "With your sceptre may you lay waste the earth. With the breath of your lips may you kill the wicked." There is reason to suspect that the phrase τῇ ἐξελθούσῃ ἐκ τοῦ στόματος αὐτοῦ, "the [sword] projecting from his mouth," is a gloss intended to emphasize the metaphorical interpretation of the sword.

The destruction of the armies opposed to God in the eschatological battle is in accordance with traditions found in Jewish apocalyptic in texts such as *1 Enoch* 38:5 (tr. Knibb): "Many kings will at that time be destroyed and given into the hand of the righteous and the holy" (see *1 Enoch* 46:4; *2 Apoc. Bar.* 40:1). According to CD^b 19:10, those who are faithful to God will escape punishment during his visitation, "but those that remain shall be delivered up to the sword when there comes the Messiah" (tr. García Martínez, *Dead Sea Scrolls*, 45).

21b καὶ πάντα τὰ ὄρνεα ἐχορτάσθησαν ἐκ τῶν σαρκῶν αὐτῶν, "and all the birds feasted on their carrion." This statement forms an inclusio with v 17, in which the birds are invited to the great supper of God. The invitation in v 17 is clearly modeled after Ezek 39:17, and this verse appears to be based on Ezek 39:4b, "I will give you to birds of prey of every sort and to the wild beasts to be devoured."

The fear of remaining unburied haunted the ancients. The statement in v 21b reflects the application of an ancient curse formula to a concrete event prophesied to occur sometime in the future. It occurs in the form of a taunt in 1 Sam 17:44, 46 and is transformed into a prophetic curse: "Any one who dies in the city the dogs shall eat; and any one who dies in the open country the birds of the air shall eat" (1 Kgs 14:11; 16:4; 21:24). A variant occurs in Deut 28:26: "And your dead body shall be food for all birds of the air, and for the beasts of the earth; and there shall be no one to frighten them away" (see 2 Sam 21:10). This Deuteronomic curse is repeated four times in stereotypical form in Jeremiah: "their dead bodies shall be food for the birds of the air and for the beasts of the earth (Jer 7:33; 16:4; 19:7; 34:20; cf. Deut 28:26; perhaps derived from the ancient taunt found in 1 Sam 17:44, 46); cf. Jer 15:3, "I will appoint over them four kinds of destroyers, says the Lord: the sword to slay, the dogs to tear, and the birds of the air and the beasts of the earth to devour and destroy" (see Gen 40:19). A similar threat is uttered by an unnamed prophet against Jezebel (2 Kgs 9:10). Ezekiel compares the pharaoh of Egypt with a dragon in the seas, which will be caught and thrown up on the land where God "will cause all the birds of the air to settle on you, and I will gorge the beasts of the whole earth with you." One of the consequences of the eschatological battle anticipated in 1QM 11:1 (tr. Vermes, *Dead Sea Scrolls*) is that the defeated dead will remain unburied: "Truly, the battle is Thine! Their bodies are crushed by the might of Thy hand and there is no man to bury them." There are a number of ancient Near Eastern treaty curses that state that the oath-breaker will not be properly buried but will be eaten by animals; e.g., the Esarhaddon treaty contains this curse: "May he give your flesh to the vulture (and) jackal to devour" (Hillers, *Treaty-Curses*, 68). Hillers (68–69) argues that the closest parallels to the treaty curses are found in Jeremiah, who used this type of curse to pronounce doom on king and people alike who had broken the covenant with Yahweh. That fallen soldiers are carrion for carnivorous birds means primarily that they are denied burial, an ancient means for hurting and humiliating an enemy even after death, sometimes accompanied by the mutilation of the corpse (Sophocles *Antigone* 21–38; Tob 1:16–20; see Fustel de Coulanges, *Ancient City*, 9–11; Parker, *Miasma*, 43–48, esp. 45 n. 47; C. P. Segal, "The Theme of Mutilation of the Corpse," *Mnemosyne*, Suppl. 17 [1971]). In ancient Greek literature, and the *Iliad* in particular, the prospect of being eaten by dogs and birds sometimes occurs in a variety of contexts (J. Griffin, *Homer on Life and Death* [Oxford: Clarendon; New York: Oxford UP, 1980] 115–19): as an expression of pathos (*Iliad* 1.1–5; 11.814; 16.837) and as a warning (*Iliad* 18.270), most often expressed in the form of a threat (*Iliad* 2.393; 22.66, 86, 335; 13:831: Hektor to Ajax, "You shall glut the dogs and birds of Troy with your fat and your flesh, falling by the Achaean ships"). In the *Iliad*, birds and dogs who eat the raw flesh of the slain are called ὠμησταί, "eaters of raw flesh" (7.256; 11.454, 479; 15.592; 16.157; 22.67).

Explanation

John has emphasized the structural and thematic importance of 19:11–21:8 by framing it between a pair of angelic revelations (17:1–19:10 and 21:9–22:9), which begin and end with numerous verbal and thematic similarities. Both framing texts use antithetical female imagery; Babylon the whore is the central concern of 17:1–19:10, while the bride, the New Jerusalem, is the focus of 21:9–22:9.

From the vantage point of earth, John sees the heavens opened (a metaphor for revelation found only here in Revelation, but equivalent to the open door in heaven in 4:1) and Christ riding forth as a divine warrior leading the armies of heaven against the beast and the false prophet, who are defeated and punished in reverse order of their appearance in chaps. 12–13. Though this scene depicts the Parousia (fulfilling the prophecy of 1:7), many motifs typical of traditional descriptions of the Parousia are missing, including the motif of Christ returning to gather the saints. The reason is twofold: (1) the emphasis here is on the *judicial* function of the Parousia, and (2) in Revelation the eternal messianic kingdom is placed on a renovated earth so that Christ comes to his people on earth rather than gathering them to a heavenly abode.

In describing Christ as a victorious warrior, the author piles up descriptive epithets and attributes in a manner similar to the description of the exalted Christ in the Patmos vision in 1:9–20. He is faithful and true; he judges righteously (v 11). He wears many diadems (v 12), symbolizing his sovereignty as "King of kings and Lord of lords" (v 16). He alone knows his secret name, perhaps corresponding to Rome's secret name (17:5). The single apparent allusion to his redeeming death is his robe, which has been dipped in blood (see 1:5; 5:9; 7:14; 12:11), actually a Christian reading of a traditional conception of the divine warrior understood as the Messiah. His public name is "the Word of God" (v 13), a phrase usually referring to the gospel (see 1:2, 9; 20:4) but used here in Revelation as a title for Christ (see John 1:1–3; 1 John 1:1).

An angel announces the imminent destruction of the earthly opponents of God (vv 17–18), followed by a brief narrative of the decisive defeat of the beast and the slaughter of his client kings and their armies by the armies of Christ. After the beast and the false prophet are captured, they are consigned to the eternal torment of the lake of fire (vv 19–21). Since the beast and his allies have already destroyed "Babylon" in accordance with God's will (17:16–17), this victory seems to represent the conquest and destruction of all human opponents of God and the Lamb (but see 20:7–9).

2. The Final Defeat of Satan (20:1–10)
3. Vision of the Judgment of the Dead (20:11–15)

Bibliography

Alföldy, G. *The Social History of Rome.* Tr. D. Braund and F. Pollock. Baltimore: Johns Hopkins UP, 1988. **Alfrink, B.** "L'idée de résurrection d'aprés Dan. XII 1.2." *Bib* 40 (1959) 355–71. **Astour, M.** "Ezekiel's Prophecy of Gog and the Cuthaean Legend of Naram-Sin." *JBL* 95 (1976) 567–79. **Badina, J.** *Le millénium d'Apocalypse 20:4–6: Etat de la question: Proposition d'interprétation.* Collonges-sous-Salève: Faculté Adventiste de Théologie, 1983. **Bailey, J. W.** "The Temporary Messianic Reign in the Literature of Early Judaism." *JBL* 53 (1934) 170–87. **Bauckham, R.** "Resurrection as Giving Back the Dead: A Traditional Image of Resurrection in the Pseudepigrapha and the Apocalypse of John." In *The Pseudepigrapha and the New Testament*, ed. J. H. Charlesworth and C. A. Evans. Sheffield: JSOT, 1993. 269–91. **Bauer, W.** "Chiliasmus." *RAC* 2:1073–78. **Bietenhard, H.** "The Millenial Hope in the Early Church." *SJT* 6 (1953) 12–30. ———. *Das Tausendjährige Reich.* 2nd ed. Zürich: Zwingli, 1955. **Böcher, O.** "Die heilige Stadt im Völkerkrieg: Wandlung eines apokalyptischen Schemas." In *Josephus-Studien: Untersuchungen zu Josephus, dem Antiken Judentum und dem Neuen Testament.* FS O. Michel. Tübingen: Mohr-Siebeck, 1974. **Bogaert, P.-M.** "La 'seconde mort' à l'époque des Tannaïm." In *Vie et survie dans les civilisations orientales.* Leuven: Peeters, 1983. 199–207. **Brockmeyer, N.** *Socialgeschichte der Antike.* Stuttgart: Kohlhammer, 1972. **Budge, E. A. W.** *The Egyptian Book of the Dead.* New York: Dover, 1967. **Clifford, R. J.** *The Cosmic Mountain in Canaan and the Old Testament.* Cambridge: Harvard UP, 1972. **Comblin, J.** "La ville bien-aimée: Apocalypse 20:9." *Vie Spirituelle* 112 (1965) 631–48. **Deere, J. S.** "Premillennialism in Revelation 20:4–6." *BSac* 135 (1978) 58–73. **Elliott, J. H.** *The Elect and the Holy: An Exegetical Examination of 1 Peter 2:4–10 and the Phrase* Basileion Hierateuma. NovTSup 12. Leiden: Brill, 1966. **Faulkner, R. O.** *The Ancient Egyptian Coffin Texts.* 3 vols. Warminster: Aris & Phillips, 1973–78. **Fensham, F. C.** "'Camp' in the New Testament and Milhamah." *RevQ* 4 (1964) 557–62. **Gagé, J.** *Les classes sociales dans l'empire Romain.* Paris: Payot, 1964. **Garnsey, P.** *Social Status and Legal Privilege in the Roman Empire.* Oxford: Clarendon, 1970. **Glasson, T. F.** "The Last Judgment—in Rev. 20 and Related Writings." *NTS* 28 (1982) 528–39. **Gourges, M.** "The Thousand Year Reign (Rev. 20:1–6): Terrestrial or Celestial?" *CBQ* 47 (1985) 676–81. **Grant, R. M.** "The Social Setting of Second-Century Christianity." In *Jewish and Christian Self-Definition*, ed. E. P. Sanders. Philadelphia: Fortress, 1980. 1:16–29. **Greenfield, J. C.** "Baʿal's Throne and Isa 6:1." In *Mélanges bibliques et orientaux.* FS M. M. Delcor, ed. A. Caquot, S. Légasse, and M. Tardieu. Kevalaer: Butzon & Bercker; Neukirchen: Neukirchener, 1985. 193–98. **Hasel, G. F.** "Resurrection in the Theology of Old Testament Apocalyptic." *ZAW* 92 (1980) 267–84. **Heinemann, K.** *Thanatos in Poesie und Kunst der Griechen.* Munich: Kastner & Callwey, 1913. **Héring, J.** "St. Paul a-t-il enseigné deux résurrections?" *RHPR* (1932) 187ff. **Hiebert, T.** "Theophany in the OT." *ADB* 6:505–11. **Hughes, J. A.** "Revelation 20:4–6 and the Question of the Millennium." *WTJ* 35 (1973) 281–302. **Hughes, P. E.** "The First Resurrection: Another Interpretation." *WTJ* 39 (1977) 315–18. **Jeremias, Jörg.** *Theophanie: Die Geschichte einer alttestamentlichen Gattung.* Neukirchen: Neukirchener, 1965. ———. "Theophany in the OT." *IDBSup*, 896–98. **Kellermann, U.** *Auferstanden in den Himmel: 2 Makkabäerbuch und die Auferstehung der Märtyrer.* SBS 95. Stuttgart: Katholisches Bibelwerk, 1979. ———. "Das Danielbuch und die Märtyrertheologie der Auferstehung." In *Die Entstehung der jüdischen Martyrologie*, ed. J. W. van Henten. SPB 38. Leiden: Brill, 1989. 51–75. **Kline, M. G.** "The First Resurrection." *WTJ* 37 (1975) 366–75. **Kuebler, E.** "Lictor." *RE* 13:507–18. **Ladd, G. E.** "Revelation 20 and the Millennium." *RevExp* 57 (1960) 167–75. **Lambgerits, S.** "Le sens de QDWŠYM dans les textes de Qumran." *ETL* 46 (1970) 24–39. **Latte, K.** "Todesstrafe." *RESup* 7:1599–1619. **Levey, S. H.** *The Messiah: An Aramaic Interpretation.* Cincinnati: Hebrew Union College–Jewish Institute of Religion, 1974. **Levy, E.** *Die römische Kapitalstrafe.* Heidelberg: Winter, 1931. **Mealy, J. W.** *After the Thousand Years: Resurrection and Judgment in Revelation 20.* Sheffield: Sheffield Academic, 1992. **Mell, U.** *Neue Schöpfung: Eine traditionsgeschichtliche und exegetische Studie zu einem soteriologischen Grundsatz paulinischer Theologie.* Berlin; New York: de Gruyter, 1989. **Michaels, J. R.** "The First Resurrection: A Response." *WTJ* 39 (1976) 100–109. **Mommsen, T.** "Die Todesstrafe." In *Römisches Straatsrecht.* Leipzig: Hirzel, 1899. 911–44. **Nickelsburg, G. W.** "Eschatology in the Testament of Abraham: A Study of the Judgment Scene in the Two Recensions." In *Studies on the Testament of Abraham*, ed. G. W. Nickelsburg. Missoula, MT: Scholars, 1976. 23–64. **Ostella, R. A.** "The Significance of the Deception in Revelation 20:3." *WTJ* 37 (1975) 236–38. **Page, S. H. T.** "Revelation 20 and Pauline Eschatology." *JETS* 23 (1980) 31–43. **Poythress, V. S.** "Genre and Hermeneutics in Rev 20:1–6." *JETS* 36 (1993) 41–54. **Prigent, P.** "Le millénium dans l'Apocalypse johannique." In *L'Apocalyptique*, ed. F. Raphaë. Paris: Geuthner,

1977. 139–56. **Rinaldi, G.** "Il Targum palestinese del Pentateuco." *BeO* 17 (1975) 75–77. **Rochais, G.** "Le règne de mille ans et la seconde mort: Origines et sens Ap. 19,11–20,6." *NRT* 103 (1981) 831–56. **Rubinkiewicz, R.** *Die Eschatologie von Henoch 9–11 und das Neue Testament.* Klosterneuburg: Österreiches Katholisches Bibelwerk, 1984. **Schüssler Fiorenza, E.** "Die tausendjährige Herrschaft der Auferstandenen (Apk. 20:4–6)." *BibLeb* 13 (1972) 107–24. **Schweitzer, A.** *The Mysticism of Paul the Apostle.* New York: Holt, 1931. **Segal, A. F.** *Two Powers in Heaven: Early Rabbinic Reports about Christianity and Gnosticism.* Leiden: Brill, 1977. **Shepherd, N.** "The Resurrections of Revelation 20." *WTJ* 37 (1974) 34–43. **Smith, D. C.** "The Millennial Reign of Jesus Christ: Some Observations on Rev. 20:1–10." *ResQ* 16 (1973) 219–30. **Smith, M. S.** "Divine Form and Size in Ugaritic and Pre-exilic Israelite Religion." *ZAW* 100 (1988) 424–27. **Snyder, B. W.** "How Millennial Is the Millennium? A Study in the Background of the 1000 Years in Revelation 20." *Evangelical Journal* 9 (1991) 51–74. **Stadelmann, H.** "Das Zeugnis der Johannesoffenbarung vom tausendjährigen Königreich Christi auf Erden." In *Zukunftserwartung in biblischer Sicht: Beiträge zur Eschatologie,* ed. G. Maier. Wuppertal: Brockhaus; Giessen/Basel: Brunnen, 1984. 144–60. **Stemberger, G.** "Das Problem der Auferstehung im Alten Testament." *Kairos* 14 (1972) 273–90. **Summers, R.** "Revelation 20: An Interpretation." *RevExp* 57 (1960) 176–83. **Vögtle, A.** "'Dann sah ich einen neuen Himmel und eine neue Erde . . .' (Apk 21,1): Zur kosmischen Dimension neutestamentlicher Eschatologie." In *Glaube und Eschatologie,* ed. E. Grässer and O. Merk. Tübingen: Mohr-Siebeck, 1985. 303–33. **Wikenhauser, A.** "Die Herkunft der Idee des tausendjährigen Reiches in der Johannesapokalypse." *RQ* 45(1937) 1–24. ———. "Das Problem des tausendjährigen Reiches in der Johannes-Apokalypse." *RQ* 40 (1932) 13–25. ———. "Weltwoche und tausendjähriges Reich." *TThQ* 127 (1947) 399–417. **Zandee, J.** *Death as an Enemy according to Ancient Egyptian Conceptions.* NumenSup 5. Leiden: Brill, 1960.

Translation

[1] *Then I saw an* [a]*angel* [b]*descending* [c]*from heaven* [bc] *with the key to the abyss and a large chain* [d]*in his hand.*[d] [2]*He apprehended the dragon (* [a]*the ancient serpent* [a] *who* [b] *is the* [c] *devil and* [d]*Satan) and bound him for a thousand years.* [3]*He cast him into the abyss, which he closed and sealed over him so that he would no longer cause the nations to go astray until the* [a] *thousand years had been completed.* [b]*After this* [b] [c]*he must be released* [c] *for a short period.*

[4]*Then I saw thrones,* [a]*and* [b]*people sat* [b] *upon them, and they were given* [c]*the authority to judge,* [c] [d]*that is,*[d] [e][f]*the souls* [f] *of those who had been beheaded because of their witness to Jesus and because of the word of God, and who had not worshiped* [g]*the beast* [gh] *or his image,*[i] *and who had not*[j] *received his brand* [k] *on their foreheads or on their hands.*[l] *They* [m]*came to life* [m] *and reigned with the Messiah for a* [n] *thousand years.* [5] [ab]*The rest of the dead did not* [c]*come to life* [c] *until the* [d] *thousand years were completed.*[b] *(This is the first resurrection.* [6a]*How fortunate* [a] *and holy is the one who has a share in the first resurrection!*[b] *The second death* [b] *has no authority over these,* [c] *but* [d]*they will be* [d] *priests to God and the Messiah, and they will reign* [e]*with him* [e] *for a* [f] *thousand years.)*

[7a]*When* [b] *the thousand years are completed,* [a] *Satan will be released from his prison* [8]*and will go out to deceive the nations that* [a] *are at the four corners of the earth, Gog and Magog, to assemble them for battle. Their number* [b] *is like the sand of the sea.* [9]*They marched up across the breadth of the earth and surrounded* [a] *the encampment of the* [b]*people of God,*[bcd]*the beloved city. Then fire came down* [c]*from heaven* [e] *and devoured them.* [10]*And the devil who deceived them was cast down into the lake of fire and brimstone where* [a]*the beast and the false prophet were, so that* [b] *they were tormented day and night for ever.*

[11]*Then I saw a great white throne and One seated* [a]*upon it,*[a] [b]*from whom earth and heaven fled,*[b] *but* [c] *there was no place* [d] *for them.* [12]*And I saw the dead,* [a]*both important and*

unimportant,[a] *standing before the* [b]*throne. And books* [c]*were opened,*[c] *and another book was opened, which is the book of life, and the dead were judged on the basis of what was recorded* [d]*in the books,*[d] *according to their deeds.* [13] [a]*The sea gave up the* [b]*dead* [c]*in it,*[b] *and Death and Hades* [d]*gave up* [d] *the* [e]*dead in them;* [e] *then* [f] *each* [g]*was judged* [g] *according to their* [h] *works.* [14] *Then Death and Hades were cast into the lake of fire.*[a][b][c] *This is* [d] *the second death,*[b] *the lake of fire.*[a] [15]*And if anyone was not found recorded* [a]*in the book* [a] *of life, that person was cast into the lake of fire.*

Notes

1.a. Variant: ἄλλον before ἄγγελον] ℵ² fam 1611²⁰⁵⁰ vgᵐˢ syrᵖʰ copˢᵃᵐˢ Tyc² Tyc³ Beatus (Romero-Pose, *Sancti Beati* 1:64; 2:343, 344). The phrase ἄλλος ἄγγελος occurs ten times in Revelation in relatively secure readings (7:2; 8:3; 10:1; 14:6, 8, 9, 15, 17, 18; 18:1); this ἄλλον was probably inserted to distinguish this angel from the one mentioned in 19:17, in agreement with the usual style of Revelation.

1.b-b. Variant: ἐκ τοῦ οὐρανοῦ καταβαίνοντα] Andr d.

1.c-c. Variants: (1) omit ἐκ τοῦ οὐρανοῦ] ℵ*. (2) ἀπὸ οὐρανοῦ] 792.

1.d-d. Variant: ἐν τῇ χειρί] ℵ fam 1611¹⁶¹¹ Andr l cop syrᵖʰ arm arab eth latt.

2.a-a. Variants: (1) ὁ ὄφις ὁ ἀρχαῖος] A (𝔓⁴⁷ and C have lacunae here) Andr l; Tischendorf, *NT Graece;* WHort; B. Weiss, *Johannes-Apocalypse,* 216; Charles, 2:362; Schmid, *Studien* 2:239; Nestle-Aland²⁷; UBSGNT⁴. (2) τὸν ὄφιν τὸν ἀρχαῖον] ℵ 051 Oecumenius²⁰⁵³ Andreas Byzantine syr TR; Bousset (1906) 436; von Soden, *Text.* Reading (1) is probably original (Schmid, *Studien* 2:94, 239; *TCGNT*¹, 702; *TCGNT*², 687); it is the *lectio difficilior* since it is in the nom. but modifies the preceding τὸν δράκοντα, "the dragon." This is an example of the author's use of a nom. in apposition to a preceding oblique case, in this instance an acc. (see 1:5; 2:13; for the use of ptcps. in the nom. of apposition, see 2:20; 3:12; 8:9; 9:13; 14:12, 14; Mussies, *Morphology,* 93). Reading (2) is certainly a syntactical correction.

2.b. The neut. sing. relative pronoun ὅ is weakly attested by ℵ fam 1611²⁰⁵⁰ Andr l Byz 8¹⁸⁰. For a discussion of the idiom ὅ ἐστιν, which can refer to substantives of any gender, see BDF § 132; Turner, *Syntax,* 48; and *Note* 21:8.c.

2.c. Variants: (1) ὁ missing before Διάβολος] Andreas. (2) ὁ before Διάβολος] ℵ fam 1611¹⁶¹¹ ²⁰⁵⁰ ²³²⁹ Oecumenius²⁰⁵³ ²⁰⁶² Andr f²⁰⁷³ g²⁰⁷¹ i 194 1773 Byz 1²²⁵⁶ Byz 2²⁰⁷⁶ Byz 13¹⁷⁰⁴ ²⁰⁵⁸ Byz 17²⁰⁷⁸ Andr/Byz 3¹⁸⁹⁴ Andr/Byz 4a²⁰⁸⁴. Since the definite article is also missing from the following Σατανᾶς in some MSS (Andreas and several minuscules), it would seem that this omission was a correction based on the absence of the definite article before Διάβολος. This follows the rule that the article is not used with proper names (Schmid, *Studien* 2:190). In some cases, however, the article is used before designations that have only been partially transformed into proper names since they retain at least a vestige of their original meaning. Διάβολος and Σατανᾶς are examples of such transitional proper names (Mussies, *Morphology,* 195–97).

2.d. Variants: (1) ὁ before Σατανᾶς] ℵ A (lacuna in C) 046 fam 1611¹⁶¹¹ ²³²⁹ fam 1006¹⁰⁰⁶ ¹⁸⁴¹ 2030 2323 Oecumenius²⁰⁵³ ²⁰⁶² Andr f g²⁰⁷¹ i⁻¹⁶⁸⁵ ⁻²⁰⁴² l¹⁷⁷⁸ ²⁰²⁰ Byz 5⁻¹⁸⁹³ Byz 6 Byz 7⁻²⁰⁷⁹ Byz 8 Byz 9⁻²⁰³ ⁻⁵⁰⁶ Byz 10⁻¹⁸⁷⁰ Byz 13 Byz 14 Byz 15⁴² Byz 17⁸² ⁴⁶⁹ ⁶⁹⁹ ²⁰⁷⁸ ²⁴³⁶ Byz 18⁻²⁵⁶ ⁻²⁰¹⁷ Byz 19⁶⁶⁴ ¹⁰⁹⁴ ²⁰¹⁶ ²⁰⁷⁵ ²⁰⁷⁷ Andr/Byz 2b⁵⁸² Andr/Byz 3 Andr/Byz 4a 4b 4c. (2) omit ὁ before Σατανᾶς] 051 fam 1611¹⁸⁵⁴ Andreas. In Revelation, Σατανᾶς is used eight times (2:9, 13[2x], 24; 3:9; 12:9; 20:2, 7) and always with the definite article, indicating that the adversary is in view. In the OT the Heb. term הַשָּׂטָן *haśśāṭān* is always articular, though in the NT it is occasionally anarthrous (Mark 3:23; Luke 22:3; 2 Cor 12:7).

3.a. Variants: (1) τά before χίλια] A (lacuna in C) ℵ fam 1006 fam 1611 Oecumenius²⁰⁵³ ²⁰⁶² Andr f²⁰²³ ²⁰⁷³ Andr l 94 Byzantine; Nestle-Aland²⁷; UBSGNT⁴. (2) omit τά] 051 fam 1611¹⁸⁵⁴ Andreas. The first occurrence of χίλια ἔτη in v 2 is anarthrous as one might expect in the case of a new apocalyptic concept that the author assumes is unknown to the readers. The expression "a thousand years" occurs six times in Revelation (20:2, 3, 4, 5, 6, 7), though in v 4 the phrase is unexpectedly anarthrous, and in v 6 the presence of τά is problematic (it is bracketed in Nestle-Aland²⁷ and UBSGNT⁴).

3.b-b. Variants: (1) μετὰ ταῦτα] A (lacuna in C) ℵ 046 fam 1006 fam 1611²³²⁹ Oecumenius²⁰⁵³ᵗᵉˣᵗ ²⁰⁶² Andr l 94 Victorinus Primasius Tyc²³ Beatus. (2) καὶ μετὰ ταῦτα] 051 fam 1611²⁰⁵⁰ Andreas vg cop^bo arm eth. (3) μετὰ δὲ ταῦτα] fam 1611¹⁸⁵⁴. (4) μετὰ ταῦτα δέ] fam 1611¹⁶¹¹ syrʰ. (5) καὶ μετὰ τοῦτο] Oecumenius²⁰⁵³ᶜᵒᵐᵐ.

3.c-c. Variants: (1) λυθῆναι αὐτόν] A (lacuna in C) Oecumenius²⁰⁵³ ²⁰⁶² fam 1006 fam 1611 94 Byzantine. (2) αὐτὸν λυθῆναι] ℵ 051 Oecumenius²⁰⁵³ᶜᵒᵐᵐ Andreas latt. Reading (2) represents a simplification of the word order (Schmid, *Studien* 2:125).

4.a. καί functions as a relative pronoun here (= ἐφ᾽ οὓς ἐκάθισαν, "on which they sat"); see BDR § 442.12.

4.b-b. The translation "people sat" indicates that I have construed the 3rd pl. aor. verb ἐκάθισαν, "they sat," as an impersonal use of the 3rd pl.; see *Comment* on 20:4a.

4.c-c. κρίμα here means "the right to judge," "the authority to judge" (Louw-Nida, § 56.22); see John 5:22.

4.d-d. The καί here appears to be epexegetical or explanatory; i.e., it defines more closely those whom John saw seated on thrones (Rochais, *NRT* 103 [1981] 839 n. 18).

4.e. Variant: insert εἶδον] fam 1006 fam 1611²³²⁹ (ἰδών); Andr f²⁰⁷³ n; vg^D Beatus. A scribal correction attempting to make it clear that τὰς ψυχάς is the obj. of εἶδον in v 4a (see *Note* 20:4.f-f.). The "I saw" is sometimes repeated in translations, e.g., the NRSV, "I also saw the souls."

4.f-f. The acc. τὰς ψυχάς, "the souls," is the obj. of εἶδον in v 4a (see *Note* 20:4.e.), despite the length of the intervening clauses (see 1:20; 4:4; 7:9; 14:14; Mussies, *Morphology*, 100).

4.g-g. Variants: (1) τὸ θηρίον] אַ A (lacuna in C) 046 Oecumenius²⁰⁵³comm ²⁰⁶² fam 1611¹⁸⁵⁴ ²⁰⁵⁰ ²³²⁹ latt syr. (2) τῷ θηρίῳ] fam 1006¹⁰⁰⁶ ¹⁸⁴¹ fam 1611¹⁶¹¹ Andreas. On the use of προσκυνεῖν + dat. or acc., see *Note* 4:10.b.

4.h. Variants: (1) οὐδέ] אַ A (lacuna in C) 046 fam 1006 fam 1611 94 Andr l Byzantine cop^bo. (2) οὔτε] 051 Andreas. The weak attestation of (2) makes it virtually certain that (1) was the original reading (Schmid, *Studien* 2:224–25). The use of οὐδέ and οὔτε in Revelation is problematic: οὐ . . . οὔτε . . . οὔτε means "not . . . neither . . . nor," while οὐ . . . οὐδέ means "not . . . not even" (BDF § 445).

4.i. Variant: τῇ εἰκόνι] fam 1006 fam 1611¹⁶¹¹ Andreas Andr/Byz 2a Andr/Byz 2b Andr/Byz 3.

4.j. Variant: οὐδέ instead of καὶ οὐκ] fam 1611¹⁶¹¹ syr^h lat^gig Victorinus Cyprian Augustine Primasius Apringius eth.

4.k. On this translation, see *Note* 13:16.b.

4.l. Here the sing. noun τὴν χεῖρα, "hand," is a *generic* sing. appropriately translated as a pl. in Eng. (cf. 13:16; Turner, *Syntax*, 22–24).

4.m-m. ἔζησαν, lit. "they lived," is in ingressive aor. used with verbs that express condition or state. It emphasizes the beginning or initial entrance into that condition or state: e.g., "they began to live," or "they came to life" (Turner, *Syntax*, 71; see Rev 1:8; 2:8; 13:14). There are several other examples in the NT where ζᾶν means "to live again" (BAGD, 336; Louw-Nida, § 23.93); see Rom 14:9.

4.n. Variants: (1) omit τά before χίλια] אַ A 051 fam 1611⁻¹⁸⁵⁴ Oecumenius²⁰⁵³ ²⁰⁶² Andreas syr^ph. (2) τά before χίλια] fam 1006¹⁰⁰⁶ ¹⁸⁴¹ Andr g l n²⁴²⁹ 94 Byzantine. Reading (1) is the *lectio difficilior* since the previous use of τὰ χίλια ἔτη in v 3 is articular. The inadequate attestation of reading (2) means that reading (1) is probably original (Schmid, *Studien* 2:195). The anarthrous use of χίλια ἔτη here is perfectly plausible, however, if v 4 is a gloss.

5.a. Variant: insert καί] 046 051 fam 1006¹⁰⁰⁶ ¹⁸⁴¹ fam 1611¹⁸⁵⁴ ²⁰⁵⁰ Andrea it^a vg^mss cop^bo.

5.b-b. Variant: omit οἱ λοιποὶ τῶν νεκρῶν οὐκ ἔζησαν ἄχρι τελεσθῇ τὰ χίλια ἔτη] אַ Oecumenius²⁰⁵³ ²⁰⁶² Andr i²⁰⁴² ²⁰⁶⁶ l¹⁷⁷⁸ n²⁰⁶⁵ 94 2030 2377 Byzantine syr Victorinus Beatus. Early accidental omission probably caused by homoioteleuton; i.e., ἔτη concludes both v 4 and this sentence.

5.c-c. On ζᾶν as "to live again," see *Note* 4.m-m.

5.d. Variant: omit τά] Andr Ø⁵⁹⁸ ²⁰³⁸. The few omissions of this article underscore the genuineness of the anarthrous χίλια ἔτη in v 4 (*Note* 4.n.).

6.a-a. On the translation "how fortunate," see *Note* 1:3.b.

6.b-b. Variant: θάνατος ὁ δεύτερος] 051 Andreas (ὁ δεύτερος omitted by Andr g²⁰⁴⁵).

6.c. The pl. demonstrative pronoun τούτων modifies the sing. substantival ptcp. ὁ ἔχων, constituting a *constructio ad sensum*.

6.d-d. The subject of the 3rd pl. verb ἔσονται is ὁ ἔχων, forming a *constructio ad sensum* (see *Note* 6.c.).

6.e-e. Variants: (1) μετὰ ταῦτα] Byzantine. (2) μετ᾽ αὐτά] fam 1611²³²⁹.

6.f. Variants: (1) omit τά] A 051 fam 1006 fam 1611¹⁸⁵⁴ ²⁰⁵⁰ 2030; Andreas Byzantine arm eth; B. Weiss, *Johannes-Apokalypse*, 35, 217; von Soden, *Text*. (2) τά before χίλια] אַ 046 fam 1611¹⁶¹¹ ²³²⁹ Oecumenius²⁰⁵³ ²⁰⁶² Andr f²⁰⁷³ l 94 Byz l Byz 11 cop^sa bo; Tischendorf, *NT Graece;* [WHort]; [Bousset (1906) 438]; [Charles, 2:372]; Schmid, *Studien* 2:195; Merk, *NT;* [Nestle-Aland²⁷]; [UBSGNT⁴]; *TCGNT*¹, 762; *TCGNT*², 687. Since χίλια (used six times in Revelation, all within this context: 21:2, 3, 4, 5, 6, 7) occurred without the article when first introduced in 20:2, one would expect the use of the anaphoric article here, which the author normally uses with precision. For this reason reading (2) is preferred, though reading (1) is certainly the *lectio difficilior*. B. Weiss (*Johannes-Apokalypse*) argues that τά is present through assimilation to τὰ χίλια in vv 3 and 5. Reading (2) must be rejected primarily because of the poor attestation.

7.a-a. Variants: (1) ὅταν τελεσθῇ] *lectio originalis.* (2) μετά] 2030 Andr g Byzantine. (3) ὅτε ἐτελέσθη] Andr b. (4) ὅτε ἐτελέσθησαν] Andr a c. (5) ὅτε τελεσθῇ] Andr d l¹⁶⁷⁸ ²⁰⁸⁰.

7.b. ὅταν + subjunctive here indicates a unique event and is a functional equivalent of ὅτε; see Rev 8:1; 11:7; 12:4 (Mussies, *Morphology,* 345).

8.a. Variants: (1) τά after τὰ ἔθνη] Andreas syrʰ. (2) omit τά] ℵ fam 1611¹⁸⁵⁴ ²³²⁹ Oecumenius²⁰⁵³ ²⁰⁶² Andr e²⁰⁵⁷ syrᵖʰ arm copᵇᵒ. When an attributive (whether an adj., a pronoun, an ordinal, an adj. ptcp., or a prep. phrase) follows a noun, the article used with the noun is repeated before the attributive (Schmid, *Studien* 2:197). This rule is particularly consistent in Revelation in the case of prep. phrases used attributively (BDF § 272; BDR § 272.2), as in 20:8 (1:4; 2:24; 5:5; 7:17; 8:3, 9; 11:2, 19; 14:17; 16:3, 12; 19:14; 20:8, 13). Though reading (2) is the *lectio difficilior,* the style of Revelation, together with the relatively weak attestation of reading (2), suggests the originality of reading (1).

8.b. αὐτῶν in the pronominal phrase ὧν ὁ ἀριθμὸς αὐτῶν is a resumptive pronoun, which some have considered a Semitism (Mussies, *Morphology,* 177). However, this instance of a *pronomen abundans* is independent or parenthetical, i.e., nonessential, and should not therefore be considered a Semitism. This construction occurs nine times in Revelation (3:8; 7:2, 9; 12:6, 14; 13:8, 12; 17:9; 20:8); for a more extensive discussion see *Note* 3:8.c. Copyists have attempted to correct this phrase to conform to more ordinary Gk. usage by omitting αὐτῶν (051 fam 1611¹⁶¹¹ Andr TR). However, αὐτῶν is attested by ℵ A 046 fam 1006¹⁸⁴¹ fam 1611²⁰⁵⁰ ²³²⁹ 2063 2080 Oecumenius²⁰⁵³ Andr f²⁰⁷³ 1 n 94 and is certainly original.

9.a. Variants: (1) ἐκύκλευσαν] A 046 fam 1006¹⁰⁰⁶ ¹⁸⁴¹ Andr f²⁰²³ ²⁰⁷³ Byzantine. (2) ἐκύκλωσαν] ℵ fam 1611¹⁸⁵⁴ ²⁰⁵⁰ Oecumenius²⁰⁵³ ²⁰⁶² Andreas. κυκλοῦν (which occurs four times in the NT [Luke 21:20; John 10:24; Acts 14:20; Heb 11:30] and three times in the Apostolic Fathers [*Barn.* 6:6; *1 Clem.* 22:8; Herm. *Sim.* 9.9.6]) is a more common word than κυκλεύειν, which occurs in the NT only as a *var. lect.* in John 10:24 and in the Apostolic Fathers only in Hermas *Sim.* 9.9.6. This rare usage accounts for scribal preference for the more usual word (Schmid, *Studien* 2:125). κυκλοῦν also occurs nine times in Greco-Jewish literature (Denis, *Concordance,* 492), while κυκλεύειν occurs twice (*Jos. As.* 1.1; 9.3).

9.b-b. On translating οἱ ἅγιοι, lit. "saints," as "God's people," see *Comment* on 5:8.

9.c. Variant: insert καὶ τὴν πόλιν τῶν ἁγίων] 046 syrᵖʰ.

9.d. The καί linking τὴν παρεμβολὴν τῶν ἁγίων with τὴν πόλιν τὴν ἠγαπημένην may possibly be epexegetical or explanatory, with "the beloved city" as an alternate way of describing "the camp of the people of God."

9.e-e. Variants: (1) ἐκ τοῦ οὐρανοῦ] A (lacuna in ℵ and C) Oecumenius²⁰⁵³ᶜᵒᵐᵐ vgᵐˢˢ copᵇᵒᵐˢˢ Andr i l 94 Tyc²ᵐˢˢ Tyc³ (lacuna in Primasius); Augustine (*Civ. Dei* 20); Tischendorf, *NT Graece;* WHort; B. Weiss, *Johannes-Apokalypse,* 217; Charles, 2:373; Nestle-Aland²⁷; UBSGNT⁴. (2) ἀπὸ (ἐκ Andr c) τοῦ θεοῦ] fam 1611¹⁸⁵⁴ vgᵐˢ. (3) ἐκ τοῦ οὐρανοῦ ἀπὸ τοῦ θεοῦ] 046 Andr l²⁰²⁰ Byzantine itᵍⁱᵍ syrᵖʰ copˢᵃ ᵇᵒ arm Victorinus (Vogels, *Untersuchungen,* 178; Tyc²; Bousset (1906) 439 [ἀπὸ τοῦ θεοῦ]). (4) ἐκ τοῦ θεοῦ ἀπὸ [ἐκ Andr i] τοῦ οὐρανοῦ] Andreas vg syr Beatus. (5) ἀπὸ τοῦ θεοῦ ἐκ τοῦ οὐρανοῦ] ℵ² 025 fam 1006¹⁰⁰⁶ fam 1611¹⁶¹¹ Oecumenius²⁰⁵³ᵗᵉˣᵗ 1773; Merk, *NT.* The phrase ἐκ τοῦ οὐρανοῦ ἀπὸ τοῦ θεοῦ also occurs in Rev 21:2, where it is attested by A (lacuna in C) ℵ Byzantine), and in 21:10, where it is attested by the Byzantine text (ἐκ τοῦ θεοῦ). It is probably original in both places (see *Notes* 21:2.b-b. and 21:10.e-e.). Reading (3) can be regarded as an expansion of the phrase found in reading (1) based on Rev 21:2, 10 (*TCGNT*¹, 762–63; *TCGNT*², 687–88), though the weight of the external evidence is in favor of reading (1). Reading (1) is also preferable on the basis of the principle *lectio brevior potior est,* "the shorter reading is preferable." Since reading (4) is supported by some versions, either it or reading (3) may be original; since Andreas also switches the order of the same clauses in 21:2, the Byzantine text might be preferable (Schmid, *Studien* 2:81–82). The absence of the phrase ἀπὸ τοῦ θεοῦ from A can be considered a transcriptional error.

10.a. Variant: omit καί after ὅπου] ℵ Andreas. The phrase ὅπου καί also occurs in 11:8, where the καί is omitted by 𝔓⁴⁷ ℵ¹ fam 1611¹⁶¹¹ Andreas.

10.b. καί functions here as a particle introducing a consecutive or result clause and so is translated "so that" (see Aune, *Revelation,* WBC 52A, cxciii; Zerwick, *Greek,* § 455; Ljungvik, *Syntax,* 62–63; Mussies, *Morphology,* 342; Aejmelaeus, *Parataxis,* 15–18); see *Notes* 2:23.c.; 3:7.d., 10.d.; 11:3.d-d.; 14:10.h-h.

11.a-a. Variants: (1) ἐπ' αὐτόν] 046 051 fam 1611²⁰⁵⁰ Andreas Byzantine. (2) ἐπ' αὐτοῦ] A (lacuna in C) fam 1006¹⁰⁰⁶ ¹⁸⁴¹ fam 1611¹⁶¹¹ ²³²⁹ Oecumenius²⁰⁵³ ²⁰⁶². (3) ἐπάνω αὐτοῦ] ℵ (the same variant occurs in 9:7, supported by 𝔓⁴⁷ and ℵ). (4) ἐπ' αὐτῷ] fam 1611¹⁸⁵⁴ itᵍⁱᵍ (*in illa*); Irenaeus (*in eo*). The grammatical rule in Revelation is that in the phrase ὁ καθήμενος ἐπί τ. θρον. (which occurs twenty-six times), if ὁ καθήμενος is in the nom. (4:1) or acc., then τ. θρον. is in the acc.; if ὁ καθήμενος is in the gen. (4:10; 5:1, 7) or dat. (5:13; 7:10), then τ. θρον. is also in the gen. or dat. (Schmid, *Studien* 2:209–10), though this rule is not observed with complete consistency.

11.b-b. Variant: αὐτοῦ inserted after οὗ ἀπὸ τοῦ προσώπου] (lacunae in 𝔓⁴⁷ and C) ℵ fam 1006 fam 1611²³²⁹

Oecumenius²⁰⁵³ ²⁰⁶² Andr e²⁰⁹¹ f²⁰³¹ ²⁰⁵⁶ h²⁰⁶⁰ ²²⁸⁶ l²⁰⁸⁰ Byz 1²²⁵⁶ Byz 5⁸⁰⁸ Byz 17⁴⁹⁶. Though this reading is rejected by all modern editions, it has a strong claim to originality. N.b. that two major witnesses have lacunae at this point, 𝔓⁴⁷ and C. Further, two of the most valuable minuscules, Oecumenius²⁰⁵³ and ²⁰⁶², have the reading, as do fam 1006 and fam 1611²³²⁹ (close to 𝔓⁴⁷ and ℵ). While the absence of αὐτοῦ is certainly the *lectio difficilior*, of the sixteen instances of προσώπου in the NT, *only in this text is it not followed by a gen.*

The syntax of this phrase is problematic: οὗ ἀπὸ τοῦ προσώπου ἔφυγεν ἡ γῆ καὶ ὁ οὐρανός. Normally in LXX Greek ἀπὸ [τοῦ] προσώπου is followed by a gen. A syntactic parallel to this clause is found in LXX Jer 22:25, ὧν σὺ εὐλαβῇ ἀπὸ προσώπου αὐτῶν, lit. "of whom you were afraid of them." In Rev 20:11, the gen. relative pronoun οὗ functions to transform the common OT phrase ἀπὸ τοῦ προσώπου σου, "from your presence," i.e., "from you," into the 3rd sing., though one might have expected οὗ ἀπὸ τοῦ προσώπου αὐτοῦ, i.e., the addition of the pleonastic pronoun as in Jer 22:25. Cf. Jer 49:16, ὁ λιμός, οὗ ὑμεῖς λόγον ἔχετε ἀπὸ προσώπου αὐτοῦ, "the famine of which you have word of it," i.e., "the famine of which you have heard." While the insertion of αὐτοῦ could be considered a correction, it is the kind of Semitism that copyists tended to eliminate. The idiom φεύγειν ἀπὸ προσώπου τινός, "to flee from the presence of someone," occurs frequently in the LXX (e.g., Exod 14:25; Josh 10:11; Judg 9:40; 2 Sam 10:13–14; 2 Kgs 3:24; 1 Chr 10:1, 1 Macc 5:34; Jdt 14:3), where ἀπὸ προσώπου τινός = מִפְּנֵי *mippĕnê* (Helbing, *Kasussyntax*, 28). ἀπὸ προσώπου is particularly Hebraistic in instances where the reference is an abstract thing (Isa 2:10; 57:1; Deut 5:5; 2 Sam 15:14; R. Sollamo, *Semiprepositions*, 86). For a detailed discussion of ἀπὸ προσώπου, see *Note* 6:16.b.

11.c. καί is used here adversatively.

11.d. Here the aor. pass. εὑρέθη, lit. "was found," may reflect the Heb. niphal of מָצָא *māṣā'*, "to find," which can mean "to be," "be present" (BDB 594), so here "and a place was not found for them" means "there was no place for them." The phrase in which this verb occurs is derived verbatim from Theod Dan 2:35.

12.a-a. Variant: omit τοὺς μεγάλους καὶ τοὺς μικρούς] 2030 Andr a Byzantine.

12.b. Variants: (1) τοῦ θρόνου] RSV; NRSV; NIV. (2) τοῦ θεοῦ] Andr a b d; AV; NAV. (3) τοῦ θρόνου θεοῦ] Andr c; *throni dei* (*De prom.* 851C; Vogels, *Untersuchungen*, 217). (4) *throni domini*] Ps.-Cyprian *Ad Novatianum* 17 (Vogels, *Untersuchungen*, 215). Variant (3) is a scribal amplification of (1) based on the phrase ὁ θρόνος θεοῦ, which occurs three times elsewhere in Revelation (7:15; 22:1, 3).

12.c-c. Variants: (1) ἠνοίχθησαν (3rd pl. aor. ind. pass.)] 025 Andr i; 1773. (2) ἤνοιξαν (3rd pl. aor. ind. active)] fam 1611¹⁸⁵⁴ ²³²⁹ 2030 Byzantine Ambrose (*aperuerunt*). (3) ἠνεώχθησαν (3rd pl. aor. ind. pass.)] Andreas. (4) ἀνεῴχθησαν (3rd pl. aor. ind. pass.)] Andr b e f l. (5) ἠνεῴχθη (3rd sing. aor. ind. pass.)] ℵ. Reading (5) is a correction so that the neut. pl. subject βιβλία will have a sing. verb in accordance with Attic and subsequently Hellenistic usage (BDF § 133).

12.d-d. Variants: (1) ταῖς βίβλοις] ℵ 94. (2) τοῖς βίβλοις] Byz 9²⁰³ ⁵⁰⁶ Byz 17¹⁸⁵². While βίβλος is normally fem. in gender, as in reading (1) (Gignac, *Grammar* 2:38), reading (2), which is either masc. or neut. pl. dat., suggests that it either varied in gender or (more likely) that the change from βιβλίοις to βίβλοις results from the omission of an accented -ι- before a back vowel and following a liquid consonant (Gignac, *Grammar* 1:302–3).

13.a. Variant: omit καί] Oecumenius²⁰⁵³ ²⁰⁶² Irenaeus cop^sa.

13.b-b. Variant: ἐν αὐτῇ νεκρούς] 051 fam 1611¹⁸⁵⁴ Andreas.

13.c. On the attributive use of prep. phrases in Revelation, see *Note* 20:8.a.

13.d-d. Variant: ἔδωκεν] A Andr/Byz 3²¹⁹⁶ Byz 17⁸².

13.e-e. Variant: ἐν αὐτῇ νεκρούς] 051 fam 1611¹⁸⁵⁴ 2030 Andreas. This reflects the same alteration as discussed in *Note* 13.b-b.

13.f. Here καί indicates a temporal transition from the previous clauses and takes the place of such advs. of time as τότε or εἶτα.

13.g-g. The subject of the pl. verb ἐκρίθησαν is the distributive sing. pronoun ἕκαστος (Mussies, *Morphology*, 84).

13.h. Variant: αὐτοῦ] Byzantine cop^samss. This sentence has a sing. subject with the pl. verb, ἐκρίθησαν ἕκαστος, but in this instance ἕκαστος is used in a distributive sense. This construction occurs in classical Gk. and Koine; see John 16:32 (ἵνα σκορπισθῆτε ἕκαστος, "each will be scattered"); Matt 18:35 (ἐὰν μὴ ἀφῆτε ἕκαστος τῷ ἀδελφῷ αὐτοῦ, "unless each forgives his brother"); other examples in BAGD, 236; Turner, *Syntax*, 198.

14.a-a. Variant: omit οὗτος . . . πυρός] 051 Oecumenius²⁰⁵³txt ²⁰⁶²txt Andr 94 598.

14.b-b. Variants: (1) οὗτος ὁ θάνατος ὁ δεύτερός ἐστιν] *lectio originalis*. (2) οὗτος ὁ θάνατος δεύτερός ἐστιν] fam 1611¹⁶¹¹ Andr i m²⁰³⁷ ²⁰⁴⁶ lat. (3) ὁ δεύτερος θάνατος] ℵ Andr l. (4) ἐστὶν ὁ θάνατος ὁ δεύτερος] Andr e²⁰²⁶ f²⁰²³ 1773 Andr/Byz 3.

14.c. Variant: insert καί] ℵ. The mechanical insertion of καί is based on the frequency with which sentences begin with καί in Revelation (73.79 percent).

14.d. Explanatory remarks made within the context of visions regularly make use of the present tense (Mussies, *Morphology*, 333).

15.a-a. Variant: τῷ βιβλίῳ] fam 1006$^{1006\ 1841}$ 2030 2377 Andr f^{2073} 94 Byzantine.

Form/Structure/Setting

I. OUTLINE

2. The final defeat of Satan (20:1–10)
　　a. Vision of Satan's temporary thousand-year imprisonment (vv 1–3)
　　　　(1) John sees an angel (v 1)
　　　　　　(a) Descending from heaven
　　　　　　(b) Holding a key to the abyss
　　　　　　(c) Holding a great chain
　　　　(2) The angel seizes the dragon with several names (v 2a)
　　　　　　(a) the ancient serpent
　　　　　　(b) the devil
　　　　　　(c) Satan
　　　　(3) The angel binds the dragon for a thousand years (v 2b)
　　　　(4) The angel throws the dragon into the abyss (v 3a)
　　　　　　(a) He locks the abyss
　　　　　　(b) He seals the abyss
　　　　(5) Purpose and length of imprisonment (v 3b)
　　　　　　(a) Purpose: to keep the dragon from deceiving the nations any longer
　　　　　　(b) Length: one thousand years
　　　　(6) The necessity of the dragon's temporary release after a thousand years (v 3c)
　　b. Vision of Christ's thousand-year reign (vv 4–6)
　　　　(1) Vision of thrones (v 4)
　　　　　　(a) Resurrected martyrs sit on them (v 4a)
　　　　　　(b) They have been beheaded (v 4bc)
　　　　　　　　[1] Positive reasons (v 4b)
　　　　　　　　　　[a] For their testimony to Jesus
　　　　　　　　　　[b] For the word of God
　　　　　　　　[2] Negative reasons (v 4c)
　　　　　　　　　　[a] They did not worship
　　　　　　　　　　　　{1} The beast
　　　　　　　　　　　　{2} The beast's image
　　　　　　　　　　[b] They did not receive the mark of the beast
　　　　　　　　　　　　{1} On their foreheads
　　　　　　　　　　　　{2} On their hands
　　　　　　(c) The first resurrection: the reward of the martyrs (v 4d)
　　　　　　　　[1] They come to life
　　　　　　　　[2] They reign a thousand years with Christ

(2) Commentary on the first resurrection (vv 5–6)
    (a) The fate of the rest of the dead: not resurrected until the thousand years are over (v 5a)
    (b) The resurrection of martyrs: the first resurrection (v 5b)
    (c) Beatitude: fortunate and holy are those who share in the first resurrection (v 6a–c)
        [1] The second death has no power over them (v 6b)
        [2] They will be priests of God and of Christ (v 6c)
        [3] They will reign a thousand years with Christ (v 6c)

c. Satan's release, defeat, and punishment (vv 7–10)
  (1) The release of Satan (v 7)
    (a) At the end of one thousand years
    (b) Satan is loosed from his prison
  (2) The mission of Satan (v 8)
    (a) He goes out to deceive the nations (v 8a)
    (b) He assembles the nations for war (v 8a–c)
        [1] Located at four corners of the earth (v 8a)
        [2] They are called Gog and Magog (v 8a)
        [3] The troops are innumerable (v 8c)
  (3) The onslaught of the assembled army (v 9a)
    (a) Marches over the broad earth.
    (b) Surrounds the camp of the people of God (camp = beloved city)
  (4) The divine destruction of the hostile army (v 9b)
    (a) Fire falls from heaven
    (b) The hostile army is incinerated
  (5) The final punishment of the devil (v 10)
    (a) He had deceived the nations
    (b) He is thrown into the lake of fire
    (c) The beast and the false prophet are already there
    (d) They will all be tormented for ever

3. Vision of the final judgment (vv 11–15)
  a. The majesty of the Enthroned One (v 11)
    (1) Seated on a great white throne (v 11a)
    (2) Theophanic effects of his presence (v 11bc)
      (a) Earth and heaven flee
      (b) No place found for earth and heaven
  b. The final judgment of the dead (vv 12–15)
    (1) The dead stand before the throne (v 12a)
    (2) Two sets of heavenly books are opened (v 12bc)
      (a) The books are opened
      (b) The book of life is also opened
    (3) The basis of judgment (v 12d)
      (a) By what was recorded in the books
      (b) In accordance with their works
    (4) The resurrection of the dead (v 13a)
      (a) The sea gives up its dead
      (b) Death and Hades give up their dead

(5) Reiterated basis of judgment: works (v 13b)
(6) The punishment of Death and Hades (v 14)
    (a) They are thrown into the lake of fire
    (b) They experience the second death
(7) The punishment of those not written in the book of life: the
    lake of fire (v 15)

II. LITERARY ANALYSIS

A. The Temporary Imprisonment of Satan (20:1–3)

The conquest of Satan narrated in this section has a general parallel earlier, in 12:7–9, where the same series of names mentioned here in 20:2 (dragon, ancient serpent, devil, Satan) appears in 12:9. The forced confinement of Satan in the abyss has parallels in the motif sequence of other ancient combat myths. In Hesiod's *Theogony,* the conquest of the Titans by Zeus and his allies is followed by the confinement of the vanquished below the earth (lines 711–19) and thereafter by a description of the underworld (lines 720–819).

The single OT passage that appears to exhibit the motifs found in the traditional scene incorporated into Rev 20:1–10 is Isa 24:21–22, which describes the eschatological judgment of God:

> On that day the Lord will punish the host of heaven in heaven, and on earth the kings of the earth. They will be gathered together like prisoners in a pit; they will be shut up in a prison, and after many days they will be punished.

The relevant motifs found in this passage include: (1) the imprisonment of the malefactors, (2) the vague designation of the period of imprisonment as "many days," and (3) the ending of the period of imprisonment with a final punishment. Two other texts closely parallel to Rev 20:1–10 (specifically vv 1–3 and 7–10) also show the influence of Isa 24:21–22. They are *1 Enoch* 10:4–6 and 10:11–13, which contain many of the same constituent motifs (Rubinkiewicz, *Eschatologie*).

First let us list the constituent motifs of Rev 20:1–3, 7–10: (1) An angel descends from heaven with a key and a chain (v 1). (2) The angel seizes and binds Satan (v 2a). (3) Satan will be imprisoned one thousand years (v 2b). (4) Satan is cast into a pit that is locked and sealed (v 3). (5) Satan is released for an unspecified period (vv 3b, 7–9). (6) Satan and his associates are cast into the lake of fire for eternal torment (v 10).

1 Enoch 10:4–6 contains the following motifs: (1) God sends an angel (Raphael). (2) Azazel (an alias for Satan) is bound by the angel. (3) Azazel is thrown into darkness and imprisoned "forever." (4) The time of imprisonment, however, will actually end at the great day of judgment. (5) On the great day of judgment Azazel is thrown into the fire. A similar sequence is evident in *1 Enoch* 10:11–13: (1) God sends an angel (Michael). (2) The angel binds Semyaza (another alias for Satan) and his associates. (3) They are imprisoned under the earth. (4) The period of imprisonment is limited to seventy generations. (5) On the day of judgment they are thrown into the abyss of fire.

Since the narrative pattern found twice in Rev 20:1–10 (i.e., in vv 1–3 and 7–10) also occurs twice in *1 Enoch,* it seems likely that both authors are dependent on a traditional eschatological scenario. The enumeration of motifs found in these three passages exhibits a striking similarity, though John has introduced the innovation of the temporary release of Satan.

B. The Judgment Scene (20:4–6)

This scene has a peculiar character and appears to belong to the final redaction of Revelation (Bousset [1906] 438). It was written expressly to be sandwiched into this particular location. It contains what might be described as three clichés that appear to have been derived from other parts of the composition: (1) "because of their witness to Jesus and because of the word of God" (v 4b; cf. 1:2, 9; 6:9; 12:17; 19:10; 20:4); (2) "who had not worshiped the beast or his image, and they had not received his brand on their foreheads or on their hands" (v 4c; cf. 13:12, 15; 14:9, 11; 19:20); and (3) "they will be priests to God and Christ" (v 6b; cf. 1:6; 5:10).

Though it appears to be a judgment scene (and thus is a compositional parallel to the more typical judgment scene in 20:11–15), it lacks many of the typical features of such an eschatological type scene. First, nothing remotely connected with κρίμα, "judgment," is found in the narrative; i.e., the right to judge given to those enthroned is apparently not exercised within this pericope. Second, the enthronement motif itself in v 4a is problematic, for it remains unclear just who is enthroned. Third, the "first resurrection" is abruptly described in past tenses in v 4d and appears to be the primary reason for the creation of this artificial judgment scene.

This textual unit is framed at the beginning by the phrases "until the thousand years had been completed. After this he must be released for a short period" (v 3bc), which serve to introduce it, and at the end by the statement "When the thousand years are completed, Satan will be released" (v 7a), which formally indicates that the unit has concluded.

C. The Eschatological War (20:7–10)

The assembly of the heathen and their concerted attack on the people of God constitute an episode or type scene that occurs frequently in early Jewish eschatological tradition. The presence of the names Gog and Magog suggests that this textual unit is patterned in part after the Gog and Magog oracle in Ezek 38–39 (as is the textual unit in Rev 19:17–21). Hartman has labeled this motif "The Tumult and Assault of the Heathen" (*Prophecy*, 77–101), a motif that can consist of indiscriminate wars and misery in the last days (*1 Enoch* 99:4; *4 Ezra* 13:30–31) or of antagonism toward an apostate Israel (*Jub.* 23:23; *1 Enoch* 90:13–19). The author of Revelation has taken this traditional eschatological scene and adapted it to a larger narrative of eschatological events that is essentially his own creation. The type scene in Rev 20:7–10 (which has two parallels in Rev 16:12–16 and 19:17–21; see *Form/Structure/Setting* on Rev 16 and Rev 19) contains the following sequence of motifs:

1. The release of Satan (v 7).
   a. He is released at the end of one thousand years.
   b. Satan is loosed from his prison.
2. The mission of Satan (v 8).
   a. He goes out to deceive the nations.
   b. He assembles the nations for war.

    (1) They are located at four corners of the earth.
    (2) They are called Gog and Magog.
    (3) The troops are innumerable.
3. The onslaught of the army (v 9a).
    a. The assembled army marches over the broad earth.
    b. The army surrounds the camp of the people of God.
    c. The camp is the beloved city.
4. The divine destruction of the army (v 9b).
    a. Fire falls from heaven.
    b. They are incinerated.
5. The final punishment of the devil (v 10).
    a. He had deceived the nations.
    b. He is thrown into the lake of fire.
    c. The beast and the false prophet are already there.
    d. All three will be continually tormented for ever.

In *1 Enoch* 56:5–8, which contains an eschatological scenario very similar to that in Rev 20:7–10, the angels incite the Parthians and Medes to leave their thrones and invade Palestine. When they reach the holy city, they will slaughter each other and then Sheol will open and swallow the sinners in the presence of the righteous. In another passage reminiscent of Rev 20:9, Lactantius *Div. Inst.* 7.17.10–11, the final victory of the righteous is described (tr. McDonald, *Lactanius,* 519):

Upon hearing of this the impious one, inflamed with wrath, will come with a great army and, with all the troops he has summoned, he will surround the mountain in which the just are staying in order to seize them. And when they see themselves surrounded and besieged on all sides, they will cry out to God with a loud voice and will beg heavenly aid. God will hear them and will send a great king from heaven who will save them, and set them free, and destroy all the impious with fire and sword.

A shorter version is found in Lactantius *Epitome* 71 (tr. Blakeney, *Epitome*):

Void of reason, frenzied with implacable rage, he [the wicked king] will bring his army to besiege the mountain where the saints have fled, and when they see themselves hemmed round, they will cry aloud in supplication to God for His aid; and He will give ear to their cry, and send down a Deliverer.

A similar scene is found in 4 Ezra 13:5–11, which describes the assembly of an innumerable host to make war on the man from the sea, who carved out a great mountain and flew up on it. The assembled army attacked but were incinerated with a stream of fire that proceeded from the lips of the man from the sea. A doublet is found in the interpretation in 4 Ezra 13:33–35:

And when all the nations hear his voice, every man shall leave his own land and the warfare that they have against one another; and an innumerable multitude shall be gathered together, as you saw, desiring to come and conquer him. But he will stand on the top of Mount Zion.

The passage goes on to interpret the destructive fire from his lips as his reproof of the assembled nations for their ungodliness.

D. Scene of Judgment (20:11–15)

This unit of text is a type scene, which consists of two subunits, v 11 and vv 12–15, each introduced with καὶ εἶδον, "then I saw." The first introduces the entire vision unit (vv 11–15), while the second emphasizes the focus on a particular scene within the vision. The first unit in v 11 is an abbreviated example of the "theophany form" (*Theophanie-Gattung*), which consists of two elements: (1) the coming of the deity and (2) the reaction of nature. Examples of this form are found in both the OT (Judg 5:4–5; Pss 18:7–15; 68:7–8; Amos 1:2; Mic 1:3–4) and early Jewish literature (Sir 16:18–19; 43:16–17; Jdt 16:15; *T. Mos.* 10:3–6; 1QH 3:32–36). The central motifs of this type scene include the enthronement of the divine judge, the opening of the heavenly books, and the execution of judgment (J. J. Collins, *Comm. Daniel*, 108). Examples of similar judgment scenes include Dan 7:9–12; *1 Enoch* 90:20–38; *T. Abr.* [Rec. A] 12. The composition of this pericope is problematic, for "the dead" are depicted as standing before the throne of God in v 12 (i.e., their resurrection is presupposed), which goes on to narrate how the two sets of books are opened and the dead are judged by what is written in the first set, i.e., by their works. V 13 appears to be a doublet or reduplication of v 12, but here the resurrection itself is explicitly referred to as if the sea and Death and Hades are two separate realms of the dead. Some scholars argue that v 13 originally came before v 12, while others contend that v 13 is an elaboration of v 12. The mention of the book of life in v 15 accounts for the interpolation of the phrase "and another book was opened, which is the book of life" into v 12.

Comment

1 καὶ εἶδον ἄγγελον καταβαίνοντα ἐκ τοῦ οὐρανοῦ ἔχοντα τὴν κλεῖν τῆς ἀβύσσου καὶ ἅλυσιν μεγάλην ἐπὶ τὴν χεῖρα αὐτοῦ, "Then I saw an angel descending from heaven with the key of the abyss and a large chain in his hand." The introductory formula καὶ εἶδον, "then I saw," introduces a new vision report (see *Comment* on 5:1). The phrase καὶ εἶδον ἄγγελον καταβαίνοντα ἐκ τοῦ οὐρανοῦ, "then I saw an angel descending from heaven," occurs with slight variation in 10:1 and 18:1. The use of chains to bind Satan and his host is an apocalyptic motif (*1 Enoch* 54:3–5; *2 Apoc. Bar.* 56:13; *Sib. Or.* 2.289; Jude 6; 2 Pet 2:4) derived from earlier Greek traditions (which in turn appear to have been influenced by the Hittite succession myth) of the chaining of the Hekatonchaires, or "hundred-handed ones" (Apollodorus 1.1.2), and the Titans in Tartarus (Hesiod *Theog.* 718; Hyginus *Fabulae* 150); an analogous tradition of the chaining of Prometheus is also preserved (*Odyssey* 11.293; Hesiod *Theog.* 522; Aeschylus *Prom.* 52–56).

A supernatural being in charge of the abyss is mentioned in *PGM* XIII.169–70, 481–83: "A god appeared, he was given authority over the abyss." Similarly, a magical procedure heavily influenced by Judaism begins "I call on you who sit over the Abyss, Bythath" (*PGM* XXXV.1). In this magical papyrus, which calls upon supernatural beings who sit in each of the six heavens, presiding angels are addressed. In Jewish thought, God does not expel or restrain demons himself but leaves that to an angel assigned to the task. In the Jewish magical papyrus called the "Recipe of Pibeches" (*PGM* IV.3007–3086 = J. van Haelst, *Catalogue* no. 1074), the magician prays (lines 3024–26), "Let your irresistible angel descend and imprison the demon flying about." The articular phrase ὁ ἄγγελος ὁ ἀπαραίτητος, "the irresistible angel," refers to a special angel whose task it is to oppose the particular demon mentioned in the magical procedure (Eitrem, *Demonology*, 17).

2a καὶ ἐκράτησεν τὸν δράκοντα, ὁ ὄφις ὁ ἀρχαῖος, ὅς ἐστιν Διάβολος καὶ ὁ Σατανᾶς, "He apprehended the dragon (the ancient serpent who is the devil and Satan)." The phrase in parentheses appears to be a gloss added to ensure the reader's proper identification of the dragon (see 12:9 and *Comment* there). In magical procedures intended to control supernatural beings, all of the known names of the being are listed in the adjuration. A relatively close parallel is found among the Aramaic incantation texts; e.g., text 27.2–3 (Isbell, *Incantation*, 79) reads "Bound and sealed [וחתימי אסירי *'syry wḥtymy*] are the demon, the devil, the satan, the curse, and the e[vil] liliths." The dragon was first introduced in Rev 12, where he is mentioned no less than eight times (12:3, 4, 7[2x] 9, 13, 16, 17) in a narrative that continues into Rev 13, where he is mentioned twice (13:2, 4). The aliases of the dragon, the ancient serpent, the devil, and Satan are listed in 12:9 as they are here.

2b καὶ ἔδησεν αὐτὸν χίλια ἔτη, "and bound him for a thousand years." For the combination of "arrest" (κρατεῖν) and "bind" (δεῖν) as part of the metaphor of capturing a felon, see Mark 6:17 (of John the Baptist). The notion of "binding" (δεῖν), particularly when used of supernatural beings, is drawn from the world of magic (see under v 3 below). The metaphor of "binding," i.e., imprisoning Satan or demons, particularly until the day of judgment, occurs frequently in Judaism (*1 Enoch* 10:4, 11–12; 13:1; 14:5; 18:16; 21:3–6; *Jub.* 5:6; 10:7–11; *2 Enoch* [Rec. J and A] 7:2; *2 Apoc. Bar.* 56:13; see Jude 6). In Isbell's collection of inscriptions from Aramaic incantation bowls, text 18.4 speaks of "the binding of Bagdana their king and their ru[ler], the king of dem[ons and devils, and the great] ru[ler of liliths]" (Isbell, *Incantation*, 58; parallel formulas are found in 17.4–5, p. 56, and 20.4, p. 64). See also Tob 8:3 (MSS A and B), "And when the demon smelled the odor he fled to the remotest parts of Egypt and the angel bound him [καὶ ἔδησεν αὐτὸ ὁ ἄγγελος]." According to *1 Enoch* 10:10–12 (see 4QEn^b 1:4, 11; Milik, *Enoch*, 175), it is Michael who is commanded to bind evil angels for seven generations until "the great day of their judgment."

3a καὶ ἔβαλεν αὐτὸν εἰς τὴν ἄβυσσον καὶ ἔκλεισεν καὶ ἐσφράγισεν ἐπάνω αὐτοῦ, "He cast him into the abyss, which he closed and sealed over him." On the term "abyss," see *Comment* on 9:1b. The two terms meaning "bind" (v 2b) and "cast" (v 3a) are often associated in combat myths. Ouranos, who had children by Gaia, had them bound (δήσας) and cast (ἔρριψε) into Tartarus (Apollodorus 1.1.2). Early Judaism knew of an analogous tradition involving the binding and imprisoning of evil angels or demons until the day of judgment. In *Jub.* 10:1–14, in response to the prayer of Noah, nine-tenths of the demons are bound in the place of judgment. A redacted version is found in *Jub.* 10:7, frag. (Denis, *Fragmenta*, 86), which reads, "The Lord commanded the archangel Michael to cast them into the abyss [βαλεῖν αὐτοὺς εἰς τὴν ἄβυσσον] until the day of judgment." Another parallel is found in 4Q511 (4QShir^b) 30:3 (M. Baillet, *Qumran Grotte 4*, DJD 7 [Oxford: Clarendon, 1982] 3:236). Referring to [ארץ שכי ומח[ותהומות שמים ה]שמי ושמי ה] [*haššāmayim ûšmê ha*]*ššāmayim ûthômôt wĕmaḥă*[*šakkê 'ereṣ*], "the heavens and the heavens of heavens and the abysses and the depths of the earth" (line 2), the author says "[It is] you, my God, who has placed a seal on them all, and there is no one who opens them." The sealing of the pit is mentioned in Rev 20:3. Similarly, *Pr. Man.* 3 refers to God ὁ κλείσας τὴν ἄβυσσον καὶ σφραγισάμενος τῷ φοβερῷ καὶ ἐνδόξῳ ὀνόματί σου, "who has closed the deep and sealed it with thy terrible and glorious name." Three common terms are found in Rev 20:3 and *Pr. Man.* 3: (1) ἄβυσσος, "deep, abyss," (2) κλείειν, "close," and (3) σφραγίζειν, "seal"; this suggests a traditional formulation of this protological scene (understood eschatologically by John). In a Gnostic variation on this conception, the *Hypostasis of the Archons* mentions that an "angel bound Yaldabaoth and cast him down into Tartaros below the abyss" (Evans et al., *Nag Hammadi*, 182). There are also many parallels from the world of Jewish magic, in which evil spirits of various types are "bound" (אסר *'āsar*) and "sealed" (חתם *ḥātam*) so that they cannot harm people. Text 27.2–3 (Isbell, *Incantation*, 79) reads, "Bound and sealed [אסירי וחתימי *'syry wḥtymy*] are the demon, the devil, the satan, the curse, and the e[vil] liliths." Note how in this magical text many names for evil beings are recited, in a way not dissimilar to the mention in v 2 of "the dragon (the ancient serpent who is the devil and Satan)." The combination of the terms "bind" (δεῖν) and "seal" (σφραγίζειν) occurs here in Rev 20:3 and also in Aramaic Jewish incantation texts. These paired terms indicate that the demon is conquered: 5.1 (Isbell, *Incantation*, 27), "Now you are conquered, you are bound, bound, you are bound and sealed [אסיריתון וחתימיתון *'syrytwn wḥtymytwn*]" (see 10.1, p. 40; 57.1, p. 129; see also Naveh-Shaked, *Amulets*, bowl 8; bowl 12a, line 1: "Bound and sealed are you [אסירת בחתימת אנתי *'syrt bḥtymt 'nty*] the evil Mevakkalta"). The world of the dead, of course, is frequently considered a prison (Pss 18:6; 116:3; Isa 24:22; 1 Pet 3:18).

3b ἵνα μὴ πλανήσῃ ἔτι τὰ ἔθνη ἄχρι τελεσθῇ τὰ χίλια ἔτη, "so that he would no longer cause the nations to go astray until the thousand years had been completed." The term πλανᾶν, "cause to go astray, deceive," and related words in the same semantic domain (such as πλάνη, "deception," πλάνος, "deceitful," ἀποπλανᾶν, "deceive," ἀπατᾶν, "deceive," ἀπάτη, "deception," ἐξαπατᾶν, "deceive," φρεναπατᾶν, "deceive," φρεναπάτης, "deceiver"; see Louw-Nida, § 31.8–13) frequently occur in eschatological contexts in both early Judaism and early Christianity (Matt 24:4; Mark 13:22; 2 Tim 3:13; 1 John 4:6). The role of deceiver is closely associated with Satan (Rev 12:9; 20:10) as well as with the eschatological antagonist (Rev 13:14; 19:20; 20:8; Matt 24:5 = Mark 13:6). According to 1QS 3:21, "because of the Angel of Darkness all the sons of righteousness go astray [תעות *tāʿût*]." The phenomenon of "going astray" (often connected with the metaphor of sheep) occurs because of external influence combined with ignorance (1QS 3:21; 1QH 2:14–16; 4:16–17) or as a consequence of internal desires and impulses (CD 3:4, 14). This is extremely important from a theological perspective, for the notion of deception presupposes that a person or group previously held the correct views or behaved in the appropriate manner *until they were tricked or deceived and in consequence led astray.* This purpose clause is an example of the author's insertion of an explanatory comment into a vision narration. Obviously the motivation of the angel who has descended from heaven cannot be presented in the vision itself.

The last phrase, "until the thousand years had been completed," refers to vv 7–10, in which the consequences of Satan's release are narrated. This phrase is repeated in v 5a, and the repetition is used to frame the insertion into the narrative found in v 4 (Bousset [1906] 438).

3c μετὰ ταῦτα δεῖ λυθῆναι αὐτὸν μικρὸν χρόνον, "After this he must be released for a short period." Victorinus understood this *breve tempus*, "short period," to be three years and six months (*Comm. in Apoc.* 20.3) since it was widely believed (based on Dan 7:25; 8:14; 9:27; 11:7, 11–12) that the period of the Antichrist's dominion would last three and one-half years (Justin *Dial.* 32; Irenaeus *Adv. haer.* 5.25.3; 5.30.4; Hippolytus *de Ant.* 61.9; *Asc. Isa.* 4:12; *Apoc. Elijah* 2:52; Victorinus *Comm. in Apoc.* 11.2).

4a καὶ εἶδον θρόνους καὶ ἐκάθισαν ἐπ᾽ αὐτοὺς καὶ κρίμα ἐδόθη αὐτοῖς, "Then I saw thrones, and people sat upon them, and they were given the authority to judge." καὶ εἶδον, "then I saw," introduces a new vision report; see *Comment* on 5:1. It is not evident whether this scene takes place in heaven or on earth (for neither is mentioned in vv 4–6), though it is usually assumed that the millennial reign of Christ occurs on the *earth*. That those who were beheaded for their testimony are *resurrected* and *reign* with Christ (v 4b–d) suggests that the scene occurs on earth.

The third-person plural aorist verb ἐκάθισαν, "they sat," is used here without a subject, so exactly *who* sat upon the thrones remains unspecified. This is an example of the impersonal use of the third-person plural (see M. Black, *Aramaic*, 126–28, with lists of occurrences in the Gospels; Mussies, *Morphology*, 231), which can be used in place of the passive voice and which occurs in Hebrew with some frequency (GKC § 144f). The impersonal third-person plural can also be used with third-person masculine plural verbs and masculine plural participles in Aramaic (see Dan 4:22; Rosenthal, *Aramaic*, § 181) and third-person plural verbs in Syriac (R. D. Wilson, *Elements of Syriac Grammar* [New York: Scribner, 1891] § 122); it can be translated "people sat." The same impersonal use of the third-person plural is reproduced literally in the LXX (Gen 29:2; 35:5; 41:14; 49:31; Esth 2:3). Further, the use of the finite verb ἐκάθισαν here, instead of an expected subordinate participial form, is an example of the author's tendency to favor parataxis over hypotaxis; see Ljungvik, *Syntax*, 80; BDR § 471.

At first sight, it is not at all clear how those seated on the thrones should be identified. Some have thought that these mysterious figures should be identified with the twenty-four enthroned elders of Rev 4–5, while most commentators understand them to represent the entire Christian church (cf. Matt 19:28; 1 Cor 6:2). This looks like the beginning of a judgment scene that is fragmentary, for the judgment itself does not occur (i.e., κρίμα, "judgment," has no real function in this textual unit). There is, to be sure, a judgment scene in the larger context (vv 11–15), but it is implied that God alone is the judge, though the scene is extremely abbreviated. Charles deals with the unintelligibility of the text by suggesting that it was originally a marginal gloss based on Dan 7 (2:182). The solution to identifying those seated on the thrones in v 4a is clear once vv 4–6 are recognized as a single (though extremely difficult) textual unit that focuses on the theme of "the first resurrection," mentioned near the conclusion in v 5b. The identity of those seated on the thrones is surely connected with the resurrected martyrs who are twice said to reign with Christ (the verbs ἐβασίλευσαν, "they reigned," and βασιλεύσουσιν, "they will reign," occur in vv 4 and 6); according to 3:21, the one who conquers will sit with the exalted Christ on his throne. The narrative order of this pericope is not in proper temporal sequence, for John first sees the thrones and those seated on them, i.e., the souls of the martyrs who had been beheaded and who had experienced the first resurrection, an instance of *hysteron-proteron* (Allo, 285). The disorganized character of this pericope results both from the author's tendency to use the literary device *hysteron-proteron*, i.e., reversing the logical order of narrative events (a device he frequently uses elsewhere; see Rev 3:3, 17; 5:5; 6:4; 10:4, 9; 20:4–5; 22:14), and from his tendency to describe *where* an individual or group of people sits before describing them (Rev 4:2, 4; 14:14; 20:11; see *Comment* on 4:2). Charles's view that the identity of those seated on the thrones *cannot* be the glorified martyrs (2:182) is simply wrong, for he did not recognize the peculiar stylistic feature just mentioned. The author has also amplified or interpolated a narrative by adding the commentary on the narrative found in vv 5–6. The entire section in vv 4–6 has characteristic features of the author, and Bousset sees this pericope as stemming from the final hand ([1906] 442).

The enigmatic reference to thrones is probably an allusion to Dan 7:9–10, "As I looked, thrones were placed [or 'a huge throne was placed'] and one that was ancient of days took his seat . . . the court sat in judgment and the books were opened." The plural term כרסון *korsāwān,* "thrones," may simply be for the purpose of emphasis, i.e., "a huge throne," since the multitude of heavenly beings *stands* in God's presence (7:10; see Goldingay, *Daniel,* 165). However, Dan 7:9 was probably construed as a reference to those associated with God in judgment, and it is this conception that is presupposed in Rev 20:4 (though not further developed here or elsewhere in Revelation). According to a tradition in *b. Ḥag.* 14a, in a debate between R. Akiba and R. Yosi the Galilean on the meaning of "thrones" in Dan 7:9a and "his throne" in Dan 7:9b, Akiba reportedly said, "One (throne) for Him, and one for David" (see Segal, *Two Powers,* 49). The judgment theme is also mentioned in Dan 7:22, "and judgment was given for the saints of the Most High, and the time came when the saints possessed the kingdom" (see Dan 7:26, "the court shall sit in judgment"). Here, as well, an actual scene of judgment is not depicted. Ps 122:4 mentions that "thrones for judgment were set, the thrones of the house of David," as if the king were not alone when rendering judicial decisions. In the ancient Near East, the gods were imagined as seated in groups to make decisions (*Enuma Elish* 1.33–34, 151–57; 2.126–27; 2.8–10).

Elsewhere in Revelation the twenty-four elders are depicted as sitting on thrones (Rev 4:4; 11:16), though there is no hint anywhere that they exercised a judicial function. According to 3:21, those who conquer are promised that they will share the throne of Christ. There are traditions in both early Judaism and early Christianity that the righteous will function as judges of the nations: 1QpHab 5:4 (tr. Vermes, *Dead Sea Scrolls*), "God will execute the judgment of the nations by the hand of his elect"; Wis 3:8, "They will govern other nations and rule over peoples, and the Lord will reign over them for ever" (see also Matt 19:28; 1 Cor 6:2; Rev 3:21). The scene presupposed by Rev 20:4, though not made explicit, must be that reflected in *Midr. Tanḥuma, Qĕdôšîm* 1 (tr. Winston, *Wisdom,* 128–29):

> In the future age, the Holy One, blessed be He, will be seated, while the angels will place crowns upon the exalted ones of Israel, and they will be seated, and the Holy One, blessed be He, will sit among them as Court President and they will judge the nations of the world.

It is possible that the major purpose of depicting the enthroned figures in Rev 20:4 is to emphasize their exaltation.

4b καὶ τὰς ψυχὰς τῶν πεπελεκισμένων διὰ τὴν μαρτυρίαν Ἰησοῦ καὶ διὰ τὸν λόγον τοῦ θεοῦ, "that is, the souls of those who had been beheaded because of their witness to Jesus and because of the word of God." Since there were several means of inflicting the death penalty under Roman law (see the discussion below), it seems extremely unlikely that all of the martyrs would have been executed by decapitation. The term "decapitated" (πεπελεκισμένων, a perfect passive substantival participle) is from the verb πελικίζειν, meaning "to behead with a πέλεκυς [axe]."

The Roman legal system knew two forms of the death penalty: the *summum supplicium* was a more vindictive form involving burning alive, crucifixion, and exposure to wild animals, while the *capite puniri* involved a simple death by decapitation (Garnsey, *Status*, 124; A. Berger, *Roman Law*, 633). Further, two types of *decollatio*, "decapitation," or *capitis amputatio*, "beheading," were distinguished: that by the sword and that by the axe (*Digest* 48.19.8.1–2; Mommsen, *Römisches Staatsrecht*, 916–25). Provincial governors had the right to execute by sword only, not by the axe, javelin, club, or noose (*Digest* 48.19.8.1). Capital penalties were graded in accordance with degrees of extremity; the most extreme penalty was condemnation to the gallows, then burning alive, then beheading (*Digest* 48.19.28).

Roman legal practice exhibited a dual penalty system, which meant that punishments were meted out not only in accordance with the nature of the offense but also in accordance with the *dignitas*, "status," of the offender (Garnsey, *Status*, 103–80; Gagé, *Les classes*, 283; Latte, *RESup* 7:1612; A. Berger, *Roman Law*, 633). Harsher punishments, including more violent forms of the death penalty, were inflicted on members of the lower classes (later designated *humiliores*), while the death penalty was rarely used for members of the upper classes (later called *honestiores*). For the upper classes various forms of exile or deportation were customarily used (see *Comment* on Rev 1:9). Decurions, for example, could not be executed (*Digest* 48.19.15; 48.19.27.1). Thus those who were beheaded with the axe referred to in v 4 in all probability belonged to the *honestiores* (the *honestiores/ humiliores* distinction became more common in the second and third centuries, but the distinction in status that these terms describe did exist in the first century A.D. [Garnsey, *Status*, 221–76]).

In the Acts of the Christian Martyrs, there are several instances of death by decapitation (*Acts Scill.* 14, 17; *Martyrdom of Potamiaena* 6; *Ep. Lugd.* 47 [all those thought to be Roman citizens were beheaded]; *Acts of Cyprian* 5.1; *Mart. of Felix* 31; *Mart. of Crispina* 4.1 [with sword]). In two instances Christian soldiers are beheaded with the sword in accordance with the military *ius gladii*, "law of the sword" (*Martyrdom of Maximilian* 3.1; *Martyrdom of Julian* 3.1). Yet the record indicates that most martyrs were executed through burning or exposure to wild animals, suggesting that they were executed as *humiliores*. It appears that the distinction between citizens of Rome and noncitizens and the distinction between *honestiores* and *humiliores* were not the same, for both citizens and noncitizens were found among either the *honestiores* or *humiliores* (Garnsey, *Status*, 266–68). Another example of a Christian martyred by decapitation comes from the relatively late legend (ca. A.D. 160) about Paul's death in the *Acts of Paul* 11.5 (Hennecke-Schneemelcher, *NTA* 2:267; see Eusebius *Hist. eccl.* 2.25.5; H. W. Tajra, *The Martyrdom of St. Paul*, WUNT 2/67 [Tübingen: Mohr-Siebeck, 1994] 23). In commenting on Pliny *Ep.* 10.96.3, Sherwin-White observes that Christians who do not sacrifice are led off to immediate execution by the sword, though the text says nothing of the manner of execution (*Letters*, 698).

A number of questions can be raised about the significance of this text in Rev

20:4 for understanding the social status of Christians in Asia Minor. Have a number of Christians already been beheaded, or is John thinking of events that will occur in the *future* but have not yet occurred? Since the only Christian martyr that John explicitly mentions is Antipas (2:13), had this Christian suffered decapitation? While no confident answers to these questions can be given, it appears probable that several Christians, including Antipas, had *already* been executed by decapitation and that more were expected to follow (see Rev 2:10). Further, since the author himself is Jewish (and has in all probability suffered exile rather than capital punishment; see *Comment* on 1:9), the problem of the social status of Jews in Asia Minor is a pertinent issue, along with questions of the relationship between Jews and Gentiles in the Christian communities to whom John writes. It was not until the reigns of Severus and Caracalla (between A.D. 198 and 211) that Jews were permitted to hold city offices (*Digest* 50.2.3.3). On some of these issues, see *Excursus 2B: Anatolian Jewish Communities and Synagogues.*

Several more observations can be made with regard to John's use of the verb πελεκίζειν, "to behead (with an axe)." First, the plural noun πελέκεις, "axes," is used to translate the Latin term *fasces,* i.e., a bundle of rods and axes carried by *lictores* or civil servants who accompanied Roman officials as bodyguards and who used the *fasces* to beat and to execute offenders (Mason, *Greek Terms,* 75; see Plutarch *Aem.* 4; Dionysius of Halicarnassus *Ant. Rom.* 2.29.1; 2.28.1; Plutarch *Publ.* 10). In one instance, a praetor is called a ἐξαπέλεκυς, i.e., one accompanied by *six lictores* with *fasces* (Polybius 3.106.6; Mason, *Greek Terms,* 43, 156, 158). The normal Greek term for *fasces,* however, was ῥαβδοῦχος (Kuebler, *RE* 13:507–18). In historical times, *lictores* acted as executioners only *outside* of Rome (Kuebler, *RE* 13:513). Josephus uses the verb πελεκίζειν to describe executions by Roman generals or officials (*Ant.* 14.39; 15.8–9; 20.117). Similarly, the noun πέλεκυς is used in connection with Roman executions in Palestine (Jos. *J.W.* 1.154, 185, 357; 2.242; *Ant.* 11.205; 14.73, 125, 140). Many other texts describe executions by *lictores* with axes (Livy 1.26; 26.15, 16; 28.29.10; 8.7.20; 8.32.10; 36.28.6; Cicero *Verr.* 3.67.156; 5.54.142; 5.45.118; Polybius 11.30.2). The procedure may be briefly summarized as follows (Mommsen, *Römisches Staatsrecht,* 915–16; Latte, *RESup* 7:1617): a beheading ordered by a Roman magistrate usually occurred outside, and a signal on a horn summoned the populace to witness the execution; the magistrate, wearing mourning apparel (i.e., a toga inside out), mounted the tribunal and gave a hand signal for the executioner to complete his task.

There are several verbal similarities between v 4 and 6:9, which suggests that the passages are doublets:

Rev 6:9	*Rev 20:4*
εἶδον	καὶ εἶδον . . .
I saw	Then I saw
ὑποκάτω τοῦ θυσιαστηρίου	
underneath the altar	
τὰς ψυχὰς	τὰς ψυχὰς
the souls	the souls

τῶν ἐσφαγμένων
of those slain

τῶν πεπελεκισμένων
of those beheaded

διὰ τὸν λόγον τοῦ θεοῦ
because of the word of God

διὰ τὴν μαρτυρίαν Ἰησοῦ
because of their witness to Jesus

καὶ διὰ τὴν μαρτυρίαν
and because of the witness

καὶ διὰ τὸν λόγον τοῦ θεοῦ
and because of the word of God

ἣν εἶχον
which they bore

The striking similarities between these passages are such that they should be considered variants of the same (literary) tradition: (1) both visions are introduced with the formulaic εἶδον, "I saw"; (2) the object of εἶδον in both instances is the souls of slain martyrs; (3) the reason they were executed is explained in two parallel causal clauses, both introduced with διά, "because"; (4) the reason is expressed in a parallel couplet, though the order of the lines is reversed; (5) the phrase διὰ τὸν λόγον τοῦ θεοῦ, "because of the word of God," occurs verbatim in both passages; and (6) the phrase διὰ τὴν μαρτυρίαν, "because of the witness," also occurs in both passages, though in 20:4 it is followed by the objective genitive "to Jesus." The source-critical problem is difficult to solve. The absence of the phrase "to Jesus" in 6:9 might suggest that the tradition was secondarily repeated in 20:4, though the fact that 6:9–11 seems awkward in its present location (see *Comment*) might suggest that it originally was at home in 20:4 and then secondarily replicated in an apocopated form in 6:9. A third possibility is that both 6:9 and 20:4 were derived from a common literary tradition, but 6:9 reflects a less Christianized formulation. No clear decision is possible. It is, in any event, rather significant theologically that the names of God and Jesus are linked several times in Revelation in couplets in which faithfulness is emphasized: one such pattern, the couplet "because of the word of God and [because of] the testimony [of Jesus]," occurs three times (1:9; 6:9; 20:4; cf. 12:11; see *Comment* on 1:9), while another, "those who keep the commands of God and maintain the witness to [or 'faithfulness to'] Jesus," occurs twice (12:17; 14:12; see *Comment* on 12:17).

4c   καὶ οἵτινες οὐ προσεκύνησαν τὸ θηρίον οὐδὲ τὴν εἰκόνα αὐτοῦ, καὶ οὐκ ἔλαβον τὸ χάραγμα ἐπὶ τὸ μέτωπον καὶ ἐπὶ τὴν χεῖρα αὐτῶν, "and who had not worshiped the beast or his image, and who had not received his brand on their foreheads or on their hands." This relative clause appears to be an analeptic interpolation (i.e., a "back reference"), which the author used to link this section with the same motifs found earlier in the narrative in Rev 13:4, 8, 12, 15; similar analeptic interpolations occur in 14:11 and 16:2 (see *Comments* on those passages). One problem is whether two types of martyrs are in view in v 4bc, as Bousset ([1906] 437) claims, or just a single group. It is more natural to construe the text as referring to a single group of martyrs, who had been executed for both positive reasons (v 4b: their obedience to the commands of God and their witness to Jesus) and negative reasons (v 4c: their refusal to worship the beast or its image and to receive its brand on their foreheads and right hands).

Charles finds the use of οἵτινες, "who," problematic and suggests that it was added by the final redactor of Revelation (2:183). In Hellenistic Greek, however, the classical distinction between ὅστις, meaning "whoever," and ὅς, "who [referring to a definite and particular entity]," became blurred, and they were used with no distinction in meaning (Mussies, *Morphology*, 174; Turner, *Syntax*, 47). In Revelation, ὅστις occurs nine times (1:7, 12; 2:24; 9:4; 11:8; 12:13; 17:12; 19:2; 20:4) in ways indistinguishable from the author's more frequent use of ὅς (sixty-nine times), except that ὅστις is always used in the masculine and feminine nominative forms (the rule in Hellenistic Greek).

4d καὶ ἔζησαν καὶ ἐβασίλευσαν μετὰ τοῦ Χριστοῦ χίλια ἔτη, "They came to life and reigned with the Messiah for a thousand years." This passage is chiefly famous in Christian tradition for mentioning the thousand-year reign of Christ. The period of a thousand years is used in Ps 90:4 (quoted in 2 Pet 3:8, "with the Lord one day is as a thousand years, and a thousand years as one day"), encouraging the figurative interpretation of a thousand years. The term "millennium," referring to this thousand-year reign, is based on the Latin words *mille*, "thousand," and *annus*, "year," derived from the reference in this verse to χίλια ἔτη, "thousand years."

There are a number of theological positions that are keyed to this passage: *amillennialism* holds that the thousand-year reign of Christ is a symbol for the period of the Christian church (Augustine; Roman Catholic; Reformed; Presbyterian); *postmillennialism* holds that the kingdom of Christ is a reality in the hearts of Christians and that the conversion of all nations will occur before the return of Christ, though the term "thousand years" refers to the quality of life and not to a literal length of time (Lutheran); *premillennialism* holds that the return of Christ will occur before the beginning of the millennium, which is understood as a literal period of a thousand years (Dispensationalism).

There have been two major ways of interpreting the thousand-year reign of Christ, the *literal* or *realistic* way and the *spiritual* way. The *literal* interpretation of the thousand-year millennium characterized many of the early fathers of the church (e.g., Justin, Irenaeus, Melito, Tertullian, Hippolytus, Methodius). Since the venue of the vision segment in 20:1–3 and the prophetic segment in 20:7–10 is apparently the *earth*, the author may be implying that the reign of the resurrected martyrs with Christ also occurs on the earth. This, however, is not made explicit. The verb ζᾶν, "to live," is used here with the meaning "raised [from the dead], resurrected" (see v 5; 3 Kgdms 17:23; Matt 9:18; Acts 9:41); in 2:8 ζᾶν is used of the resurrection of Christ (see *Comment* on that passage). According to 2 Macc 7:9, 14 (based on Dan 12:2), those who have died for the laws of the king of the universe will be raised from the dead. Kellermann argues that this reflects the belief that immediately after death the martyr is transferred to the heavenly realm in a transformed mode of existence. A similar conception is found in *Pistis Sophia* 2.99 (tr. Schmidt-MacDermot), which (because of its late date) may be dependent on Revelation:

> Nevertheless at the dissolution of the All, namely when the number of perfect souls is completed [cf. Rev 6:11], and the mystery, for the sake of which the All came into existence, is quite completed, I will spend 1000 years, according to years of light, as ruler (king) over all the emanations of light, and over the whole number of perfect souls which have received all the mysteries.

The second line of interpretation may be called the *spiritual* view, maintained by both Clement of Alexandria and Origen. Augustine popularized the view, now called amillennialism, that the reign of the saints with Christ was not a future expectation but rather the present situation of Christians who had been "raised with Christ" and "enthroned in heavenly places with Christ" (Col 3:1; Eph 2:6; Augustine *De civ. dei* 20.6–20). According to Wikenhauser (*RQ* 40 [1932] 21), the millennial reign of Christ is primarily a means of indicating that the martyrs are worthy of a special reward.

The term τοῦ Χριστοῦ, "the Anointed One," is used in Revelation three times in combination with Ἰησοῦς (1:1, 2, 5) and is used independently four times, always with the definite article (11:15; 12:10; 20:6), indicating that it means "the Anointed One," "the Messiah," rather than "Christ" (i.e., in the Second Edition of Revelation).

5a οἱ λοιποὶ τῶν νεκρῶν οὐκ ἔζησαν ἄχρι τελεσθῇ τὰ χίλια ἔτη, "The rest of the dead did not come to life again until the thousand years were completed." This parenthetical remark refers to the brief narrative in Rev 20:12–13, where the dead (apparently the wicked dead) have come back to life and stand before the great white throne, i.e., the second resurrection (although the author does not explicitly enumerate it). However, the use of the verb ζᾶν, "to live," rather than the noun ἀνάστασις, "resurrection," for the resurrection of Jesus (1:18; 2:8) increases the likelihood that the *resurrection* of the rest of the dead is in view here and that this event is enigmatically narrated in 20:12–13. However, since it appears that only *martyrs* experience the first resurrection (cf. 20:4; see Charles, 2:184–85), it is important to determine whether the resurrection referred to in 20:12–13 is a general resurrection that includes both the remaining righteous and the wicked or this resurrection involves the wicked alone (see *Comments* on 20:12–13). Since this clause interrupts the thought of the passage, it may have been an annotation added at a final stage of composition.

5b αὕτη ἡ ἀνάστασις ἡ πρώτη, "(This is the first resurrection." The term "resurrection" occurs just twice in Revelation, here and in v 6a; in both contiguous contexts it is designated ἡ ἀνάστασις ἡ πρώτη, "the first resurrection." The resurrection of Jesus is referred to by means of the verb ζᾶν, "to live" (1:18, "I was dead and now I am living [ζῶν] for ever"), rather than as an ἀνάστασις, "resurrection." A *second* resurrection, briefly narrated in 20:12–13, is not explicitly labeled such. Antithetically, though a *second* death is mentioned four times (2:11; 20:6, 14; 21:8), no mention is made of a *first* death. It is likely that the notion of the "first resurrection" was in fact modeled, as a kind of counterpoint, after the notion of the "second death." πρῶτος, "first," in Hellenistic Greek often has the sense of πρότερος, "former," in classical Greek, i.e., the first of two (BDF § 62; BDR § 62) or the first of a series involving time, space, or a set (Louw-Nida, § 60.46). There are some, however, who find the conception of *two* resurrections problematic and who argue that the eschatological conception of Revelation in fact includes only one resurrection (Kraft, 257–61; Prigent, 311–12). Ford (350) somewhat improbably suggests that the phrase "this is the first resurrection" really means "this is the first group to enjoy resurrection." However problematic the conceptions of two resurrections might be, it is difficult to avoid the conclusion that precisely such an innovation has been formulated by the author.

There is no trace of the conception of a first and a second resurrection in rabbinic texts (Str-B, 3:828). Among early Christian authors, Irenaeus (*Adv. haer.* 5.35.2–36), certainly aware of and dependent upon the resurrection schema in Revelation, mentions a resurrection of the just followed by a general resurrection. There is, however, a reference in John 5:28–29 that could be construed as referring to two resurrections: "All who in their graves will hear his voice and those who have done good will come out to the resurrection of life [εἰς ἀνάστασιν ζωῆς], and those who have done evil to the resurrection of judgment [εἰς ἀνάστασιν κρίσεως]." Of course, this refers to a single general resurrection that has two aspects, the fate of the righteous and the fate of the wicked. There are some references in early Jewish and early Christian literature to the resurrection of the just (2 Macc 7:9 [the righteous martyrs as in Rev 20:4]; *Pss. Sol.* 3:12; Luke 14:14; John 3:36; Rom 6:5; 8:11; 1 Thess 4:16; *Did.* 16:7 [which polemicizes against a general resurrection]; Ign. *Trall.* 9:2; Pol. *Phil.* 2:2; *3 Cor.* 3:24), while other texts refer to the resurrection of all the dead, both the righteous and the wicked (Dan 12:2; John 5:29; Acts 24:15; 2 Cor 5:10; *2 Apoc. Bar.* 50:2–4; 4 Ezra 7:32; *1 Enoch* 51:1–2; *m. 'Abot* 4.22); see Str-B, 4:1166–98; Schürer, *History* 2:539–44. In some texts that appear to refer to the resurrection of the righteous, it is not always clear whether the resurrection of the *body* or the immortality of the *soul* is intended (e.g., *Pss. Sol.* 3:12; Matt 25:46; Rom 2:5). Schweitzer argued that Jesus and the book of Daniel placed the resurrection at the *beginning* of the messianic kingdom, while apocalypses such as 4 Ezra and *2 Apocalypse of Baruch* placed it at the *end* (*Paul*, 88). Paul, he claimed, joined these two conceptions by supposing that there would be *two* resurrections (*Paul*, 93–97), and it is precisely this harmonizing conception that was later incorporated into Rev 20:4–6.

6a μακάριος καὶ ἅγιος ὁ ἔχων μέρος ἐν τῇ ἀναστάσει τῇ πρώτῃ, "How fortunate and holy is the one who has a share in the first resurrection!" This is the fifth of seven beatitudes in Revelation (1:3; 14:13; 16:15; 19:9; here; 22:7, 14; for a discussion of the form see *Form/Structure/Setting* on 1:1–3), though it is the only beatitude in Judeo-Christian Greek literature with a double predicate (i.e., "blessed and *holy*"). This suggests that the beatitude was created for this particular literary setting, a view confirmed by the unique reference here to the "first resurrection."

6b ἐπὶ τούτων ὁ δεύτερος θάνατος οὐκ ἔχει ἐξουσίαν, "The second death has no authority over these." The phrase ὁ δεύτερος θάνατος, "the second death," is mentioned four times in Revelation; here the adjective is in an ascriptive attributive position; elsewhere it is a restrictive attributive: ὁ θάνατος ὁ δεύτερος (2:11; 20:14; 21:8). The concept does not occur in the rest of the NT, in second-century Christian literature, or in pre-Christian Greek literature. The notion appears twice in nearly contemporary Greek literature. First, in Plutarch *De facie* 942F (who is very familiar with Egyptian myth and ritual; see J. Hani, *La religion Égyptienne dans la pensée de Plutarque* [Paris: Société d'Édition "Les belles lettres," 1976]), the phrase ὁ δεύτερος θάνατος occurs in a positive sense for the death of the ψυχή, "soul," on the moon (preceded by the death of the σῶμα, "body," on earth), which frees the νοῦς, "mind," to ascend to a blissful existence on the sun (see G. Soury, *La démonologie de Plutarque* [Paris: Société d'Édition "Les belles lettres," 1942] 196–203). Second, the conception of two deaths was promulgated by various philosophical traditions; see Macrobius in *Comm. in Somn. Scip.* 1.11.1 (Macrobius, *Commentary on the Dream of Scipio*, tr. W. H. Stahl [New York: Columbia UP, 1990]):

[T]he followers of Pythagoras and later those of Plato declared that there are two deaths, one of the soul, the other of the creature, affirming that the creature dies when the soul leaves the body, but that the soul itself dies when it leaves the single and individual source of its origin and is alloted to a mortal body.

This doctrine of the *commentatio mortis*, i.e., "the practice of dying," is also referred to in Macrobius *Comm. in Somn. Scip.* 1.11.12; 1.13.5–6; see P. W. van der Horst, "Macrobius and the New Testament," *NovT* 15 (1973) 220–32. For a more extensive discussion of the theme of *commentatio mortis* or μελέτη θανάτου, see D. E. Aune, "Human Nature and Ethics in Hellenistic Philosophical Traditions and Paul," in *Paul in His Hellenistic Context,* ed. T. Engberg-Pedersen (Minneapolis: Fortress, 1994) 305–12.

In Epictetus 1.5.4, it is said that while most people fear the deadening of the body, few care about "the deadening of the soul [τῆς ψυχῆς δ᾽ ἀπονεκρουμένης]." While the "deadening of the soul" might be construed as a sort of second death (the first being the death of the body), in actuality the "deadening of the soul" is a metaphor for the person who avoids acknowledging the truth. In *Odyssey* 12.22 the term δισθανής, "twice dead," is used to refer to Odysseus' trip to Hades (the so-called *Nekuia* in *Odyssey* 11) along with his future physical death. In Achilles Tatius 7.5.3, the hero Clitophon says of his love Leucippe (tr. J. J. Winkler, in *Collected Ancient Greek Novels,* ed. B. P. Reardon [Berkeley: University of California, 1989]), "But now you have died twice over [τέθνηκας θάνατον διπλοῦν]—soul and body [ψυχῆς καὶ σώματος] both are gone." In Lucian *De mort.* 7.2, Menippus, speaking to the ψυχή, "soul," of Tantalus in Hades, contests the notion of a second Hades or a second death (θάνατος ἐντεῦθεν). In *Bib. Ant.* 51:5 (which probably originated during the first century A.D. in Palestine), the first line of the following antithetical couplet might be construed to imply a second death:

> And when the wicked have died, then they will perish.
> And when the just go to sleep, then they will be freed.

The source of this notion in the Hellenistic world, even though the means of transmission is not known, is the Egyptian conception of the second death (Morenz, *Egyptian Religion,* 254; Bergman, *Ich bin Isis,* 57). The phrase "to die the second death" (*mt m whm*) occurs frequently in the Coffin Texts and the Book of the Dead (Zandee, *Death,* 186–88; Faulkner, *Coffin Texts* 1:88 [spell 83]; 1:134 [spell 156]; 1:267 [spell 203]; 2:69 [spell 423]; 2:76 [spell 438]; 2:88 [spell 458]; 2:308 [spell 787]), referring to the *total destruction* of the *ba,* "soul," after bodily death (Zandee, *Death,* 14; Morenz, *Egyptian Religion,* 207), a fate to be avoided at all costs. The ultimate Egyptian origin of this concept in Greek, Christian, and Jewish literature is supported by the pairing of the notions of the second death and the lake of fire in Rev 20:14 and 21:8, which also occurs in Egyptian texts (e.g., *Book of the Dead* 175.1, 15, 20; Budge, *Book of the Dead,* 184, 186–87) and once in the relatively late *Tg. Isa.* 65.6.

Philo (*Praem.* 70) speaks of two kinds of death, death itself and existence in a continued state of dying. The Hebrew expression for second death is שני מות *māwet šēnî,* first occurring in the ninth-century A.D. work *Pirqe R. El.* 34, while the Aramaic expression מיתא תניינא *mîtā' tinyaynā',* "second death," occurs only in the targums, from which six texts are discussed by McNamara (*Targum,* 118–24: *Tg. Jer.* 51:39; 51:57; *Tg. Deut.* 33:6; *Tg. Isa.* 22:14; 65:6, 15). *Tg. Jer.* 51:39 and 57 are phrased identically (tr. Hayward, *Targum of Jeremiah*): "and they shall die the second death, and shall not live for the world to come, says the Lord." McNamara, who does not mention the parallels in Lucian and in Egyptian sources, thinks that "the expression must have come from Judaism, unless it was coined by Christianity" (McNamara, *Targum*, 118), and Bogaert ("La 'seconde mort,'" 199–207) makes the same assumption. There are two possible meanings for "second death" in Judaism: (1) exclusion from the resurrection, i.e., remaining in the grave, or (2) assignment to eternal damnation (Str-B, 3:830). The Egyptian significance of second death and the lake of fire, i.e., complete and total destruction, cannot be meant in Revelation, as Rev 14:9–11 and 20:10 make clear. Rather, as in Philo and *Tg. Isa.* 65:6, *eternal torment* is signified, so that what we have is an adaptation of Egyptian underworld mythology to Judeo-Christian tradition.

On the general links between Egyptian religion and Asia Minor, see R. Salditt-Trappmann, *Tempel der ägyptischen Götter in Griechenland und an der Westküste Kleinasiens*, EPRO 15 (Leiden: Brill, 1970), and G. Höbl, *Zeugnisse ägyptischer Religionsvorstellungen für Ephesus*, EPRO 73 (Leiden: Brill, 1978).

6c ἀλλ' ἔσονται ἱερεῖς τοῦ θεοῦ καὶ τοῦ Χριστοῦ καὶ βασιλεύσουσιν μετ' αὐτοῦ τὰ χίλια ἔτη, "but they will be priests to God and the Messiah, and they will reign with him for a thousand years.)" There is a likely reference here to Exod 19:6 (see *Comments* on 1:6; 5:10; cf. Fekkes, *Isaiah*, 113–16) and a possible reference to Isa 61:6, "But you shall be called the priests of the Lord, the ministers of the holy one" (argued by Schüssler Fiorenza, *Priester für Gott*, 336–38, and Elliott, *Elect*, 116). ἱερεύς, "priest," occurs three times in Revelation (1:6; 5:10; 20:6), always (with the possible exception of 20:6) in the context of an allusion to Exod 19:6; see *Comment* on 1:6. The phrase "they will be priests to God and Christ" appears to have been derived from parallel statements in 1:6 and 5:10, except here *Christ* is mentioned in addition to God, suggesting that it at least is a gloss, though it is probable that 20:4–6 is part of the last revision of Revelation. The idea that believers will *reign* (βασιλεύειν), however, is quite different from the notion that they will constitute a βασιλεία, "kingdom." The reigning of believers is also mentioned in 5:10; 20:4; 22:5. Only in 20:4, 6 is the reigning restricted to a period of time (one thousand years) and to a specific group, the resurrected martyrs (elsewhere in the NT only in 1 Cor 4:8, where there is an extremely heavy use of irony, are believers said to reign).

7 καὶ ὅταν τελεσθῇ τὰ χίλια ἔτη λυθήσεται ὁ σατανᾶς ἐκ τῆς φυλακῆς αὐτοῦ, "When the thousand years are completed, Satan will be released from his prison." The similarity of this clause to that found in v 5a suggests that it is a "framing repetition" that functions to make a transition to the narrative after the interpolation in vv 5b–6. E. Schüssler Fiorenza correctly characterizes vv 4–6 as an "interlude" (*Priester für Gott*, 295–96). The future passive verb λυθήσεται, "will be released," can be construed as a passive of divine activity and therefore can be understood to mean "God will release Satan from his prison." According to a widespread ancient tradition, demons released from the place of their confinement are much more dangerous than they were before (Luke 11:24–26; Audollent, *Defixionum Tabellae*, no. 25; Minucius Felix *Oct.* 26; Lactantius *Div. Inst.* 2.16.4; see Eitrem, *Demonology*, 16–17).

8a καὶ ἐξελεύσεται πλανῆσαι τὰ ἔθνη τὰ ἐν ταῖς τέσσαρσιν γωνίαις τῆς γῆς, τὸν Γὼγ καὶ Μαγώγ, "and he will go out to deceive the nations that are at the four corners of the earth, Gog and Magog." The previous destruction of the hostile nations in Rev 19:11–21 has apparently been forgotten. In Ezekiel 38–39, it is not explicitly Satan who deceives Gog; rather the conflict is an evil scheme that God claims originated with Gog himself (Ezek 38:10). The phrase "Gog and Magog" is in apposition to "the nations" and may be a gloss. It is clearly an allusion to Ezek 38–39, where it is predicted that a hostile nation from the north (Ezek 38:6, 15; 39:2) will attack the peaceful and unsuspecting inhabitants of Palestine "in the latter days" (38:8–16), but the nation will be completely defeated (38:17–23; 39:1–6). In Jeremiah (upon whom Ezekiel is probably dependent; see Zimmerli, *Ezekiel* 2:299–300), repeated mention is made of an enemy from the north (Jer 1:13–15; 3:18; 4:6; 6:1, 22). Jer 6:22 predicts the coming of a hostile nation "from the farthest parts of the earth [LXX ἀπ' ἐσχάτου τῆς γῆς]." In the OT and early Jewish tradition, Gog and Magog are understood in a bewildering variety of ways. In Ezekiel, Gog is the name of the prince of Meshech and Tubal (Ezek 38:2–3; 39:1–16), whose land was called Magog; the names Meshech and Tubal are also found associated with Magog in the table of nations in Gen 10:2 (see 1 Chr 1:5; *Jub.* 7:19). Elsewhere in the OT, Gog is a personal name (1 Chr 5:4), while Magog refers to the eponymous ancestor of a people (Gen 10:2; 1 Chr 1:5). In *Jub.* 8:25 Gog is used in a strictly geographical sense. In Rev 20:8 Gog and Magog serve as symbols for the hostile nations who will make war on God and his people. In *Sib. Or.* 3.319 Gog and Magog are names for the Ethiopians or Nubians who accompanied Antiochus IV when he captured the temple in Jerusalem. In Josephus *Ant.* 1.123 Magog is regarded as a name for the Scythians (see Herodotus 1.103, 107; 4.1). In early Jewish literature, Gog and Magog are leaders of the gentile nations who will attack Israel in the eschaton (*3 Enoch* 45:5; *Sipre Deut.* 343; *b. 'Abod. Zar.* 3b; *b. Ber.* 7b); for an overview of rabbinic views of Gog and Magog, see Str-B, 3:831–40; Kuhn, *TDNT* 1:789–91. In *Tg. Neof.* Num 11:26 (Macho, *Neophyti* 4:540; McNamara-Clarke, *Tg. Neof. Num.,* 74; a parallel version occurs in M. L. Klein, *Fragment-Targums* 2:66, 152), there is a prophecy by Eldad and Medad about the future messianic war:

> And both of them prophesied together, saying: At the very end of the days Gog and Magog ascend on Jerusalem and they fall at the hand of King Messiah, and for seven years the children of Israel shall kindle fires from their implements of war: and the carpenter(s) will not have to go out.

An expanded form of this prophecy is found in *Tg. Ps.-J.* Num 11:26 (Clarke, *Tg. Ps.-J. Num.,* 220–21; K. Berger, *HCNT,* no. 969):

> Behold a king will come forth from the land of Magog at the end of the days. He will assemble kings who wear crowns, and commanders that bear armor, and all nations will follow him. They will instigate a battle in the land of Israel against the children of the dispersion, but the Lord will be ready to burn the breath of life out of them with the flame of fire that comes forth from beside the throne of his glory. Their dead bodies will fall on the mountains of the land of Israel, and the wild animals of the field and birds of the sky will come and devour their remains. Afterwards all the dead of Israel will be raised and enjoy the good things that have been secretly preserved for them since the beginning, and they will receive the reward for their works.

The eschatological scenario in Rev 20, in contrast to the similar scenario in the *Targum Neofiti* quoted above, makes no mention of the Messiah.

The judgment of Gog and Magog is referred to cryptically as lasting just twelve months in *m. ʿEd.* 2:10, and judgment is also predicted for Gog and Magog in *Sib. Or.* 3.512. In rabbinic sources the eschatological war is called "the war of Gog and Magog" (*b. Sanh.* 97b; Str-B, 4:831–40). In *Tg. Ezek.* 39:16, Gog is equated with Rome: "There, too, shall be flung the slain of Rome, the city of many boisterous crowds" (Levey, *Tg. Ezek.*, 108); see also *Pesiq. R.* 17:8; S. H. Levey, *The Messiah*, 86; P. Churgin, *Targum Jonathan to the Prophets* (New Haven: Yale UP, 1907) 26.

The motif of hostile nations at the four corners of the earth, i.e., the nations of the world, is found in OT prophecy. The attack of the Gentiles on Israel and Jerusalem was also a stock motif in the OT (Isa 5:26; Jer 25:32; 50:41; Zech 14:2–5; see *Comment* on 16:14). 4 Ezra 13:5 speaks of gathering an innumerable multitude "from the four winds of heaven" to fight the man from the sea (see 4 Ezra 13:33–34). Rissi's argument that the phrase "the four corners of the earth" indicates the location of entrances to the underworld from which a demonic army is summoned is forced (*Future*, 35–36).

The identification of "the nations, Gog and Magog" in the view of the author-editor of Revelation is problematic. It is difficult to reconcile the destruction inflicted on the nations described in 19:17–21 with the subsequent existence of nations at the four corners of the earth mentioned in 20:7–10, following the millennial reign of Christ referred to in 20:4–6 (Beckwith, 745). Interpreters have understood 20:7–10 in several different ways: (1) Gog and Magog are a *demonic* army (Wikenhauser, 75–80; Schüssler Fiorenza, *Priester für Gott*, 311–12; Lohse, 105; Rissi, *Future*, 34–35; Roloff [ET] 228; Kraft, 259; Sweet, 290–91). (2) Gog and Magog represent the rest of the dead who are resurrected and judged (Mealy, *Thousand Years*, 140–42). (3) The destruction narrated in 19:17–21 does not include *all* the inhabitants of the earth, so the forces led by Gog and Magog are the *rest* (Beasley-Murray, 297). (4) The use of mythical metaphoric language in 20:7–10 means that one need not necessarily follow the logic of the narrative (Roloff [ET] 228).

8b συναγαγεῖν αὐτοὺς εἰς τὸν πόλεμον, "to assemble them for battle." This phrase occurs verbatim in 16:14. Satan, not an earthly king, is presented as the one who gathers the nations for battle against the people of God (as in 16:12–16). The motif of the gathering of the hostile nations for an attack on Israel, and particularly on Jerusalem, is a stock motif in Jewish apocalyptic, though it is used in a variety of ways (Joel 3:2; Zech 12:1–9; 14:2; 4 Ezra 13:5, 34–35; *1 Enoch* 56:7; 90:13–19; *Sib. Or.* 3.663–68; 1QM 1:10–11; 15:2–3; Lactantius 7.17.10–11; see *Comment* on 16:14). However, in Ezek 38:14–17 and *Jub.* 23:22–25 it is God who motivates the gathering and advance of Israel's enemies. In *1 Enoch* 56:5–8 a group of angels incites the Parthians and Medes to attack Israel. In 1QM the force opposed to the sons of light is sometimes called חיל בליעל ḥêl bĕliyyaʿal, the "army of Belial" (1QM 1:1, 13). In Lactantius 7.17.10–11 a wicked king gathers together forces hostile to the people of God. This motif occurs several times in Revelation (16:14, 16; 19:17, 19; 20:8; see *Comments* on 16:14, 16).

8c ὧν ὁ ἀριθμὸς αὐτῶν ὡς ἡ ἄμμος τῆς θαλάσσης, "Their number is like the sand of the sea." The sand of the sea is used in biblical tradition as a metaphor for great abundance (Gen 41:49; Job 29:18; Ps 139:18; Jer 15:8; Hab 1:9; *Pr. Man.* 1:9; *Jos. As.* 1:2; *Gk. Apoc. Ezra* 2:32; 3:2) and is frequently used, as here, for an enormous army (Josh 11:4; Judg 7:12; 1 Sam 13:5; 1 Macc 11:1). On the analogous comparison of an invading army with a plague of locusts, see *Comment* on 9:7. In biblical tradition the simile "like the sand of the sea" is particularly associated with God's promise to Abraham that his descendants would be innumerable, like the sand of the sea and the stars of the heaven (Gen 22:17; 32:12; Pr Azar 1:13; Rom 9:27; *Gk. Apoc. Ezra* 3:10; *T. Abr.* [Rec. A] 1:5; 4:11; 8:5). The "sand of the sea" is used as a metaphor for the population of Israelites (2 Sam 17:11; 1 Kgs 4:20; Isa 10:22; 48:19; Hos 1:10) or the descendants of David (Jer 33:22). The motif of an *innumerable* hostile army that attacks Jerusalem or Israel in the eschaton, based on the Zion traditions reflected in Pss 46, 48, 76 and the Gog and Magog oracle in Ezek 38–39, is also found in 4 Ezra 13:5, which refers to "an innumerable multitude of men [*multitudo hominum*]" who were "gathered together from the four winds of heaven" to fight the man from the sea (the phrase "innumerable multitude" is repeated in v 34a: *multitudo innumerabilis*). Ezek 38:15 speaks of "you and many peoples with you . . . a great host, a mighty army."

9a καὶ ἀνέβησαν ἐπὶ τὸ πλάτος τῆς γῆς καὶ ἐκύκλευσαν τὴν παρεμβολὴν τῶν ἁγίων καὶ τὴν πόλιν τὴν ἠγαπημένην, "They marched up across the breadth of the earth and surrounded the encampment of the people of God, the beloved city." The verb ἀναβαίνειν, "to go up," is used here in three overlapping senses: (1) In Israelite and early Jewish idiom, people always went *up* (never *down*) to Jerusalem (Ezra 1:3; Ps 122:4; Isa 2:3; Jer 31:6; Obad 1:21; Mic 4:2). This reflects the topographical reality that one must travel along a gradient when going to or from Jerusalem, though the steepness of this gradient is exaggerated in rabbinic sources (Str-B, 2:239–40). The elevation of Jerusalem ranges between 2,100 and 2,526 feet above sea level, though many of the surrounding hills are even higher (e.g., Mount Scopus is 2,690 feet, and the Mount of Olives is 2,684 feet). The verb ἀναβαίνειν, "to go up, ascend," is frequently used if the traveler's goal is Jerusalem (or the temple), which must be the meaning here of the phrase "beloved city" (1 Esdr 2:5; 4:63; 1 Macc 6:48; 13:2; Mark 10:32 [= Matt 20:17, 18; Luke 18:31]; Luke 2:4, 42; 19:28; John 2:13; 5:1; 11:55; Acts 11:2; 15:2; 21:12, 15; 24:11; 25:1, 9; Gal 2:1). Other verbs are used the same way (e.g., ἀνέρχεσθαι, Gal 1:17–18). Perhaps the notion of Jerusalem as the "navel of the world" (Ezek 38:12; Jos. *J.W.* 3.52; *Jub.* 8:19) has influenced this language of "going up" to Jerusalem (Joachim Jeremias, *Jerusalem*, 51–52). One could, by contrast, καταβαίνειν, "go down," to Capernaum (John 2:12), to Egypt (Acts 7:15), to Attalia (Acts 14:25), to Troas (Acts 16:8), to Antioch (Acts 18:22), or to Caesarea (Acts 25:6). When returning from Jerusalem, one must καταβαίνειν, "come down" (Mark 3:22; Luke 2:51; 10:30; Acts 8:26; 25:7).

(2) This idiom is also used when approaching the land of Israel from outside (Str-B, 3:840); cf. the modern Hebrew term *ʿăliyyâ*, "ascent," used for a trip to Israel.

(3) This idiom can be used in the context of the attack of the nations against Jerusalem in the final eschatological war (*1 Enoch* 56:6; Ethiopic ya ʿarregu, "they shall go up"); Eichhorn (2:294) makes the important point that the verb עלה *ʿālâ*, "to go up," is used in the OT in a technical military sense (see Judg 12:3; 1 Sam 7:7; 2 Sam 11:1; 1 Kgs 20:1; Isa 36:10). The theme of a repulsed enemy attack upon Jerusalem is part of a Zion theology that surfaces frequently in the OT (Pss 46, 48, 76; Isa 17, 29; Joel 2, 4[MT 3]; Zech 12, 14). In the Gog and Magog oracle in Ezek 38–39, the phrase "the center of the earth" (Ezek 38:12) may refer to Jerusalem. The motif of battle at the sacred mountain occurs both in Canaanite texts (at Mount Zaphon) and in the OT and early Jewish texts (at Mount Zion and Mount Hermon); see H.-J. Kraus, *Worship*, 201–3; id., *Psalms*, 78–84; Clifford, *Cosmic*

Mountain, 185–89. The term κυκλεύειν, "to surround," reflects the central strategy of ancient warfare, to surround a city and besiege it until it surrendered (2 Kgs 6:14; Isa 29:3; 36:1–3; Jdt 7:19–20; 1 Macc 15:14; Luke 19:43; 21:20). The story of the siege of Jerusalem by Sennacherib of Assyria during the reign of Hezekiah (2 Kgs 18:13–19:37; Isa 36–37) appears to have become a model in later apocalyptic literature for the eschatological defeat of hostile nations intent on destroying Jerusalem. The Assyrians attempted to force the surrender of cities by starvation or conquer them through the use of battering rams, scaling ladders, and undermining of the walls. The attempt of kings with their armies to surround and conquer Jerusalem and the temple is a motif also found with some frequency in the OT, early Jewish literature, and early Christian literature (Joel 2:1–11; Ps 2:1–3; Ezek 38–39; *Sib. Or.* 3.657–68; *1 Enoch* 56:5–8; 4 Ezra 13:5–11, 33–38; Luke 19:43–44; 21:20). Jesus' prediction in Luke 21:20 of the time just before the end when Jerusalem will be surrounded by army camps is usually thought to be a historicizing interpretation of Mark 13:14 in light of the events of A.D. 68–70, the Roman siege and conquest of Jerusalem (Fitzmyer, *Luke* 2:1343; see Jos. *J.W.* 5.47–97; 6.93, 149–56).

The phrase τὸ πλάτος τῆς γῆς, "the breadth of the earth," is a problematic phrase found three times in the LXX (Hab 1:6 [ἐπὶ τὰ πλάτη τῆς γῆς; *var. lect.* A: τὸ πλάτος τῆς γῆς]; Dan 12:2; Sir 1:3), but the phrase as used here in v 9 is not demonstrably an allusion to any of these passages. It is often suggested that the author really means ὁ ὀμφαλὸς τῆς γῆς, "the center of the earth," alluding to the enemy attack on Jerusalem narrated in Ezek 38:11–12 (Loisy, 356; Kraft, 259; Rissi, *Future*, 35). Since the nations hostile to God are assembled from the four corners of the earth, they must march a very long distance to besiege the camp of the saints. For this reason the phrase ἐπὶ τὸ πλάτος τῆς γῆς very probably means "across the breadth of the earth," emphasizing the distance that must be traveled. There is also a close parallel in *1 Enoch* 56:6 (tr. Knibb, *Enoch*), "And they [the Parthians and Medes] will go up and trample upon the land of my chosen ones, and the land of my chosen ones will become before them a tramping-ground and a beaten track."

To what does the phrase ἡ παρεμβολὴ τῶν ἁγίων, "the army [or 'encampment'] of the holy ones," refer? Several possibilities have been suggested: (1) the heavenly city (Charles, 2:190); (2) the encampment of the people of God, which is identical to "the beloved city" (Swete, 269; Bousset [1906] 739; Beckwith, 746; Loisy, 356). According to 4Q394–398 = 4QMMT (see Eisenman-Wise, *Scrolls*, 192–96), part 2, lines 34–35, "Jerusalem is the camp [מחנה היא (ם) ירושלי(ו) *(w)îrûšālayi(m) maḥăneh hîʾ*]," and part 2, line 63, "Jerusalem is the holy camp [ירושלים היאה מחנה הקדש *yĕrûšālayim hîʾh maḥăneh haqqādāš*]"; (3) the encampment of the people of God stationed outside the city in expectation of the impending attack (Zahn, 2:596–97); (4) the martyrs with Christ in Jerusalem (Rev 14:1–5; see Rist, "Revelation," 522); or (5) an army of angels (perhaps the force mentioned in 19:14) now bivouacked in the vicinity of Jerusalem for the protection of the city (Eichhorn, 2:294, translates the phrase ἡ παρεμβολὴ τῶν ἁγίων as *castra angelorum*, "camp of angels"), a conception similar to the cavalry of Yahweh that protects Elisha in 2 Kgs 6:17. In this connection it is worth noting that in 1QM 7:6 and 19:1, the holy angels are said to be with the army of the sons of light (cf. 1QM 1:10; 4QM^b frag. 1, line 1), though in Revelation there is never a hint that human beings and angels fight together in any eschatological battle.

The term ἡ παρεμβολή is a noun related to the verb παρεμβάλλειν, "to surround," and has three related meanings: (1) "army barracks, fortified camp," a technical military term (Louw-Nida, § 7.22; Acts 21:34, 37; 22:24; 23:10, 16, 32; Ezekiel *Exogoge* 215, 223; on fortified army camps in the Greek world, see W. K. Pritchett, *The Greek State at War* [Berkeley: University of California Press, 1974] 2:132–46; the Roman camp is described at length in Polybius 6.27–42; see comments by Walbank, *Polybius* 1:709–23); (2) "camp, encampment," in the sense of a temporary population center where people live in tents (Louw-Nida, § 1.94; Heb 13:11, 13 [here "outside the camp" is a phrase found in Exod 29:14]; Lev 9:11; 16:17), possibly an allusion to the Israelites before they entered the land of Canaan; or (3) "army, armed forces," found with this meaning in both the singular (1 Macc 3:15, 23, 27; 4:34; 5:28; 10:49; *1 Enoch* 1:4; *T. Sim.* 5:5; Ezekiel *Exogoge* 81) and the plural (Heb 11:34; *T. Levi* 3:3). παρεμβολή (a term frequently used by Polybius and a synonym of στρατοπεδεία and στρατόπεδον, "encampment," the latter occurring in Luke 21:20) is used in the LXX to translate the Hebrew term מחנה *maḥăneh*, "camp," about 180 times and is frequently used for the camp of Israel. The term מחנה *maḥăneh* also occurs some fourteen times in two documents from Qumran, CD and 1QM.

The phrase שלום אל במחני קדושיו *šĕlôm ʾēl bĕmaḥănê qĕdôšayw*, "peace of God in the camps of his saints" (1QM 3:5), an inscription to be written on the camp trumpets just before the eschatological war, is the plural Hebrew equivalent of the singular ἡ παρεμβολὴ τῶν ἁγίων and suggests that it originated in early Judaism within the context of speculation about the eschatological war (Fensham, *RevQ* 4 [1964] 562). Here, however, it is not clear whether קדושים *qĕdôšîm* refers to angels or God's people; perhaps it includes both (Lambgerits, *ETL* 46 [1970] 24–39). The phrase צבא קדושיכה *sĕbāʾ qĕdôšeykâ*, "the host of your holy ones" (1QH 10:35), here referring to angelic beings, is another close equivalent. There are several contexts in which the term παρεμβολή is clearly used in eschatological contexts, such as in *1 Enoch* 1:4 [tr. Knibb, *Enoch*], "and the Eternal God will tread from there upon Mount Sinai, and he will appear with his host [ἐκ τῆς παρεμβολῆς αὐτοῦ], and will appear in the strength of his power from heaven." In *T. Levi* 3:3, the phrase "the powers of the hosts" (αἱ δυνάμεις τῶν παρεμβολῶν) refers to "hosts" or "armies" of angels. Here it should be borne in mind that οἱ ἅγιοι, "holy ones," can refer to angels; in the OT קדושים *qĕdôšîm*, "holy ones," is frequently used of angels (Ps 89:6; Job 5:1; 15:15; Zech 14:5; Dan 4:14; 7:27; 8:13; see also Tob 12:15; *T. Levi* 3:3; *Pss. Sol.* 17:49; Job 31:14). On the term οἱ ἅγιοι, "holy ones," as Christians, see *Comment* on 5:8. According to 1QM 3:4, there will be four camps of Israel, each made up of three tribes. 1QM indicates that the members of the sect were expected to adhere rigorously to certain rules of purity in preparation for the eschatological battle (Fensham, *RevQ* 4 [1964] 559). The phrase ἡ παρεμβολὴ τῶν ἁγίων, "the army of the saints," implies that "the saints" form an army, though unlike 1QM, the text is silent about their part in battle. Their role is completely passive, as it is in Lactantius *Div. Inst.* 7.17.10–11.

Another interpretive problem is whether the phrase τὴν πόλιν τὴν ἠγαπημένην, "the beloved city," refers to the *earthly* or the *heavenly* Jerusalem. The phrase πόλις ἠγαπημένη, "beloved city," occurs in Sir 24:11, where it refers to Jerusalem, though similar ideas are expressed in Pss 78:68 ("Mount Zion which he loves"), 87:2 (LXX 86:2) ("the Lord loves the gates of Zion"), and Jer 11:15; 12:7, where Jerusalem is referred to as "my beloved" (Zion is often used in the OT as an equivalent of Jerusalem or of the people of Jerusalem). Since the heavenly Jerusalem does not make its appearance until 21:10 (aside from 3:12), it would appear that "the beloved city" cannot be the New Jerusalem but must be the earthly Jerusalem. However, Charles argued that the heavenly Jerusalem descends *before* the destruction of heavens and earth described in 20:11–15, maintaining that the text of Revelation was disarranged after 20:3. He proposed to place 21:9–22:2, 14–15, 17 immediately after 20:3 (2:150–51). Charles maintained that Jerusalem can hardly be designated as "Sodom and Egypt" in 11:8 and then be called "the beloved city" in 20:9 (2:150). Caird dismisses this radical textual surgery by simply claiming that wherever the people of God are, there the city of God is (257). According to 17:14 (a gloss possibly based on this passage; see *Comment* on 17:14), the ten allied kings waged war with the Lamb and were conquered, while those with the Lamb are described as "called and chosen and faithful."

9b καὶ κατέβη πῦρ ἐκ τοῦ οὐρανοῦ καὶ κατέφαγεν αὐτούς, "Then fire came down from heaven and devoured them." This passage combines allusions to the Gog and Magog oracle in Ezek 38–39, where God judges Gog by sending torrential rains, hailstones, fire, and brimstone down upon Gog and his host (Ezek 38:22; 39:6), with the punitive miracles performed twice by Elijah in which fire fell from heaven and consumed the troops sent by Ahaziah (2 Kgs 1:9–12; here the phrase "fire came down from heaven and consumed him and his fifty" occurs twice). These phrases are verbally similar to Rev 20:9 in the LXX 4 Kgdms 1:10, 12, 14, καὶ κατέβη πῦρ ἐκ τοῦ οὐρανοῦ καὶ κατέφαγεν αὐτὸν καὶ τοὺς πεντήκοντα αὐτοῦ, "then fire came down from heaven and devoured him and his fifty." The traditional character of this eschatological scene is suggested by Zeph 3:8 (see Zeph 1:18), where Yahweh decides to gather the nations together on the day of judgment and consume them and the earth with fire. Allusions to 2 Kgs 1:10, 12 occur elsewhere in Jewish and Christian literature (*T. Abr.* [Rec. A] 1:11; [Rec. B] 12:3–4; *Jos. As.* 25:6; *Vit. Proph.* 21.12; Sir 48:3; Luke 9:54). The same motif is also found in Job 1:16, where it says that "The fire of God fell from heaven and burned up the sheep and the servants, and consumed them" (alluded to in a fragment of the lost work by Aristeas, *Concerning the Jews*, quoted in Eusebius *Praep. evang.* 9.25.431a; see Holladay, *FHJA* 1:261–75). According to Luke 12:49, Jesus claimed that he came "to cast fire upon the earth," a metaphor for judgment (for other versions of this saying, see *Gos. Thom.* 10, 16, and Stroker, *Extracanonical*, 183). The author of Revelation links this allusion to the punitive miracle of Elijah with Ezek 39:6, "I will send fire on Magog [see Rev 20:8 where Gog and Magog are named] and on those who dwell securely in the coastlands; and they shall know that I am the Lord." According to Ezek 38:22, fire and brimstone are rained on Gog and Magog, perhaps an allusion to the brimstone and fire that rained upon Sodom according to Gen 19:24 (see also *Comment* on v 8a and the quotation from *Tg. Ps.-J.* on Num 11:26, which mentions fire from the throne of God destroying Gog and Magog). Fire, hail, and blood are said to rain upon the earth in Rev 8:7 as the result of the sounding of the first trumpet. In 4 Ezra 13:8–11 an innumerable hostile force has come to wage war with the man from the sea, who burns them up with a stream of fire from his mouth (see *Comment* on Rev 11:5); this vision is interpreted allegorically in 4 Ezra 13:21–56, where fire is said to represent the Law. In several passages in the *Sibylline Oracles*, a cataract of fire from heaven destroys the enemies of God (*Sib. Or.* 2.196–205; 3.84–87, 543; 4.175–78; 5.274, 377–78; 7.119–25; 8.225–26), e.g., *Sib Or.* 3.53–54 (tr. Collins, *OTP* 1:363), "All men will perish in their own dwellings / when the fiery cataract flows from heaven." According to Justin *Apol.* 1.20, "both Sybil and

Hystaspes declared that there will be a destruction of corruptible things by fire" (*Oracles of Hystaspes,* frag. 6; Bidez-Cumont, *Mages* 2:361); that coheres with the Stoic view of ἐκπύρωσις, "[cosmic] conflagration," as Justin indicates (a view of Heraclitus, according to Diogenes Laertius 9.8, and a part of early Stoic doctrine; see Arnim, *SVF,* vol. 1, §§ 97–114; vol. 2, §§ 596–632). According to Commodian (*Carmen* 995–96, 1008–41; *Instr.* 45), God will judge the world with fire, which will destroy only the sinners and not the righteous.

10a καὶ ὁ διάβολος ὁ πλανῶν αὐτοὺς ἐβλήθη εἰς τὴν λίμνην τοῦ πυρὸς καὶ θείου ὅπου καὶ τὸ θηρίον καὶ ὁ ψευδοπροφήτης, "And the devil who deceived them was cast down into the lake of fire and brimstone where the beast and the false prophet were." According to Wellhausen (*Analyse,* 32), this is an interpolation by the apocalyptist into the Jewish source he was using. This event alludes to 19:20, where the beast and the false prophet were captured and thrown into the lake of fire. This may also be an allusion to the Gog and Magog oracle in Ezek 38–39, where Gog is punished by torrential rains, hailstones, fire, and brimstone (Ezek 38:22). On the false prophet, see *Comment* on 16:13.

10b καὶ βασανισθήσονται ἡμέρας καὶ νυκτὸς εἰς τοὺς αἰῶνας τῶν αἰώνων, "so that they were tormented day and night for ever." The eternal torment of the devil, the beast, and the false prophet parallels the eternal torment of those who had worshiped the beast (14:11). The terms "day and night" form a hendiadys meaning a twenty-four-hour day, and by extension "without ceasing" or "without interruption"; see *Comment* on 4:8.

11a καὶ εἶδον θρόνον μέγαν λευκὸν καὶ τὸν καθήμενον ἐπ᾽ αὐτόν, "Then I saw a great white throne and the One seated on it." καὶ εἶδον, "then I saw," introduces a new vision report (see *Comment* on 5:1). This judgment scene begins by focusing on a throne that differs from other references to thrones in Revelation in that this throne is both "great" and "white." There was a tradition in ancient Canaan that gods such as Baal were extremely large and had palaces and thrones of enormous size (see Greenfield, "Baal's Throne," 193–98; M. S. Smith, *ZAW* 100 [1988] 424–27). Similarly, the throne of Yahweh in Isa 6:1 and the cherubim throne of God in 1 Kgs 6:23–28 were thought to be of enormous size, and it may be that the adjective μέγας, "great," refers to this tradition. The enormous proportions of the heavenly throne of God are also emphasized in Ezekiel *Exogoge* 68–69 and 4 Ezra 8:21. A parallel vision of a throne is found in Hermas (*Vis.* 1.2.2), who reportedly saw a vision of a "large white chair [καθέδραν λευκὴν μεγάλην]." The Coptic-Gnostic tractate *Apoc. Paul* 22.24–30 mentions the throne of God in the seventh heaven, a throne seven times brighter than the sun. Though there are no exact parallels to the white throne mentioned here, white is, of course, the color appropriate for heaven and is associated with purity; see Michaelis, *TDNT* 4:241–50.

The *location* of the throne is necessarily vague, since heaven and earth have been destroyed (cf. 20:11; 21:1). In scenarios in which God visits the earth for salvation or judgment, his throne is set up somewhere on earth (*1 Enoch* 25:3), though specific locations are virtually never mentioned.

This mention of the throne fits the style of the author, who often focuses on the place where someone is seated first and only then on those seated there (see *Comment* on 4:2). The author does not specify *who* is seated on this throne, though the reader is by now well aware that the participial phrase "the One who sits on the throne" (4:1, 3, 9; 5:1, 7, 13; 6:16; 7:10, 15; 19:4; 21:5) is a frequent designation of

God in Revelation. The phrase "the One seated on it [i.e., 'the throne']" is a circumlocution that avoids direct mention of the divine name. However, the absence of any mention of the Lamb in this judgment scene is striking.

11b οὗ ἀπὸ τοῦ προσώπου ἔφυγεν ἡ γῆ καὶ ὁ οὐρανός, "from whom earth and heaven fled." Here heaven and earth are personified fleeing in fear of the judgment of God (Vögtle, "Himmel," 305). This verse is metaphorical, however, and does not describe the destruction of the cosmos (Mell, *Neue Schöpfung,* 128–29; Vögtle, "Himmel," 304–6). Two basic elements of the theophany form are found in vv 11b and 11c: (1) the coming of the deity and (2) the reaction of nature (examples of this form are found in both the OT [Judg 5:4–5; Pss 18:7–15; 68:7–8; Amos 1:2; Mic 1:3–4; Hab 3:4–15] and early Jewish literature [Sir 16:18–19; 43:16–17; Jdt 16:15; *T. Mos.* 10:3–6; 1QH 3:32–36; *T. Levi* 3:9; *Sib. Or.* 3.669–81]; see Jörg Jeremias, *Theophanie*). The two-part theophany form also occurs in *T. Levi* 3:9, "Even the heavens and earth and the abysses tremble before the presence of his [God's] majesty." Another aspect of the theophany form is the claim that if a divinity reveals himself suddenly and completely to mortals, they will perish (Apollodorus 3.4.3; Ovid *Metam.* 3.259–315; *Tri. Trac.* 64.33–37). This basic theophany form is not limited to Israelite-Jewish or ancient Near Eastern texts, however, for a parallel occurs in Iamblichus *De myst.* 2.4, "Moreover, the magnificence of the appearances of the gods is such that at times the whole heaven hides, and the sun and the moon, and the earth, can no longer remain in repose when they descend." According to Greek myth, Semele (the mother of Dionysos) was incinerated when she insisted on gazing at the full glory of Zeus (Apollodorus 3.4.3).

11c καὶ τόπος οὐχ εὑρέθη αὐτοῖς, "but there was no place for them." This phrase occurs verbatim in Theod Dan 2:35 in an entirely different context (the Aramaic text is וְכָל־אֲתַר לָא־הִשְׁתְּכַח לְהוֹן *wĕkol-ʾătar lāʾ-hištĕkaḥ lĕhôn,* literally "and any place was not found for them") and in very similar form in Rev 12:8 (where αὐτῶν [a genitive of possession] is used in place of αὐτοῖς [a dative of advantage]). The Semitic character of this formulaic expression is clear (see also the Hebrew text of Zech 10:10), and it seems likely that the author derived it from a Greek translation of Dan 2:35 very similar if not identical to Theod Dan 2:35. The meaning of the phrase, however, seems clear; the author anticipates the destruction of the physical universe, a view that is repeated in Rev 21:1 (Vögtle, "Himmel," 305).

12a καὶ εἶδον τοὺς νεκρούς, τοὺς μεγάλους καὶ τοὺς μικρούς, ἑστῶτας ἐνώπιον τοῦ θρόνου, "Then I saw the dead, both important and unimportant, standing before the throne." The introductory vision formula καὶ εἶδον, "then I saw," functions to focus on the specific group named here (see *Comment* on 5:1). While the phrase "small and great" (i.e., "unimportant and important") occurs four times elsewhere in Revelation (11:18; 13:16; 19:5, 18; see *Comment* on 13:16), here the phrase is reversed to "great and small" (i.e., "important and unimportant"). While the idiom "small and great" occurs more than thirty times in the OT, "great and small," which deviates from the normal order, occurs nine times (Gen 44:12; 1 Sam 20:2; 2 Chr 31:15; 2 Chr 34:30; Esth 1:5, 20; Jer 6:16; Jonah 3:5; Amos 6:11).

The living are not mentioned, probably because of the destruction of virtually all the enemies of God narrated in 19:17–21. The author seems to presuppose the resurrection of the dead who appear before the great white throne of God, but he does not explicitly mention it. Some commentators argue that this brief reference is expanded on in v 13 (Swete, 272–73; Beckwith, 748–49), while others argue that v 13 is out of place and originally belonged before v 12 (Charles, 2:194).

12b καὶ βιβλία ἠνοίχθησαν, "And books were opened." This is an allusion to a particular aspect of the judgment scene in Dan 7:10, καὶ βίβλοι ἠνεῴχθησαν, "and books were opened." The plural in both Dan 7:10 and here probably reflects the early Jewish tradition of *two* heavenly books, one for recording the deeds of the righteous and the other for recording the deeds of the wicked (Ps 56.8; Isa 65:6; Jer 22:30; Mal 3:16; Dan 7:10; *Jub.* 30:22; 36:10; *Asc. Isa.* 9:22; *Lev. Rab.* 26 [on 21:1]; *Gen. Rab.* 81 [on 35:31]; *b. Taʿan.* 11a; see *Comment* on 3:5). Dan 7:10 may be alluded to in 4 Ezra 6:20, "the books shall be opened before the face of the firmament, and all shall see my judgment together." Reference to the books of judgment in the plural occurs frequently (*1 Enoch* 47:3; 90:20; 4 Ezra 6:20; *2 Apoc. Bar.* 24:1). Books recording *evil* deeds are mentioned in Isa 65:6; *1 Enoch* 81:4; 89:61–77; 90:17, 20; 98:7, 8; 104:7; *2 Apoc. Bar.* 24:1. *1 Enoch* 47:3 relates a very similar scenario where God is seated upon his throne and "the books of the living" are opened before him. The use of the passive voice in the verb ἠνοίχθησαν, "were opened" (cf. v 12c), implies that the books are opened by angels or by God himself.

12c καὶ ἄλλο βιβλίον ἠνοίχθη, ὅ ἐστιν τῆς ζωῆς, "and another book was opened, which is the book of life." The book of life is mentioned several times in Revelation (3:5; 13:8; 17:8; 20:12, 15; 21:17; see *Comment* on 3:5). This phrase appears to be an interpolation, which the author has inserted into the basic eschatological judgment scene that he reproduces in this section. For a discussion of the book of life motif, see *Comment* on 3:5.

12d καὶ ἐκρίθησαν οἱ νεκροὶ ἐκ τῶν γεγραμμένων ἐν τοῖς βιβλίοις κατὰ τὰ ἔργα αὐτῶν, "and the dead were judged on the basis of what was recorded in the books, according to their deeds." The books referred to are those mentioned in v 12b and probably do not include the book of life in v 12c. Since the dead are judged by their *deeds*, it is assumed that these books contain a record of a person's behavior. These ἔργα, "deeds," can be understood either as sinful deeds and the record books as records of sins (see *1 Enoch* 89:70–71; 97:6; 98:7), or they can more probably be regarded more neutrally as either righteous or wicked deeds (*2 Apoc. Bar.* 24:1; *2 Enoch* 52:1–15). On the phrase κατὰ τὰ ἔργα, "according to the deeds," in a context of judgment, which occurs four times in Revelation (2:23; 18:6; 20:12, 13), see *Comment* on 2:23.

13a καὶ ἔδωκεν ἡ θάλασσα τοὺς νεκροὺς τοὺς ἐν αὐτῇ καὶ ὁ θάνατος καὶ ὁ ᾅδης ἔδωκαν τοὺς νεκροὺς τοὺς ἐν αὐτοῖς, "The sea gave up the dead in it, and Death and Hades gave up the dead in them." The reference to the existence of the sea appears to contradict the apparent destruction of heaven and earth in v 11 (see Prigent, 316), and the disappearance of the sea is specifically mentioned in 21:1. The modern reader will also wonder how it is possible to narrate the final judgment of the dead in v 12 though their "resurrection" is not mentioned until v 13. While it is possible that all of v 13 is a later insertion by the author, it is also possible that this is yet another instance of his use of *hysteron-proteron*, i.e., the arrangement of events in the reverse of their logical order (see 3:3, 17; 5:5; 6:4; 10:4, 9; 22:14).

Ancient coastal societies (Greeks, Romans, Palestinians) were conscious of *two* abodes of the dead, the *sea*, invariably thought inappropriate and unnatural (Propertius 3.7.29; Seneca *Nat. quaest.* 5.18.8; Ovid *Amor.* 2.11.16; 3.8.45; Vergil *Eclogae* 4.38; Pliny *Hist. nat.* 19.5; see Propertius 3.7.43, "Therefore remain on land, learn to be content, and die a natural death"), and the *land,* widely regarded as appropriate and as the region below which the realm of Hades was thought located.

The popular belief that the souls of those who died at sea did not enter Hades but remained where they died in the water is expressed in Achilles Tatius 5.16.2 (*Neuer Wettstein*, ad Rev 20:13). Though one occasionally finds the sea compared to Hades (Antiphilus 4; Philip 48; both in Gow-Page, *Greek Anthology* 1:92–93, 328–29), Hades is primarily associated with those buried on the land.

Death and Hades are often equated (Heinemann, *Thanatos*, 29–32), and the pair are personified four times in Revelation (1:18; 6:8; 20:13, 14; see *Comment* on 6:8). They are always in this order, suggesting that "Death" is considered the ruler over the realm of "Hades." The final elimination of Death is mentioned in Rev 21:4 and 1 Cor 15:26. The phrase "Death and Hades gave up the dead in them" is problematic, for it is unlikely that the author conceives of Death and Hades as two separate entities. Charles has argued that the phrase τὰ ταμεῖα, "the treasuries" (i.e., the place where only the souls of the righteous were admitted), was deliberately changed to ἡ θάλασσα, "the sea," to emphasize the physical resurrection of the dead (2:195–96).

13b καὶ ἐκρίθησαν ἕκαστος κατὰ τὰ ἔργα αὐτῶν, "then each was judged according to their works." This judgment of the dead from the sea and from Hades is a doublet of the judgment of all the dead before the great white throne, a judgment briefly narrated in v 12. This phrase occurs in a similar form in v 12, καὶ ἐκρίθησαν οἱ νεκροὶ . . . κατὰ τὰ ἔργα αὐτῶν, "and the dead were judged . . . according to their deeds." On the phrase κατὰ τὰ ἔργα, "according to the deeds," which occurs four times in Revelation (2:23; 18:6; 20:12, 13), see *Comment* on 2:23.

14a καὶ ὁ θάνατος καὶ ὁ ᾅδης ἐβλήθησαν εἰς τὴν λίμνην τοῦ πυρός, "Then Death and Hades were cast into the lake of fire." The suggestion that Death and Hades (see v 13 and *Comment* on 6:8) could share the fate of the enemies of God (19:20; 20:10) seems problematic. There are at least two ways of understanding the significance of this statement: (1) It could simply be a way of referring to the eschatological elimination of death (cf. Rev 21:4; 1 Cor 15:26). (2) More probably, however, "Death and Hades" here stand for all the unrighteous dead in accord with v 15, where it is stated that all whose names were not found in the book of life were cast into the lake of fire (for Hades as the place of the unrighteous dead, see Luke 16:22; 1 Pet 3:19–20). Plutarch quotes Theopompus (*De Iside* 370C; *FrGrHist* 65) to the effect that according to the Persian sages, a succession of gods will overpower each other, each reign for 3,000 years, and then after a final conflict, "finally, Hades shall pass away [ἀπολείπεσθαι]."

14b οὗτος ὁ θάνατος ὁ δεύτερός ἐστιν, ἡ λίμνη τοῦ πυρός, "This is the second death, the lake of fire." This sentence is an explanatory gloss, which is problematic, for how can Death and Hades experience the second death when they have not experienced the first (i.e., physical) death? The phrase "the second death" is mentioned twice in Revelation (2:11 and 20:6; see *Comment* there) before the author twice links it with "the lake of fire" in explanatory glosses (20:14 and 21:8).

15 καὶ εἴ τις οὐχ εὑρέθη ἐν τῇ βίβλῳ τῆς ζωῆς γεγραμμένος ἐβλήθη εἰς τὴν λίμνην τοῦ πυρός, "And if anyone was not found recorded in the book of life, that person was cast into the lake of fire." This appended clause is also a redactional insertion into the final text. As it stands, this statement means that the only criterion of salvation is to have one's name written in the book of life, and it appears to make superfluous the rendering of judgment on the basis of the deeds recorded in the books. The punishment of the wicked by fire is a frequent motif in early Jewish and early Christian texts (CD 2:5; 1QS 2:7–8).

Explanation

The "lake of fire," mentioned six times in Rev 20–21, has no exact parallels in Jewish eschatology, though fire itself is often connected with eschatological punishment (*1 Enoch* 10:6; *Sib. Or.* 2.195–205; Mark 9:43). The next to last stage in the conquest of evil is the confinement to the bottomless pit (the abyss from whence he came) of Satan (identified by his several aliases as in 12:9) by an angel for a thousand years (20:1–3). In Jewish legend, Satan was cast down to the earth from the presence of God in primordial times (see 12:9), and in the eschaton the free rein that he and his angels have exercised on earth will be brought to an end by God's intervention. Then they will be cast into the abyss.

During the temporary restraint of Satan (20:1–3), the martyrs alone are raised from the dead in the first resurrection (20:5) and reign with Christ on earth for a thousand years (this millennial reign is also described in a variety of ways in Rev 2:26–27; 7:15–17; 14:1–5). Satan is later released for a limited period (20:3). Following Satan's release from the bottomless pit, he gathers armies from the nations of the earth to attack and destroy the millennial kingdom, apparently located on Mount Zion (20:7–9). The names Gog and Magog, derived from Ezek 38–39, are generic names for nations hostile to Israel who will unsuccessfully attempt to annihilate the people of God. Yet they will be decisively defeated by rain, hail, fire, and brimstone from heaven (Ezek 38:22). Since the names Gog and Magog occur only rarely in Jewish apocalyptic literature, John has very likely derived these code names directly from Ezekiel. After Satan's defeat, he, like the beast and false prophet before him, is perpetually confined to the lake of fire (v 10).

The final judgment is depicted in vv 11–15 in the traditional eschatological imagery derived from the role of kings as dispensers of justice. The second resurrection, implied but unmentioned, enables the rest of the dead, both righteous and wicked, to stand before the throne of God awaiting their sentence (traditional imagery). Into this traditional scene of the opening of two sets of books, John has inserted a reference to the book of life (v 12; cf. 13:8; 17:8; 21:27). The metaphor of two sets of heavenly tablets or books on which righteous and wicked deeds are recorded for reference on the day of judgment is common in early Judaism. Though v 12 presupposes the second or general resurrection, v 13 awkwardly repeats this notion with the idea that the sea and Death and Hades surrendered the dead in them. Ancients thought that those who died at sea could not enter Hades. Those not found in the book of life are thrown into the lake of fire, the second death (vv 14–15).

Excursus 20A: The Temporary and the Eternal Kingdom

Bibliography

Bailey, J. W. "The Temporary Messianic Reign in the Literature of Early Judaism." *JBL* 53 (1934) 170–87. **Cavallin, H. C. C.** *Life after Death: Paul's Argument for Resurrection of the Dead in 1 Cor. 15.* Part I: *An Enquiry into the Jewish Background.* Lund: Gleerup, 1974. **Charles, R. H.** *A Critical History of the Doctrine of a Future Life in Israel, in Judaism, and in Christianity.* London: A. & C. Black, 1899. **Davies, W. D.** *Paul and Rabbinic Judaism.* 3rd ed. London: SPCK, 1970. **Dexinger, F.** *Henochs Zehnwochenapokalypse und offene Probleme der Apokalyptikforschung.* Leiden:

Brill, 1977. **Klijn, A. F. J.** "The Sources and the Redaction of the Syrian Apocalypse of Baruch." *JSJ* 1 (1971) 65–76. **Kreitzer, L. J.** *Jesus and God in Paul's Eschatology.* Sheffield: JSOT, 1987. **Murphy, F. J.** *The Structure and Meaning of Second Baruch.* SBLDS 78. Atlanta: Scholars, 1985. **Plevnik, J.** "The Taking Up of the Faithful and the Resurrection of the Dead in 1 Thessalonians 4:13–18." *CBQ* 46 (1984) 274–83. **Russell, D. S.** *The Method and Message of Jewish Apocalyptic.* Philadelphia: Fortress, 1964. **Schoeps, H. J.** *Paul: The Theology of the Apostle in the Light of Jewish Religious History.* Tr. H. Knight. Philadelphia: Westminster, 1961. **Schweitzer, A.** *The Mysticism of Paul the Apostle.* New York: Holt, 1931. **Wallis, W.** "The Problem of an Intermediate Kingdom in 1 Corinthians 15.20–28." *JETS* 15 (1972) 229–42. **Wilcke, H.-A.** *Das Problem eines messianischen Zwischenreichs bei Paulus.* ATANT 51. Zürich: Zwingli, 1967.

The notion of a *temporary* (messianic) kingdom that would form a transition between this present evil age and the age to come, i.e., between monarchy and theocracy, is a way of harmonizing the prophetic expectation of a golden age ushered in by the restoration of the Davidic monarchy with the apocalyptic view of the climactic intervention by God into world history (Schweitzer, *Paul*, 84). This interim kingdom is transitional in that it is depicted as a synthesis or compromise between this age and the age to come, combining characteristics of both worlds or ages. The expectation of a temporary eschatological messianic kingdom is clearly expressed in Rev 20:4–6, and according to some scholars the same view is reflected in 1 Cor 15:20–28.

The expectation of a future temporary kingdom is found in just three different early Jewish apocalypses, the latter two of which are roughly contemporary with Revelation (G. F. Moore, *Judaism* 2:333–39; Kreitzer, *Eschatology,* 29–91): (1) the Apocalypse of Weeks (*1 Enoch* 93:3–10; 93:11–17), written between 175 and 167 B.C. (VanderKam, *Enoch,* 142–49); (2) 4 Ezra 7:26–44; 12:31–34 (ca. A.D. 90); and (3) *2 Apoc. Bar.* 29:3–30:1; 40:1–4; 72:2–74:3 (ca. A.D. 110). Though some have claimed that a temporary messianic kingdom is to be found in *2 Enoch* 32:2–33:1 and *Jub.* 1:27–29; 23:26–31 (Russell, *Method,* 293–94), the evidence for a temporary messianic kingdom in these texts is very weak. In *2 Enoch* 32:2–33:1, the seven days of creation become the speculative basis for anticipating seven thousand years of history concluded by an eighth period of one thousand years, which will in fact last forever (based on a speculative combination of Gen 2:2, which mentions the seven days of creation, with Ps 90:4, where a day is said to equal a thousand years). Though the notion of a millennium is found here, no distinction is made between a temporary and an eternal age, nothing is said about a Messiah, and the passage is probably a very late (medieval) interpolation into the text (this passage is found in MS A, the longer text of *2 Enoch,* which perhaps originated in the late Middle Ages [Milik, *Enoch,* 107–18], but is missing from MS B, the shorter, probably earlier and more reliable MS). *Jub.* 1:27–29 seems to refer not to a *temporary* kingdom but to the eternal rule of God on earth with no mention of a Messiah. *Jub.* 23:27 says that the righteous will live to be a thousand years old, while 23:31 ("And their bones will rest in the earth, and their spirits will increase in joy") apparently refers, though vaguely, to a kind of postmortem existence (see Cavallin, *Life after Death,* 60–72).

Each of the other three texts requires more detailed discussion. (1) In the Apocalypse of Weeks (*1 Enoch* 93:3–10; 91:11–17), an earlier work inserted into the Epistle of Enoch (*1 Enoch* 91–104), history is divided into ten weeks (ages), with a *non-messianic* temporary kingdom appearing in the eighth week and an eternal earthly kingdom arriving in the tenth week (though this view is absent from the rest of the Epistle of Enoch [*1 Enoch* 91–104]). The relevant section is *1 Enoch* 91:12–17, remarkable for its similarity to the eschatological scheme in Revelation (tr. Knibb, *Enoch;* italics those of translator):

And after this there will be another week, the eighth, that of righteousness, and a sword will be given to it that *the righteous judgment* may be executed on those who do wrong, and the sinners will be handed over into the hands of the the the righteous. And at its end they will acquire houses because of their righteousness, and a house will be built for the great king *in glory* for ever. And after this in the ninth week the righteous judgment will be revealed to the whole world, and all the deeds of the impious will vanish from the whole earth; and the world will be written down for destruction, and all men will look to the path of uprightness. And after this in the tenth week, in the seventh part, there will be the eternal judgment which will be executed on the watchers, and the great eternal heaven which will spring from the midst of the angels. And the first heaven will vanish and pass away, and a new heaven will appear, and all the powers of heaven will shine for ever (with) sevenfold (light). And after this there will be many weeks without number for ever in goodness and in righteousness, and from then on sin will never again be mentioned.

(2) 4 Ezra 7:26–30 describes the temporary messianic kingdom in which the elect who are then living will participate (tr. B. M. Metzger, *OTP* 1:537):

For behold, the time will come, when the signs which I have foretold to you will come to pass; the city which now is not seen shall appear, and the land which is now hidden will be disclosed. And everyone who has been delivered from the evils that I have foretold shall see my wonders. For my son the Messiah shall be revealed with those who are with him, and those who remain shall rejoice four hundred years. After these years my son the Messiah shall die, and all who draw human breath. And the world shall be turned back to primeval silence for seven days, as it was at the first beginnings; so that no one shall be left.

In this scenario nothing is mentioned about the Messiah's roles as warrior and judge. Following the death of the Messiah (a conception not found elsewhere in Jewish texts and therefore thought by some to be a Christian interpolation) and all other living people (v 29), and the return to seven days of primeval silence "as at the beginning" (v 30), then the resurrection will occur (v 32). The Most High will appear on the seat of judgment (v 33); hell will appear with paradise opposite it, and God will execute judgment on the nations (vv 36–43). 4 Ezra 12:31–34, on the other hand, in an interpretation of Ezra's sixth vision, refers to the Davidic Messiah whom the Most High has kept for the end of days. He will sit upon his seat of judgment, and after reproving the ungodly and the wicked, he will destroy them (v 32). The righteous remnant, however, will be delivered and made joyful "until the end comes, the day of judgment, of which I spoke to you at the beginning" (v 34). Therefore, the judgment exercised by the Messiah is preliminary to the final judgment, which will be exercised by God after the eschaton has arrived. Nowhere in 4 Ezra does the Messiah play a role in the eternal theocratic kingdom that begins with the resurrection.

(3) In *2 Apocalypse of Baruch,* three apocalyptic scenarios (29:3–30:1; 40:1–4; 72:2–74:3) are set within three visions: (a) 27:1–30:5; (b) 36:1–40:4; and (c) 53:1–76:5. Only in these sections is the Messiah mentioned. After twelve waves of tribulation (*2 Apoc. Bar.* 27:1–15), the messianic kingdom is depicted as a period of phenomenal abundance and is framed by the appearance of the Anointed One (29:3) and his return to glory (30:1; unlike 4 Ezra 7:28–29, where the Messiah dies). The elect who were alive when the messianic kingdom was inaugurated will then be joined by the deceased righteous who will be raised from the dead, but the souls of the wicked will fear judgment (30:1–5). The author assumes rather than states that those who are yet living will experience a transformation in a resurrection mode of existence like the resurrected dead (Schweitzer, *Paul,* 86; see 1 Thess 4:17, where Paul also assumed the transformation of the living at the Parousia; see Plevnik, *CBQ* 46 [1984] 282). Here a period of abundance precedes the

actual appearance of the Messiah, when the resurrection of the righteous will occur prior to the judgment of the righteous and the wicked. In *2 Apoc. Bar.* 39–40, the predicted fall of the fourth kingdom (Rome) will occur following the revelation of "the dominion of my Anointed One" (39:7). After the destruction of the armies of the last ruler of that kingdom (the Messiah as warrior), the defeated ruler will be brought bound to Zion, where the Messiah will convict him of all his crimes and execute him (40:1–2, a reversal of the Roman practice of bringing captives to Rome for display and execution); "And his [the Messiah's] dominion will last forever until the world of corruption has ended and until the times that have been mentioned before have been fulfilled" (40:3). Here the messianic kingdom is obviously temporary since the "world of corruption" has not yet ended, yet unlike 4 Ezra 7:28–29, the exact duration of this kingdom is not specified. Finally, in *2 Apoc. Bar.* 72:2–74:3, the warrior Messiah will summon all nations, sparing some and destroying others (72:2–6). Following this is a period of millennial bliss (73:1–2; tr. A. F. J. Klijn, *OTP* 1:645):

> And it will happen that after he has brought down everything which is in the world, and has sat down in eternal peace on the throne of the kingdom, then joy will be revealed and rest will appear. And then health will descend in dew, and illness will vanish, and fear and tribulation and lamentation will pass away from among men, and joy will encompass the earth.

The interim character of this period, however, is suggested by *2 Apoc. Bar.* 74:2 (tr. A. F. J. Klijn, *OTP* 1:646), "For that time is the end of that which is corruptible and the beginning of that which is incorruptible." The author clearly presupposes a break between this world and the next world (Klijn, *JSJ* 1 [1971] 75). As in 4 Ezra, the Messiah plays no role in the eternal kingdom inaugurated after he is taken up into heaven.

The relevance of 1 Cor 15:20–28 to the early Jewish and early Christian view of a temporary intermediate messianic kingdom is disputed. Schweitzer (*Paul*, 65–68, 90–100) synthesized Paul's view of the sequence eschatological events in the following way: (1) the sudden and unexpected Parousia (1 Thess 5:1–4), (2) the resurrection of deceased believers and the transformation of living believers, all of whom meet the Lord in the air (1 Thess 4:16–17), (3) the messianic judgment presided over by Christ (2 Cor 5:10) or God (Rom 14:10), either or both of whom function as judge, (4) the dawn of the messianic kingdom (not described by Paul, but perhaps hinted at in Gal 4:26), (5) during the messianic kingdom the transformation of all nature from mortality to immortality (Rom 8:19–22) along with a struggle with angelic powers (Rom 16:20) until death itself is conquered (1 Cor 15:23–28), (6) the end of the messianic kingdom (Paul does not mention its duration), and (7) a general resurrection at the end of the messianic kingdom (1 Cor 6:3), immediately followed by (8) judgment upon all men and defeated angels. According to Schweitzer (*Paul*, 94), Paul introduced *two* resurrections, although Jewish eschatology before him knew only a *single* resurrection, either at the beginning of the messianic kingdom (Daniel, *1 Enoch*, sayings of Jesus) or at the end of the messianic kingdom (4 Ezra; *2 Apoc. Bar.*). This modification was motivated by the life, death, and resurrection of Jesus the Messiah. The first resurrection enables believers who have died as well as living Christians to participate in the messianic kingdom (Schweitzer, *Paul*, 90), all enjoying a resurrection mode of existence (Schweitzer, *Paul*, 91–92).

Schweitzer's reconstruction of Pauline eschatology has been widely criticized (see Davies, *Paul*, 285–98), but it also has defenders (Schoeps, *Paul*, 97–110; Wallis, *JETS* 15 [1972] 229–42; Kreitzer, *Eschatology*, 134–45, waffles on the subject). First, there is no evidence in 1 Thess 4:13–18 or 1 Cor 15:20–28 that Paul expected an intermediate messianic kingdom (Wilcke, *Zwischenreichs;* Davies, *Paul*, 290–94). Second, there is no indication that Paul expected a general resurrection (according to Schweitzer, *Paul*, 67, it was so well known that Paul simply assumed it). Davies has three supporting arguments that 1 Cor 15:20–28 indicates that the Parousia will shortly be followed by the resurrection and judgment, which will usher in the final consummation (Davies, *Paul,* 295–97): (1) The phrase βασιλεία τοῦ θεοῦ, "kingdom of God," in Paul is an unending kingdom (1 Thess 2:12; 2 Thess 1:4–5; Gal 5:21; 1 Cor 6:9–10; 15:50; Col 4:11). (2) The only text mentioning a βασιλεία τοῦ Χριστοῦ, "kingdom of Christ," Col 1:12–13, understands it as a present fact. (3) Paul connects the Parousia with the judgment of the world (1 Cor 1:7–8; 2 Cor 1:14; Phil 1:6, 10; 2:16). In Pauline thought there is certainly an interval between the resurrection of the righteous and the Parousia of Christ.

An indefinite period is mentioned in *2 Apoc. Bar.* 40:3 and 4 Ezra 12:34 (cf. 1 Cor. 15:24–28). Later rabbinic literature attributes a variety of opinions to various sages (here the traditional dates of the sages mentioned have no necessary relationship to the dates of the traditions associated with their names, and often are much later): R. Akiba (died A.D. 135) reportedly proposed a messianic kingdom lasting forty years; R. Eliezer b. Hyrcanus (ca. A.D. 90) proposed two thousand years (the most widely held opinion); R. Jehoshua (ca. A.D. 90) proposed seven thousand years; and R. Abbahu (ca. A.D. 300) also proposed seven thousand years. John is the first author who anticipates a messianic interregnum of one thousand years, a number symbolic for a lengthy yet limited period of time (see *Apoc. Elijah* 5:36–39).

What is the function of such a temporary messianic kingdom? John and the author of 4 Ezra, independently of each other, were trying to reconcile the expectation of a messianic kingdom with the notion of the final realization of the eternal reign of God. Since the Messiah was not a supernatural being in Jewish thought, there was no problem in conceiving of his death (as in 4 Ezra 7:29). Yet for Christians, the messianic kingdom could obviously not conclude in that way. At a relatively early date, therefore, the earthly messianic kingdom of Christ, after lasting an indefinite period, is concluded by a transition of sovereignty from Christ to God (1 Cor 15:24–28). In order to accommodate such a provisional state, John had to reduplicate (somewhat awkwardly) the final eschatological events and insert the temporary millennial kingdom in the middle. He narrates two final wars (19:11–21 and 20:7–10), two victories over Satan (20:1–3 and 20:10), two resurrections (20:4–6 and 20:12–13), two judgment scenes (20:4 and 20:12–13), and two states of blessedness (20:4 and 20:12). Jewish messianic expectation was based on the hope of the restoration of house of David (see *Pss. Sol.* 17). Yet Jewish eschatological expectation tended to focus not on the restoration of a dynasty but on a single messianic king sent by God to restore the fortunes of Israel. However, as a theocratic symbol, the Messiah was dispensable, since a Messiah was not invariably part of all Jewish eschatological expectation (cf. the absence of such a figure in Joel, Isa 24–27, Daniel, Sirach, *Jubilees,* the *Assumption of Moses,* Tobit, 1 and 2 Maccabees, Wisdom, *1 Enoch* 1–36, 90–104, *2 Enoch*). A preliminary and temporary messianic kingdom solves the problem of how to conceive of the transition from the Messiah to the eternal reign of God. A messianic interregnum, therefore, functions as an anticipation of the perfect and eternal theocratic state that will exist when primordial conditions are reinstated for ever.

4. The Transition to the New Order　　(21:1–8)

Bibliography

Banks, R. *Jesus and the Law in the Synoptic Tradition.* SNTSMS 28. Cambridge: Cambridge UP, 1975. **Bergmeier, R.** "'Jerusalem, du hochgebaute Stadt.'" *ZNW* 75 (1984) 86–106. **Black, M.** "The New Creation in 1 Enoch." In *Creation, Christ and Culture.* FS T. F. Torrance, ed. R.

McKinney. Edinburgh: T. & T. Clark, 1976. 13–21. **Boismard, M.-E.** "Notes sur l'Apocalypse." *RB* 59 (1952) 161–81. **Bousset, W.** *The Antichrist Legend: A Chapter in Christian and Jewish Folklore.* Tr. A. H. Keane. London: Hutchinson, 1896. **Driver, G. R.,** and **Miles, J. C.** *The Babylonian Laws.* 2 vols. Oxford: Clarendon, 1952–55. **García Martínez, F.** "The 'New Jerusalem' and the Future Temple of the Manuscripts from Qumran." In *Qumran and Apocalyptic: Studies on the Aramaic Texts from Qumran.* Leiden: Brill, 1994. 180–213. **Glasson, T. F.** *Greek Influence in Jewish Eschatology.* London: S.P.C.K., 1961. **Greengus, S.** "The Old Babylonian Marriage Contract." *JAOS* 89 (1969) 505–32. **Gundry, R. H.** "The New Jerusalem: People as Place, Not Place for People." *NovT* 3 (1987) 254–64. **Hugenberger, G. P.** *Marriage as Covenant.* VTSup 52. Leiden: Brill, 1994. **Kalluveettil, P.** *Declaration and Covenant: A Comprehensive Review of Covenant Formulae for the Old Testament and the Ancient Near East.* AnBib 88. Rome: Biblical Institute, 1982. **Kloos, C.** *Yhwh's Combat with the Sea: A Canaanite Tradition in the Religion of Ancient Israel.* Leiden: Brill; Amsterdam: G. A. van Oorschot, 1986. **Luz, U.** *Das Evangelium nach Matthäus.* Vol. 1. Neukirchen: Benziger, 1985 (ET *Matthew 1–7.* Minneapolis: Fortress, 1989). **Mayer, R.** *Die biblische Vorstellung vom Weltenbrand.* Bonn: Selbstverlag des orientalischen Seminars der Universität, 1956. **McKelvey, R. J.** *The New Temple: The Church in the New Testament.* Oxford: Oxford UP, 1969. **Prigent, P.** "Une trace de liturgie judeo-chretienne dans le chapitre XXI de l'Apocalypse de Jean." In *Judéo-Christianisme: Recherches historiques et théologiques.* FS J. Daniélou. Paris: Recherches de science religieuse, 1972. 165–72. **Reader, W. W.** "Die Stadt Gottes in der Johannesapokalypse." Diss., Göttingen, 1971. **Rordorf, W.** "Beobachtungen zum Gebrauch des Dekalogs in der vorkonstantinischen Kirche." In *The New Testament Age.* FS B. Reicke, ed. W. C. Weinrich. Macon, GA: Mercer UP, 1984. 2:431–42. **Ruiten, J. van.** "The Intertextual Relationship between Isaiah 65,17–20 and Revelation 21,1–5b." *EstBib* 51 (1993) 473–510. **Taeger, J.-W.** *Johannesapokalypse und johanneischer Kreis: Versuch einer traditionsgeschichtlichen Ortsbestimmung am Paradigma der Lebenswasser-Thematik.* BZNW 51. Berlin; New York: de Gruyter, 1989. **Unnik, W. C. van.** *Het godspredikaat 'Het begin en het einde' bij Flavius Josephus en in de openbaring van Johannes.* Amsterdam: Noord-Hollandsche Uitgevers Maatschappij, 1976. **Vögtle, A.** "'Dann sah ich einen neuen Himmel und eine neue Erde . . .' (Apk 21,1)." In *Glaube und Eschatologie.* FS W. G. Kümmel, ed. E. Grässer and O. Merk. Tübingen: Mohr-Siebeck, 1985. 301–33.

Translation

¹*Then I saw a new heaven and a new earth. For the first heaven and the first earth* ᵃ*passed away,*ᵃ ᵇ*and the sea no longer existed.*ᵇ ²*I saw the holy city, New Jerusalem,*ᵃ *descending* ᵇ*from heaven from God,*ᵇ *prepared as a bride adorned for her husband.* ³*I heard a loud voice from the* ᵃ*throne:* ᵇ

> *"Behold the dwelling of God is with people, and he* ᶜ*will dwell* ᶜ *with them, and they will be* ᵈ*his people, and God himself* ᵉ ᶠ*will be with them as their God,*ᶠ ⁴*and* ᵃ*he will wipe away every tear* ᵇ*from their eyes, and* ᶜ*death will no longer exist, nor will grief or crying or pain exist* ᵈ*any longer, for* ᵉ *the previous things* ᵈ ᶠ*have passed away."*ᶠ

⁵*Then* ᵃ *the One sitting on the throne said,*ᵇ

> *"Behold,* ᶜ*I am making everything new."* ᶜ

*He also said,*ᵈ

> *"Write, for* ᵉ *this message* ᶠ *is trustworthy and true."*

⁶*He also said to me,*

> ᵃ*"It is finished.*ᵃ

> ᵇ*I am* ᵇ ᶜ*the Alpha and the Omega,*ᶜ *the Beginning and the End.*

> *I will freely give* ᵈ*some water* ᵈ *to the one who is thirsty*

> ᵉ*from the well of living water.*ᵉ

7   *Those* ^a *who conquer* ^b*will inherit* ^b *these things,*
    for ^c *I will be* ^a*their* ^d *God and* ^e*they* ^a *will be my* ^a*children.*^e

8   *But as for the cowards and unbelievers and the abominable* ^a *and murderers and the*
    immoral and sorcerers and idolaters and all who lie, they will experience ^b *the lake*
    that burns with fire and sulphur, ^c*which is* ^c *the second death.* "

Notes

1.a-a. Variants: (1) ἀπῆλθαν] A (lacuna in C) ℵ fam 1611²³²⁹. (2) παρῆλθεν] Andreas. (3) ἀπῆλθον] 046 Byzantine. (4) ἀπῆλθεν] 025 fam 1611¹⁸⁵⁴ 2030. The differences in these variants primarily result from unintentional changes of the Hellenistic α-vocalization of the second aor. toward the classical and Atticistic o/ε-vocalization of the second aor. (Mussies, *Morphology*, 16–17), though older MSS have both types of vocalization side by side. It is interesting to observe here that the original reading (1) has been corrected independently by both the Andreas (2) and Byzantine (3) texts. The aor. verb ἀπῆλθαν, a 3rd pl. second aor. form from ἀπέρχεσθαι, means "to go out of existence, to cease" (Louw-Nida, § 13.93) and occupies the same semantic subdomain as παράγειν, παρέρχεσθαι, and ἐξέρχεσθαι.

1.b-b. Variant: καὶ τὴν θάλασσαν οὐκ ἶδον ἔτι] A.

2.a. On the problem of the orthography of Ἰερουσαλήμ in Revelation, see *Note* 3:12.g.

2.b-b. Variants: (1) ἐκ τοῦ οὐρανοῦ ἀπὸ τοῦ θεοῦ] A ℵ 046 fam 1006¹⁸⁴¹ fam 1611 Oecumenius²⁰⁵³ ²⁰⁶²ᶜᵒᵐᵐ Andr d e²⁰²⁶ f²⁰⁷³ l n²⁴²⁹ 94 syrᵖʰ cop eth. (2) ἀπὸ τοῦ θεοῦ ἐκ τοῦ οὐρανοῦ] 051 Andreas. (3) omit ἀπὸ τοῦ θεοῦ] Andr n⁻²⁴²⁹ lat arm¹. The exact phrase that occurs in reading (1) is found twice elsewhere in textually secure readings (3:12; 21:10) and as a *var. lect.* in 20:9.

3.a. Variants: (1) θρόνου] A (lacuna in C) ℵ 94 vg Irenaeusᴸᵃᵗ Ambrose Tyc³. (2) οὐρανοῦ] 025 046 051 Oecumenius²⁰⁵³ Andreas Byzantine itᵍⁱᵍ syrᵖʰ Tyc² Beatus. The context (21:5) favors reading (1), while the origin of (2) can be explained as a mechanical repetition of the phrase ἐκ τοῦ οὐρανοῦ in 21:2 (see Schmid, *Studien* 2:83; *TCGNT*¹, 763; *TCGNT*², 688).

3.b. The ptcp. λεγούσης, "saying," modifies the noun φωνῆς but is omitted in the translation as a redundant Septuagintism, functioning to introduce direct speech much like ὅτι *recitativum*.

3.c-c. Variants: (1) σκηνώσει] *lectio originalis*. (2) ἐσκήνωσεν] ℵ fam 1611¹⁶¹¹ ²⁰⁵⁰ itᵍⁱᵍ vgᵐˢˢ syrʰ.

3.d. Variants: (1) λαοί] ℵ A 046 2030 fam 1611²⁰⁵⁰ ²³²⁹ Oecumenius²⁰⁵³ ²⁰⁶²ᵗᵉˣᵗ Andreas itᵃ Irenaeusᴸᵃᵗ; von Soden, *Text*; Nestle-Aland²⁷; UBSGNT⁴; NRSV. (2) λαός] 025 fam 1006¹⁰⁰⁶ ¹⁸⁴¹ fam 1611¹⁶¹¹ ¹⁸⁵⁴ Oecumenius²⁰⁶²ᶜᵒᵐᵐ Andr d f²⁰³¹⁻²⁰⁵⁶ g n Byzantine lat syr Tyc² Tyc³ Beatus Ambrose; B. Weiss, *Johannes-Apokalypse*, 101 (*TCGNT*¹, 763; *TCGNT*², 688, erroneously cite E, which does not contain Revelation). Reading (1) is the *lectio difficilior*, for reading (2) conforms to OT covenant statements, "They shall be my people, and I will be their God" (Lev 26:12; Jer 24:7; 30:21; 31:1, 33; Ezek 11:20; 14:11; 36:28; 37:23, 27–28; Zech 2:14; 8:8).

3.e. This is the only instance in Revelation in which the intensive pronoun αὐτός is used with a substantive.

3.f-f. Variants: (1) μετ᾽ αὐτῶν ἔσται αὐτῶν θεός] ℵ Oecumenius²⁰⁵³ᶜᵒᵐᵐ ²⁰⁶² (Oecumenius²⁰⁵³ᵗᵉˣᵗ: μετ᾽ αὐτῶν ἔσται αὐτῶν ὁ θεός); 2030 fam 1611²⁰⁵⁰ ²³²⁹ 1778ᵐᵃʳᵍ Andr l¹⁶⁷⁸ ¹⁷⁷⁸ᵐᵃʳᵍ⁻²⁰⁸⁰ itᶜ itᵈᵉᵐ itᵈⁱᵛ itʰᵃᶠ vg syrᵖʰ syrʰ eth Irenaeusᴸᵃᵗ Tyc² Tyc³ (*cum eis erit eorum deus;* Vogels, *Untersuchungen*, 189); Ambrose *De excessu fratr. sui satyr.* 2.121–22 (*cum illis erit illorum deus;* R. W. Muncey, *The New Testament Text of Saint Ambrose*, TextsS 4 [Cambridge: Cambridge UP, 1959] 115); Apringius Beatus (*cum eis erit eorum deus;* Romero-Pose, *Sancti Beati* 2:382); B. Weiss, *Johannes-Apokalypse*, 155; WHortᵐᵃʳᵍ; Charles, 2:377; [Nestle-Aland²⁷]; [UBSGNT⁴]. (2) μετ᾽ αὐτῶν· καὶ ἔσται αὐτῶν θεός] syrᵖʰ (modified version of Gwynn, *Apocalypse*, 43). (3) μετ᾽ αὐτῶν ἔσται θεὸς αὐτῶν] 025 051 fam 1006¹⁸⁵⁴ Andreas itᵃʳ arm. (4) μετ᾽ αὐτῶν ἔσται θεός] fam 1611¹⁶¹¹; copˢᵃ. (5) μετ᾽ αὐτῶν ἔσται] Byzantine itᵍⁱᵍ (*cum illis erit*); Ambrose *De Abr.* 2.5.22 (*cum illis erit;* Vogels, *Untersuchungen*, 229); WHort; Merk, *NT*. (6) ἔσται μετ᾽ αὐτῶν] ℵ 1 1778 2081 Andr a b c d f l 94 copᵇᵒ eth Augustine (*erit cum eis;* Vogels, *Untersuchungen*, 226); Tischendorf, *NT Graece;* Bousset (1906) 444 nn. 2, 3. (7) αὐτῶν θεὸς ἔσται or ἔσται θεὸς αὐτῶν or θεὸς αὐτῶν ἔσται] conjectures that assume the original text has not been transmitted and must be reconstructed: Charles, 2:208, 377, 444; Lohmeyer, 166; Reader, "Stadt Gottes," 312–13 n. 159.

There are two major readings attested in these five variants: a longer reading, (1), (2), and (3), and a shorter reading, (4) and (5). Charles (2:207–8) rejects the shorter readings because they are poorly attested and because they violate the parallelism of vv 3b and 3c; i.e., the inclusion of αὐτῶν θεός, "their God," corresponds to λαοὶ αὐτοῦ, "his people," frequently found as parallels in the OT (Lev 26:12; Jer

24:7; 30:22; 31:1, 33; 32:38; Ezek 11:20; 14:11; 36:28; 37:23, 27; Zech 2:1; 8:8; cf. 2 Cor 6:16; Heb 8:10). It is possible that αὐτῶν θεός was omitted as a later scribal correction because it appeared redundant (B. Weiss, *Johannes-Apokalypse,* 115). Of the two longer readings, reading (3) fits the style of Revelation since pronouns in the gen. *always* follow θεός elsewhere (3:2, 12[3x]; 4:11; 5:10; 7:3, 10, 12; 12:10[2x]; 19:1, 5), but it is too poorly attested to be anything other than a scribal correction. Though reading (1) has the best external attestation, the emphatic position of αὐτῶν is not found elsewhere in Revelation and therefore is not characteristic of the author's style (*TCGNT*[1], 763–64; *TCGNT*[2], 688–89). Schmid (*Studien* 2:125), however, argues, primarily on the basis of the OT parallels (Ezek 37:27; Jer 31:33[LXX 38:33]; Zech 8:8), that A, reading (1), has the correct reading.

4.a. Variants: (1) omit ὁ θεός] ‭א‬ 025 051 fam 1611 Oecumenius[2053] Andreas cop eth it[gig] Irenaeus Beatus Tertullian Tyc[2(MsS)] Augustine Ambrose. (2) ὁ θεός] A l fam 1006[1006 1841] Andr a b c d n Tertullian Tyc[2] Tyc[3] Beatus Apringius vg. (3) ἀπ' αὐτῶν] Andr[g 2045] Byzantine. Reading (2) may have been assimilated from Rev 7:17 and Isa 25:8.

4.b. Variants: (1) ἐκ] A (lacuna in C) ‭א‬ fam 1006[1841]; Tischendorf, *NT Graece;* Nestle-Aland[27]; UBSGNT[4]. (2) ἀπό] Andreas Byzantine; WHort[mg]; von Soden, *Text.* Variant (2) may have arisen through assimilation to LXX Isa 25:8.

4.c. Variant: omit ὁ before θάνατος] ‭א‬ fam 1611[2050 2329].

4.d-d. Variants: (1) ἔτι τὰ πρῶτα] A fam 1006[1006 1841] fam 1611[1611 2329] Oecumenius[2053 2062] 2030 2377 Andreas. (2) ἔτι γὰρ τὰ πρῶτα] Andr i 94[text]. (3) ὅτι τὰ πρῶτα] ‭א‬[1] 046 fam 1611[1854] Augustine. (4) ἔτι τὰ πρόβατα] ‭א‬*.

4.e. Variants: (1) omit ὅτι] A ‭א‬* 025 051 fam 1006[1006 1841] fam 1611[1611 2329] Oecumenius[2053 2062] 2030 2377 Andreas ; Charles, 2:376. (2) ὅτι before τά] Andr a b d c f[2023] g Byzantine; B. Weiss, *Johannes-Apokalypse,* 219; Bousset (1906) 444; von Soden, *Text;* [Nestle-Aland[27]]; [UBSGNT[4]]. It is very possible that ὅτι, following ἔτι (e.g., ETIOTI), was omitted through an error in transcription (B. Weiss, *Johannes-Apokalypse,* 134; *TCGNT*[1], 764; *TCGNT*[2], 689).

4.f-f. Variants: (1) ἀπῆλθαν] A. (2) ἀπῆλθεν] ‭א‬ 046 fam 1611[1854 2050 2329] Oecumenius[2053 2062] Byzantine. (3) ἀπῆλθον] 025. (4) παρῆλθον] fam 1611[1611] (Nestle-Aland[27] lists syr[ph] as a witness to this reading, even though it could also be listed as a witness for readings [1] and [3]). On the morphological variation between the second aor. α-vocalization and the ο/ε-vocalization, see *Note* 21:1.a-a.

5.a. Variant: omit καί] Byzantine Irenaeus[Lat] Apringius.

5.b. Variant: λέγει] fam 1611[1854] 2030 2377.

5.c-c. Variants: (1) καινὰ ποιῶ πάντα] ‭א‬ A 025 Andr b f g l n 1773. (2) πάντα καινὰ ποιῶ] 94 Byzantine. (3) καινοποιῶ] Andreas (Andr a b[2059] c d); 2030 2377.

5.d. Variants: (1) omit μοι] A 046 94 Byzantine. (2) insert μοι] ‭א‬ 025 051 fam 1006[1006 1841] fam 1611[2050] Andreas it[a] vg syr[ph] cop[sa bo] arm eth. Reading (1) is shorter and therefore preferable (*TCGNT*[1], 764–65).

5.e. The ὅτι following the imper. γράψον can be construed three ways: (1) ὅτι used as a marker to introduce causal clauses: "Write, *for* these words are faithful and true" (more than forty times; e.g., 3:4, 16; 14:15); (2) ὅτι *recitativum* used to introduce direct discourse: "Write, 'These words are faithful and true'" (cf. 3:17; 10:6); and (3) ὅτι used to introduce a substantive clause: "Write *that* these words are faithful and true." The first possibility seems more appropriate in the context and is reflected in the *Translation.*

5.f. Variant: insert τοῦ θεοῦ] fam 1611[1854 2329] Byzantine syr[h].

6.a-a. Variants: (1) γέγοναν] A (lacuna in C); ‭א‬[1] Andr l[1678 1778] Irenaeus[Lat] it[gig] Primasius (*factum est. ego sum*); vg syr[ph] (Gwynn, *Apocalypse,* 44, reconstructs the Gk. text to read γέγοναν. ἐγὼ τὸ A κ.τ.λ.); Tischendorf, *NT Graece;* WHort; B. Weiss, *Johannes-Apokalypse,* 219; Bousset (1906) 445; Nestle-Aland[27]; UBSGNT[4]. (2) γέγονα] ‭א‬* 025 046 051 fam 1611[1611 1854 2050 2329] Andreas Byzantine Tyc[2] (*ego sum*); Beatus (*ego sum;* Romero-Pose, *Sancti Beati* 2:383); syr[h] arm; Bousset (1906) 445 (in parentheses). (3) γεγόνασιν] fam 1006 Oecumenius[2053 2062] Andr l[2020 2080] n cop[bo] it[gig] vg Tyconius Primasius Irenaeus[Lat]; von Soden, *Text.* (4) omit γέγοναν] Byzantine. (5) γέγονεν] emendation by Bousset (1906) 445, based on parallel in 16:17; see it[gig] vg Primasius: *factum est. ego sum.* (6) γέγονε] Andr c.

This variant reading must be discussed with that in *Note* 6.b-b., for when reading (2), γέγονα, occurs in MSS, either εἰμί or ἐγώ εἰμι is missing. γέγοναν of reading (1) is a 3rd pl. pf. verb from γίνεσθαι, with a rare second aor. ending that probably encouraged correction (*TCGNT*[1], 765). Reading (2) is therefore a scribal correction using the common second pf. endings. The verb γέγονα (1st sing. pf.) presupposes the absence of εἰμί, so γέγονα ἐγὼ τὸ ἄλφα is understood to be the beginning of a divine pronouncement: "I am the Alpha . . ." (Schmid, *Studien* 2:94). For the originality of εἰμί, see Rev 1:8; against it, see Rev 22:13. Yet εἰμί could have been interpolated through the influence of 1:8. Reading (1), γέγοναν, uses the first aor. 3rd pl. ending -αν instead of the normal pf. 3rd pl. ending -ασι (BDR § 83; Gignac, *Grammar* 2:354–55; Moulton-Howard, *Accidence,* 221; Mussies, *Morphology,* 265).

6.b-b. Variants: (1) ἐγώ εἰμι] A fam 1006 Andr l n; B. Weiss, *Johannes-Apokalypse,* 219; Charles, 2:379 (omits γέγοναν); [Nestle-Aland[27]]; [UBSGNT[4]]. (2) omit εἰμί] ℵ 025 046 051 fam 1611[1611 1854 2050 2329] Andreas ; Tischendorf, *NT Graece;* von Soden, *Text;* Bousset (1906) 445. (3) omit ἐγώ εἰμι] Andr a b c d f[2023] 94 Byzantine. See the discussion in *Note* 6.a-a. Reading (2) is possible since the pronoun ἐγώ frequently occurs when εἰμί is omitted (BDR § 128.2).

6.c-c. See *Note* 1:8.a-a. on the corresponding phrase in 1:8.

6.d-d. The partitive gen. ἐκ τῆς πηγῆς is the obj. of the verb δώσω, and therefore the phrase "some water" has been supplied in the translation.

6.e-e. The prep. phrase ἐκ τῆς πηγῆς τοῦ ὕδατος τῆς ζωῆς, "from the well of living water," is a partitive gen. (intensified by the prep. ἐκ) that functions as the obj. of the verb δώσω, "I will give"; see BDR § 164. For other similar uses of the partitive gen. as obj. of the verb, see 2:7, 10, 17 (simple partitive gen.); 5:9. For an example of ἀπό + the partitive gen. functioning as the obj. of the verb, see 22:19.

7.a. Plurals added for inclusive language: "those," "their," "they," and "children" (for "son").

7.b-b. Variant: δώσω αὐτῷ] 046 94 Byzantine.

7.c. Since the context makes it clear that inheritance (v 7a) is dependent on the father-child relationship (v 7b), the καί should be construed as providing the reason for the previous clause and has therefore been translated "for" (Aejmelaeus, *Parataxis,* 23–24; GKC § 158).

7.d. Variants: (1) αὐτῷ] ℵ fam 1611[1611 1854] Oecumenius[2053] Andr d f[2023 -2073] g l n 94 Byzantine. (2) αὐτῶν] A fam 1611[1854] 2030 2377 Andreas Tertullian. (3) αὐτοῖς] Andr h[2286].

7.e-e. Variants: (1) ἔσται μοι υἱός] A fam 1006 cop[sa]. (2) αὐτοὶ ἔσονταί μοι υἱοί] 051 fam 1611[1854] 2030 2377 Andreas Tertullian.

8.a. ἐβδελυγμένοις may refer to sexual perverts (Louw-Nida, § 25.186).

8.b. μέρος here is used in the sense of sharing or experiencing something together with others; see W. S. Vorster, "New Testament Sample Studies," in *Lexicography and Translation with Special Reference to Bible Translation,* ed. J. P. Louw (Cape Town: Bible Society of South Africa, 1985) 144.

8.c-c. In the phrase ὅ ἐστιν, "which is," ὅ is a neut. sing. nom. relative pronoun that can be construed as congruent in number and gender with the preceding articular noun τὸ μέρος, "the portion." In relative clauses that contain a predicate nom., as here, the relative pronoun is attracted sometimes to the gender of the predicate nom. (which in this case would be the masc. sing. noun ὁ θάνατος) and sometimes to the gender of the substantive modified by the relative clause (Schmid, *Studien* 2:206). Logically, ὅ ἐστιν could also modify τῇ λίμνῃ τῇ καιομένῃ πυρὶ καὶ θείῳ, "the lake burning with fire and sulphur." In fact, ὅ ἐστιν (or ἅ ἐστιν) is an indeclinable idiom frequently used to modify substantives of any gender (BDF § 132; BDR § 132; Turner, *Syntax,* 48 [where Rev 20:12 is incorrectly cited as an example]). The only other instances of this idiom in Revelation are found in 20:2 and in 21:17, though in 20:2 the reading ὅ ἐστιν is weakly supported by ℵ and five minuscules: fam 1611[2050] Byz 8[180] Andr l[1678 1778 2080]. The idiom occurs frequently in Colossians and Ignatius; see Col 1:24, 27; 2:17, 23; 3:14 (since this is a construction missing from undoubtedly genuine Pauline letters, it has been used as an argument for the pseudonymity of Colossians; see M. Kiley, *Colossians as Pseudepigraphy* [Sheffield: JSOT, 1986] 56); Ignatius *Eph.* 17:2; 18:1; 20:2 (*var. lect.* preferred by G. Snyder, "The Text and Syntax of Ignatius ΠΡΟΣ ΕΦΕΣΙΟΥΣ 20:2C," *VC* 22 [1968] 8–13; ὅς ἐστιν, on the other hand, is preferred by Wehr, *Unsterblichkeit,* 92–94); *Magn.* 7:1; 10:2; *Trall.* 8:1[2x]; *Rom.* 5:1; 7:3[2x]; *Smyrn.* 5:3.

Form/Structure/Setting

I. OUTLINE

5. The new heaven and new earth (21:1–8)
   a. Summary of the vision (vv 1–2)
      (1) The new heaven and the new earth (v 1a)
         (a) The first heaven and and the first earth had passed away (v 1b)
         (b) The sea no longer existed (v 1b)
      (2) John sees the New Jerusalem (v 2)
         (a) Descending from heaven (v 2a)

         (b) Adorned like a bride (v 2b)
    b. Audition of a voice from the throne (vv 3–4)
         (1) Introduction to audition (v 3a)
         (2) God dwells with people (v 3bc)
         (3) Human troubles no longer exist (v 4ab)
         (4) The former things are gone (v 4b)
    c. Audition of a speech of God consisting of seven sayings (vv 5–8)
         (1) "Behold, I am making everything new" (v 5a)
         (2) "Write, for this message is trustworthy and true" (v 5b)
         (3) "It is finished" (v 6a)
         (4) "I am the Alpha and the Omega, the Beginning and the End" (v 6b)
         (5) God will provide living water for the thirsty (v 6c)
         (6) The conqueror will inherit this (v 7)
         (7) The second death for wicked (v 8)

II. Literary Analysis

Rev 21:1–8 is the third and last subsection within 19:11–21:8, a section framed by two parallel angelic revelations in 17:1–19:10 and 21:9–22:9. 21:1–8 consists of two subordinate units of text, (1) 21:1–4 (an angelic speech from the throne) and (2) 21:5–8 (a speech of God, seated on his throne). This section is a textual unit framed at the beginning by the καὶ εἶδον, "then I saw," formula (v 1), which is used here to introduce a new vision (see *Comment* on 5:1), and at the end by the appearance of one of the seven bowl angels in v 9. V 9 serves as an introduction to a new text unit (21:9–22:6), which is carefully framed in a way parallel to 17:1–19:10.

The first subunit of 21:1–8, vv 1–4, is framed by the verbal parallels in v 1, "the first [πρῶτος] heaven and the first [πρώτη] earth had passed away [ἀπῆλθαν]," and in v 4, "the former things had passed away [τὰ πρῶτα ἀπῆλθαν]." Rev 21:5a, however, serves as a transition, for it both concludes vv 1–4 and introduces vv 5b–8. Rev 21:1–4 consists of two main elements. (1) Vv 1–2 consist of a brief introductory description of John's vision, in which (a) and (d) succinctly portray the two foci of his vision, while (b) and (c) enigmatically refer to the disappearance of the first creation: (a) the new heaven and the new earth (v 1a), (b) the first heaven and the first earth have passed away (v 1b), (c) the sea no longer exists (v 1b), and (d) the holy city Jerusalem descends from heaven adorned like a bridegroom (v 2). (2) Vv 3–4 contain an audition (not a vision) from an unidentified voice from the throne (v 3a), which provides a commentary on the three foci of John's vision, in reverse order, forming a chiasmus: (a) the dwelling of God is with people (v 3b), so that (b) death and all human troubles no longer exist (vv 3b–4a), (c) because the former things, i.e., heaven, earth, and the sea have passed away (v 4b), and (d) God then announces, "Behold, I have made everything new" (v 5a). These elements fall into a chiastic schema in which the four terms or phrases καινός, "new" (v 1a), πρῶτος, "first" (v 1b), ἀπῆλθαν, "passed away" (v 1b), and οὐκ ἔστιν ἔτι, "no longer exists" (v 1b), occur in reverse order in vv 4b and 5a (this is an expansion of van Ruiten, *EstBib* 51 [1993] 475–77):

a   new [καινός] heaven and the new [καινή] earth (v 1a)
  b   first [πρῶτος] heaven, earth, and sea have passed away [ἀπῆλθαν] (v 1b)
    c   the sea exists no longer [οὐκ ἔστιν ἔτι] (v 1b)
      d   the holy city descends from heaven (v 2)
      d'   God dwells with people (vv 3–4a)
    c'   death exists no longer [οὐκ ἔσται ἔτι] (v 4b)
  b'   former things [τὰ πρῶτα] have passed away [ἀπῆλθαν] (v 4b)
a'   God creates everything new [καινά] (v 5a)

This chiastic structure indicates that a new unity has been imposed on this passage following the insertion of 21:5–22:2 between 21:1–4 and 22:3–5 (an original poetic unity; see above). The structure of this passage is now intended to direct the reader to focus on the importance of the descent of the holy city since the longest description in this text unit is devoted to the significance of that event (vv 3–4a). In 21:1, the new heaven and the new earth are the objects of καὶ εἶδον, "then I saw," normally used to introduce a vision narrative or to focus on one aspect of a vision narrative in progress. This verse, however, provides no narration and remains as an abbreviated description of a vision that is not narrated.

The second subunit, vv 5–8, is also an audition but a very special one because it is attributed to God, who is seated on his throne (elsewhere in Revelation only in 1:8 is God clearly the speaker). This speech is striking because it is essentially a collection of *seven* sayings (the number is probably intentional, like the seven beatitudes scattered throughout the book), the first three of which exhibit a formal similarity in contrast to the last four, thus producing a 3 + 4 pattern (the first three are introduced with verbs of saying, while the last four are not). While each of the sayings will be discussed in more detail in *Comment,* it is appropriate here to list them:

(1) Then the One sitting on the throne *said,*
     "Behold, I am making everything new" (v 5a).

(2) He also *said,* "Write, for this message is trustworthy and true" (v 5b).

(3) He also *said* to me, "It is finished" (v 6a).

(4) "I am the Alpha and the Omega,
     the Beginning and the End" (v 6b).

(5) "I will freely give some water to the one who is thirsty
     from the well of living water" (v 6c).

(6) "Those who conquer will inherit these things,
     for I will be their God and they will be my children" (v 7).

(7) "But as for the cowards and unbelievers and the abominable and murderers
     and the immoral and sorcerers and idolaters and all who lie,
     they will experience the lake that burns with fire and sulphur,
     which is the second death" (v 8).

The first saying in v 5a, as we saw above, forms a conclusion to vv 1–4 as well as an introduction to vv 5–8. A linguistic feature that links vv 5–8 with vv 1–4 is the

pronoun ταῦτα, "these things," which probably refers to the eschatological blessings enumerated in v 4.

III. Source-Critical Analysis

In order to make sense of the present order of the text, it is necessary to propose
that that 21:3–4 was originally linked with 22:3–5 and that 21:5–22:2 was subsequently
inserted into this passage. A number of NT scholars have correctly argued that 21:3–
4 and 22:3–5 originally belonged together (e.g., J. Weiss, *Offenbarung*, 107). But the
sometimes concomitant view that all or part of the material inserted in 21:5 to 22:2
was an originally coherent Jewish apocalyptic composition (Bergmeier, *ZNW* 75
[1984] 90–101) does not seem correct. The arguments for the original unity of 21:3–
4 and 22:3–5 are these: (1) These units form a poetic composition with four strophes,
each consisting of four lines. (2) Twelve of the thirteen verbs in this unit are in the
future tense (except ἔχουσιν in 22:5b, which functions as a futuristic present). (3)
This poetic text has the formulaic expression οὐκ ἔσται ἔτι, "there will no longer be"
(21:4b, 4c; 22:3a, 5a), which occurs nowhere else in Revelation. (4) The phrase "and
the Lamb" is bracketed because it is probable that the phrase was added to the text
when 21:5–22:2 was added since the term "Lamb" occurs no less than *seven* times in
21:1–22:5 (21:9, 14, 22, 23, 27; 22:1, 3) and always appears to be tangential and
secondary. When the intervening text in 21:4d ("the former things have passed
away") through 22:2 is removed, the resultant text unit looks like this:

21:3b	Behold the dwelling of God [is] with people,
3c	and he will [σκηνώσει] dwell with them,
3d	and they will [ἔσονται] be his people,
3e	and God himself will be [ἔσται] with them as their God.
21:4a	And he will wipe away [ἐξαλείψει] every tear from their eyes,
4b	and death will no longer exist [οὐκ ἔσται ἔτι],
4c	nor will grief or crying or pain exist any longer [οὐκ ἔσται ἔτι],
22:3a	and "the curse of war" will no longer exist [οὐκ ἔσται ἔτι].
22:3b	The throne of God [and of the Lamb] will be [ἔσται] in the city,
3c	and his servants will worship [λατρεύσουσιν] him.
4a	And they will see [ὄψονται] his face,
4b	and his name [will be] on their foreheads.
22:5a	There will [ἔσται] no longer be any night,
5b	and people will have [ἔχουσιν] no need for lamp light or sunlight,
5c	because the Lord God will illuminate [φωτίσει] them,
5d	and they will reign [βασιλεύσουσιν] for ever and ever.

Comment

1a καὶ εἶδον οὐρανὸν καινὸν καὶ γῆν καινήν, "Then I saw a new heaven and a new
earth." (On the various functions of the introductory vision formula καὶ εἶδον,

"then I saw," see *Comment* on 5:1.) This vision of the new heaven and the new earth, which succeed the first heaven and the first earth that have "passed away" (v 1b), is introduced abruptly and enigmatically. This allusion to Isa 65:17 appears to be more closely related to the LXX than to the MT for three reasons: (1) the LXX has no equivalent for the Hebrew term ברא *bārāʾ*, "create"; (2) the term οὐρανόν, "heaven," is singular here and in the LXX, while the plural form שמים *šāmayim*, "heavens," occurs in the MT (the allusion to Isa 65:17 in 2 Pet 3:13 has the plural form); and (3) the LXX phrase τῶν προτέρων, "the former things," is reflected in the choice of the terms ὁ πρῶτος and ἡ πρώτη, "the first," in Rev 21:1. The absence of the definite articles with οὐρανὸν καινόν, "new heaven," and γῆν καινήν, "new earth" (also absent in the allusion to Isa 65:17 in 2 Pet 3:13), however, may suggest either the independent translation of Isa 65:17 (or 66:22) by the author or dependence on a Greek version other than the LXX. The articles are absent from the MT and the Hexapla but present in the LXX.

While throughout earlier vision narratives the reader can identify the perspective of the seer as either heaven or earth, the indeterminable perspective in this verse suggests the literary rather than the visionary origin of the passage. By using the introductory vision formula καὶ εἶδον, "and I saw," the author has transformed an oracle of Yahweh in Isa 65:17 (cf. 66:22), "For behold, I create new heavens and a new earth; and the former things shall not be remembered or come into mind," into a vision narrative.

The theme of the re-creation or renewal of creation in ancient Judaism is not limited to Isa 65:17 and 66:22 but is referred to in a variety of ways in Jewish apocalyptic literature as the final eschatological act. This view is reflected in *1 Enoch* 91:16, part of the Apocalypse of Weeks, written ca. 170 B.C. (Knibb, *Enoch* 2:220): "And the first heaven will vanish and pass away, and a new heaven will appear, and all the powers of heaven will shine for ever (with) sevenfold (light)." Based on this parallel, Milik (*Enoch*, 199) and M. Black ("New Creation," 17–18) argue that John was dependent on *1 Enoch*. Similarly, *1 Enoch* 45:4 speaks of the transformation of heaven. This view is reiterated in *Bib. Ant.* 3:10, a document that originated in Palestine during the first century A.D. It contains a description of the events that will follow the general resurrection and judgment presided over by God (tr. D. J. Harrington, *OTP* 2:307): "And the world will cease, and death will be abolished, and hell will shut its mouth. . . . And there will be another earth and another heaven, an everlasting dwelling place."

A number of other passages in early Jewish apocalyptic literature refer to the re-creation or transformation of an eternal heaven or an eternal earth or both (though the ambiguity of some texts often makes it difficult to distinguish between creation and transformation): (1) *creation of a new heaven and/or earth* (2 Peter 3:13; *1 Enoch* 72:1; 91:16; *Sib. Or.* 5.212 [καινὴ φύσις, "new nature"]; *Jub.* 1:29 ["new creation"]; *Jub.* 4:26 ["new creation"]; *Bib. Ant.* 3:10 ["there will be another heaven and another earth"]; *Apoc. Elijah* 5:38 [dependent on Rev 21:1]; see 2 Cor 5:17; Gal 6:15) and (2) *transformation or renewal of heaven and/or earth* (*1 Enoch* 45:4–5; *2 Apoc. Bar.* 32:6; 44:12 ["new world"]; 49:3; 57:2; *Bib. Ant.* 32:17; *Jub.* 1:29; 4 Ezra 7:30–31, 75; *Tg. Jer.* 23:23; Matt 19:28; Rom 8:21). According to 1QS 4:25 there will be an equal allotment of the spirits of truth and error "until the determined end, and until the Renewal [עד קץ נחרצה ועשות חדשה *ʿad qēṣ neḥěrāṣâ waʿăśôt ḥădāšâ*]" (tr. Vermes, *Dead Sea Scrolls*). Here the phrase ועשות חדשה *waʿăśôt ḥădāšâ*, literally "the making of the new," probably refers to the new creation (Leaney, *Rule,* 160–61). The apocalyptic notion of the re-creation of the heaven and the earth is given an anthropological application by Paul, who refers to Christians as a "new creation" (2 Cor 5:17; Gal 6:15), and by the author of 1QH 11:13, who speaks of humans as "renewed together with all the living" (tr. Vermes, *Dead Sea Scrolls,* 195).

1b ὁ γὰρ πρῶτος οὐρανὸς καὶ ἡ πρώτη γῆ ἀπῆλθαν καὶ ἡ θάλασσα οὐκ ἔστιν ἔτι, "For the first heaven and the first earth passed away, and the sea no longer existed." This statement, taken together with that in 20:11b, makes it difficult to avoid the conclusion that the author has in view the *complete destruction* of the physical universe (Vögtle, "Himmel," 304–6), though there are a number of scholars who think that a renewal or transformation of the universe is in view (Caird, 260, 265–66; Prigent, 324–25; Bauckham, *Theology,* 49–50). One of the striking features of this laconic statement is the fact that a destruction of the cosmos by *fire* is not mentioned here or anywhere else in Revelation (Bousset, *Antichrist,* 244). In early Judaism there was a tradition of *two* destructions of the world whereby God judges the human race, once by water and once by fire (*Adam and Eve* 49:3; Jos. *Ant.* 1.70; *b. Zebaḥ.* 116a; cf. Philo *Abr.* 1.1; 2 Pet 3:5–7). The alternating destruction of the world, first by fire and then by water, is also found in Greek sources (Plato *Timaeus* 22c–d). Berossus speculated that cycles of great years, consisting of 432,000 years, each had a "summer," which brought a fiery conflagration of the world, and a "winter," which brought a universal flood (Seneca *Quaest. nat.* 3.29.1; Cumont, *Oriental Religions,* 176; Glasson, *Greek Influence,* 74–80).

In the OT and early Judaism there is a link between divine judgment and fiery destruction (cf. Mayer, *Weltenbrand,* 79–99; *TDNT* 6:936–41), though it is often difficult to determine whether *partial* or *complete* destruction of the world is in view. In Isa 51:6 and Ps 102:25–26, the eternity of God is contrasted to the temporary existence of the heavens and the earth, which will eventually wear out and pass away. The destruction of the earth by fire in the day of judgment is predicted in Zeph 1:18–2:2 and 3:8. The phrase "the entire earth will be consumed by the fire of his/my passion" occurs twice (Zeph 1:18; 3:8), but it probably refers to God rising to destroy the nations, not to the literal destruction of the earth itself (Berlin, *Zephaniah,* 133). A literal cosmic destruction is sometimes said to precede the restoration of earth, though it is frequently difficult to determine whether the authors intend partial or complete destruction (Isa 65:17; 66:22; *Jub.* 23:18; *1 Enoch* 10:2; 91:16; 1QH 11:32–33 [3:32–33]; 14:18 [6:18]). At least a partial destruction of the world by fire is expressed or implied in Isa 51:6 and 66:15–16 (Mayer, *Weltenbrand,* 104–14). In *Sib. Or.* 5.447 the drying up of the sea is an event predicted for the "last time." According to *1 Enoch* 96:16 (which also alludes to Isa 65:17, though as a prophecy, not a vision), "The first heaven will vanish and pass away, and a new heaven will appear." The phrase "will vanish and pass away" occurs in both *1 Enoch* 96:16 and Rev 21:1, suggesting either literary dependence or dependence on a common apocalyptic tradition.

There are several early Jewish apocalyptic texts in which the complete destruction of the cosmos is clearly in view (Ps.-Sophocles [Clement Alex. *Strom.* 5.14.121–22; Ps.-Justin *De monarchia* 3; text in Denis, *Fragmenta,* 167–68]; *Sib. Or.* 2.196–213; 3.8–92; 4.171–92; 5.155–61; 1QH 11:32–33 [3:32–33]; 14:18 [6:18]; LXX Isa 34:4; Jos. *Ant.* 1.70). The earliest such passage is in Ps.-Sophocles (tr. H. Attridge, *OTP* 2:826):

> For there will, there will indeed, come that period of time
> when the gold-faced sky will split apart
> the treasury filled with fire, and the nurtured flame
> will in its rage consume all things on earth
> and in the heavens.
> And when the universe gives out,
> the whole wavy deep will be gone;
> the land will be empty of dwelling; the air,
> in flames, will not bear winged flocks.

Since these texts originate from the second century B.C. and later, it is possible that the fiery destruction of the cosmos has been influenced by Stoicism (see below), though the infinitely repeated destructions of the cosmos advocated by Stoicism were never adopted (cf. Tatian *Oratio* 25.2). Theophilus (*Ad Autolycum* 2.37–38) accused the Greek authors of stealing the notion of the conflagration of the universe from the prophets. According to the eschatological scenario in *Gk. Apoc. Ezra* 3:38 (tr. M. E. Stone, *OTP* 1:576), "Then the heaven and the earth and the sea will perish." According to *Apoc. Elijah* 2:1, the dissolution of heaven and earth is part of the eschatological scenario. In *2 Apoc. Bar.* 3:7, the question is asked, "Will the universe return to its nature and the world go back to its original silence?" The fiery destruction of the heavens is even part of the eschatology of the Coptic-Gnostic tractate *Orig. World* 126.29–35. This dominant view, that in the eschaton heaven and earth must either be recreated or transformed, appears to be contradicted by *2 Apoc. Bar.* 19:2 (tr. A. F. J. Klijn, *OTP* 1:627), "heaven and earth will stay forever." The same perspective is reflected in *Tg. Jer.* 33:25 (tr. Hayward), where the idea that heaven and earth will pass away is opposed:

> Thus says the Lord: Just as it is not possible that my covenant which I swore with the day and with the night should cease, so is the covenant of the heaven and the earth: I have made them that they should not pass away.

The apocalyptic theme of the destruction of the heavens and the earth occurs occasionally in early Christianity (see Heb 12:26–27 [based on Hag 2:6]; 2 Pet 3:12; Justin *1 Apol.* 20.1–4; 60.8–9; *2 Apol.* 7.2–3; *2 Clem.* 16:3; *Apoc. Peter* 5; Minucius Felix *Oct.* 11.1–3; 34.1–4; Lactantius *Div. Inst.* 7.21). This theme is particularly associated with a logion of Jesus concerning the disappearance of heaven and earth, which is found in three major versions, one from the Q-tradition, where it is linked with the issue of the validity of the Torah, a second in the eschatological discourse (Mark 13 and par.), in which it is linked with the permanent validity of the words of Jesus, and a third in *Gos. Thom.* 11. Let us first examine the version preserved in the Q-tradition in Luke 16:17:

εὐκοπώτερον δέ ἐστιν τὸν οὐρανὸν καὶ τὴν γῆν παρελθεῖν
But it is easier for heaven and earth to pass away

ἢ τοῦ νόμου μίαν κεραίαν πεσεῖν
than for one part of a letter to drop out of the law.

To this may be compared a variant of this logion found in a secondary context in Matt 5:18:

ἔως ἄν παρέλθῃ ὁ οὐρανὸς καὶ ἡ γῆ,
until heaven and earth pass away

ἰῶτα ἓν ἢ μία κεραία οὐ μὴ παρέλθῃ ἀπὸ τοῦ νόμου.
not one letter or one part of a letter will disappear from the law.

It is probable that Luke's version of this saying represents a more original version of Q in which the disappearance of heaven and earth is a metaphor for the permanence of the Torah. Though Matthew's version *may* be understood to mean that the validity of the Law will end with the eschaton (the view of patristic exegesis), it is nevertheless probable that Matthew is using the phrase as an idiom meaning "never" (Luz, *Matthäus* 1:237 [ET 265]; for references see Banks, *Law*, 215 n. 1). Another version of this logion is found in the eschatological discourse (Mark 13:31 = Matt 24:35 = Luke 21:33; Mark 13:31 and Luke 21:33 are identical, while only insignificant changes are introduced in Matt 24:35):

Mark 13:31:   ὁ οὐρανὸς καὶ ἡ γῆ παρελεύσονται,
                              Heaven and earth will disappear,

                              οἱ δὲ λόγοι μου οὐ μὴ παρελεύσονται.
                              but my words will not disappear.

Matt 24:35   ὁ οὐρανὸς καὶ ἡ γῆ παρελεύσεται,
                              Heaven and earth will disappear,

                              οἱ δὲ λόγοι μου οὐ μὴ παρέλθωσιν.
                              but my words will never disappear.

A third major version of this logion is preserved in *Gos. Thom.* 11a:

Jesus said, "This heaven will pass away,
and the one above it will pass away,
and the dead are not alive
and the living shall not die."

In this passage the two heavens apparently include the lower created one consisting of the sun, moon, and stars as well as the upper one where God dwells (J. É. Ménard, *L'Évangile selon Thomas* [Montélimar: Marsanne, 1974] 37, 96). The context has completely changed, for there is no mention of the words of the Torah or the words of Jesus.

Though the destruction of the sea is mentioned in Rev 21:1, it is noteworthy that the sea is not mentioned in connection with the new heaven and the new earth. This may be because the sea was a negative symbol for chaos and even for the abyss (cf. Rev 13:1 with 11:7). The motif of the disappearance of the sea reflects the ancient Israelite tradition of the opposition of Yahweh and the sea. The antipathy between Yahweh and the sea is expressed in a variety of ways in the OT and early Judaism (Kloos, *Combat*, 81–83): (1) Yahweh establishes a border or sets a guard on the sea (Jer 5:22; Job 7:12). (2) Yahweh rebukes or is angry with the waters (Isa 1:2; Nah 1:4; Hab 3:8; Pss 18:6; 29:3; *1 Enoch* 101:7). (3) Yahweh dries up the waters (Isa 1:2; 19:5; Jer 1:38; 51:36; Ezek 30:12; Nah 1:4; Ps 18:16; Job 12:15; *Sib. Or.* 5.447; *1*

Enoch 101:7). Some of these motifs are combined in individual passages: (1) *1 Enoch* 101:7 (God rebukes the sea so that it dries up), (2) Ps 18:16 = 2 Sam 22:16 (God rebukes the sea so that its beds become visible), (3) Nah 1:4 (God rebukes the sea and dries up the sea and all the rivers), and (4) Isa 1:2 (God rebukes the sea, dries it up, and turns the rivers into desert).

In Greek philosophical thought one tradition held to the eternity and indestructibility of the cosmos, while another maintained that the destruction (and restoration) of the cosmos would occur repeatedly. The eternity of the cosmos was maintained by Heraclitus, who claimed that the cosmos "always was and is and shall be, an ever-living fire, kindling in measures and going out in measures" (Diels-Kranz, *FVS* 22B, 30; from Clement Alex. *Strom.* 5.104.2). The language Heraclitus uses is that normally reserved for the one God in Greek philosophical thought, indicating that Heraclitus considered the cosmos to be divine. Plato and Aristotle, and the philosophical schools that traced their intellectual descent from them, consistently maintained the eternality of the cosmos. The eternity of the world was also held by Philo (*Aet.* 117–49).

Early in the fourth century B.C. the Stoic doctrine of ἐκπύρωσις, "conflagration," the periodic destruction of the world by fire (see Arnim, *SVF* 1:98), was developed. A fragment of Zeno reports that "The universe will be destroyed by fire. Everything which has something to burn, shall burn up its fuel" (P. W. van der Horst and J. Mansfield, *An Alexandrian Platonist against Dualism: Alexander of Lycopolis' Treatise 'Critique of the Doctrines of Manichaeus'* [Leiden: Brill, 1974] 74). This conflagration is dramatized by Seneca in *Hercules Oetaeus* 1102–18, where the dying Herakles anticipates the fall of the southern and northern heavens upon the earth, the fall of the sun, and the destruction of everything. A new world comes into existence out of the total destruction of the previous world (with the exception of the gods), though the new world is exactly like the old one in every respect (Arnim, *SVF* 2:625), so the destruction of the previous world was not caused by moral degeneration of human beings. The conflagration, however, was not a single culminative event but was part of an infinite cycle of conflagrations and was looked upon in a positive light (*SVF* 1:510–11, 536–38); i.e., the resolution of the cosmos into fire was considered a state of perfection.

In Rev 21:1, just two levels of the usual ancient Israelite and ancient Near Eastern three-level cosmos are mentioned: (1) the heaven and (2) the earth and the sea (on the three-level cosmos in Revelation, see *Comments* on 5:3, 13 and 10:6).

2a καὶ τὴν πόλιν τὴν ἁγίαν Ἰερουσαλὴμ καινὴν εἶδον καταβαίνουσαν ἐκ τοῦ οὐρανοῦ ἀπὸ τοῦ θεοῦ, "I saw the the holy city, New Jerusalem, descending from heaven from God." This entire phrase, less καινὴν εἶδον, "I saw a new," is repeated verbatim in v 10. Since it is improbable that the author intended to imply that he saw the holy city descend from heaven *twice*, it is clear that vv 1–2 function as an introduction to the more detailed description in 21:9–22:9, i.e., as a superscription or title (see *Comments* on 15:1 and 17:1–2). Here the formula καὶ εἶδον, "then I saw," functions to focus attention on a new aspect of the vision (see *Comment* on 5:1). The style of this clause is unusual, for of thirty-three uses of the phrase καὶ εἶδον in Revelation, this is the only instance in which the object of a vision, in the accusative, is inserted between καί and εἶδον. For the verbal similarities between 21:2, 10, and 3:12, see *Comment* on 3:12.

The mention of Jerusalem here is part of a number of allusions to Isa 65:17–20 in

Rev 21:1–5. The earliest occurrence of the phrase "Jerusalem the holy city" is found in Isa 52:1, and of "holy city" in Isa 48:2. Thereafter there is an increasing tendency to use the term "the holy city" to mean "Jerusalem" (see *Comment* on 11:2). Jerusalem is occasionally called "the holy city Jerusalem" in early Jewish literature (LXX Isa 66:20; LXX Joel 4:17; Tob 13:10 [MSS A B]; Dan 3:28; Pr Azar 5; *Pss. Sol.* 8:4). The phrase "Jerusalem the holy" (in paleo-Hebrew script ירושלם הקדושה *yrwšlym hkdwš*) occurs on silver shekels minted during the first Jewish revolt in A.D. 66–70; see Matthiae and Schönert-Geiss, *Münzen*, 84–85, plate 38. Apart from *T. Dan* 5:12, the phrase "New Jerusalem" does not occur in the OT or early Jewish literature. In fact, there is a strikingly widespread reluctance to call the heavenly or eschatological city "Jerusalem." In Ezek 40–48, the name "Jerusalem" does not occur, though it is found nineteen times in Ezek 1–39. The eschatological city is renamed יהוה שמה *YHWH šämmâ*, "Yahweh is There" (Ezek 48:35). (On "heaven" as a circumlocution for the name of God [suggesting that "from God" here is redundant], see *Comment* on 3:12.) Rome is called "the heavenly city [οὐρανοπόλις]" in Athenaeus *Deipn.* 1.20C.

The phrase καταβαίνειν ἐκ τοῦ οὐρανοῦ, "descending from heaven," is used of the New Jerusalem (in Rev 3:12; 21:10), as well as of an angel (10:1; 18:1; 20:1), fire (13:13; 20:9), and hailstones (16:21). In no other early Jewish or early Christian texts is the heavenly city said to "descend from heaven," but the city is variously described as "coming," "appearing," or "is revealed" (4 Ezra 7:26; 13:36; 10:54).

2b ἡτοιμασμένην ὡς νύμφην κεκοσμημένην τῷ ἀνδρὶ αὐτῆς, "prepared as a bride adorned for her husband." The term νύμφη, "bride," is used of the Church here and in 21:9 and 22:17 in Revelation, but not elsewhere in early Christian literature. The metaphorical *topos* "as an adorned bride," however, is found in a variety of forms in ancient literature, primarily inspired by Isa 61:10, which uses the simile "as a bride adorns herself [ככלה תעדה *kakkallâ ta'deh*] with her jewels" (see also Isa 49:18; van Ruiten, *EstBib* 51 [1993] 489–92).

Here are several examples of this *topos*: (1) Aseneth is described as κεκοσμημένην ὡς νύμφην θεοῦ, "adorned as the bride of God" (*Jos. As.* 4.1), a view that M. Philonenko takes not as metaphorical but as suggesting that she will marry a future king of Egypt who is in reality a god in disguise (*Joseph et Aséneth* [Leiden: Brill, 1968] 141). (2) The only possible allusion to Revelation in Hermas is to this verse, an allusion that occurs in *Vis.* 4.2.1, ἰδού, ὑπαντᾷ μοι παρθένος κεκοσμημένη ὡς ἐκ νυμφῶνος ἐκπορευομένη, "Behold, a virgin met me adorned as though emerging from the bridal chamber." Even though this figure is interpreted as the Church (*Vis.* 4.2.2), the proverbial character of the saying together with the fact that no other allusions to Revelation occur suggests that it is probably independent of Revelation. (3) The character of this description as a *topos* is further suggested by the parallel in Irenaeus *Adv. haer.* 1.13.3 (Harvey, *Sancti Irenaei* 1:118), where the Gnostic Marcus reportedly says, εὐπρέπισον σεαυτὴν, ὡς νύμφη ἐκδεχομένη τὸν νυμφίον ἑαυτῆς, "Adorn yourself as a bride expecting her bridegroom." (4) A further parallel occurs in Achilles Tatius 3.7.5, ὥσπερ Ἀϊδωνεῖ νύμφη κεκοσμημένη, "as a bride adorned for Hades" (a metaphor for Persephone). (5) Again, in *Ep. Lugd.* 1.35 (tr. Musurillo, *Acts*), where there does not seem to be an allusion to Rev 21:2, the martyrs in their chains are referred to metaphorically "as a bride adorned [ὡς νύμφη κεκοσμημένη] with golden embroidered tassels."

For the use of ἑτοιμάζειν, "to prepare," of the bride = New Jerusalem, see Rev 19:8. The combination of bride and city is mentioned in *b. Soṭa* 49b (tr. Epstein):

"What means 'crowns worn by brides'?—Rabbah b. Bar Hanah said in the name of R. Johanan: A [miniature] golden city." In *b. Šabb.* 59a the crown is described as a golden crown in the form of Jerusalem (S. Krauss, *Talmudische Archäologie* 1:662 n. 961). In the OT, Israel is often described with female metaphors: as a young royal bride (Ezek 16:8–14), as a harlot (Ezek 16:15–22; Hos 2:2–3:5; Jer 2:1–2; 3:1; Ezek 16:11), and most commonly as the "mother" (Isa 50:1; Hos 4:5; 4 Ezra 10:7–8; 2 Bar 3:1–3), who has "children" (Isa 49:20–22, 25; 51:18–20; 54:1; Ezek 16:20). Jerusalem is described as a captive woman in *Pss. Sol.* 2:19–21, an image repeated in the various series of *Iudaea capta* coins minted under Vespasian after the fall of Jerusalem on 7–8 September A.D. 70 (Mattingly-Carson, *CREBM* 2:5–7, nos. 31–44; 115–18, nos. 532–47; 185, nos. 761–65; Cayón, *Compendio* 1:213–14, nos. 93–96) and Titus (Mattingly-Carson, *CREBM* 2:256–57, nos. 161–70; Cayón, *Compendio* 1:243, no. 49). The bridal metaphor is applied to the returning Jewish exiles in Deutero-Isaiah (Isa 49:18) and Trito-Isaiah (Isa 61:10; 62:5). In late first-century A.D. Jewish apocalyptic literature, the New Jerusalem is occasionally called a "mother" (4 Ezra 10:7–8; 2 *Apoc. Bar.* 3:1–3; cf. 4 Ezra 9:43–47; 10:17). In Valentinian teaching, according to Hippolytus (*Ref.* 6.34.3–4; ed. Marcovich, *Hippolytus;* cf. Irenaeus *Haer.* 1.5.3; 1.7.1), the heavenly Jerusalem is another name for Sophia, and the bridegroom (ὁ νυμφίος) of Jerusalem is "the common fruit of the pleroma."

In the Greek world, the adornment of the bride, i.e., her trousseau, consisted primarily of clothing and jewelry (Blümner, *Greeks,* 138–39). Pliny *Ep.* 5.16.7 mentions the money that the father of a bride had set aside for her clothing, pearls, and jewels. *T. Jud.* 13.5 refers to a king who "adorned with gold and pearls" (αὐτὴν κοσμήσας ἐν χρυσῷ καὶ μαργαρίταις) his daughter who was about to be married. 1 Tim 2:9, however, recommends that women should adorn themselves (κοσμεῖν ἑαυτάς) not with braided hair, gold, pearls, or expensive clothes (though this has nothing to do with the bridal trousseau; adornment with pearls and silk garments is a metaphor for virtues in Plutarch *Con. prae.* 145E). The adornment of the bride = New Jerusalem is in conscious antithesis to the adornment of the whore = Babylon (Rev 17:4).

One significant interpretive issue lies in the significance of the symbolism of the New Jerusalem. One widespread view is that the New Jerusalem symbolizes the saints (McKelvey, *Temple,* 167–76; Holtz, *Christologie,* 191–95; Gundry, *NovT* 3 [1987] 254–64). Schüssler Fiorenza, however, argues that the New Jerusalem is distinguished from the saints (Schüssler Fiorenza, *Priester für Gott,* 348–50): (1) Rev 21:2 *compares* the city to a bride; the city cannot be that bride. (2) Rev 21:7 mentions that the saints will inherit the city; they cannot be the city. (3) The city is described as a *place* where the saints dwell (21:24–26).

3a καὶ ἤκουσα φωνῆς μεγάλης ἐκ τοῦ θρόνου λεγούσης, "I heard a loud voice from the throne." Though the speaker is not explicitly identified, it is not necessarily God or Christ (Lohmeyer, 151; Kuhn, *Offenbarungsstimmen,* 79 n. 49) since the voice refers to God in the third person (see v 3b). On the motif of the unidentified heavenly voice, see *Comment* on 10:4.

3b ἰδοὺ ἡ σκηνὴ τοῦ θεοῦ μετὰ τῶν ἀνθρώπων, καὶ σκηνώσει μετ' αὐτῶν, καὶ αὐτοὶ λαοὶ αὐτοῦ ἔσονται, "Behold, the dwelling of God is with people, and he will dwell with them, and they will be his people." This is almost certainly an allusion to Ezek 37:27, "My dwelling place [MT משכני *miškānî*] shall be with them; and I will be their God, and they shall be my people" (Schüssler Fiorenza, *Priester für Gott,* 351;

see Ezek 34:30; 36:28; Ezek 37:27 [quoted in 2 Cor 6:16]; cf. Zech 2:11a[MT 2:15a]). *Tg. Ezek.* 37:26–27 (tr. Levey) reads, "and I will bless them and make them numerous, and I will place My sanctuary in the midst of them forever. I will make My Shekinah dwell among them."

There are also a number of other relevant OT passages that contain similar themes: (1) Lev 26:11–12 reads, "And I will make my abode [Hebrew מִשְׁכָּנִי *miškānî*] among you, and my soul shall not abhor you. And I will walk among you and will be your God, and you shall be my people" (Rissi, *Future*, 57, sees this as the passage alluded to in Rev 21:3; cf. van Ruiten, *EstBib* 51 [1993] 498). (2) Zech 2:10b–11 (MT 2:14b–15; LXX 2:14b–15) is also pertinent: "for lo, I come and I will dwell [MT וְשָׁכַנְתִּי *wěšākantî*; LXX κατασκηνώσω] in the midst of you, says the Lord. And many nations shall join themselves to the Lord in that day, and shall be my people; and I will dwell [וְשָׁכַנְתִּי *wěšākantî*] in the midst of you, and you shall know that the Lord of hosts has sent me to you." It is probable that since "many nations" are mentioned in Zech 2:11, Rev 21:3 should read λαοί, "peoples," rather than simply λαός, "people"; see *Note* 21:3.d. (3) In Ps 46:4 (MT 46:5) the phrase "city of God" (עִיר אֱלֹהִים *ʿîr ʾělōhîm*) is parallel to "dwelling place of the most high" (מִשְׁכְּנֵי עֶלְיוֹן *miškěnê ʿelyôn*). (4) Ezek 43:7 ("where I will dwell in the midst of the people of Israel for ever") and 43:9 ("and I will dwell in their midst for ever") use the verb שׁכן *šākan* (= σκηνοῦν) as does the second clause in Rev 21:3b, while the phrase "among men" (בָּאָדָם *bāʾādām*) could have been derived from Ps 78:60 (see van Ruiten, *EstBib* 51 [1993] 499–500). (5) The covenant formula is also found in Exod 29:45 in connection with the establishment of the tabernacle: "And I will dwell among the people of Israel, and will be their God." According to *Tg. Exod.* 29:45 (tr. Grossfeld), "And I will rest My Presence among the Israelites and be God to them." The term σκηνή, "dwelling," occurs three times in Revelation, and all three occurrences are articular since the author apparently assumes that his readers are acquainted with that institution (13:6; 15:5; 21:3). The statement "I will be their God, and they shall be my people" (Jer 31:33[LXX 38:33]) is a covenant formula, perhaps based on the *verba solemnia* associated with adoption (cf. *Comment* on 21:7), which occurs with some frequency in the OT and early Jewish literature (Lev 26:11–12; Jer 7:23; 31:1[LXX 38:1]; Zech 8:3, 8; Ezek 37:26–27; 43:7; Ps 95:7; *T. Mos.* 4:2; 11QTemple 59:13). (6) Ezek 37:27 is also alluded to in 11QTemple 29:7–8a, "And I will accept them, and they shall be my people, and I will be theirs forever; [and] I will dwell with them for ever and ever." This covenant language is significant because it is applied to all people universally (n.b. the term λαοί), not just to a specific group. Emphasis on a specific group, i.e., the righteous in Israel, is found in *T. Jud.* 25:3 as well as in the many OT passages in which the covenant formula occurs referring to Israel as *the* people (Lev 26:12; Jer 24:7; 30:22; 31:1, 33; 32:28; Ezek 11:20; 14:11; 36:28; 37:23, 27–28; cf. 2 Cor 6:16; Heb 8:10).

3c καὶ αὐτὸς ὁ θεὸς μετ' αὐτῶν ἔσται αὐτῶν θεός, "and God himself will be with them as their God." This text appears to be corrupt (see *Note* 21:3.f-f.; cf. Charles, 2:207–8; *TCGNT*[1], 763–64). There is a close parallel in 11QTemple 29:7b–8a (tr. García Martínez, *Dead Sea Scrolls*, 161–62), "They shall be for me a people and I will be for them for ever." The phrase "God is with someone" is a metaphor for the presence of God reflecting victory in battle (Deut 7:21; 20:4; 23:14; 1 Chr 22:18; Isa 8:10; Zeph 3:17; Jos. *J.W.* 5.368; *Ant.* 15.138; *Bib Ant.* 35:5) or for a variety of other spiritual and temporal advantages and blessings (Gen 21:20; 31:5; 48:21; Exod 3:12;

Num 23:21; Deut 20:1; 31:6; Josh 1:5, 9; 1 Sam 16:18; 1 Chr 17:2; 2 Chr 9:8; 15:9; 26:23; Neh 3:8; Isa 8:10; 41:10; 43:5; 45:14; Jer 42:11; Hos 11:9; Amos 5:14; Zeph 2:7; Zech 8:23; Job 29:3–5; Rom 15:33; Ign. *Pol.* 6:12; Jos. *Ant.* 3.15; 4.182), and occasionally it is affirmed that God was "with" Jesus (John 3:2; Acts 10:38). It can also be a wish or prayer, "May God be with you," which perhaps became as formalized as the English expression "good-bye," i.e., "God be with you" (Gen 48:21; Josh 1:17; 1 Sam 20:42; 2 Sam 14:17; 1 Chr 22:11; 2 Chr 36:23; Ezra 1:3; cf. 1 Chr 28:20). Here the eschatological reality of the presence of God is no longer just metaphorical but actual. It has been suggested that an allusion to Rev 21:3 is found in Ign. *Eph.* 15:3, ἵνα ὦμεν αὐτοῦ ναοὶ καὶ αὐτὸς ἐν ἡμῖν θεὸς ἡμῶν, "that we might be his temples and he might be our God in us" (T. Zahn, *Ignatii et Polycarpi Epistolae Marytia Fragmenta,* vol. 2 of *Patrum Apostolicorum Opera* [Leipzig: Hinrichs, 1876] 20–21), though this covenant formula is found so frequently in the OT that a direct link between Ign. *Eph.* 15:3 and Rev 21:3 can hardly be proved.

The proclamation made by the unidentified voice from the throne serves to interpret the significance of the vision that follows in 21:9–22:5 (see Schüssler Fiorenza, *Priester für Gott,* 351, who sees 21:1–22:5 as the textual unit explicated by the proclamation in 21:3b–4).

4a καὶ ἐξαλείψει πᾶν δάκρυον ἐκ τῶν ὀφθαλμῶν αὐτῶν, "and he will wipe away every tear from their eyes." This statement is a verbatim repetition of Rev 7:17 (where, however, the subject ὁ θεός, "God," is made explicit), as well as a clear allusion to Isa 25:8, "He will swallow up death for ever, and the Lord God will wipe away tears from all faces [LXX καὶ πάλιν ἀφεῖλεν ὁ θεὸς πᾶν δάκρυον ἀπὸ παντὸς προσώπου, 'And again, God will take away every tear from every face']." On the motif of the eschatological cessation of weeping and mourning, see Isa 35:10; 51:11; 65:19; Matt 5:4 = Luke 6:21 (perhaps alluding to Isa 61:2); cf. Ps 116:8. Matthew uses the descriptive term "weeping and gnashing of teeth" to describe the fate of those cast into outer darkness (Matt 13:42, 50; 22:13; 24:51; 25:30), a fate for which there is no respite. The Epicurean view of the gods was that they lived in perfect peace and tranquility, free from all grief, sorrow, and pain (Lucretius *De rerum nat.* 1.44–49 = 2.646–51; cf. Bailey, *Titi Lucreti* 2:601–4), and served as models for human aspirations. For the Epicurean, death also functioned as the cessation of pain and sorrow (Lucretius *De rerum nat.* 3.905), a common *topos* in ancient consolation literature.

4b καὶ ὁ θάνατος οὐκ ἔσται ἔτι οὔτε πένθος οὔτε κραυγὴ οὔτε πόνος οὐκ ἔσται ἔτι ὅτι τὰ πρῶτα ἀπῆλθαν, "and death will no longer exist, nor will grief, or crying, or pain exist any longer, for the previous things have passed away." The first part of this clause is an allusion to Isa 25:8, "he will swallow up death forever" (continuing in a different order the allusion to Isa 25:8 in v 4b), a passage also cited in 1 Cor 15:54. The phrase "the previous things have passed away" is an apparent allusion to the term הראשנות *hāri'šōnôt,* "the first things," in Isa 65:17b, which refers to the troubles connected with the earlier fate of Jerusalem, whereas "the former things" in Rev 21:1–5b refer to conditions obtaining during the existence of the first heaven and first earth. The cessation of an *untimely* death (i.e., death in one's youth) is mentioned in Isa 65:20b, though this is quite different from the notion of the complete cessation of death (NRSV): "for one who dies at a hundred years will be considered a youth, and one who falls short of a hundred will be considered accursed." However, in *Tg. Isa.* 65:20, it is precisely the *complete cessation of death* for the righteous that is in view (tr. Chilton, *Isaiah Targum;* cf. van Ruiten, *EstBib* 51 [1993] 504–5): "for a youth who sins shall be dying a hundred years old, and the sinner a hundred years old shall be expelled." The ultimate annihilation of death is an apocalyptic theme (Isa 25:8; 4 Ezra 8:53; *2 Apoc. Bar.* 21:23; *Bib Ant.* 3:10; 33:3), and in early Christian literature the notion that death has ultimately been conquered through Christ is a recurring *topos* (1 Cor 15:26; 2 Tim 1:10; Heb 2:14; Ign. *Eph.* 19:3; *Barn.* 5:6). This reversal of the negative aspects of human experience is also reflected as characteristic of life in paradise according to *T. Abr.* [Rec. A] 20:14 (tr. E. P. Sanders, *OTP* 1:895), "Paradise . . . where there is no toil, no grief, no moaning, but peace and exultation and endless life." In *1 Enoch* 25:6, it is said of those in paradise that "sorrow and pain and toil and punishment will not touch" them. In Hellenistic consolation literature, death (the separation of soul from body) is referred to as a state in which there is no longer pain or sorrow (Plutarch *Consolatio ad uxorem* 611C). These Hellenistic consolation *topoi* were adapted by Christianity, as in *2 Clem.* 19:4, where the author speaks of postmortem existence: "he [the pious person] will live again with the fathers above and rejoice in a sorrowless eternity." In Hellenistic consolation literature, however, the cessation of death was never envisaged, though one common *topos* regards death not as an evil but as a blessing, a remedy for evils (see Moran, *Consolations,* 31–39); but see *b. Sanh.* 100b, "'Do not worry about tomorrow's sorrow, for you do not know what a day may bring forth' [Prov. 27:1]. Perhaps tomorrow you will no longer exist and it will turn out that you will worry about a world that is not yours."

The phrase ὅτι τὰ πρῶτα ἀπῆλθαν, "for the previous things have passed away," refers back to the disappearance of the first heaven, the first earth, and the sea in v 1. This particular phrase might allude to three passages in Isaiah: (1) Isa 65:17 (which has clearly influenced the content of Rev 21:1–4), "For behold, I create new heavens and a new earth; and the former things shall not be remembered [LXX καὶ οὐ μὴ μνησθῶσιν τῶν προτέρων] or come into mind"; (2) Isa 65:16c, "because the former troubles are forgotten [ἐπιλήσονται γὰρ τὴν θλῖψιν αὐτῶν τὴν πρώτην]"; and (3) Isa 43:18 (v 19 is alluded to in Rev 21:5a), "Do not consider the former things [μὴ μνημονεύετε τὰ πρῶτα], or consider the things of old." A similar allusion to Isa 43:18 is found in 2 Cor 5:17 (the contrast between old and new also occurs in Isa 42:9, where the subject is prophecy). The rabbinic conception of בריה חדשה *bĕriyyâ ḥădāšâ,* "new creation," deals not with cosmic renewal but with various aspects of the renewal of the individual or the renewal of the individual's external situation or relationship to God (Str-B, 2:421–23).

5a καὶ εἶπεν ὁ καθήμενος ἐπὶ τῷ θρόνῳ ἰδοὺ καινὰ ποιῶ πάντα, "Then the One sitting on the throne said, 'Behold, I am making everything new.'" This is a clear allusion to Isa 43:19, "Behold, I am doing a new thing." The apocalyptic theme of cosmic renewal may be reflected in 1QH 13:11–12 (tr. Vermes, *Dead Sea Scrolls,* 199), "For Thou hast shown them that which they had not [seen by removing all] ancient things and creating new ones [ולברוא חדשות *wĕlibrô' ḥădāšôt*]." A microcosmic application of the apocalyptic notion of the recreation or renewal of the world is found in 2 Cor 5:17, where Paul says that those in Christ are a καινὴ κτίσις [cf. Gal 6:15]· τὰ ἀρχαῖα παρῆλθεν, ἰδοὺ γέγονεν καινά, "new creation; what is old has disappeared; behold, it has become new" (see D. E. Aune, "Zwei Modelle der menschlichen Natur bei Paulus," *TQ* 176 [1996] 28–39). This is probably also an allusion to Isa 43:18–19 (cf. Isa 65:17). It is clear that the short speech in vv 5–8 is attributed to God himself and is the only such speech in Revelation, with the exception of the brief self-disclosure in 1:8.

5b καὶ λέγει· γράψον, ὅτι οὗτοι οἱ λόγοι πιστοὶ καὶ ἀληθινοί εἰσιν, "He also said, 'Write, for this message is trustworthy and true.'" This is the last of several commands to write that apparently have the entire composition in view (Rev 1:11, 19; 21:5; cf. 10:4) rather than just the partial texts that are the objects of the commands to write in 14:13 and 19:9. The phrase οὗτοι οἱ λόγοι πιστοὶ καὶ ἀληθινοί, "this message is trustworthy and true," occurs again verbatim in 22:6 (in both passages πιστοὶ καὶ ἀληθινοί, "trustworthy and true," is a hendiadys, i.e., one idea expressed through two different words), while in 19:9 we find the parallel phrase οὗτοι οἱ λόγοι ἀληθινοὶ τοῦ θεοῦ εἰσιν, "these are the true words of God." In Greco-Roman divinatory charms there is a major concern, as there is here, with emphasizing the truthfulness of the revelation, implying the obvious possibility of unreliable revelations (*PGM* I.320; II.10, 115; III.288; IV.913, 1033, 2504; V.421; VII.248, 571; XIV.6–7; cf. Daniel-Maltomini, *Supplementum Magicum* 2:65, line 67 [commentary]).

6a καὶ εἶπέν μοι· γέγοναν, "And he said to me, 'It is finished.'" The subject of γέγοναν, "it is finished," a third-person plural perfect verb, is unexpressed, though it may imply πάντα ταῦτα, "all these things" (cf. Matt 24:33–34), i.e., the eschatological events that are part of the eternal plan of God (Taeger, *Johannesapokalypse*, 38). John uses plural verbs with neuter plural nouns almost as frequently as he uses singular verbs with neuter plural nouns (Charles, 1:cxli). Beckwith (752) construes οὗτοι οἱ λόγοι, "these words," as the subject of γέγοναν. The verb γέγοναν has a close parallel with 16:17, where a voice from the throne (see 21:3a) announces, after pouring out of the seventh bowl, "It is finished [γέγονεν]!" Here, γέγονεν is a third-person singular perfect verb. According to John 19:28, Jesus' final utterance on the cross before his death was τετέλεσται, "it is finished." It has been suggested that this is an attempt to translated the Hebrew "amen" into Greek (Kraft, 265).

6b ἐγώ εἰμι τὸ ἄλφα καὶ τὸ ὦ, ἡ ἀρχὴ καὶ τὸ τέλος, "I am the Alpha and the Omega, the Beginning and the End." The divine title "Alpha and Omega" occurs several times in Revelation (1:8a; 21:6; 22:13). In 1:8a and 21:6 it is used of God, while in 22:13 (part of the Second Edition) it is used of Christ. In each context the title is not used alone but is juxtaposed with other titles, each of which emphasizes the absolute power and sovereignty of God (in 1:8 and 21:6) or of Christ (in 22:13), and each of which also serves to define and expand the others (see *Comment* on 1:8a).

The title "Beginning and End" occurs just twice in Revelation, here (where it is used of God) and in 22:13 (where it is used of Christ). The divine title "the Beginning and the End [and the Middle] of all things" is drawn from Hellenistic religious and philosophical tradition and has a cosmological rather than a temporal significance, as the detailed study by W. C. van Unnik (*Het godspredikaat*) makes clear. The Derveni papyrus, found carbonized in Macedonia and dating from ca. 350 B.C., contains lines from an Orphic poem that is probably much earlier (col. 13, line 12): Ζεὺς κεφαλή, Ζεὺς μέσσα, Διὸς δ᾽ ἐκ πάντα τελεῖται, "Zeus is the beginning, Zeus is the middle, all things are fulfilled by Zeus." This is virtually identical to the saying found in Ps.-Aristotle *De mundo* 7 (Diels-Kranz, *FVS* 1:8, lines 19–20; O. Kern, ed., *Orphicorum Fragmenta* [Berlin: Weidmann, 1922] 91, frag. 21a). This saying is alluded to in Plato *Leg.* 4.715e, "God . . . holds the beginning and the middle and the end of all things which exist [ἀρχήν τε καὶ τελευτὴν καὶ μέσα τῶν ὄντων ἁπάντων ἔχων]," a saying quoted by a number of early Christian writers, including Ps.-Justin *Cohort.* 25; Irenaeus *Adv. haer.* 3.25.5; Hippolytus *Ref.* 19.6 (ed. Marcovich, *Hippolytus*); Clement of Alex. *Strom.* 2.22; and Origen *Contra Celsum* 6.15. The Jewish writer Aristobulus also refers to this saying in a fragment preserved in Eusebius *Praep. evang.* 13.12 (666a), referring to God as "Himself the beginning, the middle and the end [ἀρχὴν αὐτὸς ἔχων καὶ μέσσην ἠδὲ τελευτήν]" (Kern, *Orphicorum Fragmenta*, 247; see Holladay, *FHJA* 4:170). Hippocrates, imitating Heraclitus, refers to the beginning and end as a kind of unbroken circle (Diels-Kranz, *FVS* 1:189): "The beginning of everything is one and the end of everything is one and the end and the beginning are the same [ἡ αὐτὴ τελευτὴ καὶ ἀρχή]." The Stoic emperor Marcus Aurelius reflects the view that the soul that "knows the beginning and the end [ἡ εἰδυῖα ἀρχὴν καὶ τέλος]" knows the Logos that penetrates the universe (i.e., God) (*Meditations* 5.32). See *Sib. Or.* 8.375–76 (tr. J. J. Collins, *OTP* 1:425), "Beginning and end I know [ἀρχὴν καὶ τέλος οἶδα]; I who created heaven and earth / for all things are from him, he knows what is from the beginning to the end [τὰ ἀπ' ἀρχῆς εἰς τέλος οἶδε]." Macrobius (*Comm. in Somn. Scip.* 1.6.8) refers to the Monad (i.e., *summum deum*, the supreme God) as *initium finisque omnium*, "the beginning and end of all things." "Beginning and End" is a divine epithet also found in the magical papyri (*PGM* IV.1125, 2836–37) and in other magical texts (Delatte, *Anecdota Atheniensia*, 26.12, 28; 35.10; 36.9; 45.28–29; 51.28–29; 61.28; 418.27; 419.13; 460.6; 498.6; 585.17; these twelve magical formulas are all of Christian origin, and the titles α [ἄλφα] καὶ ω, ἀρχὴ καὶ τέλος, "alpha and omega, beginning and end," are juxtaposed in each text, making dependence on Rev 21:6 probable). *PGM* IV.2836–37 is part of a hexameter hymn to Hekate that reads, in part, "Beginning and end [ἀρχὴ καὶ τέλος] are you, and you alone rule all. For all things are from you and you alone rule all." God is referred to as "the Beginning and End of all things" by Josephus (*Ant.* 8.280) and Philo (*Plant.* 93). Josephus also uses a threefold formula: "He is the beginning, the middle, and the end of all things" (*Ag. Ap.* 2. 190). Apart from the frequency with which Plato *Leg.* 4.715e is quoted (see above), the divine title "Beginning and [Middle and] End" is rarely found in early Christian writers; Clement of Alex. quotes Rev 21:6, which he links with John 1:3 (*Strom.* 6.16). The Beginning and End motif is also stated negatively; *Tri. Trac.* 52.34–41 describes the Gnostic God as "without beginning or end."

6c ἐγὼ τῷ διψῶντι δώσω ἐκ τῆς πηγῆς τοῦ ὕδατος τῆς ζωῆς δωρεάν, "I will freely give some water to the one who is thirsty from the well of living water." This is an allusion, with the addition of the motif of "the well of living water," to Isa 55:1 (NRSV), "Ho, everyone who thirsts, come to the waters . . . . Come, buy wine and milk without money and without price [LXX πίετε ἄνευ ἀργυρίου, 'drink without money']." Isa 55:1, applied to Wisdom, is also alluded to in Sir 55:23–25 and *Tg. Isa.* 55:1. The "I" of v 6c makes it clear that God is the one who makes living water freely available to the thirsty, whereas in Rev 7:17 it is the Lamb who leads people to the fountains of living water. The same combination of motifs (the invitation to the thirsty to come and drink [freely]; the well of living water) also occurs in Rev 22:17, John 7:37–38, and *Odes Sol.* 30:1–2. A synoptic comparison will reveal the similarities:

Rev 21:6	*Rev 22:17*
ἐγὼ τῷ διψῶντι δώσω	καὶ ὁ διψῶν ἐρχέσθω
I will give to the thirsty	And let the thirsty come,

ὁ θέλων λαβέτω
let the one who wishes receive

ἐκ τῆς πηγῆς τοῦ ὕδατος τῆς ζωῆς
from the well of living water

ὕδωρ ζωῆς
living water

δωρεάν
freely.

δωρεάν
freely.

John 7:37–38

Odes Sol. 30:1–2

ἐάν τις διψᾷ ἐρχέσθω
If anyone thirsts, let that one come

²And come all you thirsty

πρός με
to me

καὶ πινέτω . . . .
and drink . . . .

and take a drink . . . .

ποταμοὶ ἐκ τῆς κοιλίας αὐτοῦ
rivers from the belly of that one

ῥεύσουσιν
shall flow

¹Fill for yourselves water
from the living fountain.

ὕδατος ζῶντος.
of living water.

The combination of the invitation to drink (without cost) and the mention of living water links these four passages and suggests a traditional formulation in three versions: (1) Rev 21:6 and 22:17 are similar versions of the same tradition and are relatively close to Isa 55:1. (2) *Odes Sol.* 30:1–2 omits the "without cost, freely" motif and reverses the two motifs found in Rev 21:6 and 22:17. (3) John 7:37–38, which also omits the "without cost, freely" motif, contains the two motifs found in Rev 21:6 and 22:17 in the proper order but has developed the tradition into a christological formulation in which Jesus is the source of living water provided for those who come to him to drink. John 7:37–38 is therefore the most heavily developed form of this traditional formulation.

The phrase ὕδωρ ζωῆς, literally, "water of life," is ambiguous in that it can mean "flowing water" (e.g., *Did.* 7:1, 2), or it can be used in a religious sense of "living water," i.e., "water of [eternal] life" (construing ζωῆς, "of life," as a descriptive genitive) or "water, that is, [eternal] life" (construing ζωῆς as an appositional genitive). The imagery of this verse has several motifs in common with John 4:4–16, including (1) the πηγή, "well," in 4:6a, 6b, 14 (used interchangeably with φρέαρ, "well," in 4:11, 12), (2) the phrase ὕδωρ ζῶν, "living water" (4:10, 11, 14; cf. 7:38; always as an adjectival participle in John, whereas in Revelation the noun ζωή, "life," is always used with ὕδωρ as a descriptive or appositional genitive), (3) the emphasis on "living water" as a gift from God, τὴν δωρεὰν τοῦ θεοῦ (4:10), and (4) the use of the verb διδόναι, "to give" (4:14, 15). Particularly close grammatically is the sentence in John 4:14, where a partitive genitive is used as the object of the verb δώσω, "I will give": ὃς δ' ἂν πίῃ ἐκ τοῦ ὕδατος οὗ ἐγὼ δώσω αὐτῷ, οὐ μὴ διψήσει εἰς τὸν αἰῶνα, ἀλλὰ τὸ ὕδωρ ὃ δώσω αὐτῷ γενήσεται ἐν αὐτῷ πηγὴ ὕδατος ἁλλομένου εἰς ζωὴν αἰώνιον, "Whoever drinks some of the water which I will give him will never thirst for ever, but the water which I will give him will be in him a well of water springing up into eternal life." For other references to living water see LXX Zech 14:8; *Barn.* 11:2 (πηγὴ ζωῆς, "well of life"); *Odes Sol.* 11:6 (ἀπὸ πηγῆ ζωῆς, "from a well of life"); Ignatius *Rom.* 7:2; *Odes Sol.* 11:7 (Syriac *mn my' hy'*, "from the waters of life"; the Greek text has no equivalent to *hy'*, i.e., ζωῆς); Justin *Dial.* 69.6 (πηγὴ ὕδατος ζῶντος, "well of living water," is an allusion to John 4:10, 14); 114.4. Though some have argued that the phrase ὕδωρ ζῶν (or its equivalent) indicates that Ignatius was dependent on John (P. Dietze, "Die Briefe des Ignatius und das Johannesevangelium," *TSK* 78 [1905] 563–603), most scholars now concede that the use of this phrase suggests only a common background (C. Maurer, *Ignatius von Antiochien und das Johannesevangelium* [Zürich: Zwingli, 1949] 43; Wehr, *Unsterblichkeit*, 36).

7a ὁ νικῶν κληρονομήσει ταῦτα, "Those who conquer will inherit these things." The substantival participle ὁ νικῶν, "the one who conquers," introduces a promise-of-victory formula similar to the seven formulas found at the conclusion of each of the seven proclamations (2:7b, 11b, 17b, 26f.; 3:5, 12, 21; see *Comment* on 2:7b). Even though ὁ νικῶν is singular, it is certainly restricted not to a single person who conquers but to all those who conquer. Hence it can reasonably be understood to mean, with the NRSV, "those who conquer." The pronoun ταῦτα, "these things," refers to the blessings of eschatological salvation enumerated in v 4 (i.e., no sorrow, death, mourning, tears, or pain).

7b καὶ ἔσομαι αὐτῷ θεὸς καὶ αὐτὸς ἔσται μοι υἱός, "for I will be their God and they will be my children." (For the inclusive language translation, see *Note* 7.a.) This is probably a metaphor based on ancient adoption law, providing an appropriate basis for the right of inheritance mentioned in v 7a. The father-child (father-son) imagery in this phrase reflects the adaptation of adoption language in the Davidic covenant tradition reflected in 2 Sam 7:14 ("I will be his father and he shall be my son") and several other passages in the OT (Pss 2:7; 89:26–27[MT 27–28]; Jer 3:19; 31:9c ["For I am a father to Israel, and Ephraim is my firstborn"]; 1 Chr 17:13; 22:10; 28:6). This covenant formula based on the metaphorical use of adoption language is also found in *Jub.* 1:24 (tr. O. S. Wintermute, *OTP* 2:54), "And I shall be a father to them, and they will be sons to me." This may be based on an ancient Israelite adoption formula, i.e., the *verba solemnia*, "solemn words," used to publicly formalize the legal relations of marriage and adoption (see Greengus, *JAOS* 89 [1969] 505–32), though the OT contains no legislation explicitly related to the subject of adoption and there are very few possible examples of such a legal procedure (Gen 48:5–6; Exod 2:10; see also Gen 15:3; 2 Kgs 11:20; Esth 2:7, 15). Some scholars have argued that the institution of adoption was unknown in ancient Israel (H. Haag, *TDOT* 2:155). The oral declaration of relationship could be part of a pact or covenant, as in the treaty in 2 Kgs 16:7 (Ahaz to Tiglathpileser: "I am your servant and your son") and in a treaty between the Hittite king Skuppiluliuma and his vassal Sattiwazza: "When I conquer the land of Mittanni I shall not reject you, I shall make you my son" (M. Weinfeld, "Covenant, Davidic," *IDBSup*, 190); cf. Pss 89:27; 116:16; 1 Sam 25:8; Isa 63:16; 64:8; Jer 31:9b. Kalluveettil has suggested that the complete covenant formula would consist of two parts: (1) I am your servant and your son, and (2) you are my master and my father

(*Declaration*, 129–35, esp. 130). The covenant adoption formula in 2 Sam 7:14 is interpreted in a messianic context in 4Q*174* = 4QFlor 1–3 i 11 (tr. García Martínez, *Dead Sea Scrolls*, 136):

> I will be a father to him and he will be my son to me. This (refers to the) 'Branch of David,' who will arise with the Interpreter of the law who [will rise up] in Zi[on in] the last days.

In Babylonian laws pertaining to adoption (Driver-Miles, *Laws* 1:383–405), there is evidence of *verba solemnia* for dissolving the adoptive relationship, such as "'You are not my father' (or) 'You are not my mother'" (Driver-Miles, *Laws* 2:77, § 193), or "You are not my son" (Driver-Miles, *Laws* 1:403), and an example of the public recognition of the sons of a female slave as legitimate sons and heirs of her master: "(You are) my sons" (Driver-Miles, *Laws* 2:65, § 170). Given the nature of the sources (OT and ancient Near Eastern law codes), it is not surprising that the positive versions of these public formulas are extremely rare since the largely negative formulations cited above deal with the problem of inheritance rights in unusual situations. These strongly suggest that corresponding positive formulas, in Babylonia as well as Israel, were in use even though poorly attested (Hugenberger, *Marriages*, 219).

8a τοῖς δὲ δειλοῖς καὶ ἀπίστοις καὶ ἐβδελυγμένοις καὶ φονεῦσιν καὶ πόρνοις καὶ φαρμάκοις καὶ εἰδωλολάτραις καὶ πᾶσιν τοῖς ψευδέσιν, "but as for the cowards and unbelievers and the abominable and murderers and the immoral and sorcerers and idolaters and all who lie." Prigent has argued that the setting for this vice list (it is actually a list of various categories of sinners who specialize in particular vices) was a baptismal liturgy, which he attempts to demonstrate by tracing a pattern of parallels in Rev 7:13–17; 22:16–20; 1 Cor 16:20–24; 2 Cor 6:16–18; *Did.* 10:6. None of these passages, however, has an indisputable link to a baptismal setting. The two parallel vice lists that occur in 9:20–21 and 22:15 also invite comparison (see *Comment* on 9:20–21); square brackets indicate that a motif is out of sequence:

Rev 9:20–21	*Rev 21:8*	*Rev 22:15*
προσκυνήσουσιν . . . τὰ εἴδωλα They worship . . . idols	[εἰδωλολάτραι idolaters]	[εἰδωλολάτραι idolaters]
	δειλοί cowards	
	ἄπιστοι unfaithful	
	ἐβδελυγμένοι abominable	κύνες dogs
φόνοι murders	φονεῖς murderers	[φονεῖς murderers]
φάρμακα sorceries	[φάρμακοι sorcerers]	φάρμακοι sorcerers

πορνεία	πόρνοι	πόρνοι
immorality	immoral	immoral

κλέμματα
thefts

	πάντες οἱ ψευδεῖς	πᾶς φιλῶν καὶ ποιῶν ψεῦδος
	all liars	everyone who both loves and practices lying

Though this list is slightly longer than that in 22:15, it is natural to understand ἐβδελυγμένοις, "abominable," and οἱ κύνες, "the dogs," as parallels, suggesting that both may refer to sodomy or homosexuality (see *Comment* on 22:15). While 21:8 begins with two categories missing in 22:15, "the cowards" and "the unbelievers," the lists are extremely similar, though οἱ φάρμακοι, "the sorcerers," and οἱ φονεῖς, "the murderers," are reversed in 22:15. The term "cowards" here seems to be intentionally used as the antonym of "the conquerer" in v 7a. There appears to be a close relationship between the catalogues of sins (or sinners; sins and sinners are combined in Rom 1:29–31, Eph 5:3–5, *Barn.* 20:1–2; *Did.* 2:1–3:10) in early Christian literature (Matt 15:19; Mark 7:21–22; Rom 1:29–31; 13:13; 1 Cor 5:10–11 [sinners]; 6:9–10 [sinners]; 2 Cor 12:20–21; Gal 5:19–21; Eph 4:31; 5:3–5; Col 3:5–8; 1 Tim 1:9–10 [sinners]; 6:4–5; 2 Tim 3:2–5 [sinners]; Tit 1:7; 3:3 [sinners]; 1 Pet 2:1; 4:3; Rev 9:21; 21:8; 22:15; *Barn.* 20:1–2; *1 Clem.* 3:2; 30:1, 3, 8; 35:5; *2 Clem* 4:3; *Did.* 2:1–3:10; see Vögtle, *Lasterkataloge*, 1; Mussies, *Dio*, 67) and the traditional associations of the Ten Commandments (Rordorf, "Dekalogs," 435–36).

The list of various categories of sinners in Rev 21:8 has parallels with the Ten Commandments and traditional applications of the Ten Commandments, including other early Christian vice lists: (1) *murder or murderers* (Exod 20:13 = Deut 5:17; Rev 9:21; 21:8; 22:15; Matt 5:22; 15:19; 19:18 = Mark 10:19 = Luke 18:20; Mark 7:21; Rom 1:29; 13:9; Jas 2:11; 1 Pet 4:15; *Barn.* 20:1; *Did.* 2:2), (2) *sexual immorality* (Exod 20:14 = Deut 5:18; Matt 5:27; 15:19; 19:18 = Mark 10:19 = Luke 18:20; Mark 7:21–22; Rom 13:9; 1 Cor 5:9–10; 2 Cor 12:21; Gal 5:19; Eph 5:5; Col 3:5; 1 Tim 1:10; Jas 2:11; *Barn.* 20:1; *Did.* 2:2), (3) *sorcerers or sorcery* (absent from Decalogue; Rev 9:21; 21:8; 22:15; Gal 5:20; *Barn.* 20:1 [φαρμακεία, μαγεία, "sorcery, magic"]; *Did.* 2:2; 3:4), (4) *idolaters or idolatry* (Exod 20:4–6 = Deut 5:8–10; Rev [9:20]; 21:8; 22:15; 1 Cor 5:10; 6:9; Gal 5:20; [Eph 5:5]; 1 Pet 4:3; *Barn.* 20:1; Did. 5:1; Aristides *Apol.* 15.2 [Syrian text]; Clement Alex. *Paed.* 3.89.1; Tertullian *Scorp.* 2.2), and (5) *liars* (Exod 20:16 = Deut 5:20; Rev 21:8; 22:15; Matt 15:19; Mark 10:19 = Matt 19:18 = Luke 18:20; 1 Tim 1:9–10; *Barn.* 20:2 [ἀγαπῶντες ψεῦδος, "lovers of falsehood"]; *Did.* 3:5).

The two words δειλοί and ἄπιστοι, "cowards" and "unbelievers," occur only here in Revelation and are found in no other vice lists in the NT. There may be an allusion to the saying of Jesus in Matt 8:26, τί δειλοί ἐστε, ὀλιγόπιστοι; "Why are you acting like cowards, you of little faith?" This is a Matthaean rewriting of Mark 4:40, τί δειλοί ἐστε οὕτως; πῶς οὐκ ἔχετε πίστιν; "Why are you acting thus like cowards? How is it that you have no faith?" "Cowardice" was a designation in the Greek world for general moral degradation (Plato *Republic* 395E–396A; 411A; 486B; Dio Chrysostom *Or.* 23.8; for further references, see C. R. Hutson, "Was Timothy

Timid? On the Rhetoric of Fearlessness [1 Corinthians 16:10–11] and Cowardice [2 Timothy 1:7]," *BR* 42 [1997] 69–70 n. 55).

The term φάρμακος, "sorcerer," occurs twice in Revelation (21:8; 22:15), both times in the plural and both times in the context of a vice list (on the cognate noun φαρμακεία, "sorcery," see *Comment* on 9:21). In both 21:8 and 22:15, the sorcerers belong to a group that is *excluded*. An ancient Greek purification ritual, the expulsion of the *Pharmakos*, is discussed in Burkert, *Greek Religion*, 82–84. In an inscription from a private religious association in Philadelphia from the first century B.C., the list of prescribed activities (though more discursive) is remarkably similar to the lists in Rev 21:8 and 22:15. This similarity suggests that a common core of ethical concerns could characterize morally sensitive pagan religious societies as well as Christian congregations. The inscription from Philadelphia reads (text taken from Sokolowski, *Lois,* 54; translation modified from Boring et al., *HCNT,* no. 771):

> When men and women, whether free or slave, enter this building they should swear by all the gods that they bear no lies against man or woman, perform no malevolent magic [φάρμακον πονηρόν] or malevolent charms [ἐπωιδὰς πονηράς] against others, that they neither participate themselves nor advise others to participate in love philtres, abortions, contraception, nor anything else that kills children. . . . Except for sexual relations with his own wife, a man must not defile a foreign woman whom a man has, whether free or slave, and a man must not corrupt a boy or a virgin or advise others to do so. . . . A woman or man who violates these prescriptions may not enter this building.

In summary, the categories of prohibitions include: (1) lying or deceit, (2) various forms of magic, (3) various forms of illicit sexual activity, and (4) abortion defined as infanticide. All of these sins exclude the individual who commits them from access to temple worship, just as the offenders in Rev 21:8 and 22:15 are excluded from the holy city.

8b τὸ μέρος αὐτῶν ἐν τῇ λίμνῃ τῇ καιομένῃ πυρὶ καὶ θείῳ, "they will experience the lake that burns with fire and sulphur." The lake of fire (and sulphur) is mentioned six times in Revelation (19:20; 20:10, 14[2x], 15; 21:8); see *Comment* on 19:20. It is striking that vice lists often formally consist of two main sections, the list of vices (v 8a) and the penalty for those who do such things (v 8b). Such penalty clauses following vice lists are found in Rom 1:32a; 1 Cor 6:10; Gal 5:21b; Eph 5:5; Col 3:6; 1 Pet 4:5; Rev 22:15a.

8c ὅ ἐστιν ὁ θάνατος ὁ δεύτερος, "which is the second death." The second death is mentioned four times in Revelation (2:11; 20:6, 14; 21:8); see *Comment* on 20:6. Here it is of interest that Isa 65:17–20 has exerted demonstrable influence on Rev 21:1–5 and that the conception of the second death found here also occurs in *Tg. Isa.* 65:6, 15 (van Ruiten, *EstBib* 51 [1993] 506–8).

Explanation

John sees a new heaven and a new earth in place of the first heaven and earth and the sea that had "passed away" (21:1) or had "fled away" (20:11) from the presence of God. It is peculiar that such an important cosmic cataclysm is passed over with just two oblique references. The destruction of heaven and earth was part of the Synoptic tradition (Matt 5:18 = Luke 16:17; Mark 13:31 = Matt 24:35 = Luke 21:33) and occasionally appears in second-century Christian literature (2 Pet 3:10–13; *Did.* 10:6). The prophetic conception of a new heaven and a new earth in which Edenic conditions prevail is found in Isa 65:17–25. This idea is based on the supposition that a transformation of creation is necessary so that the perfect life of the eternal kingdom will be set within a perfect environment.

The descent of the New Jerusalem is accompanied by an explanation from the throne that God now dwells with people and that all death and suffering are now eliminated from human experience (vv 3–4) since primordial conditions of bliss and perfection have been reinstated. In some strands of Jewish eschatology the heavenly Jerusalem descends to earth to replace the earthly Jerusalem, or a heavenly temple becomes a replacement for the earthly temple. The climactic statement of God found in vv 5–8 succinctly summarizes the central message of Revelation. It is introduced with a commission to John to write, accompanied by an oath formula: "Write, for this message is trustworthy and true" (v 5). The reliability of the words to follow are guaranteed by the self-disclosure of the speaker, God himself, as the Alpha and the Omega (cf. 1:8) and the Beginning and the End (a widespread Hellenistic divine title emphasizing cosmic sovereignty and lordship). The ensuing message states that those who conquer, i.e., hold fast to the word of God and the testimony of Jesus, will be children of God and enjoy eternal blessedness; those who do not turn from their sinful ways will be punished with eternal torment. The role of God as presented by John is analogous to popular conceptions of the role of the emperor: his main task is to dispense justice by punishing the disobedient and rewarding the obedient.

G. The Vision of the New Jerusalem (21:9–22:9)
1. Introduction to the Vision (21:9–10a)
2. The Seer Visits the New Jerusalem (21:10b–22:5)
3. Transitional Conclusion (22:6–9)

Bibliography

Aalen, S. *Die Begriffe 'Licht' und 'Finsternis' im Alten Testament, im Spätjudentum und im Rabbinismus.* Oslo: Dybwad, 1951. **Amiran, R.** "Water Supply at Ancient Jerusalem." In *Jerusalem Revealed: Archaeology in the Holy City 1968–74,* ed. Y. Yadin. New Haven; London: Yale UP; The Israel Exploration Society, 1976. 75–78. **Baillet, M.** "Description de la Jerusalem nouvelle." *RB* 62 (1955) 222–45. ———, **Milik, J. T.,** and **Vaux, R. de.** *Les "petites grottes" de Qumran.* DJD 3. Oxford: Clarendon, 1962. **Barthélemy, D.,** and **Milik, J. T.,** eds. *Qumran Cave I.* DJD1. Oxford: Clarendon, 1955. **Baumgarten, J. M.** "The Duodecimal Courts of Qumran, Revelation, and the Sanhedrin." *JBL* 95 (1976) 59–78. **Bergmeier, R.** "'Jerusalem, du hochgebaute Stadt.'" *ZNW* 75 (1984) 86–106. **Black, M.** "The New Creation in 1 Enoch." In *Creation, Christ and Culture.*

FS T. F. Torrance, ed. R. McKinney. Edinburgh: T. & T. Clark, 1976. 13–21. **Böcher, O.** "Die Bedeutung der Edelsteine in Offb 21." In *Kirche in Zeit und Endzeit: Aufsätze zur Offenbarung des Johannes.* Neukirchen: Neukirchener, 1983. 144–56. **Bruetsch, C.** "La nouvelle Jerusalem (Ap. 21:10–14, 22–23)." *AsSeign* 27 (1970) 30–36. **Burrows, E.** "The Pearl in the Apocalypse." *JTS* 43 (1942) 177–79. **Chavasse, C.** *The Bride of Christ: An Enquiry into the Nuptial Element in Early Christianity.* London: Faber & Faber, 1939. **Chyutin, M.** "The New Jerusalem: Ideal City." *DSD* 1 (1994) 71–97. ———. *The New Jerusalem Scroll from Qumran: A Comprehensive Reconstruction.* JSPSup 25. Sheffield: Sheffield Academic, 1997. **Collins, T.** *Apocalypse 22:6–21 as the Focal Point of Moral Teaching and Exhortation in the Apocalypse.* Rome: Pontificia Universitas Gregoriana, 1986. **Comblin, J.** "La liturgie de la nouvelle Jérusalem." *ETL* 29 (1953) 5–40. **Coune, M.** "La Jerusalem celeste (Ap 21:2–5)." *AsSeign* 91 (1964) 23–28. **Deutsch, C.** "Transformation of Symbols: The New Jerusalem in Rv 21:1–22:5." *ZNW* 78 (1987) 106–26. **Dölger, F. J.** *Sol Salutis: Gebet und Gesang im christlichen Altertum.* 2nd ed. Münster: Aschendorff, 1925. **Donaldson, T. L.** "Proselytes or 'Righteous Gentiles'? The Status of Gentiles in Eschatological Pilgrimage Patterns of Thought." *JSP* 7 (1990) 3–27. **Draper, J. A.** "The Twelve Apostles as Foundation Stones of the Heavenly Jerusalem and the Foundation of the Qumran Community." *Neot* 22 (1988) 41–63. **Driver, G. R.,** and **Miles, J. C.** *The Babylonian Laws.* 2 vols. Oxford: Clarendon, 1952–55. **Eisenman, R. H.,** and **Robinson, J. M.** *A Facsimile Edition of the Dead Sea Scrolls.* Washington, DC: Biblical Archaeology Society, 1991. **Fitzmyer, J. A.,** and **Harrington, D. J.** *A Manual of Palestinian Aramaic Texts.* Rome: Pontifical Biblical Institute, 1978. **Flusser, D.** "No Temple in the City." In *Judaism and the Origins of Christianity.* Jerusalem: Magnes, 1988. 454–65. ———. "Qumran und die Zwölf." In *Judaism and the Origins of Christianity.* Jerusalem: Magnes, 1988. 173–85. **García Martínez, F.** "The 'New Jerusalem' and the Future Temple of the Manuscripts from Qumran." In *Qumran and Apocalyptic: Studies on the Aramaic Texts from Qumran.* Leiden: Brill, 1992. 180–213. **Georgi, D.** "Die Visionen vom himmlischen Jerusalem in Apk 21 und 22." In *Kirche.* FS G. Bornkamm, ed. D. Lührmann and G. Strecker. Tübingen: Mohr-Siebeck, 1980. 351–72. **Giblin, C. H.** "Structural and Thematic Correlations in the Theology of Revelation 16–22." *Bib* 55 (1974) 487–504. **Glasson, T. F.** "The Order of Jewels in Revelation xxi. 19–20: A Theory Eliminated." *JTS* 26 (1975) 95–100. **Grappe, C.** "Le logion des douze trônes: Eclairages intertestamentaires." In *Le Trône de Dieu,* ed. M. Philonenko. WUNT 69. Tübingen: Mohr-Siebeck, 1993. 204–12. **Greengus, S.** "The Old Babylonian Marriage Contract." *JAOS* 89 (1969) 505–32. **Gruenwald, I.** "From Priesthood to Messianism: The Anti-Priestly Polemic and the Messianic Factor." In *Messiah and Christos: Studies in the Jewish Origins of Christianity,* ed. I. Gruenwald, S. Shaked, and G. G. Stroumsa. Tübingen: Mohr-Siebeck, 1992. 75–93. **Gundry, R. H.** "The New Jerusalem: People as Place, Not Place for People." *NovT* 3 (1987) 254–64. **Hanson, A.** "The Treatment in the LXX of the Theme of Seeing God." In *Septuagint, Scrolls and Cognate Writings: Papers Presented to the International Symposium on the Septuagint and Its Relations to the Dead Sea Scrolls and Other Writings,* ed. G. J. Brooke and B. Lindars. Atlanta: Scholars, 1992. 557–68. **Heitzmann Pérez, M. L.** "Laturquesa, octava piedra del pectora del sumo sacerdote." *Anuario* 6 (1980) 149–58. **Hermann, A.** "Edelsteine." *RAC* 4:505–52. **Horst, P. van der.** "Moses' Throne Vision in Ezekiel the Dramatist." *JJS* 34 (1983) 21–29. **Hugenberger, G. P.** *Marriage as Covenant.* VTSup 52. Leiden: Brill, 1994. **Jart, U.** "The Precious Stones in the Revelation of St. John 21:18–21." *ST* 24 (1970) 150–81. **Jourdain, E. F.** "The Twelve Stones in the Apocalypse." *ExpTim* 22 (1910–11) 448–50. **Kloos, C.** *Yhwh's Combat with the Sea: A Canaanite Tradition in the Religion of Ancient Israel.* Leiden: Brill; Amsterdam: van Oorschot, 1986. **Knopf, R.** "Die Himmelsstadt." In *Neutestamentliche Studien.* FS G. Heinrici. Leipzig: Hinrichs, 1914. 213–19. **Kuhaupt, H.** *Der neue Himmel und die neue Erde: Eine theologische Auslegung Apk 21:1–22:5.* Münster: Regensberg, 1947. **Levine, B. A.** "The Temple Scroll: Aspects of Its Historical Provenance and Literary Character." *BASOR* 232 (1978) 5–23. **Licht, J.** "The Ideal Town Plan from Qumran: The Description of the New Jerusalem." *IEJ* 20 (1979) 47–50. **Loewen, J. A.** "A Suggestion for Translating the Names of Precious Stones." *BT* 35 (1984) 229–34. **Luz, U.** *Das Evangelium nach Matthäus.* Vol. 1. Neukirchener: Benziger, 1985 (ET: *Matthew 1–7.* Minneapolis: Fortress, 1989). **Maier, J.** "Das Gefärdungsmotiv bei der

Himmelsreise in der jüdischen Apokalyptik und 'Gnosis.'" *Kairos* 5 (1963) 18–40. **Mazzolani, L. S.** *The Idea of the City in Roman Thought.* Bloomington: Indiana UP, 1970. **McCready, W. O.** "The Sectarian Status of Qumran: The Temple Scroll." *RevQ* 42 (1983) 183–91. **McKelvey, R. J.** *The New Temple: The Church in the New Testament.* Oxford: Oxford UP, 1969. **Michael, J. H.** "East, North, South, West (Apoc 21:13)." *ExpTim* 49 (1937–38) 141–42. **Michl, J.** "Selige Menschen in einer neuen Schöpfung nach Apokalypse 21:1–5." *BK* 16 (1961) 113–15. **Milgrom, J.** "'Sabbath' and 'Temple City' in the Temple Scroll." *BASOR* 232 (1978) 25–27. ———. "Studies in the Temple Scroll." *JBL* 97 (1978) 501–23. **Müller, W.** *Die heilige Stadt: Roma quadrata, himmlisches Jerusalem und die Mythe vom Weltnabel.* Stuttgart: Kohlhammer, 1961. **Olson, D. C.** "'Those Who Have Not Defiled Themselves with Women': Revelation 14:4 and the Book of Enoch." *CBQ* 59 (1977) 492–510. **Petraglio, R.** "Des influences de l'Apocalypse dans la 'Passio Perpetuae' 11–13." In *L'Apocalypse de Jean: Traditions exégétiques et iconographiques,* ed. Y. Christe. Geneva: Librairie Droz, 1979. **Pfleiderer, O.** *Das Urchristentum: Seine Schriften und Lehren in geschichtlichen Zusammenhang beschrieben.* 2nd ed. 2 vols. Berlin: Reimer, 1902. **Porteous, N. W.** "Jerusalem-Zion: The Growth of a Symbol." In *Living the Mystery: Collected Essays.* Oxford: Blackwell, 1967. 93–111. **Prigent, P.** "Une trace de liturgie judéo-chrétienne dans le chapitre XXI de l'Apocalypse de Jean." In *Judéo-Christianisme: Recherches historiques et théologiques.* FS J. Daniélou. Paris: Recherches de Science Religieuse, 1972. 165–72. **Rand, J. A. du.** "The Imagery of the Heavenly Jerusalem (Revelation 21:9–22:5)." *Neot* 22 (1988) 65–86. **Reader, W. W.** "Die Stadt Gottes in der Johannesapokalypse." Diss., Göttingen, 1971. ———. "The Twelve Jewels of Revelation 21:19–20: Tradition History and Modern Interpretations." *JBL* 100 (1981) 433–57. **Roetzel, C. J.** "*Oikoumene* and the Limits of Pluralism in Alexandrian Judaism and Paul." In *Diaspora Jews and Judaism.* FS A. T. Kraabel, ed. J. A. Overman and R. S. MacLennan. Atlanta: Scholars, 1992. 163–82. **Ruiten, J. van.** "The Intertextual Relationship between Isaiah 65,17–20 and Revelation 21,1–5b." *EstBib* 51 (1993) 473–510. **Sabatier, A.** *Les origines littéraires et la composition de l'Apocalypse de S. Jean.* Paris: Librairie Fischbacher, 1888. **Schille, G.** "Der Apokalyptiker Johannes und die Edelsteine (Apk 21)." *SNTU* 17 (1992) 231–44. **Schnackenburg, R.** "Apostles before and during Paul's Time." In *Apostolic History and the Gospel: Biblical and Historical Essays.* FS F. F. Bruce, ed. W. W. Gasque and R. P. Martin. Grand Rapids, MI: Eerdmans, 1970. 287–303. **Schoen, H.** *L'origine de l'Apocalypse de Saint Jean.* Paris: Librairie Fischbacher, 1887. **Simons, J.** *Jerusalem in the Old Testament: Researches and Theories.* Leiden: Brill, 1952. **Smith, J. Z.** *To Take Place: Toward Theory in Ritual.* Chicago: University of Chicago, 1987. **Stuhlmacher, P.** "'Siehe, ich mache alles neu.'" *LR* 18 (1968) 3–18. **Thüsing, W.** "Die Vision des 'Neuen Jerusalem' (Apk 21,1–22,5) als Verheissung und Gottesverkündigung." *TTZ* 77 (1968) 17–34. **Topham, M.** "The Dimensions of the New Jerusalem." *ExpTim* 100 (1989) 417–19. ———. "A Human Being's Measurement, which is an Angel's." *ExpTim* 100 (1989) 217–18. **Unnik, W. C. van.** *Het godspredikaat 'Het begin en het einde' bij Flavius Josephus en in de openbaring van Johannes.* Amsterdam: Noord-Hollandsche Uitgevers Maatschappij, 1976. **Wacholder, B. Z.** "The Fragmentary Remains of 11QTorah (Temple Scroll), 11QTorah[b] and 11QTorah[c] plus 4QparaTorah Integrated with 11QTorah[a]." *HUCA* 62 (1991) 1–116. **Wahl, O.** "Göttliches und menschliches Messen: Zur Botschaft von Sacharja 2,5–9." In *Künder des Wortes: Beiträge zur Theologie der Propheten,* ed. L. Ruppert, P. Weimar, and E. Zenger. Würzburg: Echter, 1982. 255–73. **Walther, F. E.** "Vollendung (Offenbarung 21:9–22:5)." *TBei* 3 (1972) 145–51. **Wilcox, M.** "Tradition and Redaction of Rev 21,9–22,5." In *L'Apocalypse,* ed. J. Lambrecht. 205–15. **Windisch, H.** "Die Sprüche vom Eingehen in das Reich Gottes." *ZNW* 27 (1928) 163–92. **Yadin, Y.** *The Temple Scroll.* 3 vols. Jerusalem: The Israel Exploration Society, 1983.

Translation

[9]*Then came one of*[a] *the seven angels with the seven libation bowls full*[b] *of the*[c] *seven last plagues and spoke to me, saying,*[d] *"Come, I will show you*[e] *the bride, the wife of the Lamb."*[e] [10]*He then transported me in a prophetic trance*[a] *to a great and*[b] *high mountain*

and showed me the ᶜ*holy city Jerusalem* ᵈ *descending* ᵉ*from heaven from God* ᵉ ¹¹ ᵃ*with the glory of God.*ᵃ ᵇ*Its radiance was like a precious stone,* ᶜ*like jasper transparent as crystal.* ¹²*The city had* ᵃ *a* ᵇ*wide and high* ᵇ *wall with twelve* ᶜ *gates. Twelve angels were at the gates, and names* ᵈ *were inscribed* ᵉ *on the gates,* ᶠ*the names* ᶠ *of the twelve tribes of the sons* ᵍ *of Israel.* ¹³*There were three gates on the east* ᵃ *and* ᵇ *three gates on the north* ᶜ*and* ᵇ *three gates on the* ᵈ*south* ᶜ ᵉ*and* ᵇ *three gates on the* ᶠ*west.*ᵉ ¹⁴*The* ᵃ *wall of the city has* ᵇ *twelve foundation stones, and upon them are the names of the twelve apostles of the Lamb.*

¹⁵ ᵃ*The one who spoke to me* ᵃ *had a golden measuring rod to measure the city and its gates and its wall.* ¹⁶*The city is arranged with four equal sides; that is,* ᵃ *its length and width are the same. He measured the city with the measuring rod, at* ᵇ *12,000* ᶜ *stadia;* ᵈ *its length and width and height are the same.* ¹⁷*He measured* ᵃ *its wall, 144 cubits,* ᵇ*the unit measure used by a person,* ᶜ*that is,*ᶜ *an angel.*ᵇ

¹⁸*The* ᵃ*material used in the construction* ᵃ *of its wall was jasper, while the city itself was pure gold, like clear glass.*ᵇ ¹⁹ ᵃ*The foundations of the city wall were adorned with every type of precious stone. The first foundation was jasper, the second, sapphire, the third, chalcedony, the fourth, emerald,*ᵇ ²⁰*the fifth, onyx, the sixth, carnelian, the seventh, yellow topaz,*ᵃ *the eighth, beryl, the ninth, topaz, the tenth, chrysophrase, the eleventh, jacinth, the twelfth, amethyst.* ²¹*The twelve gates were twelve pearls;*ᵃ*each individual* ᵃ *gate was made of a single pearl. The main square* ᵇ *of the city was pure gold, like transparent crystal.*

²²   *I did not see a temple in the city,*
        for the Lord God Almighty and the Lamb are its ᵃ*temple.*
²³   *The city has no need of the sun or of the moon to illumine* ᵃ*it,*
        ᵇ*for the* ᵇ *glory of God illumines it,*
        and its lamp is the Lamb.
²⁴   *The nations will walk in its light,*
        and the kings of the earth will bring ᵃ*their glory* ᵃ *to it.*
²⁵   *The gates of the city will never close during the day,*
        for there will be no night there.
²⁶   ᵃ*People will bring* ᵃ *the glory and the honor of the nations to it.*
²⁷   *But* ᵃ *nothing* ᵇ *unclean will enter into it,*
        *that is,*ᶜ *anyone* ᵈ *who does what is abhorrent or false,*
        except those inscribed in the Lamb's ᵉ *book of life.*

²²:¹*He showed me a river* ᵃ ᵇ*of living water,*ᵇ *sparkling like crystal, flowing from* ᶜ*the throne* ᶜ *of God and of the Lamb,* ²*down the center of the main street of the city.*ᵃ ᵇ*On each side* ᵇ *of the river there were trees* ᶜ *of life* ᵈ*producing* ᵉ ᶠ*twelve kinds* ᶠ *of fruit,*ᵈ *each* ᵍ *yielding* ʰ *its fruit each month.*ⁱ *The leaves* ʲ*of the tree* ʲ *were for the healing of the* ᵏ *nations.* ³*And* ᵃ *"the curse of war"* ᵃ *will no longer* ᵇ *exist.*ᶜ *The* ᵈ *throne of God and of the Lamb will be in the city, and his servants* ᵉ*will worship* ᵉ *him.* ⁴*And they will see his face, and his name* ᵃ*will be on their foreheads.* ⁵*There will no longer* ᵃ *be any night, and people* ᵇ*will have no need* ᵇ *for lamp light* ᶜ *or sunlight,*ᵈ *because the* ᵉ *Lord God will illumine* ᶠ*them, and they will reign for ever and ever.*

⁶*Then* ᵃ*he said* ᵃ *to me, "These words are faithful and true, and the* ᵇ *Lord, the God of the* ᶜ*spirits of* ᶜ *the prophets, sent* ᵈ *his angel* ᵉ*to reveal to his servants* ᵉ *what must soon happen.* ⁷ ᵃ*Indeed, I will come soon.* ᵇ*Blessed is the one who obeys* ᵇ ᶜ*the message of this prophetic book."*ᶜ

⁸*It was I,*ᵃ *John, who* ᵇ*heard and saw* ᵇ *these visions. And when I heard and saw* ᶜ *them, I fell to worship before the feet of the angel who revealed them to me.* ⁹*But he said* ᵃ *to me, "Don't do* ᵇ *that! I am a fellow servant with you and your brothers and sisters* ᶜ *the prophets and* ᵈ *those who obey the commands* ᵉ *in this book. Worship* ᶠ ᵍ*God!"*

Notes

9.a. Variants: (1) ἐκ] ℵ A 025 046 fam 1006[1841] fam 1611 Oecumenius[2053 2062text] Andr e[2026] f[2023] n 94 syr[ph h] it[gig] (*de*); vg Primasius (*ex*); Beatus (*ex*). (2) omit ἐκ] 051 fam 1006[1006] Andreas.

9.b. Variants: (1) τῶν γεμόντων] ℵ[1] (ℵ*: τῶν γεμουσῶν) A (lacuna in C) Andreas syr[ph? h?]. (2) γεμόντων] 025. (3) τὰς γεμούσας] 046 fam 1006[1006 1841] fam 1611[1611 1854] 2030 2377 Andr a c l[1778] n syr[ph? h?]; B. Weiss, *Johannes-Apokalypse*, 137. (4) γεμούσας] Andr d f[2023] g Byzantine. Reading (3) is linguistically correct since it conforms in gender and number to its antecedent, τὰς ἑπτὰ φιάλας. Yet since this reading is supported only by a few minuscules, it must be regarded as a correction of τῶν γεμόντων. This reading, variant (1), is a grammatical solecism and therefore the *lectio difficilior*. However, since it has relatively strong attestation, it must be considered the correct reading (Schmid, *Studien* 2:248).

9.c. Variant: omit τῶν] Andr e[2057] h[2060] i 598 Byzantine.

9.d. On the Septuagintism λαλεῖν μετ' ἐμοῦ, see *Note* 1:12.b-b.

9.e-e. Variants: (1) τὴν νύμφην τὴν γυναῖκα τοῦ ἀρνίου] ℵ A (lacuna in C) 025 fam 1006[1006 1841] fam 1611[1611 1854 2329] 2030 2377 Andr l n Andr/Byz 4a Andr/Byz 4b lat syr cop Primasius (*nuptam uxorem agni*); it[gig] Tyc[2] Beatus (*sponsam uxorem agni*; *nuptam uxorem agni*; von Soden, *Das lateinische Neue Testament*, 588). (2) τὴν νύμφην τοῦ ἀρνίου τὴν γυναῖκα] 051 Andreas. (3) τὴν γυναῖκα τὴν νύμφην τοῦ ἀρνίου] fam 1611[2050] Andr f[2023] 94 Byzantine. (4) τὴν γυναῖκα τοῦ ἀρνίου] Oecumenius[2053 2062] Andr l[1678 1778]. Readings (2) and (3) are instances (of which there are a number of other examples in Revelation; see Schmid, *Studien* 2:70–71) of identical corrections made in the primitive text independently by the Andreas and Byzantine tradition. In reading (4) τὴν νύμφην appears to have been accidentally omitted through haplography.

10.a. For a detailed discussion of the meaning and translation of ἐν πνεύματι, lit. "in the spirit," see *Note* 1:10.a. and *Comment* on 1:10.

10.b. Variant: omit καί] fam 1611[1854] 2030 2377 Andreas.

10.c. Variants: (1) omit μεγάλην καί] 025 Andr l 94. (2) add μεγάλην καί] fam 1611[1854 2030] Andreas.

10.d. On the problem of the orthography of Ἰερουσαλήμ in Revelation, see *Note* 3:12.g.

10.e-e. Variants: (1) ἐκ τοῦ οὐρανοῦ ἀπὸ τοῦ θεοῦ] A (lacuna in C) ℵ Andreas. (2) ἀπὸ τοῦ οὐρανοῦ ἐκ τοῦ θεοῦ] Oecumenius[2053 2062]. (3) ἐκ τοῦ οὐρανοῦ ἐκ τοῦ θεοῦ] Byzantine. Parallel phrases occur in 3:12; 20:9; 21:2, indicating that reading (1) is the *lectio originalis* (Schmid, *Studien* 2:214–15).

11.a-a. Variant: omit ἔχουσαν τὴν δόξαν τοῦ θεοῦ] A Oecumenius[2062] Andr/Byz 2a[680] Andr/Byz 3[1328 1894] Andr/Byz 4c[2305] Byz 3[429 522].

11.b. Variant: insert καί] fam 1611[2329] Andr a b c d g l it[t] vg[cl] syr[ph] Primasius.

11.c. Variant: omit ὡς λίθῳ] 051 Andreas.

12.a. τὴν πόλιν (v 10) is the antecedent of the present fem. nom. ptcp. ἔχουσα.

12.b-b. μέγα can be construed as referring to the width of the wall (see *Comment* on v 12), or μέγα καὶ ὑψηλόν could be construed as a hendiadys meaning "extremely large."

12.c. Variant: δεκαπέντε, "fifteen," instead of δώδεκα, "twelve"] Oecumenius[2053 2062text]; see *Note* 13.e-e.

12.d. Variant: insert αὐτῶν] ℵ syr[ph].

12.e. Variant: γεγραμμένα] ℵ Andr l[1678 1778] n. The pf. ptcp. ἐπιγεγραμμένα is in apposition to ὀνόματα, which in turn is the obj. of the present ptcp. ἔχουσα; the pattern ἔχειν + obj. + pf. ptcp. (adj.) occurs several times in Revelation (12:6; 14:1; 19:12, 16; 21:12). In none of these instances does ἔχειν + ptcp. constitute a periphrastic construction (see W. J. Aerts, *Periphrastica* [Amsterdam: Hakkert, 1965] 161–62); see *Note* 12:6.d.

12.f-f. Variants: (1) τὰ ὀνόματα] A fam 1611[1611 (2020) 2329] fam 1006[1841] 2030 Oecumenius[2053] 2377 Andr n[2432] Primasius it[gig] Beatus arm[2] arm[4]; Bousset (1906) 447; Charles, 2:364; [UBSGNT[4]]; [Nestle-Aland[27]]. (2) ὀνόματα] Andr l Byzantine. (3) τὸ ὄνομα] Andr n[2065]. (4) omit τὰ ὀνόματα] ℵ 051 Andreas arm[1]; Tischendorf, *NT Graece*; WHort; Merk, *NT*. Reading (1) conforms to the style of Revelation (the repetition of the article τά; see Bousset [1906] 447 n. 2) and is confirmed by the virtually unanimous evidence of the versions (Schmid, *Studien* 2:126).

12.g. Here υἱῶν is a gen. of apposition, lacking an article because it reflects the Heb. construct state, which never has an article; but see 2:14 (Mussies, *Morphology*, 191).

13.a. Variant: ἀνατολῶν] Byzantine.

13.b. Variant: omit καί] Andreas it[t] vg Primasius Beatus.

13.c-c. Variant: omit ἀπὸ νότου πυλῶνες τρεῖς] ℵ Oecumenius[2053] Andr a b[2081*] c.

13.d. Variant: δυσμῶν for νότου] A Andr h i[2042] 94 cop[sa].

13.e-e. Variant: add καὶ ἀπὸ μεσημβρίας πυλῶνες τρεῖς] Andr c m[2037] (both families omit ἀπὸ νότου πυλῶνες τρεῖς; see *Note* 13.c-c.). There has been some confusion in the enumeration of the twelve gates.

While Oecumenius²⁰⁵³ᶜᵒᵐᵐ ²⁰⁶² gives the total number as fifteen, in 21:13 Oecumenius²⁰⁵³ᵗᵉˣᵗ enumerates only *nine* gates, eliminating καὶ ἀπὸ δυσμῶν πυλῶνες τρεῖς, "and on the west three gates," a reading also absent from ℵ. 2037, on the other hand, actually enumerates fifteen gates in 21:13 by inserting καὶ ἀπὸ μεσημβρίας πυλῶνες τρεῖς, "and on the south three gates," using μεσημβρία in addition to νότος. None of these readings, despite the interesting agreement of Oecumenius²⁰⁵³ with ℵ, has any claim to authenticity. They all simply reflect confusion in transmission (see Hoskier, *Oecumenius*, 15).

13.f. Variant: νότου for δυσμῶν] A Andr h i²⁰⁴² 94 copˢᵃ.

14.a. The καί with which this sentence begins is left untranslated since it lacks semantic value and functions as a discourse marker indicating the beginning of a new sentence or clause.

14.b. The present masc. sing. ptcp. ἔχων, "having," is intended to modify τὸ τεῖχος, "the wall," which is a neut. sing. nom.; however, because of the possible interchange between o = ω (BDR § 28; Thackeray, *Grammar*, 89–91, 194, 198–99; Gignac, *Grammar* 2:275–77), ἔχων *might* have been confused with ἔχον (neut. sing. nom. ptcp.). Here it functions as the finite verb ἔχει, "has" (Mussies, *Morphology*, 325).

15.a-a. On the Septuagintism λαλεῖν μετ᾽ ἐμοῦ, see *Note* 1:12.b-b.

16.a. καί is used here in an explanatory or epexegetical manner; see *Note* 21:27.c.

16.b. ἐπί + acc. of extent, meaning "at, to the extent of."

16.c. δώδεκα χιλιάδων is a gen. phrase (δώδεκα is indeclinable) functioning as a gen. of *measure*. Similar constructions appear in Mark 5:42, ἦν γὰρ ἐτῶν δώδεκα, "for he was twelve years old" (see Luke 2:42), and Acts 4:22, ἐτῶν γὰρ ἦν πλειόνων τεσσεράκοντα ὁ ἄνθρωπος, "the man was more than forty years old."

16.d. Variants: (1) σταδίους] A 046 fam 1006¹⁰⁰⁶ ¹⁸⁴¹ fam 1611¹⁶¹¹ ²⁰⁵⁰ ²³²⁹ 2030 Andr b²⁰⁸¹ f²⁰²³ 1 n 94 1773 Byzantine lat syrʰ ; WHortᵐᵃʳᵍ; Bousset (1906) 448; Charles, 2:365. (2) σταδίων] ℵ* 051 Oecumenius²⁰⁵³ ²⁰⁶² Andreas; WHort; Merk, *NT;* Nestle-Aland²⁷; UBSGNT⁴. (3) σταδίου] ℵ². Though reading (2) is the *lectio difficilior*, its origin was perhaps the result of a mechanical assimilation to χιλιάδων (Schmid, *Studien* 2:126), so reading (1) is the *lectio melior*.

17.a. Variants: (1) ἐμέτρησεν] A ℵ 025 2030 Andr f²⁰³¹ h²⁰⁶⁰ Andr Ø²⁰³⁸. (2) ἐμέτρησε] fam 1006 fam 1611¹⁶¹¹ ²³⁴⁴ Andreas Oecumenius²⁰⁵³ ²⁰⁶². (3) ἐμέτρισεν] fam 1611²⁰⁵⁰ ²³²⁹. (4) omit ἐμέτρησεν] fam 1611¹⁸⁵⁴ Andr g Byzantine. Variant (3) probably originated through the η = ι interchange (Gignac, *Grammar* 1:235–39) and actually supports reading (1). Reading (1) involves the use of moveable ν, an extremely problematic issue in NT textual criticism because of its irregular use (BDF § 20). In A it is absent from the endings of only seven words where it might have been used (7:10, κράζουσι; 9:4, ἔχουσι; 10:5, ἦρε; 17:16, μεισήσουσι; 19:17, πᾶσι; 21:8[2x], φόνευσι πᾶσι [Mussies, *Morphology*, 28–28; see Gignac, *Grammar* 1:114–16]). Only in 9:4 does Nestle-Aland²⁷ omit the final ν.

17.b-b. For this translation, see Louw-Nida, § 81.1.

17.c-c. On ὅ ἐστιν, see *Note* 21:8.c.

18.a-a. ἡ ἐνδώμησις can mean "foundation" (Louw-Nida, § 7.41) or "building material" (Louw-Nida, § 7.77). The spelling and derivation of the word are problematic because of the phonological confusion between o and ω. MM, 212, spells the word both ways: ἐνδό(-ώ-)μησις. Moulton-Howard (*Accidence*, 73) regard the spelling with -o- as the result of a false etymology; the word is derived from δωμᾶν, "to build" (*Accidence*, 307). Since θεμέλιοι (τοῦ τείχους), "foundations (of the wall)," are referred to twice (21:14, 19), the ἐνδώμησις τοῦ τείχους, "foundation of the wall" (21:18), probably refers to the superstructure built upon the foundations.

18.b. ὕαλος can mean either "glass," or "crystal" (Louw-Nida, § 2.46; 6.222).

19.a. Variant: insert καί] ℵ* Oecumenius²⁰⁵³ ²⁰⁶² Andreas itᵗ syr copᵇᵒ.

19.b. This is green, "like a ciandela beetle" (see Exod 28:18; Ezek 27:16; see Loewen, *BT* 35 [1984] 229–34).

20.a. This is a yellow topaz, "yellow like an imperial moth" (see Exod 1:16; 28:13); Loewen, *BT* 35 (1984) 229–34.

21.a-a. In the phrase ἀνὰ εἷς ἕκαστος, the prep. ἀνά functions as a distributive (= κατά); see BDF §§ 204, 305. Variant: ἵνα for ἀνά] A Andr/Byz 4b⁻¹⁷² ⁻¹⁸²⁸ Andr/Byz 4c⁻²⁰²² Byz 4¹⁷¹⁹ Byz 17¹⁸⁵² Byz 18⁹¹.

21.b. On ἡ πλατεῖα as "main square," see *Comment* on 21:21.

22.a. Variants: (1) insert ὁ] A (lacuna in C); Andr 1¹⁶⁷⁸ ²⁰⁸⁰ 1773 Byz 17⁴⁶⁹ ¹⁸⁵²; B. Weiss, *Johannes-Apokalypse*, 107; Charles, 2:367. (2) omit ὁ] ℵ Andreas Byzantine; Tischendorf, *NT Graece;* von Soden, *Text;* Bousset (1906) 451; Nestle-Aland²⁷; UBSGNT⁴. Since the presence of the article conforms to the style of Revelation, which regularly uses the article with predicate noms. (see Rev 1:8, 17; 2:23; 3:17; 7:14; 11:4 18:23; 20:5, 14; 21:6; 22:13, 16), reading (1) is probably original (Schmid, *Studien* 2:95, 198).

23.a. Variants: (1) αὐτῇ] *lectio originalis.* (2) ἐν αὐτῇ] ℵ² 2030 2377 Andr f⁰⁵¹ ²⁰²³ ²⁰⁷³ n itᵃ vgᴬ copᵇᵒ. (3) αὐτήν] Andr b²⁰⁵⁹ d f²⁰⁵⁶ h i⁻²⁰⁷⁴.

23.b-b. Variants: (1) ἡ γάρ] *lectio originalis.* (2) γὰρ ἡ] fam 1611¹⁶¹¹ ¹⁸⁵⁴ Byzantine.

24.a-a. Variants: (1) τὴν δόξαν αὐτῶν] A (lacuna in C) ℵ 025 051 fam 1006¹⁰⁰⁶ ¹⁸⁴¹ fam 1611²³²⁹ Andreas. (2) τὴν δόξαν καὶ τὴν τιμὴν αὐτῶν] Oecumenius²⁰⁵³ fam 1611¹⁶¹¹ ¹⁸⁵⁴ ²⁰⁵⁰ Andr f²⁰²³. (3) αὐτῷ δόξαν καὶ τιμὴν τῶν ἐθνῶν] fam 1611¹⁶¹¹ ¹⁸⁵⁴ Andr f²⁰⁷³ 1773 Byzantine. (4) αὐτῇ δόξαν καὶ τιμὴν αὐτῶν] Andr g. Variants (2), (3), and (4) have all been influenced by the doublet in v 26.

26.a-a. οἴσουσιν is either an indefinite pl., for which the subject "people" has been supplied in the translation (see Rev 2:24; 12:6; 13:16; 16:15; 18:14; 20:4; see esp. *Note* 2:24.a-a.), or the subject is οἱ βασιλεῖς τῆς γῆς, "the kings of the earth," mentioned in v 24 but interrupted by v 25.

27.a. The coordinating conjunction καί is used here in an adversative sense.

27.b. For a discussion of the idiom οὐ μὴ . . . πᾶν as a substitute for the more proper μηδέν, see *Note* 7:1.g-g.

27.c. καί is used here in an epexegetical or explanatory way since the coordinate clause it introduces defines πᾶν κοινόν more closely; see *Note* 16.a. Variant: οὐδέ instead of καί] 2030 2377.

27.d. Variants: (1) omit ὁ before ποιῶν] A (lacuna in C) fam 1006 fam 1611²⁰⁵⁰ ²³²⁹ 2030 2377 Andr n; B. Weiss, *Johannes-Apokalypse;* Charles, 2:369; von Soden, *Text.* (2) insert ὁ] ℵ* fam 1611¹⁸⁵⁴ Andr f²⁰⁷³ g l Byzantine; Tischendorf, *NT Graece;* [WHort]; [Bousset (1906)]; [Nestle-Aland²⁷]; [UBSGNT⁴]. (3) ποιοῦν] Andreas. Here it is probable that ὁ was added because of the difficult construction πᾶν κοινὸν καὶ ποιῶν βδέλυγμα, though Schmid (*Studien* 2:134) argues that the presence of the article corresponds to the typical style of Revelation.

27.e. Variant: οὐρανοῦ] ℵ.

22:1.a. Variants: (1) omit καθαρόν] ℵ A (lacuna in C); Oecumenius²⁰⁵³ 025 046 Byzantine eth. (2) insert καθαρόν] 051 2030 2377 Andreas.

1.b-b. ὕδατος ζωῆς, "of living water" (see 21:6), is an ambiguous expression that can mean "running water," or ζωῆς can refer to "life," i.e., "eternal life," and be construed as an epexegetical gen. so that the phrase means "of water, that is, [eternal] life."

1.c-c. Variants: (1) omit τοῦ before θρόνου] ℵ. (2) τοῦ στόματος] fam 1611¹⁶¹¹ ²³²⁹ Byz 16⁶¹.

2.a. The Gk. text can be punctuated in one of two ways. Some place a period after "Lamb" at the end of v 1 (Tischendorf, *NT Graece;* Bousset [1906] 452; Merk, *NT;* Nestle-Aland²⁷; UBSGNT⁴) and punctuate v 2 as a single independent sentence beginning with ἐν μέσῳ τῆς πλατείας . . . , "Down the middle of the street . . . ." This punctuation is dubious because the author usually begins new sentences with καί and rarely does so with a prep. phrase (exceptions: μετὰ ταῦτα εἶδον in 4:1; 7:9; 18:1; see μετὰ ταῦτα ἤκουσα in 19:1; διὰ τοῦτο in 7:15; 12:12; 18:8; various other preps. in 9:18; 22:15). The passage is best understood if vv 1–2a constitute a single sentence (WHort).

2.b-b. Variants: (1) ἐντεῦθεν καὶ ἐκεῖθεν] A (lacuna in C) 046 Oecumenius²⁰⁵³ ²⁰⁶²ᶜᵒᵐᵐ fam 1006⁻⁹¹¹ fam 1611¹⁸⁵⁴²³²⁹; B. Weiss, *Johannes-Apokalypse,* 222; von Soden, *Text.* (2) ἐντεῦθεν καὶ ἐντεῦθεν] 051 2030 fam 1611²⁰⁵⁰ 2377 syrᵖʰ Andreas TR. (3) ἔνθεν] ℵ. ἐντεῦθεν καὶ ἐκεῖθεν means lit. "from here and from there," i.e., "on both sides" (John 19:18 has ἐντεῦθεν καὶ ἐντεῦθεν). This idiom is found in Theod Dan 12:5, εἷς ἐντεῦθεν τοῦ χείλους τοῦ ποταμοῦ καὶ εἷς ἐντεῦθεν τοῦ χείλους τοῦ ποταμοῦ, "one on one side of the river and one on the other side" (see Num 22:24). The more normal expression is ἔνθεν καὶ ἔνθεν, "on one side and on the other" (see LXX Ezek 47:12 [MT מזה ומזה *mizzeh ûmizzeh*]; Dan 12:5; 1 Macc 6:38; 9:45). A corresponding idiom, מכא ומכא *mikka'an ûmikka'an,* "on both sides," occurs in *t. Soṭa* 8.9 (ed. Bietenhard).

2.c. Variant: ξύλα] Byz 3³⁸⁵ arm¹ Cassiodorus (*arbores*). This correction makes grammatically explicit that ξύλον is a collective noun.

2.d-d. Forestell (*Targumic Traditions,* 124; see Turner, *Style,* 43) insists that καρπὸν ποιεῖν, "to produce fruit," is a Heb. and Aram. idiom (citing *Tg. Gen.* 1:11–12 and *Tg. Jer.* 17:8). M. Black (*Aramaic,* 138–39; followed by Turner, *Style,* 157) argues that the Heb. עָשָׂה פְרִי *'āśâ pĕrî,* "to make fruit," i.e., "to yield fruit," is rendered literally in the LXX by the Gk. phrase καρπὸν ποιεῖν (Gen 1:11, 12; 4 Kgdms 19:30; Jer 12:2; 17:8; Ezek 17:23), that it is also found in Aram., perhaps in imitation of the Heb., and that in Gk. it is a Semitism that may have originated as a Septuagintism. However, καρπὸν ποιεῖν is also idiomatic Gk. (LSJ, 1428; Bauer-Aland, 1366–67; Aristotle *Plant.* 1.4.819b; 2.10.829a; Dioscorides *Materia medica* 2.195).

2.e. Variants: (1) ποιοῦν (nom. or acc. neut. present ptcp.)] *lectio originalis.* (2) ποιῶν (nom. masc. present ptcp.)] A Byz 2¹⁸. Reading (2) may simply be the result of the merging of ου with ω in some ptcps. (Mussies, *Morphology,* 282) since A uses the masc. ποιῶν and the neut. ἀποδιδοῦν together.

2.f-f. Here the cardinal δώδεκα is used for the multiplicative δωδεκάκις, which has been regarded as a Hebraism (BDF § 248.3; Turner, *Syntax,* 188; Mussies, *Morphology,* 217), although the same phenomenon occurs in Hellenistic Gk.

2.g. Variants: (1) ἕκαστον] *lectio originalis.* (2) ἕνα ἕκαστον] 051 Andreas. (3) ἕκαστον after ἀποδιδούς] 94 Byzantine. (4) ἕκαστος] fam 1611¹⁶¹¹ ¹⁸⁵⁴ Andr l 1773. (5) ἑκάστῳ] 046.

2.h. Variants: (1) ἀποδιδοῦν (nom. or acc. neut. sing. present ptcp. from the putative ἀποδιδόω)] A (lacuna in C) Oecumenius²⁰⁵³ ²⁰⁶² Andr a²¹⁸⁶ b c d g⁻²⁰⁴⁵; B. Weiss, *Johannes-Apokalypse*, 113. (2) ἀποδιδούς (nom. sing. masc. present ptcp. from ἀποδίδωμι)] ℵ 94 Andreas Byzantine; Tischendorf, *NT Graece;* WHort^mg; Bousset (1906) 452; von Soden, *Text;* Charles, 2:369. Reading (1) is the *lectio difficilior* and certainly original since it is based on the putative form ἀποδιδόω (the neut. ptcp. of ἀποδίδωμι is ἀποδιδόν, as in Andr i²⁰⁷⁴), of which the analogous form διδῶ from the putative διδόω (or δίδω) is found in 3:9 (see BDF § 94; Schmid, *Studien* 2:95, 248–49); but see διδόασιν (instead of διδοῦσιν) in 17:13. δίδωμι and other athematic -μι verbs were moving into the thematic -ω verb conjugation in the Hellenistic period (Mussies, *Morphology*, 280–84). The origin of the masc. form ἀποδιδούς (formed from ἀποδίδωμι; if formed from ἀποδιδόω it would be ἀποδιδῶν) is difficult to explain, though Moulton-Howard regard ἀποδιδοῦν as a correction to achieve concord (*Accidence*, 205).

2.i. Orthographical variant: μῆναν] A Andr h²²⁸⁶. On the addition of -ν to acc. sing. third-declension nouns in the imperial period, see *Note* 12:13.c-c.

2.j-j. Variants: (1) τοῦ ξύλου] *lectio originalis;* Primasius^R. (2) τῶν ξυλῶν] ℵ arm¹. (3) omit τοῦ ξύλου] Primasius^F. (4) αὐτοῦ] Tyc² (*suum*); syr^ph cop^sa. A scribal correction based on understanding ξύλον ζωῆς as a collective noun phrase meaning "trees of life."

2.k. Variant: omit τῶν] ℵ Oecumenius²⁰⁵³ ²⁰⁶².

3.a-a. On the translation of πᾶν κατάθεμα as "the curse of war," see *Comment* on 22:3. Variants: (1) κατάθεμα] ℵ¹ A 025 046 051 Oecumenius²⁰⁵³ᵗᵉˣᵗ Andreas. (2) κάταγμα] ℵ*. (3) κατάμαθε] Oecumenius²⁰⁵³ᶜᵒᵐᵐ (an error of metathesis). (4) ἀνάθεμα] fam 1611²⁰⁵⁰. (5) κατανάθεμα] fam 1006 fam 1611⁻²⁰⁵⁰ Byzantine.

3.b. Variants: (1) ἔτι] Andr e²⁰²⁶ n 025. (2) ἐκεῖ] 051 fam 1611²³²⁹ Andreas syr^ph. (3) omit ἔτι] ℵ*.

3.c. Variant: ἐστίν] fam 1611¹⁶¹¹.

3.d. Variant: omit ὁ] ℵ.

3.e-e. Variant: λατρεύουσιν] 046 Oecumenius²⁰⁶² fam 1611¹⁶¹¹ ¹⁸⁵⁴ Andr d²⁰⁶⁷ e f²⁰³¹ ²⁰⁵⁶ l¹⁶⁷⁸ ²⁰²⁰ n 1773.

4.a. Variant: καί] ℵ.

5.a. Variants: (1) ἔτι] ℵ A 025 Oecumenius²⁰⁵³ᵗᵉˣᵗ ²⁰⁶²ᵗᵉˣᵗ fam 1006¹⁰⁰⁶ ¹⁸⁴¹ fam 1611²⁰⁵⁰ ²³²⁹ 2030 2377*. (2) ἐκεῖ] 051 2377^varlect syr^h cop latt Andreas syr^ph. (3) ἐκεῖ ἔτι] Andr g²⁰⁷¹ Irenaeus^Gk. (4) omit ἔτι] 046 Oecumenius²⁰⁶²ᶜᵒᵐᵐ fam 1611¹⁶¹¹ ¹⁸⁵⁴ Byzantine.

5.b-b. Variants: (1) οὐκ ἔχουσιν χρείαν] Andr l 94. (2) οὐχ ἔξουσιν χρείαν] A fam 1006¹⁰⁰⁶ ¹⁸⁴¹ fam 1611²⁰⁵⁰ ²³²⁹ Oecumenius²⁰⁵³ ²⁰⁶² it^gig vg cop^sa Ambrose Primasius. (3) οὐ χρείαν] fam 1611¹⁶¹¹ ¹⁸⁵⁴ Byzantine. (4) χρείαν οὐκ ἔχουσι] Andreas.

5.c. Variants: (1) φωτός] ℵ A Andr b²⁰⁸¹ f²⁰⁷³ l 94. (2) φῶς] 2030 fam 1611²⁰⁵⁰ ²³²⁹ Oecumenius²⁰⁵³ ²⁰⁶² 2377 Andr i. (3) omit] 051 Andreas Byzantine [von Soden, *Text*].

5.d. Variants: (1) φωτός] ℵ Andreas Byzantine. (2) φῶς] A 025 051 2030 fam 1611²⁰⁵⁰ ²³²⁹ Oecumenius²⁰⁵³ ²⁰⁶² 2377 Andr b⁻²⁰⁸¹ f²³⁰² h i 598.

5.e. Variant: ὁ before κύριος] [von Soden, *Text*].

5.f. Variants: (1) ἐπ'] ℵ A fam 1006¹⁰⁰⁶ ¹⁸⁴¹ fam 1611²⁰⁵⁰ ²³²⁹ 2030 2377 Andr l 94 it^gig Ambrose Primasius. (2) omit ἐπ'] 051 Andreas Byzantine lat [von Soden, *Text*].

6.a-a. Variant: λέγει] fam 1611¹⁶¹¹ ¹⁸⁵⁴ 94 Andr f²⁰²³ Byzantine.

6.b. Variants: (1) ὁ before κύριος] A (lacuna in C) ℵ fam 1006¹⁸⁴¹ fam 1611¹⁶¹¹ ²³²⁹ Oecumenius²⁰⁵³ ²⁰⁶² 2377 it^gig Primasius. (2) omit ὁ] 051 Andreas Byzantine WHort^mg. Reading (2) is the result of assimilation to such passages as 1:8; 4:8; 18:8; 19:6; 22:5 (B. Weiss, *Johannes-Apokalypse*, 7; Schmid, *Studien* 2:83, 192).

6.c-c. Variants: (1) ἁγίων] 051 Andreas. (2) πνευμάτων καὶ τῶν] fam 1611²⁰⁵⁰ 2030 2377. (3) πνευμάτων τῶν ἁγίων] Andr f²⁰⁷³.

6.d. Variants: (1) με] ℵ* fam 1006¹⁰⁰⁶ ¹⁸⁴¹ Andr l syr^h cop^sa. (2) μοι] Andr n.

6.e-e. Variants: (1) omit δεῖξαι τοῖς δούλοις αὐτοῦ] fam 1611¹⁸⁵⁴. (2) διδάξαι τοὺς δούλους αὐτοῦ] Andr i.

7.a. Variant: omit καί] 051 Oecumenius²⁰⁵³ ²⁰⁶² Andreas it^t Primasius Beatus.

7.b-b. Variant: μακάριοι οἱ τηροῦντες] Oecumenius²⁰⁵³ ²⁰⁶².

7.c-c. The phrase τοὺς λόγους τῆς προφητείας τοῦ βιβλίου τούτου, lit. "the words of the prophecy of this book," is a Hebraic concatenation of gens. in which τῆς προφητείας is in apposition to τοὺς λόγους, so the whole phrase should be translated "the words that constitute this prophetic book," i.e., "the *message* of this prophetic book."

8.a. The crasis κἀγώ (καί + ἐγώ) introduces this sentence and functions as an emphatic use of the pronoun ἐγώ. It has therefore been translated "It was I."

8.b-b. Variant: βλέπων καὶ ἀκούων] ℵ fam 1006¹⁰⁰⁶ ¹⁸⁴¹ fam 1611²³²⁹ Andreas syr^ph cop^bo Primasius;

Tischendorf, *NT Graece;* Bousset (1906) 456; von Soden, *Text.* The change is probably based on the notion that the author is primarily a "seer" and only secondarily a "hearer."

8.c. The aor. ἔβλεψα, "I saw," is preferred by Nestle-Aland[27] and UBSGNT[4]. Yet John does not use the aor. of βλέπειν elsewhere (he prefers the aor. form εἶδον, a suppletive verb functioning as the aor. of ὁρᾶν, which he uses forty-five times). It is interesting that Hermas *Vis.* 1–4, the oldest part of the Shepherd of Hermas, similarly avoids the aor. form of βλέπειν but does use the impf. once (3.2.9), though he uses various other forms of βλέπειν thirteen times. The more nearly original reading is probably the impf. ἔβλεπον, which is supported by A (C has a lacuna), Oecumenius, attested by the very important minuscules 2053 and 2062 (equal in text to A and C), as well as 2329 (which reads ἔβλεπων, i.e., reflecting an interchange between o and ω; see BDR § 28). This is the reading preferred by Bousset, (1906) 456, and Charles, 2:384. ἔβλεπον is the *lectio difficilior* since it is easier to imagine a correction in agreement with the tense of the preceding ἤκουσα than the reverse (Schmid, *Studien* 2:126). The aor. verb εἶδον is read by the Koine texts and is obviously a correction (in Johannine style) of the original ἔβλεπον. This presents an interpretive problem, however, for why would the author place an aor. and an impf. side by side in this way? It appears that the aor. ἤκουσα, "I heard," summarizes John's revelatory experience as an event or series of events completed in the past, while the impf. ἔβλεπον is a consequential impf. in which, though the action of the verb is completed, the results are considered part of that action (Rijksbaron, *Syntax,* 17–19). The consequence of John's vision is that he falls prostrate to the ground in worship. The impf. verb ἔλεγον is used in a similar way in 5:14.

9.a. λέγει, a historical present meaning "says," is here rendered as a past tense following Eng. style.

9.b. Variant: insert ποιήσῃς] fam 1006[1006 1841] Andr n latt Cyprian. The same variant occurs in a similar context in 19:10.

9.c. "And sisters" added for inclusive language since ἀδελφοί, though masc., can be used as a collective term for both men and women.

9.d. Variant: omit καί] Andreas Primasius. This omission equates the two groups: "your brothers the prophets" and "those who obey the commands in this book."

9.e. Variant: insert τῆς προφητείας] Andr[2020] l it[g].

9.f. The aor. imper. προσκύνησον, "worship," can refer either to a general attitude of worship or to ritual acts of worship; see Louw-Nida, § 53.56. With the former meaning, προσκύνησον could be understood as "be a worshiper" of God, while with the latter meaning (construing the aor. in an iterative sense) it could be translated "direct your acts of worship" to God; see K. L. McKay, "Aspect in Imperatival Constructions in New Testament Greek," *NovT* 27 (1985) 208.

9.g. On the use of προσκυνεῖν + dat. or acc. in Revelation, see *Note* 4:10.b.

Form/Structure/Setting

I. OUTLINE

G. The vision of the New Jerusalem (21:9–22:9)
1. Introduction to the vision (21:9–10a)
   a. Angelic guide appears (v 9a)
   b. The seer is invited to see the bride, the wife of the Lamb (v 9b)
   c. Angel transports the seer (v 10a)
      (1) Means: a prophetic trance
      (2) Destination: a great high mountain
2. The vision of the New Jerusalem (21:10b–22:5)
   a. Object of vision: New Jerusalem (v 10b)
      (1) Descending from heaven
      (2) Descending from God
   b. External description of the city (vv 11–21)
      (1) General appearance (v 11)
         (a) It has the glory of God (v 11a)
         (b) It has a jewel-like radiance (v 11a)

          [1] Like jasper
          [2] Clear as crystal
  (2) The wall of the city (vv 12–14)
  (3) Measuring of the external features of the city (vv 15–17)
  (4) Materials out of which the city is built (vv 18–21)
     (a) Wall of jasper (v 18a)
     (b) City is made of pure gold (v 18b)
     (c) The twelve foundations of the wall adorned with various
        precious stones (vv 19–20)
        [1] First foundation: jasper (v 19b)
        [2] Second foundation: sapphire (v 19b)
        [3] Third foundation: chalcedony (v 19b)
        [4] Fourth foundation: emerald (v 19b)
        [5] Fifth foundation: onyx (v 20)
        [6] Sixth foundation: carnelian (v 20)
        [7] Seventh foundation: yellow topaz (v 20)
        [8] Eighth foundation: beryl (v 20)
        [9] Ninth foundation: topaz (v 20)
       [10] Tenth foundation: chrysophrase (v 20)
       [11] Eleventh foundation: jacinth (v 20)
       [12] Twelfth foundation: amethyst (v 20)
     (d) The twelve gates of the wall (v 21a)
        [1] Twelve pearls
        [2] Each gate a single pearl
     (e) The main square of the city (v 21b)
        [1] Made of pure gold
        [2] Transparent as glass
c. Internal description of the city (21:22–22:5)
  (1) Focus on the missing temple (v 22)
     (a) No temple in the city (v 22a)
     (b) Its temple is the Lord God Almighty and the Lamb (v 22b)
  (2) The illumination of the city (v 23)
     (a) What is unnecessary for illumination (v 23a)
        [1] The sun
        [2] The moon
     (b) The actual sources of illumination (v 23b)
        [1] Glory of God is its light
        [2] Its lamp is the Lamb
  (3) The city as the center of the world (vv 24–26)
     (a) Nations walk in its light (v 24a)
     (b) Kings bring their glory to it (v 24b)
     (c) Its gates will never close (v 25a)
     (d) There is no night there (v 25b)
     (e) People will bring the glory and the honor of the nations into
        it (v 26)
  (4) What can enter the city (v 27)
     (a) Nothing unclean (v 27a)
     (b) No one who practices wickedness (v 27b)

         (c) Only those written in the Lamb's book of life (v 27b)

     (5) New Jerusalem as Paradise (22:1–5)

         (a) The river of life (vv 1–2a)

            [1] Appearance: bright as crystal (v 1a)

            [2] Source: flows from the throne of God and the Lamb (v 1b)

            [3] Direction: flows through the middle of the street (v 2a)

         (b) The trees of life (v 2a–c)

            [1] Location: both sides of the river (v 2a)

            [2] Fruit: twelve kinds: one kind produced each month (v 2b)

            [3] Leaves: for the healing of the nations (v 2c)

         (c) Those present in the city (vv 3–4)

            [1] No one or no thing accursed (v 3a)

            [2] The throne of God and the Lamb (v 3b)

            [3] The servants of God (vv 3c–5)

               [a] They will worship God (v 3c)

               [b] They will see God's face (v 4a)

               [c] God's name will be on their foreheads (v 4b)

               [d] They need neither lamp light nor sunlight (v 5a)

               [e] The Lord God will be their light (v 5a)

               [f] They will reign forever (v 5b)

  3. Transitional conclusion (22:6–9)

    a. The angelic guide speaks (v 6)

     (1) The foregoing message is true (v 6a)

     (2) God has sent his angel to reveal imminent events (v 6b–d)

    b. The exalted Christ speaks (v 7)

     (1) Promise to return soon (v 7a)

     (2) Blesses those who obey the prophetic words in this book (v 7b)

    c. John and his angelic guide (vv 8–9)

     (1) John claims that he saw and heard this revelation (v 8a)

     (2) He worships the angelic guide (v 8b)

     (3) He is rebuked by the angel (v 9)

         (a) Angel forbids John's worship (v 9a)

         (b) The role claimed by the angel (v 9b)

            [1] A fellow servant of John

            [2] A fellow servant of John's brothers the prophets

            [3] A fellow servant of those who obey the commands in this book

         (c) Angel directs John to worship God (v 9b)

II. LITERARY ANALYSIS

Rev 21:9–22:9 is a relatively extensive textual unit in which the framing portions have close parallels with the literary framework of 17:1–19:10. There are three major sections within 21:19–22:9: The first two are (1) 21:9–10a (introduction to the vision of the New

Jerusalem) and (2) 21:10b–22:5 (the New Jerusalem), which consists of three main subunits: (a) 21:10b (a general mention of the New Jerusalem), (b) 21:11–21 (external description of the New Jerusalem), and (c) 21:22–22:5 (description of internal features of the New Jerusalem). The second of these subunits, 21:10c–21, in turn is composed of three shorter units of text: (i) 21:11–14 (the general external description of the New Jerusalem), (ii) 21:15–17 (the measuring of the external features of the New Jerusalem), and (iii) 21:18–21 (a description of the materials out of which the New Jerusalem was constructed). The third subunit, 21:22–22:5, also consists of three constituent textual units: (i) 21:22–23 (the absence of a temple), (ii) 21:24–27 (prophecy of the future), and (iii) 22:1–5 (the New Jerusalem as Paradise). (3) The third major section, 22:6–9, is a concluding angelic speech, which is a transitional section that serves as both a conclusion to 22:1–22:5 and an introduction to the epilogue in 22:10–20.

The overall structure of 21:9–22:9 must first be considered in relation to the parallel structure in 17:1–19:10, both of which have been carefully and convincingly analyzed as paired angelic revelations by Giblin (*Bib* 55 [1974] 487–504). This can best be done by providing a synoptic comparison of the parallel texts that frame these units, i.e., Rev 17:1–3; 19:9–10, and 21:9–10; 22:6–9:

Rev 17:1–19:10	*Rev 21:9–22:9*
17:1καὶ ἦλθεν εἷς ἐκ τῶν ἑπτὰ Then came one of the seven	21:9καὶ ἦλθεν εἷς ἐκ τῶν ἑπτὰ Then came one of the seven
ἀγγέλων τῶν ἐχόντων τὰς ἑπτὰ angels with the seven	ἀγγέλων τῶν ἐχόντων τὰς ἑπτὰ angels with the seven
φιάλας bowls	φιάλας τῶν γεμόντων τῶν ἑπτὰ bowls full of the seven
	πληγῶν τῶν ἐσχάτων last plagues
καὶ ἐλάλησεν μετ' ἐμοῦ λέγων and spoke with me, saying,	καὶ ἐλάλησεν μετ' ἐμοῦ λέγων and spoke with me, saying,
δεῦρο, δείξω σοι "Come, I will show you	δεῦρο, δείξω σοι "Come, I will show you
τὸ κρίμα τῆς πόρνης τῆς μεγάλης. . . . the judgment of the great whore. . . ."	τὴν νύμφην τὴν γυναῖκα τοῦ ἀρνίου the bride, the wife of the Lamb."
17:3καὶ ἀπήνεγκέν με He then transported me	21:10καὶ ἀπήνεγκέν με He then transported me
εἰς ἔρημον to the desert	
ἐν πνεύματι in a prophetic trance.	ἐν πνεύματι in a prophetic trance
	ἐπὶ ὄρος μέγα καὶ ὑψηλόν to a great and high mountain

καὶ εἶδον. . . .
And I saw . . . .

[Body of vision]

19:9bκαὶ λέγει μοι
Then he says to me,

οὗτοι οἱ λόγοι ἀληθινοὶ
"These are the true words

τοῦ θεοῦ εἰσιν.
of God."

19:10καὶ ἔπεσα ἔμπροσθεν
Then I fell before

τῶν ποδῶν αὐτοῦ
his feet

προσκυνῆσαι αὐτῷ.
to worship him,

καὶ λέγει μοι·
but he said to me,

ὅρα μή·
"Don't do that!

σύνδουλός σού εἰμι
I am a fellow servant with you

καὶ τῶν ἀδελφῶν σου τῶν ἐχόντων
and your brothers who maintain

τὴν μαρτυρίαν Ἰησοῦ·
the testimony concerning Jesus.

τῷ θεῷ προσκύνησον.
Worship God."

καὶ ἔδειξέν μοι. . . .
and showed me . . . .

[Body of vision]

22:6καὶ εἶπέν μοι
Then he said to me,

οὗτοι οἱ λόγοι πιστοὶ καὶ ἀληθινοί . . . .
"These words are faithful and true . . . ."

22:8bκαὶ ὅτε ἤκουσα καὶ ἔβλεψα
And when I heard and saw them,

ἔπεσα προσκυνῆσαι ἔμπροσθεν
I fell to worship before

τῶν ποδῶν τοῦ ἀγγέλου
the feet of the angel

τοῦ δεικνύοντός μοι ταῦτα.
who revealed them to me.

22:9καὶ λέγει μοι·
But he said to me,

ὅρα μή·
"Don't do that!

σύνδουλός σού εἰμι
I am a fellow servant with you

καὶ τῶν ἀδελφῶν σου τῶν προφητῶν
and your brothers the prophets

καὶ τῶν τηρούντων τοὺς λόγους
and those who obey the commands

τοῦ βιβλίου τούτου
in this book.

τῷ θεῷ προσκύνησον.
Worship God!"

These two extensive textual units use antithetical female imagery: the first (17:1–19:10) focuses on Rome-Babylon under the dominating metaphor of a prostitute, while the second (21:9–22:9) focuses on the eschatological city of God, the New Jerusalem, under the metaphor of the bride, the wife of the Lamb. It is clear that since both texts are introduced by referring to an angelic guide who is explicitly said to be one of the seven bowl angels (17:1; 21:9), the final editing of these texts took place after the section on the seven bowl plagues in Rev 15:1–16:20 had been completed. Since the similarities between 17:1–19:10 and 21:1–22:9 involve only the beginning and ending sections of both passages, it is likely that the texts they frame were composed earlier (and independently) of those frameworks. Further, in my judgment, Rev 21:9–22:9 was consciously structured in imitation of 17:1–19:10 *after* Rev 21:5–22:2 had been inserted between 21:3–4 and 22:3–5. There are several reasons for this judgment: (1) Rev 22:6–9 was clearly formulated to serve not only as a conclusion to 21:9–22:5 (in the same way its parallel, 19:9–10, serves as a conclusion to 17:1–19:8) but also as a transition or bridge from 21:9–22:5 to 22:10–20 (19:9–10, which mentions the marriage supper of the Lamb, similarly functions as a transition to 19:11–21:8). (2) Rev 22:6–9 exhibits many striking parallels with 1:1–3, suggesting that 22:6–9 was formulated, along with 1:1–3, at the last stage in the revision of the text of Revelation. (3) The female metaphor pervades 17:1–19:10, while it occurs just once in 21:9–22:9 (and twice in earlier sections: 19:7–8 and 21:2).

While the similarities between the framing portions of 17:1–19:10 and 21:9–22:9 are evident, there are material differences between these two textual units as well. First, while the angelic guide in 17:1–19:10 functions as an *angelus interpres,* "an interpreting angel," the angelic guide in 21:9–22:6 only speaks at the *beginning* (21:9) and at the *end* (22:6) of that unit. Though the angel of 21:9–22:9 measures the holy city, unlike the angelic guide in 17:1–19:10, he provides no commentary on the vision John sees. Second, the metaphor of Babylon-Rome as a prostitute is much more central to 17:1–19:10 than is the metaphor of the New Jerusalem as the bride and wife of the Lamb in 21:9–22:9, which is used only superficially just three times, once in 21:9 and twice earlier in 19:7–8 and 21:2.

The current textual unit (21:9–22:9) narrates the vision of the New Jerusalem as follows:

1. Rev 21:9–10a functions as an introduction to the vision of the New Jerusalem and begins a new unit of text, as does its close parallel in 17:1–3 (see the synoptic comparison above). 21:9–10b also contains an invitation by one of seven bowl angels to come and see the bride, the wife of the Lamb (= the New Jerusalem), just as 17:1–3 contains an invitation by one of the bowl angels to see the great whore.

2. Rev 21:10b–22:5, which contains an external and internal description of the New Jerusalem, is the central and largest unit of text in this section. There are several parallels between this section and 4QpIsa^d = 4Q*164,* frag. 1, a commentary on Isa 54:11–12 (tr. Horgan, *Pesharim,* 126; the capitalized words are lemmata from Isa 54:11c, 12a, and 12b, respectively):

[1] [   ]k all Israel like mascara around the eye. AND I SHALL ESTABLISH YOU AS LAPIS [LAZULI.   The interpretion of the passage is]

[2] [that] the council of the community was established [among the] priests and the p[eople in the midst of]

[3] the congregation of his chosen one, like a stone of lapis lazuli in the midst of the stones [AND I SHALL MAKE (OF) RUBY (?)]

[4] ALL YOUR PINNACLES. The interpretation of it concerns the twelve [men of the council of the community, who]

[5] give light by the decision of the Urim and Thummim[   ]

[6] the ones that are absent from them, like the sun with all its light. AND A[LL YOUR GATES AS STONES OF BERYL (?)]

[7] The interpretation of it concerns the heads of the tribes of Israel at the e[nd of days   ]

[8] his lot, the offices of [   ]

Some of the more striking parallels between 4QpIsa[d] and Rev 21:9–21 are as follows (see Grappe, "Le logion," 207–8): (1) Both texts concern the heavenly Jerusalem. (2) Both texts describe the foundations of the city as represented by a precious stone. (3) In 4QpIsa[d], the twelve (priestly?) leaders of the community render judgment by using the Urim and Thummim; in Rev 21:9–21 the names of the twelve apostles are inscribed on the walls constructed of precious stones, which evoke the pectoral of the Israelite high priest (Exod 28:17–20).

a. Rev 21:10b first mentions the New Jerusalem. The main part of the vision formally begins here with the phrase καὶ ἔδειξέν μοι, "and showed me," a phrase repeated in 22:1 to introduce that aspect of the internal description of the city that centers on Paradise imagery.

b. Rev 21:11–21 provides the external description of the New Jerusalem, including measurements and materials.

i. Rev 21:11–14 is the initial external description of the New Jerusalem. The central interest in this section is the connection of the twelve tribes of Israel with the twelve gates and the twelve names of the twelve apostles of the Lamb with the twelve foundations. The description of the wall, the gates, and the foundations seems interrupted by 21:15–17 since these items are further described in 21:18–21.

ii. Rev 21:15–17 describes the measuring of the external features of the New Jerusalem. This segment interrupts the general external description of the New Jerusalem by mentioning the new fact that the angelic guide (καὶ ὁ λαλῶν μετ᾽ ἐμοῦ, "then the one who was speaking to me," a phrase used in v 9b) has a measuring rod with which to measure the city. The measuring activity is mentioned only in vv 15–17 and functions chiefly to convey to the audience the enormous size of the New Jerusalem. John seems to know what the measurements are without being told by the angel. There is a peculiarity in this section in that while the measuring of the city, the gates, and the wall is mentioned in v 15, the gates are omitted in the measuring process in vv 16–17. Further, this section seems to interrupt the description of the wall and foundations of the city, a narrative that is picked up again in 21:18–21.

iii. Rev 21:18–21 is a description of the materials out of which the wall, the city itself, the foundations of the wall, and the gates are constructed. While this unit is not introduced by any particular literary devices, it appears to pick up the threads of the description of the city begun in 21:10c–14 and interrupted by 21:15–17, the scene in which the angel with the measuring rod reveals the enormous proportions of the city.

c. Rev 21:22–22:5 centers on the description of the various internal features of the New Jerusalem.

i. Rev 21:22–23 is introduced with the phrase καὶ ... εἶδον, "then ... I saw," typically used to introduce new aspects or subjects within a vision narrative (see *Comment* on 5:1), though this is the only occurrence in Revelation in which the phrase is *negative* and refers to what John did *not* see, namely, a temple in the New Jerusalem. This section is also characterized by an antithetical structure in which conditions are first described *negatively* in terms of what is *not* to be found in the city (no temple, no need of the sun or the moon) and then in positive terms (the Lord God and the Lamb is its temple; the glory of God and the lamp of the Lamb illumine it).

ii. Rev 21:24–27 is essentially a prediction of future conditions in the New Jerusalem. In this brief section, the few visionary features that generally characterize 21:9–22:5, e.g., εἶδον, "I saw" (21:22), or ἔδειξέν μοι, "he showed me" (21:10; 22:1), are absent. In their place is a prophecy about those who will and those who will not have access to the New Jerusalem, described with a series of future tenses with two aorist subjunctives: v 24, περιπατήσουσιν, "they will walk"; φέρουσιν, probably a futuristic present, "they will bring"; v 25, κλεισθῶσιν, an aorist subjunctive, "they will [not] close"; ἔσται, "it shall be"; v 26, οἴσουσιν, "they will bring"; εἰσέλθῃ, an aorist subjunctive, "it shall [not] enter in."

iii. The section Rev 22:1–5 is introduced with the phrase καὶ ἔδειξέν μοι, "he showed me," indicating the beginning of a new subsection, repeated from 21:9, 10. In this section the New Jerusalem is described with imagery associated with the garden of Eden or Paradise.

3. The transitional section Rev 22:6–9 serves both as a conclusion to 21:1–22:5 (and is parallel to the concluding section of the parallel text in 17:1–19:9, i.e., 19:9–10) and as an introduction to 22:10–20. One striking feature is the number of verbatim verbal parallels that are evident when 26:6–21 is compared with 1:1–3:

Rev 1:1–3	*Rev 22:6–21*
[1:1]δεῖξαι τοῖς δούλοις αὐτοῦ to show his servants	[22:6]δεῖξαι τοῖς δούλοις αὐτοῦ to show his servants
ἃ δεῖ γενέσθαι ἐν τάχει . . . . what must soon happen	ἃ δεῖ γενέσθαι ἐν τάχει . . . . what must soon happen . . . .
[1:3]μακάριος . . . Blessed . . . [are]	[22:7]μακάριος Blessed [is]
οἱ ἀκούοντες those who hear	ὁ τηρῶν the one who obeys
τοὺς λόγους τῆς προφητείας the prophetic words	τοὺς λόγους τῆς προφητείας the prophetic words
καὶ τηροῦντες τὰ and obey the things	
ἐν αὐτῇ γεγραμμένα written herein,	τοῦ βιβλίου τούτου . . . . of this book . . . .
	[22:9]τοὺς λόγους the words

τοῦ βιβλίου τούτου . . . .
of this book . . . .

²²˸¹⁰τοὺς λόγους τῆς
the words of this

προφητείας τοῦ βιβλίου τούτου . . . .
prophetic book . . . .

²²˸¹⁸τοὺς λόγους
the words

τῆς προφητείας τοῦ βιβλίου τούτου . . . .
of this prophetic book . . . .

ὁ γὰρ καιρὸς ἐγγύς.   ²²˸¹⁰ὁ καιρὸς γὰρ ἐγγύς ἐστιν.
for the time [is] near.   For the time is near.

III. Source-Critical Analysis

Several scholars have suggested that 21:3–4 was originally linked with 22:3–5 and that 21:5–22:2 was inserted into this text. The arguments for the original unity of 21:3–4 and 22:3–5 are these: (1) These units form a poetic composition with four strophes, each consisting of four lines. (2) All the verbs in this unit (except ἔχουσιν, "they have," in 22:5b) are in the future tense. (3) This poetic text has the formulaic expression οὐκ ἔσται ἔτι, "there will no longer be" (21:4b, 4c; 22:3a, 5a), which occurs nowhere else in Revelation. The complete text unit looks like this:

21:3b	Behold the dwelling of God is with people,
3c	and he will dwell with them,
3d	and they will be his people,
3e	and God himself will be with them, as their God.
21:4a	And he will wipe away every tear from their eyes,
4b	and death will no longer exist,
4c	nor will grief or crying or pain exist any longer,
22:3a	and "the curse of war" will no longer exist.
22:3b	The throne of God and of the Lamb are in the city,
3c	and his servants will worship him.
4a	And they will see his face,
4b	and his name will be on their foreheads.
22:5a	There will no longer be any night,
5b	and people will have no need for lamp light or sunlight,
5c	because the Lord God will illumine them,
5d	and they will reign for ever and ever.

Rev 21:1–22:5 has been widely regarded as an essentially Jewish source with a relatively light Christian revision (Vischer, *Offenbarung;* Pfleiderer, *Urchristentum;*

Weyland, *Omwerkings;* Sabatier, *Les origines littéraires;* Schoen, *L'origine;* Wellhausen, *Analyse;* J. Weiss, *Offenbarung;* Charles). The presence of several doublets has suggested to many earlier critics the use of sources:

Rev 21:18b	*Rev 21:21b*
And the city itself was pure gold, like clear glass.	and the main square of the city was pure gold, like transparent glass.
Rev 21:23	*Rev 22:5b*
And the city has no need of the sun or of the moon to illumine it, for the glory of God illumines it, and its lamp is the Lamb.	people will have no need for lamp light or sunlight, because the Lord God will illumine them.
Rev 21:25	*Rev 22:5a*
and there will be no night there.	There will no longer be any night.
Rev 21:27	*Rev 22:3*
But nothing unclean will enter it.	And "the curse of war" will no longer exist.

Rev 21:15–17, as it stands, appears to be an intrusion into the description of the New Jerusalem. Here the process of measuring has a function completely different from that which the divine voice commanded the author-editor himself in 11:1. Since 21:16–17 contains the only specific dimensions of the New Jerusalem, v 15 functions as a literary device, revealing how the author knows the dimensions he reports. Further, if vv 15–17 are removed from the text, v 18 appears to follow naturally after v 14. This suggests either that vv 15–17 are an interpolation or that they are parenthetical. In this case it is likely that they are an interpolation, i.e., an expansion of the description of the New Jerusalem reported in 21:9–22:5.

Comment

9a καὶ ἦλθεν εἷς ἐκ τῶν ἑπτὰ ἀγγέλων τῶν ἐχόντων τὰς ἑπτὰ φιάλας τῶν γεμόντων τῶν ἑπτὰ πληγῶν τῶν ἐσχάτων, "Then came one of the seven angels with the seven libation bowls full of the seven last plagues." The phrase καὶ ἦλθεν εἷς ἐκ τῶν ἑπτὰ ἀγγέλων τῶν ἐχόντων τὰς ἑπτὰ φιάλας, "then one of the seven angels with the seven libation bowls," is found verbatim in 17:1a (a second phrase, in v 9b, is found verbatim in 17:1b). This angel could be identical with the one mentioned in 17:1, but since the author does not make such a connection explicit, the assumption must be that he is referring, for whatever reason, to a *different* angel. As in Rev 17:1, the function of these two attributive participial phrases (τῶν ἐχόντων τὰς ἑπτὰ φιάλας, "having the seven libation bowls," and τῶν γεμόντων τῶν ἑπτὰ πληγῶν τῶν ἐσχάτων, "full of the seven last plagues") is simply to link visionary episodes formally within the composition.

9b καὶ ἐλάλησεν μετ' ἐμοῦ λέγων, δεῦρο, δείξω σοι τὴν νύμφην τὴν γυναῖκα τοῦ ἀρνίου, "and spoke to me, saying, 'Come, I will show you the bride, the wife of the Lamb.'" This angelic figure, unlike the *angelus interpres* in 17:1–18, has very little to explain to the author-editor, none of which can in any way be considered interpretive. In fact, the only statement attributed to this angel (unless he is also the speaker in 22:6, 10–11) is this invitation issued to the seer in v 9b. The angel's principal task is to "show" the author-editor certain things, and this is emphasized by the phrase καὶ ἔδειξέν μοι, "then he showed me," which occurs twice (21:10a; 22:1a).

The various Qumran fragments of the *Description of the New Jerusalem* have many parallels to Rev 21:15–21, not least of which is the repeated phrase "he showed me" (2Q*24* = 2QNJ ar frag. 1, line 3; 4Q*554* = 4QNJ[a] ar 1 ii 15; 3:20; 4Q*555* = 4QNJ[b] ar frag. 1, line 3; 5Q*15* = 5QNJ ar 1 i 2,15; 2:6; 11Q*18* = 11QNJ ar frag. 16, line 6; frag. 18, line 1). The phrase καὶ ἐλάλησεν μετ' ἐμοῦ λέγων, δεῦρο, δείξω σοι, literally "and he spoke with me, saying, 'Come, I will show you'" (which also occurs verbatim in 17:1; cf. *Comment* on 9a), is also closely parallel to the phrase καὶ ὁ λαλῶν μετ' ἐμοῦ, "and the one who was speaking to me," in v 15, though v 15 does not reveal what the angel might have said.

This invitation is followed by the transportation of John "to a high mountain" (v 10). Cf. *Apoc. Zeph.* 3:1–3, "The angel of the Lord said to me, 'Come, let me show you the [place (?)] of righteousness.' And he took me [up] upon Mount Seir and he [showed me] three men, as two angels walked with them rejoicing and exulting over them." According to Slavonic *3 Apoc. Bar.* 10:1, the angel transported Baruch to a mountain, which then became the setting for visionary revelations.

On Israel as the bride of God, see Isa 54:5 and Hos 2:19–20. The phrase "the wife of the Lamb" is probably a later expansion of the text (Bousset [1906] 446; Charles, 2:156; Loisy, 372), and it may be that the term γυναῖκα, "wife," was introduced expressly to underline the parallels between the γυνή, "woman, wife" = Rome in Rev 17:3, 4, 6, 7, 9, 18 and the γυνή = the holy city in Rev 19:7; 21:9; see Wilcox, "Tradition," 206. The Lamb is mentioned *seven* times in Rev 21:1–22:5 (21:9, 14, 22, 23, 27; 2:1, 3), which may be part of the author's conscious design to exploit the number seven (see *Excursus 5A: Christ as the Lamb*).

10a καὶ ἀπήνεγκέν με ἐν πνεύματι ἐπὶ ὄρος μέγα καὶ ὑψηλόν, "He then transported me in a prophetic trance to a great and high mountain." This is an allusion to Ezek 40:2, where Ezekiel is brought "in the visions of God" (here interpreted as "in ecstasy" or "in the spirit") to a very high mountain, where the prophet saw something "like the structure of a city" (MT כמבנה־עיר *kĕmibnēh-ʿîr*; LXX ὡσεὶ οἰκοδομὴ πόλεως); this structure is then described as the eschatological temple. In both Ezek 40:2 and the Zion tradition reflected in Ps 48:1–3, the city is presented as already situated on the top of the mountain. In Rev 21:10, on the other hand, John sees the holy city Jerusalem in the process of descending from God (καταβαίνουσαν, "descending," is a present participle) and from heaven from the vantage point of a high mountain.

The proximity of high mountains to the celestial world makes them appropriate settings for revelations and visionary experiences; see Deut 34:1–4 (Moses climbed Mount Nebo, where God showed him the land of Canaan); *1 Enoch* 17:2 (Enoch is taken to a mountain whose summit reaches heaven); *T. Levi* 2:5 (Levi sees a high mountain just before the heavens are opened and, analogous to Rev 4:1, he is invited to enter in); 4Q*213–14* = 4QTLevi ᵃᵇ 2 ii 19–20 (tr. Eisenman-Wise, *Scrolls*, 140): "I saw Hea[ven opened and I saw the mountain] beneath me, as high as to reach to Heav[en, and I was on it]"); *2 Apoc. Bar.* 13:1; Mark 9:1 = Matt 17:1 = Luke 9:28 (Jesus on the mount of transfiguration); Mark 13:3 = Matt 24:3 (Jesus delivers an apocalyptic discourse on the Mount of Olives overlooking the temple). In Matt 4:8 (see the parallel in Luke 4:5 where the reference to a high mountain is eliminated), the devil transports Jesus to an exceedingly tall mountain where he then shows Jesus all the kingdoms of the world and their glory, the devil functioning as a kind of *diabolus interpres*, a counterpart of the more typical *angelus interpres* of apocalypses. While it is possible that *Mart. Perpetua* 11:2–3 contains an allusion to Rev 21:10 (Petraglio, "Des influences," 18–19), it is probable that the two motifs of transport by angels and ascending a hill are derived from common apocalyptic tradition (tr. Musurillo, *Acts*): ". . . we began to be carried [*coepimus ferri*] towards the east by four angels . . . as though we were climbing up a gentle hill [*mollem cliuum ascendentes*]." According to the Cologne Mani Codex 53.13–16 (R. Cameron and A. J. Dewey, eds., *The Cologne Mani Codex* [Missoula, MT: Scholars, 1979]), "The Spirit snatched me [Mani] up and carried me off to the mountain in silent power. There many great [visions] were revealed to me."

Revelatory encounters are frequently set on mountains in Greco-Roman literature because, as in Judaism, mountains were thought to be the dwelling places of the gods. The literary convention of "the poet's dream" (Skutsch, *Ennius*, 148; see *Comment* on 1:11) begins with Hesiod's *Theogony* 22–34 (the Muses appear in a *vision*, not a dream, as many interpreters have assumed, to Hesiod on Mount Helicon and inspire him to write) and thereafter becomes a frequent literary convention: (1) Aeschylus apparently claimed that Dionysius had commanded him to write poetry (Pausanias 1.21.2). (2) According to *Anth. Pal.* 7.42, a dream caught up Callimachus and carried him from Libya to Mount Helicon, where the content of his work *Aitia* was revealed to him. (3) In Ennius *Annales* 1, frags. 2–10, first Homer, then the Muses, appeared to Ennius in a dream on an unnamed mountain (Skutsch, *Ennius*, 150, 375), which in later speculation became Mount Helicon or Mount Parnassus. Ennius then became "Homer incarnate," i.e., what might be referred to as "literary affiliation through metempsychosis," probably a Pythagorean notion. Ennius may be following Stesichorus, who claimed to possess the soul of Homer (in Antipater of Sidon *Anth. Pal.* 7.75), with the scene in general modeled after Hesiod *Theog.* 22–34 and Callimachus *Aitia* 1.1.21–22. For references to Ennius's dream in later Latin literature, see Skutsch, *Ennius*, 150–53. (4) In Vergil *Eclogues* 6.64–73, Gallus was led to Mount Helicon by the Muses and received the gift of song. (5) In Propertius 3.3.1–52 (an imitation of Ennius), Propertius first met Apollo, rather than Homer, and then the Muses on Mount Helicon. For other references, see West, *Theogony*, 159. (6) In *Corp. Herm.* 13.1, Tat came down from the mountain where he had received a revelation from Hermes Trismegistus.

10b καὶ ἔδειξέν μοι τὴν πόλιν τὴν ἁγίαν Ἰερουσαλὴμ καταβαίνουσαν ἐκ τοῦ οὐρανοῦ ἀπὸ τοῦ θεοῦ, "and showed me the holy city Jerusalem descending from heaven from God." The phrase τὴν πόλιν τὴν ἁγίαν Ἰερουσαλὴμ [καινὴν εἶδον] καταβαίνουσαν ἐκ τοῦ οὐρανοῦ ἀπὸ τοῦ θεοῦ, "[I saw] the holy city, [the new] Jerusalem, descending from heaven from God," with the addition of καινὴν εἶδον,

"I saw [the] new" (indicated in brackets), is found verbatim in 21:2 (on the phrase "Jerusalem the holy city," see *Comment* on 21:2; on "the holy city," see *Comment* on 11:2). The notion of a heavenly Jerusalem is found throughout early Judaism and rabbinic Judaism. A close parallel, which includes the descent of the heavenly city to Zion, is found in 4 Ezra 13:35–36:

> But he will stand on the top of Mount Zion. And Zion will come and be made manifest to all people, prepared and built, as you saw the mountain carved out without hands.

Similarly in *2 Apoc. Bar.* 4:2–7 Jerusalem is a preexistent reality, which God showed to Adam, Abraham, and Moses and which "will be revealed." Elsewhere in the NT the conception is found in Gal 4:26; Heb 11:10, 14–16; 12:22; 13:14; cf. Phil 3:20. In Gal 4:25–26 Paul somewhat awkwardly contrasts ἡ νῦν Ἰερουσαλήμ, "the present Jerusalem," with ἡ ἄνω Ἰερουσαλήμ, "Jerusalem above." The first phrase, using the adjective of time νῦν, "now," presupposes the *eschatological* dualistic framework of present/future, while the second phrase, using the adjective of place ἄνω, "above," presupposes a *spatial* dualistic framework of above/below. Paul nowhere speaks of the descent of this heavenly Jerusalem; presumably those who will live in it must ascend to it (Betz, *Galatians,* 246); see *Par. Jer.* 5:35, "May God guide you to Jerusalem the city which is above [τὴν ἄνω πόλιν Ἰερουσαλήμ]." Similarly, the author of Hebrews speaks of a heavenly Jerusalem but nowhere suggests that it will descend to earth (Heb 11:10, 14–16; 12:22; 13:14).

The conception of an "ideal city" is also found in Platonism, Stoicism, and Christianity in late antiquity (for the latter, see Mazzolani, *Idea,* 242–79). An important source of this conception in later philosophical literature is Plato *Republic* 9.13 (592A–B; LCL tr.):

> "I understand," he said; "you mean the city whose establishment we have described, the city whose home is in the ideal; for I think that it can be found nowhere on earth." "Well," said I, "perhaps there is a pattern of it laid up in heaven [ἐν οὐρανῷ ἴσως παράδειγμα ἀνάκειται] for him who wishes to contemplate it and so beholding to constitute himself its citizen."

Platonic influence is evident in Hermas *Sim.* 1.1–6, where the metaphor of two cities with their respective systems of law is used to illustrate the obligations Christians have to their own "city" (heaven) and the often conflicting demands of their earthly "city" (see *Ap. Jas.* 11.20 and Anaxagoras in Diogenes Laertius 2.7). Among Stoics the ideal city is referred to by Marcus Aurelius (9.29), and Philo too reflects this conception (*Som.* 2.250–51). Clement of Alexandria quotes the Stoic view in a passage that concludes with an explicit reference to Plato's city, though only the first part is quoted here (*Strom.* 4.26; see Arnim, *SVF* 3:80–81): "For the Stoics say that heaven is properly a city [τὸν μὲν οὐρανὸν κυρίως πόλιν], but places here on earth are not cities; for they are called so, but are not."

On the phrase "Jerusalem descending from heaven from God" as an editorial link between the earlier and later editions of Revelation, see *Comment* on 3:12. On "heaven" as a circumlocution for "God" (rendering "from God" superfluous), see *Comment* on 3:12.

11 ἔχουσαν τὴν δόξαν τοῦ θεοῦ, ὁ φωστὴρ αὐτῆς ὅμοιος λίθῳ τιμιωτάτῳ ὡς λίθῳ ἰάσπιδι κρυσταλλίζοντι, "with the glory of God. Its radiance was like a precious stone, like jasper transparent as crystal." In v 18b the city is alternatively described as "pure gold, like clear glass." The phrase "the glory of God" occurs three times in Revelation (15:8; 21:11, 23; see *Comment* on 15:8). Since the New Jerusalem exhibits the "glory of God," jasper is an appropriate choice to symbolize the overall appearance of the city, for in Rev 4:3 God is compared to jasper (along with carnelian) in a passage that resists anthropomorphism. Since jasper is normally an opaque stone, the description of it being like crystal underlines its purity and value.

12a ἔχουσα τεῖχος μέγα καὶ ὑψηλόν, ἔχουσα πυλῶνας δώδεκα, "The city had a wide and high wall with twelve gates." In ancient Near Eastern descriptions of cities, the walls that surround, protect, and define those cities are usually mentioned first (see the invitation to look at the walls of Uruk at the beginning and end of the Gilgamesh epic in 1.1.11–19 and 11.303–7; see J. Z. Smith, *To Take Place*, 49). During the Roman empire, city gates were the most popular expression of imperial triumphal architecture in Greece as well as in Asia Minor (C. C. Vermeule, *Roman Imperial Art*, 16). The wall surrounding the city has twelve gates, each one named after one of the twelve tribes of the sons of Israel, though specific names are not mentioned (see 7:5–8), undoubtedly because the author is primarily interested in the symbolic significance of the number twelve as a whole. Certainly there is no thought that each gate is reserved for use only by members of the tribe after which it is named. The unusually large number of gates emphasizes the importance of entering and leaving the city. The mention of the twelve tribes implies that the New Jerusalem is not simply a city but rather the focal point of the entire land. This arrangement corresponds to Ezekiel's vision of the square outer walls of the New Jerusalem with three gates on each side, supposedly named after the *tribes* of Israel (Ezek 48:31), though they are in fact named after the *sons* of Jacob (thus Joseph and Levi are mentioned rather than Ephraim and Manasseh); see *Comments* on Rev 7:4–8.

12b καὶ ἐπὶ τοῖς πυλῶσιν ἀγγέλους δώδεκα, "Twelve angels were at the gates." Why should it be necessary to have angels posted at each gate to guard access to the holy city? In tension with 19:17–21 and 21:1–4 (where the enemies of God have been destroyed and a new heaven and earth have been created), there are still *nations* in existence (21:24, 26; 2:2), as well as *kings* (21:24) and *wicked people* (21:27) outside the holy city. Because the gates are always open (21:25), guards are presumably necessary to keep those opposed to God on the outside. This passage is often thought to allude to Isa 62:6, which mentions watchmen (שׁמרים *šōmrîm*) posted on the walls of Jerusalem (though this allusion is doubted by Fekkes, *Isaiah*, 264–65). These watchmen were understood to be the angels Michael and Gabriel in rabbinic Judaism (*Exod. Rab.* 18.5; *Pesiq. Rab Kah.* 6.2; cf. Schlatter, *Apokalypse*, 102), and if that exegetical tradition was sufficiently ancient (for which there is no corroborative evidence) it might have influenced John. Perhaps the model here is the temple of Solomon, which had a huge contingent of gatekeepers: four thousand are mentioned in 1 Chr 23:5, while ninety-three are mentioned in 1 Chr 26:1–9. Later rabbinic tradition was much more modest in counting twenty-four guards, three priests in charge of guarding the sanctuary and twenty-one Levites to guard the rest of the temple complex (*m. Mid.* 1:1).

According to Gen 3:24 and Ezek 28:14, 16 (see *Adam and Eve* 29:1–2; *Apoc. Moses* 28:3; *2 Enoch* 8:8; *T. Levi* 18:10), cherubim or angels were thought to act as the guardians of Eden, the garden of God, and since the New Jerusalem is the eschatological counterpart of Eden (see 2:7; 22:1–5), angelic guards at its gates seem appropriate. Cherubim were prominent in the decoration of the Solomonic temple (1 Kgs 6:29–35; 2 Chr 3:7; cf. Ezek 41:17–25), and their presence on the *doors* of the temple (1 Kgs 6:32) may reflect their role as the mythical guardians of the garden of God. Angels are occasionally depicted as armed (Josh 5:13; Num 22:23; 1 Chr 21:16, 30; *3 Enoch* 22:6) and therefore as capable of protecting the temple of God (4 Macc 4:10) or the people of God (3 Macc 6:18–19; *Adam and Eve* 33:1). Similarly, in some apocalyptic visions and Merkavah traditions, angels serve to protect the heavenly court from human intrusion (*Asc. Isa.* 9:1–4; *Ma'aseh Merkavah* § 565 [ed. Swartz, *Prayer*, 237–38]; *3 Enoch* 6:2–3), though the visionaries themselves are protected from these angelic bouncers by uttering passwords that consist of secret names and prayers (*Ma'aseh Merkavah* § 568; ed. Swartz, *Prayer*, 239); see Schäfer, *Rivalität*, 219–24, Maier, *Kairos* 5 [1963] 18–40). A group of twelve angelic beings who control the movements of the stars is described in *1 Enoch* 82:10–20.

12c καὶ ὀνόματα ἐπιγεγραμμένα, ἅ ἐστιν τὰ ὀνόματα τῶν δώδεκα φυλῶν υἱῶν Ἰσραήλ, "and names were inscribed on the gates, the names of the twelve tribes of the sons of Israel." The unusual phrase "the tribes of the sons of Israel" was used earlier in 7:4, suggesting that the two phrases belong to the same editorial level of Revelation. While there is a widespread eschatological tradition in early Judaism that the gates of the eschatological Jerusalem would be named after the twelve sons of Israel, nowhere apart from Revelation are the names actually said to be *inscribed* on the gates. Here υἱῶν, "sons," is a genitive of apposition, lacking an article because it reflects the Hebrew construct state, which never has an article; but see Rev 2:14 (Mussies, *Morphology*, 191).

The association of the names of the twelve tribes of Israel with the gates of the New Jerusalem implies the realization of one of the central concerns of Jewish eschatology, namely, *the restoration of the twelve tribes of Israel*, which is repeatedly mentioned in post-exilic OT and early Jewish literature (Isa 49:5–6; 56:1–8; 60:3–7; 66:18–24; Jer 31:10; Ezek 34, 37; Zeph 3:20; Zech 8:7–8; Tob 13:5, 13; 14:6–7; 2 Macc 1:27–29; 2:7, 18; *Jub.* 1:15–17; *T. Benj.* 9:2; Philo *Praem.* 94–97, 162–72; Bar 4:37; Sir 36:11; 48:10; *Pss. Sol.* 11; 17:28–31, 50; 11QTemple 18:14–16; see Sanders, *Jesus*, 95–98). In the *War Scroll* from Qumran (1QM), which depicts the eschatological wars between the children of light and the children of darkness, all twelve tribes are represented in temple service (1QM 2:2–3), and all twelve will supply troops for the battle (1QM 2:7–8).

In Ezek 48:30–35, the walls of the eschatological Jerusalem are described as forming a gigantic square 4,500 cubits on each side, with three gates on each side named (clockwise) after the tribes of Israel: north, Reuben, Judah, Levi; east, Joseph, Benjamin, Dan; south, Simeon, Issachar, Zebulon; and west, Gad, Asher, Naphtali. 11QTemple from Qumran certainly reflects a familiarity with the biblical accounts of Solomon's temple and Ezekiel's eschatological temple. Nevertheless, the author-editor of 11QTemple chose to conflate the twelve gates of Ezekiel's city wall with the outer and middle walls surrounding the future temple, each of which had twelve gates named (clockwise) after the twelve sons of Jacob, not the tribes of Israel (11QTemple 39:12–13; 40:11–14): east, Simeon, Levi, Judah; south, Reuben, Joseph, Benjamin; west, Issachar, Zebulon, Gad; and north, Dan, Naphtali, Asher. The same order, though without the mention of directions, is found in the fragmentary text 4Q364–65 = 4QRP[b c] 28 ii 1–4 (García Martínez, *Dead Sea Scrolls*, 223). Rev 21:13 does not specifically name the gates on each side, nor does it describe the gates in a clockwise or counterclockwise manner; rather it mentions three gates on the east, north, south, and west. This suggests that John is not using a source or tradition that actually named the gates, nor can it be assumed (as some do) that the names would conform to his mixed list of tribes of Israel and sons of Jacob in 7:4–8.

In Ezek 48:30–35, the reason for naming each gate after one of the tribes of Israel might be to give them access to the city, though the gates do not fully correspond to the tribal allotments in Ezek 48:1–7, 23–29 (Levi and Joseph are gates with no allotments; Manasseh and Ephraim have allotments but no gates). Num 2:1–31 prescribes the locations for the camps of the twelve tribes around the tabernacle, three on each side named clockwise: east, Judah, Issachar, Zebulun; south, Reuben, Simeon, Gad; west, Ephraim, Manasseh, Benjamin; and north, Dan, Asher, Naphtali. The Aramaic composition called the *Description of the New Jerusalem* (4Q554 = 4QNJ^a ar = J1 [Beyer, *Ergänzungsband*, 95–97]) appears to be inspired by Ezek 40–48, though the sequence of the names of the gates in Ezek 48:30–35 is very different from 4Q554. The city has twelve gates, each named after one of the sons of Jacob, named in the following order (the names of seven gates survive in the text): south, Simeon, [Levi], Judah; west, Joseph, [Benjamin], Reuben; north, [Issachar, Zebulon, Gad]; and east, Dan, Naphtali, Asher (4Q554 = 4QNJ^a ar 2:12–3:9). This order conforms generally to that of 11QTemple 39:12–13; 40:11–14 (see above).

13 ἀπὸ ἀνατολῆς πυλῶνες τρεῖς καὶ ἀπὸ βορρᾶ πυλῶνες τρεῖς καὶ ἀπὸ νότου πυλῶνες τρεῖς καὶ ἀπὸ δυσμῶν πυλῶνες τρεῖς, "There were three gates on the east and three gates on the north and three gates on the south and three gates on the west." The twelve gates of the New Jerusalem have often been understood to reflect the tradition of the twelve gates of heaven or the twelve signs of the zodiac (Boll, *Offenbarung*, 39; Charles, 2:158; Lohmeyer, 171; Beasley-Murray, 310, 320–21), though the tradition of twelve tribes or sons of Israel is certainly the primary reason that the number twelve was deemed appropriate by the author-editor. *1 Enoch* 75:4 mentions twelve gates of the sun from which the rays of the sun come out, and a different set of twelve gates is mentioned in *1 Enoch* 75:6 (tr. Knibb, *Enoch*):

> I saw twelve gates in heaven, at the ends of the earth, from which the sun, and the moon, and the stars, and all the works of heaven go out in the east and in the west.

These are coordinated with the six gates in the east from which the sun rises and the six gates in the west through which the sun sets (*1 Enoch* 72.2–32 [for suggestions of Babylonian origin, see O. Neugebauer in M. Black, *Enoch*, 393–96]; cf. *1 Enoch* 82:4–6).

14 καὶ τὸ τεῖχος τῆς πόλεως ἔχων θεμελίους δώδεκα, καὶ ἐπ' αὐτῶν δώδεκα ὀνόματα τῶν δώδεκα ἀποστόλων τοῦ ἀρνίου, "The wall of the city has twelve foundation stones, and upon them are the names of the twelve apostles of the Lamb." In the narrative of the construction of the Solomonic temple, it is reported that huge, costly stones were used for its foundation (1 Kgs 5:17; 7:10). According to Rev 21:12, the names of the twelve tribes of Israel were inscribed on the twelve gates, and now the names of the twelve apostles are said to be engraved on the twelve foundation stones. This verse is probably a gloss in the sense that it is an addition or expansion of an earlier version of the text (Satake, *Gemeindeordnung*, 133; Bergmeier, *ZNW* 75 [1984] 92).

This verse reflects the idea found in Eph 2:20 that the Church is built ἐπὶ τῷ θεμελίῳ τῶν ἀποστόλων καὶ προφητῶν, "on the foundation of the apostles and prophets" (cf. Matt 16:18; see Lohse, 109–10). The phrase in Eph 2:20 may be understood to mean "the foundation that consists of apostles and prophets" (taking the genitive as a genitive of apposition), i.e., a single foundation that consists either of the apostles and prophets as *persons* or in terms of their *activity* (the latter view is defended by Sandnes, *Paul*, 227–29). Here the emphasis is apparently on their *persons*, for analogous texts emphasize persons as founders, not their activities. Paul, for example, speaks of Jesus Christ as the basic θεμέλιος, "foundation" (1 Cor 3:11). However, it is awkward to resort to the notion of twelve *separate* foundations, a feature nowhere even remotely paralleled in early Jewish descriptions of the eschatological Jerusalem. Hippolytus maintained that the twelve disciples were chosen from the twelve tribes of Israel (*Ref.* 5.8.12; ed. Marcovitch, *Hippolytus*), a tradition that may have arisen to explain why the twelve disciples will sit on thrones and judge the twelve tribes of Israel according to Matt 19:28 and Luke 22:30 (see Ps 122:3–5 and *Gos. Eb.* frag. 3). According to Epiphanius *Pan.* 30.13.3, the twelve apostles were chosen to be a testimony to Israel. There is a similar focus on the foundations of the walls of Uruk in the Gilgamesh epic, in which they are attributed to the activity of seven wise men (Heidel, *Gilgamesh*, 16–17):

> Climb up upon the wall of Uruk [and] walk about;
> Inspect the foundation terrace and examine the brickwork,
> If its brickwork be not of burnt bricks,
> [And] if the seven [wise men] did not lay its foundations.

The seven gates of Thebes are given an astrological association by comparing their number to that of the seven planets (Nonnos *Dionysiaca* 5.70–71).

The phrase "the names of the twelve apostles of the Lamb" is striking for several reasons and is often used as part of an argument for dating Revelation late in the first century. First of all, the term "Lamb" is used in a unique way here, for it is a *historical* reference to an aspect of the ministry of Jesus of Nazareth, comparable only to the relatively frequent references to the death of the Lamb (Rev 5:6, 9, 12; 7:14; 12:11; 13:8) and *perhaps* to the possible reference to the life, resurrection, and exaltation of Jesus in 1:5 (see *Comment* there). The apparent parallel to the 144,000 who follow (οἱ ἀκολουθοῦντες) the Lamb (14:4) is in fact a post-Easter extension of the discipleship motif (see *Comment* on 14:4).

The phrase τῶν δώδεκα ἀποστόλων, "the twelve apostles," occurs *only* in Matt 10:2 in the NT in a closely parallel phrase (τῶν δὲ δώδεκα ἀποστόλων τὰ ὀνόματα, "the names of the twelve apostles"). Elsewhere οἱ δώδεκα ἀπόστολοι, "the twelve apostles," occurs only as *variae lectiones* in Luke 9:1 (οἱ δώδεκα [ἀπόστολοι]) and 22:14 (οἱ [δώδεκα] ἀπόστολοι), though the parallel phrase οἱ δώδεκα μαθηταί, "the twelve disciples," does occur in Matt 10:1 and 11:1 (and as *variae lectiones* in Matt 20:17; 26:20). The phrase οἱ δώδεκα ἀπόστολοι also occurs in both the short and long titles of the *Didache* (short title: Διδαχὴ τῶν δώδεκα ἀποστόλων, "Teaching of the Twelve Apostles"; long title: Διδαχὴ κυρίου διὰ τῶν δώδεκα ἀποστόλων τοῖς ἔθνεσιν, "Teaching of the Lord through the Twelve Apostles to the Nations"), though these were probably added relatively late and may originally have been even shorter, e.g., Διδαχὴ τῶν ἀποστόλων, "Teaching of the Apostles" (Niederwimmer, *Didache*, 81).

The phrase οἱ δώδεκα ἀπόστολοι in Matt 10:2 and Rev 21:14, in which δώδεκα is used as an adjective, is not a pleonasm (Rengstorf, *TDNT* 1:425). While the phrase οἱ δώδεκα, "the twelve," was a technical term that originated before Easter (cf. 1 Cor 15:5) and is used in the synoptic Gospels (T. Holtz, *EDNT* 1:363), οἱ ἀπόστολοι, "the apostles," was not, a fact that is underlined through the adjectival use of δώδεκα, "twelve," in the phrase οἱ δώδεκα ἀπόστολοι, i.e., the *twelve* apostles, not other apostles (here δώδεκα points to the existing technical phrase οἱ δώδεκα). In Matt 10:2, on the other hand, δώδεκα may refer to the list of twelve apostles that follows in Matt 10:2–4, just as δώδεκα in Rev 21:14 may have been included not only to define the term οἱ ἀπόστολοι more closely but also under influence of the phrase τῶν δώδεκα φυλῶν υἱῶν Ἰσραήλ, "the twelve tribes of the sons of Israel," just preceding in 21:12. The phrase οἱ δώδεκα became increasingly infrequent (in the Apostolic Fathers, it occurs only in *1 Clem.* 43:2). The equation of "the twelve" with "the apostles" is clearly a part of the Lukan redaction, though there is evidence to suggest that this equation did not originate with Luke (Mark 6:7, 30; Matt 10:2; Rev 21:14; see Holtz, *EDNT* 1:363).

The evidence in the Pauline letters suggests that ἀπόστολος, "apostle," was used with various connotations in Paul's day (Georgi, *Gegner,* 39–49; Schnackenburg, "Apostles," 296, 301), though Paul clearly understood himself to be an apostle and part of a cohesive group of apostles (1 Thess 2:7; 1 Cor 4:9; 9:5; 15:7, 9; Gal 1:17; Ysebaert, *Amtsterminologie,* 11; Schnackenburg, "Apostles," 291). There is, therefore, tension between Luke's conception of οἱ ἀπόστολοι and Paul's conception. οἱ ἀπόστολοι occurs in later epistolary literature, but it is not always possible to determine whether it means "the [twelve] apostles" or "the apostles [including Paul]" (Eph 2:20; 3:5; 4:11; 2 Pet 3:2; Jude 17), though in the case of Eph 2:20 and 3:5, Paul is almost certainly included (Sandnes, *Paul,* 232). However, the term οἱ ἀπόστολοι in *1 Clement* (5:3; 42:1–2; 44:1; 47:4) must include Paul since the author calls him an ἀπόστολος in *1 Clem.* 47:1. Similarly, Polycarp *Phil.* 6:3 has the phrase "apostles and prophets," and since he specifically refers to "Paul and the other apostles" (9:1), he must understand οἱ ἀπόστολοι to include Paul. Ignatius, too, includes Paul among οἱ ἀπόστολοι, for he frequently refers to "the apostles" (*Eph.* 11:2; *Magn.* 6:1; 7:1; 13:1, 2; *Trall.* 3:3; 7:1; 12:2; *Pol.* 5:1) and specifically designates Paul as well as Peter as apostles (*Rom.* 4:3).

The term ἀπόστολος occurs just three times in Revelation in three very different ways (2:2; 18:20; 21:14); see *Comment* on each passage.

15 καὶ ὁ λαλῶν μετ᾽ ἐμοῦ εἶχεν μέτρον κάλαμον χρυσοῦν, ἵνα μετρήσῃ τὴν πόλιν καὶ τοὺς πυλῶνας αὐτῆς καὶ τὸ τεῖχος αὐτῆς, "The one who spoke to me had a golden measuring rod to measure the city and its gates and its wall." The phrase "the one who spoke to me" has a close parallel in v 9, where the angel's words are given as direct address in the form of an invitation to see the bride, the wife of the Lamb. Here the angel's words to John are not mentioned, suggesting that this phrase refers only to the initial invitation of the angel in v 9. This angelic guide is hardly an *angelus interpres,* "interpreting angel," in the same way that the angel of Rev 17:1–18 is. Since the angel here plays such a taciturn role in the vision, it appears that he is essentially a literary figure added to make 21:9–22:5 conform in a formal way to 17:1–19:10.

There is a parallel to this passage in Rev 11:1, where the seer was given a measuring rod and commanded to measure "the sanctuary and the altar and those who worship there," though no measurements are given there (nor does John actually carry out the command to measure the temple), suggesting that the procedure was metaphorical, symbolizing the protection of what was to be measured. Here, however, it is the *angel* and not the seer who does the measuring, and he does it with a measuring rod of *gold*, appropriate for measuring a city of heavenly origin. While to my knowledge no measuring instruments from ancient Israel have yet been discovered, a cubit measuring stick from Egypt, overlaid with gold, contains the name of Amen-hotep II, from the Eighteenth Dynasty, 1570–1310 B.C. (pictured in *IDB* 4:836).

The act of measuring the city is a literary device to enable the author to communicate the enormous size of the holy city to the hearers and readers. However, the measuring of the city is only mentioned in vv 15–17 and is described as involving only the measuring of three entities, the city, its gates, and its wall. No further mention is made of the size of the gates, which the author apparently forgot to include or chose to omit.

An interpreting angel with a measuring rod is mentioned in Ezek 40:3 and in recently published fragments from Qumran of an apocalypse concerning the heavenly Jerusalem (the seven fragments that have been published are referred to in Beyer, *Texte*, 214–22, and published with a German translation in Beyer, *Ergänzungsband*, 95–104; the largest fragment, 5Q*15* = 5QNJ ar, is translated in Vermes, *Dead Sea Scrolls*, 271–73; Fitzmyer-Harrington, *Aramaic Texts*, 54–61; and García Martínez, *Dead Sea Scrolls*, 131–33). In the fragment (the following summary is based on Beyer, *Texte*, 214–16), an unnamed visionary has been transported to the heavenly world and stands before the heavenly Jerusalem with an angel who has a measuring rod. The narrative is written in the first person singular of the visionary. The interpreting angel measures the rectangular wall enclosing the city at 140 *res* by 100 *res* (singular רס or ריסא; plural ר[א]סין). The Mishnah uses the term *res* for *stadion* (equivalent to the length of a stadium, which the Greeks divided into 600 feet or 400 cubits). However, in the *Description of the New Jerusalem* texts, the *res* measurement is different from the Greek measurement and is divided into 352 royal or long cubits (Chyutin, *New Jerusalem Scroll*, 75). The units of measure in the *Description of the New Jerusalem* texts are normally the reed followed by the equivalent in cubits, with seven cubits per reed. The precise metrical length of this cubit, however, is not known (García Martínez, "'New Jerusalem,'" 190–91). The exact length of the *res*, therefore, is uncertain, and scholars have had to resort to speculation to determine its length. M. Broshi uses a rounded figure of 1 cubit = 50 centimeters, close to the average of two estimates of the short and long cubits, and estimates that the city wall of 140 x 100 *res* is (rounded) 21 kilometers x 30 kilometers = 6,300 square kilometers, clearly a mathematical error for 630 square kilometers ("Visionary Architecture and Town Planning," in *Time to Prepare the Way in the Wilderness: Papers on the Qumran Scrolls by Fellows of the Institute for Advanced Studies of the Hebrew University, Jerusalem, 1989–1990,* ed. D. Dimant and L. H. Schiffman, STDJ 16 [Leiden: Brill, 1995] 12). García Martínez ("'New Jerusalem,'" 192–93) calculates that 1 *res* = 63 reeds = 441 cubits = 229 meters, so that the length and width of the rectangular wall surrounding the New Jerusalem would be 32 kilometers x 23 kilometers = 736 square kilometers. The wall has twelve strong gates, three on each side (cf. Ezek 48:33–34; 11QTemple 39:12–13; 40:11–14; 4Q*554* = 4QNJ[a] ar). The city is orthogonal (i.e., the streets intersect at right angles), a design with origins in ancient Egypt and with more immediate antecedents in Hellenistic town planning introduced by Hippodamus (see Chyutin, *DSD* 1 [1994] 71–97).

Six groups of fragments of the document called the *Description of the New Jerusalem* have been published: (1) 1Q*32* = 1QNJ ar (DJD 1:134–35, plate XXXI); (2) 2Q*24* = 2QNJ ar (M. Baillet, "Fragments araméens de Qumrân 2: Description de la Jérusalem Nouvelle," *RB* 62 [1955] 222–45; DJD 3:84–89, plate XVI); (3) 4Q*554* = 4QNJ[a] ar (J. Starcky, "Jérusalem et les manuscrits de la Mer Morte," *Le Monde de la Bible* 1 [1977] 38–40); (4) 4Q*555* = 4QNJ[b] ar (Eisenman-Robinson, *Facsimile*, 1541); (5) 5Q*15* = 5QNJ ar (DJD 3:184–93, plates XL–XLI); and (6) 11Q*18* = 11QNJ ar (B. Jongeling, "Publication provisoire d'un fragment provenant de la grotte 11 de Qumrân [11QJérNouv ar]," *JSJ* 1 [1970] 58–64). Texts and translations may be found in Beyer, *Texte*, 214–22; Beyer, *Ergänzungsband*, 95–104; Fitzmyer-Harrington, *Aramaic Texts*, 46–55; and a translation only in F. García Martínez, *Dead Sea Scrolls*, 129–35. These six groups of fragments (representing many parts of at least six copies of the *Description of the New Jerusalem* text) have been reconstructed into a single composition of twenty-two columns by M. Chyutin, *The New Jerusalem Scroll from Qumran* (see pp. 144–46 for notes on the reconstruction of the scroll).

In Syria-Palestine, cities were characteristically enclosed by irregular walls because of the uneven topography. In the plains of Egypt and Babylonia, however, cities could be enclosed with square or rectangular walls (e.g., Babylon). During the Hellenistic period, rectangular or gridiron form was common in town planning (supposedly influenced by Hippodamus of Miletus, born ca. 500 B.C.). Alexandria was the largest Hellenistic city constructed in this orthogonal form. However, even such large ancient cities as Babylon and Alexandria were surrounded by walls just 15 kilometers or 9 miles in circumference. While Nineveh is described in Jonah 3:3 as "an exceedingly great city three days' journey in breadth," excavations indicate that the city had a circumference of 7.75 miles (12.5 kilometers).

16a καὶ ἡ πόλις τετράγωνος κεῖται καὶ τὸ μῆκος αὐτῆς ὅσον καὶ τὸ πλάτος, "The city is arranged with four equal sides; that is, its length and width are the same." This alludes to Zech 2:2(LXX 2:6), where the angel with the measuring stick tells Zechariah that he is going to measure the width and length of Jerusalem. The New Jerusalem, however, is not only square but cubical (see v 16b). In both Ezek 40–48 (41:21; 43:16; 45:1; 48:20) and 11QTemple, the *square* is certainly the dominant shape (see Yadin, *Temple Scroll* 1:190). According to Ezek 42:20 (cf. *m. Mid.* 2:1), the temple mount of the eschatological temple will measure 500 cubits on each side (i.e., ca. 175–280 meters). The holy of holies or *dĕbîr* in the temple of Solomon was reportedly square, i.e., 20 cubits in length and width (1 Kgs 6:20; 2 Chr 3:8–9 [the height is omitted]), while the vestibule of the temple is given as 20 cubits wide and 120 cubits high (2 Chr 3:4). The breastplate of the high priest, which contained twelve precious stones (see below on v 19), is similarly described as square. On the other hand, the city described in the New Jerusalem texts from Qumran is an enormous rectangle 140 by 100 *res*, or 32 by 23 kilometers, with a total perimeter of 110 kilometers or nearly 70 miles (García Martínez, "'New Jerusalem,'" 194). A rabbinic tradition in *b. B. Bat.* 75b describes the future Jerusalem as a cube, three parasangs (i.e., 17 kilometers) in each direction. Many ancient cities are described as square, including Nineveh (Diodorus 1.3), Babylon (Herodotus 1.178), and Nicaea (Strabo 12.4.7). According to Roman tradition, Romulus founded *Roma quadrata* on the Palatine hill, and Greek writers translated the term *quadrata* with τετράγωνος, "square" (Dionysius Hal. *Ant. Rom.* 2.65.3; Plutarch *Romulus* 9.4; Appian *Bas.* frag. 1a.9 [ed. P. Viereck and A. G. Roos, *Appiani historia Romana*, 2 vols. (Leipzig: Teubner, 1905–39)]), though *quadrata* almost certainly referred to the four quarters into which the city was divided (Müller, *Die heilige Stadt*, 22–35). On Rome as a gigantic square of 300 x 300 parasangs (*b. Meg.* 6b), see *Comment* on v 16b.

16b καὶ ἐμέτρησεν τὴν πόλιν τῷ καλάμῳ ἐπὶ σταδίους δώδεκα χιλιάδων, τὸ μῆκος καὶ τὸ πλάτος καὶ τὸ ὕψος αὐτῆς ἴσα ἐστίν, "He measured the city with the measuring rod, at 12,000 stadia; its length and width and height are the same." The στάδιον, "stadium," varied from 190 to 210 meters and equaled 600 Greek feet (the Attic *stadion* was 607 feet, while the Olympic *stadion* was 630.8 feet). The Roman *stadium* equaled 625 Roman *pedes*, "feet," or 125 *passus*, "steps" or "paces" (Pliny *Hist. nat.* 2.85; Herodotus 2.149; *Kleine Pauly* 5:336–38). While the *stadion* was in origin a Greek measure, it was used in early Judaism and early Christianity (LXX Dan 4:12; 2 Macc 11:5; 12:9–10, 16–17, 29; Matt 14:24; Luke 24:13; John 6:19; 11:18).

The city is depicted as an enormous cube measuring ca. 1,416–1,566 miles in each direction. Since the fantastic size of Jerusalem is atypical of the author's tendency elsewhere in Revelation, Topham proposes several possible alterations (Topham, *ExpTim* 100 [1989] 417–19): (1) He proposes that 12,000 might be the total length of all four sides, thus making each side 3,000 stadia long. (2) Another alternative is the deletion of the word χιλιάδων, "thousand," with a figure remaining of 12 stadia. (3) The emendation he finds most attractive is the emendation of "stadia" to "cubits," with the result that the city would measure a more modest 3.5 miles each direction. These are all highly speculative emendations, however, and there is no convincing reason to reject the author's intention to depict a city of gigantic dimensions.

There is some evidence to suggest that the second Jewish temple was intended to be cubical in shape (dedicated ca. 516 B.C.). In Ezra 6:2–3, a letter of Cyrus is quoted authorizing the rebuilding of the Jerusalem temple and specifying that its height and width should be 60 cubits (perhaps a limitation to avoid cost overruns). While the *length* is missing, the dimensions of the first temple were reportedly 60 cubits long, 20 wide, and 30 high (1 Kgs 6:2; cf. 2 Chr 3:3). If these two texts are correlated, it is possible that the second temple was intended to be a large cube measuring 60 cubits (ca. 90 feet or 27.4 meters) in length, width, and height (see J. Blenkinsopp, *Ezra-Nehemiah: A Commentary* [Philadelphia: Westminster, 1988] 123–25). The cubical shape also occurs in the Gilgamesh Epic 11.28–30, 57–59, where the boat used by Utnapishtim to survive the flood is 120 cubits (ca. 60 meters) in length, width, and height, forming a huge cube (see Heidel, *Gilgamesh*, 82 n. 173, for Babylonian cubits).

The fantastic dimensions of the eschatological Jerusalem were an occasional subject for speculation in early Judaism. According to *Sib. Or.* 5.252, in the future the wall around Jerusalem will reach to Joppa (a Mediterranean coastal city), while in *Cant. Rab.* 7.5.3 it is said that Jerusalem will extend to the gates of Damascus (eschatological urban sprawl?), and it will expand and ascend until it reaches the throne of glory. According to *b. B. Bat.* 75b, the future Jerusalem will have a thousand gardens, towers, palaces, and mansions, each the size of Sepphoris, and Jerusalem will be elevated to a height of three parasangs (the size of the original Jerusalem). Very close to the enormous dimensions of the New Jerusalem are the talmudic dimensions of Rome, described as a square, 300 x 300 parasangs (*b. Meg.* 6b). Since the παρασάγγης, "parasang," is a unit of measure derived from Persia, equal to 30 *stadia*, the dimensions of Rome would then be 9,000 *stadia*, 75 percent of the size of the New Jerusalem at 12,000 *stadia*. Given the antithesis that the author of Revelation posits between the New Jerusalem and Babylon-Rome, it is possible that he has been influenced by this tradition in his depiction of the enormous size of the holy city.

17 καὶ ἐμέτρησεν τὸ τεῖχος αὐτῆς ἑκατὸν τεσσεράκοντα τεσσάρων πηχῶν μέτρον ἀνθρώπου, ὅ ἐστιν ἀγγέλου, "He measured its wall, 144 cubits, the unit of measure used by a person, that is, an angel." The Hebrew cubit, called אמה *'ammâ*, a term meaning both "forearm" and "cubit," corresponds to the Greek term πῆχυς, which also means both "forearm" and "cubit," though the English word "cubit" itself is derived from the Greek word κύβιτον, "elbow" (cf. *cubitum*, a Latin loanword from Greek). This verse is in part inspired by Ezek 40:5, in which the length of the six-cubit-long rod used to measure the new temple follows the archaic long cubit (seven palms breadth = 28 fingers = 20.6 inches), rather than the "newer" Egyptian short cubit (six palms breadth = 24 fingers = 17.5 inches); in Ezek 41:8 this archaic long cubit is called a "noble" cubit. The *Vitae Prophetarum* preserves an interesting tradition that Ezekiel, like Moses, saw the heavenly model of the temple, "where the walls would be and the wide outer wall [τὸ τεῖχος καὶ περίτειχος πλατύ], just as Daniel said that it will be built." This can only refer to Theod Dan 9:25, καὶ οἰκοδομηθήσεται πλατεῖα καὶ τεῖχος (Codex A: περίτειχος), "and the streets and the wall [Codex A: outer wall] will be built" (see Schwemer, "Vitae Prophetarum," 260–61).

Rev 21:17 presents several interpretive difficulties. (1) The size of the wall appears to be ridiculously small when compared with the gigantic size of the cubical city that it encloses (Charles, 2:164). However, it is not immediately evident whether the *height* or the *width* of the wall is described as measuring 144 cubits. Rev 21:9–22:5 is modeled in part after Ezek 40–48, and in Ezek 40:5 the "man" in Ezekiel's vision measured both the *height* and the *width* of the wall surrounding the temple area, while in Ezek 41:5, 9, 12, only the *widths* of the temple walls are measured. In descriptions of ancient cities, the *thickness* of the walls is often emphasized (Neh 3:8; 12:38; Jer 51:58 [Babylon]; Herodotus 1.178 [Babylon's walls are 50 cubits wide]; Jdt 1:2 [Ecbatana's walls are 50 cubits wide and 70 cubits high]) since walls of sufficient thickness were less liable to be undermined or breached during a siege. The translation of the two adjectives μέγα and ὑψηλόν in v 12 as "wide and high" reflects the judgment that both the width and height of the wall are referred to, and in the present case it appears likely that it is the *width* of the wall that measures 144 cubits, not the height (the size of which is unmentioned).

(2) A second problem is whether μέτρον, "measure," refers to πῆχυς, "cubit," only or to both στάδιον, "stadium" (v 16c), and πῆχυς. If μέτρον refers to πῆχυς, it could be because the cubit (= ca. 0.5 meters) was usually calculated as the distance between a man's elbow and the end of his forefinger, i.e., six or seven palms' breadth. If the cubit is measured by an *angel*, however, since angels and other supernatural beings were often perceived as having gigantic stature and therefore much larger arms and hands than ordinary human beings (Rev 10:2, 5; *2 Enoch* 1:4; 18:1; *3 Enoch* 9:2–3; 21:1; 22:3; 25:4; 26:4; 48C:5; POxy 1381, lines 117–18; *Corp. Herm.* 1.1), one could expect that the "angelic" cubit might be much larger than the conventional cubit used in human society. The specification that it is a *human* measure in v 17 would assure the reader that the cubit used is the conventional one. A parallel is found in the description of the enormous bed of the giant Og, king of

Bashan in Deut 3:11, which was nine cubits long and four cubits wide "by the cubit of a man," i.e., "by the common cubit" (MT בְּאַמַּת־אִישׁ *bĕ'ammat-'îš;* LXX ἐν πήχει ἀνδρός), a phrase meant to emphasis the large size of the iron bed. These passages suggest that it was conventional to specify the type of measure used. In Ezek 40:5 it is explicitly stated that the "long cubit" used consisted of a cubit and a palmbreadth in length. On the other hand, if μέτρον refers to *both* στάδιον and πῆχυς, it might be because of a possible suspicion that the author-editor anticipates on the part of the readers that the size of the city has been exaggerated or that it is a fantasy unrelated to human realities.

(3) The meaning of the phrase μέτρον ἀνθρώπου, ὅ ἐστιν ἀγγέλου, "the unit of measure used by a person, that is, an angel," is also problematic because it appears contradictory. There are several possible ways of understanding this phrase. (a) The simplest solution is to assume that the author has followed the model of Ezek 40–48, where the person who measures the eschatological Jerusalem is referred to simply as an אִישׁ *'îš,* "man," though it seems evident that an angel is in view. The author wants to make it clear that the "man" of Ezek 40–48 is actually an angel. There are other biblical texts in which the term "man" is used of an angelic being (Gen 18:2, 16 [cf. 4Q*180* = 4QAgesCreat 2–4 ii 3 (tr. García Martínez, *Dead Sea Scrolls,* 212): "The three men [who] appeared to [Abra]ham in the oak wood of Mambre are angels"]; 19:5, 8; Ezek 9:2, 3; Mark 16:5). (b) Following the argument used above under (2), the author may have wanted to stress that the cubit measure used was the one used in human society. (c) The author may have wanted to emphasize the mysterious or symbolic significance of the number 144, perhaps similar to the number 666 in 13:18. In line with the rabbinic attempt to link the name "Menahem" with "Messiah" because of the numerical equivalence of the letters of those terms, Dornseiff (*Alphabet,* 92) has suggested that 144 is the number of the messianic deliverer who will restore Jerusalem. Following this approach, Topham has suggested that here the number 144 represents the Hebrew spelling of "son of God" (בן אלוהים *bn 'lwhym,* a designation for the Messiah (ב = 2; נ = 50; א = 1; ל = 30; ו = 6; ה = 5; י = 10; ם = 40; total = 144). (d) Since no human measuring tool held in the hand could possibly reach 12,000 stadia (v 16), the author needs to mention that the measuring was done by an angel (Zahn, 2:610 n. 54). (e) Behind this statement may lurk the ancient view that two different systems were operative in the world of mortals and the world of the gods (on the notion that the gods have special names for themselves and aspects of the cosmos unknown to humans, see *Comment* on 19:12).

18a καὶ ἡ ἐνδώμησις τοῦ τείχους αὐτῆς ἴασπις, "The material used in the construction of its wall was jasper." The tradition that the walls of the New Jerusalem would be constructed of precious stones is found in Isa 54:11–12, Tob 13:16, and the New Jerusalem texts from Qumran, where rubies and sapphires are prominent. Lucian (*Verae historiae* 2.11) describes a city of gold surrounded with an emerald wall with seven gates, each made of a single plank of cinnamon; see *Excursus 21B: Ancient Utopias and the Paradise Myth,* where the text is cited in translation. This city also has a river of the best myrrh flowing through it, one hundred royal cubits wide and five royal cubits deep.

18b καὶ ἡ πόλις χρυσίον καθαρὸν ὅμοιον ὑάλῳ καθαρῷ, "while the city itself was pure gold, like clear glass." Note the close verbal parallel in v 21b, καὶ ἡ πλατεῖα τῆς πόλεως χρυσίον καθαρὸν ὡς ὕαλος διαυγής, "and the street of *the city was pure gold,* *like clear glass.*" Lucian (*Verae historiae* 2.11) has a striking parallel to the description of the New Jerusalem when he describes a city all of gold (Jewish sources do not usually describe the eschatological Jerusalem as constructed out of gold, though the expression "Jerusalem the golden" has arisen from the uniform color of the yellow sandstone out of which most of the city was and is constructed). Tob 13:16–17, probably based on Isa 54:11–12, mentions that the towers and battlements of the future Jerusalem would be made of gold. In antiquity, Alexandria was called "the golden [τὴν χρυσῆν] city" (Athenaeus *Deipn.* 1.20b). Parts of the temple of Solomon as well as the eschatological temple were often described as being overlaid with gold (11QTemple 36:11; 39:3; 41:15), as were parts of the Herodian temple (Jos. *J.W.* 5.201, 205, 207–8; *m. Mid.* 2:3).

19a οἱ θεμέλιοι τοῦ τείχους τῆς πόλεως παντὶ λίθῳ τιμίῳ κεκοσμημένοι, "The foundations of the city wall were adorned with every type of precious stone." This may be an allusion to Ezek 28:13, "every precious stone was your covering" (כל־אבן יקרה מסכתך *kol-ʾeben yĕqārâ mĕsukātekā;* LXX πᾶν λίθον χρηστὸν ἐνδέδεσαι), though it is obviously used in a completely different way. Several early Jewish texts, such as Isa 54:11–12 (elaborately interpreted in *Pesiq. Rab Kah.* 18.4–6), Tob 13:16–17, and the New Jerusalem texts from Qumran (García Martínez, "'New Jerusalem,'" 199), expect Jerusalem to be embellished with various kinds of jewels and precious metals. Fragments of Tobit, nearly the entire book of Tobit in Aramaic from Qumran, have been published (4Q*196–99* = 4QTob ar [4Q*200* = 4QTob hebr]; Beyer, *Ergänzungsband,* 137–47), including 13:16–17, in a text closer to the longer text in codex א than to the shorter text in codices A and B. In the Qumran fragment of Tob 13:16–17, the precious stones sapphire (ספיר[ב] *[b]spyr*), gold (הב[בד] *[bd]hb*), and ophir (אופיר[די ובאבן *wbʾbn dy ʾ[wpyr*) are mentioned, though the Aramaic terms for "gates," "walls," and "streets" are missing. The phrase "And I shall lay your foundations in lapis lazuli" from Isa 54:11 is quoted and interpreted in 4QpIsa^d (J. M. Allegro, ed., *Qumran Cave 4*, DJD 5 [Oxford: Clarendon, 1968] 27–28), to refer to the "congregation of his elect, like a stone of lapis lazuli among the stones," i.e., as a metaphor for the Qumran community itself.

Isa 61:10 uses the simile of the bride adorned with jewels for the returning Jewish exiles. In Rev 21:18–21 the description of the New Jerusalem is a combined image of the adorned bride and a description of a utopian city. Note that the verb κεκοσμημένοι, "adorned," in 21:19 is a term used of the bride image in 21:2. *Jos. As.* 18:6 describes Aseneth dressing in her bridal trousseau:

> And she girded a golden and royal girdle around (herself) which was (made) of precious stones. And she put golden bracelets on her fingers and on her feet golden buskins, and precious ornaments she put around her neck in which innumerable costly (and) precious stones were fastened, and a golden crown she put on her head, and on that crown, in front on her brow, was a big sapphire stone, and around the big stone were six costly stones.

The relationship between Joseph and Aseneth has a deeper significance, which the text itself explicates (C. Burchard, *OTP* 2:189–90). Aseneth's name is changed to "City of Refuge," behind whose walls people find shelter (*Jos. As.* 15:7; 16:16; 19:5). The seven maids who attend Aseneth receive a blessing from the heavenly man (*Jos. As.* 17:6; tr. C. Burchard, *OTP* 2:231): "May the Lord God the Most High bless you. And you shall be seven pillars of the City of Refuge, and all the fellow inhabitants of the chosen of that city will rest upon you for ever (and) ever." Aseneth is a model for later converts to Judaism. E. Stauffer, however, went too far when he claimed that the marriage of Joseph to Aseneth was "allegorically exploited in Judaism with reference to the marriage of the Messiah to the city of God" (*TDNT* 1:657).

The twelve foundation stones of vv 19–20 can be compared with the twelve precious stones arranged in four rows of three stones each on the breastplate of the high priest (Exod 28:16–20; 39:9–13); on each stone was engraved the name of one of the twelve tribes of Israel (Exod 28:21; 39:14). Ezek 28:13 describes the nine jewels covering the king of Tyre. However, in the LXX, an identical list of *twelve* jewels is found in Exod 28:16–20; 39:9–13; Ezek 28:13, reflecting an assimilation of the Ezekiel passage to those in Exodus. The stones in the description of the heavenly Jerusalem, like those used in describing the Eden of the king of Tyre in Ezek 28:13, appear to be dependent on the pectoral of the Israelite high priest in Exod 28:17–20 and 39:10–13 (Heitzmann Pérez, *Anuario* 6 [1980] 149–58).

19b ὁ θεμέλιος ὁ πρῶτος ἴασπις, ὁ δεύτερος σάπφιρος, ὁ τρίτος χαλκηδών, ὁ τέταρτος σμάραγδος, "The first foundation was jasper, the second, sapphire, the third, chalcedony, the fourth, emerald." Jasper (mentioned earlier as a precious stone used as a symbol for God in Rev 4:3 and as the material of which the wall that surrounded the city was made in v 18) is mentioned as the first of the foundation stones of the New Jerusalem.

20 ὁ πέμπτος σαρδόνυξ, ὁ ἕκτος σάρδιον, ὁ ἕβδομος χρυσόλιθος, ὁ ὄγδοος βήρυλλος, ὁ ἔνατος τοπάζιον, ὁ δέκατος χρυσόπρασος, ὁ ἐνδέκατος ὑάκινθος, ὁ δωδέκατος ἀμέθυστος, "the fifth, onyx, the sixth, carnelian, the seventh, yellow topaz, the eighth, beryl, the ninth, topaz, the tenth, chrysophrase, the eleventh, jacinth, the twelfth, amethyst." The term χρυσόλιθος (Latin *chrysolithos*), literally "golden stone," is mentioned by Pliny *Hist. nat.* 36.126 as an export of Ethiopia, though the stones from India were particularly highly regarded. The report of Pliny and Isidor (*Orig.* 16.15.2), supplemented by Propertius (who refers to the *flavo lumine*, "tawny luster," of the stone in 2.16.44), indicates that the stone was yellow in color. The word is usually translated "topaz" or "yellow sapphire," but it can also refer to "peridot" (Casson, *Periplus*, 190, 260). The beryl was a stone favored for magical amulets and was called the "stone of Zeus" (apparently only in *Cyranides* 1.2.20–26).

21a καὶ οἱ δώδεκα πυλῶνες δώδεκα μαργαρῖται, ἀνὰ εἷς ἕκαστος τῶν πυλώνων ἦν ἐξ ἑνὸς μαργαρίτου, "The twelve gates were twelve pearls; each individual gate was made of a single pearl." Twelve gates, symbolizing the twelve tribes of Israel, are also found in the ideal conceptions of the New Jerusalem in Ezek 48:33–34, 5Q15 = 5QNJ ar 1:10, and 11QTemple (see *Comment* on 21:15). Some have rationalized that the gates of pearl referred to inlaid mother-of-pearl. Since there are (admittedly late) Jewish traditions that refer to gigantic pearls, there is no need to rationalize the details of this city, which is already fabulous in most other respects. In *1 Enoch* 18:7, a mountain of pearl is mentioned. There are several rabbinic traditions concerning enormous pearls; see Str-B, 3:851–52. R. Johanan is quoted in *b. B. Bat.* 75a, "The Holy One, blessed be He, will in the time to come bring precious stones and pearls which are thirty [cubits] by thirty and will cut out from them [openings] ten [cubits] by twenty, and will set them up in the gates of

Jerusalem" (for parallel traditions, see *b. Sanh.* 100a; *Midr. Pss.* 87.2). *Pesiq. Rab Kah.*
18.5 contains the tradition that the east gate and its two wickets would be made from
a single pearl hollowed out by the Holy One. For further references in rabbinic
literature, see Burrows, *JTS* 43 (1942) 177–79.

21b καὶ ἡ πλατεῖα τῆς πόλεως χρυσίον καθαρὸν ὡς ὕαλος διαυγής, "The main
square of the city was pure gold, like transparent crystal." The term ἡ πλατεῖα (see
also 11:8 and 22:2) presents certain interpretive problems, for it can have at least
three meanings in its present context: (1) It can refer to a specific street, perhaps
the central thoroughfare of the New Jerusalem (Hadorn, 208, 210; Wikenhauser,
159; Fekkes, *Isaiah*, 244 n. 48). (2) It can be taken as a collective singular and thus
be translated "streets," referring to all the streets in the New Jerusalem (Bousset
[1906] 450; Charles, 2:170; see the complex reconstruction of the orthogonal
street system of the eschatological Jerusalem in 5Q*15* = 5QNJ ar by Chyutin, "'New
Jerusalem,'" 71–97; id., *New Jerusalem Scroll*, 86), though this usage is not elsewhere
attested. In favor of this view, however, is the fact that Tob 13:17 specifically refers
to the αἱ πλατεῖαι, "*the* streets," of the eschatological Jerusalem. (3) More probably,
however, it can be understood as referring to an open plaza or square in the center
of the city (Schlatter, *Apokalypse*, 335; Sickenberger, *Erklärung*, 194; Reader, "Stadt
Gottes," 147–48). This understanding of ἡ πλατεῖα solves the problem of how the
complex geographical features of 22:2 should be visualized (see *Comment* on 22:2).
On the use of gold in the eschatological Jerusalem, see *Comment* on v 18b.

22a καὶ ναὸν οὐκ εἶδον ἐν αὐτῇ, "And I saw no temple in the city." This explicit
and surprising denial of the presence of a temple within the New Jerusalem
suggests that the traditions with which John was familiar expected to have an
eschatological temple as the center of the eschatological Jerusalem, for οὐκ εἶδον,
"I did not see," implies "I expected to see but did not." One important issue is
whether this extremely unusual view is possible only within early Christianity, or is
it a view compatible with the apocalyptic outlook of segments of early Judaism? It
is possible to regard the absence of the eschatological temple in this vision as part
of an anti-temple and anti-priestly polemic that existed in various segments of early
Judaism, though certainly the expectation of an eschatological temple would be
the normal expectation of Jewish eschatology.

In Judaism, the eschatological expectation of a new Jerusalem generally implied
a new temple. The explicit denial of a temple in the New Jerusalem in Rev 21:22
is, therefore, surprising and has been frequently understood to reflect an anti-
temple stance of strands of early Christianity, perhaps in dependence on anti-
temple sentiment in both Judaism and the Greco-Roman world. Some early
Christians developed a polemic emphasizing that the temple in Jerusalem was
either a temporary expedient or was never really necessary (Acts 7:47–51; John
4:21, 23–24; Heb 9:1–14; *Barn.* 16:1–2; Justin *Dial.* 22.1). One of the central reasons
for the lynching of Stephen was apparently his anti-temple stance (Acts 6:13). The
traditions of Jesus' "cleansing" of the temple and predictions of the destruction of
the temple are frequently thought to reflect an anti-temple stance. Yet Jesus' act of
"cleansing" the temple makes more sense if it is understood as a symbolic action
anticipating its destruction (though not impugning its purity and legitimacy), as
well as implying its eschatological restoration (Mark 11:15–19 = Matt 21:12–13 =
Luke 19:45–48; E. P. Sanders, *Jesus and Judaism* [Philadelphia: Fortress, 1985] 61–
76). It is striking that sayings of Jesus predicting the destruction of the existing

temple and its replacement by an eschatological temple are widespread in the tradition (Mark 13:2 = Matt 24:2 = Luke 21:6; Mark 14:58 = Matt 26:61; Mark 15:29 = Matt 27:40; John 2:18–22; Acts 6:14). The Qumran community rejected the temple but paradoxically maintained a priestly structure and regarded their community itself as a metaphorical "temple." The opposition to the temple in Qumran was not absolute; rather it was based on the conviction that the present temple had been polluted and, therefore, required cleansing or replacement. Paul, too, regarded the Christian community as the "temple of God" (1 Cor 3:16; 2 Cor 5:1–2; 6:16). It is probable that Rev 21:22a and 22b are both redactional since they contain the only indications in Revelation of the absence of a temple in the holy city (Wilcox, "Tradition," 213; Bergmeier, *ZNW* 75 [1984] 89; the latter argues that v 21 should be removed and replaced with 22:1–2 to restore a meaningful sense to the passage).

A very different view of Rev 21:22 is proposed by David Flusser, "No Temple in the City," *Judaism and the Origins of Christianity* (Jerusalem: Magnes, 1988) 454–65, who argues that Rev 21:22–23 is based not on opposition to the temple but on the combination of two midrashic units, the second based on Ps 132:17, in which the phrase "I have prepared a lamp for my Messiah" occurs, and the first on Isa 60:19, which refers to the Lord as the everlasting light of Jerusalem. Flusser argues that these two midrashic units are fused in a midrash on Exod 27:20, *Tanḥuma to Exod., Tĕṣawwēh* 6 (as they also are in Rev 21:22–23): "The Holy One said to Israel: 'In this world you needed the light of the Temple, but in the world to come because of the merit of the above mentioned lamp (Ex. 27:20) I will bring you the King Messiah, who is compared to a lamp, as it is written: "There I will make a horn to sprout for David, I have prepared a lamp for my Messiah" (Ps. 132:17).'"

Temples sometimes played no role in Hellenistic utopias because of a general opposition to all social institutions, including the temple and its priesthood (see *Excursus 21B: Ancient Utopias and the Paradise Myth*). In Zeno's lost *Politeia*, the founder of Stoicism advocated a community of wives and prohibited the building of temples, law courts, and gymnasiums (μήθ᾽ ἱερὰ μήτε δικαστήρια μήτε γυμνάσια) in his world state (Clement Alex. *Strom.* 5.12.76; Plutarch *De Stoic. rep.* 1034b; Diogenes Laertius 7.33; *SVF* 1:61–62; frags. 264–67). Temples should not be built, not only because he thought that the products of craftsmen were neither holy nor worthy of the gods, but also because men should have the divine in their mind (νοῦς) because it is immortal. Further, cities should be embellished not by offerings to the gods but by virtue (*SVF* 1:62; frag. 266).

In ancient Israel, Jeremiah was unusual in that he apparently expected no future restoration of the temple and explicitly indicated that the ark was no longer necessary; he envisioned all Jerusalem as the throne of Yahweh (Jer 3:14–18). Ezekiel and Zechariah, however, do refer to an eschatological temple (Ezek 40–48; Zech 1:16; 6:12–15). Zech 2:4–5 (= LXX 2:8–9) speaks of the eschatological Jerusalem: "Jerusalem shall be inhabited like a city without walls [פְּרָזוֹת *pĕrāzôt;* translated κατακάρπως in the LXX, i.e., 'Jerusalem will be densely populated'; see Muraoka, *Septuagint,* 125] . . . , for the Lord himself would be a wall of fire around it." Perhaps John used this passage from Zechariah as the basis for his assertion that the New Jerusalem has no temple within it because the temple is the Lord God Almighty and the Lamb.

While the notion of a heavenly or an eschatological Jerusalem was widespread in early Judaism (as we have observed above), John is unique in claiming that there will be no temple within it. It is important to ask *why* he emphasizes this fact when he has used apocalyptic traditions that connect the temple of God with the New Jerusalem (3:12; see 7:15), refers often to the temple in heaven (11:19; 14:15, 17; 15:5, 6, 8; 16:1, 17), and uses temple imagery, particularly in descriptions of the heavenly throne room. The sanctity of Jerusalem was based largely on the presence of the temple within it. The *Temple Scroll* (11QTemple) uses the expression עיר המקדש *ʿir hammiqdāš*, "temple-city" (45:7–18), and largely ignores the existence of the rest of the land of Israel within which the temple-city was to be located. The texts from Qumran (particularly 2Q*24* = 2QNJ ar and 11Q*18* = 11QNJ ar; see *Comment* on 11:2) describing the New Jerusalem follow the description of the city with a description of a temple within it (García Martínez, "'New Jerusalem,'" 199–200).

22b ὁ γὰρ κύριος ὁ θεὸς ὁ παντοκράτωρ ὁ ναὸς αὐτῆς ἐστιν καὶ τὸ ἀρνίον, "for the Lord God Almighty and the Lamb are its temple." This explanatory statement introduced by γάρ, "for," has obviously been inserted by the author into an existing composition since it contains information the author neither saw nor heard in a vision (see 21:1). Further, the phrase "and the Lamb" is a later expansion of the text (see *Comments* on similar expansions in 6:16; 7:10; 14:4, 10; 22:1, 3). The really striking feature of this passage is the affirmation that *God (and the Lamb) is/are the temple of the New Jerusalem*. While the Johannine Jesus speaks of his physical body figuratively as a ναός, "temple" (John 2:19, 21), there are few parallels to the conception of God as temple. One such passage, however, appears in 4Q*511* = 4QShir[b] 35:3 (Baillet, *Qumran*, 237–38), אלוהים לו למקדש עולמים וטהרה בנברים *ʾlwhym lw lmqdš ʿwlmym wṭhrh bnbrym*, "God himself [is] an eternal sanctuary so that there will be purity among the chosen ones." A problematic passage is found in Isa 8:14, where it is said that "he [the Lord of hosts] will become a sanctuary [MT מקדש *miqdāš;* LXX ἀγίασμα]." A relatively close eschatological scenario is found in *T. Dan* 5:9, 13–14 (tr. Hollander-de Jonge, *Testaments*, 286):

> And so when you return to the Lord you will obtain mercy, and he will bring you into his sanctuary [τὸ ἀγίασμα] proclaiming peace to you. . . . And the saints will rest in Eden and the righteous will rejoice in the new Jerusalem [ἐπὶ τῆς νέας Ἰερουσαλήμ], which will be to the glory of God for ever. And no longer will Jerusalem endure desolation nor Israel be led captive, because the Lord will be in the midst of it [ὅτι κύριος ἔσται ἐν μέσῳ αὐτῆς] living together with men, and the Holy One of Israel, reigning over them in humility and poverty.

This text combines the motif of the presence of the saints in the temple (absent from Revelation) with the motif of the immediate presence of God among his people (a notion frequently expressed in the OT: Ps 46:6; Zeph 3:5, 15; Zech 2:10; 8:3), though the phrases "New Jerusalem" and "living together with men" (i.e., Jesus Christ) betray the presence of a mini-apocalypse of Christian origin (Ulrichsen, *Grundschrift*, 104–5).

23a καὶ ἡ πόλις οὐ χρείαν ἔχει τοῦ ἡλίου οὐδὲ τῆς σελήνης ἵνα φαίνωσιν αὐτῇ, "The city has no need of the sun or of the moon to illumine it." This is an allusion to Isa 60:19, and Charles argued that it was based on the Hebrew text (1:lxxvi), though the phrase οὐ χρείαν ἔχει, "it has no need" (see the parallel phrase καὶ οὐκ ἔχουσιν χρείαν, "they have no need," in 22:5), is in fact found *neither* in the LXX nor in the MT but rather corresponds to a phrase in *Tg. Isa.* 60:19 (Chilton, *Isaiah Targum*), "You shall no longer need [לא תצטרכין *lʾ tṣtrkyn*] the sun for light by day nor even the moon for brightness by night." Wilcox proposes that Rev 21:23 is derived from an interpretive tradition similar to that found in *Tg. Isa.* 60:19 ("Tradition," 207–8).

There is a doublet to this text in Rev 22:5:

Rev 21:23	*Rev 22:5*
καὶ ἡ πόλις οὐ χρείαν ἔχει And the city has no need	καὶ οὐκ ἔχουσιν χρείαν and they will have no need
τοῦ ἡλίου οὐδὲ τῆς σελήνης of the sun or the moon	φωτὸς λύχνου καὶ φωτὸς ἡλίου for lamp light or sunlight,
ἵνα φαίνωσιν αὐτῇ to illumine it,	
ἡ γὰρ δόξα τοῦ θεοῦ ἐφώτισεν αὐτήν, for the glory of God illumines it,	ὅτι κύριος ὁ θεὸς φωτίσει because the Lord God will illumine
	ἐπ᾽ αὐτούς. them.
καὶ ὁ λύχνος αὐτῆς τὸ ἀρνίον. and its lamp is the Lamb.	

23b ἡ γὰρ δόξα τοῦ θεοῦ ἐφώτισεν αὐτήν, καὶ ὁ λύχνος αὐτῆς τὸ ἀρνίον, "for the glory of God illumines it, / and its lamp is the Lamb." This couplet consists of two synonymous lines arranged chiastically:

a   For the glory of God
   b   illumines it
   b′   and its lamp
a′   is the Lamb.

The first phrase alludes to Isa 60:19–20, which predicts that the everlasting light of the Lord will replace the sun and the moon (*Pesiq. Rab Kah.* 21.5; Justin *Dial.* 113.5; Origen *Contra Cels.* 6.51). Isa 60:19–20 has perhaps influenced one of the blessings in the Jewish order of morning prayer, "O cause a new light to shine upon Zion," and Rev 21:23 may reflect an early Jewish-Christian adaptation of such a synagogue ritual (see Dölger, *Sol Salutis,* 121; Simon, *Verus Israel,* 501 n. 83). The equation of the glory of God with light is also found in Isa 60:1, "Arise, shine, for your light has come, and the glory of the Lord has risen upon you." The tradition of the presence of the glory and the light of God in the eschatological Jerusalem is a motif that occurs in early Jewish literature in probable dependence on Isa 60 (Bar 5:1–4; *Sib. Or.* 3.787; 5.420–27; *T. Dan* 5:12–13; see Volz, *Eschatologie,* 371–72). In answer to the question regarding when light first appeared in the world, R. Samuel b. Nahman reportedly replied, "The Holy One, blessed be He, cloaked himself in it as in a white garment and illuminated the entire world from the splendor of his glory" (ed. Neusner, *Pesiqta de Rab Kahana* 2:75). According to *2 Enoch* 31:2 (tr. F. I. Andersen, *OTP* 1:154), God created an open heaven for Adam so that he could look upon the angels and "the light which is never darkened was perpetually in paradise." There is a pagan parallel in the Pantheon, a temple for all the gods, which was rebuilt by Hadrian and had an enormous vault representing the cosmos (Dio Cassius 53.27). The dome had a single source of illumination, the so-called *oculus*, "eye," at the top. Since the ancient Romans regarded the sun as the eye of Jupiter, the supreme God was illuminating the room and therefore was present like the cult statue in an ordinary temple (see Hannestad, *Roman Art,* 87–88).

The second phrase, "its lamp is the Lamb," is a possible allusion to Ps 132:17b (NRSV): "I have prepared a lamp for my anointed one," in which "Lamb" has been substituted for "anointed one," one of the clearest indicators of the basic messianic significance of the figure of the Lamb in Revelation. This passage was understood to refer to "the lamp of the Messiah" (*Lev. Rab.* 24:2; *Tanḥuma to Exod., Tĕrûmâ* 61 [Exod 25:1]; see Flusser, "No Temple," 457–58). Flusser has shown that midrashic interpretations of Ps 132:17 and Isa 60:19 have been combined in *Tanḥuma to Exod., Tĕṣawwēh* 6 (Exod 27:20) ("No Temple," 458–59):

> The Holy One said to Israel: "In this world you needed the light of the Temple, but in the world to come, because of the merit of the above mentioned lamp (Ex. 27:20), I will bring you the King Messiah, who is compared to a lamp, as it is written 'There I will make a horn to sprout for David, I have prepared a lamp for my Messiah' (Ps. 132:17). And not only this: I will make light for you, because this is what Isaiah said: 'The Lord will be your [i.e., Jerusalem's] everlasting light, and your God will be your glory' (Is. 60:19)."

The parallels with Rev 21:22–23 are three (Flusser, "No Temple," 459, 464): (1) in the world to come there will be no need of the light of the temple, (2) God will be the everlasting light of Jerusalem, and (3) the Messiah is compared to a lamp (i.e., the lamp of the Messiah supersedes the lamp of the historical temple). These midrashic traditions are all much later than Revelation, though Flusser argues that since both they and Rev 21:22–23 combine three distinctive themes, they must reflect a common antecedent source or tradition. The tradition of the lamp of the Messiah is also reflected in a lead lamella from Amorgos that contains an incantation to exorcise the demon who has caused the tumor; part of the adjuration reads, "I adjure you, malign tumour, by the name of him . . . who by his son enlightened Jerusalem with a torch [τὸν διὰ τοῦ υἱοῦ φωτίζοντα τὴν Ἰερουσαλὴμ μετὰ λύχνου]" (T. Homolle, "Inscriptions d'Amorgos: Lames de plomb portant des imprécations," *BCH* 25 [1910] 430–56; the text and translation are also included in H. Leclercq, "Amulettes," *DACL* 1:1796–99). In the Barbelognostic treatise *Pistis Sophia,* the transcendent origin of Jesus is indicated by the tremendous light that he radiates (1.3; ed. Schmidt-Till, p. 3, lines 24–36; ed. Schmidt-MacDermot, p. 5).

24–26 Rev 21:24–26 paraphrases Isa 60:3–5, 11, though in Isaiah kings have been taken captive and are led in a victory procession, while in Rev 21:24–26 kings and nations enter freely. Jerusalem and the temple are mentioned as gathering places for Israel and all nations in *T. Benj.* 9:2; *Sib. Or.* 3.772–73; *Pss. Sol.* 17:32–35; *b. ʿAbod. Zar.* 3b. Other examples of universalism include *T. Levi* 2:11; 4:4; 8:14; 14:4; 18:9; *T. Jud.* 25:5; *T. Naph.* 8:3; *T. Ash.* 7:3; Tob 13:8, 11; *Ep. Arist.* 702–31; *1 Enoch* 90:30, 37–38; *Sib. Or.* 3:16ff.; 5.492–502.

24 καὶ περιπατήσουσιν τὰ ἔθνη διὰ τοῦ φωτὸς αὐτῆς, καὶ οἱ βασιλεῖς τῆς γῆς φέρουσιν τὴν δόξαν αὐτῶν εἰς αὐτήν, "The nations will walk in its light, / and the kings of the earth will bring their glory to it." This phrase alludes to Isa 60:3, where the MT text reads, "And nations shall go [וְהָלְכוּ *wĕhālĕkû*] to your light, and kings to the brightness of your rising," while LXX Isa 60:3 reverses the clauses: "And kings will come [πορεύσονται] to your light, and nations to your splendor." While the author is apparently dependent on the MT, he has chosen to use περιπατεῖν, "to walk, live," for הלך *hālak*, "to go, walk, live," going beyond the spatial meaning of הלך *hālak* in Isa 60:3 and apparently using περιπατεῖν in the metaphorical sense of "way of living," a meaning frequently found in the NT, though περιπατεῖν + διά occurs only in 2 Cor 5:7 ("we walk by faith").

περιπατεῖν meaning "to conduct one's life" is used with the dative (Acts 21:21; 2 Cor 12:18; Gal 5:16), with various comparative particles such as ὡς, πῶς, καθώς, and οὕτως (1 Cor 7:17; Eph 4:17; 5:15; Phil 3:17; 1 Thess 4:1), with various adverbs such as ἀξίως and εὐσχημόνως (Rom 13:13; Eph 4:1; Col 1:10; 1 Thess 2:12), and with the prepositions ἐν (John 8:12; 11:9–10; 12:35; Rom 6:4; 2 Cor 4:2) and κατά (Mark 7:5; Rom 8:4; 14:15; 1 Cor 3:3).

Further, rather than having the nations "come to your [i.e., 'God's'] light," they are said to "walk by *its* [i.e., 'the city's'] light." The term "light" was frequently used in the OT and early Judaism as a metaphor for the "law of the Lord" or "Torah" (Ps 119[MT 118]:105; Prov 6:23; Wis 18:4; Sir 32:16; 45:17; *2 Apoc. Bar.* 17:4; 59:2; *Bib. Ant.* 15:6; 19:4; 33:3; 4 Ezra 14:20–21; *T. Lev.* 14:4; 19:1; see Aalen, *Begriffe*, 183–95, who finds no evidence for this metaphor in rabbinic Judaism).

The theme of the kings and nations of the world making an eschatological pilgrimage to see the light and glory of God in Jerusalem occurs several times in early Jewish literature (*Pss. Sol.* 17:31; Tob 13:11).

The phrase "the kings of the earth" occurs eight times in Revelation (1:5; 6:15; 17:2, 18; 18:3, 9; 19:19; 21:24), and only in 1:5 and 21:24 are they not hostile to God and his people. The term is synonymous with the "nations" as revealed in the parallel couplets in 18:3 and 21:24. In the OT the "nations"/"kings" synonymy often occurs paired in synonymous poetic couplets (Gen 17:6, 16; 35:11; 1 Kgs 4:34; 2 Kgs 17:8; Pss 102:15; 135:10; Isa 41:2; 45:1; 52:15; 60:3, 11, 16; 62:2; Jer 25:14; 27:7; 51:28; LXX Jer 28:20; LXX Ezek 27:33; 32:10; LXX Zeph 3:8; *Barn.* 12:34; Jos. *Ant.* 191). The reverse pattern "kings"/"nations," however, occurs only rarely (LXX Isa 51:4; 60:3; LXX Ezek 26:7; Ps 72:11). The author has apparently chosen to retain the less preferred order "nations"/"kings" found in Isa 60:3, which suggests that he is alluding to that particular passage.

The pilgrimage of the kings of the earth to the New Jerusalem presupposes the existence of the nations of the world and their rulers as well as the location of the eschatological Jerusalem on the earth (Strathmann, *TDNT* 6:532). There is, then, an apparently striking inconsistency in the eschatological scenario of Revelation introduced by this verse (and v 26) since 19:17–21 and 20:7–9 narrate the destruction of the kings of the earth and their armies and 21:1 records the destruction of the first heaven and the first earth, and yet here in vv 24–27, nations and kings of the earth still exist. There are, however, similarities between the eschatological scenario in Rev 19:11–21:27 and *Sib. Or.* 3.657–731, which narrates the final events in four stages: (1) The kings of the peoples attack the temple in Jerusalem (3.657–68; cf. Rev 20:7–9a). (2) God defends Jerusalem and annihilates the attackers (3.669–701; cf. Rev 20:9b–10). (3) Zion is restored (3.702–9; cf. Rev 21:9–21). (4) The inhabitants of all the islands and cities will recognize the sovereignty of God (3.710–31; cf. Rev 21:24–25). Nevertheless, the ancient Jewish eschatological motif of nations coming to Jerusalem in the eschaton, i.e. "Zion eschatology," was so firmly fixed in apocalyptic tradition that it is necessarily included here.

The place of the Gentiles in Jewish eschatological expectation was understood in at least four ways, though with regard to the status of these Gentiles (i.e., whether full proselytism is involved or not) many passages are admittedly ambiguous (Donaldson, *JSP* 7 [1990] 7–11; see also E. P. Sanders, *Jesus and Judaism*, 212–18): (1) Some strands of Jewish apocalyptic clearly expected the annihilation of the Gentiles, as in Rev 19:17–21 (*Jub.* 15:26; 4 Ezra 12:33; 13:38; *2 Apoc. Bar.* 40:1; *T. Abr.* 31:2; 1QM). (2) A second strand focused on the eschatological restoration of Israel to the apparent exclusion or expense of other nations (Isa 11:10–16; Philo *Praem.* 164–72). (3) A third strand saw the Gentiles as subservient to Israel and as making a pilgrimage to Jerusalem to pay tribute (Isa 18:7; 49:22–26; 55:5; 60:1–22; 61:5–6; 66:18–21; Jer 3:17–18; Zeph 3:9–10; Hag 2:7–9; Zech 2:11–12; 8:20–23; 14:16–19; Ps 72:8–11; *Pss. Sol.* 17:30–31; *Jub.* 32:19; Sir 36:11–17; *Sib. Or.* 3.772–74; 1QM 12:14; 1QpPs frag. 9; *Tg. Isa.* 16:1; 25:6–10; *Gen. Rab.* 78.12). (4) A fourth strand of tradition expected the Gentiles to participate completely in the worship of Yahweh and in eschatological salvation, though it is rarely clear whether full proselytism is expected (Isa 2:2–4; 56:6–8; LXX Isa 54:15; LXX Amos 9:12; Mic 4:1–4; Pss 22:27–28; 86:9; 138:4–6; Tob 13:11; 14:6–7; *1 Enoch* 10:21; 90:30–33; 91:14; *2 Apoc. Bar.* 72:1–6; *Sib. Or.* 3.564–70, 715–23, 757–75; Philo *Mos.* 2.43–44 [H. A. Wolfson, *Philo* (Cambridge, MA: Harvard UP, 1947) 2:415–17]; *T. Levi* 18:3, 9; *T. Jud.* 24:6; 25:5; *T. Naph.* 8:3–4; *T. Zeb.* 9:8; *T. Benj.* 10:3–11). It is important to note that the LXX translator of Isaiah exhibits a theological agenda that included the inclusion of Gentiles in the people of God; cf. Isa 23:14–24:1; 62:4 (Roetzel, "*Oikoumene*," 163–82). In Rev 21:24–26, full participation in eschatological salvation is presupposed. This eschatological expectation was based in part on historical experience (Ps 68:29; 1 Kgs 10:23–25; Jos. *Ant.* 15.402; *J.W.* 5.187; 2 Macc 5:16). Some particularly famous cults in the ancient world had an international appeal and attracted offerings from a great many different regions and peoples. In Ps.-Lucian *De Syria dea* 10, 32, the temple Atargatis at Heliopolis-Mabug, for example, in the Roman province of Syria had a widespread reputation and reportedly attracted offerings from "Arabia," the Phoenicians, Babylonians, Cappadocians, Cilicians, "Assyrioi," Egyptians, Medes, Armenians, and Babylonians.

25 καὶ οἱ πυλῶνες αὐτῆς οὐ μὴ κλεισθῶσιν ἡμέρας, νὺξ γὰρ οὐκ ἔσται ἐκεῖ, "The gates of the city will never close during the day, / for there will be no night there." The first clause alludes to Isa 60:11a, "Your gates shall always be open; day and night they shall not be shut," while the second reflects Zech 14:7, "On that day there shall be continuous day (it is known to the Lord), not day and not night, for at evening time there shall be light" (see Fekkes, *Isaiah*, 271–72). There is some difficulty with the text as it stands, for the statement that the gates of the city will not close *by day* (ἡμέρας is an adverbial genitive of time) is true of all ancient cities. The text would be more comprehensible if ἡμέρας, "by day," were omitted, for then the text would read, "The gates of the city will never close, for there is no night there" (Weiss-Heitmüller, 4:314, bracket the term [ἡμέρας]). Charles solves the problem by substituting καὶ νυκτός, "and by night," for νὺξ γὰρ οὐκ ἔσται ἐκεῖ, "for there will be no night there" (2:173, 439 n. 5), which results in this translation: "The gates of the city will never close by day and by night." The import of the adverb ἐκεῖ, "there," may be that day and night alternate as usual *outside* the holy city, but within the city itself the light from God and the Lamb mean that there is no night. There is a close parallel in 1QM 12:13–15 (tr. J. Duhaime in Charlesworth, ed., *Damascus Document, War Scroll, and Related Documents*, vol. 2 of *The Dead Sea Scrolls: Hebrew, Aramaic, and Greek Texts with English Translation* [Tübingen: Mohr-Siebeck; Louisville: Westminster John Knox, 1995] 121):

> Zion rejoice greatly! Shine forth in jubilation, Jerusalem! Be glad all you, cities of Judah! Open [your] gate[s] continually [תמיד ך (י)שער פתחי *pitḥî šĕʿāra(yi)k tāmîd*], that through them may be brought the wealth of the nations! Their kings shall serve you; all your oppressors shall bow down before you and [lick] the dust from your feet.

There are a number of reasons for arguing that Rev 21:25 may be a redactional insertion (Lohmeyer, 175): (1) it interrupts the thought of vv 24 and 26; (2) it disturbs the strophic structure of the context; (3) it reads like a correction of Isa 60:11; (4) if v 25 is removed, the repetition with 22:5a is deleted; and (5) it is framed by the verbs φέρουσιν, "bring" (v 24b), and οἴσουσιν, "will bring" (v 26a), and the subject appears to be the same, so the second use of φέρειν, "to bring," appears to be a resumption.

26 καὶ οἴσουσιν τὴν δόξαν καὶ τὴν τιμὴν τῶν ἐθνῶν εἰς αὐτήν, "People will bring the glory and the honor of the nations to it." The subject of οἴσουσιν, "will bring," is not immediately evident; it could be either the "kings of the earth" (v 24b) or the "nations" (v 24a), or both. Since "kings of the earth" is the subject of φέρουσιν, "bring," in v 24, it is probably also the subject of οἴσουσιν. The "kings of the earth" is a more probable choice of grammatical subject if the "glory and honor" they bring are considered to be material goods or wealth. Actually the phrase "glory and honor" probably has a double meaning and includes wealthy gifts as well as fame and adoration.

The two attributes "glory and honor" form a stereotypical synonymous word pair widely used in antiquity to connote fame and reputation (Ps 8:5 [MT 8:6, וְכָבוֹד וְהָדָר *wĕkābôd wĕhādār;* LXX 8:6, δόξῃ καὶ τιμῇ]; LXX Job 37:22; LXX Ps 28:1; LXX Ps 95:7; 1 Macc 14:21; Rom 2:7, 10; Heb 2:7 [quoting Ps 8:5], 9; 1 Pet 1:7; Rev 4:9, 11 [where they are the first two terms in a list of three]; *1 Clem.* 45:8; 61:1; Justin *Dial.* 73.3; Philo *Abr.* 184; *Virt.* 166; Jos. *Ant.* 2.268; 6.200; 11.217; 12.118; Plutarch *Camillus* 25.1; *Pelopidas* 34.5; *Demetr.* 8.1 [εὐδοξία καὶ τιμή]; *Mul. virt.* 254B; *De frat. amore* 486B; Fronto *Addit. epist.* 8.7; Alexander Aphr. *Prob.* 141; Polybius 2.70.5; 18.14.8; Demosthenes *De cor.* 97 [εὐδοξία καὶ τιμή]). These terms are also found in the reverse order "honor and glory" (Isa 55:5; Theod Dan 5:18; 1 Tim 1:17; 2 Pet 1:17; Rev 5:12, 13; Jos. *Ant.* 18.5; *J.W.* 7.88).

The bringing of glory and honor to the eschatological city of God is surely a sign of the conversion of the nations and the kings of the earth, reflecting the Jewish hope for the eschatological conversion of the heathen (Isa 45:20, 22, 24; Zech 2:11; 8:23; Dan 7:14; Tob 13:11; 14:6; *1 Enoch* 10:21; *T. Jude* 25:5; *T. Ash.* 7:3). See 4Q504 = 4QDibHam[a] 4:9–11 (tr. García Martínez, *Dead Sea Scrolls*, 415), "And to your great Name they [Gentiles] will carry their offerings: silver, gold, precious stones, with all the treasures of their country."

27a καὶ οὐ μὴ εἰσέλθῃ εἰς αὐτὴν πᾶν κοινόν, "But nothing unclean will enter into it." While the term "enter in" is used here of access to the New Jerusalem, it is clear that the city is a metaphor for salvation, combining the notions of the people of God as an edifice and the eschatological realization of the kingdom of God on a renewed earth. "Entering in" is therefore used here (and in 22:14) as a spatial metaphor equivalent to "entering into" the kingdom of God, a metaphor that occurs frequently in the teaching of Jesus (Matt 5:20; 7:21; 18:3; 19:23–24; 23:13; Mark 9:47; John 3:5; Acts 14:22; see Windisch, *ZNW* 27 [1928] 163–92; esp. 171). An OT antecedent for this conception occurs in Deut 23:2–9, where we find the repeated phrase בִּקְהַל יְהוָה ... לֹא יָבֹא *lōʾ yābōʾ ... biqhal YHWH,* "[So-and-so] will not enter into the congregation of the Lord" (cf. Matt 5:20; 7:21; 18:3).

The notion of the purity and sanctity of the temple was occasionally extended to include the entire city of Jerusalem as well. Isa 52:1 anticipates the day when no uncircumcised or unclean person (MT טָמֵא *ṭāmēʾ;* LXX ἀκάθαρτος) can enter Jerusalem (cf. Isa 35:8; 1QH 6:20–21). Similarly, 4Q*174* = 4QFlorilegium frags. 1–3, lines 3–4, interprets the temple (tr. García Martínez, *Dead Sea Scrolls,* 136):

> This (refers to) the house in which shall never enter [. . .] either the Ammonite, or the Moabite, or the Bastard, or the foreigner, or the proselyte, never, because there [he will reveal] to the holy ones.

The decree of Antiochus III prohibiting anyone ritually unclean from entering the temple or from bringing unclean animals or their skins into Jerusalem (Jos. *Ant.* 12.145–46; discussed by R. Marcus in *Josephus,* LCL, 7:761–64) now has a close parallel in 11QTemple 47:3–18, which extends a good measure of cultic purity of the temple to Jerusalem itself (Milgrom, *BASOR* 232 [1978] 27). According to 4QTemple 47:3–5 (tr. Vermes, *Dead Sea Scrolls*):

> The city which I will sanctify, causing my name and [my] sanctuar[y] to abide [in it], shall be holy and pure of all impurity [כול טמאה *kwl ṭmʾh*] with which they can become impure.

The phrase, כול טמאה *kôl ṭĕmēʾâ,* "all impurity," is virtually identical with the phrase πᾶν κοινόν, "anything unclean," here in Revelation (Fekkes, *Isaiah,* 274). In Rev 21:12, an angel was posted as a guard at each gate, perhaps with the implication that they will bar the entry of anything polluted or unclean, as well as anyone else unworthy of entering into the holy city (see *Comment* on 21:12). The term κοινός, used only here in Revelation, means "profane" or "ritually unclean" (*TDNT* 3:797); a close synonym is ἀκάθαρτος, "unclean, defiled," which occurs in Rev 16:13; 17:4; 18:2 (both terms occur together as synonyms in Acts 10:14). κοινός and ἀκάθαρτος denote ritual impurity, a central religious category in early Judaism (Lev 10:10; 1 Macc 1:47, 62; 4 Macc 7:6) carried over into early Christianity and eventually transformed into a exclusively moral category (Matt 15:11, 18, 20; Mark 7:2, 5, 15, 18, 20, 23; Heb 9:13; Acts 10:14, 15, 28; 11:8, 9; 21:28; Rom 14:14; Heb 10:29). In the OT the verb טָמֵא *ṭāmēʾ,* "to be unclean," is used in connection with various types of unclean animals (Lev 11; Deut 14; Ezek 4:14; Hos 9:4; see Rev 18:2), and more frequently it is used to characterize people who are unclean for a variety of reasons, including those who come into contact with a corpse (Num 19:11–22), those who have leprosy (Lev 13–14; Num 5:3), sexual intercourse (Lev 15:18), a discharge or emission of semen by a man (Lev 15:16–18, 32), and menstruation or parturition by a woman (Lev 15:19–24, 33; 4Q251 = 4QHalakhah^a frag. 3, lines 14–17; 4Q274 = 4QTohorot A 1 i 4–9). Ezekiel linked uncleanness with idols (Ezek 14:11; 20:7; 18:31; 22:3–4; 23:7, 13–17; 37:23). Various texts regard uncleanness as the result of moral transgression and not simply a ritual condition (Lev 16:16, 19; Isa 6:5; Lam 1:8–9; 4:15; Ezek 14:11; Zech 13:1–2).

Charles (2:174) argues that the phrase πᾶν κοινόν, "anything unclean," is problematic since the phrase οἱ γεγραμμένοι, "those inscribed" (in the book of life), v 27b, indicates that only *people* are intended. Thus Charles proposes that πᾶν κοινόν should really be πᾶς κοινός, "any unclean person," since כָּל־טָמֵא *kol-ṭāmē'* could be translated either "anything unclean" or "any unclean person." The discussion above, however, indicates that both ritually unclean persons and unclean things (i.e., things that are by definition unclean and transmit ritual impurity on contact) must be excluded from the eschatological temple or temple-city. Furthermore, unclean things cannot enter the city on their own volition but must be transported by people, i.e., οἱ γεγραμμένοι ἐν τῷ βιβλίῳ τῆς ζωῆς τοῦ ἀρνίου, "those inscribed in the Lamb's book of life." This line of thinking assumes, finally, that πᾶν κοινόν retains an exclusively cultic interpretation and is not used metaphorically in a moral sense, but it appears that the author uses πᾶν κοινόν in a comprehensive sense that includes both objects and persons (Lohmeyer, 176; Kraft, 273; Fekkes, *Isaiah*, 274).

27b καὶ ποιῶν βδέλυγμα καὶ ψεῦδος εἰ μὴ οἱ γεγραμμένοι ἐν τῷ βιβλίῳ τῆς ζωῆς τοῦ ἀρνίου, "that is, anyone who does what is abhorrent or false, / except those inscribed in the Lamb's book of life." If the conjunction καί functions here in an epexegetical or explanatory way (i.e., "that is"), the author is not using the phrase πᾶν κοινόν, "anything unclean," in a literal cultic sense but rather is interpreting it metaphorically in a moral sense of people who are immoral. Here the phrase ποιεῖν βδέλυγμα, "to do an abomination," reflects the OT Hebrew phrase עשׂה תועבה *'āśâ tô'ēbâ* (Lev 18:26, 27, 29; 20:13; Deut 12:31; 20:18; 1 Kgs 14:24; Jer 7:10; 32:35; 44:22; Ezek 33:26). An "abomination" usually involves illicit forms of sexual intercourse and idolatry. Similarly, the phrase ποιεῖν ψεῦδος, "to do a lie," i.e., "to lie," reflects the Hebrew phrase עשׂה שׁקר *'āśâ šeqer* (Jer 6:13; 8:8, 10; Hos 7:1). It is likely that the phrase "except those inscribed in the Lamb's book of life" was added during a final stage of composition.

22:1a καὶ ἔδειξέν μοι ποταμὸν ὕδατος ζωῆς λαμπρὸν ὡς κρύσταλλον, "He showed me a river of living water, sparkling like crystal." In vv 1–2, the New Jerusalem is described with imagery associated with the garden of Eden or Paradise in early Judaism, an association that was traditional (*2 Apoc. Bar.* 4:1–7; *1 Enoch* 90:33–36; *4 Ezra* 8:52; *T. Dan* 5:12–13, "saints shall refresh themselves in Eden, the righteous shall rejoice in the new Jerusalem"). However, the use of Paradise imagery to describe the New Jerusalem does not cohere particularly well with its earlier description as an enormous cube (Strathmann, *TDNT* 6:532).

The river of living water is based on an allusion to Ezek 47:1–12, which is elaborated in v 2. There is obviously a close connection between the "river of living water" and the "tree of life" (v 2a) located near the river. The two motifs of "trees of life" and "living waters" are also juxtaposed in 1QH 8:5–7:

> [For Thou didst set] a plantation
> of cypress, pine, and cedar for Thy glory,

trees of life [עצי חיים *ʿǎṣê ḥayyîm*] beside a mysterious fountain
  hidden among the trees by the water,
and they put out a shoot
  of the everlasting Plant.
But before they did so, they took root
  and sent out their roots to the watercourse
that its stem might be open to the living waters [למים חיים *lĕmayim ḥayyim*]
  and be one with the everlasting spring.

The phrase מין חיין *myn ḥyyn*, "living water," is found in a fragmentary context in the Qumran Aramaic document J 7, line 29 (= 11Q*18* = 11QNJ ar frag. 24), part of a description of the New Jerusalem (Beyer, *Ergänzungsband,* 103). In the gnostic *Book of Baruch,* quoted in Hippolytus *Ref.* 5.26–27, there is mention (in 5.26.2) of a ritual involving the drinking of "living water" (πίνει ἀπὸ τοῦ ζῶντος ὕδατος) from a "spring of living water" (πηγὴ ζῶντος ὕδατος), based on a distinction between the water below the firmament (στερέωμα), which is part of the evil creation, and the spiritually beneficial "living water" above the firmament (5.26.3). The two motifs of fountains of pure water and *fruit-bearing trees* are also found in Hellenistic descriptions of the afterlife; cf. Ps.-Plato *Axiochus* 371C (J. P. Hershbell, ed. *Pseudo-Plato, Axiochus* [Chico, CA: Scholars, 1981] 47), "So, then, all whom a good daimon inspired in life go to reside in a place of the pious, where the ungrudging seasons teem with fruits of every kind, where fountains of pure water flow, and where all kinds of meadows bloom with flowers of many colors."

1b ἐκπορευόμενον ἐκ τοῦ θρόνου τοῦ θεοῦ καὶ τοῦ ἀρνίου, "flowing from the throne of God and of the Lamb." The river flowing from the throne is an allusion to Ezekiel's vision of the miraculous temple river that flows east from the restored temple and is a symbol of extraordinary fecundity (Ezek 47:1–12; Zech 14:8; see Joel 3:18, which mentions "the fountain from Yahweh's house"). According to Gen 2:10 a river flowed out of Eden, and a few later texts mention a celestial river (*T. Abr.* [Rec. B] 8:3; *3 Apoc. Bar.* [Greek] 2:1), while many more texts speak of one or more rivers of *fire* (a theophanic symbol) that flow from the throne of God (see *Comment* on 15:2). An unattributed baraita says that in the world to come living water will flow from Jerusalem for the house of David and those who dwell in Jerusalem (*y. Šeqal.* 50a). The abundance of water flowing from the temple is part of several later stock descriptions of the temple (Joel 3:18[MT 4:18]; *Ep. Arist.* 89; Tacitus *Hist.* 5.12 refers to a *fons perennis aquae,* "a constant spring of water") as well as of the city of Jerusalem (Zech 14:8; Ps 46:4[MT 5]; 65:9[MT 10] refers to "the river of God"; Isa 33:21; Sir 50:3; Alexander Polyhistor, according to Eusebius *Praep. evang.* 9.35–37 [452b–453c], quotes three ancient authors who mention the abundance of water in Jerusalem, probably referring to the Siloam tunnel). Philo quotes Ps 46:4(MT 46:4; LXX 45:4), referring to the river that makes glad the city of God, to argue that since there are no rivers nor a sea near Jerusalem, the statement should be understood allegorically. According to Simons (*Jerusalem,* 48 n. 3), the "visionary springs" of the prophets (Ezek 47:1–2; Joel 4:18; Zech 13:1; 14:8) only indicate that the absence of "living water" from Jerusalem will be compensated for in the abundance in the idyllic future.

The water supply of the historical City of David was dependent upon two springs in the neighborhood of the Southeast Hill, or one spring and one well (Simons, *Jerusalem,* 47–49; Amiran, "Water Supply," 75–78). The most important were the

Spring of the Steps (referred to as Gihon in the OT; 1 Kgs 1:38; 2 Chr 33:14; Sir 48:17; Jos. *Ant.* 7.347; Simons, *Jerusalem,* 163–88; Finegan, *Archaeology,* 112–15; Amiran, "Water Supply," 75–78) and the Well of Jacob (referred to as En-Rogel or the Spring of Rogel in the OT: Josh 15:7; 18:16; 2 Sam 17:7; 1 Kgs 1:9; cf. Jos. *Ant.* 7.354; perhaps also referred to once as the Dragon Well in Neh 2:13; see Simons, *Jerusalem,* 158–63; Amiran, "Water Supply," 75–78). Since the Gihon was located outside the city walls, Hezekiah constructed an aqueduct called the Siloam Tunnel to convey the water to a pool inside the city (2 Kgs 20:20; 2 Chr 32:30; Jos. *J.W.* 5.140; John 9:7, 11). The author of Revelation cannot have the river flowing from the temple, however, since there is no temple in the New Jerusalem (21:22), so he substitutes the throne of God for the temple.

While the phrase "and from the Lamb" probably reflects an expansion of an earlier text, the present form of the text (like 3:21) presupposes the christological use of Ps 110:1, so frequently quoted or alluded to in the NT but absent from Revelation: "The Lord said to my lord, 'Sit at my right hand.'" If "and of the Lamb" is a later expansion, it may well be derived from Rev 3:21, where sharing the throne of the Father is mentioned but the Lamb imagery is absent. Here a single throne is apparently in view, shared by both God and the Lamb (on the *bisellium,* "double throne," see *Comment* on 3:21). By sharing the throne of God, the Lamb also shares the sovereignty of God. This is the second of three instances in Revelation in which the sharing of a single throne by God and Christ or God and the Lamb is mentioned (3:21; 22:1, 3). While the proleptic scene in 7:17 implies that the Lamb is seated on the throne, there is no clear reference in Revelation to the Lamb actually being seated upon a throne or enthroned (with the exception of 3:21) until this point in the narrative (n.b. that despite the attempt of some scholars to regard Rev 5 as an enthronement scene, there is no clear reference there to the enthronement of the Lamb). Beskow suggests that Revelation reflects the notion of the Parousia enthronement of Christ, for he is not given the royal titles "King of kings and Lord of lords" (Rev 17:14; 19:16) except in connection with his conquest of the enemies of God (*Rex Gloriae,* 141). However, there is no hint that these titles are conferred only at the conclusion of his conquest, and Christ has already been styled "the ruler of the kings of the earth" in 1:5.

2a ἐν μέσῳ τῆς πλατείας αὐτῆς καὶ τοῦ ποταμοῦ ἐντεῦθεν καὶ ἐκεῖθεν ξύλον ζωῆς, "down the center of the main street of the city. On each side of the river there were trees of life." This is an allusion to Ezek 47:12 (continued in vv 2b and 2c), which the author has subtly modified by changing "all kinds of trees" on both sides of the river flowing from the sanctuary mentioned in Ezek 47:7, 12 to the collective term ξύλον ζωῆς, "tree(s) of life." The term ξύλον, "tree," is a collective referring to numerous trees found along both banks of the river (Swete, 299; Beckwith, 765; Bousset [1906] 452; Charles, 2:176). Examples of the use of the singular עֵץ *ʿēṣ* or ξύλον used collectively are found in Gen 1:11–12; 3:8; Lev 26:20; 1 Chr 16:32; 2 Chr 7:13; Eccl 2:5; Jer 17:2. According to Andreas (*Comm. in Apoc.* 22:2; Schmid, *Studien* 1:253), "It is customary in many places in Scripture to use the singular ξύλον for many trees."

The tree of life is mentioned five times in Revelation (2:7; 22:2[2x], 14, 19; see *Comment* on 2:7). In *Pss. Sol.* 14:3, the "trees of life" in Paradise are metaphors for the faithful (see also 1QH 6:14–19; 10:25–26; *Odes Sol.* 11.16; *Gos. Truth* 36.35–37); Andreas understands the phrase ξύλον ζωῆς collectively of Christians who share in *the* tree of life (Schmid, *Studien* 1:251). For the metaphor of the faithful as trees, see Ps 92:12–13; Isa 61:3; *1 Enoch* 93:2; *Odes Sol.* 1.2; 11.1.

In Lucian's description of the idyllic conditions on the Island of the Blessed in *Verae historiae* 13 (LCL tr.), he observes that "The grape-vines yield twelve vintages a year, bearing every month [καὶ κατὰ μῆνα ἕκαστον καρποφοροῦσιν; note that this last phrase is almost verbally identical with Rev 22:2]; the pomegranates, apples and other fruit-trees were said to bear thirteen times a year, for in one month, the Minoan, they bear twice." Another passage influenced by Ezek 47:12 is *1 Enoch* 25:4–6 (tr. Knibb, *Enoch*):

> And this beautiful fragrant tree—and no (creature of) flesh has authority to touch it until the great judgement when he will take vengeance on all *and will bring (everything) to a consummation* for ever—*this* will be given to the righteous and humble. From its fruit life will be given to the chosen; towards the north it will be planted, in a holy place, by the house of the Lord, the Eternal King. Then they will rejoice with joy and be glad in the holy (place); they will each draw the fragrance of it into their bones, and they will live a long life on earth, as your father lived, and in their days sorrow and pain and toil and punishment will not touch them.

Olson argues that John was dependent on both Ezek 47 and *1 Enoch* 25 (*CBQ* 59 [1977] 499–500).

2b ποιοῦν καρποὺς δώδεκα κατὰ μῆνα ἕκαστον ἀποδιδοῦν τὸν καρπὸν αὐτοῦ, "producing twelve kinds of fruit, each yielding its fruit each month." This is an allusion to the trees of Ezek 47:12, "they will bear fresh fruit every month," though here the trees even more miraculously bear twelve *different* kinds of fruit, one kind each month, while in Ezek 47:12 the trees simply yield a fresh crop of fruit each month. Miraculous fecundity is often associated with the eschaton (*1 Enoch* 10:19; *2 Apoc. Bar.* 29:5; Papias according to Irenaeus *Adv. haer.* 5.33.3; *Apoc. Paul* 22). This conception is very similar to the Greek utopian notion of αὐτομάτως, in which the earth *by itself* produced nourishment for the human race without the necessity of human labor (Hesiod, *Works and Days*, 118; Diodorus 2.57.1; 2.59.1; cf. Mark 4:28).

2c καὶ τὰ φύλλα τοῦ ξύλου εἰς θεραπείαν τῶν ἐθνῶν, "The leaves of the tree were for the healing of the nations." This clause is also an allusion to Ezek 47:12 ("Their fruit will be for food, and their leaves for healing"), to which the author has added "of the nations." The allusion is simply mechanical, however, since there is no real place in the eschatological scheme of Revelation for "the healing of the nations" construed as their conversion. The two motifs of the fruit of Paradise and healing are also linked in 4 Ezra 7:123, which speaks of "paradise and its imperishable fruit, the source of perfect satisfaction and healing." In a Christian interpolation into *T. Sim.* 7.2, the one who is God and man "will save all the Gentiles and the race of Israel" (see *T. Jos.* 19:6; *T. Benj.* 3:8). Although ξύλον, "tree," was understood collectively of many trees in v 2a, here suddenly the author-editor refers to "*the* tree," recalling "the tree of life" mentioned in 2:7; 22:14, 19.

3a καὶ πᾶν κατάθεμα οὐκ ἔσται ἔτι, "And 'the curse of war' will no longer exist." A series of future verbs in vv 3–5 (a similar series was used in 21:24–27 and then interrupted by 22:1–1) indicates that the author-editor has shifted from describing what he has seen in a vision to a prophetic scenario that he expects to take place in the New Jerusalem in the future. The problem with this unexpected phrase (which is equally unexpected in the context of Zech 14:11, to which it alludes) is the meaning of κατάθεμα, which occurs only here in Revelation. It is virtually synonymous with ἀνάθεμα, "curse," and κατάρα, "curse" (κατάθεμα and ἀνάθεμα are distinguished in a late inscription from Attica, though the difference between the terms is not clear; see Horsley, *New Docs* 4:264). κατάθεμα can mean a "curse" (Audollent *Defixionum* 22.23), "accursed thing," or "accursed person" (Ps.-Clement of Rome *Contestatio* 4.3), though it is more likely that the meaning of κατάθεμα here is shaped by the allusion to Zech 14:11, καὶ οὐκ ἔσται ἀνάθεμα ἔτι, "and there is no longer any curse." This is a literal translation of the Hebrew וחרם לא יהיה־עוד *wĕḥērem lōʾ yihyeh-ʿôd*, in which חרם *ḥērem* (meaning "devoted to destruction," "accursed thing," "ban") is regularly translated by ἀνάθεμα in the LXX (*GELS*, 28). Originally חרם *ḥērem* was a ritual whereby the enemy was devoted to destruction, a major constituent element of holy-war theology (Lohfink, *TDOT* 5:180–99). According to the apocalyptic scenario in Zech 14:1–11, the nations partially succeed in destroying Jerusalem and her people but are finally repulsed by Yahweh (Zech 14:1–5). Victory is followed by an idyllic depiction of eschatological Jerusalem, from the midst of which an enormous river flows (cf. Rev 22:2) and in which "never again shall the ban of destruction be upon her" (Hanson, *Apocalyptic*, 382); i.e., never again will hostile nations attempt to destroy Jerusalem (n.b. that the phrase לא יהיה עוד *lōʾ yihyeh ʿôd*, "there will never again be," reflects the covenant language of Gen 9:11; cf. Isa 54:9). חרם *ḥērem* is therefore used in Zech 14:11 as a metaphor for a genocidal form of war that intends nothing less than the complete slaughter and destruction of the enemy (see Isa 34:2; Jer 31:40), and the promise that it will never again occur is couched in the covenantal promise language of Gen 9:11. Therefore it appears that κατάθεμα is the author's way of interpreting חרם *ḥērem*. Thus the word refers not generally to curses, accursed things, or persons but specifically to the promise that "the curse of war" will no longer exist. The phrase οὐκ ἔσται ἔτι, "will no longer exist," has a close parallel in 21:1, where it is said that the sea οὐκ ἔστιν ἔτι, "exists no longer."

3b καὶ ὁ θρόνος τοῦ θεοῦ καὶ τοῦ ἀρνίου ἐν αὐτῇ ἔσται, "the throne of God and of the Lamb will be in the city." On the throne shared by God and the Lamb, see *Comments* on 3:21 and 22:1. This phrase is somewhat redundant since "the throne of God and of the Lamb" has already been mentioned as the source of the river of the water of life in 22:1. The future indicative ἔσται, "will be," reflects the prophetic tenor of the passage. As in v 1, the phrase "and of the Lamb" is probably a later gloss.

3c καὶ οἱ δοῦλοι αὐτοῦ λατρεύσουσιν αὐτῷ, "and his servants will worship him." This is the first reference to the inhabitants of the city (only pilgrimages by kings and nations have thus far been mentioned in 21:24, 26). Access to the city by the righteous is mentioned in 22:14, and perhaps 22:17b, and the notion is expressed negatively in 22:19. A gnosticized form of this tradition is found in *Pistis Sophia* 1.32, 35 (ed. Schmidt-Till, p. 31, lines 35–38 = ed. Schmidt-MacDermot, p. 52), in which it is said that God will save the souls of the Gnostics out of all matter and a city will be prepared for them in the light and they will dwell in that city. The notion of God's *servants* giving *worship* to him occurs in Ps 22:23; Isa 49:7; Dan 3:28; it is used in a negative sense of slaves worshiping idols in *Diogn.* 2:15.

4a καὶ ὄψονται τὸ πρόσωπον αὐτοῦ, "And they will see his face." The phrase "seeing the face of God" is a metaphor in Judaism and early Christianity for a full awareness of the presence and power of God (Job 33:26; Pss 10:11; 17:15; 3 John 11), for worshiping God in the temple (Ps 42:2), or for seeing God in the context of a prophetic vision (Isa 6:1; see *TDNT* 5:329–30). In Hellenistic Judaism "seeing

God" can refer to the mystical vision of God perceived mentally or spiritually (Philo *Vit. Cont.* 11–12; *Mut.* 81–82; *Abr.* 57–58; [Philo derives this notion from Platonic tradition]; Origen *Contra Cels.* 7.33–34; see *TDNT* 5:329–40). The name "Israel" was construed as "one who sees God" because he is "the firstborn of every living being which is given life by God" (*Orat. Jos.* 189 [Denis, *Fragmenta*, 61], a midrash on Gen 32, where Jacob claims in v 30 that he has seen God face to face [cf. 4Q*158* = 4QRP^a frags. 1–2, line 10]; cf. Philo *Mut.* 81–82; J. Z. Smith, "Prayer," 253–94).

In early Judaism and early Christianity the privilege of seeing God is often considered an eschatological blessing (Ps 84:7; Matt 5:8; 1 John 3:2; Heb 12:14; *Jub.* 1:28; 4 Ezra 7:91, 98; *1 Enoch* 102:8; cf. 1 Cor 13:12), while in the Greco-Roman world mention is made of the post-mortem ability of souls to behold the gods (Plutarch *De Iside* 78). Apuleius claims that during his initiation into the mysteries of Isis he approached the gods above and below and "worshipped them face to face [*et adoravi de proxumo*]" (*Metamorphoses* 11.24; Griffiths, *Isis-Book*, 99), a phrase close to the Pauline way of expressing the eschatological vision of God in 1 Cor 13:12, "then we will see face to face [πρόσωπον πρὸς πρόσωπον]." One strand of biblical tradition insists that Moses was forbidden to see God (Exod 33:20–23; cf. 3:6), the sight of whom would be fatal (Exod 3:6; 20:19; cf. *Mart. Isa.* 3.9 [Denis, *Fragmenta*, 112]), and in the NT there is a strong insistence that no one has ever seen God (John 1:18; 1 John 4:12; 1 Tim 6:15–16). According to Isa 6:2, even the seraphim hide their faces from God (for rabbinic traditions to the effect that neither the angels nor the living creatures can see God or hear his voice, but only the pious after they die, see Ginzberg, *Legends* 3:137–38; 6:57 n. 296), though according to Matt 18:10, reflecting Jewish tradition, angels can see God.

One aspect of the transcendence and greatness of God is the difficulty or impossibility of seeing him. According to Ps.-Orpheus 21–22, 24 (the intervening line 23 is a later interpolation), "I myself cannot see him; for around him a cloud has been fixed. For all mortals have mortal pupils in their eyes, too weak to see Zeus the ruler of all" (cf. *Sib. Or.* 3.17; 4.10–11; see commentary on Ps.-Orpheus by *FHJA*, vol. 4, ad loc.). In the magical curse of Sabinus, he refers to the "Son of the great God whom man never beheld [τὸν οὐδέποτ᾽ ἔδρακεν ἀνήρ]" (see Daniel-Maltomini, *Supplementum Magicum* 2:59, line 13). In Greek mythic literary tradition, human beings found it impossible to look gods in the face (*Odyssey* 16.179; *Hymn to Aphrodite* 1.181–82), and Semele's unfortunate insistence that she see the full majesty of Zeus proved fatal (Apollodorus 3.4.3; Ovid *Metam.* 3.253–315; Hyginus *Fab.* 179). The impossibility of seeing God is ascribed to his transcendence and the resultant disparity between God and people; it is often also expressed in terms of the *invisibility* of God (Xenophon *Mem.* 4.3.13–14; Jos. *Ant.* 6.189; *J.W.* 7.346; Rom 1:20; Col 1:15; 1 Tim 1:17; Heb 11:27 [Moses "saw him who is invisible (ἀόρατον)"]; *2 Clem.* 20:5; Ign. *Magn.* 3.2; *Pol.* 3:7; *Diogn.* 7:2; Tatian *Orat.* 4; Aristides *Apol.* 4.1; Origen *De princ.* 1.2.6; cf. Deut 4:12, 15, where the Israelites are said to have heard the voice of God, although they saw no form). Yet Sir 45:5 asserts that God gave his commandments to Moses face to face (κατὰ πρόσωπον). According to Johannine thought, however, Christ alone has seen God (John 6:46), and those who have seen Christ have the possibility of seeing God (Exod 24:9–11; Num 12:8). Other strands of OT tradition refer to various individuals who have seen God (Gen 32:31 [Jacob: "I have seen God face to face"]; Exod 24:2–11; 33:11; Num 12:8; Deut 4:12; Judg 13:22; Sir 17:13), all of which are softened or avoided altogether when interpreted by Philo and the targums (Hanson, "Seeing

God," 557–68). In rabbinic literature this softening of the expression "to see God" is expressed as "to see the face of the Shekinah" or "to greet the face of the Shekinah" (see the extensive collection of material in Str-B, 1:206–15).

4b καὶ τὸ ὄνομα αὐτοῦ ἐπὶ τῶν μετώπων αὐτῶν, "and his name will be on their foreheads." Reference to the seal of God on the foreheads of the 144,000 was made in 7:3 and 14:1; cf. 3:12 (see *Comment* there). The phrase is ambiguous since the pronoun αὐτοῦ, "his," could refer to either God or the Lamb (Prigent, "Trace de liturgie," 165–72), or (less plausibly) to both (Holtz, *Christologie,* 202).

5a καὶ νὺξ οὐκ ἔσται ἔτι καὶ οὐκ ἔχουσιν χρείαν φωτὸς λύχνου καὶ φωτὸς ἡλίου, ὅτι κύριος ὁ θεὸς φωτίσει ἐπ᾽ αὐτούς, "There will no longer be any night, and people will have no need for lamp light or sunlight, because the Lord God will illumine them." This is very probably an allusion to Isa 60:19:

> The sun shall be no more your light by day,
> nor for brightness shall the moon give you light by night;
> but the Lord will be your everlasting light,
> and your God will be your glory.

Num 6:25, part of the traditional priestly blessing, contains a solar metaphor: "the Lord make his face to shine upon you" (cf. Ps 118:27, "The Lord is God, and he has given us light"). The priestly blessing is alluded to in 4Q542=4QTQahat ar 1 i 1, "And He [God] will shine as a Light upon you and He will make known to you His great Name" (tr. Eisenman-Wise, *Scrolls,* 150). In the OT, the "shining face" of God is a metaphor for divine favor (Pss 4:7; 31:17; 44:4; 67:2; 80:4, 8, 20; 89:16; 119:35; see M. Noth, *Numbers* [London: SCM, 1968] 59). The priestly blessing is written on two silver plaques or amulets from Ketef Hinnom in Jerusalem, dating to the latter half of the seventh century B.C. (A. Yardeni, "Remarks on the Priestly Blessing on Two Ancient Amulets from Jerusalem," *VT* 41 (1991) 176–85; Davies, *AHI* 4:301, 302). See also Isa 60:2. 4 Ezra 7:38–42 contains a lengthy list of twenty-seven things that will no longer exist in the day of judgment (*sun, moon, stars,* cloud, thunder, lightning, wind, water, air, darkness, evening, *morning,* summer, spring, heat, winter, frost, cold, hail, rain, dew, *noon,* night, *dawn, shining, brightness,* and *light*), "but only the splendor of the glory of the Most High, by which all shall see what has been determined for them." The italicized natural phenomena center on the theme of light (this list was very likely inspired by Gen 8:22 and Eccl 12:2 as well as by Isa 60:19–20).

5b καὶ βασιλεύσουσιν εἰς τοὺς αἰῶνας τῶν αἰώνων, "and they will reign for ever and ever." The subject of the verb βασιλεύσουσιν, "will reign," is of course the servants of God mentioned in v 3. They "reign forever" in the sense that they participate as worshiping servants in the eternal rule of God. The reign of the people of God on the earth was referred to in 5:10, and the resurrected martyrs will reign with Christ on the earth during the millennium (20:6). The participation of God's people in his eternal rule is already anticipated in Dan 7:18, 27 (cf. 1 Cor 6:2).

6a καὶ εἶπέν μοι οὗτοι οἱ λόγοι πιστοὶ καὶ ἀληθινοί, "Then he said to me, 'These words are faithful and true.'" Although many interpreters argue that 22:6–21 constitutes the concluding section of Revelation (Swete, 302; Bousset [1906] 455; Beckwith, 290–91; 771; Caird, 281–82; Kraft, 276; Prigent, 348–49; Hellholm, "Genre," 52; Roloff [ET] 248–49; Vanni, *La struttura letteraria,* 107–15, 298–302; T. Collins, *Apocalypse 22:6–21,* 10–12), the phrase καὶ εἶπέν μοι, "then he said to me," does not appear to signal the beginning of a new textual unit (22:6–9 constitutes a transitional section, which concludes 21:9–22:5 and introduces the epilogue in 22:10–20). One problem with this clause is determining whether it refers to the entire book of Revelation (Prigent, 351) or just to the previous unit of text (21:9–22:5). In the context, it seems that the speaker is the bowl angel who appears in 21:9, 15 (perhaps the same one mentioned in 17:1, 7) and provides John with a guided tour of the New Jerusalem (Prigent, 351). However, the parallelism between 22:6 and 1:1 suggests that the speaker is the *angelus interpres*, "interpreting angel," who appears in 1:1 and 22:6–9 only (Lange, 259); i.e., this is part of the last revision of Revelation, in which the author tries to equate the angelic guide of 21:9–22:5 with the *angelus interpres* of 1:1. Some have argued that the speaker is Christ (Bousset [1906] 457; Charles, 2:217; Lohmeyer, 177; Lohse, 114; Kavanagh, *Apocalypse*, 10), a proposal supported by v 7, which can only be attributed to the exalted Christ.

This statement functions as an oath formula that guarantees the truth of what has preceded. The same phrase with variations ("faithful and" is omitted in 19:9) is found three times in Revelation (here; 19:9; 21:5), though the phrase μαρτυρῶ ἐγώ, "I testify," functions in precisely the same way (see *Comment* on 22:18). A close parallel occurs toward the end of the fragmentary revelatory discourse of Parmenides *On Nature* where the unnamed goddess who has revealed philosophical truths to Parmenides concludes by expounding the doctrine of being (frag. B8, lines 50–51, ἐν τῷ σοι παύω πιστὸν λόγον ἠδὲ νόημα ἀμφὶς ἀληθείης, "Here I conclude for you my reliable account and thought concerning the truth" [Diels-Kranz, *FVS* 1:239]). It is also similar to Mark 13:31, which is arguably the solemn conclusion of the eschatological discourse in Mark 13 (Hahn, "Menschensohn," 247; Pesch, *Markus* 2:309).

6b καὶ ὁ κύριος ὁ θεὸς τῶν πνευμάτων τῶν προφητῶν, "and the Lord, the God of the spirits of the prophets." Though this phrase is not without interpretive difficulties (see below), it clearly indicates that God sovereignly determines and controls the utterances of his prophetic servants so that what they say and write is both reliable and true (thus confirming the divine legitimation of Revelation; cf. *Comment* on v 6a). πνεῦμα, "spirit," is widely used as an anthropological term for the highest faculty of human beings (1 Cor 7:34; 14:14; 2 Cor 7:1; 1 Thess 5:23; a less than satisfactory discussion is found in *TDNT* 6:434–36). Used in the plural, πνεύματα, "spirits," refers to the psychic faculty of individual prophets rather than to the Spirit of God, though it is implied that the individual human spirit is the vehicle for the prophetic activity of the Spirit of God. The meaning is, therefore, the same as in 1 Cor 14:32, where Paul claims that "the spirits of prophets [πνεύματα προφητῶν] are subject to prophets." There is an interesting parallel in 1QH 20:11–13 = 12:11–13 (tr. García Martínez, *Dead Sea Scrolls*, 356):

> And I, the Instructor, have known you, my God,
> through the spirit which you gave to me,
> and I have listened loyally to your wonderful secret
> through your holy spirit.
> You have opened within me
> knowledge of the mystery of your wisdom.

The phrase also has a relatively close verbal parallel in LXX Num 27:16 (and 16:22), κύριος ὁ θεὸς τῶν πνευμάτων καὶ πάσης σαρκός, "Lord God of the spirits and of all flesh," which differs through the addition of a καί, "and," not found in Hebrew, which reads: יְהוָה אֱלֹהֵי הָרוּחֹת לְכָל־בָּשָׂר YHWH *'ĕlōhê hārûḥōt lĕkol-bāśār,* "the Lord God of the spirits of all flesh." *Num. Rab.* 21.15 interprets this phrase to mean that God is acquainted with the spirit of each person and therefore knows the role for which they are particularly suited. Variations of the phrase from Num 16:22 and 27:16 occur only occasionally in subsequent early Jewish and early Christian literature, though always with the emphasis on divine sovereignty. In 2 Macc 3:24, God is called ὁ τῶν πνευμάτων καὶ πάσης ἐξουσίας δυνάστης, "the ruler over spirits and over every authority," using two terms for supernatural or angelic beings. In *1 Enoch* 37–71, the so-called Parables of Enoch, composed ca. mid-first century A.D., God is frequently referred to as "Lord of spirits" (e.g., 37:2; 39:12), and similarly, God is called the "Father of spirits" in Heb 12:9.

6c ἀπέστειλεν τὸν ἄγγελον αὐτοῦ δεῖξαι τοῖς δούλοις αὐτοῦ, "sent his angel to reveal to his servants." The rhetoric of this passage suggests that the angel referred to is not the bowl angel mentioned in 21:9, 15 (or, if they are identical, the bowl angel mentioned there and in 17:1, 7) since that bowl angel is the speaker. It appears more likely that the angel referred to here is the essentially literary figure of the *angelus interpres* first mentioned in 1:1, who apparently is the speaker in 22:6, 8–11.

Several scholars have argued that the term "servants" here, as elsewhere in Revelation (only in 10:7 and perhaps 11:18), is a synonym for "prophets" (on the phrase "my servants the prophets," see *Comment* on 10:7). While the phrase "servants of God" sometimes refers to Christians generally (1:1; 2:20; 7:3; 19:2, 5; 22:3), there are other places where prophets are specifically in view; 10:7 refers to OT prophets, while 11:18 probably refers to early Christian prophets. The possessive pronoun αὐτοῦ, "his," here clearly refers to God, as it probably also does in the parallel phrase "his servants" in 1:1.

Rev 22:6 and 22:16 are doublets (Spitta, 221), as this comparison reveals:

Rev 22:6	*Rev 22:16*
καὶ ὁ κύριος ὁ θεὸς And the Lord, the God	Ἐγὼ Ἰησοῦς, I, Jesus,
τῶν πνευμάτων τῶν προφητῶν of the spirits of the prophets,	
ἀπέστειλεν τὸν ἄγγελον αὐτοῦ sent his angel	ἔπεμψα τὸν ἄγγελόν μου sent my angel
δεῖξαι to reveal	μαρτυρῆσαι to attest
	ὑμῖν ταῦτα this message to you
τοῖς δούλοις αὐτοῦ to his servants	ἐπὶ ταῖς ἐκκλησίαις for the benefit of the churches.
ἃ δεῖ γενέσθαι ἐν τάχει what must soon happen.	

The major differences are that 22:6 is theocentric (just as 17:1–19:10 concludes in 19:9 that "these are the true words of *God*"), while 22:16 is Christocentric, and 22:6 is in the third person, while 22:16 is in the first person. The common features, however, are many: (1) Both passages emphasize the divine sender of revelation. (2) In both passages the divine revealer is the subject of a verb meaning "to send." (3) In both passages the means whereby the revelation was communicated is described as "my messenger." (4) In both passages the content of the revelatory message is mentioned, i.e., "what must soon happen" (22:6), while ταῦτα, "these things," is ambiguous. (5) Finally, the recipients of revelation are specified in both passages by the ambiguous expression "my servants" in 22:6 and by the more complex phrases "to you" and "for the churches" in 22:16. More broadly, when the two passages are compared, *both* have similarities with 1:1–2, where the two ultimate sources of revelation are reconciled by including *both* God and Jesus Christ in the revelatory chain.

6d ἃ δεῖ γενέσθαι ἐν τάχει, "what must soon happen." This phrase is a verbatim repetition of the corresponding phrase in 1:1 (cf. 1:19; 4:1) and is part of the final edition, which the author used to frame the book (these allusions to Dan 2:29 occur only in the Second Edition of Revelation). The phrase is also an allusion to LXX Dan 2:29, where Daniel tells Nebuchadnezzar that God alone can reveal the meaning of his dream: ὁ ἀνακαλύπτων μυστήρια ἐδήλωσέ σοι ἃ δεῖ γενέσθαι, "The one who reveals mysteries has made known to you what must happen" (cf. Theod Dan 2:29). While this passage in Daniel emphasizes the *necessity* of the eschatological plan of God, the element of the *imminence* of its fulfillment is absent, doubtless because of the pseudepigraphical character of the book (cf. Dan 12:4). The same emphasis on the necessity of the occurrence of eschatological events with the absence of imminence is found in the Olivet discourse, where Jesus (in an allusion to Dan 2:29) is presented as saying δεῖ γενέσθαι, ἀλλ᾽ οὔπω τὸ τέλος, "[these events] must happen, but the end is not yet" (Mark 13:7 = Matt 24:6 = Luke 21:9). The impersonal verb δεῖ, "it is necessary," is occasionally used in eschatological contexts in the NT for the necessity of eschatological events, including those involving the life of Jesus (Matt 26:54; Mark 9:11 = Matt 17:10; Mark 13:10; Luke 22:37; 24:25–26; *TDNT* 2: 23–24).

7a καὶ ἰδοὺ ἔρχομαι ταχύ, "Indeed, I will come soon." The demonstrative particle ἰδού, "indeed, behold," functions here as a marker to underscore the truth and reliability of the saying that immediately follows (see *Comment* on 1:7a). The focal element of this phrase, ἔρχομαι ταχύ, "I will come soon," is found only in Revelation in early Christian literature, where it occurs five times (2:16; 3:11; 22:7, 12, 20), with two overlapping meanings (see *Comment* on 2:16). The Parousia is clearly meant here and in 22:12, 20.

The ritual impatience of magicians is reflected in many ancient magical texts. Many spells end with various permutations of the formula ἤδη ἤδη, ταχὺ ταχύ, "now, now! quick quick!" (*PGM* III.123–24; IV.1245, 1593, 1924, 2037, 2098). This impatience can also accompany invocations to a god or daimon to "come quickly" (*PGM* I.89–90; IV.236–37; VI.14; VII.248–49, 329ff.), by which is meant a ritual theophany whereby the attending divinity places himself or herself at the service of the practitioner for a variety of tasks. Yet in Revelation it is not *John* who impatiently commands Jesus to come; it is the exalted Jesus who uses formulas typical of magical revelation to announce his own coming, thereby reducing John to a passive role in both the reception of revelation and in responding affirmatively to the eschatological promise of Jesus.

7b μακάριος ὁ τηρῶν τοὺς λόγους τῆς προφητείας τοῦ βιβλίου τούτου, "Blessed is the one who obeys the message of this prophetic book." This is the sixth of seven beatitudes or makarisms in Revelation (see 1:3; 14:13; 16:15; 19:9; 20:6; 22:14; for a discussion of their form see *Form/Structure/Setting* on 1:1–3). In *Apoc. Paul* 51 (tr. Hennecke-Schneemelcher, *NTA* 2:797), Christ appears to Paul and the assembled disciples and says:

> Amen, Amen, I tell you, Paul, that whoever will take care of this apocalypse, and will write it and set it down as a testimony for the generations to come, to him I shall not show the underworld with its bitter weeping, until the second generation of his seed. And whoever reads with faith, I shall bless him and his house. Whoever scoffs at the words of this apocalypse, I will punish him.

8a κἀγὼ Ἰωάννης ὁ ἀκούων καὶ βλέπων ταῦτα, "It was I, John, who heard and saw these visions." This is the concluding signature of John, who names himself three times earlier (1:1, 4, 9; see *Comment* on 1:1). The conjunction of terms for *hearing and seeing* in this guarantee of the veracity of the visions contained in Revelation reflects the widespread ancient view that the only reliable access to knowledge of past and present events is through the two senses of hearing and sight (cf. 1 John 1:1–3; Aune, *New Testament*, 81–82). Terms for "seeing" and "hearing" are frequently joined together in the OT and early Judaism as a way of summarizing sense perception (Prov 20:12; Cant 2:14; 2 Kgs 7:18; Isa 18:3; 21:3; 32:3; Jer 4:21; Jos. *J.W.* 6.213), and in prayer contexts God is often asked to "see" and "hear" the plight and request of the petitioner (2 Kgs 19:16; Isa 37:17; Neh 9:9; Dan 9:18; Job 35:13). This conjunction of terms for seeing and hearing is not common in Greek and Latin literature. Based on this usage, verbs for seeing and hearing are juxtaposed in contexts of prophetic or relevatory experiences as in Jer 23:18 (to which Rev 22:8 might be alluding), "Who has stood in the council of the Lord that he should see [וַיֵּרֶא *wĕyēreʾ*; εἶδεν] and hear [וְיִשְׁמַע *wĕyišmaʿ*; ἤκουσεν] his word?" (cf. Num 24:15–16; Deut 18:16; Acts 22:14; Jos. *Ant.* 4.43). The senses of sight and hearing also figure prominently in the introduction to Gk. *1 Enoch* 1:2 (tr. Knibb, *Enoch*):

> And Enoch answered and said: (there was) a righteous man whose eyes were opened by the Lord, and he saw a holy vision in the heavens which the angels showed to me. And I heard [ἤκουσα] everything from them, and I understood what I saw [θεωρῶν].

A similar guarantee of the authenticity of a vision occurs in the late *Apoc. Zeph.* B (Sahidic frag.) 7, "Truly, I, Zephaniah, saw these things in my vision" (tr. O. S. Wintermute, *OTP* 1:508). According to Lefort, this statement was found at the conclusion of the *Apocalypse of Zephaniah*, which has survived only in fragments (T. Lefort, *Les manuscrits coptes de l'Université de Louvain* [Louvain: Louvain UP, 1940] 79–80).

8b καὶ ὅτε ἤκουσα καὶ ἔβλεψα, ἔπεσα προσκυνῆσαι ἔμπροσθεν τῶν ποδῶν τοῦ ἀγγέλου τοῦ δεικνύοντός μοι ταῦτα, "And when I heard and saw them, I fell to worship before the feet of the angel who revealed them to me." The verbs ἀκούειν, "to hear," and βλέπειν, "to see," are repeated here in a temporal clause introduced by ὅτε, "when," though normal Greek style would require participial constructions. On

John's attempt to worship the *angelus interpres,* see *Comment* on 19:10. On the combination of the two verbs πίπτειν, "to fall," and προσκυνεῖν, "to prostrate oneself before, worship," see *Comment* on 4:10. The verb δεικνύναι, "to show, reveal" with ὁ ἄγγελος, "the angel," as subject is also used to introduce this concluding section in v 6. Elsewhere in Revelation it is used to describe the revelatory task of the *angelus interpres* in 1:1, 4:1, 21:9, 10, 22:1 (see *Comment* on 21:9). The plural pronoun ταῦτα, "them," undoubtedly refers to the entire visionary portion of Revelation (1:9–22:9).

9a καὶ λέγει μοι· ὅρα μή, "But he said to me, 'Don't do that!'" The phrase ὅρα μή, "Watch what you're doing!" is an ellipsis that involves one of two different grammatical constructions, though the missing verb makes it impossible to decide which construction is involved. The same idiom occurs in 19:10. ὅρα is a second-person singular present imperative from ὁρᾶν, "to see," while the verb with μή, "not," is not expressed. If the elided verb is understood as an aorist subjunctive, i.e., a subjunctive of prohibition (e.g., μὴ ποιήσῃς, "do not do"), then μή introduces an object clause, i.e., "Watch, lest you do [such-and-such]." If the elided verb is understood as an imperative (e.g., μὴ ποίησον, "do not do"), this might be an example of asyndeton, i.e., the juxtaposition of two imperatives without a connective particle (A. T. Robertson, *Grammar,* 949; BDR § 461; Burton, *Syntax,* § 209), i.e., "Watch! Don't do it!" (cf. Matt 24:6, ὁρᾶτε μὴ θροεῖσθε, "Watch! Don't be disturbed!").

9b σύνδουλός σού εἰμι καὶ τῶν ἀδελφῶν σου τῶν προφητῶν καὶ τῶν τηρούντων τοὺς λόγους τοῦ βιβλίου τούτου· τῷ θεῷ προσκύνησον, "I am a fellow servant with you and your brothers and sisters the prophets and those who obey the commands in this book. Worship God!" Philo considered it erroneous to worship angels as if they were divine (*Conf.* 146; *Quis Her.* 205; *Cher.* 3, 35). The tendency to worship angels occurs here and in 19:10 (see *Comment* there).

V 9 is a doublet of 19:10 (see the synoptic comparison in *Comment* on 19:10).

Rev 19:10	*Rev 22:9*
And he said to me, "Don't do that! I am a fellow servant with you and your brothers and sisters	And he said to me, "Don't do that! I am a fellow servant with you and your brothers and sisters [the prophets
[who maintain the testimony concerning Jesus]. Worship God."	and those who obey the commands in this book]. Worship God."

The bracketed portions in 19:10 and 22:9 show how distinctive statements have been intercalated into the same formulaic framework. While 19:10 suggests that John's brothers are those who maintain their testimony about Jesus, 22:9 indicates that John's brothers are the prophets and those who obey the commands in this book. It appears that the author-editor has used 19:10 as the source for 22:9 (Kraft, 227), though some commentators hold that the repetition serves as a structural framework (Karrer, *Brief,* 175).

Since Revelation contains a limited amount of material that can be construed as words or commands to be obeyed, and that material is primarily limited to Rev 1–3 and 22:6–21, it is probable that the emphasis on obeying the commands in "this book" belongs to the final redactional stage of composition. Strictly speaking, such material is generally restricted to the parenetic sections of Rev 2–3 and 22:6–21 and a few scattered commands found in the body of the work (13:9–10; 14:12; 16:15; 18:4; 21:7–8).

Explanation

In Rev 21:9, as in 17:1, a bowl angel offers to show John a special sight. While in chap. 17 the vision centered on the great whore of Babylon (i.e., Rome) and her fate, here it focuses on the bride, the wife of the Lamb (i.e., the people of God under the metaphor of a city). Rome and the Church are carefully presented as antithetical realities using feminine imagery. The New Jerusalem, which John sees descending from heaven, is then described in some detail (21:9–22:9). The contrived nature of these details indicates that the city is a transparent symbol for the people of God, the Church. The idea of a heavenly Jerusalem as a city in which Christians are enrolled as citizens is not unique to Revelation, for it is found in both early Christian (Heb 12:22–24; 13:14; Gal 4:26) and early Jewish thought (*2 Apoc. Bar.* 4:1–6; *2 Enoch* 55:2). The twelve gates of the city are labeled with the names of the twelve tribes of Israel (see Ezek 48:34; 11QTemple, in describing the eschatological temple, similarly mentions twelve gates named after the twelve tribes of Israel, gates located between the middle and outer courts).

In 21:15–21, John's angelic guide measures the city, which is twelve thousand stadia long, wide, and high (at 190–210 meters per stadium, the city would be an enormous cube 1,416–1,566 miles on each side). The eschatological temple described in Ezek 42:16–20 is *square*, in contrast to Solomon's rectangular temple (1 Kgs 6:2), though the holy of holies in the latter was cubical (1 Kgs 6:20).

In poetic eschatological descriptions, the future Jerusalem could be described as constructed of precious stones (Isa 54:11–12; Tob 13:16–17). Near Eastern kings, like Sardanapallus, embellished their capitals with precious stones to emphasize their personal grandeur and magnificence (Dio Chrysostom *Or.* 2.35). The precious stones adorning the New Jerusalem form a contrast to the jewels worn by the great whore (17:4). Each of the twelve foundations of the city (each bearing the name of one of the twelve apostles, v 14) consists of a single enormous precious stone (vv 19–20). These correspond, in a different order, to the stones mounted on the breastplate of the Israelite high priest (Exod 28:17–20; 39:10–13; LXX Ezek 28:13). The identity of the New Jerusalem with the Church suggests that the function of these stones is to emphasize the priestly status of the people of God (1:6; 5:10; 20:6). At the same time, the precious foundation stones also symbolize the presence and transcendent majesty of God who now, as in the wilderness tabernacle of old, dwells in the midst of his people (20:3). The twelve gates (v 21) are not mother-of-pearl, but each consists of one gigantic pearl, according to v 17, about 250 feet in diameter (similar traditions are found in rabbinic sources).

In 22:1–6 John is shown aspects of the city modeled on traditional Jewish conceptions of Eden with its three central features: the throne of God, the river, and the fruitful tree of life. The term "paradise" (a Persian word for "garden" or "park") was used both for the earthly Eden and for a heavenly place of bliss and perfection. According to some Jewish legends, Adam lived in a heavenly paradise (the third heaven, 2 Cor 12:4; *2 Enoch* 5:1) and was expelled to earth for his disobedience. The eschatological restoration of primal Edenic conditions found in the OT prophets (Isa 11:6–9; 65:17–25) was an important theme in later Jewish apocalyptic thought. In Rev 2:7, Paradise is where the tree of life grows. The traditional river flowing out of Eden (Gen. 2:10) is here understood as the river of *life,* and the trees of life are growing on both banks of the river (imagery drawn primarily from Ezek. 47:1–12). The final goal of salvation is now realized (vv 3–5). The servants of God are finally able to see his face (according to Jewish tradition, no one could see God and live [Exod 33:17–20; see John 1:18]), which means that they share his holiness and righteousness. His name is on their foreheads because they belong to him forever. In fulfillment of the promise made in 3:21, they will reign with him forever (v 5). Only the 144,000 martyrs shared the earlier millennial reign with Christ (20:4).

Though 22:6–9 marks a formal conclusion to the angelic revelation begun in 21:9, it also functions as a transition to the concluding section of Revelation. In fact, Rev 22:6–7 is so similar in form and content to Rev 1:1–3 that both passages obviously function as a frame or *inclusio* for the entire book. Both passages mention the revelatory channels of communication, emphasize the nearness of the end, and pronounce a blessing on those who obey the revelatory message. These are only a few of the similarities that link 1:1–8 with 22:6–21. John follows the literary conventions of Jewish apocalyptic by emphasizing the truth and importance of the foregoing revelatory message and by explaining the proper use of this prophetic book. When he claims that "It was I, John, who heard and saw these visions" (v 8), he is using a common ancient *witness formula* emphasizing the reliability of the eyes and ears in gathering direct personal knowledge (Herodian 1.2.5).

Excursus 21A: Jerusalem and the Temple in Early Judaism and Early Christianity

Bibliography

Attridge, H. W. "The Ascension of Moses and the Heavenly Jerusalem." *Studies on the Testament of Moses.,* ed. G. W. E. Nickelsburg, Jr. Cambridge: Society of Biblical Literature, 1973. 122–25. **Bachmann, M.** *Jerusalem und der Tempel: Die geographisch-theologischen Elemente in der lukanischen Sicht des jüdischen Kultzentrums.* BWANT 109. Stuttgart: Kohlhammer, 1980. **Causse, A.** "La mythe de la nouvelle Jérusalem du Deutéro-Esaïe à la IIIéme Sibylle." *RHPR* 18 (1938) 377–414. **Clifford, R. J.** *The Cosmic Mountain in Canaan and the Old Testament.* Cambridge, MA: Harvard UP, 1972. **Cullmann, O.** "L'Opposition contre le Temple de Jérusalem." *NTS* 5 (1958–59) 157–73. **Davies, W. D.** *The Gospel and the Land: Early Christian and Jewish Territorial Doctrine.* Berkeley: University of California, 1974. ———. *The Territorial Dimension of Judaism.* Berkeley; Los Angeles: University of California, 1982. **Eliade, M.** *Cosmos and History: The Myth of the Eternal Return.* Tr. W. R. Trask. New York: Harper & Row, 1959. **Flusser, D.** "Two Notes on the Midrash on 2 Sam. 7." *IEJ* 9 (1959) 99–109. **Fohrer, G.,** and **Lohse, E.** "Σιών, Ἰερουσαλήμ, Ἰεροσόλυμα, Ἰεροσολυμίτης." *TDNT* 7:292–338. **García Martínez, F.** "The 'New Jerusalem' and the Future Temple of the Manuscripts from Qumran." In *Qumran and Apocalyptic: Studies on the Aramaic Texts from Qumran.* STDJ 9. Leiden: Brill, 1992. 180–213. **Gärtner, B.** *The Temple and the Community in Qumran and the New Testament.* Cambridge: Cambridge UP, 1965. **Gundry, R. H.** "The New Jerusalem: People as Place, Not Place for People." *NovT* 29 (1987) 254–64. **Isaksson, A.** *Marriage and Ministry in the New Temple.* Lund: Gleerup, 1965. **Juel, D.** *Messiah and Temple: The Trial of Jesus in the Gospel of Mark.* Missoula, MT: Scholars, 1977. **Klinzing, G.** *Die Umdeutung des Kultus in der Qumrangemeinde und im Neuen Testament.* Göttingen: Vandenhoeck & Ruprecht, 1971. **Levine, L. I.** "Josephus' Description of the Jerusalem Temple." In *Josephus and the History of the Greco-*

Roman Period. FS M. Smith, ed. F. Parente and J. Sievers. Leiden: Brill, 1994. 233–46. **Licht, J.** "An Ideal Town Plan from Qumran—The Description of the New Jerusalem." *IEJ* 29 (1979) 45–59. **Maier, J.** *The Temple Scroll: An Introduction, Translation and Commentary.* Sheffield: JSOT, 1985. **McKelvey, R. J.** *The New Temple.* Oxford: Oxford UP, 1969. **McNicol, A. J.** "The Eschatological Temple in the Qumran Pesher 4QFlorilegium 1:1–7." *Ohio Journal of Religious Studies* 5 (1977) 133–41. **Mendels, D.** *The Land of Israel as a Political Concept in Hasmonean Literature.* Tübingen: Mohr-Siebeck, 1987. **Murphy, F. J.** *The Structure and Meaning of Second Baruch.* SBLDS 78. Atlanta: Scholars, 1985. ———. "The Temple in the Syriac *Apocalypse of Baruch.*" *JBL* 106 (1987) 671–83. **Newsom, C.** *Songs of the Sabbath Sacrifice: A Critical Edition.* Atlanta: Scholars, 1985. **Schmidt, K. L.** "Jerusalem als Urbild und Abbild." *Eranos Jahrbuch* 18 (1950) 207–48. **Schüssler Fiorenza, E.** "Cultic Language in Qumran and in the New Testament." *CBQ* 38 (1976) 159–71. **Schwartz, D. R.** "The Three Temples of 4Q Florilegium." *RevQ* 10 (1979–81) 83–91. **Volz, P.** *Die Eschatologie der jüdischen Gemeinde.* Tübingen: Mohr-Siebeck, 1934. **Wacholder, B. Z.** *The Dawn of Qumran: The Sectarian Torah and the Teacher of Righteousness.* Cincinnati: Hebrew Union College, 1983. **Wenschkewitz, H.** *Die Spiritualisierung der Kultusbegriffe: Temple, Priester und Opfer im Neuen Testament.* Leipzig: Pfeiffer, 1932. **Wentling, J. L.** "Unraveling the Relationship between 11QT, the Eschatological Temple, and the Qumran Community." *RevQ* 14 (1989) 61–73. **Yadin, Y.** *The Temple Scroll* 3:182–87. **Young, J. C. de.** *Jerusalem in the New Testament: The Significance of the City in the History of Redemption and in Eschatology.* Kampen: Kok, 1960. **Zeilinger, F.** "Das himmlische Jerusalem: Untersuchungen zur Bildersprache der Johannisapokalypse und des Hebräerbriefs." In *Memoria Jerusalem.* FS F. Sauer, ed. J. B. Baer and J. Marbock. Graz: Akademische, 1977. 143–65.

A. *Jerusalem and the Temple*

Both Jerusalem and the temple were of central religious and mythic significance for early Judaism. Together, they have a close relationship to the land. The concept of the land, according to some scholars, was "spiritualized" during the second temple period (Davies, *Territorial Dimension,* 33), though that view is disputed, at least for the second century B.C., by D. Mendels (*Land of Israel,* 4). Jerusalem and the temple were very closely connected, for the sanctity of the former was regarded as an extension of the sanctity of the latter (*m. Kelim* 1:6–9; Davies, *Land,* 150–54). Both were the subjects of extensive eschatological speculation. In the ancient Near East, important temples and cities were widely thought to be modeled after celestial archetypes (Eliade, *Cosmos,* 6–11). This notion was compatible with the Platonic emphasis on the superior reality of the archetype (Plato *Timaeus* 28A–31C, 50C), a theory adapted to Judaism by Philo. In the Greek world some intellectuals criticized the practice of constructing temples, arguing that the universe was the only temple truly appropriate for a god (Euripides frag. 968; Aristotle, quoted in Seneca *Quaest. nat.* 7.29–31; Manilius *Astronomica* 1.20–24; Dio Chrysostom *Or.* 12.33–34; Plutarch *De tranquilitate animi* 477C; see Festugière, *Hermès Trismégiste* 2:233–38).

The Hellenistic criticism of physical temples is echoed in a variety of Jewish sources, including Philo *Cher.* 99–100, Jos. *J.W.* 5.458, *Sib. Or.* 4.8–11, 23–30, and Bar 3:24–28. In ancient Israel the tabernacle and the temple symbolized the presence of God. Occasional mention is made of the inadequacy of the temple to contain the God whom even the heavens cannot contain (1 Kgs 8:27; 2 Chr 6:18; Isa 66:1–2). Philo often refers to the two true temples of God, the universe and the rational soul (*Som.* 1.215; *Plant.* 50; *Quaest. in Ex.* 2.51; *Quis Her.* 75; *Spec. Leg.* 1.66). Philo understood the design of the tabernacle and the temple, their furnishings, and the priestly vestments as symbols of the universe (*Spec. Leg.* 1.85–96; *Mos.* 2.101–8, 117–35). Josephus, responding to the Hellenistic critique of temples (*Ant.* 3.180), understood the Jewish temple as a symbol of the universe (*Ant.* 3.123, 179–87; *J.W.* 5.212–18).

B. The Tabernacle and Temple in Judaism

In the OT and early Judaism the wilderness tabernacle (which was regarded as the model for the temple of Solomon but which, at least in terms of its description in the Priestly writer, was an idealization based on the temple in Jerusalem; see de Vaux, *Ancient Israel*, 296) was thought to be patterned after a heavenly prototype (Exod 25:9, 40; 26:30; 27:8; see Wis 9:8; Acts 7:44; Heb 9:24; Philo *Mos.* 2.74–76). Aside from the enigmatic statement in 1 Chr 28:11, 19 that David gave Solomon the "plan" or "pattern" (Hebrew תבנית *tabnît*, the same term used in Exod 25:9 and Num 8:4 for the "plan" shown to Moses by Yahweh) for the temple and its vessels, only Isa 6 (and possibly Ps 150:1) reflects a possible belief in a heavenly temple; the term ההיכל *hahêkāl*, "the temple," in Isa 6:1 could refer to Isaiah's vision of the heavenly temple or to a vision of God within the setting of the temple in Jerusalem. In early Jewish literature, references to the heavenly temple become increasingly common (*1 Enoch* 14; 4QShirShabb and 11QShirShabb [see the discussion on the heavenly temple in Newsom, *Songs*, 39–58]; *T. Levi* 5:1). In the *Songs of the Sabbath Sacrifice* (4QShirShabb; 11QShirShabb), the heavenly temple is described as including seven sanctuaries, linked to seven angelic priestly orders (Newsom, *Songs*, 48–51), whereas other texts describe seven or more heavens with a heavenly sanctuary located in only one of them, usually the uppermost.

There is evidence in early Judaism for two different but related expectations of a future temple.

(1) One expectation, which goes back to Ezek 40–48, focuses on the eschatological temple that will be built by God himself. In *1 Enoch* 90:28–29 (written or revised between 164 and 160 B.C.; see Nickelsburg, *Jewish Literature*, 93), the existing temple is razed and replaced with a new one built by God himself (cf. *2 Apoc. Bar.* 31:5–32:4).

(2) An alternate expectation anticipates a future temple to be constructed by the people of Israel. This latter view is reflected in the *Temple Scroll* (11QTemple), where the term "high priest" (15:15; 23:9; 25:16) is used rather than "chief priest" or "the anointed priest" found in the eschatological literature from Qumran (Yadin, *Temple Scroll* 1:183; 2:65). There is disagreement among scholars whether 11QTemple was produced by the Qumran community or was simply used by them (there appears to be a close relationship between 11QTemple and *Jubilees*), though it originated outside the community (M. O. Wise, *A Critical Study of the Temple Scroll from Qumran Cave 11* (Chicago: Oriental Institute of the University of Chicago, 1990). The future temple and the eschatological temple both appear to be mentioned in 11QTemple 29:8–10 (Yadin, *Temple Scroll* 2:128–29):

> And I will consecrate my [t]emple by my glory, (the temple) on which I will settle my glory, until the day of blessing on which I will create my temple and establish it for myself for all times, according to the covenant which I have made with Jacob at Bethel.

B. Wacholder, however, argues that a single temple is in view here and that the temple that God commanded the Qumran community to build was the eschatological temple (*Dawn*, 21–30). Similarly, J. L. Wentling (*RevQ* 14 [1989] 61–73) argues that 11QTemple 29:3–10 was based on biblical texts such as Ezek 37:26–28 and proposes that the Qumran community, isolated from the second temple in Jerusalem, anticipated that temple's destruction and its replacement by a divinely built temple in which God's spirit would dwell forever. 11QTemple 29:3–10, therefore, reflects a single eschatological temple. The Qumran community (whose leaders were displaced priests) used the term "temple" as a metaphor for their community during the "days of Belial" when they were excluded from the temple in Jerusalem by unqualified priests (Klinzing, *Kultus*, 50–93). The *Temple Scroll* provides evidence that they anticipated the building of a new temple in the future in which the sacrificial rituals would be continued until the end of days in which God himself would build a new temple.

The various perspectives on the temple in the literature from Qumran are complex (the various origins of this literature remain a matter of dispute). In 4QFlor, three temples are referred to: (1) the third temple (alluded to in 2 Sam 7:10, according to 4QFlor), which will be built by God in the eschaton (McNicol, *Ohio Journal of Religious Studies* 5 [1977] 133–41), (2) the second temple (alluded to in 2 Sam 7:10), which the community regarded as desecrated, and (3) the first temple (alluded to in 2 Sam 7:13), which was built by Solomon (Schwartz, *RQ* 10 [1979–81] 83–91). 11QTemple 29 mentions the first and third temples but does not mention the second temple.

C. The Temple and Jerusalem in Early Christianity

There are several passages in the NT in which the term "temple" is used as a metaphor for the Christian community (1 Cor 3:16–17; 2 Cor 6:16, 19; Eph 2:19–22; 1 Pet 2:4–5; see 1 Tim 3:15; 2 Tim 2:19; see Gundry, *NovT* 29 [1987] 254–64). While the rare NT use of the temple as a metaphor for an individual (1 Cor 6:19) apparently has Hellenistic parallels, the image of the *community* as a temple is found only in the Dead Sea Scrolls and in the NT (Klinzing, *Kultus*, 168–69). For the texts in the Qumran literature that use the temple as a metaphor for the community, see 1QS 5:4–7; 8:4–10; 9:3–6; 11:8; 4QFlor 1:1–7; 4QpIsa 1; 1QHab 12:3; CD 3:18–4:10. Justin expects that Jerusalem will be rebuilt and that Christians will be gathered together in joyfulness with Christ, the patriarchs, and the prophets (*Dial.* 80.1).

D. The Eschatological Temple/Jerusalem

The NT contains a critique of the temple "made with hands" (Acts 7:48–50; 17:24) based on a contrast between the temple "made with hands," i.e., built by humans, and the one "made without hands," i.e., built by God (Mark 14:58; Heb 9:11, 24; see Philo *Spec. Leg.* 1.66–67).

The expectation of the descent of a heavenly temple or the heavenly Jerusalem in the eschaton first occurs in Revelation (3:12; 21:2, 10). In early Judaism, it was only a marginal conception that appeared only occasionally. In *Midr. Wayyōšaʿ* (eleventh- or twelfth-century A.D. midrash on Exod 14:30–15:18) we read, "When Moses saw the love of the Holy Blessed One to Israel, he said . . . Thou wilt make Jerusalem to come down for them from heaven, and will not destroy it forever, and the Exiles of Israel shall be gathered in her and they shall dwell there in security" (Flusser, *IEJ* 9 [1959] 103, from A. Jellinek, ed., *Beth Ha-Midrash* [Jerusalem, 1938] 55).

Excursus 21B: Ancient Utopias and the Paradise Myth

Bibliography

Baldry, H. C. *Ancient Utopias.* Southampton: University of Southampton, 1956. ———. "Zeno's Ideal State." *JHS* 79 (1959) 3–15. **Betz, H. D.** *Lukian von Samosata und das Neue Testament.* Berlin: Akademie, 1961. **Braunert, H.** *Utopia: Antworten griechischen Denkens auf die Herausforderung durch soziale Verhältnisse.* Veröffentlichungen der Schleswig-Holsteinischen Universitätsgesellschaft, n.s. 51. Kiel: Hirt, 1969. **Capelle, P.** "Elysium und Inseln der Seligen." *ARW* 25 (1927) 245–64. **Erskine, A.** *The Hellenistic Stoa: Political Thought and Action.* London: Duckworth, 1990. **Ferguson, J.** *Utopias of the Classical World.* Ithaca, NY: Cornell UP, 1975. **Fitch, J. G.** *Seneca's Hercules Furens: A Critical Text with Introduction and Commentary.* Ithaca, NY: Cornell UP, 1987. **Garlan, Y.** *Slavery in Ancient*

Greece. Rev. ed. Tr. J. Lloyd. Ithaca, NY: Cornell UP, 1988. **Georgi, D.** "Who is the True Prophet?" *HTR* 79 (1986) 100–126. **Herzog, R.** "Überlegungen zur griechischen Utopie: Gattungsgeschichte vor dem Prototyp der Gattung?" In *Utopieforschung: Interdisziplinäre Studien zur neuzeitlichen Utopie.* Stuttgart: Metzler, 1982. 2:1–20. **Koch, M.** "Zur Utopie in der alten Welt." In *Auf den Weg gebracht,* ed. H. Sund and M. Timmermann. Konstanz: Universitätsverlag Konstanz, 1979. **Kytzler, B.** "Utopisches Denken und Handeln in der klassischen Antike." In *Der utopische Roman,* ed. R. Villgradter and F. Krey. Darmstadt: Wissenschaftliche Buchgesellschaft, 1973. **Mendels, D.** "Hellenistic Utopia and the Essenes." *HTR* 72 (1979) 207–22. **Schofield, M.** *The Stoic Idea of the City.* Cambridge: Cambridge UP, 1991. **Thesleff, H.** "Notes on the Paradise Myth in Ancient Greece." *Temenos* 22 (1986) 129–39. **Trompf, G. W.** "Utopia." *EncRel* 15:159–62.

The term "utopia," from the Greek phrase οὐ τόπος meaning "no place" (coined by Thomas Moore in the early sixteenth century), refers to a variety of ideal times and places, either in the primordial past (e.g., the Israelite garden of Eden; Hesiod's Golden Age) or in some distant place on the earth (the Greek Islands of the Blessed; Homer's island of the Phaeacians; Euhemerus' island of Panchaea), or in the future (the restoration of Edenic conditions in Jewish apocalyptic; the transformed or re-created world of Christian millenarianism). The description of such a place contains features that make it pleasing, usually including the features of an idyllic landscape: trees, shrubs, fields, flowers, fruits, spring water, sunshine and shade (in appropriate proportions), and refreshing breezes. The Greek conception of Olympus, the dwelling place of the gods, is itself a utopian ideal; see the brief sketch of conditions on Olympus in *Odyssey* 6.43–46 (LCL tr.):

> Neither is it shaken by winds nor ever wet with rain, nor does snow fall upon it, but the air is outspread clear and cloudless, and over it hovers a radiant whiteness. There the blessed gods are glad all their days.

This description became, not unexpectedly, paradigmatic for later authors and was amplified in a variety of ways by many writers (e.g., Lucretius 3.18–22; Lucan 2.271–73; Seneca *De ira* 3.6). The language of utopia was also used by Hesiod to describe the experience of just people (*Works and Days* 230–37; LCL tr.):

> Neither famine nor disaster ever haunt men who do true justice; but lightheartedly they tend the fields which are all their care. The earth bears them victual in plenty, and on the mountains the oak bears acorns upon the top and bees in the midst. Their woolly sheep are laden with fleeces; their women bear children like their parents. They flourish continually with good things, and do not travel on ships, for the grain-giving earth bears them fruit.

Greek conceptions of the ideal state often involved the redistribution of functions within a hierarchically arranged civic body, but no provision was made for increased sources of income or any reduction of the needs of society (Garlan, *Slavery,* 127).

Greek utopias include: (1) the Elysian fields (*Odyssey* 4.561–69; 6.42–46), where Rhadamanthys is ruler and life is free from cares; there are no snow, storms, and rain, but only gentle breezes; (2) the myth of the golden age or golden race (Hesiod *Works and Days* 111–20; quoted in Diodorus 5.66.5); (3) the myth of the easy life during the reign of Kronos (linked to the Kronia festival), which existed independently of the golden-age myth and was probably even more popular (Baldry, *Utopias,* 83–92); (4) the Islands of the Blessed (Hesiod *Works and Days* 161–73; *Theogony* 215–16; Pindar *Olymp.* 2.61–78), where Cronus is king, fertile soil produces three crops annually, and heroes lead lives of ease; (5) the land of the Hyperboreans (Pindar *Olymp.* 3.13–16, 26–34); (6) Calypso's island of Ogygia (*Odyssey* 5.55–74) with lush vegetation and the natural beauty of Calypso's cave; (7) the Garden of Alcinous (*Odyssey* 7.112–32), a place of ever-bearing vines and fruit trees, flowers, two springs, and gentle breezes; and (8) the land of the Phaeacians (*Odyssey* 6.262–72; 7.108–32).

Yet these places should be distinguished from idyllic natural scenes such as the love scene between Zeus and Hera on Mount Ida (*Iliad* 14.283–360) or Sappho's description of Aphrodite's grove (frag. 2; see frag. 96; *Iliad* 2.301–21; *Odyssey* 9.116–41; *Homeric Hymn to Demeter* 6–17, 422–28). Thesleff (*Temenos* 22 [1986] 132) suggests that these examples are based on two main original schemes that soon mutually influenced each other: (1) the Elysian fields type was a flowering meadow on the banks of the river Okeanos in a land where those chosen by the gods live in unending bliss, and (2) the sacred garden or grove with trees (or a single tree) had a spring of running water, flowers and fruits, a cave or rock, sometimes a snake, the perfect setting for eating, drinking, love, and sleep.

Iambulus wrote a travel account, preserved only in Diodorus 2.55–60 (see 60.3), of his trip to the Islands of the Sun (actually a group of seven similar islands, 58.7), where he lived for seven years, a place children are held in common (58.1). The utopian conception of Iambulus is strikingly egalitarian, in sharp contrast to prevailing utopian conceptions in which ideal societies were organized hierarchically (Braunert, *Utopia*, 15–17). Though people have more than they need, they are never overindulgent (59.1). The lives and societies of the natives are depicted as primitive and yet as ideal in every respect.

Lucian's *Verae Historiae,* written shortly after the middle of the second century A.D., provides indirect evidence of the popularity of utopian views in the eastern Mediterranean world. In a parody ultimately modeled on the fantastic adventures of Odysseus (a parody that the scholiast thought was aimed at the eschatological Jerusalem [Schol. 14 on *Ver. hist.* 2.11; H. Rabe, *Scholia in Lucianum* (Stuttgart: Teubner, 1971) 21]), Lucian narrates his arrival at the Island of the Blessed (the location where certain Greek heroes enjoyed a blissful afterlife), where the breezes were both perfumed and musical (2.5). After a preliminary judgment by Rhadamanthys (2.6–10), Lucian and his party are freed and taken into the city to the table of the Blessed Ones, i.e., the gods. A description of the city then follows (2.11–13, LCL tr.):

> The city itself is all of gold and the wall around it of emerald. It has seven gates, all of single planks of cinnamon. The foundations of the city and the ground within its wall are ivory. There are temples of all the gods, built of beryl, and in them great monolithic altars of amethyst, on which they make their great burnt-offerings. Around the city runs a river of the finest myrrh. . . . Nobody grows old, but stays the same age as on coming there. Again, it is neither night among them nor yet very bright day, but the light which is on the country is like the gray morning toward dawn, when the sun has not yet risen. . . . The grape-vines yield twelve vintages a year, bearing every month; the pomegranates, apples and other fruit-trees were said to bear thirteen times a year.

The utopian views of Persian sages are preserved by Plutarch (*De Iside et Osiride* 370B; LCL tr.):

> But a destined time shall come when it is decreed that Areimanius, engaged in bringing on pestilence and famine, shall by these be utterly annihilated and shall disappear; and then shall the earth become a level plain, and there shall be one manner of life and one form of government for a blessed people who shall all speak one tongue. Theopompous [*FrGrHist* 65] says that, according to the sages, one god is to overpower . . . and finally Hades shall pass away; then shall the people be happy, and neither shall they need to have food nor shall they cast any shadow.

In Seneca's tragedy *Hercules Furens,* just before the onset of madness Herakles addresses a prayer to Jupiter in which he prays for a Golden Age free from natural and social evils (928–39; tr. F. J. Miller):

> May heaven, earth, and air their order keep,
> And the everlasting stars wheel on their way,
> Unchanged; may peace profound brood o'er the world;
> May iron be used for harmless toil alone,
> And deadly weapons vanish from the earth;
> May no unbridled tempest lash the sea;
> May angry Jove send forth no lightning bolts;
> And may no river, red by winter's snows,
> O'erflow the trouble fields; may venom fail;
> And may no noxious herb its fruitage bear;
> May fierce and cruel tyrants rule no more.
> If the pregnant earth still foster any crime,
> Let her make haste to bring it to the light;
> And if she still another monster bear,
> Let it be mine to meet.

In such descriptions of a Golden Age, several details are traditionally present (Fitch, *Hercules Furens,* 361): (1) the absence of war and weapons (lines 929–31; see Aratus *Phaen.* 107ff.; Vergil *Aeneid* 8.325ff.; Ovid *Met.* 1.98ff.); (2) temperate climate (lines 931–34; Ovid *Met.* 1.107–8; *Odyssey* 4.566; 6.43–44; Horace *Epodes* 16.53ff.); (3) absence of poisonous herbs, a less common feature (lines 934–35; see Vergil *Eclogues* 4.24–25); and (4) absence of tyrants, a feature added by Seneca.

Conceptions of the ideal city-state were frequently proposed by Greek philosophers of various schools and traditions. Plato, who was deeply critical of Athenian society and political structures, proposed an ideal *polis.* The presence of temples in Plato's ideal state (*Laws* 761c; 778cd) was one feature specifically disputed by Zeno. In addition to prohibiting the building of temples, law courts, and gymnasiums and coinage in his ideal cities, Zeno reportedly advocated community of wives and unisex clothing (*SVF* 1:62; frags. 264–71; see Erskine, *The Hellenistic Stoa,* 24).

IV. Epilogue (22:10–21)
A. Concluding Parenesis (22:10–20)

Bibliography

Acerbi, A. *L'Ascensione di Isaia: Cristologia e profetismo in Siria nei primi decenni del II secolo.* Milan: Università Cattolica del Sacro Cuore, 1989. **Albl, M. C.** "'And Scripture Cannot Be Broken': The Form and Function of the Early Christian Testimonia Collections." Ph.D. Diss., Marquette University, 1997. **Aune, D. E.** *The Cultic Setting of Realized Eschatology in Early Christianity.* NovTSup 28. Leiden: Brill, 1972. ———. "The Prophetic Circle of John of Patmos and the Exegesis of Revelation 22.16," *JSNT* 37 (1989) 103–16. ———. "The Significance of the Delay of the Parousia for Early Christianity." In *Current Issues in Biblical and Patristic Interpretation,* ed. G. F. Hawthorne. Grand Rapids, MI: Eerdmans, 1975. 87–109. ———. "The Social Matrix of the Apocalypse of John." *BR* 26 (1981) 16–32. **Balogh, J.** "'Voces Paginarum': Beiträge zur Geschichte des lauten Lesens und Schreibens." *Philologus* 82 (1927) 206–10. **Black, M.** "The Maranatha Invocation and Jude 14, 15 (*1 Enoch* 1:9)." In *Christ and Spirit in the New Testament.* FS C. F. D. Moule, ed. B. Lindars and S. S. Smalley. New York: Cambridge UP, 1973. 189–96. **Blank, S. H.** "The Curse, the Blasphemy, the Spell, and the Oath." *HUCA* 23.1 (1950–51) 73–95. **Boismard, M.-E.** "Notes sur l'Apocalypse." *RB* 59 (1952) 161–81. **Bornkamm, G.** "The Anathema in the Early Christian Lord's Supper Liturgy." In *Early Christian Experience.* Tr. P. L. Hammer. New York: Harper & Row, 1969. 169–76. **Botte, B.** "Maranatha." In *Noel-Epiphanie, Retour du Christ.* Paris: Cerf, 1967. **Brun, L.** *Segen und Fluch im Urchristentum.* Oslo: Universitetsforlaget, 1932. **Charles, R. H.** "A Solution of the Chief Difficulties in Revelation 20–22." *ExpTim* 26 (1914–15) 54–57, 119–23. **Collins, T.** *Apocalypse 22:6–21 as the Focal Point of Moral Teaching and Exhortation in the Apocalypse.* Rome: Pontifical Gregorian University, 1986. **Cuming, G. J.** "Service-Endings in the Epistles." *NTS* 22 (1975–76) 110–13. **Dautzenberg, G.** *Urchristliche Prophetie: Ihre Erforschung, ihre Voraussetzungen im Judentum und ihre Struktur im ersten Korintherbrief.* BWANT 104. Stuttgart: Kohlhammer, 1975. **Dunphy, W.** "Maranatha: Development in Early Christianity." *ITQ* 37 (1970) 294–309. **Fabre, A.** "L'Étoile du matin dans l'Apocalypse." *RB* 17 (1908) 227–40. **Gaechter, P.** "The Original Sequence of Apocalypse 20–22." *TS* 10 (1949) 485–521. **Gibbs, J. M.** "Canon Cuming's 'Service-Endings in the Epistles': A Rejoinder." *NTS* 24 (1977–78) 545–47. **Giblin, C. H.** "Structural and Thematic Correlations in the Theology of Revelation 16–22." *Bib* 55 (1974) 487–504. **Goranson, S.** "The Text of Revelation 22:14." *NTS* 43 (1997) 154–57. **Graf, F.** "Prayer in Magic and Religious Ritual." In *Magika Hiera: Ancient Greek Magic and Religion,* ed. C. A. Faraone and D. Obbink. New York; Oxford: Oxford UP, 1991. 188–213. **Grant, R. M.** "'Holy Law' in Paul and Ignatius." In *The Living Text.* FS E. W. Saunders, ed. D. E. Groh and R. Jewett. Lanham, MD: University Press of America, 1985. 65–71. **Güterbock, H. G.** "Mursili's Accounts of Suppiluliuma's Dealings with Egypt." *Revue Hittite et Asianique* 18 (1960) 59–60. **Hall, R. G.** "The *Ascension of Isaiah*: Community, Situation, Date, and Place in Early Christianity." *JBL* 109 (1990) 300–306. **Hartman, L.** "Form and Message: A Preliminary Discussion of 'Partial Texts' in Rev 1–3 and 22,6ff." In *L'Apocalypse,* ed. J. Lambrecht. 129–49. **Kamlah, E.** *Die Form der katalogischen Paränese im Neuen Testament.* WUNT 7. Tübingen: Mohr (Siebeck), 1964. **Käsemann, E.** "Sentences of Holy Law in the New Testament." In *New Testament Questions of Today.* Philadelphia: Fortress, 1969. 66–81. **Kavanagh, M. A.** *Apocalypse 22:6–21 as Concluding Liturgical Dialogue.* Rome: Pontifical Gregorian University, 1984. **Könnecke, C.** *Emendationen zu Stellen des Neuen Testaments.* BFCT 12. Gütersloh: Bertelsmann, 1908. **Lambert, W. G.** "The Fifth Tablet of the Era Epic." *Iraq* 24 (1962) 122. **Langevin, P.-E.** *Jésus seigneur et l'eschatologie: Exégèse de textes prépauliniens.*

Brugge: Desclée de Brouwer, 1967. **Leipoldt, J.**, and **Morenz, S.** *Heilige Schriften.* Leipzig: Harrasowitz, 1953. **Lietzmann, H.** *Mass and Lord's Supper: A Study in the History of the Liturgy.* Tr. D. H. G. Reeve. Leiden: Brill, 1955–79. **Mancini, A.** "'Qui nocet noceat adhuc . . . .'" *Palestra del Clero* 14 (1935) 89–91. **Moffatt, J.** "The Bright and Morning Star." *The Expositor* 6 (1920) 224–41. **Moore, M. S.** "Jesus Christ: 'Superstar.'" *NovT* 24 (1982) 82–91. **Moule, C. F. D.** "A Reconsideration of the Context of *Maranatha.*" *NTS* 6 (1959–60) 307–10. **Mueller, B.** "Die epiloog van die Openbaring aan Johannes (22:6–21)." *Scriptura* 6 (1982) 57–64. **Nestle, E.** *Einführung in das griechische Neue Testament.* 3 vols. Göttingen: Vandenhoeck & Ruprecht, 1909. **Oliver, R. P.** "The First Medicean MS of Tacitus and the Titulature of Ancient Books." *TAPA* 82 (1951) 232–61. **Olsson, B.** "Der Epilog der Offenbarung Johannis." *ZNW* 31 (1932) 84–86. **Oppenheim, A. L.** *The Interpretation of Dreams in the Ancient Near East.* Transactions of the American Philosophical Society n.s. 46/3. Philadelphia: American Philosophical Association, 1956. **Prigent, P.** "Une trace de liturgie judéo-chrétienne dans le chapitre XXI de l'Apocalypse de Jean." In *Judéo-Christianisme: Recherches historiques et théologiques.* FS J. Daniélou. Paris: Recherches de Science Religieuse, 1972. 165–72. **Robinson, J. A. T.** "Traces of a Liturgical Sequence in 1 Cor. 16:20–24." *JTS* 4 (1953) 38–41 (= "The Earliest Liturgical Sequence?" In *Twelve New Testament Studies.* London: SCM, 1962. 154–57). **Roller, O.** *Das Formula der paulinischen Briefe.* Stuttgart: Kohlhammer, 1933. **Ross, J. M.** "The Ending of the Apocalypse." In *Studies in New Testament Language and Text,* ed. J. K. Elliott. NovTSup 44. Leiden: Brill, 1976. 338–44. **Sato, M.** *Q und Prophetie: Studien zur Gattungs- und Traditionsgeschichte der Quelle.* WUNT 29. Tübingen: Mohr-Siebeck, 1988. **Schaeublin, C.** "μήτε προσθεῖναι μήτ' ἀφελεῖν." *Museum Helveticum* 31 (1974) 144–49. **Scholz, H.** *Der Hund in der griechisch-römischen Magie und Religion.* Berlin: Triltsch & Huther, 1937. **Schottroff, W.** *Der altisraelitische Fluchspruch.* WMANT 30. Neukirchen: Neukirchener, 1969. **Schulz, S.** "Maranatha und Kyrios Jesus." *ZNW* 53 (1962) 125–44. **Seeberg, R.** "Kuss und Kanon." In *Aus Religion und Geschichte: Gesammelte Aufsätze und Vorträge.* Vol. 1. Leipzig: Deichert, 1906. **Skrinjar, A.** "Ego sum a et o (Apoc 22:13)." *VD* 17 (1937) 10–20. **Speyer, W.** *Bücherfunde in der Glaubenswerbung der Antike: Mit einem Ausblick auf Mittelalter und Neuzeit.* Göttingen: Vandenhoeck & Ruprecht, 1971. ———. *Büchervernichtung und Zensur des Geistes bei Heiden, Juden und Christen.* Stuttgart: Hiersemann, 1981. **Stauffer, E.** "Der Methurgeman des Petrus." In *Neutestamentliche Aufsätze.* FS J. Schmid, ed. J. Blinzler, O. Kuss, and F. Mussner. Regensburg: Pustet, 1963. 288–91. **Thompson, E. M.** *A Handbook of Greek and Latin Palaeography.* Chicago: Ares, 1966. **Trevijano Etcheverria, R.** "'El discurso profético de este libro' (Apoc 22.7.10.18–19)." *Salmanticensis* 29 (1982) 283–308. **Turner, E. G.** *Greek Manuscripts of the Ancient World.* Oxford: Clarendon, 1971. **Unnik, W. C. van.** "De la règle μήτε προσθεῖναι μήτε ἀφελεῖν dans l'histoire du canon." *VC* 3 (1949) 1–36. **Wendel, C.** *Die griechisch-römische Buchbeschreibung verglichen mit der des vorderen Orients.* Halle: Niemeyer, 1949. **Windisch, H.** "Der Apokalyptiker Johannes als Begründer des Neutestamentliche Kanons," *ZNW* 10 (1909) 148–74. ———. "Die Sprüche vom Eingehen in das Reich Gottes." *ZNW* 27 (1928) 163–92.

Translation

[10] *He said to me, "Do not seal the words of this prophetic book,* [a] *for the time* [a] *is near.* [11] *Let the person who is unjust continue to act unjustly,* [a] *and let the person who is morally depraved* [b] *continue to be depraved,* [b a] *and let the person who is righteous act righteously, and let the person who is holy continue to be holy."*

[12a] *"Indeed, I am coming soon,* [b] *and my reward is with me to repay* [c] *to each in proportion to* [d] *his or her* [d] *behavior.* [13a] *I am* [a b] *the Alpha and the Omega,* [b c] *the First and the Last, the Beginning and the End.* [c]

[14] *"Blessed are* [a] *those who wash their robes* [a] *so that* [b] *they will* [c] *have* [d] *access to* [d] *the tree*

of life and [e] *so that they might enter into the city by the gates.* [15] *Outside are the dogs and the magicians and the fornicators and murderers and idolaters and everyone* [a] *who is fond of lying.* [a]

[16] *"I, Jesus, sent my angel to attest* [a] [b] *this message* [b] *to you* [c] *for the benefit of* [c] *the churches. I am David's descendant,* [d] *the* [e] *bright morning* [f] *star."*

[17] [a] *The* [b] *Spirit and the* [c] *bride say, "Come!" Let the one who hears say, "Come!" Let the one who is thirsty come. Let the one who desires receive the gift of the water of life.*

[18] *"I myself* [a] *testify to* [b] *everyone who hears the prophetic* [c] *words of this book: If anyone adds* [d] *to them,* [e] [f] *God* [g] *will add* [g] *to him* [f] *the* [h] *plagues described in this book;* [19] *and if anyone takes away any part* [a] *of the message* [b] *of this* [c] *prophetic* [d] *book, God will take away* [e] *that person's share* [f] [g] *of the tree* [g] *of life and* [h] *the holy city described in this book."* [20] *He who testifies to this says, "Surely, I am coming* [a] *soon."* [b] *Amen!* [c] *Come, Lord Jesus!* [d]

Notes

10.a-a. Variants: (1) ὅτι ὁ καιρός] 2377 Andreas Cyprian (*quia iam tempus*); Tyconius Primasius (*quia tempus iam*). (2) ὁ καιρός] 598. (3) ὁ γὰρ καιρός] Andr i 94. (4) καιρὸς γάρ] i.e., *tempus enim:* Apringius Tyc[2] Beatus it[gig]. Reading (3) is an assimilation to Rev 1:3, while all the variants try to correct the placement of γάρ in the third position in the sentence.

11.a-a. Variants: (1) omit καὶ ὁ ῥυπαρὸς ῥυπανθήτω ἔτι] A (lacuna in C) 2030 fam 1611[2050] Oecumenius[2062txt]; *Epistula ecclesiarum apud Lugdunum et Viennam,* written in A.D. 177 (Eusebius *Hist. eccl.* 5.1.3–5.3.3 [ed. Musurillo, *Acts*]: ὁ ἄνομος ἀνομησάτω ἔτι, καὶ ὁ δίκαιος δικαιωθήτω ἔτι [5.1.58]); Andr a[1]. (2) insert καὶ ὁ ῥυπαρὸς ῥυπανθήτω ἔτι] Primasius it[gig] Tyc[1] Tyc[2] Beatus Fulgentius.

11.b-b. Variants: (1) ῥυπαρευθήτω] (lacunae A C 025 051) 046 fam 1006[1006 1841] fam 1611[2329] Oecumenius[2053 2062comm] Andreas Byzantine; Bousset (1906) 457. (2) ῥυπανθήτω] ℵ (lacunae A and C) fam 1611[1854] Andr l[2080] Byz 17[2017] 94 792 Origen; WHort; B. Weiss, *Johannes-Apokalypse;* 224; Merk, *NT;* Nestle-Aland[27]; UBSGNT[4]. (3) ῥυπαρωθήτω] Andr e[2026] Andr g. (4) ῥυπωθήτω] 1773. (5) ῥυπαρυνθήτω] Andr n. The evidence for reading (1) is by far the strongest of the other readings, though the evidence is remarkably understated in Nestle-Aland[27]. The verb ῥυπαρεύειν (a *hap. leg.,* attested only here in Gk. literature) is a very unusual word and was perhaps coined by the author as a formation based on the preceding adj. ῥυπαρός. The uniqueness of this word is an argument for its originality (Schmid, *Studien* 2:83), and for this reason it is certainly the *lectio difficilior.* Readings (3), (4), and (5) reflect various ways in which scribes stumbled at the strange term and introduced a variety of modifications. The evidence for reading (2) is relatively weak, which makes it difficult to understand why most modern texts have selected it as the original reading. The verb ῥυπαίνειν or ῥυπαίνεσθαι is relatively common and very probably represents a scribal correction for the unique term ῥυπαρεύειν.

12.a. Variant: insert καί] fam 1611[1611] 2030 Andreas.

12.b. Variant: ταχὺ ταχύ] Oecumenius[2053 2062].

12.c. Variant: ἀποδοθῆναι] ℵ* Andr l.

12.d-d. Variant: (1) ἐστὶν αὐτοῦ] A (lacuna in C) ℵ. (2) ἔσται αὐτοῦ] 046 fam 1006 fam 1611[1854] Oecumenius[2053 2062] Byzantine. (3) αὐτοῦ ἔσται] fam 1611[1611] Andreas. (4) ἐστὶν αὐτῷ] fam 1611[2050]. Both (2) and (3) are attempts to correct the original text, (1).

13.a-a. Variant: ἐγώ εἰμι] fam 1006[1006 1841] fam 1611 Andr f[2073].

13.b-b. See *Note* 1:8.a-a.

13.c-c. Variants: (1) ὁ πρῶτος καὶ ὁ ἔσχατος, ἡ ἀρχὴ καὶ τὸ τέλος] ℵ 046 Cyprian Origen Primasius Tyconius Athanasius syr; B. Weiss, *Johannes-Apokalypse,* 224. (2) πρῶτος καὶ ἔσχατος ἡ ἀρχὴ καὶ τέλος] A. (3) πρῶτος καὶ ἔσχατος, ἀρχὴ καὶ τέλος] Oecumenius[2053text comm 2062text] lat syr. (4) ἀρχὴ καὶ τέλος, ὁ πρῶτος καὶ ὁ ἔσχατος] 2377 arm Andreas Origen Ambrose (*finus atque principium, primus et nouissimus;* R. W. Muncey, *The New Testament Text of Saint Ambrose,* TextsS 4 [Cambridge: Cambridge UP, 1959] lvii, 116); Arethas. (5) ἡ ἀρχὴ καὶ τὸ τέλος, ὁ πρῶτος καὶ ὁ ἔσχατος] Andr f[2073] l.

14.a-a. Variants: (1) οἱ πλύνοντες τὰς στολὰς αὐτῶν] ℵ A (lacuna in C) fam 1006[1006 1841 2050 (πλύναντες)]; Oecumenius[2053 2062] Andr l it[ar] vg cop[sa] Ps.-Athanasius (*Orationes contra Arianos* 4.28; *PG* 25.512: πλατύνοντες); Fulgentius (*qui laverunt stolas suas*); Apringius Ps-Ambrose; Tischendorf, *NT Graece;* B. Weiss, *Johannes-Apokalypse,* 10; Merk, *NT;* Nestle-Aland[27]; UBSGNT[4]. (2) οἱ ποιοῦντες τὰς ἐντολὰς αὐτοῦ] 046 fam 1611[1611 1854] Andreas Byzantine it[gig] (*qui faciunt mandata eius*); syr[ph h] cop[bo] Tertullian (*De pudicitia*

19.9: *qui ex praeceptis agunt*); Cyprian (*qui faciunt praecepta eius*); Tyc² (*qui servant mandata haec*); Beatus (*qui servant mandata mea*); von Soden, *Text*. Swete (307) demonstrates the similar appearance of the two variants written in uncial form and suggests that it is slightly more probable that the first arose out of the second rather than the reverse:

ΠΛΥΝΟΝΤΕΣΤΑΣΣΤΟΛΑΣ

ΠΟΙΟΥΝΤΕΣΤΑΣΕΤΟΛΑΣ

*TCGNT*¹, 765, and *TCGNT*², 690, further suggest that the variants would have sounded very similar. The phrase ἔπλυναν τὰς στολὰς αὐτῶν does occur in Rev 7:14, where it is coupled with the conception of atonement (unlike here), and this earlier use of the phrase is one argument for the originality of reading (1). The phrase τηρεῖν τὰς ἐντολάς occurs twice (12:17; 14:12; see John 14:15, 21; 15:10), whereas ποιεῖν τὰς ἐντολάς occurs only as a *var. lect.* here in 22:14 (see *2 Clem.* 4:5; Gk. *1 Enoch* 99:10), suggesting that reading (1) is more consistent with the style of Revelation (Schmid, *Studien* 2:83). In favor of reading (2), on the other hand, is the occasional use in the context of a beatitude of the motif of obeying commands (Luke 11:28; *1 Enoch* 99:10; Rev 1:3; 22:7; *2 Clem.* 19:3). However, ποιεῖν τὰς ἐντολάς occurs in 1 John 5:2, though the author normally uses τηρεῖν τὰς ἐντολάς (1 John 2:3, 4; 3:22, 24; 5:3), suggesting that the argument from style is less than conclusive. The phrase μὴ ποιῆτε τὰς ἐντολάς μου occurs in an extracanonical saying of Jesus (*2 Clem.* 4:5; cf. Matt 7:24; see Stroker, *Extracanonical*, 71). In support of reading (2), Goranson (*NTS* 43 [1997] 154–57) suggests (unpersuasively) that a theological motivation can be suggested for changing "observe his commandments" to "wash their robes" but not for the reverse change. He also claims that other ancient texts have parallels in which a blessing is pronounced on those who keep the commandments, but he mentions only *2 Enoch* 99:10 (he might have mentioned Luke 11:28 and *2 Clem.* 19:3).

14.b. ἵνα can be construed several ways (see *Notes* 14:13.f. and 16:15.c.): (1) as introducing a final or purpose clause, i.e., "in order that they will have access to the tree of life" (BDF § 369 [2]; Turner, *Syntax*, 102), (2) as introducing a causal clause, "because they will have access to the tree of life" (i.e., ἵνα = ὅτι, as the ἵνα in Mark 4:12 = Luke 8:10 becomes ὅτι in Matt 13:13), a usage that is also found in 14:13 and 16:15, or (3) as the imper. use of ἵνα: e.g., "may their right be to the tree of life."

14.c. It is unusual that ἵνα is followed here by the fut. ind. ἔσται and then by the aor. subjunctive εἰσέλθωσιν, although a similar syntactical phenomenon occurs in 3:9, where, despite textual difficulties, it appears ἵνα is followed by two fut. inds., though both are replaced by aor. subjunctives in the MS tradition. Mussies (*Morphology*, 341) is probably correct that the original MS of Revelation had a relatively large number of fut. inds. that functioned as aor. subjunctives (cf. 4:9; 8:3; 14:13; 17:17; 18:14). Though there is no serious doubt that ἔσται is original here, it is also true that subjunctive forms like ὦ and ἦς do not occur in Revelation (scribes tended to replace the fut. inds. in ἵνα clauses with aor. subjunctives).

14.d-d. The phrase ἐξουσία ἐπί, lit. "power over," occurs several times in Revelation (2:26; 6:8; 11:6[2x]; 13:7; 14:18; 16:9); see Delebecque, 77–78.

14.e. Charles (2:177) suggests that καί here means "and so" because the faithful must enter the city before they eat; he translates the relevant parts of the verse "that they may have the right to the tree of life *and so* may enter . . ." However, once it is recognized that the author uses the literary device *hysteron-proteron* (see *Comment* on 22:14), Charles's proposal becomes unnecessary.

15.a-a. Variants: (1) ποιῶν καὶ φιλῶν] ℵ 046 it^gig cop^sa. (2) ὁ φιλῶν καὶ ποιῶν] 051 fam 1611²⁰⁵⁰ 2030 Andreas. (3) ὁ βλεπὼν καὶ ποιῶν] syr^ph.

16.a. The verb μαρτυρεῖν, meaning "to attest, testify, witness," is used to emphasize the truth and reliability of the communication, i.e., "to provide information about a person or an event concerning which the speaker has direct knowledge" (Louw-Nida, § 33.262). The term occurs just four times in Revelation, all in the literary frame at the beginning (1:2) and end (22:16, 18, 20).

16.b-b. The neut. pl. pronoun ταῦτα, "these things," refers to the message constituted by the entire book of Revelation.

16.c-c. This translation of ἐπί as "for the benefit of" reflects an awkward use of the prep. in Gk. Variants: (1) ἐπί] ℵ Andr f²⁰²³ Byzantine; found in most modern editions. (2) ἐν] A (lacuna in C) fam 1006¹⁰⁰⁶ ¹⁸⁴¹ fam 1611²³²⁹ Andr f²⁰⁷³ i l 94 it^gig (*testari haec in ecclesiis*); Tyc² (*testari vobis haec in ecclesiis*), supported by WHort^mg; B. Weiss, *Johannes-Apokalypse*, 112; Charles, 2:382. (3) omit] Andreas; Primasius (*vobis septem ecclesiis*). The original reading is certainly ἐπί, which is the *lectio difficilior* because of the relatively unusual meaning of the prep. in this context. In reading (2), ἐν in A is a correction (Schmid, *Studien* 2:134), which can mean "*before* the churches," i.e., in community gatherings (Hadorn, 218). In reading (3), the omission of a prep. before ταῖς ἐκκλησίαις in Andreas is an attempt to read ταῖς ἐκκλησίαις in apposition to ὑμῖν: "to you, that is, to the churches." In reading (1), which is most probably the original reading, ἐπί, "for," is dependent on the inf. μαρτυρῆσαι and can mean "to testify *for* [the benefit of] the churches" (see Louw-Nida, § 90.40, ἐπί + dat. as a marker of persons *benefited* by an event, i.e., with the dat. of advantage) or, less probably, "to testify *to* the churches" (Louw-Nida, § 90.57, ἐπί as "a marker of the experiencer, often with the implication of an action by a superior force or agency"). Though ἐπί in Rev 10:11 is often referred to as a parallel usage (Bousset [1906] 166; Prigent, 357 n. 19; Bauer-Aland, 582.II.1.b.δ), this is possible only if ἐπί + dat. is construed as meaning "about, on the subject of," but that meaning would require ἐπί + gen. (Bauer-Aland, 580.I.1.b.β). Since John's message to the nations is primarily one of *judgment*, the occurrence of ἐπί + dat. in 10:11 is used in the sense of "to prophesy *against* the people" (Louw-Nida, § 90.34; ἐπί + dat. or acc. is "a marker of opposition in a judicial or quasi-judicial context" meaning "against"), i.e., with the dat. of disadvantage.

16.d. The Gk. phrase ἡ ῥίζα καὶ τὸ γένος is a hendiadys, which has been translated here simply "descendant" (see Bratcher-Hatton, *Revelation*, 322) since ῥίζα (lit. "root") has the figurative meaning "descendant, offspring" here (Louw-Nida, § 10.33), and γένος is very similar in meaning (Louw-Nida, § 10.32). καί functions epexegetically: e.g., "the shoot, that is, the descendant" (see *Note* 5:5.d.).

16.e. Variants: (1) omit καί] *lectio originalis;* Andr d n 94 1773. (2) καί before ὁ ἀστήρ] 051 2030 fam 1611²⁰⁵⁰ Andreas itᵃ syrᵖʰ arm copˢᵃ ᵇᵒ.

16.f. Variants: (1) ὁ πρωϊνός] ℵ C 025 046 (ὁ προϊνός); 051 Oecumenius²⁰⁵³ᵗᵉˣᵗ ²⁰⁶²ᵗᵉˣᵗ fam 1611¹⁶¹¹ ¹⁸⁵⁴ Tyc²; B. Weiss, *Johannes-Apokalypse*, 127 (ὁ προϊνός). (2) καί ὁ προϊνός] A. (3) καὶ πρωϊνός] fam 1006¹⁰⁰⁶ ¹⁸⁴¹ 209 Andr g²⁰⁴⁵ ²⁰⁷¹ Andr l¹⁶⁷⁸ ¹⁷⁷⁸ Byz 17⁴⁶⁹ ¹⁸⁵² itᵍⁱᵍ vg Primasius Beatus Apringius. (4) καὶ ὀρθρινός] Byzantine.

17.a. καί is left untranslated since it functions as a marker for the beginning of a new sentence.

17.b. Variant: omit τό before πνεῦμα] ℵ copᵇᵒ.

17.c. Variant: omit ἡ before νύμφη] ℵ 051 2377 Andreas.

18.a. In the phrase μαρτυρῶ ἐγώ, the ἐγώ is used for emphasis and can be translated "I myself testify" or even "I solemnly testify."

18.b. Variant: omit τῷ] 2377 Andreas.

18.c. The noun προφητείας is a gen. of quality reflecting a Hebraism often woodenly rendered "the words *of the prophecy* of this book." The paucity of adjs. in Hebrew necessitated the use of nouns in the construct state (functionally equivalent to the Gk. gen.) where the more natural Gk. idiom would be the use of an adj. (e.g., ὁ προφητικὸς λόγος, "the prophetic word"). This Hebraism occurs frequently in the NT (see Rom 6:6; 7:24; Phil 3:21; Matt 19:28).

18.d. Variants: (1) ἐπιθήσῃ] Andr c i l¹⁶⁷⁸. (2) ἐπιθήσει] Andr a²¹⁸⁶ l¹⁷⁷⁸.

18.e. Variant: αὐτῷ] Andr a²¹⁸⁶ c e.

18.f-f. Variants: (1) ὁ θεὸς ἐπ' αὐτόν] *lectio originalis*. (2) ἐπ' αὐτὸν ὁ θεός] ℵ 2030 2377 Andreas Ambrose Apringius. (3) ἐπ' αὐτῷ ὁ θεός] fam 1611²⁰⁵⁰. (4) ὁ θεός] A. (5) ὁ θεὸς αὐτῷ] Andr a²¹⁸⁶ c⁻²⁰⁴⁴. (6) ἐπ' αὐτῷ] Andr i.

18.g-g. Variants: (1) ἐπιθήσαι] Andr f⁰⁵¹ ²⁰²³ ²⁰⁷³ 94 Byzantine. (2) ἐπιθήσοι] Andr l.

18.h. Variant: insert ἑπτά] 046 051 2377 Andreas.

19.a. The prep. phrase ἀπὸ τῶν λόγων τοῦ βιβλίου τῆς προφητείας ταύτης, lit. "from the prophetic words of this book," is a partitive gen. (intensified by the prep. ἀπό, "from"), which functions as the *obj.* of the verb ἀφέλῃ, "remove, expunge"; see BDR § 164. An indefinite pl. obj., such as τινά, "anything," is presupposed. The author often uses the partitive gen. (most frequently with ἐκ or ἀπό) as the subject or obj. of various verbs; see Rev 2:7, 10, 17; 5:9; 11:9; 21:6; see *Introduction*, Section 7: Syntax, under "partitive genitive," pp. clxxi–clxxiii.

19.b. Variant: τούτων after λόγων] ℵ Andr l.

19.c. Variant: insert τούτου before τοῦ βιβλίου] ℵ Andr f²⁰³¹ ²⁰⁵⁶.

19.d. See *Note* 18.c.

19.e. For this translation of the fut. ind. ἀφελεῖ, see *Note* 18.b. above.

19.f. Here μέρος means "share" in the sense of experiencing something together with others; see W. S. Vorster, "New Testament Sample Studies," in *Lexicography and Translation with Special Reference to Bible Translation*, ed. J. P. Louw (Cape Town: Bible Society of South Africa, 1985) 144.

19.g-g. Variants: (1) ἀπὸ τοῦ ξύλου] *lectio originalis*. (2) ἀπὸ βίβλου] Latin versions (*de libro uitae*): itᶜ ᵈⁱᵘ ʰᵃᶠ vg ꟳᴷᴼᴨᶜᵁⱽᵂ; TR KJV. Brief discussion in *TCGNT*², 690.

19.h. Variant: omit ἐκ] A copᵇᵒ.

20.a. The present ind. verb ἔρχομαι, "I come," "I am coming," is an example of the futuristic present (BDF, § 323; N. Turner, *Syntax*, 63), frequently used in prophecies.

20.b. Variant: omit ἀμήν] ℵ fam 1611²⁰⁵⁰ ²³²⁹ Andr a²¹⁸⁶ c l 94 itᵍⁱᵍ syrᵖʰ cop Primasius Beatus.

20.c. Variant: insert ναί] 051 fam 1611¹⁸⁵⁴ ²⁰⁵⁰ 2030 2377 Andr d f²⁰³¹ ⁻²⁰⁵⁶ i Byzantine Primasius.

20.d. Variants: (1) omit Χριστέ] A (lacuna in C) ℵ fam 1611¹⁶¹¹ Oecumenius²⁰⁵³ ²⁰⁶² [WHort]; von Soden, *Text;* Nestle-Aland²⁷; UBSGNT⁴. (2) add Χριστέ] Andreas Byzantine.

Form/Structure/Setting

I. OUTLINE

V. Epilogue (22:10–21)
  A. Concluding parenesis (22:10–20)
    1. Admonitions of the angelic guide (vv 10–11)
      a. To the seer (v 10)
        (1) Command: Do not seal the book
        (2) Reason: The end is near
      b. To the unrighteous (v 11a)
        (1) Let the unjust person continue acting unjustly
        (2) Let the morally depraved continue to be depraved
      c. To the righteous (v 11b)
        (1) Let the righteous continue to act righteously
        (2) Let the holy continued to be holy
    2. Sayings of the exalted Christ (vv 12–16)
      a. The promise of his imminent return (v 12)
        (1) He brings his reward with him (v 12a)
        (2) He will repay each according to his or her behavior (v 12b)
      b. Self-predications (v 13)
        (1) "I am the Alpha and the Omega" (v 13a)
        (2) "I am the First and the Last" (v 13b)
        (3) "I am the Beginning and the End" (v 13c)
      c. Beatitude (vv 14–15)
        (1) Those who wash their robes are blessed (v 14a)
          (a) They will have access to the tree of life (v 14b)
          (b) They will enter the city by the gates (v 14c)
        (2) Those who are outside the city (those who do not wash their robes) (v 15)
          (a) "Dogs"
          (b) Magicians
          (c) Fornicators
          (d) Murderers
          (e) Idolaters
          (f) Everyone fond of lying
      d. Concluding attestation of the exalted Jesus (v 16)
        (1) The transmission of this revelation (v 16a)
          (a) The revealer: I, Jesus
          (b) The means: I sent my angel
          (c) The purpose: to attest "these things"
          (d) The primary recipients: to "you" (plural) (the prophets)
          (e) The secondary recipients: the churches
        (2) Verifying self-predications (v 16b)
          (a) I am the descendant of David

        (b) I am the bright morning star
3. Invitation to the water of life (v 17)
    a. The twofold invitation (v 17ab)
        (1) The Spirit and bride say "come" (v 17a)
        (2) Let the hearer say "come" (v 17b)
    b. The exhortation to come and drink (v 17c)
        (1) Let the one who is thirsty come (v 17c)
        (2) Let the one who wishes receive the water of life freely (v 17c)
4. Jesus addresses conditional curses to those who hear this book (vv 18–19)
    a. To those who "add" to the book: God will "add" the plagues in this book (v 18bc)
    b. To those who "take away " from the book (v 19)
        (1) God will "take away" their share of the tree of life (v 19b)
        (2) God will "take away" their share in the holy city (v 19b)
5. Jesus, who attests this revelation, promises to return soon (v 20ab)
6. Responses of the author (v 20c)
    a. "Amen!"
    b. "Come, Lord Jesus!"

II. Literary Analysis

A. *Rev 22:10–20 as a Text Unit*

Conventional analyses of the structure of the last part of Revelation frequently regard 22:6–21 as a distinct textual unit (Prigent, 276; Kraft, 276; T. Collins, *Apocalypse*, 10–12), which is frequently called an "epilogue" (Swete, 302; Beckwith, 290–91; 771; Caird, 281–82; Prigent, 348–49; Hellholm, "Genre," 52), while others use the rhetorically neutral term "conclusion" (Bousset [1906] 455; Kraft, 276; Roloff [ET] 248–49). Vanni earlier referred to 22:6–21 as an "epilogue" but later dropped the term in preference for "concluding liturgical dialogue" (*La struttura letteraria*, 298–302).

In classical rhetoric, the conclusion of a speech was called the "epilogue" (ἐπίλογος) or "peroration" (*peroratio* or *conclusio*) and formed the final part of the four-part, five-part, or six-part classical oration (Ps.-Cicero *Ad Herennium* 1.3.4). This concluding section was used to review previous arguments, often in an impassioned way (Aristotle *Rhet.* 1414b; Ps.-Cicero *Ad Herennium* 2.30.47). Therefore, the conclusion of Revelation is an "epilogue" only in the sense that it exhibits a striking thematic correspondence to the prologue in 1:1–8 (Giblin, 214), though the peroration of classical speeches normally had a particularly close connection with the exordium or *prooimion,* which functioned to catch the attention of the audience while introducing the subject of the speech.

This unit (whether it consists of 22:6–21 or 22:10–21) is like the title in 1:1–2 in that it is *metatextual* since it comments on the text of Revelation. Its primary function is to underscore the divine origin and authority of the book that it concludes. A distinctive literary form, the "liturgical dialogue," has even been proposed for 22:6–21 by Vanni (*La struttura letteraria*, 111) and argued in detail by Kavanagh (*Apocalypse*), though this proposal is extremely speculative.

The chief challenge to the view that 22:6 begins a new textual unit is the convincing demonstration by Giblin (*Bib* 55 [1974] 487–504) that 17:1–19:10 and 21:9–22:9 are structurally parallel: both sections end with John's attempting to worship the angelic messenger (19:10; 22:8–9). Just as 19:10 must be considered the conclusion of 17:1–19:9, so 22:8–9 must be considered the conclusion of 21:9–22:7. This becomes obvious when a comparison is made of the parallel texts that frame these units, i.e., Rev 17:1–3; 19:9–10, and 21:9–10; 22:6–9:

Rev 17:1–19:10	*Rev 21:9–22:9*
[17:1]καὶ ἦλθεν εἷς ἐκ τῶν ἑπτὰ Then came one of the seven	[21:9]καὶ ἦλθεν εἷς ἐκ τῶν ἑπτὰ Then came one of the seven
ἀγγέλων τῶν ἐχόντων τὰς ἑπτὰ angels with the seven	ἀγγέλων τῶν ἐχόντων τὰς ἑπτὰ angels with the seven
φιάλας bowls	φιάλας τῶν γεμόντων τῶν ἑπτὰ bowls full of the seven
	πληγῶν τῶν ἐσχάτων last plagues
καὶ ἐλάλησεν μετ' ἐμοῦ λέγων and spoke with me, saying,	καὶ ἐλάλησεν μετ' ἐμοῦ λέγων and spoke with me, saying,
δεῦρο, δείξω σοι "Come, I will show you	δεῦρο, δείξω σοι "Come, I will show you
τὸ κρίμα τῆς πόρνης τῆς μεγάλης. . . . the judgment of the great whore. . . ."	τὴν νύμφην τὴν γυναῖκα τοῦ ἀρνίου the bride, the wife of the Lamb."
[17:3]καὶ ἀπήνεγκέν με He then transported me	[21:10]καὶ ἀπήνεγκέν με He then transported me
εἰς ἔρημον to the desert	
ἐν πνεύματι in a prophetic trance.	ἐν πνεύματι in a prophetic trance
	ἐπὶ ὄρος μέγα καὶ ὑψηλόν to a great and high mountain
καὶ εἶδον. . . . Then I saw	καὶ ἔδειξέν μοι. . . . and showed me . . . .
[17:4–19:8]	[21:11–22:5]
[19:9a]μακάριοι . . . . "Blessed	
[19:9b]καὶ λέγει μοι Then he says to me,	[22:6]καὶ εἶπέν μοι Then he said to me,

οὗτοι οἱ λόγοι ἀληθινοὶ
"These are the true words

τοῦ θεοῦ εἰσιν.
of God."

οὗτοι οἱ λόγοι πιστοὶ καὶ
"These words are faithful and

ἀληθινοί . . . .
true. . . .

^{22:7}μακάριος . . . . [see 19:9a]
Blessed. . . ."

^{22:8b}καὶ ὅτε ἤκουσα καὶ ἔβλεψα
And when I heard and saw them,

^{19:10}καὶ ἔπεσα ἔμπροσθεν
Then I fell before

τῶν ποδῶν αὐτοῦ
his feet

προσκυνῆσαι αὐτῷ.
to worship him,

ἔπεσα προσκυνῆσαι ἔμπροσθεν
I fell to worship before

τῶν ποδῶν τοῦ ἀγγέλου
the feet of the angel

τοῦ δεικνύοντός μοι ταῦτα.
who revealed them to me.

καὶ λέγει μοι·
but he says to me,

καὶ λέγει μοι·
But he says to me,

ὅρα μή·
"Don't do that!

ὅρα μή·
"Don't do that!

σύνδουλός σού εἰμι
I am a fellow servant with you

σύνδουλός σού εἰμι
I am a fellow servant with you

καὶ τῶν ἀδελφῶν σου τῶν ἐχόντων
and your brothers who maintain

καὶ τῶν ἀδελφῶν σου τῶν προφητῶν
and your brothers the prophets

τὴν μαρτυρίαν᾽ Ἰησοῦ·
the testimony concerning Jesus.

καὶ τῶν τηρούντων τοὺς λόγους
and those who obey the commands

τοῦ βιβλίου τούτου.
in this book.

τῷ θεῷ προσκύνησον.
Worship God!"

τῷ θεῷ προσκύνησον.
Worship God!"

The structural problem of whether the preceding section ends with 22:5 or 22:10 can be solved satisfactorily when it is recognized that 22:6–9 functions as a transitional section that provides both a conclusion to 21:9–22:5 and an introduction to 22:10–20. Gaechter (*TS* 10 [1949] 508–13), Schüssler Fiorenza (*CBQ* 39 [1977] 364), and Michaels (*Interpreting,* 71) are among the few who correctly argue that the "epilogue" begins in 22:10, though Lohmeyer (177–78) clearly saw the problem of making a break between 22:5 and 22:6.

B. The Compositional Problems

This section gives the appearance of being so uneven and disorderly that a number of proposals have been made for rearranging and even eliminating some portions of the text in the interest of creating greater intelligibility and coherence out of the whole. One major problem in interpreting this section is determining the identity of the speakers despite the numerous abrupt shifts. The angel who showed John the holy city in 21:10–22:5 is explicitly described as one of the bowl angels (21:9), and it is presumably he who is identified in the narrative as "the one who spoke with me" (21:15) and is the subject of the verbs ἐμέτρησεν, "he measured" (21:17), and ἔδειξεν, "he showed" (22:1). In 22:6, therefore, this same bowl angel appears to be the subject of the verb εἶπεν, "he said." Yet v 7 contains a saying that can only be attributed to the risen Jesus: "And behold, I am coming soon." But 22:8, where John tries to worship the angel who showed "these things" to him, suggests that this angel should be considered the speaker of vv 6–7. It is possible that the saying of Christ in the first person in v 7 is, as it were, a prophetic utterance of the *angelus interpres* (so Kraft, 277). Then, following the sayings in 22:10–11, when the speaker is apparently still "the angel who showed these things to me" (v 8), i.e., the *angelus interpres* of 21:9, two sayings follow in vv 12–13 without hiatus and again, like v 7a, must be attributed to the risen Jesus:

> [12]Indeed, I am coming soon, and my reward is with me to repay to each in proportion to his or her behavior. [13]I am the Alpha and the Omega, the First and the Last, the Beginning and the End.

It is possible that vv 14–16 constitute a speech or collection of sayings of the risen Jesus. However, while vv 14–15 need not be attributed to the exalted Christ, v 16 certainly must since it begins "I, Jesus." In v 17, a saying is attributed to the Spirit and the bride, paired with a reiteration or response from "the one who hears." The integrity formula in 22:18–19 can be attributed either to John or to the risen Jesus, though v 20 suggests that it should be attributed to the risen Jesus: "He who testifies to this says, 'Surely I am coming soon.'" The response in v 20b and the epistolary postscript must be attributed to John.

C. Proposed Rearrangements of the Text

The central problem in any literary analysis of 22:10–20 (or the larger section 22:6–21) is whether this section can be understood as a unity in its present form or whether some form of rearrangement or surgery (minor or major) is required to make sense of the present state of the text. According to Charles (2:212), in 22:6–21, more than anywhere else in Rev 20–22, the *disjecta membra* ("scattered limbs") of the poet-seer are to be found.

C. Könnecke (*Emendationen*, 40–42) proposed the following rearrangement of pericopes in 22:6–21: (1) v 6, (2) vv 7b–11, (3) vv 14–16, (4) v 13, (5) v 12, and (6) vv 17–21; he eliminated only v 7a ("Behold, I will come soon"). Through this rearrangement, the angelic guide is the speaker in vv 6–15 (since 7a has been eliminated), the exalted Jesus speaks in vv 16, 13, 12, the Spirit and the bride speak in v 17, and John speaks in vv 18–21. This is a very simple and economical rearrangement that does solve the basic problem.

Charles (2:212–13, 379–85) suggested that this section should be reconstructed in the following order: vv 6–7, 18a, 16, 13, 12, 10, 8–9, 20–21. He prefaced the epilogue with 21:5cde, 6c–8, he regarded some of the material in 22:6–21 as displaced (22:14–15, 17 belong after 21:9–22:2), and he excised other material that he thought was added by the editor (22:11, 18b–19).

There are a number of other textual rearrangements proposed by scholars to solve the incoherent and illogical features of Rev 22:6–21 (e.g., Gaechter, *TS* 10 [1949] 485–521; Boismard, *RB* 59 [1952] 172–78). However, all such proposals are based on the dubious assumption that an originally coherent text was somehow thrown into violent disarray.

D. Advocates of the Unity of the Text

Despite the many problems discussed above under B. The Compositional Problems, there are scholars who have argued for the unity and coherence of the concluding section of Revelation (Bousset [1906] 455–60 [with the exception of 22:6–9]; Vanni, *La struttura letteraria*, 107–15; Kavanagh, *Apocalypse*, 51–53). Many of these scholars assume that this unity becomes evident once the liturgical structure of the text is perceived (see below under III. Theories of Liturgical Sequence).

E. Parallels between 22:6–21 and 1:1–3

Rev 22:6–21 exhibits several striking parallels with 1:1–3 that suggest the author has self-consciously framed the entire composition with similar motifs. We have insisted on considering 22:6–9 a transitional passage, and this transitional character becomes clear in light of the striking parallels between 1:1–3 and 22:6–10 (and 18). These parallels suggest that the entire section was part of the Second Edition of Revelation. Here the similarities are arranged in parallel columns:

Rev 1:1–3	*Rev 22:6–10, 18*
¹δεῖξαι τοῖς δούλοις αὐτοῦ to show his servants	⁶δεῖξαι τοῖς δούλοις αὐτοῦ to show his servants
ἃ δεῖ γενέσθαι ἐν τάχει. . . . what must soon happen. . . .	ἃ δεῖ γενέσθαι ἐν τάχει. . . . what must soon happen. . . .
³μακάριος . . . οἱ ἀκονόντες blessed . . . those who hear	⁷μακάριος ὁ τηρῶν blessed [is] the one who obeys
τοὺς λόγους τῆς προφητείας the prophetic words	τοὺς λόγους τῆς προφητείας the prophetic words
καὶ τηροῦντες τὰ and obey the things	τοῦ βιβλίου τούτου. . . . of this book. . . .

ἐν αὐτῇ γεγραμμένα	⁹τοὺς λόγους
written in it,	the words
	τοῦ βιβλίου τούτου. . . .
	of this book. . . .
	¹⁰τοὺς λόγους τῆς
	the words of this
	προφητείας τοῦ βιβλίου τούτου. . . .
	prophetic book. . . .
	¹⁸τοὺς λόγους τῆς προφητείας
	the prophetic words
	τοῦ βιβλίου τούτου. . . .
	of this book. . . .
ὁ γὰρ καιρὸς ἐγγύς.	¹⁰ὁ καιρὸς γὰρ ἐγγύς ἐστιν.
for the time is near.	for the time is near.

III. THEORIES OF LITURGICAL SEQUENCE

Just as some scholars believe that the epistolary greeting in NT letters may be derived from the opening greeting of a group of Christians assembled for worship (see *Comment* on 1:4), so a number of scholars have proposed that the sequence of motifs that concludes several NT letters, including Revelation, reflects a ritual series of actions and words derived from Christian worship services. Three main types of liturgical sequence theories that apply to the concluding chapter of Revelation have been proposed: (1) a liturgical sequence that leads to the celebration of the Eucharist and begins when the public reading of the letter has concluded (Lietzmann, *Mass;* J. A. T. Robinson, *JTS* 4 [1953] 38–41); (2) a liturgical sequence that reflects the conclusion of a service of the word (Cuming, *NTS* 22 [1975–76] 110–13); and (3) the hypothesis that 22:6–21 is a liturgical dialogue (Vanni, *La struttura letteraria;* Kavanagh, *Apocalypse*).

The first view was briefly proposed by Lietzmann (*Mass,* 186–87), who suggested that 1 Cor 16:20–24 reflected a liturgical dialogue. When the Corinthians heard 1 Cor 16:20 read to them, "Greet one another with a holy kiss," they kissed one another, and when they heard 1 Cor 16:23, "The grace of the Lord Jesus be with you," they responded, "And with your spirit." When the reading from the letter concluded, the Lord's Supper began.

In dependence on Seeberg ("Kuss und Kanon"), Lietzmann (*Mass*), and Hofmann (*Untersucht*), Bornkamm ("Anathema," 169–76) isolates a sequence of four liturgical formulas: (1) the summons to the holy kiss, (2) the Anathema, (3) the Maranatha, and (4) the promise of the grace of the Lord Jesus. In essential agreement with Lietzmann, though apparently independent of him, J. A. T. Robinson (*JTS* 4 [1953] 38–41), whose discussion is not as clear as it might be, apparently distinguishes five elements in the supposed liturgical sequence with which 1 Cor 16:20–24 concludes: (1) mutual greetings (v 20a); (2) exchange of the kiss of peace (v 20b); (3) the invitation, issued with the warning of exclusion (v 22): "If anyone has no love for the Lord, let him be accursed" (see *Did.* 10:6, "If anyone is holy, let him come; if anyone is not, let him repent"); (4) pronouncement of the Aramaic watchword *maranatha* (cf. 1 Cor 11:26); and (5) Paul's closing greetings, which echo the words with which the presider begins, "The grace of our Lord Jesus Christ be with you" (v 24). Since all interpretations of *Did.* 9–10 admit the presence of some type of cultic meal, whether the agape or the Eucharist, the *crux interpretum* for the foregoing theories is the comparison between *Did.* 10:6 and 1 Cor 16:22:

Did. 10:6	*1 Cor 16:22*
Let grace [χάρις] come and let this world pass away. Hosanna to the God of David. If any man be holy, let him come! If anyone is not, let him repent.	If any one has no love for the Lord, let him be accursed [ἀνάθεμα].
Maran atha, Amen.	Marana tha. The grace [χάρις] of the Lord Jesus be with you.

Bornkamm ("Anathema," 171–72) finds the same introit liturgy in 1 Cor 16:20–24 and *Did.* 10:6, but he also identifies it in the conclusion of Revelation. He thinks this conclusion has been formulated in close dependence on the Lord's Supper introit as revealed by the summons to prayer, Maranatha, in 22:20, "Amen! Come, Lord Jesus!" as well as by the invitation in v 17, "And let him who is thirsty come, let him who desires take the water of life without price."

Following Vanni (*La struttura letteraria,* 109–15, 298–302), Kavanagh has proposed that Rev 22:6–21 is a liturgical dialogue (*Apocalypse,* 97–141). His proposal is based in part on analyses of the antiphonal character of many of the hymns of Revelation (Deichgräber, *Gotteshymnus,* 46–47; Jörns, *Evangelium,* 161), on the presence of liturgical dialogue in the biblical psalms, on hymnic material from Qumran and early Christianity (*Did.* 10:6; Rev 1:4–8), and on the presence of apparently liturgical elements in Rev 22:6–21. He begins by arguing for the unity of 22:6–21, which he thinks is evident in an A-B-A structure, which he designates a "literary triptych" (*Apocalypse,* 73–94): (1) The first stage of this structure, 22:6–11, is organized in general form like 19:9–10 and 21:5–8 and can be subdivided into three speeches: (a) 22:6–7, (b) 22:8–9, and (c) 22:10–11. (2) The second stage, 22:12–16, is characterized by a series of unintroduced speeches. (3) The third stage, 22:17–21, consists of three "movements": (a) 22:17 is responsorial and centers on the word "coming"; (b) 22:18–19 is a brief speech focusing on the book and its contents; and (c) 22:20 is again responsorial, focusing on the term "coming." In addition, a wish-prayer in 22:21 concludes the section. This structural analysis serves as a basis for Kavanagh's proposal, following Vanni, that Rev 22:6–21 represents a liturgical dialogue (see below). After the preliminary discussion, the actual analysis of Rev 22:6–21 as a liturgical dialogue is relatively weak (*Apocalypse,* 131–38). The apportionment of speakers in the dialogue or "narrated conversation" occurs in a two-page appendix (*Apocalypse,* 186–87), where the "lector" is assigned 22:6–17b, 17c–20b, 21, while the "hearers" are assigned the single word ἔρχου, "Come!" in v 17b and "Amen! Come, Lord Jesus!" in v 20c. Kavanagh does argue that the lector speaks the part assigned to John in vv 6a, 8–9a, and 10a, the part of the *angelus interpres* in v 9bc, and the part of Jesus himself in vv 7a, 12, 16, 20b, and perhaps 13 also (*Apocalypse*, 131–32). Yet this hardly amounts to a liturgical dialogue. It must be concluded that the hypothesis that 22:6–21 is a liturgical dialogue, at least in the form presented by Kavanagh, has not been proved, for despite the many different voices in this passage (both those that are identifiable and those that are not), the complexity of the text remains without a satisfactory explanation.

IV. Literary Forms in 22:18–20

The concluding paragraph of Revelation (22:18–20) also constitutes the final segment of the larger section 22:10–20, which is preceded by the transitional passage 22:6–9. Since 22:6–9 is transitional, it forms part of the conclusion of 21:9–22:9 as well as part of the introduction to 22:6–20. The literary unity of this section is exhibited by several features in 22:6–7 (of the transitional section 22:6–9) and 22:18–20 that the author uses to frame the textual unit: (1) The oath formula μαρτυρῶ ἐγώ, "I testify" (v 18), corresponds to the oath formula in v 6, "these words are faithful and true." (2) The promise "Yes, I will come shortly" in v 20 corresponds to the phrase "Behold, I will come shortly" in v 7. (3) The phrase "the prophetic words of this book" occurs four times in this section (vv 18, 19 and vv 7, 10). (4) The conditional curses in vv 18b–19 correspond inversely to the conditional beatitude of v 7.

Some scholars regard vv 18–19 as an interpolation added by a later redactor rather than a statement that comes from the hand of the primary author (Charles, 2:222; Langevin, *Jésus seigneur*, 282). It is precisely because Kraft (282) regards Revelation as a prophetic book that he views vv 18–20 as a secondary interpolation, because he maintains that a prophetic book, in contrast to an apocalypse, does not envisage the cessation of revelation. This is a relatively flimsy reason, however, for regarding this paragraph as secondary, since it drives an artificial wedge between prophecy and apocalyptic.

The final paragraph of Revelation consists of three literary forms that the author has molded into a new and complex unity: (1) The *integrity formula*, usually expressed negatively in Greek literature, μήτε προσθεῖναι, μήτε ἀφελεῖν, "do not add, do not delete," is found in vv 18b–19. (2) Two conditional curse formulas that incorporate the integrity formula and the *lex talionis*, "principle of retributive justice," are found in vv 18b–19. This form has been labeled a "sentence of holy law" (E. Käsemann, "Sentences of Holy Law," 66–81). (3) A liturgical invocation, "Amen! Come, Lord Jesus!" and a response, "Yes, I will come shortly," appear in reverse order in v 20. The entire paragraph is framed by variations on the oath formula, "I testify" in v 18 and "he who testifies" in v 20.

1. *The Integrity Formula.* This formula occurs frequently throughout the ancient world in Jewish, Christian, and pagan literature. It has been misleadingly (because anachronistically) designated a "canonization formula" (Bousset [1906] 459–60; Bousset-Gressmann, *Religion des Judentums*, 148; Brun, *Segen*, 109), for there are many parallels to this formula. However, it functions as a "canonization formula"

in only a restricted number of instances. It has more correctly been designated a *Sicherungsformel*, "protection formula" (Kraft, 282). Yet the designation "integrity formula" is even more appropriate, for it encompasses the various functions the formula has in various contexts.

The integrity formula was used in connection with sacred traditions, holy texts, and divine revelations, either as a guarantee that they had not been tampered with or as an attempt to protect them from alteration by others in an era that lacked the legal protection of copyright laws. At the conclusion of an Egyptian book of wisdom called the *Instruction of Ptah-hotep* (ca. 2200 B.C.), we find this injunction: "Take no word away, and add nothing thereto, and put not one thing in the place of another" (Leipoldt-Morenz, *Heilige Schriften*, 56). More recently, Morenz has corrected this translation to read "Do not say now this and now that and confound not one thing with another" (Morenz, *Egyptian Religion*, 223–24, 251); i.e., this text can no longer be considered an example of the integrity formula. At the conclusion of the Akkadian "Epic of Irra" (late first millennium B.C.), the following statement is made in an epilogue to a dream narrative: "and when he [the author] rose in the morning, he did not miss or add a single line in writing the opus down" (tr. Oppenheim, *Dreams*, 193). Similarly, toward the end of the apocryphal gospel entitled the *History of Joseph the Carpenter* 30, we again find the formula "And whosoever shall take anything away from this narrative, or add anything to it, commits sin." The integrity formula is used in the OT in wisdom settings, where it functions to protect the integrity of the divine instructions that have been transmitted by tradition (Prov 30:5–6; Sir 18:6; 42:21). A Mesopotamian text reads "It was revealed to him in the night and he did not leave out a single line, nor did he add one to it" (W. G. Lambert, *Iraq* 2 [1952] 122). Here the formula guarantees the accuracy of a divine revelation.

The formula also occurs at the conclusion of ancient treaties, where it has a juridical function: "To this tablet I did not add a word nor did I take one out" is a statement found in a Hittite treaty (Güterbock, *Revue Hittite et Asianique* 18 [1960] 59–60). Many commentators point to Deut 4:2 (see Deut 12:32) as the OT parallel to Rev 22:18–19: "You shall not add to the word which I command you, nor take from it" (LXX οὐ προσθήσετε . . . οὐκ ἀφελεῖτε). In Deut 4:2 the formula does double duty as an injunction to protect the inviolability of a covenant treaty (the literary genre that frames Deuteronomy) and to protect a sacred text. The *Temple Scroll* from Qumran repeats the injunction of Deut 12:32: "All the words that I command you today you shall observe to fulfill them. You shall not add to them and not take anything away from them" (11QTemple 54:5–7; tr. Maier, *Temple Scroll*, 47). For the present context in Revelation, it is significant that in the following passage in Deut 13:1 and in 11QTemple 54:6 there is a stern warning against false prophets. At the conclusion of a treaty between the Romans and the Jews (1 Macc 8:30), we read:

> If after these terms are in effect both parties shall determine to add or delete [προσθεῖναι ἢ ἀφελεῖν] anything, they shall do so at their discretion, and any addition or deletion [προσθῶσιν ἢ ἀφέλωσιν] that they may make shall be valid.

Ancient treaties were more typically concluded with a series of terrible curses, both to protect the text and to insure the observance of the terms of the treaty (see

Beyerlin, *Texts*, 129–31). A variant of the integrity formula occurring in the prologue to a Hittite treaty between Suppiluliumas and Kurtiwaza contains a conditional sanction against anyone who will remove, hide, break, or change the wording of the tablet upon which the treaty is written (*ANET*, 205). Another frequently cited parallel to Rev 22:18–19 is found in *Ep. Arist.* 311, where a sanction is pronounced by an assembly of Egyptian Jews in order to protect the LXX translation (M. Hadas, ed., *Aristeas to Philocrates: Letter of Aristeas* [New York: Harper, 1951] 221–23):

> When all had assented to what had been said, they bade that an imprecation be pronounced, according to their custom, upon any who should revise the text by adding [προστιθείς] or transposing [μεταφέρων] anything whatever in what had been written down, or by making any excision [ἀφαίρεσιν]; and in this they did well, so that the word might be preserved imperishable and unchanged always.

This legend was well known and was recounted also by Philo (*Mos.* 2.34), who reproduced the formula μήτ' ἀφελεῖν τι μήτε προσθεῖναι ἢ μεταθεῖναι, "Not to delete anything nor to add anything nor to change anything." Josephus (*Ant.* 12.109), who also recounts this formula, and Philo curiously omit any reference to the curse. While this use of the formula can properly be designated a "canonization formula," we have already observed that it was used in a much broader way. Elsewhere Josephus uses the integrity formula to describe how carefully the Jews have preserved the Scriptures (*Ag. Ap.* 1.42): "For, although such long ages have now passed, no one has ventured either to add, or to remove, or to alter a syllable [οὔτε προσθεῖναί τις οὐδὲν οὔτε ἀφελεῖν αὐτῶν οὔτε μεταθεῖναι]." Though Josephus uses the formula to affirm the accuracy of his work as a historian (*Ant.* 1.17; *J.W.* 1.26), since he regarded his rewriting (and embellishment) of Jewish history as a prophetic task (J. Blenkinsopp, "Prophecy and Priesthood in Josephus," *JJS* 25 [1974] 241–42), his use of the integrity formula fits the conception he had of his prophetic role (W. C. van Unnik, *Flavius Josephus als historischer Schriftsteller* [Heidelberg: Lambert Schneider, 1978] 39, 41–47).

In rabbinic literature the integrity formula is used to refer to the inviolability of tradition (i.e., the oral law) and to the task of the methurgeman in translating portions of Scripture into Aramaic (*b. Meg.* 14a; *b. 'Erub.* 13a, 100a; *b. Sanh.* 101a; *b. Šabb.* 116b; *Midr. Ruth* 2.4 [103b]; *Num. Rab.* 10 [159b]; the rabbinic use of the formula is discussed by E. Stauffer, "Der Methurgeman des Petrus," 288–91). In *t. Soṭa* 2.1 we read "He read aloud from it [the text] and wrote, deleting nothing and adding nothing [לא חסר ולא יתר *lōʾ ḥāsēr wělōʾ yōtēr*]" (ed. Bietenhard). The relationship between prophecy and the Torah is spelled out in a baraita in *b. Meg.* 14a: "48 prophets and 7 prophetesses prophesied to Israel, and they neither took away from nor added anything to what is written in the Law, save only the reading of the Megillah."

In Jewish literature, as we have seen, there is a tendency to expand the twofold integrity formula into a threefold formula by adding the element of change (μεταθεῖναι = לשנות *lišnôt*, "to change"). In an apocalyptic literary setting, the integrity formula is combined with an oath formula in a statement similar to Rev 22:18–19: "would that they [sinners who lie and write the Scriptures in their own names] would write all my words truthfully in their names, and neither take away [μήτε ἀφέλωσιν] or change [μήτε ἀλλοιώσωσιν] anything in these words, but write truthfully all that I testify [διαμαρτυροῦμαι] to them!" (*1 Enoch* 104:10–11; M. Black, *Apocalypsis*, 43).

The integrity formula is also used to describe regularity in nature in *1 Enoch* 41:5 (tr. Knibb, *Enoch*), "And I saw the chambers of the sun and the moon . . . and their magnificent course, and (how) they do not leave the course, neither adding (anything) to, nor omitting (anything) from, their course." Similar to this is the view expressed in Eccl 3:14, "I know that whatever God does endures for ever; nothing can be added to it, nor anything taken from it [Hebrew עָלָיו אֵין לְהוֹסִיף וּמִמֶּנּוּ אֵין לִגְרֹעַ *ʿālāyw ʾên lěhôsîp ûmimmennû ʾên ligrōaʿ;* Greek ἐπ᾽ αὐτῷ οὐκ ἔστιν προσθεῖναι, καὶ ἀπ᾽ αὐτοῦ οὐκ ἔστιν ἀφελεῖν]. God has made it so, in order that men should fear before him."

The integrity formula is also used as a device to insure the inviolability of law codes. Thus the epilogue to the Lipit-Ishtar law code pronounces a curse on anyone who would damage, erase, or add his name to the clay tablets on which the code is recorded (*ANET*, 161). Similarly, the epilogue of the Code of Hammurabi curses anyone who "has distorted my words, has altered my statutes, effaced my name inscribed (thereon), and has written his own name" on the law code (*ANET*, 178). In a chreia attributed to the Spartan Agesilaus, he is made to claim that he would "make no addition, subtraction, or revision in the present laws [τοῖς γὰρ οὖσιν οὔτ᾽ ἂν προσθείην τι οὔτ᾽ ἀφέλοιμι οὔτε μεταποιήσαιμι]" (Plutarch *Apoth. Spart.* 214b).

The integrity formula occurs a number of times in early Christian literature after Revelation. In *Barn.* 19:11 (see *Did.* 4:13), the addressees are exhorted to "guard what you have received, neither adding to it nor deleting from it" (μήτε προστιθεὶς μήτε ἀφαιρῶν). Eusebius (*Hist. eccl.* 3.39.15) reported that Papias claimed that Mark had written down Peter's account of the Lord's "oracles" (λόγια), giving particular attention to one thing: "to leave out nothing [τοῦ μηδὲν . . . παραλιπεῖν] of what he had heard or to falsify [ψεύσασθαι] nothing in them," an obvious variant of the integrity formula. Eusebius also reports that the Anonymous (an unknown Christian opponent of Montanism) was hesitant to write against the Montanists lest he be guilty of adding to or deleting from (μήτε προσθεῖναι μήτε ἀφελεῖν) the word of the new covenant of the Gospel (*Hist. eccl.* 5.16.3). With regard to the Quartodecimian controversy in Asia Minor, Eusebius (*Hist. eccl.* 5.24.2) reports the words of Polycrates of Ephesus: "Therefore we keep the day undeviatingly, neither adding nor taking away [μήτε προστιθέντες μήτε ἀφαιρούμενοι]." In the 39th Festal Letter of Athanasius of Alexandria (A.D. 367; Migne, *PG*, XXVI.1438), in which he prescribes his famous list of canonical OT and NT books, he warns at the conclusion, "Let no one add to these, neither let one take anything from these [μηδὲ τούτοις ἐπιβαλλέτω, μηδὲ τούτων ἀφαιρείσθω τι]." Of all the texts referred to thus far, this comes closest to a "canonization" formula.

The integrity formula is also found frequently in Greco-Roman literature. The second-century A.D. orator Aelius Aristides claims to have quoted Plato *exactly* (*Or.* 30.20; tr. C. A. Behr, LCL, 2:151): "for somehow I happened to have quoted this from memory, neither subtracting nor adding anything [οὔτ᾽ ἀφελὼν οὐδὲν οὔτε προσθείς]." The same formula is used in connection with the importance of accurate memory in Chariton *Chaereas and Callirhoe* 3.1.5–6 (tr. from Greek text of W. E. Blake): "Dionysos said, 'Tell me her [Callirhoe's] very words. Do not add or subtract anything [μηδὲν ἀφέλῃς μηδὲ προσθῇς], but remember accurately."

Cicero, referring to the eloquence of Catulus, says (*De oratore* 3.8.29; tr. LCL), "for my own part when listening to him my regular verdict is that any addition or alteration or subtraction [*addideris aut mutaveris aut detraxeris*] you might make would be inferior—an alteration for the worse." Artemidorus (*Oneirocritica* 2.70), an early second-century A.D. dream interpreter, commends his work to the protection of Apollo and requests that "those who read my books neither add nor delete anything from the present contents [μήτε προσθεῖναι μήτε τι τῶν ὄντων ἀφελεῖν]" (tr. White, *Oneirocritica*, 137; Greek text from R. Hercher, ed., *Artemidori Daldani Onirocriticon libri V*[Leipzig: Teubner, 1864] 167, line 25; this parallel is mentioned in BAGD, xxv–xxvi). He further claims that Apollo himself commanded him to write the book. In the introduction to his lost book *De Philosophia ex Oraculis Haurienda* (ed. G. Wolff, *Porphyrii: De philosophia ex oraculis haurienda librorum reliquiae* [Berlin: Springer, 1856]), the Neoplatonist Porphyry expresses his intention to provide a philosophical explanation of the oracles. This he prefaces with an oath: "And I testify by the gods that I have neither added to nor deleted from the intention of the oracles [κἀγὼ τοῦ θεοῦ μαρτύρομαι, ὡς οὐδὲ οὐδὲν οὔτε προστέθηκα οὔτε ἀφεῖλον τῶν χρησθέντων νοημάτων]"; Wolff, *Porphyrii*, 109, based on a fragment quoted in Eusebius *Praep. evang.* 4.7 [143d]); cf. POxy 1381, lines 174–75, where essentially the same statement is made, though only the term ἀφεῖλον, "I deleted," occurs (Nock, *Essays* 1:161 n. 5). The formula also occurs in a magical context in *PGM* XXXVII.16, a fragmentary text, where the formula [ἀ]φελεῖν τι ἢ προσθεῖναι, "to [d]elete or add anything," refers to the spell itself. With regard to the Law, Dio Chrysostom *Or.* 31.140 says (LCL tr.), "For in the first place, the law is explicit and can never become worse, since it is not possible either to take away from or add to its written terms [οὐ γάρ ἐστιν οὔτε ἀφελεῖν οὔτε προσθεῖναι τοῖς γεγραμμένοις]." He also observes that chiseling even a single word from any official public inscription is a capital crime (*Or.* 31.86).

The integrity formula also occurs in the writings of a number of Greco-Roman historians who use it to affirm accuracy in the use of sources and facts (Dionysius Hal. *Ant. Rom.* 5.8; *On Thucydides* 5, 16; Lucian *Hist.* 47), though this did not really mean slavish accuracy. Rather, it meant sticking to the general sense of the sources without copying them verbatim. Josephus also uses a variation of the formula when commenting on the accuracy of his own work as a historian (*Ant.* 1.17; *J.W.* 1.26); both passages are located in prefaces. In an interesting exception to the texts discussed above, the unknown author of a Greek translation of an aretology in honor of the Egyptian god Imouthes (POxy 1381, lines 174–77) claims with obvious pride that he had carefully *revised* the original by adding what was lacking and deleting what he thought was extraneous (καὶ ἐν τῇ ὅλῃ γραφῇ τ[ὸ] μὲν ὑστερὸν προσεπλήρωσα, τὸ δὲ περ[ι]σσεῦον ἀφεῖλον, "and in the whole writing I completed what was lacking and I deleted what was superfluous").

A consideration of all of the pagan, Jewish, and Christian uses of the integrity formula discussed above leads to the following conclusions: (1) The integrity formula was so widely diffused throughout the ancient world that it would have been immediately comprehensible to people of diverse languages and cultures. (2) It was used either to guarantee that a text had not been tampered with or (when coupled with a curse) to prevent a text from being altered in any way. (3) In most instances, the integrity formula was used in conjunction with a sacred tradition, sacred text, or divine revelation, though it occasionally had other applications such as protecting the integrity of treaties. (4) The integrity formula implies that the text or tradition in connection with which it is used is *complete, definitive, and incapable of improvement.* (5) The integrity formula occurs with some frequency in the writings of Hellenistic historians to guarantee the accuracy of their use of sources. (6) Structurally, the integrity formula is generally placed at the beginning or conclusion of a text since such formulas usually have a metatextual character; that is, they describe the text to which they are attached. (7) In the case of John's use of the integrity formula, the author is not claiming canonical status for his book, i.e., equal status with the literature of the OT (against Windisch, *ZNW* 10 [1909] 159), though he does appear to be giving it the status of a divine revelation that must be safeguarded from any alteration.

2. *Two Conditional Curse Formulas.* Unlike any of the parallels discussed above (with the exception of *Ep. Arist.* 310–11), John combines the integrity formula with two *conditional curses* in such a way that the curses replace the negative particles that are almost always used with integrity formulas. Curses belong to the area of sacral law since the punishments they contain are not under the jurisdiction of human individuals or institutions but are the concern of supernatural powers or forces. Curses were widely used throughout the ancient world, and many examples can be found in ancient literature and inscriptions.

Curses generally exhibit a two-part structure in which a condition is expressed in the protasis and formulated as a conditional clause (e.g., "If anyone does X"), a relative clause (e.g., "Whoever does X"), or a participial clause (e.g., "The one who does X"), and the curse itself is found in the apodosis, which usually contains a verb in the future indicative or imperative (Greek or Latin) or in the imperfect (Hebrew, Phoenician, Aramaic). This type of curse is clearly modeled after casuistic legal formulas.

Curses, which correspond inversely to blessings (and in association with which they are commonly found; see Deut 27–28; Luke 6:20–26; C. H. Dodd, "The Beatitudes: A Form Critical Study," in *More New Testament Studies* [Grand Rapids: Eerdmans, 1968] 1–10), are found in both the OT (Schottroff, *Der altisraelitische Fluchspruch;* S. H. Blank, *HUCA* 23.1 [1950–51] 73–95; S. Gevirtz, "Curse," *IDB* 1:749–50) and the NT (Brun, *Segen;* H. Koester, "Segen und Fluch III: Im Neuen Testament," *RGG*[3] 5:1651–52; Betz, *Galatians,* 50–52, and the literature there cited).

Belief in the effectiveness of the curse is a form of magic; a conditional curse is like a land mine ready to be detonated whenever and wherever the conditions are fulfilled. Like the integrity formula, curses were used as supernatural sanctions in the absence or impotence of effective legal authority. Conditional curses, occasionally expressed in terms of *lex talionis,* "principle of retributive justice" (i.e., what you do will be done to you), were used in ancient epitaphs to protect tombs and their contents, upon inscriptions to protect them from defacement, and at the conclusion of treaties to ensure adherence to the terms of the agreement. For examples, see Lattimore, *Epitaphs;* Beyerlin, *Texts,* 129–31; Gibson, *Inscriptions* 1:24; 2:44–45, 95–98. B. Olsson (*ZNW* 31 [1932] 84–86) thought that the author of Revelation had been influenced by the form of sepulchral inscriptions found in Asia Minor (e.g., *CIG,* 2664). Such a hypothesis is unnecessary in view of the widespread use of conditional curse formulas in a variety of settings and cultures.

The closest NT parallel to Rev 22:18b–19 is Gal 1:8–9. There Paul states that if anyone preaches a gospel different from the one received from Paul, "let him or her be accursed [ἀνάθεμα ἔστω]." The gravity of the issue is emphasized by the twofold repetition of the curse, though the first curse appears to be a virtual quotation of a pronouncement made by Paul earlier in the setting of Christian worship (on this point, see Betz, *Galatians*, 50). Paul pronounced these conditional curses in the introduction of Galatians in order to protect the integrity of the oral gospel, just as John pronounced a double curse at the conclusion of Revelation on anyone who dared alter the written prophecy he had composed.

Käsemann identified Rev 22:18b–19 as a "sentence of holy law" (*Satz heiligen Rechts*), which he considers a pronouncement made by an early Christian prophet within the setting of a eucharistic celebration ("Sentences of Holy Law," 76). In his view, such sentences have five formal features: (1) chiastic structure, (2) the same verb in both parts of the pronouncement, (3) the second part related to the eschatological activity of God, often expressed in the passive voice used as a circumlocution for divine activity, (4) the *lex talionis*, "principle of retributive justice," and (5) a protasis introduced with the casuistic legal form "if anyone" or "whoever" and an apodosis exhibiting the style of apodictic law (Käsemann, "Sentences of Holy Law," 66–81). I shall consider separately below the question of whether Rev 22:18b–19 reflects part of a larger liturgical sequence.

Klaus Berger attempted to refute Käsemann's view by arguing that the "sentence of holy law" originated in Israelite-Jewish aphoristic wisdom, that the form should more appropriately be designated *Sätzen weisheitlicher Belehrung*, "sentences of wisdom instruction," and that its primary setting was ethical exhortation or parenesis (Berger, "Zu den sogennanten Sätzen heiligen Rechts," *NTS* 17 [1970–71] 10–40; id., "Die sog. 'Sätze heiligen Rechts' im N.T.: Ihre Funktion und ihr Sitz im Leben," *TZ* 28 [1972] 305–30). In view of Berger's critique, which is not entirely valid, together with other considerations, several qualifications need to be made regarding Käsemann's analysis of the form: (1) The form (as distinguished from the content) of the sentences is used in settings other than prophetic, such as juridical, sapiential, and parenetic (see Ign. *Eph.* 2:1–2; 21:1; *Trall.* 5:2; *Rom.* 8:1; on these and other texts in Ignatius and Paul, see Grant, "'Holy Law,'" 65–71). (2) The form of the sentence is not "stable" in that rarely are all five features found in any given example; Rev 22:18b–19, for example, lacks chiastic structure. The basic character of the form is the presence of the *lex talionis*, a two-part pronouncement, the protasis of which deals with the action of individuals in the present and the apodosis with the eschatological response of God. (3) Käsemann claims, but does not demonstrate, the use of this form in early Christian prophetic speech (he points only to Rev 22:18b–19 and 1 Cor 14:38 as examples). (4) Similarly, Käsemann claims but does not demonstrate the prophetic use of this form *in a eucharistic setting* as a preliminary exclusion formula (see the critique of this view in C. Roetzel, *Judgment in the Community: A Study of the Relationship between Eschatology and Ecclesiology in Paul* [Leiden: Brill, 1972] 146–49). (5) The form is one among many rhetorical forms found in prophetic speech (e.g., 1 Cor 14:38; Origen *Contra Cels.* 7.9; Herm. *Vis.* 2.2.7–8), but it is used in other settings also. (6) When the speaker is a supernatural being (the one uttering the curses in Rev 22:18b–19 is the exalted Jesus) or one who explicitly claims to speak with divine authority (e.g., 1 Cor 14:38; Origen *Contra Cels.* 7.9), the sentence can safely be understood as a prophetic speech form.

A final word needs to be said about the placement of curses at the conclusion of Revelation. When used to safeguard treaties, curses are virtually *always* placed at the end. This placement seems logical and has no bearing on the location of the concluding curse in Revelation. Curses are rarely found at the conclusion of apocalypses or revelatory literature in general during the Greco-Roman period. In one instance, at the conclusion of the Coptic Gnostic *Disc. 8–9* (J. M. Robinson, *Nag Hammadi*, 297), an oath is demanded of all who read the document, and blessing is pronounced on those who keep the oath and woe upon those who do not. Similarly, the *Apoc. Paul* ends with these words (Hennecke-Schneemelcher, *NTA*, 2:797): "And whoever reads it with faith, I shall bless him and his house. Whoever scoffs at the words of this apocalypse, I will punish him." It appears that only the combination of the two curses with the integrity formula in Rev 22:18b–19 has determined the placement of the combined form at the end of Revelation.

3. *A Liturgical Invocation and Response.* Rev 22:20 contains a final promise of the exalted Jesus, "Yes, I am coming quickly" (followed by John's response, "Amen! Come, Lord Jesus!"). In form, the second statement is a liturgical invocation or ἐπίκλησις, while the first is similar to responses typically uttered when a deity is believed present.

John's "invocation" is correctly understood by most interpreters as a modification in Greek of the Aramaic formula מרן אתא *māran ʾătāʾ* or מרנא תא *māranāʾ tāʾ*, either of which can be translated "our Lord, come!" or "our Lord has come" (Kuhn, *TDNT* 4:467–70), a phrase simply transliterated in two early Christian sources, 1 Cor 16:22 and *Did.* 10:6. In the OT and Judaism the presence of God is a religious conception of central significance; see S. Terrien, *The Elusive Presence: Toward a New Biblical Theology* (San Francisco: Harper & Row, 1978). God's presence could be experienced through various modalities: in nature, in the holy war, in the cult, in personal experience, and (by anticipation) in the eschaton. Yet liturgical invocations requesting the deity to come or to be present are rare (Pss 3:8; 44:27; 74:22; Num 10:36ff.; cf. the divine response "I will arise" in Ps 12:6; Isa 33:10). Yahweh is characterized as "the God who comes," however, for he is the subject of the verb בוא *bôʾ* some thirty-three times, though most references refer to the past in the setting of hymns of praise (see Deut 33:2; Pss 96:13; 98:9; Isa 59:19–20; Hab 3:3–4, 16; Zech 2:14). During the second temple period, cultic invocations for God to "come" occur only in Hellenized descriptions of Israelite religion (see Jos. *Ant.* 4.46; 20.90). While the anticipation of the eschatological visitation (פקד *pāqad*) of Yahweh finds expression in the later portions of the OT (Joel 2:1ff.; 3:4; Zech 14:5; Mal 3:1) and in the literature of second temple Judaism, prayers requesting that coming are rare.

In Greek religion, on the other hand, the gods were frequently invoked to "come" since they were conceptualized as existing in space and therefore must "come" in order to be present and actually hear the supplicant (Versnel, "Ancient Prayer," 29–30; Pax, *Epiphaneia*, 32ff.). These invocations were customarily expressed using imperative forms of the many Greek verbs meaning "to come": βῆθι, δεῦρο, ἐλθέ, ἐπινίσεο, ἕρπε, ἧκε, μόλε, παρίθι, etc. Such invocations were used to dedicate new images and temples of the gods and for securing their presence at sacrifices, oracular consultations, prayers, and private (magical) rituals. Zeus is the exception. In public liturgies he is never invited to come; he sees and acts from where he is. A selection of such invocations is found in the following texts: Sappho frag. 1.5, 25; *PGM* I.296–325; Homeric Hymns 24. Such invocations conclude nearly half the late Orphic Hymns (e.g., 1.9; 9.11; 11.4, 21; 12.14; 14.12; 27.11; 33.8; 34.1; 35.7; 36.13; 40.8). Invocations to come pervade the magical papyri that prescribe procedures for procuring revelations through the presence of a supernatural being (*PGM* I.163; II.2; III.51, 129, 481, 564; IV.1171, 1605; V.249; VII.961–65[5x]; LXII.25; see Hopfner, *Offenbarungszauber* 2:40ff.). Phrases very similar to Rev 22:20 include "come to me, Lord" (δεῦρό μοι κύριε, *PGM* XII.238; ἧκέ μοι κύριε, XIII.88, 603) and "Quickly, by your power now appear on earth to me, yea verily, god!" (*PGM* I.89–90). In dramatic and mythological literature the response pronounced by the invoked deity is sometimes expressed through "I have come" speeches (Athena in *Iliad* 1.207; Apollo in Euripides *Orestes* 1628; Dionysius in Euripides *Bacchae* 1; a ghost in Euripides *Hecuba* 1; Poseidon in Euripides *Troades* 1; Hermes in Euripides *Ion* 5; see O. Weinreich, "De Dis Ignotis Quaestiones Selectae," in *Ausgewählte Schriften* [Amsterdam: Gruener, 1969] 1:285ff., with other examples).

Comment

10 καὶ λέγει μοι· μὴ σφραγίσῃς τοὺς λόγους τῆς προφητείας τοῦ βιβλίου τούτου, ὁ καιρὸς γὰρ ἐγγύς ἐστιν, "He said to me, 'Do not seal the words of this prophetic book, for the time is near.'" While the speaker is not explicitly identified, it is likely that the speaker is the *angelus interpres,* "the interpreting angel," whom John attempted to worship (vv 8–9). Some interpreters, however, attribute this statement to the exalted Christ (Bousset [1906] 457; Allo, 328; Lohmeyer, 178–79).

The phraseology is based on an allusion to Dan 8:26; 12:4, 9, the only apocalypse in which the author receives a divine command to seal up his book until the end. This verse is a conscious allusion to this motif in Daniel, where the act of sealing both insures the inviolability of the message and serves to explain why a book supposedly written by Daniel in the sixth century B.C. was unknown until four centuries later.

Though it is often claimed that the motif of sealing a revelatory book in order to preserve its secrets until the eschaton is a common literary convention among Jewish apocalypses (e.g., Gruenwald, *Apocalyptic,* 12), this motif occurs in explicit form *only* in Daniel and Revelation. Closely related, however, are three passages in 4 Ezra. In 4 Ezra 12:37, "Ezra" is told to write his visions in a book that he is to *conceal,* but he is to *reveal* the secrets he has learned to those who are wise; thus there is both an esoteric and an exoteric tradition. In 4 Ezra 14:5–6 and 14:45–46 the exoteric and esoteric motif appears once more. In the latter passage "Ezra" is instructed to make public the twenty-four books that he wrote first (the Hebrew Scriptures) but to circulate privately the seventy books written last (i.e., apocalyptic revelations) only to the wise. The notion of the esoteric character of apocalyptic revelation is largely based on these passages from Daniel and 4 Ezra, though the reason for emphasizing the concealing of such books until the end is probably the result of their pseudepigraphical character; i.e., they were only known long after the supposed time of composition (see J. J. Collins, *Comm. Daniel,* 341–42).

While the notion of "sealing" an apocalyptic revelation is found only in Dan 8:26;

12:4, 9, the idea of hiding a revelatory book until the end of days is found in other apocalypses. In *Gos. Eg.* 68.1–9, it is claimed that the *Gospel of the Egyptians* was written by Seth and placed in an inaccessible high mountain called Charaxio that the truth might be revealed at the end of time. The motif of concealed revelation also occurs in *T. Mos.* 1:17–18, where Moses commands Joshua to "embalm" his revelation and place it in clay jars and put the jars in a place prepared by God where they will remain concealed until the day of repentance, i.e., the eschatological Day of the Lord (Tromp, *Assumption*, 147–48). At the conclusion of the Coptic-Gnostic treatise *Disc. 8–9* (60.10–63.32), the mystagogue instructs the initiate to write the revelation down on turquoise steles to be deposited in the temple at Diospolis and to include an oath warning readers not to misuse the book.

11 ὁ ἀδικῶν ἀδικησάτω ἔτι καὶ ὁ ῥυπαρὸς ῥυπαρευθήτω ἔτι, καὶ ὁ δίκαιος δικαιοσύνην ποιησάτω ἔτι καὶ ὁ ἅγιος ἁγιασθήτω ἔτι, "Let the person who is unjust continue to act unjustly, and let the person who is morally depraved continue to be depraved, and let the person who is righteous act righteously, and let the person who is holy continue to be holy." These parenetic phrases are apparently to be attributed to the *angelus interpres* of v 10. Each of these two couplets are isocola, i.e., phrases of approximately equal length with a corresponding structure. From the standpoint of Semitic poetic structure, these are two synonymous couplets that stand in antithetical relationship to each other:

a¹ Let the person who is unjust continue to act unjustly,
a² and let the person who is depraved continue to be depraved,

b¹ and let the person who is righteous act righteously,
b² and let the person who is holy continue to be holy.

These four lines also exhibit polysyndeton, i.e., the linking of each clause to the previous clause by means of a copula.

These lines may constitute an allusion to LXX Dan 12:10b, καὶ ἁμάρτωσιν οἱ ἁμαρτωλοί· καὶ οὐ μὴ διανοηθῶσι πάντες οἱ ἁμαρτωλοί, "and the sinners will sin, and all the sinners will be devoid of understanding," while Theod Dan 12:10 reads καὶ ἀνομήσωσιν ἄνομοι· καὶ οὐ συνήσουσιν πάντες ἄνομοι, "and the lawless will act lawlessly, and all the lawless will lack understanding"; this passage in Daniel is also alluded to in 4Q174 = 4QFlor 1–3 ii 3–4. The allusion to Dan 12:10 is likely because the continuation of past behaviors for both the righteous and the wicked is in view in both passages. The conclusion of Daniel is important for our author since he also alludes in v 10 to the angelic command to Daniel to seal the book he has written (Dan 12:4, 9). An analogous antithetical exhortation is found in Ezek 2:27, "He that will hear, let him hear; and he that will refuse to hear, let him refuse." Rev 22:11 is cited in a rather free form in *Ep. Lugd.* 58 (Eusebius *Eccl. hist.* 5.1.58), ἵνα ἡ γραφὴ πληρωθῇ ὁ ἄνομος ἀνομησάτω ἔτι, καὶ ὁ δίκαιος δικαιωθήτω ἔτι, "that the Scripture be fulfilled, 'Let the lawless one continue to be lawless, and let the one who is righteous continue to act righteously.'"

12 Ἰδοὺ ἔρχομαι ταχύ, καὶ ὁ μισθός μου μετ' ἐμοῦ ἀποδοῦναι ἑκάστῳ ὡς τὸ ἔργον ἐστὶν αὐτοῦ, "Indeed, I am coming soon, and my reward is with me to repay to each in proportion to his or her behavior." While vv 10–11 seem to be attributed to the *angelus interpres* whom John attempted to worship in vv 8–9, this abrupt saying must be attributed to the exalted Christ. It is no less abrupt than the saying in 16:15, which was similarly inserted into an existing narrative. The demonstrative particle ἰδού, "indeed, behold," functions here as a marker to indicate the truth and reliability of the saying that follows (see *Comment* on 1:7a).

The first phrase ("Indeed, I am coming soon, and my reward is with me") appears to have been loosely based on LXX Isa 40:10 (with the bracketed portions omitted), ἰδοὺ [κύριος μετὰ ἰσχύος] ἔρχεται καὶ [ὁ βραχίων μετὰ κυριείας, ἰδοὺ] ὁ μισθὸς αὐτοῦ μετ᾽ αὐτοῦ [καὶ] τὸ ἔργον [ἐναντίον αὐτοῦ], "indeed, [the Lord] comes [with strength] and [his arm with lordship; indeed,] his reward is with him [and] his behavior [before him]" (cf. Isa 62:11 and Wis 5:15). It has been reformulated from the third person to the first person and supplemented with the redactional phrase ἰδοὺ ἔρχομαι ταχύ, "indeed, I am coming soon," characteristic of the Second Edition of Revelation (2:16; 3:11; 22:7, 12, 20). The second phrase ("to repay to each in proportion to his or her behavior") is an allusion to a widespread proverbial expression found in Prov 24:12 (ὃς ἀποδίδωσιν ἑκάστῳ κατὰ τὰ ἔργα αὐτοῦ, "who will repay to each according to his or her behavior"), as well as in numerous other places in OT and early Jewish literature (Pss 27:4[MT 28:4]; 62:12[LXX 61:13]; Prov 24:12; Jer 17:10; *Jos. As.* 28:3; *Pss. Sol.* 2:16, 34; 17:8). The same saying is cited in Matt 16:27; Rom 2:6 (quoting Prov 24:12); 2 Cor 11:15; 2 Tim 4:14; Rev 2:23; 18:6; 20:12, 13. In all these passages, however, the plural form τὰ ἔργα , "the works (i.e., 'behavior')," is used. Both phrases are combined *only* here in Rev 22:12 and in *1 Clem.* 34:3: Ἰδοὺ ὁ κύριος, καὶ ὁ μισθὸς αὐτοῦ πρὸ προσώπου αὐτοῦ, ἀποδοῦναι ἑκάστῳ κατὰ τὸ ἔργον αὐτοῦ, "Behold, the Lord, and his reward is before him to repay to each according to his or her work" (also quoted in Clement Alex. *Strom.* 4.22).

The view that *1 Clem.* 34:3 is based on Rev 22:12 (J. B. Lightfoot, *Apostolic Fathers* 1/2:104; Charles, 2:221) ignores the striking verbal differences between the two texts (emphasized by D. A. Hagner, *The Use of the Old and New Testaments in Clement of Rome,* NovTSup34 [Leiden: Brill, 1973] 61–62). Yet the unusual combination of Isa 40:10 and Prov 24:12 requires explanation. The similarities, however, are too striking (including the omission of common phrases from Isa 40:10) to suggest that the authors of *1 Clement* and Revelation each combined these two passages independent of a traditional combination (Prigent, 354; Lindemann, *Clemensbriefe,* 106). Hagner correctly suggests that the combination may derive from a common source, perhaps a lost apocryphal writing (*Clement of Rome,* 62, 93, 270–71). Certainly the author's inclusion of the redactional phrase ἰδοὺ ἔρχομαι ταχύ, "indeed, I am coming soon," suggests adaptation from an existing source. Similarly, the term ἔργον, "work," occurs nineteen times elsewhere in Revelation, but only in 22:12 in the singular. This also suggests that the saying is based on a traditional proverbial formulation.

This saying of the exalted Christ clearly indicates that he functions as *judge,* for he promises to repay each person in a way proportional to his or her behavior. This saying stands in some tension with the depiction of God as judge in 20:11–14, where it is explicitly stated that "each person was judged [i.e., by God] according to their works [κατὰ τὰ ἔργα αὐτῶν]" (as in Rom 2:6; 1 Pet 1:17). The role of Christ as judge is found in a variety of passages in the NT, usually within an eschatological context (John 5:22; Acts 10:42; Rom 2:16; 2 Thess 1:7–11). The motif of judgment according to works or behavior is attributed to the exalted Christ in Revelation only here in 22:12 and in 2:23 (see *Comment* there also), though Christ as judge occurs in a variety of other ways (1:16; 2:12, 16, 22–23; 3:3; 19:15). The saying in Rev 2:23 is also formulated as an utterance of the exalted Christ: "I will give to each of you in accordance with your behavior [δώσω ὑμῖν ἑκάστῳ κατὰ τὰ ἔργα ὑμῶν]" (suggesting that both passages belong to the Second Edition). Outside Revelation, the closest parallel is Matt 16:27, where it is the Son of man who will function as judge: "For the Son of man is about to come in the glory of his Father, with his holy angels, and then he will repay each person in accordance with his or her behavior [ἀποδώσει ἑκάστῳ κατὰ τὴν πρᾶξιν αὐτοῦ]." Since the motif of the returned Son of man judging each person according to his or her behavior is found only in Matt 16:27 (but cf. Matt 13:41–42; 25:31–46), it is obviously not part of the Son of man tradition in the NT (Tödt, *Son of Man*, 84–87; Hare, *Son of Man*, 156–58), nor is it part of the Son of man tradition in the Similitudes of Enoch (Theisohn, *Der auserwählte Richter*, 260–61).

13 ἐγὼ τὸ ἄλφα καὶ τὸ ὦ, ὁ πρῶτος καὶ ὁ ἔσχατος, ἡ ἀρχὴ καὶ τὸ τέλος, "I am the Alpha and the Omega, the First and the Last, the Beginning and the End." This is a collection of three isocola in which each "I am" predication consists of two terms used antithetically to express a divine characteristic by implying that, since he is both extremes, he encompasses the continuum defined by the antithetical terms. Each of these antithetical titles has been used before in Revelation: (1) The title "the Alpha and the Omega" is used of God in 1:8 and 21:6 (in both instances as the predicate of an "I am" clause) but of Christ here (see *Comment* on 1:8). (2) The title "the First and the Last" is also used in 1:17 (as the predicate of an "I am" clause), 2:8, and here, always of Christ (see *Comment* on 1:17). (3) The title "the Beginning and the End" occurs just twice in Revelation, in 21:6, where it is used of God (also as the predicate of an "I am" clause), and here, where it is applied to Christ (see *Comment* on 21:6). This particular grouping of three antithetical titles occurs nowhere else in Revelation, though the first and third occur side by side as predicates of an "I am" saying attributed to God in 21:6. "I am" sayings occasionally occur in series, such as the series of nine in Melito *Hom.* 103 (i.e., "I am your forgiveness, I am the Passover of salvation, I am the lamb that was slain for you, I am your ransom, I am your life, I am your light, I am your salvation, I am your resurrection, I am your king"), and in connection with several of the so-called Isis aretalogies (Apuleius *Metam.* 5–6; Diodorus Siculus 1.27.3–6; see Bergman, *Ich bin Isis*).

14a Μακάριοι οἱ πλύνοντες τὰς στολὰς αὐτῶν, "Blessed are those who wash their robes." This is the last of the seven beatitudes or makarisms in Revelation (see 1:3; 14:13; 16:15; 19:9; 20:6; 22:7; for a discussion of their form, see *Form/Structure/ Setting* on 1:1–3). This beatitude and those in 14:13 and 19:9 have the plural form μακάριοι, "blessed" (like those in Matt 5:3–12, Luke 6:20–23, and three of the five in 4Q525 = 4QBéat 2 ii 1–3).

The phrase οἱ πλύνοντες τὰς στολάς, "those who wash their robes," is functionally equivalent to ὁ νικῶν, "the one who conquers," in 2:7, for in both passages the reward is access to the tree of life (Charles, 2:177). For Lohmeyer (180) this meant that the beatitude was restricted to martyrs, while Charles (1:187–88) wants to level all references to garments, eschatological or otherwise, into metaphors for the spiritual body. Here the action of washing one's robes is clearly a metaphor for moral and spiritual cleansing or reformation. It is closely parallel to the phrase καὶ ἔπλυναν τὰς στολὰς αὐτῶν, "and they washed their robes," used of the heavenly martyrs in 7:14, though there it is paradoxically stated that they made them white by (or in) the blood of the Lamb, i.e., the saving and purifying effect of the sacrificial death of Christ, appropriated through martyrdom (see *Comment* on 7:14). Another parallel is found in 3:4, where some Christians in Sardis are referred to as ἃ οὐκ ἐμόλυναν τὰ ἱμάτια αὐτῶν, "who have not soiled their clothes," i.e., a metaphor for continuing faithfulness to their original Christian commitment.

The metaphor of washing one's garments has several possible meanings: (1) Christian baptism, (2) the decision to lead a morally upright life, or (3) martyrdom. Both Rev 7:13 and 22:14 are assumed by a number of scholars to refer to *baptism,* usually without supportive arguments (Kamlah, *Paränese,* 23; Prigent, 355; id., "Liturgie," 169). There are several difficulties with this view: (1) While baptism is certainly associated with the language of purification and cleansing in early Christianity (Titus 3:5; Heb 10:22; 1 Pet 3:21), such language is not exclusively restricted to baptismal contexts and baptismal imagery (e.g., Eph 5:26). In early Christianity the washing of the (naked) *body* was associated with baptism, while the washing of *garments* was not. (2) The substantival participle οἱ πλύνοντες, "those who wash," is in the present tense, indicating continuous activity rather than a once-for-all event such as baptism. (3) It is the person owning the garments who washes them, whereas people are baptized by others, i.e., the active versus the passive sense. Wilckens (*TDNT,* 691) tries to explain away the active sense of 7:13–14, 22:14, and 3:4 by collapsing them all into the passive sense of 3:5, where the victor is promised that he will be clothed with white robes. These factors suggest that the origin of the metaphor of washing one's garments is rooted in the practice frequently attested in the OT and early Jewish literature of the *washing of garments* (and sometimes the body as well) as a *purification ritual* (πλύνειν is used of washing things that are not the body or a part of the body; e.g., LXX Lev 14:9, καὶ πλυνεῖ τὰ ἱμάτια καὶ λούσεται τὸ σῶμα αὐτοῦ ὕδατι, "and he will wash his garments and bathe his body in water"; cf. Louw-Nida, § 47.8). It must therefore be understood in the *active* sense of what a person must do, i.e., either reform his or her way of living or (less likely) die as a witness for Christ.

The metaphor of washing one's garments is appropriate in the context of the larger metaphor of entering into the holy city, as some of the following texts suggest. The people of Israel were required to wash their clothes in preparation for their appearance before God (Exod 19:10, 14), and Levites were required to wash their clothes as a ritual of consecration (Num 8:7, 21; priests, on the other hand were given entirely new garments, Lev 8:13). This tradition, with an ethical interpretation, is found in one MS of *T. Levi* in a long interpolation following 2:3 (text in de Jonge, *Testaments,* 25):

> Then I washed my garments [ἔπλυνα τὰ ἱμάτιά μου]
>   and having purified them with pure water,
> then I washed [ἐλουσάμην] my entire self in living water,
>   and I made all my paths upright.

This is close to the statement in Num 8:21: "The Levites purified themselves from sin and washed their clothes." More common, however, are the notions that there is "impurity requiring washing" (CD 11:22) and that clothing is susceptible to uncleanness (*m. Kelim* 27:1–2; 28:1–10); i.e., the washing of the clothes as a cultic procedure is required of those who are considered ritually unclean (Lev 11:25, 28, 40; 13:6, 34; 14:8, 9, 47; Num 19:10, 21; 31:24; 4Q277 = 4QTohorot B^c frag. 1, line 13 [García Martínez, *Dead Sea Scrolls*, 90]). Often the washing of *both* one's clothes and one's body is required for achieving ritual purity (Lev 14:8, 9; 15:5–13, 21, 22, 27; 16:26, 28; 17:15; Num 19:7, 8, 19; 11Q*19* = 11QTemple 45:8–9, 16; 49:17–20; 50:8, 13–15; 51:4–5; 4Q*512* = 4QRitual of Purification 10–11 x 6 [García Martínez, *Dead Sea Scrolls*, 441]; 1–6 xii 5–6 [García Martínez, *Dead Sea Scrolls*, 442]; 4Q*274* = 4QTohorot A 1 i 3,5 [García Martínez, *Dead Sea Scrolls*, 88]; 4Q*514* = 4QOrd^c 1 i 9 [García Martínez, *Dead Sea Scrolls*, 92]). In some texts the washing of one's garments was necessary for those with certain types of ritual impurity as a prerequisite for entering the wilderness tabernacle (in Num 8:7 the Levites are required to wash themselves and their clothes; in 8:15 it is said that "the Levites may go in to do service at the tent of meeting once you have cleansed them"), entering the city-temple (11Q*19* = 11QTemple 45:8–9, 16–17), or approaching the altar (*Jub.* 21:16).

Wearing soiled garments was forbidden for members of the Qumran community as CD 11:3–4 indicates (tr. García Martínez, *Dead Sea Scrolls*, 41–42): "No-one is to wear dirty clothes or (clothes) which are in the chest, unless they have been washed with water or rubbed with incense." There are also references to ritual washing alone of all or part of the body as a ritual of cleansing (4Q*414* = 4QBaptismal Liturgy frag. 12, line 5: "He will wash in water and he will be [pure]"; CD 10:11; *T. Levi* longer version following 18:2 [text in de Jonge, *Testaments*, 46]; Mark 7:2–3; John 13:10). Several texts refer to the act of washing a person's *body* as a symbol of the moral and spiritual cleansing in baptism or ritual washing (e.g., Titus 3:5; Heb 10:22).

14b ἵνα ἔσται ἡ ἐξουσία αὐτῶν ἐπὶ τὸ ξύλον τῆς ζωῆς, "so that they will have access to the tree of life." The phrase ἐξουσία ἐπί, "power over," is used with the verbs διδόναι, "to give," ἔχειν, "to have," and εἶναι, "to be," elsewhere in Revelation (2:26; 6:8; 11:6[2x]; 13:7; 14:18; 16:9). The closest parallel is 16:9, where God is referred to as τοῦ ἔχοντος τὴν ἐξουσίαν ἐπὶ τὰς πληγὰς ταύτας, "the one who has authority over these plagues."

The phrase in v 14b corresponds rather closely, though inversely, to Gen 3:22–24, which narrates the expulsion of Adam from Eden because of the possibility that he might eat from the tree of life and so live forever. According to v 14b, the ban that barred people from access to the tree of life and the immortality that it symbolizes has been lifted. Gen 3:22–24 is also alluded to in *1 Enoch* 25:24–25, extant in Greek as well as Ethiopic. The Greek version runs as follows (M. Black, *Apocalypsis*, 35):

καὶ τοῦτο τὸ δένδρον εὐωδίας, καὶ οὐδεμία σὰρξ ἐξουσίαν ἔχει
And this fragrant tree, and no flesh has authority

ἄψασθαι αὐτοῦ μέχρι τῆς μεγάλης κρίσεως, ἐν ᾗ ἐκδίκησις
to touch it until the great judgment, when the judgment

πάντων καὶ τελείωσις μέχρις αἰῶνος· τότε
and completion of all things forever occurs. Then

δικαίοις καὶ ὁσίοις δοθήσεται ὁ καρπὸς αὐτοῦ
to the righteous and holy its fruit will be given

τοῖς ἐκλεκτοῖς εἰς ζωήν.
to the elect for life.

While this Greek translation is somewhat awkward, it is very similar to the Ethiopic version as translated by Knibb (*Enoch* 2:113–14):

And this beautiful fragrant tree—and no (creature of) flesh has authority to touch it until the great judgment when he will take vengeance on all and will bring (everything) to a consummation for ever—this will be given to the righteous and humble. From its fruit life will be given to the chosen.

Tg. Neof. Gen 3:22–24 exhibits a greatly expanded version of the story of the expulsion of Adam from the garden of Eden (tr. Macho, *Neophyti* 1:505):

He [God] established the garden of Eden for the just and Gehenna for the wicked. He established the garden of Eden for the just who will eat and nourish themselves from the fruits of the tree of Life, because they observed the commandments of the Law and fulfilled its precepts.

Renewed access to the tree, or trees, of life symbolizing eternal life (mentioned again in 22:19) is an eschatological theme that occurs with some frequency in early Jewish texts (see *Comments* on 2:7 and 22:2). The fact that access to the tree of life is mentioned before access to the city (v 14c) betrays the presence of the figure of speech called *hysteron-proteron*, "last-first," i.e., placing two events in reverse order, a rhetorical phenomenon that occurs frequently in Revelation: 3:3, 17; 5:5; 6:4; 10:4, 9; 20:4–5, 12–13.

14c καὶ τοῖς πυλῶσιν εἰσέλθωσιν εἰς τὴν πόλιν, "and so that they might enter into the city by the gates." Entry by means of the gates was of course the only legitimate means of access to an ancient city (cf. John 10:1). This phrase appears to have been formulated in antithesis to the statement in 21:27, where what cannot enter or be brought into the city because of ritual or moral impurity is specified. While the term "enter in" is used here of valid access to the New Jerusalem, it is apparent that the city is a metaphor for salvation, combining the notions of the people of God as an edifice with the eschatological realization of the kingdom of God on a renewed earth. "Entering in" is therefore used here (as in 21:27) as a spatial metaphor equivalent to "entering into" the kingdom of God, a metaphor that occurs frequently in the teaching of Jesus (Matt 5:20; 7:21; 18:3; 19:23–24; 23:13; Mark 9:47; John 3:5; Acts 14:22; see Windisch, *ZNW* 27 [1928] 163–92, esp. 171).

15 ἔξω οἱ κύνες καὶ οἱ φάρμακοι καὶ οἱ πόρνοι καὶ οἱ φονεῖς καὶ οἱ εἰδωλολάτραι καὶ πᾶς φιλῶν καὶ ποιῶν ψεῦδος, "Outside are the dogs and the magicians and the fornicators and murderers and idolaters and everyone who is fond of lying." This polysyndetic list of various types of sinners who are excluded from the holy city is based in part on the Jewish tradition of the necessity of eliminating *all* foreigners from the Land (*Pss. Sol.* 17:21). "Dog" is used here as metaphor for the wicked (if understood literally, it would be the only reference in this vice list to nonhumans) and is the only instance in which this term occurs on an early Christian vice list. It may be that κύων, "dog" (and perhaps οἱ πόρνοι, "the fornicators," as well; see below), is used more specifically here for male homosexuals, pederasts, or sodomites since the term on the parallel vice list in 21:8 (see *Comment* there) is ἐβδελυγμένοι, "those who are polluted." Female and male cult prostitution is forbidden in Deut 23:17–18:

> There shall be no cult prostitute of the daughters of Israel, neither shall there be a cult prostitute of the sons of Israel. You shall not bring the fee of a prostitute or the wages of a dog into the house of the Lord your God.

Here the MT has the term כֶּלֶב *keleb*, "dog," which is used as a parallel for קָדֵשׁ *qādēš*, "male prostitute, sodomite" (see K. van der Toorn, *ADB* 5:512; Botterweck, *TWAT* 4:164; Charles, 2:178; Ford, 345, 347), though this view is not without its critics (*RAC* 16:783–84; n.b. that in *m. Tem.* 6:3 the "dog" of Deut 23:18 is understood literally). On male prostitution, see *RAC* 16:324–26.

According to 4Q*394* = 4QMMT[a] 8 iv (Qimron-Strugnell, *Qumran Cave 4*, DJD 10, 52–53, lines 58–59), "And one must not let dogs enter the holy camp, since they may eat some of the bones of the sanctuary while the flesh is still on them" (see also García Martínez, *Dead Sea Scrolls*, 78 [lines 61–62]). This ban on bringing dogs into Jerusalem is not because they are unclean animals (they are considered unclean because of their habits, but they are not eaten) but because of their tendency to dig up bones and eat the remaining meat of sacrificial victims. It seems probable that the opponents of the Qumran sect who lived in Jerusalem kept dogs, a practice the sectarians regarded as a severe transgression (Qimron-Strugnell, *Qumran Cave 4*, 162). In the OT and early Judaism, dogs were viewed ambivalently (*RAC* 16:782–83). They were economically beneficial as watch dogs and herding dogs. On the other hand, they were held with contempt for having what were judged disgusting habits (Prov 26:11; Luke 16:21), but they were not technically classified in Jewish halachic traditions as unclean (see *JE* 4:630–32). When applied to people, the term "dog" is therefore an insult (1 Sam 17:43; 24:14; 2 Kgs 8:13; Isa 56:10–11) and a term used by Jews of Gentiles (Mark 7:27–28; Matt 15:26–27; Ps.-Clement *Hom.* 2.19.1–3; see Str-B, 1:724–26; this equation is rejected by Tagawa, *Miracles*, 118–19). The proverb in Matt 7:6 and *Did.* 9:5, "Do not give that which is holy to the dogs," is applied in the latter passage to exclude the unbaptized from the Eucharist (the same proverb is quoted in *Gos. Thom.* 93, the *Liber Graduum* 30.11, and at least two Gnostic sources in Hippolytus *Ref.* 5.8.33 and Epiphanius *Pan.* 24.5.2).

In early Christian literature the term "dog" is applied to those who are unbaptized and therefore unclean (*Did.* 9:5), as well as to heretics (Phil 3:2; 2 Pet 2:22; Ign. *Eph.* 7:1). See O. Michel, "κύων," *TDNT* 3:1101–4; S. Pedersen, "κύων," *EWNT* 2:821–23. There is some evidence to suggest that Christians in late antiquity believed that demons could take the form of dogs (*Acts of Andrew*, Gregory's Epitome, 7; ed. MacDonald, 210–11).

In Deut 18:9–14 (repeated in 11QTemple 61:16–19), a passage cast as a prophecy of what will transpire when the Israelites enter into the land, there is a list of excluded professions, which includes the diviner, soothsayer, augur, sorcerer, charmer, medium, wizard, and necromancer (Deut 18:10–11). In Rev 22:15, sorcery is one of the practices that exclude one from the holy city. The list appears to have been formed on the basis of the tradition in Deuteronomy.

The term οἱ πόρνοι, "the fornicators," may (in view of the masculine gender) refer more specifically to male prostitutes; on the Jewish abhorrence of τὸ παιδεραστεῖν, "pederasty," see Lev 18:22; 20:13; Philo *Spec. Leg.* 3.37–42; Wis 14:26

(Str-B, 3:70–74). Plato, though writing in a cultural environment where homophile relationships were more routinely accepted, also regarded homosexual relationships as contrary to nature (*Phaedrus* 251a; *Leges* 1.636b–d; 8.841d–e). Some later Greek writers, and more commonly Roman writers, regarded homosexuality as similar to such sexual sins as adultery (Aeschines *Timarchos* 185 [F. Blass, ed., *Aeschines: Orationes* (Leipzig: Teubner, 1980) 92–93]; Plutarch *Bruta anim.* 990d–991a; *Amatorius* 751c–d [where Plutarch speaks of ἡ παρὰ φύσιν ὁμιλία πρὸς ἄρρενας, "intercourse with males which is against nature"]; Galen *De prop. an.* 6.9; Sextus Empiricus *Pyrrh.* 3.199; Juvenal *Satires* 2.36; Martial *Epigrams* 1.90; Ovid *Metam.* 9.715–48). The *Lex Scantinia,* a law passed in Rome in 149 B.C., legislated against *stuprum cum masculo,* i.e., pederasty (Juvenal 2.44; Ausonius *Epigr.* 92; Prudentius *Perist.* 10.204; Suetonius *Dom.* 8.3; Tertullian *De monog.* 12; see Berger, *RESup* 7:411; Weiss, *RE* 12:2413; G. Rotondi, *Leges publicae populi romani* [Hildesheim: Olms, 1966] 293; F. X. Ryan, "The *Lex Scantinia* and the Prosecution of Censors and Aediles," *CP* 89 [1994] 159–62). In Lucian *Hermotimus* 22, Virtue (ἀρετή) is compared to a city from which all vices had been forcibly driven out (LCL tr.):

> All those things that you find here—robbery, violence, cheating—they say you would find none of them ventured into that city; no, they live together in peace and harmony naturally enough; for what, I suppose, in other cities produces strife and discord, plot and counter-plot, is entirely absent. They do not any longer look on gold, pleasures, or glory as things to quarrel about—they drove them from the city long ago, thinking them unnecessary to their common life. So they live a calm and perfectly happy life with good government, equality, freedom, and the other blessings.

The phrase καὶ πᾶς φιλῶν καὶ ποιῶν ψεῦδος, literally "and everyone who loves and does falsehood," is a Semitism with a close parallel in Gk. *1 Enoch* 99:9, τὰ ψεύδη ἃ ἐποιήσατε, "the lies which you did." The phrase is analogous to the Johannine Semitism ποιεῖν τὴν ἀλήθειαν, "to do the truth" (John 3:21; 1 John 1:6; see M. Zerwick, "Veritatem facere [Joh. 3,21; I Joh. 1,6]," *VD* 18 [1938] 338–42, 373–77), an idiom based on the Hebrew phrase אמת עשׂה *'āśâ 'emet,* meaning "to keep faith," which occurs twice in the OT (Neh 9:33; 2 Chr 31:20) and several additional times in more complex expressions (Gen 47:29; Josh 2:14; 2 Sam 2:6). In the Qumran *Manual of Discipline,* עשׂה אמת *'āśâ 'emet* means "to act sincerely" or "to practice the true law" (1QS 1:5 [ולעשׂות אמת *wěla' ăśôt 'emet*]; 5:3; 8:2; see Leaney, *Rule,* 119; *DCH* 1:329). ποιεῖν ἀλήθειαν occurs frequently in Jewish and early Christian literature (LXX Isa 26:10; Tob 4:6; 13:6; *Pss. Sol.* 17:15; *T. Reub.* 6:9; *T. Benj.* 10:3; *T. Iss.* 7:5; *1 Clem.* 31:2). It has already been expressly mentioned in Revelation that the 144,000 do not lie (14:5), and ψεῦδος occurs in the brief vice list in 21:27. There is also the close parallel in the sinner list in the Two Ways source in *Did.* 5:2 and in *Barn.* 20:2, where ἀγαπῶντες ψεῦδος, "those who love falsehood," are mentioned. With Revelation, however, "everyone who loves and does falsehood" could refer to the false apostles (2:2) as well as the ψευδοπροφήτης, "false prophet" (16:13; 19:20; 20:10).

16a Ἐγὼ Ἰησοῦς ἔπεμψα τὸν ἄγγελόν μου μαρτυρῆσαι ὑμῖν ταῦτα ἐπὶ ταῖς ἐκκλησίαις, "I, Jesus, sent my angel to attest this message to you for the benefit of the churches." Though the speaker is obviously the exalted Jesus, Kavanagh argues that here the lector is speaking in the words of the person of Jesus and that the book concludes in v 21 with the lector's blessing (*Apocalypse,* 132–33).

The primary exegetical problem in this passage is that of determining to whom the plural pronoun ὑμῖν, "you," and the plural noun ταῖς ἐκκλησίαις, "the churches," refer; i.e., do they refer to the same or different groups? Many commentators understand ὑμῖν (dative of indirect object) to refer to the Christian members of the seven churches addressed by John, i.e., as a direct address to the audience; cf. 1:4 (e.g., Swete, 309; Charles, 2:219; Satake, *Gemeindeordnung*, 25; Lohse, 113; Mounce, 394; Sweet, 315, 317; Beasley–Murray, 342; Roloff, 212; Prigent, 357; Yarbro Collins, *Crisis and Catharsis*, 39). Yet the significance of the plural ὑμῖν cannot be disposed of that easily, for that would give the passage a peculiar redundancy: "I, Jesus, have sent my angel to testify to you [ordinary Christians individually] for the churches [ordinary Christians collectively]." Others (and this is the position argued here) hold that the ὑμῖν refers to a circle of Christian prophets whose task it was to transmit John's revelatory message to the churches (Bousset [1906] 459; Beckwith, 777; Charles, 2:219 [entertained as a secondary possibility]; Kiddle-Ross, 454; Lohmeyer, 180; Schüssler Fiorenza, *NTS* 23 [1976–77] 425; Vanni, *La struttura letteraria*, 80; Aune, *BR* 26 [1981] 19; id., *JSNT* 37 [1989] 103–16; Hill, *NTS* 18 [1971–72] 414–15). In Greek it is only a remote linguistic possibility that ὑμῖν and ταῖς ἐκκλησίαις refer to the same entity. The presence of the preposition ἐπί, "for," before ταῖς ἐκκλησίαις indicates that ταῖς ἐκκλησίαις is more remote from the action described by the infinitive μαρτυρῆσαι, "to attest," than is the pronoun ὑμῖν. Therefore, the view that ὑμῖν and ταῖς ἐκκλησίαις *both* refer to Christians in general is improbable (Aune, *JSNT* 37 [1989] 104–5).

Since ὑμεῖς, "you," and αἱ ἐκκλησίαι, "the churches," in Rev 22:16 refer to two *different* (though perhaps overlapping) groups, we must consider to whom the ὑμεῖς might refer. Swete (309) thinks that the ὑμεῖς refers to Christians in the seven churches, while αἱ ἐκκλησίαι refers to Christians everywhere, though this view founders on the fact that αἱ ἐκκλησίαι occurs thirteen times in Revelation and refers only to the seven churches of the province of Asia. The pronoun ὑμεῖς must therefore refer to a *different* group. There are four possibilities: (1) potential martyrs (Caird, 286), (2) lectors whose task it was to read Revelation to the congregations (Zahn, 2:626 nn. 89, 628), (3) envoys whose task it was to transmit copies of Revelation to the seven churches (suggested as a possibility in Aune, *JSNT* 37 [1989] 107–8), or (4) a group of John's prophetic colleagues (Aune, *JSNT* 37 [1989] 103–16). Though there is no inherent reason that possibilities (2), (3), and (4) cannot be combined in some way, there are strong arguments in favor of (4).

In 22:9 the angelic revealer claims that "I am [εἰμί] a fellow servant with you and your brothers and sisters the prophets and those who obey the commands in this book." In writing this statement, John clearly implies that he is a prophet, a self-conception also implied in his designation of the work he is writing as a "prophecy" (1:3) and a "prophetic book" (22:7, 10, 18, 19). Here a *plurality* of prophets is in view. While the true prophets of all ages could conceivably be referred to, the present tense of the verb εἰμί, "I am," suggests that prophets of the *present* are in view, as are ordinary Christians "who obey" (τῶν τηρούντων, a present substantival participle). Since "those who obey" are contemporaneous with John, it is also likely that "your brothers and sisters the prophets" are also John's contemporaries. Rev 22:9 has a close parallel in 19:10: "Then I fell down before his feet to worship him, but he said to me, 'Don't do that! I am a fellow servant [σύνδουλος] with you and your brothers and sisters who maintain [τῶν ἐχόντων] the testimony concerning Jesus. Worship God. For the testimony concerning Jesus is the Spirit of prophecy." Here John's "brothers and sisters who maintain the testimony of Jesus" obviously constitute a group contemporaneous with John. Their prophetic function is indicated by the gloss with which the verse concludes, which identifies ἡ μαρτυρία Ἰησοῦ, "the testimony of Jesus" (a subjective genitive), with τὸ πνεῦμα τῆς προφητείας, "the Spirit of prophecy." The glossator is trying to make it clear that John's brothers and sisters who hold the testimony of Jesus are indeed Christian *prophets*.

References to prophecy and prophets in Revelation present a number of difficult interpretive problems. Just one prophet is specifically mentioned under the pejorative code name "Jezebel" (2:20). Though she has followers (2:22–23), they are not designated prophets, though the original Jezebel was the patroness of 450 prophets of Baal and 400 prophets of Asherah (1 Kgs 18:19). The two witnesses of Rev 11 are called prophets (11:10) and have a prophetic ministry (11:3), though precisely what that ministry was is not further specified. Prophetic guilds led by master prophets are religious phenomena found in both ancient Israel and early Christianity. The prophetic schools of the OT, called "sons of the prophets," were led by master prophets who were called "father." Elisha led one such school (1 Kgs 20:35; 2 Kgs 2:3, 5, 7, 15; 4:1–38). Classical prophets such as Isaiah had disciples who may have collected, edited, and written down the oracles presented in the books bearing their names. Prophetic groups also functioned in early Christianity, though the evidence is scanty. 1 Cor 14:29–33 suggests that a group of prophets functioned in a special way in the Corinthian church (Aune, *Prophecy*, 219–22). Some scholars have argued that the Q source arose within just such a prophetic community (Sato, *Q und Prophetie*). The author of the *Odes of Solomon* also seems to represent a group of inspired singers, who constituted an identifiable group within the Odist's Christian community (Aune, *NTS* 28 [1982] 435–60). A similar prophetic school may lie behind the pseudonymous *Ascension of Isaiah* (cf. *Asc. Isa.* 6), a Jewish work with an extensive Christian addition completed in the second century A.D. (Hall, "*Ascension of Isaiah*," 300–306; see Acerbi, *L'Ascensione di Isaia*, 210–53).

16b ἐγώ εἰμι ἡ ῥίζα καὶ τὸ γένος Δαυίδ, ὁ ἀστὴρ ὁ λαμπρὸς ὁ πρωϊνός, "I am David's descendant, the bright morning star." This is one of five ἐγώ εἰμι, "I am," sayings in Revelation (1:8, 17; 2:23; 21:6; 22:16; see *Comment* on 1:8); a series of three "I am" sayings is found in 22:13, with the verb εἰμί, "I am," lacking. The self-designation here in v 16 is made up of two elements, each used elsewhere in Revelation: (1) The phrase "root of David" (an allusion to Isa 11:10) also occurs in 5:5 (see *Comment* there). This traditional messianic title is combined here with the phrase τὸ γένος Δαυίδ, "offspring of David," which also occurs in Ign. *Eph.* 20:2; *Trall.* 9:1; *Smyrn.* 1:1. (2) The phrase ὁ ἀστὴρ ὁ λαμπρὸς ὁ πρωϊνός, "the morning star" (an allusion to Num 24:17 and perhaps Isa 60:3), is referred to in 2:28 as something received by the exalted Jesus from his Father, which he in turn will give the Christian who conquers. Here it is a predicate of Jesus himself in the context of an ἐγώ εἰμι, "I am," self-disclosure formula.

In CD 7:18–19 (cf. 4QD^a 3 iv 8), alluding to Num 24:17, the star is said to be the interpreter of the Law (והכוכב הוא דורש התורה *wĕhakkôkāb hû' dôrēš hattôrâ*). Num 24:17 ("a star shall come forth from Jacob") was interpreted messianically in Judaism (Mal 4:2[LXX: 3:20]; Zech 6:12; 1QM 11:6–7; 4QTest 9–13; CD 7:18–20; *T. Levi*

18:3; *T. Jud.* 24:1; cf. *y. Ta'an.* 68d, where the would-be Messiah Shimon bar Kosiba's nickname "Bar Kochba," meaning "son of a star," is also an allusion to Num 24:17; cf. Eusebius *Hist. eccl.* 4.6.2; see Vermes, "The Story of Balaam," in *Scripture and Tradition in Judaism: Haggadic Studies,* 2nd ed. [Leiden: Brill, 1973] 165–66). Coins minted during the Bar Kochba revolt depict a star over the temple (cf. Schürer, *History* 1:544 n. 133). The messianic interpretation of Num 24:17 was taken over into early Christianity (Matt 2:2–20 [see Str-B, 1:76–77]; Justin *1 Apol.* 32.12; *Dial.* 106.4; Hippolytus *Comm. in Dan.* 1.9; Origen *Contra Cels.* 1.59–60). The term λαμπρός, "bright," reflects the belief that, apart from the sun and the moon, Venus/ Aphrodite is the brightest of all the planets (Pliny *Hist. nat.* 2.37; Martianus Capella 8.883). In Greek the morning star is called φωσφόρος, and in Latin *lucifer* (Cicero *De natura deorum* 2.20.53). Only in Rev 22:16, however, is the star metaphor used directly of Christ, and it is very probably an allusion either to Num 24:17 construed in a traditionally Jewish messianic sense or to a Christian exegetical tradition originally inspired by Num 24:17. Albl argues convincingly that Gen 49:10–11, Num 24:17, and Isa 11:1, 10 form a constellation of messianic proof-texts used in strands of pre-Christian Judaism that were taken over by Christianity (Heb 7:14; Justin *1 Apol.* 32; Cyprian *Quir.* 1.21; Eusebius *Demonstratio* 7.3.55) and even as early as Rev 5:5 and 22:16 could be used without discussion as titles of Jesus ("Testimonia Collections," 247–56). In the star hymn of Ignatius, Jesus is referred to under the metaphor of a star that exceeds all other stars in brightness (*Eph.* 19:2–3; cf. Matt 2:1–12; *Prot. Jas.* 21:2; Clement of Alex. *Exc. ex Theod.* 74; Schoedel, *Ignatius,* 91–93; J. B. Lightfoot, *Apostolic Fathers* 2/2:80–81; H. F. Stander, "The Starhymn in the Epistle of Ignatius to the Ephesians [19:2–3]," *VC* 43 [1989] 209–14). The metaphor of the star was used in astrology with political interests for the expected ruler sent by God or the gods. In the phrase "the lightbearer [φωσφόρος] arises in your hearts" in 2 Pet 1:19, the term φωσφόρος is an adjective meaning "bringing morning light," which F. J. Dölger (*AC* 5 [1936] 1–43) suggests refers to the dawn. However, used substantivally, it usually means "morning star," i.e., Venus (H. Conzelmann, *TDNT* 9:312; Spicq, *Lexicographie,* 954). This is in part confirmed by the fact that this phrase probably alludes, directly or indirectly, to Num 24:17. In *Tg. Esth.* 10.3, Mordecai is compared with the morning star (Str-B, 3:857). Twice in the Hellenistic epic *Argonautica* by Apollonius, the hero Jason is compared to a star, once to Sirius, the brightest of the stars (3.956–59), and once earlier when he approached the palace of Hypsipyle (1.774–81); see G. O. Hutchinson, *Hellenistic Poetry* (Oxford: Clarendon, 1988) 112.

17a καὶ τὸ πνεῦμα καὶ ἡ νύμφη λέγουσιν· ἔρχου, "The Spirit and the bride say, 'Come!'" The invitation to come is generally understood as the response of the Spirit and the Church to the promise of Jesus in v 12 that he will come soon, though one problem with this interpretation is the fact that ἔρχεσθαι, "to come," occurs twice more in v 17 with an apparently different meaning. The problematic juxtaposition of these sayings is partially solved, however, if it is recognized that ἔρχεσθαι is a catchword used to link two different notions. The Spirit is closely connected to prophetic inspiration in Revelation and is the subject of the verb λέγει, "says," at the conclusion of each of the seven proclamations (2:7, 11, 17, 29; 3:6, 13, 22). Since these proclamations are dictated by the exalted Christ, there is a close connection between the revelatory messages of the exalted Christ and the Spirit. Christ and the Spirit are linked by Paul in the phrase "Spirit of Christ" (Rom

8:9), and Charles identifies the Spirit here as the Spirit of Christ (2:179). It is probably more accurate to say that the Spirit is the one speaking and issuing an invitation through the prophet John (Bousset [1906] 459).

The term νύμφη, "bride," occurs twice earlier, in 21:2, 9. In 21:2 "bride" is a simile describing the appearance of the New Jerusalem descending from heaven, while in 21:9 "bride" (as well as "wife") is shifted to a metaphor for the New Jerusalem. Here the bride must be the personification of the Church (Bousset [1906] 459; Charles, 2:179).

According to Jerome *Ep.* 107, νύμφος, "male bride," was a grade in Mithraic initiation. In Firmicus Maternus *De errore prof. relig.* 19.1 (Bidez-Cumont, *Mages* 2:154; corrected by R. L. Gordon, "Reality, Evocation and Boundary in the Mysteries of Mithras," *JMS* 3 [1980] 50), the initiate is addressed, ἰ]δὲ νύμφε, χαῖρε νύμφε, χαῖρε νέον φῶς, "Behold bride, greetings bride, greetings new light." Here the Nymphus, whose symbol is the lamp and whose planet is the evening star, is the new light. The Latin term *nymphus,* the second of the seven grades of Mithraic initiation, is, as Gordon (48–50) has observed, a non-word for an impossible thing—a male bride.

17b καὶ ὁ ἀκούων εἰπάτω· ἔρχου, "Let the one who hears say, 'Come!'" The verb ἀκούειν, "to hear," is used in both a *plural* participial form (1:3: "those who hear") and a *singular* participial form (22:18: "everyone who hears") for the implied reader, i.e., those whom the author envisages as hearing the reading of the text of Revelation in the context of Christian worship. It is quite possible that the singular substantival participle ὁ ἀκούων, "the one who hears," in this verse (with an implicitly distributive meaning; cf. the NRSV translation: "everyone who hears") refers to the individual members of the same group. However, the phrase ὁ ἀκούων is ambiguous because it can refer to at least three different entities: (1) the one who hears the invitation to come spoken by the Spirit and the bride and who reiterates that invitation to others; (2) John, the hearer of the revelation (22:8), who reiterates the invitation issued by the Spirit and the bride; (3) the one who hears the reading of John's prophetic book (1:3; 22:18) and who reiterates the invitation of the Spirit and the bride. Here ἔρχου, "Come!" can also be construed as a response to the promise of Jesus in v 12; i.e., the hearer joins the Spirit and the bride (i.e., the Church), and the prophet John articulates their imperative prayer for the imminent return of Jesus.

17c καὶ ὁ διψῶν ἐρχέσθω, ὁ θέλων λαβέτω ὕδωρ ζωῆς δωρεάν, "Let the one who is thirsty come. Let the one who desires receive the gift of the water of life." Here it is clear that the verb ἔρχεσθαι, "to come," has a very different meaning from the two previous uses of ἔρχεσθαι in this verse where the coming of Jesus is in view. To whom is this invitation to come addressed? It is likely that the hearer mentioned in v 17b is also the one who thirsts for the spiritual fulfillment offered by God and is therefore encouraged to come. Here "let him come" may also function as an invitation to participate in the Eucharist. This statement, which is closely parallel to 21:6, is a probable allusion to Isa 55:1a, "Ho, everyone who thirsts, come to the waters [οἱ διψῶντες, πορεύεσθε ἐφ᾽ ὕδωρ]" (combining the three motifs of an address to the *thirsty,* an invitation to *come,* and the mention of *water*), while Isa 55:1b offers satisfaction "without money and without price," corresponding to the term δωρεάν, "as a gift" (cf. Fekkes, *Isaiah,* 260–61).

The grammatical pattern of a substantival participle followed by a finite verb in the imperative or future occurs with some frequency in the Second Edition of Revelation (2:7, 17, 11, 26; 3:5, 12, 21; 22:11, 17a); the only exception is 13:18, which the author may have added when the First Edition was revised. The imperative form of the verb "come" (לְכוּ *lĕkû*) occurs three times in Isa 55:1 (just as ἔρχεσθαι occurs three times in Rev 22:17), though in LXX Isa 55:1 only the first לְכוּ *lĕkû* is translated, again suggesting the author's dependence on the Hebrew text.

Hunger and thirst are frequent metaphors for unfulfilled moral and spiritual needs and are often used in the OT, early Judaism, and early Christianity for the need for spiritual satisfaction and fulfillment that can only be provided by God (Pss 42:2; 63:1; 143:6; Sir 24:21; *Odes Sol.* 30:1–2; cf. Jer 2:13), by the words of God (Amos 8:11; Philo *Spec. Leg.* 2.63), by Christ (John 4:14–15; 7:37; 1 Cor 10:4), or by the pursuit of righteousness (Matt 5:6). In CD [text A] 6:3–4, "well" is used as a metaphor for the Torah, while in CD [text B] 19:34, former members of the community are castigated for having departed from the well of living water (ויסורו מבאר מים החיים *wayyāsûrû mibbĕʾēr mayim haḥayyîm*), i.e., the Torah. In rabbinic literature water is a frequent metaphor for the Torah (*b. Sukk.* 52b; *b. Qidd.* 30b; *Gen. Rab.* 54.1; 66.1; 84.16; *Exod. Rab.* 2.5; 25.8; *Num. Rab.* 1.7; *Cant. Rab.* 1.2–3). The thirst of the people of God combined with God's provision of water is a frequent metaphor for salvation in Deutero-Isaiah, based on the story of the wilderness period experienced by Israel after the Exodus from Egypt (Isa 41:17–18; 43:19–20; 44:3–4; 48:21; 49:10; cf. 12:3).

18a μαρτυρῶ ἐγὼ παντὶ τῷ ἀκούοντι τοὺς λόγους τῆς προφητείας τοῦ βιβλίου τούτου, "I myself testify to everyone who hears the prophetic words of this book." The identification of the speaker is problematic, though the present text of Revelation suggests that "the one who testifies these things" (v 20) is Jesus (see *Comment* on v 20). While most commentators regard the statements in vv 18–19 as those of Jesus (Swete, 311; Charles, 2:218; Mounce, 396; Allo, 333), some insist that the speaker is John (Zahn, 2:628–29; Bousset [1906] 459; Lohmeyer, 181; Caird, 287). Kraft thinks that the original subject of the verb μαρτυρῶ, "I testify," was probably John but that the final redaction of the book has attributed the interpolated curses to Jesus (Kraft, 281–82).

The phrase "I testify" is one of several oath formulas used in Revelation to introduce or conclude prophetic pronouncements. Here it is used to introduce an integrity formula in vv 18–19 (see *Form/Structure/Setting* on Rev 22:10–20). John understood his prophetic role as that of testifying accurately to the revelatory message he had received (1:2). Another oath formula used by John to conclude oracles is οὗτοι οἱ λόγοι [πιστοὶ καὶ] ἀληθινοί, "these words are [faithful and] true" (19:9; 21:5; 22:6; see *Comment* on 19:9). Oath formulas that introduce apocalyptic speeches are found occasionally in Jewish apocalyptic literature (K. Berger, *Amen-Worte*, 20–27, has a comprehensive discussion of the oath formula in eschatological sayings in this literature; see also G. W. E. Nickelsburg, "The Apocalyptic Message of *1 Enoch* 92–105," *CBQ* 39 [1977] 309–28). Berger lists the following passages where the oath formula occurs: *1 Enoch* 98:1, 4, 6; 99:6; 103:1; 104:1; *2 Enoch* 49:1; *Asc. Isa.* 1:8; 3:18; *Apoc. Mos.* 18; *3 Apoc. Bar.* 1:7; *T. Sol.* 1:13; Rev 10:6; *1 Clem.* 58:2. The function of the oath formula in apocalyptic literature is the verification of the truth of the vision report that follows. Apocalyptists, including John, conceived of their role as witnesses to divine truth, whether they wrote under pseudonyms or not. The oath formula could therefore be more appropriately designated the "witness formula" in view of that function. Introductory oath formulas in prophetic speeches are found in Josephus (*Ant.* 18:197ff.) and in the *Odyssey* (17.154ff.; 19.302ff.; 20.229ff.). In the OT, the oath formula "Yahweh has sworn by" functions much like the messenger formula "thus says the Lord" in introducing pronouncements of judgment (see Amos 4:2; 8:7). The prophetic oath formula can be expressed in the third person (see Isa 14:24; 62:8; Jer 49:13; 51:14; Amos 6:8; Pss 110:4; 132:11) or as a first-person speech by Yahweh (Gen 22:16; Isa 45:23; 54:9; Jer 44:26). The ancient Israelite oath formula "as the Lord lives" (Judg 8:19; Ruth 3:13; Amos 8:4) was also adopted for use as a prophetic oath formula: "as I live, says the Lord" (Isa 49:18; Jer 22:24; 46:18; Ezek 5:11; 14:16, 18, 20; Zeph 2:9). In the OT, however, the prophetic oath is *always* spoken by Yahweh, never the prophet. In Jewish apocalyptic literature and in the Greco-Roman sources cited above, the oath formula is *always* used by the prophet or seer, never by the deity. The speaker using the oath formula "I testify" is the risen and exalted Jesus, as v 20 makes clear.

The reference "to all who hear the prophetic words of this book" is usually taken to refer to the liturgical setting in which John expected his book to be read aloud, a repetition of the earlier mention of the hearers in 1:3 (see *Comment* on 1:3). The use of πᾶς, "every," with an articular substantival participle, however, emphasizes the responsibility each individual has who hears this book read. Such reading could be done before individuals and groups in a variety of settings, of which Christian worship is perhaps the most obvious candidate, though the possibility of a school setting should not be ignored. Yet despite the group setting, *each individual who hears* is responsible for hearing and obeying what is heard. In antiquity books were nearly always read aloud so that the terms for "reading" and "hearing" (ἀναγινώσκειν-ἀκούειν; *legere-audire*) could be used as synonyms (Herodotus 1.48) or used together as an idiomatic expression referring to a single activity (Rev 1:3 [see *Comment* there]; Augustine *Ep.* 147; *Conf.* 10.3; Cassiodorus *Inst. divin. lect.* 1.29; see J. Balogh, *Philologus* 82 [1927] 206–10). This means that here "all who hear" can equally well refer to "all who read," and reading-hearing can be either a public or private activity.

The phrase "the prophetic words of this book" is a Semitism (see *Note* 22:18.c.), which also occurs in 22:7, 10 and 1:3 (with the omission of τοῦ βιβλίου τούτου, "this book"). Though John nowhere claims the status of a prophet, the fact that he self-consciously wrote a book he designated as "prophetic," together with the fact that his brethren are prophets (22:9), indicates that John had a prophetic self-understanding (see *Comment* on 1:3).

18b ἐάν τις ἐπιθῇ ἐπ' αὐτά, "If anyone adds to them." The Greek verb most frequently used in the integrity formula is προστιθέναι, "to add to." The two conditional clauses in vv 18b–19 are parallel constructions. The protasis of both conditions consists of the conditional particle ἐάν, "if," with the aorist subjunctives ἐπιθῇ, "add," and ἀφέλῃ, "take away," while the apodosis has the future indicatives ἐπιθήσει, "will add," and ἀφελεῖ, "will take away." This type of conditional clause refers to a future event that is possible, even probable. The event described in the protasis is pending (BDF § 373; Moulton, *Grammar* 3:114–15; Burton, *Syntax*, 104). John regards it as very possible that someone will attempt to tamper with his book, and given the MS history of the typical Jewish apocalypse, his fears appear to be well grounded.

The two verbs translated "add," ἐπιθῇ and ἐπιθήσει (v 18), and those translated "take away," ἀφέλῃ and ἀφελεῖ (v 19), are examples of paronomasia; the first of each pair of verbs is used literally, while the second occurrence of the same verb is used metaphorically (BDF § 488.1; Turner, *Syntax*, 148); for other examples of paronomasia in Revelation, see 2:2(2x), 22; 3:10; 11:18; 14:8; 18:6(3x), 20, 21. The usual formulation of the integrity formula (see *Form/Structure/Setting* on Rev 22:10–20) favors the Greek antonyms προσθεῖναι, "to add," and ἀφελεῖν, "to subtract, delete." John appears to have consciously replaced προσθεῖναι, the verb most commonly used with the integrity formula (see above under *Form/Structure/Setting*) with ἐπιθεῖναι, one of its synonyms, in order to capitalize on the fact that the latter verb can mean "to inflict" (see Luke 10:30; Acts 16:23), as well as "to add," thereby enabling him to use paronomasia in both conditional clauses. This careful composition reveals a noteworthy rhetorical ability on the part of the author.

18c ἐπιθήσει ὁ θεὸς ἐπ' αὐτὸν τὰς πληγὰς τὰς γεγραμμένας ἐν τῷ βιβλίῳ τούτῳ, "God will add to him the plagues described in this book." Here God is the subject of the verbs in the apodosis of the conditional clauses in vv 18c and 19 as the one who will bring the two curses to fulfillment should the conditions be met. In the talmudic period the divine name was no longer used explicitly in connection with either blessings or curses (Heinemann, *Prayer*, 113). Here one would have expected the verbs in the apodosis to be passives of divine activity (see Luke 12:9). In the Greco-Roman world, as in the ancient Near East, curses of a conditional nature were commonly formulated without mention of a god or gods in the apodosis. It was precisely in Asia Minor, however, where deities were more commonly appealed to by name in curses; see K. Latte, *Heiliges Recht: Untersuchungen zur Geschichte der sakralen Rechtsformen in Griechenland* (Tübingen: Mohr-Siebeck, 1920) 77ff.

John has combined the integrity formula (though not in the usual formulation with negative particles) with two conditional curses, the purposes of which are the protection and the maintenance of the integrity of his book. Why did he think it necessary to take such a precaution? Some have emphasized that John's use of this formula attests to his prophetic consciousness (Bousset [1906] 460; Lohmeyer, 182). A parallel situation is found in Hermas *Vis.* 2.1.3 and 2.4.1–4, where the ancient lady gives Hermas a little scroll containing a revelatory message, which he duly copies. When she returns and learns that he has not yet delivered his copy of the book to the elders, she replies, "You have done well, for I have words to add [προσθεῖναι]." The resultant revision is made known to all the elect, with Clement, Grapte, and Hermas serving as messengers by bringing copies and presenting them orally to various audiences (2.4.2–3). This is then an actual example of a written revelation augmented with a codicil.

The integrity formula cannot be labeled a "canonization formula" without drastically oversimplifying its function in ancient literature. Specifically, it cannot be claimed that John intended his book to be placed on an equal footing with the OT (against Bousset [1906] 460; Windisch, *ZNW* 10 [1909] 167; Moffatt, 492). John's use of the integrity formula, however, does suggest that he regarded his book as the record of a divine revelation that was both complete (and so unalterable) and sacred.

The main issue, however, is that of the *function* of the integrity formula. Did John really fear that someone would tamper with his book, or was he simply using this protective device to emphasize the sanctity and completeness of his revelatory book (the view of Lohmeyer, 182; L. Brun, *Segen*, 109). In all probability *both* possibilities were the concern of the author. There are several possible reasons that John may have feared that someone would tamper with his book: (1) The textual history of other apocalypses, both Jewish and Christian, reveals that such texts were constantly being revised and modified by those who transmitted them. (2) John was a member of a prophetic group (Rev 22:9, 16) opposed by the prophetess "Jezebel" and her prophetic circle (Rev 2:20–23) and by the Nicolaitans (Rev 2:6, 14–15); Revelation was therefore written in a setting of prophetic conflict. (3) In early Christianity there is evidence to suggest that prophetic revelations were subject to evaluation (1 Thess 5:19–22; 1 Cor 12:10; 14:29; cf. 2 Thess 2:1–2; 1 Cor 2:6–16; 12:1–3; 14:37–38; Rom 12:6), a procedure about which very little is known. Yet this process seems to have involved the interpretation of one prophet's revelations by other prophets (G. Dautzenberg, *Prophetie*, 122–48; Aune, *Prophecy*, 217–29). All this suggests that John may have had reason to believe that his revelation was in danger of being interpreted away or augmented by Christians within the various local communities who regarded themselves as prophetically gifted. This is perhaps strengthened by the proximity of a prohibition against adding and deleting in LXX Deut 13:1 with a passage cautioning against following the advice of false prophets (LXX Deut 13:2–6; cf. Philo *Spec. Leg.* 1.315). In *Phaedrus* 275e, Plato comments on the vulnerabilities of written texts (LCL tr.): "And every word, when once it is written, is bandied about, alike among those who understand and those who have no interest in it, and it knows not to whom to speak or not to speak; when ill-treated or unjustly reviled it always needs its father to help it; for it has no power to protect or help itself."

By "the plagues described in this book," John refers to the temporal punishments that will be inflicted on humankind in the future. The seven last plagues mentioned in 15:1 and described in Rev 15:1–16:21 are probably meant in addition to the three earlier plagues unleashed by the sounding of the sixth trumpet (9:18). However, John's choice of the term πληγή, "plague," is primarily governed by his decision to use paronomasia at this point, since it was one of the few choices that would have been appropriate as an object of the verb ἐπιθεῖναι, "to add, inflict."

19a καὶ ἐάν τις ἀφέλῃ ἀπὸ τῶν λόγων τοῦ βιβλίου τῆς προφητείας ταύτης, "and if anyone takes away any part of the message of this prophetic book." This is the protasis of a conditional sentence in which the condition is assumed to be possible.

19b ἀφελεῖ ὁ θεὸς τὸ μέρος αὐτοῦ ἀπὸ τοῦ ξύλου τῆς ζωῆς καὶ ἐκ τῆς πόλεως τῆς ἁγίας τῶν γεγραμμένων ἐν τῷ βιβλίῳ τούτῳ, "God will take away that person's share of the tree of life and the holy city described in this book." The tree of life has been promised to those who conquer (2:7), as has participation in the city of God (3:12), in the proclamations to the seven churches. In the final section of Revelation, the New Jerusalem is described (21:2–27), and the tree of life in its midst is mentioned (22:2). In contrast to the temporal punishment referred to in v 18, exclusion from the tree of life and the holy city must be regarded as an eternal punishment.

20a λέγει ὁ μαρτυρῶν ταῦτα, "He who testifies to this says." The identity of "he who testifies" must be Jesus since the statement in v 20b, "Surely, I am coming soon," can only be attributed to the exalted Jesus. Jesus is called a μάρτυς, "witness," in 1:5 and 3:14; in both passages his present role as a guarantor of revelation is in view, not his earthly role as a witness who completed his testimony with death. Elsewhere in early Christian literature Jesus is called a μάρτυς only in Ign. *Phld.* 7:2 (see *Comment* on 1:5). This phrase is a functional equivalent to the messenger formula (though perhaps "quotation formula" would be more appropriate) with which John introduces each of the proclamations to the seven churches. Each of these proclamations is framed by a messenger or quotation formula (see *Comment* on 2:7), and as in 2:7, 11, 17, here the messenger/quotation formula introduces a concluding statement.

20b ναί, ἔρχομαι ταχύ, "Surely, I am coming soon." ναί, "surely," is a particle of affirmation used here to indicate with solemn assurance the truth of the statement immediately following. ναί and ἀμήν, "amen," often function as synonyms (discussed fully in K. Berger, *Amen-Worte*, 6–12); see Rev 1:7, where both particles occur in conjunction (ναί, ἀμήν), and 2 Cor 1:20, where they are used as synonyms. Oecumenius (*Comm. in Apoc.* 3:14; Hoskier, *Oecumenius,* 64) observes that ἀμήν means ναί, a view repeated by Arethas (*Comm. in Apoc.* 9; Migne, *PG* CVI.560D). The phrase ναὶ λέγω ὑμῖν, "yes, I tell you," is found in Luke 7:26b (= Matt 11:9), 11:51 (= Matt 23:36, ἀμὴν λέγω ὑμῖν), and 12:5. In Rev 14:13 the phrase ναί, λέγει τὸ πνεῦμα, "yes, says the Spirit," is probably equivalent to ἀμήν, λέγει τὸ πνεῦμα, "amen, says the Spirit." Further, while ναί can be used as a prepositive or introductory particle of asseveration (Rev 22:20; 16:7) and as a responsory particle, in Revelation ἀμήν *always* has a responsory function (as in 22:20b).

"I will come soon" is a solemn promise made by the exalted Jesus that he will soon return to inaugurate the eschatological age, a promise that occurs in very closely similar phrases in 2:16; 3:11; 16:15; 22:7, 12. ἔρχομαι, "I come," is a futuristic present, a not uncommon use of the present tense in verbs of coming and going (Burton, *Syntax,* 9–10; Kühner-Gurth, *Ausführliche Grammatik* 2/1:139–40; BDF § 323), which can specifically be labeled the "oracular present" (Smyth, *Greek Grammar,* § 1882) or the "prophetic present" (Turner, *Syntax,* 63). The verb ἔρχεσθαι, "to come," is used in the prophetic present fourteen times in Revelation (1:4, 7, 8; 2:5, 16; 3:11; 4:8; 7:14; 9:12; 11:14; 16:16; 22:7, 12, 19). The verb ἔρχεσθαι, when used in the prophetic present, however, does not invariably refer to the Parousia. As G. R. Beasley-Murray has pointed out, the phrase ἔρχομαί σοι, "I will come to you," in the proclamation to the churches at Ephesus (2:5) and Pergamon (2:16) does not refer to the Parousia; rather it refers to a coming in judgment prior to the Parousia ("The Relation of the Fourth Gospel to the Apocalypse," *EvQ* 18 [1946] 173–86; cf. Aune, *Cultic Setting,* 126–33). More often, however, ἔρχεσθαι refers to the Parousia (3:11; 16:15; 22:7, 12, 20).

The phrase ἔρχομαί [σοι] ταχύ, "I will come [to you] shortly," is found five times in Revelation (2:16; 3:11; 22:7, 12, 20), and in every instance it is spoken by the exalted Jesus. This feature is quite remarkable since in the many magical invocations preserved on papyrus in which various supernatural beings are requested or commanded to act or to come, the impatient conjuror often concludes with such phrases as "now! now! quickly! quickly!" (often expressed as ἤδη ἤδη, ταχὺ ταχύ, or sometimes as ἄρτι ἄρτι, ταχὺ ταχύ; cf. *PGM* I.261; III.85, 123; IV.973, 1245, 1593, 1924, 2037, 2098; VII.248, 254, 259, 330–31, 410, 472–73, 993; VIII.52, 63; XIc.13; XII.58, 86, 143, 396; etc.); on the form and function of such invocations, see Graf, "Prayer," 188–213. Particularly relevant are these quotations from *PGM* VIII.83, ἤδη ἤδη, ταχὺ ταχύ, ἐν τῇ νυκτὶ ταύτῃ ἐλθέ, "Now! now! quickly! quickly! Come in this night!" and *PGM* XII.147, ἔρχου μοι ὡδὶ αἶψα, "Come quickly to me here!" On the other hand, Rev 22:20 forms a striking contrast to these parallels since it is not the one making the invocation who impatiently commands the imminent arrival of the deity; rather it is the one invoked who promises a speedy coming. One senses again the presence of an anti-magic polemic in which the sovereignty of the exalted Jesus is emphasized in such a way that all human attempts to control the deity are vitiated.

I have already called attention to the fact that verbs such as ἥκω, "I have come," and ἦλθον, "I came," when attributed to supernatural beings or revealers, constitute technical epiphanic language. A number of ἦλθον sayings are attributed to Jesus in the synoptic Gospels, and the Son of man is frequently the subject of such sayings (e.g., Mark 10:42–45 = Matt 20:25–28; Luke 22:25–27; see particularly E. Arens, *The HΛΘON-Sayings in the Synoptic Tradition* [Göttingen: Vandenhoeck & Ruprecht, 1976]), yet the ἦλθον sayings of the Fourth Gospel have a far more Hellenistic flavor and are *not* illuminated by the OT-Jewish religious background (see Arens, 326); see John 8;14; 9:39; 10:10; 12:27, 47; 15:22; 16:28; 18:37. The phrase "I will come shortly" in Rev 22:20 bears only a superficial resemblance to Hellenistic epiphanic language, for in this context it is not a coming in the past that is referred to, nor even an imminent cultic coming, but rather a final, decisive eschatological coming. The tense of ἔρχομαι cannot convincingly be interpreted in any other way.

20c ἀμήν, ἔρχου κύριε Ἰησοῦ, "Amen! Come, Lord Jesus!" This is not strictly a prayer, but part of a dialog in which this statement is a response to the preceding statement; see *Comment* on 1:6 for an extensive discussion of this liturgical formula. The second-person singular present imperative ἔρχου, "Come!" is unusual in that imperatives rarely occur in prayers in the NT or in early second-century Christian literature. In Koine Greek generally, the present imperative is very rare in the context of prayers, whereas the aorist imperative is relatively common. F. W. Mozley observed that in addressing God in the LXX and the NT, the aorist imperative is almost always used, though he does cite a few exceptions: 1 Kgdms 3:9, 10; Job 10:2; 13:21; 14:15; Isa 64:9: Sir 33:11; Luke 11:3 ("Notes on the Biblical Use of the Present and Aorist Imperative," *JTS* 4 [1903] 280). In Koine Greek the present imperative is used only in situations of strong emotional stress (Bakker, *Imperative*, 82–83). In Rev 22:20, the imperative ἔρχου is used in response to Christ's promise to come soon, perhaps communicating an affective urgency to the audience. The author apparently uses the present imperative to exhort Christ to keep his promise, so the entire phrase might be understood as "Yes, amen, do that, Lord Jesus" (Bakker, *Imperative*, 134). Bakker suggests that John uses the present imperative because this phrase is not so much a prayer as a conversational situation. However, it is important to recognize that the context of this concluding prayer, i.e., the entire situation presented in Revelation, is indeed a situation of extreme need and stress; therefore, the function of the present imperative in this situation of stress is clearly appropriate.

This phrase is widely regarded as a translation of the Aramaic liturgical formula *maranatha,* which indicates that the Aramaic phrase contains a verb in the imperative ("our Lord, come!") rather than in the perfect ("our Lord has come"). Since the transliterated but untranslated Aramaic formula *maranatha* is found in liturgical settings in *Did.* 10:6 and 1 Cor 10:22, it is not unreasonable to assume, particularly in view of the liturgical echoes found in 22:14–21, that "Come, Lord Jesus!" is a liturgical ejaculatory prayer that John has adopted for use at the conclusion of Revelation. S. Schulz has convincingly argued that the original meaning of *maranatha* must necessarily have been an urgent prayer for the imminent Parousia of Jesus (in which the title "Lord" was virtually synonymous with

"Son of man") and not an acclamation of the divine presence in worship (*ZNW*53 [1962] 125–44, esp. 138). He demonstrates that *marana* in the formula cannot have originally referred to God as some have claimed (e.g., Dunphy, *ITQ*37 [1970] 294–307). It is unnecessary to argue, however, that the *original* meaning of the formula cannot without further ado be regarded as determinative for *later* meanings (the polysemy of *maranatha* is in fact suggested by M. Black, "The Maranatha Invocation," 196; see *NIDNTT* 2:897). That the *maranatha* formula is translated "Come, Lord Jesus!" probably indicates that John has not translated the formula himself but is using a traditional variant of the *maranatha* formulation, another example of which is found in Phil 4:5, ὁ κύριος ἐγγύς, "the Lord is at hand." The traditional character of "Come, Lord Jesus!" is indicated by the fact that the phrase "Lord Jesus" is found only twice in Revelation, here and in the epistolary benediction in v 21, which, as we shall see, has significant traditional features. Further, the only Pauline epistolary benediction in which the name "Lord Jesus" occurs is found in 1 Cor 16:23, *immediately following the maranatha formula in 1 Cor 16:22!* The syntax of κύριε Ἰησοῦ is also unique to Revelation, since "Lord" is in the vocative case, and "Jesus," in apposition to "Lord," is also in the vocative. The view that the nominative is always used in apposition to the vocative (Zerwick, *Greek*, 11) therefore needs qualification since titles combined with proper names appear to constitute an exception; see Acts 26:2 and the comments of G. Mussies, *Morphology*, 90.

In Rev 22:20, however, "Come, Lord Jesus!" can have two distinct meanings or possibly a combination of two meanings: (1) It can refer exclusively to the *cultic* coming of Jesus, particularly if v 20 is regarded as part of a liturgical sequence and introductory to the celebration of the Lord's Supper. (2) It can refer exclusively to the *eschatological* coming of Jesus (probably the dominant view). (3) It can refer to *both* the cultic and the eschatological coming of Jesus at one and the same time; i.e., an eschatological expectation can have dimensions that are realized in present experience (Aune, "The Significance of the Delay of the Parousia," 103–9). This latter view is espoused by Audet, *Didaché*, 411–12 (particularly with reference to *Did.* 10:6), and W. Bousset, *Kyrios Christos* (Nashville, Abingdon, 1970) 352, among others.

That the author uses the formula "Come, Lord Jesus!" in an exclusively eschatological sense is suggested by the following factors: (1) Rev 22:14–21 contains liturgical *allusions* but in all probability is not a liturgical *sequence*. That is to say that while *maranatha* could easily function as an invocation for a cultic epiphany, it does not appear to function that way here. (2) The *maranatha* invocation in v 20b is qualified by v 20a; since the promise ναί, ἔρχομαι ταχύ, "Yes, I come quickly," can only bear an eschatological interpretation, the response ἀμήν, ἔρχου κύριε Ἰησοῦ, "Amen! Come, Lord Jesus!" must necessarily be given an eschatological interpretation.

While the *meaning* of the formula for the author may be eschatological, the formula may *function* in its present context in one of three ways: (1) It may focus on the eschatological dimension of the Lord's Supper (see 1 Cor 11:29; Mark 14:25; Matt 26:29; Luke 22:16), provided that the completion of the public reading of Revelation is followed by the celebration of the Lord's Supper. (2) It can function as a (possibly liturgical) formula used to reinforce or sanction the double curse in vv 18–19 (E. Peterson, *Εἷς Θεός*, 130–31; Moule, *NTS* 6 [1959–60] 307–10). (3) Finally, it can function as a reinforcement or sanction for the truth and gravity of the total message of Revelation, which emphasizes the promise of salvation for the faithful and the threat of judgment for the unfaithful and the ungodly. In view of our conclusion that Rev 22:14–21 contains liturgical allusions, though not a liturgical sequence, there is no compelling reason to suppose that the formula, "Come, Lord Jesus!" was always and only attached to the celebration of the Lord's Supper.

E. Peterson and C. F. D. Moule have suggested that *maranatha* functioned as a reinforcement of the imprecation to which it was attached. Among the supporting examples cited by Moule are: (1) A Christian sepulchral inscription from Salamis dated to the fourth or fifth centuries A.D. reads ἀνάθημα ἤτω μεράν ἀθάν, "let him be accursed; *maran athan.*" (2) Amandus pronounced a curse on those who might dare tamper with his grave: *et sit anathema maranatha, quot es perditio, in adventu Domini nostri Jesu Christi* (Migne, *PL* LXXXVII.1274). (3) Tertullian, *De pud.* 14, 13, understood the apostle Paul's use of the phrase "anathema maranatha" (1 Cor 16:22) as a malediction. The formula "Come, Lord Jesus!" it appears, can function very well as a sanction for curses such as those found in 22:18–19. The question is whether v 20 is closely tied with vv 18–19, or whether it forms a general conclusion to the whole of Revelation. First, while a close tie might be indicated by the use of the verb μαρτυρεῖν, "testify," in vv 18a, 20, it must also be noted that the formula "Come, Lord Jesus!" is separated from the curses of vv 18–19 by the phrase "Surely, I am coming soon!" (v 20a). Second, of the penalties prescribed in the curses, the inflicting of plagues and the exclusion from the holy city, only the latter can be associated with the Parousia. Third, the imperative ἔρχου, "Come!" is twice used of the Parousia in 22:17, immediately preceding the paragraph containing the curses. I conclude that John has appended the prophecy of Jesus in v 20a to the response of the Christian community represented by the author in v 20b, not specifically as a reinforcement or sanction for the curses in vv 18–19 but more generally as a sanction for the total message of Revelation.

Explanation

Rev 22:10–20 constitutes an "epilogue" in that it exhibits striking thematic similarities with the "prologue" in 1:1–8, and its central function is to emphasize the divine origin and authority of the entire book of Revelation. This section is extremely difficult to analyze for it consists of a pastiche of sayings attributed to different speakers or voices, and it is often difficult to decide the identity of the speakers. In vv 10–11, the speaker is apparently the angel who "showed these things" to John, though the two sayings that abruptly follow in vv 12–13 must be attributed to the risen Jesus. It is possible that vv 14–16 continue as a collection of sayings of the risen Jesus, even though only v 16 must clearly be attributed to him. In v 17, a saying is attributed to the Spirit and the bride, with a response from "the one who hears." The integrity formula in vv 18–19, which pronounces a curse on those who alter John's revelatory book, can be attributed to either John or Jesus, though v 20 must certainly be attributed to the risen Jesus. For this and other reasons, Vanni (*La struttura letteraria*) and Kavanagh (*Apocalypse*) have described this section of Revelation as a "concluding liturgical dialogue."

In a phrase reflecting an antithetical allusion to Daniel (8:26; 12:4, 9), the author is told *not* to seal up his prophetic book, for the time is near (v 10); that is, it is to be heard and heeded by all who have access to it. In two poetic couplets, probably to be attributed to the interpreting angel of vv 8–9, the wicked are encouraged to continue their wickedness and the righteous are enjoined to continue acting righteously, a probable allusion to Dan 12:10 (v 11).

Vv 12–13 begin with an abrupt pronouncement by the risen Jesus that he is coming soon and bringing a reward with him. This promise of the imminent return of Christ formulated in the first person is a major motif at the beginning and end of Revelation (2:16; 3:11; 22:7, 20), emphasizing the salvific aspect of the Parousia, for even though people will be rewarded in a way commensurate with their behavior, only the righteous seem to be in view. The speaker identifies himself through an "I am" saying in which the predicate consists of three titles formulated as antitheses: "the Alpha and the Omega, the First and the Last, the Beginning and the End." Together these titles underscore the strikingly high Christology of the final edition of Revelation, for the title "Alpha and Omega" is used of God in 1:8 and 21:5, "the First and the Last" is a divine title derived from Isaiah applied to Christ in 1:17 and 2:8, and "the Beginning and the End" is used of God in 21:6.

The seventh beatitude occurs in vv 14–15, where a blessing is pronounced upon those who "wash their robes" (a metaphor for salvation), for they will have access to the tree of life (the restoration of the believer to the heavenly Eden) and can enter into the holy city through its gates (reminiscent of Synoptic sayings of Jesus about "entering into" the kingdom of God). The beatitude concludes with a brief list of those who are excluded from the holy city, including dogs (a metaphor for male homosexuals), magicians, fornicators, murderers, idolaters, and liars (v 15).

Vv 16–17 open with a statement in which the divine origin of Revelation is attested: "I, Jesus, sent my angel to attest this message to you for the benefit of the churches." The pronoun "you" in this statement is plural and therefore cannot refer to John or to the churches (which would be redundant); rather it must refer to the circle of prophets whose task it was to deliver John's revelatory message to the Christian congregations. This pronouncement, like the one in v 13, is followed by an "I am" saying, this time with two predications: "I am David's descendant, the bright morning star." The first is a messianic title derived in part from Isa 11:10, while the second may be an allusion to the messianic "star" prophecy in Num 24:17.

The invitation to come issued by the Spirit and the bride may be addressed to Jesus in response to v 12, while the invitation to come attributed to "the one who hears" may represent the hearer/reader of the book who is expected to echo the invitation to come uttered by the Spirit and the bride (both uses of the verb "to come" refer to the Parousia of Jesus). In the invitation for the one who is thirsty to come (presumably the hearer who recognizes his spiritual need), the verb "come" is used in a different sense, perhaps as an invitation to participate in the Lord's Supper, reflecting the liturgical design of the closing portion of Revelation.

In vv 18–19, the exalted Jesus (though there is some question about the identity of the speaker), who had commanded John to write down the substance of the divine message that he would receive (1:11, 19; see 14:13; 19:9; 21:5), now concludes by dictating two curses. One is aimed at those who might add anything to the book, and the other is directed to those who might delete anything from the book. This formulaic prohibition against "adding to or deleting from" the book is an integrity formula, i.e., an idiomatic expression widely used in the ancient world to safeguard the contents and inviolability of tombs, treaties, and oracular revelations. John's use of this formula, combined in a unique and rhetorically skillful way with two conditional curses, indicates that the author viewed his composition as both *complete* and *inspired.* John's careful choice of words in vv 18–19 indicates that he was less concerned with the specific content of the curses or the punishments that they prescribed than with the dramatic and rhetorical effect that they would have on the readers.

Since the speaker in vv 18–20a is probably the exalted Jesus, the two sayings that compose this short section should be considered oracles that John, in his role as a prophet, is communicating to the seven Christian communities of western Asia Minor. Like a number of other prophetic sayings in Revelation, this compound saying in vv 18–20a consists of two segments, both introduced by a verb of saying or speaking, followed by what appears to be a community response in v 20b. This prophetic sanction against tampering with Revelation not only functions to underline the completeness and sanctity of the book; it also seeks to safeguard the book from John's prophetic opponents who were (he doubtless believed) perfectly capable of tampering with Revelation while exercising the prophetic gift of evaluating and interpreting the utterances of prophets like himself. Since the two curses of vv 18–19 are conditional, they are like land mines awaiting detonation. Yet, unlike a concealed mine that can be activated by an unwary foot, these curses function more like a warning posted for those who might unwittingly blunder into such dangerous territory.

In v 20a, the exalted Jesus promises that he will soon come, a prophecy that has a double edge: salvation for the faithful and judgment for the unfaithful and ungodly. In view of the common practice of Greco-Roman magicians (emulating the invocations of traditional religion) to command the appearance of an invoked deity impatiently with expressions meaning "now! now! quickly! quickly!" it appears that John has formulated this promise of Jesus in a manner that parodies magical invocations. "Surely I am coming soon!" since uttered by the exalted Jesus himself, emphasizes his sovereignty and independence over all who would invoke his coming. Belief in the imminent return of Jesus, a notion that pervaded Revelation, functioned as a strong motivation for Christians faithfully to adhere to the high moral and spiritual standards associated with the Christian way of life. John's response to the promise of the imminent coming of Jesus (here probably representing the view of the Christian congregations to whom he writes) is an enthusiastic "Amen! Come, Lord Jesus!" a phrase familiar to all Christians, either in its original Aramaic formulation *maranatha* or in the Greek translation of that formula found in v 20 (John may have avoided the *maranatha* formulation precisely because of its incomprehensibility and hence possible similarity to the *voces magicae* of pagan magicians).

B. Epistolary Postscript   (22:21)

Bibliography

Bahr, G. J. "The Subscriptions in the Pauline Letters." *BibLeb* 87 (1968) 27–41. **Doty, W. G.** *Letters in Primitive Christianity.* Philadelphia: Fortress, 1973. **Kavanagh, M. A.** *Apocalypse 22:6–21 as Concluding Liturgical Dialogue.* Rome: Pontifical Gregorian University, 1984. **Nestle, E.**

Einführung in das griechische Neue Testament. 3 vols. Göttingen: Vandenhoeck & Ruprecht, 1909. **Roller, O.** *Das Formula der paulinischen Briefe.* Stuttgart: Kohlhammer, 1933. **Ross, J. M.** "The Ending of the Apocalypse." In *Studies in New Testament Language and Text,* ed. J. K. Elliott. Leiden: Brill, 1976. 338–44. **Schnider, F.,** and **Stenger, W.** *Studien zum neutestamentlichen Briefformular.* Leiden: Brill, 1987.

Translation

²¹ᵃ*May* ᵇ *the grace of the Lord* ᶜ *Jesus* ᵃ *be with all* ᵈ *the saints.* ᵉ

Notes

21.a-a. Variant: omit ἡ χάρις τοῦ κυρίου Ἰησοῦ] fam 1611²³²⁹ cop^bo. Accidental omission (*TCGNT* ¹, 766; *TCGNT* ², 690).

21.b. In early Christian letters in which grace benedictions are used in salutations and concluding greetings, the verbs are usually lacking and must be supplied. When verbs are included (as in 1 Pet 1:2; 2 Pet 1:2; Jude 2), they are voluntative optatives and thus have the character of prayers. In the translation above, "May . . . be" has been supplied to express the optative of wish.

21.c. Variants: (1) omit Χριστοῦ] ℵ A (lacuna in C) fam 1611¹⁶¹¹ Oecumenius²⁰⁵³ ²⁰⁶² Nestle-Aland²⁷; UBSGNT⁴. (2) add Χριστοῦ] 046 051 Andreas Byzantine it^ar gig vg syr^h ph arm; [WHort]; von Soden, *Text.*

21.d. Variants: (1) μετὰ πάντων] A (lacuna in C) vg Beatus; Tischendorf, *NT Graece*; UBSGNT⁴; Nestle-Aland²⁷. (2) μετὰ τῶν ἁγίων] ℵ it^gig; WHort. (3) μετὰ τῶν ἁγίων σου] fam 1611²³²⁹. (4) μετὰ πάντων τῶν ἁγίων] fam 1006¹⁰⁰⁶ ¹⁸⁴¹ fam 1611¹⁶¹¹ ¹⁸⁵⁴ Andreas Byzantine syr cop; Bousset (1906) 460; Charles, 2:385; von Soden, *Text;* Merk, *NT.* Reading (1), "with all," is the *lectio brevior,* "shortest reading," which could have given rise to all the other readings by being expanded in six different ways: (1) "with you all," (2) "with us all," (3) "with the saints," (4) "with your saints," (5) "with all the saints," and (6) "with all his saints" (*TCGNT* ¹, 766). Yet it is difficult to accept the notion that John would have pronounced this concluding *charis*-benediction indiscriminately upon *all* without restricting its scope to Christians alone (Charles, 2:226). The distinctive phrase in reading (2), "with the saints," in this case is preferable since other variants can be accounted for through the influence of the Pauline letters (supported by Nestle, *Einführung,* 169–70; Ross, "Ending," 338–44). See discussion in *TCGNT* ¹, 766–67; *TCGNT* ², 690–91.

21.e. Variants: (1) omit ἀμήν] A fam 1006¹⁰⁰⁶ it^gig. (2) insert ἀμήν] ℵ 046 051 Andr c d e²⁰⁵⁷ f²⁰³¹ ·²⁰⁵⁶ g h i¹⁶⁸⁵ ²⁰⁴² 1 94 1773 Byzantine vg syr cop; Charles, 2:385; von Soden, *Text.* Reading (1) is the *lectio difficilior,* given the tendency to conclude NT books with "amen" (*TCGNT* ¹, 767; *TCGNT* ², 691).

Form/Structure/Setting

"The grace of the Lord Jesus be with the saints" is the concluding epistolary benediction of Revelation, which functions to remind the reader that the book is framed as a letter extending from 1:4 through 22:21 (Roller, *Das Formula,* 245; see *Comment* on 1:4–6). It is striking, in view of the complexity of the closing section of the typical Pauline letter (see Doty, *Letters,* 39–42; Aune, *New Testament,* 186–87; Schnider-Stenger, *Briefformular,* 108–67), that this epistolary closing consists of only the epistolary benediction. The conclusions as well as the introductions of ancient letters consisted of stereotyped formulas that exhibit a very narrow range of variation. The epistolary benediction "grace . . . be with you," even though it is found almost exclusively in the Pauline letters (Rev 22:21 is one of only nine exceptions through the sixth century A.D. according to Roller, *Das Formula,* 506), was probably inherited by Paul from early tradition, perhaps ultimately from Christian liturgy. The following list reveals that the epistolary benediction of v 21, like those of the Pauline letters and the epistolary tradition influenced by Paul, consists of three basic elements: (1) the use of the term χάρις, "grace," (2) the specification of the divine source of that grace,

and (3) the specification of those who are to benefit from that grace. The simpler
form of this epistolary benediction contains just the first and the third elements (Col
4:18; 1 Tim 6:21; 2 Tim 4:22b; Titus 3:15; Heb 13:25, none of which belong to the
genuine Pauline corpus of letters).

Rom 16:20:
The grace   / of our Lord Jesus Christ   / be with you

1 Cor 16:23:
The grace   / of the Lord Jesus   / be with you

2 Cor 13:14:
The grace   / of the Lord Jesus Christ   / be with you all

Gal 6:18:
The grace   / of our Lord Jesus Christ   / be with your spirit,
                                                         brothers and sisters

Phil 4:23:
The grace   / of the Lord Jesus Christ   / be with your spirit

Col 4:18:
  Grace   / be with you

1 Thess 5:28:
The grace   / of our Lord Jesus Christ   / be with you

2 Thess 3:18
The grace   / of our Lord Jesus Christ   / be with you all

Philem 25:
The grace   / of our Lord Jesus Christ   / be with your spirit

1 Tim 6:21:
  Grace   / be with you

2 Tim 4:22b:
  Grace   / be with you

Titus 3:15:
  Grace   / be with you all

Heb 13:25:
  Grace   / be with all of you

1 Clem. 65:2:
The grace   / of our Lord Jesus Christ   / be with you [etc.]

This formula is absent from Ephesians and from all the general Epistles (1–2
Peter, James, 1–3 John, Jude), as well as from the letters of Ignatius. While it is
possible to conclude that in Rev 22:21 the author is the only one to adopt Paul's
concluding grace-benediction, it is also possible to conclude that John is using a

variant of the traditional epistolary benediction that had been popularized in Asia Minor (and elsewhere) by Paul, though he customizes it by adding a distinctive touch when he refers to "the saints" (a term found thirteen times in Revelation). The traditional nature of the formula is also indicated by the phrase "Lord Jesus," found elsewhere in Revelation only in 22:20 (where it is also part of a traditional formulation) and in other epistolary benedictions only in 1 Cor 16:23 (where it is also associated with the liturgical formula *maranatha*).

Comment

21 ἡ χάρις τοῦ κυρίου Ἰησοῦ μετὰ τῶν ἁγίων, "May the grace of the Lord Jesus be with all the saints." The traditional character of this grace benediction is indicated by the presence of the term χάρις, "grace," which occurs in Revelation only in the epistolary introduction in 1:4 and here in the epistolary conclusion. χάρις is clearly not part of the author's theological vocabulary, though χάρις is also found only in the epistolary framework of 1 Thessalonians and Philemon, both of which are unquestionably Pauline letters, and χάρις was obviously an important theologoumenon for Paul. Kavanagh, who interprets 22:6–21 as a liturgical dialogue, regards v 21 as the concluding blessing of the lector (who also speaks in the name of the exalted Jesus in v 16 [*Apocalypse*, 132–33]).

Explanation

The author concludes, as he began, with a traditional feature of the ancient letter. In so doing, he uses the kind of stereotyped benediction particularly associated with the Pauline letters, just as he began with a salutation and a thanksgiving closely resembling those of Paul (1:4–6). In spite of its formulaic character, the benediction effectively conveys one of the basic convictions of the Christian faith, that the grace available only in and through Jesus Christ may be appropriated and experienced by his people.

The Subscription

Bibliography

Oliver, R. P. "The First Medicean MS of Tacitus and the Titulature of Ancient Books." *TAPA* 82 (1951) 232–61. **Thompson, E. M.** *A Handbook of Greek and Latin Paleography.* Chicago: Ares, 1966. **Turner, E. G.** *Greek Manuscripts of the Ancient World.* Oxford: Clarendon, 1971. **Wendel, C.** *Die griechisch-römische Buchbeschreibung verglichen mit der des vorderen Orients.* Halle: Niemeyer, 1949.

Translation

ᵃ*The Revelation by* ᵇ *John* ᵃ

Notes

a-a. Variants: (1) ἀποκάλυψις Ἰωάννου] A fam 1611¹⁸⁵⁴. (2) ἀποκαλύψεις Ἰωάννου] ℵ. (3) Ἰωάννου ἀποκάλυψις] Andr Ø⁹⁴. (4) ἀποκάλυψις] Byz 12⁶²⁷. (5) ἀποκάλυψις τοῦ ἁγίου Ἰωάννου τοῦ θεολόγου] Byz 6¹³⁵² Byz 14³²⁵ ⁵¹⁷ Byz 17⁹³. (6) *explicit apocalypsis iohannis apostoli*] vg^GIE. This is just a sample of the shorter subscriptions (see Hoskier, *Text* 2:647–49). Reading (2) is an itacism, and so reading (1) is very probably the most original form of the subscription. Reading (3) is simply the metathesis of readings (1) and (2), while reading (5) is an example of how the subscription was expanded by pious scribes.

b. The subscription attested in A and fam 1611¹⁸⁵⁴ contains just two words, Ἀποκάλυψις Ἰωάννου. The gen. Ἰωάννου is a gen. of source or origin, hence a gen. of authorship.

Comment

ἀποκάλυψις Ἰωάννου, "The Revelation by John." The titles of ancient books were regularly placed at the *end* of a papyrus roll (Oliver, *TAPA* 82 [1951] 243, 245; E. M. Thompson, *Handbook*, 58; Wendel, *Buchbeschreibung*, 24–29). For examples of end titles, 𝔓⁷⁵ (third century A.D.) preserves the subscriptions ΕΥΑΓΓΕΛΙΟΝ ΚΑΤΑ ΛΟΥΚΑΝ, "The Gospel according to Luke," and ΕΥΑΓΓΕΛΙΟΝ ΚΑΤΑ ΙΩΑΝΝΗΝ, "The Gospel according to John." For the end titles of two fragments of Sappho, see E. G. Turner, *Greek Manuscripts,* 46 (no. 17b), 48 (no. 18: σαπφο[ῦς μελῶν]).

Before the codex supplanted the roll book, titles (when used) usually had the simplest possible form (e.g., the title of the work in one word, if possible, and the author's name in the genitive).

Only two uncials contain the subscription ἀποκάλυψις Ἰωάννου. They are ℵ (in the form Ἀποκαλύψεις Ἰωάννου) and A. One cursive, fam 1611¹⁸⁵⁴, contains the subscription. Here the genitive is a genitive of source or origin indicating authorship.

Index of Modern Authors

Aalen, S. 1133, 1171
Aarne, A. 647, 667
Abbott, E. A. xxx, 67, B:xxx, C:xxx
Aberbach, M. xxx, B:xxx, C:xxx, 1039
Abrahams, I. xxx, 162, B:xxx, C:xxx
Abramowitz, C. 114
Abt, A. 245, 252
Acerbi, A. 1195, 1226
Achelis, F. H. cxlviii, B:xxx, 655, 770, C:xxx
Achtemeier, P. J. 319, 442
Adams, A. W. cxlviii
Adler, A. 96, 141, B:xxx, 811, C:xxx
Aejmelaeus, A. xxx, cv, cxxxiii, cl, clx, cxcii–cxcv, ccii, 66, B:xxx, 655, 787, 855, C:xxx, 1074, 1112
Aerts, W. J. clx, clxxxix, 103, 653, 784, 1137
Agnew, F. H. 132, 144–45
Aland, B. cxxxix, cliv, clvi, clxviii, clxxv, 134, 239, 258, 325, 339, 356, 368, 385, 429–30, 470, 485, 516, 549, 574, 701, 737, 790, 852, 946, 999, 1006, 1043, 1139, 1199
Aland, K. cxxxiv, cxxxvi–cxxxix, cxlii–cxlvii, cliv, clvi, clxviii, clxxv, 24, 42, 51, 63–65, 67–68, 120, 133–34, 158, 178, 229, 239, 247, 258, 270–72, 274, 322–26, 339, 356, 368, 380–82, 384–86, 426–30, 470, 483–87, 489–90, 516, 548–50, 552, 574, 579, 581–82, 633–34, 652, 654–55, 701, 716–22, 737, 750, 783–86, 788, 790, 839, 852–54, 856, 859, 908, 910, 936, 946, 965, 967–71, 973, 999, 1006, 1014, 1016–17, 1042–43, 1072–74, 1110–12, 1137–39, 1141, 1197, 1199, 1200, 1239
Albeck, C. 291, B:xliii, 462, 471, 509, C:xliii
Albl, M. C. 1195
Albright, W. F. xxx, 296, B:xxx, 640, C:xxx
Alepuz, M. clxi
Aletti, J. N. 114
Alexander, P. 152, 286, 298, 301, 538, 701, 843, 871, 994 1034, 1040, 1051
Alexiou, M. 961, 978–79
Alföldi, A. xxx, 292, 296, 358, B:xxx, 741–42, 775, C:xxx
Alföldi-Rosenbaum, E. 293, 714, 756, 906, 945
Alföldy, G. 1069
Alford, H. xxviii, lxiii, B:xxviii, C:xxviii
Alfrink, B. 1069
Allegro, J. 935, 1164
Allen, J. H. xxx, B:xxx, C:xxx
Allison, D. C. xxxiii, B:xxxiii, 480, 575, 600, C:xxxiii
Allo, E. B. xxviii, clxi, clxxxvii, 67, 325–26, B:xxviii, 440–41, 446, 551, 574, 578, 585, 596–97, 602–3, 606, 803, C:xxiii, 989, 1034, 1057, 1084, 1229
Alon, G. 194
Altaner, B. 781, 844, 905
Alter, R. 436, 737
Altink, W. 781, 827
Alzinger, W. 132, 138–39
Amiram, D. H. K. 849, 901, 1133, 1176–77
Andersen, F. I. xxx, cvii, cxc, 277, 291, 305, B:xxx, 502, 568, 570, 698, C:xxx, 968, 997, 1169
Anderson, B. H. 547
Anderson, C. P. 245, 250

Anderson, G. A. 367, 372–73, 818
Anderson, J. G. C. 737
Anderson, R. T. 647
Andiñach, P. R. 480
Andrews, D. K. 575, 629
Applebaum, S. 168
Aptowitzer, V. 647, 678
Arens, E. 1234
Argyle, A. W. clx, clxxxviii
Arieh, E. 849, 901, 1133, 1176–77
Armstrong, D. clx
Arndt, W. F. clxviii, clxxv, clxxxi–clxxxii, ccvi, 41, 51, 132, 178
Arnim, J. von 34, 48, 76, 259, 544, 1100, 1120, 1153
Arnold, C. F. lvi
Arnold, W. N. 480
Ashton, J. cv–cvi
Astour, M. 1069
Attridge, H. W. xxx, lxx, 39, 255, 301, 351, B:xxx, 458, 544, 705, 745, C:xxx, 1117, 1188
Audet, J.-P. xxx, 84, B:xxx, 640, C:xxx, 1235
Audollent, A. M. H. 284
Augrain, C. 319, 424
Aulén, G. 319, 349, 647, 669
Aune, D. E. xxx, xlvii, liv, lix, lxx, lxxiii, lxxv, lxxvii, lxxxi–lxxxii, cv–cvi, 11, 26, 52, 57, 60, 100, 106, 110, 119–20, 123, 125–26, 144, 191, 264, 280, 364, B:xxx, 453, 560, 600, 603, 610, 613, 617, 620, 639, 666, 713, 731, 781, 810–11, 822, 830, 849, 871, 886, C:xxx, 977, 981, 998, 1040, 1092, 1185, 1195, 1225–26, 1232–33, 1235, 1239
Aus, R. D. 647, 662, 688
Avemarie, F. 781, 845
Avigad, N. xxx, 175, 301, B:xxx, 575, 618, C:xxx
Avi-Yonah, M. 287, 289, 618

Bacchiocci, S. 60, 84
Bachmann, M. 377, 393–95, 575, 597, 905, 1188
Bacon, W. B. xlvii, 575, 602
Badina, J. 1069
Bagnall, R. S. 133, 136
Bahr, G. J. 1238
Bailey, C. A. xxx, B:xxx, C:xxx, 1124
Bailey, J. W. 1069, 1104
Baillet, M. xxx, 48, 314, B:xxx, C:xxx, 1082, 1132, 1133, 1160, 1168
Baines, W. G. 713
Baird, W. 266
Bakker, W. F. xxx, clx, clxvi–clxvii, ccii, 228, B:xxx, 428, 653, 657, C:xxx, 911, 1234
Balcer, J. M. 117
Balch, D. L. 708
Baldensperger, W. 377
Baldry, H. C. 1191–92
Balogh, J. 5, 20–21, 1195, 1230
Balsdon, J. P. V. D. xxx, 79, B:xxx, 545, C:xxx
Balz, H. R. xlvii, 224
Bammel, 990
Bammer, A. 132, 139
Banks, R. 1108, 1119
Barclay, W. 713

Barnard, L. W. lvi
Barnes, T. D. lvi
Barnett, P. W. 613
Barr, J. xxx, B:xxx, 547, 568, C:xxx
Barrett, A. A. 713, 736, 775
Barrett, C. K. xlvii, lii, 132, 148–49, 168, 191, 367, 369, 371, B:xxx, 410, C:xxx
Bartelink, G. J. M. 698
Barthélemy, D. 1133
Bartina, S. 60
Barton, B. H. 480
Barton, G. A. 647
Barton, J. B:xxx, 613, 887, C:xxx
Bartsch, S. 905, 923–24, 927, 938
Bastomsky, S. J. 737–38
Batey, R. A. 1012
Bauckham, R. J. xxx, lxiii, xcix, cv, cxxi, 33, 60, 83–84, 99, 214, 245, 250, 251, 264, 266, 295, 319, 355, 361–62, B:xxx, 377, 413, 424, 436, 443, 445–46, 463–64, 474, 480, 517, 547, 571, 575, 585–86, 597, 604, 606–7, 611, 628, 661, 693–94, 713, 758, 769, 771, 781, 799–802, 808, 826, 844, 847–48, 901, C:xxx, 905, 949–50, 961, 976, 1012, 1035, 1065, 1069, 1117
Bauer, W. xxx, clxviii, clxxv, clxxxi–clxxxii, ccvi, 51, 132, 134, 178, 239, 258, 325, 339, 356, 368, B:xxx, 385, 429–30, 470, 485, 516, 549, 573, 574, 606, 701, 737, 790, 852, C:xxx, 946, 972, 999, 1006, 1043, 1070, 1139, 1199
Baumann, U. 931
Baumgarten, A. I. xxx, cxcii, 266, 287, 292, B:xxx, C:xxx
Baumgarten, J. M. 818, 820, 1133
Baumgartner, W. 58, 211
Baumstark, A. 43, 266
Baus, K. 172, 781, 842
Beagley, A. J. 424, 442, 446–47, 575, 597, C:xxxi, 905, 934, 985, 997
Beagon, M. 952, 989
Beale, G. K. xxx, 73–74, 266, 336, 346, B:xxx, 713, C:xxx, 905, 941, 953–54
Bean, G. E. 132, 139, 156
Beasley-Murray, G. R. xxviii, xlvii, lii, lv, lxii, xcviii–xcix, 83, 105, 110, 186, 188, 250, 282–83, 289, 345, B:xxviii, 439, 441–43, 462, 470, 472, 586, 594, 596, 609, 700, 756, 812, 869, 882, C:xxviii, 948, 1095, 1156, 1225, 1233
Beatty, P. C. 290, 531
Beaujeu, J. lxvi
Beauvery, R. 905, 920
Beck, R. xxx, 97, 105, B:xxxi, 406, C:xxxi
Becker, A. S. 905
Becker, J. xlvii, 5, 119
Beckwith, I. T. xxviii, lvii, lxi–lxiv, lxvi, xcix, clxxiv–clxxv, cxcv, 6, 13, 33–34, 36, 65, 83, 190, 236, 251, 274, 282–83, 290–91, 297, 341, 344, B:xxviii, 400, 406, 411, 439, 441, 446–47, 471, 473, 483, 512, 586, 596, 598, 606–7, 620, 638, 645, 654, 661, 746, 757, 767, 803, 808, 812, 871–72, 876, 882, 895, C:xxviii, 910, 946–49, 990, 994, 1027, 1044, 1055, 1095, 1097, 1101, 1126, 1177, 1181, 1201, 1225
Beckwith, R. T. 60, 594, 1038
Begley, V. 962

Begrich, J. 632, 670
Behm, J. xxviii, 198, 272, B:xxviii, 441–42, 445, 594, 597, 604, 882, 889–90, 900, C:xxviii
Behr, C. A. 124, 183, 980, 1211
Beis, N. cxxxiv, 912
Bell, A. A. xxx, lvi, B:xxxi, 535, C:xxxi
Bell, H. I. cxxxiv, cxxxvii, 178
Beloch, K. J. 132
Belsheim, J. cli
Ben-Dov, M. 575, 618
Benedum, J. 173
Benko, S. lvi, lxviii
Benner, M. 117, 127–29
Benoit, P. xxx, 319, 359, 601, B:xxxi, 770, C:xxxi, 1040
Benrath, G. A. 751
Benson, I. M. 647
Bentzen, A. 781, 842, 844
Berger, A. xxx, 79, 82, 127, 163, 166, 183, 292, 342, B:xxxi, 396, 403, C:xxxi, 1086
Berger, K. xxxi, lxx, lxxiv, 23, 56, 117, 119, 125–26, 314, 317, 416–18, 462, 469, 575, 590, 592, 602, 611, 616, 620, 622, 624, 625, 627, 628, 640, 839, 874, 885, 888, C:xxxi, 1022, 1028, 1094, 1132, 1214, 1229, 1233
Berger, P. R. 245, 255, B:xxxi
Bergh van Eysinga, G. A. van den 713, 771–72
Bergman, J. xxxi, B:xxxi, 647, 680, C:xxxi, 1092, 1219
Bergmeier, R. xxxi, cv–cvi, cxvii, 319, B:xxxi, 547, 647, 713, 732, 735, 740, 781, C:xxxi, 905, 920, 1037–38, 1108, 1115, 1133, 1156, 1167
Berlin, A. xxxi, B:xxxi, C:xxxi, 1117
Bernard, J. H. xlvii, lii
Beskow, P. xxxi, 58, 355, B:xxxi, 456, 458, C:xxxi, 1177
Best, E. 41
Betz, H. D. xxxi, lxx, lxxviii, 5, 11, 73, 88, 107, 113, 191, 208, 241, 364, B:xxxi, 390, 614, 689, 697, 734, 849, 864–66, 883, 885, 887, C:xxxi, 1062, 1153, 1191, 1213–14
Betz, O. 88, 293, 560, 562, 647, 693, 695, 781
Bevan, E. 397, 762
Beyer, K. xxxi, clx, clxxxviii, cxciv, cci, 97, 199, 247, B:xxxi, 534–35, 550, 551, 787, C:xxxi, 1156, 1159–60, 1164, 1176
Beyerlin, J. xxxi, 85, 125, B:xxxi, C:xxxi, 1210, 1213
Beyerlin, W. lxxiii, 60
Bichsel, M. A. 317
Bickerman, E. 23, 51, 775, 777
Bidez, J. B:xxxi, 414, 830, C:xxxi, 1100, 1228
Bieder, W. 5
Bielmeier, P. A. 132
Bietenhard, H. xxxi, 189, 244, 266, B:xxxi, 563, 566, 696, C:xxxi, 1040, 1059, 1070, 1139, 1210
Bihlmeyer, K. xxxi, li, B:xxxi, C:xxxi
Bilabel, F. 319, 342
Bilde, P. 713, 751, 765
Billerbeck, P. 37, 112
Binder, G. 416
Bird, P. 905
Birdsall, J. N. cli, cliv, clvii, 713
Birnbaum, P. 303
Birt, T. xxxi, 176, 319, 322, 338, 340–41, 343, 354, B:xxxi, 547, 558, C:xxxi
Bishop, J. lvi, lxii, 737–38, 905, 947
Björck, B. 377, 409

Black, M. xxxi, lxxiv, clx, clxviii–clxix, clxxii, cxc, cc–cci, 10, 34–35, 60, 70, 92, 126, 195, 198, 199, 210–11, 228–29, 241, 263, 302, 363, 370, B:xxxi, 377, 379, 391, 398, 408, 430, 472, 485, 509, 553, 573, 575, 694, 728, 784, 811, 869, C:xxxi, 945, 962, 968, 1029, 1050, 1084, 1108, 1116, 1133, 1139, 1156, 1195, 1211, 1235
Blake, W. E. 1211
Blakeney, E. H. B:xxxi, 414, 418, C:xxxi, 1080
Blanchetière, F. 168
Blank, S. H. 1195, 1213
Blass, F. clxiii–clxiv, clxvii–clxxvi, clxxviii–clxxxii, clxxxv, clxxxviii–clxxxix, cxciii–cxciv, cxcv, cxcvi, cxcviii, cxcix, cc, ccii, cciv–ccvi, ccvi, 7, 25, 42, 50, 64, 65–67, 82, 157–58, 198, 1224
Blech, M. 172
Blenkinsopp, J. 1161, 1210
Blevins, J. L. lxx
Blidstein, G. 713, 762
Blinzler, J. 216, 819, 822
Bloch, R. 416
Blomqvist, J. xxxi, clx, cxciii, 134, 157, 199, B:xxxi, C:xxxi
Blümner, H. xxxi, B:xxxi, 532, 833, C:xxxi, 1000, 1032, 1122
Blundell, M. W. 962, 993–94
Boardman, J. 301
Boccaccio, P. 765
Böcher, O. xxviii, xxxi, xlvii, lvi–lvii, 323, 368, B:xxviii, B:xxxi, 478, 480, 509, 575, 599, 601, 751, C:xxviii, C:xxxi, 1070, 1134
Bochmuehl, M. 176, 187, 195
Böckenhoff, K. 191, 195
Bodenmann, R. xxxi, 91, B:xxxi, 840–41, C:xxxi
Bodinger, M. 737, 739–40
Boer, W. den 775
Bogaert P.-M. xcv, 156, 168, 1070, 1093
Bohak, G. 771
Böhlig, A. xxxi, B:xxxi, 560, C:xxxi
Boismard, M. É. cv–cvi, cx–cxii, 5, 60, 74, 575, 585, 1016, 1109, 1195, 1205
Bokser, B. 367
Bolkestein, H. 193
Boll, F. xxxi, 114, 291–92, 297, B:xxxi, 390, 406, 413, 520–21, 523, 560, 647, 680–81, 684, 686, 705, 809, 1063, 1156
Bömer, F. xxxi, 13, B:xxxi, 817, C:xxxi
Bonanno, A. 357
Bonhöffer, A. 258
Bonner, C. xxxi, clxxxii, 31, 191, 285, B:xxxi, 454, 771, 773, C:xxxi, 955
Bonnet, M. lxvi, 334, 542, 626, 1027, 1032, 1057
Bonwetsch-Achelis 383
Booth, W. C. xlvii
Borgen, P. 156, 195, 204, 214
Borger, R. cxxxiv, 132, 176, 178, 909, 962, 966
Boring, M. E. xxviii, lxx, 184, 264, B:xxviii, B:xxxi, 394, 441–42, 446–47, 461, 471, 594, 597, 819, 821, C:xxviii, C:xxxi, 1036, 1132
Börker, C. 133
Borleffs, J. W. P. lvi, 737
Bornkamm, G. xxxi, xcviii–xcix, 123, 287, 288, 344, B:xxxi, 571, 575, 585, 848, C:xxxi, 1195, 1206–7
Borsch, F. H. xxxi, 90, B:xxxii, 781, 841, 842, C:xxxii

Botha, P. J. J. 775
Botte, B. 1195
Botterweck, J. 1223
Bouché-Leclerq, A. xxxi, B:xxxii, 560, C:xxxii
Boulluec, A. Le xxxi, B:xxxii, 543, C:xxxii
Bourgeault, G. 710
Bourguignon, E. 60, 82
Bourne, F. C. 118
Bousset, W. xxviii, xxxi, li, lxii–lxiii, xcviii–xcix, cx, cxvii, cxxi, cxxxiv, clvi, clix, clxxi, clxxiv–clxxv, clxxxii, clxxxvii, cciii, 6, 33, 63, 65, 67, 78, 82, 103–5, 110, 112, 133–34, 142–43, 148, 157–58, 161, 177–78, 183, 190, 208, 216, 229–32, 235–36, 238, 242, 247, 250, 259, 266, 270, 272–73, 282, 283, 321, 322, 323–26, 332, 339, 341, 344, 352, 364, 366, B:xxviii, B:xxxii, 380–82, 384, 386, 394, 400, 410, 424, 429, 439–41, 445–47, 462, 425, 466, 469–71, 483, 486–87, 490, 512, 522, 538, 551–52, 555, 559, 562, 568, 572, 574–75, 580–82, 586, 588, 594, 596, 598–600, 603, 607, 611, 619, 623, 633, 642, 652, 654–55, 664, 670, 672–74, 681, 688, 694, 695–96, 700–702, 708, 710, 713, 716, 719, 729, 730, 732, 745, 747, 751, 753, 767, 769, 783–85, 787–88, 790, 796, 800–801, 803, 808, 812, 825, 842, 847, 850, 854, 856, 869, 876–77, 882, 888–89, 891, 895, 900, C: xxviii, C:xxxii, 908, 910, 918, 934, 948, 954, 965, 968, 970–73, 985, 990, 994, 1006, 1016–17, 1023, 1027, 1030–32, 1036, 1038, 1042–44, 1058, 1062, 1072–74, 1078, 1083, 1088, 1097, 1109–12, 1117, 1137–41, 1151, 1166, 1177, 1181–82, 1197, 1199, 1201, 1205, 1208, 1216, 1225, 1228, 1229, 1231, 1235, 1239
Bowersock, G. xxxi, B:xxxii, 759, 775, 777–78, C:xxxii, 951
Bowker, J. xxxi, B:xxxii, 708, C:xxxii
Bowra, C. M. 104
Boyd, W. J. P. 50
Bradley, K. R. 738
Brandenburger xcv
Bratcher, R. G. xxxi, 7, 65, B:xxxii, 385, 398, 548, 572, 700, 720, 757, 876–77, C:xxxii, 1199
Braude, W. G. B:xxxii, 842–43, 845, C:xxxii, 1061
Braun, F.-M. 647
Braunert, H. 1191
Braverman, J. 176
Brekelmans, C. H. W. cv, cxi, 172
Brelich, A. 905
Bremer, J. M. 314
Bremmer, J. 100
Brenk, F. E. xxxi, B:xxxii, 416–17, 442, C:xxxii
Bretscher, P. M. clx
Brettler, M. Z. xxxi, 308, 334, 365, B:xxxii, 640, C:xxxii
Brewer, R. R. lxx, 266, 272, 297
Briggs, C. A. clxxiv, 502
Brightman, F. E. 277
Briscoe, J. xxxii, B:xxxii, C:xxxii
Brock, S. P. cxlviii, 781, 819, 821
Brocke, M. 225
Brockmeyer, N. 1070
Broer 398
Brommer, F. 648, 685
Broneer, O. 172
Brongers, H. A. 156, 166, 781, 833

Brooten, B. J. 169, 195, 203
Broshi, M. 576, 618, 628, 1159
Broughton, T. R. S. 136
Brown, D. F. 905, 921–22
Brown, F. clxxiv
Brown, G. M. xli
Brown, J. P. 266, 286, 849
Brown, R. E. xxxii, lii, lv, 60, 100–101, 209, B:xxxii, 709, 752, C:xxxii
Brown, R. R. xxxvii, 356, B:xxxvii, C:xxxvii
Brown, S. 41, 228, 231, 239–40, 781, 805
Browne, G. M. 382
Brownlee, W. H. clxxviii, 108, B:xxxii, 456, C:xxxii, 912
Brox, N. 49, 132, 148, 424, 442, 849, 894
Bruce, F. F. xxxii, cxlviii, 23, 33, 36, 60, 151, B:xxxii, C:xxxii, 1012, 1039
Brückner, W. 319
Bruetsch, C. 1134
Brugsch, H. 673
Bruins, E. M. 713
Brun, L. 713, 905, 948, 1195, 1208, 1213, 1231
Brunell, J. clx
Brunner, H. 648
Bruns, J. E. 648, 905, 929
Brunt, J. 191
Brunt, P. A. 777, 874
Brunvand, J. H. 648, 667
Brütsch, C. B:xxviii, 602, C:xxviii
Buber, S. 696, 873
Buchanan, E. S. cli, cliii
Buchanan, G. W. B:xxviii, 441, 446, 466, C:xxviii
Büchler, A. 821
Büchsell, F. 31
Buckler, W. H. 214, 773, 775
Budge, E. A. 648, 673–74, 680, 683, 705, 763, 1070, 1092
Bühner, J.-A. lxiv
Bultmann, R. xxxxii, 250, 264, B:xxxii, 813, C:xxxii
Bundy, E. L. 319, 332
Burch, V. 713
Burchard, C. 189, 367, 369, 371, 811, 1056, 1164
Burchner, H. 132
Burke, D. G. 1003
Burkert, W. xxxii, 138, 192, B:xxxii, 474, 514, 566–67, 623, 672, 685, 762, 770, 814, 817, C:xxxii, 938, 1132
Burkitt, F. C. 819
Burney, C. F. xxxii, clx, clxxxv, cc, 23, 50, 256, 319, 367, 371, B:xxxii, 382, 697, 713, 719, C:xxxii
Burrows, M. 781, 1134, 1166
Burton, E. DeW. xxxii, clx, clxxxvii, 135, 159, 216, B:xxxii, 430, 551, 559, 567, 652, 655, 719, C:xxxii, 1053, 1186, 1230, 1233
Buschmann, G. 156, 162
Buttmann, A. xxxii, clxxiv, ccv, 229, 231, B:xxxii, 654, C:xxxii, 910, 967
Buttolph, P. A. 838
Buzy, D. 751
Byatt, A. 576

Cabaniss, A. 266, 304
Cadbury, H. J. xxxii, cxc, 192, 192, B:xxxii, 819, 822, C:xxxii
Cadoux, C. J. 156
Caird, G. B. xxvi, lv, lxiii, xcviii, 80, 83, 105, 148, 161, 236, 251, 283, 345, B:xxviii, 384, 410, 429, 440–41, 445, 447, 461, 470, 512, 568, 597, 604, 648, 700, 746, 767–68, 812, C:xxviii, 948,

994, 1034, 1038, 1098, 1117, 1181, 1201, 1225, 1229
Calder, W. 214, 478
Caley, E. R. xxxii, 96, B:xxxii, C:xxxii
Callan, T. 176, 187
Calza, G. 905
Cameron, R. 88, 1152
Campbell, L. A. 105, 451
Campion, L. G. 41
Capelle, P. 1191
Caquot, A. 713, 728
Carmignac, J. lxx, lxxx, 735
Carpenter, J. E. xlvii
Carr, W. xxxii, B:xxxii, 648, C:xxxii
Carson, D. A. 68
Carson, R. A. G. 906, 920, 1122
Casel, O. 319, 359, 508
Casey, M. 60, 90, 781, 789, 841–42
Caspari, W. 41
Cassem, N. H. 632, 638
Casson, L. xxxii, ccvii, B:xxxii, C:xxxii, 962, 970, 1001–1002, 1005, 1165
Castagnoli, F. 905, 920
Cathcart, K. J. xxxii, 359, 361, B:xxxii, 847, C:xxxii
Causse, A. 1188
Cavallin, H. C. C. 1104–5
Cayón, J. R. C:xxxii, 920, 1122
Cerfaux, L. 648, 775, 781, 826
Cerny, L. 377, 421, 849
Chadwick, H. 358, 508
Chaplin, T. 576
Charles, J. D. 319
Charles, R. H. xxviii, xxxii, l, lv, lviii, lxii, lxiv–lxvi, xcix xcviii, cv, cx, cxiv–cxv, cxvii–cxviii, cxxxvi–cxxxviii, clvi, clix, clxii, clxxi, clxxiii–clxxv, clxxix–clxxx, clxxxviii, cci–ccii, 6, 13, 24–25, 39, 42, 63, 65–68, 76, 78, 83, 97, 103, 105, 110, 133–34, 143, 157–158, 161, 177–78, 183, 190, 197, 205, 208, 211, 216, 229, 230–31, 236, 239, 242, 247, 250–51, 255, 264, 270–74, 282–84, 288–89, 291, 302, 309, 322–26, 339, 341, 344, 352, 368–69, B:xxviii, B:xxxii, 380–82, 384, 386, 394, 398, 400–401, 405–6, 410–11, 414, 426, 429, 439, 442, 462, 469–71, 473, 483–87, 489, 495, 507–8, 512, 521–22, 530, 533, 536, 548, 549, 557, 568, 571, 574, 578–79, 581–82, 586, 594, 596, 620, 623, 633–34, 638, 652–54, 656, 657, 663–64, 666, 681, 688, 697, 700–702, 704–6, 708, 716, 718–19, 721, 725, 732, 741, 747, 750–51, 756–58, 767–69, 783–85, 788–88, 790, 799–800, 803, 808, 810, 823–24, 848, 852–54, 856, 858–60, 864, 869, 872–73, 876–77, 882, 887–90, 894, 898, 900, C:xxviii, C:xxxii, 908, 910, 915, 918, 936, 944, 953, 956, 965–73, 983, 985, 990, 994, 1003, 1010, 1015, 1016–17, 1023, 1026–28, 1030, 1037–39, 1042–45, 1055, 1062, 1072–74, 1084–85, 1099, 1101, 1103, 1104, 1110–12, 1123, 1126, 1137–41, 1150–51, 1156, 1162, 1166, 1172, 1175, 1177, 1182, 1195, 1198, 1204–5, 1208, 1218–19, 1223, 1225, 1228–29, 1239
Charlesworth, J. 9, 47–48, 60, 72–73, 85–86, 88, 98–100, 114, 152–53, 182, 189, 197, 210, 213, 223–24, 239, 241, 285–86, 290–91, 294–95, 298, 301, 304–6, 314, 330, 363, 369, 408–9, 412, 415, 422–23, 435, 452, 456, 470, 474, 478, 496, 499–500, 507, 515, 517, 520–21,

525, 534, 538, 561, 563, 574. 588, 613, 626, 646, 681, 684, 686, 698–99, 701, 729, 738–39, 742, 755, 760, 787, 805, 811, 843, 871, 875, 881, 887, 891, 897, 900, 932, 999, 1008, 1173
Charlesworth, M. P. 775, 849, 962
Chase, S. H. lvi, lix
Chavasse, C. 1012, 1030, 1134
Chernus, I. 60, 100
Chester, A. 32–33
Childs, B. S. 648
Chilton, B. D. xxxii, 168, 235, 307, B:xxxii, 662, 804, 847, C:xxxii, 1062, 1168
Chilton, C. W. 835
Chilver, G. E. F. xxxii, B:xxxii, 417–18, 738, C:xxxii, 905
Christ, F. 1004
Churgin, P. 1095
Chyutin, M. 576, 1134, 1159–60, 1166
Clabeaux, J. J. 117, 130
Clarc, C. 762
Clark, A. C. 132
Clarke, E. G. xxxviii, B:xxxix, C:xxxix, 1094
Clemen, C. C. xxxii, 190, 368, B:xxxii, 713, C:xxxii
Cleugh, J. 929
Clifford, R. J. 1070, 1096, 1188
Cogan, M. 384
Cohen, H. 905, 920
Cohen, S. 195, 203
Coleman-Norton, P. R. 118
Colledge, M. A. R. 891
Collins, J. J. xxxii, lxx, lxxvii–lxxx, lxxxii, lxxxviii–lxxxix, cvii, 60, 71, 91, 195, 202, 336, B:xxxii, 414–15, 423, 474, 520–21, 576, 594, 599, 607, 611, 648, 684, 692, 699, 738, 739, 760, 887, 900, C:xxxii, 950, 1008, 1201, 1216
Collins, M. F. 678
Collins, T. 1134, 1181, 1195
Colpe, C. B:xxxi, C:xxxi, 1132
Comblin, J. xxxii, 372–73, B:xxxii, 424, 437, 440–41, 447–48, 450, 466, C:xxxii, 1070, 1134
Comfort, P. W. cxxxiv
Comstock 767
Considine, J. S. 377, 576, 619
Conybeare, F. C. xxxii, cxxxiii, cxxxiv, cli, clxxvi, clxxxvi, clxxxviii, cliv, cxcv–cxcvi, B:xxxii, 381, 485, 859, C:xxxii, 910
Conzelmann, H. xxxii, 13, 186, 207, 838, B:xxxii, C:xxxii, 962, 971, 1005, 1227
Cook, B. F. 173
Cook, E. M. 846
Cook, S. A. 169, 214, 219, 955
Copenhaver, B. P. xxxii, 12, B:xxxii, C:xxxii
Copley, F. O. xxxii, 94, B:xxxii, 563, 676, C:xxxii, 1067
Coppens, J. 781, 801, 842, 905, 955
Corsini, E. 424, 440, 447
Corssen, P. 713
Cortes, E. 245, 250
Cothenet, E. 576, 602, 648, 1012
Coune, M. 41, 1134
Couroyer, C. 900
Court, J. xxxii, lx, B:xxxiii, 585, 736, C:xxxiii, 948, 994
Cousar, C. B. xxxii, 349, B:xxxiii, C:xxxiii
Cowley, A. xxxii, 66, B:xxxiii, 458, 514, 611, 879, C:xxxiii
Cowley, A. E. clxxi–clxxii, cxc, cxciv, cc–cci, cciv, 159

Cowley, R. W.   xxxii, 33, B:xxxiii, 391, 394, C:xxxiii
Cowper, B. H.   cxxxiv
Craigie, P. C.   678, 852, 872
Cramer, J. C.   cxlvii
Cranfield, C. E.   xxxii, 46, 68, B:xxxiii, C:xxxiii
Crocker, R. L.   xxxvii, 356, B:xxxvii, C:xxxvii
Crone, T. M.   lxxv
Cross, F. M.   266, 303, B:xxxiii, 565, 648, 678, 820, C:xxxiii
Crossan, J. D.   xxxii, 132, 214, 221, B:xxxiii, 703, C:xxxiii
Crum, W. E.   cxxxiv, cxxxvii, 178
Cruz, V. P.   5
Culianu, I. P.   108, 266, 781, 836
Culley, R. C.   259
Cullmann, E.   xxxii, 28, B:xxxiii, 547, 568, C:xxxiii, 1188
Culpepper, R. A.   xlvi, lv–lvi
Cuming, G. J.   1195, 1206
Cumont, F.   xxxii, 295, B:xxxi, xxxiii, 414, 458, 680, 830, C:xxxi, xxxiii, 940, 1100, 1117, 1228
Curtius, C.   289
Cuss, D.   xxxii, B:xxxiii, 756, 762, C:xxxiii

Dabrowa, E.   891
Dahl, N. A.   60, 107, 117, 130
Dahlheim, W.   931
D'Alisera, S.   cxxxv
Dalman, G.   xxxiii, ccii, 60, 90, 323, 349, B:xxxiii, 427, 527, C:xxxiii
Daly, R. J.   319, 353
Danby, H.   B:xxxiii, 457, 514, 821, 839, C:xxxiii
Daniel, R. W.   xxxiii, 191, 206, 350, B:xxxiii, 534, 888, C:xxxiii, 1055, 1126, 1180
Daniélou, J.   xxxiii, 108, 256, B:xxxiii, 450, C:xxxiii, 1036
Danker, F. W.   xxxiii, clxviii, clxxv, clxxxi–clxxxii, ccvi, 51, 86, 132, 175, 178, 308, B:xxxiii, 681, 826, C:xxxiii
D'Arms, J. H.   962
Darnell   304
Darr, K. P.   648, 682
Dassman, E.   173
Dautzenberg, G.   1195, 1232
Davenport, G. L.   648, 669
Davidson, M.   905
Davidson, P. F.   172
Davies, G. I.   849
Davies, P. R.   xxxiii, 455, 510, 896, C:xxxiii
Davies, W. D.   xxxiii, 108, 111, B:xxxiii, 444, C:xxxiii, 1104, 1107–8, 1188–89
Davis, R. D.   319
Day, J.   xxxiii, B:xxxiii, 547, 560, 648, 667–68, 697, 707, C:xxxiii
Dean-Otting, M.   60, 266, 317
Debevoise, N. C.   891–92
Debord, P.   xxxiii, 13, B:xxxiii, C:xxxiii
Debrunner, A.   clxiii–clxiv, clxvii, clxx–clxxvi, clxxviii–clxxxii, clxxxv, clxxxviii–clxxxix, cxciii–cxciv, cxcv, cxcvi, cxcviii, cxcix, cc, ccii, cciv–ccvi, 7, 25, 42, 50, 64, 65–67, 82, 157–58, 198, 1224
Deer, D. S.   176–77, 781
Deere, J. S.   1070
Degrunner, A.   788
Dehandschutter, B. A. G. M.   5, 19, 76, 156, 162, 172
Deichgräber, R.   xxxiii, 39, 43, 46, 302, 309–10, 314, 360, 366, B:xxxiii, 470–71, 638, 640–41, 741, 863–65, 874, 885, 888, C:xxxiii, 1006, 1021–22, 1024, 1207
Deininger, J.   713, 756, 773–75
Deissmann, A.   xxxiii, clxiii, 34, 60, 83–84, 124, 182, 213, 216, 236, B:xxxiii, 408, 469, 701, 767–68, 772, 895, C:xxxiii, 954
Delahaye, K.   648
Delatte, A.   xxxiii, 31, 58, 191, 285, 300–301, B:xxxiii, 454, 523, C:xxxiii, 955, 1027, 1127
Delcor, M.   547
Delebecque, É.   xxviii, 216, 319, 323, 352, B:xxviii, 642, C:xxviii
Delling, G.   xxxiii, 5, 17, 28, 30, 50, 266, 306, 309, 314, B:xxxiii, 411, 480, 543, 568, C:xxxiii, 968, 997
Delobel, J.   xxxiii, cxxxiv, clix, 134, B:xxxiii, 718–19, C:xxxiii
De Moore, J. C.   849, 873
Den Boer, W.   1040, 1051
Denis, A.-M.   xxxiii, ccvi, 185, 197, 294, 306, 346, 348, 366, B:xxxiii, 382, 422, 450, 510, 526, 588, 619, 642, 656, 694, 749, 760, 828, 831, 895, C:xxxiii, 911, 968, 1015, 1032, 1054, 1074, 1082, 1117, 1180
Denniston, J. D.   xxxiii, clx, cxciii, cxcv, 66, B:xxxiii, C:xxxiii, 1003
De Puma, R. D.   962
Dequeker, L.   319, 359
Derchain, Ph.   xxxiii, 31, 191, 285, 300–301, C:xxxiii, 955 B:xxxiii, 454, 523, 1027
Derenbourg, J.   576, 615
Dessau, H.   951
De Ste. Croix, G. E. M.   714
Detienne, M.   514
Deubner, L.   172
Deutsch, C.   1134
Devine, R.   781
DeVries, L. F.   480, 514
Dewailly, L.-M.   508
Dewey, A. J.   88, 1152
Dexinger, F.   xxxiii, 10, B:xxxiii, C:xxxiii, 1104
Dibelius, M.   xxxiii, xlvii, lv–lvi, 118, 123, 150, 165, B:xxxiii, 838, C:xxxiii
DiBerardino, A.   478
Dick, K.   xxxiii, B:xxxiii, C:xxxiii
Diehl, E.   286, 993
Diel, P.   699
Diels, H.   15, 280, 451, 762, 899, 1120, 1126–27, 1182
Dieterich, A.   xxxiii, 118, 266, B:xxxiii, 560, 648, 670, C:xxxiii
Dietrich, E.   176, 187
Dietze, P.   1129
Dihle, A.   646, 993
Dijkstra, M.   lxx, lxxiii–lxxiv, 118, 125
Dik, S. C.   clx, cxcii
Dimant, D.   1159
Dindorf, W.   690, 1056
Dinkler, E.   456, 459
Diobouniotis, C.   xxxiii, cxxxiv, cxlviii, cl, clvi, B:xxxiii, 553, C:xxxiii
Dittenberger, W.   139, 234, 838, 969
Dix, G. H.   23, 456, 648
Dodd, C. H.   xxxiii, 101, 367, 368, 371, B:xxxiii, C:xxxiii, 1060, 1213
Dodds, E. R.   763
Dogniez, C.   xxxiii, B:xxxiii, 564, C:xxxiii
Dölger, F. J.   424, 452, 455, 456, 458, 1134, 1169, 1227
Donahue, J. R.   1030

Donaldson, T. L.   1134, 1172
Donfried, K. P.   214, 225–26, 456, 459
D'Ooge, M. L.   cxc, 114
Doran, R.   xxxiii, B:xxxiv, 693, C:xxxiv
Dormeyer, D.   314, 317
Dörner, F. K.   412
Dornseiff, F.   xxxiii, 292, B:xxxiv, 377, 714, 771, C:xxxiv, 1163
Dothan, M.   xxxiii, 38, 366, B:xxxiv, C:xxxiv
Doty, W. G.   lxx, lxxii, lxxx, 23, 1239
Doudna, J. C.   xxxiii, clx, cxc, B:xxxiv, 553, 573, 656, C:xxxiv
Dougherty, E. C. A.   clx, clxix–clxxi, clxxiii–clxxviii, clxxxi, clxxxv–clxxxvii, cxcvii–cxcvii, 430–31, 485
Doughty, C. M.   810
Dover, K. J.   xxxiii, clx, B:xxxiv, C:xxxiv, 993
Dow, S.   192
Downey, G.   905, 924
Draper, J. A.   424, 441, 447–50, 469, 1134
Drew-Bear, T.   921
Driver, G. R.   1109, 1130, 1134
Driver, S. R.   clxxiv, cc, 56, 390, 648, 685, 714, 771
Dschulnigg, P.   xli, 67, 147, B:xli, 759, C:xli
D'Souza, J.   367, 372–73
Duckworth, H. T. F.   773
Dugmore, C. W.   60, 84
Duhaime, J.   474, 1173
Dulaey, M.   cxlviii
Duling, D.   566
Duncan-Jones, R. P.   132, 136, 176, 181
Dundes, A.   675
Dunkerley, R.   xlvii, xlix
Dunn, J. D. G.   xxxiii, 39, 48, 194, 264, B:xxxiv, 710–11, 870, C:xxxiv, 1040
Dunphy, W.   1195, 1235
Dürbeck, H.   905, 935
Durham, J. I.   xxxiii, 47, 357, B:xxxiv, C:xxxiv
Durling, R. J.   xxxiii, 258, 260, B:xxxiv, C:xxxiv

Eastwood, C.   41, 49
Eckhardt, K. A.   xxxiii, xlvii, lvi, lviii, 77, B:xxxiv, 622, C:xxxiv
Eckstein, F.   191
Edelstein, J.   183
Edelstein, L.   183
Edgar, T.   228, 240
Edmondson, G.   lix
Ehrenberg, V.   xxxiii, 142, B:xxxiv, 773, C:xxxiv
Ehrman, B. D.   cxxxiv, cxxxvi
Eichhorn, J. G.   xxviii, 183, 290, 184, B:xxviii, 440, 448, 598, 700, 877, C:xxviii, 1032, 1097
Eisenhut, W.   156, 166
Eisenman, R. H.   xxxiii, B:xxxiv, 346, 478, 560, C:xxxiv, 1052, 1134, 1152, 1160, 1181
Eissfeldt, O.   xxxiii, B:xxxiv, 636, 642, C:xxxiv, 976–77, 985, 1022
Eitrem, S.   xxxiii, 191, 298, B:xxxiv, 480, 531, 734, 894–95, C:xxxiv, 1062, 1082, 1093
Eliade, M.   xxxiv, 152, B:xxxiv, 668, C:xxxiv, 1188–89
Ellermeier, F.   lxxiii
Elliger, W.   132, 140
Elliott, J. H.   xxxiv, 171, 308, 325, 362, B:xxxiv, 467, C:xxxiv, 1070, 1093
Elliott, J. K.   cxxxiv, cxl, cxli, cxlvi, 41, 232, 273, 962, 966

Elliott, K. 547, 552, 558
Elliott, S. M. 956, 962, 993
Eltester, W. 60
Ely, F. H. lvi
Emerton, J. A. 235, 648, 668
Endres, F. C. 114
Engberg-Pedersen, T. 1092
Engelmann, H. xxxiv, 86, 132, B:xxxiv, 874, C:xxxiv
Engnell, I. 266, 303
Enroth, A.-M. 108, 118, 150
Enslin, M. S. xxxiv, B:xxxiv, 896, C:xxxiv
Ensslin, W. 891
Epp, E. J. cxxxvi
Epstein, I. xxxiv, 92, B:xxxiv, 392, 456, 515, 562, C:xxxiv, 1034, 1121
Erbes, K. 751
Eriksson, K. clx
Ernst, J. B:xxxiv, 576, 600, 648, 714, 745, 751, 753, C:xxxiv
Erskine, A. 1191, 1194
Esler, P. F. 194
Evans, C. A. xxxiv, B:xxxiv, C:xxxiv, 1083
Evans-Pritchard, E. E. 544
Everson, A. J. 377, 422, 849
Exler, F. X. J. 23, 118, 120
Eybers, I. H. 849
Eynde, P. van den 377

Fabre, A. 1195
Fairman, H. W. 319, 334
Fanning, B. M. xxxiv, clxxxv, clxxvii, cciv, 66, 324, 349, 551 B:xxxiv, 428, 472, 487, C:xxxiv
Farnell, L. R. 192
Farrer, A. xxxiv, 57, B:xxxiv, C:xxxiv, 1046
Farris, S. 314, 317
Faulkner, R. O. 1070, 1092
Fayer, J. C. 182, 775, 905
Fears, R. 295
Fee, G. xxxiv, cxlviii, 186, 192–93, 273, B:xxxiv, 717
Fehling, D. 5, 8, 118, 121
Fekkes, J. xxxiv, cv, cx, 98, 238, 287, 322, 346, B:xxxiv, 420, 474, 620, 836, 846, 880, C:xxxiv, 985, 1010, 1012, 1029, 1040, 1053–54, 1093, 1154, 1166, 1172, 1174–75, 1228
Feldman L. H. 176
Feldmeier, R. 833
Fensham, F. C. 1070, 1098
Ferguson, E. 708
Ferguson, J. 1191
Ferrar, W. J. xxxiv, 78, B:xxxii, C:xxxiv
Festugière, A.-J. xxxiv, xl, cxciv, 32, 98, B:xxxiv, xl, 415, 521, 550, 761, 808, 809, 865, C:xxxiv, xl
Feuillet, A. 41, 60, 91, 245, 250, 266, 287–88, 290, 377, 390, 406, 425, 547, 576, 595–96, 602, 605, 607, 616, 632, 645, 648, 781, 1189
Fiedler, P. xxxiv, clx, 103, B:xxxiv, C:xxxiv
Field, F. B:xxxiv, C:xxxiv
Field, R. xxxiv
Fiensy, D. A. 266, 303
Fillmore, C. J. clx, clxviii
Filson, F. V. 132
Finegan, J. xxxiv, B:xxxiv, 425, 456, 605, C:xxxiv, 1177
Finkel, A. 60, 106
Finkelstein, L. 565, 696
Finley, M. I. xxxiv, lvii, 186, B:xxxiv, 623, C:xxxiv
Fischel, H. A. 887
Fischer, B. cli, cliii

Fischer, L. 320, 341
Fishwick, D. 775–76
Fitch, J. G. 1191
Fitzgerald, J. T. 905, 935
Fitzmyer, J. A. xxxiv, clxxxv, cci, 32–33, 221, 227, B:xxxiv, 833, C:xxxiv, 1042, 1097, 1134, 1159–60
Flowers, H. 266
Flusser, D. 266, 304–5, 315, 576, 590–91, 595, 714, 727–28, 743, 751, 768, 1134, 1167, 1170, 1188, 1191
Foerster, W. 83, 648, 751
Fohrer, G. xlii, 41, 47, B:xlii, 603, C:xlii 962, 982, 1188
Fonck, L. 648
Fontenrose, J. xxxiv, 113, B:xxxiv, 547, 648, 667, 670, 671, 683, C:xxxiv
Forbes, R. J. 96
Forbes Irving, P. M. 648, 705
Ford, J. M. xxviii, l, cvi–cvii, cxi, cxv, 23, 110, 297, 320, 323, 345–46, 368, B:xxviii, 781, 812, 849, 872, C:xxviii, 929, 934, 997, 1012, 1032, 1223
Forestell, J. xxxiv, B:xxxiv, C:xxxiv, 1139
Forstner, D. 114, 771
Forsyth, N. 648
Foss, C. 215, 218
Foster, J. 355
Fowler, A. 119
Fox, K. A. 148, 467
Fraenkel, E. xxxiv, 95, B:xxxiv, C:xxxiv
Francis, F. O. 1012, 1036
Frank, S. 819, C:xxxiv
Frank, T. xxxiv, 136, 181, B:xxxiv, 773, 989
Franke, P. R. 905, 921
Fränkel, M. 184
Frankfort, H. 320, 334, 672
Frankmölle, H. 781, 826
Fraser, P. M. xxxiv, 156, 168, B:xxxiv, C:xxxiv
Frazer, J. G. 451
Fredricksmeyer, E. 776–77
Freedman, H. xxx, xxxiv, 277, 345, 355 B:xxx, xxxiv, 502, 568, 570, 600, C:xxx, xxxiv, 968, 997
Freeman, K. 280
French, D. H. 118, 131
Frend, W. H. C. 172, 175, 467
Freudenberger, R. lvi
Freundorfer, J. 647, 686
Frey, J. lv, 214, 221, 1040, 1058
Fridh, Å. J. 118, 122, 905
Friedländer, M. 751
Friedrich, G. lxxvi, 23, 510
Friedrichsen, A. 962, 1005
Friesen, S. J. xxxiv, 139, 160, B:xxxiv, 756, 775–78, C:xxxiv
Frings, J. 60
Frisk, H. xxxiv, cxcv, ccvii, 354, B:xxxiv, C:xxxiv, 936, 1005
Fritz, K. von 79
Frost, S. B. xxxiv, B:xxxiv, C:xxxiv, 1033
Frye, R. N. 891
Fuchs, G. 921
Fuller, R. H. 710–11
Funk, R. clxx–clxxi, clxxiv, clxxviii–clxxix, clxxxi–clxxxiii, clxxxix, cxcv, cxcix, ccvi, 42, 64, 82, 157, 198
Furley, D. J. 317
Furley, W. D. 315
Fustel de Coulanges, N. D. xxxiv, B:xxxiv, 622, C:xxxiv, 1068

Gabriel, A. 556

Gaechter, P. cv, cxv, 1195, 1203, 1205
Gaertringen, F. F. H. von 309
Gagè, J. 60, 1070, 1086
Gagniers, J. des 245
Galling, K. 781, 844, 905
Gallivan, P. A. 738
Gallop, D. xxxiv, 404, C:xxxiv
Gamber, K. 89, 114
Gamble, H. 118
Gangemi, A. 132, 195, 266
Ganschinietz, R. 60
García Martínez, F. xxxiv, 98, 204, 215, 224, 237, 260–61, 346, B:xxxiv, 572, 576, 604, 615, 622, 705, 741, 745, 838, 878, 897, C:xxxiv, 945, 1060, 1067, 1109, 1123, 1130, 1134, 1155, 1159–60, 1163–64, 1168, 1173–74, 1182, 1188, 1221, 1223
Gardiner, A. 298
Gardner, P. 905
Garlan, Y. 969, 1191–92
Garnsey, P. 60, 78, 80, 399, 962, 996, 1070, 1086
Garofalo, S. 905
Garrow, A. J. P. 585
Gärtner, B. 367, 1188
Gaster, M. 99
Gaster, T. H. 317, 879
Geffcken, J. 738, 751
Gehman, H. S. clx, clxiii
Geiger, F. 776
Geissen, A. xxxiv, B:xxxiv, C:xxxiv
Gelsomimo, R. 115, 905, 944–45
Gelston, A. 632
Genette, G. xcii
Gentry, K. L. lvi
George, A. R. 788
Georgi, D. xxxiv, 144–45, B:xxxiv, C:xxxiv, 1134, 1158, 1192
Gerhard, G. A. 141
Gerhardsson, B. 118
Gerson-Kiwi, E. 356
Gerstenberger, E. 632
Gerth, B. xxxvii, clxi, clxvi, cxc, cxciii, 216, B:xxxviii, C:xxxviii, 1233
Gese, H. 60
Geva, H. 618
Gevaryahu, H. M. I. 5
Gevirtz, S. 1213
Geyser, A. 425, 464
Ghirshman, R. 891
Gibbs, J. M. 1195
Giblet, J. 60, 266
Giblin, C. H. xxviii, lxiii, xci–xcii, xcv, xcix, cv, cxxiii, B:xxviii, 442, 446–47, 547, 555, 572, 576, 596, 603, 609, 623, 819, C:xxviii, 905, 915, 947, 1012, 1020, 1134, 1144, 1195, 1201–2
Gibson, J. C. L. xxxiv, 336, B:xxxv, C:xxxv, 1213
Giesen, H. xxviii, 114, 335, 352, B:xxviii, 442, 446–47, 455, 466, 595–96, 603–4, 606, 619–20, 768, 803, C:xxviii
Giet, S. xxxiv, B:xxxv, C:xxxv, 947
Gifford, E. H. 764
Gignac, F. T. xxxiv, clxxxvi, cxcvii, B:xxxv, 429, 483, 486, 579, 582, 634, 652, 657, 719, 784–85, 852, 854, 856, 858, C:xxxv, 908, 966, 1016, 1075, 1111, 1138
Gill, D. H. 192
Gill, D. W. J. 192, 245, 251
Gillet, L. 245
Gilliam, J. F. 192, 245, 251
Gilliard, F. D. 5, 20
Gingrich, F. W. clxviii, clxxv, clxxxi–clxxxii, ccvi, 51, 132, 178

Ginzberg, L. xxxiv, 103, 189, B:xxxv, 560, 728, 897, C:xxxv, 1180
Glasson, T. F. xxviii, lxx, 352, B:xxviii, 440, C:xxviii, 1039, 1070, 1109, 1117, 1134
Glay, M. Le 299
Gnilka, J. 1012, 1030
Gnoli, G. 111
Goguel, M. 148
Gokey, F. X. 648
Golden, J. 108, 111
Goldin, J. B:xxxv, 405, 612, 849, 873, C:xxxv
Goldingay, J. E. B:xxxv, 609, C:xxxv
Goldsmith, R. W. 962, 989
Goldstein, J. A. 359
Gollinger, H. xxxiv, B:xxxv, 648, 671, 689, 691, 707–8, C:xxxv
Gollwitzer, H. 648
Gonda, I. clx
Gonzaga, M. clx
Goodenough, E. R. xxxiv, 31, 60, 152, 172, 175, 266, 293, 305, B:xxxv, 453, 536, C:xxxv
Goodman, M. 169, 171, 480, 543, 931
Goodspeed, E. J. xxxiv, lxx, lxxv, 118, 130, 320, B:xxxv, C:xxxv
Goodwin, W. W. clx
Goranson, S. 425, 1195, 1198
Gordon, C. H. 565, 714
Gordon, R. L. 299, 1228
Gordon, R. P. xxxii, 359, 361, B:xxxii, 481, 533, 847, C:xxxii
Gorman, P. 773
Gornatowski, A. 320, 354
Gourges, M. 1070
Goussen, H. cli, clv
Gow, A. S. F. xxxiv, 141, B:xxxv, 825, C:xxxv, 1103
Grabbe, L. L. 931
Graetz, H. 169
Graf, F. 1195
Grant, F. C. xxxiv, 234, 300, B:xxxv, C:xxxv
Grant, M. 169, 648, 705, C:xxxv
Grant, R. M. xxxiv, 161, 256, B:xxxv, 710, 714, 1070, 1195
Grappe, C. 134, 1147
Grassmann-Fischer, B. 416
Gray, G. B. 464–65
Grayston, K. 751
Green, E. M. B. 246, 257
Greenberg, M. 934
Greene, J. T. 176, 186
Greenfield, J. C. 1070, 1100
Greengus, S. 1109, 1129, 1134
Greenough, J. B. xxx, cxc, B:xxx, C:xxx
Greenup, A. W. 425, 448
Greeven, H. xxxiii, 165, B:xxxiii, C:xxxiii
Grelot, P. 50, 840, 1040, 1050
Grenfell, B. P. cxxxvi–cxxxvii
Grese, W. C. xxxiv, B:xxxv, 508, 809, C:xxxv
Gressmann, H. xxxv, xxxi, 110, 283, 320, 322, 356, 370, B:xxxii, xxxv, 642, 694, 729, 751, 753, C:xxxii, xxxv, 954, 1208, 1229
Greve, A. 576, 601–2
Griffin, M. T. 738–39, 1040
Griffith, G. T. 169–70
Griffiths, J. G. xxxv, 367, B:xxxv, 469, 648, 680, 683, 705, C:xxxv, 905, 954–55, 1041, 1180
Grillmeier, A. 781
Grobel, K. 962, 1002
Groningen, B. A. van 320, 331

Grosjean, P. 266, 288
Gross, W. xxxv, clxix, B:xxxv, C:xxxv
Grossfeld, B. xxx, xxxv, 32, B:xxx, xxxv, 476, 705, C:xxx, xxxv, 951, 995, 1039, 1123
Grosvenor, M. xlv, 67, 75, 167, B:xlv, 750, C:xlv
Grotius, H. xxxv, 111, 343, B:xxxv, C:xxxv
Grözinger, K.-E. 315, 538, 843, 994
Grudem, W. lxx, lxxvi
Gruen, E. S. C:xxxv, 931
Gruenwald, I. xxxv, 100, 174, 267, 278–79, 291, 301, 303, 305, 363, B:xxxv, 471, 509, C:xxxv, 1134, 1216
Grundmann, W. 172
Gry, L. 576, 602
Gsell, S. 377, 398
Guarducci, M. 826
Guelich, R. A. xxxv, B:xxxv, 828, C:xxxv
Guintella, A. M. 478
Guiraud, P. 773
Gülzow, H. 411
Gundry, R. H. 228, 231, 240, 1002, 1109, 1122, 1134, 1188, 1191
Gunkel, H. xxxv, 285, 288, 291, 332, B:xxxv, 394, 609, 632, 636, 648, 670, 885, C:xxxv, 1012, 1022, 1028
Güntert, H. 1041, 1056
Günther, H. W. 111
Gunther, J. J. xlvii
Günther, R. 416–17
Gusmani, R. 215
Gustafson, W. M. 456, 458
Guthrie, D. xxxv, lxiii, B:xxxv, C:xxxv, 948
Gutman, J. 576, 612, 714
Güttgemanns, E. 60
Guy, H. A. 769
Gwynn, J. cli, clvi, B:xxxv, C:xxxv

Haacker, K. 132
Haag, H. 1129
Haapa, E. 377
Haas 628
Habicht, C. 776
Hachlili, R. xxxv, 174–75, 291, 300–301, 612, C:xxxv
Hackett, J. A. 176
Hadas, M. xxxv, B:xxxv, 767, 878, C:xxxv, 1210
Hadas-Lebel, M. xxxv, B:xxxv, 845, C:xxxv
Hadorn, D. W. xxviii, lvi, xcviii, 183, 235, 238, 332, 341–42, 344, B:xxviii, 447, 559, 714, 769, 801, 809, 812, 900, C:xxviii, 908, 947, 998, 1166, 1198
Haelst, J. van xxxv, cxxxiv, cxxxvi–cxxxvii, 306, B:xxxv, 450, C:xxxv, 1081
Haenchen, E. xxxv, li, B:xxxv, C:xxxv
Hafemann, S. J. xxxv, 100, B:xxxv, C:xxxv
Hagedorn, D. cxxxiv, cxxxviii
Hagg, E. 267
Hagner, D. A. 202, 363, 1218
Hahn, F. xxxv, lxx, lxxv, 118, 121, 126, 132, 144–45, 150, B:xxxv, 576, 610, C:xxxv, 1182
Haines, C. P. 127
Hainsworth, J. B. xxxvi, cxciii, B:xxxvi, C:xxxvi
Hall, R. G. 267, 272, 1195, 1226
Halperin, D. L. 267, 278
Halpern, B. 320, 334
Hals, R. M. xxxv, B:xxxv, C:xxxv
Handel, P. 416
Hands, A. R. xxxv, B:xxxv, 623, C:xxxv

Hanell, K. 883
Hanfmann, G. M. A. 156, 165, 172, 215, 218, 714, 757
Hanhart, K. 714
Hani, J. 648, 672, 1091
Hänlein-Schäfer, H. 776, 778
Hannestad, N. xxxv, 95, 262, B:xxxv, 700, C:xxxv, 1170
Hansen, E. V. 176
Hanson, A. T. xxxv, 99, B:xxxv, 702, 833, 870, C:xxxv, 1134
Hanson, J. S. lxxi, lxxxii, 60
Hanson, P. D. xxxv, lxx, lxxvii, 71, B:xxxv, 648, C:xxxv, 1034, 1063, 1179
Haran, M. xxxv, 320, 356, 372, B:xxxv, 405, 481, 523–24, 678, 849, 879, C:xxxv
Hardy, E. G. lvi
Hare, D. R. A. xxxv, 156, 163, B:xxxv, C:xxxv, 1219
Harl, M. xxxiii, B:xxxiii, 564, C:xxxiii
Harlè, P.-A. 367
Harnack, A. von xxxiii, cxxxiv, cxlviii, cl, clvi, 148–49, 250, B:xxxiii, 467, 553, C:xxxiii
Harnisch, W. xxxv, B:xxxv, C:xxxv
Harrelson, W. 710
Harrington, D. J. xxxv, 103, B:xxxv, 414, C:xxxv, 1116, 1134, 1159–60
Harrington, W. J. xxviii, xxxv, lxiii, 110, 290, 345, B:xxviii, xxxv, 440, 442, 445–47, 597, 604–5, 680, 746, 801, C:xxiii, C:xxxv, 948, 990
Harris, H. A. 169, 172
Harris, M. A. 315
Harris, W. V. 962, 1002
Hartingsveld, L. van 714
Hartling, L. von 467
Hartman, L. lxxi, lxxix, clx, 5, 8, 118, 125, 632, 714, 730, 759, 849, 896, C:xxxvi, 1064, 1078, 1195
Hartman, S. S. 751
Harvey, W. W. xxxv, lix, B:xxxvi, C:xxxvi, 1121
Hasel, G. F. 1070
Hatch, E. xxxv, 231, B:xxxvi, 550, 569, C:xxxvi, 910
Hatton, H. A. xxxi, 7, 65, B:xxxii, 385, 398, 548, 522, 700, 720, 757, 876–77, C:xxxii, 1199
Hatzfeld, J. 251
Hauck, F. 1003
Haugg, D. 576, 601, 610
Hauret, C. 648
Haussleiter, J. xxxv, cxlviii, cl–cli, 25, 33, 78, 130–31, 134, 232, 289, 291, 300, 321, B:xxxvi, 380, 382, 600–601, 613–14, 737, 745, 770, C:xxxv, 948, 950, 1042
Hawkins, J. C. clxxxv
Hawthorne, G. F. 325
Hay, D. M. xxxv, 263, B:xxxvi, 689, C:xxxvi
Hayward, R. xxxviii, 32, 50, B:xxxvi, xxxix, 613, 677, 816, C:xxxvi, xxxix, 930, 957, 973, 987, 992, 1012, 1041, 1059, 1092, 1118
Head, B. V. 139, 681
Headlam, A. C. xli, 39, 68, B:xlii, C:xlii
Heckenbach, J. 60
Hedley, L. cxxxvii
Hedrick, W. K. 648, 670, 681–82, 688
Heidel, A. B:xxxvi, C:xxxvi, 1157, 1161
Heil, J. P. 377, 393
Heiler, F. 44, B:xxxvi, C:xxxvi
Heiligenthal, R. 132, 148–49
Heinemann, J. xxxv, 267, 303, 359, B:xxxvi, 425, 463, 853, C:xxxvi, 1231

Heinemann, K. 1070, 1103
Heinen, H. 350
Heintze, H. 456
Heitmüller, W. xxix, xlvii, lxii, 190, 238, 354, B:xxix, 425, 456, 459, 576, 601, 801, C:xxix, 947, 949, 956, 1006, 1172
Heitzmann Pérez, M. L. 1134, 1165
Helbing, R. xxxv, clxxv, clxxxi–clxxxii, 51, 230, B:xxxvi, 581, 657, C:xxxvi, 908–9, 971, 987, 1075
Hellholm, D. xxxv, lxxi, lxxxi, lxxxvii, xcix, 21, 344, B:xxxvi, C:xxxvi, 1181
Hellwig, A. clxi
Helmbold, A. xlvii, lii
Helyer, L. R. 23
Hemer, C. J. xxxv, lviii, lx, lxiii, 96, 110, 112, 132, 156, 160–62, 168, 176, 182–83, 190, 195, 201, 215, 220, 228, 234, 242, 245, 257, 259–60, B:xxxvi, 399–400, 530, 768, C:xxxvi
Hempel, J. 1024
Henderson, B. W. 738
Hendricksen, W. xxviii, lxiii, C:xxviii
Hendrickson, G. L. 5, 21
Hengel, M. xxxv, xlvii, liii, lv, 3, 156, 263, 293, 315, B:xxxvi, 594–95, 598, 611, 613, 625, 628, 691, 767, 813, C:xxxvi, 990
Hengstenberg, E. W. B:xxviii, C:xxviii
Henle, F. A. 151
Hennecke, E. lxvii, lxxvi–lxxvii, cxvii, 224, 362, 451, 515, 617, 626, 694, 739, 1034, 1057, 1086, 1185
Henten, J. W. van 18, 76, 648, 746
Hepper, N. 1001
Hercher, R. xxxvi, 87, 142, B:xxxvi, C:xxxvi, 1212
Hèring, J. 1070
Herion, G. A. 870
Hermann, A. 1134
Hermisson, H. J. 358
Hershbell, J. P. 1176
Herter, H. 532, 929
Herzog, R. 1192
Herzog-Hauser, G. 776
Hesseling, D. C. 172, 788
Heubeck, A. xxxvi, cxciii, B:xxxvi, C:xxxvi
Hiebert, T. 1067, 1070
Higgins, R. 172, 175
Hilgenfeld, A. 132, 148–49, 751
Hilhorst, A. xxxvi, clxi, clxxiv–clxxv, 64, 198, 271, B:xxxvi, 656, C:xxxvi, 972
Hill, C. E. 425, 463, C:xxxvi
Hill, D. xxxvi, lxxi, lxxvi, 82, 111, 264, B:xxxvi, 576, 937, 1225
Hillers, D. xxxvi, B:xxxvi, 377, 403, 714, 770, C:xxxvi, 957, 962, 968, 997, 1068
Hillyer, N. 353
Himmelfarb, M. xxxvi, lxxi, 60, 71, 267, B:xxxvi, 472–73, C:xxxvi
Hinnells, J. R. 299
Hirsch, E. 601
Hirschfeld, O. 228, 242
Hirzel, R. 547, 645, 962, 1002
Hjertén, J. 402
Hobbs, T. R. xxxvi, B:xxxvi, 384, C:xxxvi, 1026
Hockel, A. 23
Hodges, Z. C. 377, 393
Höfer 58
Hoffmann, H. 172
Hoffmann, Y. 849
Hofius, O. 748
Hofmann, J. xxxvi, cli, cliv, B:xxxvi, C:xxxvi, 1206

Hoftijzer, J. 176
Hogarth, D. G. 132
Hohl, E. 738
Hohnjec, N. 367
Hölbl, G. 132, 1093
Holladay, C. R. 745, 760, 1099, 1127
Holladay, W. L. xxxvi, 189, 341, B:xxxvi, 382, 504, 678, 833, C:xxxvi, 932
Holland, G. S. 423
Hollander, H. W. xxxvi, 165, 262, 369, B:xxxvi, 505, 511, 681, C:xxxvi, 1168
Holly, D. cxxxiv
Holmberg, B. xxxvi, 161, B:xxxvi, C:xxxvi
Holm-Nielson, S. 315, 481, 502
Holtz, T. xxxvi, lxiv, xcviii, 37, 47, 110, 132, 145, 255, 322–23, 332–34, 341–42, 344, 349, 351, 372, B:xxxvi, 466, 841, C:xxxvi, 1053, 1122, 1158, 1181
Holwerda, D. 905, 934, 949
Hommel, F. 899
Hommel, H. 906
Hommel, P. 267, 281, 649, 681
Hommolle, T. 692, 1170
Honeyman, A. M. 765
Hopfner, T. 298, B:xxxvi, 683, 763, C:xxxvi, 955, 1216
Hopkins, K. 776–77, 962
Horgan, M. P. xxxvi, 61, 106, 161, 292, B:xxxvi, 463, 608, 735, C:xxxvi, 1061, 1146
Horn, F. W. 547, 559, 562
Horner, G. cli, cliv
Horowitz, S. 565, 696
Horsley, G. H. R. clxi, cxcix, 58, 67, 84, 132, 139, 168, 190, 192, 217, 251, 485, 773–74, 785, 811, 825
Horst, J. xxxvi, 230, 235, 238, 309, B:xxxvi, C:xxxvi
Horst, P. W. van der xxxvi, 18, 29, 164, 167, 169–70, 193, 245, 261–62, B:xxxvi, 404, 411, C:xxxvi, 952, 997, 1092, 1120, 1134
Hort, F. J. A. xxviii, xliv, xlvii, lvi, cxxxv, clvi, 24, 42, 51, 63–65, 67–68, 78, 96, 133–35, 157–58, 177, 197, 216, 229, 270–72, 322, 324–26, B:xxvii, xlv, 380–82, 384–86, 426–29, 483, 485–87, 489–90, 548, 550, 579, 581–82, 633–34, 652, 653–55, 716, 718–19, 721–22, 783–85, 788, 790, 854, 856, 859, C:xxviii, xlv, 908, 910, 965–73, 1014, 1016, 1017, 1042–44, 1072–74, 1110–11, 1137–40, 1197, 1200, 1239
Hoskier, H. C. xxxvi, cxxxiv–cxxxv, cxxxix, cxli–cxliii, cxlvi, cl, cliv, clvi, ccvi, 42, 48, 64, 178, 216, 255, 297, B:xxxvi, 394, 483, 553–54, 899, C:xxxvi, 909, 912, 1016, 1042, 1138, 1233, 1242
Hotchkiss, R. V. 55
Hout M. van den 142
Houtman, C. xxxvi, 244, 320, 346, B:xxxvi, 403, 564, 565, 615, 625, 629, C:xxxvi, 992
Howard, A. A. cxc
Howard, G. 534
Howard, W. F. xxxix, clxxii, cxc, cxcii, cxciv, cc–cci, 64, 66, 96, 197, 199, 229, 232, 270, 368, B:xl, 427, 553, 558, 573, 582, 652, 654, 701, 750, 856, C:xl, 970, 1043, 1111, 1138, 1140
Howe, N. 215, 218
Hubbell, C. G. 267
Hubert, M. 118
Huffmon, H. B. lxxiii
Hugenberger, G. P. 1109, 1130, 1134

Hughes, J. A. 1070
Hughes, P. E. 108, 111, 1070
Hunt, A. S. cxxxvi–cxxxvii
Hunter, L. W. 245, 249
Hunzinger, C.-H. lvi, 781, 906
Hurtado, L. xxxvi, 267, 289, B:xxxvi, C:xxxvi, 1036
Hussey, G. B. 172
Hutchinson, G. O. 1227
Hutson, C. R. 1131
Hvalvik, R. xxxvi, lxxii, B:xxxvi, 442, 771, C:xxxvi, 947

Immerwahr, H. R. 666
Imnašvili cliv
Inan, J. 293, 714, 756–57, 906, 945
Isager, J. 962
Isaksson, A. 819, 1188
Isbell, C. D. H. xxxvi, 57, 346, B:xxxvi, 453–54, C:xxxvi, 1083
Isenberg, M. 176, 193

Jackson, H. M. 105, 299
Jacobs, I. A. 714
Jacobson, H. xxxvi, 88, 261, B:xxxvi, 503–4, 525, C:xxxvi, 1043
Jacopi, G. 556
Jacques, X. cxii
Jahnow, H. 962, 976, 1006
Jakob-Sonnabend, W. 738–39
James, M. R. xxxvi, 292, B:xxxvi, 754, C:xxxvi
Janko, R. 315
Janzon, P. 132, 148
Jart, U. 1134
Jastrow, M. xxxvi, B:xxxvi, C:xxxvi, 955
Jeansonne, S. P. 61, 91–92, 840
Jellicoe, S. xxxvi, clxi, 56, 306, B:xxxvi, C:xxxvi, 954
Jellinek, A. B:xxxvi, 625, 841, C:xxxvi, 1191
Jenks, G. C. 751–52
Jenni, E. 422
Jepsen, A. 255
Jeremias, A. xxxvi, 332, 334, 345, 364, B:xxxvi–xxxvii, C:xxxvi–xxxvii
Jeremias, C. xxxvi, B:xxxviii, 604, C:xxxvii
Jeremias, G. lxx
Jeremias, Joachim xxxvi, xcix, clxxxviii, ccii–cciii, 61, 221–22, 232, 289, 320, 333, 344, 367, 369, 371, B:xxxvii, 527–58, 547, 570, 588, 599–600, 628, 781, 826, 849, 898, C:xxxviii, 1003, 1030, 1041, 1059, 1096
Jeremias, Jörg xxxvi, 294, B:xxxvii, 891, C:xxxvii, 1070, 1101
Jeske, R. L. 36, 61, 82
Jewett, P. 203
Johanan, R. 1165
Johannessohn, J. xxxvi, B:xxxvii, C:xxxvii
Johannessohn, M. clxi, clxxii, 61, 64
Johnson, A. C. 118
Johnson, A. R. 5
Johnson, L. T. 195, 204
Johnson, M. D. 1024
Johnson, S. E. 156, 245
Johnston, S. I. 377, 394, 1012, 1053
Joly, R. 906, 924
Jonas, H. 620
Jones, A. H. M. xxxiii, xxxvi, 142, 156, 160, 163, 172, 201, 234, 249, B:xxxiv, xxxvii, 773, C:xxxiv, xxxvii, 962, 999
Jones, B. lvi
Jones, B. W. lxxi, lxxxiv, lxxxviii
Jones, C. P. xxxvi, 79, B:xxxvii, 456, 458, C:xxxvii, 936, 982

Jones, D. L. 776
Jones, H. S. clxxx, 56, 96, 178
Jonge, M. de xxxvi, 165, 225, 262, 281, 369, B:xxxvi, xxxvii, 505, 511, 649, 681, C:xxxvi, xxxvii, 1168, 1220–21,
Jongeling, B. 1160
Jörgensen, G. 850, 897
Jörns, K.-P. xxxvi, cxciii, 302, 307, 309–11, 315, 338, 347, 366–67, B:xxxvii, 633–34, 636–40, 699, 865, 885, 888, C:xxxvii, 1006, 1021, 1023, 1026–28, 1030, 1207
Jossua, J. P. 649
Joüon, P. xxxvi, 23, 61, B:xxxvii, 649, 1207
Jourdain, E. F. 1134
Judge, E. A. 714, 767
Juel, D. 1188
Juster, J. 169, 171

Kahn, C. H. xxxvi, 15, B:xxxvii, C:xxxvii
Kaibel, G. 77, 105, 401
Kaiser, O. 98, 182, 402
Kaligula, L. 320, 365
Kalimi, I. 649, 678
Kallas, J. lxxi, lxxxviii
Kalluveettil, P. 1109, 1129
Kamlah, E. 1195, 1220
Kang, S.-M. 781
Karrer, M. xxxvi, lxxi–lxxiv, 8, 37, 110, 118, 125–26, 143, 261, B:xxxvii, 439, C:xxxvii, 1037, 1186
Karwiese, S. 132, 141
Käsemann, E. 1195, 1208, 1214
Kassing, A. T. 649
Katz, P. 656
Kaufman, S. A. 32
Kaufmann, Y. xxxvii, 33, B:xxxvii, C:xxxvii
Kautzsch, E. clxxi–clxxii, cxc, cxciv, cc–cci, cciv, 159, 714
Kavanagh, M. A. xxxvii, cxii, 23, 28, B:xxxvii, C:xxxvii, 1031, 1182, 1201, 1205–8, 1224, 1236, 1238, 1241
Kavanagh, P.-E. 1195
Kearsley, R. 714, 756, 773–74, 886
Kee, K. 5, 369
Keel, O. xxxvii, 267, 298, 301, 369, B:xxxvi, 481, 523, C:xxxvii
Kees, H. xxxvii, 18, 369, B:xxxvii, C:xxxvii, 1066
Kehnscherper, G. 481, 519
Keil, B. 124
Keil, J. 132, 137, 156, 776
Kellermann, U. 576, 625, 649, 708, 710, 1070, 1089
Kelso, J. L. 320, 357
Kenyon, F. G. cxxxiv
Keresztes, P. lvi, 751
Kerkeslager, A. 377
Kern, O. 118, 1126–27
Ketter, P. 576
Kiddle, M. xxviii, lxii, 242, 251, 290, B:xxviii, 443, 445, 447, 801, 803, 841, C:xxviii, 948, 1036, 1038, 1225
Kiley, M. 1112
Kilmer, A. D. xxxvii, 356, B:xxxvii, C:xxxvii
Kilpatrick, G. D. clxi, 216, 232, 267, 273, 308
Kimelman, R. 156, 163
Kipp, T. 118, 127
Kirby, J. T. 118–19
Kirk, G. S. 342
Kittel, A. T. 169,
Kittel, B. 315, 481, 530, 632

Kittel, G. 576, 609
Kittredge, G. L. cxc
Kiuchi, N. 367
Klasse, W. 377
Klauck, H.-J. lvi, lxv, 176, 377, 405
Klauser, T. 172, 425, 479
Klein, J. 173
Klein, M. L. xxxvii, 42, 168, 306, 359, B:xxxvii, 705, 708, 812, C:xxxvii, 1049, 1057, 1094
Klein, R. xxxvii, B:xxxvii, 678, C:xxxvii
Klijn, A. F. J. 412, 422, 435, 452, 755, 1105, 1107, 1118
Kline, M. G. 1070
Klinzing, G. 241, 1188, 1190–91
Kloos, C. 649, 1109, 1119, 1134
Kloppenborg, J. S. xxxvii, 221, B:xxxvii, 813, C:xxxvii, 1033
Klostermann, E. 898
Knibb, M. A. xxxvii, 8, 35, 91, 103, 106, 263, 286, 304, 317, B:xxxvii, 391, 408, 421, 500, 538, 636, 701, 729, 824, 835, 848, 868, C:xxxvii, 994, 1033, 1038, 1061, 1067, 1097–98, 1105, 1116, 1156, 1178, 1185, 1211, 1222
Knibbe, D. 132, 138–39
Knierim, R. 864
Knohl, I. 481
Knopf, R. 1134
Knox, B. M. W. 5, 20
Kobelski, P. J. 481, 534, 535, 649, 693
Koch, G. xxxvii, 340, 371, B:xxxvi, B:xxxvii, C:xxxvii
Koch, J. E. 649
Koch, K. xxxvii, lxxi, lxxvii, 367, 369, C:xxxvii, 1022, 1028
Koch, M. 1192
Köchling, J. 173
Koehler, L. 58, 211
Koep, L. xxxvii, 215, 224, 320, 342, B:xxxvi, 547, 558, C:xxxvii
Koerte 192
Koester, C. R. 425, 476, 706
Koester, H. xxxvii, lviii, lxxxix, 132, 140, 148, 215, B:xxxvii, 547, 570, 756, C:xxxvii, 1006, 1213
Koffmahn, E. 320, 341, 342
Kohl, H. 61, 104
Koijj, G. van der 176
Könnecke, C. 1195, 1204
Koonce, K. 714, 761
Köpstein, H. 5, 13
Korn, J. 228, 240
Kornemann, E. 180, 773, 776
Korpel, M. C. A. xxxvii, 372, B:xxxvii, 649, 705, C:xxxvii
Körtner, U. H. xlvii, li
Koskenniemi, H. 142
Kosnetter, J. 649
Kraabel, A. T. xxxvii, 160, 164, 169, 170, 215, B:xxxvii, 453, C:xxxvii
Kraeling, C. H. xxxvii, 339, B:xxxvii, C:xxxvii
Kraemer, R. S. 156, 164, 757
Kraft, A. 513, 606
Kraft, H. xxviii, liv, cx, cxv, clxx, 9, 17, 75, 78, 85, 106, 110–12, 143, 148, 183, 185, 236, 250, 272, 290, 346, B:xxviii, 398, 439–40, 446–48, 469, 551, 596, 601, 603–4, 610, 612, 616, 619, 767, 784, 800–801, 807, 845, 876, C:xxviii, 1005–6, 1019, 1026–27, 1031, 1037–38, 1090, 1095, 1097, 1126, 1175, 1181, 1186, 1201, 1204, 1208–9, 1229
Kraft, R. A. C:xxxvii–xxxviii, 998

Krämer, J. 30
Krämer, H. 1045
Kranz, W. 15, 280, 451, 762, 899, 1120, 1126–27, 1182
Kraus, H.-J. xxxvii, 313, 334, 360, B:xxxvii, C:xxxvii, 1096
Kraus, T. 61
Krause, M. S. xxxvii, 114, B:xxxvii, 377, 395, 685, C:xxxvii
Krauss, F. B. xxxvii, B:xxxvii, 403, 413, 416–17, 517, C:xxxvii
Krauss, S. xxxvii, lvii, lxiii, 215, 223, 293, B:xxxvii, 377, 400, C:xxxvii, 1122
Kraybill, J. 714, 767–68
Kreitzer, L. J. xxxvii, B:xxxvii, 421, 738, C:xxxvii, 1105, 1107
Krenz, E. 315–17
Kretschmar, G. 819
Kreuzer, S. 547
Krodel, G. A. xxviii, lvi, 336, B:xxviii, C:xxviii
Kroll, J. xxxvi, 61, 104, 315, 317, B:xxxvii, 508, C:xxxvii, 955
Kropp, A. M. 58, 235, 299, 305, B:xxxvi, 450, 603, 681, 842, 884, C:xxxvii
Krueger, P. xxxix, B:xxxix, C:xxxix
Krüger, G. xxxvii, 302, B:xxxvii, C:xxxvii
Kruse, H. 639
Kubitschek 341–42
Kübler, B. 342
Kuebler, E. 1070, 1087
Kuhaupt, H. 1134
Kuhn, K. G. lvii, 228, 240, 930, 988, 1094, 1215
Kuhn, P. xxxvii, B:xxxvii, 397, 561, 882, C:xxxvii, 1122
Kuhnen, H.-P. xxxvii, B:xxxviii, C:xxxviii, 1008
Kühner, R. xxxvii, clxi, clxvi, cxc, cxciii, 216, B:xxxviii, C:xxxviii, 1233
Kuhnlat, H.-W. lxxi, 315
Kümmel, W. G. xxxvii, lviii, lxiv, 140, B:xxxviii, C:xxxviii
Kunkel, W. 127
Kuntzmann, R. 169
Kürtzinger, J. xlvii, li
Kuss, O. 29, 216, 819, 822
Kuykendall, R. M. lxxi, lxxvii
Kvideland, R. 672
Kytzler, B, 1192

Labib, P. xxxi, xxxvii, 114, B:xxxvii, xxxi, 560, 685, C:xxxi, xxxvii
Labuschagne, C. J. 714, 741
Lacy, T. A. 576, 602
Ladd, G. E. xxviii, lxiii, lxxi, B:xxviii, 442–43, 447, 462, 803, C:xxviii, 1070
Lagercrantz, O. clxi
Lagrange, M. cxxxv
Lähnemann, J. 118, 126, 195, 206
Lake, K. cxxxv
Lambert, W. G. 1195, 1209
Lambertz, M. 697
Lambgerits, S. 1070, 1098
Lambrecht, J. xxxvii, xcv, B:xxxviii, 661, 899, C:xxxviii
Lampe, G. H. W. clxxvi, cxcvii, 31, 154, 158, 256, 401, 425, 455–57, 1012, 1039
Lanahan, W. F. 995
Lancellotti, A. xxxvii, clxi, clxix, clxxxvii, 197, 199, 276, B:xxxviii, 551, 578, 654, 829, C:xxxviii
Lang, M. L. 666
Lange, J. P. xxviii, B:xxviii, C:xxviii
Lange, N. M. R. de xxxvii, B:xxxviii, C:xxxviii

Langer, P. 776, 777
Langevin, P.-E. 1195, 1208
Läpple, A. 367
Larfeld, W. 127
LaRondelle, H. K. 850
Larsen, J. A. O. 773
Latte, K. 1070, 1086–87, 1231
Lattimore, R. xxxvii, B:xxxviii, 401, C:xxxviii, 940, 1034, 1213
Lattke, M. 315
Laughlin, T. C. xxxvii, clxi, cciv, B:xxxviii, 489, 791, C:xxxviii, 909
Laumonier, A. 170
Lauterbach, J. Z. xxxvii, 255 290, 360, B:xxxviii, 407, 519, 602, 624–25, 741, 872, C:xxxviii, 1049
Lawrence, J. 738
Lawson, R. 1030
Layton, B. 896
Leaney, A. R. C. xxxvii, B:xxxviii, 695, C:xxxviii, 1117
Lebram, J. C. H. lxxxvii, 751, 754
Leclercq, H. 191, 300, 692, 1170
Le Déaut, R. 649
LeFrois, B. J. 649, 680–81, 705
Lee, D. xxxvii, B:xxxviii, C:xxxviii
Lee, G. 989
Lee, J. A. L. cv, cxxxiv, clxi, 146
Lefort, L. T. cli,
Lefort, T. 1185
Le Glay, M. 776
Lehmann-Hartleben, K. 357
Lehmann-Nitsche, R. 649
Leipoldt, J. 1196, 1209
Leiser, B. M. 267
Leitzmann, H. 1196, 1206
Leivestad, R. 649
Lemaire, A. 186
Lentzen-Deis, F. 267, 1041
Leon, A. J. 812
Leskow, T. 5
Lethaby, W. R. 132
Leudemann, G. 140
Levey, S. H. xxxvii, 91, 298, 301, B:xxxviii, 515, C:xxxviii, 1070, 1095, 1123
Levick, B. lvii, lxix, 377, 398–99
Levine, B. A. 1134
Levine, L. I. 169, 176, 193, 576, 619, 1188
Lévi-Strauss, C. 667
Levy, J. 323, 349, B:xxxviii, C:xxxviii
Levy, E. 1070
Lewis, D. xxxviii, 129, B:xxxix, C:xxxix, 955, 962
Lewis, I. M. 61, 82
Lewy, H. 763
Licht, J. 377, 409, 1134, 1189
Liddell, H. G. clxxx, 56, 96, 178
Lieberman, S. xxxvii, 262, B:xxxviii, 405, 771, C:xxxviii
Liebeschuetz, J. H. W. G. xxxvii, 310, B:xxxviii, 416–17, 776–77, C:xxxviii, 998
Lietzmann, H. 61, 90, 192, 781
Lieu, J. M. 23
Lifschitz, B. xxxviii, 58, 169, 234, 350, B:xxxviii, 534, C:xxxviii
Lightfoot, J. xxxviii, 112, 149, 244, B:xxxviii, 621, C:xxxviii
Lightfoot, J. B. xxxviii, xlvii, lvii, lxvi, 76, 150, 234, 245, 256, 258, 289, B:xxxviii, 478, C:xxxviii, 1218, 1227
Lilliebjörn, H. 457–58
Lindars, B. xxxviii, 50, 55, 210, 212, 221, 367, B:xxxviii, 662, 689, 841, C:xxxviii
Lindblom, J. xxxviii, 61, 82, B:xxxviii, 560, C:xxxviii

Lindemann, A. xxxviii, cxxvii, B:xxxviii, C:xxxviii, 1218
Lindijer, C. H. 781, 811, 812, 821
Lindsay, D. R. 781, 838
Lipsius, R. A. lxvi, 542, 626, 1027, 1032, 1057
Ljung, I. 195
Ljungvik, H. xxxviii, cxxxiii, clxi, cxcii–cxciv, ccii, 198, 229, B:xxxviii, 427, 483, 579, 655, 787, 789, 854–55, C:xxxviii, 1074, 1084
Lloyd, A. B. 672
Lloyd, G. E. R. 61, 113, 245, 317
Loasby, R. E. 850, 899
Lobeck, C. A. 198
Lo Bue, F. xxxviii, cl, 257, B:xxxviii, C:xxxviii
Lods, A. 649
Loehr, M. 481
Loenertz, R. J. lxxi
Loewen, J. A. 1134
Loewenstamm, S. E. 481, 502
Lohfink, G. 576, 600, 625–26, 1179
Lohmeyer, E. xxviii, lxii, xcviii–xcix, clxxxvii, 23, 77, 78, 83, 85, 110, 131, 133, 143, 148, 182, 190, 199, 230, 236, 238, 242, 250–51, 272, 283–84, 307, 309–10, 325, 332, 344, B:xxviii, 395, 402, 410, 439, 443, 446–47, 466, 471, 476, 483, 548, 570, 572, 585, 596, 619, 638, 649, 652–53, 688, 772, 803, 808–9, 812, 845, 871, 876–77, 882, 890, 900, C:xxviii, 948–49, 985, 1006, 1028, 1030–31, 1034, 1110, 1122, 1156, 1173, 1175, 1182, 1204, 1216, 1219, 1225, 1229, 1231
Lohse, E. xxviii, xxxviii, liv, lxii, xcviii–xcix, cv, cxxvii, cxxviii, 37, 61, 78, 83, 93, 105, 156, 236, 251, 283, 309, 332, 335, 341, 345, B:xxviii, B:xxxviii, 385, 398, 446, 585, 594, 596–97, 732, 751, 781, 800–801, 825, 869, 882, 889, C:xxviii, C:xxxviii, 948, 1012, 1061, 1157, 1182, 1188, 1225
Loisy, A. xxviii, B:xxviii, 447, 512, 586, 597, 603, 606, 628, C:xxviii, 944, 990, 1030, 1063, 1095, 1097, 1151
Long, B. O. 731
Longacre, R. E. 666
Lortzing, J. 649
Lotz, W. 833
Louw, J. P. xxxviii, clxi, clxxv, clxxvii–clxxviii, clxxx–clxxxiv, cxcii–cxcii, cxcviii, 7, 15, 39, 47, 56, 66, 121, 134, 143, 165, 199, 215–16, 229–31, 236–40, 246–47, 261, 309, 322, 325–26, 349, B:xxxviii, 381, C:xxxviii, 1015, 1112
Lövestam, E. 228–29
Lowe, A. D. 656
Luca, G. de 177
Lücke, F. xxxviii, lxxiii, B:xxxviii, C:xxxviii
Lueken, W. 649, 693–94
Lührmann, D. 61, 547, 563, 570
Lülsdorff, R. 108, 112, 351
Lunt, G. 306
Lust, J. cv, 61, 547, 564, 815
Luterbacher, F. xxxviii, B:xxxviii, 413, 416, C:xxxviii
Luz, U. 1109, 1119, 1134
Luzarraga, J. 576, 625

Maas, F. 642
Maas, M. 320, 325, 355
MacCormack, S. 267, 308, 310, 776, 1041, 1051

MacDermot, V. xli, 225, B:xlii, 412, 415, 560, 602, 684, 692, 811, C:xlii, 941, 1034, 1056, 1089, 1170, 1179
MacDonald, D. R. xxxviii, B:xxxviii, 453, 757, 810, C:xxxviii, 1223
Mach, M. xxxviii, 16, 175, 303, B:xxxviii, 842, C:xxxviii
Macho, A. D. xxxviii, B:xxxviii, C:xxxviii, 1050, 1222
Macholz, C. cciii, 481, 528
MacKay, W. M. 176, 188
MacKenzie, R. K. 425, 441, 548
MacMullen, R. xxxviii, 186, 193, 203, B:xxxviii, 467, 762, C:xxxviii
MacRae, G. 351
Maehler, H. 1056
Magi, F. 357, C:xxxviii
Magie, D. xxxviii, 139, 181, 218, B:xxxviii, 398–99, 733, 756, 773–74, 922, 1001
Maher, M. xxxviii, 370, B:xxxviii, xxxix, 677, 897, C:xxxviii, xxxix
Maiberger, P. 377, 409–10
Maier, G. xlvii, li, C:xxxviii, 1209
Maier, J. xxxviii, 100, 267, B:xxxviii, C:xxxviii, 1134, 1155, 1189
Mair, G. R. 94
Mair, L. 545
Majercik, R. 714, 763
Malalas, J. 619
Malherbe, A. J. xxxviii, 139, 147, 161, B:xxxviii, 403, 708, C:xxxviii
Malina, B. J. xxxviii, lxxi, lxxxix, 98, 106, 177, 189, 317, 353, B:xxxviii, 390, 406, 508, 511, 526, 665, C:xxxviii, 917
Maloney, E. C. xxxviii, clxi, clxx–clxxi, cxciii–cxciv, 6, B:xxxviii, 379, 655–56, C:xxxviii, 910
Maltomini, F. xxxiii, 191, 206, 350, B:xxxiii, 534, 888, C:xxxiii, 1055, 1126, 1180
Mancini, A. 1196
Mannsperger, D. 920
Mansfield, J. 1120
Marcovich, M. 149, 151, 291–92, 299, B:xxxviii, 736, C:xxxviii, 1126, 1157
Marcus, R. 132, 614
Margolies, M. 111
Margulis, B. 481, 502
Marianas, J. de 601
Markschies, C. 245, 262
Marshall, P. K. 649
Martin, A. 267, 311–12
Martin, D. B. 5, 13, 16–17
Martin, J. xxxviii, B:xxxviii, 739, C:xxxviii
Martin, R. A. clxi
Martin, R. H. lxvi, lxviii, B:xxxviii, C:xxxviii
Martin, R. P. 315, 317, 410
Martino, F. de 962, 999
Maryon, H. 556
Mason, H. J. xxxviii, 40, 142, 310, B:xxxix, 407, 695, 700, 875, C:xxxix, 946, 1087
Masson, C. L. 781, 824
Mateos, J. xxxviii, clxi, 326, B:xxxix, C:xxxix
Mathers, S. L. M. 885
Mathewson, D. le, lxxxi
Matthews, E. xxxiv, 156, 184, B:xxxiv, C:xxxiv
Matthiae, K. xxxviii, B:xxxix, 608, C:xxxix, 1121
Mattingly, H. 906, 920, 1122
Maurer, C. xxxviii, 350, B:xxxix, 460, C:xxxix, 1129
Mauser, U. W. 649
Maxfield, V. A. 173, 175

May, H. G.   133, 906, 929
Mayer, R.   1109, 1117
Mayer-Maly, T.   156
Mayser, E.   xxxviii, clxi, clxxiii, 25, 63, 65, 216, B:xxxix, C:xxxix
Mazar, B.   576, 618
Mazzaferri, F. D.   xxxviii, lxxi, lxxvi, lxxxiv, lxxxviii, xcviii, xcix, cv, cviii, 5, B:xxxix, 571, C:xxxix, 1012
Mazzini, I. G.   921–22
Mazzolani, L. S.   1135, 1153
McArthur, H.   782, 819
McBain, B.   416
McCarter, K.   481, 502, 909
McCarthy, D. J.   425, 475, 782
McCartney, E. S.   5, 902
McCready, W. O.   1135
McCumsey, E.   508
McCurdy, G. H.   267
McDermott, W. C.   lvii
McDonald, M. F.   xxxviii, B:xxxix, 590, 592, 613, 615, 617, 624, 707, 726, 743, 755, 764, 767, 830, C:xxxix, 1080
McGaughy, L. C.   68
McGinn, B.   751
McKane, W.   782, 833
McKay, K. J.   267, 324, 662
McKay, K. L.   xxxviii, clxi, clxxvi, clxxxvi–clxxxviii, cxcviii, 134–35, 148, 158, B:xxxix, 383, 430, 483, C:xxxix, 1141
McKelvey, R. J.   425, 448, 470, 1109, 1122, 1135, 1189
McKenzie, J. L.   267, 287–88
McKenzie, R.   clxxx, 56, 96, 178
McKinnon, J.   320, 325
McNamara, M.   xxxviii, 32–33, 48, 154, 185, B:xxxix, 460, 782, C:xxxix, 1092–93
McNicol, A.   576, 1189, 1191
Meade, D. G.   830
Mealand, D. L.   156
Mealy, J. W.   1041, 1047, 1070, 1095
Médebielle, P. A.   320
Meeks, W. A.   576, 708
Meier, J.   1033
Meiggs, R.   xxxviii, 129, B:xxxix, C:xxxix, 955, 962, 999–1000
Meinardus, O. F. A.   118, 133
Mell, U.   1070, 1101
Mellink, M. J.   118
Mellor, R.   xxxviii, 182, B:xxxix, 776, C:xxxix, 906, 921–23
Ménard, J. E.   xxxviii, 351, B:xxxix, C:xxxix, 1119
Mendels, D.   1189, 1192
Mendenhall, G. E.   377
Mensching, G.   481, 508
Menzies, A.   343
Merendino, R. P.   101
Merk, A.   xxxix, 24, 63, 134, 158, 247, 270–72, 322–23, 326, B:xxxix, 381, 385–86, 426, 483, 486–87, 489–90, 550, 581–82, 634, 716, 783–84, 788, 790, 853–54, 856, 859, C:xxxix, 908, 910, 973, 1016, 1042–44, 1074, 1110, 1137–39, 1197, 1239
Merkelbach, R.   118, 133, 1056
Merton, P.   1055
Merz, E.   377
Meshorer, Y.   xxxix, 300, B:xxxix, 468–69, 678, 685, C:xxxix
Meslin, M.   623
Metzger, B. M.   xxxix, lxvi, cxxxv, cxxxviii, cli, cliv, 3–4, 33, 51, 65, 78, 135, 159, 179, 183, 197–98, 267, 297, 300, 323,

B:xxxix, 380, 394, 447, 519, 562, 582, 602, 633, 716–19, 721, 784–86, 791, 853–54, 858–59, C:xxxix, 910, 965–69, 971, 1016, 1042–43, 1065, 1072–74, 1105, 1110–11, 1123, 1198, 1239
Meyer, E.   xxxix, lxii, 309, B:xxxix, C:xxxix
Meyers, C. L.   61, 300, 734
Meyers, E. M.   300
Michael, J. H.   61, 267, 377, 547, 850, 1135
Michaelis, W.   23, 38–39, 58, 181, 457, 1100
Michaels, J. R.   xxxix, B:xxxix, 644, C:xxxix, 1070, 1203
Michel, O.   293, 309, 883, 886, 1223
Michl, J.   16, 108, 267, 286, 288, 290, 300, B:xxxix, 509, 649, 708, 819, 843, C:xxxix, 994, 1134
Migne, J. P.   255, 811–12, 977, 1211, 1236
Mihelic, J.   502
Milburn, R. L.   lvii
Miles, J. C.   1109, 1130, 1134
Milgrom, J.   367, 372, 814, 1135, 1174
Milik, J. T.   xxx, xxxix, lxxiv, 10, 268, 294, 319, 359, 363, 370, B: xxxi, xxxix, 576, 699, 770, 824, C: xxxi, xxxix, 1082, 1105, 1116
Millar, F.   xxxix, lvii, lxvii, 118, 142, 308, B:xxxix, 399, 405, 738–39, 776, C:xxxix, 951, 989, 1054, 1133
Miller, A. M.   315–16, 331, B:xxxix, C:xxxix
Miller, F. J.   980, 1194
Miller, J. I.   962, 1001
Miller, P. D.   649, 1041, 1057
Milligan G.   clxxxii, clxxxvi, cxcvii, 67, 271, 426
Milne, P. J.   649, 675
Miltner, F.   133
Min, P. B.-S.   576, 585–86, 599–602
Minar, E. L.   770
Minear, P. S.   xxxix, liv, cxxii, B:xxxix, 576, 649, 661, 714, C:xxxix, 994
Mink, G.   cli
Minns, E. H.   954
Mischkowski, H.   192
Mitchell, S.   xxxix, 16, 249, B:xxxix, 399, 400, 886, C:xxxix, 1036
Mitropoulou, E.   649
Mittelstadt, M. C.   923
Mitton, C. L.   118, 130, 215
Moda, A.   cxii
Moering, E.   61, 169
Moffatt, J.   xxviii, B:xxviii, 377, 398, C:xxviii, 1196, 1231
Molitor, J.   cli, cliv
Momigliano, A.   416, 738, 776–78, 906
Mommsen, T.   xxxix, 61, 80, 156, 166, 292, B:xxxix, 396, 756, C:xxxix, 1057, 1070, 1086–87
Monceaux, P.   773
Montagnini, F.   649
Montgomery, J. A.   xxxix, clxi, 91, 337, B:xxxix, 532, 840, C:xxxix
Moore, C. A.   xxxix, B:xxxix, 896, C:xxxix
Moore, G. F.   xxxix, 297, 359, B:xxxix, 810, C:xxxix, 1105
Moore, J. M.   874
Moore, M. S.   177, 1196
Moore, R. D.   906, 935
Moore, S. D.   cv–cvi, cviii
Moran, H. E.   xxxix, B:xxxix, C:xxxix
Moran, W. L.   41, 531, 839, 1125
Morenz, S.   xxxix, 104, 190, 297, B:xxxix, 763, C:xxxix, 1092, 1196, 1209

Moret, A.   333–34
Moretti, L.   773–74
Morgan, M. A.   xxxix, xcv, 97, 278, 286, 298, 301, 305, 319, B:xxxix, 404, 514, 561, 649, 766, 809, C:xxxix, 1063
Morgenthaler, R.   ccvii, 714, 736
Morin, G.   cli
Morray-Jones, C. R. A.   267, 303
Mortley, R.   508
Morton, J. F.   481, 521–22
Morton, R.   lxxvi
Moule, C. F. D.   xxxix, clxiv, clxxv, 61, 90, B:xxxix, 377, 483, 512, 789, C:xxxix, 1196, 1235–36
Moulton, J. H.   xxxix, clxxii–clxxvi, clxxxii, clxxxvi, cxc, cxcii, cxciv, cxcvii, cc–cci, ccvi, 64, 66, 67, 96, 135, 158, 179, 197, 199, 216–17, 229, 232, 270, 271, 349, 368, B:xxxix, xl, 379, 426, 427, 483, 550, 553, 558, 573, 582, 652, 654, 701, 750, 856, 860, C:xxxix, xl, 970, 1043, 1111, 1138, 1140, 1230
Mounce, R. H.   xxviii, liii, lxiii, 83, 242, 251, 272, 283, B:xxviii, 384, 394, 410–11, 441, 447, 462, 596–97, 604, 746, 803, 882, 889, C:xxviii, 936, 948, 1027, 1053, 1225, 1229
Mourelatos, A. P. D.   267, 281
Mowinckel, S.   xxxix, B:xl, 377, 632, 643, 885, C:xl, 1022, 1028
Mowry, L.   267, 304, 309, 320, 345
Mozley, F. W.   1234
Muehsam, A.   906
Mueller, B.   1196
Mueller, T.   228
Mullen, E. T.   267, 303
Müller, C. D. J.   267, 288, 291
Müller, D.   649, 681
Müller, H.-P.   320, 481, 850, 868
Müller, K.   177
Müller, U. B.   xxviii, xxxix, lviii, lxxv, xcviii, cv, cx, cxvii, 61, 82, 110–11, 118–19, 126, 143–44, 208, 251, 259, 335–36, 344–45, 351, B:xxviii, B:xl, 420, 562, 594, 611, 649, 756, 800–801, 808, 835, 842, C:xxviii, C:xl, 934, 953, 985, 998, 1031
Müller, W.   1001, 1135, 1161
Muncey, R. W.   cxlviii, 1110, 1197
Münchow, C.   320
Munck, J.   3, 576, 601, 613, 619–20, 626
Muraoka, T.   xxxix, 271, B:xl, 858, C:xl, 936, 1167
Murmellstein, B.   714
Murphy, F. J.   xcv, 1105, 1189
Murphy-O'Connor, J.   1000
Muscovi, J. N.   377
Muse, R. L.   118
Mussies, G.   xxxix, l, cix, cxviii, clix, clxvi–clxix, clxxi, clxxxi, clxxxvi–clxxxvii, clxxxix–cxc, cxciii, cxcvi, cxcviii–cxcix, ccii, cciv–ccv, 17, 42, 63–64, 66–67, 95, 133–34, 151, 158, 177–78, 184, 196–99, 216–17, 229, 231, 237, 270–73, 276, 307, 324, 326, B:xl, 379, 402, 407, 427–31, 438, 481, 483, 484, 486, 488–89, 512, 521, 525, 538–39, 547, 551–52, 558–59, 579–81, 627, 634, 642, 651–57, 682, 684, 701, 716, 718–21, 749, 769–70, 784, 787, 790, 802, 805, 828–29, 833, 852–53, 855, 857–58, C:xl, 908, 910–12, 946, 950, 962, 966–70, 972–73, 985, 1000, 1014–15, 1017, 1035, 1042–43, 1045, 1054, 1064, 1072–76, 1084, 1089, 1110–11, 1137–40, 1155, 1198, 1235

Mussner, F. 216, 819, 822
Musurillo, H. xxxix, lii, cciv, 37, 64, 162, 206, 304, B:xl, 409, 412, 686, 702, 897, C:xl, 946, 953, 1121, 1152, 1197
Myers, J. M. xxxix, B:xl, 803, C:xl

Nabers, N. 192
Nachmanson, E. xxxix, 3–4, 9, B:xl, 516, 806, C:xl
Naldini, M. 306
Nauck, A. xxxix, B:xl, C:xl
Naveh, J. xxxix, B:xl, 421, 453, 513, 544, 559, 629, 735, C:xl, 955, 1083
Neef, H.-D. 267
Nestle, E. 24, 42, 50–51, 63–65, 67–68, 120, 133–34, 158, 178, 229, 247, 270–72, 274, 322–26, 343, 380–82, 384–86, 426–30, 483–84, 486–87, 489–90, 548, 550, 552, 579, 581–82, 633–34, 652, 654–55, 716–22, 750, 783–86, 788, 790, 839, 853–54, 856, 859, 908, 910, 936, 962, 965, 967–71, 973, 1005, 1014, 1016–17, 1042–43, 1072–74, 1110–12, 1137–39, 1141, 1196, 1197, 1200, 1238–39
Neuenzeit, P. 267
Neugebauer, F. 263, 1156
Neumann 262
Neusner, J. 203, 235, B:xl, 624, C:xl, 1169
Newmann, B. C. lvii, lxvii, 61, 63
Newport, K. G. C. clxi, clxxix–clxxx, 197, 508, 547, 574, 657, 907, 1015
Newsom, C. xxxix, 34–35, 285, 291, 315, B:xl, 471–72, 509, 649, 669, C:xl, 1189–90
Neyrey, J. 545
Nickelsburg, G. W. E. xxxix, lxxvii, cvii, 267, B:xl, 649, 669, 830, C:xl, 1070, 1190, 1229
Nida, E. clxxv, clxxvii–clxxviii, clxxx–clxxxiv, cxcii–cxcii, cxcviii, 7, 15, 39, 47, 56, 66, 121, 134, 143, 165, 199, 215–16, 229–31, 236–40, 246–47, 261, 309, 322, 325–26
Niditch, S. 267
Niederwimmer, K. xl, B:xl, C:xl, 1157
Nielsen, J. 320, 357
Nielsen, K. 481, 512, 514, 850, 880
Niggemeyer, J.-H. xl, B:xl, C:xl
Nilsson, M. P. 23, 30, 50, 318, 764, 922
Nissen, A. 710
Nitzsch, K. I. lxxvii
Noack, B. 649
Nock, A. D. xl, cxciv, 32, 58, 86, B:xl, 415, 521, 550, 761, 776–77, 809, 865, C:xl, 1212
Noort, E. lxxiii
Norden, E. xl, 12, 25, 42, 315, 317, 333–35, 360, B:xl, 649, C:xl, 1056
Norelli, E. 455, 466
North, J. L. cxlviii
North, R. 177
Noth, M. 1041, 1181
Nützel, J. M. 576, 602
Nussbaum, M. xl, B:xl, 834, C:xl

Oberweis, M. 714, 772
O'Brien, P. T. 576, 641
O'Connor, D. W. 576, 601
Odelain, O. xl, 18, B:xl, C:xl
Oden, R. A. xxx, 39, 301, B:xxx, 458, 705, C:xxx, 1117, 1188
Ogilvie, R. M. 577, 592–93
O'Hagen, A. P. 425, 474
Ohlemutz, E. 177

Oke, C. C. 61
Oliver, J. H. 773, 962
Oliver, R. P. 3–4, 1196, 1242
Olson, D. C. 782, 1135, 1178
Olsson, B. 687, 1196
Olyan, S. M. xl, 297, B:xl, 534, C:xl
O'Neill, J. C. 367
Oppenheim, A. L. 61, 71, 481, 525, 763, 1196, 1209
Orentzel, A. lvii
O'Rourke, J. J. clxxxv, 315, 632, 639
Osborne, E. F. xlvii, lii
Osiek, C. lxxi
Ostella, R. A. 1070
Osten-Sacken, P. von der 23, 649, 691, 751
Oster, R. 133, 267, 281
Oswalt, N. 277
Otto, E. 763, C:xl, 906, 958
Overbeck, J. 556
Oxtoby, W. G. 48
Ozanne, C. G. clxi, 195, 198

Paap, A. H. R. E. 782, 805–6
Page, D. L. xxxiv, 141, B:xxxv, 425, 451, 825, C:xxxv, 1103
Page, S. H. T. 1070
Paget, J. C. 710
Palm, J. 906
Palmer, L. R. xl, 96, B:xl, C:xl
Pappano, A. E. 738
Pardee, D. lxxi, lxxiv, 125
Parker, R. xl, B:xl, 622, 835, 884, C:xl, 1068
Parrot, D. M. 649
Patai, R. 577, 615
Paul, S. M. 215, 223
Paulien, J. 481
Paulsen, H. xxx, B:xxx, 606, C:xxx
Pax, E. xl, 61, 118, B:xl, C:xl, 1215
Pearcy, L. T. 61, 33
Pedersen, J. 819
Pedersen, S. 1223
Pedley, J. G. 156, 215, 219
Peek, W. 61, 77, 409
Peels, H. G. L. 377, 409–10
Peerbolte, L. J. L. xl, B:xl, 742, 751, 772, C:xl
Perdrizet, P. 453
Peri, I.d 156, 164
Pernot, H. 788
Perrin, M. xl, 50, B:xl, 592, C:xl
Perrin, N. xl, 50, 55, B:xl, 528, C:xl
Perrot, A. 133
Perry, B. E. 241
Pervo, R. I. 819, 822
Pesch, R. xl, 5, 8, B:xl, C:xl, 1182
Petersen, N. 75
Peterson, E. xl, 31, 246, 253–54, 267, 302, 310, 320, 329, 331, 350, 363–64, B:xl, 523, C:xl, 955, 1235–36
Petraglio, R. 288, 1135, 1152
Pétrement, S. xl, B:xl, 649, C:xl
Petuchowski, J. J. 225, 481, 511
Petzl, G. xl, 173, 184, 215, B:xl, 411, C:xl
Pfister, F. 61, 898
Pfitzner, V. C. 173
Pfleiderer, O. 577, 586, 1135, 1149
Pheasant, F. 929
Philipp, H. xl, B:xl, C:xl, 955
Philonenko, M. xl, 263, B:xl, C:xl, 1121
Pick, B. 133, 177, 181, 776
Pickard, M. 508
Picthall, M. M. 708–9
Pietersma, A. xl, 267, 290, 371, B:xl, 531, 588, 767, C:xl

Pietrantonio, R. 425, 463
Pines, S. 425
Piper, O. 320, 345, 751
Places, É. des 30, 1056
Platner, S. B. 906
Pleket, H. lvii, lxviii–lxix, 5, 13, 61, 86, 776, 962, 998, 1002
Plevnik, J. 1105–6
Ploeg, J. P. M. van der B:xli, 534, C:xli
Plumpe, J. 649
Pohlenz, M. xl, B:xli, 542, C:xli
Pollastri, A. 478
Pollitt, J. J. xl, B:xli, C:xli
Porten, B. xl, 98, 306, 342, B:xli, 611, 629, C:xli, 955
Porteous, N. W. 1135
Porter, S. E. xl, clxi, clxxxiv, clxxxvii, 66, 77, 216, 246, 257, B:xli, 430, 438, 629, 642, 785, 852, C:xli
Poucouta, P. 782
Power, E. 782, 810
Poythress, V. S. clxi, 1070
Preisker, H. xlvii, 645, 751
Prete, B. 714, 750
Preuschen, E. 320, 322
Preuss, H. 751
Price, M. J. 268, 281
Price, S. R. F. lxiv, 154, 714, 741, 756, 761, 776–78
Priest, J. B. 414, 1013, 1041, 1050, 1063
Prigent, P. xxviii, lvii, lxii, cx, 109, 133, 242, 304, 342, 345, B:xxxviii, 446–47, 455, 469, 475, 574, 604, 650, 689, 708, 750, 762, 769, 800–801, C:xxxviii, 948, 1013, 1053–54, 1070, 1109, 1117, 1135, 1181, 1182, 1196, 1199, 1201, 1218, 1225
Pritchard, J. B. 336, 356, 685, 1063
Pritchett, W. K. 1098
Propp, V. 650, 675–76
Provan, I. 962, 985, 990, 997
Purintun, A.-E. 513, 606
Purvis, J. D. 649, 678

Qimron, E. xl, B:xli, 819–20, C:xli, 1223
Quasten, J. 320, 325
Quispel, G. 61, 91

Rabe, H. 1193
Race, W. H. 315
Rad, G. von xl, B:xli, 377, 782, 819, 850, 864, 885, C:xli, 958, 1053
Radermacher, L. xl, B:xli, 551, 790, C:xli
Radt, W. 177, 192
Rahlfs, A. xl, 91, B:xli, C:xli
Räisänen, H. 148–50, 208, 377, 412
Rajak, T. 169
Ramirez, J. M. C. 61
Ramlot, L. 61
Ramsay, W. M. xl, lxiii, lxvi, cxxi, 80, 87, 110, 118–19, 125, 131, 161, 168, 183, 197, 220, B:xli, 394, 398, 756, 768, C:xli
Rand, J. A. du 1135
Ratté, C. T. 215, 218
Reader, W. W. xl, cv, B:xli, 577, C:xli, 1109–10, 1135, 1166
Reardon, B. P. 567, C:xli, 927, 1092
Reeves, J. C. 481
Regard, P. F. clxi, clxxix, 102
Rehkopf, F. clxiii–clxiv, clxvii–clxxvi, clxxix–clxxxii, clxxxv, clxxxviii–clxxxix, cxciii–cxciv, cxcvi, cxcviii, cc, ccii, cciv–ccvi, ccvii, 7, 25, 50, 61, 65–67, 96, 157–58, 198, 1224

Rehm, B.   xl, 360, B:xli, C:xli
Reichelt, G.   xl, 12, 14, 16–17, 322, 341, 350, 364, B:xli, C:xli
Reichelt, H.   xl, B:xli, 472, C:xli, 1032
Reichmann, V.   cli
Reicke, B.   xl, 131, 171, B:xli, 467, 710, 714, 744, 889, C:xli, 906, 948
Reif, S. C.   315–16
Reinach, S.   377, 398, 399
Reinhold, M.   906, 962
Reiser, M.   clxi, cxcii, cxcii, cxciv
Renan, E.   751
Rendtorff, R.   xl, 18, 358, B:xli, C:xli
Rengstorf, K. H.   286, 460, 809, 1158
Reymond, P.   577, 615
Reynolds, J.   xl, 18, 184, 202, 362, B:xli, C:xli, 969
Richards, K. H.   cvi
Richardson, L.   577, 620
Rickman, G.   962, 1002–1003
Ricl, M.   886
Riddle, D. W.   lxxi
Riess, E.   416
Rife, J. M.   118
Rigaux, B.   714, 745, 751
Rigsby, R. O.   814–15
Rijksbaron, A.   xli, clxi, clxxxiv, clxxxvii, clxxxix, 67, 187, 326, B:xli, 430, C:xli, 1141
Rinaldi, G.   268, 1071
Ringgren, H.   714, 735, 782, 830, 833
Rissi, M.   xxviii, xli, 37, 255, 343, 349, B:xxviii, B:xli, 377, 394, 402, 439, 442, 446–47, 473, 476, 494, 598, 689, C:xxviii, C:xli, 934, 991, 1013, 1041, 1053, 1095, 1097
Rist   1097
Robb, J. D.   23
Robbins, F. E.   114
Robert, J.   846
Robert, L.   clxxxii, 170, 201, 219, 284–85, 350, B:xli, 472, 714, 761, 846, C:xli
Roberts, C. H.   5, 320, 343, 782, 805–6
Roberts, J. J. M.   524
Roberts, W. R.   331
Robertson, A. T.   clxix–clxx, clxxiv–clxxvi, clxxix–clxxxx, clxxxvii, 63, 75, 102, 199, 217, 229, 231, B:xli, 429, 551, 634, 644, 654–55, 722, 788, 852, 857, C:xli, 910, 947, 967, 981, 1186
Robinson, D. M.   377, 398, 400
Robinson, H. S.   906, 945
Robinson, H. W.   268, 303
Robinson, J. A. T.   lvii, lix–lxi, B:xli, 400, C:xli, 1196, 1206
Robinson, J. M.   114, 153, 222, 281, B:xli, 451, 452, 566, 650, 666, 674, 748, C:xli, 953, 1055, 1134, 1160, 1215
Robinson, W. H.   773, 775
Rochais, G.   clxi, cxcv, 1071, 1073
Roetzel, C. J.   1135, 1172, 1214
Rogers, G. M.   133
Rogers, R.   lvii, lxviii
Rohde, E.   177, 182
Rohland, J. P.   693
Roller, O.   23, 320, 322, 341–42, 345, 1196, 1239
Roloff, J.   xxviii, xli, lviii, lxii, 105, 161, 183, 236, 246, 250–51, 259, 261, 282, 284, 290, 309, 332–34, 342, B:xxviii, B:xli, 384, 394, 400, 410, 447, 455, 595–96, 604, 650, 700, 726, 735, 756, 768, 800–802, 811, C:xxviii, C:xli, 1030, 1036, 1095, 1181, 1201, 1225
Romero-Pose, E.   xxviii, xli, cxlviii, 231,

B:xxviii, B:xli, C:xxviii, C:xli, 1072, 1110–11
Rönsch, H.   cli
Roos, A. G.   1161
Rordorf, W.   xli, lvii, lxvi, 61, 83–84, 239, B:xli, 479, 710, C:xli, 1109, 1131
Roscher, W. H.   xli, 58, 114, B:xli, C:xli, 920–22
Rosenbaum, E.   293, 714, 756–57
Rosenstiehl, J.-M.   B:xli, 588, 619, 751, 831, C:xli
Rosenthal, F.   xli, cxc, B:xli, 551–52, 573, C:xli, 1084
Ross, J. M.   232, 268, 273, 1196, 1239
Ross, M. K.   xxviii, lxii, 242, 251, B:xxviii, 443, 445, 447, 801, 803, 841, C:xxviii, 948, 1036, 1038, 1225
Ross, P.   1005
Rossner, M.   773–74
Rostovtzeff, M.   xli, lxiii, lxviii–lxix, B:xli, 398–99, C:xli
Rotondi, G.   1124
Roueché, C.   xli, 312, B:xli, 472, C:xli, 1025
Rougé, J.   133, 136, 962
Rousseau, F.   cv–cvi, cx–cxii
Rousselle, A.   929
Rowland, C.   xxviii, lviii, 61, 268, 285, 304, B:xxviii, 440, 447, 547, 714, 733, C:xxviii
Rowley, H. H.   377, 421
Royse, J. R.   577, 582
Rubensohn, O.   1001
Rubinkiewicz, R.   506, 1071, 1078
Rückert, K.   782
Ruckstuhl, E.   xli, 67, 147, B:xli, 759, C:xli
Rudberg, G.   118, 126–27, 133, 141, 899
Rudolf, K.   xli, B:xli, 674, C:xli
Rudwick, M. J. S.   246, 257
Ruhbach, G.   xxxvii, 302, B:xxxvii, C:xxxvii
Ruiten, J. van   1109, 1112, 1123, 1125, 1132, 1135
Ruiz, J.-P.   cxi, 963, 994
Rusam, F.   xli, 37, B:xlii, 841, C:xlii
Rush, A. C.   173
Russell, D. A.   61, 86, 315
Russell, D. S.   xli, lxxvii, B:xlii, 460, C:xlii, 1032, 1105
Russell, E.   320
Ruyt, C. du   192
Rydbeck, L.   xli, clxxxix–cxci, B:xlii, 487, 553, C:xlii
Ryle, H. E.   754

Sabatier, A.   cv, 1135, 1150
Sabourin, L.   577, 625
Saffrey, H. D.   61, 77, 650, 671
Safrai, Z.   577, 619
Sahin, S.   412
Ste. Croix, G. E. M.   lvii, lxvii
Saldarini, A. J.   xxxv, 103, B:xxxv, C:xxxv
Salditt-Trappmann, R.   1093
Salter, T. B.   62, 65
Sambursky, S.   771
Sanday, W.   xli, cxlviii–cxlix, 39, 65, 68, 229, B:xlii, 716–17, C:xlii
Sanders, E. P.   xli, lxxi, lxxviii–lxxx, cvii, 285, B:xlii, C:xlii, 981, 1125, 1166, 1172
Sanders, H. A.   714
Sanders, J. N.   xlvii, 62
Sanders, J. T.   xli, 315, 333, B:xlii, C:xlii
Sanderson, G. V.   425
Sanderson, J. E.   xlii, 306, B:xliii, C:xliii
Sandevoir, P.   xxxi, B:xxxii, 543, C:xxxii
Sandnes, K. O.   xli, B:xlii, 573, C:xlii, 1008, 1157–58

Sass, H.   16
Satake, A.   xli, 18, 37, 110–11, B:xlii, 611, 620, 650, C:xlii, 1156, 1225
Sato, M.   1196, 1226
Sattler, W.   xli, 320, B:xlii, 406, 513, C:xlii
Sauter, F.   xli, 235, 268, 311, 315–16, B:xlii, C:xlii
Schaeublin, C.   1196
Schäfer, P.   xli, 268, 278–79, 297, 305, 307, B:xlii, 481, 535, 850, 884–85, C:xlii, 1036, 1155
Schaik, A. P. van   547, 782, 800
Schalit, A.   18
Schaller, B.   455
Schattenmann, J.   315
Scheiber, A. S.   850, 891, 893
Schelkle, K.   41, 49
Scherrer, S. J.   714, 764
Schick, C.   cli
Schiffman, L. H.   xli, 195, 205, B:xlii, 535, C:xlii, 1159
Schille, G.   133, 144, 315, 317, 632, 641, 1135
Schimmel, A.   114
Schlatter, A.   xli, 18, 339, B:xlii, 900, C:xlii, 1154, 1166
Schlier, H.   xli, 28, 182, 208, 237, 255, 367, B:xlii, 398, 400, 715, 752, C:xlii
Schlosser, J.   169
Schlumberger, G.   453
Schlütz, K.   23, 33
Schmid, J.   xli, lxiii, cxxxv–cxxxix, cxlii–cxliv, cxlvii, cl, clvii clvi, clix, clxiii, clxv–clxvi, clxix, clxxiv, clxxxi, clxxxix, cc, ccii, cciv–ccv, 24–25, 34, 42, 50, 63–65, 67, 157–58, 177–78, 183, 216, 219, 229, 237, 247, 270–73, 321, 324–26, B:xlii, 380–81, 393, 427–29, 484–90, 521, 548, 552, 558, 568, 579–82, 597, 633–34, 651–52, 654–55, 716–21, 750, 752, 783–90, 853–54, 856, 859, 899, C:xlii, 908–10, 912, 965–66, 968–71, 1016–17, 1042, 1044, 1072–74, 1110–12, 1137–41, 1177–78, 1198
Schmidellio, J.   cxxxv, 68, 134, 230
Schmidt, C.   xli, 150, 225, B:xlii, 415, 560, 602, 684, 692, 708, 811, C:xlii, 941, 1034, 1056, 1089, 1170, 1179
Schmidt, F.   xli, B:xlii, 626, C:xlii
Schmidt, J. M.   lxxi, lxxvii, 62
Schmidt, K. L.   650, 1189
Schmidt, P.   293
Schmidt, T. E.   963, 990
Schmithals, W.   118
Schmitt, A.   268
Schnackenburg, R.   xli, 100, 133, 140, 145, 209, B:xlii, 469, 696, 813, C:xlii, 1135, 1158
Schneemelcher, W.   lxvii, lxxvi–lxxvii, cxvii, 19, 224, 362, 451, 515, 617, 626, 694, 739, 1034, 1057, 1086, 1185
Schneider, J.   23, 366
Schnelle, U.   xlvii, lv, 95, 393, 843, 937, 959, 992, 1006, 1062, 1103
Schnider, F.   23, 1239
Schoedel, W. R.   xli, 289, B:xlii, 508, 606, 744, C:xlii
Schoen, H.   1135, 1150
Schoeps, H. J.   887, 1105, 1107
Schofield, M.   1192
Scholem, G. G.   268, 278, 303, 377, 699
Scholer, D. M.   156, 163
Scholl, R.   963
Scholz, H.   1196
Schönert-Geiss, E.   xxxviii, B:xxxix, 608, C:xxxix, 1121

Schottroff, W.   1196, 1213
Schowalter, D. N.   xli, 295, B:xlii, 715, 776, C:xlii
Schrage, W.   156, 163, 166
Schreiber, T.   650
Schrenk, G.   xli, xcviii–xcix, 342, 344, B:xlii, 384, 447–48, 571, C:xlii
Schröder, S.   xli, B:xlii, C:xlii, 1000
Schubert, P.   577, 641
Schuller, E. M.   315
Schulz, S.   1196, 1234
Schürer, E.   xlii, 181, 249, 287, 289, 372, B:xlii, 475, 605, 622, C:xlii, 1091, 1227
Schüssler Fiorenza, E.d   xlii, xlvii, liv, lxxi, lxxv, xcviii–xcix, 23, 41, 43, 111, 133, 320, 344, B:xlii, 442, 446, 572, 782, 863, C:xlii, 1059, 1071, 1093, 1095, 1122, 1124, 1189, 1203, 1225
Schütz, J.   75, 232, 872
Schwartz, D. R.   425, 462, 1189, 1191
Schwartz, J.   cxxxv, cxxxvii, 305, 490, 552, 782, 954, 1155
Schweitzer, A.   1071, 1091, 1105–7
Schweizer, E.   24, 151, 268, 581, 620, 937, 1039
Schwemer, A. M.   xlii, B:xlii, 620, 843, 887, 891, C:xlii, 1162
Schwertheim, E.   412
Schwier, H.   577, 609
Scobie, C. H. H.   118
Scoralick, R.   268, 303
Scott, A.   318, 525
Scott, K.   lvii, 715, 739, 776
Scott, R.   clxxx, 56, 96, 178
Scott, R. B. Y.   clxi, cxcix, cci, 41, 50, 320, 322, 349
Scott, W.   xlii, 12, 98, B:xlii, 415, 763, 884, 887, C:xlii
Scullard, H. H.   xlii, B:xlii, 623, 738, C:xlii, 944, 1000
Sebeok, T. A.   667
Seeberg, R.   1196, 1206
Seesemann, L.   148–49
Sefrai, Z.   577
Segal, A. F.   62, 92–93, 268, 577, 1071
Séguineau, R.   xl, 18, B:xl, C:xl
Seibert, I.   367, 369
Seidel, H.   315
Seitz, C. R.   268
Sekki, A. E.   24, 34
Seland, T.   196
Sellheim, R.   642
Sellin, E.   xlii, B:xlii, C:xlii
Seltman, C.   782, 833
Semsdorf, H. K.   672
Sevenster, J. N.   156, 164, 169–70
Shaked, S.   xxxix, B:xl, 421, 453, 513, 544, 559, 629, 735, C:xl, 955, 1083
Sharpe, E. F.   62, 82
Shea, W. H.   118–19, 650, 850
Shear, T. L.   1000
Shelton, J. C.   534
Shepard, N.   1071
Shepherd, M. H.   xlii, 345, B:xlii, C:xlii
Sheppard, A. R.   5, 16, 886, 1013, 1036
Sherk, R. K.   xlii, 118, 127, B:xlii, 775, C:xlii
Sherwin-White, A. N.   xlii, lxviii, 127, 129, 163, 171, 192, 311, 341, B:xlii, 399, 931, C:xlii, 1086
Sichtermann, H.   xxxvii, 340, 371, B:xxxvi, B:xxxvii, C:xxxvii
Sickenberger, J. B.   62, 108, 133, B:xlii, 448, 650, C:xlii, 1166
Sieffert, A. E. F.   148

Sieg, Fr.   clxii
Siegert, F.   li
Silberman, L. H.   246, 256
Silberschlaag, E.   169
Silva, M.   clxii, 952
Simon, M.   xlii, 148, 177, 187, 188, 290, B:xxxiv, xlii, 468, 600, C:xxxiv, xlii, 1013, 1036
Simonetti, M.   141
Simons, J.   1135, 1176–77
Simpson, M.   xlii, B:xliii, C:xliii
Sirard, L.   752
Sissa, G.   782
Skard, E.   cxxxv, cxlviii, cl
Skarsaune, O.   xlii, 90, B:xliii, C:xliii
Skeat, T. C.   lxxiii, 5, 125, 320, 320, 343
Skehan, P. W.   xlii, 306, B:xliii, C:xliii, 906, 1013, 1041, 1063
Skemp, J. B.   477
Skrinjar, A.   62, 268, 288, 782, 1196
Skutsch, O.   xlii, B:xliii, C:xliii, 1152
Slater, T. B.   62, 90, 782, 906, 953, 1013
Slusser, M.   5, 19
Smalley, S. S.   xlii, xlvii, liii–liv, lxv, 33, B:xliii, C:xliii, 947, 950
Smallwood, E. M.   lvii, 129, 169, 171, 931
Smidt, J. C. de   36
Smith, C. R.   425, 462–63, 464
Smith, D.   1013, 1063
Smith, D. C.   1071
Smith, F.   989
Smith, J. Z.   xlii, lxxi, B:xliii, C:xliii, 1135, 1154, 1180
Smith, K. F.   xlii, B:xliii, C:xliii
Smith, M.   xlii, lxxi, lxxvii, 5, 12, B:xliii, 644, C:xliii
Smith, M. S.   378, 401, 684, 1071, 1100
Smith, R. L.   56, 1063
Smith, R. P.   805
Smitmans, A.   215
Smyth, H. W.   xlii, clxiv, clxxii–clxxiii, clxxvi, clxxix–clxxx, cxciv, ccvi, 66, B:xliii, 428, 485, C:xliii, 1015, 1233
Snodgrass, A. M.   98, 182
Snyder, B. W.   1071, 1112
Snyder, J. M.   320, 325, 355
Soden, H. F. von   xlii, cxxxv, cli–clii, 42, 51, 63, 65, 134, 157, 177, 229, 247, 270–71, 322, 324–26, B:xliii, 380, 385, 429, 483, 486–87, 489–90, 548, 552, 579, 582, 633, 651, 654–55, 716–21, 783–84, 790, 856, C:xliii, 936, 965, 968, 970, 1014, 1016–17, 1042–43, 1072–73, 1110–12, 1137–41, 1198, 1200, 1239
Soden, W. von   lxxi, 197, 550
Söder, R.   xlii, B:xliii, C:xliii
Söderblom, N.   108, 111
Soderlund, S.   141
Söding, T.   710–11
Soggin, A.   196, 211
Soisalon-Soininen, I.   xlii, clxii, B:xliii, 750, C:xliii
Sokoloff, M.   104
Sokolowski, F.   xlii, 118, 124, B:xliii, 766, C:xliii, 1013, 1036, 1132
Solin, H.   164
Sollamo, R.   xlii, clxii, clxiv–clxv, clxxix, B:xliii, 384, 386, 508, C:xliii, 1015, 1075
Soury, G.   1091
Souza Nogueira, P. A. de   xlii, B:xliii, 829, C:xliii, 928, 963, 991, 994
Sparks, H. F. D.   72, 530, 1054
Spengel, L.   xlii, B:xliii, C:xliii, 923

Sperber, A.   xlii, 90, B:xliii, C:xliii, 1039
Sperber, D.   62
Speyer, W.   118, 1196
Špicq, C.   xlii, B:xliii, C:xliii
Spiekermann, H.   850
Spinks, B. D.   268, 303–4
Spiro, A.   577
Spitaler, A.   cxxxv, 68, 134, 230
Spitta, F.   xxviii, cv, cx, 8, 111, 339, 350, 354, 358, 367, 370, B:xxix, 702, 783–84, 835, C:xxix, 1183
Spittler, R.   626
Staalduine-Sulman, E. van   650, 707, 849, 850, 873
Staats, R.   213
Stadelmann, H.   1071
Stadelmann, L. I.   320, 348, 366, 547, 782, 828
Stagg, F.   clxii
Stahl, M.   931
Stahl, R.   577, 609
Stahl, W. H.   1091
Stählin, W.   752
Stambaugh, J.   577, 621
Stander, H. F.   1127
Stanford, W. B.   5, 21, 50, 57, 62
Stanley, D. M.   850
Staples, P.   850, 864, 885
Starcky, J.   1160
Staritz, K.   xcviii, 320, 322, 341, 342, 344–45
Staudacher, H.   756
Stauffer, E.   119, 126, 715, 767, 771, 1030, 1165, 1196, 1210
Stearns, J. B.   62, 86, 121
Steck, O. H.   886
Stefanovic, R.   clxxxii, 320, 340, 345–46, 355
Stegemann, H.   lxii, B:xliii
Stegemann, V.   235, 288, 292
Stegemann, W.   xlii, C:xliii
Steigerwald, G.   963, 999
Steinberger, G.   782
Stemberger, G.   1071
Stendahl, K.   50, 52
Stengel, P.   xlii, B:xliii, 817, C:xliii
Stenger, W.   23, 1239
Stevenson, G. M.   173
Stewart, Z.   167, 173, 175
Stierlin, H.   cv–cvi, cx, cxii–cxiv
Stock, St. G.   xxxii, cxxxiii, clxxvi, clxxxvi, clxxxviii, cxcv–cxcvi, B:xxxii, 381, 485, 859, C:xxxii, 910
Stolle, F.   378, 397
Stolt, J.   lvii–lix
Stone, M. E.   xlii, lxxi, lxxv, lxxviii–lxxix, 213, B:xliii, 752, C:xliii, 1118
Stonehouse, N. B.   xlviii, cli, clvi
Stoneman, R.   xlii, B:xliii, C:xliii
Stott, W.   60, 62, 594, 1038
Stouannos, B.   177
Stowers, S.   24
Strand, K. A.   62, 84, 577, 602, 604, 963
Strange, J. F.   300
Strathmann, H.   19, 1171, 1175
Strecker, G.   xlviii, xlix, lv, 5, 19, 95, 315, 393, 752–753, 759, 782, 826, 843, 937, 959, 992, 1006, 1062, 1103
Strobel, A.   xxxvi, xlii, lxii, 62, 84, 333, 344, B:xxxvii, xliii, C:xxxvii, xliii, 906, 948–49
Stroker, W. D.   xlii, 221, 362, B:xliii, 415, 703, 710, C:xliii, 1099
Strugnell, J.   xl, 24, 35, B:xli, 819–20, C:xli, 1223

Stuart, M. 290, B:xxix, C:xxix
Stübe, R. 119, 124
Stuckenbruck, L. T. xlii, 91, 262, B:xliii, C:xliii, 1036
Stuhlmacher, P. 570, 782, 1135
Stuhlmann, R. xliii, B:xliii, 378, 385, 547, 826, C:xliii
Sukenik, E. L. 169
Sukutris, I. 24
Sullivan, R. D. 931, 952
Summers, R. 1071
Süring, M. L. 320
Sutherland, C. H. V. 181
Swanson, D. C. 320, 368, 547, 549, 558
Swartz, M. D. xli, xliii, 205, B:xlii, xliii, 535, C:xlii, xliii
Sweet, J. P. M. xxviii, lxiii, 33, 83, 105, 177, 250, 283–84, 289, 332, 345, B:xxix, 384, 448, 585, 597, 604, 736, 746, 756, 812, C:xxix, 948, 1036, 1225
Swete, H. B. xxviii, xliii, lvii–lviii, lxiv, lxvi, lxxii, 78, xcviii, clxxv, 24, 34, 48, 83, 105–6, 110, 133, 183, 250, 264, 282, 290–291, 326, 341, 344–45, 355, B:xxix, B:xliii, 394, 398, 447, 462, 483, 533, 549, 559, 568, 597, 602, 606, 619, 621, 628, 638, 688–89, 700, 768–69, 806, 876, 889, C:xxix, C:xliii, 908, 947, 954, 994, 1036, 1097, 1101, 1177, 1181, 1198, 1201, 1225, 1229
Sykutris, J. 119, 124
Sylva, D. D. 232
Syme, R. B:xliii, 738, 765, 893, C:xliii
Syrén, R. 1041
Szelest, H. lvii

Tabachovitz, D. clxii, ccvi, 269, 282, 972
Tabor, J. D. 268, 318, 577, 600
Tadmor, H. 384
Taeger, J.-W. xlviii, 425, 440, 442, 446–47, 478, 776, 1109, 1126
Tagawa, K. xliii, B:xliii, C:xliii, 1223
Tajra, H. W. xliii, B:xliii, C:xliii, 1086
Talbert, C. H. xxviii, 33, 111, B:xxix, 602, 756, C:xxix, 948
Talmon, S. 577, 650, 705
Tambyah, T. I. 782
Tannenbaum, R. xl, 184, B:xli, C:xli
Taran, L. 104, 268, 281
Tarn, W. W. 169–70
Tasker, R. V. G. cxxxv, 655
Tatton, C. 196
Taylor, C. 906, 924
Taylor, F. W. 378
Taylor, L. R. xliii, 295, B:xliii, 773, 776, C:xliii
Taylor, N. 481
Taylor, V. cci
Tcherikover, V. xliii, 169–70, B:xliii, C:xliii
Teixidor, J. 1013, 1036
Tengbom, L. C. 119
Terrien, S. 1215
Thackeray, H. St. J. xliii, clxii, clxiii, 141, 198, 229, B:xliii, 856, 872, C:xliii, 1138
Thayer, J. H. xliii, B:xliii, 404, 471, 706, 720, 757, 791, 871, 876, C:xliii
Theisohn, J. xliii, B:xliii, C:xliii, 1219
Theissen, G. xliii, B:xliii, 628, 736, 819, C:xliii
Theodor, J. 291, B:xliii, 462, 471, 509, C:xliii
Thesleff, H. 1192–93
Thiede, C. P. 782
Thiel, W. 196, 211
Thieme, G. 141

Thomas, D. W. 850, 852
Thomas, R. L. 378
Thompson, E. M. cxxv, 3, 1196, 1242
Thompson, J. A. 481, 532
Thompson, L. L. xliii, lvii, lxviii, cvi, cix, 143, 148, 182, 228, 239, 285, 311, 315, 352, B:xliii, 604, C:xliii
Thompson, S. xliii, clix, clxii, clxxxvii, clxxxix, cxcvii, cxcix–ccii, 66, 97, 151, 197, 199, 231, B:xliii, 395, 430, 451, 551, 553, 617, 647, 654, 667, 685, 719, 852–53, C:xliii
Thorley, J. 650
Thraede, K. 315
Thrall, M. E. 199
Thüsing, W. 1135
Till, W. xli, 150, 225, B:xlii, 415, 560, 602, 684, 692, 708, C:xlii, 941, 1034, 1056, 1170, 1179
Tilly, M. 577, 611
Tischendorf, C. xliii, cxxxv, 7, 24, 42, 51, 63, 65, 67, 134, 157–58, 177–78, 196, 216, 247, 270–72, 322, 325–26, 381–82, 385, 429, 483, 486–87, 489–90, 550, 580–82, 633, 652, 654–55, 716, 719–21, 783, 786, 788, 790, 853–54, 856, 859, C:xliii, 965, 969, 972–73, 1014–15, 1042, 1043, 1072–74, 1110, 1112, 1137, 1139–41, 1197, 1239
Tissot, Y. 782, 821
Tödt, H. E. xliii, B:xliii, C:xliv, 1219
Toit, A. du xliii, 185, B:xliv, C:xliv
Tomson P. J. 156, 162, 192
Tondriau, J. 775
Tonneau, R. 133
Toorn, K. van der 1223
Topham, M. 148, 1135, 1161
Torm, F. 656
Torrance, T. F. 850
Torrey, C. C. xliii, clxi, cxcix, 322, 349, B:xliv, 427, 551, 717, 721, 737, 791, 850, 871, C:xliv, 947, 968, 1013–14, 1041, 1044
Touilleux, P. xliii, 315–16, B:xliv, C:xliv
Tov, E. xliii, 141, B:xliv, C:xliv
Towner, W. S. 906, 950
Townsend, J. L. 228, 231, 240
Traube, L. 782, 805
Travis, S. H. 834
Trebilco, P. xliii, 20, 58, 169–71, B:xliv, C:xliv
Trell, B. L. 268, 281, 906, 921
Trenker, S. clxii, cxciv
Treu, K. cxxxv, cxxxviii, cxlii, cxliv–cxlvi
Trevett, C. xlviii
Trevijano Etcheverria, R. 1196
Trites, A. A. 5, 19, 177, 185, B:xliv, 628, C:xliv
Tromp, G. W. 1192
Tromp, J. xliii, B:xliv, 401, 413, 461, 600, C:xliv, 1217
Tromp, N. J. 378
Trudinger, L. P. clxii, 32, 41, 246, 256, 425, 475
Trudinger, P. 738
Tsevat, M. 814
Tucker, G. M. 3
Tuilier, A. xli, 83–84, B:xli, C:xli
Turcotte, L. 849, 901, 1133, 1176–77
Turner, C. H. xli, cxxxv, cxlvi, cxlviii–cxlix, 65, 229, 324, B:xliii, xliv, 716–17, C:xlii
Turner, E. G. lxxiii, cxxxvii, 3, 125, 1196, 1242
Turner, N. xliii, clix, clxiii, clxvii–clxxi,

clxxv, clxxix, clxxxix, cxcix–ccii, ccvi, 25, 42, 143, 198–99, 229, 231, 239, 427, 429–31, 470, 472, 483, 485, 548, 614, 642, 646, 654, 718, 750, 784, 828, 831, 867, 859, 871, C:xliv, 911, 969, 1008, 1072–73, 1139, 1199, 1231, 1233

Uhlig, S. 906
Ulfgard, H. 378, 411, 425, 446–50, 468–69, 473–74, 476–77
Ulrich, E. xlii, 306, B:xliii, C:xliii
Ulrichsen, J. H. xliii, lvii, lxii, 244, 367, B:xliv, 561, 632, 715, C:xliv, 906, 948, 1052, 1065, 1168
Unnik, W. C. van 32, 62, 102, 112–13, 196, 268, 304, 320, 332, 335, 360, 378, 412, 906, 952, 1109, 1126, 1135, 1196, 1210
Urbach, E. E. xliii, 292, B:xliv, 410, 610, 715, 762, C:xliv

Valgiglio, E. cli
Van Beek, G, 1001
VanderKam, J. C. xliii, 10, 268, 294, B:xliv, 820, C:xliv, 1105
Van Dijk, T. A. 666
Vanhoye, A. xliii, cv, 74, 97, B:xliv, 572, C:xliv, 985
Vanni, U. xliii, xlviii, xlix, lxxii, xcv, cxi, 6, 19, 24, 27, 50, 62, B:xliv, 378, 495, 650, 661, 687–88, C:xliv, 1181, 1201, 1205–7, 1225, 1236
Varley, D. 114–15
Vassiliadis, P. 6, 62, 81
Vaux, R. de xxx, xliii, 242, 296, 319, 334, 359, B:xxxi, xliv, 770, C:xxxi, xliv, 1190, 1133
Venetz, H.-J. 715, 743
Verdenius, W. J. xliii, cxcii
Vermaseren, M. J. xliii, 94, 97, 298, B:xliv, 451, 458, C:xliv
Vermes, G. xliii, 92, 177, 187, B:xliv, 569, 625, 682, 692, 735, 811, 819–21, 840, C:xliv, 1061, 1068, 1084, 1116–17, 1125, 1174
Vermeule, C. C. xliii, B:xliv, 402, C:xliv, 906, 920–22, 1154
Vermeule, E. 62, B:xliv, C:xliv
Vermez, P. 1013
Versnel, H. S. xliii, 296, B:xliv, 409, 623, 642, 901, C:xliv, 992, 1215
Vessey, D. lvii
Vielhauer, P. lxxvi, lxxvii, cx, cxvii, 19, B:xliv, C:xliv
Viereck, P. 1161
Villefosse, A. H. de clxxxii
Villiers, P. G. R. de 577
Violet, B. 350
Vischer, E. xliii, cv, cx, B:xliv, 639, 702, 715, C:xliv, 1037–38, 1149
Vitringa, C. 425, 448
Vlastos, G. xliii, B:xliv, C:xliv
Vogels, H. J. xliv, cxlviii, cli, B:xliv, 716–17, C:xliv, 1075, 1110
Vögtle, A. xliv, 133, B:xliv, 650, C:xliv, 1071, 1101, 1109, 1117, 1131
Voicu, S. J. cxxxv
Vokes, F. E. 710–11
Vollenweider, S. 650
Völter, D. xxix, xliv, 8, B:xxix, B:xliv, C:xxix, C:xliv
Volz, P. 189, 239, B:xliv, 460, 803, 828, 870, C:xliv, 1033, 1050, 1169, 1189
Vööbus, A. cli, 782, 819, 821
Vorster, W. S. 1112, 1199

Vos, L. A. xliv, cvi, 20, 52, 264, B:xliv, 393, 608, C:xliv
Voss, J. 62, 89–90
Votaw, C. W. xliv, clxxxix, cxcviii, B:xliv, 644, C:xliv
Vouga, F. lxxi, lxxxix, cvi
Vuyst, J. de xliv, B:xliv, C:xliv

Wacholder, B. Z. 90, 1135, 1189, 1190
Waddell, W. C. 370
Waele, F. J. de 192
Wagner, J. 412
Wahl, O. 1135
Wahlde, U. C. von cvi, cxix, 666
Wakeman, M. K. 650, 707
Walbank, F. W. xliv, B:xliv, 740, 761, C:xliv, 922, 1098
Walker, N. 268
Wallace, H. 650, 715
Wallert, I. 425, 469
Wallis, W. 1105, 1107
Walther, F. E. 1135
Walton, F. R. 108, 111
Wankel, H. 133
Wankel, I. 217
Warden, P. D. 133, 136
Wardman, A. 776
Ward-Perkins, J. B. 850, 891, 963
Warmington, E. H. 963
Waszink, J. H. 191
Waters, K. lvii
Watson, A. xliv, 79–80, 166, B:xliv, 409, C:xliv
Watson, L. 378
Watts, D. W. 899
Webb, R. L. xxxiv, B:xxxiv, C:xxxiv, 1083
Weber, H. E. cvi–cvii
Weber, R. xliv, B:xliv, C:xliv
Wehr, L. xliv, B:xliv, 607, 692, C:xliv, 1112, 1129
Weicht, W. 782, 809, 815
Weinfeld, M. 1129
Weinreich, O. 119, 268, 280, 662, 752, 762, 1216
Weinstock, J. 776
Weiser, A. xliv, 85, B:xliv, 886, C:xliv, 1022, 1028
Weiser, Z. 62
Weiss, B. xliv, cxxxv, clvi, clxxiv, cxcvi, cciv, 24–25, 42, 63, 65, 67–68, 134–35, 157–58, 177–78, 197, 216, 270–71, 324–26, B:xliv, 380, 382, 384–86, 426–29, 483, 486–88, 548, 552, 573, 581–82, 634, 652–55, 700, 716, 718–20, 722, 732, 746, 785–87, 790, 854, 856, 859, 900, C:xliv, 908, 910, 965, 968, 970–72, 1016–17, 1042–45, 1072–74, 1110–11, 1112, 1137–40, 1197, 1199
Weiss, H.-F. xliv, B:xliv, 747, C:xliv
Weiss, J. xxix, xliv, lxii, cvi, cx, 8, 238, 270, 284, 354, B:xxix, xliv, 394, 439–40, 441, 445, 452, 496, 522, 568, 573, 594, 620, 666, 688, 702, 708, 710, 725, 735, 749, 756, 758, 762, 766, 785, 801, 811, 823, C:xxix, xliv, 938, 947, 949, 953, 956, 1006, 1052, 1115, 1150, 1172
Weiss, M. 378, 421, 850, 900
Weizäcker, C. xlviii, xlix, lv
Welles, C. B. 734
Wellhausen, J. xliv, B:xliv, 400, 439, 442, 446, 466, 538, 586, 594–96, 609, 619–20, 663, 666, 710, 798, 863, 869, 871, 873, 883, 892, C:xliv, 947, 950, 1011, 1030, 1044, 1052, 1055, 1058, 1100, 1150

Wellmann, M. xliv, cxc, B:xlv, 468, C:xlv
Wendel, C. 3, 699, 1196, 1242
Wengst, K. xliv, 239, 315, B:xlv, C:xlv
Wenschkewitz, H. 367, 1189
Wentling, J. L. 1189, 1190
Werner, E. xliv, 41, 44, 268, 304, B:xlv, C:xlv
West, M. L. xliv, 86, 113, B:xlv, C:xlv, 1056, 1152
West, S. xxxvi, cxciii, B:xxxvi, C:xxxvi
Westcott, B. F. xliv, xlviii, liii, cxxxv, cxlix, clvi, 42, 51, 63–65, 67–68, 133–35, 157–58, 177, 197, 216, 229, 270–72, 322, 324–26, B:xlv, 380–82, 384–86, 426–29, 483, 485–87, 489–90, 548, 550, 579, 581–82, 633–34, 652, 653–55, 716, 718–19, 721–22, 783–85, 788, 790, 854, 856, 859, C:xlv, 908, 910, 965–73, 1014, 1016, 1017, 1042–44, 1072–74, 1110–11, 1137–40, 1197, 1200, 1239
Westermann, C. xliv, 152, 285, B:xlv, 378, 391, 407, 425, 452, 470, 565, 632, 708, 731, 873, 884, C:xlv
Wettstein, J. J. xliv, lix, B:xlv, 394, C:xlv, 902, 989, 995
Wevers, J. W. 564
Weyland, W. G. J. xliv, B:xlv, 791, C:xlv, 1045, 1150
Whale, P. 367
Whitbread, L. G. 113
White, H. J. cli, cliii
White, J. L. 24, 120
White, L. M. 905, 935
White, R. F. xcii
White, R. J. xliv, B:xlv, 413, 573, 759, C:xlv
Whiting, J. 481, 530
Whittaker, C. R. 962
Whittaker, M. 549
Wiebe, R. A. xxxiv, B:xxxiv, C:xxxiv, 1083
Wieder, N. 44
Wiesenberg, E. J. 853
Wifstrand, A. clxii, 790
Wikenhauser, A. xxix, B:xxix, 601, 650, 715, 801–2, 900, C:xxix, 998, 1071, 1090, 1095, 1166
Wilcke, H.-A. 1105, 1107
Wilckens, U. 241
Wilcox, M. clxii, cxc, 547, 553, 1135, 1151, 1167, 1169
Wilhelmi, G. 196, 199, 211, 650
Wilken, R. L. xliv, 164, 215, B:xlv, 467, C:xlv
Wilkinson, J. 577, 618–19
Wilkinson, L. P. 933
Wilkinson, R. H. 228, 242
Will, E. 192, 203, 246, 251
Willett, T. M. xci, xcv
Williams, A. L. 1013, 1036
Williams, F. xliv, 153, B:xlv, 662, C:xlv
Williams, J. cxlviii, cl
Williams, J. G. 257
Willis, G. C. 257
Willis, W. L. 192
Wilson, J. C. lvii–lviii, lx–lxii, 946–47
Wilson, N. G. 61, 86, 315
Wilson, R. D. 1084
Wilson, R. R. 62, 82
Wilson, W. T. xliv, 187, B:xlv, C:xlv
Windisch, H. 112–13, 1135, 1174, 1196, 1213, 1222, 1231
Winer, G. B. xliv, clxx, clxxiv–clxxv, clxxxi, 230–31, 272, 326, B:xlv, 431, 581, 852, 857, C:xlv, 910
Winfrey, D. G. 228, 240

Wink, W. 108, 110
Winkle, R. E. 425, 464
Winkler, J. J. 1092
Winston, D. xliv, B:xlv, 504, 677, C:xlv, 1085
Winter, P. 288–89
Winterbottom, M. 127
Wintermute, O. S. 290, 496, 588, 1035, 1129, 1185
Wise, M. O. xxxiii, B:xxxiv, 478, 560, 561, C:xxxiv, 1052, 1152, 1181, 1190
Wisse, F. cxxxv, cxxxix xxxi, B:xxxi, 560, C:xxxi
Wissowa, G. xliv, B:xlv, C:xlv
Witt, R. E. xliv, B:xlv, 469, C:xlv
Wlosok, A. 776
Wojciechowski, M. 108, 112
Wolf, G. 1212
Wolff, C. xliv, 62, 93, 207, B:xlv, 678, 782, 829, C:xlv, 930, 983
Wolff, H. W. B:xlv, 481, 502, 642, C:xlv, 987
Wolfson, H. A. 1172
Wood, P. 177, 183, 246
Wordsworth, J. cli, cliii
Wortmann, D. 62
Woude, A. S. van der lxxi, lxxiv, 119, 125, B:xli, 534, 649, C:xli
Wrede, H. 776, 779
Wright, G. E. 502
Wright, M. R. 318
Wright, W. 78, 529
Wülker, L. xliv, B:xlv, 400, 413, 415–16, C:xlv
Wünsch, R. 315

Ximénes de Cisneros, F. clviii

Yadin, Y. 292, 1135, 1160, 1189, 1190
Yamauchi, E. 119
Yarbro Collins, A. xliv, lvii, lx–lxii, lxxi, lxxii, lxxxii–lxxxiii, xci–xcii, xciv, xcix, 24, 29, 50, 52, 62, 74, 91, 114, 156, 164–65, 186, 215, 226, 268, 318, 336, B:xlv, 378, 404, 572, 585–86, 650, 666, 670–71, 673–74, 680, 688–89, 691, 704, 715, 767–68, 782, 811–12, 829–30, 841, 838, 848, 850, 864, 885, C:xlv, 940, 946, 963, 976, 985
Yarden, L. 62, 89, 577, 612
Yardeni, A. xl, 98, 306, B:xli, 611, C:xli, 955, 1181
Yate, R. 752
Yerkes, R. K. 192
York, A. D. 32
Young, D. 193
Young, J. C. de 1189
Ysebaert, J. xliv, 112, 144–45, B:xlv, 425, 453, 456–59, 715, 721, 767, C:xlv, 1158

Zahn, T. xxix, xliv, l–li, liii, lxiii, lxv, cli, clxxiv, 67, 111–12, 165, 182–83, 197, 208, 268, 270, 282, 300, 322, 338, 394, 342–43, B:xxix, B:xlv, 411, 440–41, 447, 467, 481, 512, 519, 559, 596, 600–601, 603, 801, 873, 900, C:xxix, C:xlv, 936, 994, 1097, 1124, 1163, 1225, 1229
Zalewski, W. 119
Zandee, J. 1041, 1066, 1071, 1092
Zanker, P. 577, 620
Zazoff, P. xliv, B:xlv, 468, C:xlv
Zeilinger, F. 1189
Zeitlin, S. xxxiv, 156, B:xxxiv, 896, C:xxxiv
Zellweger, E. cxxxv, 232, 722

Zeron, A.   577, 615
Zerwick, M.   xlv, clxviii, clxxi, clxxiv, cxcii,
   cxciv–cxcvi, cxcviii, 67, 68, 75, 167,
   198, 229, B:xlv, 379, 430, 579, 617,
   750, 784, 786–88, 831, 859–60, C:xlv,
   908, 966, 969, 1074, 1224, 1235
Ziegenaus, O.   177

Ziegler, J.   B:xlv, 559, 899, C:xlv
Ziegler, K.-H.   xlv, 52, 55, 91, 217, 298,
   B:xlv, 533, 850, 891–93, C:xlv
Zielinski, T.   650, 705
Zilliacus, H.   3
Zimmerli, W.   xlv, 69, 71, 297, 298, B:xlv,
   477, 515, C:xlv, 1052, 1094

Zimmermann, H.   119
Zimmern, H.   298
Zondervan, P.   782
Zwickel, W.   358, 481, 511
Zwiep, A. W.   577, 625–26

Index of Principal Topics

Abaddon 533–34, 940
Abercius epitaph 478
Abomination 1175
    of desolation 936
Abraham 186
Abyss 348–49, 525–26, 616, 732, 918, 940,
    1078, 1081, 1104
    ascent from 940
Acclamation 363–64
Accusative clxx
Accusator 163
Accuser 655, 700–701
Adam and Eve 152
Adoption 1123, 1129–30
Adscriptio 26, 29, 87, 119–22, 789
Aeolus 451
Aeschylus 86
Akiba 1085, 1108
Alexander of Abonuteichos 764
Alexander the Great 757
Allegory 89, 106, 786, 917, 927, 966, 1030,
    1165
Alliteration 1003
All the nations 688–89
Alogoi liii
Alpha and Omega (divine title) cxxv, 51,
    57, 59, 101, 1126, 1219
Altar(s) 4–5, 790
    agents of punishment 994
    of burnt offerings 536, 606–7
    constellation 406
    golden altar of incense 512–14, 606–7
    heavenly 403, 515, 536
    of incense 536
    Jerusalem temple 405–6
Amen 49, 56, 59, 255, 316, 839, 1027, 1233
    concluding function 1027
    responsory 59
    titular use 255–57
Amillennialism 1089–90
Amore (see Rome, secret name of)
Amplificatio 331
Amplified oracle 58
Amulets 189–91, 298, 453, 523, 537
Anacolouthon 379
Analeptic expansions cxxx
Analeptic gloss 928
Anaphoric article clxv
Anathema 1207
Anatolia
    inscriptions from 16
Ancient serpent 696–97
Andreas of Caesarea lxiii, clvi
Angelic action 435, 797–99, 977
Angelic epiphany 977
Angelic speech 435, 797–99, 977, 984,
    1113
Angelic speech and action 435
Angel of the sun 1063
Angelophany 434–35, 1035
Angels 34, 290
    army of 693, 1059
    authority over fire 846
    in charge of the four winds 451
    equivalent to gods 107
    flying 824, 977
    hierarchy 392, 455
    innumerable 363–64
    made of fire 295, 451

made of wind 451
messengers of the nations 692
no knees 291
of punishment 537–38
standing before God 471, 508–9
as stars 525–26, 534
Angels of the seven churches 108–12
Angelus interpres, "interpreting angel" lxxvii,
    cxx, cxxiv, cxxix–cxxx, 12, 15–16, 22,
    283, 573, 915, 919, 925, 928, 1019,
    1035, 1146–47, 1151–52, 1158–59,
    1182–83, 1186, 1204
Anger of persecutor 707–8, 732
Animation of images 762–64
Anointed one (see also Messiah) 1090
Anonymity xlviii
"Another angel" 795, 823–25, 829, 832,
    842, 845, 848, 976, 985
Antichrist lix, 213, 394, 462–63, 617, 752–
    55, 950
    Nero as 950
Antiochus Epiphanes 594, 608, 740, 745,
    754, 1094, 1174
Antiochus II 249
Antipas of Pergamon lxv, 163, 178, 184–
    85, 256
Antiphonal hymns 315–17
Anti-temple polemic 1166–68
Antithesis 157, 184, 748, 1032, 1146, 1148
Antithetical parallelism 531
Apocalypses, genre of lxxvii–lxxxii, cvii, 1216
Apocalyptic discourse 729–30
Apocalyptic language 908
Apocalyptic literature lxxvii–lxxxviii, 11
Apollo 113, 562
Apollyon 535
Aporia 329, 331–32, 741, 984
Apostles 144–45, 155, 1007–8, 1157–58
Apostolic Decree 187, 208
Apostrophe 970
Apotheosis 627
    witnesses to 627
Apotropaic amulets 453
Apsinth (see Wormwood)
Aramaism 198, 871
Archangels 109, 694
Arch of Titus 357
Argos 298
Ark of the covenant 512, 677–78, 744–45
    in heaven 517, 677
    as throne of God 677
Armageddon 898–99
Armenian version cliv
Artemis 77
Artemision 138, 281–82
Ascension of Jesus 689, 712
Ascent narratives 317–19, 625, 712
Ascent to Jerusalem 1096–97
Asceticism 810–12
Asia 29
    Jewish population 29
Assault of the heathen 1064–65, 1079–
    80, 1094–95
Assonance 1003
Astral prophecy lxxxix
Astrology 97
Atonement 475
Atticism 786
Auditions lxxxiii, 990

Augustus lxii, 154, 160, 171, 181, 202,
    295, 756, 875, 946–47, 952
    appointed client kings 952
    as first emperor 946
    Prima Porta statue of 95
Author-editor xlviii, cxxii–cxxiii
Authority 212
Authorship xlviii–lvi
Azazel 669

Baal 560, 685, 706–7
Babylon lxi, 829–32, 901, 972
    destruction of 957, 976, 983, 987–88,
        1008, 1026
    the great 831
    historical 929–30, 960
    judgment of 1019
    non-Rome interpretation 918–19, 991
    symbolic name for Rome lxix, 829–30
    wealth of 930, 1004
Babylonian adoption law 1130
Bacchus 141
Balaam 120, 185–88
Balak 178, 186
Balance scales 396
Banishment 78–80
Baptism 455, 458–59, 475
Barbelognostic 1170
Barefoot statues 95
Bar Kosiba lviii, cxxi
Barnabas, Letter of lxxii
Bat qol 85, 561
Beast 587, 589, 616–17
    biography of 941–44
Beast from the land cxvi, 660, 728, 756–
    57, 760
    commissioning of 757, 779
Beast from the sea cxvi, 660, 728, 732,
    746, 757, 758, 765, 779, 866–67, 894
    cult image of 761
    kingdom of 890
    miracles performed 759, 1065
    throne of 889
    worship of 741, 765, 795, 832, 1079
Beatitudes 8, 10–11, 19–20, 22–23, 838,
    1031, 1091, 1185, 1219–20, 1237
Before God 220, 509–10, 512
Before the throne 509–10, 512, 872
Beginning, (Middle), and End (divine
    title) cxxv, 101, 1126–27
Behemoth 728–30, 732, 755, 779, 1033
Belial, Beliar (see also Mastema, Satan)
    535, 696, 701, 707, 1061
Bellerophon 539
Benediction 40
Binding 1082–83
Birkat ha-Minim 163
Birth pangs of the Messiah 688
Bisellium, "double throne" 262, 264, 1177
Black 396
Blameless 822–23
Blasphemous names 733, 925, 934
Blasphemy 162–63, 165–66, 742–44, 889
Blind 259
Blood 383, 887–88
    to drink 887–88
    of the grape 847–48
    of the Lamb 474, 746–47
    of the martyrs lxv

of the prophets 1010, 1026
of the saints 938, 1010
vengeance 384
Boismard, M. É. cx–cxi
Book of life 223–25, 227, 345, 746, 1102–3, 1175
Bousset, W. cxvi–cxvii
Bow 394
Bowl 356–58, 879
Branch of David 350
Branding 456–59, 766–67, 832–33
Brass 96
Breath of life 624
Bride 1228
  Church as 1029–30, 1121
  crown of 1122
  Israel as 1151
  topos of adorned bride 1121, 1164
Bridegroom, Christ as 1029–30
Bronze 96, 1000
Buying and selling 768
Byzantine text clvii

Canaanite mythology 732
Canonization formula 1231
Capital punishment (see also Decapitation) 1086–87
Capite puniri (see Capital punishment)
Capitis amputatio (see Decapitation)
Carnelian 285, 314
Ceaseless praise 302
Celibacy 448, 810–11, 818–22, 848
Censer 515
Census list 434, 436, 443, 462
Ceremonial, Roman imperial court 314, 742
Cerinthus l, liii
Chaos 731–33
Charles, R. H. cxiv–cxv
Cherubim 272, 297–99, 301, 305, 318, 824
  in Ezekiel 301
Chiasm 797, 832, 1113–14, 1169
Chiliarch 386, 419, 1064
Chimaera 539
Choinix 397
Christ, Jesus (see also Messiah) 37–38, 260
  beginning of God's creation 256
  coming of 240–41
  enthronement of (see also session ad detram dei) 261, 262–63
  faithful witness 255–56
  has seven spirits of God 227
  new name of 244
Christianizing additions cxxx–cxxxii
Christian prophets 264, 1007–8
Christology cxxv
Cinnamon 1001
Circumcision 459, 837
Citizenship 170–71, 225, 227, 243
Citron wood 999–1000
Claudius lx–lxi, 95, 143
  edict of 143
Client kingship 951
Clothing 222–23, 292–93
Cloud as heavenly transport 55, 625, 690, 801, 840–41
Codex 322, 343
Cognitio, "judicial inquiry" 163
Cold 257–58
Collegia illicita 170
Colossae 249–50
Colossians 249
Colossos of Rhodes 556–57, 575
Combat myths 667–74, 695, 712, 779
  ancient versions of 667–68

Jewish versions of 668–69
Comets 511, 520
Commandments of God 709–12
Command to write 85–86, 105–6, 120–21, 838
Commentatio mortis, "the practice of dying" 1092
Commission 87, 335–36, 573
Commission visions 70–71, 277
Commune Asiae (see Koinon of Asia)
Compilation theories cx–cxiv, cxviii
Complutensian group clviii
Composition criticism cvi
Concentric circles 286
Concord, topos of 952–53, 958
Confess/deny 184, 225–27, 237
Congregation of Belial (see Synagogue of Satan) 165
Conquering 223, 227
  through death 702, 838–39
Consolation literature 1125
Constellations 665, 679, 686, 691, 869
Constitutio Antoniniana 171
Constructio ad sensum cciv–ccv, 428–29, 489, 908, 991, 994, 1014, 1016
Constructio praegnans 871
Coptic versions cliv–clv
Corona aurea 174
Coronation ritual 242
Corpus Johanneum lv
Cosmic disturbances 391–92, 678, 712
Cosmic tree 152
Cosmological dualism 165
Cosmology lxxxv, 317–19
Cosmos
  destruction of 1116–20
  transformation of 1116–17
Council of Ephesus 140
Courtesan topos (see Prostitute, prostitution)
Court of Gentiles 606
Court of the temple 606–7
Covenant formula 1123
Covenant language 1179
Covenant suzerainty treaty 119
Cowards 1131–32
Creation of the world 746, 827
Croesus tradition 218, 220
Crown imagery 172–75, 241
Crown of life 167
Crucifixion of Jesus 620, 747
Cry of victory (Siegesruf) 470, 1022
Cubit 1162–63
  common cubit 1162–63
  royal (long) cubit 1162–63
Cultic utensils, Israelite 356–58
Cult of angels 1036–37
Cup 833
Curse of war 1178–79
Curses 409–10, 1213–15, 1238
Cyrus 236

Dan, tribe of 462–63, 479, 499
Dative clxxv–clxxvi
David redivivus 351
Day 422
Day and night 836–37
Day of Christ 421
Day of the Lord 414, 421–23
  the great day 421
Day of wrath 391, 414, 421–23, 644
Dea Roma 154, 756, 920, 922–23
  and Augustus 181–82
  and Julius Caesar 154
  seated on seven hills 920–22, 961
  surviving statues of 922

Death 103, 219, 716
  conquest of 1125
  eschatological elimination of 1103
  metaphorical 219
Death and Hades 103, 389, 401–2, 1102–3
  personification of 401
Death = plague 382, 402
Death of Christ 361, 475
Death of Jesus 351
Debir 147, 318, 512
Decalogue (see Ten Commandments)
Decans 291
Decapitation 1084, 1086–87
Deceit 823
Deceiver 1083
Decemviri 951
Deception 760, 1083
Declarative hymn of praise 885–86
Decollatio (see Decapitation)
Decuriones, "provincial councilors" 172
Delator, "accuser" 163, 176
Delegations 309
Delphi 15
Delusion 1010
Demonic cavalry 538–39
Demons 542
Demonstrative explanations 472–73
Demonstrative questions and answers 472–73
Denarius 381
Deportatio 79
Descent to hell 103
Description of the New Jerusalem (Qumran text) 604, 1151, 1159–60, 1165
Desert (see also Wilderness) 933
Deserted city, topos of 986–87
Devil 166, 654, 680, 696–98, 700, 704, 736, 752, 1152
Diabolus interpres 1152, 1216–17
Diadem 158, 685, 733, 842, 1042, 1054
Dialogue lxxxiii
Diaspora Judaism 172, 447
Didyma, temple of Apollo at 562
Dietary laws 837
Dignitas, "status" 78
Digressions 605
Dike 280
Diminutives 549, 552, 558
Dio Cassius lxviii
Dionysius 86
Dionysius of Alexandria l–lii
Diptych, literary 439
Discipleship 222, 811–14
Disciplina Etrusca 417
Discipline 260
Discourse lxxxiii
Disheveled hair 532
Dispositio 122
Divi filius, "son of god" 310
Divination 1126
Divine council 277, 303
Divine passive (see Passive of divine activity)
Divinity of emperor 310–11
Divisio 765
Dogs 957, 1222–24
  male homosexuals 1131, 1223–24
Domitian lvii–lviii, lxii–lxiii, lxvi–lxviii, 154, 293, 756, 1011
  attitude toward provinces lxix
  death of 77
  edict of lxiii, 244, 398–400
  hostility to Judaism lxvii
  persecution under lxiv–lxix, cxvi
  re-evaluation of lxviii–lxix
  titles of 310–12

Door in heaven 279–80, 313, 1052–53
Double document 341–43
  from Egypt 342
  in imperial Aramaic 342
Double standard 116, 988
Doublets, literary xcv–xcii, 13–14, 452, 520, 529, 798, 928, 940, 1020–21, 1026, 1031–32, 1037, 1087–88, 1103, 1144, 1148–49, 1169, 1183–84, 1186, 1202–6
Doxologies 43–46, 49, 307, 364, 366–67, 429, 470–71, 1014
Dragon cxvi, 682–85, 692, 695, 725, 732, 746, 757, 866–67, 894, 1078, 1082
  worship of 740
Dream interpretation 106–7, 759
Dreams 71
Dual penalty system, Roman 1086–87
du-Stil, "thou style" 309, 886
Dwellers on the earth 240

Eagle 300, 523–24, 657, 704–5, 785
Earth 737
  personified 686, 707
Earthquake 294–95, 403, 413, 415–16, 518, 627, 899–900
Easter 84
Eating a book (scroll) 572–73
  in dreams 573
  in Ezekiel 572
  symbolic commission to prophecy 573–75
Ecstatic experiences 279, 284
Edict of Domitian 244, 398–400
Egypt 619–20
Eighth day 84, 950
Ekphrasis, "description" of a work of art cxx, 103, 473, 919–28, 938
  hidden meanings of 924–25, 938
  oracular character 938
  in the OT and early Judaism 924–25
Ekpyrosis (*see* Stoic cosmology)
Elders 287, 1085
Elect 955
Elements of the cosmos (earth, air, fire, water) 865, 899
Elijah 613, 615, 1099
Elijah and Enoch 589, 599–600, 610, 612
Empedocles 1036
Emperor worship lxiii–lxiv
Endless cosmos 748
Endurance 795
  of Jesus 76
Enoch 153
"Entering in" 1174
Enthronement 261–62,
  of the Lamb 332–35
Enthronement formula 643
Enthronement ritual 332–35
  Egyptian 333–35
  Israelite 334–35
Enthronement scenes 277–78
Enthymeme 10–11
Enumeration of the slain 628
Ephesus 77, 136–41, 154–55
  Christianity in 139–41
  history of 137–39
  Judaism in 139
  population of 136–37
  "temple keeper" (*neokoros*) 138–39
Ephraim, tribe of 461, 479, 1156
Epilogue cxii, 1201, 1236
Epiphanic language 94, 117, 661–62
Epiphanies lxxxiii, 71, 75, 99–100, 117
Epistolary aorist 106
Epistolary formulas 29

prescript 43
Epitaphs 940
Erasure 225, 227, 747–48
er-Stil, "he/she style" 360, 470, 642, 886
Eschatological antagonist (*see also* Antichrist) 213, 617, 698, 729–30, 735, 751–55, 761
  claims to be divine 755
  performs signs and wonders 753, 759, 894
Eschatological judgment 383, 801–2, 827–28, 846
Eschatological scenarios xciii, cxxii, 279, 445, 636, 679, 736, 835, 848, 953, 1080, 1094, 1118, 1171
Eschatological temple 1166–68, 1191
Eschatological warrior-king 1048–50
  blood-stained garment of 1057
Essenes (*see also* Qumran Community) 293
Eternal kingdom of God 1104–8
Eternal message 825–26, 849
Eternal torment 795, 835, 1066, 1093, 100
Ethiopic version clv
Eucharistic prayers 640–41
Euphrates 890–91, 929
Execution of Christians 765
Ex eventu prophecy lxxxv
Exile 79–80, 461
Exodus motif 891
Exodus plagues 496, 499–506, 546, 616
Expiatory sacrifice, Israelite-Jewish 353
Exploitation 960
Expulsion from heaven 698–99
Eye medication 259–60
Eyes 95, 301, 353–54

Faded diminutives 552
Faithful witness 37
Falling stars 415, 520–21, 525, 534
Fall of Babylon (= Rome) 829, 901, 915, 976, 983, 987–88, 1008
False apostles 143–46, 753
False Christ 752, 759
False prophet 729, 753, 756, 760, 866–67, 894
Famine 397–400, 402
Fasces, "axes" 292, 1087
Fear God 827
Feast of Booths 439–40, 448–50, 468–70, 477
Feast of Tabernacles (*see* Feast of Booths)
Feet 95
Female figures as personifications 681, 933, 936, 991, 1054, 1122
Fine flour 1002
Fire 516–17, 613–14
  falling from heaven (*see also* Lightning) 759–60, 1099
  as means of punishment 1066
Fire-breathing monsters 540
First and Last 101–2, 160–61
Firstborn from the dead 38
First death 1090, 1092
First Edition lxxxix, cxx, 103, 168, 202
First fruits 441, 448, 802, 814–18
First-person narrative 9, 19
First resurrection 1090
Fiscus Iudaicus 171
Five 530
Flaccus 181
Flaviales 293
Flavius Philostratus lxviii
Flight 419–20
Formalist analysis 674–76

Fornication = apostasy 204
Forty-two months 609–10, 742–43
Forum Romanum 618
Foundation of the world 747–48
Four archangels 537
Four cavaliers 389–90, 393–403
  astrological interpretation 390
Four evangelists, symbols for 299–300
Four quarters of the earth 450
Four winds 450
Four-winged deities 301
Fragmentary theories cxvi–cxviii
Frankincense 1001
Frogs 894
Fruit 1003
Fulfillment of God's word 958–59

Gabriel 557, 884
Gaechter, R. cxv
Gaia 1082
Gaius (Caligula) liii, 736–37, 741–42, 755, 949, 951
  assassination of 949
Galba lxi
Garden of Eden 152, 154
Garden of God 152
Garment (*see also* Clothing, White garments) 222–23, 227, 259–60, 293, 410
  washing of 1220–21
Gematria 770–73
Genitive clxxi–clxxv
Genitive absolute clxxxviii
Genre criticism lxxi–lxxii
Gentiles in the eschaton 1172
Georgian version
Gift exchange 623
Gigantomachy 527
Gladius 98
Glaukon-Asklepios 764
Glorify God = conversion 628–29
Glory 365, 985, 994–95
Glory and honor 308, 365, 1173
Glory of God 304, 881, 1154, 1169
  illuminates New Jerusalem 1168–69
Gnosticism 207–8
God
  circumlocutions for name of (*see also* Passive of divine activity) 244, 420, 467, 476, 510, 808, 1121
  creator of heaven and earth 312–13, 564–66, 827–28
  "the living God" 454, 566
  "the one who comes" 940
  righteous judgment of 876
  sight of 1179–81
  as temple or sanctuary 1168
God fearers 645
God of heaven 629
Gog and Magog 535, 616, 1061, 1093–95, 1099, 1104
Gold 879
Gold crown 293, 801, 842
Gold wreath 801, 842
Good Shepherd 477–78
Gospels, order of 300
Go up to Jerusalem (*see* Ascent to Jerusalem)
Grace and peace wish 26–28
Grace benediction 1239–41
Grain harvest 799–803, 844–46, 849
Grape harvest 799–800, 844–46, 849
Great city 619, 621, 831, 900, 959, 997, 1006
Great tribulation 76, 245, 445, 472–74
Great years 1117

Guardian angels 110
Guilds 768

Hades 401–2, 835, 1066
  personification of 401
  rivers in 1067
Hadrian 154, 922
  and the cult of *dea Roma* 922
Hallelujah 316, 1022, 1024, 1026, 1028
  concluding function 1024, 1027
  introductory function 1024
  spelling of 1014
  summons to praise 1028
Harklean version clvi
Harlot 733, 1122
  Israel as 1122
Harmagedon 1
Harmony, miraculous 918, 952–53, 958
Harvest 844
Heaven 967, 1116
  as abode of the righteous 626
Heavenly ascents cxxiv, 71, 278–79, 281,
    284, 313, 317–19
Heavenly battle 691
Heavenly books 224–25, 1102, 1104
Heavenly court 313, 638, 808, 836
Heavenly Jerusalem 285, 437, 1099, 1153
Heavenly letter 124, 329–30
Heavenly temple 241, 405, 475–76, 545,
    596–97, 661, 712, 789, 842, 879–80,
    1133
Heavenly throne 285, 545, 871
Heavenly throne-room scenes xcvii–
    xcviii, 313, 863, 869
Heavenly voices, unidentified 397, 561–
    62, 571, 624, 638, 798, 838, 857, 882,
    977, 1027
Hebraisms 120, 198, 269, 282, 429, 485,
    687, 750, 859, 972, 1015, 1139–40
Hecataeus of Abdera 111
Hekalot literature 277–79, 305
Hekate 104–5, 117
Hekatonchaires 1081
Helel ben Shachar (*see* Morning Star)
Helios 58, 681, 889
Hendiadys 75, 302, 1199
Herakles cycle 708–9
Hermas, Shepherd of lx, cvii
Hermes 58
Hermetica 763
Hierapolis 263
Hippodamus 1160
Hippolytus of Rome cxlix
Historical Jesus 255–56
Holiness 243
Holy and true 407
Holy angels 836
Holy city 588, 594, 608–9, 743
Holy ones 1098
Holy Spirit (*see also* Spirit of God) 33, 36,
    46, 283
Holy war traditions 808, 956
Homer 160
honestiores 79–80, 1086
Honor 365
Horai 280
Horn of the Messiah 354
Horns 353–54, 757, 779
Hot 257–58
Humiliores 79, 1086
Hybris 220, 685–86, 742–44, 995
Hybris soliloquy 258, 978, 995–96
Hymn of praise 331–32, 355–56, 742, 874,
    1022, 1028
Hymn of thanksgiving 312, 635–37

Hymns xcvii–xcviii, 314–17, 873–74
  chanting of 317
  imperial 317
Hypostatic voice 88
Hypotaxis 483
Hysteron–proteron 258–59, 347, 349, 396,
    562, 572, 1084, 1102

Iamblichus 763
"I am" formula 100–101, 1226
Iao 31, 58, 453
Idolatry = sexual immorality 148, 188,
    907, 929–31, 960, 988
Idol meat 186–87, 191–94, 208, 936
Idols, idolatry 541–44
  denunciations of 542–44
  Hellenistic critique of 543–44
Ignatius of Antioch 160
"I know" clause 121, 142–43, 236
Imminence (of the end) 8–9, 20–21, 53,
    1184, 1218
Imperator = king 875, 946
Imperial cult 235, 242, 756, 775–79
Imperial edict 126–27
Imperial virtues 874–75
Imperium 700
Implied audience xlix
Implied author xlix
Imprecatory prayers 408–10
Imprecatory psalms 407–8
Imprisonment 166
Incense offering 508
  heavenly 508, 511
  in Jerusalem temple 513–14
Incense pan 355
Inclusio 540, 1067
Inhabitants of the earth 932, 940
Innumerable multitude 445–46, 466, 474,
    1080, 1096
Inscriptio 3
Integrity formula 1208–13, 1231–32
Interludes cxxix
Intermediate state 410–11
Intermezzo 1022
Intermissions cxxii
Interpolations in Revelation 106, 593,
    683, 722, 917–18, 953, 984, 1055, 1100
Interpretatio Judaica 679
Intertextuality cvi
Intoxication 931–32, 938, 960, 966, 987
Investiture
  of the beast 726
  of the Lamb 332–38
Invitation 1034
Invocation 1215–16
Ioudaios 164
Iris 557
Irony 220
Isis 468, 680–81, 1180
Isis-Osiris-Horus-Typhon myth 672–74
Israel 460
Israel of God 442
Itinerant missionary 145
Iudaea capta coins 1122
Ius gladii, "right of the sword" 396, 403,
    1086
Ius talionis (see *Lex talionis*)
Ivory 1000–1001

Jasper 285, 314
Jeremiah 1167
  influence of 983
Jeremiah-Baruch tradition 678
Jerusalem lx, cxxii, 232, 588–90
  destruction of lxi, lxix, 619, 740, 995–96

"the holy city" 1121
  as a *polis* 619
  population of 628
  streets of 618–19, 1166
  temple of lx, cxxiii, 876, 1188–91
  water supply of 1176–77
Jesus Christ (*see also* Christ) 37–38
  blood of 47
  as faithful witness 37
  firstborn from the dead 38–39
  ruler of the kings of the earth 40
Jew 164
Jewish eschatology 152, 189, 237–39
Jewish exorcists 191
Jewish magic 1083
Jewish revolt 1011
Jezebel 186, 196–98, 203–6, 213–14, 957,
    1025–26
Johannine circle lv–lvi
John in Ephesus 140–41
John Mark l–li
John of Ephesus l
John of Zebedee l, liii–liv
John the Apostle li, liii–liv
John the author of Revelation xlix–l, lvi,
    18–19
  leader of circle of prophets cxxi, 1224–26
  Palestinian origin xlix–l, cxxi
John the Baptist l
John the Disciple li
John the Elder l, lii–liii
Joseph, tribe of 461, 464, 1156
Josephus 111–12
Judah, tribe of 462, 479, 499
Judaism
  in Anatolia 168–72
  population of 164
Judgment 828
  of the dead 644
  doxology (*Gerichtsdoxologie*) 864–66,
    885–86, 888, 1022, 1026
Julian the Theurgist 763
Julius Caesar lxi, 736, 741–42, 946–47,
    949, 961
  assassination of 949
  as first emperor 946–47, 950, 961
Jupiter 293, 937

kai adversativum cxcii–cxciii, 122, 134,
    230, 716, 720
Kalends 623
Keeping one's garments 896–97
Keeping the commandments cxxv, 11,
    237, 239, 709, 795, 837, 1186
Keret myth (Ugaritic) 335–36
Key of David 103, 235
Keys possessed by God alone 103–4
Keys to Death and Hades 102, 280
King
  of demons 535
  = emperor 875, 946
  of kings 735, 911, 918, 953–55, 1044,
    1054, 1062–63, 1069
Kings 419
  of Rome 946, 948, 962
  of the whole world 895–96, 1064, 1171
Kiss of peace 1207
Kithara 355–67, 807–8, 852, 872, 879, 1008
Kittim 735, 830, 896
Koine Greek 141
Koinon of Asia 729, 773–75, 779
Kraft, H. cxv–cxvi
Kronos-Zeus succession myth 687

Lake of fire 866, 1066, 1103–4, 1132

Lake of Hades 1067
Lamb cxxxi, 323, 352, 367–73, 392
  Christ as 367–73
  conquers enemies 952–53
  Egyptian traditions of 370–71
  as lamp 1169–70, 1173
  sacrificial 371–73
  slaughtered 353
  standing 352–53, 803
Laodicea 249–50
  Christian community at 249–50
  earthquake of A.D. 17 249
  earthquake of A.D. 60 lxiii, 249, 259, 263
  medical school at 260
  Pergamene control of 249
  water at 257, 263
  wealth of 259
Laodiceans, Letter to the 250
Latinisms 872
Lawless one (*see* Eschatological antagonist) 735
League of Asia 180–81
Leontocephaline 299
Lernaean hydra 685
Lesser to greater (*qal wahomer*) 406–7
Letter l, 40, 1239–40
Levi, tribe of 463, 499, 1156
Leviathan 540, 684–85, 698, 728–30, 732, 754–55, 780, 1033
Leviathan-Behemoth myth 728–30, 732
Levitical singers 293
Lex talionis 207, 646, 847, 993, 1008, 1012
Libations 883
Lictors 292, 1087
Lifting up the hand 564
Lightning 294–95, 517, 561, 760–61
Linen 998–99
Linen garments 293, 854, 878
Lion of the tribe of Judah 350, 369
Lists of cosmic catastrophes 506–7
Liturgical sequence 1206–8
Liturgical setting 28–29
Liturgy
  early Christian 11, 265, 304, 317, 345
  heavenly 305, 314, 331–32, 345, 356
  Jewish 304, 359
Living creatures 297–98
Living God 102
Living water 436, 479, 1127–29, 1139, 1176, 1179
Locusts, locust plagues 527, 529–33
Long hair 532
Lord, title for Jesus 620
Lord and God 310
Lord God Almighty 306, 642, 1028, 1168
Lord of lords 734, 918, 953–55, 1054, 1062–63, 1069
Loud voice 559
Love of life 703
Lucifer 691
Lukewarm 257–58
Lupus, lupa, "wolf," "she-wolf" 925, 929
Luther, Martin 49
Luxury products 980–82
Lynching 586
Lyre 355–56

Macarisms (*see* Beatitudes)
Macellum, "meat market" 192
Magical formulas and texts 305, 453, 1063
Magical gems 453–54
Magic spells 1010, 1063
Magic square 299
Main square (*see* Public square)

Manasseh, tribe of 463, 478, 1156
Mani 1152
Manna 189
Many waters 929–30
Maranatha 1234–36
Marble 1001
Marcionite Prologues 130
Mark of the beast 767
Martyr, martyrdom 167, 184–84, 290, 390–91, 406, 443, 938
  resurrection of 410, 1084
Mary 680, 686
  in Ephesus 140
Mastema (*see* Satan) 669, 693
Materia magica 191, 763
Maxim 730
Measuring 585, 593, 603–5
Medusa 685
Megiddo 858–59, 898–99
Melchiresa 701
Melito of Sardis lii
Menorah(s) 65, 88–89, 108, 147, 172, 357, 612
Merchants 998, 1010
Merismos 765
Merkavah mysticism 278–79, 330, 1155
Messalina 969
Messiah 210, 393–94, 398, 420–21, 462, 477–78, 639, 643–44, 660, 663, 688–89, 712, 754, 835, 843, 849, 1057, 1061, 1063, 1065, 1107, 1170
  appearance of 1107
  authority of 700
  death of 1106
  interpretation of Ps 2:7 211–12
  lamp of 1170
  Morning Star of 212–13
  scepter, crook, rod of iron of 210
  as warrior 1107
Messianic banquet 251, 1063–64
  parody of 1063
Messianic interpretation of OT 212
Messianic titles 350
Messianic woes 239–40, 275, 444
Metamorphosis stories 704–6
Metonymy 645
Michael 514, 654, 666, 692–95, 700–701, 712, 741, 1053, 1059
Mighty angel 347
Miletus 77
Military census 443
Millennium 831, 1089, 1093
Millstone 1008
Minuscule manuscripts cxxxix–cxlviii
Miracles 679, 874, 894, 1065
Mithraism 105, 297–99
Mithras Liturgy 73, 282, 300
Monologue 978
Monotheism 543
Montanism liii, 201
Moon 385, 414
  darkening of 413, 523, 890
  turns red 523
Moral purity 810
Morning Star 107–8, 212–13
Moses 85–86, 261–62, 613, 863, 872, 881
Moses and Elijah 600, 610, 612
Mother of whores 916, 936
Mountains, settings for revelation 1151–52
Mount Zion (*see also* Jerusalem) 437, 445, 689, 803–4, 1098–99, 1151
  inviolability of 1047
  Zion eschatology 1171–72
Muratorian Canon 250

Myrrh 1001
Mystery 106–7, 569–70, 939, 958–59
Mythological narratives 664–65

Nakedness 897–98
Name of the Lamb and his Father 804–5, 848
Narratio 121, 128
Narrative criticism cvi
Nations of the world 212, 638–39
Nebuchadrezzar 761
Neokorate 155, 778
Neoplatonism 763
Nepos lii
Nero lx–lxi, lxvi, 78, 249, 259, 535, 736–37, 769, 957
  death of lxi, 762
  as eighth king 950
  length of reign 743
  persecution by 466, 1011
Nero *redivivus,* "living again," or *redux,* "returned," legend lxii, lxix, cxvii, 726, 730, 737–40, 780, 918, 934, 957, 961
Nerva 78, 947–50
New cosmology 403–4
New creation 1116–17
New earth 1113–16
New heaven 1113–16
New Jerusalem 915, 919, 1099, 1113, 1122
  descent of 1133, 1151, 1153
  description of 1144, 1146–47, 1153–54, 1160–66
  dimensions of 1161–62
  future conditions 1148
  gates of 1155, 1172–73, 1222
  miraculous fecundity 1178
  as Paradise 1144, 1148, 1154, 1175
New song 359–60, 796, 808–9, 848, 873
Nicolaitans 120, 143, 147–49, 178, 188, 207, 213–14
Nicolaus 149
Noachide laws 187, 543
Nomina sacra 805–6
Nominative absolute clxix
Nominative of apposition clxix
Nudity 293
Number
  of the beast 769–71
  of a person 769
Numenius 30
Numerus iustorum, "number of the just" 391, 412
  number of the elect 412
  number of the saved 412
Numerus martyrum, "number of the martyrs" 391, 411–12
Numerus praedestinatorum, "number of the predestined" 412

Oath 255, 559, 564–67
Obedience 237
Obeying the commandments (*see* Keeping the commandments)
Oil 398
Olympian gods 557
One hour 952, 968, 998, 1004
144 1163
144,000 cxxix, 47, 292, 436, 439–48, 459–60, 466–67, 477, 479, 604, 785, 796, 804–12, 848, 952, 1157, 1181
1,260 days 594, 605, 609–10, 621, 666, 691, 743
Opanim 297, 301
Open door 236, 280–82, 661–62, 1069
Opening of the mouth 763

Open scroll 558, 571
Open the mouth 744
Ophites
    astrology 300
    ritual 153
Opisthograph 339, 341–42
Oracle of assurance 100
Oracle of Hystaspes 592–93, 727–28, 743, 830, 951, 1099–100
Oracles 58–59, 764
Oratio obliqua 307, 410
Otherworldly journey lxxxiii
Ouranos 1082

Palestine 588
Palm fronds 468–69
    and Feast of Booths 469–70
    symbolic of victory 468–69
Pantheon 1170
Papias li, liii, cxlix
Papyri of Revelation cxxxvi–cxxxviii
Papyrus rolls 3–4
Paradise 152–54, 1191–94
Paradox 122
Paranomasia 143, 238–39, 786, 1230–31
Parasang 1162
Parataxis cxxxiii, 120, 483, 854
Paredros daimon 252–53
Parenesis lxxxvii–lxxxviii, cxxv, cxxvii, 147, 1217
Parenetic salvation-judgment oracle 126
Parenthetical nominative clxix
Parmenides 280–81
Paroket 147, 612
Parousia 188, 221–22, 254, 275, 1053, 1069, 1108, 1177
Parthians 533, 866, 891–94, 918, 957, 1080, 1095
Partitive genitive clxxi–clxxiii, 158
Passive of divine activity cii–ciii, 361, 394–95, 410–11, 527–28, 603, 607, 743, 760, 847, 870
Patmos lx, 76–82
Paul in Ephesus 139–40
Pauline eschatology 1107
Pauline influence cxxvii, 30, 37
Pax Romana, "Roman peace" 395
Pectoral of Israelite high priest 1165
Peregrinus 155
Perfection 220
Pergamon 136, 143, 180–81, 192, 194, 201, 736
    great altar of Zeus 182
    history of 180
    imperial cult in 183
    Jews in 181
    library at 180
    population 181
    temple of Asklepios 183
Periphrastic constructions 216
Periphrastic participles clxxxviii–clxxxix
Peroration 1201
Persecution of Christians lxiv–lxvii, lxxxv, 166, 474, 838
Persephone 104
Perseverance 837
Philadelphia 234–35
    Christian community at 234–35
    earthquake of A.D. 17 234, 244
    guild organization 234
    weakness of 229, 236
Philoxenian version clvi
Phylactery 767
Pilgrimage of the nations 876
Pillar 241–42, 245
Pillars of fire 557–58

Plagues 418–19, 495
    eschatological 499–500
    seven 502–6
Pleiades 98
Pliny lxviii
Pluto 687
Poet's dream (literary convention) 1152
Poll tax 171
Pollution 810
Polycarp li, 167
Polysyndeton 145–46, 364, 981, 1064
Population, Christian 467
Porphyry 763
Port 1005
Poseidon 687
Possession trance 82, 933, 960
Post-tribulation rapture 240
Poverty 161
Praescriptio 26, 43, 128
Praise 366
Prayer 359, 512–14, 545–46, 1234
    and incense 513–14
Prayer of Joseph 224
Prelude (Vorspiel) 494
Premillennialism 1089
Pretribulation rapture 240
Priest, priesthood 47–49
Priestly blessing 1181
Priestly garments 93–94
Prigent, P. cxvi
Primasius clii
Primeval waters 296–97
Prince of Darkness 701
Prince of fire 884
Prince of Gehinnom 535
Prince of the world 884
Proclamation formula 123–24, 150, 213
Proclamations to the churches 119–24
Proclus liii
Proconsul of Asia 733
Procurator 180
Prodigy, prodigies 397, 403, 413, 415, 416–19, 518–20, 522–23, 679, 876, 884
    in early Christianity 418
    in early Judaism 418
    expiation of 416–17
    lists of 417–18, 507
    sighting of 416–18
Progymnasmata 923
Prohibition to write 562–63
Prometheus myth 669
Promise to Abraham 1096
Promise-to-the-victor formula 124, 261, 1129
Pronomen abundans clxvi–clxvii, ccii, 229, 427–28
Prooimion 1201
Prophecy and apocalyptic lxxv, cxxv
Prophetic action 565, 603
Prophetic book xcviii, cxxiv–cxxv
Prophetic call narrative 70–73
Prophetic circle 206
Prophetic commission 573, 594
Prophetic curse 1068
Prophetic guilds liv
Prophetic letters lxxiv, 124–25
Prophetic narrative 586
Prophetic necessity 573–74
Prophetic oracle 51–53, 126, 150
Prophetic signature 123, 150
Prophetic speech forms 119
Prophetic spirit 34, 1182–83
Prophetic taunt song 976–78, 1024
Prophetic trance (see Trance, prophetic)
Prophets
    Christian liv, 111, 1008, 1226

OT liv, 1007, 1226
    persecution of 163
Prostitute, prostitution
    female 909
    in the Greco-Roman world 929
    literary topos 925, 934, 937
    male 909
    symbol for Babylon-Rome (see also Whore, great) 1146
    symbol for godless cities 929, 988
Prostration 355, 430, 471, 640, 741–42, 1022, 1040
Protection 604
Protevangelium 697
Protology lxxxiv, 728, 748
Proverb 260
Pseudonymity lxxxiv, lxxxviii
Public reading 12
Public square 580, 617–18, 1166
Punishment and revenge 993–94
Purple 934–35, 999
"Put into their hearts" 958
Puzzled narrator 927
Pythagoreanism 115
    number symbolism 115
Python-Leto-Apollo myth 670–72, 713

Quaestiones, "sitting juries" 163
Queen of the cosmos 680
Qumran community 287, 691, 706, 1164

Rahab 753, 780
Rainbow 285–86, 557
Raining blood 519
Raising the hand (see Lifting up the hand)
Ram 368–70, 719, 757
Rapture story 625–26
Rational sacrifice 359, 511
Rearrangements of text 1204–5
Recapitulation theory xci–xciii
Red 683
Redactional features 666, 725, 732, 749, 766
Redemptive death 337, 361
Regathering of twelve tribes 442, 460, 1034
Reign of God 638–40, 642–43, 699, 870, 1028
Relegatio 80
Relegatio ab 79
Relegatio ad insulam 79
Relegatio in insulam 79
Religious fraud 764
Remembering 147, 221
Repentance 122, 195, 197, 204–5, 495–96, 499, 586, 611–12, 827, 889
Resumptive pronoun (see also Pronomen abundans) 428
Resurrection lxxxvi, 39, 102–3, 1081, 1089, 1102, 1107
    general resurrection 1090
    of the just 1091, 1107
    of martyrs 410
    of the wicked 1090
Revelation of John
    as an apocalypse lxxvii–xc
    date of lvi–lxx
    First Edition of cxx, cxxiii–cxxxii
    genre of lxx–xc
    as a letter lxxii–lxxv
    literary structure xc–cv
    outline of c–cv
    Pauline influence on cxxvi–cxxvii
    as prophecy lxxv–lxxvi
    Second Edition of cxx, cxxxii–cxxxiv, 103, 837, 928

source criticism of cv–cxxxiv, 74–5, 438–39, 588–93, 664–66, 917–19, 983–84, 1052, 1115, 1149–50
stages of composition cxxii–cxxxiv
unity of cvii–cx
Revelatory dialogue 349
Revelatory letter 119
Revision, literary 917
Revision theories cx, cxiv–cxvi, cxviii
Reward 644–45
Rhea 687
Rhetoric 923
Riddle 941
Righteous as agents of divine retribution 956, 993–94
Right hand 338–40, 354, 558–59
Ritual impatience of magicians 1184–85
Ritual lament (*Leichenlied*) 976, 978
for cities 979
Ritual purity 810
Roll (papyrus) 322
Roma (goddess; see *Dea Roma*)
Roman citizenship 171
Roman emperors 734, 947–48
ways of counting 947–48
Roman fear of the sea 988–89
Roman imperial power 735
Roman roads 131
Roman triumphs 296, 468, 1050–52
Rome 734, 829–30
contacts with Judaism 931
secret name of 926–27
wealth of 990
Romulus and Remus 920, 925
Root of Jesse 350
Royal investiture 365
Ruler cults 734
Rumplestilskin 1056

Sackcloth 413, 611
Sacred fire 295
Sacred meals 186, 192–93, 251–53
Sacred mountain 1096–97
Sacrifice 814–15
Sacrificial meat 186–87, 191–94, 208
Sacrificial victims 823
Saeculum 961
Saints 359, 1007
angels 359
Israelites 359
Salutation, epistolary 26–27
Salvation 259
Sanctus 288, 302–7, 316, 1024
Sanhedrin 293
Sarapis 192, 251, 681
Sardis 169, 218–22, 1220
earthquake of A.D. 17 218
history of 218
synagogue at 170, 218–19
Satan (*see also* Belial, Devil, Mastema, Synagogue of Satan) 185, 534–35, 616–17, 664, 668, 680, 686, 693, 695, 700–702, 704, 735–36, 780, 1059, 1078, 1094, 1104
deep things of 207–8, 214
eschatological expulsion from heaven 735
member of the heavenly court 701
protological expulsion from heaven 696, 1104
release 1083
temporary imprisonment of cxxiv, 1078–79, 1081
throne of 182–83
Satanail 697
Satanism 207

Saturnalia 623
Sayings of Jesus cxxvi, 221–22, 264–65
Scepter 210
Scorpions 530–31
Scripta exterior xcix, 339, 342–44
Scripta interior xcix, 339, 342, 344
Scroll as symbol of imperial power 341
Scroll of Rev 5 xcviii–xcix, 571–72
Scroll of Rev 10 xcviii–xcix, 571–72
Sea (*see also* Abyss) 732
negative symbol 1119–20
Seal, sealing 441, 448, 452–55, 479–80, 530, 1083, 1216–17
God 453–55
ring 453–54
Second death 159, 168, 645, 1090–93, 1103, 1132
Second Edition lviii, cxx, 182, 444
Second resurrection 1090
Second Sophistic 924
Secret names 190, 1055–57
Secret plan of God 568–69
Seed 708
Seizure motif 689–90
Semitic idioms 717, 766, 910, 1003, 1101
Semitic interference cxcix–cciii
Semitisms 379, 382, 720, 911, 1075, 1139, 1224
Senatorial aristocracy lxvii–lxviii
Senatus consultum 951
Sepphoris 172
Septimus Severus 922
Septuagintism 859, 907, 912, 967, 972, 1139
Seraphim 297–98, 305, 809, 824
Serpent 706, 1083
"Servant" = "lamb" 371
Servant of God 1, 17–18
Servants the prophets 13, 106, 569–70
Sessio ad dextram dei, "session at the right hand of God" 262–63, 332–33, 689
Seth (= Typhon) 683, 686, 704–5
Seven xciii–xcv, 29, 114–15, 365, 392
Seven angels 852
Seven archangels 109, 509
Seven churches 24, 130–32, 219
situation of lxx
Seven heads 683–84, 733, 736, 779, 917
symbol for hills 926
symbol for kings 945
symbol for rulers 733, 736
Seven heavens 318–19, 511, 560
Seven Hills (of Rome) 921, 944–45, 961
Seven kings of Rome 948, 961
Seven mountains (*see* Seven Hills)
Seven planets 97, 112, 406, 560
Seven seals 322, 336, 344, 346–47
Seven spirits 33–35, 219, 296, 354
Seven stars 97–98, 112, 141, 219
Seven thunders 559–60, 562
Seventy 362
Seven torches 295
Seven vowels 57, 560
Sexual immorality = idolatry 148, 188, 907, 929–31, 960, 988
Shekinah 476
Sheol 401
Shepherd 369, 477–78, 812
Shepherd's crook 210
Shutting heaven 615
Sickle 843–45
Sign 679, 863
Silence in heaven 507–8
Silent reading 20–21
Silk 999
Silk route from China 999

Sinai tradition 85, 294–95, 517–18
Six days of creation 421
666 770–73, 837, 1163
Slave, servant 455, 970, 1002–3, 1027
Small and great 766
Smoke 881–82
Smyrna lviii, 136, 159–61, 175, 922
destruction by Lydians 161
earthquake of A.D. 178 161
legendary visit by John 160
legendary visit by Paul 160
Snake 299
Solecisms 269–70, 428, 484, 841
Solomon 90, 262, 454
Song
of the Lamb 360, 872–73
of Moses and the Lamb 863, 872–83
of thanksgiving 635–37, 646
of victory 635, 638, 646, 663–64
Son of man 54–55, 59, 90–92, 221–22, 299, 338, 421, 800–801, 839–42, 849
Sophia 1122
Sorcery 1010, 1130–32
Soul 404–5, 1091, 1103
Source criticism cv–cxxxiv, 74–75, 917–19, 983–84, 1052, 1149–50
Spirit in Revelation 36, 151
Spirit(s) of God 33, 35, 83, 283
Spirit of prophecy 1039
Spirits of the prophets 1182–83
Stand before the Lord 612–13
Stars 415, 1226–27
as angels 525–26, 534
Statue, Greek words for 761
Stoic cosmology 1118, 1120
Stoicism 76
Stoic paradox 161
Storm phenomena 294
Strength 365
Subscriptio 3
Succession myth 687
Suetonius lxviii
Suffering for the name 146
Suffering servant 373
Summons to flight (*Afforderung zur Fluch*) 990–91
Summons to praise 1027–28
Summum supplicium (*see* Capital punishment)
Sun 99, 413–14
darkening of 413, 523, 890
Sunday 83–84
Superscriptio 26, 29
Swearing by heaven and earth 564–65
Sword cxxvi, 98–99, 181–82, 189, 395, 1058, 1060–61, 1067
Symbolic action 593, 603, 976, 982
Symbolic description 73, 1047
Synagogue of Satan (*see also* Congregation of Belial) 157, 164–65, 230
Synagogue messenger 112
Synagogues 157, 164–65, 168–72
Beth Alpha synagogue at Sardis 218–19
Synoptic tradition 264
Syrian versions clvi

Tabernacle 744–45
in heaven 876–78
Israelite 877–78, 881
Tabitha 589–90
Table fellowship 194
Tablets of heaven 345
Tacitus lxviii
Tamid offering 272, 514
Tanin 668

Tattooing   456–59
Taxo   409
Tefillin   767
Temple   318–19, 877
   cosmic interpretation of   318–19, 597
   court of   lx
   precinct of   lx
   symbolic interpretation of   597–98
Temple in Jerusalem   546, 589, 594, 596,
   604–6
Temple of Janus   395, 878
Temple of Onias in Leotopolis   546
Temple of Solomon   745, 881, 1154
Temple slaves   13
Temporary messianic kingdom   1104–8
Temptation   231
Ten Commandments   85–86, 710–12,
   1131
Ten horns   683–84, 733, 917
   symbol for rulers   684, 733, 950–51, 961
Ten kings = Roman client kings   951
Tepid   258
Testing   231
Thanksgiving   635, 640–41
Theocracy   1105
Theologia crucis   352
Theologia gloriae   352
Theophany   c, 85, 294–95, 314, 518, 557,
   880–81, 1066
Theophany form   (*Theophannie-Gattung*)
   413, 1081, 1101
Theurgy   763
Thief   53, 221–22, 896
Third day   624
Third-person imperatives   151
Three-level cosmos   348–49, 366, 403–4,
   526, 565
Three woes   495, 524, 536, 587–88, 630
Threnody   978–79
Threshing   803, 845
Throne   262–63, 272–72, 284, 292, 309
   of the beast   889
   as circumlocution for God   284
   of the dragon   736
   of God   284–85, 352, 373, 404, 476, 545
   of Satan   182–84, 194
Throne theophany   337–38
Throne vision   70–71, 261–62, 276–78,
   337–38, 389, 436–38, 635
Thunder and lightning   517, 561
Thunderbolt   295
"Thus says" formula   121
Thyatira   148–49, 201, 204, 213
Tiber   920–22, 926, 929
Tiberias   172
Tiberius   160, 175, 249
Time, times, and half a time   587, 609,
   706, 743
Titans   1078, 1081
Title   9–10, 22
Titus   1011
Torah   154, 220, 710–12, 837
Trade guilds   186
Trajan   lviii
Tralles   172
Trance, prophetic   63, 82–83, 933, 960,
   1151
Tree = elect community   153
Tree(s) of life   151–54, 1177–78, 1221–22
Triangular numbers   770–71
Tribulation   166, 239–40, 245, 472–74

Tripartite oath formula   566–67
Tripartite prophecy formula   112–14
Trisagion   288, 302–7, 316, 809, 1024
True Israel   442
Trumpets   510–11
   in eschatological scenarios   510–11
   as prodigy   519
   seven trumpet plagues   496
   as structuring device   497
Tübingen school   144
Twelve apostles   lxiv, 292, 444, 461, 1147,
   1157–58
Twelve stars   681
Twelve Tables   646
12,000   436, 441, 479
Twelve tribes   441–42, 444, 460–61, 1154–
   55
   lists of   443, 464–65
   regathering of   442, 460
Twenty-four elders   287–92, 314
Twenty-four priestly courses   288–89
Twenty-four prophets   292
Two-level cosmos   349, 565
Two-powers heresy   92
Two witnesses   586–87, 598–603, 610, 746
   ascension of   587, 625–26
   identification of   599–603
   lynching of   586
   origin of   611
   prophetic ministry of   613
   punitive miracles of   615
   resurrection of   587
Tyconius   clii
Type scene   436–38, 1079
Typhoeus   707
Typhon (= Seth)   683, 686, 704–5

Unburied   622, 1068
Uncial manuscripts   cxxxviii–cxxxix
Unclean (ritually)   1174–75, 1221
Unclean spirits   894
Underworld (*see also* Abyss, Hades, Sheol)
   526
Underworld journeys   281
Unidentified speaker(s)   585, 857, 882,
   991, 1027
Universality   361–62, 809–10, 954
Untimely death   1124–25
Utopias (ancient)   1191–94

Varro (*see also* Seven Hills)   944–45
Vengeance   390–91, 408–9
   divine   992–93
   prayer for   408–10
Venue of visions   275, 439, 585–86, 1116
Venus   212
Vespasian   lxi–lxii, 920–22, 1122
   Iudaea capta coins   1122
   sesterius of   920–22, 925–27, 929
Vesuvius, eruption of   519–20, 527
Vice lists   204, 1130–32
   penalty clauses   1132
Victorinus of Petau   78
Victory   699–700, 872, 1025, 1170
Vigilence   216, 219
Vilification   185
Vindication   407
Vineyards   398–99
Violent death of the prophets   163, 610,
   620, 886–87
Virginity   810–12, 848

Virtue   242
Vision narratives   c
   episodic character of   c
Vision report   82, 329, 919
   static character   919
Visions   lxxxii, 70–73
Vision trance   82, 283
Voice(s)   85, 88
Volcanic activity   519
Vulgate   cliii

Walk = conduct   222–23
War, eschatological   443, 463, 691, 847
Watchers   302, 668–69
Water of life   431, 479, 1127–29, 1139,
   1176, 1179
Wealth   161
Wedding feast of the Lamb   1031–32
Wedding of the Lamb   1029
White   293
White garments   223, 227, 259–60, 292–
   93, 424, 429, 468, 474–75
   symbolizing purification   474
   symbolizing salvation and immortal-
   ity   424
Whore, great   lxv, 915, 929, 1025
   judgment of   916, 925, 956–57, 960,
   1019
   representive of Babylon   959
   representive of Jerusalem   934, 959
   representive of Rome   929, 934
   seated   934
Widowhood   996
Wife of the Lamb   1029
Wilderness   598, 690–91, 705–6
   place of refuge   933
Wine   398, 832, 1002
   unmixed   833
Winepress of God's wrath   799, 846–47
Wings   301
Winnowing   803
Wisdom   365, 471, 941
Witness formula   1230
Woe   524, 536, 704
Woes of the Messiah (*see* Messianic woes)
Women leaders   203, 214
Wood   1000
Word of God   81, 239, 1058–59
Works   207, 209, 645, 839, 1102
Works of the law   711
World   638
World market, *topos* of   979–80
Wormwood (*see* Apsinth)   484, 495, 520
Worship   230, 273, 308
   of angels   1035–38
   heavenly   356
Worthiness   222, 347, 360, 364
Wreath imagery   172–75, 241
Wreath of immortality   167

Zealot oracle   593–95
Zealots   767
Zephyrinus   liii
Zeugma   605
Zeus   99, 295, 527, 557, 561, 690, 707,
   1078, 1126
Zeus-Ammon   141
Zion (*see* Mount Zion)
Zodiac   291, 681, 713, 1156
   Hebrew names   681

Index of Biblical and Other Ancient Sources

The Old Testament

(* = Septuagint)

Genesis

1:1	256–57, 565, 828
*1:2	348, 526
1:3–25	748
1:5	379
1:7	296
1:8	379
*1:9	cxciii
*1:11	1139
1:13	379
1:14–19	523
*1:14	679
1:19	379
*1:20	855
1:21	728, 733
1:23	379
1:26–27	349
*1:26	748
1:26	277
*1:30	400, 855
1:30	623
1:31	379
2–3	154
*2:1	656
2:2	379, 1105
*2:5	400
2:7	623, 894
2:8	154, 978
2:9	152, 154
2:10–14	871
2:10	154
2:11–14	379
2:15	154
*2:16	clxxii
2:16	154
*2:17	clxxii, 198
*2:19	969
*2:23	969
2:25	897
3	697
*3:2	clxxii
3:3–6	187
*3:3	clxxii
*3:4	198
*3:5	clxxii
3:7	897
3:9–10	897
3:10–11	897
*3:12	clxxii
3:15	696, 708
3:18	153
*3:20	1043
3:21	897
3:22–24	152
3:23–24	152
3:24	152, 1154
4:3	224
*4:4	clxxii
*4:8	cxcv
4:10	408
4:15	452
4:18	379

*5:13	88
5:22	222, 626
5:24	277, 599, 626
6:1–4	668
*6:1	cxcv
6:9	222
*6:12	cxcv
6:17	623
*7:6	cxciv
*7:11	348, 526
7:11	296
7:15	623
*7:20	cxciii
7:22	623
8:1	992
*8:2	348
8:2	296
8:5	379
8:13	379
*8:18	cxciv, 655
*8:20	405
8:22	302, 1181
9:5–6	407
9:6	887
9:11	1179
*9:12	679
9:13–16	286
9:13	285
*9:17	679
9:20–24	897
*9:21	987
10	362
10:2	137, 1094
10:4	137
10:5	361
*10:13–14	clxvii
*10:14	229
10:20	361
*10:32	460
*11:2	427
11:3–4	737
11:4	992
11:7	277
*11:19	1043
11:30	153
12:5	1002
12:7	679
*12:17	910
*13:4	ccii, 653
*13:10	154
*13:11	427
13:12	153
13:16	466
14:14	772
14:18	828
14:19	565, 566
14:22	564–66, 828
*15:1	ccvi, 269, 282
*15:2	407
15:3	1129
*15:4	ccvi, 153, 269, 282
15:5	466
*15:8	407
15:18	890
*16:1	382

*16:2	clxxxvi, cxcvii, 381
16:6–14	705
*16:7	431
16:10	466
*16:11	1043
*16:13	1043
*16:15	1043
17:1	222
17:3	772
17:4–6	466, 467
*17:5	1043
17:5	244
*17:11	679
*17:15	1043
17:16	466
17:17	244
*17:19	1043
*17:20	230
18:16–19:29	620
19:11	766
*19:12–17	679
19:17	420
*19:22	1043
*19:23	cxciv
19:24	516, 541, 760, 835
*19:36	clxxx
*19:37	1043
*19:39	1043
*20:12	859
*20:13	ccii, 229, 653
*20:21	ccii, 653
*21:10	217
21:20	1123
*21:23	1043
22:1	255
22:12	827
22:17–18	466
22:17	364
*22:20	ccvi, 269, 282
*22:24	382
*22:30	ccvi
23:6	852
24:3	828
24:7	629
24:9	564
*24:13	431, 855
*24:29	clxxxvi, 382
*24:30	cxciv, 550
*24:49	cxcvii
24:55	166
*24:56	cxciv
*25:1	382
*25:26	1043
*25:30	1043
26:2	679
26:4	466
*26:19	479
*26:27	cxciv, 655
*27:5	379
*27:6	379
*27:19	clxxii
*27:21	cxciii
*27:28	clxxii
*27:31	clxxii
*27:34	85, 347, 882

27:34	347	49:10	350	9:8–12	501, 505, 883
*28:13	229	49:11	475, 847, 938, 1049	9:9	903
28:13	clxvi	49:17	462	9:12	496, 541, 889
28:14	466	49:24	478	9:13–35	505, 901
28:17	280, 313	*49:31	1084	*9:15	382
*28:22	clxxii	50:19	1038	9:18	900
29–30	465			9:22–26	495, 501, 546
*29:2	1084	*Exodus*		9:22–24	903
*29:8	cxciii			9:23	294
*29:32	1043	1:2–4	464	9:24	900–901
*29:33	1043	1:7	908	9:26	480
*29:34	1043	1:15	379	9:27	886
*29:35	1043	1:21	cciv, 489	9:28	294, 852
30:8	852	*2:1	clxxii	9:29	294
*30:14	clxxii	*2:2	652	9:33	294
*30:22	992	2:10	1129	9:34–35	496, 541, 889
*31:13	ccii, 653	2:15	706	9:34	294
*31:30	198	2:17	cciv, 489	10:1	496, 541, 889
*31:53	550	2:23	620	10:3–20	505
32:12	364, 466	2:24	677	10:4–20	495, 546
32:23–33	675	3:1–22	70	10:12–20	501, 527, 533
32:27–28	244	3:1–12	115	10:20	406, 541, 889
32:29	1055	3:2–4:23	88	10:21–29	501, 505, 890
32:31	1180	3:2	679	10:21	495, 546, 866, 903
*33:1	393	3:6	1180	10:23	480
*33:15	clxxii	30–32, 40		10:27	496
*34:29	1002	3:14	302	11:6	cciv, 489
*35:11	1084	3:16	287	11:9–10	541, 889
35:11	466, 467	3:18	287	11:15	1009
*35:13–15	clxxiv	4:1–17	70	12:1–28	499
*35:13	64	*4:12	744	12:1–20	372
*35:14	64	*4:15	744	12:5	372
35:14	879	*4:17	229	12:7	456
*35:15	64	*4:21	cxciii	*12:13	679
35:17	189	*4:22	38	12:21	287
35:22–26	464	4:29	287	12:29–36	815
*36:6	1002	*5:3	382	12:29–32	501
37:9–11	680	6:2–12	70	12:43–49	372
*37:17	379	*6:3	cxcii	12:47	372
37:34	611	6:3	679	13:2–16	815
*38:1	382	6:6	620	*13:9	679
*38:4	ccvi	*6:25	clxxii	*13:19	cxciv
*38:13	ccvi, 269, 282	7–14	496, 545	13:21	558
*38:24	269, 282	7–13	500, 502, 503, 504	14:4	541, 889
*39:13	cxcv	7–12	480, 495, 499, 502, 505, 546	14:6	496
*40:2	clxxxii, 657	7–10	631	*14:10	cxcv
40:8	769	7:1–7	70	14:13	470, 700
*40:17	clxxii	7:3–4	495	14:21	891
40:19	1068	*7:3	679	14:24	625, 841
*40:30	ccii, 653	7:8–13:16	500, 546	*14:25	1075
*41:14	1084	7:8–12:36	499	14:30	470, 700
41:15–16	769	*7:9–12	683	14:31	872
*41:19	229	7:13	541, 889	15	872, 1057
41:42	854	7:14–11:10	616	15:1–18	863, 872
41:45	244	7:14–24	884	15:1–8	668, 903
41:46	640	7:14–19	615, 884	15:1	863
*42:8	cxciii	7:17–21	500	15:2	365, 470, 700, 863
*42:22	cxcii	7:20–21	495, 546, 903	15:3–4	1048, 1049
42:22	cciii, 528	7:22–23	496	*15:3	382
42:28	cciii, 528	7:22	541, 889	15:6	340
43:14	731	8:1–7	500	15:8	872
*44:3	cxciv	*8:4	cxciii	15:11	277, 332, 741, 875
44:12	1101	8:15	496, 541, 889	15:12	340, 707
*45:16	ccvi	8:16–19	501	15:13	365
*45:18	clxxii	8:17	908	*15:14	643
*45:24	643	8:19	496, 541, 889	15:16	624
46:8–27	464	8:20–32	505	*15:18	639–40
*48:4	230	8:20–24	501	15:18	640, 873
48:5–6	1129	8:22–26	506	*15:23	clxxx
48:15	478	8:22	480	*15:27	431, 855
48:19	466, 467	8:32	496, 541, 889	16:1–36	195
48:21	1123	9:1–7	501, 505, 506	16:7	881
49	465	*9:3	382	16:10	625, 679, 841, 881
49:5–7	465	9:4–7	480	16:15	189
49:9	350, 373	9:7	496, 541, 889	16:19	1175

16:32	706	25:7	93
*17:5	clxxii	25:9	476, 597, 677, 878
*18:6	ccvi, 269, 282	25:12	379
18:12	287	25:22	1027
18:19	613	25:29	357–58
*18:25	230	25:31–40	89, 295
19	1066	25:31	969
19:4	705	25:35	969
19:5	45	25:36	969
*19:6	42, 88	25:37–39	357
19:6	45, 47–48, 337, 362, 1093	25:40	476, 597, 677, 878
*19:9	379	26:30	476, 597, 677, 878
19:9	882	*26:33	877
19:10–15	819, 822	27:2	489
19:10	474, 1220	27:3	357, 879
19:12–13	882	27:8	476, 677, 878
19:13	510	27:20–21	295
19:14	474, 1220	27:20	1167, 1170
19:16–20:1	88	*27:21	745
19:16–19	294	27:21	88, 90
19:16–18	294, 314, 517	*28:4	94
*19:16	483	28:4	93, 223, 293
19:16	85, 294, 510, 880, 882	28:5	854
19:18	517, 880	28:15	93
19:19	510, 560	28:17	1147
20:2–17	711	28:22	93
20:4–6	827	28:31	93
20:4	349	28:36–38	242
20:7	567, 744, 889	28:36–37	174
20:11–16	171	*28:39	94
20:11	349, 565	28:39	93, 854
*20:12	cxcvii	*28:40	94
20:12	158	28:40	93
20:13–15	544	*29:1	823
20:16	823	*29:4	745
20:18–20	314	29:5	93
*20:18	87	29:6	174
20:18	85, 88, 510, 560	29:8	93
20:19	100	*29:9	94
*20:22	87	29:12	clxxii, 475, 489
*21:12	198	29:14	1098
*21:13	ccii, 653	29:16	475, 879
21:18	205	29:20–21	475
21:19	624	*29:20	clxxii
21:23–25	993	29:20	879
21:24–45	834	29:38–46	372
21:24–25	992	29:38–42	514
21:24	646	29:42	372
*22:19	198	30:1–10	357
22:25	cciv, 489	30:1–8	514
*22:27	543	30:7–9	514
*22:28	815	30:8	89, 513
22:28	543	30:11–16	436
*22:29	815	*30:20	cxciii
*23:16	815	30:34–38	513
*23:19	815	31:8	357
23:19	815	*31:15	198
23:21	890	32:1–43	903
*23:27	230	32:1–6	188
23:29	814	*32:13	550
24	261	32:15–16	188
24:6	879	*32:19	cxcv
24:8	879	32:20–28	1180
24:9–11	96, 288, 1180	32:20	762
24:9–10	287	32:28	949, 985
*24:10	ccii, 653	32:32–33	224, 227
24:10	297	32:32	223–24
24:12	1180	*33:11	197, 1180
24:16–17	881	34:5	880
24:16	625, 841, 880	34:6	407
25–27	903	34:13	762
25:1–8	188	34:15	193, 345
25:1–2	188	*34:22	815
25:1	1170	34:22	814
*25:3	815	34:25	372

*34:26	815
34:26	815
34:27–28	85
34:28	711
34:29	99, 711
34:30	557
35:9	93
35:19	93
35:30–35	958
36:2	clxxviii, 912
*36:6	94
37:16	357–58
37:23–24	357
37:25–39	357
38:3	357, 879
38:24	815
*39:1	815
39:27	93
39:30	174
39:36	357
39:37	357
40–48	1167
40:2	877
40:6	877
40:10	357
40:14	93
40:16–38	881
40:29	877
40:34–35	880–82
45:16	269, 282
Leviticus	
*1:1	745
*1:3	823
2:1	513
*2:14	815
2:15	513
4:1–5:13	372
4:2	clxxii
*4:3	823
4:7	489
4:18	406, 489
4:25	489
4:30	489
4:32	373
4:34	489
*5:15	823
6:3	93
6:8	cciv, 489, 513
6:14–15	513
7:6	194
*8:7	94
8:9	174
*8:13	94, 1220
*8:31	269, 282
8:35	302
*9:6	cxciii
9:6	881
*9:9	1043
9:11	1098
9:22	564
9:23	881
9:24	760
10:1–3	513
10:1–2	513
*10:1	517
10:1	513
10:6	532
*11:32	1043
*11:36	431, 855
12–15	372
13:45	532
*14:5	479
*14:9	1220

14:10–14	372
14:19	372
*14:36	cxciii
*14:51	1043
*14:52	475
14:52	475
15:16–18	1175
15:16	812
15:18	810, 812
15:19–24	1175
15:24	810
15:33	1175
16	604
16:1–2	510
16:2	625, 841, 880, 882
*16:4	94
16:4	223, 293, 878
16:10	878
16:11–14	514
16:12–13	880
16:12	513
16:16	1175
16:17	1098
16:23	878
*16:32	229
16:33	604
*17:5	353
17:7	930, 988
17:11	373, 475
*18:21	clxxiii
*18:22	1223
18:25	258
18:26	1175
18:28	258
18:29	1175
19:12	823
*19:13	217
*19:18	cxcii, 711
*19:28	230, 457
19:28	457
*19:33–34	711
*20:2	clxxiii, 198
*20:3	clxxiii
20:5–6	930, 988
20:13	1175, 1223
*20:15	198
21:9	957
21:10	532
*22:21	823
*22:22	clxxiii, 258
23:5	372
23:9–14	802, 814
23:12	372
23:14	815
*23:17	815
*23:20	815
23:40	469
23:42–43	476
23:43	476, 477
24:1–4	89, 295
24:2–4	88, 90
24:5–7	358
24:6	357
24:16	744, 889
24:19–20	992, 834
25:9	510
26	502
26:8	530
26:11–12	1123
26:11	476
26:12	1110
26:14–33	505
26:22	403
*26:25	382
26:26	396

27:9	
27:12	352
27:26–27	815
Numbers	
1	462
*1:1	745
1:2–46	436
1:2	216
1:4–15	464
1:5–15	464, 465
1:18	216
1:20	216
1:49	463
2:1–31	1156
2:3–31	35
2:3	462
2:33	463
3:14–4:49	436
3:14–39	463
3:27	cciv, 489
3:33	cciv, 489
*3:38	427, 877
3:40	216
3:43	216
3:44–51	815
4:7	357
4:9–10	357
4:14	357, 879
4:20	cciii, 528
4:26	cciii, 528
4:31	cciii, 528
4:35	cciii, 528
*5:3	217
5:6	cciii, 528
5:10	cciii, 528
5:13	cciii, 528
5:16	cciii, 528
5:18	cciii, 528, 532
*5:21	230
5:22	255
5:26	cciii, 528
5:31	871
6:1–12	532
6:12	372
6:22	189
6:25	1181
7:12	462
7:13	879
7:19	879
7:25	879
7:31	879
7:89	561
8:1–4	89
8:7	1220
*8:14	cxciii
8:21	1220
9:2–5	372
9:15	877
10:1–8	877
*10:9	510
10:14	cxciii, 510
*10:15	462
*10:16	460
*10:19	460
*10:20	460
*10:23	460
*10:24	460
*10:26	460
*10:27	460
10:33	677
11:12	256
11:14–17	287

ccivk, 489	
11:19	
11:26	
12:5	
12:7	
12:8	
13:2–14	
*13:2	
13:4–16	
13:4–14	
*13:20	
14:10	
*14:21	
*14:28	
14:33	
14:44	
*15:32	
15:39	
*16:3	
16:3	
16:6–7	
16:6	
16:19	
*16:22	
16:22	
16:23–35	
16:30–35	
16:32–34	
16:33	
16:40	
16:42	
16:46–47	
17:11–12	
17:11	
*18:1	
18:8–24	
18:12–13	
*18:12	
18:13–17	
*18:13	
19:19	
*20:4	
20:4	
20:6	
21:17–18	
*21:29	
22–24	
22:22	
22:23	
22:24	
23:24	
24:14	
24:15–17	
24:17	
24:20	
*24:27	
25:1–5	
25:1–2	
26:1–56	
26:1–51	
*26:9	
26:9	
26:53	
26:55	
26:57–62	
*26:65	
*27:16	
27:16	
*27:20	
28:2–8	
28:3–8	
28:9–10	

Reference	Page
28:11–14	372
28:16	372
28:19–24	372
28:26–29	372
28:26–27	814
*28:26	815
29:1–3	372
29:7–8	372
29:12–14	372
31:4–6	443
31:6	510
*31:14	clxxxii, 657
*31:16	157
31:16	165, 187–88
31:19–20	474
31:24	474
*32:10–12	567
32:14	870
*33:9	431, 855
34:19–28	462
*34:23	460
*34:24	460
*34:26	460
*34:27	460
35:30	602, 631
*35:33	217
35:33	407
*36:3	460
36:6	cciv, 1009, 489

Deuteronomy

Reference	Page
*1:3	cxcv
1:7	890
1:10	466
*1:13	cxciii
1:17	766
1:28	992, 999
1:31	705
1:33	625, 841
*1:34–36	567
*1:42	cxciii, 998
2:9	clxxiii, 1001
*2:34–35	199
*4:12	88
4:13	677, 711
4:26	565, 566
*4:30	cxciv
*4:33	454
*4:41	427
*4:42	cxciv
*5:5	1075
5:6–21	711
5:6	620
5:8	349, 565
5:11	744, 889
5:16	158
5:17–19	544
5:22–27	100, 988
5:26	102, 454
*6:8	679
6:12	620
6:13	566
*6:14	217
*6:16	cxcvii
7:5	762
7:9	677
7:12	677
*7:16	217
*7:18	874
8:5	260
*8:7	348, 526
8:8	816
*8:19	565
9:1	992
*9:14	cxcii, 874
*9:27	550
*10:3	858
10:4	711
10:5	711
10:8	352, 677
10:12–15	827
*10:17	953
10:18	613
*10:19	711
10:20	566
*10:21	874
10:22	466
*11:18	679
11:24	890
11:25	624
*11:25	229
12:3	762
12:7	194
12:15	1003
*12:16	815
*12:20	969, 1003
12:20	1003
*12:21	969, 1003
12:21	1003
13	759
13:1–11	214
13:1–6	753
13:1–3	759
*13:1	1232
*13:2–6	1232
13:2–6	753, 759
13:10	617
*13:14	730
13:14	730
14:22–28	194
14:23–26	815
*14:26	969, 1003
14:26	1003
*14:29	clxxxvi, cxcvii
15:21	372
16:1–8	372
16:2–3	372
16:9–12	814
*16:9	844
*16:18	230
17:1	372
17:6	602
17:12	352
17:14	689
17:17	346
17:18–20	345
18:1–4	194, 1109
18:4	815
18:5	352
18:7	352, 613
18:15	600
18:18–19	204, 600
18:18	600
*19:6	cxciv
19:10	887
19:15	602, 631
19:21	992, 834
19:29	992
21:15–17	38
22:23–24	1029
*21:23	217
23:9–14	819
23:9–10	812
23:17–18	1223
*23:25	844
24:1–3	345
24:6	1009
26:1–11	814
26:2	816
*26:10	815
27:5	cciv, 489
27:15	255
28	502
28:26	1068
*28:30–31	217
28:38	403, 529
28:39	403
28:42	403, 529
*28:59	869
28:59	869
28:62	466
28:66	302
*29:19	217
29:20	882
29:23	541, 620, 825
30–32	872
30:3–5	436
30:12–13	348
30:19	565
31:9	677
*31:16	907, 737
31:16	930, 988
31:19	85
31:21	85
31:24–27	86
31:28	565
31:29	541
31:30–32:43	863, 872
31:30–32:42	872
32:1–43	86
32:1	123, 150
32:3	994
*32:4	874–75
32:4	886
*32:8	110, 691
32:8	691
32:10–14	705
32:14	938, 397, 847
32:17	542
32:23–25	394, 402
32:24	403
32:33	733
32:39	93, 302, 564
*32:40	550, 564, 567
32:40	564
32:41	1061
*32:42	908
32:42	394
*32:43	703
32:43	408
33	1057, 465
33:1	10
33:2–3	277
33:2	364
33:3	359
33:8–11	600
*33:13	348
33:17	354
33:22	350
33:26	625
*33:34	1043
34:5–6	600
34:5	872

Joshua

Reference	Page
1:1	872
1:4	890
*1:15	427
1:15	872
*2:12	679
*2:13	clxxx, 231
2:17	871

2:19 408
2:20 871
3:3 677
3:10 102, 454
*3:15 1043
3:17 891
4:7 677
5:10–12 372
5:13 1061, 1155
*5:14 407, 694
5:14 99, 693
6 510
6:6 677
*6:20 99
6:21 98, 182
*6:24 199
7:6 287
7:19–21 885–86
7:19 994
8:10 287
*8:20 99
8:20 836
8:31 872
*9:18 550
*9:19 550
9:24 17, 872
*10:11 1075
10:11 901
11:14 1095
*12:1 427
13–19 604
*13:5 427
14:7 17
15:7 1177
*15:9 431, 855
*17:3 230
*17:11 858
18:16 1177
*19:8 460
*19:9 460
*19:16 460
*19:23 460
*19:27 427
*19:34 427
21:4–7 462
*22:19 229
23:3 689
24:2 890
24:8 302
24:9 17
*24:17 679
24:17 620
24:31 290

Judges

1:7 646
*1:8 99
*1:25 99
*1:27B 58
2:7 290
2:8 17
2:11–23 xcii
*2:17 907, 930
2:17 988
*3:10 1042
*3:16 98, 182
4:6–16 898
*4:15 99
*4:16 99
5 1057
5:4–5 1081, 1101
5:4 518
5:5 416
*5:19 858
5:19 898

5:20 212, 525
5:31 99
6:2 420
6:5 531
6:8 620
6:11–17 115
6:12 679
6:15–16 70, 397
*6:17 clxxiv
6:25–26 762
7 898
7:8–22 510
7:12 1095, 531
7:13 397
8:14 287
*8:19 567
8:19 102, 566
8:27 930, 988
*9:40 1075
9:53 1009
9:56–57 646
11:3 287
11:34 489
*13:2 382
13:3 679
13:5 532
13:17–18 1055
13:20 626
*13:22 198
13:22 1180
15:11 646
*15:13 567
*16:4 382
16:17 532
16:21 1009
*16:23 910
16:28 992
*17:1 382
18:2 530
*18:6 229
18:7 530
*18:10 ccii, 653
18:14 530
18:17 530
*18:18 ccii
18:30 462
19:24 489
*19:26 ccii, 653
*20:22 653
*20:28 508
*20:37 99
20:40 836
*21:1 567
*21:7 550, 567
21:12 489
*21:10 99, 1125
*21:18 567
*21:20 ccii

Ruth

1:4 379
*1:7 ccii, 653
1:8 cciv, 489
1:19 439, 737
*2:1 382
*2:14 1043
*3:2 229
*3:4 ccii, 653
3:13 102, 566
4:1–4 287
4:2 290

1 Samuel (1 Kingdoms)

*1:1 382

1:2 379
1:11 532
1:26 352
2:8 878
2:9 890
2:10 365, 639, 678
2:35 639
3:3 89
*3:14 567
4:3 677
4:4 272
4:6–9 737
*4:8 524, 615, 656
4:8 742
4:10 949, 985
*4:19 859
5:7 737
6:7 cciv, 489
6:20 423
*7:6 883
7:6 737
7:10 560, 678
7:26 454
8:5 689
*8:20 1042
8:20 689
*9:1 382
*9:2 382
*9:10 ccii, 653
9:21 70
9:24 302
*10:4 815
10:8 cciv
10:18 489
10:25 510
10:27 742
12:3 639
12:5 639
12:17 294
12:18 294
13:5 1095
*13:9 570, 825
13:13 640
13:16 420
*14:11 ccii, 653
14:11 420
14:15 852
*14:27 1043
14:39 102, 566
15:6 977
*15:11 237
15:21 815
16:1–13 334
*16:1 clxxxii, 51
*16:2 51
16:7 206
16:21–22 640
*16:22 508
*17:6 548
17:6 548
17:26 102
17:36 102
17:40 530
17:43 976
17:44 976, 1068
17:46 1068
18:5 13
18:7 628
18:30 13
19:4 13
*19:6 567
20:2 1101
20:3 566
*20:42 567
21:4–5 819
21:5–6 819

Reference	Page	Reference	Page	Reference	Page
21:5	812	12:30	308	*6:17	877
21:11	628	*13:37	clxxxii, 51	6:20-21	357
22:1-2	706	*14:2	clxxxii, 51	6:20	1160
22:5	977	*14:10	217	6:23-28	1100
*23:22	ccii, 653	14:19-20	13	6:33-35	877
24:6	639	14:20	206	6:36	605
*24:10	379	14:22	13	7:2-12	924
*24:13	384	15:21	102	*7:7	ccii, 653
24:13	384	*15:14	1075	7:9	605
*24:22	550, 567	*15:31	ccvi, 269, 282	7:10	1156
25:16	302	*15:32	ccii, 653	7:12	605
*26:5	ccii, 653	*16:1	51	7:15-50	924
26:9	639	17:11	466	7:15-21	241
26:11	639	18:16	510	7:15-20	242
26:15	332, 741, 875	*18:19	570, 825	7:23-26	296
26:16	639	18:20	826	7:23	296
26:23	639	18:22	826	7:24	296
*28:10	567	18:25	826	*7:31	877
28:20	302	18:27	826	7:48	357
29:1	898	*19:1	clxxxii, 51	7:49	89-90, 147
*29:4	ccii, 653	19:7	550, 567	8:1-66	881
29:5	628	*19:8	550, 567	8:1-3	287
*29:7	217	*19:24	550	8:9	711
*29:10	ccii, 653	*20:1	382	8:10-12	880-81
*30:5	550	20:22	510	8:10-11	881-82
31:1-7	898	21:10	1068	8:11	881
		*21:17	567	8:28	17
2 Samuel (2 Kingdoms)		21:22	949, 985	8:29	302
		22:4	ccii, 528	8:33-37	502
1:10	308	22:5	348	8:35	615
*1:12	clxxxii, 51	22:8	518	8:37	529
1:16	408	22:9	614, 882	8:39	206
1:17-27	978	22:11	272, 297-98	*8:47	ccii, 653
1:19	949, 985	22:14	393, 559, 678	8:53	872
1:25	949, 985	22:51	639-40	8:56	17
1:27	949, 985	*23:7	909	8:59	510
2:22	66	23:7	909	*10:4	815
*2:23	ccii, 653	*23:16	883	10:8	640
2:28	510	23:17	887	*10:10	30
3:1-3	978	24:1-9	436	10:24	clxxviii, 912
*3:9-10	567	24:2	224	*11:9	clxxxii, 657
3:28-29	407	24:9	224	*11:34	229
3:28	871	24:17	564	11:36	88, 147
3:31	611	25:8	1129	12:6	640
*3:33	clxxxii, 51			12:11	531
*3:35	567	*1 Kings (3 Kingdoms)*		12:14	531
3:38	949, 985			*12:24	533
*4:4	382	1:9	1177	13:30	524
4:9	566	*1:13	567	14:1	622
4:10	826	*1:17	550, 567	14:11	957, 1068
5:10	642-43	1:29	566	*14:39	198
6:2	272	*1:30	567	*15:8	99
6:4-5	510	1:32-48	334	16:4	957, 1068, 622
6:14	510	1:38	1177	16:7	541
6:15	85	*1:51	ccvi, 269, 282, 567	16:28-19:3	214
6:16	510	*2:3	381	16:31	203-4
6:17	510	*2:4	clxxxvi, cxcvii	17-18	615
6:21	510	*2:8	550, 567	17:1-7	706
6:22	cciv, 489	2:16	969	*17:1	509
7:7	477	*2:23	567	17:1	615, 631
*7:8	642	2:33	408	17:2-3	691
7:11	364	2:37	408	*17:20	clxxvi
7:13-16	640	2:45	640	*17:21	clxxvi
7:14-15	260	3:8	466	*17:25	910
7:14	1129	3:15	677	*18-21	203
7:20	17	*3:28	876	18:1	615, 621
*7:25 (MS B)	642	4:2	364	18:4	203, 214
*7:26 (MS A)	642	4:20	466	18:12	934
*7:27	642	4:21	890	18:15	613
8:2	604	4:28	397	*18:18	509
*10:13-14	1075	*5:4	286	18:19	203, 214
11:7	clxxii	5:13-18	436	18:35	clxxii
11:11-12	819	5:17	1156	18:36-39	760
11:11	812	5:21	397	18:38	759-60
11:21	1009	*6:5	877	19:1-3	203
*11:26	clxxxii, 51	6:14-36	924	19:3-4	691

19:4–8	706	9:36–37	957	15:25–26	677
19:9	88	10:26–27	762	*16:8–36	827
19:10	642, 886	11:12–20	334	16:15	677
19:11	518	11:12	173	16:27–28	365
19:14	163, 642, 886	11:14	242	16:31	875
19:18	628	11:20	1129	*16:36	clxxv, 1027
*20:8	346	13:14–19	982	*16:42	852
*20:9	282	13:21	624	16:42	clxxv
20:31–32	611	13:23	677	17:13	1129
20:35	liv	15:19–20	436	*17:24	642
21:1–16	203	*16:10–15	405	18:8	296
21:8	345	16:13	879	18:18	150
21:9	282	16:14	510	20:2	308
21:10	602	16:15	879	20:28	949
21:23–24	957	16:17	296	21:1–17	667
21:23	203, 957	17:13	18, 570	21:1–6	436, 466
21:24	622, 1068	17:23	18, 461, 570	21:1	697, 701
22	279, 336	18:12	872	21:6	463
22:1–38	335	18:13–19:37	1099	*21:12	382
22:10	353	18:18	235	21:12	1061
22:11	603, 982	18:30	ccii, 528	21:16	564, 611, 824, 1058
22:17–23	313	19:1–2	611	21:26	760
22:19–23	303, 894	19:2	289	22:10	640, 1129
22:19–22	70, 277	*19:4	744	22:19–20	278
*22:19	99	19:4	454	23:1–6	316
22:19	123, 150, 155, 286, 290,	*19:6	744	*23:5	clxxv
	352–53, 363, 640, 693, 701, 967	*19:15	875	23:6	289
22:20	335, 373	19:15	272, 828	23:24–32	316
22:21	290	*19:28	clxxxii, 643, 657	24:4	289
22:27–29	611	*19:32	ccii, 653	24:7–18	289
22:31	766	20:3	992	25:1–31	289, 293
25:13	296	20:20	1177	25:1–8	316
*30:22	clxxii	21:8	872	25:8	766
		21:10	18, 570, 1088	26:3	1, 18
2 Kings (4 Kingdoms)		21:13	604	26:13	766
		22:13	870	27:1–24	436
1:9–16	631	22:17	541	27:23	466
1:10	407, 516, 759–60	23:1–2	287	28:4	640
1:12	407, 516, 760	23:2	766	28:5	262
1:14	516, 760	23:3	242	28:6	1129
2:1–11	599	23:6	762	28:9	206
2:1–12	626	23:11–15	762	28:11–19	597
2:2	102	23:20	762	28:11	877
2:3	liv	23:29–30	898	28:15	89–90
2:5	liv	*23:29B	858	28:18	272
2:7	liv	24:2	18, 570	28:19	677
2:11–12	626, 631	24:7	890	29:10	309
2:11	625, 841	25	lxi	*29:11	49
2:15	liv	25:3	1, 18	29:11	44, 49, 364–65
2:16	934	25:13–17	678	29:23	262
3:14	613	25:26	766	35:15	289, 293
*3:24	1075				
4:1–38	liv	**1 Chronicles**		**2 Chronicles**	
*4:42	815				
4:42	397, 814	1:5	137, 1094	*1:3	ccii, 653
*5:16	509	1:7	137	*2:8	874
5:16	613	3:5	232	2:12	828
6:14	1099	5:4	1094	*2:13	878
6:17	693, 1099	5:10	949	2:14	878
7:1	397	5:25	930	2:17–18	436
*7:6	533	5:26	461	3:14	878
7:9	826	*6:49	405	3:15–16	241
7:16	397	6:49	17	4:2	296
*8:15	1043	*7:29	858	4:7	295
9	203	9:8	262	5:1–7:10	881
9:6	643	*9:25	654, 750	5:7	677
*9:7	384, 1025, 1026	*9:29	512	5:10	711
9:7	clxxix, 18, 384, 408, 570, 1026	9:33	302	5:11–14	881–82
9:10	622	*10:1	1075	5:12–13	881
9:13	510, 643	11:19	887	*5:13	clxxv
9:22	203–4, 930	12:14	766	5:14	881
*9:27 B	858	12:23–37	462	6:12–42	881
9:30–37	203	13:6	272	6:16	640
9:30	203	14:7	689	6:20	302
9:33–37	622	15:16–22	316	6:26	615

Ref	Page	Ref	Page	Ref	Page
*6:28	529	36:10	89	10:36	814–15
6:30	206	36:14	289	10:37	815
*6:35	876	36:15–16	111, 610	11:1	608
*6:37	ccii, 653	36:16	870, 886	11:18	608
6:42	992	36:18	89, 766	12:22	l, 18
7:1–3	881	*36:23	142	13:29	901
7:1–2	881–82	36:23	629		
7:1	760			**Esther**	
*7:3	clxxv	**Ezra**		*1:1	85, 295, 347, 518, 662, 678, 882
*7:13	382	1:2	629	1:6	854
7:13	527, 529	1:7	89	1:14	35
7:18	640	2	436	2:6	232
*8:11	ccii, 653	2:36	289	2:7	256
8:12	877	2:41	289, 293	2:17	173
9:8	262	2:62	224	*3:13	142
9:23	clxxviii, 912	3:10	289, 293	4:1	611
10:11	531	3:11	347	4:16	302, 750
10:14	531	4:13	784	*4:17	740, 864, 886
12:6	865, 886	4:15	223	4:17	731, 886
13:5	640	5:11	629, 828	*6:13	454
13:11	357, 912	5:12	629	5:1–2	353
13:12	510	6:9	629	6:1	223
15:3	407	6:10	629	7:10	646, 845
*15:8	21	6:19–21	372	*8:13	454
15:8	877	*7:12	953	*8:15	685
16:9	354	7:12	955, 629	8:15	72
*18:15	clxxxvi, cxcvii	7:14	35	8:17	624
18:18–22	277	7:21	75, 629	9:2	624
18:18	352	7:23	629	9:22	623
18:30	766	7:27	958	*9:30	29
20:6	423	8:24	289	*10:3	662
*20:19	clxxv	8:29	289	*11:5–8	896
20:27–28	808	9:5–15	513	13:14	740
21:4	clxxii	9:6	992	*16:16	102
21:11	930	9:11	18		
21:12–15	lxxiv, 125	9:13–15	628	**Job**	
*21:23	323	9:15	865, 886	1–2	303
22:22	407	10:6	l, 18	1	279
23:11	173	10:16	379	1:6–12	277–78, 693, 701
*23:13	393	11:43	992	*1:6	700
24:9	17, 872			1:6	277, 288, 290, 516, 613, 697
24:19	610	**Nehemiah**		*1:7	700
24:20–22	621	1:4	629	*1:9	700
24:21	617	1:5	629	1:9	697
25:1	232	1:6	302, 475	*1:12	700
26:16	357, 1000	1:8	872	1:12	697
28:18	357	2:4	629	1:16	760, 852
29:7	877	2:6	353	2:1–7	701
29:11	613	2:8	154	2:1–6	277–78, 693
29:17	877	2:12	clxxviii, 912, 958	2:1	277, 288, 290, 613
30:1–27	372	2:20	629	2:3	697
*30:24	815	4:4–5	407	2:4	697
31:15	1101	4:9	302	2:6	530, 697
31:20	1224	5:18	166	2:7	697
32:6	17	*6:12	21	3:19	766
32:30	1177	6:14	901	3:21	53
*32:32	21	6:18	l, 18	4:10	532
32:33	365	7	436	4:16	507
*33:3	693	7:5	clxxviii, 912, 958	5:1	836, 1098
*33:5	693	7:39	289	*5:8	407
33:14	1177	7:44	289, 293	5:17–18	260
34:21	870	*8:12	229	7:7	992
34:25	541	8:15	469	*7:12	683
34:30	766, 1101	9:1	611	7:12	667, 733, 1119
34:31	242	*9:6	693, 875	9:7	453
35:1–19	372	9:6	407, 565	9:9	98
35:3	678	9:8	886	*9:31	1043
*35:7	815	9:15	189	9:34	210
35:7	372	9:17	cciii, 528, 620	10:2	1234
*35:8	815	9:26	163, 610, 886	10:9	992
*35:9	815	9:33	865, 886	11:8–9	366
35:22–24	898	10:29	17	*12:6	643
*35:24	clxxxii, 51	10:35	814	12:15	1119
*35:25	clxxxii, 51				
36:7	89				

Ref	Page	Ref	Page	Ref	Page
13:6	123, 150	2:1–2	419, 644, 896	22:28	875
13:21	1234	2:1	875, 1061	23:1	210, 478
*14:10	985	2:2	639, 1061	23:3	478
14:15	1234	2:6	803, 848	23:4	210
14:18	416	2:7	210–11, 334, 1129	24:3	352
15:8	277, 303	*2:8–9	209	*24:14	654
15:15	836, 1098	*2:8	688	25:7	992
16:19	255	2:8	1061	25:10	677
18:13	401	*2:9	199, 211, 652, 688, 1043	25:14	654, 677
18:15	835	2:9	53, 210–16, 663, 672, 676,	26:8	878
19:11–12	364		688–89, 712,	*27:4	207, 993
20:5	704		1060, 1061	*27:8	639
21:9	210	*3:9	429, 470	27:9	17
22:8–9	996	3:9	429, 470, 1024	28:1	365
24:2–3	996	*4:4	643	28:2	564
24:31	996	4:7	1181	28:4	207, 541
25:2–3	364	6:3–4	407	28:8	365, 639
26	667	6:3	875	29	929, 560, 678
26:5–6	348	7	407	29:1–2	308
*26:6	534, 940	7:7–8	692	29:1	277
26:6	534	7:11	8, 65, 886, 888	29:3–9	393, 559, 560, 678
26:11	241	*7:12	888	29:3	559, 561, 706, 929, 1119
26:14	562	7:13–14	394	29:4	559
28:10	354	8:3	313	29:5	559
*28:14	526	8:4	789, 875	29:7	559
*28:22	534	8:5	1173	29:8	559
28:22	534, 940	8:6	277, 365, 542, 1173	29:9	559
29:18	1095	9:4	865	29:10	296
30:6	420	9:7–8	875	30:11	611
31:11	1098	9:12	408	30:12	611
31:12	534	9:13	408	*31:2	823
32:8	623	*9:37	639–40	31:17	1181
33:1–2	744	10:6	833	*32:2–3	355
33:1	123, 150	10:7	409	32:2	823
33:4	623	10:12	564	32:4	302
33:31	123, 150	10:13	875	*32:6	656
34:2	123, 150	10:16	639–40	32:6	929
34:16	123, 150	*11:6	833	*32:19	clxxx, 231
35:16	744	11:6	516, 541, 760, 833, 835	33:2–3	355
36:7	262	11:13	875	33:2	1028
*36:16	526	13:1–2	407	33:3	359
37:2–5	393, 559	13:2	875	33:6–9	313
37:2	560	14:4	875	33:19	clxxx, 231
37:3	450	15:1	875	34:9	359
37:4	560	15:10	230	34:10	359
37:5	560	16:10	230	34:11	827
*37:22	1173, 1175	*17:6–16	294	34:15	354
38:1–42:6	15	*17:7	416	35	407
38:7	213, 525	17:13	1061	35:2	1049
38:8–11	667	*17:50	639	35:3	1049
38:16	828	18:1–3	353	35:9	909
38:22–23	902	18:2–4	clxvii	35:10	332, 741, 875
38:31	98	18:4	ccii, 528	35:13	611
38:32	98	18:5–18	668, 707	35:17	407
40:9	560	18:5–6	348, 401	36:7	clxxv, 852
40:10	365	18:6–16	294	36:9	909
40:15–24	728	18:6	1119	38:13	744
*40:25	683	18:7–15	1081, 1101	39:9	744
41:1–34	728	18:7–9	880	40:3	359
41:10	423	18:7	416, 901	40:6	358
*41:11–13	540	18:8	882	*41:2	454
41:18–21	614	18:11	297–98, 1049	41:13	43, 255
41:19–21	540	18:13	393, 559, 561, 614	42:2	454
*41:22	526	18:31	741	42:3	102
*41:23	526	18:35	340	*42:4	355
41:24	1009	18:50	639	42:7–8	348
*42:3	874	19:1	542	43:4	355
		19:10	572	44:4	1181
Psalms		19:14	871	44:21	206
		20:6	340, 639	45	1046, 1047
1:1	11	21:2	220	45:6	640
1:2	302, 475	22:1	875	45:7–8	1047
1:3	153	22:2	220	45:7	210
2	210, 952, 1061	22:4	285	46	1047
2:1–3	1064	22:21	735	46:2–3	416

Ref	Pages	Ref	Pages	Ref	Pages
46:2	901	72:18–19	43	*86:2	1098
46:3–4	668, 707	72:19	255	86:9–10	875–76
*46:3	875	*73:2	992	*86:10	875
46:3	901	*73:13	683	87:4	668, 732, 754
46:4	878, 1176	*73:14	683	87:6	224
46:5	878	74:2	992	*87:12	534
46:6	644, 1168	74:7	878	88:1	302, 475
*46:9	643	74:9–10	407	88:3–7	348
46:10	1123	*74:9	833	88:11	534
47:5	85, 510	74:9	833	*88:11	940
47:8	643, 875	74:12–17	667	88:12	534
47:9	643	74:13–14	667	88:18	353
48:1–8	1047	74:13	683, 733	*88:28	37, 39
48:7	682	74:14	1033, 683–84, 732, 754	*88:38	37–39, 255
48:14	653	74:15	706–7	*88:50	992
49:1	123, 150	*75:5	990	*89:1	872
*49:3	296	*75:8	833	89:3–4	640
49:14	401	75:9	833	89:5–7	701
49:15	401	75:10	353	*89:6	277
*50:1	427	75:11	353	89:6	407, 741, 875, 1098
50:3	296	76:7	423	89:7	277, 288, 302
50:10	852	*76:19	294	89:8	277, 642, 741, 875
50:12–14	372	77:16	706	89:9–14	667
50:14	636	77:17	706	89:9–10	667
50:23	636	77:18	294, 518	89:9	642
51:15–17	358	77:19	929	89:10–15	667
51:16–17	358	*77:25	189	89:10	684
51:17	358	*77:43	679	89:16	1181
52:2	98, 182	*77:51	815–16	89:17	353
55	407	78:2	744, 1098	*89:18	407
55:7–8	705	78:23	280, 313	89:26–27	1129
*55:13	clxxx, 231	78:25	189	89:28	37–39
*56:7–9	355	78:31	870	89:35–37	640
56:8	224, 1102	*78:41	407	89:38	37, 255
56:13	clxxx, 231	78:43–52	502, 505, 546	89:52	43, 255
57:4	98, 182, 532	78:43–51	499, 506	89:53	255
57:7–9	355	78:44	502, 884	90	872
58	407	78:45	503	90:4	1089, 1105
58:6	533	78:46	503, 527, 529	90:17	541
59	407	78:47	503, 902	*91:1–3	355
59:13	409	78:49–51	503	91:4	1049
59:18	365	78:50	504	91:6	359
61:7	640	78:51	815	*92:1–3	355
*61:13	207, 993	78:52	705	*92:1	643
62:1	508	78:60	1123	92:10	353
62:5	409	78:68	1098	92:11	353
62:12	207, 365, 488	79	407	93:1	365, 643
62:13	207	79:1–3	621–22	93:3	706
63:5	564	79:2–3	621	93:4	706, 929
63:8	340	*79:2	284	*94:11	567
65:7	644	79:5	407	94:12–15	260
66:6	706–7	79:10	408	*95:2	826
67:1	420	79:12	993	*95:3	826
67:2	1181	*80:1–3	355	*95:5	542
*67:24	1043	80:1	210, 272, 297, 478	95:5	313
68:4	625, 841	*80:2	356	*95:7	1173
68:7–10	478	80:4	407, 1181	95:7	365, 1123
68:7–8	1081, 1101	80:8	1181	*95:10	643
68:8	517, 518	80:11	852	*95:11	656
68:17	539	80:20	1181	95:11	567
68:18	364, 539	81:1–3	355	*96	827
68:23	1043	81:2	356	*96:1	643, 1029
68:33	561	81:3	85	96:2	826
68:34	625	81:16	397	96:3	826
*68:35	656	82:1–8	277	*96:6	656
69	407	82:1	277, 303, 692, 701	96:10	643, 875
69:27–28	224	*82:4	207, 359	96:11	703, 1007
69:28	224	82:5	277, 890	97:1	643, 1029
*70:22	355	82:6	277, 302	97:2	880
71:19	741	83	407	*97:4–6	355
*71:20	526	*83:2	454	97:5	901
*71:22	407	*83:18	875	97:7	277
71:22	355	84:2	454, 878	97:8	880
72:11	308, 1027, 1120	84:3	102	*98:1	284, 636, 642–63
72:14	408	*85:9–10	875–76	98:1	359

98:4–6	355	114:6–7	518	139:18	1095
99	303	114:6	368, 370	139:23	206
99:1	272, 297, 636, 642–43	*115:1	1024	141:2	358, 513
99:2	875	115:3–8	543	141:3	358
102:1	366	115:4–7	544	141:14	397
102:15	1171	115:4–6	542, 544	142:5	542
102:25–26	1117	115:4	541	143:3	890
102:25	313	115:13	645	144:5–7	668, 707
103:1	366	115:15	828	144:7	929
*103:4	202	*116:1	1024, 1028, 1083	144:9–10	808
103:7	561	116:3	401	144:9	359
103:20	316	116:5	886	*144:13	640
*103:26	683	116:19	1034	*144:17	874–75
104	1024	*117:1	688, 1024, 1026, 1028	*145:1	1024
104:2	259	117:2	1024	145:6	565
104:3	296, 625, 841	*117:9	580	*145:10	639–40
104:4	34, 451, 846	*117:19	clxxxi, 581	145:13	640
104:6–9	667	117:22	874	145:17	874, 886
104:13	296	*117:24	1029	146:1	1024
104:25–26	728	117:24	874	146:6	98, 182, 565, 828
104:25	297	*118:1	1024	*146:7	356
104:26	683	118:9	580	*146:10	1024
104:32	880	118:19	clxxxi	146:10	640
104:35	1024	118:24	1029	147:1	1024
*104:36	815–16	118:25	470	147:2	436
105	502	118:27	489	147:7	356
105:1	1028	*118:37	886	148:2	316
105:6	17	*118:46	574	147:20	1024
105:26	872	*118:137	864	148	1027, 1177
105:27–36	499, 502, 505, 506, 546	119:1	1071	148:1	1024
105:28	502	119:35	1181	148:4	296
105:29	503, 884	119:46	574	148:14	1024
105:30	503	119:100–103	572	*149:1	359–60
105:31	502, 503	119:103	572	149:1	1024
105:32–33	503, 901	*119:137	886	149:9	1024
105:34–35	503, 527, 529	119:137	864, 886	150	1026
105:36	503, 815	*120:5	clxxxii, 321, 339	150:1	1024, 1028
105:37	542	121:2	828	150:3–5	356
105:40	189	122:3–5	292	150:6	1024
105:42	17	124:8	828		
105:45	1024	125:1–2	416		
*105:48	1027	130:4	ccii, 528	*Proverbs*	
106:1	1024, 1028	*131:2–5	567		
106:26	564	131:17	353	*2:3	85, 347, 882
*106:37	542	132:2–5	567	2:13	890
106:47	436	132:5	878	*2:14	623
106:48	43, 1024	132:7	878	2:16–19	935
*107:1–3	356	*132:17	353	3:9–10	814–15
107:22	636	*132:17	757, 1167, 1170	*3:12	260
108:1–3	356	134:1	352	3:12	260
109	407	134:2	564	4:1	123, 150
109:17	409	134:3	828	5:3	935
109:28	409	*134:15	541	5:4	98, 522
110	334	135:1	1024	5:6	935
*110:1	841	135:2	352	*5:18	clxxx
110:1	263, 334, 689, 841	135:7	450	*6:7	407
*110:2	874	135:10	1171	6:24–35	935
110:2	210	135:15	541	*6:30	clxxxvi, cxcvii
110:3	334	*136:4	875	7:5–27	935
110:4	334	136:5–9	313	7:24	123, 150
111:1	1024	*136:8	993	8:13	827
111:2	874	136:26	629	*8:22	256
111:10	827	137	407	8:22	39, 256
112:1	1024, 1026	137:7	901, 992	8:29	667
113	1026	137:8	993	8:30	256–57
113:1	1024	*138:7	386	9:1–6	1064
*113:2	541	*138:8–9	348	10:27	704
113:4	368, 370	138:8	542	11:1	396
113:5	332, 741, 875	*138:14	874	13:4	401
113:6	368, 370	139	407	13:24	260
113:9	1024	139:1–6	206	14	257
*113:21	645	139:7	386	*14:5	37
*114:1	1024	139:8–9	348	14:5	257
114:4–7	518	139:14	874	14:25	257
114:4	368, 370	139:16	224, 354	15:3	354

*15:11	534, 940	3:16-26	990	12:5	863
15:11	534	4:3	224	*12:6	407
15:18	257	5:8-10	990	12:32	692
16:4	257	*5:8	524, 656, 968	13:1-22	830, 870
16:11	396	*5:11	524, 656, 968, 997	13:1	88
16:24	572	*5:18	968, 997	13:6	422
17:27	257	*5:19	407	13:8	682
19:19	257	*5:20	524, 656, 968, 997	13:9-10	414, 506
20:23	396	*5:21	524, 656, 968, 997	13:9	422
*21:16	411	*5:22	524, 656, 968, 997	13:10	413, 890
21:16	411	*5:24	407	13:21	986
*21:23	clxxx, 231	5:25	416, 901	*13:22	235
21:28	823	5:26	1095	14	742
22:5	703	5:27-28	753	14:1-2	876
22:14	935	6	277, 279, 303, 336, 880	14:4-23	978
22:24	257	6:1-13	liv, 87, 115, 277, 335	14:10-15	668
23:12-14	260	6:1-8	70	*14:10	471
*23:14	231	6:1-7	313	14:12-15	695-96
*23:24	clxxx	6:1-4	880	14:12	107, 212-13
*23:29	524, 656	6:1	640, 1100	14:13-14	740, 742, 745
24:7	744	6:2	290, 297-98, 301, 352,	14:13	742, 852, 899
*24:12	207		640	*14:14	840
*26:25	85, 347, 882	*6:3	304	14:14	840
27:4	257, 423	6:3	302-6, 316, 363	14:22-23	830
27:20	534	*6:4	880	14:30	400
*28:9	643	6:4	880	15:3	611
29:17	260	6:5	99, 1175	15:9	884
31:8	744	6:6	515, 516	17:4-5	753, 800, 845
31:21	935	*6:8	379	17:5-8	628
31:22	854	6:8	373	17:5	802, 844
		*6:10	cxcviii	*17:7	407
Ecclesiastes		6:13	627	17:8	541
		7:10-17	982	17:12-14	668, 929
*1:3	526	*7:14	679, 682, 688	17:12	1028
2:5	154	8:1-4	603, 982	18:3	85
2:14	890	*8:2	37	18:4-5	802, 844
*3:15	654	8:5-8	668	*19:1	840
9:8	468	8:6-8	956	19:1	620, 625, 840-41
*9:10	ccii, 653	8:6-7	929	19:4	364
11:2	950	8:7	956	*19:17	657
*16:18	526	8:8-9	753	*19:18	550
		8:16-18	liv	20:1-6	603
Song of Songs (Canticles)		8:18	206	20:2-6	982
		8:23	898	20:2	611
*1:5	cxciii	9:1	898	*20:4	897
3:4	184	9:3	422	20:4	897
4:13	154	9:4	422	21:1-10	830
5:15	854	9:7	640	21:3	682
7:2	256	9:8	614	*21:9 (MS B)	829
		*9:12	427	21:9	901
Isaiah		9:18-21	882	21:15-16	976
		10:1-2	996	21:17	394
1:2	1119	*10:1	524, 656	22:1-14	422
*1:4	407	10:5-19	830	22:12	611
1:9-10	620	*10:5	524, 656	22:15-20	235
1:9	620	10:5	210, 891	22:21	235
*1:18	475	10:13-19	830	22:22	235-36, 244
*1:21	clxvii, 929	10:20-22	628	23-24	976
*1:24	968, 997, 407, 524, 656	*10:20	407	23:1	986
1:26	244	10:22	364, 466	23:8	1010
2:1	88	10:26	210	23:16-17	929
2:2-4	876	11:1	350, 373	23:17	930, 931, 988, 997
2:2	689	11:2-3	33	24-27	lxxvii
*2:4	844	11:4	614, 1060, 1061	24:6	240
2:7-9	990	11:10	350, 373	24:8	1008
2:8	541	11:11-16	436, 628, 863	24:13	802, 844
*2:10	1075	*11:11	427	24:17	240
2:10	419	*11:12	450	24:18-23	413
*2:11	875	11:12	450	24:18-20	518
2:12-17	422	11:14	99, 210	24:21-22	686, 1078, 1083
*2:17	875	11:15	891	24:21	419
*2:19	420	12:1-6	863	24:23	287, 290, 803-4
2:19-21	419	12:1-2	863	25:1	255
*3:9	524, 656	12:2	863	25:6-8	1033, 1063
*3:11	524, 656	12:4-6	863	25:8	349, 401, 431, 479, 1111

Ref	Page	Ref	Page	Ref	Page
26:9	240	40:9–11	804	49:23	238
*26:13	875	40:9–10	825	49:25	1122
26:16–27:6	1057	*40:9	825	49:26	887, 937
26:16–19	240	40:9	804	50:1	937, 1030, 1122
26:17–18	682	40:11	368, 478, 804, 812	50:2	891
26:17	682	40:12	396	50:3	413, 611
26:18	240	40:18–20	543	50:26	706–7
*26:20	clxxxi, 581	40:25	741, 875	51:2	466
26:20	870	41:2	891, 1171	*51:3	154
26:21	240	41:4	92, 101, 116, 161	51:4	123
*27:1	683	41:9	123	51:6	1117
27:1	668, 684, 697–98, 1061	41:10	340	51:9–11	668
27:3	302, 511	*41:14	407	51:9–10	668
27:12–13	436	41:24	969	51:10	706
27:13	85, 510	42:8	994	51:13	257
28:1	898	42:10	359–60	51:17–23	903, 932
28:5	173, 628	42:14	682	*51:17	833
28:15	401	42:15	901	51:17	833, 937, 987
28:17	929, 902	42:17	420	51:18–20	1122
28:18	401	*42:24	230	51:20	870
28:19	302	42:26	111	*51:22	833
28:23	123, 150	*43:3	230	51:22	833, 937
28:28	397	43:4	238	52:1	608, 1121
29:3	1099	*43:5	427	*52:5	688, 744
29:5–6	900	43:7	243	52:5	744
29:6	294, 313, 393, 413, 559	*43:10	37	52:7–9	825
29:11	346, 349	*44:5	456, 458	*52:7	643, 825
*29:19	407	44:5	455, 458	52:7	643
30:7	668, 732, 754	44:6	92, 101, 116, 161	52:11	990, 991
*30:8	85	44:9–20	543	52:15	1171
30:8	85–86	44:21	147	53	372–73
30:17	530	*44:23	656	53:7–8	371
30:21	85	44:23	703	53:7	368, 371, 744
30:30–31	393, 559	44:28	477	53:12	371
30:30	561, 900	45:1	236, 1171	54:1–6	1030
30:31	210	45:2	901	54:1	1122
30:33	541, 835, 870	*45:6	427	54:4	996
*31:1	524, 656	45:11	542	54:7–10	436
31:1	968, 997	45:14	238, 876	*54:9	550
31:4	803	45:16	543	54:10	416, 901
*33:1	524, 656	45:20	543, 1173	54:11–12	1146
33:21	1176	45:22	1173	55:1–2	259, 1063
34:1–7	422	*45:24	364	55:1	1128
34:2	870	45:24	1173	*55:4	37
*34:4	656, 1117	46:5	741, 875	55:11	614
34:4	415, 506	46:6	396	56–66	lxxvii
34:5–7	1063	46:8–9	147	56:1	1155
34:5–6	1061	*46:11	427	*56:7	688
34:6	394	46:11	891	56:10	1223
*34:7	909	47	974, 996	*57:1	1075
34:9–10	835	*47:3	897	*57:6	883
34:9	541	47:3	897	59:15–20	1057
34:10	836, 882, 1026	*47:4	382	57:15	308
34:11–15	986	*47:8	996	58:1	510
34:11	604	47:9	996, 1010	59:17	1049
34:14	986	*48:1	550	*59:19	427
34:17	cciv, 489	48:2	608, 1121	60:1–3	876
*35:7	431, 855	*48:6	106	60:2	1181
*35:9	901	48:12	101, 116, 161	60:3–7	1155, 1170
35:9	297, 403	48:13	340	60:3	1171
36:1–3	1099	48:19	466	60:14	237–38, 244, 1043
36:3	235	48:20	13, 990	60:19	1167, 1168, 1170, 1181
36:15	ccii, 528	49:1–6	1060	60:21	153, 542
37:4	454	49:2	98, 182, 1060	61:1–3	422
*37:16	875	49:3	237	*61:6	48, 1193
37:16	272, 297, 828	49:5–6	436, 1155	61:10	1023, 1029, 1030, 1121
37:17	454	49:6	460	*62:2	244
*37:20	875	49:9	66	62:2	190, 244
37:22–29	976	*49:10	431, 477, 478, 855	*62:3	685
37:31–32	628	49:10	478, 889	62:5	1030
40:1–11	liv	*49:13	656	*62:6	302
40:1–2	313	49:13	703	62:6	1154
*40:2	42	49:18	1030, 1121	*62:8	567
40:3	705–6	49:20–22	1122	63:1–6	800, 846, 1049, 1050, 1057
40:4	901	49:22	564	63:1–3	1048

63:2–3	846, 1061	3:18	1094	*12:2	1139
63:2	1962	3:20	1029	12:7	1098
63:3	791, 845–46	*4:2	clxxv, 323, 393	12:12	1061
63:16	1129	4:2	566	*12:16	550
63:17	460	*4:3	524, 656	13:3–11	603
*63:18	608	4:4–5	977	*13:7	ccii, 653
64:1	416, 901	4:4	1026	*13:13	827
64:3	517, 901	4:6	891, 1094	13:14	420
64:8	1129	*4:7	827	13:16	994
65:5–6	882	4:8	611	*13:18	167, 173
65:6	1102	*4:10	30	13:21	682
65:13–14	1063	4:11	422	13:22	957
*65:15	244	4:13	753	13:26	957
65:15	244	4:19	573	13:27	188, 812, 930, 935
*65:16	550	4:24	416	14:10	901
65:16	255	4:26–27	986	14:12	402, 502
65:17	1116, 1117	4:31	682	*14:13	30
65:19	407	5:2	566	*14:16	883
65:22	541	5:3	260	14:16	622
66:1	566	5:6	403	14:17	302
66:6–14	689	5:7	930	14:21	309
*66:6–7	679	5:11	930	15:1	352
66:6–7	662	5:14	613, 642	*15:2	718, 730–31, 749–51
66:6	882	5:12	995	15:2	382, 719, 730–31, 749–51
*66:7	651	5:15	753	15:3	402, 1068
66:7	682, 687–88, 708	5:18	422	15:8	1095
66:8	708	5:22	1119	15:15	407
*66:10	clxxxii, 51	5:26–28	990	*15:16	509
66:15–16	1117	6:1	977, 1094	15:16	572, 642
66:16	1061	6:3	211, 653	15:19	352
66:18–24	1155	6:11	573	15:27	531
*66:18	362, 876	*6:12	827	16:4	1068
66:18	1065, 1155	6:13	766, 1175	16:9	983, 1009
66:19	137	6:16	1101	16:13	302, 475
*66:20	608, 1121	*6:22	1094	16:14–15	566
66:22	1116, 1117	6:22	753, 891, 1094	16:16	420
66:24	1026	6:24	682	16:18	983, 992
		6:26	611	16:19	876
Jeremiah		7:2	150	17:1	489
		*7:6	883	17:10	206–7
1:1–10	87	7:6	887	17:12	677
1:1–3	8	7:8–9	711	17:18	407
1:1–2	9	7:10	206, 352, 1175	17:21	703
1:2	19	*7:20	883	18:21–23	407
1:4–10	liv, 70	7:23	1123	18:21	382
1:4	19	7:25	18, 570	19:1–5	982
*1:6	30	7:33	1068	19:1	289
1:11–13	15	7:34	1009	19:3	150
1:11	19	8:1–2	622	*19:13	693
1:13–15	1094	8:1	422	19:17	1068
1:14	240, 827	*8:6	clxxx, 205	*20:3	clxxv
1:15	753, 891	8:8	1175	20:7–10	895
1:16	541	8:10	1175	20:7–9	573
1:38	1119	8:14	522	20:12	407
2:1–2	1122	8:16	462, 531	*20:15	652, 687
2:2	705	8:17	403	20:15	687
*2:3	407, 816	9:1	289, 302	20:16	510
2:3	815, 818	9:10–12	986	21:7	502
2:4	123, 150	9:11	986, 987	*21:9	985
2:6	705	9:15	522	21:9	402, 502
*2:13	479	9:21	401	*22:5	567
2:20	930	*9:25–26	688	22:5	986
2:24	1003	10:1–16	543	22:8	619, 831
2:30	260	10:7	874–75	22:11	150
3:1	1122	10:10	102, 407, 454, 853	22:14–15	976
3:2	188, 812, 930	*10:19	clxx, 524, 656	*22:18	968
3:6–10	929	10:21	477	22:22	653
3:9	930	10:25–26	870	22:23	682
3:13	930	*10:25	883	22:24	453
3:14–18	1167	11:5	255	*22:25	1075
3:15	477	11:15	1098	22:30	224, 1102
3:16–18	422	*11:19	368	*23:3	ccii, 653
*3:16	407	11:20	407, 886, 1054	23:5	350–51
3:16	678	*12:1	864, 886	23:6	244
3:17	243–44	12:1	886	23:7–8	566

*23:8　ccii, 653
23:14　620
23:15　522
23:18　88, 277, 303, 313, 352, 701
23:22　277, 352, 701
*23:31　21
23:36　102, 454
24:7　1123
24:8　628
*24:9　230
*24:10　382
24:10　402
25:4　18, 570
25:6–7　541
25:9　689
25:10　983, 1009
25:12–14　830
25:13　clxxxii, 574
25:14　clxxxii, 574
25:15–29　932
25:15　833
*25:16　450
25:29　240, 827
25:30–31　800
*25:30　clxxxii
25:30　240, 393, 559, 574, 827
25:32　1095
25:34–36　477
26:5　18, 570
26:8　232
*26:10　909, 937
*26:18　567
26:20–23　620
27:1–28:16　603
*27:8　402, 990
*27:9　207
27:12　937
27:13　402
*27:45　368
*28:2　clxx, 524, 656
*28:6　983, 990
*28:7–8　829
*28:7　786, 832, 926, 930, 932, 983, 987
*28:8　901, 983, 985
*28:9　983
28:10–11　982
*28:13　926, 929
*28:14　567
*28:32　754
*28:34　686, 733
*28:36　891
*28:37　983, 986
*28:49　983
*28:63–64　1008
*28:64　983
29　lxxiv, 125, 141
29:1–23　829
*29:2　827
29:4–23　lxxiv, 125
29:17–18　402
29:19　18, 570
29:20　123, 150
29:24–32　lxxiv, 125
29:24–28　lxxiv, 125
29:30–32　lxxiv, 125
30:6　652, 682
*30:7　567
30:7　473, 900
30:9　351
30:32　1123
*31:1　524, 656
31:1　422
31:2　705
31:7–14　436
31:9　38, 1129

31:10　1155
31:16　479
31:29　422
31:33　1123
31:34　766
32:6–44　982
32:9–15　341
*32:15　833, 987
*32:17　987
32:24　402
*32:30　clxxxii, 574, 827
32:30　541
32:35　1175
32:36　402
32:40　827
*33:7　379
33:11　983
*33:15　350
33:16　244
33:17　640
34:13　620
34:20　1068
34:32　996
35:15　18, 570
35:17　642
*36:1–23　829
*36:4–23　lxxiv, 125
36:21　353, 640
*36:24–28　lxxiv, 125
*36:30–32　lxxiv, 125
*37:6　652
38:2　402
38:3　679
38:4–6　621
*38:9　38
38:11　240
*38:16　479
38:16　566, 567
38:17　642
*38:24　766
*39:17　30
40:8　l, 18
40:9　567
40:11　1009
*42:5　37
42:5　407
42:7　166
42:15　150, 155
42:17　402
43:8–13　731
43:11　382, 402, 718, 730–31, 749
44:7　642
44:13　402, 827
44:22　402, 1175
44:26　550, 566, 827
*45:16　567
46:10　422, 887, 909, 937
46:23　531
46:28　865
47:2　827, 929, 956
47:6　1061
*47:9　567
48:1　clxx, 524, 656
48:6–8　977
48:6　705
48:25　353, 757
48:26　932
49:12　833
49:13　567
*49:16　1075
49:18　620
49:19　423
49:24　682
49:30　420
49:35　815

49:36　450, 451
50–51　976
50:1–51:64　830
50:8–10　977
50:8　990
*50:11　718, 730–31, 749
50:12　937, 986
50:16　844
50:19　478
50:25　891
*50:29　407
50:29　394, 983, 992
50:32　983
50:34　983
50:41　1095
50:43　682
50:44　423
50:45　368
51　925, 957, 986
51:2　clxx, 524, 656
51:3　394
*51:5　407
51:6–10　977
51:6　983, 990, 991
51:7–8　829
51:7　786, 832–33, 926, 930, 932, 983, 987
51:8　983, 985
51:9　983, 992
*51:13　827
51:13　926, 929
51:14　532, 567
51:16　450
*51:26　550, 827
51:27　531
51:30　983
51:32　983
51:33　800, 802–3, 844–45
51:34　668, 686, 732–33, 754
51:36　891
51:37　983, 986
51:39　932
51:43　986
51:45–48　977
51:48　983
51:49　983, 1011
51:63–64　983, 1008
51:64　983
52:17–23　678
52:17　296
52:18　357
52:19　89

Lamentations

1–2　422
1　978, 995, 996
*1:1　clxxxii, 51
1:8　957, 1175
1:11c–16　995
1:13　760
1:15　800, 846
1:18–22　995
*1:19　clxxxvi, cxcvii, 995
1:21　422
2　978, 995
2:2　644
*2:4　883
2:8　604
2:10　611
*2:15　167, 173, 997
2:16　744
2:18　302
2:20–22　995
3:1　210, 891

3:10–11	403	*4:3	679	13:5	422
3:12–13	394	4:4–8	982	13:9	224
3:15	522	*4:7	574	13:16	clxxxii, 574
3:19	522	4:7	clxxxii, 573	*13:17	574
3:44	625, 841	4:9–17	982	14:9	895
*3:64	207	4:16	396	14:11	1111, 1123
4	978	5:1–17	982	*14:19	883
4:5	256	5:2	519	14:21	402
*4:11	883	*5:9	936	16:8–14	1122
4:12	240	*5:11	936	16:9–13	977
4:15	1175	5:12	519	16:11	1122
*4:21	833	5:16–17	394, 402	16:13	854
4:21	833	5:17	403	16:15–58	188, 812
5:3–4	996	*6:2	574	16:15–22	929, 1122
5:8	742	6:3	150	*16:17	clxxiii
5:19	640	6:9	930, 936	16:18	513
		6:11–12	400, 502	16:20	1122
Ezekiel		6:11	402	*16:25	548
		*6:12	198	16:25	548
1–39	1121	6:14	986	*16:34	907
1–3	74, 297	6:16	930	*16:36	897
1–2	336	7:7	240	16:37–38	957
1	71, 261, 279, 330	*7:8	883	*16:38	897
1:1–3:27	87, 575	7:13	1003	16:46	620
1:1–3:15	cxvii, 70	7:16	419	16:49	620
1:1–3:11	liv, 115	7:19	422, 644, 870	16:63	744
1:1–3	9	*7:26	clxx	17:14	677
1:4–3:11	277	8–11	74	*17:23	1139
1:4–28	314	*8:2	280	*17:24	400
*1:4	280, 323, 393	8:2	338	20:5–6	564
1:4	338, 679, 753	8:3	933	20:6	564
1:5–25	297, 314	*8:7	323, 393	20:7	620
1:5–14	298	8:10–11	513	*20:8	883
1:5	314	*8:10	323, 393	*20:13	883
1:6	301	9	530, 767	20:15	564
*1:7	548	9:1–7	537	*20:21	883
1:7	291, 471, 509, 548	9:2–6	767	20:23	564
1:10	298–99	9:2	93, 878	20:25–26	815
*1:15	280, 323, 393	9:3–8	530	20:28	564
1:18	297	9:3	93, 878, 985	*20:31	815
1:22	285, 296	9:4–8	434	20:42	564
1:24	97, 1028	9:4–6	452	20:48	1026
1:26–28	117	*9:4	455	*21:2	574
1:26	91–92, 272	9:4	440, 455, 456	21:3	150
1:27–28	285, 1014	*9:8	883	*21:17	340
1:28	99, 285, 561, 881	*9:11	472	21:26	308
2–3	575	9:11	93, 878	21:31	883
2:1	679	*10:1	280, 323, 393	*21:36	883
2:2	379, 933	10:1	679	*22:10	897
2:8–3:7	70	*10:2	515	*22:22	883
2:8–3:4	115	10:2	878	22:24	870
2:8–3:3	liv, cxvii, 570, 571, 572, 575	10:4	985, 881	23:1–49	188, 812, 929
2:8	571, 572	10:6	878	*23:10	897
2:9–10	xcviii–xcix, 321–22,	10:7	878	23:10	957
	339–42, 345–46, 558, 571, 573	*10:8	323	*23:18	897
*2:9	280, 323, 393	*10:9	280, 323, 393	23:25	257
2:9	338, 340, 572	10:12	297	23:26–29	956, 957
*2:10	322, 536	10:14	298	*23:29	897
2:10	572–73	10:18	881	23:29	957
3:1	575	10:20	272, 297	23:31–33	833
*3:3	572	*11:1	283	23:41	513
3:3	97, 572	11:1	933, 934	23:49	cciv, 489
*3:10	clxxiv, 64	*11:4	574	24:3	603
*3:12	84, 933, 934	11:4	clxxxii, 573	25–32	xcix, 131, 344
3:12	303, 305, 881	11:5	283	*25:2	574
3:13	338	*11:18	936	25:2	clxxxii, 574
3:14	933, 934	11:20	1111, 1123	26–28	979
*3:18	198	11:23	881	*26:7	953, 955
3:18	408	12:6	502	26:15–18	976, 978
3:20	408	*12:16	ccii, 653	*26:16	clxxxii, 51
3:23	881	12:16	402	26:17	979
3:24	624	13:1–9	422	26:18	416
3:27	123, 744	13:1	338	27	109, 990
4–24	xcix, 344	*13:2	574	27:1–8	976
4:1–3	982	13:2	150	27:2	979

27:5–24	980	37:19	463	*46:24	ccii, 653
27:12–24	978	*37:21	ccii, 653	47	1178
27:13	137, 1002	37:22	1111	47:1–12	1175, 1176
27:17	397, 979	37:24	478	47:6–12	153
27:25–36	976, 980	*37:25	ccii, 653	*47:12	1139, 1177
27:25–32	1004	37:25	640	47:12	1177, 1178
27:29–36	978	37:26	1123	47:13	460
*27:29	1005	*37:27	476	47:21–23	460
27:33–35	1004	37:27	476, 1123	48	465
28:1–19	153	38–39	lxxvii, 1047, 1078, 1093, 1094,	48:1–29	461, 465
28:1–9	668		1097, 1099, 1100, 1104	48:1–7	1156
28:2–5	742	38:1–23	1047	*48:4	427
28:2	740, 742, 745, 754, 995	38:1–6	896	48:23–29	1156
28:3	754	*38:2	574	48:30–35	442, 460, 461, 465, 1156
*28:13	154, 1165	38:2	1094	48:35	244
28:13	854, 897	38:6	1094		
28:14	1154	38:7–17	952	*Daniel* (** = Theodotion)	
28:16–20	1165	38:7–8	1065		
*28:19	clxxxii, 51	38:8–16	1094	1–6	cvii, 675
*28:21	574	38:8	898	1:1–8	830
*28:25	ccii, 653	38:10	1094	1:2	89
*29:2	574	38:11–12	1099	1:4	941
29:3–5	668	38:15	1094	1:5	353
29:3	732–33, 754	38:17	18	1:7	244
*29:13	ccii, 653	38:20	416, 420, 901	1:12–15	166
29:21	757	38:22	541, 760, 902, 1100, 1104	1:12	clxxiii
30:1–9	422	39:1–6	1047, 1064, 1094	1:17	769, 941
*30:15	883	*39:1	574	1:19	353, 640
31:2–9	152–53	39:2	898, 952, 1094	2:2	353, 640
*31:8	154	39:4	1067, 898	*2:13	cxc
*31:9	154	39:6	760	2:17	569
32:2–8	668	39:9–13	1165	2:18	106, 629
32:2–4	754	39:9	1032, 1064	2:19	106, 569, 629, 769
32:2–3	732	39:17–20	1064	*2:22	207
32:2	733	39:17–19	887	**2:22	207
32:3	979	39:17–18	1047	*2:23	clxxv
32:4	1033	39:17	898, 1063, 1067	2:27	106, 569
32:7–8	414, 506	39:18–19	937, 1064	2:28	106, 569
32:7	415	39:20	908	*2:29	282
32:13	929	*39:29	883	**2:29	282
*32:16	clxxxii, 51	40–48	15, 473, 603, 678, 1121	2:29	106
32:16	979	40–42	604, 605	2:30	106, 569, 769
*32:18	clxxxii, 51	40:1–42:20	596	**2:35	1101, 654, 695
33:3–6	510	40:1–6	604	2:35	1101
33:4	408	40:1–4	603	*2:37	953, 954, 955
*33:11	clxxx	40:3–42:20	603, 604	**2:37	365
33:21–22	422	*40:3	603	2:37	364–65, 629
*33:27	198	40:3	603, 604	2:40	211
33:27	420	40:5	604	*2:43	91
33:31–32	20	40:17–20	605	*2:44	639
34	1155	40:23	605	2:44	629
*34:2	574	41:21–25	877	*2:45	282
*34:3	353	41:21–22	357, 877	2:46	1034
34:4	219	42:40	604, 1160	*2:47	953, 954
34:12	422	43	74	2:47	106, 569
34:23	477, 478, 812	43:2	96–97, 572	*3:2	954
34:25	705	43:4	985, 881	3:3–18	710
34:30	1123	43:5	933, 934	*3:4	361
*35:2	574	*43:6	269	3:4	361, 467, 574, 761
35:6	408	43:7	188, 640, 812, 930	3:5	308
36:7	564	43:9	930	3:6	308, 1027
*36:20	ccii, 653	43:15	489	*3:7	361, 467, 574
*36:21	ccii, 653	43:20	489	3:8–12	830
*36:22	ccii	*43:22–23	823	3:10	308, 1027
36:28	1111, 1123	*44:4	323, 389, 393	3:11	308, 1027
37	115	44:4	338, 881	3:13	708
37:1	934, 1123	*44:5	clxxiv	3:15	308, 627, 1027
37:3	472	44:12	564	**3:16	472
*37:8	280, 323, 389, 393	44:15	613	3:19	708
37:8	338	44:30	815	**3:25	744
37:9	450	*45:18	877	*3:26	309
37:10	624	45:21	372	*3:27	864
37:15–28	463	46:1–3	475	*3:28	608, 1121
37:15–23	436	46:13–15	372	3:29	361, 467, 574, 744
37:16	463	*46:20	ccii, 653	*3:55	284

*3:96	clxxxvi, cxcvii, 361, 381, 467, 574, 744	7:11–12	353	9:14	885–86
4	954	*7:11	87	9:17	17
4:3	640	7:11	87	9:21	513, 539
4:6	106	7:12	461, 668	*9:22	clxxiv, 64
*4:9	106	7:13–14	73, 277, 668	***9:22	clxxiv
4:11	875	*7:13	54, 91–92, 840–41	9:22	941
4:14	836, 1098	**7:13	54, 840–41	**9:24	608
*4:17	668, 836, 997	7:13	52, 54–55, 59, 73, 90–93, 116–17, 337–38, 539, 625, 700, 789, 800–801, 840–42, 849, 870, 1061	9:26–27	594
*4:19	938, 968			9:27	936, 1084
4:22	609, 784, 1084			10	74
4:23	244	7:14	337, 361, 467, 574, 1173	10:1–22	70
*4:27	831	7:15	xlix, 18, 75, 938	*10:1	clxxiv
4:28–29	784	7:16	cxxv, 472	10:2–9	72
*4:30	937	7:18	73, 261, 337, 362	10:2–3	82
**4:30	937	7:19–27	734	10:2	xlix, 18, 75
4:30	92	7:20–21	353	10:5–14	117, 1035
4:31–32	561	**7:20	742	10:5–9	72
*4:32	609	7:20	684, 733–34, 950	10:5–6	90, 285
**4:32	609	7:21–22	359	*10:5	280,
*4:33	92	*7:21	359	10:5	93, 338, 878
*4:34	628	**7:21	746	**10:6	1054
**4:34	103, 308	7:21	617, 746	10:6	95–96, 99, 538, 693, 695–96
4:34	640	**7:22	21, 359	10:7	75
4:35	240	7:22	21, 73, 1084, 1085	10:9–10	99
*4:37	953, 954	7:24–25	754	10:9	280
4:37	836	7:24	684, 733–34, 769, 941, 950	10:10	100
5:5–6	757	7:25	359, 587, 609, 611, 621, 630, 706, 742–44, 1084	*10:11	64
5:5	627			10:13–21	693
5:11–12	769	*7:27	639	10:13	110
**5:18	1173	7:27	73, 261, 337, 359, 362, 1098, 1181	10:15–17	72
5:18	995	8:1	xlix, 18, 679	*10:15	clxxiv, 64
5:19	361, 467, 574	8:2–8	369	**10:15	clxxiv
5:20	995	8:2	338, 539	10:16	90, 744, 841
5:23	542, 544, 629	8:3–4	353	10:18	90, 100
**5:27	220	*8:3	757	*10:19	clxxiv, 64
6:2–24	830	**8:3	757	**10:19	clxxiv
*6:4	874	8:3	323, 368, 485, 757	10:20–21	538
6:20	17, 454	*8:4	280	10:20	137, 692–93
6:21	347	8:4	297	10:21	110, 693, 695–96
6:25	361, 467, 574	8:8	450, 757	11:1	110
*6:26	467, 574	8:9–14	743	*11:2	910
6:26	361, 454, 640	8:10–11	742	11:2	137
*6:27	103	8:10	525, 685	11:4	450
**6:27	103	8:11–14	594, 607	11:7	1084
6:27	102		694	11:13	936
7–12	lxxvii, lxxxviii, xciii, cvii, 15, 830	8:11	372, 607	**11:19	901
7–10	xcii	8:13	1098	11:29–39	754
7	cx, 73–74, 117, 262, 336, 338, 668, 733–34, 954, 1081, 1084	*8:13	379, 608	*11:30	830
		8:14	742, 1084	11:30	708
7:1–9	734	8:15	75, 539, 769	*11:31	769
7:1–8	732, 734, 754	8:16	561	11:31	745
7:1	539, 830	8:17	99	11:33	941
7:2–7	779	*8:18	clxxiv, 64	11:35	446, 474
7:2	xlix, 18, 450	**8:18	clxxiv	11:36–39	729
*7:3	616, 732	8:20–21	369	11:36–37	740, 755
**7:3	732	8:20	757	*11:36	742–45, 954
7:4	734, 870	8:21	137	*12:1	231, 694, 900
7:5	734	8:23–25	754	**12:1	900
7:6	734	*8:24	359	12:1	110, 224, 239, 446, 473, 474, 693–96, 900
7:7–8	353, 734, 769, 941, 950	8:24	359		
7:7	539, 684, 733–34, 870	8:26	xcviii, 345, 563, 1236	12:2–3	625
*7:8	359, 746	*8:27	938	12:2	1089, 1091, 1099
**7:8	742	8:27	75	12:3	99, 406, 557
7:9–18	338, 472	**9:1	clxxiv	**12:4	346
7:9–14	72, 116, 336–37	9:1	379	12:4	lxxxix, 563, 1217, 1236
7:9–13	71, 92–93	9:2	xlix, 18, 75	12:5–7	556, 557
7:9–12	277, 1081	9:3	82, 611	*12:5	280, 389
7:9–10	73, 91–92, 223, 288, 1084, 1085	9:6	18, 570	12:5	75, 338
7:9	73, 91–92, 94, 116–17, 223, 293, 337, 468, 640, 1084, 1085	**9:7	ccii, 653	12:6–9	571
		9:9	ccii, 528	12:6	878
*7:10	336	9:10	18, 570	*12:7	103, 550, 566, 567, 609
7:10	73, 286, 304, 352, 363–64, 538, 640, 835, 870, 1066, 1102	*9:11	clxxiv	**12:7	308, 550, 609
		9:11	17	12:7	564, 575, 587, 609, 611, 621, 706, 743, 878
		**9:12	1042	**12:9	346

12:9	lxxxix, xcviii, 345, 1217, 1236
*12:10	231, 769
**12:10	1217, 769
12:10	474, 769, 941, 1237
*12:11	745, 769, 936
12:12	444

Hosea

1:1	19
1:2	930, 988
1:10	102, 364, 454, 466
1:11	422
2:1	102, 466
2:2–5	937, 1122
2:2	422
2:3	986
2:4	930, 988
2:5	957
2:10	897
2:12	957
2:16–17	705
2:19–20	1030
2:20	403
4:2	711
4:5	1122
4:12–13	929
*4:15	550
4:15	566, 930, 988
5:3	420, 929
5:4	188, 812
5:8	510
6:10	188, 812
6:11	802, 844–45
7:2	901
*7:13	524, 656
8:1	510
8:13	901
9:1–6	109
9:1	930, 988
9:4	879
9:9	901
*9:12	524, 656
*9:13	654
*10:5	clxxxii, 51
10:6	420
10:8	391
*10:15	657
11:1	706
11:10–11	436
11:10	559
12:5	642
12:6	306, 420, 642
12:7	396
*12:8	398
12:9	258
*13:2	clxxx, 969
*13:4	693
13:7–8	403
13:13	240
13:14	401
13:15	891
14:1–3	109

Joel

1–2	532
1:1	19
1:4	529
1:6	532
*1:10	398
1:13	611
1:15	422
2:1–14	495, 546
2:1	422, 510
2:2–3	510

2:2	890, 900
2:4–9	533
*2:4–5	533
2:10	413, 414, 415, 890
2:11	421, 422
2:15	85, 510
2:20	753
2:25	529
2:30–31	506
2:31	413, 421
2:32	80
3–4	lxxvii
3	cx
3:1–17	1047, 1049
*3:1–2	clxxii
3:2	689, 847, 896, 898, 1095
3:4	413, 415, 422
3:6	137
*3:7	ccii, 229, 653
*3:10	844
3:12	847
*3:13	843–44
3:13	799–800, 802, 843–46, 849
3:15	414, 415, 890
3:16	413, 559
3:17–21	1057
3:19	930
4:7	137
4:10	844
4:13	799, 802, 843–46
4:14	422
4:15	414, 415
4:16	413
*4:17	608, 1121

Amos

1:1	9, 19, 88
1:2	393, 559, 561, 1081, 1101
2:10	705
3:6	510
3:7–8	573
*3:7	568
3:7	18, 277, 568, 570
3:8	559
*3:13	642
3:13	58, 306, 642
*4:2	567
4:6–13	502, 505, 546
4:6–11	499, 502, 506
4:6	502
4:7–8	502, 503
4:7	392
4:9	502, 503, 527, 529, 532
*4:10	382
4:10	502, 503
4:11	502, 503, 620
*4:13	642
4:13	306, 642
5:1–3	976, 977, 978, 987
5:3	627
5:7	522
5:8	306
5:11	990
5:14	306, 642
5:15	306, 642
*5:16	642
5:16	306, 642
5:18–20	422
5:18	997
5:20	890
5:27	642
6:3	422
6:4–6	990
6:6	815
*6:8	567

6:8	642
6:11	1101
6:12	522
6:14	642
7:1–6	628
7:2	529
7:7–9	604
7:14–17	87
7:14–15	277
7:14	206
7:15	277
7:16	123, 150, 155
7:17	407
8:4–6	990
8:5	396, 766
*8:7	567
8:9	413, 414, 506, 522, 890
8:10	611
8:14	566
*9:5	642
9:5	306, 642
9:6	296
9:9	689
9:10	422
*9:12	229
*9:15	642

Obadiah

1–14	870
12–14	422
15	422
16	833

Jonah

1:1	19
1:2	992, 619, 831
1:3–4	1081
1:9	629
2:1–6	348
2:9	470, 1025
2:10	636
3:2	619, 831
3:3	619, 831, 852, 1160
3:5	766, 1101

Micah

1:1	19, 88
1:3–4	1101
1:4	413, 416
1:7	930, 988
1:18–25	1029
2:11	1027
2:13	977
2:19–20	977
*3:5	486
*3:8	82
*4:3	217, 844
4:7	640, 803
4:9–10	240
4:9	682, 1027
4:10	682
4:12–13	802–3, 844
4:13	800
5:4	478, 653, 950
*5:5	211
5:6	211
5:8	1180
5:13	541
5:18	1118, 1119, 1133
5:20	1222
5:22	1066
5:38–42	993
*6:2	123, 150

6:2	995
6:4	620
6:5	147
6:10–12	990
6:11	396
6:24	990
7:1–2	993
7:6	957, 1223
7:14	210
7:18	741, 875

Nahum

1:1	88
1:2	870
1:4	706, 891, 956, 1119
1:5	413, 416
1:6	423
3:4–7	988
3:4	929, 930, 931, 988, 1010
*3:5	642
3:5	306, 957

Habakkuk

1:1	19, 88
*1:6	1099
1:6	416
1:9	1095
2:3	568
2:5	401
2:6	997
2:12	997
2:15–16	833
2:18–19	542
2:19	217, 997
2:20	508
3	1057
3:4–15	1101
3:8	707, 1119
3:9	394, 1049
*3:11	559
3:11	890, 1049
3:12	803, 844
3:13	707
3:15	668, 707, 929

Zephaniah

1:1	19, 1117
*1:7–18	231
1:7	507
1:14–18	422
1:14–16	510, 519
1:14	421
1:15	413, 870, 890
1:16	510
1:18–2:2	1117
1:18	240, 644, 870
2:1–5	109
2:2–3	422, 644, 870
2:2	422
2:5	997
2:9	620
2:13	986
2:14	986
3:6	997
3:8	870, 1117
*3:13	823
3:13	1034
3:14–20	109
3:20	1155

Haggai

1:12–13	111

2:6–7	413, 518
2:6	240
2:17	902
2:21–22	413
2:21	518
2:23	453

Zechariah

1–8	473
1–6	15
1:1	19
*1:2	643, 910
1:6	18, 570
1:7–11	390
1:8–11	424
*1:8	381
1:8	390
*1:10	471
1:11–17	393
*1:14	910
*1:15	910
1:16	1167
1:18–21	757
2:1–5	604
2:1–4	757
2:1–2	604
*2:1	280
2:1	1111
2:2	1160
2:3–5	392
2:4–5	1167
*2:5	280, 286, 524, 656
2:5	604
*2:6	1160
2:6	450
*2:8–9	1167
2:10	1168
2:11	1173
2:13	507
3:1–7	277
3:1–5	222, 313
*3:1	700
3:1	613, 697, 701
3:2	697
*3:4	471
3:4	93, 222, 599, 611
*3:8	350
4	89, 586, 612
4:1–14	89, 585, 631
4:1–10	314
4:1–2	117
4:2–3	612
4:2–14	579
4:2	89, 227, 295, 353
4:3	89, 586, 612
4:6	227
4:10	89–90, 227, 353–54
4:11–14	89
4:11	612
4:14	586, 612
*5:1–5	843
5:1–5	843
*5:1	280, 844, 987
5:1	844
*5:4	550
*5:9	280
6:1–8	390, 424
6:1–3	390
*6:1	280
*6:2	381
6:2	396
*6:3	401
6:3	393, 400
6:5	450, 613
6:6	396

*6:7	401
6:7	400
6:9–14	599, 611
*6:12	350
7:3	66
*7:9	972
*8:2	910
*8:3	244
8:3	1168
8:7	1155
8:8	1111
*8:16	972
8:20–23	238, 876
8:22	362
9–14	lxxvii
9:1	460
*9:7	936
9:13	137
9:14–15	510
9:14	85, 519
9:15	879, 887, 1063
*10:3	642
11:5	258
12:1–9	422, 896, 1047, 1064, 1095
12:2–6	595
12:2	833
*12:3	608
12:10–12	52, 461
*12:10	clxxxii, 51, 55
12:10	lii, 56, 59
*12:11	858, 899
12:11	899
12:12	56
12:13	1065
13:1	1176
13:4	611
13:7	477
13:17	1061
14	448, 449, 450
14:1–21	422
14:1–14	cxx
14:1–11	1047, 1179
14:1–5	449, 1179
14:2–4	847
14:2	896, 898, 1064, 1065, 1095
14:4–5	803
14:4	416
*14:5	277
14:5	420, 836, 1098
*14:8	479
14:8	1176
*14:9	639
14:11	1178, 1179
14:16–21	449
14:16–19	449

Malachi

*1:1	111
1:3–4	986
*2:7	111
*2:16 (MS A)	642
*3:1	111, 235
3:2	423
*3:5	550
3:13–24	422
3:16	225, 1102
3:22	872
3:23–24	626
3:23	422
4:1	1061
4:4	872
4:5	421, 599, 626

The New Testament

Matthew					
		8:12	890	13:24–30	802, 844–45
		8:13	627	13:30	802, 844
1:1	351	8:19–20	813	13:33	397
1:6	351	8:19	485	13:35	744, 748
1:18	682	8:27	628	13:36–43	801–2, 844–45
1:20	280	8:29	22	13:38	845
1:23	cxc, ccvii, 682	8:31	542	13:39	748, 801, 843, 845
2:2	213	9:2	cxc, 784	13:40	199, 748
2:3	439	9:3	744	13:41–42	1219
2:6	478	9:4	206	13:42	1066
2:10	213	9:5	604	13:43	99, 150–51, 155, 557, 802, 844
2:11	308, 623	9:8	994	13:46	clxxxvii, 324
2:13	280	9:9	907	13:49	748
2:15	706	9:15	1030	13:50	1066
2:19	280	9:16	368	14:25	907, 1235
3:2	803, 844	9:17	cxc	14:27	100–101, 158
3:7–10	lxxvi	9:18	1089	15:2	287
3:7	870	9:24	535	15:3–4	711
3:11–12	clxvii, 229, 802, 844	9:27	351	15:11	895
3:12	800–801	9:28	888	15:15	471
3:16–17	211	9:35	825	15:18	895
4:1–11	736	9:37–38	800, 802, 844	15:22	351
4:3	211	10:1	lxiv, 1157	15:24	477
4:4	895	10:2	lxiv, 144–45, 1158	15:26	1223
4:5	608	10:11	229, 1190	15:27	888
4:7	57	10:15	422, 620, 828	15:31	994
4:8	638, 736	10:16–23	474	15:36	640
4:9	308	10:18	574	16:1	679
4:10	57	10:19	cxc, 627	16:2	287
4:23	825	10:22	146, 1039	16:3	679
5:2	744	10:28	158	16:4	599
5:3–12	11, 838	10:29	clxxix	16:7	212
5:3–10	788	10:31	158	16:13	825
5:3	161	10:32–33	184, 1039	16:14	601
5:4	cciii, 528	10:32	cxxvi, 212, 225–27, 264–65	16:16	102, 454
5:6	cciii, 528	10:33	212, 237	16:18	1157
5:7	cciii, 528	10:37–38	811, 822	16:19	66, 235, 244
5:9	cciii, 528	10:38	813	16:21	623
5:11–12	163, 610, 886	10:39	703	16:24–25	813
5:12	645	10:42	766	16:25	703
5:15	cxc, cxciii, 617, 784, 855	11:1	lxiv, 1157	16:27	207, 693, 1219
5:17–20	711	11:2–6	570	17:2	99, 223, 468, 557
5:23	146	11:2–3	373	17:3–4	600
5:23–24	405	11:2	209	17:4	471
5:33–37	567	11:4	599	17:5	625, 841
5:34–35	566	11:5	825	17:6	628
5:35	566	11:9	56	17:9–13	599
5:38–42	835	11:11–13	599	17:10–13	610
5:39	409	11:14	602, 610	17:10–12	599
5:44	409	11:15	cxxvi, 150–51, 155, 264, 990	17:11	clxxxv, 50
5:48	220	11:21	611	17:14	clxxiii, 66
6:4	206	11:22	422, 828	17:17–19	530
6:6	206	11:23	620	17:17	158
6:9–21	161	11:24	422, 620, 828	17:20	416
6:13	245	11:25–27	12	17:21	895
6:18	206	11:25	471, 629, 828	17:23	623
6:24	258, 990	11:26	clxxvi	17:24	171
7:1–2	993	11:27	212, 364	17:27	cxc, 784
7:6	957, 1223	12:4	877	18:3	1222
7:11	623	12:23	351	18:4	995
7:12	325, 998	12:24	535	18:6	clxviii, 430, 766 1008
7:15–23	143	12:27	191	18:8	1026
7:15	145, 753, 757, 894	12:36	422, 828	18:9	1066
7:16	cxc	12:38	471	18:10	110, 766
7:21	212, 1222	12:40	199	18:12–14	478
7:24–27	20	12:43	986	18:12	clxxix
7:24	11, 23, 710	12:50	212	18:16	602
7:26	11, 23	13:9	cxxvi, 150–51, 155	18:20	229
7:27	1223	13:14	21	18:23–35	17
8:11–12	1033	13:17	887	18:23	17
8:11	1033, 1063	13:19	264	18:26	17, 308, 1027

18:27 — 17
18:28 — 17
18:32 — 17
18:35 — 324
18:44 — 222
19:5 — 859
19:7 — 345
19:12 — 150, 769
19:17–19 — 711
19:17 — 237, 709, 711, 837
19:21 — 220
19:23–24 — 990, 1222
19:27–29 — 822
19:28–30 — 277
19:28 — cxxvi, 261, 264, 292, 362, 436, 461, 813, 1085, 1116, 1157, 1158
19:29 — 811, 822
20:1–16 — 397
20:3 — 952
20:5 — 952
20:6 — 952
20:9 — 952
20:17 — lxiv, 1157
20:19 — 623
20:20–28 — 601
20:22–23 — 833
20:28 — 46
20:29 — 429
20:30 — 351
21:5 — 804
21:8 — ccv, 469
21:12–13 — 606, 1166
21:12 — 606
21:18–21 — 409
21:19 — 907
21:23 — 287
21:25 — 244
21:33–51 — 17
21:34–36 — 17
21:35 — 617
21:42 — 859
22:1–14 — 811, 822
22:1–10 — 1032
22:1 — 471
22:13 — 890
22:14 — 955
22:16 — 235
22:23–33 — 822
22:23–24 — 83
22:32 — 100
22:34 — clxxix
22:36–40 — 711
22:37 — 57
22:38 — 325
22:43 — 283
22:49 — 146
23:5 — 767
23:12 — 995
23:13 — 1222
23:16 — 877
23:17 — 877
23:18–20 — 405
23:21 — 185, 877
23:26 — 56, 839
23:30–31 — 802
23:31–35 — 406
23:34–36 — 610
23:34 — clxxiii, 886
23:35 — 405, 621, 1011
23:37–39 — 610, 886
23:37 — 232, 617
24 — 730
24:2 — 594
24:3 — 679, 748

24:4 — 1083
24:5 — 100, 730
24:6–28 — 473
24:7 — 400, 518
24:8 — 240
24:9–22 — 440, 474
24:9 — cxc, 688
24:11 — 144–45, 894
24:14 — 394, 688, 825–27
24:15–31 — 239
24:15–22 — 691
24:15 — ccv, 745 936
24:16 — 420
24:21 — 474, 900
24:23 — 679
24:24 — cxcviii, 679, 720, 730, 752–53
24:27 — 199
24:29 — 413, 415, 424, 890
24:30–31 — 801, 843
24:30 — cxxvi, 52, 55–56, 213, 264
24:31 — 436, 450, 510, 519, 693, 845
24:33 — cxxvi, 264
24:34 — 1133
24:35 — 1119
24:36 — 952
24:37 — 199
24:38 — 199
24:42–44 — 221, 227
24:42–43 — cxxvi, 264
24:43–44 — 265
24:43 — 265
24:44 — 952
24:45–51 — 17
24:45 — 17
24:46 — 17
24:48 — 17
24:50 — 17, 952
25:1–13 — 1030
25:8 — clxxiii
25:10 — 1032
25:13 — 227, 952
25:27 — 785
25:29 — 150
25:30 — 890
25:31–46 — 277
25:31 — 1219
25:32 — 477, 688
25:34 — 748
25:41 — 409, 1026, 1066
26:3 — 287
26:20 — lxiv
26:21 — clxxix
26:22 — 100
26:25 — 100
26:26 — 572
26:29 — 788, 1033
26:31–32 — 477
26:31 — 478
26:45 — cxciv
26:47 — 287
26:48 — 679
26:52 — cxxvi, 264–65
26:53 — cxciii, 693
26:57 — 287
26:59–60 — 602
26:61 — 594
26:63 — 102, 454, 566
26:64 — 55, 625, 788, 840–41
26:65 — 744
26:69 — 485
26:74 — 567
27:1 — 287
27:3 — 287
27:11–14 — 37, 1038
27:12 — 287

27:20 — 287
27:22–23 — 162
27:25 — 408
27:33 — 847
27:34 — 856
27:40 — 594
27:41 — 287
27:45 — 890, 952
27:46 — 220
27:48 — clxxix
27:51 — 518, 627
27:53 — 608
27:54 — 628
27:57–61 — 617
27:60 — 623
27:66 — 346
28:1 — 379
28:2 — 518
28:3 — 223, 293, 468
28:4 — 100, 1035
28:5 — 471
28:10 — 158
28:12 — 287
28:18–20 — 333
28:18 — 12, 364
28:19 — 688
28:20 — 748

Mark
— 265
1:2 — 610
1:6 — 611
1:7 — clxvii, 229
1:10–11 — 211
1:10 — 656
1:11 — 656
1:14–15 — 570
1:14 — 825
1:15 — 21, 828
1:19 — cci
1:24 — 235
1:27 — 628
1:32 — cxc
2:3 — cxc
2:5 — cciii
2:7 — 744, 875
2:9 — 604
2:11 — 604
2:12 — 628, 994
2:15 — cxciv
2:18 — 784
2:20 — 1030
2:26 — 877
3:1 — 653
3:3 — 604
3:11 — 627
3:14 — 144
3:17 — 244
3:22 — 535
3:23 — 1072
3:30 — 144
3:32 — cxc
4:9 — 150–51, 155
4:20 — cxciii
4:21 — 855
4:23 — 150–51, 155, 787
4:27 — cxciv, 910
4:29 — 800, 802, 842–44
4:41 — 628, 910
5:5 — 302
5:10 — 986
5:15 — cxciii
5:18–19 — cxcii
5:21 — 429
5:26 — cxcii

5:31	cxcii	10:42	1234
5:35	clxxiii, cxc	10:45	46
5:36	158	10:47–48	351
5:42	628	10:49	605
6:7	145, 1158	11:8	469
6:14	cxc	11:14	471
6:15	613	11:15–17	606
6:17	1082	11:15–16	606
6:19	cxcii	11:15	1166
6:21	1064	11:17	688
6:23	567	11:25	146
6:30	145	11:27	287
6:33	cxcii	11:29	clxviii, 430, 485
6:38–41	530	11:30–31	244
6:39	400	12:2	clxxiii
6:43	clxxiii, cxc	12:8	622
6:45	cci	12:12	cxcii
6:50	cxxviii, clxxiv, 64, 100–101, 158	12:13	cxc, 711
6:51	628	12:18–27	822
6:56	785	12:19	cxcii, 1099
7:1–23	194	12:23	cxcviii
7:3	287	12:24–25	822
7:5	287	12:25	656
7:9–10	711	12:28–31	711
7:15	895	12:28	clxxix, 379
7:16	150	12:29	57
7:18	972	12:35–37	351
7:19	895	12:35	351, 471
7:20	895	12:40	996
7:21–22	544	12:42	ccvii
7:21	895	13	lxxxix, cxxii, cxxxiii, 276, 394, 730, 753
7:23	895	13:2	594, 1167
7:24	cxcii	13:3–8	424
7:25	clxvii, 229	13:5–6	394
7:32	cxc	13:6	100–101, 730, 753, 1083
8:3	287	13:7–20	239
8:6	640	13:7–19	473
8:11	679	13:8	240, 400, 518
8:16	cxcii	13:9	clxvii, 229, 574, 900
8:17	653	13:11	1039
8:22	cxc	13:13	146, 444
8:24	cxciii	13:14–20	691, 706, 977
8:25	cxciii, 617	13:14	ccv, 420, 745, 749, 753, 768–69, 936, 941
8:28	265		
8:31	623	13:19	273
8:34–35	813	13:21–23	759
8:34	cxciii	13:22	145, 679, 730, 752–53, 894, 1083
8:38	227, 693, 836		
9:2	223	13:24–27	424
9:3	clxvii, 229, 468	13:24–25	413
9:4–5	600	13:24	424, 890
9:5	471	13:25	415, 656
9:7	clxxix	13:26–27	801–2, 843
9:8	cxc	13:26	cxc, 55, 625, 840–41
9:11–13	599, 610	13:27	436, 450, 845
9:14	429	13:29	cxxvi
9:15	ccv	13:31	1119, 1133
9:18	cxcii	13:32	801
9:31	623	13:33–37	227, 250, 261, 264
9:34	1104	14:8	clxxix
9:38–41	191	14:12	cxc, 361
9:39	cxciii	14:22	572
9:42	766, 1008	14:25	1033, 1235
9:43	1026, 1066	14:27–28	477
9:48	1026, 1066	14:27	478
10:4	345	14:36	clxxvi, 833
10:13	cxc	14:43	287
10:19	711	14:49	cxcii
10:24	471	14:53	287
10:28–30	822	14:56	cxcii
10:29	811, 822	14:58	379, 594
10:34	623	14:59	cxcii, 1038
10:35–40	601	14:62	55, 100, 625, 840–41
10:38–39	833	14:71	567
10:38	856		

15:1–5	37, 1038		
15:1	287		
15:12–14	162		
15:12	471		
15:16	ccvii, 325		
15:22	847		
15:25	cxciv		
15:27	cxc		
15:29	162, 594		
15:33	890		
15:34	clxxvi, 220		
15:36	516		
15:42–47	617		
15:43	clxxxi, 581		
16:2	379		
16:5	223, 293, 468		
16:9–20	689		
16:9	379		
16:11	161		
16:18	628		
16:20	679		

Luke

1–2	602		
1:5	289		
1:8–10	514		
1:8	289		
1:12	624		
1:13	158		
1:16	57		
1:17	83, 283, 599, 610		
1:19	clxx, 35, 100, 472, 509, 551, 826		
1:26	382		
1:27	382		
1:28	clxxxi, 581		
1:30	158		
1:32	351		
1:33	640		
1:35	235, 472		
1:46–55	317		
1:59	cxciv, 550		
1:65	624		
1:69	351		
1:71	clxxix		
1:72	677		
1:77	230		
2:1	736		
2:4	351		
2:7	38		
2:9	628		
2:10	158, 826		
2:13	ccv, 693		
2:21	cxciv, 550		
2:25	382		
2:26	639		
2:27	83, 283		
2:28–30	cxxxvi		
2:29–32	317		
2:29	17, 407		
2:37	302		
3:7–9	lxxvi		
3:7	870		
3:16	clxvii, 229, 472		
3:17	clxvii, 229, 800–801, 803, 844		
3:18	clxx, 551		
3:21–22	211, 666		
3:31	351		
4:1–13	735		
4:1	83, 283, 666		
4:5–8	736		
4:6	736		
4:12	472		
4:16–30	570		
4:21	345		

4:22	895	10:12	620, 800
4:25	610, 615, 621	10:13	611
4:29	607	10:18	415, 525, 695-97
4:33	895	10:19	697
4:34	235	10:20	224
4:36	628	10:21-22	11
5:1	cxciii, 617	10:21	clxxvi, 629, 828
5:5	472	10:24	887
5:10	158	10:25	clxxix
5:12	clxviii, 430	10:27	703
5:17	clxviii, 430	10:32	212, 786, 1157
5:23-24	605	11:4	245
5:35	1030	11:13	623, 1234
6:8	605	11:15	535
6:20-23	11, 838, 1219	11:19	191
6:20-21	788	11:20	23
6:20	161, 990, 1219	11:24	986
6:22-23	610, 886	11:26	185
6:23	645	11:28	cxxvi, 11, 20, 237, 264-65
6:24-25	990	11:30	199
6:26	894	11:37	clxxxv
6:27-31	835, 993	11:40	322, 339
6:37	993	11:44	cxciii, 855
6:44	cxc	11:45	clxxxv, 1007
6:47-49	20	11:47-51	163
6:47	11, 23	11:49-51	610
6:49	11, 23	11:49	clxxiii, 471, 886 1007
7:3	287	11:50-51	621
7:4	309	11:50	748
7:5	165	11:51	56, 405, 839
7:16	570, 613, 628	11:52	66
7:18-23	373	12:1	161
7:21	627	12:5	56
7:22	825, 990	12:6	clxxix, 530
7:26	56	12:8-9	184
7:40	clxxxv	12:8	cxxvi, 225-27, 264
8:4	429	12:9-10	237
8:8	150-51, 155	12:11	cxc, 518, 574, 1039
8:12	clxvii, 229	12:12	627
8:13	231	12:13	990
8:15	150	12:16-25	990
8:16	855	12:20	cxc, 784
8:20	cxc	12:21	150
8:21	20	12:28	265
8:34-35	cxc	12:30	638
8:35	clxx, 551, 628	12:33-34	161
8:41	382	12:35-38	cxxvi, 250-51, 264
8:47	628	12:35-37	261
8:49	clxxiii, clxxxv	12:35ff.	cxxvi
8:50	158	12:36	1032
9:1	lxiv, 1157	12:37	250
9:3	750	12:39-40	cxxvi, 221, 227, 264
9:6	227	12:40	222
9:8	599	12:41-46	17
9:12	ccv	12:43	clxvii, 17, 229
9:17	cxc	12:45	17
9:19	599	12:46	17
9:20	639	12:47	20
9:22	287, 624	12:48	cxc
9:23-24	813	12:54-55	clxxxv, 50
9:24	703	13:8	clxxxv, cxcviii
9:26	265, 836	13:9	150
9:29	223, 468	13:13	628
9:30-33	600	13:16	47, 717
9:34-45	625, 841	13:17	628
9:36	cxc	13:19	859
9:41	clxxxi, 580	13:21	397
9:43	628	13:24	236
9:46	clxxxi	13:28	cci, , 607 1033
9:49-50	191	13:29	cxc, 1033, 1063
9:54	759-60	13:33	620, 631
9:57-58	813	13:34-35	610, 886
9:57	813	13:34	617
10:2	802, 844	14:3	471
10:3	368, 558	14:8	1032

14:10	cxcvi, cxcviii, 158, 381
14:11	995
14:15-24	811, 822
14:15	1032, 1033, 1063
14:18-19	653
14:20	811
14:26-27	811
14:26	822
14:27	813
14:33	972
14:35	cxc, 150-51, 155
15:4-7	478
15:4	clxxix
15:16	516
15:18	244
16:4	cxc
16:7	clxxxv
16:9	cxc, 999
16:17	1118, 1133
16:19-31	835
16:21	1223
16:22	411, 1103
16:23	clxxxv, 835
16:24	1043
16:29	clxxxv, 600
17:2	clxviii, 430, 766
17:18	628
17:20-37	cxxii
17:23	cxc
17:24	199
17:27-28	cxc
17:27	199
17:28	199
17:29	541, 835
17:33	703, 813
17:37	clxxxv
18:1-5	996
18:3	384
18:6-8	411
18:7	302, 407, 475, 853
18:11	clxxvi, 641
18:13	clxxvi
18:14	995
18:15	cxc
18:20	711
18:24	990
18:28-30	822
18:29	811, 822
18:31	870
18:33	cxc
18:34	623
18:36	379
18:38-39	351
18:43	628
19:8	993
19:10	477
19:12	911
19:13-16	530
19:14	1097
19:20	653
19:22	clxxxv
19:23	785
19:37	ccv
19:41-44	1047
19:43	cxciv
19:45-48	1166
19:45-46	606
19:45	606
19:47	606
20:1	287
20:4-5	244
20:10	clxxiii, cxcvi, 158, 381 938
20:27-40	822
20:34-36	822
20:35	810

21:4	150	1:2–3	256	5:17	212
21:6	594	1:3	32	5:20	874
21:8	21, 100, 730	1:4	31	5:22	421
21:11	400, 403, 679	1:6–7	222, 382	5:27	12, 90, 421, 700, 789
21:12–24	440, 474	1:8	31	5:28	1091
21:12	cxc, 394, 574	1:10	55	5:29	1091
21:15	742	1:12	221	5:31	37, 256
21:16	cxc	1:13	973	5:35	612
21:17	146	1:16	clxxiii	5:36	209, 874
21:20–24	691, 1047	1:18	12, 1180	5:43	221
21:20	1064, 1074, 1098	1:19–28	610	5:44	995
21:21	420	1:20	184, 227	5:45	711
21:24	608, 688	1:26	472	6:2	429, 759
21:25	413, 679	1:27	clxvii, 229	6:8	clxxix, clxxxiv
21:26	415	1:29	353, 368–69, 371, 373	6:9	397
21:27	55, 625, 840–41	1:36	353, 368–69, 371, 373	6:11	640
21:33	1119, 1133	1:39	147	6:13	clxxxiv, 397
21:35	786	1:40	clxxix	6:14–15	613
21:36	67	1:42	244	6:14	759
22:3	185, 669, 1072	1:46	380	6:20	101, 158
22:5	287	1:47–48	236	6:23	640
22:6	cciii	1:48	654	6:30	679, 759
22:7	cxc, 361, 371	1:49	211	6:31–34	195
22:15	198	1:51	55, 788	6:31–33	189
22:16	528, 1063, 1235	2:6	222	6:32	212
22:18	788, 1033	2:7	516	6:35	101, 478
22:28–30	264, 277, 813, 1033, 1063	2:11	222, 679	6:39–40	423
22:29	212	2:13	cxciv	6:39	22, 972
22:30	261, 292, 436, 461, 907, 1042	2:18	471	6:40	22, 423
22:37	870	2:19	1168, 594	6:44	423
22:42	833	2:20	717	6:48	101
22:52	287	2:23	759	6:49–51	195
22:66	287	2:24	654	6:50–51	189
22:69	788, 841	2:25	206, 236	6:51	101, 308
22:70	100	3:1	382	6:54	22
23:1–12	1038	3:2	759, 1180	6:57	102, 995
23:1–5	37	3:3	lii, 1222	6:58	308
23:1	ccv	3:5	lii, 1222	6:61	236
23:14	382	3:11	221	6:64	236
23:20–23	162	3:16	46, 972	6:65	528
23:28	clxxxii, 51	3:21	1223	6:69	235, 454
23:29–31	cxc	3:25	516, 528	6:70	clxxix
23:30	362, 420	3:27	244	6:71	clxxix
23:33	847	3:29	220	7:3	cxcvi, 158, 209, 381, 874
23:34	409	3:32–33	221	7:7	37, 256, 809
23:43	154	3:32	37, 256	7:13	407
23:44	cxciv, 890	3:35	12	7:17–18	478
23:47	628	3:36	870, 1062, 1091	7:18	235, 995
23:49	852	4:4–16	1128	7:21	209, 874
23:50–56	617	4:7	856	7:31	cxcviii, 759
23:56	711	4:9	856	7:33	cxciv
24	625, 631, 689	4:10	265, 1129	7:37–38	1128
24:1	379	4:12	1180	7:37	265, 1128
24:4	293	4:14	478, 1128, 1129	7:40	clxxiii
24:5	99, 161	4:16–19	236	7:42	351
24:7	623	4:21	1166	7:49	ccv
24:12	clxxxv	4:23–24	175, 1166	7:50	clxxix
24:19	209	4:23	83, 283	7:57	199
24:21	436, 623	4:24	83, 283	8:12	101, 222
24:23	161	4:27	cxxviii, clxxiv, 64	8:13–18	631
24:25–27	345	4:28	147	8:14	37, 256, 1234
24:26	cxciii, 617	4:29	206	8:17	602
24:30–31	251	4:30	clxxiii	8:18	37, 256
24:36–54	666	4:35–38	802, 844	8:24	101
24:36	clxxxv	4:35	cxciv, 1166	8:28	12, 101
24:39	100	4:39	206	8:38	212
24:46	623	4:44	37, 256	8:41–43	823
24:47	688	4:48	679	8:44	164
24:49	212	4:53	627	8:49	212
24:51	626	4:54	759	8:51	209, 237
		5:2	533	8:52	209, 237, 887
John		5:5	717	8:54	209
		5:6	803	8:55	209, 237
1:1–14	317	5:7	471	8:58	101
1:1–3	1069	5:8	605	9:3	874

9:4	874	13:36	813	19:13	533
9:7	147, 1177	14:2-3	403, 691	19:14-15	162
9:14	381	14:3	clxxxv, 50	19:17	533, 847
9:16	759	14:6	101	19:20	533
9:22	163, 227	14:10	12	19:26	47
9:24	628, 994	14:11	209, 874	19:27	lii
9:34-35	607	14:12	209, 874	19:31-37	617
9:37	clxxiv, 64	14:15	209, 237, 709, 837	19:35	381
9:39	1234	14:19	55, 206	19:37	55-56
10:1-16	478	14:21	47, 209, 237, 709, 837	19:38-42	617
10:2	477	14:23	209, 237	20:1	379
10:4	477	14:24	209, 237	20:2	cxc, 147
10:7-9	236	14:25-26	36	20:6	147, 533
10:7	101	14:30	cxxviii, clxxiv, 64, 613, 639	20:8	147
10:9	101	15:1	101	20:12	223, 293, 468
10:10	212, 1234	15:5	101	20:19	379
10:11	46, 101	15:6	cxc	20:24	clxxix, 87
10:12	477	15:8	cxcvii	20:28	clxxvi, 57
10:14	101, 477	15:9	47	20:30	759
10:15	46	15:10	209, 237, 709, 837	21:1	907
10:17	46	15:11	220	21:7	47
10:23	606	15:12	47	21:9	15
10:24	ccviii, 1074	15:15	12	21:10	clxxiii
10:25	209, 874	15:18-19	809	21:15	368
10:32	209, 874	15:20	209, 237	21:16	clxxiii, 368
10:33	874	15:22	1234	21:17	206, 220, 236, 368
10:37	209, 874	15:24	209, 874	21:18-19	601, 813
10:38	874	15:25-16:2	cxxxvii		
10:41	759	15:26-27	1039	*Acts*	
11:5	47	15:26	cxcviii, 36		
11:17	31	16:2	163	1:1-5	666
11:24	22, 423	16:5	31	1	631, 689
11:25	101	16:11	613, 639, 696	1:3	161
11:26	972	16:13-14	36	1:4	383
11:37	381	16:14	clxxiii	1:5	83, 283
11:41	640-41	16:15	clxxiii	1:6	436
11:47	759	16:17	clxxiii	1:7	801
11:49	clxxix	16:20	859	1:9-10	468, 626
11:52	381	16:21-23	cxxxvii	1:9	625, 841
12:4	clxxix	16:24	220	1:10	223, 280, 293
12:7	197	16:28	1234	1:11	626, 689
12:9	381	16:30	206	1:15	216
12:10	381	16:32	324	1:23	689, 697
12:12	ccv, 429	16:33	349-50, 838	1:24	206
12:13	469	17:2	12, 700	2:2	786
12:15	158, 804	17:3	407	2:3	553
12:18	759	17:5	654	2:5-11	621
12:25-26	813	17:6	209, 237	2:5	621
12:25	703	17:8	12, 221	2:9	29
12:26	813	17:12	534	2:11	379
12:27	clxxx, 231, 1234	17:13	220, 653	2:15	952
12:28-29	561	17:14	12, 809	2:17-18	clxxii
12:31	607, 613, 639, 695-96	17:15	clxxx, 231, 239	2:19	679
12:32	696	17:21	381	2:20	413, 890
12:33	15	17:24	403, 748	2:23	747
12:37	759	17:25	886	2:26-27	210
12:40	cxcviii	18:4	206, 236	2:27	230
12:42	163, 227	18:5	101	2:30-32	351
12:43	995	18:6	101	2:45	785
12:46	972	18:8	101	3:2	cxc
12:47	19, 23, 1234	18:10	147	3:6	191
12:48	22, 221, 423	18:11	833, 853	3:9	628
12:49-50	12	18:12-13	147	3:12	471
13:1	47, 238	18:16	147	3:13	371
13:3	12, 700	18:19-24	1038	3:14	235
13:6	145	18:21	1064	3:15	39
13:12	11	18:26	clxxix	3:18	639
13:16	144	18:32	15	3:20	clxv, 386
13:17	11	18:33-38	37, 1038	3:21	626
13:19	101, 654, 788	18:33	147	4:5	287
13:20	221	18:37	37, 256, 1234	4:8	287
13:21	clxxix, 37, 256	19:1-2	173	4:10	191
13:23	clxxix, 47	19:3	clxxvi	4:21	628
13:27	185	19:6-7	162	4:23	283, 287, 952
13:34	47, 381	19:11	528	4:24	407, 565, 828

4:25–26	210, 419	10:11	clxxxv	14:21	clxx, 551
4:26	639	10:18	697	14:22	1222
4:27	235, 371	10:21	100	14:23	287
4:30	235, 371	10:22	645, 827, 836	14:27	236
4:32	952	10:25	308, 1027, 1035	15	165, 187, 208
4:35	785	10:27	clxxxv	15:8	206
4:36	697	10:28	194	15:9	475
5:3	185	10:30	280	15:12	379
5:5	624	10:31	clxxxv, 859	15:17	688
5:16	ccv	10:32	697	15:19–21	543
5:31	clxv, 386	10:34	744	15:20	186–88, 193
5:32	431	10:35	645	15:22	697
5:33	708	10:40	230	15:23–29	208
5:36	859	10:42–43	19	15:23	26
5:39	220	10:42	421, 644	15:28–29	543
5:42	972	10:43	623	15:28	208
6:1–6	149	10:45	441	15:29	clxxx, 186–88, 193, 195, 231
6:3	287	10:46	379	15:37	697
6:5	149, 155	11:1	441	16:10	clxx, 551
6:9	157	11:3–10	194	16:12	325
6:11	379, 744	11:5	82, 271, 338	16:13	170
6:12	287	11:6	338, 389	16:14–15	201
6:13	744, 746, 1166	11:7	379	16:14	645
6:14–15	149	11:10	1237	16:17	17, 785, 825
6:14	379, 594	11:13	697	16:18	191
7:1–8:3	163	11:18	628	16:37–38	171
7:2	679	11:19–20	441	16:37	171
7:5	199	11:28	clxxxix, 15, 67	16:40	201
7:35	852	11:29	l, 324	17:1	157
7:38	111	11:30	287	17:4	645
7:41	541	12:1–2	601	17:5–9	163
7:42	693	12:2	601, 602	17:6	736
7:44	677, 745	12:6	67	17:13	163
7:45	clxv, 386	12:7	280	17:17	645
7:47–51	1166	12:8	clxxxv	17:22–31	827
7:48	185	12:11	clxxix	17:24	185, 828
7:49	566	12:12	697	17:29	542
7:50	312	12:15	110	17:31	421
7:51–52	163	12:23	628, 995	17:34	629
7:52	610, 886	12:25	697	18–20	155
7:53	111	13:1	697	18:2	203
7:54–60	601	13:5	157	18:5	19
7:54	708	13:6	382, 827, 894	18:6	162
7:55	881	13:9	697	18:7	645
7:56	55, 803, 841, 1060	13:10–11	409	18:8	203
7:58–60	617	13:14	170	18:9	158
7:58	607	13:16–17	441	18:10	100
8:1	l, 149, 474	13:16	645	18:12–17	162
8:10	766	13:19	cxciv, 550	18:14	744
8:17	459	13:20	717	18:15	216
8:20	409	13:22–23	351	18:18	532
8:22	clxxx, 197, 205	13:25	385	18:19–28	139
8:25	clxx, 551	13:26	441, 645, 827	18:19–21	139
8:30	379	13:29	870	18:19	170
8:32–33	371	13:32	clxx, 551	18:24–26	139
8:32	353, 368, 373	13:33	201, 210–11	18:26	139, 170, 203
8:35	744	13:35	230	19	140
8:36	clxxxv	13:43	645	19:1–40	140
8:39	690	13:44–52	163	19:1–7	cxi, 140
8:40	clxx, 551	13:45	162	19:1	139
9:1–9	163	13:48	628–29	19:6	459
9:5	100, 1166	13:50	645	19:8	139–40, 170
9:6	573	14:1–7	163	19:10	lviii, 140, 250, 441
9:13	359	14:1	157, 170	19:11–20	140, 191
9:15	574	14:8	379	19:12	895
9:22	852	14:2	162	19:15	210
9:24	302	14:3	230	19:17	624
9:31	827	14:4	145	19:19	cxc, 553
9:32	359	14:11–15	1035	19:21	83, 283
9:34	191	14:13	174	19:23–41	138–40
9:41	359, 1089	14:14	145	19:23	544
10:2	645, 827	14:15–17	827	19:26	lviii, 544
10:5	697	14:15	102, 454, 565–66, 828, 1038	19:31	756, 774
10:9–16	194	14:19	163	19:35	clxxxv, 138, 155
10:10	82	14:20	1074	19:38	146

Reference	Page	Reference	Page	Reference	Page
20:5	130	**Romans**		10:6–7	348
20:6	530			10:7	526
20:7	84, 379	1:1–6	29	10:11	972
20:16–17	139	1:1	17	10:12–13	441
20:17–38	77, 140, 144	1:3	201, 351	10:12	259
20:17	140, 287	1:5	688	11:1–10	441
20:19	231	1:7	26, 28	11:3	405, 886
20:21	19	1:8–17	641	11:5	441, 628
20:28	140, 478	1:16	441	11:7–8	628
20:29–30	140	1:18–23	543	11:7	441, 460
20:29	144–45	1:18	870, 1062	11:16	817–18
20:30	145	1:23–25	188	11:25–32	238
20:31	140, 302	1:32	876, 1132	11:25–27	441
21:5	193	2:1	clxxvi, 1023	11:25–26	107, 629
21:10	clxxiii, 66	2:4	259	11:25	412
21:11	141, 603	2:5	423, 870, 1054, 1091	11:26	804
21:20	441, 467, 628	2:6	207, 1193	11:33–36	317
21:24	cxcvi, 158, 381	2:7	1173	11:33	207, 259
21:25	186–88	2:8	870	11:35	cxciii
21:27–36	163	2:10	1173	11:36	44, 49, 995
21:28	744	2:13	20	12:6–8	202
21:31–33	1064	2:16	206, 421, 423	12:13	359
21:31	66	2:24	744	12:14	409
21:34	1098	2:26	876	12:15	750
21:36	ccv, 179	2:27–28	709	12:17	835, 993
21:37	clxxxv, 1064, 1098	2:28–3:1	162, 164	13:1–2	743
21:39	170	2:28–29	442	13:4	396
22:2	clxxxv	2:29	83, 283	13:8–10	711
22:3	100	3:3	407	13:8–9	711
22:7	379	3:4	823	13:9	544
22:8	100	3:5	870	14:9	161, 644, 1073
22:13	627	3:8	162	14:10	421, 1107
22:17	82	3:19	711	14:15	46
22:20	601	3:20	711	14:17	82
22:24	1064, 1098	3:26	886	14:21	856
22:25–29	171	3:29–30	441	15:11	688
22:25	171	4:11–17	442	15:12	351
22:26–29	1064	4:11	441, 459	15:15	147
23:9	220	4:16–18	466, 467	15:19	232
23:10	1064, 1098	4:20	994	15:25	232
23:12	856	5:3–4	75	15:26	232, 359
23:15	1064	5:3	76	15:31	232
23:16	1098	5:8	46	16:1–2	203
23:17–19	1064	5:9	870	16:2	359
23:18	clxxxv	5:16	876	16:3–4	203
23:22	1064	5:17	363	16:5	818
23:21	856	5:18	859	16:7	145, 203
23:26	26	6:5	1091	16:15	359
23:27	171	7:7–25	711	16:20	696, 1107, 1240
23:28	cxc	7:7–11	711	16:25–27	44–46, 49, 107
24:1	530	7:8	711	16:27	49
24:15	clxxxix, 67	7:12	711		
24:19	146	8:4	876	**1 Corinthians**	
24:24	clxxxv	8:9	82–83, 283		
25:5	clxxxv	8:11	1091	1:3	26, 28, 40
25:8	744	8:15	clxxvi	1:4–9	641
25:13–26:32	574	8:18	67	1:5	259
25:19	146	8:19	1107	1:7–8	1108
25:22	clxxxv	8:21	1116	1:8	421
25:23	1064	8:23	817–18	1:10	952
25:27	15	8:27	359	1:23–24	352
26:6–7	461	8:29	39	1:24	441, 471
26:7	302, 475	8:34	689	1:25	996
26:10	359	9–11	441	1:26	161
26:11	163, 744	9:5	45–46	1:27–28	216
26:22	766	9:6–13	466	2:6–16	569
26:23	39	9:6–8	441	2:7	107, 471, 748
26:24	clxxxv	9:6	441, 442	2:10	207
26:29	100	9:13	46	3:6	185
27:1	clxxvi	9:24–29	628	3:16–17	241, 597
27:2	1005	9:26	102, 454	3:16	1167
27:6	1005	9:27	466	4:5	22, 206
27:10	clxxxix, 67	9:29	364, 620	4:6	722
27:24	158, 573–74	9:33	804	4:8	258–59, 1093
28:15	640	10:4	711	4:9	1158

Ref	Page	Ref	Page	Ref	Page	Ref	Page
4:12	409	14:24–25	206	8:18	6
5:5	421	14:25	206, 308, 1027	8:22	6
5:7	353, 361, 371, 373	14:26	317	8:23	145
6:1–2	359	14:29	59, 144	9:2	clxxx, 157
6:1	146	14:33	359	9:3	6
6:2–3	956, 994	14:37–38	123, 150	9:7	46
6:2	360, 1085	14:38	1214	9:11	259
6:3	1107	15:1	147	10:1	75
6:7	835, 993	15:3	46	11:1	258
6:9–11	188, 1108	15:4	623	11:2	812, 1029, 1030
6:10	1132	15:5	lxiv, 1158	11:3	145, 697
6:20	47, 361	15:7	145	11:5	144
7:1	822	15:9	163	11:13	144
7:19	709, 711	15:15	220	11:14	697
7:22	12	15:20–28	1105, 1107, 1108	11:15	207
7:23	47, 361	15:20–23	39, 1107	11:17	995
7:25–27	811	15:20	817–18	12:1–10	278
7:26	473	15:23	818	12:1–5	318
7:28	811	15:24–28	1109	12:2–4	319
7:29–31	822	15:25	689	12:2–3	152, 154, 279, 404
7:33–34	822	15:26	1103	12:2	655, 690
7:34	811	15:32	139, 155	12:4	562, 563, 690, 809
7:36–38	811	15:50	1108	12:11	144
8:1	186, 193	15:51–52	107	12:17	1072
8:1–13	193	15:52	510, 519	13:1	602
8:4–13	195	15:54	349	13:4	161
8:4	186, 193, 542	15:57	350	13:12	359
8:7	186, 193	16:2	82, 379	13:14	1240
8:10	186, 193	16:3	232		
8:11	46, 542	16:8–9	139	*Galatians*	
9:4	856	16:8	139, 155		
9:5	145, 822	16:9	236, 244	1:3	26, 28
9:13	194, 405	16:10	1132	1:4	46
9:16–17	573	16:15	818	1:5	44, 49, 836
9:18	cxcvi, 158, 381	16:19	203	1:6–9	147
9:21	711	16:20–24	1206	1:8–9	409, 826, 1213
9:25	167, 175	16:20	1206	1:10	13
10:6–8	188	16:22	409, 1207, 1215	1:13–14	163
10:7	856	16:23	1235, 1240	1:17	232
10:11	748			1:18	232
10:14–11:1	195	*2 Corinthians*		1:23	163
10:16	475			2:1	232
10:18	162, 194, 405, 949	1:1	359	2:4	cxcvi, 145, 158, 381
10:19–20	542	1:2	26, 28, 40	2:7–8	441
10:19	186, 193	1:3–4	317	2:9	241
10:20	cxc, 542	1:12	clxxv, 852	2:10	clxvii
10:22	996, 1234	1:14	421, 1108	2:11–18	194
10:23–11:1	193	1:20	44, 56, 839	2:11–14	194
10:28	186	1:21–22	459	2:20	46, 229, 238
10:30	162	1:22	459	3:1	clxxvi, 545
10:32	362	2:2	cxciv, 550	3:2–3	147
11:3	183	2:8	161	3:7	442
11:9	273	2:12	130, 236, 244	3:8	688
11:10	110	2:18	952	3:13	47, 361
11:11	199	3:3	102, 454	3:16	325, 466, 708
11:14	532	3:7	558, 711	3:17	717
11:15	532	3:14	711	3:19	111
11:20	83	3:15	345	3:23	67
11:26	231, 1207	4:4	639	3:28	441
11:29–30	214	5:1–5	410	4:5	47, 361
11:29	1235	5:1–2	1167	4:6	clxxvi
11:32	260	5:1	403, 431	4:17	722
12:1	544	5:2–4	223	4:25	232
12:2	785	5:3	220	4:26	232, 937, 1153
12:3	1039	5:8	403	5:2	75
12:4–6	202	5:10	421, 1107	5:3	711
12:13	441	5:17	1116, 1117	5:7	147
12:23	897	6:4	75–76	5:12	258
12:28	145, 1007	6:9	103	5:14	711
12:29	145, 1007	6:10	161, 259	5:19–21	188
13:2	206, 416, 1080	6:15	165	5:21	1108, 1132
14:6	12, 59, 83, 283	6:16	241, 454, 597, 1111, 1167	6:2	711
14:7	355	6:17	991	6:7–9	800
14:15	83, 283, 543	6:18	58, 642	6:8	1240
14:16	83	7:1	475	6:15	1117
14:19	530	7:5	322	6:16	162, 175, 442, 460

Ephesians		1:22		cxciv, 550	4:16	lxxii, 21, 38, 249, 256

Ephesians

	1:22
	1:23
1:2	27–28
1:3–14	317
1:4	748, 823, 940
1:7	475
1:13	459
1:14	325
1:15	359
1:18	359, 836, 996
1:20	689
2:2	639
2:4	46, 259
2:6	689, 1090
2:11–19	441, 460
2:11	147
2:13	475
2:14–16	317
2:14	605
2:15	273, 711
2:18	82
2:19–22	597
2:19–20	241
2:20	li, 1007, 1008, 1157, 1158
2:22	82–83, 283
3:1	75
3:3–5	82
3:5	83, 107, 283, 1007, 1008, 1158, 570
3:9–10	107, 570
3:9	312, 748
3:17	185
3:18	359
3:20–21	45
3:21	44–45, 836
4:1	222
4:3	82
4:7	19
4:11	145, 1007
4:12	359
4:29	972, 895
4:30	459
5:2	46–47, 238
5:3	359
5:5	972, 1132
5:6	870, 1062
5:8	908
5:11	992
5:14	317, 605
5:18	82–83, 283
5:19	317
5:22–33	1030
5:25	clxxvi, 46–47, 1029
5:27	823
5:28	703
5:33	199, 788
6:1	clxxvi
6:2	711
6:3	cxcvi–cxcvii, 158, 381
6:4	clxxvi
6:5	clxxvi
6:6	13
6:9	clxxvi
6:10–17	617
6:12	639
6:17	98, 182
6:18	82–83, 283, 359
6:22	6

Philippians

1:1	17
1:2	27–28
1:3–11	421, 641
1:6	1108
1:10	421, 1108

1:22	
1:23	
1:27	952
2:2	220, 952
2:5–11	333, 335, 367
2:6–11	317
2:9–11	333
2:9	351
2:10	348, 367
2:15	823
2:16	167, 421, 1108
2:17	883
2:20	952
2:25	6, 145
2:28	6
2:30	431
3:2	957, 1223
3:3	175
3:6	163
3:14	167
3:16	199, 750
3:20	362, 1153
4:3	224
4:14	199
4:19	259
4:20	44, 49, 836
4:22	359
4:23	1240

Colossians

1:1	ccvii
1:2	26, 28, 130, 1108
1:3–8	641
1:4	359
1:6–7	250
1:7	ccvii, 411
1:8	83, 283
1:10	222
1:12–14	317
1:12	359, 836
1:13	201, 231
1:15–20	39, 317
1:15	ccvii, 38–39, 256, 263
1:16	273, 287, 312
1:18	ccvii, 25, 38–39, 41, 256
1:19	185
1:22	823
1:24	1112
1:26–27	107, 570, 1116
1:27	325, 1112
2:1	249–50
2:11	223
2:17	1112
2:19	clxxv, 852
2:23	1112
3:1–3	689
3:1	1090
3:6	870, 1062
3:14	1112
3:16	317
3:18	clxxvi
3:19	clxxvi
3:20	clxxvi
3:21	clxxvi
3:22	clxxvi
4:1	clxxvi
4:3	235
4:7	411
4:8	6, 1240
4:9	140
4:11	1108
4:12–13	250
4:12	13
4:13	130, 249, 263
4:15	249

4:16	lxxii, 21, 38, 249, 256

1 Thessalonians

1:1	26, 28–29, 40
1:2	641
1:3	142
1:4	46, 1108
1:5–10	147, 1108
1:9–10	201, 827
1:9	102, 188, 454
1:10	870
2:6	995
2:9	147, 302
2:12	222, 1108
2:13–14	147
2:14–16	163
2:15	610, 886
2:20	995
3:10	302, 475
3:13	359, 403, 836
4:1–2	147
4:3	188
4:9	147, 711
4:13–18	1107
4:14	403, 614
4:16–17	436, 802
4:16	clxxv, 510, 519, 852, 1107
4:17	625, 690, 845, 1106
5:1–4	1107
5:2	221, 227, 421
5:3	682
5:9–10	46
5:15	409
5:21	144
5:38	1240

2 Thessalonians

1:2	27–28
1:4–5	1108
1:7–10	1060
1:8	516
1:9	clxv, 386, 420
1:10	359, 836
1:11	220
2	730
2:1–12	276
2:1	436, 802, 845
2:2	421
2:3–12	753
2:3	534, 742, 753
2:4–7	730
2:4	740, 742, 745, 755
2:5	742
2:8	730, 753
2:9–11	760
2:9–10	679, 753, 759–60
2:9	421, 730, 735–36, 753
2:8	1060
2:13	47, 785, 818
2:16	47
3:5	76
3:8	302
3:18	1240

1 Timothy

1:2	27–28
1:3	139, 141
1:8–11	711
1:17	44–45, 180, 317, 366, 836, 853, 875
1:20	744
2:2	946
2:6	46
2:9	1122

Ref	Page	Ref	Page	Ref	Page
3:15	241, 325, 454	1:2	22	10:37	568
3:16	83, 112, 283, 317, 333, 689	1:3	231, 317, 689	11:2	290
4:1–5	145	1:5–14	333	11:4	406
4:1	839	1:5	201, 210–11	11:5	599, 626
4:3	821–22	1:6	38	11:10	1153
4:10	102, 454	1:7	202, 451, 846	11:12	466
5:1	287	1:8–9	1047	11:14–16	1153
5:5	302, 475	1:8	clxxvi, 640	11:27	1180
5:8	184, 237	1:12	415	11:28–12:17	cxxxvii
5:10	359	1:13	689	11:28	1003
5:17	287	1:14	35, 110	11:29	1074
5:19	287, 602	2:2	111, 1003	11:30	1074
5:21	34, 112	2:6	90, 789	11:32–38	887
6:1	407, 744	2:7	366, 1173	11:33	735
6:11	clxxvi	2:9	169, 366	11:34	1098
6:13	38	2:11–13	708	11:37–38	706
6:14	237	2:14–5:5	cxxxvii	11:37	611, 617
6:15–16	875	2:18	231	12:1–2	167
6:15	911, 953	3:3	366	12:2	76, 689
6:16	44	3:11	567	12:6	47, 260
6:20	clxxvi	3:12	102, 454	12:7–11	260
6:21	1240	3:21	49	12:11	1003
		4:3	567, 748	12:14	1180
2 Timothy		4:10	839	12:18	437
		4:12–13	206	12:19	510
1:2	27	4:12	98, 182, 1060, 1067	12:22–24	277, 436
1:3	302, 475	4:13	354	12:22	102, 232, 454, 803–4, 1153
1:9–10	107, 570	4:16	309	12:23	39, 224, 227, 644
1:13	852	5:5	201, 210–11	12:24	406
1:18	139	5:7	clxxx, 231	12:26–27	1118
2:5	167	6:1	clxxx, 205	12:26	518
2:8	351	6:2	459	13:2	1035
2:12	214, 237, 261	6:10	359	13:10	194, 405
2:18	49	6:13–17	255	13:11	745, 1098
2:20	407	6:13	567	13:13	1098
3:1	22	7:7	216	13:14	1153
3:8	185	7:12	ccvii	13:15	358
3:13	1083	7:13	405	13:21	44, 49, 836
3:16	351	7:14	351	13:22	6
4:1	421, 644	7:28	211	13:24	359
4:6	883	8:1–5	677	13:25	1240
4:7–8	167, 175	8:1	309, 689		
4:7	838	8:2–5	903	**James**	
4:8	167, 173, 888, 1054	8:2	476, 745, 878		
4:12	139	8:10	1111, 1123	1:1	17, 441, 442, 460
4:14	207, 993	8:11	766	1:2–4	155
4:17	688, 735	9:1–14	1166	1:3	76
4:18	44, 49, 836	9:2	745	1:12	175
4:19	203	9:3	745	1:18	818
4:20	77	9:4	677, 711	1:22	20
		9:6	745	1:27	996
Titus		9:7	745	2:2	165
		9:8	745	2:5	161, 259
1:1	17	9:11–12	476	2:7	744
1:2–3	107, 570	9:11	878	2:8	711
1:4	27	9:12	745	2:10	711
1:5	141	9:13–14	373	2:20	clxxvi
1:16	184, 237	9:13	475	2:21	405
1:22	823	9:14	102	4:10	995
2:9	407	9:15	clvi	4:15	cxciv, 550
2:14	45–46	9:21	745	4:17	621
3:15	1240	9:22	475	5:1	clxxv
		9:24	677, 745	5:3	22
Philemon		9:25	745	5:10	887
		9:26	748	5:11	852
3	27	10:1	cxc	5:12	566, 567
4	641	10:2	785	5:13	317
5	359	10:7	clxxvi	5:14	287
7	359	10:8–22	cxxxvii	5:17	198
8–9	75	10:12	689	5:20	clxxx, 231
10	140	10:19	475		
11	6	10:22	1220	**1 Peter**	
		10:23	184		
Hebrews		10:28	602	1:1	442, 829
		10:29–11:13	cxxxvii	1:2	26, 475
1:1	1003	10:31	102, 454	1:3–5	317

1:5 22
1:6 231
1:6–7 155
1:7 220, 1173
1:17 207, 227, 362
1:18–20 747
1:18–19 361, 371
1:18 47, 361
1:19–20 747
1:19 353, 368–69, 475, 823
1:20 22, 107, 570, 748
2:4–10 241
2:4 1081
2:5 48, 597
2:6 804
2:9–10 175
2:9 48, 422, 442, 460
2:11–18 155
2:11 362
2:13 946
2:16 13
2:18 407
2:19–20 835
2:21–25 317
2:21–24 76
2:21 813
2:23 823, 1054
2:25 477, 478
3:1 cxcvi
3:4 ccvii
3:7 422
3:9 835
3:10 703
3:12 354
3:13–4:6 155
3:18 46, 1083
3:19–20 1103
3:20 689
4:4 162
4:5 644
4:11 44–45, 49, 836
5:1 287
5:2 478
5:4 167, 173, 175, 477
5:5 287
5:11 44
5:13 829–30

2 Peter

1:1 17
1:2 27
1:9 475
1:12–13 147
1:14 223, 601
1:16–17 1003
1:17 366
1:19 212, 612
1:20 972
2:1 47, 145, 237, 361, 407, 753, 894
2:2 744
2:6 620
2:9 47, 828
2:15–16 186
2:15 185
2:17 890
3:1–2 147
3:1 147
3:2 431, 1007
3:3 22
3:5–7 1117
3:7 421, 828
3:8 413, 421, 901, 1089
3:10 221, 227
3:12 421, 1118
3:13 1116

3:14 220
3:18 49

1 John

1:1 1058, 1069
1:4 220
1:7 475
1:9 227, 475
2:3–5 237
2:3 209, 237, 709, 837
2:4–5 711
2:4 209, 237, 709
2:5 209, 237
2:8 325
2:13 839
2:16 972
2:18 22, 199, 752
2:20 235, 459, 752
2:21 972
2:22 237
2:23 184, 227
2:27 459
3:6 972
3:8 752
3:9 972
3:10 752, 972
3:13 809
3:15 972
3:18 209
3:22 209, 237, 709, 837
3:24 clxxii, 209, 237, 709, 837
4:1–3 144, 753, 894
4:1 145, 894
4:2–3 752, 1039
4:2 227
4:3 227, 752, 894
4:6 1083
4:10 47
4:13 clxxii
4:15 227
4:17 421, 422, 828
5:2 709
5:3 209, 237, 709, 837
5:4–5 839
5:8 859
5:19 639
5:20 407, 722

2 John

3 27
4 clxxiii
7 227, 752, 760
8 645
9 972
12 220

3 John

5–8 155

Jude

1 17
2 26
3 359
4 237, 407
5 147
6 698, 1081, 1082
7 620
9 654, 693–95
11 185–86
13 415, 525, 890
14 363
18 22

24–25 45–46, 49
25 748, 875

Revelation

1–16 xcv
1–3 lxxxi, xc, xciv, cx–cxi, cxxviii, 76, 284, 1148
1 73
1:1–20:13 cxiv
1:1–16:11 cxxxix
1:1–14:16 cliii
1:1–3:22 lxxxvii, lxxxix
1:1–3:21 xlix, 19
1:1–2:1 cliii, clv
1:1–20 cxxxii
1:1–8 xciv, c, clv, 5, 7, 16, 928, 1236
1:1–6 cxxiv
1:1–3 lxxx, cxii–cxiii, cx, cxxxii, 8, 12, 58
1:1–2 c, 3, 5, 6–8
1:1 xlix, l, lxxvii, lxxxiv, cxiii, cxxiv–cxxv, cxxxviii, clxiii, clxx–clxxi, clxxv, clxxvii, clxxxix, cxciv, 7–8, 12–15, 17–18, 22, 63, 75, 106, 282–83, 557, 919, 928, 1019
1:2–3:19 cxxxix
1:2 lxxxiv, cxiii, cxxv, cxxvii–cxxviii, clviii, clxxi, cxcv, 7, 19, 22, 41, 80–81, 239, 383, 1038, 1058, 1069, 1079
1:3–14 896
1:3 liii–liv, lxxv, lxxxvii, xciv, c, cxiii, cxxiv–cxxvii, clxxi, cxclv, 5, 7, 10–12, 20–21, 28, 264–65, 555, 582, 798, 838, 896, 1031, 1073, 1091
1:4–3:22 8
1:4–20 lxxv, 130
1:4–8 cxii–cxiii
1:4–7 cxxxvi–cxxxvii, cxxxix
1:4–6 lxxxii, cxx, 49, 1241
1:4–5 lxxii, lxxiv, c, cxxvii, 23, 25–27, 29, 40, 125
1:4 xlix, lxxii–lxxiii, lxxv, lxxxi, lxxxiv, xciv, cxii, cxiv, cxxv, cxxvii–cxxviii, clxvi, clxxvii, 18, 25, 30–36, 40, 50, 57, 73, 75, 87, 112, 130, 219, 296, 354, 509, 510, 633, 637, 758, 853, 856, 864, 886, 918, 939, 940, 1239, 1206, 1241
1:5–7 cxii
1:5–6 c, 29, 41, 43, 45–46, 51, 237, 366–67, 429, 470
1:5 lxxxvi, cxxv–cxxvi, cxxviii, clxix, clxxi, clxxv, clxxxi, 25–26, 37–43, 45–47, 66, 121, 178, 184, 238, 255, 353, 535, 1038, 1057, 1069, 1157, 1177
1:6 cxxviii, clix, clxxviii, 29–30, 43, 45, 47–49, 73, 116, 236, 261, 362, 442, 631, 805, 836, 1079, 1093
1:7–12 cxx, cxxiv, cxxvi
1:7–8 c, 50, 51
1:7 lii, cxxvi, clxxxii–clxxxiii, clxxxv, 29, 50–53, 55–56, 73, 93, 241, 264, 337, 352, 454, 589, 625, 839–41, 888, 1069, 1089
1:8–20 74

1:8 lxxiii, cxiv, cxxv, cxxvii,
clxix, clxxxv, clxxxviii,
ccviii, ccx, 25, 30–33,
40, 50–51, 57–58,
75, 93, 100–101, 112,
271, 335, 633, 637, 642,
852, 856, 864, 886, 918,
939, 940, 1073, 1111, 1112,
1114, 1126, 1127
1:9–22:20 xciii
1:9–22:9 lxxxii, lxxxiv, c
1:9–3:22 lxxxii–lxxxiv, lxxxvii,
xciv, c, cxii, 51, 60, 67, 98
1:9–20 liv, lxxxiii–lxxxiv, c,
cxiii–cxxiv, cxxx, 60, 65,
67, 70–72, 74, 100, 105–6,
115, 121, 202, 263, 282, 919
1:9–19 71
1:9–11 74–75
1:9–10 lxxxiv, xciii, 71, 116
1:9 xlix, l, lxv, lxxxiv–lxxxv,
xcii, cxxvii–cxxviii, cxxxiv,
clviii, clxiii, clxv, clxix–clxxi,
clxxviii, clxxxix, 9, 18, 25, 41,
69, 73, 75–76, 80–81, 114–15,
202, 239, 383, 406, 474,
703, 1058, 1069, 1086, 1088
1:10–3:22 xciii
1:10–20 71, 282
1:10–11 cxxiv, 69, 282
1:10 lxxxiv, cxxix, clxxxi,
36, 69, 71, 75, 82–83,
85, 87–88, 116, 274, 283–84,
313, 347, 510, 559, 582,
882, 933, 1123
1:11–20 116
1:11 lviii, xciv, xcviii, cxxiv,
cxxviii, clxiii, clxv, clxx, clxxviii,
cciii, 40, 69, 73–75, 85, 87,
105, 109, 116, 120, 160,
234, 344, 838, 1126, 1237
1:12–3:22 cxx, cxxiv–cxxvi, cxxxi
1:12–20 cxxiv, 58, 69, 74–75, 105
1:12–18 74
1:12–16 69, 73, 800, 1047
1:12–13 142
1:12 xciv, cxxvi, cxxviii, clxiv,
clxxxiii, clxxxv, clxxxix, 64, 67,
69, 75, 87–88, 108, 269,
907, 1089
1:13–20 cxxxviii–cxxxix
1:13–16 69, 72, 93, 576, 789, 800
1:13–15 90
1:13–14 cxxv
1:13 clv, clxxxiv, ccix–ccx,
54, 59, 65, 89–90, 92–93,
108, 293, 299, 324, 487, 789,
796, 800–801, 840–42, 849, 879
1:14 cxiv, cxxxiii, clxiv, cxcv,
69, 121, 1054
1:15 clxxiii, ccx, 69, 202, 572, 789
1:16–20 227
1:16 xciv, cxxvi, clxiii–clxv, clxxxii,
cc, ccvi, 69, 98, 121, 181, 271,
299, 321, 340, 490, 551, 557,
784, 789, 895, 1060
1:17–20 70, 74, 282
1:17–18 70–71, 116, 121, 237
1:17 lxxxiv, cxxv–cxxvi, clxiv,
clxvi, clxx, 25, 38, 57,
59, 65–66, 70, 74, 92,
99–101, 158, 161, 166,
271, 1237

1:18 cxxvi, clxvi, clxxi, clxxviii,
clxxxviii, cxciii, cxcv, 43,
53, 66, 100–101, 103–4,
121, 157, 161, 216, 280,
313, 401, 836, 1103
1:19–20 70
1:19 liii, cxvi, cxxiv, cxxviii,
cxxxiii, clxxxix, cxcv, 25, 67,
70, 74, 85, 105–6, 116, 282–83,
488, 838, 858, 860, 970, 1237
1:20 xciv, cxxviii–cxxix,
clxiv–clxv, clxxxii, 65–66, 70–72,
108–10, 112, 116–17, 142,
219, 321, 340, 509, 569,
919, 936, 939, 1030, 1073
2–5 526
2–3 541, 552, 790, 839, 871
2:1–3:22 lx, lxiii, xliv, lxv, lxxii,
lxxiv–lxxvi, lxxxiii, lxxxvii,
xciv, c, cxv–cxvi, cxxxiv–cxxxv,
cxxviii, cxxxii–cxxxiv, cxcv,
36, 40, 58, 66, 74, 87, 105–6,
108–11, 115, 117, 130, 142,
145–47, 151, 158, 183–84,
202, 240–41, 867, 896
2:1–3:21 75
2:1–3:20 70
2:1–7 lxxvi, c, cxiii, 126, 132, 135, 140
2:1 xciv, cxxviii, cxxxii, clxiv–clxv,
clxviii–clxix, ccx, 68, 85, 89,
106–9, 120–21, 134–35, 160,
340, 509, 657, 717, 789
2:2–4 135
2:2–3 109, 122, 142, 155, 213
2:2 cxxviii, cxxxiv, clxx, clxxxix,
cxciii, cxciv, cxcv, cxcviii, 25,
76, 122, 135–36, 142–44, 157,
198, 202, 220, 236–37, 239–40,
633, 646, 753, 831, 839, 1158,
1177, 1224
2:3 cxxviii, cxxxiv, clxiv, clxxxvii,
25, 76, 136, 146, 202, 229,
236, 383
2:4–6 136
2:4–5 142
2:4 lxxvi, cxxxiii–cxxxiv, cxcv,
cxcviii, 120, 122, 126, 135–36,
146, 185, 199, 202, 786
2:5–6 122
2:5 lxxvi, lxxxvii–lxxxviii, cxiv,
cxxv, cxxviii, cxxxii–cxxxiii,
cxxxviii, clxxvi, clxxxv, cxcv, 25, 50,
67, 108, 120, 122, 126, 136,
147, 155, 179, 216, 221, 241,
245, 541, 614, 1054
2:6 cxxxiii, cxcv, cxcviii, 109, 120,
122, 135–36, 140, 143–46,
148–49, 155, 178, 188
2:7 lxxxvi–lxxxvii, cxxv–cxxvi,
cxxviii, cxxxii, clxvii, clxxi–clxxiii,
clxxv, clxxix, clxxxi, clxxxix, ccvii,
36, 109, 123–24, 136, 151–52,
158, 168, 179, 199, 208, 213,
264–65, 324, 516, 645, 702,
730, 749, 787, 859, 1034,
1129, 1177, 1188, 1199
2:8–11 lxxvi, c, cxiii, 126, 156, 159
2:8 lviii, cxxv–cxxvi, cxxviii,
clxv–clxvi, 38, 57, 66, 83, 85,
101, 107–8, 116, 121, 134, 141,
146, 159–61, 283, 509, 717,
789, 1038, 1073, 1237
2:9–10 lxv, 474

2:9 cxxxii–cxxxiii, clxviii,
clxx, clxxx, cxciii, cxcv,
120, 122, 134, 142, 145–46,
159–60, 164–65, 170, 207,
236–37, 460
2:10 lxv, lxxxv, lxxxviii, cxxv,
cxxxii, clxx, clxxii–clxxiii,
clxxv, clxxxviii–clxxxix, clxxxvi,
clxxxix, cxcvi–cxcvii, 37,
53, 67, 109, 120, 122, 159,
163, 167, 169, 175, 179, 185,
216, 240, 324–25, 381,
486, 516, 654, 703–4, 1087
2:11 lxxxvii, cxxv–cxxvi, cxxxviii, clxxx,
ccvi, 36, 83, 109, 123–24, 150–51,
158–59, 190, 265, 28336,
398, 645, 702, 730, 749, 1129
2:12–17 lxv, lxxvi, c, cxiii, 126,
155, 176, 179, 183, 213
2:12–13 cxxxvii, cxxxix
2:12 cxxxvi, cxxxviii, clxv, ccvi,
85, 98, 107–9, 121, 134,
141, 146, 179, 189, 509, 717,
789, 1060
2:13–15 179
2:13 lxv, lxxxv, cxxxviii, cxxxxii,
cxxxiv, clxiii, clxix, clxxi, clxxxi,
clxxxiii, ccii, 25, 37, 41–42, 120,
122, 135, 142, 147, 157, 163,
176, 179, 182, 202, 207, 237,
256, 653, 736, 780, 837–38, 1199
2:14–15 143, 148–49, 179, 213
2:14 cxxxiii, clxiii, clxxxv, clxxxix,
cxcv, cxcviii, 109, 120, 122,
146, 149, 179, 186–87, 193,
208, 251, 543, 936
2:15 clix, 109, 120, 143, 148–49,
155, 165, 178–79, 186, 195,
270, 580, 1054
2:16–16:14 cxliv
2:16 lxxxviii, cxxv–cxxvi, cxxviii,
cxxxiii, clxv, clxxi, clxxv–clxxxvi,
clxxxi, clxxxiii, clxxxv, cxcv, 50,
67, 98, 120, 122, 135, 147, 155,
179, 181, 188, 221, 241, 245,
541, 1054, 1060, 1237
2:17 lxxxvii, cxxv–cxxvi, cxxviii,
clxvii, clxxi, clxxiii, cci,
ccvi, 83, 109, 123–24, 135, 150–51,
158, 168, 179, 191, 199, 208, 265,
283, 324–25, 516, 645, 702, 749,
859, 1034, 1129
2:18–29 lxxvi, c, cxiii, 126, 195, 200
2:18 cxxviii, clxix, clxxi, cci, ccvi,
ccx, 85, 96, 107–9, 121, 134,
141, 146, 200, 509, 717, 787,
789, 1054, 1073
2:19–29 957
2:19–21 200
2:19–20 185
2:19 cxxviii, cxxxiv, clxviii, 76, 122,
135, 142, 157, 200, 202, 837,
839, 957, 1030
2:20–24 148
2:20–23 143
2:20–22 120
2:20–21 200
2:20 cxxxiii, clxiii, clxviii–clxx,
clxxxix, cxcv, cxcviii, cciii, 13,
25, 63, 120, 122, 134, 145–46,
149, 165, 178, 185, 187, 193,
200, 207, 237, 251, 543, 698,
936, 1030, 1226

2:21 clxxx, clxxxix, cxciii,
cxcvii, 6, 146, 197, 200, 205, 541
2:22–25 122, 200
2:22–23 200, 214, 1226
2:22 cxiv, cxxxii, clxxxviii, clxxx,
clxxxv–clxxxvi, cxcvi–cxcvii,
53, 122, 143, 158, 197, 205,
239, 486, 541, 614, 646, 831
2:23–24 185
2:23 cxxxviii, clxxxiii, clxxxv,
cxciii, cxcviii, ccix, 100–101,
119, 122, 146, 200, 205, 207,
237, 271, 324, 579, 645, 787,
993, 1102, 1103
2:24–25 200
2:24 cxxxviii, cxxxiii, clxx, cxci,
cxcv, 120, 147, 149, 200, 207,
216, 553, 633, 721, 853, 1054,
1089, 1139
2:25 lxxxviii, cxxv, clxxxvi,
cxcvi–cxcvii, 147, 158, 199–200,
207, 221, 241, 486, 580, 912
2:26–28 151, 200
2:26–27 124, 264, 645
2:26 lxxxvii, cxxv, cxxxii, clxix,
68, 124, 135, 146, 200–201,
212, 382, 700, 702, 807, 1104
2:27 cxiv, clxxv, clxxxi, cxcv, ccviii,
25, 30, 201, 210–11,
271, 477, 653, 688, 858, 860
2:28 cxxxviii, clxiii–clxiv, ccix,
135, 201, 805
2:29 cxxxviii, ccvi, 36, 83, 109,
123, 150–51, 265, 283, 730, 749
3 cxvi
3:1–6 lxxvi, c, cxiii, 126, 214, 217
3:1 xciv, cxii, cxxxviii, clxv–clxvi,
clxviii, cxciii, cxcv, cxcviii, ccvi,
33, 35–36, 65, 85, 107–9, 121–22,
134, 141–42, 146, 157, 216–17, 236,
296, 354, 509, 717, 789
3:2–4 122, 217
3:2–3 cxxvi, 264, 896
3:2 lxxxvii, cxxv, clxviii, clxxxv,
clxxxviii–clxxxix, cxcv, 25, 67,
102, 122, 217, 220, 509, 758, 839,
858, 860
3:3 lxxxvii–lxxxviii, cxxv, cxxxviii,
cxxxii–cxxxiii, clxx, clxxxvii,
cxciv, 67, 122, 147, 158, 216–17,
221–22, 245, 259, 265, 347, 396,
486, 541, 550, 562, 572, 614,
896, 1085, 1102
3:4–5 259
3:4 clxxxiii, cxcii, cxcv, 25, 120,
122, 146, 217, 223, 271, 468,
646, 810, 857–58, 860, 888,
897, 1111, 1220
3:5 lxxxvi–lxxxvii, cxxv–cxxvi,
clviii, clxv–clxvi, 30, 108,
124, 151, 158, 212, 217, 220,
223–27, 264–65, 271, 292,
345, 410, 468, 486, 509, 558,
645, 702, 718, 758, 805, 970, 1102,
1129, 1220
3:6 cxxviii, ccvi, 36, 83, 109, 123,
150–51, 265, 283, 730, 749
3:7–13 c, cxiii, 126, 228, 233
3:7 cxxxviii, cxlix, clxv, clxix,
cxciii, 66, 85, 103, 107–9, 134,
141, 146, 233–35, 509, 717,
787, 789, 1111
3:8 lxxxvii, cxiv, cxxv, cxxxii,

clxvi–clxvii, clxxxix, cxcviii,
53, 122, 142, 157, 233, 427,
657, 720, 911, 1074
3:9–14:3 cxxxix
3:9–11 122
3:9 lxv, cxxxii, clxx–clxxi,
clxxix, clxxxvi–clxxxvii, cxciii,
cxciii, cxcv, cxcvi–cxcviii, 47,
53, 120, 122, 134, 146, 148, 158,
162, 164, 170, 207, 230, 233,
238, 381, 460, 483, 486, 720, 1198
3:10 lxxxvii, cxxviii, cxxxiv, clxxi,
clxxx, clxxxix, cxcviii, 67,
76, 135, 143, 198, 202, 229,
231, 239–40, 410, 579, 646,
716, 758, 787, 810, 831, 932
3:11 lxxxviii, cxxv, cxxxviii, clxxxv,
cxcvi–cxcvii, 50, 53, 59, 135,
147, 167, 175, 188, 207, 221,
233, 1237
3:12 l, lxxxvii, cxxv, clxix–clxx,
clxxv, clxxvii, ccii, 25, 42,
68, 124, 135, 151, 158, 178,
190, 199, 220, 232–33, 241,
243, 382, 475, 597, 645, 702,
718, 805, 807, 877, 919, 1098,
1110, 1120, 1121, 1181, 1191
3:13 cxxviii, ccvi, 36, 83, 109,
123, 150–51, 265, 283, 730,
749
3:14–22 lxxvi, c, cxiii, 126, 245, 247
3:14 lxxxv, cxii, cxxv, cxxxviii,
clviii, clxix, clxxi, clxxxi, 37, 39,
41, 57, 107–9, 121, 134, 141, 146,
247, 255, 257, 312, 407, 509, 717,
789, 1220
3:15–17 248
3:15–16 257, 263
3:15 cxcv, cxcviii, ccviii, 122, 152,
157, 236, 248, 839
3:16–20 122
3:16 clxxxix, ccx, 67, 122, 248,
580, 1111
3:17 lxiii, clxvi, cxciii, cxcviii, 161,
221, 248, 258, 263, 271, 312,
347, 396, 562, 572, 995, 1085,
1102
3:18–20 248
3:18 clxviii, clxxi, clxxx, clxxxiii,
clxxxix, cxciii, cxcvi–cxcvii,
ccviii, 223, 248, 271, 292–93,
410, 897
3:19–4:3 cxxxviii
3:19 lxxxviii, cxxv, cxxxviii, cxxxiii,
cxcv, ccviii, 67, 216, 248, 260,
541, 580
3:20–5:14 cxxxviii
3:20 cxxvi, clxx, clxxiv, clxxxi,
clxxxiii–clxxxix, cci, 53, 248,
250–54, 264, 280, 907
3:21 lxxxvii, cxxv–cxxvi, clxix,
clxxxiii, clxxxix, 30, 42, 68,
124, 135, 151, 199, 212, 248,
264, 277, 284, 332, 335,
369, 382, 473, 645, 689, 702,
805, 807, 838, 1084, 1085,
1177, 1179
3:22 lxxxvi, cxxxviii, ccvi–ccvii, 36,
83, 109, 123, 150–51, 248,
265, 283, 730, 749
4–22 xcii, cxxiv, 552, 790
4–11 cxii
4–9 284

4–7 xciv
4–6 2766
4–5 34, 73–74, 288, 338, 345
4 cxii, 278–79, 288, 351
4:1–22:9 lxxxii–lxxxiv, lxxxvii,
lxxxix, c, cxxii–cxxiii, 266,
274, 278, 282, 805
4:1–22:5 xlix, lxxxvii, cxx,
cxxiv–cxxvi, cxxviii, cxxxi,
19, 76, 105, 115, 148, 541, 836
4:1–19:10 275
4:1–16:21 c, cxxiii
4:1–11:19 cxi
4:1–9:21 lxxxiii, cxi
4:1–8:6 xcii
4:1–8:5 xciv
4:1–8:1 cxxiii, 276, 282
4:1–6:17 74, 276, 278, 450
4:1–5:14 lxxxvii, xcvii, 313, 360,
494, 545, 863, 869–70, 881,
902
4:1–11 cxxxi, 329, 373
4:1–8 cxiii
4:1–4 cxiii
4:1–2 ci, 266, 274–75, 280, 284
4:1 lxxxii, xciii, c, cxii, cxvi,
cxxiv, cxxviii–cxxx, cxxxii,
clxx–clxxi, clxxiv, clxxxiii,
clxxxix, cciv, ccvi, 12, 53, 64, 66,
71, 75, 83, 87–88, 103, 106, 274–76,
280–83, 323, 349, 379, 385, 428–29,
450, 488–89, 510, 582, 617, 624,
633, 789, 795–96, 853, 863, 928,
1052, 1069, 1074, 1100, 1139, 1152
4:2–22:9 cxxx, 275
4:2–7:17 ci, 266
4:2–6:17 275, 278
4:2–5:14 ci, 266, 274
4:2–11 ci, 266, 274, 389
4:2–3 274
4:2 clxv, clxxxi, clxxxv, cc, 34, 36,
53, 71, 82–83, 103, 116, 274, 276,
283–84, 428, 429, 490, 551, 784,
789, 933, 1085, 1100
4:3 ccviii–ccx, 274, 285–86,
539, 548, 1100, 1154, 1165
4:4–7 274
4:4 lxxxvii, clix, clxiv–clxv, clxxxi,
cc, ccix, 223, 259, 270–71, 274,
286, 288, 337, 429, 471, 490,
548, 551, 633, 784–86, 842, 1073,
1085
4:5–6 274
4:5 xciv, cxii, cxiv, cxxix, clviii,
clxv–clxvi, cxcii, 33–36, 40,
88, 227, 274, 276, 294, 296,
325, 354, 483, 484, 509, 510,
517, 551, 661, 678, 758, 859,
899, 902, 919, 1030
4:6–8 cxiii, 274
4:6–7 300
4:6 cxiv, clxiv–clxv, clxxiv, clxxvi,
clxxxiii, ccviii, cccx, 34, 271, 274,
285–86, 322, 339, 381, 510, 758,
784–85, 852, 869–72
4:6b–10 lxxxvii
4:7–8 ccv, 379
4:7 clix, clxiv–clxv, clxxi, ccvi,
ccix, 272, 274–75, 299, 323,
490, 551
4:8–11 275, 288, 315
4:8–10 438
4:8–9 275

4:8   xcvii, cxiv, cxxv, cxxvii,
          clix, clxiv–clxv, clxix, clxxiv,
          clxxix, clxxxiii, cc, ccvi, ccix,
          25, 30, 32–33, 50, 57–58, 112,
          269, 271–72, 275–76, 282,
          286, 299, 301, 306–7, 315–16,
          323–24, 326, 338, 379, 475, 490,
          551, 633, 637, 642, 796, 836,
          852, 856, 858, 860, 864, 874,
          880, 886, 888, 918, 939, 940, 970
4:9–11   cxiii, 338, 367, 970
4:9–10   366 565
4:9   cxxxvi, clxv, clxxi, clxxviii,
          clxxxi, clxxxvi, cxcvi–cxcviii, cciii,
          25, 43–44, 103, 271–73, 275–76,
          284, 312, 324, 326, 366–67, 429,
          470–71, 483, 486, 580, 635, 640,
          809, 836, 912, 970, 1100
4:10–11   275
4:10   lxxxvii, cxxvi, clxv, clxxi,
          clxxviii, clxxxi, clxxxvi,
          cxcvi–cxcvii, 34, 43, 103, 230,
          238, 270–71, 273, 275–76, 284, 288,
          290, 307, 355, 467, 471, 486, 510, 597,
          633, 640, 758, 808, 836, 842,
          970, 1026, 1034, 1074
4:11–12   808
4:11   lxxxiii, lxxxv, xcvii, clxix–clxx,
          clxxvi, clxxviii, clxxxvii, clxxxix,
          cxcviii, 25, 57, 275, 309–10, 315–16,
          336, 360, 365–66, 471, 637, 640,
          642, 970, 981, 1023
4:13   1023
4:14   1073
5   lxxxi, xcix, cxvii, 329–30,
          332–33, 335–36, 338–39,
          344–45, 571, 575, 726, 779
5:1–8:1   lxxxiii, lxxxvii, xciv, xcviii,
          342, 434
5:1–6:17   cxxxi
5:1–14   ci, cxxxi, 282, 319, 327,
          329–30, 333, 389
5:1–11   cxiii
5:1–10   cxlix
5:1–9   571
5:1–8   xciv
5:1–5   329
5:1   xcvii, clxiv–clxv, clxxiii, clxxv,
          clxxxi–clxxxii, cxciv, ccviii, 66,
          68, 276, 284, 304, 324, 327,
          329, 338, 340–43, 351, 354, 558,
          571, 585, 934, 1052, 1063, 1074,
          1081, 1100, 1116, 1120
5:2–5   347
5:2   clxv, clxxxix, 85, 312, 322–23,
          327, 329–31, 335, 338, 347, 354,
          364, 389, 555, 557, 571, 741,
          882, 965, 1044
5:3–7   346, 355
5:3–4   331–32, 342
5:3   clxxxv, clxxxix, 318, 327, 329–30,
          348, 366
5:4–5   lxxxiv, 351
5:4   clxxxv, clxxxix, cxcviii, 327,
          329–30, 351, 364, 427
5:5–14   lxxxvii
5:5–8   cxxxvii, cxxxix
5:5–6   352, 443, 474
5:5   clxiii, clxv, clxviii, clxxi, clxxiv,
          clxxix, clxxxiv–clxxxv, clxxxix, 53,
          221, 259, 288, 312, 322, 327, 329–31,
          333, 347–48, 369, 373, 396, 430,
          462, 562, 572, 633, 702, 789, 838, 853,

879, 1085, 1102
5:6–10   327, 329
5:6–7   329, 333
5:6   lxxxvii, xciv, cxii, cxxix,
          clix, clxiv–clxvi, clxx–clxxi,
          clxxvii, ccvi–ccvii, ccx, 33–36, 40,
          53, 65, 227, 272, 276, 296, 323–24,
          327, 331, 333, 338, 352–53,
          361, 368, 370–71, 389, 551,
          633, 726, 783–84, 795, 854, 870,
          919, 1038, 1157
5:7   clxiv–clxv, clxxiii, clxxxi,
          clxxxvii, 11, 66, 216, 284, 327,
          331, 333, 336, 340, 364, 430,
          516, 557, 643, 726, 1074, 1100
5:8–14   329, 333
5:8–12   355
5:8–10   327
5:8   cxiv, cxxix, clxv–clxvi, clxxi,
          clxxiv, ccvii, ccx, 270–72,
          288–89, 291, 296, 324, 326, 329,
          331, 355–56, 358, 374, 471, 514,
          758, 808, 879, 882, 919, 937, 1010,
          1026, 1051, 1059
5:9–14   315, 374
5:9–12   873
5:9–10   lxxxiii, xcvii, 288, 315,
          327–28, 331, 336–37, 360,
          374, 741
5:9   xciv, clxv, clxxiii, clxxv, clxxix,
          clxxxi, clxxxiv, clxxxix, cxcviii,
          47, 51, 66, 158, 179, 212,
          309–10, 316, 322, 324, 327–28,
          331, 346, 351, 353, 360–61, 364,
          371, 467, 516, 574, 642–43, 726,
          795, 809–10, 814, 818, 1057, 1069,
          1157
5:10   cxxviii, clix, clxx, 47–49,
          116, 214, 261, 327, 442, 471, 617,
          631, 853, 1093, 1181
5:11–14   288, 329
5:11–12   327, 336
5:11   lxxxvii, cxiv, clxv, clxxi,
          clxxvi, cc, 272, 286, 314,
          326–27, 329, 331, 336–38,
          363, 365
5:12–13   369
5:12   lxxxiii, xcvii, clxv, clxxxix,
          cc, ccvi, 85, 269, 282, 309–10,
          315–16, 326–27, 331, 336, 338,
          346–47, 353, 360–61, 364–66,
          371, 965, 981, 998, 1044, 1157, 1173
5:13–14   cxiii, 44, 307, 327, 336
5:13   lxxxiii, xcvii, clxv, clxxi,
          clxxviii, clxxxi, ccvi, 43, 46, 262,
          284, 312, 315–16, 318, 326–27, 329,
          331, 336–38, 348, 365–67, 374, 981,
          1074, 1100, 1173
5:14   lxxxvii, cxiii, clxv, clxxxv, cciii,
          25, 230, 238, 271–72, 288, 307–8,
          324, 329, 331, 337, 970, 1026
6–19   240
6:1–22:6   xcviii, 344
6:1–22:5   lxxxi
6:1–19:10   xci
6:1–8:5   xci, 115
6:1–8:1   lxxxv, xci, xcviii–xcix, cxxiii,
          313, 345, 389, 392, 423, 557,
          571, 863
6:1–7:17   xcix, 344, 507
6:1–7:13   cxxxix
6:1–17   ci, 245, 282, 377, 394, 868–69
6:1–8   ci, 330, 392, 395, 402,

423, 495, 496
6:1–2   380
6:1   xcviii, clxv, clxxiv, clxxix,
          clxxxix, 65, 272, 322, 329, 338, 344,
          483, 559, 560, 582, 806, 863, 1028
6:2–17   240
6:2–8   390
6:2   clxxxi, cxciv, cxcvi–cxcvii,
          cc, ccix, 53, 103, 167, 280, 299,
          323, 338, 381, 382, 385, 389, 411,
          428, 429, 490, 551, 789, 795–96, 801,
          842, 858
6:3–8   380
6:3   clxiii, clxv, clxxiv, cxcii,
          272, 322, 379, 392, 402,
          483, 582
6:4–7   865
6:4   cxxxviii, clxvi–clxvii, clxx,
          clxxxi, clxxxvi, clxxxix, cxciv,
          cxcvi–cxcvii, ccix, 135, 158, 221,
          230, 259, 312, 347, 381, 382, 393,
          486, 559, 562, 572, 720, 786,
          851, 859, 1085, 1102
6:5–8   cxxxvii, cxxxix
6:5–6   395
6:5   clxiv–clxv, clxxiv, clxxxi, cc,
          53, 103, 272, 280, 299, 322–23,
          338, 379, 382, 385, 389, 392, 393,
          428, 429, 483, 490, 551, 582, 683,
          789, 795–96, 858
6:6–14   879
6:6   lxiii, lxx, clxv, clxxi, ccviii, ccx,
          66, 272, 419, 582, 784, 870, 883
6:7   clxv, 272, 322, 392, 420, 483, 582
6:8   cxiv, clxvi, clxix, clxxxi,
          clxxxiii–clxxxv, clxxxix, cxcii, 42,
          53, 103, 198–99, 280, 323, 338,
          382, 385, 389, 393, 394, 419, 429,
          484, 488, 530, 653, 789, 795–96,
          858, 1103
6:9–17   392, 423
6:9–11   lxv, lxxxv, ci, cxii–cxiv,
          cxlix, 176, 410, 424, 443, 780, 838,
          1088
6:9–10   495, 515
6:9   cxxxvii, clviii, clxv, clxx, clxxviii,
          clxxxv–clxxxvi, ccix, 19, 41, 63,
          80–82, 239, 322, 361, 392, 408, 483,
          511, 536, 597, 606, 703, 845, 1058,
          1087, 1088, 1089
6:10–11   82
6:10   clxix, clxxvi, ccvi, 40, 66, 85,
          235, 240, 245, 273, 316, 347, 513,
          795, 810, 882, 888, 965, 1025, 1044
6:11   clxxv, clxxxvi, clxxxix, cxcvi–cxcvii,
          cxcix, 67, 158, 223, 230, 259,
          324, 381, 468, 486, 568, 719–20, 833,
          932, 1089
6:12–17   ci, 439
6:12–14   523
6:12–13   415, 419, 421
6:12   clxiii–clxv, cxciv, ccix, 53, 322,
          338, 379, 389, 392, 416, 419, 483,
          550, 611, 627, 716, 868
6:13   clxx, clxxviii, clxxxiv, ccix, 414,
          418, 653
6:15   cxxxviii, clxv, clxxviii, 13,
          40, 574, 1064
6:16–17   424
6:16   clxiv–clxv, clxx, clxxvii,
          clxxxi, clxxxiv–clxxxv, 262, 284, 369,
          386, 531, 706, 1075, 1100
6:17   clxxi, clxxxix, 420, 828

7   cxvi, 424, 443, 446, 449, 450, 452, 459, 977
7:1-17   xcv, ci, cxxii, 72, 389, 423, 424, 449, 479, 555, 574, 598, 605, 630, 796-99
7:1-12   cxxxi, 72
7:1-8   ci, cxvii, cxx, 240, 245, 449, 479, 529, 796
7:1-7   cxix, cxxiii
7:1-4   805
7:1-3   cxv, 459, 529, 537
7:1-2   884
7:1   lxxxvii, xciii, cxiii, clxx, clxxxiii, cxcvi-cxcvii, 280, 528, 536, 537, 797, 823, 846, 863
7:2-8   455, 459, 530, 780, 796
7:2-3   392, 435, 797, 977
7:2   cxiii, cxxxviii, clviii, clxiii, clxv, clxvii, clxxv, clxxvii, clxxxix, cxcii, 85, 102, 229, 338, 347, 389, 398, 451, 486, 528, 565, 657, 718, 720, 755, 768, 797, 823, 882, 911, 965, 977, 1044, 1072, 1074
7:3-8   cxiii, 596, 598, 604, 804, 848
7:3   cxxix, clxiii, clxviii, cxcix, ccix, 13, 66, 232, 309, 398, 452, 454, 479, 487, 528, 529, 537, 721, 768, 795, 797
7:4-17   437
7:4-8   cxv, cxx, 443, 446, 459, 461, 464, 466, 467, 474, 479, 796, 802, 819, 1154
7:4   cxx, clxiii, clxxi, cciv, 165, 452, 466, 487, 539, 582, 768, 784-85, 795-96, 804
7:5-8   443, 460, 461
7:5-6   465
7:5   clxxiv, 452, 487, 768
7:6   clxxiv, 464
7:7   clxxiv, 462
7:8   clxxiv, 452, 463, 465, 768
7:9-17   lxxxvii, xcvii, ci, cxiv, 278, 440, 466, 473-74, 480, 802, 814
7:9-12   cxii, 277, 315, 480, 796
7:9-10   262, 369, 469, 480, 808, 827
7:9   lxv, lxxxv, xciii-xciv, cxxxi, clxiv-clxv, clxvii, clxix-clxx, clxxxiii, clxxxv, clxxxix, ccii, ccv, 25, 51, 53, 103, 212, 223, 229, 259, 271, 280, 292, 323, 352, 362, 385, 393, 410, 427, 440, 450, 471, 480, 484, 489, 657, 718, 720, 758, 789, 795-96, 803, 808, 858, 873, 911, 1014, 1074, 1139
7:10   xcvii, cxxxi, clxv, clxxxi, clxxxiv, 66, 85, 284, 315-16, 347, 467, 471, 559, 638, 640, 700, 873, 882, 965, 1014, 1025, 1044, 1074, 1100
7:11-12   288, 367, 480, 808
7:11   lxxxvii, cxxxi, clxiv-clxv, clxxv-clxxvi, clxxxvii, 230, 272-73, 286, 308, 352, 355, 363, 464, 510, 597, 633, 640, 758
7:12   lxxxiii, xcvii, clxxi, clxxviii, 43-44, 238, 315-16, 326, 336, 365-67, 429, 470, 471, 640, 836, 429, 470, 471, 640, 836, 981, 1014
7:13-17   lxxxiii, lxxxvi, 16, 72, 480, 796
7:13-14   222, 919
7:13   cxxxi, clxv, clxxix, cxcii, 66, 223, 259, 271, 288, 349, 410,

429, 468, 473, 633, 788, 810, 879, 1220
7:14-17   cxxxviii, 288
7:14   lxv, lxxxv, clxv-clxvi, clxxvi, clxxxi, clxxxvii, cxcii, 47, 76, 237, 239, 259, 271, 273, 324, 353, 371, 410, 466, 472, 645, 788, 810, 827, 839, 1057, 1069, 1157, 1177, 1220
7:15-17   472, 645
7:15   clxv, clxx, clxxxi, 220, 262, 284, 302, 597, 633, 758, 877, 1100, 1104, 1139
7:16-8:12   cxxxviii-cxxxix
7:16   clxiii, ccviii, ccx, 427, 478, 889
7:17   clxv, cxcviii, 262, 332, 352, 369, 431, 474, 477, 812, 827, 848, 855, 1111, 1127, 1177
8:1-22:5   xcix, 344
8:1-11:19   497, 498, 500, 546
8:1-11:14   ci, 480
8:1-9:21   480, 497, 499, 527, 531, 555, 635, 646, 869
8:1-5   cxiii, 869
8:1-4   xcvii, cxxxix
8:1   xcv, xcviii-xcix, ci, clxv, cxcii, ccviii, ccx, 273, 282, 307, 322, 344, 392, 423, 480, 488, 507, 571, 580, 785, 868-69
8:2-22:6   xcviii
8:2-22:5   507
8:2-14:20   xcviii
8:2-11:19   xcii, xciv
8:2-11:18   xciv-xcv, cxxiii, cxxx, 389, 863
8:2-11:14   xciv
8:2-9:21   lxxxv, ci, 392, 423, 510, 519, 541, 568
8:2-13   cxii
8:2-6   ci, 494
8:2-5   lxxxvii, 313, 545, 661, 863, 870, 881, 902
8:2   xciv, xcix, ci, cxiv, clxv-clxvi, cxciv, 35, 40, 109, 219-20, 227, 338, 352, 395, 435, 494, 509, 511, 518, 613, 758, 797, 823, 863, 879
8:3-9:21   lxxxvii
8:3-5   ci, 291, 507, 508, 511, 518, 536
8:3-4   l, 358, 515, 912, 1030, 1072
8:3   clxv, clxxxvi, cxcvi-cxcvii, ccix, 158, 230, 284, 359, 381, 405-6, 411, 435, 467, 483, 486, 510, 514-15, 536, 597, 606, 633, 705, 720, 755, 758, 785, 796-97, 808, 823, 829, 845, 853, 882
8:4   clxiv, clxv, 220, 359, 509, 512-13, 515, 880-81
8:5-9:16   cxxxviii
8:5   cxiii, clviii, clxxviii, clxxxvii, ccix, 216, 294, 324, 405-6, 418-19, 430, 511, 513, 515, 536, 597, 606, 627, 661, 678, 796, 845, 859, 899, 902
8:6-11:15   xci
8:6-9:21   240, 244
8:6   ci, clxv-clxvi, cxcvi-cxcvii, 494, 511, 854
8:7-15:8   xcii
8:7-9:22   868
8:7-9:21   494, 495, 511, 545, 865
8:7-9:19   541, 686
8:7-9:12   cliii
8:7-12   ci, 496, 500, 519, 522, 545, 546
8:7-10   cxiii

8:7   ci, clxiii-clxiv, clxxviii, clxxxi, cxciii, ccx, 25, 379, 418, 495, 498, 500, 519, 528, 546, 637, 868, 976, 1066
8:8-11:19   115
8:8-9   ci, 495, 546, 864, 903
8:8   clxxv, clxxxviii, cxciii, 381, 418, 488, 498, 500, 520, 637, 868, 870
8:9   clxix, cc, ccv-ccvi, 25, 42, 178, 309, 419, 428, 489, 498, 500, 519, 615, 853, 884, 1072
8:10-11   ci, 495, 520, 521, 546, 864
8:10   clxiii-clxvi, clxxi, 415, 418, 431, 484, 488, 498, 501, 519, 637, 855, 976
8:11-12   cxiii
8:11   clxv, clxix, clxxviii, clxxx, cxcviii, 382, 496, 498, 501, 519, 537, 859, 868
8:12   ci, clxiii-clxiv, clxvi, cxcvi-cxcvii, ccix, 270, 419, 454, 485, 488, 495, 498, 501, 519, 546, 637, 866, 890, 976
8:13-9:21   ci, 496
8:13   ci, cxii-cxiii, cxxxii, clxiii, clxv-clxvi, clxix, clxxi, clxxiv, clxxx, clxxxix, ccix, 67, 85, 240, 299, 312, 338, 347, 379, 410, 430, 488, 495, 523, 536, 545-46, 582, 630, 656-57, 795, 810, 824, 882, 932, 965
9   cxii
9:1-17:2   cxxxix
9:1-21   cxii
9:1-12   ci, 495, 546, 890
9:1-11   cxiii, 496, 497, 498, 501, 526, 536
9:1-10   526
9:1-6   497, 529
9:1-2   525, 526
9:1   clxiii, clxv-clxvi, clxxviii, ccix, 66, 318, 338, 348, 389, 415, 488, 496, 534, 536, 559, 637, 696, 976, 1082
9:2-15   cxxxviii-cxxxix
9:2   clxiii, clxvi, 318, 348, 497, 525, 881, 890
9:3-21   240
9:3-11   lxxxvii, 525
9:3-5   527
9:3-4   cxxxviii
9:3   clxv, clxxviii, ccii, 532
9:4-6   438
9:4-5   497
9:4   cxxix, clxiv-clxv, clxxxvi, cxciii, cxcvi-cxcvii, ccix, 158, 230, 1089
9:5   clxxxvi, cxcvi-cxcvii, cxcviii, ccviii, 158, 230, 273, 323, 381, 486, 527, 531, 607, 720
9:6   clix, clxxi, clxxvii, clxxxvi, clxxxix, 158, 217, 158, 496, 627, 970
9:7-11   496, 539
9:7-10   497, 533
9:7-9   532
9:7   cxxxviii, clxiv-clxv, clxxviii, cci, 299, 381, 390, 533, 548, 784, 842, 870
9:8   clxxxv, cci, 532
9:9-10   12
9:9   clix, clxxviii, clxxxv, cci, 531
9:10-17   cxxxvii
9:10   clxxxiv, clxxxix, cxciii, ccix,

398, 497, 527, 533
9:11   cxiv, cxxviii, clv, clxvi,
           clxix–clxx, clxxxiv, 109, 318,
           348, 382, 484, 495, 525, 526, 527,
           546, 846, 899, 940
9:12–21   cxiii
9:12   clxx, clxxxiii, clxxxv, cciv,
           50, 53, 106, 283, 379, 488, 495–96,
           522, 524, 539, 582, 630, 1054
9:13–21   ci, cxxx, 555, 574, 866, 903
9:13–19   495, 497, 498, 501, 547, 892
9:13–16   497, 539
9:13–14   514
9:13   cxii, clxiv, clxvi, clxviii–clxix,
           clxxix, 25, 42, 178, 220, 269,
           397, 405, 406, 430, 485, 488,
           489, 496, 509, 511, 582, 597, 606,
           633, 637, 758, 845, 883, 888, 976,
           1072, 1073
9:14–15   497, 537, 538
9:14   cxii, clxiii–clxvi, clxix, cciv,
           ccvi, 63, 427, 545, 890
9:15–19   890
9:15–16   497
9:15   clxv, cxcvi–cxcvii, 496, 519,
           522, 530, 538, 541, 843, 854
9:16–19   538
9:16–17   cxiv
9:16   clxxi, ccviii, 363, 459, 538, 582
9:17–10:9   cxxxix
9:17–19   539
9:17–18   540–41, 614
9:17   clxiv–clxv, clxxxi, clxxxiv,
           cc–cci, ccviii, ccix, 299, 490,
           497, 536, 551, 580, 835
9:18   clxv, clxxvii, clxxx, ccv, 428,
           484, 496, 519, 530, 537, 538, 540,
           835, 870
9:19–10:1   cxxxvii, cxxxix
9:19   cxiv, clxiv–clxv, clxxxiv, cxcv,
           cc, 299, 398, 490, 497, 551,
           617, 853
9:20–21   419, 495, 498, 501, 541–42,
           545, 711, 827
9:20   clxiv, clxxv, clxxx, clxxxvi,
           clxxxix, cxcvi–cxcvii, ccx, 25, 158,
           197, 238, 273, 381, 486, 541, 720,
           858, 860, 869, 1130
9:21   clxxx, ccviii, ccx, 197, 205,
           427, 541, 630, 728, 1130, 1131,
           1132
10–11   571
10   xcvii–xcix, cxvii, 224, 342,
           557, 568, 571
10:1–11:14   635
10:1–11:13   xcv, cxxx, 499, 568, 588, 630
10:1–11:6   497
10:1–11:2   610
10:1–11   liv, lxxv, lxxxiii, lxxxvii,
           ci, cxix–cxx, cxxii–cxxiii, cxxx,
           100, 547, 555, 568, 574, 630, 646
10:1–7   435, 558, 570, 797, 977
10:1–6   557
10:1–3   ci, 555, 574
10:1–2   ci, 585
10:1   cxi–cxiii, clxiii–clxiv, clxvi, cci,
           ccviii, 99, 271, 292, 338, 347, 429,
           435, 571, 596, 625, 755, 797,
           841, 851, 863, 977, 1072, 1121
10:2–11   558
10:2–3   ci
10:2   lxxxiv, xcix, cxi–cxiii, cxxxiii,
           clviii–clxv, cxcii, cxcv, cc, ccvi,

ccviii, ccx, 135, 299, 321,
           339–40, 490, 551, 552, 555, 557,
           559, 564, 571, 1162
10:3–5   ccii, 559
10:3–4   xciv, ci, cxi, cxiii, 555, 559,
           564, 574
10:3   cxxviii, clxvi, ccii, ccix, 65, 85,
           347, 435, 797, 882, 965, 977, 1044
10:4   cxxviii, clxxxv, clxxxix, cxcii,
           65–67, 221, 259, 312, 347, 396,
           397, 561, 570, 572, 582, 585, 638,
           795–96, 838, 1014, 1027, 1102, 1122
10:5–9   cxxxvii, cxxxix
10:5–7   ci, cxi, cxiii, 555, 574
10:5–6   cxii, 564
10:5   clxiv, clxxviii, ccii, 66, 135,
           349, 429, 556, 558, 559, 585, 1162
10:6–7   568
10:6   lxxxv, cxxvi, clix, clxxi,
           clxxviii, clxxxi, 25, 43, 103, 273,
           307, 312–13, 326, 349, 454, 526, 559,
           565, 566, 836
10:7   cxii, cxxvii, cxxx, clxx–clxxi,
           clxxxi, clxxxiii, clxxxvii, clxxxix,
           cxciv–cxcv, cxcviii, 13, 17, 67,
           106, 247, 273, 307, 454, 555,
           567–69, 638, 785, 825, 852,
           870, 958
10:8–11:2   610
10:8–11   lxxxiv, ci, cxi, cxiii, 115,
           555, 558, 570, 574, 585, 594,
           603, 630
10:8–10   70, 555, 558, 570,
           571, 919
10:8   xcix, cxxviii, clviii, clxiv–clxv,
           clxix, clxxiv, clxxxiii, cxcii,
           cc, ccx, 64, 66, 216, 269, 282,
           321, 339–40, 397, 490, 551, 557–58,
           561, 571, 575, 582, 585, 638,
           784, 796, 807
10:9–10   571
10:9   clviii, clxv, clxviii, clxx,
           clxxxiv–clxxxv, ccviii, 221, 259,
           312, 347, 396, 549, 552, 558,
           562, 575, 788, 790, 1102
10:10–11:3   cxxxviii
10:10–11   575, 585
10:10   clviii, clxiv–clxv, ccviii, ccix,
           97, 354, 549, 552, 558
10:11   liv, xciv, xcix, cxxviii, clxx,
           clxxxii, clxxxiv–clxxxv, clxxxix,
           cxci, 212, 467, 555, 571, 574,
           585, 594, 604, 629, 719, 788, 795
11   lx, cxvi, 571, 601, 608, 610,
           617, 625
11:1–15:4   xcix, 572
11:1–19   585
11:1–18   cxxxi
11:1–14   lx, ci, 574, 575, 582, 646
11:1–13   lxxxiii, xcix, cxi, cxv, cxvii,
           cxix–cxx, cxxii–cxxiii, 555, 568,
           571, 585–86, 588, 590, 593,
           620, 630, 726–28
11:1–3   585, 610
11:1–2   l, lx, ci, cxii–cxiii, 555, 582,
           585–86, 588, 593–98, 603–4, 607,
           610–11, 620, 627, 630, 877
11:1   216, 230, 238, 405, 406,
           511, 536, 555, 582, 585, 596,
           604, 790
11:2   l, cxciii, cxcviii, ccx, 66, 212,
           299, 551, 583, 587–88, 594, 605,
           610–11, 623, 630, 691,

706, 717, 743
11:3–16   583
11:3–14   593, 635
11:3–13   lxxxii, lxxxv, ci, 586,
           588–90, 592–94, 597, 602–4,
           610–11, 616, 620, 625–26, 630–31
11:3–12   591
11:3–10   586
11:3–7   cxlix
11:3–6   ci, 583, 586
11:3–5   cxiii
11:3–4   583
11:3   clxvi, cxcii–cxciii, 37, 198,
           229, 247, 271, 292, 429, 555, 559,
           583, 585–87, 592, 594, 603–4, 607,
           609, 613, 616, 621, 623, 630,
           691, 706, 743
11:4–16:2   cxxxix
11:4–13   cxxxii, 585, 675
11:4   cciv–ccv, 89, 108, 220, 271, 428,
           473, 489, 509, 583, 585–86, 610,
           758, 854
11:5–6   586, 600
11:5   cxiv, clviii, clxv, clxx, clxxxix,
           cxciv, cxcix, 323, 398, 579, 583,
           591, 615, 719
11:6–8   cxiii
11:6   clxiv, clxxi, clxxviii, clxxxi,
           clxxxix, cxcvi–cxcix, 216, 555,
           580, 583, 588, 591, 610, 616, 644
11:7–13   611
11:7–10   ci, 583, 586, 621
11:7–9   589, 596
11:7–8   lxv
11:7   lxxxvii, cxx, cxxvii, cxxx,
           cxxxii, clxvi, clxxxiii, cxcviii,
           19, 81, 176, 273, 307, 318, 323,
           348, 483, 525, 526, 527, 580, 583,
           587–88, 590, 604, 610, 631, 683,
           709, 732, 746, 755, 779, 846,
           853, 930, 940, 942, 943, 1065, 1119
11:8–10   583, 620
11:8   l, lx, cxiv, cxx, cxxxvi, clxiii,
           clxvi, ccii, 37, 270, 581, 583–88,
           601–2, 608, 610, 619, 621–22,
           627–28, 631, 653, 831, 901,
           936, 1038, 1089
11:9–13   cxiii
11:9–10   clxxxv, 584, 587
11:9   xciv, clxv, clxx, clxxxiii,
           clxxxviii–clxxxix, cxciii, 51, 179,
           212, 324, 362, 467, 516, 555,
           574, 581, 584, 592, 601, 609,
           622, 629
11:10–11   601
11:10   clxxxvii, 240, 245, 410, 551,
           555, 584, 594, 609–10, 615, 795,
           810
11:11–13   586–87
11:11–12   ci, 584, 623, 625
11:11   clxx–clxxi, clxxxi, clxxxiii,
           cxciii, 581, 584, 589, 592, 609,
           621, 624, 657, 899
11:12   clxxiv, clxxviii, cxciv, 85,
           347, 397, 545, 561, 584, 589,
           624–26, 631, 638, 840–41,
           882, 1014
11:13–14   cxii
11:13   lx, ci, cxii, clxxxi, cxciii,
           216, 486, 574, 584–87, 592, 612,
           627, 787, 827, 970
11:14–13:18   495
11:14–12:18   726

11:14–12:17 592
11:14–18 cxi, 496, 497, 661, 728
11:14 ci–cii, cxiii, cxxxviii, cxxx,
cxxxii, clxxxv, 50, 53, 135, 488,
495, 522, 524, 536, 582, 584–85,
587, 630, 646, 919
11:15–16:21 cii, 632
11:15–14:20 xciv
11:15–13:1 cxxxviii–cxxxix
11:15–19 cxii, 278, 495, 865, 868
11:15–18 lxxxiii, lxxxv, xcvii, cii,
cxiii, cxxx, 278, 315–16, 392,
423, 494–95, 498–99, 501, 510–11,
517, 545, 547, 555, 568, 574, 585,
630, 632, 635–37, 646, 660,
661, 869
11:15 lxxxvii, xcvii, cxiv, cxxv,
cxxxviii, clxvi, clxxi, clxxviii, cxciv,
cciv, ccvi, 43, 85, 269, 282, 315,
334, 347, 397, 489, 496, 559, 635,
640, 642, 646, 699, 700, 785, 836,
882, 976, 1028, 1090
11:16–12:14 cliii
11:16–18 lxxxvii
11:16 lxxxvii, cxxxi, clix, clxv, clxx,
clxxv, 220, 230, 238, 270–71,
273, 288, 308, 355, 367, 471, 509,
758, 853, 1023, 1026, 1085
11:17–18 xcvii, 288, 312, 315, 635,
637, 640–41, 643, 646
11:17 cxxxvi–cxxxviii, clxix,
clxxvi–clxxvii, clxxxvii, 9, 30, 40,
57–58, 112, 135, 272–73, 306,
336, 365, 383, 636–37, 639, 643,
647, 796, 852–53, 856, 864, 874,
886, 888, 918, 1023, 1028
11:18 liv, cxiv, clviii, clxx–clxxi,
clxxv, clxxxix, cxciii, 6, 13, 17,
21, 25, 143, 212, 239, 359, 420, 555,
570, 580, 636–37, 640–42, 647, 766,
828, 858, 860, 1101
11:19–12:18 728
11:19–12:17 lxxxiii, cii, cxix, 635,
647, 660–61, 663–65, 674–75,
716, 725, 732, 754, 779
11:19–12:5 662
11:19 l, cii, cxi, cxiii, cxxxii, clviii,
clxvi, clxxxi, ccx, 294, 475, 483–84,
517, 559, 597, 605, 627, 633, 660–62,
665, 677, 679, 712, 853, 859, 876–78,
899, 902
12–14 cxii
12 xcix, cxvii, cxxix–cxxx, 77, 572,
660, 666–67, 669–76, 680, 702,
705, 708, 712, 803, 1042
12:1–22:5 xcix, 572
12:1–19:2 cxi
12:1–16:21 cxi
12:1–15:4 xcii, xciv
12:1–14:20 cxii
12:1–18 cxix, cxxxiii
12:1–17 cxv, cxvii, cxxii, cxxix–cxxxi,
517, 661, 679, 725, 732, 735
12:1–8 497
12:1–6 lxxxiii, cxvii, cxlix, 661, 663,
665–66, 689, 691, 712, 803
12:1–5 689
12:1–4 cii, 661, 663, 665, 675, 680, 712
12:1–3 cxiii, 690
12:1–2 cii, cxlix, 675, 682
12:1 clxiii–clxv, clxix, clxxi, clxxxi,
cci, 271, 292, 429, 548, 661, 665,
682–83, 688, 713, 794, 863, 869,

902, 1078
12:2 clxxxiv, clxxxix, cxciii, cxcv,
cc, 237, 490, 551, 565, 665,
671, 675
12:3–4 cii, 675, 682
12:3 xciv, cxx, cxxx, clxiv, clxxi,
cci, ccviii–ccix, 53, 103, 158, 429,
651, 665, 671, 679, 683, 692, 713,
733, 762, 789, 794, 842, 863, 869,
902, 934
12:4–17 661
12:4–6 cii, cxiii, cxlix, 661, 663, 665,
670, 679, 712
12:4–5 lxxxvii, 708
12:4 cxiii, clxiii, clxv–clxvi, clxxi,
clxxviii, clxxxiii, clxxxiv, clxxxix,
cxcvi–cxcviii, ccviii–ccix, 67, 307,
415, 483, 580, 652, 663, 665, 671,
675, 680, 683, 1082
12:5–7 cxvii
12:5 cii, clxv, clxx, clxxxiv, clxxxix,
67, 210–12, 262–63, 284, 477,
657, 662–63, 665, 671, 675–76,
686, 691, 704, 708, 712–13, 831,
876
12:6 cii, clxiv–clxv, clxvii, clxxvii,
clxxxiv, cxc–cxci, cxcvi–cxcvii,
ccii, 199, 229, 427, 553, 587, 590,
598, 604, 609, 611, 657, 663–64, 666,
671, 691, 705–6, 720–21, 743,
784, 911, 933, 1044, 1074, 1139
12:7–12 cii, cxvii, 527, 661, 663–64,
666, 705–6, 803
12:7–9 lxxxiv–lxxxv, lxxxvii, cii,
661, 663–64, 666, 670–71, 675,
691–96, 712, 1078
12:7–8 cxiii, 617
12:7 clxix, clxxxiii, clxxxix, ccviii,
81, 109, 671, 683, 693, 702, 721,
750, 1059, 1082, 1088
12:8 427, 1101
12:9–11 cxiii
12:9–10 696
12:9 lxxxvii, cxiii, cxix, clxix,
clxxviii, clxxxiii, ccviii, 109,
182–83, 239, 382, 484, 495,
525, 534, 546, 616, 663, 665,
668, 680, 683, 691, 698–99,
704, 706, 708–9, 716, 729–30,
758, 760, 1078, 1082, 1083
12:10–17 691
12:10–12 lxxxiii, lxxxv, lxxxvii, xcviii,
cii, cxix, 315–16, 561, 638, 663,
665, 671, 676, 699, 701–2,
758, 808
12:10–11 702
12:10 cxxv, cxxxviii–cxlix, clxvi, clxix,
clxxi, clxxxiii, cxcviii, ccviii, 85, 220,
302, 316, 334, 347, 397, 429, 470–71,
509, 559, 582, 638–39, 642, 661,
664–65, 702, 796, 882, 1014
12:11 lxv, lxxxv, cxvii, cxxvii,
cxxx–cxxxi, clxv, clxx, clxxviii,
cxciv, cci, 19, 41, 81, 353, 371,
406, 474, 475, 664–65, 676,
700–701, 710, 813, 827, 839, 871,
1038, 1057, 1069, 1088, 1157
12:12–17 671
12:12 clxix–clxx, clxxvi, clxxviii,
lxxxiv, cxcviii, 273, 349, 485,
495, 524, 526, 664–65, 680, 700,
713, 758, 762
12:13–18 666, 679

12:13–17 lxxxiii, cii, cxvii,
cxlix, 240, 661, 663–66, 670,
712, 735, 803
12:13–14 590, 666
12:13 cii, cxix, clxiv–clxv, clxxviii,
cxcviii, ccviii, 652, 663–66, 683, 686,
696, 708, 1082, 1089
12:14 cii, clxiv–clxvii, clxxvii–clxxviii,
clxxxiii, clxxxiv, cxcvi–cxcvii,
ccii, ccix, 6, 183, 229, 386, 395,
427, 587, 598, 604, 609, 653, 664,
666, 671, 674, 680, 691, 706, 708,
720, 743, 911, 1074
12:15–17 cxiii
12:15–16 cii, 664
12:15 clxiv–clxv, cxcvi–cxcvii, ccix,
183, 664, 707–8, 1082
12:16 clxv, clxxxiv, ccviii, 671, 676,
683, 686, 1082
12:17–13:18 795
12:17 lxxxvi, cii, cxvii, cxxv, cxxvii,
clxv, clxxi, clxxxii–clxxxiii, clxxxix,
ccviii, 9, 81, 237, 383, 406,
590, 616–17, 664–65, 683, 691,
702–3, 712, 716, 730, 746, 795–96,
837, 1082, 1088
12:18–13:18 cii, 635, 660, 713,
716, 725, 728–29, 779
12:18–13:11 779
12:18–13:10 726, 728
12:18–13:4 732
12:18 cii, cxiii, cxxx, cxxxii, clv,
661, 665, 725, 732, 735, 779
13–16 cxxxii
13 lxi, cxvi, cxxix, 73–74, 616,
631, 660, 676, 708, 726, 729,
733, 779, 784, 795, 833, 837,
848, 866, 894, 1053
13:1–18 lxxxiii, cxix, cxxxi–cxxxiii,
cxxx–cxxxi, 592, 716, 725, 730,
732, 734–35, 941, 942, 943, 944
13:1–10 lxxxvii, cii, cxxix–cxxx,
592, 616, 676, 725, 729, 732,
740, 753, 757–58
13:1–9 cxxx
13:1–8 lxxxiii, cxiii, 749, 769
13:1–7 746
13:1–4 732
13:1–2 cii
13:1 xciii–xciv, cii, cxx, cxxx, cxxxii,
clxiv–clxv, clxx–clxxi, cxcii–cxciii,
cci, ccviii, 158, 338, 348, 548,
616, 661, 683–85, 692, 716, 728,
734–36, 842, 863, 908, 934,
951, 960, 1054, 1119
13:2–4 726
13:2 cii, cxxix, cxxxii, clxv,
ccviii–ccix, 182, 683, 700, 720,
725–26, 740, 743, 757, 780, 866,
870, 889, 903, 908, 1082
13:3–22:21 cxxxviii–cxxxix
13:3–4 cii, ccv, 429, 484, 489, 827, 940
13:3 lxi–lxii, cii, cxxix–cxxx, cxxxii,
clxiv–clxv, clxxi, clxxviii–clxxix,
65, 231, 239, 353, 683, 717,
725–26, 758, 780, 950, 960
13:4 lxiii, cxxix–cxxx, cxxxii–cxxxiii,
clxv, clxxv, clxxxiii, clxxxix,
ccviii, 230, 238, 273, 332, 543,
683, 700, 725–26, 730, 735, 737,
780, 832, 837, 883, 1082, 1088
13:5–10 cii
13:5–7 411, 743

13:5   cxiv, cxxviii, clxxxix, ccx,
          587, 609, 631, 691, 706,
          727, 730, 970, 995
13:6   clxv, clxx, clxxviii, clxxxi,
          clxxxiv, clxxxix, cxcviii, 162,
          742, 889, 1030
13:7-10   708
13:7-8   617, 853
13:7   lxv, lxxxv, xciv, clv, clxxi,
          clxxxiii, clxxxix, 51, 85, 210,
          212, 240, 359, 362, 467, 616-17,
          717, 726, 750, 765, 780, 795,
          819, 839, 849
13:8   cxxx, clviii, clxv-clxvii,
          clxxv, clxxvii, cxciii, ccii, 224,
          227, 229-30, 238, 240, 245, 273,
          323, 345, 353, 361, 369, 410,
          427, 638, 657, 719-20, 730, 741,
          747, 768, 795, 810, 827, 832,
          837, 883, 910, 911, 919, 932, 940,
          1074, 1088, 1102
13:9-10   cxxxii, 730, 768-69
13:9   cxxxiii, cxcix, 52, 58, 123,
          150-51, 265, 730, 751
13:10   lxxxviii, cxxxv-cxxxviii, cxxxiv,
          clxii, clxx, clxxv, clxxviii, clxxxv,
          clxxxix, cxcix, 76, 202, 265,
          316, 359, 411, 718, 730-31, 749,
          795-96, 798, 837
13:11-18 cii, cxvii, cxxix-cxxx, cxlix,
          676, 725, 728-29, 736, 740, 753,
          755, 757-59, 795, 894, 1065
13:11-17 lxxxvii, 769, 894
13:11-16 726-28
13:11-14 cxiii
13:11   xciii, cii-ciii, cxxviii, cxxxi,
          clxiv, clxxxv, cc, cciv, ccviii, 323,
          338, 373, 487, 533, 580, 683,
          720, 725, 728, 732, 908, 1065
13:12-18 757, 779
13:12-17 ciii
13:12-16 720
13:12-13 729
13:12   lxi, ciii, cxxix-cxxx,
          cxxxii, clxv, clxvii, clxxv, clxxxvi,
          cxcii, cxcv-cxcvii, ccii, 158,
          229-30, 238, 240, 273, 381,
          427, 452, 486, 657, 718, 720,
          736, 741, 755, 810, 832, 837,
          883, 911, 950, 1074, 1079,
          1080, 1088
13:13-15 780
13:13-14 679
13:13   clxx, clxxviii, clxxxix, cxcvi,
          419, 720, 730, 753, 755, 758, 1121
13:14-18 cxiii
13:14-15 543, 730
13:14   lxi, cxxxii, clxv, clxx, clxxvi,
          clxxviii, clxxxix, cxciii, cciv, ccvi,
          25, 85, 240, 245, 323, 410, 419,
          580, 656, 698, 720, 736, 743,
          755, 758, 795, 810, 858, 860,
          932, 950, 1073, 1083
13:15-18 832
13:15-17 743
13:15-16 lxiii, 730, 903
13:15   cxxviii, cxxx, cxxxii, clxv,
          clxxxix, cxcvi-cxcvii, 230, 238,
          273, 381, 580, 720-21, 727, 741,
          743, 755, 764, 795, 795, 832,
          837, 864, 883, 1079, 1088
13:16-18 458
13:16-17 827

13:16   clviii, clxiv-clxv, clxx,
          clxxxii, cxcv-cxcvi, ccviii-ccix,
          13, 66, 68, 135, 161, 419, 573,
          592, 637, 721-22, 728, 734, 755,
          766, 768, 772, 787, 796, 832-33,
          864, 1064, 1073
13:17   cxxxii, clxv, clxx, clxxxix,
          cxciv-cxcvi, ccvi, 381, 728, 732,
          734, 768, 833, 837
13:18   ciii, cxxxvii-cxxxviii, cxxxii,
          clxiv-clxv, cxcv, ccvi, ccviii,
          123, 150-51, 749, 751, 769-70,
          772-73, 798, 941, 1062
14   794-95, 829, 831, 848
14:1-20   ciii, cxix, cxxii, cxxiii, 635,
          660, 781, 794-95
14:1-13   794
14:1-5   lxxxiii, lxxxvii, xcvii, ciii,
          cxix, cxxii, cxxxi, 277-78, 369,
          436, 439, 440, 442-45, 459, 460, 477,
          660, 795-96, 798, 802-4, 811,
          813-14, 819, 825, 848, 956, 1104
14:1-3   cxiii, 804, 810
14:1   lxxxiii, xciii, cxx, clxiii-clxv,
          clxx, clxxxiii, cci, cc, ccix,
          30, 53, 103, 232, 278, 280, 323,
          338, 385, 393, 429, 452, 459,
          477, 490, 551, 653, 721, 734, 789,
          794-96, 806, 814, 827, 848,
          858, 863, 1044, 1181
14:2-5   lxxxiii
14:2-3   237, 278, 796, 803
14:2   ccviii, 97, 355-56, 393,
          559-61, 582, 638, 795-96, 803,
          806, 809, 870, 1028
14:3-5   278
14:3-4   307, 436
14:3   lxxxvii, cxxxi, clxv, clxix,
          clxxvii, clxxxiv-clxxxv, clxxxix,
          cxcii, cciv, 272, 288, 359, 361,
          381, 444, 477, 510, 633, 758,
          795, 804, 808, 814, 1091
14:4-5   cxiii, cxxix, 796, 803,
          810, 822, 827, 848
14:4   clxv, clxxvii, clxxxiii-clxxxiv,
          cxcv, cc, ccii, 6, 47, 222, 412,
          428, 443, 473, 477, 490, 580,
          653, 785, 795, 802, 810, 819,
          822-23, 873, 919
14:5   clxv, clxxxi, 818-19
14:6-20   795, 800, 848
14:6-18   795
14:6-13   794
14:6-12   ciii, cxix, cxxii, 2, 660,
          795-96, 848
14:6-11   lxxxiii
14:6-7   lxxxiii, cxiii-cxiv, 435, 628,
          795-97, 825-27
14:6   lxi, xciii-xciv, cxxxvii, clxiii,
          clxxxi, clxxxix, ccix, 51, 212,
          240, 338, 349, 362, 435, 467,
          485, 523, 548, 551, 570, 657,
          784, 795, 797, 800, 808, 810,
          840, 977, 1072
14:7   lxxxv, clxxi, ccvi, 85, 238,
          271, 273, 312, 318, 347, 431,
          435, 526, 559, 565, 597, 797,
          802, 825, 852, 855, 882,
          977, 1044
14:8-11   803
14:8   lxxxiii, cxi, cxiii, cxxx, clviii,
          clxviii, clxxi, clxxxvii, cciii, ccvii,
          66, 143, 203, 205, 212, 239, 405,

          435, 511, 646, 688, 787, 795-97,
          800, 802, 823, 825, 834, 849, 851-52,
          876, 901, 932, 960, 966, 977, 1011,
          1044, 1072
14:9-11   lxiii, lxxxiii, cxiii, 435,
          795-98, 827, 833, 836-37,
          848-49, 903, 1093
14:9-10   cxciv, cxcix, 550
14:9   cxxxii, clxiv-clxv, clxx, clxxxv,
          cxcv, ccix, 85, 230, 238, 273,
          326, 339, 347, 435, 543, 559,
          721, 734, 741, 766, 768, 786-87,
          795-97, 800, 833, 851, 864,
          882, 941, 1072, 1079
14:10-11 798
14:10   clviii, clxv, clxxi, clxxiii,
          lxxv, clxxxi, cxciii, cxcix, cci-ccii,
          ccvii-ccviii, 198, 229, 247, 318,
          326, 420, 541, 579, 758, 786,
          796, 802, 810, 831-32, 870, 873,
          966, 1062
14:11   cxxx, cxxxii, clxv, clxxi,
          clxxv, clxxviii, cxcix, ccviii,
          43, 230, 238, 273, 288, 302, 543,
          734, 741, 766, 768, 787, 796-98,
          832-33, 864, 883, 1079
14:12-13 cxiv, cxxxii
14:12   lxxxvii, lxxxviii, cxxv,
          cxxxvii-cxxxviii, cxxxiv, clxix, clxxi,
          25, 42, 76, 81, 177-78, 202, 237,
          359, 709, 712, 749, 751, 769, 795-96,
          798, 848, 1038, 1088
14:13-20 660
14:13   lxv, lxxxiii, lxxxv, xciv, ciii,
          cxxii, cxxvi-cxxvii, cxxxi, clix,
          clxxi, clxxiv, clxxxiii, clxxxvi,
          cxcv-cxcvii, 7, 10-11, 19, 22,
          36-37, 52, 56, 58, 83, 85, 158,
          230, 283, 381, 486, 561, 582,
          620, 638, 720, 795-96, 798, 848-49,
          854, 858, 860, 888, 896, 970,
          1023, 1031, 1237
14:14-20 ciii, cxvii, cxix, cxxii,
          435, 794-95, 798-800, 843,
          845, 848-49, 1052
14:14-16 lxxxiii, ciii, 435, 625,
          797-802, 839-41, 844-45,
          849, 977
14:14   xciii, cxiii, clxiv, clxix-clxx,
          clxxxi, ccvi, 25, 50, 53-54, 59,
          65, 90, 92-93, 103, 270, 280,
          284, 299, 323, 338, 385, 393,
          429, 435, 487, 548, 551, 784, 790,
          794-96, 798-801, 842, 846, 849,
          858, 912, 977, 1052, 1073
14:15-20 844
14:15-17 cxiv, 799-800
14:15-16 cxiii, 801-2
14:15   clxv, clxxxi, clxxxix, cxciii,
          85, 284, 347, 392, 435, 475, 559,
          597, 721, 795-97, 799-802, 823,
          28, 841, 844-45, 882, 977, 1072
14:16   clix, clxx, clxxxi, 284, 435,
          704, 796, 799, 801, 840, 842
14:17-21 802
14:17-20 lxxxiii, ciii, cxiii, 435,
          798-802, 840, 844-45, 849
14:17   cci, 435, 475, 597, 789-90,
          795-96, 799-800, 802, 823,
          833, 841-42, 846, 853, 1072
14:18-20 435, 797, 800-801, 803,
          844, 976
14:18   cxiv, clix, ccvi, ccviii,

85, 347, 392, 406, 435, 455, 536,
552, 559, 597, 606, 795–800,
823, 841, 843, 845, 882, 884,
965, 977, 1044

14:19-20   435, 799, 847

14:19   clxxi, clxxviii, 796, 834, 49, 870, 1062

14:20   clxxvii, ccviii, 796, 798, 847–48

15–22   cxii

15–18   xciv

15–16   xciv, 495, 500, 546, 869, 928

15:1–22:9   xcix, 572

15:1–16:21   lxxxiii, lxxxv, xci–xcii, xciv–xcv, xcviii, ciii, cxxxiii, cxxx–cxxxi, 115, 392, 495, 498–99, 500, 546, 647, 660, 863, 867, 902, 959

15:1–16:20   xcvii

15:1–16:1   lxxxvii, 849

15:1–8   313, 494, 545, 881

15:1–4   ciii

15:1   xciii, cxii–cxiv, clxv, clxxi, clxxxi, clxxxvii, 338, 435, 551, 644, 679, 794, 797–98, 848, 854, 863, 870, 881, 886, 899, 903, 1120

15:2–16:21   863, 869, 902

15:2–8   xcvii, 278, 869–70

15:2–4   cxii–cxiii, 373, 511, 814, 863, 869

15:2–3   237, 853, 863

15:2   lxiii, cxxxii, clxv, clxxi, clxxv, cxcv, ccx, 271, 297, 338, 355–56, 435, 475, 766, 786, 797, 808, 869–72, 874, 941, 1066

15:3–4   xcvii, 315–16, 808, 863, 872–73

15:3   cxiv, cxxxviii, cxxx–cxxxi, clxiii, clxv, clxix, clxxiv, clxxvi, clxxxiv, ccvi, 13, 40, 57–58, 66, 209, 212, 272–73, 306, 383, 526, 637, 642, 852, 863, 869, 872, 888

15:4   cxiv, clxxvi, clxxxvi, cxciii, cxcvi–cxcvii, cciii, 25, 158, 212, 220, 230, 238, 273, 316, 486, 510, 617, 688, 758, 831, 858, 860, 874, 876, 886, 1031

15:5–16:1   868

15:5–8   ciii, cxii, 863, 869, 881

15:5–6   cxiii, 863

15:5   xciii, clxx, clxxiv–clxxv, clxxxiii, ccii, 53, 280, 450, 475, 597, 661, 745, 863, 877

15:6   cxiv, clxv, clxx, clxxxiii, 93, 109, 293, 475, 597, 796, 852, 869, 877

15:7–8   cxiii

15:7   cxxvi, cxxx–cxxxi, clxv, clxxi, clxxiv, clxxviii–clxxix, ccx, 43, 103, 272, 307, 326, 356, 454, 565, 834, 836, 852, 863, 868–70, 879–80, 886

15:8–16:2   cxxxvii, cxxxix

15:8   clxv, clxx–clxxi, clxxviii, clxxxi, clxxxv, clxxxix, cxcix, 65, 427, 475, 581, 597, 852, 869, 877, 880, 882, 912

16   cxii, 867, 884, 928

16:1–22:11   xcii

16:1–21   ciii, 240, 863, 865, 868, 889

16:1   ciii, cxii–cxiii, clxv, clxxi, clxxiv, clxxviii, ccx, 85, 347, 356, 379, 397, 455, 475, 559, 561, 582, 597, 834, 852, 854, 864, 868, 870, 877, 879, 882–83, 889, 899, 902

16:2–21   ciii, 902–3

16:2–8   902

16:2   lxiii, ciii, cxii–cxiv, cxxx, cxxxii, clxv, clxxviii, cxciii, ccx, 230, 238, 273, 356, 379, 498, 500, 543, 734, 741, 768, 795–96, 832–33, 837, 854–55, 863–66, 868, 879, 888, 899, 903, 941

16:3–7   cxiii

16:3–4   903

16:3   ciii, cxii, clxv, clxix, clxxi, clxxviii, cxciii, ccx, 65, 356, 419, 495, 498, 500, 546, 753, 854, 864–65, 868, 879, 884, 899, 903

16:4–7   ciii, 864–65

16:4   clix, clxiv–clxv, clxxiv, clxxviii, cxciii, ccx, 356, 419, 431, 498, 501, 615, 854–55, 864, 868, 879, 884, 899, 903

16:5–7   xcviii, cxii, cxiv, 315–16, 864–66, 888, 903

16:5–6   864–65, 885, 888

16:5   cxiv, cxxvii, clxxiv, cxcviii, 40, 112, 316, 379, 582, 637, 875, 918, 939, 1023, 1024, 1040

16:6–7   887

16:6   liv, lxxxv, cxxxviii, cxxxi, clix, 359, 555, 646, 785, 888, 938, 1023, 1024

16:7–20   903

16:7   clxix, clxxii–clxxiv, clxxvi, 56–58, 272–73, 306, 379, 383, 405–6, 477, 511, 561, 582, 597, 606, 637, 642, 828, 852–53, 64–65, 874, 886, 888, 968, 1024, 1025, 1028, 1040

16:8–9   ciii, cxii–cxiii, 495, 546, 866, 890, 903

16:8   cxliii, clxv, clxxv, clxxxix, ccx, 356, 498, 501, 854, 868, 879, 899

16:9–19:10   866

16:9   clxv, clxx, clxxiv, clxxxix, cxciii, ccviii, ccx, 162, 419, 495, 541, 628, 744, 830, 868–69, 889, 902, 909, 910

16:10–16   942, 943

16:10–11   ciii, cxii–cxiii, 498, 501, 866

16:10   cxiii, cxv, cxxxviii, cxxxii, clxv, clxxxi, clxxxv, cxc, cxciii, ccii, ccix–ccx, 182, 356, 495, 546, 736, 854, 857, 868, 879, 890, 899, 903, 941

16:11   clxxx, 162, 197, 205, 495, 541, 629, 744, 868–69, 889–90, 902

16:12–16   445, 498, 501, 814, 866–67, 90, 894, 953, 956, 1047, 1079, 1095

16:12–14   cxiii, 538

16:12–13   ciii, 941

16:12   cxii–cxiii, cxxvii, cxxxviii, cxxxviii, clviii, clxiv–clxv, clxx, clxxvii, cxciii, cxcvi–cxcvii, ccx, 63, 356, 495, 574, 854, 867–68, 879, 890–92, 895, 899, 903, 953, 956, 1047, 1095

16:13–18:2   cxxxviii

16:13–14   cxiii–cxiv, 34, 866–67, 890, 895–96, 903

16:13   lxxxvii, clxv, clxxi, ccviii, 65, 338, 389, 683, 729, 755, 759–60, 780, 858, 866–67, 894–95, 1065, 1100, 1174, 1224

16:14   cxxxviii, clxvi, clxxiv, clxxviii, clxxxix, cxcv, 57, 239, 419, 421, 542, 559, 574, 642, 644, 679, 716, 753, 758–59, 858, 867, 894, 953, 959, 1065, 1095

16:15–17   cxi, cxiii

16:15   lxxxiii, lxxxvii, xciv, cxii, cxiv, cxvi, cxxv–cxxvii, cxxxii, clxxxv, cxc–cxci, cxcvi–cxcvii, 10–11, 19, 22, 30, 50, 52, 54, 58–59, 188, 222, 227, 241, 264–65, 553, 573, 721, 788, 798, 838, 846, 858, 867, 890, 897, 1023, 1031, 1091, 1139

16:16   l, lxv, cxiii, clxiii, clxxviii, 533, 645, 867, 890, 894, 896, 937, 1095

16:17–21   ciii, cxii, 498, 501, 866–67, 903

16:17–19   cxxxviii

16:17   xcv, cxiii, clix, clxiii, clxv, clxxvii, ccx, 85, 347, 356, 397, 475, 536, 597, 845, 854, 868, 877, 879, 882–83, 889, 903, 1126

16:18–21   294, 517, 518, 661, 899, 902

16:18–20   cxiii

16:18   cxiii, clviii, clxxvii, 294, 418, 419, 483, 484, 517, 627, 678, 868, 901

16:19–21   495, 546

16:19–20   294

16:19   lxi, cxiv, cxxx, clviii, clxxi, clxxviii, clxxxix, cxcviii, 212, 220, 420, 510, 619, 758, 796, 829, 831–32, 834, 852, 866–68, 903, 59, 960, 1062

16:20   419

16:21   cxiii, clxv, clxxi, clxxx, clxxxiv, cxcii, ccix–ccx, 162, 744, 68–69, 889, 1121

17–18   xciv, cxvii, , 959

17   lxxxv, xcix, cxvi–cxvii, cxx, cxxix, cxxxi–cxxxii, 73–74, 103, 572, 616, 631, 680, 919, 920, 923, 924, 925, 926, 927, 928, 929, 938, 939, 985, 988, 1051
xcv, cxxxii, 1113

17:1–22:9   928, 1146

17:1–19:10   xcii, xciv–xcv, xcvii, c, ciii, cxxxviii, 832, 849, 867, 903, 905, 918, 932, 953, 956, 959, 984, 1020, 1040, 1068, 1069, 1143, 1144, 1145, 1146

17:1–19:8   524, 1019

17:1–18:24   cxv, cxvii, cxlix, 867, 899, 1019, 1158

17:1–18   lxxxiii–lxxxi, cxix–cxx, cxxii–cxxiv, cxxx–cxxxi, 16, 22, 72, 288, 919, 959, 1016, 1019, 1040, 1146

17:1–10   918

17:1–9   cxi

17:1–7   cxvi, 918

17:1–6   72, 924, 938

17:1–3   xcv, 732, 927, 1144

17:1–2   ciii, cxiii, cxv, 869, 905, 915, 916, 1034, 1120

17:1   xcvii, cxiv, cxxxviii, cxxx, cxxxviii, clxv–clxvi, clxviii, clxxiv, clxix, clxxxi, clxxxiii, ccx, 12, 64, 6, 83, 205, 269, 282–83, 349, 356, 430, 616, 709, 732, 796, 846, 852, 854, 879, 905, 906, 907, 912, 913, 914, 915, 928, 956, 985, 1011, 1025, 1034, 1182, 1187

17:1b–6	925	
17:2–19:20	cxxxix	
17:2–19:10	916	
17:2	cxxviii, clviii, clxxi,	
	clxxxiii, cxciv, ccii, 40,	
	204–5, 240, 574, 718, 795, 810,	
	832, 905, 906, 907, 912,	
	913, 914, 916, 930, 932, 1010	
17:3–19:10	732, 925, 960, 1158	
17:3–18	ciii, 905, 916	
17:3–17	941, 942, 943, 944	
17:3–7	cxiii	
17:3–6	ciii, cxv, 916	
17:3	xciii–xciv, ciii, cxx, cxxx–cxxxi,	
	clix, clxiv–clxv, clxx–clxxi, clxxiv,	
	clxxviii, clxxxi, cxcii, cciv–ccvi,	
	36, 71, 82–83, 116, 283, 323,	
	338, 389, 489, 616, 683–84, 692, 716,	
	733, 736, 795, 908, 909, 916,	
	933, 985	
17:3b–6a	916	
17:4	lxi, cxx, cxxx, clxiv–clxv,	
	clxxiv–clxxv, cci, ccx, 205, 271,	
	292, 369, 429, 832, 908, 909,	
	919, 926, 930, 935, 970, 1003,	
	1034, 1122	
17:5	xciv, cxiv, clxiv, clxix–clxx,	
	cci, ccix, 106, 205, 212, 232,	
	467, 569, 721, 795, 832, 852,	
	907, 936, 937, 939,	
	1025, 1069	
17:6–7	ciii, 908, 909, 910	
17:6	lxv, lxxxiv–lxxxv, cxvii, cxxxi,	
	clxv, 37, 41, 81, 240, 338, 359,	
	389, 829, 838, 857, 887, 889,	
	908, 909, 910, 924, 937, 938	
17:6b–18	lxxxiii, ciii	
17:7–18	72, 916 917	
17:7–11	lxxxvii	
17:7	xciv, cxv, cxxx, clxiv–clxv,	
	clxxviii, 106, 569, 788, 831,	
	846, 908, 909, 910,939, 985, 1182	
17:8–18	ciii, 917	
17:8–17	ciii	
17:8–10	cxv	
17:8	cxiii, cxvii, clviii, clxv–clxvi,	
	clxxiii–clxxiv, clxxvii–clxxviii,	
	clxxxv, clxxxviii–clxxxix, cxcviii,	
	25, 65, 67, 223–24, 227, 240,	
	245, 318, 345, 348, 410, 526–27,	
	616, 638, 718, 737, 739, 746–48,	
	795, 810, 846, 908, 910, 932,	
	939, 940, 941, 950, 956, 1104	
17:9–17	919	
17:9–14	919	
17:9–11	lxii, lxxxv, cxvii, 918, 946, 991	
17:9–10	ciii, 736	
17:9	xciv, cxiii–cxiv, cxvii,	
	cxxxvii–cxxxviii, cxxx, cxlix,	
	clxiv–clxv, clxvii, ccii, 229, 427,	
	574, 657, 720, 749, 751, 768–69,	
	798, 910, 911, 920, 941, 944,	
	945, 1030, 1074	
17:9b–11	lxi	
17:9c–11	lxx, 948, 949	
17:10–12	892	
17:10	cxi, cxxiii, clix, clxx, clxxxix,	
	cxcviii, 273, 307, 704, 719, 911,	
	949, 951	
17:11–18	918, 939, 950	
17:11	lxii, cxv, cxvii, clxv, clxxviii,	
	clxxxv, cci, 288, 323, 580, 720,	
	730, 772, 833, 846, 908, 911	
17:12–17	918	
17:12–16	918	
17:12–14	lxxxv, cxi, cxiii, cxvii,	
	895, 911, 951, 953, 959	
17:12–13	cxv, 892	
17:12	cxiii, cxxviii, cxxx, clxiv–clxv,	
	clxviii, clxxxiii, 430, 574, 908,	
	911, 939, 950, 951, 953, 959,	
	1030, 1065	
17:13	clxv, clxviii, 288, 430, 810,	
	908, 911, 915, 952, 1140	
17:14–17	cxiv	
17:14–15	cxvii	
17:14	lxxxvii, cxiv, cxxxvi, cxxxviii,	
	cxxx–cxxxi, clxv, clxxi, clxxxiii,	
	cxcviii, cci, 37, 40–41, 350, 369,	
	445, 447, 574, 617, 620, 644,	
	803, 810, 866, 895, 903, 911,	
	918, 944, 952, 953, 954, 955,	
	956, 1065, 1174	
17:15–18	lxxxv, cxi, cxvii, 917, 918	
17:15–17	919	
17:15	ciii, cxiii–cxiv, cxvi, clxvi,	
	clxxviii, clxxxiv–clxxxv, 205, 362,	
	788, 907, 911, 917, 918, 939,	
	956, 985, 1025, 1030	
17:16–17	cxiii, 830, 895, 908, 1069	
17:16	cxiv–cxv, cxxx, clxiv–clxvi,	
	clxv, clxxxi, 205, 323, 429, 907,	
	908, 911, 912, 916, 939, 956,	
	957, 958	
17:17	cxiv–cxv, cxxxviii, clxiv–clxv,	
	clxviii, clxxxviii, clxxxvi, clxxxix,	
	cxcv–cxcvii, 19, 81, 158, 239,	
	427, 430, 486, 795, 812, 870,	
	908, 912, 952, 958	
17:18	ciii, cxiii, cxv, cxxxviii, clxv–clxvi,	
	40, 619, 831, 854, 900, 912, 956,	
	957, 959, 1030	
18	cxvii, 859, 912, 915, 917,	
	961–65, 970, 975, 976, 982,	
	984, 1011, 1012, 1034	
18:1–19:10	lxxxv	
18:1–19:8	1019	
18:1–24	lxxxiii, lxxxvi, ciii, cxix,	
	cxxii, cxxxi, 830, 916, 961, 961–65,	
	973, 974, 975, 977, 1022, 1040	
18:1–3	ciii, cxi, cxiii, 435, 797, 976,	
	977, 984, 986, 1024, 1034	
18:1	xciii, clxx–clxxi, clxxxiii,	
	97, 280, 435, 450, 572, 755,	
	797, 863, 965, 976, 977, 1139	
18:2–23	cxv, 983	
18:2–8	983	
18:2–3	cxxx, 435, 797	
18:2	lxi, clix, clxxi, cxcii, ccix, 34, 66,	
	435, 542, 559, 795, 797, 829, 831–32,	
	852, 854, 901, 965, 977, 986, 1041,	
	1174	
18:2a	977	
18:2b	977	
18:3–19:4	cxxxix	
18:3	cxxviii, cxxx, clviii–clix, clxxi,	
	clxxxiii, clxxxvii, cxciv, cxcviii,	
	cci, cciii, ccix, 40, 204–5, 212, 318,	
	483, 574, 655, 688, 786, 795, 831,	
	834, 849, 876, 907, 916, 930,	
	32, 965, 966, 986, 988,990,	
	1025, 1171	
18:4–24	919	
18:4–20	ciii, 1034	
18:4–15	438	
18:4–8	ciii, cxi, cxiii, 561, 977	
18:4	ciii, clxix, clxxvi, cxcvi–cxcvii,	
	ccv, 273, 397, 429, 484, 489,	
	582, 638, 796, 883, 967, 971,	
	976, 991, 1010	
18:5	clxviii, cxcviii, 552, 790, 901,	
	967, 992	
18:6–7	645, 956	
18:6	clxxv, clxxxiii, cci–ccii, ccviii,	
	143, 198, 206, 239, 271, 646,	
	831, 833, 889, 967, 993, 994, 1103	
18:7	clxix, cxcviii, ccviii–ccix,	
	158, 967, 979, 994, 996, 1073	
18:8–9	957	
18:8	clxviii–clxx, clxxviii, clxxxi,	
	cxcviii, 57, 430, 852, 957, 967,	
	968, 996, 997, 1010, 1072, 1139	
18:9–20	ciii	
18:9–19	979	
18:9–13	cxi, cxiii	
18:9–10	ciii, 836, 957, 976	
18:9	cxxviii, clxxxiii, ccix, 40,	
	205, 273, 574, 616, 709, 796,	
	907, 916, 930, 968, 976, 988,	
	990, 1026	
18:10	lxi, clxviii–clxx, clxxvi,	
	clxxviii, cxcviii, ccviii, 273,	
	430, 524, 619, 656, 828–29,	
	831–32, 852, 900, 952, 959, 968,	
	970, 971, 982, 984, 991, 998, 1006	
18:11–17	ciii	
18:11	clxxxii, clxxxiv, 51, 968, 998, 1026	
18:12–13	980, 981, 984	
18:12	cxxxviii, clxviii, clxx–clxxi,	
	clxxx, ccviii–ccix, 196, 878, 969,	
	980, 998, 999, 1000, 1001, 1030	
18:13	cxiv, clv, clxx, ccvi–ccix,	
	3, 969, 1001, 1002, 1003	
18:14–23	cxiv	
18:14	cxi, cxiii–cxiv, clxviii,	
	clxxvii, clxxxvi, cxc–cxci, cxciii,	
	cxcvi–cxcvii, ccix, 25, 158, 199,	
	217, 486, 552, 553, 721, 788,	
	790, 858, 860, 912, 969, 970,	
	976, 984, 1003, 1139	
18:15–19	cxi, cxiii–cxiv	
18:15	clxxvii–clxxviii, ccviii, 616,	
	709, 796, 970, 1003, 1004	
18:16–17	cxxxviii–cxxxix,990	
18:16	cxx, cxxx, clix, clxx, clxxxi,	
	ccviii, ccx, 271, 273, 292, 429,	
	524, 619, 656, 831, 878, 900,	
	909, 934, 959, 970, 971, 976,	
	982, 984, 991, 1004, 1030	
18:17–20	ciii	
18:17	clxviii, clxx, ccx, 365, 430,	
	952, 968, 971, 976, 1004,	
	1005, 1006	
18:18	clxxi, clxxxv, 66, 198	
	430, 524, 548, 619, 656	
	831, 836, 900, 959, 971, 976	
18:18b–20	976, 977, 978, 1006	
18:19	clxiv, clxviii–clxx, clxxvi,	
	clxxxv, ccix, 273, 952, 959, 968,	
	971, 990, 991, 1006	
18:20	li, liv, cxi, cxiii–cxiv, clxix,	
	clxxvi–clxxvii, 143–44, 198, 239,	
	273, 359, 555, 646, 831, 853, 968,	
	971, 972, 983, 984, 991, 1006, 1007	
18:21–24	civ, cxi, 983, 1034	
18:21	lxi, civ, cxiii–cxiv,	
	clxvii–clxix, clxxviii, ccix,	
	143, 158, 198, 239, 347, 430, 485, 488,	
	555, 580, 619, 646, 829,

831, 832, 852, 900–901, 959,
972, 976, 982, 983, 991
18:22–23   civ, cxi, cxiii, 983, 1009
18:22   cxiv–cxv, ccviii–ccix,
158, 355, 427, 972, 1009
18:23–24   cxiv, 973, 984, 1009
18:23   civ, cxiv, clxvi, cciii, 158,
212, 271, 544, 688, 698, 876,
972, 973, 983, 1009, 1010
18:24   liv, lxv, lxxxv, civ, cxiii, cxxxi,
359, 361, 555, 645, 887, 973,
83, 984, 1010
19–22   xciv
19:1–10   xcvii, cxi, cxvi, 1017, 1039,
1052
19:1–8   lxxxiii, lxxxvii, 278, 288,
16, 1012, 1013, 1017, 1019,
1020, 1021, 1023, 1040
19:1–4   civ, 315, 1022, 1040
19:1–3   cxiii, 808
19:1–2   lxxxiii, xcvii, civ, 315–16,
864
19:1   xciii, clxx–clxxi, clxxxiii,
ccv–ccvi, ccviii, 44, 85, 316, 336,
347, 365, 381, 429, 470–71, 484,
489, 559, 582, 638, 699, 700,
784, 882, 1013, 1014, 1017,
1018, 1023, 1024, 1028
19:2   clxiv, clxvi, clxxvi, clxxix,
clxxxi, cxcviii, 13, 204–5, 828,
888, 915, 916, 929, 930, 932,
1013, 1014, 1017, 1023
19:3   lxxxiii, xcvii, civ, clxxi,
clxxviii, clxxxvii, cxciv, cci,
ccviii, 315, 429–30, 483, 655,
836, 1013, 1014
19:4–8   367
19:4–6   cxxxviii–cxxxix
19:4–5   cxiii
19:4   civ, cxxxi, clxv, clxxv, clxxxi,
cviii, ccx, 230, 238, 270–73, 284,
288, 324, 326, 355, 471, 633,
786, 864, 888, 1013, 1026,
1027, 1100
19:5–21:21   cxxxviii
19:5–8   civ, 315–16, 1019,
1022
19:5   xcvii, civ, cxiv, clviii–clix,
clxv, clxix, clxxi, clxxvi–clxxxvii,
cxcii, 13, 273, 315, 397, 471,
561, 637, 766, 883, 1013,
1022, 1027, 1028, 1101
19:6–10   cxxxi
19:6–8   xcvii, civ, cxiii, 315,
808, 827
19:6   cxxxviii, clix, clxix, ccv–ccvi,
ccviii, 57–58, 97, 317, 381, 393,
471, 484, 489, 559–60, 582, 637,
39–40, 642, 784, 795, 806–7,
852, 870, 874, 968, 1013, 1014,
1028
19:7   clx, clxiii, clxv–clxvi, clxxi,
316, 369, 918, 1013,
1023, 1029
19:8   cxiv, clxxi, cxcv–cxcvi,
ccviii, 259, 271, 292, 359, 876,
878, 484, 489, 559–60, 582, 637,
1034, 1121
19:9–10   xcv, civ, cxii, cxiv,
919, 1012, 1013, 1017, 1019,
1032, 1040
19:9   lxxxiii, xciv, cxiii, cxxxvii, clx, clxv,
clxx, clxxviii, clxxxiv–clxxxv,

11, 19, 22, 52, 58, 81,
85, 239, 369, 717, 788–89, 810,
838, 896, 898, 918, 1013, 1014,
1031, 1032, 1034, 1058, 1091, 1182,
1186
19:10   lxxxiv, xcvi, cxii–cxiii,
cxxvii–cxxviii, clxvi, clxxi,
clxxxiv–clxxxv, clxxxix, cxciii,
cxcv, 9, 81, 83, 99, 230, 238,
273, 283, 308, 383, 411, 485,
555, 703, 734, 779, 788, 1014, 1019,
1034, 1035, 1036, 1037, 1038, 1039,
1069, 1186
19:11–21:8   xcii, xciv–xcv, c, civ, cxxxiii,
cxxxi, 1022, 1040, 1068
19:11–21:4   cxvii
19:11–21   lxxxiii, lxxxvii, xcii, civ,
cxxiv, cxxxvi, 98, 350, 445, 802,
848, 894, 953, 1019, 1040, 1045,
1046, 1052, 1093, 1108
19:11–20   cxi, 848
19:11–17   1047
19:11–16   civ, cxii, cxix–cxx, cxxxii,
59, 393, 866, 953, 1045, 1046,
1047, 1048, 1049, 1051, 1058, 1059
19:11–12   cxiii, 1019, 1057
19:11   cxiii, clviii, clx, clxxxi,
clxxxiv, clxxxviii, 37, 53, 103,
56, 280–81, 284, 323, 338, 393,
429, 551, 789, 795–96, 863,
1041, 1042, 1045, 1049, 1052,
1053, 1054, 1058, 1108
19:12   cxxxiii, clx, clxiv, cxcv, cc–cci,
ccviii, 158, 190, 232, 299, 384,
393, 490, 548, 551, 653, 685,
734, 769, 784, 833, 842, 1040, 1041,
1042, 1044, 1045, 1054, 1055, 1056
19:13   cxiii, clxv, ccx, 19, 43, 81,
271, 312, 324, 352, 382, 484,
551, 1040, 1041, 1042, 1043,
1057, 1058, 1059
19:14–16   438
19:14   lxxxvii, cxiii, clxxxv, ccviii,
25, 223, 259, 293, 597, 788,
848, 853, 858, 860, 878, 1040,
1042, 1055, 1059
19:15–16   cxiii
19:15   cxiii, cxxxvi, clxv, clxxi,
clxxiv, clxxxi, clxxxiv, cxcvi–cxcvii,
cci, 57, 98, 181, 210–12, 420, 477,
642, 645, 653, 688, 796, 833–34,
846–47, 860, 870, 895, 1040,
1043, 1044, 1060, 1061, 1062
19:16   cxiv, cxxvi, cxxviii, clxiv, clxix,
clxxi, clxxxv, ccix, 37, 40–41,
484, 620, 653, 734, 784, 805,
944, 953, 1040, 1044, 1055,
1062, 1063, 1177
19:17–21   lxxxv, civ, 847, 849, 941,
942, 944, 1032, 1046, 1047, 1063,
1079, 1095, 1101, 1171
19:17–20   1079
19:17–18   cxiii, 435, 541, 797, 977,
1047, 1064
19:17   clx, clxiii, clxviii, clxxxviii,
ccvi, ccix, 66, 85, 338, 347, 429–30,
435, 485, 488, 523, 559, 657,
797, 882, 896, 941, 977, 1040, 1044,
1063, 1064, 1065, 1072, 1073,
1095, 1171
19:18   cxxxviii, clv, clviii, clxxxi,
cxcvi–cxcvii, 13, 419, 637, 766, 1040,
1044, 1064, 1065, 1066

19:19–21   866–67, 903
19:19–20   617
19:19   cxiii, cxvii, cxxviii, clxv,
clxxxi, clxxxiii, clxxxix,
10, 40, 211, 284, 338, 644, 798,
867, 896, 944, 952, 1040, 1044,
1045, 1064, 1065, 1066, 1067, 1095,
1171
19:20   lxiii, lxxxvi–lxxxvii, cxiii,
cxxxviii, clxv–clxvi, clxxi, clxxxviii,
clxxxiii, clxxxviii, cciv, 65, 230,
238, 273, 318, 419, 541, 543,
616, 679, 709, 729, 753, 755,
758–60, 766, 768, 780, 795–96,
832–33, 835, 849, 864, 866, 871,
94, 940, 1007, 1040, 1045,
1067, 1100, 1007, 1040, 1045,
19:21   lxxxvi, cxiii, cxxxvi, cxxxviii,
clxv, clxxxi, cciii, ccix, 98, 181,
271, 284, 324, 326, 420, 944, 1040,
1045, 1058, 1060, 1065, 1066,
1067, 1068
20–22   xcix, cxi, cxv, 572
20–21   1104
20:1–15   lxxxiii, 1079, 1070, 1082
20:1–10   civ, cxix, cxxii, 1069, 1070,
1071, 1076, 1077, 1078, 1078
20:1–6   xcii, cxi, 1071
20:1–3   xcii, civ, cxi, cxv, cxxix,
435, 526, 527, 797, 1071,
1072, 1078, 1089, 1104
20:1–2   cxiii, 1071, 1082
20:1   cxiii, clxiv, clxvi, clxxi, 66,
318, 338, 340, 348, 435,
525, 526, 534, 755, 797, 863,
1071, 1072, 1076, 1080, 1081,
1082, 1096
20:2–3   lii
20:2   cxiii, clxix, ccvii–ccviii, 25,
42, 178, 184, 382, 534, 536, 654,
683, 698, 704, 1071, 1072, 1078,
1082, 1112
20:3   cxiii, clxx, clxxviii, clxxxiii,
clxxxix, cxcvi–cxcvii, cxcix, 212,
318, 348, 427, 526–27, 568,
698, 704, 719, 743, 912, 1071,
1072, 1078, 1079, 1082, 1083,
1084, 1085, 1104
20:4–22:21   cxiv, 1071
20:4–7   438
20:4–6   lxxxvi, lxxxvii, civ, cxi,
cxiv–cxv, cxxiv, cxxix, 277,
1079, 1095, 1105
20:4–5   cxiii–cxiv, 221, 259, 347,
396, 562, 572, 1071, 1084
20:4   lii, lxiii, lxv, lxxxv, cxiii,
cxxv, cxxvii–cxxviii, cxxx,
clviii, clx, clxxv, clxx–clxxi,
clxxv, clxxxiii, clxxxiii,
cxc–cxci, cxciv, ccix, 9, 19, 63,
81–82, 161, 176, 199, 214,
230, 237–39, 261, 273, 288,
334, 338, 354, 383, 404, 406,
410, 435, 543, 553, 703, 721,
734, 741, 766, 768, 780, 795–97,
832–33, 837, 864, 883, 1038, 1071,
1073, 1073, 1079, 1084, 1085,
1087, 1088, 1089, 1093,
1139, 1188
20:5   clxvi, cxcix, 271, 473,
88, 810, 912, 919, 970,
1071, 1073, 1090, 1104
20:6–8   cxiii

20:6   lxxxiii, xciv, cxxv,
                 cxxxvii–cxxviii, cxlix, clxvi,
                 clxxxiii, ccvi, 10–11, 19, 22,
                 48–49, 168, 261, 325, 334,
                 337, 362, 442, 798, 838, 896,
                 1031, 1066, 1071, 1073, 1091,
                 1092, 1093, 1103, 1181
20:7–15   cxi
20:7–10   xcii, civ, cxi, cxv, cxxiv,
                 814, 942, 943, 953, 1047, 1065,
                 1078, 1079, 1080, 1089, 1095
20:7–9   847, 1069, 1104, 1171
20:7–8   617
20:7   clxxi, 273, 307, 616, 788, 970,
                 1071, 1074, 1093, 1171
20:8–9   952
20:8   clxvii, clxx–clxxi, clxxviii,
                 clxxxi, clxxxix, ccii, 212, 229,
                 271, 450, 657, 698, 718, 720,
                 853, 896, 899, 1065, 1071, 1074,
                 1075, 1083, 1093, 1094,
                 1095, 1096
20:9–10   cxiii
20:9   l, cxiii, cxxxviii, ccviii, 359,
                 617, 644, 760, 898, 1059, 1071,
                 1074, 1080, 1096, 1097, 1098, 1099,
                 1100, 1121
20:10–22:5   cxxxix
20:10   lxxxvi–lxxxvii, clxv–clxvi,
                 clxx–clxxi, clxxviii, cxciii, ccii,
                 43, 198, 302, 318, 510, 541, 579,
                 617, 653, 698, 704, 729, 753,
                 759–60, 780, 787, 796, 835–37,
                 853, 871, 894, 941, 1066, 1071,
                 1074, 1083, 1100, 1103, 1224
20:11–15   lxxxvi, civ, cxv, cxix,
                 cxxii, cxxiv, 277, 644, 1069,
                 1070, 1071
20:11–13   592
20:11   lxxxvi, civ, cxiii–cxiv, clx,
                 clxiv–clxv, clxvii, clxx,
                 clxxvii, clxxxi, cxciii, 284,
                 318, 386, 416, 652, 654, 695, 706,
                 1007, 1071, 1074, 1075, 1081,
                 1085, 1100, 1101, 1117,
                 1132, 1133
20:12–15   civ, 223, 1072, 1075
20:12–13   221, 259, 347, 396, 442,
                 562, 572
20:12   cxiii–cxiv, clviii, clxv–clxvi,
                 clxxxi, clxxxiii, ccvii, 206,
                 224, 338, 345, 637, 644, 671,
                 18, 758, 766, 1071, 1072,
                 1079, 1081, 1090, 1102, 1103,
                 1112, 1218
20:13–15   cxi
20:13   cxiii–cxiv, clxvi, clxxxi,
                 clxxxiii, cxcix, 206–7, 324, 401,
                 645, 698, 853, 993, 1075, 1102, 1103
20:14–15   1066, 1076
20:14   cxiii–cxiv, clxvi, clxix–clxx,
                 clxxviii, 168, 176, 271, 318,
                 401, 473, 810, 871, 919, 1075,
                 1092, 1103
20:15   cxiii, clviii, clxvi, clxxxviii,
                 cxcix, 224, 227, 318, 345,
                 558, 604, 718, 827, 871, 1070,
                 1076, 1102
21   cxvii, 1110
21:1–22:9   1146
21:1–22:5   cxvii, 437, 448, 1115,
                 1149, 1150
21:1–8   lxxxiii, xcvii, civ, cxxiv,

                 1108, 1109, 1112, 1113, 1114
21:1–4   cxi, cxv, cxvii, 1113,
                 1114, 1125
21:1–2   civ, cxiii
21:1   lii, lxxxvi, cxii, clxiii, cxcv,
                 318, 338, 349, 526, 565, 566,
                 63, 1074, 1100, 1101, 1102,
                 1109, 1110, 1113, 1115, 1116,
                 1117, 1118,1119, 1120
21:2–22:5   245
21:2–4   lxxxvi, cxii, 1103
21:2   l, cxii, clxiii, clxx, clxxvii, clxxix,
                 75, 232, 243, 338, 608, 812,
                 1029, 1030, 1110, 1113, 1120, 1121,
                 1122, 1153, 1191
21:3–4   lxxxvi, xcvii, civ, cxiii, 1115, 1149
21:3   cxii, clxv, clxiv, clxxxiii,
                 cx, 53, 85, 347, 379, 397, 437,
                 76, 559, 561, 582, 745, 789,
                 833, 882, 1027, 1102, 1111,
                 1113, 1115, 1122, 1123, 1124,
                 1146, 1147
21:4   lii, cxi–cxiii, cxv, clxiv, ccvi,
                 144, 427, 431, 437, 479, 551,
                 1103, 1111, 1113, 1115,
                 1124, 1125
21:5–22:2   xcvii, 1149
21:5–8   lxxxiii, civ, cxi–cxii, cxv–cxvi,
                 52–53, 58–59, 335
21:5–7   cxi
21:5   cxi, cxiii–cxv, cxvii, clviii, clxv,
                 clxxxi, clxxxiv–clxxxv, 37, 53, 85, 239,
                 256, 284, 312, 810, 838, 1034,
                 1100, 1111, 1113, 1114, 1125,
                 1126, 1146, 1182, 1237
21:6–8   cxiii
21:6   cxiv, cxxv, clxix, clxxii–clxxiii,
                 ccviii, ccx, 51, 57, 59, 100–101,
                 135, 179, 256, 271, 284, 324,
                 431, 437, 478, 479, 483, 516,
                 788, 855, 859, 1112, 1126,
                 1127, 1128, 1129, 1199
21:7   clxix, cci, ccx, 199, 227,
                 833, 871, 1112, 1122, 1129,
                 1150, 1163
21:8   lxxxvi, cxxxiii, clxv–clxvi,
                 cxcv, ccvii, ccx, 168, 205, 318,
                 429, 484, 541, 542, 544, 545,
                 835, 871, 1054, 1066, 1092, 1103,
                 1112, 1222, 1130, 1131,
                 1132, 1133
21:9–22:18   xcvii, cxii–cxiii
21:9–22:9   lxxxiii, xciv–xcv, xcvii,
                 c, civ, cxxiii, 915, 919, 1020, 1040,
                 1068, 1069, 1113, 1120, 1133,
                 1141, 1142, 1143, 1144, 1145,
                 1187, 1202, 1203
21:9–22:6   lxxxiv, 22
21:9–22:5   lxxxvi, xcii, xciv,
                 cxv–cxvii, cxix, cxxii, cxxiv,
                 cxxx–cxxxi, 16, 915, 919, 939,
                 1148, 1162
21:9–22:2   cxi, cxv
21:9–27   cxvii
21:9–21   1147, 1171
21:9–10   xcv, civ, 603, 680, 732,
                 852, 916, 1020, 1133, 1146
21:9   cxxxviii, cxxx, clxv–clxvi,
                 clxviii, clxx, clxxiv, clxxix,
                 clxxxiii, ccx, 12, 66, 83, 269,
                 282–83, 285, 349, 356, 369,
                 430, 616, 709, 732, 796,
                 846, 854, 869, 879, 915,

                 928, 1029, 1112, 1121, 1133,
                 135, 1136, 1137, 1146, 1150,
                 1151, 1187
21:10–22:7   732
21:10–22:5   civ, 1133
21:10–27   604
21:10–11   cxiii
21:10   l, xciii, xcvi, civ, clxx, clxxvii,
                 12, 36, 71, 82–83, 116, 154,
                 32, 243, 283, 285, 608, 755,
                 19, 928, 933, 1074, 1098,
                 1110, 1112, 1136, 1137, 1144,
                 1147, 1148, 1151, 1152, 1153
21:11–21   civ, 1147
21:11–14   1147
21:11   cxiii, clxviii, ccviii, 285,
                 933, 985, 1136, 1137, 1144,
                 1153, 1154
21:12–14   460
21:12–13   461
21:12   cxiii, clx, clxiii–clxix, clxxiv,
                 cc–cci, ccvii, 25, 165, 271,
                 299, 460, 490, 551, 653, 784,
                 919, 1044, 1136, 1137, 1154,
                 1155, 1158, 1174
21:13   cxiii, clviii, clxxvii, 1136,
                 1137, 1138, 1155, 1156
21:14   li, lxiv, lxx, cxiii, clxv, cc,
                 145, 323, 490, 551, 784, 1007,
                 1115, 1136, 1138, 1156,
                 1157, 1158
21:15–17   603, 1147, 1150
21:15   cxiii, cxxviii, clxx, clxxiv,
                 clxxxiii, clxxxv, cxcvi–cxcvii,
                 ccx, 616, 709, 796 1136, 1138,
                 1147, 1150, 1158, 1159, 1160,
                 1165
21:16–21   cxiii
21:16   cxiii, clx, clxxv, cxcv, ccix,
                 265, 1136, 1138, 1160, 1161
21:17   ccvii, 36, 769, 1102, 1112,
                 1136, 1138, 1162, 1163
21:18–21   1029, 1030, 1075, 1115, 1147
21:18   ccviii, ccx, 285, 1136, 1138,
                 1150, 1163
21:19   clv, clxv, ccviii–ccx, 285,
                 379, 551, 1115, 1136, 1138, 1164,
                 1165
21:20   clv, ccviii–ccx, 619, 831,
                 1136, 1138, 1150, 1165
21:21–23   cxiii, 1150, 1169
21:21   clxviii, ccviii, ccx, 430,
                 1136, 1138, 1150, 1165,
                 1166, 1167
21:22–22:21   cxxxix
21:22–22:5   civ, 968, 1147
21:22–26   438
21:22–23   369, 1170
21:22   cxv, clx, clxv, clxix, cxcv,
                 57–58, 271, 306, 338, 437,
                 439, 637, 642, 746, 852, 873–74,
                 77, 888, 968, 1028, 1115, 1136,
                 1138, 1147, 1148, 1154, 1166,
                 167, 1168, 1169, 1170, 1177
21:23   clxiii–clxv, cxcv–cxcvi,
                 427, 437, 785, 873, 1136,
                 1138, 1150, 1167, 1168,
                 169, 1170
21:24–27   cxiii, 919, 1148, 1178
21:24–26   1122, 1170
21:24   cxxxviii, clxxvii–clxxxviii, clxxxv,
                 cciii, 40, 212, 1136, 1139,
                 1154, 1171, 1179

21:25   cxvi, cxcv, 158, 1136,
1139, 1150, 1154, 1172, 1174,
1174, 1204
21:26   clxxviii, 212, 366, 1136,
1139, 1172, 1179
21:27   clviii, clx, clx, clxvi, clxxviii,
clxxxi, cxciii, cxcv, 158,
224, 345, 427, 542, 581, 718,
1007, 1104, 1115, 1136, 1139,
1174, 1174
22   858
22:1–15   1148, 1154, 1155
22:1–10   xcii
22:1–4   cxiii
22:1–2   cxvii, 153, 1140
22:1   cxxxi, clxiv–clxv, clxxi,
ccviii, 12, 262–63, 283–85,
369, 467, 478, 479, 633, 873,
19, 928, 1075, 1136, 1139,
175, 1176, 1177, 1178, 1179
22:2   clxiv, clxxviii, clxxxiii,
ccx, 152, 154, 212, 656, 919,
115, 1136, 1139, 1140,
1177, 1178
22:3–5   lxxxvi, xcviii, cxi–cxii,
cxv, cxvii, 919, 1115
22:3–4   645
22:3   cxii, cxxxi, clxv, ccviii,
13, 262–63, 284, 369, 427, 467,
475, 633, 873, 1075, 1115,
1136, 1140, 1150, 1178,
179, 1184
22:4   clxiv, ccix, 232, 452, 456,
721, 734, 795, 805, 1136,
1140, 1179, 1180, 1181
22:5–21   cxxxii, 867, 896
22:5–8   lxxxi, cxii
22:5–6   75
22:5   cxiii, cxvii, cxxviii, clxiii,
clxix, clxxi, clxxviii, clxxxv,
3, 57, 214, 261, 276, 362, 639,
785, 836, 852, 1115, 1136,
1140, 1146, 1150, 1169, 1173,
1181, 1203, 1204, 1205, 1206
22:6–21   xlix, lxxxvii, xciv, c,
cxvi, cxx, cxxiv–cxxv, cxxxi,
6, 19, 58, 1035, 1038, 1148,
1149, 1181, 1201, 1206, 1207
22:6–15   cxi
22:6–10   1205
22:6–9   xcv, civ, cxii, 1020, 1032,
1133, 1144, 1145, 1146, 1182
22:6–7   cxi, cxiii, 1188
22:6   liv, xcvi, civ, cxii–cxiii, cxvii,

cxxiv, cxxxviii, clxix–clxx, clxxxix,
13–14, 37, 57, 106, 239, 256, 282–83,
555, 788, 810, 852, 919, 928, 1032,
1034, 1126, 1136, 1140, 1181, 1182,
1201, 1202, 1205
22:7–8   1
22:7   liv, lxxv, lxxxvii, xciv, xcviii,
civ, cxi, cxv, cxxxv, cxxxvii–cxxxviii,
clxv, clxxi, clxxxv, 7, 10–12, 19–23,
50, 54, 59, 103, 135, 188, 241,
245, 265, 344, 798, 838, 896,
1031, 1091, 1136, 1140, 1225, 1237
22:8–16   lxxxiv, 12
22:8–13   cxi
22:8–9   lxxxiv, civ, cxiii, cxxiv, 238,
919, 1036, 1037
22:8   xlix, lxxxiv, lxxxvii, xcvi,
cxxiv–cxxvi, clxix, clxxxv, clxxxix,
18, 75, 99, 135, 230, 283, 308,
82, 928, 1034, 1136, 1140, 1141
22:9   liv, xcviii, cxxiv, cxxxviii,
clxv, clxxi, clxxiv, clxxxiv–clxxxv,
3, 230, 273, 344, 374, 411, 555,
788, 916, 1035, 1036, 1037, 1038,
1040, 1141, 1186, 1187,
1218, 1225
22:10–21   lxxxvii, lxxxix, civ,
1195, 1200, 1201
22:10–20   xc, 1144, 1182, 1195,
1200, 1201, 1236
22:10–15   cxii
22:10–13   cxv
22:10–11   civ
22:10   liv, lx, lxxv, lxxxviii, xciv,
xcviii, cxxv, cxxxviii, clxv, clxxi,
clxxxiv–clxxxv, cxcv, 7, 12, 21,
66, 122, 344, 549, 788, 1195, 1196,
1197, 1203, 1204, 1205, 1216,
1217, 1225
22:11   lii, lxxxviii, cxxv, cxxxviii,
clx, ccix–ccx, 151, 412, 768,
1196, 1197, 1217, 1218
22:12–21   lxxxvii
22:12–15   52, 58
22:12–13   civ, cxiii
22:12   cxiv, cxxv, cxxxviii, clxxv,
clxxxiii, clxxxv, clxxxix, 50, 54,
59, 135, 188, 206–7, 241, 271,
644–45, 1196, 1217, 1218
22:13   cxxv, clxix, ccviii, ccx, 51,
57, 59, 101, 116, 161, 256,
271, 1111, 1126, 1196,
1219, 1226
22:14–21   1235

22:14–15   civ, cxi, cxiii, cxv
22:14   lxxxvi, xciv, cxxxvii, clxx,
clxxviii, clxxxi, clxxxvi,
cxcvi–cxcviii, 7, 11, 19, 22, 152,
158, 221–22, 230, 259, 347,
381, 396, 410, 474, 486, 562,
572, 581, 645, 709, 720, 788,
798, 838, 912, 1031, 1085, 1091,
1102, 1174, 1179, 1196, 1198,
1219, 1220, 1221, 1222, 1223
22:15   188, 205, 542, 543, 544,
545, 1130, 1131, 1132, 1197,
1198, 1223, 1224
22:16–21   cxii, cxvi
2:16   liv, civ, cxi, cxiii, cxv, cxxiv,
cxxviii, clxiii–clxix, clxxi, clxxiv,
clxxxii, clxxxix, ccix, 13–14, 19,
63, 75, 100–101, 212, 271,
350, 557, 574, 1197, 1198, 1199,
1224, 1225, 1226, 1227
22:17   civ, cxi, cxiii, cxv, 83, 151,
265, 283, 478, 479, 812, 1127,
1128, 1129, 1179, 1197, 1199,
1227, 1236
2:18–20   52, 58, 1204, 1208
22:18–19   lxxx, xcviii, civ, cxi,
cxiv–cxvi, 12, 344, 409, 1204,
1210, 1213, 1214, 1236
22:18   liv, lxxv, cxxv, cxxviii, clxv, clxxi,
7, 19, 143, 198, 239, 582, 614,
646, 831, 870, 1197, 1198,
199, 1204, 1205, 1208, 1225,
1227, 1228, 1229, 1230,
1231, 1232
22:19   liv, lxxv, cxxv, clxv,
clxxi, clxxxiii, clxxxvii, 143, 152,
179, 198, 239, 324, 516,
614, 646, 831, 1179, 1197,
1222, 1225, 1232
22:20–21   cxiii
22:20   xciii, civ, cxi, cxv,
cxxv–cxxvi, cxxviii, clxxvi,
lxxxiv–clxxxv, 19, 21, 37, 41,
50, 54, 56, 59, 135, 188, 241,
245, 255, 620, 839, 1199, 1216,
1206, 1207, 1208, 1215,
1232, 1233, 1234, 1235, 1236,
1237, 1241
22:21   lxxii, lxxiv, lxxxii, civ,
xi, cxv, cxxvi–cxxvii, clxxiv,
37, 40, 63, 125, 620, 1233,
238, 1239, 1240, 1242, 1241
22:22   1240, 1241, 1242

Old Testament Apocrypha

Baruch
1:4   287
1:20   17, 872
2:4   ccii, 653, 998
2:13   ccii, 653
2:17   876
2:20   18
2:23   983
2:24   18
2:28   17, 1199
2:29   ccii, 653
3:32   206
3:36   17

4:37   427
5:5–9   436

Bel and the Dragon
1:5   565
7   954
14:5   102
14:25   102
32   1002

1 Esdras
1:54   766
2:13   852

2:3   142
3:5   clxvii
3:11   85, 347, 882
4:40   49
4:46   629
4:50   clxxxvi, cxcvii
4:54   clxvii
4:58   629
4:59   49
4:63   clxvii
5   436
5:64   85, 347, 882
6:5   287

6:8	287	5:6	240
6:13	565	5:9	521
6:27	17, 287	5:20–30	83
6:32	clxvii	5:31–6:34	15
6:33	ccii, 653, 999	5:41	444
7:2	287	6:5	452
8:25	875, 958	6:18	240
8:82	18	6:20–24	418
8:90	352	6:23	510, 519
9:2	51	6:24	240
9:8	629	6:25	444
9:10	85, 347, 882	6:26	240, 599
10:6	clxxxii	6:31–59	83
		6:35–9:25	xcv
2 Esdras		6:39	507
1:4	ccii, 653	6:47–54	755
1:32	18	6:47–52	728, 732
2:1	18	6:49–52	728
2:18	18	6:51	728
3:11	clxxv	6:52	728–29, 1033
3:23	17	6:58	38
5:1	21	7:1–8:19	15
5:56	17	7:26	1121, 1105
6:14	21	7:27	444
7:102	17, 999	7:28	1106, 1107
8:24	17	7:29	1108
10:6	51	7:30	507, 1116
14:3	620	7:31	1116
15:8	408	7:32	1091
19:6	565, 693	7:35	839
21:1	608	7:36	154, 411, 422. 828
21:18	608	7:38	411, 422, 828
		7:39	414
4 Ezra (4 Ezra 1–2 = 5 Ezra;		7:72	240
4 Ezra 15–16 = 6 Ezra)		7:74	240
1–2	xcv	7:75	411
1:19	189	7:77	839
1:25	958	7:88–99	411
1:32	1101	7:91	411
2:8	620	7:95	411
2:33	xlix, 18	7:97	99, 557
2:34	411	7:100–101	410
2:38	1033	7:102	422, 828
2:39	223	7:104	422, 828
2:42–48	277, 436	7:113	422, 828
2:42–45	277, 290, 437	7:123	153
2:42	xlix, 18	7:125	99, 557
2:45	223	7:127–28	151
3–14	804	8:5	704
3:1–9:22	xcii	8:7	875
3:1–5:20	xcv	8:21–22	295
3:1–36	82	8:21	1100
3:1–2	lxi, 830	8:22	451
3:1	xlix, 18, 75	8:33	839
3:5	623	8:37–9:25	15
3:7	361	8:52	153, 411
3:12	240	8:53	401, 452
3:28–31	lxi, 830	9:7–8	444
3:34	240	9:11	163
3:35	240, 1000	9:23–37	83
4:1–5:13	15	9:26–10:59	xcv
4:11	99	9:43	1122
4:16	760	10–13	827
4:21	240	10:7–8	1122
4:28–32	802, 844	10:21–23	595
4:29	213	10:22	89, 678
4:35–37	391, 408	10:30	100
4:35	407, 802, 844	10:44–48	473
4:36	412	10:59	240, 423
4:39	240	11:1–12:51	xcv
4:52–5:13	418	11:1–12:39	734
5:1–6:34	xcv	11:1	734
5:1	240	11:5	240
5:4–13	418, 507	11:7–8	523
5:5	415	11:32	240
11:34	240		
11:36–46	350, 734		
11:37	870		
11:43	742		
12:3	737		
12:11	734		
12:22–26	736		
12:24	240		
12:31–34	350		
12:31	1105, 1106		
12:32–33	420		
12:32	350		
12:33	1172		
12:34	422, 444, 828, 1108		
12:37	1216		
13:1–58	xcv		
13:3	55, 625, 841		
13:5–50	277, 436		
13:5–11	1047, 1080, 1095, 1096, 1121		
13:5	450, 1153		
13:8–11	420		
13:10–11	1061		
13:10	614		
13:12–13	436, 460		
13:15	444		
13:16–19	473		
13:20–56	15		
13:26	444		
13:29–50	803		
13:29	240, 1047		
13:30–31	644		
13:30	240, 1079		
13:31	1079		
13:33–36	804		
13:33–35	847, 1080		
13:34–45	896		
13:34–35	898		
13:35	803		
13:36	1131		
13:37–38	420, 614, 1061, 1064		
13:38	1172		
13:39–50	461		
13:39–49	460		
13:39–47	436		
13:48–49	444		
13:48	444		
13:50–51	83		
14	85, 115		
14:1–48	xcv		
14:5–6	563, 1216		
14:7–9	625		
14:9	626		
14:11–12	507		
14:20	890		
14:22	423		
14:26	563		
14:37–48	563		
14:39	870		
14:45–46	1216		
14:50	625		
15–16	xcv		
15:5	400		
15:35–36	848		
15:20	419		
15:42	901		
15:49	400		
16:18–22	400		
16:34	400		
16:44	830		
16:46	400, 830		
16:74	422		
Judith			
1:1	619, 831		

Ref	Page
2:2	107, 569
2:5	142
2:20	532
3:2	13
3:8	361
4:14	352
5:5	823
5:8	629
5:18	859
5:19	ccii, 653
6:3	13
6:16	287
6:19	629
7:11	949, 985
7:19	1097
7:30	530
8:3	205
8:9	530
8:15	530
8:25	641
8:27	260
9:12	565, 629
9:13	349, 565
11:4	13
11:7	629
11:16	737
11:17	475
11:34	cciv
13:4	766
13:13	766
13:17	737
13:18	565
14:3	1075
16:13	874
16:15	1081
16:17	422, 524, 656, 828, 896
18:24–27	231
19:24	cciv
21:12	cciv

1 Maccabees

Ref	Page
1:5	205
1:8–9	173
1:11	737
1:20–61	729, 754
1:20–24	745
1:21	89
1:26	287
1:46	359
1:54	745, 936, 985
1:60–63	710
2:7	608
2:11	859
2:23–28	543
2:28–29	691
2:37	737
2:40–41	737
2:43	859
2:58	599
3:15	1098
3:18–19	244
3:23	1098
3:24	949, 985
3:25	624
3:27	1098
3:32	890
3:43	737
3:45	608
3:50	244
3:51	608
3:54	510
3:58	859
3:60	244
4:10	244
4:15	949
4:30	17
4:34	949, 985, 1098
4:40	510
4:43	823
4:49–50	89
4:54–55	316
4:54	356
4:60	608
5:45	766
5:57	737
5:68	543, 762
6:1–5	745
6:14–15	173
6:22	407, 408
6:34	847, 938
6:48	clxxii
7:6–7	737
7:15	567
7:16–18	621
7:18	624
7:30	567
7:33	clxxii, 287, 1098
7:36	352
7:38	901, 992
8:1–32	931
8:8	clxxii
9:4	539
9:27	900
10:20	174, 935
10:37	clxxii
10:42	877
10:49	1098
10:62	935
10:64	935
10:65	clxxii
11:1	858, 1095
11:8	293
11:13	733, 1054
11:23	clxxii, 287
11:58	935
12:1–4	931
12:16	931
12:35	287
13:5	1095
13:32	685
13:33–34	1095
13:36–37	469
13:47–48	762
13:51	468, 808
14:21	365
14:35	935
14:39	clxxii
15:14	1097

2 Maccabees

Ref	Page
1:2	17
1:11	641
1:14–17	745
1:19	clxxii
1:24–25	875
2:1	clxxii
2:3	542
2:4–8	678
2:4–6	189
2:5	711
2:7	436
2:8	625, 841
2:10	760
2:17	48
2:21	693
3:1	608
3:2	877
3:24	34, 624
3:25–26	693
4:7–20	172
4:41	clxxii
5:2–4	693
5:2	418
5:11–6:11	729, 754
5:16	1172
5:20	766
5:27	691
6:7	193
6:10	167, 1089
6:12–17	260
6:12	193
7:1–3	710
7:3	708
7:9	625, 1091
7:11	625
7:14	625
7:23	625
7:29	625
7:33	102
7:36	408
7:37	875
7:38	373
7:39	708
7:42	193
8:2–4	408
8:3	408
8:4	901
8:11	1002
8:19–20	693
9:5	206
9:8	167
11:6	693
11:8	223, 468
11:20	167
11:34–38	931
12:6	888
12:16	884
12:22	624
12:27	clxvii
12:34	949, 985
13:4	934
13:13	287
13:21	107, 569
13:25	510
14:4	167, 468
14:37	287
15:4	102
15:12–16	601
15:14	608
15:22–23	693
17:11–16	167

3 Maccabees

Ref	Page
1:8	287
1:23	710
2:2	629
2:3	865, 886
2:5	620
2:11	256
2:18	608
3:1	708
3:28–29	767
4:12–13	708
4:15	427
4:16	542, 544
5:1–5	646
5:1	708
5:2	833
5:3	512
5:21	646
5:35	954
5:38	646
6:5	608
6:9	359
6:18–21	693

6:18–19	878	17:19	354	28	clxxxvi, cxcvii, 381
6:21	646	17:22	453	42	206
6:28	102, 629	18:1	102, 312		
7:3	1005	21:2–3	532	*Tobit*	
7:6	629	21:3	98, 182	1:16–20	1068
7:13	1003, 1024	22:6	260	2:2	323
7:16	641	23:9–11	567	2:3–10	622
7:23	44	23:13	475	2:16–17	110
		23:14	147	3:2	864, 886
4 Maccabees		23:19	354	3:8	535
1:11	76, 702	24:4	625, 841	3:17	536
2:1	1003	26:29–27:3	990	4:6	543
3:14	516	27:8	93	4:13	937
3:17–18	702	27:23	572	5:4–5	110
5:1	286	28:6–7	147	5:14	397
5:2–3	195	29:23	766	6:12	687
5:2	186, 193	30:1	260, 1155	7:18	629
5:16–17	710	30:17	411	8:3	535, 536, 1082
5:29	710	30:19	544	10:10	1002
6:10	167, 702	32:23	709	10:11	629
6:18	710	35:19	207	10:12	629
6:29	373, 999	36:10	460	11:14	836
6:33	702	36:11	38, 1155	12:7	107, 569
7:4	702	36:12	608	12:11	107, 569
7:8	710	36:17	17, 436, 1155	12:12	291
7:9	76	37:11	990	12:15	35, 291, 359, 509, 694, 836
7:19	625	38:10	475	12:20	85
8:1	702	38:22	147	12:22	679, 869, 874
8:2	708	38:23	411	13:5	1155
9:1–2	710	39:19	354	13:7	629, 853
9:6	702	39:26	397, 847, 938	13:10	609, 1121
9:8	76, 625	39:30	531	13:11	629, 853
9:10	708	40:4	173, 935	13:13	436, 1155
9:30	76, 702	40:8–11	505	13:16	1163
11:20	167, 702, 1010	42:5	900	13:18	43
13:7	702	42:18–19	206	14:6–7	1155
13:15	167, 1029	43:16	1081	14:15	44, 1024
15:29	167	43:17	561		
15:30	76	44:3	206	*Wisdom of Solomon*	
16:14	702	44:16	cciii, 528, 599, 626	2:1	704
16:16	167	44:17	220	2:22	107, 569
16:25	625	44:18	cciii, 528	2:24	697
17:4	76	44:19	466	3:1	404
17:5	625	44:20	220	3:5	231, 360
17:11–16	167	44:21	466	3:8	461, 639–40, 1085
17:12	76	45:12	174, 990	4:2	151
17:15	175, 702	45:16	511	4:7	411
17:17	76, 999	45:20	815	4:10–11	599
17:18	309	45:24	cciii, 528	5:16	167, 175, 992
17:19–23	76	45:81	93	6:7	766
17:23	76	46:8	cciii, 528, 985	7:1	206
18:16	153	47:8–10	316	7:29	99
18:24	44, 49, 76	47:22	350	9:1	312–13
		47:23	411	9:4	263
Sirach		48:1–14	613	9:8	476, 677
1:3	1087	48:2	615	9:10	309
1:8	284	48:3	760	10:16	760
1:16	909	48:9	599	11:1–19:9	506
1:30	206	48:10	599	11:1–14	504
2:1	231	48:12	599	11:10	231
5:15	766	49:1	572	11:15	504
7:28	147	49:6	608	11:18	540
11:12	354	49:7	cciii, 528	12ff.	865
12:16	572	49:8	272	13–15	543
13:13	990	49:9	901	13:2	865
13:39	990, 1095	49:14	599	14:12–21	188
14:12	401	50:13	286	14:12	188
14:17	198	50:15	847, 938	14:27	188
15:8	206	50:16	85, 347, 882	15:8–9	542
16:12	207	51:12	clxxv	15:15	544
16:14	207			16:1–4	504
16:18–19	1080	*Susanna* (** = Theodotion)		16:9	504, 527, 533
17:15	354	**1:2	382	16:15–19	504
17:17	110	**1:45	382	16:20	189

17:1–18:4	890	18:5–25	504
17:1–20	504	18:9	359, 1058
18:3	558	18:15–16	98, 182, 1058

18:21	511
18:24	93
19:1–9	504
24:9	39

Pseudepigrapha and Early Jewish Literature

Adam and Eve

2:2	879
4:2	189
5:2	85, 347, 854, 882
7:2	836
8:1	407
9:1–11:13	697
10:3	744
12–16	695
13:1	695
16:2	695
16:3	697
16:5	158
18:3	158
19:2	407
21:3	744
21:4	158
22:1	694
25:1–3	154, 1117
27:5	886
29:11	85, 347, 854, 882
33:4	879
33:5	542
36:2	153
37:4	284, 694
38:1	694
38:3	450
40:1–3	153
40:1–2	154
40:1	694
40:2	347
47	696
47:3	736

Apocalypse of Abraham

8:1	561
8:2	561
8:6	561
9–19	278
9:1–10	88
9:1	561
10:1	561
10:3	561
10:12	99
11:2–3	73, 1024
11:2	94
13:10 (A)	884
17:1	97
17:6–21	316
18	298, 301
18:1	97
18:3	316
19:1	561
19:6	846
20–31	15
21–32	827
23	696
23:7	733
27	595
27:5–7	597
29:2	507

29:19	646
30:3–8	506
30:8	294
30:14–16	499
31:1	519

2 Apocalypse of Baruch

1:1–12:4	xcv
1:1–9:2	xcv
1:1–2	8
1:3–4	597
2:1	297
3:1–3	1122
3:7	507, 1118
4:3	476
4:5	476
6:3–9	595
6:4–6	435
6:4–5	452
6:5–9	678
8:1–2	561
8:3	75, 1082
9:1	75
10:1–20:6	xcv
10:1–3	lxi
10:2	830
10:5	75
10:10	1002
11:1	lxi, 75, 830
11:3	85, 347, 393, 882
12:3	995
13:1–20:6	xcv
13:1–2	561
13:1	75
13:10	1121
14:1–2	393
15:8	167
19:1	565
19:2	1118
21:1–34:1	xcv
21:6	295, 352, 846
21:7–29:21	924
21:9	102
21:10	102
22:1–30:5	15
22:1	561
23:5	412
25:1	240
27:1–15	239, 473, 507
27:1–13	418
29:1–2	444
29:3–30:1	1106
29:4	728–29, 732, 755, 1033
29:8	189, 195
29:17	994
29:20	994
30:1	507
30:2	412
32:1	444
32:8	75
34:1	319

35:1–47	xcv
35:1	319
39:1–43:3	15
39:5–7	734
40:1–3	755, 804
40:1	847, 1067
40:2	444
40:3	1108
41:1–4	803
44:1	75
47:2–52:7	xcv
48:8	846
48:10	352
48:32	240
48:40	240
48:47	422
49:2	422
50:1–51:16	15
50:2–4	1081
51:3	99
51:7–16	439
51:11	297
53–57	827
53:1–77:17	xcv
54:1	240
55:6	422
57:13	1081
66:2	359
67:2	608
67:7	742, 830
70:2	240
70:7–10	896
70:10	240
70:20	802, 844
71:1	444
75:6	412
76:1–5	626
76:2	626
77:17–26	461
77:17–19	lxxiv, 125
77:18–87:1	xcv
77:19–26	523
78–87	lxxiv, 125, 830, 1064
78:2	29
78:5–7	436
80:2–3	595
83:2–3	206

3 Apocalypse of Baruch

praef. 1–2	10
praef. 2	319
1:1	xlix, 18
1:3	58, 306, 642
1:6	569
1:7	xlix, 18, 422, 563, 566, 828
1:8	569
2:6	569
4:1	xlix, 18
4:1 (Gk.)	874
4:3–5	683
4:6	401

4:9 xlix, 18
4:15 859
5:1 xlix, 18
6:2 174, 1063
8:1 644
8:4 537
8:5 188
8:14 561
8:14 (Syr.) 561
9:7 697
11:2 105
11:2 (Slav.) 695
11:3 514, 561, 854, 1028
11:4 291
11:4 (Gk.) 694–95
11:4 (Slav.) 695
11:6 (Gk.) 695
11:7 (Gk.) 694
11:8 (Gk.) 694
13:4 clxxxi
14:1–2 1028
14:1 561
16:3 500, 527
27:1 1106
29:3 1106
36:1–40:4 1106
39:7 1107
40:1–4 1106
53:1–76:5 1106
72:2–74:3 1106, 1107

Apocalypse of Daniel
13:1–13 753, 759
14:1–3 600

Apocalypse of Elijah
1:8 167, 175, 287
1:10 287, 753
1:13 21
2:1 1118
2:4–5 290
2:5 531
2:7–8 767
2:32 531
2:52 743
3:1 753
3:5–13 753, 759
3:5 753
3:13 753
3:18 753
3:31 619
4:2 753
4:7–19 588–89
4:7 600
4:8–12 590, 742, 753
14:9–15:7 589
4:10 287
4:11 415, 525
4:13–14 589
4:13 619, 831
4:15 753
4:20 753
4:28 753
4:31 753
5–7 884
5 153
5:6 152
5:36–39 1108
5:38 1111
9:1–7 531

2 Apocalypse of Enoch
29:4 (J) 736, 740

Apocalypse of Moses
5:3 clxxxi, 581

9:3 153
13:2–3 153
16:4–5 697
17:1 697
20 897
20:4 897
22:1–29:6 277
22:1–3 511
22:3 511
27:5 308, 864, 1025, 1927
27:7 886
28:2 153
28:4 152
29:11 786
38:2 355
39 696
39:2 736
40:3 694
40:4 537
42:1 453
43:4 1024

Apocalypse of Sedrach
2:1–4 561
2:1 88
2:2 88
2:3 88
5:4 742
8:6 clxxvii
8:7 clxxvii
9:1 154
11:19 85
12:1 154
14:1 694
16:6 154
16:10 49

Apocalypse of Zephaniah
frag. A 316
2:10–12 72
3:8–9 701
4:1–4 496
4:1 337
4:4 532
5:6 562
6:8 532, 701
6:11–13 72
6:11 99, 557
6:17 701
8:1 337
8:5 21
9–12 497
9:1–5 497
9:12–10:9 117
12 1062
12:1 511
12:7 422

Aristeas, *Hist.*
frag. 1 760

Aristobulus, *Fragmenta*
3 510

Demetrius, *Fragmenta*
2 465
21.5 382

1 Enoch
1–36 lxxvii, lxxxii, xciii, 71, 473, 669, 811
1:1–2 8
1:1 10, 423
1:4 656, 1059
1:5 302
1:9 363, 836, 954
2:113–14 1222

5:1 103, 365, 454
6–11 668, 686
6:6 698
7:1 810
7:5 887, 888
7:6 865, 887
8:1 836
8:2 107
8:3 869
8:4–11:12 408
8:4 408
9:1–11 408
9:1 537, 694, 887, 1011
9:2 865
9:4 853, 953, 954
9:5 312
9:8 810
9:9 1011
10:1–15 408
10:1–6 669
10:2 669
10:4–6 1078
10:4 1082
10:6 421, 422, 693, 828, 1104
10:7 302, 1119, 1120
10:11–14 669
10:11–13 1078
10:11–12 1082
10:11 810
10:12–11:2 669
10:12 422, 828
10:13 1066
10:16–11:2 408, 669
10:21 238
12:2 836
12:3 75, 853
12:4 698
13:8 561
14 278
14:5 698
14:6 949, 985
14:8–16:3 71, 277, 1066
14:8–25 liv, 436
14:8 625, 841
14:12 484
14:14–15 280–81, 313
14:14 99
14:18–22 71
14:19 870
14:20 223, 468
14:21 99
14:22 337, 352, 363
14:24 99
15:2–7 810
15:3 698, 810
16:1 422, 669, 828
17:6 890
17:7 526
17:8 526
17:12 1151, 1152
18:1 450
18:2 450, 451
18:6–8 945
18:8 945
18:11 558
18:13–16 107, 112
18:13 520
18:14 473, 686
18:15 473
18:16 704
18:21 526
19:1 35, 422, 542, 669, 828
20:1–7 694
20:1 509, 537
20:2–8 35
20:2–7 836

20:5	110, 694	49:4	421	69:27	12, 421, 700, 841
20:7	35	50:1	359	70–71	71
21:1–6	112	50:2	702	70:1–71:17	71
21:3–6	35, 107	51:1–2	1091	70:1–4	599
21:3	484, 520	51:2	359	70:1	240
21:5–10	15	51:3	263	70:2–4	410
21:5	836	52:1	625, 841	70:2	625, 841
21:6	473, 704	52:9	421	70:3	154
21:7	526, 558	53:1	240	71	278
21:9	836	53:3	538, 843, 994	71:1	836
21:10	473	54:3	1081	71:2	870
22:1–14	15	54:6	240, 694	71:4	359
22:3	473, 836	54:7	296	71:5–17	277
22:4	422, 828	55:2	240	71:6–8	286
22:7	472, 473	55:4	263, 419, 421	71:7	297
22:9	472, 473	55:5–6	644	71:8	363, 694, 836
22:11	422, 828	55:6	1064	71:9	694, 836
22:13	422, 828	56:1	538, 843, 994, 1047	71:10	94
23:1–4	15	56:5–8	1080	71:11	302
23:4	473, 836	56:5–6	538	71:13	694
24–25	154, 1221	56:5	538, 891, 1047, 1095	72–82	lxxvii, xciii
24:1–25:7	15	56:7	896, 898	72:1	836, 1116
24:1–25:3	945, 1082	56:8	1065, 1097	74:2	836
24:3–4	154	57	436	75:3	884
24:6	836	57:2	359	75:5	34
25:3	277, 472, 473, 853	58:3	359	76:1–14	450
25:4–6	154	58:5	359	77:3	154
25:4	ccii, 473, 528, 669, 886	60:1–6	71	80:2–8	418, 507
25:5	152	60:1–3	71	81:2–3	xcviii, 345
25:7	44, 853	60:1	363	81:2	224, 345
26:1–27:5	15	60:2	288	81:3	44
27:2–3	835	60:4	359	83–90	lxxvii, 369
27:2	836	60:5	240	83:7	206
27:3	422, 636, 828	60:7–11	728, 732, 755	83:11	44
27:4	422, 828	60:8	154	84:1–4	43
27:5	44	60:12–23	728	84:2–3	317
32:2–6	153	60:12–22	884	84:2	954
32:3	154	60:24	728–29, 732, 755	84:4	422, 828
32:6	473, 836	61:1–5	604	85–90	xciii, 369–70
36:4	44	61:1	824	86:1–3	107, 686
37–71	lxxvii, xciii, 34, 94,	61:8	263, 359	86:1	415, 525
	412, 419, 824	61:9–13	302	86:3	525
37:2	240	61:10	359, 884	88:1–3	415
37:5	240	61:11	33	88:1	525
38:4	99, 359	61:12	34, 410	88:3	107, 686, 1082
38:5	359, 419, 994, 1067	62:1–6	277	89:7	346
39:3	625–26, 841	62:1	240, 419	89:11–12	370
39:4–9	411	62:3	419	89:16	370
39:4–5	410	62:4	682	89:22	370
39:9	44	62:6	419	89:26	370
39:10	44	62:8	359	89:29	370
39:12–13	304	62:9	419	89:33	1062
39:12	302	62:11	538, 843, 994	89:42	clxxix, 370
39:13	44	62:12–13	835	89:45–46	370
40:1–10	537, 701	62:12	870	89:52	71, 599
40:1	337, 363	62:14	1033, 1034, 1035, 1063	89:55	423
40:4–7	302	63:1	419, 538, 843, 994	89:56–58	608
40:6	240	63:2	419, 954	89:61–64	224
40:7	240, 693, 701	63:4	954	89:66	423
40:9	694	63:12	419	89:67	423
41:2	359, 410	65:6	240	89:72–77	346
43:4	359	65:10	240	89:76–77	346
45:3	263, 277	65:12	240, 359	90:5	853
45:4	1116	66:1	240, 537, 538, 843	90:6	370
46:1–8	71	66:2	885	90:9	323, 368, 370
46:1–3	71	67:7	240	90:13–19	896, 1079
46:1	91, 94, 836, 1067	67:8	240, 419	90:13–15	370
46:4–6	421	67:12	419	90:13	1064, 1095
47:2–3	288	69:5	810, 836	90:16–19	896
47:2	359, 410	69:6	697	90:16	1065
47:3–4	277	69:10	1056	90:17	224, 346
47:3	363	69:13	359	90:18	370
47:4	391, 408, 412	69:14	1056	90:19–20	370
48:1	359	69:22	884	90:19	370, 956, 994
48:5	240	69:25	302	90:20–39	71
48:9	835	69:26–29	277, 335	90:20–38	277

90:20–23	71, 1081
90:21	509
90:24	415, 525
90:26–27	835
90:28–29	241
90:31–33	71
90:31	599
90:33	436
90:37–38	71
90:37	323, 353–54
90:40	43
91–108	lxxiv, 125
91–105	lxxvii
91–104	lxxx, 1105
91:1–19	506
91:1–3	224
91:3–10	lxxvi
91:7–9	500
91:12–17	xciii, 10, 956
91:12	994
91:15	506
91:16	1116
93	xciii, 1105
93:1–15	344
93:1–10	10
93:1–3	10
93:2	836
93:3–10	499
93:8	599
94:3–5	lxxxvii
94:8	990
94:9	422, 828
95:3	956, 994
95:7	956, 994
96:1	956, 994
96:2	705
97:3	422, 828
97:8–9	258, 990
98:2–3	990, 994
98:5	ccii, 528
98:8	422, 828
98:10	422, 828
98:12	956, 994
98:13	622
99:1	365
99:4	644, 896, 1064, 1079
99:7	542
99:10	20
99:13	524
99:14	524
99:15	422, 828
99:16	359, 1062
100:1	1047
100:3	848
100:4	422, 828
100:5	359, 836
100:6	lxxiv, 125
100:9	541
101:7	1120
102:8	856
103:1	106
103:2	206
103:5–6	11
103:9	422
104:5	421, 422, 828
104:6	158
104:7	224
104:10	106, 206
104:12	106, 206, 886
104:13	1029
106:1	422
106:2	94, 99
106:3	clxxix, 744
106:5–6	94–95
106:9	472

106:10	94
106:13	15, 472
106:19–107:1	345
106:19	206, 224
107:1	224
107:2	1
108:3	224
108:5	836
108:7	224
108:12	287, 290

2 Enoch

1:5 (A)	99, 557, 613
1:5 (J)	99, 613
1:7	99
3:1	625, 841
3:3 (J)	296
4–6	884
4:1	291
4:2 (A)	296
7:1	890
7:2	1082
8:1–3	153
8:1	152, 154
11:45	1063
12:2 (J)	34
16:7	34
17	1059
17:1	302
17:9	302
18:3–4	698
18:6 (J)	422
18:8–9	316
19:1–4	884
19:1 (J)	557
19:2	99
19:3 (J)	224, 316
19:6	302
20:1 (J)	287
20:4	302
21:1 (J)	305
21:6	681
22:6 (A)	695
22:12 (J & A)	224
27:3	112
29:2–3	846
29:4–5	696, 698
29:4 (J)	755
30:2–3	112
30:4–6	681
31:6 (J)	698
32:2–33:1	1105
33:10 (A)	940
36:1–2	599
39:5	846
40:10 (J)	450
42:4	316
49:1 (J)	566
53:2 (J)	224
67	626

3 Enoch

1:6–12	278
1:8	297
1:12	305
2:1	297, 524
6:1	599
6:2	297
7:1	278, 297
14:4	451, 560, 1063
15B:2	174, 309
16	291, 471, 509
16:1	842
17:1	509
17:8	842

18	309
18:19	870
18:24	352
18:25	842
19:4	870
19:25	613
20:2	305, 316
21:1–3	298
21:4	842
22B	305
22:4	613
23:18	152
24–40	316
24:11	524
25:5–7	297
25:6	301
26:3	524
26:12	701
28:7–10	277
31:2	538, 843, 994
32:1–2	277
32:1	538, 843, 994
33:1–34:2	286
33:1	538, 843, 994
33:3	297–98
33:4	871
35	1059
35:1–6	277
36:1–2	871
37:1	871
39:2	297, 316
40:2	305
44:3	535
44:5	524
44:10	696
48A:1	297
48A:10	1033
48B:1	174, 309

Epistle of Aristeas

12	644
32	461
33	357, 879
39	461
42	357, 879
46	461
50–82	357
73–79	357
79	880
95	508
96	93
98	243
129	748
134–39	543
155	874
158	814
159	767
176	805
185.2	58
188	205
256	644
280	173

Epistle of Jeremiah	lxxiv, 125
6:63	760
8–9	542, 544
8	174
9	174
30	542
50	542
57	542
70	542
71	854

Eupolemus *Fragmenta*
2 — 745
2.7–8 — 90
30.5 — 382
39.2 — 382

Ezekiel Trag. *Exagoge*
68–82 — 261, 277, 436
71 — 309
74–76 — 262
83 — 15
85 — 525
89 — 114
117 — 504
132–51 — 502, 503, 527
133–34 — 884
247 — 558

5 Ezra
1–2 — xcv, 803
1:19 — 189
2:4 — 167
2:18 — 601
2:33 — xlix, 18
2:38 — 452
2:39 — 223
2:40 — 452
2:42–48 — 277, 803
2:42–45 — 175, 277, 290
2:42 — xlix, 18
2:45 — 223

6 Ezra
15–16 — 803

Apocalypse of Ezra
2:19 — 620
4:43 — 693
6:14 — 606
7:6 — 599
7:12 — 620

Greek Apocalypse of Ezra
1:6 — clxxxi, 581
1:7 — 690
1:9 — 485, 524
1:10 — 542
1:12 — 411
1:14 — 644
1:24 — 485, 524
2:19 — 760
2:23 — 407
2:27 — 422, 828
2:29 — 422, 828
3:3 — 422
3:10 — 466
4:5 — 407
4:12 — 485, 524
4:24 — 694
4:26–27 — 753, 759
4:36 — 511, 519
4:38 — 565
5:1 — 407
5:6 — 407
5:7 — 690
5:16 — 407
6:3–15 — 894
6:5 — 894
6:7 — 894
6:17 — 167
7:11 — 422, 828
7:16 — 49

History of the Rechabites
13:2 — 189

Joseph and Aseneth
1:27–29 — 1105
2:6 — 653
3:6 — 878
4:9 — 811
4:10 — clxxvi
5:5 — 72, 173, 653
5:6 — 117
8:1 — 811
8:3 — clxxvi
8:5 — 189, 454
8:6 — 454
8:9 — clxxvi, 749
8:11 — 411
9:2 — clxxx, 197
10:16 — 323, 393
11:7 — clxxvi
11:9 — 629
11:10 — 454
11:15–18 — 744
12:1 — clxxvi, 312–13
12:2 — 348–49, 526
12:11 — clxxix
13:12 — clxxvi
14:8–11 — 117
14:8–9 — 842
14:9 — 73, 99, 323, 393, 1054
14:10 — 99
15:3 — 227
15:4 — 224, 748
15:7 — cciii, 411
15:12 — 526, 1056
16:14 — 154, 189
16:15 — 572
16:16 — 853
16:17 — 363
17:6 — 241
17:8 — 1054
18:6 — 173
18:9 — 99, 154
18:11 — 629, 874
19:5 — 640
19:8 — 639–40
21:5 — 174
21:8 — 875
21:15 — 629
21:21 — 856
22:7 — 94–95
22:13 — 411
23:15 — 1054
24:20 — 859
26:2 — 158
26:5 — 99
27:9 — 653
27:10 — clxxvii, clxxix
27:11 — clxxix
28:3 — 207
28:4 — clxxix
28:7 — 158
28:9 — 854, 027

Jubilees
1:4 — 86, 114
1:5–7 — 86
1:11 — 542
1:12 — 163, 610, 886
1:20 — 669, 693
1:25 — 34, 102
1:26 — 114
1:27–29 — 111, 1116
1:28 — 803
2:1 — 111
2:2 — 34, 294, 348, 451, 509, 526, 560, 565, 846, 884
2:4 — 296

2:8 — 294
2:16 — 366, 526, 565
2:18 — 509
2:19–20 — 749
2:20 — 38
3:26 — 897
3:30 — 897
4:15 — 302, 698
4:19 — 669
4:23 — 599, 690
4:26 — 1116
5:6–11 — 669
5:6 — 111, 1082
5:12–19 — 224
5:12–13 — 224
5:13 — 111
5:14 — 890
7:20–29 — lxxvi
7:20 — 187
8:3 — 302
8:19 — 1096
9:15 — 669
10:1–3 — 669
10:5 — 302
10:7 — 526, 1082
10:9 — 627
10:11 — 669
10:17 — 669
10:22 — 669
11:4–6 — 542
12:4 — 629
13:20 — 466
15:27 — 509
15:31–32 — 34
15:33 — 165, 1062
16:9 — 224
16:18 — 47
16:31 — 470
16:33 — 669
17:11 — 359, 836
17:15–16 — 277–78, 693
18:15 — 466
20:7 — 629
21:4 — 102
21:10 — 669
22:17 — 542
23 — xciii, 622
23:11–21 — 239, 473
23:18 — 398
23:23 — 622, 644, 896, 1064
23:30–32 — 224
23:30 — 625, 956, 994, 1078
23:32 — 224
24:30 — 422, 828, 870
25:16 — 466
27:23 — 466
28:17–24 — 465
30:18 — 613
30:20–23 — 224
30:20–22 — 227
30:22 — 224
31:4 — 359
31:14 — 836
32:3 — 465
32:19 — 461
32:20–21 — xcviii
32:20 — 626
32:21–22 — 224
33:12 — 836
33:20 — 48
33:22 — 464
35:1 — 110
36:3–11 — lxxvi
36:7 — 1056
36:10 — 224, 422

48:5–8   504
48:5   527
48:15–18   693
49:1–17   372
49:1–7   372

Jubilees (fragmenta)
3:9   422, 828
10:7   422, 694, 828

Ladder of Jacob
1:10   466
2:6–22   305
2:7–22   277
2:8   297
2:18–19   305

Martyrdom of Isaiah
1:9   185
2:7–11   706
2:7   740
2:12   382
6:1–11:43   318
9:2   88
10:9   534

Paralipomena Jeremiae
1:5   clxxvi, 58, 306, 642
1:6   clxxix, 608
1:8   597
2:2   85, 347, 882, 984
2:5   516
2:10   606
3:2   511, 854
3:8–11   678
3:10–11   595
3:10   346
3:18–19   595
4:1   347, 511
4:3   66
4:7–8   597
5:21   644
5:24   644
5:32   411, 629, 828, 854, 984
6:13   17
6:15–7:36   524
6:15–7:4   lxxiv, 125
6:19   17
7:15–16   523
7:15   854, 984
7:20   524
7:24–35   lxxiv, 125
9:1–4   513
9:1   152
9:3–6   304
9:5   694
9:6   clxxvi, 58, 306
9:7–14   623
9:7   606
9:17   639
9:18   521
9:21–22   620
9:21   617
9:29   67, 107
15:7   1024
23   lxxxix

Prayer of Azariah
1:13   364, 466
1:32   272
4   885
5   608
12   17

Prayer of Manasseh
2   828

2.22.12   clxxvi, 58
3   453
22:13   clxxvii

Psalms of Solomon
2:2   608, 1064
2:6   458
2:16   207
2:18   886
2:19   608
2:25–29   754
2:25   733
2:34–35   207
2:34   207, 993
3:12   1091
3:14   242
4:16   541
5:1   clxxv, clxxvii
5:28   368
6:2   541
8:1   510
8:4   608, 1121
8:12   608
8:20   887
9:4   542
9:9   689
10:1–3   260
10:5   clxxv, 886
10:8   429, 470
11:1   510
11:2–7   436
12:6   429, 470
13:2–3   402
13:2   382
13:9   38
14:1   260
14:3   153–54
14:9   890
14:19   901
15:3   360, 815
15:4–9   530
15:6   452
15:7   382, 402
15:8   456
15:9–10   767
15:9   452
15:10   456
15:12   422, 423
16:2   401
16:9   542
17–18   827
17:8–9   207
17:8   207, 993
17:11–25   1047
17:16–17   691
17:16   157
17:19   526
17:21–25   420, 803
17:21   351
17:22–23   1064
17:22   608
17:23–24   210–11, 688
17:23   653
17:24–25   1053, 1058, 1060
17:24   211
17:26–28   460
17:26   436, 1054
17:29   362, 1054
17:34   689
17:35   420
17:40–42   812
17:40   478
17:43–44   460
17:43   836
17:44   423
18:1   542
18:4   38
18:5   639
18:6   423

Ps.-Philo Biblical Antiquities
3:3   240
3:9   240
3:12   240
4:16   240
8:6   464, 465
8:11–14   465
10:1   504, 527
10:3   465
10:7   189
11:4   295, 518
11:5   518
12:8   153
14:2   466
16:1–7   185
16:3   890
18:13   188
19:13   414, 890
25:4   462, 465
25:9   462
25:9–13   462, 465
26:10–11   465
28:8   561
38:2   710
38:3   846
48:1–2   626
48:1   615, 617
48:2   626
51:1   890
53:3–5   561
57:2   185
60:2   507
64:6   223, 293

Questions of Ezra
21   277

Sepher ha-Razim
praef. 15–16   561
pref. 18   809
1.9–10   846
1.135–40   766
2.43–44   561
2.148   1063
3.23   846
3.28   846
3.57–58   846
4.9   846, 1063
4.10   97, 885
4.31–67   1063
5.3–4   286
7   278, 871
7.1–2   298
7.1–3   405
7.16–17   305

Sibylline Oracles
1.66   58, 1117
1.137–46   772
2.6–26   507
2.15–19   996, 1027
2.23   403
2.34–38   679
2.35   418
2.39–55   167, 175
2.89   1081
2.96   186
2.154–64   507
2.167   753, 759
2.171   461
2.187–89   599
2.195   1104

Reference	Page
2.196–213	506
2.196–205	1066
2.196–200	760
2.215	694
2.230	58
2.243	689
2.286	1066
2.334–38	1066
3	xcii
3.20–23	565
3.20	312
3.35	565
3.47–48	826
3.52–62	996
3.53–61	541
3.53–54	760
3.54	1066
3.55	422
3.63–74	730, 739, 753, 760
3.63–67	753, 759
3.81–92	506
3.82–83	415
3.84–85	760, 1066
3.132–41	686
3.147–55	687
3.156–61	687
3.162–64	573–74
3.175–76	934
3.179–82	990
3.186	422
3.206	422
3.250	558
3.273–79	597
3.298	574
3.307–13	408
3.311–12	645, 887
3.311	887
3.312	993
3.313	408
3.315	382
3.316–17	402
3.317	382
3.319	1094
3.320	887
3.332	403
3.334	418
3.335	402
3.380	422
3.387–400	934
3.393	401
3.396–400	684
3.397	684
3.457	418
3.480	401
3.491	574
3.497	744
3.531–32	990
3.544	541
3.545–72	543
3.556–61	423
3.601–7	543
3.606	541
3.607	419
3.632	1062
3.643	622
3.657–701	1047
3.657	990
3.660–68	644
3.663–68	896, 898
3.663	419, 875
3.669–701	506
3.669–81	1101
3.669	85, 854, 882, 1064
3.675	422
3.689–92	541, 900
3.690–92	835
3.691	902
3.714	422
3.716–20	238
3.722	541
3.725–31	238
3.750	990
3.763	102, 1097
3.779	422
3.783	990
3.796–808	507, 679
3.798	418
3.805	418
4.28	541
4.47	506
4.61	418, 884
4.82	619, 831
4.93	831
4.107–8	263
4.119–22	738
4.120	891
4.124	519
4.130–34	520
4.137–39	738
4.138–39	739
4.139	891
4.159–60	1062
4.171–78	506
4.174–75	511
5	xcii
5.1–51	772
5.12–51	946
5.28–34	739
5.33–34	740, 745, 755
5.38–39	900
5.63	85, 854, 882
5.74	22
5.101–10	595
5.137–54	738
5.138–53	739
5.143	830
5.154	619, 831
5.155–61	520, 525
5.158–61	525, 996
5.159	830
5.161	359
5.165	1010
5.173	995
5.201	520
5.214–27	738
5.215–24	739
5.226	619, 831
5.243	422
5.248	422
5.252	1161
5.286	941
5.290–91	263
5.344–49	890
5.344–45	561
5.346–51	414
5.348	22
5.351	422
5.361	22
5.363–70	739
5.377–80	519
5.413	619, 831
5.414–33	803
5.432	359
5.434	830
5.447–83	507
5.454	527
5.477–82	414
5.512–31	681, 699
5.512–13	691
5.516	212
5.528–29	699
7.118–29	506
7.120	1066
7.125	414
7.149	189
7.200	1066
8.36–42	957
8.68–72	738
8.70–72	739
8.85	733
8.88	834
8.113–19	1008
8.140–47	739
8.178–93	507
8.190	415
8.225–43	506
8.233	415
8.239	519
8.243	760, 1066
8.253	510
8.336–58	506
8.341	415
8.353	531
8.413	415
10.55	418
11.29–32	772
11.91	772
11.92	772
11.114	772
11.189–90	772
11.208	772
11.256	772
11.266	772
12.39	772
12.49–50	772
12.68	772
12.78–94	738
12.78	772
12.96	772
12.101	772
12.121	772
12.125	772
12.144	772
12.148	772
12.189	772
12.207	772
12.246	772
12.250	772
12.258	772
13.83–84	772
13.118	531
14.21	772
14.28	772
14.44	772
14.59–60	772
14.79	772
14.95	772
14.106	772
14.126	772
14.137	772
14.150	772
14.163	772
14.227	772
14.248	772

Testament of Abraham

Reference	Page
1:4 (A)	407, 694
1:5 (A)	466, 809
1:6 (A)	694
1:7 (A)	407
2:2 (A)	694
2:6 (A)	619, 831
3:3 (B)	269
3:9 (A)	694
3:12 (A)	240
4:2–3 (A)	981
4:5 (A)	352, 407
4:5 (B) (MS B)	694

4:7 (A)	694	17:11 (A)	454	5:6	814
4:9 (A)	485	17:12–19	684	5:7	1062
4:10 (A)	clxxix	17:14	683–84	5:8	ccii
4:11 (A)	842–43	17:14 (A)	685	7:7	629
5:1 (A)	694	17:16	684		
5:9	85, 347	18:11 (A)	624	*Testament of Jacob*	
5:9 (A)	854, 882	19:4 (A)	694	2:24	152
5:12	306	19:6–7	683–84	7:27–28	224
6:5 (A)	clxxix	19:6–7 (A)	685		
6:6 (B)	240	19:7	683	*Testament of Job*	
7:1 (A)	clxxxi	19:7 (A)	419, 685	2:4	565
7:3–4 (A)	557	20:10 (A)	694	3:1	561, 854
7:9 (B)	411	20:12	316	4:4	182, 530, 617
7:11 (A)	694	20:15 (A)	49	4:10	167, 173
7:14–16 (B)	626			5:1	455
7:16–17 (B¹)	626	*Testament of Adam*		7:9	407
7:16 (B)	685	1:1–2:12	291	8:1–3	701–2
8:1 (A)	352	1:4	316	14:1–3	356
8:2–3 (A)	407	1:5	296	16:2–4	701–2
8:3 (A)	58	1:12	508	16:4	889
8:3 (B)	296–97, 625, 841	4:3	560	16:7	994
8:5 (B)	363	4:8	287, 298	18:5	617
8:7 (B)	284, 363			20:1–3	701–2
8:9 (A)	842–43	*Testament of Asher*		20:3	530
8:10 (A)	842–43	1:8–9	698	23:5	472
9:1 (A)	100	2:10	224	25:7	653
9:2 (A)	886	3:2	698	26:4	clxxix
9:3 (B)	clxxxi, 581	6:4	697	27:2	617
9:4 (B)	clxxxi, 581	7:1	620	27:3–9	702
9:7 (A)	352	7:2	450	27:3–5	167
9:8 (A)	625, 694, 841	7:3	688	31:5	99
9:15 (A)	485	7:5	224	32:11	859
10–15	lxxxix			33:1–9	262
10:1 (A)	625, 694, 841	*Testament of Benjamin*		33:3	290
10:2 (B)	154, 625, 841	2:3	clxxix	33:5	290
10:6–7 (A)	403	3:1	629	33:7	290
10:9 (B)	174	3:8	369	37:2	454
10:11 (A)	760	4:1	167, 173	38:1	407
10:12 (A)	270, 561, 694	4:4	995	39:9–40:5	690
10:15 (B)	744	6:4	185	39:12–13	625
11:4 (A)	284	7:1–4	505, 506	39:12	626
11:6 (A)	284	9:2	cciii, 441, 689	40:3	174, 625
12 (A)	1081	10:10	188	40:6	308
12:1 (B)	625, 841	11:2–3	157	43:11	clxxxii, 51
12:3–18 (A)	277			43:13	886
12:3 (B)	760	*Testament of Dan*		46:7–47:11	191
12:4–6 (A)	285	3:6	697	47:9	114
12:4 (B)	760	5:1	185	51:1–4	316
12:5 (A)	557	5:4–8	462	52:8–10	626
12:9 (B)	625, 841	5:5–6	697	52:12	316
12:10–11 (B)	403	5:8	499	53:4	clxxxii, 51
12:11 (A)	284	5:9–13	462	53:5–6	622
12:13	clxxx	5:9	499	53:10	49
12:14 (A)	846	5:10–11	693, 754		
13–14 (B)	401	5:11–12	359	*Testament of Joseph*	
13:2 (A)	284	5:12	411	3:2	407
13:6	461	5:13	362	3:7	652
13:6 (A)	292	6:1	697	8:5	994
13:8 (A)	602			9:3	368
13:10 (A)	846	*Testament of Gad*		10:2–3	185
14 (AB)	695	2:5	clxxix	10:3	995
14:5 (A)	694	4:7	697	10:19	995
14:9 (B)	49	5:2	698	10:2–3	185
14:12 (A)	694			19	896
14:13–15 (A)	561	*Testament of Isaac*		19:4	436
14:13 (A)	854	2:13	411	19:6	369, 688
15:1 (A)	694	2:15	411	19:8	369
15:2 (A)	625, 841	6:1–6	316		
15:4 (A)	641	6:24	316	*Testament of Judah*	
15:5	994			9:4	clxxxi
15:11 (A)	352	*Testament of Issachar*		12:4	685
15:12 (A)	clxxvi, 58, 642, 786	1:9	994	19:4	698
15:12 (B)	565	4:45	1062	21:5	814
16–20 (A)	401	5:4	359	23:1–3	597
16:6 (A)	557	5:5	ccii	23:1	542

24:1	213	18:59–60	225
24:2	281		
24:4–6	350	*Testament of Moses*	
25:3	693	1:13	748
		1:14	748
Testament of Jude		1:15	600
9:4	clxxxi, 581	2:4	629
21:6	852	3:1	531, 891
22:2	688	3:2	678
25:5	994	3:12	565, 566
		4:9	461
Testament of Levi		4:21	1123
1:1	422, 828	8	754
2–5	lxxxii, lxxxix	8:1	40, 239
2:2	384, 528	9:1	694
2:6	281, 313	9:6–7	408, 409
2:7	296	10:3–6	1081
2:9	656	10:5–6	414, 415
2:10	352	10:5	413, 890
3:1	656	10:8	705
3:3	693	10:9–10	681
3:4–9	277	10:14	600
3:4	476	12:9	453
3:5–6	476, 511		
3:5	422	*Testament of Naphtali*	
3:8	287, 302	2:3	clxxix
3:9	348, 526	3:1	698
4:1	414	3:4	620
4:4	ccii, 528, 688	4:1	620
5:1	277, 281, 313, 476	5:4	681
5:4	224	8:4	698
6:5	99	8:6	698
6:11	1062		
6:26	194	*Testament of Reuben*	
8:2–10	93	1:6	629
8:2	174, 223, 293, 468, 509	1:10	clxxxii, 51
8:9	174	2:1–9	34
8:10	512	2:4	165
8:14	244, 688	3:1–8	34
9:7	814	3:15	clxxxii, 51
9:14	814	4:1	827
10:3	597	4:4	1062
11:1	382	4:6	188
13:1	827	6:9	629
13:9	262	6:12	853
14:1	688		
14:4	cciii, 688	*Testament of Simeon*	
14:6	620	2:8	clxxix
15:4	clxxix	3:2	856
16:3	887	3:4	827
18:2	35, 173, 225	3:5	698
18:3	213, 225	5:3	188
18:5	656	6:6	ccii, 528, 693
18:6	476, 561	7:2	688
18:9	cciii		
18:11	152, 359	*Testament of Solomon*	
18:12	693	title	9
18:30	879	1:6–7	454
18:52	clxxix	1:8	629

1:9	393		
1:11	393		
2:9	535, 629, 639		
3:1	393		
3:5–6	535		
3:5	58		
3:6	629, 639		
5:1–13	535		
6:1	535, 639		
6:6	562		
6:8	58		
7:4	685		
13:1	532		
14:4	704		
16:3	348		
17:4	456, 629		
18:41	629		
20:14–17	525		
20:16	415		
20:21	629		
Testament of Zebulon			
2:2	887		
4:7	422		
7:3	644		
8:2	185		
9:8	688, 693		
Vitae Prophetarum			
1.1	610, 620		
1.2	856		
1.5(8)	ccii		
2.1	610, 617		
2.10	689		
2.11–19	678		
3.2	610		
3.6–7	842–43		
3.7	891		
3.17–20	462		
4.21B	484, 689		
6.1	610		
7.1	610		
10.3	619, 831		
10.8	621, 689		
10.8b	859		
12.12	745		
18.1	745		
21.3	610		
21.4–5	615		
21.4	615		
21.10	760		
21.12	599		
21.15	599		
22.11	844		
23.1	621, 887		

Dead Sea Scrolls

CD (*Damascus Document*)		5:2	346	10:9	240
1:4–5	628	5:18–19	694	10:11	1221
1:4	444	5:18	694	12:1–2	819, 822
1:21	870	6:2	992	12:12	820
1:49	992	6:8	287	12:22–23	599, 611
2:5–6	846	7:6–7	820	13:20–22	599, 611
3:4	1083	7:18–19	1226	14	1083
3:8	870	8:10	733	14:18–19	599, 611

15:1 567
19:9–11 599, 611
19:10–12 455
19:12 452
19:12 456
19:34–20:1 599, 611
20:16 870

1QH (*Thanksgiving Hymns*)
1:8–13 884
1:10–11 451, 846
1:21 569
1:25 875
2:13 569
2:14 1083
2:20–22 641
2:20 641
2:22 165
2:27 97
2:31 641
3:4 1098
3:5 1098
3:7–12 682
3:8–9 682
3:16–19 534
3:19–22 303
3:19–21 641
3:19 641
3:23–24 875
3:29 707
3:32 707
3:37 641
4:5 641
4:16–17 1083
4:25 359
4:27–29 569
5:5–6 641
5:5 641
6:8 628
6:13 509
6:14–18 153
6:17–18 152
7:6 641
7:26 641
7:28–29 875
7:28 741
7:34 641
8:5–6 153
8:7 479
8:16 478–79
9:25 167, 173
9:37 641
10:5–6 875
10:35 1098
11:3 641
11:13–14 303
11:32–33 1117
13:18 17
14:8 clxxviii, 956, 1065
15:17 870
15:28 741
17:7 641
16:3 304
17:25 17

1QM (*War Scroll*)
1:1 1095
1:1–3 691
1:2 463
1:10–11 896, 1064
1:10 896, 1097
1:11–12 474
1:12 900
1:13 1095
2:1 292
2:2–3 460, 1155

2:2 289, 463
2:7–8 1155
2:10–14 896
2:16–3:11 510
3:9 870
3:12–13 460
3:14–15 460
4:1 870
4:4–5 808
4:9 165
5:11–14 99
5:19 165
6:3 870, 1061
6:6 359
6:11 443
7:3–7 812
7:3–6 819–20
7:3–4 820
7:3 820
7:6 1097
7:12–9:3 510
7:14 510
9:5–6 693
9:12–15 35
9:15–16 537, 694
10:8–9 741
10:10 359
10:12 359
11:2 17
11:6–7 1226
11:11–13 693
12:1–5 303
12:1–2 224
12:1 359
12:8–9 34
12:11 1061
12:14–15 237
12:14 1172
12:15 362
13:10–12 695
13:10 694
13:13 741
14:2–3 474
15–19 693
15:1 474, 896
15:2–3 1064
15:2 896
15:3 564, 1061
16:1 359
17:2 185
17:4ff. 696
17:6–8 694
17:6 692
17:7 693
18:1 564, 754
18:3 564
19:6 237
19:11 1061

1QpHab (*Pesher on Habakkuk*)
2:8–10 569
2:8 clxxviii, 912, 958
2:9 18
5:4 461, 955, 1085
7:1–5 569
7:4–5 106
7:5 18, 106, 569–70
7:8 106
7:14 106
8:1–3 837
9:12 955, 1221
12:14 422, 828
13:2 422, 828

1QS (*Rule of the Community*)
1:3 18

1:8 220
1:13 237
1:15 1224
1:17–18 694
2:2 220
2:22 220
3:3 220
3:9 220
3:18–19 694
3:20 694–95
3:21 1083
3:24 694
4:7 167, 173
4:9 823
4:12 870
4:18–19 754
4:24 1116
5:1–2 165
5:8 153
6:5–6 814
6:8 287
8:1 292
8:12–14 706
8:20 220
8:21 220
9:2 220
9:6 220
9:8 220
9:9 220
9:10–11 599, 611
9:19–21 706
9:19 220
10:22 823
11:5 153
11:7–9 303
11:7–8 359
11:15 309
11:16 17

1Q15 (1QpZeph *Zephaniah Pesher*)
4 422

1Q20 (1QapGen *Genesis Apocryphon*)
2 iv 6–7 566
2:7 853
19:14 280
20:10–11 198
21:13 466
22:27 280

1Q22 (1QDM *Sayings of Moses*)
2:10 615

1Q28a (1QSa *Rule of the Congregation*)
1:15 460
1:29 460
2:11–12 212
2:18–19 814

1Q28b (1QSb *Blessings*)
1:5 359
4:26 509
5:24 1061
5:24–25 1067
5:26 354

1Q35 (1QHHymns[b] *Thanksgiving Hymns*)
frag. 1, line 2 741

2Q24 (2QNJ ar *New Jerusalem*)
frag. 1, line 3 1151

4Q24 (4QLeviticus[b])
frag. 20.4 306

4Q28 (4QDeuteronomyᵃ)
32:43   308

4Q88 (4QPsalmsᶠ)
10:5   703

4Q158 (4QReworked Pentateuchᵃ)
frag. 6, line 8   205

4Q159 (4QOrdinancesᵃ)
2 iv 3–4   292

4Q161 (4QpIsaᵃ)
7–10 iii 26   1061
8 iii 15–19   1060
8–10 iii 11–13   33

4Q163 (4QpIsaᶜ)
6–7 ii 4   830

4Q164 (4QpIsaᵈ)   292
frag. 1   1146–47

4Q166 (4QpHosᵃ)
2:12–13   897

4Q167 (4QpHosᵇ)
2:5   18, 570

4Q168 (4QpMic)
10:6–7   422, 828

4Q169 (4QpNah)
frags. 1–2   956
1:3–4   608
frags. 3–4   608, 956

4Q171 (4QpPsᵃ)
1–10 ii 1   402
1–10 ii 10–11   161
1:5   955
2:5   955
3:15   569
3:15–16   612

4Q174 (4QFlorilegium)
1:2–6   597
1–3 i 12   350
1–3 ii 3–4   1217

4Q175 (4QTestim)
1–20   599, 600, 611
5–8   204

4Q176 (4QTanḥumin)
1–2 i 1–4   622
1–2 ii 1–2   703

4Q180 (4QAges of Creation)
frag. 1, line 3   224
2–3 ii 3   1163

4Q216 (4QJubᵃ)   294

4Q252 (4QpGenᵃ = 4QPatriarchal
Blessings)
5:3–4   350

4Q255 (4QSᵃ Rule of the Community)
frag 2, line 5   220

4Q256 (4QSᵇ Rule of the Community)
frag. 8, line 2   220

4Q257 (4QSᶜ Rule of the Community)
1 ii 5   220

4Q258 (4QSᵈ Rule of the Community)
3 ii 3   220
frag. 3, line 3   220
frag. 3, line 8   220

4Q266 (4QDamascus Documentᵃ)
frag. 1, line 16   259

4Q267 (4QDamascus Documentᵇ)
frag. 2, line 2   185
frag. 2, lines 5–6   150
3 iv 1–2   900

4Q268 (4QDamascus Documentᶜ)
3 i 17   822

4Q269 (4QDamascus Documentᵈ)
frag. 2, line 2   185

4Q274 (4QTohorot A)
1 i 3 1   221
1 i 5 1   221

4Q277 (4QTohorot B)
frag. 1, line 13   1221

4Q280 (4QTohorot E)
10 ii 7   534

4Q285 (4QWar Scrollᵍ)
frag. 5, lines 2–3   350

4Q372 (Apocryphon of Joseph)
frag.1, line 13   745

4Q375 (Apocryphon of Moses)
1:3   901
1.4–5   204

4Q381 (4QNon-Canonical Psalms B)
frag. 15, line 6   741

4Q385 (4QPs.-Ezekielᵃ)
frag. 4, lines 8–9

4Q390 (4QPs.-Moses Apocalypse)
2 i 5   570

4Q394 (4QMMTᵃ)
8 iv 1223
32–35   878

4Q394–98   1097

4Q400 (4QShirShabbᵃ)
2:1   472
3 ii 5   472
3–4:4   35

4Q401 (4QShirShabbᵇ)
35:1   472

4Q403 (4QShirShabbᵈ)
1 i 31   472
1 i 43   35
1 ii 8   35
1 ii 9   35
1 ii 10   878
1:23   509
2:10–27   509

4Q404 (4QShirShabbᶜ)
frag 1:1   509
frag 2:4–5   509
5:5   35

4Q405 (4QShirShabbᶠ)
3 ii 15   509
17:3   35
20 ii 2   291, 471, 509
20 ii 21–22 11   35
20–22 i 10–11   285
20–22 ii 7   878
23 i 8   472
23 i 8–9   35
23 i 9–10   35
19ABCD 4   35

4Q414 (4QBaptismal Liturgy)
frag. 12, line 5   1221

4Q416, 418
frag. 2, line 5   478

4Q418 (4QSapiental Work Aᵃ)
frag. 9, line 17   572

4Q436 (4QBarki Nafshiᶜ)   98

4Q491 (4QMᵃ War Scroll)
frag.11   693

4Q504 (4QDibHamᵃ)
3:5–7   260
3:12   18
frag. 4, line 10   47–48
frag. 6, lines 6–7   705
7:8   534

4Q512 (4QRitual of Purification)
10–11 x 6   1221

4Q521 (4QMessianic Apocalypse)
2 ii 7   261

4Q525 (4QBéat)
2 ii 1–3   11

4Q534 (4QMess ar)
1:8   206

4Q537 (4QApocryphon of Jacob)
frag. 1, lines 3–4   224

4Q544 (4QAmramᵇ)
3:2   695

4Q550 (4QProto Estherᵃ)
4:5   346

4Q554 (4QJNᵃ ar New Jerusalem)
1 iii 15   1151
2:12–3:9   442, 461
3:20   1151

6Q15 (6QDamascus Document)
frag. 3, line 2   185

11Q10 (11QtgJob Targum on Job)
31:12   534

11Q13 (11QMelchizedek)
9–15   692

11Q18 (11QJN ar New Jerusalem)
frag. 16, line 6   1151
frag. 18, line 1   1151

11Q19 (11QTempleᵃ)
3–48   604
13:8–16   373
18:4   1155

24	465	44–45	465	54:10–15	205
29:7–9	1123	44:18–20	203	57:11–13	292
38–39	606	45:8–9	1221	59:13	1123
39–41	465	45:16–17	1221	61:1–2	205
39:12	1156, 1159–60	46:16–18	820	61:6–7	602
39:12–13	442, 461	47:5–12	820	61:16–19	1223
40	606	47:13	608	64:8	602
40:11–14	442, 461, 1155				

Josephus

Against Apion		3.32	189	7.43	838
1.22	139	3.83	558	7.95	308, 1027
1.141	154	3.88–90	88	7.146	687
1.164	302	3.90–92	711	7.154	611
1.172	689	3.90	563	7.158	687
1.193	543	3.91	567	7.243	687
1.197–98	619	3.96	600	7.305–6	356
1.197	619, 628, 831	3.123	319	7.347	154
1.199	302	3.131	300	7.356	362
1.209	619	3.140	357	7.365–66	289
1.248–50	543	3.142–43	357	7.367	289, 302
1.282	608	3.143	357–58	8.45–49	191
2.12	745	3.153–54	878	8.46–49	894
2.39	170	3.153	93	8.47	454
2.75	762	3.157	174	8.63–98	924
2.83–84	745	3.172	174	8.77–78	241
2.103–4	605	3.178	243	8.79–80	296
2.108	289	3.181	319	8.90	90
2.119	876–77	3.185	878	8.133–40	924
2.184–203	740	3.199	89	8.151	898
2.218–19	625	3.221	368	8.186	154
2.236–37	543	3.226	368	8.197	623
		3.237–47	372	8.316–59	203
Antiquities		3.234	883	8.317	203
1.26	379	3.245	470	8.319	615
1.37	154	3.251	368	8.328	615
1.52	687	3.318–19	194	8.330	203
1.70	1117	3.271	687	8.334	203
1.85	88, 599, 626	4.70	608, 814–15	8.335	407
1.103	286	4.75	194	8.337	407
1.104	30	4.115–16	467	8.338	407
1.123	1094	4.126–30	188, 194	8.343	407
1.185	561	4.128	1124	8.347	203
1.193	641	4.154	117	8.350	30
1.240	697	4.171	117	8.352	88
1.304	687	4.200	608	8.355–59	203
1.321	838	4.207	543	8.362	611
2.123	597	4.209	608	8.402	407
2.142	1036	4.213	767	9.11	308, 1027
2.181	597	4.218	608	9.13.2	163
2.205	371	4.227	608	9.28	599
2.267–69	88	4.270	1009	9.47	203
2.274	302	4.303	872	9.65	687
2.276	30	4.326	600, 625	9.99–101	lxxiv, 125
2.293–314	503	5.26	815	9.108	203, 384, 1026
2.294–95	866	5.39	17, 872	9.122–24	203
2.295	496	5.60	302	9.122–23	203
2.299	496	5.150	833	9.225	154
2.304	496	5.220–21	397	9.256	407
2.305	496, 901	5.282	826	9.265	886
2.306	527	5.284	626	9.273	814
2.309	496	6.99	420	10.3.1	163
2.312	261	6.116	420	10.8	534
2.320	496	6.211	895	10.11	611
2.346	872	6.223	302	10.37	886
2.409	748	6.301	1009	10.38	621
2.417	748	6.332	401	10.46	154
3.8	711	6.344	703	10.79	830
3.15	1124	7.24–38	740	10.84	543
3.26–32	189	7.40	611	10.97	838

10.101	838	14.261	193, 219	1.650-51	300
10.210	563	14.304	173	1.571	544
10.213	308, 1027	14.429	420	1.581-83	544
10.216	609	14.488	174, 309	1.596	401
10.226	154	15.37	206	1.650	625
10.230	838	15.40	1172	1.671	173, 685
10.263	407	15.89	138, 544, 1087	2.101-10	740
10.276-77	830	15.136	111	2.119	164
11.5	875	15.138	1123	2.120-21	820
11.55	407, 888	15.268-73	172	2.121	820, 838
11.90	13	15.339	778	2.123	223, 293
11.101	13	15.341	172	2.137	223, 293
11.133	442, 446, 460, 461	15.391	877	2.138	360
11.159	534	15.396	606	2.142	1036
11.205	1087	15.410-17	605	2.153-55	625
11.215	689	15.411-16	606	2.156	401
11.327	223	15.417	605	2.160-61	820
11.331	223	16.160	170	2.167	697
12.8	838	16.162-68	171	2.184-85	745, 755
12.39	461	16.162-65	165	2.236-37	611
12.40	357, 879	16.171-73	171	2.261-63	613
12.45	174	16.171	169, 219	2.305	619
12.49	461	16.172	817	2.315	619
12.56	461	16.235	169	2.339	619
12.60-84	357	16.260	302	2.389	893
12.78-82	357	16.296	173	2.397	608
12.82	880	17.1.3	184	2.400	606
12.89	805	17.148	833	2.457	998
12.109	1210	17.151-55	300	2.457-86	1011
12.119	170	17.180	703	2.530	697
12.125-26	139, 170	17.197	173	2.599	172, 1011
12.147-53	219, 263	17.220	911	2.266-70	170
12.148-53	169	18.21	820	2.461-65	170
12.166-68	139	18.85-87	678	2.466-76	170
12.172-73	139	18.198	206	2.477-79	170
12.233	154	18.228	735	2.487	170
12.241	172	18.256-309	740	2.599	172
12.250	89	18.257-61	755	2.618-19	172
12.272-75	420	18.261	745	3.95	844
12.285	697	18.263	931	3.174	302
12.300	611	18.270	931	3.225	844
12.301	703	18.277-78	755	3.375	401
12.344	543	18.280	755	3.377	622
12.358-59	745	18.312-13	171	3.392	111
12.396	838	18.312	947	3.539	172
12.407	clxxx, 231	18.374-79	170	4.171	608
12.421	420	19.280-84	128	4.214	608
13.113	1004	19.281	143	4.261	608
13.163-65	931	19.290	543	4.281	877
13.169	931	19.335-37	172	4.289-300	417
13.198	703	19.349	611	4.314-17	602, 622
13.200	clxxx	20.12	174	4.317	617, 622
13.207	838	20.17	1087	4.381-84	622
13.217	302	20.92	687	4.467	154
13.292	290	20.97-99	613	4.491-99	947
13.320	697	20.101	399	4.536	532
13.372	470	20.118	608	4.546	875
13.415	838	20.123	611	5.14	48
14.1.3-4	184	20.144	520	5.16	48
14.22	615	20.168-72	613	5.31	302
14.35	173	20.216-18	223, 292	5.47-97	1097
14.37-39	931	20.241	685	5.100-111	1011
14.39	1087	20.256	1	5.137	619
14.65-66	372			5.187	1172
14.72	89	*Jewish War*		5.190-99	606
14.73	1087	1.5	875	5.193-94	605
14.110-13	171	1.12	900	5.198-99	605
14.125	1087	1.26	1210	5.202	876-77
14.140	1087	1.99	697	5.207	877
14.153	173	1.154	1087	5.209	877
14.213-16	170	1.284	911	5.211	877
14.235	219	1.307	420	5.216	406
14.241-43	249	1.357	174, 309	5.217	90
14.247-55	181	1.414-15	778	5.225	406
14.259-61	169, 219	1.415	172	5.227	819, 822

Ref.		Ref.		Ref.	
5.235	174, 243	6.288	418	7.105	173
5.368	1123	6.289	415, 679	7.124	174
5.378	360	6.289–300	418, 507	7.148	89
5.409	875	6.293–96	876	7.185	895
5.413	206	6.293	876–77	7.189	835
5.442	900	6.299–300	882	7.218	162, 171
5.458–59	595	6.300	397, 450, 561, 562	7.223–24	1011
6.6	154	6.301	302	7.323	886, 888
6.7	398	6.345	838	7.344–60	625
6.93	1097	6.370	420	7.410–19	1
6.98	595	6.406	848	13.113	733
6.122	595	6.420	1011		
6.124–26	605	6.426–27	194	*Life (Vita)*	
6.149–56	1097	6.429	900	2	289
6.258	1060	6.434	166	39	838
6.274	302	7.17	893	43	838
6.283–84	595	7.46–53	170	92	172
6.285–87	595	7.71	364	93	838
6.286	630	7.105–6	893	132	172
				349	838

Philo

Ref.		Ref.		Ref.	
Abr.		46	608	*Mos.*	
1.1	1117			1.4	290
56	48	*Fug.*		1.39	622
121	30	17	161	1.74–75	30
				1.75	30–31
Aet.		*Jos.*		1.90–146	505
117–49	1120	25	622	1.90	505
				1.96	505
Agr.		*Leg.*		1.98–101	505, 866
111–20	76, 1033	14–21	736	1.103–5	505
111–17	172	103	174	1.107–12	505
		116–17	742	1.118–19	505
Apol. (Hyp.)		116	308, 741	1.120–22	505, 527
11.14–17	820	119	765	1.123–25	505
11.14	820	120	170	1.123	413, 527, 529
		139	543	1.126–29	505
Cher.		188	745, 755	1.130–32	505
22	318	197–337	740	1.133	505
42	360	207–8	745	1.134–39	505
		212	605	1.143–46	480
Conf.		225	608	1.255	360
5	318	245	169	1.263–304	194
78	410	290	543	1.294–99	188
		299	608	2.24	48
Congr.		315–16	171, 990	2.44	543
118	504, 505	346	755	2.55–58	541
177	260	352	742	2.56	835
		353	310	2.68–69	821
Decal.		362	368	2.70	557
46–49	561	369	703	2.72	608
46–47	87			2.109–10	93
64	1038	*Leg. All.*		2.114–15	242, 1056
72–79	543	1.34	259	2.114	174
74	542	1.43	39	2.116	685
82–95	567	1.50	823	2.118–21	94
110	711	1.80	167	2.131	685
		2.42	114	2.203–5	543
Det.		2.48	38	2.213	87
145	260	2.56	93	2.228	410
146	260	2.90	260	2.229	48
160	30	3.163	259	2.34	1210
				2.288	600
Ebr.		*Mig.*		96–146	865
75	365	45	13		
		47–48	87	*Mut.*	
Flacc.		49–50	88	11	30–31
4.23	407	103	243	12	30
25ff.	170	124	241	46	13

Op.
7 — 748
35 — 379
58–59 — 418
69 — 206
153–54 — 154
172 — 30

Plant.
12 — 525
69 — 161

Praem.
52 — 76
95 — 1050
104 — 161
128 — 529

Prov.
95 — 1050
106 — 76
120 — 76

Quaest. in Gn.
1.6 — 154
1.86 — 599
4.51 — 154

Quaest. in Ex.
1.21 — 241
2.5 — 543
2.47 — 614
2.73 — 90
2.78 — 90
2.81 — 90
2.95 — 90
2.104 — 90

Quis Her.
27 — 259
205 — 515
216–25 — 90
274 — 410

Quod Deus
12 — 839
110 — 30

Quod Omn. Prob.
8 — 161
9 — 259
26 — 173

Sac.
8 — 600
19 — 38
72 — 815
91–92 — 255
119 — 38
136 — 817

Sob.
16 — 290
21 — 38
56 — 161
66 — 48

Som.
1.87 — 206
1.179 — 161

1.231 — 30
1.256 — 410
2.114–15 — 691, 692
2.246 — 608

Spec. Leg.
1.28 — 543
1.53 — 543
1.77–78 — 171
1.92 — 418
1.121–22 — 194
1.166 — 372
1.169–70 — 372
1.315–17 — 204–5
1.315–16 — 214
1.334 — 114
2.2 — 567
2.5 — 566
2.145 — 48
2.229–30 — 172
3.27–42 — 1223
4.40 — 567
138 — 817

Virt.
11.72.75 — 872
95 — 816

Vit. Cont.
18 — 820, 822
32–33 — 822
68 — 820
68–69 — 822
83ff. — 822

Rabbinic Literature

'Abot de Rabbi Nathan
2 — 1000
12 — 404
26 — 405
32 — 1063
34 — 111, 612

Hekalot Rabbati
15:8–16:2 — 846

Ma'aseh Merkavah
548.2 — 741
548.4 — 741
548.7 — 741

Masseket Hekalot
4 — 846

Mekilta Exodus
15:1 — 873

Mekilta de Rabbi Ishmael

Beshallah
5 — 872
7 — 518

Kaspa
3 — 602

Nezikin
4 — 602
9 — 624

10 — 290
18 — 407

Shirata
1 — 360
6 — 625
8 — 741

Midrashim

Genesis Rabbah (Bereshit Rabbah)
1.1 — 256
1.6 — 296
2.4.97 — 33
12.1 — 562
22.12 — 696
38.1 — 662, 688
49 — 243
55.7 — 677
63.13 — 897
65.21 — 352, 471, 509, 1063
73.3 — 103
78.1 — 846
81 — 224
82.8 — 189
97.9 — 462

Exodus Rabbah
3.14 — 32
5.9 — 560
8.1 — 842
9.1–3 — 504
19.7 — 38

28.6 — 560
29.4 — 100, 934
29.9 — 518
30.18 — 701
34.1 — 100

Leviticus Rabbah
6.3 — 352
11.2 — 1064
12.2 — 662, 688
19 — 609
24.2 — 701
26 — 224
32.4 — 599

Numbers Rabbah
2.10 — 694
10.1 — 100
11.2 — 189, 1009
13.11 — 33

Deuteronomy Rabbah
3.17 — 600
11.10 — 345, 354

Ruth Rabbah
7.2 — 33

Ecclesiastes Rabbah (Qoheleth Rabbah)
1.9 — 873
7.32 — 599
8.1 — 573

Canticles Rabbah
1.9 — 189
1.11 — 290
3.11 — 885
4.4 — 677
5.2 — 236
5.16.3 — 100

Midrash on Psalms
8.1 — 802, 844–45
8.1.73 — 843
21.1 — 842
21.5 — 92
78.5 — 104
104.27 — 1024

Lamentations Rabbah
2.2.4 — 848

Tanḥuma Exodus
30b — 873

Mishnah

'Abot
1:17 — 257
3:1 — 934, 1024
4:11 — 700
4:17 — 174
4:22 — 1091
5:8 — 505, 506
5:19 — 186
6:9 — 839

'Arak.
2:5 — 356

'Aboda Zara
2:3 — 193, 195

Baba Batra
10:1–2 — 342, 345

Berakot
5:3 — 641
6:4 — 816

Bikkurim
1:3 — 816
1:9 — 816
2:1 — 816
2:4 — 816
2:10 — 816
3:2 — 816

Kelim
1:8 — 605

Ma'aśerot
5:6 — 816

Makkot
3:6 — 457

Menaḥot
11:5–8 — 358
11:7 — 358

Middot
1:8 — 289
2:3 — 605
2:5 — 605

Pe'a
1:1 — 816

Roš Haššana
3:3–4 — 510

Sanhedrin
4:5 — 954
7:2 — 957
9:1 — 957
10:3 — 436

Šebi'it
4:13 — 565, 566
4:14 — 566

Šebu'ot
3:8 — 767
3:11 — 767

Sukka
3:1–8 — 469
4.5 — 470
5.4 — 510

Ta'anit
2:4 — 615
3:8 — 615
4:2 — 289

Tamid
1:1 — 289
5:1–6 — 508
5:1–6:3 — 514
7:3 — 510

Yoma
1:5 — 289
5 — 514, 880
5:1 — 514

Pesiqta Rabbati
20.4 (96b) — 841
22.6 — 352
46 — 694
197a — 504

Pesiqta de Rab Kahana
20.4 (96b) — 625
23.1 — 623

Pirqe Rabbi Eliezer
4 — 451, 694
15 — 110
34 — 168

Shemonah Esreh
10 — 436, 460

Sipre Leviticus
103a — 476

Sipre Numbers
12:1 — 821

Sipre Deuteronomy
32:1 — 565
32:33 — 696
171 — 188, 1001
343 — 1094

Talmud Babli

'Arakin
12b — 289

Baba Batra
14b–15a — 291
74b–75a — 728, 732, 755
75a — 729
75b — 243
160a — 345, 1023
160b–161a — 342

Baba Meṣi'a
59b — 519
83b — 843

Baba Qamma
97b — 608

Berakot
9b — 696
17a — 99, 290, 557

Giṭṭin
20b — 457
31b — 884
57a — 848
68a — 454

Ḥagigah
12b — 189, 297, 507, 512, 677, 694–95
13b — 298, 301
14a — 92
14b — 297
15a — 291, 352, 471, 509

Horayot
12a — 678

Ketubot
13b — 188
77b — 278

Megilla
17b — 392
25a — 188

Menaḥot
1 — 695
85a — 185
98b — 90
110a — 512, 694

Nedarim
32a — 772

Pesaḥim
54a — 476
110a — 535
112b — 539

Qiddušin
29b   684

Sanhedrin
38b   701
50a   957
51a   957
51b   957
52b   957
56b   187
66b   957
76a   957
82a   188
93ab   33
97a   392
97b   610
107b   608
113a   103, 615

Šebiʿit
34a   566
35a   565

Šabbat
17b   188
55a   456, 537, 538, 843
87a   821
88a   538, 539, 843
88b   100
114a   223
120b   456
152b   404, 405, 411

Soṭa
49b   397, 398

Sukka
45b   292

Taʿanit
2a   103
6b   641
11a   224
24b   615
25b   885

Ṭebul Yom
20b   885

Yoma
4a   625, 841
8a   456
39b   677
52b   678
53b   615
75b   189
77a   515

Zebaḥim
62a   512, 695

Talmud Yerušalmi

ʿAboda Zara
3.1, 42c   278

Berakot
2c   291, 471, 509
2c.23   352
5.9b   615

Peʾa
1.1   561

Šabbat
7.2   609

Sanhedrin
10.28b   615
28cd   188
38b   1036

Šeqalim
6.1   678

Taʿanit
1.63d   615
4.8   848
68a   289

Targums

Tg. Exodus
29:45   1123
32:19   700

Tg. 1 Samuel
17:43   873

2 Tg. Esther
1.1   995

Tg. Job
2–117   322

Tg. Psalms
118:22   322

Tg. Isaiah
6:3   304, 307
6:22   1033
11:1–6   1053
11:1   351
11:10   351
22:13   149
22:14   168
22:22   235
22:25   235, 1092
24:23   804
31:4   804
63:2–3   1062
63:3–4   847
65:6   1092
65:15   168, 190, 1092
65:20   1124
66:6–8   662
66:7   662, 688

Tg. Jeremiah
2:3   816
2:13   479
7:34   973
10:7   853
10:10   853
25:10   1009, 1032
33:25   1118
51:7   926, 930, 935, 987
51:39   168, 1092
51:55   957
51:57   168, 1092

Tg. Ezekiel
1:1   427
1:6   298
1:8   515
1:22   296
1:24   301
1:26   91
3:12   301
22   91

Tg. Joel
4:13–14   847

Targum Neofiti I
Gen 3:24   154
Gen 30:22   104
Gen 50:19   1038
Gen 51:9   992
Exod 12:42   1094
Num 1:5–15   460
Num 1:21   460
Num 1:29   460
Num 1:31   460
Num 1:35   460
Num 9:15   877
Num 11:26   1094
Deut 33:6   168

Targum Onqelos
Gen 30:19   1038
Gen 41:32   1039
Gen 49:11   1040
Exod 19:16   295, 518
Exod 24:10   297
Exod 34:30   557
Lev 23:42–43   476
Num 11:25   1039
Num 11:26   1039
Num 11:29   1039
Num 24:2   1039
Num 27:18   1039
Deut 32:10–14   705
Deut 33:6   168

Targum Ps.-Jonathan
Gen 3:10   897
Gen 3:15   708
Gen 32:26   302
Gen 41:38   1039
Gen 50:19   1038
Exod 1:15   370–71
Exod 15:17   677
Exod 19:16   295, 518
Num 9:15   877
Deut 32:1   565
Deut 32:39   32
1 Sam 2:6   103
2 Kgs 9:22   203

Targum Yerušalmi I
Gen 3:6   535

Tosepta

ʿAboda Zara
8.4   187
8.4–6   543

Baba Batra
11.1   342

Berakot
1.9   303

Ḥullin
2.13   193

Megilla
32a   85

Soṭa
4.71   696

Taʿanit
2.1–2   289

Tamid
32b   278

Early Christian Literature

Acts of Andrew
14 — 810
27 — 453
31 — 707

Acts of Bartholomew
6 — 542

Acts of Carpus (Greek)
1–23 — 182
24–34 — 206
47 — 44

Acts of Carpus (Latin)
7 — 44

Acts of John
18–19 — 77, 809
37 — 77
38 — 293
41 — 191
90 — 95

Acts of Justin
6 — 44

Acts of Maximilian
2 — 457

Acts of Paul
1.1 — 534
5 — 821
5.13 — 534
7 — 84, 110
11.2
11.5 — 1086
12 — 810
21 — 477, 563
25 — 459, 813
26–39 — 756

Acts of Peter
12 — 759
5 — 459
24 (Latin) — 840
25 — 601
29 — 84

Acts of Pilate
15.1 — 599
16.7 — 600
20–24 — 401
25 — 600, 617

Acts of the Scillitan Martyrs
2 — 40
12 — clii
14 — 1086
15 — 625
17 — 1086

Acts of Thomas
4–5 — 1032
5 — 174
7 — 1032
13 — 1032
26–27 — 459
30 — 644
49–50 — 459
79 — 757
82 — 150

87 — 459
99 — 212
108–13 — 620
120 — 459
121 — 56, 839
131 — 459
136 — 362
137 — 362–63
143 — 207
169–70 — 626

Ambrose *De Cain et Abel*
1.2.8 — 600

Andreas of Caesarea
Comm. in Apoc.
6.8 — 403
10.6 — 568
11.3–4 — 599
17.9 — lxiii

Apocalypse of Paul
12 — 557
14 — 694
20 — 600, 626
21 — 296
21.22–24 — 281
22 — 1066
31 — 1066
34 — 1066
36 — 1066
38 — 223
43 — 515, 694
44 — 511
51 — 626

Apocalypse of Peter
1 — 55, 557, 1033
1–2 — 759
2 — 753, 759
2 (Ethiopic) — 600
6 — 55, 263, 689, 842
4 — 4, 1032
14 — 1066
17 — 224

Apocalypse of Thomas — 223, 990

Apostolic Church Order
18 — 286

Apostolic Constitutions
2.25 — 48
3.15 — 244
6.9.6 — 144, 753
6.11 — 351
7.26.2 — 641
7.32.3 — 519
7.35.3 — 303
7.38.4 — 641
8.12.8 — 287
8.12.26 — 189
8.12.27 — 287, 304
8.15.9 — 46
8.40.2 — 814
8.40.4 — 46
8.41 — 599
8.41.5 — 46
15.3 — 412
20.3 — 685

Arethas *Commentarii in Apoc.*
9 — 255

Aristides *Apologia*
15.2–5 — 711
15.5 — 193

Arnobius *Adversus nationes*
1.46 — 191

Ascension of Isaiah
1:3 — 613, 639
1:8 — 535
2:4 — 535, 639, 735
2:10 — 611
3:10 — 620
3:13–4:22 — 729, 761
3:15 — 110–11
4:1–14 — 739
4:1–13 — 761
4:1–7 — 753
4:2–12 — 729
4:2–3 — lxvi
4:2 — 535, 730, 739
4:6 — 740, 742, 745, 755
4:10–11 — 753
4:10 — 759
4:11 — 745, 761
4:12 — 742–43
4:13 — 691
5:1–14 — 886
5:2–15 — 535
5:2 — 623
5:13 — 833
6–11 — lxxxii
6–9 — 278
6 — 1226
7:12–22 — 1034
7:14 — 286
7:19 — 286
7:21 — 1034
7:22 — 175, 290
7:24 — 286
7:27 — 287
7:29 — 286
7:31 — 286
7:33 — 286
7:35 — 286
8:5 — 1035
8:9 — 286
8:14–15 — 223
8:26 — 290
8:45 — 1038
9:7–9 — 626
9:7 — 404
9:9 — 626
9:10–11 — 167, 173
9:10 — 286
9:12 — 290
9:14–15 — 692
9:21–23 — 224
9:24–26 — 223
9:24 — 175, 286
9:25 — 167
9:30 — 290
10:1–16 — 277
10:29 — 613, 639
10:35 — 223
10:40 — 223
11:16 — 692
11:40 — 286, 290

51:1–5 620

Athenagoras
Leg.
3.31 162
17.3 541
26.3–4 764
33.1 822
De res.
23 711

Augustine
Confessions
8.12 20
10.3 21
De civitate Dei
3.11 762
18.42 461
Epistulae
29.9 192, 1000
147 21
193.3 599, 600, 617
193.5 599, 617
De Gen.
9.5 599, 600, 617
Haer.
5 149
Sermons
40.6 1030

Ps.-Augustine
Quaest. Vetus et Novum Test.
76.2 lix

Books of Jeu
2.42 560
2.44 560
2.45 560
2.47 560

Letter of Barnabas
1:1 47
1:3 259
1:7 114, 817–18
1:8 75
2:5 clxxix
2:10 358
4:4–6 769
4:4–5 734
4:6–7 175
4:6 941
4:9 75, 423, 995
4:11 597, 710
5:3 114
5:5 748
5:11 610
5:12 477
5:13 165, 1024
6:2 804
6:3 308
6:4 874
6:9 clxv
6:15 597
7:2 644
7:5 611
7:9 423
7:12 611
8:3 461
8:5 308
9:2 308
9:5 688
9:6–8 441
9:7 82
9:8 772, 806
9:9 360

9:41 677
10:2 82
10:9 82
11:7 clxv
11:11 83
12:9 87, 423
12:10 351, 689
13:4–6 463
14:1 360
14:2 82, 989
14:4 360
15:5 413, 414, 421
15:9 625, 950
16:5 608
16:8 185, 625, 973
16:9 236
16:10 597
17:2 114
18:1 698
19:2 259
19:37 302

Basil *Commentarii in Is.*
1.46 110

Canon Muratori
57–59 lxxii
71–72 4, 12
171–72 29

Cassiodorus *Inst. div. lec.*
1.29 21

Chariton
3.2.16 174

Chronicon Paschale
1.466 398

1 Clement
inscr. 58
1:1 lxvii
2–3 237
2:3 58
2:4 412
4:8 clxv, 386
4:10 clxv, 386
4:17 872
5 lxvi
5:1–7 167
5:2 241
5:4–7 601
5:4 626
5:7 626
6:1 445, 466
6:2 167
8:3 clxxx, 197, 205, 611
8:4 475
9:3 626, 695
9:4 599
11:1 541, 760, 835
11:2 859
14:1 886
15:6 677
16:1 477, 478
16:7 353, 368
16:10 823
18:11 386
20:2 102, 302
20:12 44–45, 49
21:9 clxvii, 229
23:5 235
24:1 818
24:4 302

26:1 874
27:1 888
27:7 clxvii
28:3 348, 386
29:3 818
32:4 44, 49, 58
34:3 207, 1218
34:6 304, 337, 363
35:1–2 822
36:3 202
36:5 689
37:3 1064
38:2 822
38:4 44, 49
39:7 836
40:1 208
41:2 232, 405
42:1–2 1158
42:4 818
43:2 1158
43:2–3 745
43:3 66
43:6 44, 49
43:14 407
44:1 1158
44:3 478
44:5 839
45:7 44, 49
45:8 366
46:8 clxviii, 430
47:1 1158
48:2 clxxxi, 581
48:3 clxxxi, 581
50:1 874
50:7 44, 49
51:5 872
51:8 872
53:1 146
53:3 874
53:4 224
54:2 478
56:4 47, 260
56:6 58
56:9 clxxix
57:1 748
57:2 478
58:2 44, 49, 412, 566
59:2 412
59:4 688
60:1 273, 888
60:4 58
61:1 366
61:2 366
61:3 44–45
62:2 58
64:1 34, 45, 49
64:2 44
65:2 49, 364, 366

2 Clement
1:1 644
3:2 225–27
4:5 710
5:2–4 368
5:3 698
5:5 874
7:1–5 175
7:3 167
7:6 459
8:6 459
9:3 597
11:6 207
13:2–4 744
13:2 688
14:2 1030

15:1 822
16:3 423
17:3 287
17:4 207, 688
17:5 287
17:6 423
19:1–3 11, 23
20:2 454
20:5 44, 49

Ps.-Clement *Diamart.*
1 479

Ps.-Clement *Epistle of James*
2 47
6 47

Ps.-Clement *Epistle of Peter*
1.2 360
3.1 360

Ps.-Clement *Homilies*
2.6.1 114
2.6.2 206
2.10.1 114
2.17.1 599
2.19.1–3 1223
2.32 764
3.72.1 478
7.8 193
9.22 224
16.21 144
54.2 47

Ps.-Clement, *Recognitions*
1.21.7 114
2.19.1–3 1223
3.47.2 764
4.36 193

Clement of Alexandria
Eclogae ex scripturis propheticis
4.1 256
Excerpta ex Theodoto
27.2 291
29 208
63 84
74 213
80.3 459
80.83 459
Paedagogus
1.5 244
1.7 235
2.1 193
2.8 174–75
2.10.108 cxlix
2.19.3 847
2.29.1 847
2.108 li
2.119 li
2.19.3 938
2.29.1 938
3.12 711
3.101.3 477
Protrepticus
2 542
Quis div. salv.
3 519
42 li, lix, 78, 81, 116
Stromata
2.5 937
2.20 149
3.4 149
3.5 99
3.6 1030

3.25.5–26.3 149
4.16 193
5.6 32, 90, 97
5.8.48.8 847
5.11.77 290, 842
5.12.76 544
5.14.96 363
5.88.5 208
5.88.48 938
5.104 1120
6.3 542
6.11 806
6.16 115
6.58.1 256
6.106 li
7.1 256
7.7 48
7.16 479
17.12 84

Commodian
Carmen
810–11 535
827–32 729
833–64 729
Instructiones
1.41 729
41.7 739
41.8 739
43.1 519

Cyprian
Epistulae
3.5 40
15.1 40
20.3 48
59.3 742
70.3 752
Ad Quirinum
1.22 244

Ps.-Cyprian *De mont. Sina et Sion*
8 40

Cyril of Jerusalem
Procatechesis
14 20

Didache
1:2 711
2:1–3 711
6:3 193, 1086
7:1–2 479
8:244–45 309, 1086
9:3–4 309
9:5 clxxiii
9:244–45 1086
9:344–45 640, 1086
10:2–5 640
10:244–45 309, 1039
10:358 312
10:444–45 309
10:544–45 309
11–13 140, 145, 155, 1024
11 145
11:1–2 144–45
11:3–6 144–45
11:5–10 145, 894
11:6 155, 1025
11:7–12 144
11:7 82
11:8 82
11:9 82, 155, 1025
11:12 82
12:1–5 144

12:1–4 155
12:1 145
13:3–7 815
13:3 818
13:5 818
13:6 818
13:7 818
14:1 84
16 cxxii, 276
16:2 22
16:3 145, 423, 730, 757, 894, 1083
16:4–5 473
16:4 698, 730, 742, 759–60
16:5 239, 440, 474
16:6 510, 519, 679, 869
16:8 52, 54–55, 1017

Didascalia
11.5.6 753

Didymus *Trin.*
2.22 479

Diognetus, Epistle of
5–6 362
5:13 259
6:1–9 404
7:2 58
8:9 407
9:2 235

Ps.-Dionysius Areopagita
De caelesti hierarchia
9.2 694

Epiphanius
Haereses or *Panarion*
1.5 599
1.26.5.12 153
11.24 141
19.6.2 566, 567
25.2.2–7.3 149
26.13.4 599
27.6.6 lxvi
28.7.5 811
29.2 163
29.7 977
29.7.7–8 706
30.2 977
30.2.7 706
42.9.4 250
42.12.3 250
51.3–6 liii
51.12.1–2 78
51.13.33 lx
51.33.1 201
51.33.3–4 201
78.11 141

Ps.-Epiphanius *Testimonia*
5.23 351
5.27 351
11 662, 688
71.3 350

Epistula apostolorum
18 (Coptic) 84

Ep. Lugd.
1:6 241
1:11 175
1:17 175, 241, 708
1:36 175

1:41	175
1:48	175
2:3	38
2:7	174
10	412, 813
13	412
36	167
38	167
42	167
57	412

Esaias Abbas *Orationes*

5.3	48

Eusebius
Chronicon

PG XIX.551–52	lix
3.160	398

Commentarii in Ps.

47	110
50	110

Demonstratio evangelica

2.3.80	244
3.5	78, 82
3.6	191, 1086

Historia ecclesiastica

1.4.3–4	244
2.4–5	lxvi
2.15.2	829
2.22.4	735
2.23.10–18	602
2.23.21–24	601
2.25.5–7	liii
2.25.6–7	601
2.25.8	601
3.1	lxvi, 140–41
3.4.5	141
3.5.3	706, 977
3.17	lxvii
3.18	lxvii, 81, 1086
3.18.1	li
3.18.3	lxix
3.18.4	lxvii
3.19–20	lxvii
3.20.8–9	lix, 78
3.23.1	78
3.23.2–3	78
3.23.3–4	lix–lx
3.23.5–19	78
3.23.5–9	lix
3.28.1–2	liii, 939
3.28.2	liii
3.28.3	lii
3.29.2–4	liii, 149
3.31.4	liii
3.39.4	li
3.39.5–6	140
4.7.7	193
4.18.6	141
4.18.8	li
4.22.6	144, 752–53
4.23.8	84
4.26.2	lii, 4, 84
4.26.5–11	lxvii
4.26.9	lxvi
4.29.3	822
5.1.3–5.3.3	lii
5.1.10	813
5.1.13	412
5.8.4	140
5.16.2	163
5.17.3–4	214, 235
5.24.3	140
5.25.1–5	753
5.28.1–4	753
5.30.3	lxix
6.7	753
6.20.3	liii, 1025
6.38	224
7.24	lii, 999
7.24.3	lii
7.25	li
7.25.1–5	liii
7.25.6–8	lii
7.25.9–10	lxxii
7.25.11–14	li
7.25.12–16	li, liii
7.25.15	l
7.25.22	lii
7.26	cxcix
9.8.11	403
10.4.2	174

Onomasticon

14.31	898
28.26	898
58.1	898
70.10	898
90.12	898
100.10	898
108.6	898
108.13	898
110.21	898
116.21	898
140.1	898

Praeparatio Evangelica

1.10.2	cciii
1.10.4	517
1.10.10.36–37	301
3.11.38	281
4.7	1212
5.19.1	403
5.21.5	542
5.21.213c	764
8.11	820
9.21.3–10	465
9.21.17	465
9.27.1–37	504
9.27.28–29	504
9.27.32	504, 527
9.27.33	504
9.27.34	504
9.30.1	745
9.30.5	382
9.34.7	745
9.34.14	745
9.35	398
9.39	678
9.39.5	189

Filastrius
Diversarum haereseon liber (Haer.)

89	250

Gospel of Bartholomew

4.29	694
31–36	451
52–55	695–96

Gospel of Mary (BG 8502)

7:9	150
8:10–11	150

Gospel of Peter

3.5	935
6.23	623
8.33	346
10	625
12.50	84
14.60	75
35	84
50	84, 1011

Gospel of the Nazoraeans

frag. 13	608

Gregory of Nazianzus *Orationes*

42	110, 405

Hermas
Mandates

1.1	312
2.2	146
2.4	clxxiii
3.1	185, 895
3.3	205
4.3.4	698
4.3.6	698
5.1.3	698
5.2.4–8	185
6.2.3	clxxiv
7.2	698
7.3	698
7.7.5	837
8.6	224
9.9	698
9.11	698
10.1.6	185
10.3.2–3	405
10.3.2	972
11.1–2	145, 894
11.2	cxxviii, clxxiv, 64
11.3	698
11.4	145, 894
11.7	145, 894
11.9	157, 1039
11.12	155
11.13	157
11.14	157
11.17	698
12.2.2	698
12.3.4	837
12.4.2	273
12.4.6	698
12.4.7	698
12.5.1	698
12.5.2	167
12.6.1	698
12.6.2	698
12.6.3	837
12.6.4	698

Similitudes

1.9–11	259
2.9	224
5.1.5	837
5.3.2–3	282
5.3.2	cxxviii, clxxiv, 64
5.3.3	837
5.4.5	cxxviii, clxxiv, 64, 282
5.5.2	312
5.5.3	836
5.7.4	58
6.1.5	clxxiv
6.2.2	102, 454
6.3.2	cxxviii, clxxiv, 64
6.9	924
6.3.6	629
8.2.1–4	175
8.2.1	468
8.2.3	223
8.2.5	405
8.3.3	110–11, 693
8.3.6	167, 175, 698
8.6	459
8.6.3	459, 629
8.6.6	205

8.7.3	198
9.1.1	cxxviii, clxxiv, 64, 282
9.4.6	190
9.9.6	ccviii
9.11.1	cxxviii, clxxiv, 64
9.13.5	859
9.15.4	145
9.15.5	145
9.16.2	459
9.16.3–5	459
9.16.3	459
9.16.4	459
9.17.1	441, 442
9.17.4	459, 688
9.22.2	145
9.23.2	146
9.28.3	146
9.28.4	184
9.28.7	184

Visions

1–5	clxxxv
1–4	lxxxix
1.1.2	99, 1100
1.1.3	933
1.1.4	656, 702
1.1.6	1153
1.2.1	99, 656
1.2.2	253, 344
1.2.4	822
1.3.2	224
1.3.3–4	21, 224
1.4.3	cxxviii, clxxiv, 64
2.1.1	82, 690
2.1.3–4	344
2.1.3	549, 552, 558
2.1.4	552
2.2.1	clxxv, 83
2.2.5	567
2.2.7	473, 474, 836
2.2.8	567
2.3.2	102, 454
2.3.4	clxxxv
2.4.1–3	558
2.4.1	552
2.4.2–3	344
2.4.2	287, 552
2.4.3	21, 87, 287, 549, 552
3	924
3.1.4	253
3.1.7	clxxxv
3.2.1	146
3.2.4	clxxxv
3.3.1–2	83
3.3.5	58
3.6.1	972
3.4.1	836
3.4.2	836
3.7.2	102, 454
3.8.2	242
3.8.4	822
3.8.5	937
3.10.1	cxxviii, clxxiv, 64
4	924
4.1.1	474
4.1.6	527, 894
4.1.10	683
4.2.1	223
4.2.1–2	812
4.2.2	clxxxv
4.2.4	474
4.2.5	474
4.3.3	683
4.3.5	223
4.3.6	474
5, praef.	12
5.1	253
5.5	clxxxv, 11, 23, 87

Hilary *Tractatus*
super Psalmos (Ps.)

2	257

Hippolytus
Commentarii in Dan.

1.9	213
3.4	761
4.5.3	733
4.7.1	760
4.11.1	840
4.16.1	760
4.21.3	760
4.22	cxlix, 383
4.34	cxlix, 229, 321–22
4.35.3	599
4.50.1–2	599
4.50.2	616
4.50.3	753
4.56.6	1065
34.3	345
34.4	88

De antichristo

2	114
8	351
6	760
14.5–6	463
16.2	742, 753
17.6–7	742, 753
18.1–4	742, 753
22	840
25	733
25.1–3	617, 734
26	840
28.1	617, 735
29	cxlix
36–42	li, cxlix
40	965, 966, 967
44	840
46	599
46.3–4	599
47	cxlix, 580
48	cxlix, 720–22
49–50	cxlix
49	720
50	770
52	745
53	742, 753
56.1	753
58.4	753
59	110
60	cxlix, 651–52, 656–57, 666
61	652, 657, 680
61.9	691, 743, 753, 1084
65	cxlix

Frag. in Gen.

34	cxlix, 655

Refutatio or *Haer.*

1.2	115, 989
1.5.3	1122
1.7.1	1122
4.41	764
4.43	115
4.51	115
5.3	461
5.6.4	208
5.7.41	620
5.8.12	292
5.8.39	508
5.10.2	12
5.16.5	620
5.26.1–6	291
5.26.21	736
5.28.2	759
6.30.7	207
6.38.4	256
6.34.3–4	1122
7.24	155
7.36.3	149
9.19	223

Theoph.

4	686

Ps.-Hippolytus
De consummatione mundi

28	770

Ignatius of Antioch
Ephesians

inscr.	29, 313
1:3	140
2:1	140, 411
2:2	287
3:1	76, 957
4:1–2	355
4:1	222, 287, 957
5:2–3	606, 790
6:1	508
6:2	140
7:1	140, 145, 957
7:2	317
9:1	6, 145
9:2	47
9:3	703
10:3	698
11:1	22
13:1	692, 698
13:2	692
15:1–2	508
15:3	597
17:1	613, 639
18:2	351
19:1–3	317, 680
19:1	213, 613, 639, 686, 692
19:2	332
20:2	287, 351

Magnesians

1:1	143
1:2	639
1:3	613
2	411
2:1	222, 287
3:1	287
6:1	287, 289
7:1	287
7:7	597
8:1	579
8:2	508, 1058
9:1	84
10 (long rec.)	244
10:1	244
10:3	362
11:3 (long rec.)	207
12:1	222

Philadelphians

inscr.	234
1:1	508
1:2	355
2:1–2	757
2:1	478, 813
4	411
5:1	37
6:1	232, 234
6:3	234
6:2	613, 639
6:9 (long rec.)	766
7:1	206

7:2	37, 597	1.21	140	16.13	757
7:3	141	1.24.5	193	20.1.4	1118
8:1	289	1.26.3	li, 4, 149, 155	20.5	541
Philippians		1.28.2	193	21.3	627
2:1	644	2.6.2	191	23.2	39
11:6–7	698	2.7.4	363	26.1	829
Polycarp		2.21.1	145	26.7	162
1:2	175	2.22.1	208	27	107
2:3	167, 175	2.22.5	lix–lx, 78	28.1	lii, 698
3:1	167	2.28.9	148	31	163, 1039
3:2	76	2.32.1	567	31.5	163
5:2	822	2.32.4	191	31.6	237
8:3	cxxvii, 216, 839	2.49.3	191	33.3	39
Romans		3.1.1	li	40.1	107
inscr.	29, 47, 313	3.3.4	lix–lx, 78, 140	42.1	638
1:1	37	3.11.1	li, 149, 155	44.2	107
2	175	3.11.8	272, 300	46.2	39
4	175	3.16.5	li	51	55
4:3	411, 601	3.16.8	li	51.9	55, 90, 840–41
5:2	302	3.18.2	33	52.3	54
5:3	698	3.18.3	lviii	52.12	56
7:1	613, 639	3.19.2	840	53.2	39
7:2	479	3.23.5	897	58.3	541
9:1	478	4.8.3	48	60.8	1118
10:3	76	4.14.2	li	61.4	lii
17:3	351	4.14.12	4	63.15	39
Smyrnaeans		4.20.2	346, 364	67	11
1:1	351	4.18.6	405	68.6	107
1:2	359	4.20.11	li, 276	78.9	107
4:2	833	4.21.3	393	120.4	54
5:1–2	184	4.30.4	4	*2 Apology*	
6:1	150, 769	4.33.1	114, 840	6.6	191
8:17	813	4.33.11	840	7.2–3	1118
9:1	698	4.40.3	696	12	162
10:1	641	5.5.1	599	32.12–13	351
12:1	258	5.25.1	735, 742, 745, 753	*Dialogue with Trypho*	
12:2	76, 411	5.25.3	735, 743, 753, 1084	1.3	lviii, cxxi
13:1	216	5.25.4	742, 753	2–8	141
Trallians		5.26.1	li, 733	9.3	lviii
inscr.	47	5.28.2	742, 753, 756	10.3	710
1:1	76, 143	5.30.1	722	10.4	645
3:1	287	5.30.3	lviii–lix, lxvii, lxix, 770, 1065,	11.5	176, 460, 466
4:2	613, 617, 639		1084	14.1	479
5:2	692	5.30.4	743, 745	14.8	53, 55–56, 840
7:1	287	5.33.3	lix, 3	16.4	163, 886
7:2	606, 790	5.33.4	li	17.1	162–63
8:1	698	5.35.2	cxlix, 3	17.2	744
8:2	744, 746	*Dem.*		24.1	950
9:1	348	3	459	24.3	441
12:2	289, 1058	*Epideixis*		30.3	191
12:3	6, 948	97	191	31.1	55, 90, 840
13:3	823			31.3	90, 840–41
		Jerome		32	1084
Ps.-Ignatius		*Commentary on Daniel*		32.1	90
Antioch		7:2–3	451	32.2	lii, 56
12.3	766	*Commentary on Matthew*		32.3–4	743
Philippians		3.57	599	32.3	609, 841
15.1	766	*De vir. illustr.*		32.4	742, 753
Ephesians		9	li, lix	32.6	841
5	757	10	81	34	193
Hero		24	lii	35	193
2	757	74	cl	35.3	144, 753, 757, 759
		Epistulae		35.6	193, 541
Irenaeus		53	130	39.2	33
Adversus haereses				41.4	950
1	757	**Justin**		45.5	lii
1.5.3	1122	*1 Apology*		47.4	163
1.5.4	639	5.2	542	49.2	599
1.6.3	193	6	33	49.3	610
1.7.1	1122	6.2	1039	49.5	610
1.13.3	1039, 1121	9.1	542	52.2	350–51
1.16.3	li	13.3	1039	55.1	1039
1.18.1	256	15.6	822	55.2	312, 542
1.20.2	461	15.7	445, 466	61.1	256
		16.5	567	61.6	210

62.4	256
64.7	lii, 56
69.6	479
72.3	353
76.1	90, 841
76.6	191
76.7	90
79.2	90, 841
80.1	441
80.5	lii
81	cxlix
81.4	li–lii, lviii, 4
82.1	145, 460
82.2	753
85	191
85.2	191
85.8–9	662, 688
86.4	351
87.2	33
88.8	210
93.2	711
93.4	163
95.4	163
96.2	163
100.3	90
106.4	213
108.2	162–63
108.3	163
109.1	clxxx, 197
110	742
110.2	753
110.5	163
111.13	353
114.2	353
116.1	235
117.3	162–63
118.1	lii, 56
118.2	358
119–20	467
119	362
119.4	466
120.4	55, 840
120.5	620
121.3	clxxx
122.6	210
126.1	90
126.2	461
131.2	163
131.6	lii
133.6	163
135	191
137.2	163
138.1	950
139.4	359

Lactantius
Divinae Institutiones

2.16	191, 1093
2.17	1057
4	592
4.27	191, 1080
7	592
7.15.11	830
7.16	519
7.16.1–14	729
7.16.8	414
7.16–17	729
7.17	590, 592, 745, 1047, 1080
7.17.1–8	591, 726–27
7.17.1–3	590, 726–27, 729
7.17.1–2	729
7.17.2–11	729
7.17.2	613, 615
7.17.3	617, 623
7.17.4–8	726–28
7.17.4	740, 755

7.17.5	764
7.17.7	592, 767
7.17.8	728, 743
7.19	418
7.21	1118
7.26.5–7	592
7.169	413

Epitome

66.9	592
71	414, 415, 418, 745, 1080

John Malalas *Chronographia*

10.18	619
10.23	619
10.26	882
10.32	619
10.33	626
10.37	601
10.52	627

Martyrdom of Agape

7.2	44

Martyrdom of Apollonius

47	44

Martyrdom of Carpus
Greek recension

4	765
9	708
35	167, 175

Latin recension

3.5	167, 175

Martyrdom Conon

6	44

Martyrdom of Crispina

4.2	44

Martyrdom of Dasius

7	761
12.2	44

Martyrdom of Felix

31	1086

Martyrdom Fruct.

2.2	765
5	625
7.2	44, 625

Martyrdom of Irenaeus

6	44

Martyrdom Julius

3.1	1086
4.5	44

Martyrdom of Justin

5	625
5.8	765
6.1	629

Martyrs of Lyons (see Ep. Lugd.)

Martyrdom Marian

12.7	409
13.5	44

Martyrdom of Montanus

14:5	167

Martyrdom of Paul

4	626
5	459

Martyrdom of Perpetua and Felicitas

1	44
10.13–14	702
11	44
11.7–8	625
12	288, 304
12.2	302

Martyrdom of Pionius

5.2	761
12	686
18.4	174
23	44

Martyrdom of Polycarp

1:1	185
3:1	698
9:1	397, 624
9:2–3	237
9:2	184
12:2–3	162
12:2	708
13:1	162
14	306, 412
14:2	58, 185, 833
17–19	167, 175
17:1	167
17:2	162
18:1	162
18:3	167
19:1	235
19:2	58, 167
21	44, 364

Martyrdom of Ptoamiaena

6	1086
alternate ending	
5	64

Melito *Pass.*

22	401
55	401
102	401

Methodius
Sym. et Ann.

3	662, 688

Symposium

7	662, 688
8.5	680
8.7	393

Minucius Felix *Oct.*

31	822

Odes of Solomon

3:10–11	123, 150, 953
6:1	356
7:16b–20	liv
7:17	356
8:16	459
9:1	150
9:3	639
9:6	239
9:11	223
11:16–21	153, 1027
11:19	152
14:8	356, 99
17:17	46
22:5	684
23:5–22	330
23:5–6	329
23:5	329
23:7–8	329
23:7	329
23:8–9	329

23:10	329	8.24	542	1.3	461
23:11–16	330	8.28–30	193	6.2	461
23:13–15	330	8.41	542		
23:17–19	330	*De principiis*		*Protevangelium of James*	
23:17	329	1.8.1	291, 694	21.2	213
23:19–20	330	2.3.6	319		
23:21–22	330	3.2.1	697	*Quest. Barth.*	
23:21	329	*Epis. ad Afric.*		1.17	599
26:3	356	11.61	534		
29:6	639	11.80	534	*Quest. Esdr.* (Rec. B)	
29:8	210	*Fragmenta in Ps.*		11	510, 519
31:3	360	2.2	243		
36	277–78, 436	*Homiliae in Ex.*		*Second Book of Jeu*	
38:9–14	932	12.4	345	43	360
39:6–7	459	*Homiliae in Ez.*			
39:7	805	14.2	345	*Sophia Jesu Christi* (CG III)	
41:3	639	*Homiliae in Lc.*		97:21–23	150
41:6	360	23	110	98:21–22	150
42:17	104, 991	*De orat.*		105:10–12	150
42:20	805	14.1	cxci	107:18–108:1	150
		Philocalia			
Oecumenius		2.1	345	*Sulpicius Severus*	
Commentarius in Apocalypsin		5.5	345	*Chr.*	
3:14	255, 1233			2.29	lxvi
4:6–8	297	**Polycarp** *Philippians*			
5:10	48, 965, 966	inscr.	27, 58	**Tatian** *Oratio ad Graecos*	
12.1	680	2:1	689	4.2	543
15.3	872	5:1	222	5	39
		5:3	lviii	5.1	256
Olympiodorus *Frag. in Jer.*		6:2	354	8.1–4	542
52:1	811	7:1	698, 752	12.4	542
		8:2	146	16.2	542
Origen		9:2	167	25.2	1118
Commentarii in Gen.		10:3	744		
PGXII.73B	224	13	6	**Tertullian**	
1.1	256			*Adversus Marcionem*	
Commentarii in Io.		*Pistis Sophia*		1.29.2	149
1.19	256	1.1	560	1.3	1039
2.10	48	1.10	415, 560	3.14	cxlix
5.4	345	1.17	150	3.14.3	li, 4
12.31	38	1.18	150	3.24.4	li
13.17	1036	1.23	412	4.5	li
Commentarii in Mt.		1.26	412	4.5.2	4
11.12	193	1.27	412, 692, 1034	4.24.1	145
16.6	lix, 78	1.33	150, 225	5.11.12	250
27	752	1.41	811	*Adversus nationes*	
Comm. in Joh.		1.42	150	1.7	lxvi
2.10	48	1.43	150, 602	1.7.8–9	lxvi
12.31	38	1.45	412	1.8	362
13.26.161	534	1.50	412	1.14	162, 900
Contra Celsum		1.55	708	*De anima*	
1.6	191	2.66	684	6	404
1.24	191	2.68	150	8	404
1.25	191, 1036	2.70	684	37.4	711
1.27	445	2.71	684	50	599
1.59–60	213	2.80	708	50.7	753, 759
1.67	191	2.86	150, 412, 560	*Apologia*	
2.50	753, 759	2.87	150	4.11	162, 1034
3.24	191	2.96	412, 811	5	950
3.28	542	2.98	412	5.3–4	lxvi
4.33	191	2.99	1089	5.4	lxvii
4.34	191	3.124	150	9	193
5.6	1036	3.125	150, 412	10	778
5.45	191	4.143	560	10.1	765
6.17	39	106	360	21.1	170
6.27	153, 162			22.8	824
6.30	300	*Passion of Montanus*		23.4	542
6.32	534	(see *Mart. Montanus*)		47.12	1067
6.45	753, 759	**Philastrius**		*De baptismo*	
6.46	742, 753	33.1	149	17.4	lxvi
7.6	542			*De carne Christi*	
7.9	1214	**Primasius**		15.1	840
7.62	543, 762	*PL* 68:407–936	cl	*De corona*	
8.2	362			7	174
8.17	358, 405	*Protevangelium Jacobi*		13	718
8.22	84	1.1	461	15	395

De exhort. cast.
7   48
9–10   822
12   40
De fuga in persec.
10   40
13   1236
14   1236
Ad Hermog.
34   415
De idol.
4   542
14   744
15.5   542
Ieiun.
11   752
Adv. Iud.
14.4   840
Ad. Marcionem
1.14.3   459
1.28.3   459
3.7.4   840
3.8   752
3.14   cxlix
3.14.3   li, 4
3.23.4   744
3.24.4   li
4.5   li, 601
4.5.2   4
4.10.12   840
4.14.16   744
4.16–17   711
4.22.1   600
4.34   466
4.39.11   840
5.3   466
5.13.7   744
5.16   753
De modestia
7.1–4   477

De monogamia
6   466
7   48
Ad nationes
1.7   lxvi
1.7.8–9   lxvi
Oratione
3   304
De oratore
28.1–2   48
36   82
De praescriptione
3.12–4.5   752
26.6   163
33   149
36   80, 601
40   458
De pudicitia
9   897
De resurrectione
7   897
Ad Scap.
2   542
Scorpiace
10.10   163
12   158
15   163, 601
20   468
De spect.
9   542
De test. an.
2   542
Ps.-Tertullian
Ad uxorem
1.3–4   822
Adversus haer.
1.6   149
Carmen adv. Marc.
4.198–210   291

Testament of the Forty Martyrs
3   44
Theodoret *Haer.*
3.1   149
Theophilus *Ad Autolycum*
1.8   764
1.9–10   543
1.10   542
1.14   114
2.2   543
2.9   114
2.10   256
2.24   154, 534
2.33   114
2.34   711
3.4   162
3.19   534
Treat. Res.
48.6   600
Victorinus of Pettau
Commentarius in Apocalypsin
2   351
1.1   33
1.7   130–31
4.3–4   300
4.3   289–90
4.4   300
5.1   345
10.3   78, 578
10.11   lix
11.2   614, 743
11.3   600
11.4   613, 617
13   737, 745
17.3   737
17.4   745
17.10   lix

Nag Hammadi Tractates

Apocalypse of Adam
6:1   153
10:2   422
12:2   422, 828
13.3   421
26:4   422, 828
33:4   515
37.5   421
43:2   422
77.26–83.4   674
78.6–26   674
84.4–24   561

First Apocalypse of James
14.30–31   263
28.16–17   222

Apocryphon of James
4.1   822
14.29–30   360
14.30   689
15.11–13   510
15.19–22   360

Apocryphon of John
2.1.16–17   liii
2.11.29–31   685
2.16   114

3.18.1–2   685
4.3.10–12   liii
4.18.18–20   685
4.21–24   479
21.16–22:9   153
21.24   153
29.12   1154
31.22–25   452

Concept of Our Great Power
41.7–8   281
44.25–26   222

Dialogue of the Savior
143.11–15   223

Discourses on the Eighth and Ninth
63.15–23   566

Gospel of the Egyptians
3.42   560
3.43.8–44.9   57
4.52   560
68.1–9   1217
173   57

Gospel of the Hebrews
frag. 4b   362

Gospel of Philip
53.8–9   748

Gospel of Thomas
2   362
7   150–51
11   1110
11a   1119
21   150–51, 222
24   150
33a   151
52   292
53   811
54.507   1055
63   150, 1032
64   811
65   150
73   800, 802, 844
86   813
96   150, 1103
103   222
111   415

Gospel of Truth
19.34–20.27   351
20.12   354
21.3–5   224
36:35–37   153

38.16–32	1056	*Paraphrase of Shem*		*Thunder, Perfect Mind*		
		1.16–17	561	13.16		102
Hypostasis of the Archons		27.26–27	451	14.12		88
88.17–18	561	40.6	561			
				Second Treatise of the Great Seth		
Letter of Peter to Philip		*Teaching of Silvanus*		65.33–37		748
134.13	561	104.1–14	104			
134.17	561	105.13–16	222	*Trimorphic Protennoia*		
135.3	561	110.19–30	104, 998	36.4		104
137.19	561	116.3	206	40.8–9		88
138.21	561			42.4		88
		Testimony of Truth		42.9–16		88
On the Origin of the World		32.24	104			
104.19	35	33.8	104	*Tripartite Tractate*		
104.35–106.11	277	47.5–6	697	89.25–28		526
105.10	35	69.10–11	459	95.17–19		114
121.30–35	699			119.3		561
123.2–15	699			138.8–12		510

Greek and Latin Literature

Achilles Tatius		42.52	138	Ammianus Marcellinus		
1.1.10	549	43.7	312	22.12.6		192
1.2.1	567	43.16	997			
2.2.5	847	47–52	331	*Anthologia Graeca*		
2.36.4	690	47.1–4	331	9.223.1–2		523
2.37.2	690	47.78	124	9.778		824
5.20.5	811	48.2	86			
		48.3	86	*Anthologia Palatina*		
Acta Alexandrinorum		48.8	86	6.171		556
7.101–7	897			7.161		523
		Aeschines *Against Ctesiphon*		9.408		524
Aelian		10	173	10.25		875
De natura animalium		45	173	14.20		772
6.63	757	46	173	14.105		772
10.48	757	77	293	Garland of Philip		
11.32	790	147	173	36.2		141
12.3	370	164	174			
13.38	190	179	173	Antoninus Liberalis		
15.21	757	258	173	19.2		cxci
16.39	757					
Varia historia		Aeschylus		Appian *Bella civilia*		
4.17	770	*Agamemnon*		1.83		413
		160	1056	3.1.2		740
Aelius Aristides *Orationes*		537	993	4.1.4		416, 417
17	16	1080–82	535	5.9		892
17.3–5	159	*Choephoroe*				
17.11–13	979	309–14	1193	Apollodorus		
18	160, 979	577–78	887	*Bibliotheca*		
18.2	159	*Eumenides*		1.1.5–7		687
18.3	831	39	174	1.3.5		699
19	160	653	887	1.4.3		699
19.5	40	741	190	1.4.4		690
20	160	*Persians*		1.5.1		690
20.15	40	40	445	1.6.1–2		667
21	160–61	87–92	956	1.6.1		527
21.3–4	159	249–52	979	1.6.3		683, 686, 696, 705
21.10	159	*Prometheus Vinctus*		1.7.3		137
23.13	182	172	cxciii	1.7.4		667
23.15	183	271	cxciii	1.9.1		690
25.56	40	569	298	1.9.23		540, 690
26.11–13	980	678	833	2.1.3		298
26.23	40	747–51	531	2.3.1–2		667
26.107	40	978	298	2.3.1		539
27.36	167	1007	cxciii	2.4.9		95
36.40	379			2.5.2		685
39.5	183	Alcinous *Did.*		2.5.8		540
39.6	183	14	318	2.7.7		690
42.4	183			2.8.1		708
42.6	183			3.5.3		690

3.10.7	690	660–62	95	2.28.4–7	413
3.11.2	690	*Plutus*		3.10.1–17	115
3.12.2	690	39	174	6.4	174
3.12.4	690	*Ranae, Frogs*			
3.12.6	105, 707	330–31	95	Aurelius Victor *De viris illustribus*	
3.14.8	706	1283	cxciii	2.13	627
3.15.4	690	1392	401		
73.1.1	690	1508–14	458	Caesar *De bello civili*	
Epitome		*Thesmophoriazusai*		3.33	138, 890
1.9	690	295–97	508	3.105	519
3.22	690	*Vespae*		Callimachus	
4.7	707	1428	clxxii	*Aetia*	
				1.1.21–22	86
Apollonius Rhodius		Aristotle		*Hymns*	
Argonautica		*De caelo*		4.35–38	673
2.679–80	518	1.10	748	*Hymn to Apollo*	
2.680	662	2.13 (292ab)	318	1–2	678
3.1302–5	540	2.14	824	1–8	518, 662
4.57	699	298a	824	2.3	95
4.640–42	559	304B.22	cxciii	32–35	94
4.1286	413	*Ethica Nicomachea*		*Hymn to Artemis*	
		8.11 (1160a)	817	204	138
Apollonius of Tyana *Epistulae*		*Politica*		240	138
65	138	1276a	619	*Hymn to Zeus*	
		Rhetorica		91–92	331
Appian *Bella civilia*		3.3 (1406A.9–10)	833		
4.2.8	128	1361a.36	308	Calpurnius *Eclogues*	
4.2.8–11	142	1367a	993	1.84	311
4.2.8	128, 967	1377B	cxci		
14.1.2	938, 997	*Nic. Ethics*		*Catullus*	
		993	1132	34.9	104
Apuleius		*Top.*		61.9–10	95
Apologia		113a	993		
90	185			Cebes *Tabula*	
Metamorphoses		Arrian		4.3	473
9.4	468	*Anabasis*		5.1	284
11.2	680	1.17.3–6	218	5.3	473
11.3	174	3.4.2	257	6.2	473
11.4	680	3.16.4	831	7.2	473
11.9	293, 469	7.5.4–6	173	8.2–3	473
11.10	293	7.17.2	831	12.3	473
11.24	174	*Indica*		15.3	473
		1.8	831		
Aratus *Phaenomena*				*Chaldaean Oracles*	
10	679	Artemidorus *Oneirocritica*		frag. 224	763
26–27	98	1.77	173, 175		
45–70	683	2.3	415	Cicero	
96–146	680, 706	2.5	189	*Academica priora*	
225	373	2.9	759	2.16.51	86
238	373	2.16	732	*Ad Atticum*	
357	373	2.24	844	5.15	249
403	406	2.36	413, 520, 525	*In Catilinam*	
515–16	373	2.45	573	4.4	839
549	373	4.23	415	*De divinatione*	
709	373	5.23	520, 525	1.42.93	416
713	373	5.26	190	1.43.97	884
				1.43.98	519, 762
Archilochus *Fragmenta*		Athenaeus *Deipnosophistae*		2.27.58	519, 884
30D	535	1.25e	360	*Pro Flacco*	
		3.98e	397	27	29
Aristophanes		5.6.1–27	173	28.68	181, 263
Aves		5.194–95	533	*Leges*	
760–61	458	5.195a	174	23	174
1281–82	532	5.197f	174	24	16
Equites		5.198a	174	*De natura deorum*	
116–27	20	6.272c	397	1.22	679
521	871	8.361	137	2.17	762
1369	225	10.437b	174	2.42	680, 683
Knights		14.619b	138	2.44	406
116–27	20	1.208b	959	2.53	212
Nubes, Clouds		2.38c	987	3.17.44	401
821	cxciii	3.93 998		3.40	406
Pax		3.98c	959	*De Officiis*	
1180–81	225			1.150	10
Persians		Aulus Gellius *Noctes Atticae*		2.7.25	457
659–60	95	2.28.1–3	413		

Orationes Philippicae
1.13 — 777
2.86 — 741
2.110 — 777
De republica
1.16.25 — 413
2.10.17 — 627
Tusculan Disputations
3.34 — 80
4.70 — 898
In Verrem
3.81.188 — 397

Claudian *Eutrop.*
2.141–16 — 843

Cleanthes *Hymn to Zeus*
10 — 99

Cleomedes
1.8–9 — 318
2.9 — cxci

Cologne Mani Codex
56–57 — 88
57.12–16 — 88

Cornelius Gallus *Elegies*
1 — 531

Corpus Hermeticum
I.16 — 107
I.26 — 318, 809
I.30 — 508
I.31 — 508, 511
I.32 — 12, 700
II.381.218 — 415
X.5 — 508
X.25 — 525
XIII.1 — cxciv, 550
XIII.15–16 — 809
XIII.17–20 — 809
XIII.18–19 — 511
XIV — lxxiv
XVI — lxxiv
XVI.5 — 348
XXIII — 865
XXIII.54–63 — 865
XXIII.54–70 — 887
XXIII.58 — 866
Asclepius
3.23b — 763
3.24a — 763
3.24b — 884
3.25 — 415
3.37 — 763
3.38 — 763
14.17–18 — 32
25 — 531
29.5–7 — 32
72.18 — 531
134.25–26 — 32
Fragmenta
6.13 — 98

Cynic Letters
Diogenes
27 — 76
47 — 76
Hippocrates
15 — 87

Cyranides
1.2.6 — 189

Demosthenes
De corona
15 — 308
54–55 — 173
84 — 173
108 — 312
116 — 173
De fals. leg.
163 — 568
Orationes
8.41 — 216
23.93 — 568
60.28 — 703

Dio Cassius
1.5.12 — 627
4.1 — 316
4.3 — 627
36.3.2–3 — 892
36.45.2–3 — 892
37.6.1 — 892
37.17.1 — 164
37.25.2 — 417
40.47.2 — 415
41.61 — 762
42.27 — 396
42.27.2 — 396
44.19.1–5 — 736
47.40.2 — 413, 519
48.24.2 — 138
51.20.6–7 — 138
51.20.6 — 181
51.20.7–8 — 774
54.7 — 762
55.10a.4 — 893
56.29.2–6 — 418
56.45.2 — 418
56.46.2 — 627
58.25 — 740
59.8.1–2 — 736
59.19.5 — 742
59.24.4 — 741–42
59.24.5 — 316
59.27.4–6 — 742
59.28.1 — 774
59.28.5 — 310
60.5.4 — 742
60.24.3 — 821
62.1.1–2 — 562
62.20.5 — 20
63.9.3 — 738
65.2 — 162
65.2.3 — lxviii
65.5.4 — 595
65.6.1–3 — 595
65.9.4–5 — lxviii
66.1 — 418
66(64).8.2 — 676
66.19.3 — 738
66.21–23 — 520
66.22.2 — 527
66.22.4 — 527
66.23.1 — 520, 527
66.23.2 — 520
66.23.4–5 — 527
66.26.2 — lxviii
67.1.1 — lxviii
67.2.6 — lxviii
67.3.5 — lxviii
67.4.2 — lxviii
67.4.3 — 292
67.4.6 — 171
67.4.7 — 311
67.5.7 — 310
67.6.3 — lxviii
67.13.1–3 — lxvii

67.13.4 — 310–11
67.14 — lxvii
69.1–2 — 402
72.35.5 — 295
73.16 — 817
73.23.2 — 86
79.10.1–2 — 86
80.17–19 — 740
80.18.1–3 — 740

Dio Cassius
51.20 — 922
55.27.1–3 — 996
55.31.3–4 — 996
68.30 — 987
76.4.4–5 — 987

Dio Chrysostom *Orationes*
1.13 — 477
1.58–84 — 684
1.67 — 684
1.78–82 — 1054
1.79 — 684
2.75 — 955
3.41 — 684
3.73–85 — 117
4.23 — 805
4.25 — 684
4.41 — 477
4.44–45 — 477
10.23 — 1056
11.29–30 — 996
12.60 — 174
12.60–61 — 762
12.84 — 762
13 — 79
13.34 — 979, 982
14.22 — 684
17.2 — 147
21.10 — 738
31.54–55 — 138
31.84–85 — 227
31.84 — 225
31.140 — 1212
32.60 — 40
33.23 — 982
34.7 — 946, 947
34.48 — 136
36.42–53 — 390
37.34 — 40
38.20 — 402
45.1 — 407
46 — 399
77/78.39 — 147
78.31 — 218

Diodorus Siculus
1.11.2 — 298
1.21.2 — 672
1.21–22 — 672
1.88.4–7 — 672
1.88.4 — 683
2.31.4 — 291
2.47.1–3 — 808
2.47.2 — 808
4.3.4 — 987
4.11.5 — 685
4.15.3 — 540
4.49.8 — 879
4.66 — 817
9.3.2 — 113
11.14.3–4 — 693
12.32.2 — 748
19.45.2 — 902
28.3 — 745
29.15 — 745

31.18 745
32.17.1–7 740
40.3.5–6 111

Diogenes Laertius
1.28 113
1.33 113
2.51 138
4.27 526
4.46 458
4.64 413
6.102 681
7.119 48
8.18 397
10.76–77 834
10.139 835

Diogenes Oenoandensis
Fragmenta
24 835

Dionysius Antiochenus
Epistulae
39 142

Dionysius of Halicarnasus
Roman Antiquities
1.77.2 413, 557
2.7 51
2.56.2 627
6.17.3 400
7.72.15 817
8.56.2 762
10.2.3 517
De comp. verb.
24 286

Dioscorides Materia medica
1.12.6 cxc
1.13.9 cxc
1.25.14 cxc
1.28.8 cxc
1.40.16 cxc
1.59.21 cxc
1.88.12 cxc
1.109.1–2 468
1.109.2–3 468
2.127.12 cxc
2.164.2 cxc
2.171.10 cxc
2.210.7–8 cxc
2.226.6 cxc
2.252.20 cxc
3.23.1–4 521
3.23.5–6 521
3.23.6 521

Empedocles Fragmenta
(M. R. Wright)
14.9 31
(Diels and Kranz)
B96 899
B98 899
B107 899
B115 899

Epictetus (Arrian Discourses)
1.9 236
1.19.29 173
1.20 236
1.28.17 198
2.2.12 258
2.2.13 76
2.23.28 766
3.7.29 258
3.8.6 236

3.13.14 236
3.22.23 111
3.22.34 236
4.2.4–10 258
4.7.6 312
Encheiridion
33 567

Euripides
Alcestis
493 540
Andromache
812 324
Bacchae
223–24 204
237–38 204
260–61 204
353–54 204
487 204
686–87 204
957–58 204
Electra
474–75 539
Fragmenta
(Nauck, Trag. graec.)
689 95
Hecuba
348 703
Hercules
518 703
531–34 703
Hippolytus
856–74 20
Ion
203–4 539
206–18 415
401–2 817
1146–58 679
1046–47 834
1157 679
Iphigeneia Aulidensis
905–6 174
Iphigeneia Taurica
57 241
Medea
807–10 834
Orestes
96 817
Phaethon (frag. 781)
11–12 535
Phoenissae
116 298
857 817
1524 817
Rhesus
528–33 679

Ennius Annales
5 86

Frontinus Strat.
2.11.7 lxix

Fronto, M. Cornelius
Epistula ad Verum
2.1 127

Fulgentius Mythologies
17 113

Gaius Institutes
2.147 342

Galen
De anatomicis administrationibus
1.2 183

2.600 324
16.5 549
De cognoscendis
9 181
De propriorum animi
9 181
De san. tuend.
6.12 263

Heliodorus Aethiopica
3.3 190
7.8 174

Ps.-Heraclitus Ep.
4 544

Hermogenes Progymnasmata
1 cxci
10 923

Herodas
5.65–67 458
5.77–79 458

Herodian
1.7.5 95
1.8.4 295
1.16.2 623
1.16.4 295
2.3.2 295
2.8.6 295
3.8.5 821
4.2 777
7.6.2 295
7.9.1 295
8.4.9–10 835
8.7.2 309

Herodotus
1.1 8
1.3.5 cxciii
1.14 160
1.26 137
1.48 20–21
1.76–84 220
1.76–77 220
1.82 532
1.85 929
1.92 817
1.148 138
1.159.3 562
1.178–89 619
1.178 929, 1162
1.183 877
1.207 833
2.15 619
2.42 369
2.44 241
2.46 369, 534
2.59 672
2.79 534
2.106.2 cxci
2.113.1 458
2.130.1 cxci
2.142 clxxx, 231
2.152 672
2.155 672
2.156 534, 673–74
3.40 141
3.83 clxxx, 231, 992
4.52 572
4.71 817
4.161 379
4.181.3–4 257
5.6 457
5.24 clxxx, 231

5.49 824
6.16 877
6:98 415
6.109 900
6.119.2 cxci
7.37.2 522
7.140 50
7.141 50, 985
7.171 403
7.187 397
8.37–39 693
8.115 403
9.67 985

Heron *De mens.*
60.4 534
61.4 534

Hesiod
Eoiae
frag. B.3–34 668
Fragmenta
204.113 113
Theogony
22–34 86
31–32 113
34 102
38 113
48 102
178–87 755
211–12 401
211 401
319–24 539
381 108
412–17 104
427 104
453–91 687
455 401
507–616 669
522 1081
536–41 192
553–57 192
632 699
711–19 1078
718 1081
720–819 1078
756–57 401
820 699
820–68 667
Works
236 989
709–11 992

Ps.-Hesiod *Scutum Herculis*
72 95

Hierocles *On Duties*
1.3.54 403

Hipparchus
1.8.14–15 406
1.11.6 406

Hippocrates
De articulis
10 198
Epidemics
1.11 113
Epistulae
14 142
Morb. sacr.
4 47
Progn.
1 113
2 400

Historia Augusta
6.5 628
7.2 628

Homeric Hymns
1.181 95
2.314–15 557
3.147 137
3.403 518, 662
6.1 174
6.7 174
6.18 174
21 102
32.6 174

Homeric Hymn to Apollo
19 331
19–29 331
207 331
317–20 699

Homeric Hymn to Demeter
73–75 673

Horace
Carm.
1.12.53 893
4.3.13 619, 831, 959
Epistles
2.1.255 395, 878
2.2.171–79 843

Hyginus
Fabulae
57.2 539
140 670, 705
Odes
1.3.23 989
Poetica Astronomica
2.25 680
2.3 683

Iamblichus
De mysteriis
5.23 763
6.7.11 12
De vita Pythagorica
82 770
85 96
105 96

Iliad
1.1–7 86
1.1.5 1068
1.70 113
1.247–49 572
1.494 cxciv
1.586–94 699
2.243 477
2.353 561
2.261–62 898
2.416 29
2.484–93 331
2.786–87 557
3.121 557
3.276–80 566
3.397 95
4.49 542
5.853 cxciii
5.867 841
5.897 cxciv, 550
6.119–236 623
6.181–82 539
7.479 400
8.41–46 94

8.67 985
8.69 cxciv, 550
8.398 557
8.409 557
9.171 508
9.236 561
9.409 894
9.500 542
10.200 985
11.27–28 557
11.67–71 845
11.99–100 898
11.157 985
11.185 557
11.218–19 331
11.218 331
11.632–35 923
11.814 1068
13.20–27 94
13.445–47 1056
13.474 95
14.121 clxxii
14.130 clxxx, 231
14.231 401
14.508 331
15.36–40 567
15.144 557
15.158–59 557
15.188 401
16.672 401
16.682 401
16.837 1068
17.51 487
18.182 557
18.394–99 699
18.478–608 923
19.366 95
20–21 707
20.234 689
20.375–80 559
22.510 898
23.21–23 622
23.183 622
23.226 108
23.244 401
24.15–21 622
24.70 542

Isocrates
Archidamus
96 817
Ad Dem.
26 834
Epistulae
2 142
Evagoras
57 761

Joannes Lydus *De mensibus*
3.32 234

Justinian *Institutes*
2.10.2–3 342
2.10.12 342

Juvenal *Satires*
1.73 79
4.38 739
5.30 532
6.116–24 929
9.130 944
14.298–300 218

Ps.-Libanius *Epistolary Styles*
63 142
92 142

Livy

1.16.1–2	627
1.19.2–4	395, 878
1.32.10	348
2.39.9	445, 466
4.6.5	872
4.15.6	397
4.33.2	445, 466
5.7.2	445, 466
5.13.6	252
5.15.11	872
6.20.7	173
9.23.16	445, 466
10.7.9	468
10.47.3	468
21.46.8	872
25.39.17	872
26.11.9	817
27.11	417
27.37.13	174
29.9.5	872
34.29.5	445, 466
34.45.6–8	417
35.9.2–5	417
35.21.2–6	417
36.37	417
37.3.1–6	417
37.44.4	201
37.46.4	174
38.37.2	872
38.37.4	174
39.7.1	174
40.37.3	174
43.13.1–2	417
43.13.1	417
43.13.6	416
43.13.8	174

Longinus *De sublimate*

10.2	400

Longus

1.20	646

Lucan

1.522–83	417, 520
1.536–43	522
1.547–48	520
1.578	519
5.79–81	670

Lucan *Pharsalia*

3.209–10	218

Lucian

Alexander

11	223, 772
12–26	764
48	310

Dialogi deorum

8.1–2	690
10.1	690
25	889

Dialogi meretricii

9	190
286	935
294	935, 937
321	935

Dialogi mortuorum

6(20)	473
9	670

Adversus indoctum

20	738, 740

De luctu

19	173–74

De mercede conductis

13	218

De morte Perigrini

11–13	155
16	155, 193
29	29
40	223

Nigrinus

27	458

Philopseudes

25	223

De sacrificiis

6	699
8	281
12	174

De saltatione

38	670

Saturnalia

10	128

De Syria dea

4	690
10	764
42	223
58	174
59	458

Timon

4	174

Trag.

33	281

Vit. auct.

9	339

Zeuxis

2	360
4	549

Lucretius *De rerum natura*

2.705	539
3.915ff.	839
5.29	540
5.905–7	539
6.71–79	834
6.848–78	257

Lycophron Trag.

Alexandra

281	241

Macrobius

Commentarii in Somnium Scipionis

6.5–82	115

Saturnalia

1.7.18ff.	623
1.9.17–18	395, 878
1.17.9	535
1.23.14–16	129
1.23.21	58
5.22.4–6	138

Manetho *Aegyptiaka*

frag. 64	370
frag. 65	370

Manilius *Astronomica*

1.32–43	297
1.34	679
1.109	679
1.177–78	212
1.215	679
1.255	679
1.263–64	353
1.295	679
1.343–45	523
1.384–86	525
1.421	406
1.427	415
1.431	406
1.506	679
1.779–804	777
1.799	525
1.814–75	415
1.892–926	520
2.61	566
5.18	406

Marcus Aurelius *Meditationes*

3.4.3	48
3.5.1	40

Martial

1.1.62	311
1.4.2	317
2.92.1	316
2.92.4	311
3.3.103	311
3.3.110	311
4.2.6	311
4.67.4	311
5.1.7	316
5.1.42	311
5.1.112	311
5.1.190	316
5.1.261	311
5.2.6	311
5.2.177	316
5.5.1	311
5.5.3	311
5.5.4	311
5.8.1	311
6.64.5–6	311
6.64.14	311
7.5	311
7.8.1	311
7.8.2	311
7.12.1	311
7.34.8	311
7.40.2	311
7.45.7	311
7.55	317
7.99.5–8	311
8.1.1	311
8.15	lxviii
8.31.3	311
8.32.6	317
8.78	lxviii
8.82.1–4	311
8.82.2	311
9.16.3	311
9.20.2	311
9.23.3	311
9.24.6	311
9.28.5	311
9.28.7	311
9.66.3	311
9.78.8	311
9.79.7	316
9.84.2	311
9.101.23–24	311
10.34.1	311
10.72.3	311
10.72.8	311
10.93.2	311
14.47	311

Menander

Perikeiromene

440	535

Rhetor

1.342	31
2.17	86, 121

Samia
321–24	458

Minucius Felix *Octavius*
23	762
27	763
32.1	405

Musonius Rufus
25.8–9	76

Nicolaus of Damascus
Fragmenta
65	138

Nonnos *Dionysiaca*
1.163–205	686
2.53–59	707
2.68–76	707
2.126	706
2.175	281
2.277–80	707
2.558–59	85
2.655	680
2.672–73	683
10.311	690
11.144–46	699
12.29–32	667
29.19	540
154–218	683

Numenius *Fragmenta*
(É. des Places)
2.23	30
3.1	30
3.8	30
3.9	30
4a.7	30
4a.9	30
4a.12	30
5.5	30
5.6	30
5.14	30
5.18	30
6.7	30
6.8	30
6.15	30
7.2	30
7.13	30
7.14	30
8.2	30
12	30

Odyssey
1.170	472
1.319–23	705
1.351–52	360
1.420	705
3.371–72	705
4.606	cxciii
6.127–29	898
6.221–22	898
7.38	94
7.84–132	923
9.12–16	331
9.544–45	94
10.1–76	451
11.43	400
11.51–78	622
11.633	400
14.112	cxciv
14.169	cxciii
14.188	472
14.422	817
15.250–51	690

16.16–18	623
16.57–58	472
19.7	clxxx, 231
19.446	95
20.101–4	561
20.341–44	623
22.481	835
22.493	835
24.529–53	559

Orphic Hymns
1.2	104
1.7	104
18.4	103
25.4–5	113
29.4	104
34.26	457
55.5	104
62.2	262
73.6	104
87	401

Orphica Fragmenta
316	104

Ovid
Artis amatoriae
1.655–56	646

Fasti
1.121–24	395, 878
2.63	316
2.127	316
2.481–509	627
2.520	817
6.810	316

Ibis
123–24	531

Metamorphoses
1.517–18	113
1.625–27	298
1.749–79	889
2.1–366	889
2.139	406
2.235–38	889
2.254–56	902
5.158	704
5.321–31	706
6.667–74	540
7.104–5	540
7.350–51	706
7.354–56	706
7.371–72	706
7.382–83	706
7.384–85	706
8.25–36	393
8.274	817
8.289	540
9.69ff.	685
10.243–97	764
14.805–51	627
14.816–17	627
15.41–42	190
15.785	413

Palatine Anthology
(see *Anthologia Palatina*)

Pausanias
1.9.7	138
1.14.3	563
1.17.3	174
1.18.6	556
1.19.3	cxci
1.20.3	cxci
1.21.1	cxci

1.21.2	86
1.23.8	cxci
1.26.5	cxci
1.26.6	cxci
1.27.7	cxci
1.27.10	cxci
1.28.5	cxci
1.29.4	cxci
1.34.2	cxci
1.37.1	cxci
1.38	563
2.17.4	174
2.17.6	174
2.26.8	182–83
2.36.9	160
2.37.4	685
4.7.1	398
4.31.8	138
5.11.7	281
5.13.8	182
5.20.3	103
5.24.5	690
6.25.2	401
7.2.6	138
7.2.7	137
7.2.8	138
7.5.1–3	159, 161
7.5.1	160
7.5.2	160
7.5.4	138
7.5.9	160
7.5.12	160
8.48.1–2	468
10.4.1	829
10.12.10	31
10.23.1–10	693
73.18.11	690

Periplus Maris Rubri
4	cxcv
13.8	ccx
16.22	ccx
18.18	ccx
18.22	ccx
42	cxcv
48	cxcv

Petronius *Satyricon*
103	458
103.2	458
105	458

Philo of Byzantium
De septem orbis spec.
4.1–6	556

Philostratus
Vita Apollonii
1.12	13
1.15	399
1.27	764
1.28	764
3.27	189
4.7	168
4.16	678
4.34	183
5.13	736, 945
6.37	218
6.42	399
7.1	40
8.5	lxvi
8.7	532
18.19–20	86
8.30	625, 627

Vitae sophistae	
1.21	399
1.532	396
2.23	310
552	95

Ps.-Phocylides *Sententiae*	
3	186
3–8	187
13	838
212	532
631	193

Pindar	
Fragmenta	
87–88	673
Isthmia	
6.60–61	871
7.21–22	871
7.43–47	699
Nemean Odes	
3.78	572
Olympia	
1.19	572
1.40	690
1.65	699
2.81–82	241
3.29–30	768
9.48–48	360
Pythia	
2.83–85	834
4.23	561
4.225	540

Plato	
Alcibiades	
2.149b	141
Apologia	
40c	531, 839
Cratylus	
404D–E	535
405E	535
Crito	
48B	834
49B–C	993
Laws	
642	993
Leges	
1.636b–d	1224
4.715e	31
8.841d–e	1224
9.854D	458
9.864e	876
11.931A	762
840C	871
898D–899D	525
Meno	
71E	993
Phaedo	
4.60e–61b	86
62a	839
81C–D	404
89B–C	532
111d	836
112E–113C	1067
113D	1066
Phaedrus	
251a	1124
265c	198
Politicus	
271e	477
Protogoras	
324A–B	993
Republic	
4.440d	477

9.13 (592A–B)	1153
10.13(6:14c–d)	836
328C	174
363C	12
424b–c	360
613e–621d	278
Symposium	
202e	513
203b	909
221B	cxci
Theatetus	
176D	cxci
Timaeus	
21E	534
29d–30c	748
37B	525
37E	31
22C–D	1117
40A–B	525

Plautus *Bacchides*	
312	138

Pliny the Elder *Naturalis historia*	
2.17	1004
2.22.90	520
2.25.96	520
2.36–38	212
2.37	212
2.46.119	450
2.57.147	519
2.58	1060
2.58.148	418
2.86.200	218
2.118	989
2.148	1060
3.38	959
3.66–67	944
4.12.69	78
5.14.70	619
5.15	820
5.17	820
5.30	233–34
5.126	194, 1122
5.3.7	1000
8.187	523
9.54	928, 1004
9.124–41	999
12.41	998
12.51	1001
12.65	1001
12.70	1001
12.82	1001
12.87	989
13.91	1000
14.2.9	281
14.9	234
14.58	938
14.121	341
14.148	937
16.3.7	173–74
16.5.14	173
18.2.6	174
18.2.8	817
18.30.119	817
18.63–70	397
18.71–75	397
18.74	397
18.82	1002
19.3–6	989
19.9	997
19.36	898
22.4.6–8	173
30.2.11	185
30.12	341

33.66	218
34.1	1000
34.18	898
34.18.41	556
34.36	1000
34.139	948
36.62	1001
36.97	281
37.204	981

Pliny the Younger	
Epistulae	
1.5	78
1.10	78
1.12.6–8	lxviii
2.13.8	311
3.5.4	86
3.5.17	339, 341
3.11.3	lxviii
3.13.1	311
4.11.6	lxviii
6.16.11	519
6.16.17	523, 527
6.16.20	520
6.20.9	520
6.20.14	531
6.20.15	523, 527
7.27.14	lxviii
9.13.5	78
10.2.1	311
10.3A.1	311
10.5.1	311
10.53	950
10.6.1	311
10.8.1	311
10.56	79–80
10.96	176, 317
10.96.5–6	761
10.96.5	765
10.96.9–10	171
10.96.10	192–93
10.97.1	765
10.116	137
Panegyricus	
1.6.3	311
2.3	311
2.7	311
10.4	777
24.5	777
33.3–4	lxviii
33.4	310
42	171
48.3–4	lxviii
52.1	777
52.7	777
88.4	311
88.8–9	311
89.2	777
90.5–7	lxviii
96	163

Ps.-Plutarch *De fluv.*	
16	894

Plutarch	
Aemelius	
34.5	174
32–34	1051
Alexander	
31	416
678D	cxci
De Alexandri magni fortuna	
340A	20
Amatorius	
25.771	875

Antony
25.2 — 892
60 — 762
Apoth. Spart.
214b — 1211
Brutus
5.3 — 20
Caesar
66.4–14 — 736
68 — 322
Cicero
14 — 413
Convivium septem sapientium
149C — 416
Coriolanus
37.3 — 764
38.1 — 761
38.2 — 764
Crassus
21.6 — 533
23–28 — 892
24.1–2 — 533
24.2 — 532
25.4 — 533
De defectu oraculorum
415B–C — 895
419b–c — 562
421C–E — 542
De exilio
604B — 79
De facie
928B — 297
942F — 526
Flam.
16 — 922
De fortuna Alexandri
6 — 467
329A–B — 477
340A — 20
340B — 685
De frat. amore
488d — 308, 685
De garrulitate
6.504e — 833
504a — 508
505–6 — 508
De genio Socratis
509d–f — 836
590B–592E — 526
591A–C — 526, 836
De Herodoti malignitate
855D — 665
De Iside et Osiride
352a — 31
352C — 878
355D–358F — 672
357F — 673
354c — 31
354f–355a — 298
358C–D — 704
358D — 672
358E — 672
358F — 672
359E — 683
361c — 513
363B — 683
364B — 683
366A — 672
372f–373a — 31
375F — 534
379C–D — 544
Lycurgus
16 — 199
23.2–4 — 87

Lysander
1 — 532
Marcellus
14.7 — 127
22.1–2 — 174
28 — 417
Moralia
186F — 190
Numa
2.3 — 627
Otho
4.5 — 417
Pelopidas
31 — 413
Pericles
12.1–2 — 737
17.1 — 766
Pompey
38.2 — 892
57.1 — 766
Praecepta gerendae reipublicae
807b — 183
De Pythiae oraculis
145e — 1122
395 — 1000
397E–398B — 762
402a — 817
404E — 15
Quaestiones convivales
3.1–2 (645d–649f) — 174
4.6.2 — 470
8.4 — 468
8.8.2–3 (729c) — 186
730a — 766
Quaestiones Graecae
298f — 817
Quaestiones Romanae
26.270D–F — 223, 293
167B — 532
Quomodo adulescens poetas audire debeat
70d — 147
Romulus
18 — 199
27.6 — 627
27.6–8 — 627
28.1–3 — 627
Septem sapientium convivales
161F — 297
De sera numinis vindicta
563b–68 — 278
Solon
4.2 — 113
Sulla
7 — 417
7.3 — 519
7.3–4 — 519
De Superstitione
168D — 611
Theseus
16.2 — 817
De tuenda sanitate praecepta
123d — lxii

Ps.-Plutarch
De proverbuus Alexandrinorum
21 — 370

Polyaenus
4.9.4 — 218

Polybius
1.19.7 — 996
1.36.8 — 748
2.15.1 — 397
3.49.7 — 199, 922

3.106.6 — 1087
3.421–42 — 922
6.39.13–15 — 397
6.39.13 — 397
6.56.13 — 838
6.345 — 838
10.37.9 — 838
13.6.2 — 748
24.8.9 — 748
30.25 — 1051
30.25.9 — 533, 892
31.9 — 745
32.15 — 182, 201
32.16 — 9
36.10.1–7 — 740

Porphyry *De abstinentia*
2.56.6 — 405
11 — 542
42 — 542

Proclus *In Timaeus*
1.76.21–30 — 692
3.6.13 — 763

Propertius
3.3 — 86
3.7.3 — 989

Ptolemy *Math. synt.*
1.3 — 318

Ptolemy *Tetrabiblos*
2.90–91 — 511
28 — 406
29 — 450, 451

Quintilian *Institutiones*
3.3.1 — 122
4.3.12 — 665
10.1.91 — lxviii
11.32–34 — 20

Quintus Smyrnaeus
2.598 — 281
4.554 — 405

Res Gestae Divi Augusti
13 — 395, 878
27.2 — 893
29.2 — 893
34.2 — 874

Ps.-Sallust
Epistula ad Caesarem Secunda
13.6 — 831

Scholia in Aristophanem Plutum
594 — 104

Seneca
De beneficiis
2.12.1–2 — 742
Epistulae moraliae
62.3 — 161
67.10 — 76
86.1–7 — 1004
94.21 — 147
102.22 — 404
Marc.
19–20 — 839
Medea
328 — 989
361 — 989
605 — 989

668 989
Quaestiones naturales
6.1.13 218
Troad
954 531

Servius
In Aeneidem
1.294 395, 878
3.92–93 562
3.366 416
3.538 395
In Vergilii Carmina Commentariorum
4.511 104

Sextus Empiricus
Adversus mathimaticos
7.107 556
Outlines of Pyrrhonism
1.148 457
3.202 457

Silius Italicus *Pun.*
3.607 lxviii
6.228 540

Sophocles
Aias
14–18 559
Ajax
17 85
Antigone
21–38 1068
463–64 531
1144 95
Electra
149 523
1007–8 531
1417–21 887
Oedipus Coloneus
6 cxciii
622 887
1362 262
Oedipus Rex
410 13
1320 992
Oedipus Tyrannus
410 13
Philoctetes
79 198
391–95 218
Trachiniae
183 817
761 817
1048 cxciii

Statius *Silvae*
1.1.62 311
1.1.103 95, 316
3.3.103 311
3.3.110 311
3.3.171 lxviii
4.3.11–12 399
5.1.60–61 981
5.1.120–26 981
3.4.21–25 183
3.4.53 317
4.2.5 316
4.2.6 311
4.3.159 lxviii
5.1.42 311
5.1.112 311
5.1.187 316

5.1.261 311
5.2.91–92 lxix
5.2.177 316

Stobaeus *Ecl.*
2.67.20 48
3.120 839

Strabo
1.2.28 824
3.2.10 998
7.5.4 457
8.3.14 401
11.5.4 159
12.3.21 159
12.3.27 160
12.8.16 249
12.8.18 218, 234, 236, 244, 249
12.8.20 160
13.4.2 740
13.4.5 218
13.4.10 234, 236
13.4.11 244
13.4.14 249, 257
14.1.2 159
14.1.3 137
14.1.4 159–60
14.1.15 160
14.1.20 138
14.1.21 138
14.1.23 138
14.1.24 136, 774
14.1.37 160–61
14.1.42 756
14.2.5 556
14.2.29 159, 249
14.3.3 774
14.38 201
15.2.10 831
16.1.5 929
16.1.9 929
16.1.28 893
16.2.23 998

Suetonius
Divus Augustus
32.1 170
52 774
79.2 95
94.1–4 418
100.4 96, 627
Caligula
14.2 736, 893
22.1 310
22.2 310
27.3 458
57.1–4 418
57.1 764
Claudius
19 399
Domitian
1.3 lxviii
2.2 893
2.3 lxviii
3.1 lxviii
4 292
4.4 292–93, 756
7.2 lxiii
8.2 lxix
12.1 lxviii
12.2 162, 171
12.3 lxviii
13.2 310–11
14.2 lxiii

15 lxvii
18 lix
22.1 lxviii
Galba
11 396
Divus Iulius
37.2 296
42.3 170
81.1–3 418
82 736
88 761
Nero
16.2 lxvi
20.3 316
38 lxvi
49 762
49.3–4 737
57 738, 893
57.2 738
Tiberius
20 742
48.2 218
Titus
3.5 1220
8.3–4 520
8.5 79
9.3 lxviii
Vespasian
5 418
5.7 417
23.4 418
Vitellius
2 742
11.2 311

Synesius *Epistulae*
54 12

Tacitus
Agricola
2–3 lxviii
7 lxviii
Annals
1.1 947
1.10.4.98 1011
2.47 218, 234
2.47.3–4 244
2.87.12.11 311
3.52.1–54.3 1004
3.53 998
3.60–63 138
3.63 160
3.66–69 774
4.15 774
4.37–38 160
4.37 181, 774, 922
4.55–56 160, 175, 774
4.56 160, 922
4.67 520
5.10 740
5.29 308
11–16 417
11.31 929
12.43 397, 399, 417
12.64 417
13.10 739
13.33 774
13.43 774
14.12 417
14.15 316
14.27 249
15.38.44 lxvi
15.44 445, 466
15.47 417

History
1.3.3   417
1.86   417
2.8   738
2.8.1   739
2.8–9   738
2.50   418
2.78   418
3.68   396
4.51   893
4.52   lxviii
5.5   404, 761
5.9   745, 755
5.13   397, 418, 561, 562, 676
5.13.1   882

Theocritus
2.152   833
21.25   568

Theognis
1.3   102

Theon of Smyrna
Progymnasmata
148.6–7   318

Theophrastus
Characteres
17.8   190
Historia plantarum
1.12.1   522

Thucydides
1.1.1   6
1.21   900
1.23.3   403
1.129.3   128
2.8   415
2.11.5   cxci
2.56   clxxii
2.56.4   clxxii
2.56.5   clxxii
2.56.6   clxxii
2.93.4   cxciv, 550
3.38.1   568
3.45.1   cxci
3.85   817
4.16.1   397
4.80.4   174
4.130.2   cxci
6.32.1   508
7.3.3   cxciii
7.28.3   cxciii
7.69   cxci
8.70   199

  History
  3.72   948
  4.52   lxviii
  5.13   1060

The Twelve Tables
8.2   646

Ulpian *Digest*
1.18.6.8   396
2.1.3   403
27.1.6.2   774
27.1.6.14   756
37.11.4   339, 341
47.2.57.8   835

47.9.4.1   80
47.14.3.3   79
48.14.1   79
48.19.8.9   166
48.19.9.10   835
48.19.28.13   80
48.19.29   166
48.19.35   166
48.22.5   79
48.22.6   79–80
48.22.7   80
48.22.7.1   80
48.22.7.2   79
48.22.7.17   79
48.22.10–22   79
48.22.14.3   79
48.22.15   79
50.2 79

Valerius Flaccus
1.11   316

Varro
De lingua Latina
5.122   358, 879
5.128   262
5.165   395, 878
6.16   817
De re rustica
2.2.13   523

Velleius Paterculus
2.10.2   872
2.101   893

Vergil
Aeneid
1.60–66   959
1.294   395, 878
1.589–94   94
3.90–96   676
3.93   562
3.377–80   563
3.537–47   395
5.88   286
6.111   468
6.265   1007
6.300   95
6.529–30   409
6.621   473
6.623   473
6.711–12   472
6.781–82   996
6.783   945
7.135   174
7.272–82   959
7.606   893
9.112   562
9.638–39   841
10.76   252
10.539   293
11.197   401
12.102   95
Eclogues
4.392–93   113
Georgics
1.6   311
1.57   1001
1.438–65   413
1.463–68   413
1.466–97   417
1.475   518

2.7–8   95
2.98   234
2.140   540
2.192   358, 879
3.85   540

Vettius Valens
13.27   98
140.6   450

Vita Aesopi
107   383
G 106   241

Vitruvius
1.1.4   138
9.4.3   523
9.5.1   406

Xenophon
  Anabasis
  1.2.7   154
  1.3.14   154
  1.5.5–6   397
  1.5.7   clxxii
  2.4.25   619
  2.14.4   154
  4.5.27   833
  4.5.35   clxxii
  4.6.11   clxxii
  4.6.15   clxxii
  5.4.32   457
  6.1.31   567
  6.6.17   567
  7.1.40   174
  7.3.23   397
  Cyropaedia
  1.1.2   477
  2.5   51
  1.4.24   949
  8.3.13   685
  14.24   959
  3.3.20   clxxvi
  3.3.34   174
  Hellenica
  2.1.8   cxci
  2.3.20   225
  2.3.51   225, 227
  6.4.7   676
  Memorabilia
  2.1.21–34   933
  3.13.3   258
  Resp. Lacedaem.
  6.4   322
  De Vectigalibus
  4.21   457

Xenophon of Ephesus
Ephesiaka
1.1–3   138
4.4   646

Zonaras
11.15, p. 45, 11–16D   738

Papyri

Corpus Papyrorum Judaicarum (CPJ)
1:28.20	184
1:29	184
1:29.10	184
1:80–82	171
1:125.2	184
2:119–36	171
2:153	172
2:202.1–2	184
2:206.1	13
2:207.1–2	184
2:439.6	551
3:111–16	171
3:157	105
3:407.3	184
3:439	785

P. Chester Beatty
2018	531, 589, 884

Papyri Demoticae Magicae
iv.125	614
xii.6–20	191
xii.70	253
xii.90	253
xiv.55ff.	253
xiv.60ff.	252
xiv.340	253
xiv.550ff.	253
xiv.780	253

P. Enteux
24.14	516

P. Flor.
20.19	450
50.104	450

Papyri Graecae Magicae (PGM)
I	107, 252
I.1–3	252
I.1–42	252, 264
I.37–38	252
I.40	252
I.41–42	252
I.42–95	264
I.65–66	252
I.72	107, 347
I.73–81	16
I.74–75	525
I.76	252
I.77	252
I.78	252
I.84–87	252
I.84	253
I.86	252
I.87	252
I.88–90	253
I.88	252
I.89	252
I.90	252
I.92	252
I.93	252
I.96–195	264
I.96–131	252
I.97	252
I.146	191, 195
I.160–61	252
I.167	252
I.168–70	252
I.172	16, 252

I.173–77	252
I.176	16, 252
I.179	401
I.181–88	253
I.304	662
I.305	518
I.306	453
I.309	453
I.327	254
I.332–33	253
II.128	773
III.71	347
III.192–93	253
III.218	58
III.226	453
III.229	453
III.252–53	662
III.255	518
III.266–67	453
III.273	450
III.291–95	253
III.334	253
III.496	450
III.541	154
III.661	57, 560
III.665	514
IV.59	253
IV.210	514
IV.224	358, 879
IV.272	58
IV.341–42	104
IV.411	57
IV.475–834	300
IV.487–88	57
IV.528	57
IV.559	102
IV.617	614
IV.625–28	282
IV.634–37	73
IV.676–77	560
IV.679–84	560, 627
IV.692–704	73
IV.698	174
IV.937	190
IV.959	102
IV.968	58
IV.970	208
IV.978	208
IV.992	57
IV.993	57
IV.1002	254
IV.1007	254
IV.1012–13	284
IV.1015	254
IV.1019	254
IV.1023	254
IV.1027	174
IV.1030	254
IV.1039	102
IV.1045	254
IV.1048	190
IV.1057	190
IV.1110	284
IV.1116–21	348
IV.1121	254
IV.1182–83	57
IV.1219–22	89
IV.1224	57
IV.1310	514
IV.1375	58
IV.1466	104

IV.1485–86	453
IV.1534–45	453
IV.1550–52	102
IV.1552	58
IV.1561	453
IV.1606	450
IV.1621	453
IV.1636	697
IV.1709–10	312–13
IV.1830	514
IV.1840–70	264
IV.1851–67	253
IV.1859–60	252–53
IV.2041	253
IV.2176	544
IV.2315	453
IV.2317	401
IV.2326	453
IV.2351	57
IV.2374	253
IV.2594–95	887
IV.2640	514
IV.2656–57	887
IV.2768–69	284
IV.2836–37	104
IV.2870	514
IV.2891	514
IV.3007–86	450
IV.3024–25	16
IV.3027–28	154
IV.3038–39	895
IV.3039–40	cxciii
IV.3045	213
IV.3046–47	206
IV.3053	453
IV.3065–66	895
IV.3066	450
IV.3068	213
IV.3075	895
IV.3077	313
IV.3081	895
IV.3166	16
IV.3191	516
IV.3197ff.	253
IV.3210	358, 879
IV.3220	253
IV.3238–39	57
V.99	566
V.209–10	213
V.220	514
V.256–60	113
V.285–97	113
V.363	57
V.367	57
V.395	514
V.459–63	349, 566
V.475	534
VII.220	453
VII.261	349, 566
VII.264	284
VII.270–71	566
VII.311	453
VII.476	57
VII.490	835
VII.535	514
VII.541	253
VII.583	453
VII.595–96	453
VII.633	284
VII.668	58
VII.720	57

VII.796–801	107	XIII.253	544	LXXI.1–5	58
VII.823	102	XIII.449–53	107	LXXI.3–4	30
VII.833–36	16	XIII.454–55	524	LXXII.3	58
VII.839–41	16	XIII.481–84	349, 885	LXXXVIII.1	253
VII.891	16	XIII.481–83	526	LXXXVIII.12	213
VII.898	16	XIII.571	313	CII.5	614
VII.925	514	XIII.585	16	21.21	766
VII.962	58	XIII.595	534		
VII.1014	254	XIII.596	534	*P. London*	
VIII.8	450	XIII.608–11	16	I.113.11b	406
VIII.33	544	XIII.608	254	1.1	58
VIII.40–41	242	XIII.618	789	5a.11	102
VIII.55	514	XIII.637	17	5b.25	102
VIII.89–91	86	XIII.646	86	5c.5	102
X.25–26	701	XIII.705	96	8.1	58
XII.6–20	195	XIII.761–62	58	13a.1	58
XII.14–95	763	XIII.763–64	191	21.1	58
XII.18–20	253	XIII.845	191	21.5	284
XII.20–23	252	XIII.849–59	57	21.43–45	58
XII.45	523	XIII.931	57	24.1	58
XII.71	17, 58	XIII.975–96	534		
XII.79	102	XIII.1020	31	*Papyrus Oxyrynchus*	
XII.87–88	284	XIII.1048	31	20–21	151
XII.111	31	XIV.17	58	100	261
XII.118	16	XIVa.9	58	115	clxxxii
XII.155–58	208	XIVc.17	58	115 lines 3ff.	51
XII. 209	190	XIV.415	514	117.15	229
XII.238	58	XV.15–16	895	301	3
XII.247	853	XV.15	629	472	544
XII.250	58	XV.18	766	523	261
XII.261	895	XVI.1	629	717	406
XII.280	190	XVI.8	401	848	859
XII.367–69	789	XVI.17	401	939	clxxxvi
XIII.1	514	XVI.25	401	939.19	cxcvii, 158
XIII.6	253	XXI.11–14	57, 560	1068	clxxxvi
XIII.8	253	XXI.42	853	1068.5	cxcvii, 158
XIII.12	254	XXIIa.19	58	1068.19	cxcvii, 158
XIII.15	514	XXIIb.10–13	285	1070.22	229
XIII.25	514	XXXV	285	1230	381
XIII.39	57, 560	XXXV.1–12	285	1381.8.	86
XIII.62–63	313	XXXV.7–10	885	1380.120–21	341
XIII.73	16	XXXV.17–19	766	1381.160–70	86
XIII.82	534	XXXV.37–41	566	2396	3
XIII.84	534	XXXVI	734	2433	3
XIII.90	86	XXXVI.4	285	2753	614
XIII.104ff.	253	XXXVI.77	285	3407.15–16	84
XIII.144–47	107	XXXVI.295–96	835	3693	192
XIII.146–47	524	XXXVI.302	835		
XIII.169–70	349, 526, 885	XXXVIII.5	253	*P. Ross*	
XIII.207	57	XLIV	57	III.4.9	488
XIII.210	254	LXII.34	254		
XIII.210–11	252	LXII.44	358, 879		
XIII.211	86	LXII.48	358, 879		
XIII.225	514	LXIII.15	253		

Inscriptions

Ancient Greek Inscriptions		3416	234	769	844
in the British Museum (IBM)		3417	289	1:296	164
3:587b	838	3424	234	1:378	287
3:676–77	170	3427	234	1:650c	287
		3428	234	1:650d	287
British Museum Inscriptions		3:933, no. 6298	105	1:653b	287
481.4	139			1:663	287
		Corpus Inscriptionum Iudaicarum		1:678	164
Corpus Inscriptionum Graecarum		*(CIJ)*		1:680	164
(CIG)		81	811	1:697	164
1068	234	242	811	1:710	164
2:2953b	138	361	876	1:711	164
2:2972	138	688	411	1:731	287

1:732	287
2:738	170, 175
2:741	170
2:742	164
2:742.29	160, 164
4:744	170
2:748	164, 170
2:754	170
2:755	164, 170
2:756	170
2:766	170
2:774	170
2:775	170
2:800	287
2:803	287
2:829	287
2:931	287
2:944	178
2:1007	178
2:1085	178
2:1086	178
2:1277	287
2:1400	605
2:1404	287
2:1510	38
2:1537	366
2:1538	366

CTA
| 2 | 707 |
| 3.IIID.35–36 | 707 |

Die Inschriften von Ephesos (I. Eph.)
Ia.24	138
2.223	778
2.232	778
2.232a	778
2.233	778
2.234	778
2.235	778
2.237	778
2.239	779
2.240	779
2.241	779
2.242	778
4.125	139
5.1498	778
6.2048	778
951	136–37
VI.2040	155

Inscriptiones Graecae (IG)
| 155 | 168 |

Inscriptiones Graecae ad res Romanas pertinentes (IGRom)
1:861	310
3:739	173
4:834	170
4:1431.29	160, 164

Orientis Graeci Inscriptiones Selectae (OGIS)
1:339, line 47	838
338	179
339.96	173
383.138–40	174
438	774
598	605

Res Gestae Divi Augusti
| 21 | 174 |

Supplementum Epigraphicum Graecum (SEG)
4:247.2	252
4:250.2	252
26:482.4	13
26:1817.80	190
32:1202.5	6
1068.2	77

Sylloge Inscriptionum Graecarum (SIG)
1.22 129	
83.55	817
200.10	817
372.27	174
398.36	174
455.2	817
502.40	817
739.5	817
867.35	281

Other Ancient Texts

Ahiqar
| 100b (2.18) | 98 |

Enuma Elish
1.33–34	1085
1.151–57	1085
2.126–27	1085
2.8–10	1085
6.69–94	1063

Gilgamesh Epic
9.266–95	152
11.28–30	1161
11.57–59	1161
16–17	1157

Cebes Tabula
| 2.1 | 927 |

| 5.1–3 | 926, 936 |
| 22–23 | 934 |

Egyptian *Book of the Dead*
17.40–42	1066
175.15	1066
175.20	1066